American Diaries

American Diaries

An Annotated Bibliography of Published
American Diaries and Journals

FIRST EDITION

Volume 2:
Diaries Written from 1845 to 1980

Laura Arksey, Nancy Pries, and Marcia Reed

GALE RESEARCH COMPANY • BOOK TOWER • DETROIT, MICHIGAN 48226

Laura Arksey, Nancy Pries, and Marcia Reed

Gale Research Company

Amy Marcaccio, *Editorial Coordinator*

Aided by:
Linda George, John Krol, Prindle LaBarge, Jennifer Mossman,
Helen Sheppard, Kathryn Tanis, Julie Towell

Mary Beth Trimper, *External Production Supervisor*
Darlene K. Maxey, *External Production Assistant*
Linda Davis, *External Production Assistant*
Arthur Chartow, *Art Director*
Laura Bryant, *Internal Production Supervisor*
Louise Gagné, *Internal Production Associate*
Sandy Rock, *Senior Internal Production Assistant*

Frederick G. Ruffner, *Publisher*
Dedria Bryfonski, *Editorial Director*
Ellen T. Crowley, *Associate Editorial Director*

Library of Congress Cataloging-in-Publication Data
(Revised for volume 2)

Arksey, Laura.
    American diaries.

    Expansion and revision of a work by William
Matthews: American diaries: an annotated bibliography
of American diaries written prior to the year 1861.
    Bibliography: v. 1, p.
    Includes indexes.
    Contents: v. 1. Diaries written from 1492 to 1844--
v. 2. Diaries written from 1845-1980.
    1. American diaries--Bibliography. 2. Auto-
biographies--Bibliography. 3. United States--History,
Local--Sources--Bibliography. I. Pries, Nancy.
II. Reed, Marcia. III. Matthews, William, 1905-
American diaries. IV. Title.
Z5305.U5A74 1983 [CT214]   016.92'0073   83-8860
ISBN 0-8103-1800-8 (v. 1)
ISBN 0-8103-1801-6 (v. 2)

Photocomposition by
Typetext
Algonac, Michigan

Printed in the United States of America

Contents

Preface

A diary is a verification, proof that a person has lived and has cared enough about a life to describe it. Many have spent time on this planet, but few have made the effort to record their stay. The diarist is saying that at a particular time and place, a life has been lived and feelings have been felt and thoughts crossed a mind. The very act of recording has provided a unique attachment to surroundings and self, an opportunity to examine life. Just as Plato said, "The life which is unexamined is not worth living," one might ask, with the inveterate diarist, Emerson, "How can an unrecorded life BE examined?"

My own interest in diaries is as a collector and diarist. Both efforts go back to my ninth year. At that time I lived in a house that had a library, and the man who formed that library, my father, was a diarist. His library was in a small room at the foot of the stairs that led to my bedroom. I walked through a world of books every day of my life. I saw a person recording a life. At age nine I endeavored to record mine.

I also began collecting books on natural history. My home was on the edge of the bluff overlooking the Mississippi River in St. Paul, Minnesota, just one mile from Fort Snelling. It was a wonderful place in which to grow up and a wonderful way to live, with the downtown part of the city just a ten-minute streetcar ride and yet a relatively undisturbed wilderness out the back door. Describing nature seemed necessary.

I recorded my adventures "below the bluff" in a nature journal and also made an attempt to keep a diary that described my fourth grade experiences. I managed to keep the latter until summer vacation began, and then the days were nearly identical. There were no distinct happenings like the progress of classes, but only an idyllic swim in the river every day.

The next year I began another diary, but that, too, was not carried beyond June. The "bird journal", however, continued to receive the descriptions that nature provided. Then in my early teens, the nature journal gave way to a diary which I have kept regularly for thirty years, and my collecting of nature books, to a diary collection eventually numbering some 7000 volumes.

Although the terms tend to be used somewhat interchangeably, a diary is to me separate and distinct from a journal. A diary is for every day and tells what one did and thought, in the random, nonthematic fashion of real life. A journal is more formal, usually a book of observations on particular events, situations, or preoccupations of the writer. It may have an official purpose, such as the great exploration journals of Lewis and Clark, Zebulon Pike, and others. Of the journals dealing with particular themes or preoccupations, the nature journals of Audubon and John and William Bartram and the religious journals of Michael Wigglesworth, David Brainerd, and Mildred Ratcliff are notable.

Recordings of literary men and women often exemplify both journal and diary characteristics, with a certain thematic unity provided by the consuming interest in literature coupled with a zeal to record the welter of everyday life. Good examples are the diaries of Margaret Fuller and of Bronson Alcott, who asked:

> Was it the accident of being shown, when a boy, in the old oaken cabinet, my mother's little journal, that set me out in this chase of myself, continued almost uninterruptedly, and now fixed by habit as a part of the day, like the rising and setting of the sun? Yet it has educated me into whatever skill I possess with the pen. I know not to how much besides; has made me emulous of attaining the art of portraying my thoughts, occupations, surroundings, friendships; and could I succeed in sketching to the life a single day's doings, should esteem myself as having accomplished the chiefest feat in literature.

True diaries, especially of people who had no idea their private lives would ever be made public through the publishing of their diaries, provide an astonishing picture of the variety of human experience. Some diaries are little more than account books or records of the weather. Others are voluminous and comprehensive works of such compulsive diarists as Samuel Sewall and George Templeton Strong. Some are practical, telling of the running of a household, business, or plantation, or of labor conditions, prices, or the progress of technology and invention. Occupations of all kinds and periods are revealed through diaries. Archaeologists, farmers, whalers, teachers, doctors, missionaries, artists, and fur traders have all, either incidentally or intentionally, recorded details of their work. Leisure as well as work activities emerge through diaries. The notes of play and concertgoers are entertaining and informative, as are the enthusiasms and experiences of hunters, fishermen, mountaineers, book collectors, photographers, etc. The diaries of tourists and travelers range from feeble and conventional descriptions of buildings, scenes, or countries, to the excellent and exuberant records of Francis Parkman, Richard Henry Dana, and Louisa Lord.

Some diaries have been kept for a specific duration of time in order to record significant events or circumstances. War, pioneer, and prison diaries are examples. The anonymous "Cholmley's batman" kept an outstanding account of Braddock's defeat in the French and Indian wars, while a good picture of civilian experience during war can be found in Grace Galloway's diary of Philadelphia during the Revolution. Both men and women were amazingly prolific recorders of the pioneer experience, and the diaries of Mary Richardson Walker and James Clyman are representative. Prison and prisoner-of-war diaries are of great interest, not only for their content, but for the heroic efforts often required to keep them. For example, a World War II prisoner used the pins in blackout curtains to prick words on rolls of toilet paper, which he then dropped through a grate and recovered years later. Of course, the American Revolution and Civil War provide many examples from the more distant past.

Finally, there are fascinating introspective diaries, such as Emerson's and Thoreau's, often with more attention devoted to reflections than events. Such diarists have followed Emerson's injunction to "Pay so much honor to the visits of truth to your mind as to record them." They ask, "Why am I here and what am I doing with my life?" One sees here that the search for a meaningful life becomes meaningful by reason of recording. In fact, the life and the diary may have an unusual symbiotic effect, with the diarist living a good life to record a good life.

Diaries, as primary sources, are obviously grist for the historian's mill. But they are also a too often overlooked source of enjoyment and enlightenment for the ordinary reader, for from them, we can learn so much about people, events, and ourselves. Therefore, I welcome the new *American Diaries* as a means of making published diaries more accessible to all categories of users. I, myself, shall continue to be an avid keeper, reader, and collector of diaries.

James Cummings
Stillwater, Minnesota

Introduction

American Diaries: An Annotated Bibliography of Published American Diaries and Journals to 1980, now complete in two volumes, guides librarians, scholars, students, and general readers to more than 6000 published diaries and journals. Volume 2, *Diaries written from 1845-1980,* annotates over 3000 diaries and journals. Together these two volumes supersede the previous authoritative work in this field, William Matthews' *American Diaries: An Annotated Bibliography of American Diaries Written Prior to the Year 1861* (University of California Press, 1945), more than doubling the number of citations, while adding subject and geographic indexing, an expanded name index, and augmented bibliographic citations.

Need for Revision and Expansion of Matthews' Work

The bibliographic treatment of diaries as a distinct genre has a short but distinguished history. In 1923 Harriette M. Forbes published her *New England Diaries, 1602-1800.* In the same year, Arthur Ponsonby performed a similar service for English diaries with the first of his series of works combining bibliography with extensive diary extracts. In both countries, however, the prodigious activity of William Matthews greatly advanced the bibliographic coverage of diaries. A professor of English linguistics, he began the study of diaries as a means of analyzing linguistic change but quickly discovered in them such antiquarian, historical, and human interest values as to claim his attention for the remainder of his life. Matthews' work with American material resulted in not only his aforementioned *American Diaries*, but also in *American Diaries in Manuscript, 1850-1954: A Descriptive Bibliography* (University of Georgia, 1974), still the definitive source on American manuscript diaries. However, the decades that have elapsed since the 1945 appearance of his work on published diaries and its original restrictions in scope, made the need for a major new work apparent.

Interest in Personal and Local History

The decision to undertake such a project now was prompted partly by the evident interest in personal and local history among users of both public and academic libraries. People seem to want to know about others' lives; not just the lives of the famous, the individual makers of history, but the legions of unknown people who helped shape the events of history, or who were, in turn, affected by them. Thus, readers are seeking out, through diaries and other personal narratives, the experiences of Civil War soldiers, pioneers of the westward migration, the history of a particular town, or the stories of their own immigrant forebears. At the same time, interest has not waned in the lives of the famous or infamous. However, readers are also curious about the famous as "ordinary" people, about the day-to-day events and influences surrounding the achievements for which they are known. But rather than relying entirely on the biographer or historian to select from and organize such material, some readers want to do such sifting of detail for themselves and turn to published diaries, letters, and other personal records for this purpose. Whether dealing essentially with persons or events, they would agree with William Matthews that:

> The historian can give you an orderly. . .account of major social practices and general events at particular times, but only a good diary can give you the fine detail and the wondrous confusions of daily life and the feelings and momentary reflections that reveal the living reality of the period.

Interest in personal history is paralleled by the growing field of local history, and the contribution of diaries to historical research on counties, towns and villages is obvious.

Publishing, too, reflects this heightened interest in the history of individuals and places. Not only are many diaries being published for the first time, but many useful diaries long out of print have been reprinted or entirely reedited, and multivolume anthologies, such as Kenneth L. Holmes' *Covered Wagon*

Women (Glendale, Calif., 1983- in progress), are being launched. Although the reprint boom of recent memory has waned, it has left many libraries stocked for years to come with diaries previously held only in the largest research libraries, or at best, available in fragile old copies in rare book rooms. A major purpose of the present *American Diaries* is to make such recently published, reprinted, or reedited diaries more widely known and therefore more easily accessible to the reader.

Value of Diaries in Study of History

Although we assume, as did William Matthews, the value of diaries to the study of history, it is not an unqualified assumption. A single diary of a particular event, period, or phenomenon is fragmentary and anecdotal, but the study of many such diaries can lead to new conclusions or, more often, to further confirmation of existing ones. It is interesting to note, for example, after reading hundreds of diaries of the westward migration, that pioneers crossing the Plains in the 1850s had far more to fear from cholera than from Indians, or to rediscover, through an immersion in Civil War diaries, that Northern soldiers regarded themselves as fighting more to preserve the Union than to free the slaves. And yet, occasionally, even a single diary can provide some fact, date, or perspective the historian is seeking. In either case, no history student or scholar uses diaries as the sole source of evidence, but in balance with other resources. Nor is the claim made that diaries very often provide new and startling information. But what may be commonplace to history professors is often new to their students, and there is obvious value in encouraging them to make some of their own discoveries through diaries and other primary materials, using them to test or corroborate the established knowledge delivered through textbooks and class lectures.

Still, for many diaries, no claim of historic importance of any kind can be made. Yet many of these diaries are valuable as human documents and sometimes leave the most lasting impression. The diary of a homesick young Maryland cavalryman stationed at a desolate Southwest outpost sheds no historic light on the Indian wars in which he was fighting, but the picture of him riding away after mail call, empty-handed and in tears, remains indelibly impressed on the reader's mind. In fact, for many readers, a *mixture* of human interest, personal, and historic motivations will lead them to diaries for answers to such questions as: What was it like for my forbears to come over steerage from Sweden? What was life like in my home town a hundred years ago? What was it like to travel across the West in a stagecoach?

Present Work More Comprehensive than Matthews

Another factor prompting the decision to expand and revise Matthews' *American Diaries* was the incompleteness of some aspects of the original work. Not only have many diaries appeared since his 1945 publication, but because of his cut-off date, his work excluded an enormous body of material available to him. Thus, because Matthews carried his work only through the diaries begun prior to 1861, the period of the Civil War was omitted. As he explained, "So numerous are the diaries of Americans who took part in the Civil War that when I was making my bibliography of American diaries, my courage failed me and I called a halt at 1860." Volume 2 of the present work rectifies that massive omission. Furthermore, Matthews' definition of American, while in accord with the lights of the time, dictated the omission of all Alaskan, Hawaiian and much Spanish-American material. Colonial America, to him, was largely the English-speaking eastern seaboard, and the diaries of the Spanish explorers and settlers of the Southwest, in territory once under Spanish domain, were excluded. By his own choice, he also omitted the diaries of American missionaries serving in foreign countries. The present work not only goes back to pick up diaries published during Matthews' time and omitted for the above reasons, but incorporates, as well, the results of much recent publishing of Hawaiian, Alaskan, Spanish, French, Russian, and missionary material. We do not fault the thoroughness of Matthews' coverage within his intended scope, for it was thorough indeed, but rather point out the importance of diaries which must now be included because of the addition of two new states and a long-needed recognition of American backgrounds other than English.

Scope of This Book

We have accepted Matthew's definitions of diaries and journals as expressed in his preface to *American Diaries:*

I understand a diary to be a day-by-day record of what interested the diarist, each day's record being self-contained and written shortly after the events occurred, the style being usually free from organized exposition. Between 'diary' and 'journal' I have generally made a conventional distinction, that a diary is written for personal reasons, and that a journal, although otherwise similar to a diary, is kept as part of a job; in practice, there is often little or no difference, for journals are rarely altogether impersonal, many official journals being filled with private opinions and affairs of the writers...I believe the diary to be a unique kind of writing; all other forms of writing envisage readers, and so are adapted to readers, by interpretation, order, simplification, rationalization, omission, addition, and the endless devices of exposition. Although many diaries, too, are written with readers in mind, they are in general the most immediate, truthful, and revealing documents available to the historian. A comparison of a diary with a narrative based upon it, or of letters and diaries on the same subjects, will quickly show the essential differences.

While accepting Matthews' definitions, we have tried, in our selection of diaries and journals for inclusion, to abide by them more strictly. For some reason, Matthews included considerable material that violates his own definitions, items we would consider narratives or memoirs. While we have not removed these items, we have tried not to add such material to the present work. There are admittedly borderline cases and some have been included because of their importance, especially Spanish, French, and Russian exploration journals (in Volume 1) and many Civil War diaries that were polished to varying degrees for publication (in Volume 2). Our emphasis, then, is on works that record immediate experiences, events, impressions, and reflections, rather than on later reconstructions of them. Our use in annotations of the terms "diary" or "journal" is based on the term used in the citation or the term that best fits the above definitions. Our concern has been more to exclude material that does not fit either term than to make fine distinctions between the two terms.

We have defined as "American" any diary or journal kept by an American, whether in America or elsewhere, or kept in America by a foreigner, or foreign diaries related to events which took place primarily on American soil or record a major event conventionally regarded as American. Thus the diary of an American diplomat living abroad would be included, while the diary of a German soldier fighting Americans and their allies in World War II would not. We have also defined as "American" any area that is now part of the fifty United States, regardless of its original or territorial colonial status. We have cited and described only diaries that are available in English, either as the original language or in translation, and only those that are published as printed books or periodical articles. Scholars seeking manuscript diaries will find Matthews' *American Diaries in Manuscript* of continued usefulness. The premise behind the new *American Diaries* is that published diaries and journals are the province not only of scholars but of the reading public as well. Thus, our emphasis has been on published, largely loanable material of use equally to the research scholar, the student, and the ordinary reader.

Omissions From This Volume

There have been some intentional omissions. Ship logs have not been included unless they contain distinctly personal diary content. Travel accounts of the highly narrative travelogue variety have been excluded even if entitled "diary" or "journal." Also omitted were war correspondents' newspaper dispatches, although some have been published recently as "diaries." Unintentional omissions must surely occur. We have cited and described only those diaries we were able to lay hands on, aware that others do exist. Furthermore, there are obscure published diaries that give no clue in the title or subtitle that they are diaries; nor do they appear in major bibliographies of important historical topics. No doubt some diaries were missed in our scouring of historical and other periodicals, indexes, and abstracts. Finally, no attempt was made to present a complete publishing history of every diary cited.

Criteria Used in Annotating

Our concern in examining and annotating a diary has been to discover and call to the reader's attention whatever events, conditions, circumstances, attitudes, places, and people emerge as significant. Obviously, judgment of significance is perilously subjective, but we trust that common sense and intuition on the one hand, and our backgrounds in American history and reference librarianship on the other, did not lead us too far astray. The impossibility of doing justice in a short annotation to such monumental diaries as those of Mary Chesnut, George Templeton Strong, Charles Dawes, or Anne Morrow Lindbergh must be admitted with regret. We tried in annotating to draw out the following elements.

1. Whatever the diarist emphasized heavily, e.g., religion, nature, illness, social life, even the weather.

2. Conditions of categories of persons, e.g., women, the aged, the very young, minorities, the handicapped, etc.

3. Occupations or professions

4. Historic events

5. Modes of travel

6. Religious affiliations or denominations

7. Names of specific people, places, ships, etc.

8. Customs, social milieu, attitudes and values

9. Such broad generic categories as travel, religion, exploration, military, etc. Some annotations may exhibit a number of these emphases, while others contain only one brief reference to a historic event or place, largely depending on the length and content of the diary.

Coverage of Volume 2

In Volume 2, depth and breadth of coverage of certain groups of diaries differs because of the presence or absence of definitive bibliographies for those areas. For instance, more Civil War diaries are cited, and described in greater detail, because recent, comprehensive, descriptive coverage is unavailable elsewhere. On the other hand, one turns to the three-volume work of Steven E. Kagle for the most serious treatment extant of American literary diaries and to the extensive work of Davis Bitton for thorough description of Mormon diaries.

Furthermore, as was the case with Volume 1, there are important groups in America whose experience and perspective unavoidably do not appear in the present work, especially those who, for various reasons, did not keep diaries. The westward migration and Indian wars emerge strictly from the perspective of pioneers and military personnel, not Indians. Similarly, in diaries, the subject of slavery emerges from the writings of slave traders, slave owners, visitors to the South, and abolitionists, but not, of necessity, from the slaves themselves. The student of these perspectives must seek other kinds of historical materials. No claim can be made, then, that *American Diaries* provides more than a partial, though important, access to personal narratives of the American experience. Furthermore, the prejudiced honesty of diaries must be taken as it is. Unrevised diaries reflect what their authors saw and felt, not what the hindsight of history or enlightenment indicate they should have seen and felt or how they should have interpreted their experiences. Also, because we are limited to those diaries that first have survived as manuscripts and, of these, diaries that someone has deemed worthy to publish, the puzzle of America as revealed through this medium does indeed have many gaps.

Format of Volume

The diaries are arranged chronologically, with diaries beginning in the same year arranged alphabetically by diarist's name. Diaries or portions of diaries published more than once have been arranged by date of publication. Although the chronological arrangement of *American Diaries* ensures that there is no overlap of beginning dates between the two volumes, the user must be cautioned that there is unavoidable overlap of some material, because many diaries begun prior to 1845 continued well into the period covered by Volume 2. The two volumes are intended to be used together, and for this reason, numbering of entries continues from Volume 1 to Volume 2. As in most current annotated bibliographies, citation is given first, followed by annotation. Occupation, rank, and place of birth or residence of the diarist are mentioned in the citation or annotation when applicable to the diary described. For diaries covering twelve months or less, months are specified and all indication of days are dropped. Disputed authorship is mentioned in the annotation.

Name, Subject, and Geographic Indexes Included

Each volume contains its own indexes; they are not cumulated. Citations in the indexes refer to entry numbers rather than page numbers.

Name Index—contains names of diarists as well as names of persons mentioned prominently in diaries. Citations appearing in boldface type refer to diarist entries.

Subject Index—used together with Volume 1, the researcher can trace interests related to women's lives, religious experience, travel, social life, leisure pursuits, the arts, education, maritime history, intellectual life, immigrant and ethnic experience, slavery, American Indians, occupations, foreign impressions of America, observance of holidays, and so on. Topics unique to Volume 2 include armed conflicts from the Mexican War through two world wars to the Vietnam War (with the Civil War predominating as the single largest category in the volume), the westward migration and pioneer experience, various gold rushes, Indian wars of the West, the abolition of slavery, the opening of Japan, changing attitudes and roles of women, and more.

Geographic Index—includes those place-names that figure in the diary, but not the diarist's birthplaces unrelated to the contents of the diary. Major place-names are given in their present form, e.g., Hawaii, rather than Sandwich Islands.

Preparation of This Volume

Volume 2 of *American Diaries*, like Volume 1, is an equal collaboration of its three authors, but with each concentrating on a particular area of interest or expertise. Marcia Reed specialized on women's diaries, Nancy Pries on the Civil War, and Laura Arksey on the westward movement, while all three annotated and indexed a wide variety of other diaries. The assistance of many libraries, near and far, must be acknowledged with gratitude. Locally, we are indebted to Seattle Pacific University, Seattle Public Library History Department, and the University of Washington, especially its Northwest Collection and staff. The work of Volume 2 would not have been completed without considerable travel, and we are grateful for the outstanding diary collections and helpful library staffs at Duke University, Princeton University, the Library of Congress, the Bancroft Library of Berkeley, the University of Michigan libraries and Clements Library at Ann Arbor, the University of North Carolina, and state historical societies of California, Oregon, and Utah. Special thanks go to Seattle Pacific University for several research grants which helped defray the expense of these travels. Extraordinary interlibrary assistance of Seattle Public Library, the Wisconsin Historical Society, Duke University, and the Library of Congress also deserve mention.

Acknowledgments

In addition, certain individuals should be singled out for acknowledgment: at Seattle Pacific University, Library Director George McDonough for flexible time and unfailing encouragement, Ann Hill for heroic interlibrary loan service, Betty Fine for valuable help with proofreading, Mary Massey and Nancy Risdon for cheerfully rising to various emergencies, and Gary Fick and Roger Miller for willingness to trade reference hours to suit our convenience, and to James Cummings, foremost private collector of diaries in the United States, for generosity in sharing his unique collection for this project and for contributing the preface. We also appreciate the expert work and patience of Amy Marcaccio of Gale Research Company and Keith Irvine of Reference Publications. Finally, to our long-neglected families, our thanks for your help, ungrudging forbearance, and encouragement.

Frequently Cited Sources

Andrews, Matthew Page, comp. *The Women of the South in War Times.* Baltimore: Norman, Remington, 1920.

Angle, Paul McClelland and Miers, Earl S. *Tragic Years, 1860-1865: A Documentary History of the American Civil War.* New York: Simon & Schuster, 1960. 2 vols.

Bary, Helen Valeska, comp. *The Course of Empire: First Hand Accounts of California in the Days of the Gold Rush of '49.* New York: Coward-McCann, 1931.

Berger, Josef and Berger, Dorothy, eds. *Diary of America: The Intimate Story of Our Nation Told by 100 Diarists.* New York: Simon & Schuster, 1957.

Berger, Josef and Berger, Dorothy, eds. *Small Voices.* New York: P.S. Ericksson, 1967, c1966.

Bettersworth, John K. and Silver, James W., eds. *Mississippi in the Confederacy.* Baton Rouge: Published for the Mississippi Dept. of Archives and History, Jackson, by Louisiana State University Press, 1961. 2 vols.

Bieber, Ralph Paul, ed. *Southern Trails to California in 1849.* Glendale, Calif.: Arthur H. Clark, 1937; Philadelphia: Porcupine, 1974.

Brown, Leonard. *American Patriotism: or, Memoirs of "Common Men."* Des Moines: Redhead and Wellslager, 1869.

Brownlee, W. Elliot and Brownlee, Mary M. *Women in the American Economy: A Documentary History, 1675 to 1929.* New Haven: Yale University Press, 1976.

Carter, Kate B., comp. *Treasures of Pioneer History.* Salt Lake City: Daughters of Utah Pioneers, 1952-1957. 6 vols.

Clifton, James M., ed. *Life and Labor on Argyle Island: Letters and Documents of a Savannah River Rice Plantation, 1833-1865.* Savannah: Beehive Press, 1978.

Commager, Henry Steele, ed. *The Blue and the Gray: The Story of the Civil War as Told by Participants.* Indianapolis: Bobbs-Merrill, 1950. 2 vols.

Culley, Margo, ed. *A Day at a Time: The Diary Literature of American Women from 1764 to the Present.* New York: Feminist Press, 1985.

Dickey, Luther Samuel. *History of the 103D Regiment, Pennsylvania Veteran Volunteer Infantry, 1861-1865.* Chicago: L.S. Dickey, 1910.

Dunaway, Philip, ed. *A Treasury of the World's Great Diaries.* Garden City, N.Y.: Doubleday, 1957.

Garrett, Jill K. and Lightfoot, Marise P. *The Civil War in Maury County, Tennessee.* Columbia? Tenn.: 1966.

Godfrey, Kenneth W., Godfrey, Audrey M., and Derr, Jill M., eds. *Women's Voices: An Untold History of the Latter-Day Saints.* Salt Lake City: Deseret Book Company, 1982.

Hafen, Le Roy R. and Hafen, Ann W., eds. *Fremont's Fourth Expedition: A Documentary Account of the Disaster of 1848-49, with Diaries, Letters and Reports by Participants in the Tragedy.* The Far West and the Rockies, vol. 11. Glendale, Calif.: Arthur H. Clark, 1960.

Hafen, Le Roy R. and Hafen, Ann W., eds. *Handcarts to Zion: The Story of a Unique Western Migration, 1856-1860.* The Far West and the Rockies, vol. 14. Glendale, Calif.: Arthur H. Clark, 1960.

Hafen, Le Roy R. and Hafen, Ann W., eds. *Journals of Forty-Niners: Salt Lake to Los Angeles, with Diaries and Contemporary Records.* The Far West and the Rockies, vol. 2. Glendale, Calif.: Arthur H. Clark, 1954.

Hafen, Le Roy R., ed. *Overland to the Gold Fields, 1859, From Contemporary Diaries.* The Southwest Historical Series, vol. 11. Glendale, Calif.: Arthur H. Clark, 1942.

Hakola, John W., ed. *Frontier Omnibus.* Missoula: Montana State University Press, 1962.

Hall, Carroll Douglas, ed. *Donner Miscellany, 41 Diaries and Documents.* San Francisco: Book Club of California, 1947.

Hart, Albert Bushnell. *American History Told by Contemporaries.* New York: Macmillan, 1896-1929. 5 vols.

Hellerstein, Erna O., Hume, Leslie P. and Offen, Karen M., eds. *Victorian Women: A Documentary Account of Women's Lives in Nineteenth-Century England, France, and the United States.* Stanford, Calif.: Stanford University Press, 1981.

Hickerson, Thomas Felix. *Echoes of Happy Valley.* Chapel Hill, N.C.: Distributed by Bull's Head Bookshop, 1962.

Hine, Robert V. *The Frontier Experience: Readings in the Trans-Mississippi West.* Belmont, Calif.: Wadsworth, 1963.

History of the American Field Service in France, "Friends of France", Told by its Members. Boston and New York: Houghton Mifflin, 1920. 3 vols.

Hoffman, Nancy. *Woman's "True" Profession: Voices from the History of Teaching.* Old Westbury, N.Y.: Feminist Press; New York: McGraw-Hill, 1981.

Holmes, Kenneth L., ed. *Covered Wagon Women: Diaries & Letters from the Western Trails, 1840-1890.* Glendale, Calif.: Arthur H. Clark, 1983-in progress.

Huser, Verne, ed. *River Reflections: An Anthology.* Charlotte, N.C.: East Woods Press, 1984.

Illinois Infantry. 73d Regt. *A History of the Seventy-Third Regiment of Illinois Infantry Volunteers.* Springfield, Ill.: 1890.

Johnston, Abraham Robinson. *Marching with the Army of the West, 1846-1848.* Edited by Ralph P. Bieber. The Southwest Historical Series, vol. 4. Glendale, Calif.: Arthur H. Clark, 1936.

Jones, Katharine M., ed. *Heroines of Dixie: Confederate Women Tell Their Story of the War.* Indianapolis: Bobbs-Merrill, 1955. Reprint. Westport, Conn.: Greenwood, 1973.

Jones, Katharine M., ed. *Ladies of Richmond, Confederate Capitol.* Indianapolis: Bobbs-Merrill, 1962.

Jones Katharine M., ed. *When Sherman Came: Southern Women and the 'Great March.'* Indianapolis: Bobbs-Merrill, 1964.

Koury, Michael J., ed. *Diaries of the Little Big Horn.* Papillion?, Neb.: Old Army Press, 1968.

Leyda, Jay, ed. *The Melville Log: A Documentary Life of Herman Melville, 1819-1891.* New York: Harcourt, Brace and World, 1951. Reprint with supplement. Gordian Press, 1969. 2 vols.

Lifshin, Lyn, ed. *Ariadne's Threat: A Collection of Contemporary Women's Journals.* New York: Harper & Row, 1982.

Luchetti, Cathy. *Women of the West.* St. George, Utah: Antelope Island Press, 1982.

McCord, Shirley S., comp. *Travel Accounts of Indiana, 1679-1961.* Indianapolis: Indiana Historical Bureau, 1970

McFarling, Lloyd, ed. *Exploring the Northern Plains, 1804-1876.* Caldwell, Id.: Caxton Printers, 1955.

McMillan, Malcolm Cook, ed. *The Alabama Confederate Reader.* University, Ala.: University of Alabama Press, 1963.

Maddow, Ben. *A Sunday Between Wars: The Course of American Life from 1865 to 1917.* New York: Norton, 1979.

Marcus, Jacob Rader. *Memoirs of American Jews, 1775-1865.* New York: Ktav Publishing House, 1974.

Massachusetts Artillery. 5th Battery, 1861-1865. *History of the Fifth Massachusetts Battery.* Boston: L.E. Cowles, 1902.

Matthews, William and Wecter, Dixon. *Our Soldiers Speak, 1775-1918.* Boston: Little, Brown, 1943.

Meier, Peg, comp. *Bring Warm Clothes: Letters and Photos from Minnesota's Past.* Minneapolis: Minneapolis Tribune, 1981.

Merrill, Catharine. *The Soldier of Indiana in the War for the Union.* Indianapolis: Merrill, 1866-1869. 2 vols.

Merrill, James M., ed. *Uncommon Valor: The Exciting Story of the Army.* Chicago: Rand McNally, 1964.

Moffat, Mary Jane and Painter, Charlotte, eds. *Revelations: Diaries of Women.* New York: Random House, 1974. Reprint. Vintage Books, 1975.

Moore, Frank, ed. *The Rebellion Record.* New York: G.P. Putnam, 1861-1863. Suppl., 1864; D. Van Nostrand,   1864-1868. 11 vols.

Morgan, Dale Lowell, ed. *Overland in 1846: Diaries and Letters of the California-Oregon Trail.* Georgetown, Calif.: Talisman Press, 1963. 2 vols.

Myres, Sandra L., ed. *Ho for California! Women's Overland Diaries from the Huntington Library.* San Marino: Huntington Library, 1980.

New Jersey Infantry. 12th regt., 1862-1865. *History of Men of Company F.* Edited by William P. Haines. Camden, N.J.: C.S. McGrath, Printer, 1897.

New York State Bureau of Military Statistics. *Annual Report. 5th.* Albany: C. Van Benthuysen and Sons Steam Printing House, 1868.

Our Women in the War. Charleston, S.C.: News and Courier Presses, 1885.

Pennsylvania Infantry. 124th regt., 1862-1863. *History of the One Hundred and Twenty-Fourth Regiment, Pennsylvania Volunteers.* Compiled by Robert McKay Green. Philadelphia: Ware Bros. Co., Printers, 1907.

Poe, Clarence Hamilton, ed. *True Tales of the South at War.* Chapel Hill: University of North Carolina Press, 1961.

Quaife, Milo Milton, ed. *Pictures of Gold Rush California.* Chicago: Lakeside Press, 1949. Reprint. New York: Citadel Press, 1967.

Ramey, Emily G. and Gott, John K., comps. *The Years of Anguish, Fauquier County, Virginia.* Warrenton? Va.: 1965.

Rubin, Michael, comp. *Men Without Masks: Writings from the Journals of Modern Men.* Reading, Mass.: Addison-Wesley, 1980.

Schlissel, Lillian, comp. *Women's Diaries of the Westward Journey.* New York: Schocken Books, 1982.

Smith, George Winston and Judah, Charles, eds. *Chronicles of the Gringos: The U.S. Army in the Mexican War.* Albuquerque: University of New Mexico Press, 1968.

Stanyan, John Minot. *A History of the Eighth Regiment of New Hampshire Volunteers.* Concord: I.C. Evans, Printer, 1892.

Stevens, William Burnham. *History of the Fiftieth Regiment of Infantry, Massachusetts Volunteer Militia.* Boston: Griffith-Stillings Press, 1907.

Straubing, Harold Elk, ed. *Civil War Eyewitness Reports.* Hamden, Conn.: Archon Books, 1985.

Tourgee, Albion W. *The Story of a Thousand: Being a History of the Service of the 105th Ohio Volunteer Infantry.* Buffalo, N.Y.: S. McGerald & Son, 1896.

Reid, Robert Leonard, ed. *A Treasury of the Sierra Nevada.* Berkeley: Wilderness Press, 1983.

U.S. Naval War Records Office. *Official Records of the Union and Confederate Navies in the War of the Rebellion.* ser. 1, vol. 1-27; ser. 2, vol. 1-3. Washington, D.C. Government Printing Office, 1894-1922. 30 vols.

U.S. War Dept. *Report of the Secretary of War Communicating the Several Pacific Railroad Explorations.* Washington: A.O.P. Nicholson, Printer, 1855, 4 vols.

U.S. War Dept. *Reports of Explorations and Surveys, to Ascertain the Most Practicable and Economical Route for a Railroad from the Mississippi River to the Pacific Ocean.* Washington: A.O.P. Nicholson, Printer, 1855-60, 12 vols.

Vining, Donald, ed. *American Diaries of World War II.* New York: Pepys Press, 1982.

Virginia Artillery. Richmond Howitzers. *Contributions to a History of the Richmond Howitzer Battalion.* Pamphlet nos. 1-4. Richmond, Va.: C. McCarthy, 1883-1886.

Walcott, Charles Folsom *History of the Twenty-First Regiment, Massachusetts Volunteers.* Boston: Houghton Mifflin, 1882.

Weygant, Charles H. *History of the One Hundred and Twenty-Fourth Regiment, N.Y.S.V.* Newburgh, N.Y.: Journal Printing House, 1877.

White, Helen McCann, ed. *Ho! For the Gold Fields: Northern Overland Wagon Trains of the 1860's.* St. Paul: Minnesota Historical Society, 1966.

Willert, James. *Little Big Horn Diary: Chronicle of the 1876 Indian War.* La Mirada, Calif.: Willert, 1977, 1982.

Williams, C. Fred, ed. *A Documentary History of Arkansas.* Fayetteville: University of Arkansas Press, 1984.

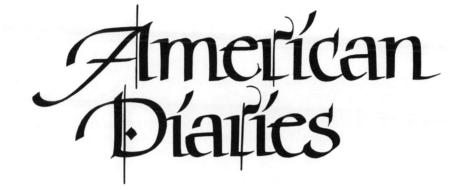

AMERICAN DIARIES

1845

ANON.   **2783**

Woolworth, Nancy L. "Captain Edwin V. Sumner's Expedition to Devil's Lake in the Summer of 1845." NORTH DAKOTA HISTORY 28 (1961):79-105.

> Jun-Jul 1845. Extracts from the records of several diarists within an article on military expedition dispatched to the Red River of the North because of United States-British boundary antagonisms, especially competing fur trade interests; the march of Capt. James Allen's company from "Traverse des Sioux" to "Lac qui Parle"; description of councils held with the Sioux; references to Métis involved in the fur trade.

ANON.   **2784**

In SKETCHES OF MISSION LIFE AMONG THE INDIANS OF OREGON, by Zachariah A. Mudge, pp. 52-54. New York: Carlton & Porter, 1854. Reprint. Fairfield, Wash.: Ye Galleon, 1983.

> Sep 1845. Attempt by a missionary from The Dalles Mission to climb Mount Adams; a few notes on the conducting of services for Indians of the area.

ABERT, JAMES WILLIAM, 1820-1897   **2785**

In MESSAGE FROM THE PRESIDENT OF THE UNITED STATES COMMUNICATING A REPORT OF AN EXPEDITION LED BY LIEUTENANT ABERT ON THE UPPER ARKANSAS AND THROUGH THE COUNTRY OF THE COMANCHE INDIANS IN THE FALL OF THE YEAR 1845, by United States Army Corps of Topographical Engineers. 29th Cong., 1st sess., 1847, S. Exec. Doc. 438, pp. 1-75. Washington, D.C.? 1846.

GUADAL P'A, THE JOURNAL OF LIEUTENANT J.W. ABERT, FROM BENT'S FORT TO ST. LOUIS IN 1845. With introduction and notes by H. Bailey Carroll. Canyon, Tex.: Panhandle-Plains Historical Society, 1941. 121 pp.

In THROUGH THE COUNTRY OF THE COMANCHE INDIANS IN THE FALL OF THE YEAR 1845, by United States Army Corps of Topographical Engineers, edited by John Galvin, pp. 1-77. San Francisco: J. Howell, 1970.

> Aug-Oct 1845. Topographical engineer's journal of party detached from Fremont expedition to survey Purgatory Creek, the waters of the Canadian and False Washita; sketching Cheyenne Indians at Bent's Fort, council between Delawares and Cheyennes and Indian ceremonies; notes on Kiowa and Crow Indians; return journey, meeting emigrants on road from Fort Gibson to Texas.

In REPORT OF THE SECRETARY OF WAR, COMMUNICATING, IN ANSWER TO A RESOLUTION OF THE SENATE, A REPORT AND MAP OF THE EXAMINATION OF NEW MEXICO, MADE BY LIEUTENANT J.W. ABERT, by United States Army Corps of Topographical Engineers. 30th Cong., 1st sess., 1848, S. Exec. Doc. 23, pp. 1-132. Washington, 1848.

In 30th Cong., 1st sess., 1848, H. Exec. Doc. 41, pp. 386-405, 417-546.

In ABERT'S NEW MEXICO REPORT, 1846-'47, by United States Army Corps of Topographical Engineers, pp. 1-182. Albuquerque: Horn & Wallace, 1962.

WESTERN AMERICA IN 1846-1847: THE ORIGINAL TRAVEL DIARY OF LIEUTENANT J.W. ABERT, WHO MAPPED NEW MEXICO FOR THE UNITED STATES ARMY. Edited by John Galvin. San Francisco: J. Howell, 1966. 116 pp.

> Jun-Sep 1846. At Bent's Fort recovering from illness; studying and sketching rare plants and minerals; notes on Cheyennes, their language, use of plants and meeting with Cheyenne chief Nah-co-mense, or Old Bark, and Yellow Wolf; exploring and surveying New Mexico, Indian villages and gold mines; returning to Fort Leavenworth.

In THE UNITED STATES CONQUEST OF CALIFORNIA, pp. 386-405. New York: Arno, 1976.

In NOTES OF TRAVEL IN CALIFORNIA, app., pp. 72-83. New York: D. Appleton; Philadelphia: G.S. Appleton, 1849.

> Jun-Jul 1846. Extract of natural history notes on birds, plants and animals from Fort Leavenworth to Bent's Fort; references to William H. Emory, Doniphan and Kearny.

ANDREWS, PERSIS SIBLEY, 1813-1891   **2786**

In VICTORIAN WOMEN, edited by Erna O. Hellerstein, pp. 306-308.

> Aug-Dec 1845. Extracts from rural New England housewife's journal; joys and trials of household management; finding and keeping hired help; spinning and dyeing wool, weaving, quilting, mending; drawing for pleasure and working as "drawing master" at school.

BARCLAY, ALEXANDER, 1810-1855   **2787**

In THE ADVENTURES OF ALEXANDER BARCLAY, by George P. Hammond, pp. 135-182. Denver: Old West, 1976.

> 1845-1850. Brief daily notes of an energetic English immigrant, mountain man and fur trader turned landowner in New Mexico; farming, trading and contacts with travelers on the Santa Fe Trail, including Kit Carson and other famous traders, Indians, Spaniards, pioneers and the military; common-law marriage to Taos woman kept secret from relatives in England.

BROWN, WILLIAM REYNOLDS, 1816-1874　　**2788**

In MINNESOTA FARMERS' DIARIES, with an introduction and notes by Rodney C. Loehr, pp. 37-82. Minnesota Historical Society Publications, Narratives and Documents, vol. 3. St. Paul: Minnesota Historical Society, 1939.

Extracts in DIARY OF AMERICA, edited by Josef and Dorothy Berger, pp. 194-197.

> Oct 1845-Jun 1846. Minute details of farming near Red Rock; notes on crops, livestock, prices and agricultural equipment; work as justice of the peace; names of other settlers in the area; a valuable record of pioneer farming.

CHAPLIN, THOMAS B., 1822-1890　　**2789**

In A DOCUMENTARY HISTORY OF SLAVERY IN NORTH AMERICA, edited by Willie Lee Rose, pp. 210-212, 253-254, 375-377. New York: Oxford University Press, 1976.

> May-Jun 1845, Feb-Apr 1849. Extracts from the journal of a St. Helena Island, South Carolina, cotton planter; routine daily work of slaves and master; serving on an inquest jury regarding a slave's death resulting from his master's brutality, with graphic description of succession of cruelties which caused his death; the diarist's outrage over this incident and regrets over the necessity of selling some of his own slaves to pay debts; his suspicion that one of his own slaves was harboring runaways.

Rosengarten, Theodore. "Tombee: From the Life Story and Plantation Journal of Thomas B. Chaplin." SOUTHERN EXPOSURE 12 (November/December 1984): 25-31.

> Feb 1849. Brief extract covering a few details of daily plantation work and the inquest regarding slave's death.

COLTON, WALTER, 1797-1851　　**2790**

Plumb, Robert J. "The Alcalde of Monterey." UNITED STATES NAVAL INSTITUTE PROCEEDINGS 95, no. 1 (1969): 72-83.

> 1845-1849. Extracts within article describing journey to California and the unusual assignment of a navy chaplain to serve as mayor of the Monterey district; notes on the voyage on the CONGRESS during which he organized the ship's library, confident that "sailors will read if you furnish them with books suited to their tastes and habits"; graphic description of rounding Cape Horn; the effectiveness of his weekly prayer meetings; once in California, appointment by Stockton to govern Monterey and a good picture of his duties and problems bringing order to the newly acquired territory; effects of the gold rush and his own two months in the diggings, but prediction that the wealth of California would lie in "wines, figs, dates and almonds" rather than gold.

THREE YEARS IN CALIFORNIA. New York: A.S. Barnes; Cincinnati: H.W. Derby, 1850. 456 pp. Reprint. New York: Arno, 1976. Introduction and notes by Marguerite E. Wilbur. Stanford: Stanford University Press, 1949. 376 pp.

THE LAND OF GOLD; OR THREE YEARS IN CALIFORNIA. New York: D.W. Evans, 1860. 456 pp.

THE CALIFORNIA DIARY. Foreword by Joseph A. Sullivan. Oakland, Calif.: Biobooks, 1948. 261 pp. Diary, pp. 1-208.

Extracts in DIARY OF AMERICA, edited by Josef and Dorothy Berger, pp. 319-321; PICTURES OF GOLD RUSH CALIFORNIA, edited by Milo M. Quaife, pp. 158-172; CALIFORNIA GOLD, edited by Edwin R. Heath, pp. 1-13. Boston: Heath, 1959.

> 1846-1849. California journal covering his experiences as mayor of Monterey and work as publisher of California's first newspaper, the CALIFORNIAN; notes on life and customs, including social and religious observances during carnival, Lent and Christmas; military affairs in California during the Mexican War, noting movements of ships along coast, arrival of Fremont and march south; news of the gold discovery; traveling to and reporting on work and conditions at mines; a valuable historical account embellished with anecdotes, moralistic sketches and recollections of persons, places and events.

DOWNEY, JOSEPH T., b. 1820　　**2791**

THE CRUISE OF THE PORTSMOUTH, 1845-1847: A SAILOR'S VIEW OF THE NAVAL CONQUEST OF CALIFORNIA. Edited by Howard Lamar. Western Historical Series, no. 4. New Haven, Conn.: Yale University Press, 1958. 246 pp.

> 1845-1847. Dated entries soon abandoned for narrative by a humorous and mischievous enlisted man who kept the journal to be read aloud for the entertainment of his shipmates; life on the PORTSMOUTH under Capt. John B. Montgomery, with amusing sketches of ordinary seamen during the Mexican War; notes on the Bear Flag Revolt and the march from San Diego under Stockton and Kearny to recapture Los Angeles; a journal which editor compares to Melville's WHITEJACKET; muster roll appended.

DUERST, MATHIAS　　**2792**

Luchsinger, John, trans. "Diary of One of the Original Colonists of New Glarus." WISCONSIN HISTORICAL SOCIETY COLLECTIONS 15 (1900):292-337.

> Apr-Aug 1845. Swiss immigrant's difficult travel in Europe with his own and a number of other families; across the Atlantic with bad conditions and wretched food on board ship; arrival at Baltimore, thence to Pittsburgh, Cincinnati and Wisconsin, with good descriptions of canal, river boat and land travel; lodgings in taverns; a number of births and deaths during sea and overland journey; references to Nicholas Duerst and others. Translated from the German.

DUNLOP, ALEXANDER GRAHAM, 1814-1892　　**2793**

THE NEW WORLD JOURNAL OF ALEXANDER GRAHAM DUNLOP. Edited by David Sinclair and Germaine Warkentin. Toronto: Dundurn Press; Edinburgh: Paul Harris, 1976. 121 pp.

> Apr-Aug 1845. Englishman's travel journal; on sailing ship MARY WALKER from Jamaica to New Orleans; comparison of slavery in both places; on riverboat CHAMPLAIN up the Mississippi River, seeing Natchez, Vicksburg, Memphis, St. Louis and Chicago; traveling on Lake Michigan and Lake Huron on the ST. LOUIS to Detroit; comments on the fresh and prosperous look of towns, American manners and women, politics and slavery; afterthoughts during return to England on the sailing ship WELLINGTON.

EWBANK, THOMAS, 1792-1870　　**2794**

LIFE IN BRAZIL; OR, A JOURNAL OF A VISIT TO THE LAND OF THE COCOA AND THE PALM. New York: Harper & Brothers, 1856. 469 pp.

> Dec 1845-Aug 1846. Journey of prominent English-born inventor to Rio de Janeiro aboard the MAZEPPA; ship travel; copious notes, in narrative style, on people of all classes; customs, the

arts, business, social life and dress; particular emphasis on Roman Catholic practices and the horrors of Brazilian slavery.

FRANKLIN, WILLIAM BUEL, 1823-1903　　　　**2795**

MARCH TO SOUTH PASS: LIEUTENANT WILLIAM B. FRANKLIN'S JOURNAL OF THE KEARNY EXPEDITION OF 1845. Edited by Frank N. Schubert. Washington, D.C.: Historical Division, Office of Administrative Services, Office of the Chief of Engineers; United States Government Printing Office, 1979. 41 pp.

May-Aug 1845. Young topographical engineer's account of expedition of First Dragoons to secure safe route for Oregon emigrants and to map area from Fort Laramie to Bent's Fort; departure from Fort Leavenworth with rapid trek across plains to South Pass and return via Santa Fe Trail; scenic and topographical notes; frequent encounters with wagon trains; good description of buildings and layout of Fort Laramie where 1200 Sioux assembled for council; important Oregon Trail document.

GOODNOUGH, EZRA　　　　**2796**

Aink, David L. "Who Was ANN PARRY's Jonah?" AMERICAN NEPTUNE 32 (1972):34-44.

1845-1847. Extracts within article from journal begun by Ezra Goodnough and continued by John Joplin, seamen on an unprofitable and trouble-plagued whaling voyage to the Indian Ocean; desertions, deaths, accidents, inept leadership, quarrels and boredom, leading to frequent speculation as to who might be the Jonah aboard.

HARRITT, JESSE, b. 1818　　　　**2797**

"Diary of Jesse Harritt." OREGON PIONEER ASSOCIATION TRANSACTIONS (1910-1911):506-526.

Apr-Oct 1845. Indiana man's journey from the Missouri River to The Dalles; notes of stages and difficulties as well as sights "interesting and singular" en route; some Oregon prices.

McNary, Lawrence A. "Route of the Meek Cut-Off." OREGON HISTORICAL QUARTERLY 35 (1934):1-9.

Aug-Oct 1985. Extract.

HEATH, JOSEPH THOMAS, 1805-1849　　　　**2798**

WITH AN EAGLE'S QUILL: THE JOURNAL OF JOSEPH THOMAS HEATH. Edited by L.F. Ramsey. N. p., n.d., 104 leaves.

JOSEPH THOMAS HEATH DIARY. Edited by L.F. Ramsey. Tacoma: City Print Shop, 1976. 140 leaves.

MEMOIRS OF NISQUALLY. Edited by Lucille MacDonald. Fairfield, Wash.: Ye Galleon, 1979. 180 pp.

1845-1849. Englishman's attempt at farming near Fort Nisqually as a member of the Puget Sound Agricultural Company, a Hudson's Bay Company subsidiary; carving a farm out of the wilderness with the uncertain help of Indian labor; problems with weather, wolves, pests, etc., and the frequent Indian raids on stock; struggles with ill health, loneliness and homesickness; frequent acrimonious dealings with Dr. William F. Tolmie, superintendent at Nisqually, but pleasant relations with English neighbor, John Edgar; notes on Indian customs and ships in the area.

HENRY, WILLIAM SEATON, 1816-1851　　　　**2799**

CAMPAIGN SKETCHES OF THE WAR WITH MEXICO. New York: Harper & Brothers, 1847. 331 pp. Reprint. New York: Arno, 1973.

1845-1847. Long narrative diary of military service in Mexican War; from New Orleans by steamer to Matagorda and Corpus Christi; Mexican villages; fishing and hunting; relations with Mexicans; hot, dusty march to Colorado River and on to Rio Grande; skirmishes, desertions, brutal deaths, military funerals, details of troops and officers, movements and lines of battle; praise for medical officers and General Taylor; battle of Resaca de la Palma, entering Matamoros, march to Camero on San Juan River in terrible heat with lack of water; disgust with primitive transportation; fandangos and gambling at Mier; lengthy description of taking Monterrey; battle of Buena Vista; many tributes to brave and gallant fellow officers in an exalted, florid style for the "dear reader."

HICKS, ELIJAH　　　　**2800**

"Journal of Elijah Hicks." CHRONICLES OF OKLAHOMA 13 (1935):68-99.

Dec 1845-June 1846. Official journal, kept by missionary, of treaty expedition under Pierce M. Butler and M.G. Lewis to the Comanches; company made up of government commissioners, Seminole and Chickasaw delegates and assorted adventurers; travel through Oklahoma; work and council among Comanches; substance of speeches, especially diarist's; restoring of some captives; conclusion of peace treaty.

HILL, TIMOTHY　　　　**2801**

Hill, John B., ed. "A Missionary Enters Missouri." PRESBYTERIAN HISTORICAL SOCIETY JOURNAL 25 (1947):1-13, 113-129, 175-186.

1845-1857. Article containing extracts of Presbyterian seminarian's diary of travel to work as a missionary in Missouri in response to an appeal from Rev. Artemas Bullard of St. Louis; train and riverboat travel to Missouri; itinerant preaching, especially in Monroe County, with interesting notes on frontier families and local ministers, past and present, including the eccentric Dr. David Nelson; strong antislavery views and refusal to have his ordination in Missouri because he did not want slaveholding ministers to lay hands on him; a pastorate at St. Charles, then at the Fairmont Presbyterian Church in St. Louis.

HOWELL, JOHN EWING, 1806-1885?　　　　**2802**

"Diary of an Emigrant of 1845." WASHINGTON HISTORICAL QUARTERLY (1907):138-158.

Apr-Oct 1845. Journey from Jackson county, Missouri, to Oregon City; notes mainly on route, distances, scenery and condition of land and timber, by a settler who later returned to Clark County, Missouri.

KERN, EDWARD MEYER, 1823-1863　　　　**2803**

"Artist's Journal of a Pioneer Trip." LIFE, 6 April 1959, pp. 96-104.

Aug 1845-Feb 1846. Extracts from the journal of artist and topographer with Fremont's third expedition; exploration and mapping from Great Salt Lake to Humboldt Sink and across the Sierra Nevada; forced by dwindling supplies to a diet of horsemeat, acorns and lizards; notes on trapper Bill Williams and on Indians encountered.

In REPORT OF EXPLORATIONS ACROSS THE GREAT BASIN OF THE TERRITORY OF UTAH by United States Engineer Department, pp. 447-486. Washington, D.C.: Government Printing Office, 1876.

In THE EXPEDITIONS OF JOHN CHARLES FREMONT, by John C. Fremont, edited by Donald Jackson and Mary L. Spence, vol. 2, pp. 48-68. Urbana: University of Illinois Press, 1973.

Hanson, Meri, ed. "From Walker Lake to Walker Pass with Fremont's Third Expedition." NEVADA HISTORICAL SOCIETY QUARTERLY 21 (1978):56-65.

> Nov 1845-Feb 1846. Segment covering exploration of Humboldt River, Carson Lake and Owens River and Lake with a party under Theodore Talbot, part of Fremont's larger expedition; topographical features, camps, route and distances along the grueling route from Walker Lake through Owens Valley to Walker Pass; a few references to guide Joseph Walker.

In FREMONT'S FOURTH EXPEDITON, edited by Leroy R. and Ann W. Hafen, pp. 289-295.

> Oct-Nov 1848. Brief diary covering early part of the disastrous fourth expedition; through Kansas with Benjamin and Richard Kern, Laklin Godey and others; buffalo hunting, camps, distances, trouble with "wild mules," bad weather and difficult travel conditions.

KINZIE, JOHN HARRIS   2804

Hamaker, Terry, ed. "John Harris Kinzie, American Voyageur." HISTORICAL SOCIETY OF MICHIGAN 20 (1984):2-8.

> Aug-Oct 1845. Journal of Chicago entrepreneur, agent of the American Fur Company and owner of the Kinzie Forwarding Company; from Chicago to Copper Harbor on the steamer GREAT WESTERN, conveying geologists and copper prospectors to the Upper Peninsula; references to many boats plying the lakes; people and activities at Copper Harbor, thence on sailing vessels to look for copper in the Pigeon River, Fort William, Isle Royale and Agate Harbor areas; notes on various minerals found as well as interesting contrast between steam and sail travel on the Great Lakes.

LAUB, GEORGE   2805

England, Eugene, ed. "George Laub's Nauvoo Journal." BRIGHAM YOUNG UNIVERSITY STUDIES 18 (1978):151-178.

> 1845-1846. Mostly review of diarist's conversion to Mormonism and the deaths of Joseph and Hyrum Smith but with current account of events subsequent to Joseph Smith's death; persecution of the Mormons and expulsion from Nauvoo; some of Smith's sermons; earliest account of Brigham Young's "transfiguration and assumption of authority."

LYMAN, CHESTER SMITH, 1814-1890   2806

AROUND THE HORN TO THE SANDWICH ISLANDS AND CALIFORNIA. Edited by Frederick J. Teggart. New Haven: Yale University Press, 1924. 328 pp.

> 1845-1850. Travel diary of eminent scientist, soon to be professor of astronomy and physics at Yale; voyage around Cape Horn to Hawaii aboard the MARIPOSA; notes on scores of important people in Hawaii at that time; Hawaiian royalty, missionaries and administrators; keen interest in work of missionaries, progress of education, particularly the Hawaiian Chiefs' Children's School; diarist's own efforts in both causes; detailed scientific observations, including an excellent report on Mauna Loa volcano; notes on local customs and impact of Christianity; voyage to California aboard the EUPHEMIA; life in San Francisco, San Jose and Monterey; extensive observation of Spanish society, gold rush, ranching, trade, religion and mores; many personal, place and ship names; a varied, informative and intelligent diary.

Teggart Frederick J., ed. "The Gold Rush: Extracts From the Diary of C.S. Lyman." CALIFORNIA HISTORICAL SOCIETY QUARTERLY 2 (1923-1924):181-202.

> 1848-1850. Interesting extracts describing his efforts in the gold fields near Sutter's Fort; his own and others' earnings and accounts of less fortunate gold seekers, some penniless and starving.

MERIWETHER, ANNE KINLOCH, 1830-1867   2807

Brydon, Anne P. "A Small Diary of 1845." ALBEMARLE COUNTY HISTORICAL SOCIETY MAGAZINE 33/34 (1975-1976):141-162.

> Jan-Jul 1845. Fifteen-year-old Virginia girl's almost daily visits from her home, Kinloch, to relatives at neighboring plantations Belvoir, Keswick, Cloverfields, Castalia, Cismont, Castle Hill and Music Hall; a special trip to Charleston, South Carolina, by train and steamboat to visit other relatives; such activities as sewing, music lessons, reading, attending church; a home visit of the dentist "to fix our teeth" and mention of her physician father, Thomas Warner Meriwether, away all night with a patient. Two brief entries, February 1865, appended by her nine-year-old daughter, Anne Nelson Page, after reading her mother's diary, concluding with "Oh when will this war be over and Pa can come home?"

MONTGOMERY, JOHN BERRIEN, 1794-1873   2808

"The Navy on the Pacific Coast." MILITARY SERVICE INSTITUTION OF THE UNITED STATES JOURNAL 30 (1902):708-720.

> Sep 1845-Jul 1846. Extracts from journal of the commander of the PORTSMOUTH, with entries beginning at Monterey and continuing at Mazatlan, Acapulco and return; events at Sonoma; references to Thomas Larkin, the American consul, and José Castro, Commandant General of California; news of Fremont's movements.

MOORE, NATHANIEL FISH, 1782-1872   2809

DIARY: A TRIP FROM NEW YORK TO THE FALLS OF ST. ANTHONY IN 1845. Edited by Stanley Pargellis and Ruth L. Butler. Chicago: Published for the Newberry Library by the University of Chicago Press, 1946. 101 pp.

> Jul-Sep 1845. Vacation diary of the president of Columbia College of New York; an arduous six weeks of travel by train, stagecoach and the lake and riverboats EMPIRE, CECILIA and ATLAS; interesting notes on fellow passengers, trade and commerce and river ports, mainly along the Mississippi.

NEWTON, ALONZO, 1822-1891   2810

In THE COLCHESTER, CONN., NEWTON FAMILY, compiled by Claire A. Newton, pp. 109-114. Naperville, Ill., 1911.

    Jan-Jul 1845. Religious journal kept while attending theological seminary at Lima, New York; studies, religious work and illnesses.

PALMER, JOEL, 1810-1881   2811

JOURNAL OF TRAVELS OVER THE ROCKY MOUNTAINS TO THE MOUTH OF THE COLUMBIA RIVER. Cincinnati: J.A. & U.P. James, 1847. 189 pp. Reprint. 1851. 1852. Ann Arbor, Mich.: University Microfilms, 1966. Fairfield, Wash.: Ye Galleon, 1983. 186 pp.

In EARLY WESTERN TRAVELS, edited by Reuben G. Thwaites, vol. 30. Cleveland: Arthur H. Clark, 1907.

    1845-1846. Emigrant journey to Oregon from Laurel, Indiana, of a pioneer who became an Oregon legislator; observations of Nez Perce Indians and helpful notes for emigrants; descriptions of Willamette, Umpqua and Clamet Valley; references to Dr. McLoughlin, Rev. H.H. Spalding, Dr. Whitman and other Hudson's Bay personnel and missionaries; a good Oregon Trail narrative written up from notes.

PEABODY, CHARLES, b. 1816   2812

Smith, William E. and Ophia D., eds. "The Diary of Charles Peabody." HISTORICAL AND PHILOSOPHICAL SOCIETY OF OHIO BULLETIN 11 (1953):274-292; 12 (1954):119-139.

    Oct 1845-May 1846. Religious travels of Congregational minister and secretary for the American Tract Society; on the CHESAPEAKE, with colorful notes on towns, people and mores along the river and canal route; the condition of religion in Ohio, including conflict between Old and New School Presbyterians and status of other denominations; the slavery question; visits to Cincinnati, Dayton, Hamilton, Marietta, etc., with horseback itineration throughout Ohio, staying in homes and taverns: detailed references to ministers and other residents throughout the area; an outstanding picture of Ohio life during a period of rapid change.

POLK, JAMES KNOX, 1795-1849   2813

THE DIARY OF JAMES K. POLK DURING HIS PRESIDENCY. Edited by Milo M. Quaife. Chicago Historical Society Collections, vols. 6-9. Chicago: A.C. McClurg, 1910. 4 vols. Reprint. New York: Kraus, 1970.

Abridgement. POLK: THE DIARY OF A PRESIDENT. Edited by Allan Nevins. London and New York: Longmans, Green, 1929. 412 pp. Reprint. New York: Capricorn Books, 1968.

    1845-1849. Personal and political diary of the eleventh president; deliberations with the cabinet, particularly over conduct of the Mexican War; negotiations with Britain on the Oregon boundary question; dealings with Sen. Thomas Hart Benton, Secretary of State James Buchanan, generals Winfield Scott, Zachary Taylor and others; an intimate picture of Polk's likes and dislikes and an important political document.

Extracts in THE FRONTIER EXPERIENCE, by Robert V. Hine, pp. 178-183.

    1846-1848.

Extracts in AMERICAN HISTORY TOLD BY CONTEMPORARIES, edited by Albert B. Hart, vol. 4, pp. 32-34.

    Sep 1847-Feb 1848.

POOR, JOHN A.   2814

Baxter, James Phinney. "Reminiscences of a Great Enterprise." MAINE HISTORICAL SOCIETY COLLECTIONS AND PROCEEDINGS, 3d ser. 3 (1892):247-263.

    Feb 1845. Extract within article describing Portland man's journey to Montreal to promote the construction of the proposed Atlantic and St. Lawrence Railroad.

PREUS, CAROLINE DORTHEA MARGRETHE KEYSER, 1829-1880   2815

LINKA'S DIARY, ON LAND AND SEA. Translated and edited by Johan C.K. and Diderikke M. Preus. Minneapolis: Augsburg Publishing House, 1952. 288 pp.

    1845-1864. Personal diary of happy girlhood in Norway with a loving family; romance and marriage to Lutheran minister Herman Preus; their difficult decision to emigrate in 1851 to a Norwegian Lutheran congregation at Spring Prairie, Wisconsin; good humored account of journey on sailing ship COLUMBUS, an uncomfortable overland trip to Wisconsin, adjustment to the details of pioneer life and management of their farm during frequent absences of Pastor Preus on synod business; evidence of maturing faith.

Extract in A DAY AT A TIME, edited by Margo Culley, pp. 105-110.

    May-Jul 1851. "Taking leave of girlhood" for marriage; arrival in America, first impression of Americans and bustling, noisy New York.

SMITH, EPHRAIM KIRBY, 1807-1847   2816

TO MEXICO WITH SCOTT: LETTERS OF CAPTAIN E. KIRBY SMITH TO HIS WIFE. Prepared by Emma J. Blackwood. Cambridge: Harvard University Press, 1917. 225 pp.

    1845-1847. Letter-diary of a career army officer under Taylor and then Scott, recording action at Palo Alto, Matamoros, Saltillo, Vera Cruz, Monterrey, Perote, Puebla and Mexico City; graphic descriptions of marches, battles, condition and conduct of troops, including diarist's total dissatisfaction with volunteer regiments; references to generals Twiggs, Pillow and Worth in addition to Scott and Taylor; movements of Santa Anna; sensitive notes on scenery and customs of Mexico amid the horror of war.

SNYDER, JACOB R., 1812-1878   2817

"The Diary of Jacob R. Snyder Written while Crossing the Plains to California in 1845." SOCIETY OF CALIFORNIA PIONEERS QUARTERLY 8 (1931):224-260.

    May-Oct 1845. Emigrant journey from Independence, Missouri, to California, with "the party all in high spirits" on the day of departure; expenses, route, camps and conditions; some quarrels and resort to weapons; amicable encounters with Plains Indians, including one occasion when emigrants gave them a feast, but harrassment by Diggers in the Humboldt region.

STEELE, JOHN, 1821-1883?   2818

"Extracts from the Journal of John Steele." UTAH HISTORICAL QUARTERLY 6 (1933):3-28.

    Sep 1845-May 1877. Mormon diary of an Irish immigrant; with the Nauvoo Legion; defense against mob; journey to Salt Lake and building of city; service with the Mormon Battalion; plague of crickets; references to Jim Bridger; mission to England.

In TREASURES OF PIONEER HISTORY, compiled by Kate B. Carter, vol. 2, pp. 40-44.

1847-1850 (with gaps). Arrival in the Salt Lake valley, where he developed a prosperous farm after a period of near starvation; making adobes; eventually selling his farm when ordered on a mission for the church.

WALKER, WILLIAM, 1800-1874   **2819**

In THE PROVISIONAL GOVERNMENT OF NEBRASKA TERRITORY AND THE JOURNALS OF WILLIAM WALKER, PROVISIONAL GOVERNOR OF NEBRASKA TERRITORY, edited by William E. Connelley, pp. 153-406. Nebraska State Historical Society Proceedings and Collections, 2d ser., vol. 3. Lincoln: State Journal Co., Printers, 1899.

1845-1854. Private diary of influential Wyandot Indian, a member of legislative council and the provisional governor of Nebraska Territory in 1853; valuable information on Wyandots and relations with other tribes; supplying information to Henry Schoolcraft and reaction to his publication on Indians; comment on passing of Kansas-Nebraska Act; frequent mention of correspondence with delegates in Washington to look after Indian interests; family and social life, farming, weather, health, reading and community affairs; Methodist meetings; notes on slavery and, as a slaveholder, his outrage at Methodist abolitionists.

WARD, HENRY DANA   **2820**

Carpenter, Charles, ed. "Henry Dana Ward: Early Diary Keeper of the Kanawha Valley." WEST VIRGINIA HISTORY 37 (1975):35-48.

1845-1847. Extracts within article from the diary of an Episcopal minister; a few parish notes, social life, outings, domestic life, etc.; brief references to many longtime families in the area.

WARRE, HENRY JAMES   **2821**

OVERLAND TO OREGON IN 1845. Edited by Madeleine Major-Fregeau. Ottawa: Public Archives of Canada, 1976. 149 pp.

1845-1846 (with gaps). Diary and sketches of English naval officer and painter, actually on a secret reconnaissance to Oregon Territory for military purposes but traveling as a gentleman on an excursion to the West; details of his dress and provisions; from Montreal to the Columbia River, accompanied by Sir George Simpson as far as the Red River settlement and by Peter Skene Ogden, "a fat, jolly good fellow reminding me of Falstaff"; by horse and canoe stopping at Hudson's Bay Company posts, forts Garry, Ellice, Colville, Vancouver and Carlton House; meeting and gaining valuable information from Father De Smet; notes on Cree, Assiniboin and Bannock Indians; wild and magnificent scenery, including Mounts Hood, Rainier and St. Helens which produced a plume of smoke and ash; attending a festive ball at Fort Victoria with details of a circle dance performed with Indian women; exhausting his provisions on return over Rocky Mountains and being supplied by Father De Smet who was taking food to isolated Indians.

WATKINS, HARRY, d. 1894   **2822**

In ONE MAN IN HIS TIME: THE ADVENTURES OF H. WATKINS, STROLLING PLAYER, by Maud and Otis Skinner, pp. 1-258 passim.

Philadelphia: University of Pennsylvania Press, 1938.

1845-1863. Biography containing substantial extracts from actor's diary beginning in Texas at age twenty-one and covering his theater experiences throughout the southern and eastern states, with long engagements in Cincinnati and Boston; learning from veteran actors and becoming one himself; assessments of plays and actors, backstage incidents and gossip about suchstars as Junius Brutus Booth and Edwin Forrest; struggles as an itinerant actor to support himself and eventually a family; an interesting diary providing a virtual catalog of the mostly forgotten plays and actors popular at the time.

WOOD, WILLIAM, 1809-1894   **2823**

AUTOBIOGRAPHY OF WILLIAM WOOD. New York: J.S. Babcock, 1895. 2 vols. Diary, vol. 2, 39-79, 249-298.

Apr-Oct 1845, 1846-1848. Travel diaries of New York City school commissioner; journey from Fort Smith, Arkansas, to New Orleans and New York; scenery, towns, hotels and meals; life in New York City; death of his wife; trip to and travel in England; remarriage.

1846

ANON.   **2824**

In CHRONICLES OF THE GRINGOS, compiled by George Winston Smith, pp. 115-119.

Aug 1846. Extracts from journal of officer with the Army of the West; in New Mexico; unopposed march to Santa Fe; Kearny's pacification speeches in towns along the way.

ANON.   **2825**

"Santa Fe: Diary of an Officer of the Army of the West." NILES NATIONAL REGISTER 71 (1846):90-92.

Aug 1846. Marches from Santa Fe and the conquest of New Mexico by an army which, according to the diarist, "marched nearly 900 miles over a desert country, and conquered a province of 80,000 souls, without firing a gun—a success which may be attributed mainly to the skill and ability with which General Kearny has managed this arduous and delicate business."

ADAMS, J.J.   **2826**

In A JOURNAL OF THE TWELVE MONTHS CAMPAIGN OF GEN. SHIELDS' BRIGADE IN MEXICO IN THE YEARS 1846-7, compiled by W.W. Bishop, pp. 3-46. St. Louis: Cathcart, Prescott & Co., Printers, 1847.

1846-1847. Combined diaries of lieutenants J.J. Adams and H.C. Dunbar of Company D, Third Regiment, Illinois Volunteers, during the Mexican War; descriptions of people and country; siege and surrender of Vera Cruz; much editorial summarizing.

ALLRED, REDDICK NEWTON, 1822-1905   **2827**

In TREASURES OF PIONEER HISTORY, compiled by Kate B. Carter, vol. 5, pp. 297-372.

1846?-1903. Mormon journal beginning with an autobiographical account; life in Nauvoo, going with Mormon Battalion to California and returning to Winter Quarters and then to Salt Lake City; difficult journey to California on way to a year of mission work in Hawaii; return to everyday life in Spring City and Chester, Utah; going to aid handcart companies; serving prison term for polygamy; family, church and community affairs.

BACKUS, ELECTUS   2828

In CHRONICLES OF THE GRINGOS, compiled by George Winston Smith, pp. 79-82, 176-178.

Sep 1846, Mar 1847. Extracts from officer's journal describing battle of Monterrey; naval operations off Vera Cruz.

BARBOUR, MARTHA ISABELLA HOPKINS, 1824-1888   2829

In JOURNALS OF THE LATE BREVET MAJOR PHILIP NOR-BOURNE BARBOUR ... AND HIS WIFE, MARTHA ISABELLA HOPKINS BARBOUR, by Philip Norbourne Barbour, edited by Rhoda van Bibber T. Doubleday, pp. 111-166. New York and London: G.P. Putnam's Sons, 1936.

Jul-Oct 1846. Journal kept while diarist was staying with her aunt and uncle, Lucy and Levi Jones, at Galveston, Texas; pleasant notes of domestic and social life and longings for her husband's safety during the war with Mexico.

BARBOUR, PHILIP NORBOURNE, 1813-1846   2830

JOURNALS OF THE LATE BREVET MAJOR PHILIP NORBOURNE BARBOUR ... AND HIS WIFE, MARTHA ISABELLA HOPKINS BAR-BOUR. Edited by Rhoda van Bibber T. Doubleday. New York and London: G.P. Putnam's Sons, 1936. 187 pp. Diary, pp. 17-108.

Mar-Sept 1846. Daily life and military activities of officer in war with Mexico; long entries written especially for his wife; frequent indications of his love and devotion to her and of his dedication to his country; kept until night before battle of Monterrey where he was killed.

BARRY, CHARLES EDWARD, 1811-1851   2831

In DEAR SARAH: NEW ENGLAND ICE TO THE ORIENT AND OTHER INCIDENTS FROM THE JOURNALS OF CAPTAIN CHARLES EDWARD BARRY TO HIS WIFE, by Norman E. Borden, Jr., pp. 1-204 passim. Freeport, Maine: Bond Wheelwright, 1966.

1846-1847. Biography containing long extracts from journals of a clipper ship captain from Charlestown, Massachusetts; voyage to the Orient and back on the DELPHI, with ice as the main cargo on the outward journey; interesting details of work, dealings with crew and his functions as captain and ship's doctor.

BIGLER, HENRY WILLIAM, 1815-1900   2832

CHRONICLE OF THE WEST: THE CONQUEST OF CALIFORNIA, DISCOVERY OF GOLD, AND MORMON SETTLEMENT, AS REFLECTED IN HENRY WILLIAM BIGLER'S DIARIES. By Erwin G. Gudde. Berkeley: University of California Press, 1962. 145 pp.

1846-1848. Grueling march to California via Santa Fe with the Mormon Battalion in Company B under Jesse D. Hunter; frequent references to colonels Cooke and Kearny; diarist's last months of service in California during which time "the Mormon Battalion are without clothes, shoes, salt and all kinds of general provisions save beef"; upon his discharge, employment at Sutter's Coloma sawmill, where he recorded James Marshall's discovery of gold; his own subsequent prospecting and the influx of gold-seekers; meetings with eminent Mormons and pioneers, including

Samuel Brannan. Editor describes and draws upon six versions of Bigler's diaries.

Bigler, Adelbert, ed. "Extracts from the Journal of Henry W. Bigler." UTAH HISTORICAL QUARTERLY 5 (1932):35-64, 87-112, 134-160.

1846-1891. Extracts, chiefly from 1846-1850.

"Diary of H.W. Bigler in 1847 and 1848." OVERLAND MONTHLY, 2d ser. 10 (September 1887):233-244.

1847-1848. Extracts covering his last months with the Mormon Battalion in California, the gold discovery at Sutter's Mill and beginnings of gold rush.

"Discovery of Gold in California: From Henry W. Bigler's Journal." HEART THROBS OF THE WEST 7 (1946):169-171.

1847-1848. Extracts including the discovery of gold: "this day some kind of metal that looks like gold was found in the tail race...our metal has been tried and proves to be gold."

In THE CALIFORNIA GOLD DISCOVERY, edited by Rodman W. Paul, pp. 61-62. Georgetown, Calif.: Talisman Press, 1966.

Jan-Feb. Extracts describing the discovery of gold at Sutter's Mill.

In JOURNALS OF FORTY-NINERS, edited by Le Roy R. and Ann W. Hafen, pp. 142-180.

Oct 1849-Jan 1850. Extract covering return to California to mine gold; being outfitted by John Smith, uncle of Joseph Smith, for half share of profits; forming Flake-Rich Company; working briefly at Williams Ranch; visit to San Gabriel Mission.

BLISS, ROBERT STANTON, 1805-1851   2833

Alter, J. Cecil, ed. "The Journal of Robert S. Bliss, with the Mormon Battalion." UTAH HISTORICAL QUARTERLY 4 (1931):67-96, 110-128.

1846-1848. March from Kansas via Santa Fe to San Diego; garrison duty there and other marches within California; shock of coming upon remains of some of the Donner party, "their bones bleaching in the sun"; return to Missouri River and back again to Utah; notes on Indians, religious and personal affairs.

"From Sutter's Fort to Valley of Great Salt Lake." HEART THROBS OF THE WEST 7 (1946):172-179.

Aug-Oct 1847. Brief entries covering return journey from California to Utah; route, terrain, camps and conditions of animals; remains of the Donner party; trade with Indians; grief at learning his family was not at Salt Lake.

Cooley, Everett L., ed. "The Robert S. Bliss Journal." UTAH HISTORICAL QUARTERLY 27 (1959):380-403.

Jan-May 1848. Wintering in Salt Lake City while anxiously awaiting return to his family; sawmill operations, wolf hunts, etc.; appreciation for counsel of Mormon leaders and constant praise for the benefits of living in Zion; notes on Indian customs and dealings with settlers; march across the plains with journal ending just short of Winter Quarters.

BOND, WILLIAM CRANCH, 1789-1859   2834

Jones, Bessie Z., ed. "Diary of the Two Bonds: First Directors of the Harvard College Observatory." HARVARD LIBRARY BULLETIN 15 (1967):368-386; 16 (1968):49-71, 178-207.

1846-1849. Joint diary kept by father and son, William Cranch Bond and George Phillips Bond during the early years of

Harvard's "Great Refractor"; fitting and maintaining telescopes and other equipment, reporting observations, fund raising and customs problems on imported scientific equipment; references to Harvard presidents Edward Everett and Jared Sparks and a host of scientists, professors, distinguished visitors and benefactors, including Samuel A. Eliot, Truman Henry Safford, Benjamin Peirce, John Quincy Adams and Josiah Quincy; much news of national and international developments in astronomy of the time.

BREEN, PATRICK, d. 1868   **2835**

Teggart, Frederick J. "Diary of Patrick Breen, One of the Donner Party." ACADEMY OF PACIFIC COAST HISTORY PUBLICATIONS 1 (1910):271-284.

THE DIARY OF PATRICK BREEN, RECOUNTING THE ORDEAL OF THE DONNER PARTY SNOWBOUND IN THE SIERRA. Introduction and notes by George R. Stewart. San Fransisco: Book Club of California, 1946. 38 pp.

In WHAT I SAW IN CALIFORNIA, by Edwin Bryant, pp. 256-260. New York; D. Appleton; Philadelphia: G.S. Appleton, 1848; edited by Marguerite E. Wilbur. Santa Ana, Calif.: Fine Arts Press, 1936.

In ORDEAL BY HUNGER, new ed., by George R. Stewart, pp. 323-325. Boston: Houghton Mifflin, 1960.

In OVERLAND IN 1846, edited by Dale L. Morgan, vol. 1, pp. 310-322.

Extracts in DIARY OF AMERICA, by Josef and Dorothy Berger, pp. 306-314.

Nov 1846-Mar 1847. Snowbound with Donner party in Sierra Nevada at Truckee Lake; weather, hunger, suffering and deaths; arrival of ten men with provisions from Bear Valley; another attempt to travel prevented by more snow.

In A TREASURY OF THE SIERRA NEVADA, edited by Robert L. Reid, pp. 77-82.

Jan-Mar 1847. Extracts.

BRYANT, EDWIN, 1805-1869   **2836**

WHAT I SAW IN CALIFORNIA. New York: D. Appleton; Philadelphia: G.S. Appleton, 1848. 455 pp. Reprint. Lincoln: University of Nebraska, 1985. Edited by Marguerite E. Wilbur. Santa Ana, Calif: Fine Arts Press, 1936. 481 pp.

ROCKY MOUNTAIN ADVENTURES. New York: Hust, 1885. 452 pp.

1846-1847. Lexington, Kentucky, journalist's emigrant journey from Louisville to California with a party originally under William H. Russell; from Independence over Platte route, thence from Fort Bridger via Hastings' Cutoff; confrontation with large numbers of Mormon emigrants; notes on Shawnee, Potawatomi, Sioux, Digger, Shoshoni and Utah Indians; description of scenery, plants, soil, landmarks, etc.; Mexican War news; separation of emigrants bound for Oregon and references to Lansford W. Hastings and James M. Hudspeth; hardships, illnesses and injuries throughout journey; good descriptions of mirages on the Salt Desert; in California, meeting with John Sutter; activities at New Helvetia and San Francisco; march with Fremont to Santa Barbara, meeting with California peace commissioners, terms of peace and capitulation; a detailed journal in somewhat narrative style.

Korns, J. Roderic, ed. "The Journal of Edwin Bryant." UTAH HISTORICAL QUARTERLY 19 (1951):43-107.

Jul-Aug 1846. Extract covering Wyoming, Utah and Nevada segment of the journey.

CARRIGER, NICHOLAS, 1816-1885   **2837**

In OVERLAND IN 1846, edited by Dale L. Morgan, vol. 1, pp. 150-158.

Apr-Sep 1846. Brief entries of journey from Missouri to California, apparently with first wagon party to go by way of the "Old Fort Kearny" route; deaths and other disasters reported laconically.

COGSWELL, BEN   **2838**

Phillips, Josephine E. "Flatboating on the Great Thoroughfare." HISTORICAL AND PHILOSOPHICAL SOCIETY OF OHIO BULLETIN 5, no. 2 (1947):11-24. Diary, pp. 23-24.

Nov-Dec 1846. Fragment from diary and log of a Marietta boatman on the Ohio.

CORNISH, JOHN HAMILTON, 1815-1878   **2839**

Bartram, R. Conover, ed. "The Diary of John Hamilton Cornish." SOUTH CAROLINA HISTORICAL MAGAZINE 64 (1963):73-85, 145-158.

1846-1860. Diary kept by the minister of the Church of St. Thaddeus at Aiken; a meeting with John C. Calhoun and later attending his funeral in Charleston; references to many local people, their births, weddings, funerals, etc., including the funeral of John C. Fremont's mother, Ann Whiting Pryor Fremont; parish duties; mention of his own congregation at times composed of white and "coloured" worshipping together; ceremonies in Aiken to celebrate secession.

COULTER, RICHARD   **2840**

"The Westmoreland Guards in the War with Mexico." WESTERN PENNSYLVANIA HISTORICAL MAGAZINE 24 (1941):101-126.

1846-1848. Extracts from the Mexican War diaries of Pvt. Richard Coulter, Lt. Thomas J. Barclay and Pvt. Israel Uncapher of the Westmoreland Guards from Greensburg, incorporated into the Pennsylvania Volunteers as Second Regiment, Company E; departure from Greensburg for mobilization at Pittsburgh, with cheering citizens along the route; on the NORTH CAROLINA from Pittsburgh to New Orleans, thence a fourteen day voyage to Island of Lobos and on to Vera Cruz with notes on the siege; march to Mexico City, with brief descriptions of the battles of Cerro Gordo, Contreras, Churubusco, Molino del Rey and Chapultepec; at Jalapa and Perote; the last few days in Mexico City and brief extracts of return journey; unofficial roll of the Westmoreland Guards with ages, occupations and service records.

CRAVEN, TUNIS AUGUSTUS MACDONOUGH,   **2841**
1813-1864

A NAVAL CAMPAIGN IN THE CALIFORNIAS, 1846-1849: THE JOURNAL OF LIEUTENANT TUNIS AUGUSTUS MACDONOUGH CRAVEN, U.S.N., UNITED STATES SLOOP OF WAR, DALE. Edited by John Haskell Kemble. San Francisco: Book Club of California, 1973. 124 pp.

1846-1849. Private journal of naval officer serving in the United States Pacific Squadron during the Mexican War; voyage around South America with stops at various ports; details of life in California; United States takeover there and discovery of gold; diarist's opinions and prejudices amply evident; anti-Catholic and anti-Spanish attitudes; bemoaning of his circumstances as a sailor who preferred dry land.

Kemble, John Haskell, ed. "Naval Conquest in the Pacific." CALIFORNIA HISTORICAL QUARTERLY 20 (1941):193-234.

Jun 1846-May 1847. Extracts omitting passages of an entirely personal nature.

Kemble, John Haskell, ed. "Amphibious Operations in the Gulf of California." AMERICAN NEPTUNE 5 (1945):121-136.

1847-1848. Narrative extract covering certain activities of Pacific Squadron ship DALE during Mexican War; maneuvers in the area of La Paz, Loreto and Mulege; assignment to command of the LIBERTY; action at Guaymas, La Paz, Mazatlan and San Jose del Cabo.

DUVALL, MARIUS, 1818-1891   2842

A NAVY SURGEON IN CALIFORNIA. Edited by Fred Blackburn Rogers. San Francisco: John Howell, 1957. 114 pp.

Apr 1846-Mar 1847. Surgeon's tour of duty on the warship PORTSMOUTH in California waters and activities ashore; news of movements and engagements of American units and ships and progress of the war; extensive comment on John C. Fremont, Robert Stockton, John Sutter, Gen. Mariano Vallejo, Dr. John Marsh, Ezekiel Merritt, Samuel Neal and Capt. Charles M. Weber; medical treatment of civilians as well as military personnel; fairly detailed notes on Indians, settlers and ranchers.

DUVALL, ROBERT CARSON, 1819-1862   2843

"Extracts from the Log of the U.S. Frigate SAVANNAH Kept by Robert Carson Duvall." CALIFORNIA HISTORICAL SOCIETY QUARTERLY 3 (1924):104-125.

Jul 1846-Mar 1847. Midshipman's diary and log of naval activities in the Monterey area; action at San Diego and Robert F. Stockton's first expedition to Los Angeles; information shedding light on the actions of John D. Sloat and Stockton; dated entries followed by narrative.

EDWARDS, MARCELLUS BALL, b. 1828   2844

In MARCHING WITH THE ARMY OF THE WEST, edited by Ralph P. Bieber, pp. 107-280.

Jun 1846-Apr 1847. Military journal of Saline County private with Capt. John W. Reid's company of mounted Missouri volunteers under Doniphan; march from Fort Leavenworth via Bent's Fort to New Mexico, where he engaged in campaigns against the Ute and Navaho; buffalo hunting en route and concern over slaughter beyond need to supply food; privation and hardship for man and beast and the sad necessity to shoot failing horses; arrival at Santa Fe, with description of city, its inhabitants and their customs; activities of Kearny and Doniphan and frequent references to William Gilpin, David Waldo and others; extensive account of New Mexico Indian campaigns and activities in and around Zuni.

EMORY, WILLIAM HEMSLEY, 1811-1887   2845

In NOTES OF A MILITARY RECONNAISSANCE, FROM FORT LEAVENWORTH, IN MISSOURI, TO SAN DIEGO, IN CALIFORNIA, INCLUDING PARTS OF THE ARKANSAS, DEL NORTE AND GILA RIVERS, by United States Army Corps of Engineers, pp. 15-126, by 30th Cong., 1st sess., 1848, H. Exec. Doc. 41. Washington, D.C.: Wendell and Van Benthuyse, Printers, 1848. Reprint. Albuquerque: University of New Mexico Press, 1951.

In NOTES OF A MILITARY RECONNAISSANCE, by United States Army Corps of Topographical Engineers, pp. 1-230. New York: H. Long, 1848.

In THE UNITED STATES CONQUEST OF CALIFORNIA. New York: Arno, 1976.

In NOTES OF TRAVEL IN CALIFORNIA, pp. 3-72. New York: Appleton, 1849.

Aug 1846-Jan 1847. Topographical engineer's journal of marches from Bent's Fort along the Little Cimarron to Santa Fe with Kearny and Doniphan; reconnaissance with advance guard of the Army of the West; notes on Armijo's movements; some description of Spanish customs; march to California along the Gila, with notes on Apaches and Pimas, as well as detailed description of terrain, scenery and animal and plant life; engagements and troop movements in California, including the battle of San Pasqual; events narrated with considerable flourish.

"General Kearny and the Army of the West." NILES NATIONAL REGISTER 71 (1846):138-140, 157-159, 174-175.

Aug-Sep 1846. Extracts covering journey from Bent's Fort to Santa Fe, from a diary kept by topographical engineer who was chief of engineering staff with Kearny's command.

In CHRONICLES OF THE GRINGOS, compiled by George Winston Smith, pp. 159-165.

Jan 1847. Extract covering battle of San Gabriel.

FOOTE, SARAH   2846

"A Wagon Journey from Ohio to Wisconsin in 1846." WISCONSIN HISTORICAL SOCIETY PROCEEDINGS 59 (1911):188-200.

Apr-May 1846. Teenage girl's journey with her father, Percival Foote, and other family members from Wellington, Ohio, to Winnebago County, Wisconsin, via Chicago Turnpike; lodgings and expenses at taverns and a "temperance house, which we have not usually found on our route"; arrival at Nepeuskun "ready to begin life in the woods."

FORBUSH, MARY JOSEPHINE FAXON, 1834-1870   2847

In OUR OWN DAY, by Elsie P. Mitchell, pp. 15-37 passim. Boston: Branden Press, 1976.

1846-1870? Biography containing extracts from the diary of an intellectual young Boston society woman; early teens, European travels, marriage, family life of unrelieved childbearing until just before her death; highly reflective and rather unconventional; especially revealing of her girlhood.

FORD, ANN JEANNETTE TOOKER, 1824-1882   2848

"Missionary's Bride in 1846." LONG ISLAND FORUM 36 (1973):156-160.

Nov-Dec 1846. Letter-diary of a young Patchogue woman's voyage to India on the FLAVIO with her missionary husband, George Ford; mostly weather, including a severe storm; prayers, etc., with diary ending at sea.

FURBER, GEORGE C.   2849

THE TWELVE MONTHS VOLUNTEER. Cincinnati: J.A. & U.P. James, 1848. 624 pp. 1849. 1857. 640 pp.

Sep 1846-May 1847. Military journal of lawyer with Tennessee Volunteers in war with Mexico; rigors of march from Memphis to the Rio Grande, through area between Brazos and Colorado

River to Matamoras; long descriptions of country interpolated with history; military camps, manner and customs of Mexicans; worn out horses, some left to die suffering want of forage; much sickness; military funerals; occasional entertainments in cities; march to Tampico embarking on steam ships for Vera Cruz with horses to follow; seasickness and storm causing damage to ships in harbor; battles of Vera Cruz and Cerro Gordo, moving on to Jalapa, leaving destruction and great casualties from both illness and violence; return to Vera Cruz and by ship to New Orleans.

GAINES, JOHN POLLARD, 1795-1857   2850

Winfrey, Dorman H., ed. "Diary of Major John Pollard Gaines." TEXANA 1 (1963):20-41.

Jun-Sep 1846. Mexican War diary of prominent lawyer and planter who organized the First Regiment of Kentucky Volunteer Cavalry; entries beginning at Camp Oakland near Memphis, where "bustle and confusion" were the "order of the day"; march with Col. Humphrey Marshall's command and diarist's complaint about Marshall's unwillingness to delegate authority or to control troops' stealing food from the local populace on their march through Arkansas and Texas; notes on scenery, towns, plantations, etc; indignation over appropriation of Cherokee lands by Texans; with General Wool at San Antonio and carrying his "discretionary" orders back to Marshall; much illness and many deaths, including that of his friend Moses V. Grant; terrible march through chaparral, almost dying from thirst, to Carmage on the Rio Grande.

GERDEMANN, HERMANN PHILIPP WILHELEM   2851

In FINDING THE GRAIN: PIONEER JOURNALS, FRANCONIAN FOLKTALES, ANCESTRAL POEMS, by Norbert Krapf, pp. 47-53. Jasper, Ind.: Dubois County Historical Society and Herald Printing, 1977.

Jun-Dec 1846. Brief account of trip from Germany to settle in Cincinnati. Translated from the German.

GIBSON, GEORGE RUTLEDGE, 1810?-1885   2852

JOURNAL OF A SOLDIER UNDER KEARNY AND DONIPHAN. Edited by Ralph P. Bieber. Southwest Historical Series, 3. Glendale, Calif.: Arthur H. Clark, 1935. 371 pp. Reprint. Philadelphia: Porcupine Press, 1974.

Jun 1846-Apr 1847. War journal of a Missouri volunteer, a lawyer and publisher of the WESTON JOURNAL at Weston, Missouri; march from Fort Leavenworth to New Mexico; encampment at Santa Fe, with considerable detail on its citizens and their customs; marches and action in El Paso del Norte and Chihuahua, including the battle of Sacramento; references to his company commander, Woldemar Fischer, as well as Kearny and Doniphan; full dated entries in narrative style.

OVER THE CHIHUAHUA AND SANTA FE TRAILS. Edited and annotated by Robert W. Frazer. Albuquerque: University of New Mexico Press, 1981. 111 pp.

Apr-May 1847. From Chihuahua to Santa Fe via El Paso with a group of thirty traders; a gruesome return to site of battle of Sacramento; colorful notes of scenes, terrain, incidents of travel, especially over the desolate "Jornada del Muerto," dreaming of mint juleps; references to many individuals and unflattering notes on Mexicans.

Apr-May 1848. From Santa Fe to Fort Leavenworth over the Santa Fe Trail with a party of seven carrying government mail; difficulties

ranging from desert terrain to danger from Indians; a buffalo hunt; many references to Maj. William Singer.

GRIFFIN, JOHN STROTHER, 1816-1898   2853

Ames, George Walsott, ed. "A Doctor Comes to California: The Diary of John S. Griffin, Assistant Surgeon with Kearny's Dragoons." CALIFORNIA HISTORICAL SOCIETY QUARTERLY 21 (1942):193-224, 333-357; 22 (1943):41-66.

A DOCTOR COMES TO CALIFORNIA. California Historical Society Special Publications, no. 18. San Francisco: California Historical Society, 1943. 97 pp. Reprint in THE UNITED STATES CONQUEST OF CALIFORNIA, pp. 1-97. New York: Arno, 1976.

Sep 1846-Aug 1847. Diary of surgeon with General Kearny's Army of the West; harrowing march from Santa Fe over the Santa Fe-Gila River Trail to California and the "conquest" of California; historically important diary providing information on terrain, privations; accounts of battles and medical treatments.

HAMMOND, WILLIAM GARDINER, 1829-1894   2854

REMEMBRANCE OF AMHERST: AN UNDERGRADUATE'S DIARY. Edited by George F. Whicher. New York: Columbia University Press, 1946. 307 pp.

Extracts in THE PACIFIC ERA, by Hawaii University, Honolulu, edited by William W. Davenport, pp. 109-124 passim. Honolulu: University of Hawaii Press, 1948.

1846-1848. Private record of college years at Amherst, giving a vivid daily account of the studies, social life and intellectual growth of a serious student; copious references to faculty and students, including Julius H. Seelye, William J. Rolfe, Edward Hitchcock, John M. Emerson and Aaron Warner; religious life, leisure reading, amusements, flirtations, debates and campus politics described in an outstanding student diary.

Fuess, Claude M. "An Amherst Student of the 1840's." AMHERST GRADUATES QUARTERLY 23 (1933):1-10.

May-Aug 1847. Extracts within article; mainly the trial of the Oliver Smith will case at Northampton, with Daniel Webster and Rufus Choate on opposing sides, for which students were dismissed from classes; good description of oratorical style of both.

HOLLAND, JAMES K., 1822-1898   2855

"Diary of a Texas Volunteer in the Mexican War." SOUTHWESTERN HISTORICAL QUARTERLY 30 (1926):1-33.

May-Nov 1846. Harrison County man's account of march to the Rio Grande with the Seventeenth Rangers, Mounted Company of Texas Volunteers, under Bird Holland; camps and route; humorous incidents and remarks until volunteers began dying of cholera; action at Monterrey; return home.

HOLLINGSWORTH, JOHN MCHENRY, 1823-1889   2856

Cowan, R.E., ed. "Journal of John McHenry Hollingsworth, a Lieutenant in Stevenson's Regiment." CALIFORNIA HISTORICAL SOCIETY QUARTERLY 1 (1922-1923):207-270. Reprint. THE JOURNAL OF LIEUT. JOHN MCHENRY HOLLINGSWORTH OF THE FIRST NEW YORK VOLUNTEERS. San Francisco: California Historical Society, 1923. 61 pp.

1846-1849. Military diary of a Baltimore soldier; voyage on the SUSAN DREW to California, during which a mutiny was quelled; in port at Rio de Janeiro and Valparaiso; service in California, with a secondhand account of the battle of San Pasqual, which had occurred while the diarist was at sea; adventures, flirtations and social life; a dinner and conversations with Kit Carson; some experiences in the mining country; an interesting and lively diary.

HOLT, THOMAS, 1815-1896   2857

In OVERLAND IN 1846, edited by Dale L. Morgan, vol. 1, pp. 191-198.

Dec. 1846-Jan 1847. Diary of a fifty-day trip made by a settler in Santiam Valley, Oregon, to relieve emigrants on Applegate's Cutoff; encounters with Indians; appeal to public to help share the expenses he incurred for purely humanitarian concern.

HUGHES, JOHN TAYLOR, 1817-1862   2858

DONIPHAN'S EXPEDITION AND THE CONQUEST OF NEW MEXICO AND CALIFORNIA. By William E. Connelley. Topeka, Kan.: The author, 1907. 670 pp. Diary, pp. 59-111.

Aug 1846-May 1847. Soldier's record of Doniphan's expedition; in Texas, New Mexico and Mexico; notes on topography, dealings with Indians and camp life.

IVES, WILIAM, b. 1817   2859

Gilchrist, Marie E., ed. "William Ives' Mountain Huron Survey." MICHIGAN HISTORY 50 (1966):323-340.

May-Nov 1846. Surveyor's record of an expedition to subdivide townships in the Huron Mountains for sale to copper and iron prospectors; difficulties of chain and compass work in rugged, forested area; log entries of camps, locations and weather.

Gilchrist, Marie E. "Isle Royale Survey." INLAND SEAS 24 (1968):179-192, 303-304, 315-325; 25 (1969):25-40.

1847-1848 (with gap). Surveyor's journal, quoted within article, of two surveys conducted as part of the United States Linear Survey; from Detroit to Sault Sainte Marie on the SAMUEL WARD and to Isle Royale on the INDEPENDENCE; technical notes, weather, camps, difficulties of terrain and suffering from insects; return to Detroit on the ST. CLAIR and SARATOGA; second trip to Isle Royale aboard DETROIT and SWALLOW.

JOHNSTON, ABRAHAM ROBINSON, 1815-1846   2860

In MARCHING WITH THE ARMY OF THE WEST, edited by Ralph P. Bieber, pp. 73-104. Glendale: Arthur H. Clark, 1936.

Jun-Aug 1846. Military journal of Upper Piqua, Ohio, man who was regimental adjutant of the New Mexico First Dragoons under Kearny and later his aide-de-camp; march from Fort Leavenworth with a combination of dragoons, topographical engineers and Doniphan's Missouri volunteers; concerns about inappropriate balance of horse to foot troops, inadequate supplies and volunteers' lack of training and experience; Kearny's activities in New Mexico; geological observations.

In 30th Cong., 1st sess., 1848, H. Exec. Doc. 41, pp. 567-614.

Sep-Dec 1846. Military journal of march from Santa Fe to San Diego; meeting Kit Carson who had news of Fremont and Stockton in California; distances, vegetation and ruins; Apache, Pima, Maricopa and other Indians.

JONES, NATHANIEL VARY, 1822-1863   2861

"The Journal of Nathaniel V. Jones, with the Mormon Battalion." UTAH HISTORICAL QUARTERLY 4 (1931):3-23.

1846-1847. March with the Mormon Battalion to San Diego via Santa Fe in Nelson Higgins' company; severe privations of food and water, mainly attributed to mismanagement; descriptions of missions in California; burial of some of the Donner party skeletons, apparently leaving another group unburied; references to Cooke and Kearny; return to Missouri as a member of Fremont's guard.

"The Round Trip Journey from Fort Leavenworth to California." HEART THROBS OF THE WEST 7 (1946):164.

Sep 1846-Aug 1847. Extracts.

KANE, PAUL, 1810-1871   2862

WANDERINGS OF AN ARTIST AMONG THE INDIANS OF NORTH AMERICA, FROM CANADA TO VANCOUVER'S ISLAND AND OREGON, THROUGH THE HUDSON'S BAY COMPANY'S TERRITORY AND BACK AGAIN. London: Longman, Brown, Green, Longmans and Roberts, 1859. 445 pp. Masterworks of Canadian Authors, vol. 7. Toronto: Radisson Society of Canada, 1925. 329 pp. Reprint. Rutland, Vt.: C.E. Tuttle, 1967; Edmonton: M.G. Hurtig, 1968.

PAUL KANE'S FRONTIER. Edited by J. Russell Harper. Austin: Published for the Amon Carter Museum, Fort Worth, and the National Gallery of Canada by the University of Texas Press; Toronto: University of Toronto Press, 1971. 350 pp. Diary, pp, 47-157.

1846-1848. Diary of Canadian artist kept to explain his sketches of Indians; by horseback through Mackinaw, Sault Sainte Marie, Fort William, Kaministikwia route to Fort Alexander, Winnipeg, Saskatchewan River, Edmonton and Athabasca Pass; hazardous winter crossing of Rocky Mountains on snowshoes to Columbia River, Fort Vancouver and Oregon City; painting and sketching Flathead, Chinook, Colville, Cowlitz, Klackamas, Clallum and Nez Perce Indians during trips on Willamette, Cowlitz and Nisqually rivers with extensive descriptions of lodges, customs, costumes, legends, games and superstitions; visiting Hudson's Bay trading posts, the Whitman Mission, only days before massacre, and the Walker and Eells Presbyterian Mission; sketching Mount St. Helens and hearing of eruption and superstitions about the volcano from the Indians; spending winter months in amusements with British officers of the MODESTE anchored at Fort Vancouver.

KENLY, JOHN REESE, 1822-1921   2863

MEMOIRS OF A MARYLAND VOLUNTEER. Philadelphia: J.B. Lippincott, 1873. 521 pp. passim.

1846-1848. Mexican War diary of a Baltimore volunteer serving with the Eagle Artillery Company of the Maryland Infantry; presented as memoirs but, according to author, mostly notes made as the events occurred.

KREITZER, JOHN   2864

In CHRONICLES OF THE GRINGOS, compiled by George Winston Smith, pp. 46-49.

Dec 1846. Diary extracts of soldier with the First Pennsylvania Regiment of Volunteers en route to Mexican War; train and canal boat travel through Pennsylvania; rowdy behavior of some troops in towns.

LANE, HENRY S., 1811-1881   2865

Barringer, Graham A. "The Mexican War Journal of Henry S. Lane." INDIANA MAGAZINE OF HISTORY 53 (1957):383-434.

Jun 1846-Jun 1847. Journal of Crawfordsville lawyer and Whig congressman, later governor and senator, who raised a company of volunteers from Montgomery County and served as its captain; brief entries on journey to Mexico, then full details of march through Mexico, with great depletion of troops through sickness, lack of provisions and medicine rather than battles; constant boredom, low morale and homesickness, both of the volunteers and the diarist who cursed the Polk administration and himself for "bringing northern troops here in the most sickly season of the year and when we were not needed and could not be used"; meetings with General Taylor and news of war developments elsewhere in Mexico.

LANMAN, CHARLES, 1819-1895   **2866**

A SUMMER IN THE WILDERNESS. New York: D. Appleton; Philadelphia: G.S. Appleton, 1847. 208 pp.

Jun-Aug 1846. Monroe, Michigan, man's diary of a canoe voyage up the Mississippi and around Lake Superior via St. Louis, Sault Sainte Marie, etc; literary touristic descriptions.

A TOUR TO THE RIVER SAGUENAY, IN LOWER CANADA. Philadelphia: Carey and Hart, 1848. 231 pp.

May-Aug 1847. A tour across New York, in the Catskills and Adirondacks, to Lake Champlain, Montreal, Quebec and Saguenay River; fishing and sealing on the St. Lawrence; thence to Labrador, New Brunswick, St. John's River and Penobscot River.

LARCOM, LUCY, 1824-1893   **2867**

In LUCY LARCOM: LIFE, LETTERS, AND DIARY, by Daniel D. Addison, 295 pp. passim. Boston and New York: Houghton Mifflin, 1894. Reprint. Detroit: Gale Research, 1970. Freeport, N.Y.: Books for Libraries, 1971.

1846-1893. Former Lowell mill girl's irregularly kept diary; trip to and teaching in one room log school at Lookingglass Prairie, Illinois; return to Norton, Massachusetts, to teach at Wheaton Seminary; occasional entries on subjects she was teaching, nature, writing, religion, reading and thoughts on literature, slavery, abolition, the Civil War and lectures by Ralph Waldo Emerson and Charles Sumner; great friendship with John G. Whittier and his sister Elizabeth; end of the war, Lincoln's assassination and the memorial service at Old South Church, Boston; worshipping at Trinity Church, hearing sermons of Phillips Brooks and finally joining the Episcopal church.

LATTIE, ALEXANDER, 1802-1849   **2868**

"Alexander Lattie's Fort George Journal." OREGON HISTORICAL QUARTERLY 64 (1963):197-245.

Feb-Jul 1846. Hudson's Bay Company journal of Scottish-born pilot on the Columbia; semi-official record of ship movements, weather, arrivals and departures of officials, traders and Indians; growing hostilities between Hudson's Bay personnel and American settlers, especially John McClure, with whom Lattie came to blows; references to his superior James Birnie.

LEE, JOHN DOYLE, 1812-1877   **2869**

Brooks, Juanita, ed. "Diary of the Mormon Battalion Mission." NEW MEXICO HISTORICAL REVIEW 42 (1967):165-209, 281-332.

Aug-Nov 1846. Mormon leader's account of trip from Winter Quarters to Santa Fe with the Mormon Battalion to collect part of their pay to help finance Mormon migration to Utah; journey with James Pace and Howard Egan to overtake the battalion; comments on many Mormons settled along route to Fort Leavenworth; upon reaching the battalion, diarist's dismay over forced march conditions and treatment of sick leading to continuous disagreements with the "wolfish" Lt. Andrew Jackson Smith; notes on Spanish in New Mexico; activities of the battalion and Lt. Col. Philip St. George Cooke in Santa Fe; references to Samuel Gully, Jefferson Hunt and others; return to Atchison County, Missouri, with Indian encounters en route.

JOURNALS OF JOHN DOYLE LEE. Edited by Charles Kelly. Salt Lake City: Privately printed for R.B. Watt by Western Printing, 1938. 244 pp. Reprint. Introduction by Charles S. Peterson. Salt Lake City: University of Utah Press, 1984.

Nov 1846-Jul 1847. Life at Winter Quarters and record of personal missions for Brigham Young; council meetings and addresses by Young and others; plural marriages; operation of a store with A.P. Rockwood; emigration to Utah.

Jul 1859 (with gaps). Fragmentary "underground" journal kept after the Mountain Meadows Massacre, for which he was executed in 1877; visits to his families; worry about his farm at Harmony.

A MORMON CHRONICLE: THE DIARIES OF JOHN D. LEE. Edited by Robert G. Cleland and Juanita Brooks. San Marino, Calif.; Huntington Library, 1955. 2 vols.

Extracts in DIARY OF AMERICA, by Josef and Dorothy Berger, pp. 358-372.

1848-1876. Extensive diary of dissident Mormon leader who was originally Brigham Young's helper and confidant but eventually was excommunicated and finally executed for his part in the Mountain Meadows Massacre of 1857; leadership and problem-solving ability demonstrated from Nauvoo, Illinois, through emigration of 1848 to settlement in Salt Lake and colonization of southern Utah, where for twenty-five years he energetically developed farms, founded settlements, established mills and irrigation systems and maintained a large polygamous household; final years of lonely exile after expulsion from Mormon community, as a fugitive from justice and as a prisoner awaiting trial and execution; a valuable diary of a complex man and almost obsessive chronicler of his experiences, thoughts, faith and even dreams and visions.

Fife, Austin E. "Folkways of the Mormons from the Journals of John Doyle Lee." WESTERN FOLKLORE 21 (1962):229-246.

1848-1876. Extracts, within article, which illustrate folkways and folklore relating to religious beliefs and practices; polygamy, legends, medicine, agriculture, etc.

Larson, Gustive O., ed. "Journal of the Iron County Mission, John D. Lee, Clerk." UTAH HISTORICAL QUARTERLY 20 (1952):109-134, 253-282, 353-383.

Dec 1850-Mar 1851. Official journal of a mission under George A. Smith to settle and develop iron resources in southern Utah; outfitting and departure from Salt Lake; diarist's reluctance to leave family and business "to endure the sufferings and hardships which necessarily attend a mission of this kind"; organization of militia and names of officers; route, distances, terrain, snow and sub-zero temperatures; prospects for settlement along the way; some incidents with Indians, including the adoption of an Indian boy by William Empy; councils and sermons; the founding of Parowan and electing county officers, allocating land and organizing church activities; references to countless individuals.

LIENHARD, HEINRICH, 1822-1903   2870

Korns, Roderic J., ed. "The Journal of Heinrich Lienhard." UTAH HISTORICAL QUARTERLY 19 (1951):108-176.

Jul-Sep 1846. Extract from a narrative journal of a Swiss immigrant traveling with the Harlan-Young party whose use of the Hastings' Cutoff induced the Donner party to adopt that route; from Fort Bridger via the Great Salt Lake and Salt Desert; references to Lansford W. Hastings, T.H. Jefferson and Jacob D. Hoppe; good notes on Nevada Indians. Translated from the German.

LINDSEY, ROBERT, 1801-1863   2871

TRAVELS OF ROBERT AND SARAH LINDSEY. Edited by One of their Daughters. London: S. Harris, 1886. 189 pp. American diary, pp. 11-53.

1846-1851. Extracts from the journals of an English Quaker missionary traveling throughout the east and midwest with colleague Benjamin Seebohm.

Jones, Louis T., "The Quakers of Iowa in 1850: Journal of Robert Lindsey." IOWA JOURNAL OF HISTORY AND POLITICS 12 (1914):262-286.

Dec 1849-Feb 1850. Iowa portion of Lindsey's religious travels, with notes on many Iowa Quakers, including Joseph D. and Amos Hoag and others with whom he lodged; meetings at Salem, Oakley, Pleasant Plains, etc.; difficulties of horseback travel over poor roads in winter; religious reflections.

LUDVIGH, SAMUEL, 1801-1869   2872

Trautmann, Frederick, ed. and trans. "Maryland through a Traveler's Eyes." MARYLAND HISTORICAL MAGAZINE 78 (1983):67-71.

Sep 1846. Extract covering travel from Baltimore to Frederick to Cumberland, with notes on train, canal and stagecoach travel and fares; descriptions of cities and towns, local mores and religious practices, which he regarded from his customary skeptical position.

Trautmann, Frederic, ed. "Ohio through a Traveler's Eyes." OLD NORTHWEST 9 (1983):59-76.

Oct-Nov 1846. Ohio extracts from Austro-Hungarian immigrant's diary of travel to promote freethinking and to observe American religious and social attitudes; lecturing and debating; distributing his radical journal DIE FACKEL; interviews with a number of doctors and diarist's low opinion of the state of American medicine; concern about the poverty, ignorance and ready adoption of American materialist values he found among German immigrants; interesting conversations in stagecoaches, always engineered by the diarist to elicit attitudes; notes on Cleveland, Cincinnati, etc., where he enjoyed plays and commented on customs and intellectual life.

LYMAN, ELIZA MARIE PARTRIDGE SMITH, 1820-1886   2873

In TREASURES OF PIONEER HISTORY, compiled by Kate B. Carter, vol. 2, pp. 213-284.

1846-1885. Diary of plural wife of Joseph Smith and then of Amasa Mason Lyman; trip west to Nauvoo and on to Salt Lake City; difficult traveling, birth of first child while in Winter Quarters, childbed fever and death of baby at five months; birth of second child in wagon before reaching Salt Lake City; personal hardships and strenuous pioneer life of gardening, spinning, sewing and housework in San Juan County, Utah, with her only comfort in religion.

In WOMEN'S VOICES edited by Kenneth W. Godfrey, Audrey M. Godfrey and Jill Derr, pp. 248-260.

1848-1849. Extracts beginning upon arrival in Salt Lake; managing in "log room" with eight people, later in a "wagon box and tent" while her husband was on a mission; scarcity of the basic necessities, with much sharing and mutual support among Lyman's seven wives, who were obliged to be mostly self-sustaining as they established households in Utah.

MCCLELLAN, GEORGE BRINTON, 1826-1885   2874

THE MEXICAN WAR DIARY OF GEORGE B. MCCLELLAN. Edited by William S. Myers. Princeton: Princeton University Press, 1917. 97 pp. Reprint. New York: Da Capo, 1972.

Sep 1846-Apr 1847. Summary of journey from West Point to Mexico; by ship to Brazos, thence overland to the mouth of the Rio Grande, with dated entries describing marches to Matamoros, Victoria and Tampico, the siege of Vera Cruz and battle of Cerro Gordo; much detailed complaint against the conduct of the war, privations of the soldiers and poor performance of volunteers; frequent references to generals Patterson, Pillow, Worth, Twiggs and to lieutenants Gustavus W. Smith and J. G. Foster; notes on Mexico and its people; an important source on McClellan's early military career.

Extract in THE FRONTIER EXPERIENCE, by Robert V. Hine, pp. 183-185.

Dec 1846-Jan 1847.

MCCLINTOCK, WILLIAM A., d. 1847   2875

"Journal of a Trip through Texas and Northern Mexico in 1846-1847." SOUTHWESTERN HISTORICAL QUARTERLY 34 (1930-1931): 20-37, 141-158, 231-256.

Sep 1846-Jan 1847. Bourbon County man's letter-diary of his service, with Company Two of the First Kentucky Volunteer Cavalry; a long stay at San Antonio working in the appalling government hospital, where "suffering and neglect which if told, would scarce be believed"; description of the city and its inhabitants; unflattering comments on General Wool and his leadership and diarist's relief at being transferred to Taylor; a few military details.

MCCLURE, ELIZABETH ANN COOLEY, 1825-1848   2876

Jervey, Edward W. and Moss, James E., eds. "From Virginia to Missouri in 1846." MISSOURI HISTORICAL REVIEW 60 (1966):162-206. Diary, pp. 171-206.

1846-1848. Extracts, beginning upon her marriage to James W. McClure, covering Carroll County, Virginia, girl's last two years of life; wagon and riverboat journey to Texas and Missouri during which, although she loved her husband "to distraction," she was often depressed because of homesickness, her husband's illness and fears for their uncertain future; settling near Pleasant Hill, Missouri, where she and her husband taught school; baptism into the Methodist church and religious reflections; a few entries by her husband, including her death of typhoid.

MCKINSTRY, GEORGE, 1810?-1890?   2877

In OVERLAND IN 1846, edited by Dale L. Morgan, vol. 1, 203-215.

May-Jun 1846. Emigrant's diary of journey from Independence, Missouri, in company commanded by William H. Russell; route, encampments, distances and some descriptions;; complaints of delays caused by women, children and stray cattle; notes on decision-making processes and disciplinary actions of company committee, with diary ending after Fort Laramie.

MAGOFFIN, SUSAN SHELBY, 1827-1855   2878

DOWN THE SANTA FE TRAIL AND INTO MEXICO. Edited by Stella M. Drumm. New Haven, Conn.: Yale University Press; London: H. Milford, Oxford University Press, 1926. 294 pp. Reprint. Santa Fe, N. Mex.: W. Gannon, 1975.

1846-1847. Bride's expedition with her trader husband, Samuel, from Independence, Missouri, to Mexico; details of wagons, meals, their tent, members of traveling group and delays caused by mules and horses wandering off; annoying mosquitoes, howling animals at night, wind, rain and heat; waiting at Pawnee Fork for a government escort; sorrow over miscarriage at Bent's Fort; through San Miguel and ancient Pecos to Santa Fe where as a white woman she was quite a curiosity; delightful description of people, the house where they lived, entertainment, social life with other Americans and attentions from officers; great interest in Mexican customs, food, etc.; hasty departure on receiving news of insurrection at Taos; harbored by Don Agapita and Ramon Ortiz at El Paso del Norte; living in suspense of being harmed or imprisoned until receiving news of battle of Sacramento and taking of Chihuahua; dismay at manner of treatment of Chihuahuans by Missouri Volunteers; on to Saltillo, Monterrey and meeting General Taylor with whom she was favorably impressed; account reflecting a lively and adventurous spirit.

Extracts in DIARY OF AMERICA, by Josef and Dorothy Berger, pp. 299-306.

Jun-Aug 1846. Travel conditions and sights until reaching Santa Fe.

Extracts in CHRONICLES OF THE GRINGOS, compiled by George Winston Smith, p. 139.

Apr 1847. Colonel Doniphan's occupation of Chihuahua.

MATHERS, JAMES, 1790-1870   2879

In OVERLAND IN 1846, edited by Dale L. Morgan, vol. 1, pp. 225-236.

Jul-Nov 1846. Emigrant's notes of distances covered, weather and conditions of travel on route from North Platte River to San Jose, California, via Salt Lake.

MILLER, HIRAM OWENS, b. 1818   2880

In DONNER MISCELLANY, edited by Carroll D. Hall, pp. 5-27.

May-Oct 1846. Diary, formerly attributed to Milford Elliott, but kept by Hiram Miller and James Frazier Reed, important as the only record of the Donner party prior to their disastrous winter in the Sierra Nevada; bare notes of Miller, chiefly itinerary through July 2, when he withdrew from the party and gave the diary to Reed, who continued it until his expulsion in October for killing teamster John Snyder.

In OVERLAND IN 1846, edited by Dale L. Morgan, vol. 1, pp. 257-259.

May-Jul 1846.

OSWANDEL, J. JACOB   2881

NOTES OF THE MEXICAN WAR. Philadelphia, 1885. 642 pp. passim.

1846-1848. Military journal of member of First Pennsylvania Volunteers; everyday camp life; possibly an embellished version of John Kreitzer's diary.

Extracts in UNCOMMON VALOR, edited by James M. Merrill, pp. 132-133.

Dec 1846. A river boatman enlists and starts off for the Mexican War.

Extracts in CHRONICLES OF THE GRINGOS, compiled by George Winston Smith, pp. 297-299.

Apr-May 1847. The deplorable conditions at "Camp Misery" on outskirts of Jalapa.

PRINGLE, VIRGIL KELLOGG, b. 1804   2882

"Diary of Virgil K. Pringle." OREGON PIONEER ASSOCIATION TRANSACTIONS (1920):281-300.

In OVERLAND IN 1846, edited by Dale L. Morgan, vol. 1, pp. 163-188.

Apr-Nov 1846. Emigrant journey to Salem, Oregon, with the first party to take Applegate's Cutoff; notes on division of the company, birth, deaths, illnesses, route, distances, camps, weather, etc.; great suffering in getting through Umpqua Canyon on depleted provisions; meetings with Pawnees and a feast "with our Sioux brethren"; satisfaction with "the society and location of Salem."

QUITMAN, JOHN ANTHONY, 1798-1852   2883

In LIFE AND CORRESPONDENCE OF JOHN A. QUITMAN, by John F.H. Clairborne, vol. 1, pp. 236-240. New York: Harper & Brothers, 1860.

Jul 1846. Brief diary extract of newly appointed brigadier general's train trip with other young officers from Washington, D.C., to Pittsburgh and by riverboat to New Orleans; on to site of war where General Taylor assigned him to Third Brigade, Second Division Volunteers; note of Taylor's plans with hint of discontent.

REED, JAMES FRAZIER, 1800-1874   2884

In OVERLAND IN 1846, edited by Dale L. Morgan, vol. 1, pp. 259-268.

In HISTORY OF THE DONNER PARTY, by Charles McGlashan, pp. 153-158. Truckee, Calif.: Crowley & McGlashan, 1879. New ed. San Francisco: T.C. Wohlbank, 1934. 234 pp. Ann Arbor: University Microfilms, 1966. 193 pp.

In ORDEAL BY HUNGER, by George R. Stewart, pp. 341-347. New ed. Boston: Houghton Mifflin, 1960.

Korns, J. Roderic, ed. "The Journal of James Frazier Reed." UTAH HISTORICAL QUARTERLY 19 (1951):186-223.

Jul-Oct 1846. Donner party diary, originally begun by Hiram M. Miller, with Reed portion beginning with embarkation on the Hastings' Cutoff; brief notes of route, distances and conditions through Wasatch Mountains and across the Salt Desert; abrupt end of diary on the Humboldt, apparently upon Reed's expulsion from the party, which fortunately enabled him to travel ahead and later organize rescue of the snowbound emigrants.

In OVERLAND IN 1846, pp. 342-350.

In DONNER MISCELLANY, edited by Carroll D. Hall, pp. 60-75.

Extracts in DIARY OF AMERICA, by Josef and Dorothy Berger, pp. 314-319.

Feb-Mar 1847. Record of second Donner relief expedition; the struggle to reach members snowbound at Starved Camp; distribution of food; description of cannibalized dead and starving survivors.

RICHARDS, MARY HASKIN PARKER, 1823-1860   2885

In WOMEN'S VOICES, edited by Kenneth W. Godfrey, Audrey M. Godfrey and Jill Derr, pp. 166-181.

Nov. 1846-Feb 1847. Extract from diary kept at Winter Quarters by a young English Mormon awaiting the return of her husband, Samuel Whitney Richards, from a mission; life and domestic chores in the home of her in-laws; social life with Jane Snyder Richards and other friends and relatives; notes on the sermons and counsels of Heber C. Kimball, Ezra T. Benson, Brigham Young, Orson Pratt, etc.; longing for her husband's return "to the safty of my bosem."

RICHARDSON, WILLIAM H.   2886

JOURNAL OF WILLIAM H. RICHARDSON. Baltimore: Printed by J. Robinson, 1847. 84 pp. 2d ed. Baltimore: J.W. Woods, Printer, 1848. 96 pp. 3d ed. New York: W.H. Richardson, 1849.

McGroarty, William B., ed. "William H. Richardson's Journal of Doniphan's Expedition." MISSOURI HISTORICAL REVIEW 22 (1928):193-236, 331-360, 511-542.

Aug 1846-Jul 1847. Anne Arundel County, Maryland, soldier's account of march with a company of Missouri volunteers raised at Carrollton; from Fort Leavenworth via Santa Fe into Mexico with good details of camp life, chores and hardships; on the Rio Grande, with interesting notes on Spanish customs; nursing his friend Elias Barber, one of many sick and exhausted soldiers neglected by their officers and surgeons; the battles of Bracito and Sacramento and general movements in Chihuahua; references to Doniphan, Gen. John Wool and Col. David Mitchell; fairly long, narrative entries with considerable humor and sarcasm.

In CHRONICLES OF THE GRINGOS, compiled by George Winston Smith, pp. 135-138.

Mar 1847. Extract of account of battle of Sacramento.

ROBINSON, JACOB S.   2887

SKETCHES OF THE GREAT WEST. Portsmouth, N.H.: Portsmouth Journal Press, 1848. 71 pp.
MAGAZINE OF HISTORY, extra no. 128, 4 (1927):1-58.
A JOURNAL OF THE SANTA FE EXPEDITION UNDER COLONEL DONIPHAN. Princeton: Princeton University Press, 1932. 95 pp. Reprint. New York: Da Capo, 1972.

1846-1847. A Portsmouth, New Hampshire, man's account of service with the First Regiment of Missouri Mounted Volunteers; notes on Indians, traders, Spanish, camp life, conditions of travel, etc., between St. Louis and Santa Fe; difficult desert marches in extreme heat, with sufferings of men and horses; a badly managed campaign with "no medicines and wagons provided for the sick" and the question "why the government has seen fit to starve this detachment remains yet to be explained"; interesting notes on Zuni and Navaho customs.

ROGERS, WILLIAM P., 1819-1862   2888

Pace, Eleanor D., ed. "The Diary and Letters of William P. Rogers." SOUTHWESTERN HISTORICAL QUARTERLY 32 (1929):257-299. Diary, pp. 257-285.

Jul 1846-May 1847. Diary of a lawyer serving with Zachary Taylor's army in Mexico; his command of Company K of the Mississippi Rifles; battles of Monterrey and Buena Vista, with heavy losses for which diarist blamed chief officers; marching through chaparral barefoot with his feet "literally torn to pieces"; criticism of Jefferson Davis and A.K. McClung, low morale, disgust with army life and conviction that volunteers "will never do for an invading army"; religious and ethical reflections including wondering whether the honesty required of a Christian is compatible with the practice of law; notes on Mexican civilians and the surprising hospitality shown him on visits to their ranches.

ROPER, JOSEPH F.   2889

"Joseph F. Roper Diary." ALABAMA HISTORICAL QUARTERLY 19 (1957):395-404.

1846-1853. Extracts from the diary and expense account of a Methodist circuit rider serving various Alabama circuits; preaching and working among blacks and whites; the death of his wife; a visit to Stone Mountain, Georgia, a "stupendous monument of the wisdom and power of God."

SAFFORD, DANIEL, 1792-1856   2890

In A MEMOIR OF DANIEL SAFFORD, by Anne Eliza B. Safford, pp. 172-217. Boston: American Tract Society, 1861.

1846-1853. Bostonian's tour in Europe as a delegate to the World's Evangelical convention in London; travels in Scotland, England, France, Germany and Switzerland, with general touristic notes; later travels in Canada and again Europe for his health.

SANBORN, FRANCIS GREGORY, 1838-1884   2891

Dickinson, Thomas A. "Francis Gregory Sanborn." WORCESTER SOCIETY OF ANTIQUITY PROCEEDINGS 6 (1884):155-168.

1846-1858. Article on the life of Harvard entomology professor, with extracts from his early diaries; mainly notes of school life at Phillips Academy and his burgeoning scientific interests; a few references to his family at Andover, Massachusetts.

SCRIBNER, BENJAMIN FRANKLIN, 1825-1900   2892

CAMP LIFE OF A VOLUNTEER. Philadelphia: Grigg, Elliot; New Albany, Ind.: J. R. Nunemaker, 1847. 75 pp.
A CAMPAIGN IN MEXICO. Philadelphia: J. Gihon, 1850. 75 pp.

Jul 1846-Jun 1847. Diary of a New Albany soldier, a member of the Spencer Greys, Second Indiana Regiment; down the Mississippi to New Orleans and on to Brazos and Santiago; the march to Monterrey and Saltillo; lengthy description of battle of Buena Vista; notes on officers, customs and characteristics of Mexicans; hardships of campaigning, sightseeing in Matamoros and Monterrey, features of towns and landscapes, etc.; several letters inserted to bridge gaps between entries.

Extracts in OUR SOLDIERS SPEAK, by William Matthews and Dixon Wecter, pp. 132-137.

Feb 1847. The battle of Buena Vista.

SHANE, CARLOS W.   2893

"Being an Account of a Journey to the Territory of Oregon, with Some Account of the Soil and Climate." PRESBYTERIAN HISTORICAL SOCIETY JOURNAL 21 (1943):1-33.

Apr-Sep 1846. Cincinnati Presbyterian's journey to Clackamas, Oregon; from Independence, with notes on scenery, travel conditions, landmarks, fellow emigrants and Indians; sorrow for neglect of the Sabbath en route.

SINCLAIR, JOHN   **2894**

In JOURNAL OF A TRIP TO CALIFORNIA, by John F. Riker, pp. 19-32. Urbana? Ohio, 1855?

Nov 1846-Jan 1847. Extract by member of the Donner party making futile attempt to travel through Sierra Nevada snowstorms.

SMITH, JESSE NATHANIEL, 1834-1906   **2895**

JOURNAL OF JESSE N. SMITH. Compiled and edited by Nephi Jensen. Salt Lake City: Stevens & Wallis, 1940. 136 pp.

JOURNAL OF JESSE NATHANIEL SMITH: SIX DECADES IN THE EARLY WEST: DIARIES AND PAPERS OF A MORMON PIONEER. Edited by Oliver R. Smith. Provo, Utah: J.N. Smith Family Association, 1970. 556 pp. passim.

1846-1870 (with gaps). Diary of a Mormon leader; journey by wagon train to Utah; two missions to Scandinavia and the subsequent conducting of European converts to Salt Lake by ship, railroad and wagon; pioneer life in Utah, Arizona and Mexico where he exercised both spiritual and civic leadership; family life, including plural marriage.

STANDAGE, HENRY, 1818-1899   **2896**

In THE MARCH OF THE MORMON BATTALION FROM COUNCIL BLUFFS TO CALIFORNIA, by Frank A. Golder, pp. 138-238. New York and London: Century, 1928.

1846-1847. Military journal of Englishman who enlisted as private in Mormon Battalion at Council Bluffs; journey to Los Angeles and long account of settlement; abundant details and many personal items; a good, simple journal.

STEVENS, ISAAC INGALLS, 1818-1862   **2897**

In THE LIFE OF ISAAC INGALLS STEVENS, by Hazard Stevens, vol. 1 passim. Boston and New York: Houghton Mifflin, 1900.

1846-1847. Extracts from diaries of Mexican War service under Gen. Winfield Scott; ship voyage to Mexico; engineering activities and military action at Vera Cruz, Plano del Rio, Cerro Gordo, Jalapa, Puebla, Mexico City, etc., with detailed, articulate notes on scenes, people, marches and condition of troops.

1853-? Scattered but substantial extracts of diaries kept during his period as Indian agent and later governor of Washington Territory; his controversial treaty negotiations with various tribes and explorations of the Northwest as chief of the Northern Pacific Railroad survey.

TAYLOR, WILLIAM E., 1820-1905   **2898**

In OVERLAND IN 1846, edited by Dale L. Morgan, vol. 1, 123-130.

Apr-Sep 1846. Emigrant's account of the first wagon crossing of the Sierra Nevada from Missouri to California; brief entries of party headed by John Craig and Tarkin Stanley; distances and campsites.

TENNERY, THOMAS DOUTHIT, 1819-1891   **2899**

THE MEXICAN WAR DIARY OF THOMAS D. TENNERY. Edited by

D.E. Livingston-Little. Norman: University of Oklahoma Press, 1970. 117 pp.

1846-1847. Military diary kept from the day he left Effinghon County, Illinois, to join Company E of the Fourth Regiment of Illinois Volunteers; military life, companions, conditions and movements of the troops, continual illnesses, skirmishes and the battle of Cerro Gordo where he was wounded; details of the countryside, Mexican towns and the church at Jalapa, the town where he stayed until sufficiently recovered to return home.

Livingston-Little, D.E., ed. "Mutiny during the Mexican War: An Incident on the Rio Grande." JOURNAL OF THE WEST 9 (1970):340-345.

Aug-Sep 1846. Extract covering a riot within Georgia regiment aboard the CORVETTE anchored near Camp Belknap on the Rio Grande; fighting, with some fatalities, within a unit under Henry R. Jackson; attempt by Illinois commander, Edward D. Baker, to quell the riot, which led to his own wounding.

TURNER, HENRY SMITH, 1811-1881   **2900**

THE ORIGINAL JOURNALS OF HENRY SMITH TURNER WITH STEPHEN WATTS KEARNY TO NEW MEXICO AND CALIFORNIA. Edited by Dwight L. Clarke. Norman: University of Oklahoma Press, 1966. 173 pp.

Jun-Dec 1846. Personal Mexican War diary covering the march with General Kearny's Army of the West from Fort Leavenworth to Santa Fe, then the arduous desert crossing to California; weather and conditions of travel; privations of men and animals; homesickness and prayers of diarist.

May-Aug 1847. Official report of the return expedition from Monterey via Fort Laramie to Fort Leavenworth; distances, terrain, wagon trains and numbers of emigrants encountered; lacking the personal content of the 1846 diary.

WARNER, WILLIAM H., 1812-1849   **2901**

Russell, John R., ed. "Excerpts from the Last Diary." UNIVERSITY OF ROCHESTER LIBRARY BULLETIN 15 (1962):12-18.

1846-1849. Topographical engineer's trip to and work in California; mostly camps and marches, with diary ending just before his death in an Indian ambush.

WHEATON, ELLEN DOUGLAS BIRDSEYE, 1816-1858   **2902**

THE DIARY OF ELLEN BIRDSEYE WHEATON. Boston: Privately printed, 1923. 419 pp.

1846-1857. The private release of thoughts and events in the life of a sensitive, intelligent Syracuse, New York, woman, overworked with twelve children; frequent longing for just a few minutes to call her own; cultural and social concerns, especially slavery; disappointment over meager accomplishments of Anti-Slavery Convention of 1850; involvement of her husband, Charles Augustus Wheaton in the "Jerry Rescue" in opposition to the fugitive slave law of 1850; interest in women's rights, entertaining Susan B. Anthony and Amelia Bloomer; attending lectures whenever her many domestic demands allowed and hearing Horace Mann, Henry Ward Beecher, Horace Greeley and Ralph Waldo Emerson; much mental anguish over her husband's business failure.

WHITEFIELD, EDWIN, 1816-1892   2903

Norton, Bettina A. ''Sketching America: The New York Public Library's Sketchbook of the Nineteenth Century American Artist and Traveler Edwin Whitefield.'' BULLETIN OF RESEARCH IN THE HUMANITIES 81 (1978):169-178.

Aug-Sep 1846, Jan 1848. Extracts, within article, from diary of an itinerant topographical artist, an English immigrant who produced lithographs of many American cities and scenes; brief notes of travel in the east and Ohio, seeking ''views'' to sketch.

WHITWORTH, ROBERT W.   2904

Gracy, David B. and Rugeley, Helen J.H., eds. ''From the Mississippi to the Pacific.'' ARIZONA AND THE WEST 7 (1965):127-160.

Aug 1846-Jul 1847. Record of a teenage English adventurer who, with his friend William Biddome, rather unwittingly enlisted in the Mormon Battalion; travel from New Orleans to St. Louis on OLD HICKORY, with jaunty descriptions of what he saw en route; thence up the Missouri intent on joining the American Fur Company as a trapper; instead, joining the battalion at Fort Leavenworth, ''siezed with the desire to live in one of the little white tents''; the march, with diarist's sufferings from thirst, hunger, blistered feet and extremes of heat and cold borne with considerable fortitude; comments on Santa Fe, Sonora and San Diego; interesting notes on Indians, particularly their food; in California quarters at San Luis Rey, where diary ends abruptly.

WILBUR, JAMES HARVEY, 1811-1887   2905

TRAVELS OF J.H. WILBUR. Edited by Gertrude W. Johnson. Salem, Oreg.: Willamette University Friends of the Library, 1975. 159 pp.

1846-1848. Diary of a northern New York Methodist circuit preacher appointed to Methodist Mission on Willamette River in Oregon Territory; sailing on the WHITON; seasickness and shipboard life; constant concern for his soul and those of the passengers and crew; frequent remonstrances to himself to read, study and spend more time in devotion; falling overboard while helping paint the ship; stopping in San Francisco, distressed by moral state of the city and establishing a Sunday school there; making trip to Sonoma Valley, noting bountiful wheat; visiting Monterey and Carmel Catholic missions, observing Corpus Christi celebration; seeing Kearny and Fremont start for the United States and being surprised at provisions required, manner of packing the mules, etc.; receiving news of Whitman massacre just after taking up work at Oregon Institute, predecessor of Willamette University.

WISLIZENUS, ADOLPHUS, 1810-1889   2906

MEMOIR OF A TOUR TO NORTHERN MEXICO, CONNECTED WITH COL. DONIPHAN'S EXPEDITION. 30th Cong., 1st sess., 1848. S. Misc. Doc. 26. Washington, D.C.: Tippin & Streeper, Printers, 1848. 141 pp.

1846-1847. Account of a German immigrant's scientific exploration of northern Mexico and California while attached to Santa Fe trader A. Speyer's party; extensive notes on creeks and streams, rock formations, soil and vegetation; Mexican villages, a deserted Pecos village, Ciboleros on a buffalo hunt and encounter with Comanches while riding alone; being detained for six months after mob attack on American Hotel at Chihuahua; receiving appointment as surgeon and leaving with Colonel Doniphan's troops after battle of Sacramento; continuing scientific

observations on return trip through Monterrey, Brazos and via ship to New Orleans.

Extract in CHRONICLES OF THE GRINGOS, compiled by George Winston Smith, pp. 139-142.

Apr-May 1847. Travel with Doniphan and Missouri Volunteers from Chihuahua to Saltillo.

YOUNG, LORENZO DOW, 1807-1895   2907

Little, James Amasa, ed. ''Diary of Lorenzo Dow Young.'' UTAH HISTORICAL QUARTERLY 14 (1945):133-170.

1846-1852 (with gaps). Mormon diary begun by Lorenzo Dow Young but mainly kept by his wife, Harriet Page Wheeler Decker Young, as though dictated by him; journey from Nauvoo, Illinois, to Salt Lake as one of the original Mormon pioneers; accidents, sickness and a number of deaths; references to Brigham Young, Parley P. Pratt, etc.

1847

ARMITAGE, THEODORE   2908

''Flatboating on the Wabash.'' INDIANA MAGAZINE OF HISTORY 9 (1913):272-275.

Mar-Apr 1847. Brief notes of a trading journey by flatboat from Pittsburg, Indiana, to New Orleans; cargo, such as flour, oats, corn, pork, etc., loaded at various towns along Wabash and-Mississippi; weather and navigational details.

ATKINSON, GEORGE HENRY, 1819-1889   2909

In BIOGRAPHY OF REV. G.H. ATKINSON: JOURNAL OF A SEA VOYAGE TO OREGON IN 1848, compiled by Nancy B. Atkinson, pp. 34-65, 71-105, 113-124. Portland: F.W. Baltes, 1893.

Oct 1847-Jul 1848. Letter-journal of a Congregational missionary to Oregon; voyage from Boston around Cape Horn to Hawaii on the SAMOSET, with detailed, formal notes on the voyage; a stay in Hawaii, where he described missionaries and their educational work; news there of the Whitman massacre; to Oregon on the COWLITZ; notes on Hudson's Bay Company activities and personnel at Fort Vancouver, as well as on renowned Oregon missionaries such as Spalding, Eells and Walker; beginnings of work at Oregon City.

Rockwood, E. Ruth, ed. ''Diary of Rev. George Henry Atkinson, D.D.'' OREGON HISTORICAL QUARTERLY 40 (1939):52-63, 168-187, 265-282, 345-361; 41 (1940):6-33, 212-226, 288-303, 386-404.

1848-1858. Extracts covering voyages to Hawaii and Oregon, organization of missions and schools, sermons; his eventual pastorate of the First Congregational Church in Portland; some good descriptions of people and places.

BAILEY, THOMAS   2910

''Diary of the Mexican War.'' INDIANA MAGAZINE OF HISTORY 14 (1918):134-147.

Oct 1847-Jul 1848. Diary kept by a musician in Company C, Fifth Regiment of Indiana Volunteers; by steamboats WAVE, SOPHIA and ALABAMA down Mississippi; march to Mexico City, with notes on villages en route and positions of other regiments; return to the United States and mustering out.

BEAUREGARD, PIERRE GUSTAVE TOUTANT 2911

In CHRONICLES OF THE GRINGOS, compiled by George Winston Smith, pp. 250-251.

Aug-Sep 1847. Lieutenant's brief account of incidents from signing of the armistice at Tacubaya to the resumption of the Mexican War.

BERNARD, JESSE TALBOT, 1829-1909 2912

"A Diary of Jesse Talbot Bernard." FLORIDA HISTORICAL QUARTERLY 18 (1939):115-126.

1847-1853. Scattered extracts of trip to Philadelphia and travels within Florida; teaching and farming at Newnansville; membership in both the Methodist church and the Masons; taking up a career in law.

BLACKWELL, ELIZABETH, 1821-1910 2913

PIONEER WORK IN OPENING THE MEDICAL PROFESSION TO WOMEN. London and New York: Longmans, Green, 1895. 265 pp. passim.

PIONEER WORK FOR WOMEN. London: J.M. Dent; New York: E.P. Dutton, 1944. 236 pp. passim.

1847-1851. Extracts from woman student's journal of trials of acquiring a medical education; applying without success to four medical schools in Philadelphia; being accepted at Geneva University in New York State and successfully completing course of study despite amusing discriminations; continuing studies in Paris and London; a picture of a woman dedicated to the ideal of medical education for women.

In WOMEN IN THE AMERICAN ECONOMY, by W. Elliot Brownlee, pp. 273-276.

Nov 1847-Jan 1848. Extracts on her discouraging reception as a woman in anatomy class.

BLAKE, LILLIE DEVEREUX UMSTED, 1835-1913 2914

In CHAMPION OF WOMEN: THE LIFE OF LILLIE DEVEREUX BLAKE, by Katherine D. Blake and Margaret L. Wallace, 224 pp. passim. New York: Fleming H. Revell, 1943.

1847-1904. Scattered diary entries interspersed with letters, quotations from her autobiography and the author's narrative; youthful indignation at discrimination against women; frustrations, disappointments and joys of an aspiring author; tragedy of widowhood at age twenty-six; active participation in National American Woman Suffrage Association and presidency of New York State Woman Suffrage Association in 1887.

BLANCHET, AUGUSTINE MAGLOIRE ALEXANDRE, 1797-1887 2915

JOURNAL OF A CATHOLIC BISHOP ON THE OREGON TRAIL. Translated and edited by Edward J. Kowrach. Fairfield, Wash.: Ye Galleon, 1978. Journal, pp. 21-116.

1847-1851. Journal kept by the newly appointed bishop of Walla Walla on a journey from Montreal to St. Louis and along the Oregon Trail to Fort Walla Walla; notes on places, missions,

people, entertainments, scenery and difficulties of travel; a report on the Whitman massacre and its aftermath, including burial of victims by Father Brouillet and councils conducted by Blanchet and Peter Skene Ogden to help avoid war with the Cayuse; a cultivated French priest's reactions to the pioneer West, Indians, American Catholics and Protestants.

Hamilton, Ropahel N., ed. "The Journey of the Bishop of Walla Walla." ILLINOIS CATHOLIC HISTORICAL REVIEW 9 (1927): 208-222.

Apr-Sep 1847. Extracts covering journey to Walla Walla.

BROADHEAD, JOHN ROMEYN, 1814-1873 2916

In THE MELVILLE LOG, edited by Jay Leyda, vol. 1 passim.

1847-1849. Extracts from the diary of a member of the American Legation in London and Melville's London agent after the death of Gansevoort Melville; arrangements for publishing of OMOO and MARDI; dealings with publisher John Murray.

BURGE, DOLLY SUMNER LUNT LEWIS, 1817-1891 2917

Robertson, James I., Jr., ed. "The Diary of Dolly Lunt Burge." GEORGIA HISTORICAL QUARTERLY 44 (1960):202-219, 321-338, 434-455; 45 (1961):57-73, 155-170, 257-275, 367-384; 46 (1962):59-78. Reprint. THE DIARY OF DOLLY LUNT BURGE. Edited by James I. Robertson, Jr. Athens: University of Georgia Press, 1962. 141 pp.

1847?-1879 (with gaps). Diary of widowed schoolteacher, a devout Methodist, a native of Maine who moved to Madison, Georgia; marriage in 1850 to Thomas Burge, settling at his plantation near Social Circle in Newton County; birth of daughter Sarah and death of husband; plantation management through the war years and the havoc wrought by Sherman's march; adjusting to the end of slavery; marriage to the Rev. William J. Parks, living in Oxford until his death; return to her plantation; Sarah's marriage; a single entry on her sixty-second birthday; notes on weather, local events and social engagements; religious services, activities and reflections with much self-examination and castigation; war news, prices and shortages; contracts with outstanding clergymen and pioneers of Emory College.

A WOMAN'S WARTIME JOURNAL. With an introduction and notes by Julian Street. New York: Century, 1918. 54 pp. Macon, Ga.: J.W. Burke, 1927. 65 pp.

1864-1865. Extracts covering the impact of Union invasion, plantation matters and the problems of the postbellum period.

Extracts in THE BLUE AND THE GRAY, edited by Henry S. Commager, vol. 2, pp. 955-958; TRAGIC YEARS, by Paul M. Angle and Earl S. Miers, vol. 2, p. 936; TREASURY OF THE WORLD'S GREAT DIARIES, edited by Philip Dunaway, pp. 283-284; WHEN SHERMAN CAME, edited by Katharine M. Jones, pp. 8-14.

COLLINS, FRANCIS, 1820-1882 2918

Collins, Maria Clinton, ed. "The Journal of Francis Collins, an Artillery Officer in the Mexican War." HISTORICAL AND PHILOSOPHICAL SOCIETY OF OHIO QUARTERLY PUBLICATIONS 10 (1915):37-109.

Jan 1847-Aug 1848. Journal of Columbus, Ohio, lieutenant who was aide-de-camp to General Shields; service with the Fourth Artillery Regiment, beginning at Tampico; marches and action; social and camp life, scenery, Mexican customs and towns;

references to generals Scott, Twiggs, Patterson, etc.; well written and readable, in a largely narrative style.

COX, LEANDER M., 1812-1865   2919

Hinds, Charles F., ed. "Mexican War Journal of Leander M. Cox." KENTUCKY HISTORICAL REGISTER 55 (1957):29-52, 213-233; 56 (1958):47-70.

Nov 1847-Apr 1848. Journal of a lawyer who commanded a company of volunteers from Fleming County, eventually Company B of the Third Kentucky Foot; march and river travel to New Orleans, thence by ship to Mexico, with trip described in detail; long march from Vera Cruz to Mexico City after the main fighting had ended, but with guerrilla attacks and insurrections continuing; diarist and men devastated with typhus and other illnesses and many deaths; reading of Bible and classic literature, with much religious and philosophical reflection; news of peace negotiations and return to Kentucky; references throughout to Manlius Thomson, Thomas Crittenden and Winfield Scott.

DIEDERICHS, JOHANNES F.   2920

Baensch, Emil, trans. "Letters and Diary of Joh. Fr. Diederichs." WISCONSIN MAGAZINE OF HISTORY 7 (1923-1924):218-237, 350-368. Diary, pp. 223-237.

Aug 1847-May 1848. Diary of German immigrant from Eberfeld who eventually settled at Manitowoc, Wisconsin; travel from Bremen to New York aboard the FLORIAN; nursing his wife and children through seasickness, while personally finding the storms exhilarating; fruitless complaints to the captain about bad food and conditions for steerage passengers; Reformed religious views, with a constant sense of God's providences; disgust in New York with German "leeches" exploiting newly arrived immigrants.

DODGE, ROBERT, 1820-1899   2921

DIARY, SKETCHES AND REVIEWS, DURING AN EUROPEAN TOUR. New York: Printed for his friends, 1850. 304 pp. Diary, pp. 5-210.

Apr 1847-Mar 1849. Travel diary of a cultivated, wealthy American on the "Grand Tour"; rather prosaic descriptions of the tourist attractions of Britain, France, Belgium, Netherlands, Germany, Switzerland, Greece, Italy, Austro-Hungary, and Turkey; little reflection or direct social commentary.

DUYCKINCK, EVERT AUGUSTUS, 1816-1878   2922

In THE MELVILLE LOG, edited by Jay Leyda, 2 vols. passim.

1847-1860 (with gaps). Extracts from the diary of a prominent critic, literary friend of Melville's and reviewer of his works; visits and correspondence with Melville and comments on his writing.

Yannella, Donald and Kathleen M., eds. "Evert A. Duyckinck's Diary." In STUDIES IN THE AMERICAN RENAISSANCE, 1978, edited by Joel Myerson, pp. 207-258. Boston: Twayne, 1978.

May-Nov 1847. Diary of recently dismissed editor of LITERARY WORLD, kept during a period of unemployment while he searched for work; an enforced leisure during which he read even more avidly than usual and enjoyed plays, operas, art galleries and walks about New York; visits with Poe and Melville; reactions to the acting of Edwin Forrest; an interview with President Polk;

Mexican War news and opinions; literary and local anecdotes and the diarist's wry amusement at the foibles of humanity.

EGAN, HOWARD, 1815-1878   2923

PIONEERING THE WEST. Edited by William M. Egan. Richmond, Utah: Howard R. Egan Estate, 1917. 302 pp. Diary, pp. 21-136, 169-181, 191-197.

1847-1855 (with gaps). Mormon's journeys; from Winter Quarters to Salt Lake, with good travel and camp details and frequent mention of the counsel of Heber C. Kimball; return trip, noting the illness of Brigham Young; from Fort Utah to California with distances, water, grass and suitable camp sites carefully recorded for a future guidebook; cattle business in California; traveling by mule from Salt Lake to Sacramento in ten days through the desert and searching out Egan Trail for a mail route from Placerville to Salt Lake.

In JOURNALS OF FORTY-NINERS, edited by Le Roy R. and Ann W. Hafen, pp. 307-319.

Nov 1849-Jan 1850. Portion of journal kept while captain of wagon train from Fort Utah to California; chiefly weather, roads, distances, water and grass supply; joining Captain Rich and the Hunt train at Williams ranch; provisioning and starting to gold mines.

EMPEY, WILLIAM ADAM, 1808-1890   2924

Morgan, Dale L. "The Mormon Ferry on the North Platte." ANNALS OF WYOMING 21 (1947):110-167. Diary, pp. 124-136, 138-146.

May-Aug 1847. Record of the Mormon ferry operated at the Upper Crossing of the North Platte to assist Mormon and Oregon emigration; logistics of ferrying numbers of wagons and fees collected; prayers and admonitions, including those of Brigham Young.

FALLON, WILLIAM   2925

In OVERLAND IN 1846, edited by Dale L. Morgan, vol. 1, pp. 361-366.

Apr 1847. Extracts from diary of leader of the fourth Donner relief attempt which brought out the last survivor remaining at the site of the Donner tragedy, Lewis Keseberg, who had acquired a taste for human flesh because of cannibalism to which the Donner party was reduced; gruesome descriptions of remains of the dead; Keseberg's sequestering of money and property of his dead comrades and lying to his rescuers.

FERGUSON, PHILIP GOOCH, b. 1824   2926

In MARCHING WITH THE ARMY OF THE WEST, edited by Ralph P. Bieber, pp. 283-361.

1847-1848 (with gaps). Potosi, Missouri, newspaper publisher's diary of service with the Third Regiment, Missouri Mounted Volunteers, organized to replace troops in New Mexico; march from St. Louis to Santa Fe perceived as an adventurous lark rather than a military undertaking; buffalo hunting; people and customs of Santa Fe; a meeting with Kit Carson; marches through New Mexico to Chihuahua; news of Armijo's movements; frequent references to Alton Rufus Easton and Sterling Price.

FIELDS, JAMES THOMAS, 1816-1881   2927

BIOGRAPHICAL NOTES AND PERSONAL SKETCHES. Boston: Houghton Mifflin, 1881. 285 pp. passim.

1847-1876? Biography containing substantial extracts from the diary of Portsmouth, New Hampshire, author and publisher, a founder of the firm Ticknor and Fields and longtime editor of ATLANTIC MONTHLY; many references to literary figures of the day including an acquaintance with Dickens whose lecture tours inspired him to take up lecturing upon his retirement from publishing; references to such New England intellectuals as Louis Agassiz and Edwin P. Whipple; European travels; a lifelong passion for books.

FOSTER, BENJAMIN BROWNE, 1831-1903   **2928**

DOWN EAST DIARY. Edited by Charles H. Foster. Orono: University of Maine at Orono Press, 1975. 377 pp.

1847-1853. Witty and precocious diary of a Maine teenager; work as an apprentice shop clerk, chiefly at Bangor, with periods of time spent in Orono and Weston, Maine, and Newburyport and Ipswich, Massachusetts; amusing anecdotes of local events and people; extensive reading, with notes on books; some serious reflections and a skeptical attitude toward religion; reactions to national events and politics; attendance at the Newburyport Lyceum; interest in phrenology; many flirations and a short-lived attempt to quell "fierce and virulent passions" by abstinence from meat; student life at Bowdoin, where he distinguished himself; a wonderful diary by a young man who declared, "I could hardly exist without this journal of mine."

GILMER, JULIANA PAISLEY   **2929**

In CHRONICLES OF THE GRINGOS, compiled by George Winston Smith, p. 11.

Jan 1847. Greensboro woman's notes about recruiting Regiment of North Carolina Volunteers for Mexican War.

GORDON, ROBERT, 1825-1877   **2930**

Stuart, Reginald R. and Grace D., eds. "Journal of a Voyage from Baltimore to San Francisco." PACIFIC HISTORIAN 6 (1962):93-110, 147-160; 7 (1963):45-57, 79-93, 124-137, 190-195.

May-Jun 1847. Emigration from Ireland on the R.H. DOUGLASS, with brief notes of ship travel and finding employment in Baltimore.

1849-1852. Well described gold rush voyage from Baltimore on the XYLON around Cape Horn to San Francisco; such miseries of steerage as cold, dampness, wretched food, bullying by officers, drunkenness and fights among crew and passengers; in port at Rio de Janeiro and Valparaiso; continuing under new captain, with log entries; the madness and suicide of a passenger and rescue of a seaman who fell overboard; in San Francisco and Sacramento, thence to the diggings, with good account of his activities at Auburn, where he settled and became a merchant; an especially good diary of the gold rush journey by sea and the frantic, often disappointing search for gold in California.

GREENING, JOHN   **2931**

Croft, Josie Greening, ed. "A Mazomanie Pioneer of 1847." WISCONSIN MAGAZINE OF HISTORY 26 (1942):208-218.

1847-1849. Extracts from English immigrant's letter-diary; mainly settlement with his family in Wisconsin and description of the country, weather, farming and social life there.

HALLECK, HENRY WAGER, 1815-1872   **2932**

THE MEXICAN WAR IN BAJA CALIFORNIA: THE MEMORANDUM OF CAPT. HENRY W. HALLECK CONCERNING HIS EXPEDITIONS IN LOWER CALIFORNIA. Edited by Doyce B. Nunis, Jr. Los Angeles: Dawson's Book Shop, 1977. 208 pp. Diary, pp. 89-130.

May 1847-Apr 1848. Field diary interspersed with narrative of a talented young officer in Army Corps of Engineers during confused and unsuccessful Mexican War campaigning in Baja California; vituperation against Mexican commander Manuel Pineda and "lawless vagabonds" who opposed United States presence and praise for "respectable inhabitants" who welcomed it; detailed descriptions of terrain, villages and people; reconnaissance missions and battle of La Paz; life aboard INDEPENDENCE, CYANE and LEXINGTON.

Yates, Dohn D. "Insurgents on the Baja Peninsula: Henry Halleck's Journal of the War in Lower California." CALIFORNIA HISTORICAL QUARTERLY 54 (1975):221-244.

1847-1848. Extracts within article.

HARMON, APPLETON MILO, 1820-1877   **2933**

APPLETON MILO HARMON GOES WEST. Edited by Maybelle H. Anderson. Berkeley, Calif.: Gillick Press, 1946. 204 pp.

THE JOURNALS OF APPLETON MILO HARMON, A PARTICIPANT IN THE MORMON EXODUS FROM ILLINOIS AND THE EARLY SETTLEMENT OF UTAH. Edited by Maybelle H. Anderson. Glendale, Calif.; Arthur H. Clark, 1946. 208 pp.

1847-1853. Combination diary and narrative of Mormon pioneer and missionary; life in Nauvoo; repeated overland journeys to Salt Lake; mission to England, where he saw the Great Exhibition of 1851; return to pioneer life in southern Utah; detailed comments on all aspects of his varied experience, revealing keen observation, sensitivity and resourcefulness.

Morgan, Dale L. "The Mormon Ferry on the North Platte." ANNALS OF WYOMING 21 (1947):110-167. Diary, pp. 136-138.

Jun-Jul 1847. Diary extracts giving names of people, including Jim Bridger, and companies ferried across the North Platte; numbers of wagons and fees collected.

HARTMAN, GEORGE W., b. 1828   **2934**

A PRIVATE'S OWN JOURNAL. Greencastle, Pa.: Printed by E. Robinson, 1849. 35 pp.

Extracts in OUR SOLDIERS SPEAK, by William Matthews and Dixon Wecter, pp. 138-142.

1847-1848 (with gaps). Military journal of private from Westmoreland County, serving with the Second Pennsylvania Regiment; notes on New Orleans, Vera Cruz, Perote and battles of Churubusco, Molino del Rey and Mexico City.

HASTINGS, LOREN B., 1819-1881   **2935**

"Diary of Loren B. Hastings, a Pioneer of 1847." OREGON PIONEER ASSOCIATION TRANSACTIONS (1923):12-26.

Apr-Dec 1847. Emigrant journey from Hancock County, Illinois, to The Dalles and Portland; notes on stages and conditions of journey, encounters with Indians, activities and capabilities of his fellow emigrants; difficulties getting wagons and cattle down the Columbia, with particular problems at Cascade Falls and diarist's ingenious solutions.

HAVEN, ALICE BRADLEY, 1828-1863   **2936**

In COUSIN ALICE: A MEMOIR OF ALICE B. HAVEN, by Cornelia H.B. Richards, pp. 1-392 passim. New York: D. Appleton, 1868.

     1847-1863. Scattered journal entries, not all dated, in memoir of author of prose and verse, sometimes published under names Alice G. Lee and Clara Cushman, mainly for children; chiefly a confessional with written prayers, much self-reproach and resolutions to deepen her spiritual life; suffering early widowhood followed by a severe illness.

HILL, DANIEL HARVEY, 1821-1889   **2937**

In CHRONICLES OF THE GRINGOS, compiled by George Winston Smith, pp. 239-242, 261-264, 419-423.

     Aug-Sep 1847, Jan 1848. Extract from officer's journal describing skirmish during Scott's march across Mexico to Mexico City; storming of Chapultepec; ferreting out guerillas after Mexican surrender.

HOFFMAN, VIRGINIA HAVISIDE HALE, 1832-1856   **2938**

In LIFE OF MRS. VIRGINIA HALE HOFFMAN, LATE OF THE PROTESTANT EPISCOPAL MISSION TO WESTERN AFRICA, by George D. Cummins, pp. 1-256 passim. Philadelphia: Lindsay & Blakiston, 1859.

     1847-1856. Extracts from religious and missionary journal; self-abasing reflections; impressions of first communion while living with her sister's family in Norfolk, Virginia; teenage desire to go to Africa as a missionary; marriage to the Rev. Cadwallader Colden Hoffman and returning with him to African Mission of the Protestant Episcopal Church at Cavalla, Liberia; adjusting to missionary life, learning language and teaching in missionary school; birth and death of daughter.

HONE, PHILIP, 1780-1851   **2939**

Angle, Paul M., ed. "The Western Trip of Philip Hone." ILLINOIS STATE HISTORICAL SOCIETY JOURNAL 38 (1945):277-294.

     Jun-Jul 1847. Extract covering part of a trip to Illinois and Wisconsin, mainly to attend the Harbor and River Convention in Chicago; notes on travel by Mississippi steamboats DOMAIN, etc.; stay in Chicago, "truly the wonder of the western world"; speeches and deliberations of the convention; travel in Wisconsin to inspect his property there; Great Lakes excursion on the NIAGARA, DETROIT, etc.; a rigorous journey for an elderly man in declining health.

HULIN, LESTER, 1823-1897   **2940**

DAY BOOK OR JOURNAL: OREGON TRAIL AND APPLEGATE ROUTE. Eugene, Oreg.; Lane County Pioneer-Historical Society, 1959. 1 vol. unpaged.

     Apr-Nov. 1847. Emigrant journey from Iowa to Willamette Valley; route, camps, landmarks, roads, distances and an Indian attack; notes on losing cattle, deaths in the party and Pawnee Indians.

HURLY, KEALING   **2941**

O'Connell, Lucille, ed. "Kealing Hurly's Scrip Book." EIRE-IRELAND 15 (1980):105-112.

     1847-1848. An Irish immigrant's brief notes on journey from Galway on the BETHEL to New Brunswick, thence to Boston and immediately on to Alvarado, Mexico, as a servant to an officer in the Mexican War; descriptions of Alvarado and its inhabitants; return to Boston.

HUTTON, WILLIAM RICH, 1826-1901   **2942**

GLANCES AT CALIFORNIA, 1847-1853, DIARIES AND LETTERS OF WILLIAM RICH HUTTON. San Marino: Huntington Library, 1942. 86 pp. Diary, pp. 3-6, 8-12.

     Jul-Nov 1847, Apr. 1849. Diary of clerk to army paymaster; brief travels in California; natural history notes on trip up Sacramento River and in area of Sutter's Fort and Mormon Diggings.

JAMIESON, MILTON   **2943**

JOURNAL AND NOTES OF A CAMPAIGN IN MEXICO. Cincinnati: Ben Franklin Printing House, 1849. 105 pp.

     Sep 1847-Jul 1848. A seminarrative journal of a Batavia, Ohio, man's service with Company C of the Second Ohio Volunteers; military details; notes on countryside, roads, forts, towns, etc., along the southern line of the United States army in Mexico; description of Mexican customs and agriculture.

JOHNSON, WILLIAM S., d. 1880   **2944**

Moore, John H., ed. "Private Johnson Fights the Mexicans." SOUTH CAROLINA HISTORICAL MAGAZINE 67 (1966):203-228.

     1847-1848. Diary of a Columbia man serving with Company H of the Palmetto Regiment; from Mobile on several ships including the FLOYD, where "our accommodations would be second choice to a pig sty"; siege of Vera Cruz, with description of the city after its capture; severe illnesses of troops, but no accommodation for the sick; very unpleasant march to Puebla, enduring hunger, heat and cold; notes on garrison life there, with continued privations and rampant sickness; description of inhabitants; the taking of Mexico City; frequent references to generals Scott and Twiggs, and diarist's disgust with some of his officers.

JOHNSTON, WILLIAM PRESTON, 1831-1899   **2945**

Shaw, Arthur Marvin, ed. "Student Life at Western Military Institute." FILSON CLUB HISTORICAL QUARTERLY 18 (1944):78-108.

     Nov 1847-Jul 1848. Extracts from a youthful journal kept by the future president of Louisiana State and Tulane universities; an engaging record of his life, attitudes and studies at Western Military Institute in Georgetown, Kentucky; considerable leisure reading, sports, social life and church activity; disturbing death of his fellow student Frank Hopkins and of his beloved grandmother Caroline H. Preston; many references to his father, Gen. Albert Sidney Johnston, and other relatives; entries for August through October summarized at a later date.

JUDAH, HENRY MOSES   **2946**

In CHRONICLES OF THE GRINGOS, compiled by George Winston Smith, pp. 231-232, 304, 401-403.

     Apr, Jun, Aug 1847. Extracts from soldier's diary; incident of camp woman resisting order to remain behind during army's march to Mexico City; hostilities while camped near Puebla; meeting Mexican robber chief Manuel Dominguez and his company of spies serving Gen. Winfield Scott.

KEMPER, JAMES LAWSON, 1823-1895   2947

Jones, Robert R., ed. "The Mexican War Diary of James Lawson Kemper." VIRGINIA MAGAZINE OF HISTORY AND BIOGRAPHY 74 (1966):387-428.

> Jan-Mar 1847. Madison County lawyer's diary with entries beginning at Washington, D.C., where, with his companion B.D. Fry, he was seeking a commission in the Mexican War; an endless round of calls on Secretary of War William L. Marcy, President Polk and others; attending many sessions of Congress, where he was not impressed with the oratory; hasty, somewhat acerbic notes on people and social life; having a tooth pulled under ether; finally receiving a commission as quartermaster with the Virginia Regiment of Volunteers; to Richmond and Fort Monroe, where he assumed his duties; voyage to Brazos on the EXACT, during which he was desperately ill with yellow fever.

KIMBALL, HEBER CHASE, 1801-1868   2948

"The Pioneer Journal of Heber C. Kimball." UTAH GENEALOGICAL AND HISTORICAL MAGAZINE 30 (1939):7-19, 76-85, 140-149, 204-211; 31 (1940):18-24, 80-87, 150-158, 211-218.

> Apr-Jun 1847. Mormon elder's full and excellent notes kept during the journey of the Pioneer Company from Winter Quarters to Salt Lake with Brigham Young; names of emigrants and their organization into companies of ten, as well as other aspects of Young's regimen for the journey; Indian incidents and a buffalo hunt; struggles of the Mormon pioneers.

KURZ, RUDOLPH FRIEDRICH, 1818-1871   2949

JOURNAL OF RUDOLPH FRIEDERICH KURZ. Translated by Myrtis Jarrell, edited by J.N.B. Hewitt. Smithsonian Institution Bureau of American Ethnology Bulletin 115. Washington, D.C.: United States Government Printing Office, 1937. 382 pp. Reprint. Fairfield, Wash.: Ye Galleon, 1969; Lincoln: University of Nebraska Press, 1970.

Extracts in Bushnell, D.I. "Friedrich Kurz, Artist-Explorer." SMITHSONIAN INSTITUTION ANNUAL REPORT (1927):507-527.

> 1847-1852. Extracts from private diary of Swiss painter with an incurable fascination with "aboriginal forests, the wild animals that inhabited them, and the Indians"; visiting and painting at western trading posts of fur companies on the Mississippi and upper Missouri rivers; many interesting incidents, described in long narrative entries, of Crow, Arikara, Assiniboin, Blackfoot, Cree, Crow, Fox, Gros Ventre, Mandan, Omaha, Potawatomi and Dakota Indians; sometimes employed as clerk at forts Union and Berthold, fleeing from the latter because Indians regarded him as source of cholera which was striking the area; sympathetic views of Indians and their plight; opinions on George Catlin, Mormons, Mexican War, gold rush, American artists and other aspects of American culture; a valuable diary.

LEWIS, JANE VOORHEES   2950

"The Journal of Jane Voorhees Lewis." NEW JERSEY HISTORICAL SOCIETY PROCEEDINGS 65 (1947):83-92.

> Apr-Jun 1847. Young woman's wagon journey from Hopewell, New Jersey, to settle at White Hall, Illinois, with her husband, David G. Lewis, father, Abraham J. Voorhees, and other family members; brief notes of travel, route, people, accommodations and towns: prices of food along the way.

Extract in TRAVEL ACCOUNTS OF INDIANA, compiled by Shirley McCord, pp. 194-195.

> May-Jun 1847. Indiana segment of the journey with brief notes on Indianapolis, etc.

MCWILLIAMS, WILLIAM JOSEPH, 1817-1902   2951

Larner, John William, ed. "A Westmoreland Guard in Mexico." WESTERN PENNSYLVANIA HISTORICAL MAGAZINE 52 (1969):213-240, 387-413.

> 1847-1848 (with gaps). Murrysville carpenter's detailed record of service with the Westmoreland Guards of Greensburg, mustering at Pittsburgh as Company E of Second Pennsylvania Volunteers; on the NORTH CAROLINA to New Orleans; thence to Island of Lobos and Vera Cruz, with notes on siege and casualties; the battle of Cerro Gordo, march to Puebla and battles of Contreras, Churubusco, Molino del Rey and Chapultepec; activities in Mexico City, including theater and bullfight; notes on Mexican customs; tedious parades, guard duty, etc., while waiting for declaration of peace; references, at various points, to generals Robert Patterson, David E. Twiggs and Winfield Scott; return to Pennsylvania.

MARRAST, JOHN CALHOUN, 1825-1863   2952

"Col. John C. Marrast." CONFEDERATE VETERAN 13 (1905):162-163.

> Feb 1847. Brief extract from diary of Alabamian scouting with Capt. Ben McCullough's rangers around Buena Vista.

MARTIN, E.C.   2953

"Leaves from an Old Journal: Lake Superior in 1847." MICHIGAN PIONEER AND HISTORICAL COLLECTIONS 30 (1906):405-409.

> May 1847. Account of a government surveying party under William A. Burt to establish the western boundary of the Upper Peninsula and to lay out town lines; travel on several lake steamers, thence over Indian trails with pack ponies in difficult terrain and bad weather; dealings with Indians; surveying details, including use of "solar compass," and names of members of the party.

MORRELL, PRUDENCE, 1794-1855   2954

Johnson, Theodore E., ed. "Prudence Morrell's Account of a Journey to the West in the Year 1847." SHAKER QUARTERLY 8 (1968):37-70, 82-96.

> May-Oct 1847. Shaker woman's record of visits to Shaker communities in Ohio, Kentucky and New York, where she observed the religious vitality and community enterprises of the period; detailed notes on preaching, singing, dancing and "gifts from the holy angels," as well as farms, mills, etc.; travel with Sister Eliza Sharp by train, stagecoach and riverboat, with descriptions of countryside and towns; notes on individuals at Watervliet, Union Village, Whitewater, etc., rejoicing at their simplicity and goodness but regretting the apostasy of some "Seceeding Shakers"; reactions of unbelievers to Shakers and their ways.

NEWCOMB, CHARLES KING, 1820-1894   2955

THE JOURNALS OF CHARLES KING NEWCOMB. Edited by Judith Kennedy Johnson. Brown University Studies, vol. 10. Providence, R.I.: Brown University, 1946. 299 pp.

1847-1870. Extracts, which are dated but arranged topically, from the massive introspective journals of a minor New England thinker and disciple of Emerson; thoughts on religion, with inclinations toward Swedenborg, nature, society and morals; extensive and varied opinion on books and literary figures; reactions to opera and drama, with many references to Shakespeare; occasional mention of Providence and Philadelphia where he lived, but mainly a journal of thought rather than events.

NOBLE, Mr.   2956

In FLORIDA PLANTATION RECORDS FROM THE PAPERS OF GEORGE NOBLE JONES, by George Noble Jones, edited by Ulrich B. Philips and James D. Glunt, pp. 209-328. St. Louis: Missouri Historical Society, 1927.

Jan-Dec 1847. Overseer's daily record, kept by Noble through August and then by Joshua N. Sanders, at El Destino plantation in Leon and Jefferson counties, near Tallahassee; weather and assignment of tasks; names of sick and runaway slaves.

PAINE, CHARLES SMITH, 1819-1895   2957

In HISTORY OF SAMUEL PAINE, JR. AND HIS WIFE PAMELA CHASE PAINE, by Albert P. Paine, pp. 135-159. Randolph Center, Vt., 1923.

1847-1879. Extracts from the diary of a Randolph, Vermont, farmer; notes on personal, family and town affairs; visits to neighboring towns; details of farming, religion, morals and natural history.

PARSONS, JOHN E., 1829-1915   2958

"A Student at N.Y.U. in 1847: Excerpts from the Diary of John E. Parsons." NEW YORK HISTORICAL SOCIETY QUARTERLY 38 (1954):325-344.

Jan-Jun 1847. Brief entries on studies and activities at New York University in the days when it had a faculty of seven; church and university chapel services; pleasure reading, such as NICHOLAS NICKLEBY, "to the neglect of my studies"; skating and skiing; references to faculty, students and such incidents as "Barker exposed Big Catlin for plagiarism."

"Through the Atlantic States to Cuba in 1852: Excerpts from the Journal and Letters of John E. Parsons." NEW YORK HISTORICAL SOCIETY QUARTERLY 42 (1958):367-385.

Mar-Apr 1852. Lawyer's travel diary; mainly narrative, touristic descriptions of Washington, D.C., Charleston and Havana, as well as train and ship travel; return on the NASHVILLE to Nashville, with excitement over racing another riverboat "for seven or eight hundred miles...night and day, part of the time neck and neck"; visit to Mammoth Cave and stay in Cincinnati.

PIERCE, FRANKLIN, 1804-1869   2959

In LIFE OF FRANKLIN PIERCE, by Nathaniel Hawthorne, pp. 68-94. Boston: Ticknor, Reed and Fields, 1852.

Jun-Aug 1847. Extracts from general's private military journal; march from Vera Cruz to Castle of Perote by the Ninth Regiment of Infantry, volunteers from Massachusetts; sickness among soldiers, loss of mules due to carelessness of quartermaster's department and excessive heat; march to San Juan requiring more breaking of mules than marching; brief skirmish, constructing a bridge over Plan del Rio in four hours, under direction of

Captain Bodfish, to replace old Spanish bridge that had been destroyed; camps, guerillas, increasing sickness, resting troops, hospitalizing the ill and repairing damage at Castle of Perote.

Extracts in UNCOMMON VALOR, edited by James M. Merrill, pp. 146-150.

Jul 1847. Extracts describing Mexican guerilla tactics.

POINT, NICOLAS, 1799-1868   2960

Barrette, Paul A., trans. "A Journey in a Barge on the Missouri from the Fort of the Blackfeet (Lewis) to That of the Assiniboines (Union): Particulars Edifying or Curious." MID-AMERICA 13 (1931):238-254.

Garraghan, G.J., ed. "A Journey in a Barge on the Missouri from Fort Lewis to Fort Union, 1847." FRONTIER AND MIDLAND 15 (1935):241-250.

May-Jun 1847. French Jesuit's journal of travel with Father De Smet from Fort Lewis, via the Missouri River, as far as Fort Union at the mouth of the Yellowstone; notes on Blackfoot Indians and French settlers; data about the American Fur Company, its officials, Indian relations, etc.; a formal narrative style.

PRESTON, WILLIAM, 1816-1887   2961

JOURNAL IN MEXICO. Paris, France: Privately printed, 192-? 45 pp. passim.

Nov. 1847-May 1848. Journal of lieutenant colonel of the Fourth Kentucky Volunteer Infantry, future prominent politician and diplomat; voyage to Mexico; battles of Vera Cruz and Cerro Gordo and other military operations; nice description of natural surroundings, Mexico City, etc.; a few dated entries but mostly a retrospective narrative.

RAVENEL, THOMAS P.   2962

In PLANTATION AND FRONTIER DOCUMENTS: 1649-1863, by Ulrich B. Phillips, vol. 1, pp. 195-203. Documentary History of American Industrial Society, vol. 1. Cleveland, Ohio: A.H. Clark, 1909. Reprint. New York; B. Franklin, 1969.

1847-1850. Extract covering work on Woodboo, a plantation north of Charleston, South Carolina; planting and harvesting cotton, peas and corn; ginning cotton.

RITCHIE, M.D.   2963

In HISTORY OF THE DONNER PARTY, by Charles McGlashan, pp. 119-120. Truckee, Calif.: Crowley & McGlashan, 1879. New ed. San Francisco: T.C. Wohlbank, 1934. 234 pp. Ann Arbor: University Microfilms, 1966. 193 pp.

In OVERLAND IN 1846, edited by Dale L. Morgan, vol. 1, pp. 331-332.

In DONNER MISCELLANY, edited by Carroll D. Hall, pp. 52-55.

Feb. 1847. Very brief, but the only known diary of the first Donner relief attempt, a record started by M.D. Ritchie and continued by R.P. Tucker; desperate traveling conditions of relief group and worse plight of starving Donner party snowbound in the Sierra Nevada.

ROBERTS, GEORGE B., 1816-1883   2964

"The Round Hand of George B. Roberts: The Cowlitz Farm Journal." OREGON HISTORICAL QUARTERLY 63 (1962):101-174.

1847-1851 (with gaps). Account kept by Hudson's Bay Company official, later to become an American citizen, of work at Cowlitz Farm of the Puget Sound Agricultural Company; weather, farming methods and implements, crops and livestock; supervision of Indian, French-Canadian and Hawaiian labor; activities of Sir James Douglas and Peter Skene Ogden; measles epidemic which devastated Indian population; news of Whitman massacre; a businesslike but descriptive journal.

ROODS, JOHN Q.   2965

Pomeroy, Earl S., ed. "Wisconsin in 1847." WISCONSIN MAGAZINE OF HISTORY 33 (1949):216-220.

Oct. 1847. Newark, Ohio, resident's brief notes while on a trip to evaluate Wisconsin farm land; quaint and outspoken reactions to people, especially women, and the quality of the country: "If only I had my money back and was at home, Wisconsin might go to the Devil."

SEARS, JOSHUA, b. 1817   2966

In SHIPMASTERS OF CAPE COD, by Henry C. Kittredge, pp. 157-220 passim. Boston: Houghton Mifflin, 1935. Reprint. Hamden, Conn.: Archon, 1971.

Extracts in DIARY OF AMERICA, edited by Josef and Dorothy Berger, pp. 482-485; TREASURY OF THE WORLD'S GREAT DIARIES, edited by Philip Dunaway, pp. 77-80.

1847-1859. Extracts from the diaries and logs of a captain noted for risking ship and crew in the race for profits; voyages on the BURMAH and clipper WILD HUNTER, with brief entries describing boredom and homesickness, storms and calms and frequent damage to ships.

SESSIONS, PATTY BARTLETT, 1795-1892   2967

In WOMEN'S VOICES, edited by Kenneth W. Godfrey, Audrey M. Godfrey and Jill Derr, pp. 183-198.

Jan-Jun 1847. Mormon midwife's diary extract from Winter Quarters; constant round of births, including a woman "put to bed" with her twentieth child, and attending the sick; meetings in which speaking in tongues occurred; her own domestic chores amid tireless work for others.

In COVERED WAGON WOMEN, edited by Kenneth L. Holmes, vol. 1, pp. 157-187.

Jun-Sep 1847. Driving wagon from Winter Quarters in Nebraska to Salt Lake City; order of march with First Fifty Company; hunting and dividing the kill; picking and drying currants and berries; record of births in the company; cheerful acceptance of hardships and indication of steady faith.

SKELLY, JAMES, b. 1823   2968

Greer, James K., ed. "Diary of a Pennsylvania Volunteer in the Mexican War." WESTERN PENNSYLVANIA HISTORICAL MAGAZINE 12 (1929):147-154.

Jan-Dec 1847 (with gaps). Journey to Mexico with the Cambria Guards of Cambria County; by steamboat WISCONSIN to New Orleans, thence on the GENERAL VEAZIE to Tampico area, with smallpox raging among troops at sea and on land; camping on Isle of Lobos; to Vera Cruz, Perote and Mexico City, with diary ending abruptly.

SMITH, AZARIAH, b. 1828   2969

"Diary of Azariah Smith in 1847 and 1848." OVERLAND MONTHLY, 2d ser. 11 (February 1888):123-127.

Sep 1847-Jul 1848. Diary of a former Mormon Battalion member employed at Sutter's Coloma sawmill to earn money for his return to Salt Lake; his report that "Mr. Marshall has found some pieces of (as we all suppose) gold, and he has gone to the fort for the purpose of finding out what it is"; continuing his mill work as well as picking up gold; trouble getting his pay from Sutter.

In THE CALIFORNIA GOLD DISCOVERY, edited by Rodman W. Paul, pp. 65-69. Georgetown, Calif.: Talisman Press, 1966.

Oct 1847-May 1848. Extracts.

SMITH, ELIZABETH DIXON, 1809?-1855   2970

"Diary of Mrs. Elizabeth Dixon Smith Geer." OREGON PIONEER ASSOCIATION TRANSACTIONS (1907):153-176.

In COVERED WAGON WOMEN, edited by Kenneth L. Holmes, vol. 1, pp. 111-155.

Apr 1847-Feb 1848. Journey from La Porte, Indiana, to Oregon with her husband, Cornelius Smith, and their seven children; distances and conditions of travel, including hardships, especially during her husband's illness when she was forced to "carry my babe and lead, or rather carry, another through snow, mud and water, almost up to my knees"; her husband's death upon their arrival in Oregon.

SMITH, LEVI LATHROP   2971

Tanis, James Robert, ed. "The Journal of Levi Lathrop Smith." PACIFIC NORTHWEST QUARTERLY 43 (1952):277-301.

1847-1848 (with gaps). Farming diary of the original settler of present Olympia, Washington; brief notes on weather, livestock and crops; references to Indians, his claim partner, Edmund Sylvester, and to the few Puget Sound settlers; loneliness and a sense of isolation, perhaps contributing to strange, fanciful ramblings in the diary.

SNOW, ERASTUS, b. 1818   2972

Creer, Leland H., ed. "Journey to Zion from the Journal of Erastus Snow." UTAH HUMANITIES REVIEW 2 (1948):107-128, 264-284.

Apr-Oct 1847. Extract covering Mormon's journey from Winter Quarters with the first pioneer party under Brigham Young; detailed notes on quasi-military organization, with names of "Captains of Tens," elders, etc.; camps, route, incidents and problems of travel; buffalo hunting; encounters with Sioux and Oregon emigrants; rafting across the Platte; lectures and admonitions of Brigham Young; the founding of Salt Lake City.

SUTTER, JOHN AUGUSTUS, 1803-1880   2973

THE DIARY OF JOHANN AUGUST SUTTER. With an introduction by Douglas S. Watson. San Francisco: Grabhorn Press, 1932. 50 pp.

NEW HELVETIA DIARY; A RECORD OF EVENTS KEPT BY JOHN A. SUTTER AND HIS CLERKS AT NEW HELVETIA, CALIFORNIA. San Francisco: Grabhorn Press in arrangement with the Society of California Pioneers, 1939. 138 pp.

1847-1848. Daily events at Sutter's Fort; some entries by clerks John Bidwell, William F. Swasey and William N. Loker; construction of sawmill and discovering gold.

In THE CALIFORNIA GOLD DISCOVERY, edited by Rodman W. Paul, pp. 56-61. Georgetown, Calif.: Talisman Press, 1966.

Aug 1847-Mar 1848. Extracts relating to discovery of gold.

THAYER, Rev. Dr.   **2974**

"Excerpts from a Diary Written by Dr. Thayer." NEWPORT HISTORICAL SOCIETY BULLETIN, no. 79 (1931):7-15; no. 80 (1931):14-23.

May-Aug 1847. Extracts from Newport, Rhode Island, Protestant clergyman's diary of travel in Europe; briefly in Belgium and along the Rhine; sojourning in Geneva and reflecting on the influence of its residents such as Calvin, Voltaire and Rousseau; commentary on temperance, woman's place, the Anglican church and, especially, Roman Catholicism; trip to Mont Blanc and overnight stay at a convent; description of a diligence and notes on the natural beauty of the countryside and mountains.

TOLMAN, SUSAN L.   **2975**

In YEARS AND HOURS OF EMILY DICKINSON, by Jay Leyda, vol. 1, pp. 122-149. New Haven: Yale University Press, 1960.

Sep 1847-Jul 1848. Extracts from official journal kept for the enlightenment of missionaries sent out from Mount Holyoke Seminary; revealing of the religious, academic and social climate to which Emily Dickinson was exposed during her brief period as a student there; references to conversions of various students.

TUCKER, REASIN P.   **2976**

In OVERLAND IN 1846, edited by Dale L. Morgan, vol. 1, pp. 332-334.

In DONNER MISCELLANY, pp. 52-55.

Feb-Mar 1847. Continuation of M.D. Ritchie's diary of the first Donner relief expedition; brief description of coming upon the starving survivors and attempt to lead them out; several deaths even at this point.

VAIL, REBECCA WORDEN, d. 1872   **2977**

Wagner, Joyce S. "A Nineteenth Century Woman Diarist or Rebecca of Green Brook Farm." RUTGERS UNIVERSITY LIBRARY JOURNAL 46 (1984):76-83.

Jun-Jul 1847. Article containing extracts from diary of a Quaker farm woman at Green Brook, New Jersey; a record of work days beginning at five and filled with washing, cooking, cleaning, sewing, milking and care of children; the obvious importance to her of female relatives as a support system.

VAN EYCK, HENDRIK   **2978**

In DUTCH IMMIGRANT MEMOIRS AND RELATED WRITINGS, selected by Henry S. Lucas, vol. 1, pp. 470-480. Assen, Netherlands: Van Gorcum, 1955.

1847-1856. Dutch immigrant's journey from the Netherlands on the SNELHEID to the New World; sightseeing and visiting old friends and making new ones in New York and New Jersey; canal and riverboat trip after making decision to move to Michigan; good descriptions of farming and industry on Ohio River and in Michigan.

WHITE, WILLIAM N., d. 1867   **2979**

Irvine, William Stafford, ed. "Diary and Letters of Dr. William N. White." ATLANTA HISTORICAL BULLETIN, no. 10 (1937):35-50.

Oct 1847-Jan 1848. Diary of New York resident, recently graduated from Hamilton College, who came south looking for improved health and a career; description of early Atlanta; organizing a school and worrying about competition from others; his feelings about teaching; concern for lack of churches and preaching, especially Presbyterian; meetings to organize city government; writing for local publications; decision to move to Athens for partnership in book business and editorship of the SOUTHERN LITERARY GAZETTE; notes on reading, agriculture, railroad development, moving the state capital, Masons, etc.; no clear distinction between diary and letters but mostly appears to be the former.

1848

ANON.   **2980**

"The Upper Des Moines Valley—1848." ANNALS OF IOWA, 3rd ser. 9 (1909-1910):94-104.

Jun-Jul 1848. Travel along the Des Moines River and surrounding valley and tributaries; detailed notes on scenery, timber and prospects for farming.

BARTLETT, JOHN RUSSELL, 1805-1886   **2981**

PERSONAL NARRATIVE OF EXPLORATIONS & INCIDENTS. London and New York: D. Appleton, 1854. 2 vols.

1848-1853. Commissioner's extensive journals of eight journeys in connection with United States and Mexican boundary commission; botanical and zoological data; natural history observations in Texas, New Mexico, California Sonora and Chihuahua; visiting copper and quicksilver mines, ruins and California missions; topographical information for purpose of possible railway route; customs and habits of numerous Indian tribes.

BRALEY, SAMUEL TRIPP, 1817-1870   **2982**

Miller, Pamela A. "Captain Samuel Tripp Braley: Life at Home, Life at Sea." ESSEX INSTITUTE HISTORICAL COLLECTIONS 119 (1983):5-17.

1848-1853. Extracts, within article, from logs and diaries of Rochester, Massachusetts, captain of the New Bedford whaler ARAB; loneliness for his wife, Mary Ann, whom he had married two weeks before a three year voyage; a second voyage, during which he kept a journal for her containing outspoken comments on sex, marriage and fatherhood as well as worries about money and the success of his whaling ventures.

BREWSTER, MARY LOUISA BURTCH, 1822-1878   **2983**

Lipton, Barbara. "Yankee Woman on an Arctic Whaler." ALASKA JOURNAL 7 (1977):50-55.

1848-1849. Extracts from diary of wife of Capt. William Eldredge Brewster on the TIGER, first ship known to carry a woman through the Bering Sea into Arctic waters; often lonely but preferring to be with her husband rather than spending long years at home alone; notes on their cabin, seamen, homesickness, moving into the ice and trading with Eskimos.

BRITTON, WILLIAM   2984

In CHRONICLES OF THE GRINGOS, compiled by George Winston Smith, p. 400.

Mar-Apr 1848. Extract from young soldier's diary of social life and friendliness of Mexicans while stationed at Puebla at close of Mexican War.

CABOT, JAMES ELLIOT, 1821-1903   2985

In LAKE SUPERIOR: ITS PHYSICAL CHARACTER, VEGETATION AND ANIMALS, by Louis Agassiz, pp. 9-133. Boston: Gould, Kendall and Lincoln, 1850.

Jun-Aug 1848. Expedition with Louis Agassiz to study natural history of the northern shore of Lake Superior; from Boston via Albany and Niagara Falls to Sault Sainte Marie; interesting descriptions of traveling by Mackinaw boat, a cross between a "dorp and mud scow," and by canoe with voyageurs singing French chansons and Indians singing a "low monotonous chant"; Professor Agassiz's lectures, which he illustrated on a portable "blackboard" of painted linen on a roller; at St. Joseph's Island, meeting a former British major, now a frontier farmer, living with his large family in a primitive dwelling containing the works of Shakespeare, Scott, etc.; an interesting diary of experience in "practical investigation of natural phenomena" shared with college students, museum personnel and other interested people.

CHAVANNES, ANNA   2986

Robinson, Emma S., ed. "The Journal of Madame Chavannes." NEW JERSEY HISTORICAL SOCIETY PROCEEDINGS 62 (1944):83-98.

May-Jul 1848. Extracts from affluent Swiss immigrant's journal of travel from Lausanne to settle at Wartburg, Tennessee, with her husband, Adrian Chavannes, and their five children; ship travel, experiences in New York and Chattanooga and train and wagon travel to their destination; a few notes on American customs and manners; prices and conditions at Wartburg. Translated from the French.

COCKE, JOHN HARTWELL, 1780-1866   2987

In A DOCUMENTARY HISTORY OF SLAVERY IN NORTH AMERICA, edited by Willie Lee Rose, pp. 446-448. New York: Oxford University Press, 1976.

Jan 1848. Extract from diary of master of Bremo Bluff plantation located in central Virginia on the James River; visiting his Alabama plantation established as "School for Ultimate Liberian Freedom," believing all Negroes were destined to return to Africa to spread Christian religion; finding shocking moral conditions and much venereal disease; arranging marriages.

COFFIN, ELIJAH, 1798-1862   2988

THE LIFE OF ELIJAH COFFIN. Edited by Mary C. Johnson. Cincinnati? E. Morgan & Sons, 1863. 307 pp. Diary, pp. 23-262.

1848-1861. New Garden, North Carolina, clergyman's journal; meetings and religious work in Indiana and Kansas; visits to New England.

CONGDON, JOHN REMINGTON   2989

Clarkson, A. Collins and Skillin, Rebecca C., eds. "The Wreck of the Bark MONTGOMERY." RHODE ISLAND HISTORY 24 (1965):97-116.

Sep 1848. Extracts from diary of an East Greenwich captain describing mainly the wreck of his ship the MONTGOMERY three hundred miles east of Nantucket; bad weather, with ship taking on water and having to be pumped constantly; failure of pumps, continued battering by high seas and the gradual realization that the ship would be lost; all hands taking to lifeboats and their sufferings from exposure, hunger and thirst; captain's faith and prayers for deliverance; rescue by the ELIJAH SWIFT.

COOPER, SUSAN FENIMORE, 1813-1894   2990

RURAL HOURS. New York: G.P. Putnam; London: Putnam's American Agency, 1850. 521 pp.

JOURNAL OF A NATURALIST IN THE UNITED STATES. London: R. Bentley, 1855. 2 vols.

Abridgement. RURAL HOURS. New and rev. ed. Boston and New York: Houghton Mifflin, 1887. 337 pp. Reprint. Syracuse, N.Y.: Syracuse University Press, 1968.

1848-1850. Quiet, meticulous nature diary kept at Cooperstown and Lake Otsego, New York, by James Fenimore Cooper's daughter; notes on plants, trees, animals and the changing seasons; neighborhood customs; the disappearing Indian.

COUTS, CAVE JOHNSON, 1821-1874   2991

HEPAH, CALIFORNIA! THE JOURNAL OF CAVE JOHNSON COUTS FROM MONTEREY, NUEVO LEON, MEXICO, TO LOS ANGELES, CALIFORNIA. Edited by Henry F. Dobyns. Tucson: Arizona Pioneers' Historical Society, 1961. 113 pp.

Jan-Dec 1848. Extract from military officer's diary of march over Gila Trail to provide strength for weak garrisons in newly acquired California; notes on land, water and agricultural products; social, economic and moral conditions of Mexicans; interactions with Indians, especially Apaches and Pimas; of special value for actions and movements of the First and Second Dragoons and revealing the relations and conduct of career military men; biting remarks about his commander, the usually intoxicated Maj. Lawrence P. Gresham.

FROM SAN DIEGO TO THE COLORADO IN 1849: THE JOURNAL AND MAPS OF CAVE J. COUTS. Edited by William McPherson. Los Angeles: A.M. Ellis, 1932. 77 pp.

Scharf, Thomas L., ed. "Pages from the Diary of Cave Johnson Couts: San Diego in the Spring and Summer of 1849." JOURNAL OF SAN DIEGO HISTORY 22, no. 2 (1976):9-19.

Sep-Nov 1849. The military escort for party making boundary survey after war with Mexico; conflicts with Amiel Weeks Whipple, who plainly demanded recognition for all accomplishments of the party; being annoyed by the constant barrage of requests from emigrants wanting maps and provisions; incidents with Indians, chiefly Colorados, Cuchans and Maricopas; colorful notes on other officers and their abilities.

COWLES, HELEN MARIA, 1831-1850   2992

In GRACE VICTORIOUS; OR, THE MEMOIR OF HELEN M. COWLES, by Henry Cowles, pp. 41-205. Oberlin, Ohio: J.M. Fitch, 1856.

1848-1850. Extracts from the diary of an Austinburg, Ohio, woman; religious and moral reflections, lectures, teaching, visits, social and family affairs, weather, etc.

FARWELL, JOHN VILLIERS, 1825-1908   2993

In REMINISCENCES OF JOHN V. FARWELL, by Abby F. Ferry, vol. 1, pp. 99-174. Chicago: R.F. Seymour, 1928.

1848-1851, 1853. Extracts from young man's personal diary written in a formal style; working as bookkeeper in Chicago dry goods firms of Hamilton and White, Hamlin and Day, and Wadsworth and Phelps; happy marriage and settling in own home; cholera epidemic; private and religious thoughts; family affairs; enjoying a panorama of the Mississippi River from St. Louis to the Falls of St. Anthony; attendance at Clark Street Methodist Church; joy over birth of daughter; painful entry noting death of his wife followed by single entry two years later.

FORBES, CLEVELAND, d. 1857   2994

In CALIFORNIA GOLD RUSH VOYAGES, compiled by John Edwin Pomfret, pp. 179-244. San Marino, Calif.: Huntington Library, 1954. Reprint. Westport, Conn.: Greenwood, 1974.

Oct 1848-May 1849. Log and diary of the captain of the steamer CALIFORNIA on a voyage from New York to Panama via Rio de Janeiro, Valparaiso, Callao and Peyta, then from San Francisco to Panama via Monterey, Santa Barbara, San Diego, Mazatlan and Acapulco; first journey made difficult by his health, requiring a change of command at Panama; Forbes' criticisms of his replacement John Marshall's handling of the ship, difficulties with crew and supplies.

GAILLARD, MAURICE, 1815-1877   2995

Burke, James M., ed. "Early Years at St. Mary's Pottawatomie Mission." KANSAS HISTORICAL QUARTERLY 20 (1953):501-529.

1848-1850. Official record, kept by a Swiss-born priest, of Jesuit mission located at present St. Marys; references to Pawnee-Potawatomi warfare; building the mission, learning Potawatomi and preparing dictionary and prayer book; confessions, catechism classes, masses and baptisms; frequent and difficult travel to visit the sick; a cholera epidemic with many deaths; visit of Father De Smet and references to fathers Christian Hoecken, Felix L. Verreydt and others.

GARFIELD, JAMES ABRAM, 1831-1881   2996

THE DIARY OF JAMES A. GARFIELD. Edited by Harry J. Brown and Frederick D. Williams. East Lansing: Michigan State University Press, 1967-1981. 4 vols.

1848-1881 (with gaps). President's personal and political diary begun in his teens at Orange, Ohio, and continuing through a life of public service which culminated in his shortlived presidency; interesting details of college experiences at what later became Hiram College and at Williams College; a teaching career in Ohio and his life as a young man there; church activities with the Disciples of Christ for whom he was a lay preacher; descriptions of "protracted" and tent meetings; religious reflections; copious and varied reading, which became a lifelong habit; participation in lectures and debates; much information on Ohio towns, events and people; law studies and practice; marriage to Lucretia Rudolph; three brief entries from Civil War service; European travels; his long career in Congress with comments on a virtually encyclopedic range of people, issues and events; extensive material on presidents Grant and Hayes, as well as Charles Sumner, Henry L. Dawes, James G. Blaine, Salmon P. Chase and a host of other important figures; his election and brief presidency; an outstanding diary which presents a vivid picture of the man and his times.

Holmes, Oliver Wendell, ed. "James A. Garfield's Diary of a Trip to Montana in 1872." FRONTIER AND MIDLAND 15 (1934):159-168. Reprint. Sources of Northwest History, no. 21. Missoula: State University of Montana, 1934. 12 pp. FRONTIER OMNIBUS, edited by John W. Hakola, pp. 347-357.

Holmes, Oliver Wendell, ed. "Peregrinations of a Politician: James A. Garfield's Diary of a Trip to Montana in 1872." MONTANA: THE MAGAZINE OF WESTERN HISTORY 6, no. 4 (1956):34-45.

Aug-Sep 1872. Extract covering a trip from Fort Leavenworth, Kansas, to Montana on a mission to persuade the Flathead Indians to accept removal to the Jocko reservation; well described train and stagecoach travel; activities in Helena, Virginia City and Missoula; negotiations with Flatheads, who were opposed to the removal; references to Gov. Benjamin F. Potts, stagecoach drivers and interesting Montana characters.

GUTHRIE, ABELARD, 1814-1873   2997

In THE PROVISIONAL GOVERNMENT OF NEBRASKA TERRITORY AND THE JOURNALS OF WILLIAM WALKER, PROVISIONAL GOVERNOR OF NEBRASKA TERRITORY, edited by William E. Connelley. pp. 101-152. Nebraska State Historical Society Proceedings and Collections, 2d ser., vol. 3. Lincoln: State Journal Co., Printers, 1899.

1848. Fragment covering march from Vera Cruz under command of Colonel Williams of the Michigan Volunteers to bury Georgia Volunteers killed by guerrillas.

1858-1862. Extracts on expanding holdings in Quindaro, Kansas, which he expected to become the great city of the West; dealings with Gov. Charles Robinson over business of the Quindaro Company and eventual financial failure due to Robinson's deceit; defending rights of Shawnees and Wyandots; in Washington as delegate from Nebraska Territory; promoting bill to establish territorial government for Indian territory south of Kansas and failure of bill, at least partly due to James H. Lane's neglect; also trying to get Quindaro named as point on Pacific railroad; opinions on slavery, Lincoln, prominent political figures, the state of the nation and the Civil War.

HALL, LINVILLE JOHN   2998

JOURNAL OF THE HARTFORD UNION MINING AND TRADING COMPANY. Printed on board the HENRY LEE, 1849. 88 pp.

AROUND THE HORN IN '49. Wethersfield, Conn.: Reprinted by L.J. Hall, 1898. 252 pp. Reprint. With an introduction by Oscar Lewis. San Francisco: Book Club of California, 1928. 127 pp.

Dec 1848-Sep 1849. Journal of a Bloomfield, Connecticut, printer who set up his press and began printing a journal on board the HENRY LEE; sailing from New York to San Francisco under Capt.

David P. Vail; debating club, Sunday services and the work of sailors; an elaborate Fourth of July; in port at Rio de Janeiro and a stormy passage of Cape Horn; log entries of weather, position, ships encountered, etc., with diary ending at San Francisco; names and occupations of all members of his gold rush company included. Diary has been attributed to George B. Webster and Hall's name is listed variously as John Linville and Linville John.

HASSLOCK THEKLA DOMBOIS, b. 1824   **2999**

Mayfield, George R., trans. and ed. "The Diary of a German Immigrant." TENNESSEE HISTORICAL QUARTERLY 10 (1951):249-281.

Nov 1848-Feb 1849. Travel with her husband and children, including a newborn baby, to settle in America; from Wiesbaden and Mainz by carriage, boat and train to Le Havre, enjoying the sights and pleasant hotels en route; to New Orleans on the GIRONDE after an irksome delay at Le Havre, where she observed the French with some amusement and disdain; departure, terrible storms, a fire, frequent seasickness and shortened rations; births and deaths, especially in steerage; an excellent picture of difficulties of ocean travel even for cabin passengers far removed from the "stench" and "vileness" of steerage.

HEALY, JAMES AUGUSTINE, d. 1900   **3000**

Lucey, William L. "College Life in Worcester." NEW ENGLAND GALAXY 10, no. 3 (Winter 1969):54-60.

Dec 1848-Aug 1849. Georgia student's notes on senior activities in Worcester, Massachusetts, at Holy Cross College; preparing for school; interest in national politics; recreation and entertainments; music and dancing lessons; the town Fourth of July celebration; being valedictorian of first graduating class.

HUTCHINGS, JAMES MASON, 1820-1902   **3001**

SEEKING THE ELEPHANT: JAMES MASON HUTCHINGS' JOURNAL OF HIS OVERLAND TREK TO CALIFORNIA. Edited by Shirley Sargent. American Trails Series, 12. Glendale, Calif.: A.H. Clark, 1980. 203 pp.

1848-1849 (with gaps). A cultivated English immigrant's gold rush adventures; from Liverpool on the GERTRUDE, with excellent descriptions of the voyage, during which he conducted religious services and assisted the captain, David S. Sherman, in various capacities; references to his cabin mate, Walter Millard; his life in New York, where he worked as a carpenter, with interesting notes on churches of various denominations; Fourth of July; from New Orleans on the GRAND TURK, thence on the ST. JOSEPH to Independence; from Duncan's Ferry overland with John J. Wilson and a military escort under Robert M. Morris; joining the army temporarily as a wheelwright; colorful notes on hazards, hardships, humorous incidents, fellow argonauts, Indians, forts, etc., and a meticulous record of graves; a glimpse of rowdy life at Placerville.

KANE, ELISHA KENT, 1820-1857   **3002**

ADRIFT IN THE ARCTIC ICE PACK, FROM THE HISTORY OF THE FIRST U.S. GRINNELL EXPEDITION IN SEARCH OF SIR JOHN FRANKLIN. Edited by Horace Kephart. New York: Outing, 1915. 402 pp. passim.

Aug 1848-May 1849. A mixture of narrative and diary describing the first of several American-sponsored attempts to rescue Sir

John Franklin and his company, who had failed to return from an expedition to search for the Northwest Passage; months with ships wedged into pack ice and helplessly adrift; sufferings from scurvy, snow blindness, cold and hunger; a graphic survival diary kept by the medical officer and scientist of two-ship rescue party.

ARCTIC EXPLORATIONS: THE SECOND GRINNELL EXPEDITION IN SEARCH OF SIR JOHN FRANKLIN. Philadelphia: Childs & Peterson, 1856. 2 vols. passim.

1853-1855. Commander's narrative, quoting extensively from his own diaries, of the harrowing second attempt to rescue Franklin; difficult trek to Upernavik, Greenland, after the ship was frozen in at Rensselaer Bay, which resulted in the gathering of important information on Greenland Eskimos, Moravian settlements, wildlife, etc.; references to his medical officer, I.I. Hayes.

KERN, BENJAMIN J., b. 1818   **3003**

In FREMONT'S FOURTH EXPEDITION, edited by LeRoy R. and Ann W. Hafen, pp. 79-108.

Oct 1848-Jan 1849. Diary of the doctor who, with his two brothers, accompanied Fremont's disastrous fourth expedition to locate passes for a transcontinental railroad across the Sangre de Cristo and San Juan mountains; route from St. Louis via the Kansas and Arkansas rivers to Big Timber; great suffering from snow and cold; loss of mules and men, which necessitated return of survivors to seek shelter at Taos.

KERN, RICHARD, 1821-1853   **3004**

In WHEN OLD TRAILS WERE NEW: THE STORY OF TAOS, by Blanche C. Grant, pp. 119-141. New York: Press of the Pioneers, 1934.

In FREMONT'S FOURTH EXPEDITION, edited by LeRoy R. and Ann W. Hafen, pp. 109-133.

Oct 1848-Feb 1849. Diary of artist with Fremont's fourth expedition; sketches as well as account of the fateful trip and sheltering at Taos.

KIDDER, HARRIETTE SMITH   **3005**

Harrison, Victoria G. "Little Matters and a Great Mission." RUTGERS UNIVERSITY LIBRARY JOURNAL 46 (1984):58-75.

1848-1849. Article containing extracts from the nearly lifelong diary of a New Jersey Methodist minister's wife; articulate religious and domestic notes; child rearing, church and philanthropic work, including organizing Sunday schools and an orphanage; private and public protest against the limited role allowed women in American Methodism; surprisingly few references to her husband, Daniel P. Kidder.

KNAPP, HANNAH FROST, b. 1833?   **3006**

Massi, Barbara S. "Hannah Knapp's Diary." WESTCHESTER HISTORIAN 51 (1975):86-90.

1848-1849. Extracts from North Castle, New York, teenager's diary embedded in summarizing narrative describing diary's contents; a family outing to the beach; her uncle, Arnell F. Dickinson.

LEWIS, HENRY, 1819-1904   **3007**

Heilbron, Bertha L., ed. "Making a Motion Picture in 1848; Journal of a Canoe Voyage from the Falls of St. Anthony to St. Louis." MINNESOTA HISTORY 17 (1936):131-158, 288-301, 421-436.

MAKING A MOTION PICTURE IN 1848. With introduction and notes by Bertha L. Heilbron. Minnesota Historical Society Publications. Saint Paul: Minnesota Historical Society, 1936. 58 pp.

Jun-Aug 1848. Artist's canoe journey along the Mississippi; making sketches for his enormous panorama of the upper Mississippi; high-flown romantic narrative and descriptions of natural history, Indians, etc.

LONG, JOHN DAVIS, 1838-1915   3008

AMERICA OF YESTERDAY. Edited by Lawrence S. Mayo. Boston: Atlantic Monthly Press, 1923. 250 pp.

JOURNAL. Edited by Margaret Long. Rindge, N.H.: R.R. Smith, 1956. 363 pp.

1848-1915 (with gaps). Extracts from personal diary; charming boyhood entries on growing up in Buckfield, Maine, with occasional admonitions inserted by his father; school at Hebron Academy where he was desperately homesick; entering Harvard at age fifteen, lonely first year until he moved into a dormitory; good notes on academic life, honors, election to Phi Beta Kappa and speaking at commencement; teaching at Westford Academy; a visit to a Shaker village; attending Harvard Law School; selected extracts during public life in House of Representatives and as secretary of the navy under McKinley; views on McKinley, Theodore Roosevelt, other public figures, the Philippine question and the Spanish-American War; a few reflections after his retirement at Buckfield.

Mayo, Lawrence Shaw, ed. "The America that Used to Be." ATLANTIC MONTHLY 130 (1922):721-730.

Feb-Aug 1848. Precocious diary of a nine-year-old; school work and other lessons imposed by his father; extensive reading, especially of the Bible, with amusing comments on some passages; opinions on local, national and world events; a lively picture of family and village social life, intellectual and moral values.

MCGAVOCK, RANDAL WILLIAM, 1826-1863   3009

PEN AND SWORD: THE LIFE AND JOURNALS OF RANDAL W. MCGAVOCK. Edited by Herschel Gower and Jack Allen. Nashville: Tennessee Historical Commission, 1959. 695 pp.

1843-1862 (with gaps). Diaries kept by member of prominent Tennessee family; student days at Harvard Law School; reading, lectures, visits and visitors, theater and opera in Boston; trips to Washington, D.C., and through New York State, visiting Niagara Falls, to Canada; "Grand Tour" to Europe upon graduation, dining with President Fillmore and his family before departure; to England aboard the WATERLOO in a party including Episcopal bishop James Harvey Otey and former Tennessee congressman Edwin Hickman Ewing; touring the British Isles with visits to the Crystal Palace Exposition and glimpses of Queen Victoria; then to the Continent and Egypt; upon return, law practice in Nashville and marriage to Seraphine Deery; attendance at 1856 and 1860 Democratic national conventions; Fourth of July celebrations; visits to Washington, D.C., and a meeting with President Buchanan; successful term as mayor of Nashville; service as lieutenant colonel of the Tenth Tennessee; description of defense of Fort Henry and Fort Donelson, where he was captured, and criticism of Confederate generalship; briefly held at Camp Chase and then confined at Fort Warren; notes on prison conditions, activities and fellow inmates; exchange and journey to Mississippi

where regiment was reorganized; a full, rich diary covering family, social and civic affairs and local, state and national political events and issues.

MOERENHOUT, JACOB ANTOINE, 1796?-1879   3010

THE INSIDE STORY OF THE GOLD RUSH. Translated and edited by Abraham P. Nasatir, in collaboration with George E. Dane. California Historical Society Special Publication, no. 8. San Francisco: California Historical Society, 1935. 91 pp. Diary, pp. 4-40.

Jul-Aug 1848. Report by the French consul at Monterey of a tour of placer mining country; careful and official observations.

NORSTROM, CARL EDWARD   3011

Celsing, Mrs. Fredrik, ed. and trans. "A Swedish View of St. Louis." MISSOURI HISTORICAL SOCIETY BULLETIN 27 (1971):147-150.

Aug 1848. Extract from account of Swedish engineer's trip to study railroad construction; from Chicago to La Salle on the Michigan and Illinois Canal, where he "was met with the news that previous steamer had just exploded," killing forty passengers; on to St. Louis by riverboat with references to other serious accidents; disapproving comments on American ways, especially egalitarian treatment of servants.

OBER, MERRILL, 1832-1853   3012

Clough, Wilson O., ed. "A Journal of Village Life in Vermont in 1848." NEW ENGLAND QUARTERLY 1 (1928):32-40.

Sep-Nov 1848. Life of a precocious boy in Monkton; studies, including Greek, Milton and Shakespeare, reading and music; a lecture by George Perkins Marsh with offer of the use of his library; Free Soil Party activities; religious reflections.

PEREZ ROSALES, VICENTE, 1807-1886   3013

In WE WERE 49ERS! CHILEAN ACCOUNTS OF THE CALIFORNIA GOLD RUSH, translated and edited by Edwin A. Beilharz and Carlos U. Lopez, pp. 1-59. Pasadena, Calif.: Ward Ritchie Press, 1976.

Dec 1848-Mar 1849. Long, sporadically kept entries of a Chilean's voyage from Valparaiso on the STAUELLI; "a mixed lot on this little Tower of Babel: Frenchmen, Englishmen, Germans, Italians, Chileans, nabobs and beggers," with the diarist's highly entertaining anecdotes of them; shipboard diversions and an uprising of steerage against cabin passengers; in San Francisco, with good sketches of life and milieu there, especially its international character; a trip to Contra Costa, which was "amusing enough"; equally entertaining accounts of his adventures in various diggings; literary and classical allusions throughout.

"We Were Forty-Niners: The Gold Rush through Chilean Eyes." AMERICAN WEST 13, no. 3 (1976):48-52.

Mar 1849. Undated extracts covering journey from Sacramento to the northern mines, some luckless experiences on the American River and an equally unsuccessful venture as a merchant in Sacramento.

PERKINS, AROZINA, 1826-1854   3014

In WOMEN TEACHERS ON THE FRONTIER, by Polly W. Kaufman, pp. 55-152. New Haven: Yale University Press, 1984.

1848-1851. Substantial diary of a young New England teacher, one of many who went west under auspices of the National Popular Education Board; teaching in New Haven, working in the

Baptist Sabbath School and distributing tracts for the American Tract Society; an interval at Marshfield, Massachusetts, then training at the Board's institute at Hartford under Nancy Swift and Lucy Tappan Grosvenor, with lectures by Thomas Gallaudet, Samuel S. Greene, etc.; good notes on curriculum and routine; an exhausting journey to Fort Des Moines, Iowa, where she was poorly received by the settlers and had to teach under impossible conditions; improved circumstances at Fairfield Female Seminary, but entries end abruptly; a sad diary of an idealistic young teacher whose ardor to go west was rewarded with unrelenting work, loneliness and disappointment.

PRATT, ORVILLE C., 1819-1891   **3015**

In OLD SPANISH TRAIL, by Le Roy R. Hafen, pp. 341-359. Glendale, Calif.: A.H. Clark, 1954.

Aug-Oct 1848. Daily entries for a complete trip over the Old Spanish Trail from New Mexico to California made by order of the War Department to report on some confidential matter; weather, camping and trail conditions; food and water supply; contact with Indians; first news of discovery of gold.

RAYMOND, HENRY JARVIS, 1820-1869   **3016**

Raymond, Henry W., ed. "Extracts from the Journal of Henry J. Raymond." SCRIBNER'S MONTHLY 19 (1879-1880):57-61, 419-424, 703-710; 20 (1880):275-280.

1848-1866 (with gaps). Extracts from the desultorily kept journal of editor and politician, founder of the NEW YORK TIMES; his first visit to Washington, D.C., where he interviewed Daniel Webster and Georgia congressman Butler King and reported on strategies and aspirants for the Whig presidential nomination of 1848; recollections of Martin Van Buren's reaction to a train accident; practices in the New York State Assembly; ruminations on zeal and discretion; a visit to the Army of the Potomac in January, 1863, conversing with generals Wadsworth, Burnside, Sumner and Parks; conflicting opinions on the "Mud March"; Burnside's problems with subordinates; talks with Lincoln, Seward, Stanton and Chase; discussions with prominent men about French intervention; account of origin of and diarist's involvement in the National Union Convention held at Philadelphia in 1866.

ROBERTSON, WILLIAM H., 1823-1898   **3017**

"Robertson Diary." WESTCHESTER COUNTY HISTORICAL BULLETIN 23 (1947):26-39.

Oct 1848-Jun 1849. Extracts from Whitlockville lawyer's diary; his nomination and election to the New York legislature; Whig county convention and 1848 presidential election; journey to Albany by sleigh and train; inauguration of Hamilton Fish as governor; politics and social life in the state capital; a gala dinner celebrating Washington's Birthday at the Troy House; detailed description of the William P. Van Rensselaer mansion on east bank of the Hudson River; notes on his Albany accommodations; references to Thurlow Weed and William H. Seward; travel around New York state by boat, train and wagon; a visit to Niagara Falls; long, highly descriptive entries.

ROOT, RILEY   **3018**

JOURNAL OF TRAVELS. Galesburg, Ill.: Gazetteer and Intelligencer Printers, 1850. 143 pp. Oakland, Calif.: Biobooks, 1955. 130 pp.

Apr-Sep 1848, Mar-May 1849. Knox County, Illinois, traveler's factual record kept from St. Joseph to Oregon City with travel guide in mind; accurate account of organizing at St. Joseph; distances, camp sites, feed for cattle, fuel, water, landmarks, geologic features and crossings of the Platte and Snake rivers to Fort Boise; at Burnt River injecting a note of despair: "Oh! when shall I view once more, a verdant landscape!"; along John Day and Deschutes rivers noting destitute Deschutes Indians; arrival of first public mail in Oregon City by mail steamer from San Francisco; description of fledgling Astoria and gold rush San Francisco where there were many ships in the bay, their crews having deserted for the mines; a narrative summary containing Spalding's account of Whitman massacre, news of discovery of gold, description of mines, and diarist's return to St. Louis via Panama and New Orleans.

SHAW, JOSEPH COOLIDGE   **3019**

"The 'Yankee Priest' Says Mass in Brattleboro." VERMONT HISTORY 44 (1976):198-202.

Jul 1848. Boston priest's stay in Brattleboro to "take the water cure" and minister to Irish laborers.

SIBLEY, JOHN LANGDON   **3020**

In CHRONICLES OF THE GRINGOS, compiled by George Winston Smith, pp. 451-452.

Jul 1848. Extract from private diary of assistant librarian at Harvard; return of ragged and fatigued Massachusetts Regiment at end of war with Mexico, their hostility toward Gen. Caleb Cushing, especially at dinner in their honor at Faneuil Hall.

STOKES, JOHN   **3021**

Rice, F. Andrew. "John Stokes's Diary in America." NATIONAL ENGLISH REVIEW 110 (1938):78-86.

1848-1849. Extracts within article on English immigrant's travel from Bradford-on-Avon, intending to settle at Rockville, Connecticut; on the QUEEN OF THE WEST to New York; work at mill owned by George Kellogg and lodging with the family of Enoch Bound; constant homesickness and longing for British food, customs and working conditions, which led to his eventual return.

THORNE, SAMUEL, 1835-1915   **3022**

THE JOURNAL OF A BOY'S TRIP ON HORSEBACK. New York: Privately printed, 1936. 47 pp.

Extracts in SMALL VOICES, edited by Josef and Dorothy Berger, pp. 140-147.

Apr-Jun 1848. A twelve-year-old boy's diary of travel by horseback from Charleston, South Carolina, to New York with his teenage friend; an ingenuous mixture of notes on bad roads, kind farmers, a reception with President and Mrs. Polk and how to relieve a constipated horse!

THORNTON, JESSY QUINN, 1810-1888   **3023**

OREGON AND CALIFORNIA IN 1848. New York: Harper & Brothers, 1849. 2 vols. Reprint. Arno, 1973. 393, 397 pp.

May-Nov 1848. Seminarrative journal of travel from Quincy, Illinois, to Oregon via Fort Laramie, Green River and Applegate's Cutoff; a retelling of the Donner tragedy; conventional details of route, sights and Indians.

TORBERT, JAMES MONROE, b. 1822   3024

Brannon, Peter A., ed. "James M. Torbert's Daybook." ALABAMA REVIEW 1 (1948):226-235.

1848-1859. Extracts from the diary of a Macon County, Alabama, planter; brief entries of weather and agricultural tasks performed by himself and his slaves.

"James M. Torbert's Journal." ALABAMA HISTORICAL QUARTERLY 18 (1956):218-280; 22 (1960):1-76.

1856-1875. Owner's diary of events at his plantation near the village of Society Hill; the multitudinous tasks of farm life; business dealings, legal matters, politics and social activities; crops and livestock; weather and its consequences; buying, selling and punishing slaves; overseers; health of diarist, his family and slaves; births and deaths; setting up and operating lumber and grist mill; trips to Columbus, Georgia; daily entries for 1856-1857 and part of 1860 but only annual summations for other years; financial and family history notes, list of fifty-nine slaves and recipes for medicine appended.

WHITMAN, WALT, 1819-1892   3025

Scattered throughout Whitman's complete prose works are many diary fragments, memoranda, daybooks, sketches, jottings, etc., some of which are difficult to identify absolutely as diaries. Major editions of his works are:

COMPLETE WRITINGS OF WALT WHITMAN. Issued under the editorial supervision of his literary executors, Richard Maurice Bucke, Thomas B. Harned, and Horace L. Traubel. New York and London: G.P. Putnam's Sons, 1902. 10 vols. Reprint. Grosse Pointe, Mich.: Scholarly Press, 1968.

COLLECTED WRITINGS. General editors: Gay Wilson Allen and E. Sculley Bradley. New York: New York University Press, 1961. 18 vols.

In addition, diaries and diary fragments are contained in the following:

THE UNCOLLECTED POETRY AND PROSE OF WALT WHITMAN. Collected and edited by Emory Holloway. Garden City, N.Y.: Doubleday, Page, 1921. 2 vols. Diary, vol. 2, pp. 77-78. Reprint. Gloucester, Mass.: P. Smith, 1972.

1848 (with gaps). A fragment of what was once apparently a diary for the year; in New Orleans publishing the CRESCENT, where disenchantment soon set in and he departed; brief account of return to Brooklyn via Great Lakes and Niagara Falls; only one dated entry, March 18.

SPECIMEN DAYS AND COLLECT. Philadelphia: R. Welsh, 1882-1883. 314 pp. SPECIMEN DAYS IN AMERICA. Newly revised by the author. London: W. Scott, 1887. 317 pp. Philadelphia: David McKay, 1892. Reprint of the text of the 1892 edition. Boston: David R. Godine, 1971. 197 pp. passim.

PROSE WORKS, 1892. Edited by Floyd Stovall. The Collected Writings of Walt Whitman. New York: New York University Press, 1963-1964. 2 vols. SPECIMEN DAYS, vol. 1.

COMPLETE POETRY AND COLLECTED PROSE. Edited by Justin Kaplan. New York: Literary Classics of the United States, 1982. SPECIMEN DAYS, pp. 675-926.

1860-1887? (with gaps). A collection drawn together late in his life of memoirs, Civil War memoranda and diaries, travel diaries and nature notes; work as a volunteer nurse in Washington, D.C., and field hospitals, with accounts of the sick, wounded and dying, possibly unsurpassed in war annals; his life in and around

Camden, New Jersey, travels to Niagara Falls, Canada, Long Island, etc.; descriptions of Abraham Lincoln and memories of a visit with Emerson; wide-ranging reflections and sympathies.

WALT WHITMAN: REPRESENTATIVE SELECTIONS. Edited by Floyd Stovall. New York: American Book, 1934. 426 pp. Diary, pp. 363-367. Rev. ed. New York: Hill and Wang, 1961.

Apr-Oct 1861. Civil War extracts.

MEMORANDA DURING THE WAR. Camden, N.J.: Author's publication, 1875-1876. 68 pp.

MEMORANDA DURING THE WAR & DEATH OF ABRAHAM LINCOLN. Edited by Roy P. Basler. Bloomington: Indiana University Press, 1962. 1 vol. Reprint. Westport, Conn.: Greenwood, 1972.

1862-1865. Memoir containing notes kept while tending the sick and wounded in Washington hospitals and Virginia, mostly "verbatim renderings from such pencillings on the spot"; graphic pictures of wounded and dying soldiers and something of their lives and backgrounds; some routine of Civil War hospitals and the poet's efforts to be of service and comfort.

WALT WHITMAN'S CIVIL WAR. Compiled & edited by Walter Lowenfels. New York: Knopf, 1960. 333 pp.

WALT WHITMAN AND THE CIVIL WAR. Edited by Charles I. Glicksberg. Philadelphia: University of Pennsylvania Press, 1933. 201 pp. Diary, pp. 131-144. Reprint. New York: A.S. Barnes, 1963.

1862-1864 (with gaps). Whitman's brief, irregularly kept Civil War diaries; mainly volunteer work at Armory Square Hospital in Washington, nursing both Union and Confederate sick and wounded; a reference to his love for Lincoln; voluminous correspondence; a moving glimpse of what he saw and felt as a Civil War nurse.

Extracts in DIARY OF AMERICA, edited by Josef and Dorothy Berger, pp. 468-472.

1862-1865. Selections relating to the Civil War.

DAYBOOKS AND NOTEBOOKS. Edited by William White. The Collected Writings of Walt Whitman. New York: New York University Press, 1978. 3 vols. DAYBOOKS, vols. 1, 2.

1876-1891. Dated entries containing names, dates, activities and ideas; a few tax and book sale records.

WALT WHITMAN'S DIARY IN CANADA, WITH EXTRACTS FROM OTHER OF HIS DIARIES AND LITERARY NOTEBOOKS. Edited by William Sloane Kennedy. Boston: Small, Maynard, 1904. Reprint. Folcroft, Pa.: Folcroft Press, 1970. Norwood, Pa.: Norwood Editions, 1977. 73 pp. Diary, pp. 1-45.

DAYBOOKS AND NOTEBOOKS. Edited by William White. The Collected Writings of Walt Whitman. New York: New York University Press, 1978. 3 vols. DIARY IN CANADA, vol. 3.

Jun-Aug 1880. Travels in Canada, where he made the friendship of Dr. Richard Maurice Burke; experiences and observations in Ontario, Montreal and Quebec.

1849

ANON.   3026

In THE ARGONAUTS AND PIONEERS, by Verna I. Shupe, pp. 12-18. Pocatello, Idaho: Graves & Potter, Tribune Press, 1931.

1849-1853 (with gaps). Brief, scattered notes of a gold rush journey with an Iowa company; mining at Placerville, with prices and earnings; return by ship and overland via Panama.

ANON.   **3027**

In JOURNAL OF A VOYAGE FROM BOSTON TO SAN FRANCISCO IN 1849, edited by Carroll D. Hall, pp. 1-37. Redwood City, Calif., 1933.

> Jan-Oct 1849. Gold rush voyage on the EDWARD EVERETT of a member of the Boston and California Mining and Trading Joint Stock Company; notes on crew and passengers, "a great diversion of characters aboard here"; amusements, food and Sunday services; ships encountered throughout voyage; selling his share in the company in California and heading for the diggings; passenger list appended.

ANON.   **3028**

In SOUTHERN TRAILS TO CALIFORNIA IN 1849, edited by Ralph P. Bieber, pp. 259-280.

> Apr-Sep 1849. Brief daily notes on travel from Austin, Texas, to gold mines at Mariposa, California; distances, scenery, climate and vegetation.

ANON.   **3029**

"Journal of a Voyage on the Raging Canal." WESTERN PENNSYLVANIA HISTORICAL MAGAZINE 63 (1980):273-276.

> Oct 1849. Canal boat journey on the INDIANA from Pittsburgh to Johnstown as first phase of a trip on the Pennsylvania Canal and Portage Railroad; humorous anecdotes about passengers and the chaotic but festive atmosphere on board; by train from Johnstown and finally on the packet KISHACOGWILLAS to Lewistown.

ALDRICH, LORENZO D., 1818?-1851   **3030**

A JOURNAL OF THE OVERLAND ROUTE TO CALIFORNIA. Lansingburgh, N.Y.: Alexr. Kirkpatrick, Printer, 1851. 48 pp. Reprint. March of America Facsimile Series, no. 87. Ann Arbor, Mich.: University Microfilms, 1966. Los Angeles: Dawson's Book Shop, 1950. 93 pp.

> 1849-1850 (with gaps). Journal of gold rush; travel from Albany, New York, to California; riverboat travel on Ohio River; an early record of southern route or Santa Fe Trail from Fort Smith, Arkansas, across Oklahoma, panhandle of Texas and along Canadian River to San Diego by wagon and pack mule; hardships of travel; difficult river crossings; notes on Mexican, Pima and Maricopa Indians and villages; a bullfight in San Diego; by ship BELFAST to San Francisco and brief account of return to Panama on the REPUBLIC.

ARMSTRONG, J. ELZA, 1826?-1905   **3031**

In THE BUCKEYE ROVERS IN THE GOLD RUSH: AN EDITION OF TWO DIARIES, edited by Howard L. Scamehorn, 195 pp. Athens: Ohio University Press, 1965.

> 1849-1852. Interspersed diary entries of two observant young forty-niners of the Buckeye Rovers Company of Ohio; literate, developed and religiously introspective notes of John Edwin Banks contrasting with economical details of J. Elza Armstrong; overland crossing via the Humboldt and experiences in the diggings; the usual mixture of hardship, disease, quarrels, heroism and depravity, plus the awesomeness and beauty of the West described in a valuable gold rush source.

ATHEARN, PRINCE ALLEN, 1811-1867   **3032**

Athearn, Lovelia, ed. "The Log Book of P.A. Athearn," PACIFIC HISTORIAN 2, no. 2 (1958):6-7; no. 3, 13-16; no. 4, 9-12; 3, no. 1 (1959):21-23; no. 2, 39-42; no. 3, 68, 71-72.

> Apr-Sep 1849. Gold rush journey from Switzerland County, Indiana, by riverboats SOUTH AMERICA and TINCON to St. Joseph; overland to the Mother Lode via present Carson Pass; brief notes of distances and conditions of travel.

> Jan 1852. Return east on the NORTH AMERICA via Nicaragua, thence on the PROMETHEUS, with diary ending immediately upon departure; scant information.

AUDUBON, JOHN WOODHOUSE, 1812-1862   **3033**

AUDUBON'S WESTERN JOURNAL. Introduction, notes and index by Frank H. Hodder. Cleveland: A.H. Clark, 1906. Reprint. Glorieta, N.M.: Rio Grande Press, 1969. 249 pp.

Extracts in THE COURSE OF EMPIRE, compiled by Helen V. Bary, pp. 98-130.

> 1849-1850. Journal of the famed ornithologist's son and naturalist in his own right; with Col. Henry L. Webb's California Company by the almost impossible Mexican border route; travel from New York to New Orleans, Brazos and Brownsville on a succession of steamers; devastation of the company from cholera in Texas; the desertion of Colonel Webb and near abandonment of the project until reorganized under Audubon; to Saltillo, Pantilla, etc., with notes on Mexicans, scenery, terrain and natural history; difficulties on the Gila Desert, where Audubon had to abandon his carefully garnered specimans of birds and mammals; in San Diego, Los Angeles, San Francisco, Stockton, etc., and at various diggings and missions; good vignettes of life among the miners; frequent references to his friend Robert Layton.

BACHMAN, JACOB HENRY   **3034**

Van Nostrand, Jeanne S. "Audubon's Ill-fated Western Journey: Recalled by the Diary of J.H. Bachman." CALIFORNIA HISTORICAL SOCIETY QUARTERLY 21 (1942):289-310.

> Mar-Nov 1849. Article containing generous extracts, beginning on the Rio Grande, of gold rush journey undertaken by a party of affluent New York greenhorns under the incompetent leadership of Col. Henry L. Webb; cholera and desertions, including that of Webb, leaving John W. Audubon in charge; difficult travel along route through northern Mexico chosen by Webb.

Van Nostrand, Jeanne Skinner. "Diary of a 'Used Up' Miner." CALIFORNIA HISTORICAL SOCIETY QUARTERLY 22 (1943):67-83.

> 1849-1878. Extracts within article, with entries beginning near San Francisco, where Bachman has been sent by ship from San Diego to recuperate from the grueling overland journey; work in San Francisco unloading freight; to the diggings in Calaveras County; work, violence, disorder and some peculiar mining camp justice; very infrequent entries from 1851-1878 covering his life as a farmer and prospector in Calaveras County.

BAKER, GEORGE H., 1827-1906   **3035**

"Records of a California Residence." SOCIETY OF CALIFORNIA PIONEERS QUARTERLY 8 (1931):39-70.

> 1849-1850. Extracts containing colorful descriptions, in rather elevated style, of life in gold rush California; an unsuccessful mining venture with partner John H. Keyser; observations and activities in Sacramento, San Francisco and San Jose; some

inconclusive attempts at becoming a merchant; on the AURORA to Oregon, from which he returned ''grievously disappointed,'' but Oregon notes are omitted from these extracts; continuing to seek his fortune in California and finding most reports of easy gold to be ''humbug.''

BARNES, LAURA A. LANGWORTHY   3036

Bailey, Joe H., ed. ''Journals of Trek of Barnes Family.'' ANNALS OF IOWA, 3d ser. 32 (1953-1955):576-601.

Jun-Sep 1849. Journals kept by a Bureau County, Illinois couple, Laura and Julius Barnes, of their unsuccessful attempt to migrate to Oregon; mainly difficult wanderings in Iowa and eventual settlement in Mills County; description of countryside and occasional farms; much religious sentiment and longing for a proper place of worship; the plotting of California City, Iowa.

BENNETT, JAMES AUGUSTUS, 1831-1909   3037

Brooks, Clinton E. and Reeve, Frank D., eds. ''James A. Bennett: A Dragoon in New Mexico.'' NEW MEXICO HISTORICAL REVIEW 22 (1947):51-97, 140-176. Reprint. FORTS AND FORAYS. Albuquerque: University of New Mexico Press, 1948. 85 pp.

1849-1856 (with gaps). Cavalryman's diary; enlistment at Rochester, New York; complaints of grueling drills, near starvation diet and severe military discipline during training on Governors Island; by train and riverboat to Jefferson Barracks at Fort Leavenworth, where men were dying of cholera; humorous descriptions of learning to ride; the march to New Mexico, with good notes on Spanish customs; forays against the Apaches with Kit Carson as guide; Indian depredations, including the murder of J.M. White, a Santa Fe trader, and his wife; the killing of an Indian baby and scalping of Indians by soldiers; activities at forts Defiance, Union and Webster; continuous marches, winter and summer, under extreme conditions of cold, heat and hunger; long convalescence from a nearly fatal bullet wound; march with William H. Emory to fix the boundary between the United States and Mexico; activities at Fort Fillmore and a ghastly march during which thirsty men were left to die by Col. Daniel T. Chandler; a graphic picture of the harsh life of Indian fighters and brutalities of both sides.

BERRIEN, JOSEPH WARING   3038

Hinckley, Ted and Hinckley, Caryl. ''Overland from St. Louis to the California Gold Field in 1849.'' INDIANA MAGAZINE OF HISTORY 56 (1960):273-352.

May-Aug 1849. Belleville, Illinois, man's full and articulate gold rush diary; colorful details of riverboat travel from St. Louis to St. Joseph, thence by mule wagon; descriptions of scenery, camp life, problems and such processes as ferrying wagons across rivers and lowering them down cliffs; good notes on the Humboldt and Sierra Nevada crossing; nothing of his experience in the gold fields.

BOOTH, EDMUND, 1810-1905   3039

EDMUND BOOTH, FORTY-NINER: THE LIFE STORY OF A DEAF PIONEER. Stockton, Calif.: San Joaquin Pioneer and Historical Society, 1953. 72 pp. Diary, pp. 8-16.

Jul-Oct 1849. Fragment of a longer lost diary of the gold rush journey of a man from Anamosa, Iowa, with entries beginning west of Independence Rock; route via South Pass, with condi-

tions of travel and progress, or lack of it, of other emigrant companies, particularly the Washington City Company; advice from Chief Truckee; failure of oxen on the Humboldt; coming upon the Pioneer Line wagons ''standing in and by the road.''

BOWMAN, E.I.   3040

In WAGONS WEST, by Elizabeth Page, pp. 333-335. New York: Farrar & Rinehart, 1930.

Mar-May 1849. Brief notes of stages of journey from Illinois with the emigrating Jerseyville Company as far as the Missouri River.

BOYDEN, SETH, 1788-1870   3041

''Seth Boyden's Day in California, 1849-51.'' NEW JERSEY HISTORICAL SOCIETY PROCEEDINGS, n.s. 12 (1927):309-318, 455-461; 13 (1928):70-76.

1849-1851. Newark inventor's gold rush diary, beginning at Panama upon his arrival on the FALCON; thence on the OREGON to San Francisco, up the Sacramento to the diggings, with a good account of mining methods, amounts of gold mined, earnings and expenses; return via Panama and Havana on the BOHEMIA and FALCON.

BROWN, JOHN EVANS, 1827-1895   3042

MEMOIRS OF A FORTY-NINER. By Katie E. Blood. New Haven, Conn.: Associated Publishers of American Records, 1907. 27 pp.

''Memoirs of an American Gold Seeker: Experiences of a 'Forty-Niner' during His Journey across the Continent on Horseback.'' JOURNAL OF AMERICAN HISTORY 2 (1908):129-154.

Mar-Aug 1849. Gold rush journey from Asheville, North Carolina; on horseback and riverboat with several friends to St. Louis, which diarist found to be ''increasing rapidly in population and bad morals''; cholera, etc., treated with laudanum and morphine; good notes in the race for position of various companies along the trail; interesting comments on other forty-niners; a serious gun accident; encounters with Indians.

BRUFF, JOSEPH GOLDSBOROUGH, 1804-1889   3043

GOLD RUSH: THE JOURNALS, DRAWINGS AND OTHER PAPERS OF J. GOLDSBOROUGH BRUFF, CAPTAIN, WASHINGTON CITY AND CALIFORNIA MINING ASSOCIATION. Edited by Georgia W. Read and Ruth Gaines. New York: Columbia University Press, 1944. 2 vols. Abridgement. California Centennial ed. New York: Columbia University Press, 1949. 794 pp.

1849-1951. Copious diary kept by the captain of the Washington City and California Mining Association from Washington, D.C.; to the gold fields and back; a careful chronicle of the journey and its hardships of hunger, scurvy, cholera, danger from Indians and quarrels among the forty-niners; route via Lassen's Cutoff with frequent references to Peter Lassen and others prospecting in the Gold Lake area; an excellent diary containing evidence of both nobility and brutality among those racing for gold.

BRYAN, FRANCIS T.   3044

In United States. 31st Cong., 1st sess., 1850, S. Exec Doc. 64, pp. 14-24.

Jun-Jul 1849. Report of topographical engineer; from San Antonio to El Paso via Fredericksburg; reconnaissance for permanent military road; terrain, water, wood, grass and soil; record of distances and necessary wells.

''Report of Lieut. F.T. Bryan Concerning His Operations in Locating a Practicable Road between Fort Riley to Bridger's Pass.'' ANNALS OF WYOMING 17 (1945):24-55.

Jul-Oct 1856. Official report of Army Corps of Topographical Engineers expedition; route, camps and distances; notes on topography, water, grass, etc.

BURBANK, ARTHUR R.   **3045**

Davis, Charles A. and McDonald, Lucile, eds. ''The Arthur R. Burbank Diary and Journal.'' COWLITZ COUNTY HISTORICAL QUARTERLY 5, no. 4 (1964):13-28; 6, no. 1 (1964):12-29; no. 2 (1964):15-28; no. 3 (1964):16-28; no. 4 (1965):16-28.

1849-1879 (with gaps). Methodist merchant's gold rush journey from Naples, Illinois; outfitting in St. Louis; down Mississippi aboard the HAMILTON; from St. Joseph, Missouri, with a ''Sabbath observing company'' led by Methodist missionaries; church attendance wherever possible and services in camps; weather, conditions of travel and route; notes on emigrants and Indians; across desert by Truckee route; comments on the site of Donner tragedy; reports of Hudspeth's Cutoff disasters; life in gold camps and mining towns, especially Nevada City; subsequent sporadic notes of travel in Oregon and settlement at Monticello, Washington; an extensive and colorful diary.

CALDWELL, T.G.   **3046**

In GOLD RUSH: THE JOURNALS, DRAWINGS AND OTHER PAPERS OF J. GOLDSBOROUGH BRUFF, edited by Georgia W. Read and Ruth Gaines, vol. 2, pp. 1247-1268. New York: Columbia University Press, 1944.

May-Oct 1849. Physician's journey via Fort Hall and Lassen's Cutoff, traveling with J. Goldsborough Bruff, who found and copied Caldwell's journal; terrain, camps and conditions of travel; tending the injured and sick, including his friend Allen McLane who died of dysentery.

CHAMBERLIN, WILLIAM H.   **3047**

Bloom, Lansing B., ed. ''From Lewisburg (Pa.) to California in 1849.'' NEW MEXICO HISTORICAL REVIEW 20 (1945):14-57, 144-180, 239-268, 336-357.

Feb-Sep 1849. Gold rush journey of a group from Lewisburg, Pennsylvania, by wagon and riverboat to Memphis, with observations on countryside and slavery, including a slave market; overland via Canadian River, Santa Fe and ''southern route'' being opened by Randolph B. Marcy; full notes on route, camps, conditions, distances and hardships; references to Capt. Frederick T. Dent and to being ahead of his advance road-building detachment; encounters with the unfortunate Knickerbocker Company and with Indians.

CHAPELL, DANIEL A.   **3048**

Dorsett, E. Lee, ed. ''The Whale Ship BENJAMIN TUCKER of New Bedford.'' AMERICAN NEPTUNE 10 (1950):298-300.

1849-1851. Brief extracts from diary of cooper aboard the BENJAMIN TUCKER; whales taken and ships encountered; floggings of crew; quarrels between captain and first mate; desertions at Honolulu; a matter-of-fact picture of dangers and brutalities of whaling life.

CHAPMAN, HORATIO DANA, 1826-1910   **3049**

CIVIL WAR DIARY. DIARY OF A FORTY-NINER. Hartford, Conn.: Allis, 1929. 115 pp. 16 pp.

Apr-Oct 1849. Extracts from travel diary of a Connecticut voyager's trip from New York around the Horn on the SELINA as member of the Fremont Mining and Trading Company bound for California; shipboard adventures and clues to character of various crew members and passengers; city excursions in Rio de Janeiro and Valparaiso during stopovers; dangerous episode during foul weather sailing with irresponsible captain and first mate; delays in entering San Francisco harbor and abrupt end of record after arrival in San Francisco.

1863-1865. Diary of service in Company C, Twentieth Connecticut; battle of Chancellorsville, Gettysburg campaign and operations along the Rappahannock; awful physical conditions of troop transport but welcome show of civilian support during train trip from Virginia to Alabama; stationed in Tennessee and Alabama; the Atlanta campaign, march across Georgia and fall of Savannah; Carolinas campaign; notes on hard marches, countryside and towns, execution of deserters, an April Fool's joke, the Chickamauga battlefield, foraging, Union troops, pillaging and destruction, attitudes of Georgia civilians, etc.; sporadic but lengthy and detailed entries, probably revised to some extent after the war.

CHAPMAN, W.W.   **3050**

''Chapman Diary.'' WYOMING HISTORICAL DEPARTMENT QUARTERLY BULLETIN 1, no. 2 (1924):7-9.

1849-1850. Gold rush diary of travel from Illinois to Sacramento, etc.; brief notes describing journey and several deaths from cholera, including that of James Whitlock; a few later entries in California relating to timber trade and mining.

CHRISTMAN, ENOS, 1828-1912   **3051**

ONE MAN'S GOLD: THE LETTERS & JOURNAL OF A FORTY-NINER. Edited by Florence M. Christman. New York: McGraw-Hill, 1930. 277 pp. passim.

1849-1852. West Chester, Pennsylvania, apprentice printer's journal, kept for his fiancée, Ellen Apple; around Cape Horn on the EUROPE with others of the California Gold Mining Association of Philadelphia, with details of its organization and outfitting; excellent notes of ship life and passengers, other vessels met and sailors' diversions and songs; in port at Valparaiso; account of his life at Happy Valley and in the Mariposa diggings; work for the SONORA HERALD, with notes on people and events there, including murders and subsequent actions of the Vigilance Committee; home via Panama on the WINFIELD SCOTT and UNITED STATES; a fine journal of a born writer.

CLARK, BENNETT C., 1819-1890   **3052**

Bieber, Ralph P., ed. ''Diary of a Journey from Missouri to California in 1849.'' MISSOURI HISTORICAL REVIEW 23 (1928-1929):3-43.

Extracts in DIARY OF AMERICA, edited by Josef and Dorothy Berger, pp. 322-328.

Apr-Aug 1849. Boonville, Missouri, man's gold rush journey with a group from Cooper County; difficulties of the trip; a few personal items, with entries ending in Nevada when he was taken sick.

CLARK, STERLING B.F., 1825-1852   3053

HOW MANY MILES FROM ST. JO? San Francisco: Privately printed, 1929. 56 pp. Diary pp. 7-30.

Mar-Aug 1849. Brief notes of distances from Hollidaysburg, Pennsylvania, in the company of Capt. Joseph Taylor and from St. Joseph in the Evans Wheeling Company; leaving his books behind with officers at Fort Kearny; selling wagons at Fort Laramie and packing through to Sacramento.

CLARKE, ASA BEMENT   3054

TRAVELS IN MEXICO AND CALIFORNIA. Boston: Wright & Hasty, Printers, 1852. 138 pp.

1849-1850. Voyage from New York on sailing ship JNO. CASTNER to Brazos Santiago; overland via Brownsville, Chihuahua, Janos, Guadalupe Pass and Colorado River to Los Angeles; Mexican villages, trade and mining; a bullfight; delay at Janos with a bad knee, thus leaving Hampden Mining Company and being carried in another company's wagon; reading Bryant's WHAT I SAW IN CALIFORNIA; notes on Pima and Maricopa Indians; taking coastal route to mines and working with modest success.

CLIFTON, JOHN   3055

In MORE THAN GOLD IN CALIFORNIA, by Mary B. Ritter, pp. 31-43, 69-86. Berkeley: Professional Press, 1933.

Apr-Oct 1849. Extracts of Niles, Michigan, man's gold rush diary; laconic notes of travel conditions and vicissitudes, including dust like "hot ashes"; coming upon huts of the Donner party.

May-Jan 1872. Wagon journey from Gilroy, California, to Los Angeles, camping en route, with notes on property and hospitality of ranchers; visit with A.L. Bush in Los Angeles and return trip.

COGSWELL, MOSES PEARSON, 1822-1850   3056

Hunt, Elmer Munson, ed. "The Gold Rush Diary of Moses Cogswell of New Hampshire." HISTORICAL NEW HAMPSHIRE (December 1949):1-59.

Mar-Aug 1849. Canterbury man's voyage via Cape Horn on the SWEDEN as a shareholder in the Roxbury Sagamore Mining Company; from Boston, with a blessing on board by the famous "Father" Taylor; a detailed picture of life among gold rush passengers, including such amusements as a glee club, "sparring" matches and magic shows; frequent confrontations with Capt. Jesse G. Cotting over wretched fare, including tea with an old shoe boiled up in it; diarist's musings about human nature and its various manifestations among passengers and crew, but basically admiration for courage and decency of the Yankee sailors; log notes, weather and ships encountered, including a race with the MAGNOLIA; Fourth of July; in San Francisco, with full descriptions of life while awaiting decision of where to take claims; arrest of the "Hounds" for attack on Chileans; an outstanding gold rush diary by a promising young man who did not survive the experience.

"San Francisco in August, 1849." PACIFIC HISTORIAN 10, no. 3 (1966):12-18.

Aug 1849. Extract providing an excellent picture of gold rush San Francisco, including "the most motley collection of human beings that was ever seen in one place"; the "Hounds" incident; prevalence of disease and misery among gold seekers; names

of ships in the harbor; assessment of business, maritime and agricultural potential of the area; diarist's preparations for the diggings.

COKE, HENRY JOHN, 1827-1916   3057

A RIDE OVER THE ROCKY MOUNTAINS TO OREGON AND CALIFORNIA. London: R. Bentley, 1852. 388 pp.

1849-1851. English traveler's long narrative entries of trip to America via West Indies; finding "super abundance of snobbism" in New York; overland trip, visiting St. Louis, Fort Leavenworth and Fort Laramie where he had "a capital feed with intelligent officers"; experiencing the illness, heat, and loss of animals typical of travel over South Pass; Fort Hall, "a real nom de guerre for a very ordinary mud edifice"; visits by Bannock Indians; nearly losing his life in crossing Snake River to reach Fort Boise; comparing scenery around The Dalles and along the Columbia River to that of the Danube or Elbe; from San Francisco to Hawaii; attending reception given by Kamehameha III; adventures and incidents recounted with great flourish.

COOK, ELLIOTT WILKINSON, 1818-1877   3058

LAND HO! THE ORIGINAL DIARY OF A FORTY-NINER. Edited by Jane J. Cook. Baltimore: Remington-Putnam Book Co., 1935. 43 pp.

1849-1850. Diary of a man from Lockport, New York, a member of the Niagara and California Mining Company; from New York to Chagres on the CRESCENT CITY, with brief but good notes of ship travel and life and difficulties in Panama; thence on the NIANTIC to San Francisco and the diggings, with some detail of life, prices and earnings.

COX, CORNELIUS C., b. 1825   3059

Martin, Mabelle E. ed. "From Texas to California in 1849." SOUTHWESTERN HISTORICAL QUARTERLY 29 (1925-1926): 36-50, 128-146, 201-223.

Apr 1849-Feb 1850. Gold rush diary; from Harrisburg, Texas, to California with Thomas Smith's company, traveling with Lewis B. Harris and James McAllister; gradual disintegration of the party; notes on hunting, camps and Indians; arrival at Stockton, where diary ends abruptly.

CRANDALL, HENRY SARGENT, 1826-1909   3060

LOVE AND NUGGETS. Edited by Ronald D. Crandall. Old Greenwich, Conn.: Stable Books, 1967. 208 pp. passim.

1849-1853. Letters and journals of Henry Crandall and his wife, Mary Caroline, which have been interspersed in sequence to tell their story; life in Washington County, New York, and Henry Crandall's gold rush journey and experiences at Nevada City, California.

CROSS, OSBORNE, 1803-1876   3061

A REPORT, IN THE FORM OF A JOURNAL, TO THE QUARTERMASTER GENERAL, OF THE MARCH OF THE REGIMENT OF MOUNTED RIFLEMEN TO OREGON. 31st Cong., 2nd sess., 1850, S. Exec. Doc. 1, part 2, pp. 126-244. Washington, D.C., 1850.

THE MARCH OF THE MOUNTED RIFLEMEN. Edited by Raymond W. Settle. Glendale, Calif.: Arthur H. Clark, 1940. 380 pp. Journal, pp. 31-272.

MARCH OF THE REGIMENT OF MOUNTED RIFLEMEN TO OREGON. Fairfield, Wash.: Ye Galleon, 1967. 218 pp.

May-Nov 1849. Quartermaster's military journal of expedition of Mounted Riflemen from Fort Leavenworth to Fort Vancouver to garrison posts along emigrant overland route; problems with unbroken mules and untrained teamsters; daily marches, topography, scenery and natural history.

DALLAS, FRANCIS GREGORY, 1824-1890   3062

THE PAPERS OF FRANCIS GREGORY DALLAS. Edited by Gardner W. Allen. Naval History Society Publications, vol. 8. New York: Printed for the Naval History Society by the De Vinne Press, 1917. 303 pp. passim.

1849-1859 (with gaps). Diary of Boston naval seaman dismissed from United States Navy over a duel; service with German Navy, traveling from New York to Liverpool and sightseeing in London before reaching Bremen and first assignment on the UNITED STATES later renamed HANSA; displeasure over Belgians advancing in rank over him by influence in court; given command of the corvette HAMBURG, having readily acquired fluent German for both work and social life; monotony of life when confined to ship but enjoyment of sightseeing in northern Germany and balls and amateur theater in Brake; reinstatement in United States Navy; serving on the DECATUR, ordered to the Pacific; chiefly log notes at sea but also descriptive notes of ports at Honolulu, San Francisco, Vancouver Island, Port Townsend and Whidbey Island; requisitioned by military district of Puget Sound for field duty fighting Indians in Seattle; return to East Coast and duty in Philadelphia with some interesting family notes; scattered entries of service on the RELEASE and in command of the ORION suppressing slave trade along the western coast of Africa.

DAMON, SAMUEL CHENERY, 1815-1885   3063

A TRIP FROM THE SANDWICH ISLANDS TO LOWER OREGON AND UPPER CALIFORNIA. Honolulu: Printed at the Polynesian Office, 1849. Pp. 41-96. Reprint. MAGAZINE OF HISTORY, extra no. 97 (1923):1-86.

A JOURNEY TO LOWER OREGON & UPPER CALIFORNIA. San Francisco: J.J. Newbegin, 1927. 86 pp.

Apr-Jul 1849. Diary of Honolulu clergyman and chaplain of American Seamen's Friend Society; traveling to Columbia River on MASSACHUSETTS, the second steam ship to visit Hawaii, meeting Catholic missionaries at Astoria and supplying Methodist mission with SEAMAN'S HYMN BOOK; on to Fort Vancouver and offices of Hudson's Bay Company; at Portland and Oregon City where he met with important local clergy; traveling to Salem with the Rev. Cushing Eells, principal of Tualatin Academy; on to San Francisco, which he thought disappointing; preaching at Benicia and Stockton; joining a party going to Sutter's Fort where he gave the prayer at a public function in celebration of Fourth of July; visiting some mines and Hawaiians mining in California and then returning to Honolulu; good narrative describing scenery, social and moral conditions.

DAVENPORT, SARAH, 1839-1888?   3064

"A Journal - Sarah Davenport." NEW CANAAN HISTORICAL SOCIETY ANNUAL 2, no. 4 (1950):26-89.

1849-1852. A little girl's diary of weather, school, farm and household duties; attending baby brother and gathering berries; visits to and by relatives.

DAY, GERSHOM BULKLEY, 1804-1852   3065

In PIONEER DAYS: THE LIFE STORY OF GERSHOM AND ELIZABETH DAY, by Mary E.D. Trowbridge, pp. 90-139 passim. Philadelphia: American Baptist Publication Society, 1895.

1849-1852. Letter-diary of itinerant Baptist minister who left his Sturgis, Michigan, home and family to preach to emigrants on the overland trip and to miners in California; hardships of journey; Baptist Association meeting in Sacramento; preaching to miners at Feather River and in the mountains until killed by Indians.

DECKER, PETER, 1822-1888   3066

THE DIARIES OF PETER DECKER: OVERLAND TO CALIFORNIA IN 1849 AND LIFE IN THE MINES. Edited by Helen S. Giffen. Georgetown, Calif.: Talisman, 1966. 338 pp.

1849-1851. Well written gold rush diary kept by a man of apparent education; valuable description of the strenuous trip from Columbus, Ohio, as a member of the Columbus and California Industrial Association, with notes on people and gold rush companies, route, terrain, sicknesses, injuries, weather, prices, etc.; a church service which he attended upon his arrival in Sacramento; life at the mines on Feather River.

DELANO, ALONZO, 1806-1874   3067

LIFE ON THE PLAINS AND AMONG THE DIGGINGS. Auburn and Buffalo, N.Y.: Milner, Orton & Mulligan, 1854. 384 pp. passim. Reprint. New York: Arno, 1973.

ACROSS THE PLAINS AND AMONG THE DIGGINGS. New York: Wilson-Erickson, 1936. 192 pp. passim.

May-Sep 1849. Dated but long narrative entries of Ottawa, Illinois, man's journey to Shasta County, California; from St. Joseph via Fort Laramie, South Pass and Fort Hall in a company led by Jesse Greene; route, conditions of travel, individuals and emigrant trains; difficulties and sufferings of man and beast from dust, thirst and hunger; encounters with Indians and traders; a narrative account of his life in California.

Extracts in AMERICAN HISTORY TOLD BY CONTEMPORARIES, edited by Albert B. Hart, vol. 4, pp. 43-48.

May 1849.

Extracts in PICTURES OF GOLD RUSH CALIFORNIA, edited by Milo M. Quaife, pp. 253-287.

Sep 1849. Life, appearance and customs of Oleepa Indians near his proposed townsite on the Feather River twenty miles above Marysville.

DEWOLF, DAVID, 1822-1862   3068

"Diary of the Overland Trail and Letters of Captain David Dewolf." ILLINOIS HISTORICAL SOCIETY TRANSACTIONS 32 (1925):184-222.

May-Oct 1849. Gold rush diary of a Nova Scotian who later settled at Wyoming, Illinois; entries beginning en route with death from cholera of company member Andrew Moodie; good details of travel conditions, terrain, camps and distances; buffalo hunting and enjoyment of the meat, which he found to be sweeter and juicier than beef; notes on other emigrants and on Mormons at Salt Lake; such hardships as twenty-two miles without water or grass for stock; references in bad situations to "seeing the elephant"; description of California mining experiences in letters to his wife.

DORE, BENJAMIN, 1825-1906   **3069**

"Journal of Benjamin Dore." CALIFORNIA HISTORICAL SOCIETY QUARTERLY 2 (1923-1924):87-139. Reprint. JOURNAL OF BENJAMIN DORE. Berkeley, Calif.: Press of the Courier, 1923. 54 pp.

1849-1852. Bangor, Maine, carpenter's voyage around the Horn to San Francisco on the CANTERO with a cargo of lumber; log entries and lively notes of shipboard diversions, including mock trials; in port at St. Catherine, Brazil, and Valparaiso; work as a carpenter in San Francisco and Vancouver, Washington, and as a shipbuilder at Portland, Oregon; several poems, gold rush and sea songs, some by Everett F. Crocker, a fellow passenger and argonaut from Maine; list of CANTERO passengers and members of his gold rush company.

DOTEN, ALFRED R., 1829-1903   **3070**

THE JOURNALS OF ALFRED DOTEN. Edited by Walter Van Tilburg Clark. Reno: University of Nevada Press, 1973. 3 vols.

1849-1903. Massive and important diary of a Plymouth, Massachusetts, forty-niner, frontier journalist and colorful figure of the California gold and Nevada silver mining regions; long and difficult voyage around Cape Horn on the YEOMAN as a member of the Pilgrim Mining Company, with good descriptions of ship travel and the port of Talcahuano, Chile, and references to Capt. James M. Clark and others; California mining experiences, social life and milieu in Stockton, Calaveras County, Spanish Gulch, etc.; work as a correspondent for the PLYMOUTH ROCK, reporting back particularly on Vigilance Committee lynchings in San Francisco and elsewhere; several years of farm and ranch work at Mountain View and Milpitas; dances, parties, a camp meeting of 2,000 with "preaching, shouting and groaning, etc.," and other social phenomena of the region; to Nevada for the Comstock silver boom, where he met Mark Twain; newspaper work for the COMO SENTINAL, VIRGINIA DAILY UNION, TERRITORIAL ENTERPRISE and GOLD HILL EVENING NEWS as a colleague of Dan De Quille; notes on all aspects of the colorful and violent life there, as well as politics, plays, concerts, church functions, circuses, meetings of the Pacific Coast Pioneers, illnesses, injuries and medical treatment of the populace, the doling out of frontier justice for murders, etc.; marriage to Mary Stoddard and births of children; his slide into reckless speculation, drinking and whoring; decline of the Gold Hill Mine and remains of his fortunes; move to Austin as editor of the REESE RIVER REVEILLE, with failure there and destitution of his family; final years in Virginia City and Carson City, a debt-ridden alcoholic, but still observing and noting everything "about town" and referring to scores of individuals prominent in mining, journalism, politics or local lore.

"My Adventures in the California Diggings." LIFE, 27 April 1959, pp. 89-103.

1851-1852. Colorful extracts illustrating mining, vigilante justice and camp life.

DOUGAL, WILLIAM H., 1822-1895   **3071**

OFF FOR CALIFORNIA: THE LETTERS, LOG AND SKETCHES OF WILLIAM H. DOUGAL, GOLD RUSH ARTIST. Edited by Frank M. Stanger. California Centennial Edition, no. 22. Oakland: Biobooks, 1949. 62 pp.

Apr-Nov 1849. Good notes, which surpass the usual log, of enterprising artist and ship owner aboard the GALINDO, carrying merchandise and argonauts to California via Cape Horn; notes on

storms, seamanship and social life in ports of Rio de Janeiro and Valparaiso; his life in San Francisco, where he engaged in grocery and livery business while staying on the ship.

DRAPER, SETH   **3072**

VOYAGE OF THE BARK ORION FROM BOSTON AROUND CAPE HORN TO SAN FRANCISCO. Providence, R.I., and Cambridge: Printed by H.O. Houghton, 1870. 80 pp.

Nov 1849-May 1850. Excellent picture of pleasures and trials of a voyage from Boston around the Horn to San Francisco; shipboard activities, including use of the library presented by Seaman's Friend Society of Dorchester, religious services and Thanksgiving, complete with mince pies made by women passengers; in port at Rio de Janeiro, where he saw churches, gardens, a bullfight and many other ships bound for California; storms, a death and burial at sea; capture of an albatross; report of ship's surgeon being put in irons for poisoning cake intended for crew; visiting Robinson Crusoe's cave on Juan Fernandez.

DUNDASS, SAMUEL RUTHERFORD, 1819-1850   **3073**

JOURNAL OF SAMUEL RUTHERFORD DUNDASS. Steubenville, Ohio: Printed at Conn's Job Office, 1857. 66 pp. Journal, pp. 7-56.

THE JOURNALS OF SAMUEL RUTHERFORD DUNDASS & GEORGE KELLER: CROSSING THE PLAINS TO CALIFORNIA IN 1849-1850. Fairfield, Wash.: Ye Galleon, 1983. 106 pp. Journal, pp. 9-52.

Mar 1849-Jan 1850. Overland journal of member of Steubenville Company, or California Mining Company, as Dundass calls it in his journal; conventional descriptions of laborious journey from Steubenville, Ohio, to Independence, Platte River, Sweetwater and California; last of trip through desert made on foot; after little success at mining, taking discouraging position as inspector of the port of San Francisco.

DURIVAGE, JOHN E.   **3074**

In SOUTHERN TRAILS TO CALIFORNIA IN 1849, edited by Ralph P. Bieber, pp. 159-255.

Mar-Sep 1849. Articles in journal form, written for the DAILY PICAYUNE of New Orleans; travel by southern route through Mexico to California gold fields with Hampden Mining and Trading Company; cholera epidemic in Texas and colorful religious ceremony in Mier to protect inhabitants from cholera; advice on forming traveling parties and obtaining provisions.

DWINELLE, JOHN W., 1816-1881   **3075**

"The Diary of John W. Dwinelle." SOCIETY OF CALIFORNIA PIONEERS QUARTERLY 8 (1931):105-129, 141-183.

Aug-Oct 1849. Rochester, New York, lawyer's diary of travel from New York to San Francisco via Panama, with extracts beginning on the EMPIRE CITY at sea near Chagres; a brief stay there and description of the town as "filled with muck and every kind of animal and vegetable filth"; interesting account of canoe travel to Cruces, description of that town and its inhabitants, then his dangerous and uncomfortable mountain journey by horseback to Panama City, where he was stranded for weeks waiting passage to California; his own illness and many deaths there and aboard ship from "Isthmus Fever"; in port at San Diego, thence to San Francisco where, upon meeting overland argonauts, he concluded "in comparison with what those poor fellows had undergone, we began to think our sufferings had been light''; establishing a law practice, enjoying social life and observing manners and mores of gold rush San Francisco; an outstanding diary of the Panama route to California.

EASTLAND, THOMAS B. 3076

Watson, Douglas S. and Huggins, Dorothy H. "To California through Texas and Mexico: The Diary and Letters of Thomas B. Eastland and Joseph G. Eastland, His Son." CALIFORNIA HISTORICAL SOCIETY QUARTERLY 18 (1939):99-135, 229-250.

Apr-Dec 1849. Journey from New Orleans by steamships FANNY and DE ROSSET to Lavocca, Texas, for outfitting; then to San Francisco over the unusual southern route, which diarist declared to be impracticable for general emigration; initially traveling in the wake of army engineers and road builders, with notes on Col. Jack Hays and other officers; departure from army route to cross Mexico; from Mazatlan to San Francisco on steamer OREGON.

EASTON, LANGDON C., 1814-1884 3077

Mattes, Merrill J., ed. "Fort Laramie to Fort Leavenworth via Republican River in 1849." KANSAS HISTORICAL QUARTERLY 20 (1952-1953):392-416.

Aug-Sep 1849. Official journal of an exploration by First United States Dragoons to determine if the Republican River would offer a better route than the Platte for military and emigrant purposes; camps, route, distances, terrain, water and grass; problems with worn-out horses and mules; encounters with Cheyennes and a Sioux village ravaged by cholera; references to Lt. N. George Evans.

ECCLESTON, ROBERT, 1830-1911 3078

OVERLAND TO CALIFORNIA ON THE SOUTHWESTERN TRAIL. Edited by George P. Hammond and Edward H. Howes. Berkeley: University of California Press, 1950. 256 pp.

Apr-Dec 1849. Nineteen-year-old's gold rush journey with Fremont Association of New York under escort of Col. John C. Hays; ocean trip from New York to Galveston aboard the BENJAMIN R. MILAM; opening of the Lower Road from San Antonio to El Paso and cutoff from Burro Mountains in New Mexico to Tucson, both to become important shortcuts on the Southwestern Trail and parts of major emigrant, stage and mail routes; hazards and monotony of wilderness journey, vignettes of colorful participants, encounters with Apaches, democratic workings of the Fremont Association, pious introspections and youthful enthusiasms of diarist in an unusually detailed and articulate gold rush record.

THE MARIPOSA INDIAN WAR, 1850-1851: DIARIES OF ROBERT ECCLESTON: THE CALIFORNIA GOLD RUSH, YOSEMITE AND THE HIGH SIERRA. Edited by C. Gregory Crampton. Salt Lake: University of Utah Press, 1957. 168 pp.

1850-1851. Life at the Mariposa mines at Agua Frio, with mining processes, problems and prices; influx of prospectors leading to Indian depredations and eventually war, during which diarist was a volunteer in the Mariposa Battalion; activities of trader James D. Savage, who led the volunteers against Miwok, Yokut and Yosemite Indians; marches and camps in the Yosemite, Fresno, Merced and San Joaquin river areas and the Sierra Nevada; efforts of the Federal Indian Commission and frequent references to John Boling, John Kuykendall, Francis Laumiester, James Burney and Gov. John McDougal.

ELLIS, CHARLES HENRY 3079

In CALIFORNIA GOLD RUSH VOYAGES, 1848-1949, edited by John E. Pomfret, pp. 11-94. San Marino, Calif.: Huntington Library, 1954. Reprint. Westport, Conn.: Greenwood, 1974.

Jan-Jul 1849. Straightforward account of voyage from Boston to San Francisco aboard the NORTH BEND with his son Hiram; recreations of passengers and their service to crew; nautical observations and descriptions; birds and fish; thirty-two days passing through Straits of Magellan.

ESBJORN, LARS PAUL 3080

Nordstrom, O.L., ed. "Diary Kept by L.P. Esbjörn when Making a Trip from Gelfe to New York on the Steamship COBDEN." AUGUSTANA HISTORICAL SOCIETY PUBLICATIONS 5 (1935):11-34.

Jun-Aug 1849. Shipboard diary of Swedish immigrant and leader of the Augustana Lutheran church; death of his little son en route; preaching to passengers and crew and his concern about "worldliness" and drunkenness; a "crazy girl" whose condition was treated by frequent duckings in water by the diarist and others as well as whippings by her parents; entries ending at Newfoundland.

EVANS, GEORGE W.B., 1819-1850 3081

MEXICAN GOLD TRAIL: THE JOURNAL OF A FORTY-NINER. Edited by Glenn S. Dumke. San Marino, Calif.: Huntington Library, 1945. 340 pp.

1849-1850. An exceptionally fresh and vivid gold rush diary of a man from Defiance, Ohio, traveling as a member of the Defiance Gold Hunters' Expedition; by steamboat down the Mississippi to New Orleans and by ship to Port Lavaca, Texas; overland through Texas, northern Mexico, Arizona, etc.; mining practices and camp life in California; conditions at Sacramento.

EVERSHED, THOMAS, 1817-1890 3082

Barns, Joseph W., ed. "The Gold Rush Journal of Thomas Evershed, Engineer, Artist, and Rochesterian." ROCHESTER HISTORY 39, no. 1-2 (1977):1-44.

May-Aug 1849. Account by English immigrant, a member of the Lockport Mining Company of Lockport, New York; full entries describing conditions and incidents of travel from Independence, including some of their company foolishly firing on Indians; problems with sick mules; descriptions of scenery, flowers and wildlife; notes on Salt Lake and a long account of the Humboldt ordeal; a few experiences in California, with diary ending shortly after his arrival in Sacramento, where he reported the breakup of many large mining companies.

FARNHAM, ELIJAH BRYAN, 1825-1898 3083

Mattes, Merrill J. and Kirk, Esley J., eds. "From Ohio to California in 1849." INDIANA MAGAZINE OF HISTORY 46 (1950):297-318, 403-420.

Apr-Sep 1849. Cumberland, Ohio, man's gold rush journey; route, scenery and camps; notes on emigrants, Mormons and Indians, Sioux, whom he admired, and Diggers, whose habits he described with disgust; much death from cholera; fairly long description of Fort Laramie and its inhabitants; several bad gun accidents; sad description of men, who had lost stock and wagons, struggling on foot; the usual problems about oxen, grass, water, etc.

FARRER, WILLIAM, 1821-1906   3084

In JOURNALS OF FORTY-NINERS, edited by Le Roy R. and Ann W. Hafen, pp. 193-218.

Oct-Dec 1849. Diary of a Mormon on journey to California mines with Flake-Rich Company under Captain Smith; distances and camps; concerns for water and grass; detailed descriptions of country; separating from Captain Smith's company and rejoining Jefferson Hunt wagon train; diary ending after Cajon Pass.

FLINT, ISAAC A., 1816-1892   3085

Van Arsdol, Ted, ed. "Golden Gate to Columbia River on the Bark KEOKA." OREGON HISTORICAL QUARTERLY 63 (1962):41-54.

Nov 1849-Jan 1850. Adventurous minister's trip from San Francisco to the Columbia, where contrary winds kept the ship from entering the river; passengers' sufferings from cold, hunger, thirst and sickness; diarist's assistance to "green" and desperate captain faced with mutinous crew and angry passengers; rescue by Columbia pilot Cornelius White and successful crossing of the bar; diarist's further harrowing experience in a whale boat.

FORSHEY, CALEB GOLDSMITH   3086

Terres, John, ed. "Caleb Forshey at the Memphis Railroad Convention." WEST TENNESSEE HISTORICAL SOCIETY PAPERS, no. 37 (1983):82-87.

Oct 1849. Account by Louisiana delegate, a civil engineer, of a convention held to discuss transcontinental railroad funding and routes; convention events, political aspects and the diarist's contributions; social life in Memphis; meetings with Matthew Fontaine Maury.

FOSTER, ISAAC, 1790-1868   3087

In THE FOSTER FAMILY, CALIFORNIA PIONEERS, by Lucy A. Foster Sexton, pp. 15-142 passim. Santa Barbara: Schauer Printing Studio, 1925.

1849-1857 (with gaps). Gold rush and repeated overland trips of Presbyterian minister from Plainfield, Illinois; brief notes of route and conditions of travel, mainly with the Iowa Company of California Emigrants under Joseph M. Knight; some Indian incidents; scenery and terrain; references to his friend Nathan Burr; final trip via Panama and eventually settling his family at San Jose, where he became a judge.

GALE, FREDERICK W.   3088

Hoyt, Edward A. and Brigham, Loriman S. "Glimpses of Margaret Fuller." NEW ENGLAND QUARTERLY 29 (1956):87-98. Diary, pp. 97-98.

Dec 1849. Extracts describing social encounters with Margaret Fuller as Marchioness of Ossoli in Florence.

GARRETT, THOMAS MILES, 1830-1864   3089

Hamilton, John Bowen, ed. "Diary of Thomas Miles Garrett at the University of North Carolina." NORTH CAROLINA HISTORICAL REVIEW 38 (1961):63-93, 241-262, 380-410, 534-563.

Jun-Nov 1849. Student diary of a scholarly and reflective young man, later a promising lawyer killed in the Civil War; studies in rhetoric, French, Bible, Latin, mathematics and science; notes on textbooks and additional reading; lectures by college president David L. Swain, professor Elisha Mitchell and others; rivalry between literary societies; reactions to and participation in debates; some student uproars; temperance society meetings and diarist's disgust at the drunkenness prevalent in Chapel Hill; thoughts on the growing discord between North and South and opinions on national and local politics.

GEIGER, VINCENT EPLY, 1824?-1869   3090

TRAIL TO CALIFORNIA: THE OVERLAND JOURNAL OF VINCENT GEIGER AND WAKEMAN BRYARLY. Edited by David Morris Potter. Yale Historical Publications, Manuscripts and Edited Texts, 20. New Haven: Yale University Press, 1945. 245 pp. Reprint. 1962.

Feb-Aug 1849. Gold rush diary started by Geiger and continued by Bryarly with no explanation for change; account of a well planned organization, the Charlestown Virginia Mining Company, including the constitution establishing a co-partnership with economic, military and governmental functions; extensive entries in colorful, vigorous language; roster of members.

GIBBS, GEORGE, 1815-1873   3091

In MARCH OF THE MOUNTED RIFLEMEN, by Osborne Cross, pp. 275-327. Glendale, Calif., Arthur H. Clark, 1940.

May-Jun 1849. Record of civilian artist with an expedition of the Mounted Riflemen commanded by Osborne Cross; march from Fort Leavenworth to Fort Laramie; difficulties with unbroken mule teams; conditions of emigrant parties on the trail; a buffalo hunt; extensive natural history notes.

In DRAWINGS BY GEORGE GIBBS IN THE FAR NORTHWEST, by David I. Bushnell, pp. 3-21 passim. Smithsonian Miscellaneous Collections, vol. 97, no. 8. Washington D.C.: Smithsonian Institution, 1928.

Jun-Sep 1849. Extracts covering travel from Fort Laramie to the Snake River with enthusiastic descriptions of scenery, waterfalls, etc.

Aug-Oct 1851. Journal of an expedition through northwestern California led by Indian agent Col. Redick M'Kee; notes on the Clear Lake Indians and treaty negotiations.

GORDON, ANDREW   3092

In THE WAY OUR PEOPLE LIVED: AN INTIMATE AMERICAN HISTORY, edited by William E. Woodward, pp. 244-277. New York: E.P. Dutton, 1944. Reprint, Liveright, 1963.

In A TREASURY OF THE WORLD'S GREAT DIARIES, edited by Philip Dunaway, pp. 65-68.

Apr-Sep 1849. Extracts from gold rush diary containing graphic details of the hardship and psychological strain of a cross-country trek under Jacob Birdsall; brief glimpses of San Francisco.

GOULD, CHARLES, 1824-1913   3093

In THE BOSTON-NEWTON COMPANY VENTURE: FROM MASSACHUSETTS TO CALIFORNIA IN 1849, compiled by Jessie G. Hannon, pp. 1-224 passim. Lincoln: University of Nebraska Press, 1969.

Apr-Sep 1849. Interspersed entries of the diaries kept by Charles Gould and David Jackson Staples; from Boston to Independence by train, Great Lakes and river steamers; overland with theBoston-Newton Joint Stock Association via the Platte and Humbolt to Sutter's Fort; amiable, sometimes humorous entries of sober, God-fearing young men on a well organized expedition remarkably free of dissension and hardship; a contrast with more typical accounts of gold rush haste, greed and disaster; highly enjoyable.

GRAY, CHARLES GLASS, b. 1820   3094

OFF AT SUNRISE: THE OVERLAND JOURNAL OF CHARLES GLASS GRAY. Edited by Thomas D. Clark. San Marino, Calif.: Huntington Library, 1976. 182 pp.

May-Nov 1849. Journey from Independence to San Francisco with the Newark Overland Company under John Stevens Darcy; route via Platte River Road, South Pass, Salt Lake City, Humboldt River Road and Lassen's Cutoff; terrain, camps, distances and conditions of travel; problems with wagons and oxen; illnesses and deaths of many emigrants; a graphic account of the hardships of overland travel with good notes on scenery and people; many literary allusions.

GREEN, ROBERT B., 1821-1849   3095

ON THE ARKANSAS ROUTE TO CALIFORNIA IN 1849: THE JOURNAL OF ROBERT B. GREEN OF LEWISBURG, PENNSYLVANIA. Edited by J. Orin Oliphant. Lewisburg, Pa.: Bucknell University Press, 1955. 87 pp.

Feb-Sep 1849. Gold rush journey with William H. Chamberlin and others from Lewisburg along Kearny's route via Fort Smith, Santa Fe and the Gila and Colorado rivers to Los Angeles; initially, by stage and boat to Little Rock; from Fort Smith along army road being marked by Capt. Frederick T. Dent, traveling with or behind Dent's troops; disagreements with Chamberlin who "still keeps his sullen disposition," and other dissension; disgust with morals of the citizens of San Miguel and Santa Fe; arduous travel to the Gila and Colorado over the "Devil's Turnpike" and deserts beyond, where they nearly died; coming upon the Knickerbocker Company in "truly appalling" condition; some good notes on Indians; an ingenuous journal, funny and sarcastic in places.

GUNN, LEWIS CARSTAIRS, 1813-1892   3096

RECORDS OF A CALIFORNIA FAMILY: JOURNALS AND LETTERS OF LEWIS C. GUNN AND ELIZABETH LE BRETON GUNN. Edited by Anna L. Marston. San Diego, Calif., 1928. 279 pp. Journal, pp. 21-84.

1849-1850. Travel from New Orleans by steamboat to Brazos, Texas, crossing the Rio Grande to Matamoras, Mexico; a circuitous horseback trip to Mazatlan and voyage on the COPIAPO to San Francisco; clear details of route, prices of food, mules etc. baggage, people, ranches, villages, cholera and trouble with Comanche Indians; brief stopover at Durango, Mexico, "a civilized town," for Corpus Christi celebration; discouraging attempts at prospecting around Jamestown followed by successful work as physician.

HACKNEY, JOSEPH   3097

In WAGONS WEST, by Elizabeth Page, pp. 110-193. New York: Farrar & Rinehart, 1930.

May-Sep 1849. Journal of member of Jerseyville Company from St. Joseph to California; substantial entries of company organization and management, route, camps, landmarks, hunting, emigrants encountered and arrival at gold mines.

HALE, ISRAEL F., 1804-1891   3098

"Diary of a Trip to California in 1849." SOCIETY OF CALIFORNIA PIONEERS QUARTERLY 2 (1925):61-130.

May-Sep 1849. Gold rush diary beginning at St. Joseph; detailed description of route, camps and sights along the way; diarist's objection to Sunday travel; some difficulties with Indians; a few notes on Mormons; arrival in the Sacramento Valley.

HALE, RICHARD LUNT, 1828-1913   3099

THE LOG OF A FORTY-NINER. Edited by Carolyn H. Russ. Boston: B.J. Brimmer, 1923. 183 pp.

1849-1854. Voyage from Newburyport, Massachusetts, around Cape Horn to San Francisco on the GENERAL WORTH under Capt. Samuel Walton; exciting, literary-style notes on ship life, crew and passengers, their relationships, work and amusements; in port on Juan Fernandez, with fascinating account of diarist's explorations in the "footsteps of my hero" Robinson Crusoe; in San Francisco briefly; to Portland to recover from illness; adventures there with Peter Loudine, who died following the prediction of his death by the ghost of his sister; return to San Francisco and thence to the gold fields around Yuba and Tuolumni with Newburyport men Leonard Noyes, Alexander Coffin and Joseph Tucker; on the BEATRICE to Callao, Peru, and from there on the PAULINE, with a detour to pick up guano on the Chincha Islands, where he described appalling slave conditions of Chinese workers; evils of impressment as means of engaging crew; return to Newburyport; one of the best gold rush sea voyage accounts.

HALL, WILLIAM HENRY HARRISON, 1823-1907   3100

THE PRIVATE LETTERS AND DIARIES OF CAPTAIN HALL: AN EPIC OF AN ARGONAUT IN THE CALIFORNIA GOLD RUSH, OREGON TERRITORIES, CIVIL WAR AND OIL CITY. Edited by Eric Schneirsohn. Glendale, Calif.: London Book, 1974. 270 pp. passim.

1849-1861 (with gaps). Warren, Vermont, man's diaries of a voyage via Cape Horn on the NEW JERSEY with the Suffolk and California Trading and Mining Association; mostly log entries of the voyage and fragmentary notes of his references to many boats, including the LOT WHITCOMB; notes on his Vermont friends John O. and W.A. Waterman and on Charles and Jacob Kamm of Oregon; return to Vermont; Civil War service and residence at Oil City, Pennsylvania.

HALSEY, GAIUS LEONARD, d. 1891   3101

In THE PIONEERS OF UNADILLA VILLAGE, by Francis W. Halsey, pp. 289-302. Unadilla, N.Y.: Sold by the vestry of St. Matthew's Church, 1902.

Feb-Nov 1849. Plainville, Connecticut, doctor's brief travel notes; from New York to Panama, San Diego and San Francisco; delay in getting up Sacramento River; walking to Sutter's Mill in extreme heat; success in mining and decision to return to New York since there was little demand for doctors in San Francisco in winter; his severe illness at San Blas.

HAMELIN, JOSEPH P., b. 1823   3102

In THE FAR WEST AND ROCKIES: GENERAL ANALYTICAL INDEX TO THE FIFTEEN VOLUME SERIES AND SUPPLEMENT TO THE

JOURNALS OF FORTYNINERS, SALT LAKE TO LOS ANGELES, prepared and edited by Le Roy R. and Ann W. Hafen, pp. 77-101. The Far West and the Rockies Historical Series, vol. 15. Glendale, Calif.: A.H. Clark, 1961.

Aug 1849-Feb 1850. Diary kept by a member of Pomeroy wagon train from Salt Lake City to Los Angeles; finding messages from Hunt party with advice about route to avoid; meetings with Utes who wounded and stole horses and mules; abandoning wagon and heavy goods as oxen gave out; crossing desert, noting magnificent sunrises; going on foot to secure cattle for relief of train; finally acquiring cattle which then vanished in night on the return trip; expecting poor reception and being surprised at good spirits of comrades in spite of bad news; arriving at Los Angeles and visiting decaying San Gabriel Mission; an entertaining gold rush diary.

HAVENS, CATHERINE ELIZABETH   3103

DIARY OF A LITTLE GIRL IN OLD NEW YORK. New York: H.C. Brown, 1919. 101 pp.

Extracts in DIARY OF AMERICA, edited by Josef and Dorothy Berger, pp. 212-215; SMALL VOICES, edited by Josef and Dorothy Berger, pp. 207-223.

1849-1850. Childhood diary of New York merchant's daughter; life and scenes of New York City and country estate on Long Island; social and school activities; music lessons and family events; charming and articulate diary.

HAWKS, JAMES D.   3104

"Hawks Diary." SOCIETY OF CALIFORNIA PIONEERS QUARTERLY 6 (1929):83-98.

Aug-Oct 1849. Travel from Baja California to San Diego, with good account of hardships, hunger and thieves; brief description of voyage from San Diego to San Francisco.

HAYES, BENJAMIN IGNATIUS, 1815-1877   3105

PIONEER NOTES FROM THE DIARIES OF JUDGE BENJAMIN HAYES. Edited by Marjorie T. Wolcott. Los Angeles: Privately printed, 1929. 307 pp. Reprint. New York: Arno, 1976.

1849-1875 (with gaps). Emigrant journey with the Clay Company of Liberty, Missouri, via Santa Fe and Warner's Ranch, with notes on J.J. Warner; account of life in southern California, where he became the first judge of the Southern District; journeys between courts at Los Angeles, San Diego and San Bernardino by carriage, horseback and steamer SENATOR; social life, judicial matters and local events; notes on many people, including Father Blas Raho, Juan Bandini, José Castro, Col. Cave J. Couts, General Kearny, etc.; dated entries interspersed with narrative.

HESLEP, AUGUSTUS M., b. 1806   3106

In SOUTHERN TRAILS TO CALIFORNIA IN 1849, edited by Ralph P. Bieber, pp. 353-386.

May 1849-Jan 1850. Emigrant physician's articles for the DAILY MISSOURI REPUBLICAN of trip from Independence, Missouri, to San Jose, California, to regain health; travel with the Morgan County and California Rangers of Illinois party over the Santa Fe Trail and down the Gila River; cholera; argument against use of pack mules rather than wagons; notes on Kansa, Arapaho,

Kiowa and Cheyenne Indians; Catholic missions along route from Los Angeles to San Jose.

HESTER, SALLIE, b. 1835   3107

In COVERED WAGON WOMEN, edited by Kenneth L. Holmes, vol. 1, pp. 231-246.

Extracts in SMALL VOICES, edited by Josef and Dorothy Berger, pp. 67-74.

1849-1850. Teenage girl's diary of eventful overland trip from Bloomington, Indiana, to San Jose, California; travel by carriage to New Albany, Indiana, and by riverboat on the Ohio and Missouri to St. Joseph to lay in supplies: weekly entries made on Sunday when the wagon train rested during arduous trip via the Platte River, Fort Laramie and Black Hills; her obvious adaptability to hardships, new experiences and separation from friends.

"The Diary of a Pioneer Girl." THE ARGONAUT 96, A-97 (September-October 1925):3.

Mar-Jul 1849. Extracts.

HIGGINSON, THOMAS WENTWORTH, 1823-1911   3108

LETTERS AND JOURNALS OF THOMAS WENTWORTH HIGGINSON. Edited by Mary T. Higginson. Boston and New York: Houghton Mifflin, 1921. 358 pp. passim. Reprint. New York: DaCapo, 1969; New York: Negro Universities Press, 1969.

1849-1906. Scattered extracts from journals arranged and edited so that document sources are mostly obscured; Boston literary and social life; travels; Civil War service.

ARMY LIFE IN A BLACK REGIMENT. Boston: Fields, Osgood, 1870. 296 pp. New ed. Boston and New York: Houghton Mifflin, 1900. 413 pp. With an introduction by Howard Mumford Jones. East Lansing: Michigan State University Press. 1960. 235 pp. Diary, pp. 5-47, 83-84, 88-90, 182-188. Many later editions.

Nov 1862-Jan, Mar 1863, Feb 1864. Extracts from diary he kept while serving as colonel of the First South Carolina Volunteers, the first regiment of former slaves mustered into the Union army; arrival at Camp Saxton near Beaufort, South Carolina; camp life and the customs, character, religious spirit and performance of black recruits and comparison to white troops; a beautiful description of New Year's Day celebration of emancipation, hearing "the choked voice of a race at last unloosed" as freedmen spontaneously sing "My Country 'Tis of Thee"; occupation of Jacksonville, Florida; return to Camp Shaw at Beaufort; frustrated hopes of joining campaign in Florida; lengthy, articulate entries reflecting the diarist's developing perceptions and appreciation of the black soldiers under his command.

"Leaves from an Officer's Journal." ATLANTIC MONTHLY 14 (1864):521-529, 740-748; 15 (1865):65-73.

Nov 1862-Jan 1863.

Extracts in THE BLUE AND THE GRAY, edited by Henry S. Commager, vol. 1, pp. 329-334; TRAGIC YEARS, by Paul M. Angle and Earl S. Miers, vol. 1, pp. 459-461.

HILLIARD, MIRIAM BRANNIN   3109

In THE PLANTATION SOUTH, edited by Katharine M. Jones, pp. 323-337. Indianapolis: Bobbs-Merrill, 1957.

Dec 1849-Apr 1850. Extracts from diary of mistress of cotton plantation at Grand Lake, Chicot County, Arkansas; sewing, cooking, social life and family matters; down the Mississippi aboard the MAGNOLIA for a visit to New Orleans, Leonidas Polk's sugar plantation at Bayou Lafourche and to Jackson, Mississippi.

HILLYER, EDWIN, 1825-1908   **3110**

Holzhueter, John O., ed. "From Waupun to Sacramento in 1849." WISCONSIN MAGAZINE OF HISTORY 49 (1966):210-244.

Mar-Aug 1849. Gold rush journal of a newly married Wisconsin man; organization and rules of the company of which he became "colonel"; policy of Sunday rest; excellent details of interactions with Indians, including diarist's concern for their plight: "Where will the poor red man find a home free from the intrusion of the whites?"; the usual account of suffering and death on the Humboldt; arrival at Sacramento; a mixture of reminiscence and dated entries, partly in narrative style.

HOFFMAN, BENJAMIN   **3111**

Ambler, C.H. "West Virginia Forty-Niners." WEST VIRGINIA HISTORY 3 (1941):59-75. Diary, pp. 63-75.

Jul-Sep 1849. Shepherdstown, West Virginia, man's gold rush journey, with diary beginning at the Platte River; brief notes of travel.

HOSFORD, BENJAMIN FRANKLIN, 1817-1864   **3112**

In A MEMORIAL OF THE LIFE, CHARACTER, AND DEATH OF REV. BENJAMIN F. HOSFORD, edited by Leander Thompson, pp. 25-47. Cambridge, Mass.: Printed at the Riverside Press, 1866.

1849-1852. Clergyman's religious reflections, illnesses, reading and sermons.

HOSPERS, JOHN, b. 1801   **3113**

Van der Zee, Jacob, trans. "Diary of a Journey from the Netherlands to Pella, Iowa, in 1849." IOWA JOURNAL OF HISTORY AND POLITICS 10 (1912):363-382.

May-Aug 1849. Dutch immigrant's account of travel with many others from Holland to join the religious community at Pella; long, interesting notes on difficult Atlantic crossing on the FRANZISKA, with much sickness and death from scarlet fever; burials at sea of many children, including his daughter; constant religious activities at sea and on land; stay in Albany; Fourth of July celebration; by lake and canal boats, including the LOUISIANA, and stagecoach to Iowa.

ISHAM, GILES S., d. 1864   **3114**

G.S. ISHAM'S GUIDE TO CALIFORNIA AND THE MINES AND RETURN BY THE ISTHMUS. New York: A.T. Houl, Printer, 1850. 32 pp.

GUIDE TO CALIFORNIA AND THE MINES. Fairfield, Wash.: Ye Galleon, 1972. 62 pp.

Apr 1849-Mar 1850. Lyons, Michigan, man's gold rush journal and emigrant guide; from St. Joseph with William Fitch; terrain, camps, distances and provender for stock along route via Fort Kearny, Green River and the Humboldt; a few incidents of the journey and references to fellow travelers; notes on California, particularly Sacramento; return on the PAOLI to Panama; description of the Isthmus; to New Orleans on the ALABAMA.

JENKINS, FOSTER HOOKER, 1830-1910   **3115**

JOURNAL OF A VOYAGE TO SAN FRANCISCO. Northridge: California State University, Northridge Libraries, 1975. 91 pp.

Nov 1849-May 1850. Journal of a successful, relatively pleasant voyage on the ORION under Capt. Henry C. Bunker; good descriptions of Rio de Janeiro, rounding of Cape Horn and Juan Fernandez Island; names of ships encountered; activities such as reading, games, music and church services; notes on crew and passengers, including a doctor clapped in irons for poisoning the crew's gingerbread.

A GOLD RUSH VOYAGE ON THE BARK ORION FROM BOSTON AROUND CAPE HORN TO SAN FRANCISCO: A UNIQUE RECORD BASED UPON THE JOURNALS OF FOSTER H. JENKINS, HENRY S. BRADLEY, SETH DRAPER AND EZEKIEL I. BARRA. Edited by Robert W. Wienpahl. Glendale, Calif.: Arthur H. Clarke, 1978. 298 pp., passim.

Nov 1849-May 1850. Mainly Jenkins's journal with entries from Draper's journal, Bradley's log and Barra's later narrative interspersed.

JOHNSTON, WILLIAM GRAHAM, 1828-1913   **3116**

EXPERIENCES OF A FORTY-NINER. Pittsburgh, 1892. 390 pp. Diary, pp. 23-247. Reprint. New York: Arno, 1973.

OVERLAND TO CALIFORNIA. Oakland: Biobooks, 1948. 272 pp. Diary, pp. 5-166.

Mar-Jul 1849. Pittsburgh man's diary written up from notes of the first gold rush wagon train to reach California; from Independence under famous guide Jim Stewart, who "tells us to be in no haste...the parties starting this early are making woeful mistakes and that when once we take up the line of march, he will engage to pass every mother's son of them"; route via South Pass, with detailed notes on outfitting, standing watch, meals, difficulties and solutions, Indians, of whom he had a poor opinion, Mormons and other emigrants; admiration for fellow argonaut Crawford Washington; highly entertaining throughout.

In THE COURSE OF EMPIRE, compiled by Helen V. Bary, pp. 74-94.

Apr-Jul 1849. Extracts.

JOSSELYN, AMOS PIATT, 1820-1885   **3117**

THE OVERLAND JOURNAL OF AMOS PIATT JOSSELYN. Edited by J. William Barrett II. Baltimore: Gateway Press, 1978. 129 pp. Journal, pp. 13-50.

Apr-Sep 1849. Gold rush journal of secretary and financial clerk of the South Zanesville Company; along the Old National Road and by riverboat from Zanesville, Ohio; overland from Independence via South Pass, Salt Lake and the Lassen route; camps, distances and road conditions; references to the Newark Company and to James MacDonald and others of the diarist's group.

KAMEHAMEHA IV, King of the Hawaiian Islands   **3118**

THE JOURNAL OF PRINCE ALEXANDER LIHOLIHO: THE VOYAGES MADE TO THE UNITED STATES, ENGLAND AND FRANCE IN 1849-1850. Edited by Jacob Adler. Honolulu: University of Hawaii Press for the Hawaiian Historical Society, 1967. 153 pp.

1849-1850. Erudite journal of fifteen-year-old Crown Prince Alexander of Hawaii on a "Grand Tour" with his brother Lot and Finance Minister Gerrit P. Judd; visits to San Francisco, New York and other American cities, where the young princes were entertained by the wealthy and powerful; voyage to Europe and enjoyment of ship travel; in London and Paris for Dr. Judd's diplomatic endeavor to seek restitution for an attack on Honolulu by French warships; sightseeing and social life among European aristocracy and royalty; the diarist's evident preference for European over American manners, mores and racial attitudes; a rather conventional tourist record kept at Dr. Judd's request, but with charming flashes of boyish enthusiasm and frankness.

KELLAM, ROBERT F., b. 1825   **3119**

Taylor, Orville W., ed. "Journal of a Trip from Camden to Texas." ARKANSAS HISTORICAL QUARTERLY 10 (1951):285-294.

Jun-Sep 1849 (with gaps). Camden, Arkansas, merchant's horseback journey with Mandeville Wallace to visit his parents in Rush County, Texas, lodging and dining with frontier families; good times with relatives and friends, although such enjoyments as dances and sings were marred by his suffering from "Texas sore eyes"; a brief but colorful diary, with expenses appended.

KENDALL, JOSEPH, 1803-1864   **3120**

A LANDSMAN'S VOYAGE TO CALIFORNIA: BEING AN ACCOUNT COMPILED FROM THE LETTERS AND THE JOURNAL OF JOSEPH KENDALL. San Francisco: Printed by Taylor & Taylor, 1935. 137 pp. passim.

May-Oct 1849. English immigrant's voyage around Cape Horn from New York to San Francisco on the CANTON, with entries beginning after a month at sea; Old Neptune's festivities and other diversions of passengers and crew; suffering from heat, cold, seasickness, bedbugs, etc.; Sunday services and diarist's daily Bible reading and entrusting his fate to God; around the Cape where, "I cannot describe the roaring and whistling of the raging ocean," with diary ending at sea.

KERR, THOMAS, 1825-1888   **3121**

Camp, Charles L. "An Irishman in the Gold Rush." CALIFORNIA HISTORICAL SOCIETY QUARTERLY 7 (1928):205-227, 395-404; 8 (1929):17-25, 167-182, 262-277.

1849-1852. Long extracts covering journey from Liverpool to San Francisco aboard the LONDON with friend Alexander Mills; travel as a cabin passenger, but concern for steerage passengers "treated like dogs"; in port at Valparaiso; amusing notes on sailors and passengers; once in California, a long period of work at Eliza City, later at Sutter's establishment and as a builder in San Francisco, but always unable to raise enough money to outfit himself for the mines; distress over gambling and other forms of "vice and folly" prevalent in gold rush California; illness, despair and regret that he ever left Ireland.

KINGSLEY, NELSON, d. 1852   **3122**

DIARY OF NELSON KINGSLEY, A CALIFORNIA ARGONAUT OF 1849. Edited by Frederick J. Teggart. Publications of the Academy of Pacific Coast History, vol. 3, no. 3. Berkeley: University of California, 1914. 179 pp.

1849-1851. New Milford, Connecticut, man's gold rush voyage around the Horn on the ANNA REYNOLDS to seek "temporal and intellectual gain" as a member of the California and New Haven Joint Stock Company; fairly detailed log entries of voyage; experiences in the diggings, with names of many fellow argonauts; a good account of everyday life in California.

KNAPP, AUGUSTA MURRAY SPRING, 1822-1885   **3123**

In GIDEON LEE KNAPP AND AUGUSTA MURRAY SPRING HIS WIFE, by Gideon L. Knapp, 66 pp. passim. N.p.: Privately printed, 1909.

Jan, Aug-Dec 1849, Jan 1850, 1874-1879, 1882. Journal extracts of New York City woman interspersed with letters focusing on family and religious concerns; her efforts to cope with widowhood; notes on reading.

LASSELLE, STANISLAUS   **3124**

In A HISTORY OF TRAVEL IN AMERICA, by Seymour Dunbar, vol. 4, app., pp. 1427-1443. Indianapolis: Bobbs-Merrill, 1915. New ed. New York: Tudor, 1937.

Mar-Aug 1849. Overland journey from Logansport, Indiana, along or near Santa Fe Trail to Williams Ranch in California, partly in company with a New York party referred to as the Knickerbockers; treachery of Indians hired to help cross Colorado River; notes on places William Emory camped and the cutoff he identified to avoid Devil's Turnpike; good observations on Pueblo villages, Choctaw, Pawnee, Kickapoo, Commanche, Creek, Apache, Maricopa and Pima Indians, and both the selfish and generous acts of exhausted travelers.

LOOMIS, THADDEUS LEVI, b. 1825   **3125**

Anderson, Niles, ed. "Grandfather Was a Forty-Niner." WESTERN PENNSYLVANIA HISTORICAL MAGAZINE 50 (1967):33-50.

Mar-Oct 1849. A few dated entries within letters home of a young Illinois lawyer bound for the gold fields; a good description of a Sioux war party returning from despoiling the Pawnees.

LORD, ISAAC   **3126**

Holliday, J.S. "In the Diggings." CALIFORNIA HISTORY 61 (1982):168-187. Diary, pp. 182-185.

Dec 1849-Jan 1850. Extract describing Sacramento, "the utter confusion and total disorder that prevail on every hand," and condition of gold seekers wintering there; commerce and amusements; a severe flood, which submerged most of the city, and its effects on the inhabitants.

LYMAN, ALBERT   **3127**

JOURNAL OF A VOYAGE TO CALIFORNIA. Hartford, Conn.: E.T. Press; New York: Dexter, 1852. 192 pp.

1849-1850. Diary of Hartford merchant, a member of the Connecticut Mining and Trading Company; voyage on their schooner, the GENERAL MORGAN, around Cape Horn to California, stopping to see the sights of Rio de Janeiro and to hunt in Patagonia; notes on weather, ship's position, vessels encountered, Fourth of July celebration, inhabitants of Tiera del Fuego, etc.; briefly in San Francisco; establishing stores at Sacramento City and Mormon Island; searching for gold; hauling freight and passengers on the schooner; voyage to Hawaii and visiting the various islands;

interesting description of congregations of Congregational and Catholic churches in Honolulu; long narrative descriptions of California and Hawaii.

LYMAN, ELLEN BANCROFT LOWELL, 1837-1894 3128

In ARTHUR THEODORE LYMAN AND ELLA LYMAN: LETTERS AND JOURNALS, by Arthur T. Lyman, prepared by Ella Lyman Cabot, vol. 1, pp. 242-245, vol. 2 passim. Menasha, Wis.: Privately printed, 1932.

1849-1892 (with gaps). Extracts, some arranged topically; girlhood studies, marks, friends, reading, piano lessons and concern for her "faults"; later accounts of pleasant days, noting her children's development, activities and sayings; family affairs; observations on marriage, friends and deaths, especially of her two infant sons; religious thoughts.

MCCALL, ANSEL JAMES 3129

THE GREAT CALIFORNIA TRAIL: WAYSIDE NOTES OF AN ARGONAUT. Bath, N.Y.: Steuben Courier Printers, 1882. 86 pp.

Apr-Sep 1849. Bath, New York, lawyer's long, literary entries describing his gold rush journey from St. Joseph to Sacramento via South Pass and Lassen's Cutoff; some events at St. Joseph; notes on Indians, emigrants and Mormons; descriptions of scenery, with an eye for the "picturesque"; an interview with Jim Bridger; coming upon the "cannibal cabins" of the Donner party and a retelling of the story, with diarist's opinion that the survivors were "ghouls."

PICK AND PAN. Bath, N.Y.: Steuben Courier Printers, 1883. 46 pp.

Sep-Nov 1849. Prospecting in California, mainly at Johnson's Ranch and Sutter's Fort; notes on mining procedures, character of miners, their lives and fortunes; colorful, in narrative style.

MCCORD, HENRY J., b. 1827 3130

Roper, Sylvia F., ed. "Sea Voyage by a Forty-Niner." MISSISSIPPI VALLEY HISTORICAL REVIEW 28 (1941-1942):413-422.

Dec 1849-Sep 1850. Extracts of an Erie County, Ohio, man's gold rush journey by sea on the ORLEANS; from New York to San Francisco via Cape Horn and Chile; disturbances first by crew and then passengers, especially over lack of provisions; a few colorful details of life at sea and in unidentified ports.

MCCOY, SAMUEL FINLEY, 1820-1898 3131

In PIONEERING ON THE PLAINS, 32 unnumbered pp. Kaukauna, Wis.: Printed not published, 1924.

May 1849-Jan 1850. Chillicothe, Ohio, man's overland travel with his brother Alexander to California via the Santa Fe Trail; dissension between members driving ox wagons and those driving mule wagons, resulting in division of the company; homesickness for wife and family; sensitivity to scenery and small beauties such as sparks from campfire against night sky; encounter with friendly Snake Indians and traveling in company with two Wyandots; return home by ship after success at mining.

MCDOUGAL, JANE 3132

In HO FOR CALIFORNIA! edited by Sandra L. Myres, pp. 9-33.

"A Woman's Log of 1849: From the Diary of Mrs. John McDougall." OVERLAND MONTHLY, 2d ser. 16 (September 1890):273-280.

May-Jun 1849. Woman's shipboard diary kept during her return from San Francisco to her home in Indianapolis; daily life and entertainments; the management of the ship CALIFORNIA by Capt. Cleveland Forbes; descriptions of Santa Barbara, San Diego, Mazatlan, San Blas, Acapulco and Panama.

MCLANE, ALLEN, d. 1849 3133

In GOLD RUSH: THE JOURNALS, DRAWINGS AND OTHER PAPERS OF J. GOLDSBOROUGH BRUFF, edited by Georgia W. Read and Ruth Gaines, vol. 2, pp. 1269-1271. New York: Columbia University Press, 1944.

Sep 1849. Fragmentary gold rush journal of a doctor from Platte County, Missouri, who died of dysentery on the trail; notes kept after McLane became separated from his friend Dr. T.G. Caldwell, describing experiences on Lassen's Cutoff; discovered by J.G. Bruff and copied into his own records.

MARCY, RANDOLPH BARNES, 1812-1887 3134

In REPORTS OF THE SECRETARY OF WAR...ALSO, THE REPORT OF CAPTAIN R.B. MARCY'S ROUTE FROM FORT SMITH TO SANTA FE, by United States Army, Corps of Topographical Engineers, pp. 169-227. 31st Cong., 1st sess., 1850, S. Exec. Doc. 64. Washington, D.C.: Printed at the Union Office, 1850.

Extracts in MARCY AND THE GOLD SEEKERS: THE JOURNAL OF CAPTAIN R.B. MARCY, WITH AN ACCOUNT OF THE GOLD RUSH OVER THE SOUTHERN ROUTE, by Grant Foreman, pp. 152-371 passim. Norman: University of Oklahoma Press, 1939.

Apr-Nov 1849. Official journal of a military escort accompanying forty-niners over the less traveled southern route from Fort Smith through present Oklahoma, Texas, New Mexico and Arizona; scenery, terrain and conditions of travel; notes on various gold rush companies, including the hapless Knickerbockers; description of Cherokee and Comanche customs and diarist's councils with Comanches on behalf of the "Great White Father in Washington."

Richardson, Rupert N., ed. "Documents Relating to West Texas and Her Indian Tribes: Marcy's Reconnaissance through Northern and Western Texas." WEST TEXAS HISTORICAL ASSOCIATION YEAR BOOK 1 (1925):30-54.

Sep-Oct 1849.

In EXPLORATION OF THE RED RIVER OF LOUISIANA, by United States War Department, pp. 10-82. 32nd Cong., 2nd sess., 1853, S. Exec. Doc. 54. Washington, D.C.: R. Armstrong, Public Printer, 1853; 33rd Cong., 1st sess., 1854, S. Exec. Doc. Washington, D.C.: O. Tucker, Senate Printer, 1854.

In ADVENTURE ON RED RIVER, by United States War Department, edited by Grant Foreman, pp. 1-199. Norman: University of Oklahoma Press, 1937.

May-Jul 1852. Official journal of an expedition to the unexplored source of the Red River as part of a broader military effort to protect settlers and emigrants from Indians; departure from Fort Belknap, with articulate and detailed notes on scenery, geology, terrain, vegetation and wildlife of a large area in present Oklahoma and Texas. considerable description of Comanche, Kiowa and Wichita Indians and their customs by a sympathetic observer.

"Captain R.B. Marcy's Reconnaissance of the Headwaters of the Red River." WEST TEXAS HISTORICAL ASSOCIATION YEAR BOOK 3 (1927):78-117.

May-Jun 1852.

Ristor, C.C. "Documents Relating to General W.T. Sherman's Southern Plains Indian Policy." PANHANDLE-PLAINS HISTORICAL REVIEW 9 (1936):7-27.

Apr-Jun 1871. Extracts from journal of a tour undertaken by Sherman to investigate unrest among Plains Indians consigned to reservations; from New Orleans through Texas, inspecting many forts en route, with notes on their condition and efficiency; abandoned ranches and other evidences of Indian depredation; arrest at Fort Sill of Kiowa chief Satanta; diarist's opinion that the "benevolent civilizing peace policy" briefly tried by the United States government was not working and that only force would subdue the Indians.

MARCY, WILLIAM LEARNED, 1786-1857   3135

"Diary and Memoranda of William L. Marcy." AMERICAN HISTORICAL REVIEW 24 (1918-1919):444-462, 641-653.

1849-1851, 1857. Extracts from the diary of lawyer and statesman who was governor of New York, secretary of war under Polk and secretary of state under Pierce; notes made sporadically after these periods, but with reflections on them; Washington politics, particularly the slavery question; much on the Whig party; extensive references to Zachary Taylor, including an assessment of his character and views; the early months of Buchanan's administration.

MARSTERS, WOODBURY, 1822-1882   3136

Leighton, Albert C., ed. "The Diary of Woodbury Marsters." NEW ENGLAND HISTORICAL AND GENEALOGICAL REGISTER 137 (1983):218-234.

Jan-Apr 1849. New Hampshire man's gold rush journey by sea on board the MARIA under Capt. J.F. Baker; outfitting at Boston, including prices; weather and log entries; activities, merriment and quarrels among crew and passengers; rescuing survivors from the wrecked LAMERTINE; sightseeing in Rio de Janeiro; an entertaining diary which ends abruptly at sea.

MASSEY, ERNEST DE   3137

A FRENCHMAN IN THE GOLD RUSH: THE JOURNAL OF ERNEST DE MASSEY, ARGONAUT OF 1849. Translated by Marguerite E. Wilbur. California Historical Society Special Publications, no. 2. San Francisco: California Historical Society, 1927. 183 pp.

Extracts in "A Frenchman in the Gold Rush: Translated from the Journal of Ernest de Massey." CALIFORNIA HISTORICAL SOCIETY QUARTERLY 5 (1926):3-43; 6 (1927):37-57.

1849-1851. Letter-journals of a French gold seeker; stormy and dangerous arrival at San Francisco on the CERES; extensive descriptions of the people and life at San Francisco and apparent effects of the gold rush; wonderful gossip on members of the French community, including "fine fellows from Paris" now doing the most menial tasks in order to survive; work as a merchant and editor, but little on mining; later material undated.

MELVILLE, HERMAN, 1819-1891   3138

JOURNAL OF A VISIT TO LONDON AND THE CONTINENT. Edited by Eleanor Melville Metcalf. Cambridge: Harvard University Press, 1948. 189 pp.

In THE MELVILLE LOG, edited by Jay Leyda, vol. 1 passim.

Extracts in HERMAN MELVILLE, MARINER AND MYSTIC, by Raymond M. Weaver, pp. 284-304 passim. New York: George H. Doran, 1921; TREASURY OF THE WORLD'S GREAT DIARIES, edited by Philip Dunaway, pp. 409-415.

Oct-Dec 1849. Journal of a voyage to England, the Continent and back; Atlantic crossing on the SOUTHAMPTON, with anecdotes of fellow passengers, including Prof. George J. Adler, ship social life and Melville's unsuccessful attempt to save a man who had jumped overboard; sightseeing, concerts, plays and social life in London as well as contacts with his publishers and other literary people; public hanging of a husband and wife, "a most wonderful, horrible and unspeakable scene"; brief notes of tourist experiences in Paris, Brussels and Cologne before return to London and homeward journey on the INDEPENDENCE; references to his own writing and reading throughout.

JOURNAL UP THE STRAITS. Edited by Raymond Weaver. New York: Colophon, 1935. 182 pp. Reprint. New York: Cooper Square, 1971.

JOURNAL OF A VISIT TO EUROPE AND THE LEVANT. Edited by Howard C. Horsford. Princeton Studies in English, no. 35. Princeton, N.J.: Princeton University Press, 1955. 299 pp. Reprint. Westport, Conn.: Greenwood, 1976.

In THE MELVILLE LOG, vol. 2 passim.

Oct 1856-May 1857. Tour in England, Europe and Asia Minor; contact while in England with Hawthorne; analytic notes on such places as Syria, Greece, Egypt, Constantinople, Jerusalem, Rome, etc., and on books read.

Konvitz, Milton R. "Herman Melville in the Holy Land." MIDSTREAM: A MONTHLY JEWISH REVIEW 25, no. 10 (1979):50-57.

Jan 1857. Extracts within article on Melville's observations in Palestine, which contributed years later to his "Clarel: a Poem and Pilgrimage in the Holy Land."

"Journal of Melville's Voyage in a Clipper Ship." NEW ENGLAND QUARTERLY 2 (1929): 120-125.

In THE MELVILLE LOG, vol. 2 passim.

Jun-Aug 1860. A diary fragment of part of Melville's voyage from Boston to San Francisco around Cape Horn on the METEOR, commanded by his brother Thomas; weather and sailing notes; distress over the death of a young sailor who fell from the rigging.

MILLET, SAMUEL   3139

A WHALING VOYAGE IN THE BARK WILLIS. Boston: Privately printed, 1924. 44 pp. Diary, pp. 1-23.

1849-1850. Whaling diary kept aboard the WILLIS of Mattapoisett, Massachusetts, during a very successful voyage; exciting details of the chase and its dangers; routines of seamen's work; complaints about miserable fare, including "water so thick it can hardly be sucked through the teeth" and totally insufficient food to sustain their hard work; ships encountered.

MINOR, CLORINDA   3140

MESHULLAM! OR, TIDINGS FROM JERUSALEM. Philadelphia: For the author, 1850. 100 pp. 2d ed. rev. 1851. 139 pp. Reprint. New York: Arno, 1977.

1849-1850. Travel diary, kept for her friends, of a devout Protestant woman's pilgrimage to the Holy Land; Atlantic crossing and the ports of Marseilles and Jaffa; travel to Bethlehem, Bethany, the Mount of Olives and Jerusalem, where she stayed in the hotel of John Meshullam, a Christian Jew, whose story she narrates; detailed description of scenes and people; much religious introspection, her illnesses and God's providences, all in florid style.

MOORE, EDWIN MARSHALL   **3141**

Bakken, Lavola, ed. "Pioneer-Style Patriotism." UMPQUA TRAPPER 8 (1972):36-37.

Jul 1849, Jul 1859. Extracts describing two Fourth of July celebrations, one aboard the EDWIN en route to the gold rush and the other in Roseburg, Oregon.

MORGAN, MARTHA M.   **3142**

A TRIP ACROSS THE PLAINS IN THE YEAR 1849, WITH NOTES OF A VOYAGE TO CALIFORNIA BY WAY OF PANAMA. San Francisco: Printed at Pioneer Press, 1864. 31 pp. Reprint. Fairfield, Wash.: Ye Galleon, 1983. 37 pp.

May-Jun 1849. Bare notes, beginning at St. Joseph and ending at Pleasant Valley, of gold rush journey via Salt Lake; terrain, camps, distances and difficulties.

Jan-Feb 1854. Voyage to California; on the OHIO to Panama and then on an unnamed ship with diary ending at sea; some hymns or religious poems appended.

MORGAN, WILLIAM IVES, 1826-1869   **3143**

Muzzy, Florence E.D., ed. "The Log of a Forty-Niner." HARPER'S MAGAZINE 113 (1906):920-926.

1849-1853. Extracts from a Bristol, Connecticut, man's voyage around Cape Horn on the J. WALLS, JR. as a member of the Brothers Mining and Trading Company; illness and bad luck in the mines at Volcano, etc.; notes on politics and trade; return on the INDEPENDENCE.

MORISON, JAMES, 1818-1882   **3144**

BY SEA TO SAN FRANCISCO. Edited by Lonnie J. White and William R. Gillaspie. Memphis: Memphis State University Press, 1977. 61 pp.

Nov 1849-Jun 1850. A doctor's perceptive journal, undated during later months, of a voyage on the SARAH SANDS from New York to California to set up a medical practice and to escort his sister-in-law Ellen Smith Morison to her husband; keen interest in ports visited, including Rio de Janeiro, Valparaiso, Callao, Lima, Panama City and Acapulco, and many prominent people whom he met; observations of political situations in South America.

NUSBAUMER, LOUIS, 1819-1878   **3145**

VALLEY OF SALT, MEMORIES OF WINE: A JOURNAL OF DEATH VALLEY. Edited by George Koenig. Berkeley, Calif.: The Friends of Bancroft Library, 1967. 67 pp. passim.

In THE LOST DEATH VALLEY '49ER JOURNAL OF LOUIS NUSBAUMER, by George Koenig, pp. 1-80 passim. Death Valley, Calif.: Death Valley '49ers, 1974.

In SHADOW OF THE ARROW, by Margaret Long, pp. 294-299. Caldwell, Idaho: Caxton Printers, 1950.

1849-1850. Extensive extracts from gold rush diary of a German immigrant who attempted an unknown route and became lost in what is now Death Valley with a group of about one hundred, including the heroic William L. Manly, who eventually led them to safety; retrospective account of the journey from New York into Nevada, with frequent dated entries of the days leading to and including period in Death Valley; from Salt Lake with the Jayhawkers and other companies newly regrouped for an autumn attempt on a southern route under Mormon guide Jefferson Hunt; to Mount Misery and into Death Valley, with breakup of the company into smaller groups, each seeking its own way out of the desert.

OSBUN, ALBERT GALLATIN, 1807-1862   **3146**

TO CALIFORNIA AND THE SOUTH SEAS: THE DIARY OF ALBERT G. OSBUN. Edited by John H. Kemble. San Marino, Calif.: Huntington Library, 1966. 233 pp.

1849-1851. Entertaining diary of an Ohio doctor's unsuccessful gold rush venture abandoned in favor of an attempt to establish trade between San Francisco and islands of the South Pacific; ship travel from New York to California via Panama on the CRESCENT CITY, EUREKA and OREGON; mining at Yuba River and eventually dissolving of his Shannon Mining Company; trading voyage of the RODOLPH, mainly in the Samoan group, with good descriptions of seafaring life and Samoan customs; return home via Mexico where diary ends.

PALMER, ROBERT H.   **3147**

A VOYAGE AROUND CAPE HORN. Philadelphia: W.S. Young, Printer, 1863. 31 pp.

Aug-Dec 1849. Philadelphian's gold rush diary of voyage on the MARIA from Delaware Bay around Cape Horn to San Francisco; description of San Francisco followed by letter giving narrative of a five-weeks "voyage of discovery" up the Pacific coast.

PARRY, CHARLES CHRISTOPHER, 1823-1890   **3148**

Ross, Earle D., ed. "A Travelogue of 1849." MISSISSIPPI VALLEY HISTORICAL REVIEW 27 (1940-1941):435-441.

Mar-Apr 1849. Travel journal of an English immigrant who was both a doctor and a botanist; hectic journey to join Maj. W.H. Emory's Mexican boundary expedition; from Davenport, Iowa, by stage, canoe and riverboat to New Orleans, where cholera was "secretly known to be raging"; failure there of attempt to get a ship to Panama; by train to New York to seek ship passage to California; meeting with his mentor, botanist John Torrey.

PERKINS, ELISHA DOUGLASS, 1823-1852   **3149**

GOLD RUSH DIARY: BEING THE JOURNAL OF ELISHA DOUGLASS PERKINS ON THE OVERLAND TRAIL IN THE SPRING AND SUMMER OF 1849. Edited by Thomas D. Clark. Lexington: University of Kentucky Press, 1967. 206 pp.

May 1849-Feb 1850. Outstanding gold rush diary of a young man from Marietta, Ohio, a member of the Marietta Gold Hunters; full entries covering descriptions of terrain, plants and animals, details of camp and trail, problem solving, relations with his own and other companies; religious reflections; very humorous in places, but with bouts of homesickness and discouragement over the enormous difficulties, even folly, of the undertaking.

PERKINS, WILLIAM, 1827-1893   3150

THREE YEARS IN CALIFORNIA: WILLIAM PERKINS' JOURNAL OF LIFE AT SONORA, 1849-1852. Introduction and annotations by Dale L. Morgan and James R. Scobie. Berkeley: University of California Press, 1964. 424 pp.

1849-1852. Highly narrative gold rush diary; scant on trip via Mexico, but extensive on life in the diggings at Sonora and depiction of a society often characterized by gambling, lynchings, duels, murders and callousness toward violence; notes on Indians, the prominent Spanish-speaking population and a variety of foreigners lured to the gold rush; mining techniques and the activities of John A. Sutter, Daniel A. Enyart, Hiram W. Theall and others.

PHELON, HENRY A.   3151

In IN A SPERM WHALE'S JAWS: AN EPISODE IN THE LIFE OF CAPTAIN ALBERT WOOD OF NANTUCKET, MASS., edited by George C. Wood, pp. 1-16. Hanover, N.H.: Friends of the Dartmouth Library, Dartmouth College, 1954.

Mar-Apr 1849. Extracts from an account of a harrowing incident involving crew of the whaling ship PLOUGH BOY; the crushing of a whale boat by the jaws of a sperm whale, with some of the men inside and others scattered into the water; the nursing of Wood, severely wounded by the whale's teeth, and his remarkable recovery.

PIERCE, HIRAM DWIGHT, b. 1810   3152

A FORTY-NINER SPEAKS. Edited by Sarah W. Meyer. Oakland, Calif.: Keystone Inglett Printing Co., 1930. 74 pp.

1849-1851. Troy, New York, blacksmith's gold rush voyage by unnamed ship to Panama, with a good description of Chagres, old Panama and Tecamos and his experiences while awaiting passage to California; on the SYLPH to San Francisco; observations on bad manners of passengers; in the diggings near Sacramento City; return to San Francisco and the dissolving of the R.C.E.C. Mining Company, of which he was a member; continued unsuccessful work in the gold fields, with notes on prices and earnings, health, Fourth of July, etc.; return home via Nicaragua; reflections throughout of a devout Presbyterian.

POOLE, FITCH, 1803-1873   3153

Poole, Mary E. "Fitch Poole." DANVERS HISTORICAL SOCIETY COLLECTIONS 14 (1926):41-62. Diary, pp. 50-59.

1849-1870 (with gaps). Extracts from diary of businessman, city official and librarian of the Peabody Institute; brief entries concerning politics, local events, his writing, his work on behalf of the Mechanics Institute Library and the Peabody Institute, social and cultural activities and Civil War news; notes on reading and Memorial Day.

POWELL, H.M.T.   3154

THE SANTA FE TRAIL TO CALIFORNIA, 1849-1852: THE JOURNAL AND DRAWINGS OF H.M.T. POWELL. Edited by Douglas S. Watson. San Francisco: Book Club of California, 1931. 272 pp.

1849-1852. Record of a Greenville, Illinois, man traveling with the Illinois Company; route via St. Louis, Santa Fe, Guadalupe Pass, Santa Cruz, Tucson, Gila, Colorado River and San Diego; his experiences at Mariposa, travels in California and return to Illinois; an interesting gold rush account.

POWNALL, JOSEPH   3155

Cleland, Robert Glass, ed. "From Louisiana to Mariposa." PACIFIC HISTORICAL REVIEW 18 (1949):24-32.

Jun-Sep 1849. Gold rush journey from De Soto Parish via northern Mexico, with entries beginning at the Rio Grande; route through Texas, Chihuahua, Sonora, down the Gila, across the Colorado and the desert to Los Angeles, eventually to the Mariposa diggings; a few notes on Mexicans and Indians.

PRATT, ADDISON, 1802-1872   3156

In JOURNALS OF FORTY-NINERS, edited by Le Roy R. and Ann W. Hafen, pp. 66-112.

Oct-Dec 1849. Account of travel with the Jefferson Hunt wagon train to southern California; good descriptions of country and conditions; disagreements as to route and separating with a large number from Hunt train; difficulty of getting food and water, particularly for cattle; through Cajon Pass; Christmas dinner at Williams Ranch.

In THE SHADOW OF THE ARROW, by Margaret Long, pp. 152-162. Caldwell, Idaho: Caxton Printers, 1941. Rev. and enl. ed., 1950.

Oct 1849.

PRICE, LEWIS RICHARD, b. 1817   3157

Jackson, W. Turrentine, ed. "Mazatlan to the Estanislao." CALIFORNIA HISTORICAL SOCIETY QUARTERLY 39 (1960):35-52.

Sep-Oct 1849. Young Englishman's almost entirely narrative account of travel on the OREGON to San Diego; life there and at San Francisco, San Jose and Stockton, as well as in the diggings at Wood's Creek and Hawkins's Bar.

Jackson, W. Turrentine, ed. "Journal of Richard Lewis Price: Voyage From London to San Francisco." PACIFIC HISTORIAN 4 (1960):97-112.

Apr-Jul 1871. Extracts from board chairman's trip to inspect London-owned mines of the Sierra Buttes Gold Mining Company; on the JAVA to New York with George T. Coulter; by train to Utah, where he had an interview with Brigham Young and observed the Mormons; travels in California and Nevada, taking him to Sierra mines, Napa Valley, the Mother Lode, the redwoods and Virginia City; time spent with Adolph Sutro and enthusiasm for construction of his tunnel; return east by train; interesting notes throughout on people, scenes, mining and transcontinental rail travel.

PRITCHARD, JAMES AVERY, 1816-1862   3158

THE OVERLAND DIARY OF JAMES A . PRITCHARD FROM KENTUCKY TO CALIFORNIA IN 1849. Edited by Dale L. Morgan. Denver: F.A. Rosenstock, 1959. 221 pp.

1849-1850. Gold rush diary of a man from Petersburg, Kentucky, apparently captain of his company; travel to St. Louis on the steamer CAMBRIA; frequent and detailed entries of the overland journey; conditions of travel, encounters with other wagon trains, Indians, landmarks and individual forty-niners; California portion summarized.

"Diary of a Journey from Kentucky to California in 1849." MISSOURI HISTORICAL REVIEW 18 (1924):535-545.

Apr-May 1849. Extract covering arrival at St. Louis on the CAMBRIA and travel across Missouri, with descriptions of towns and countryside.

Williamson, Hugh P., ed. "An Overland Journey in 1849." KENTUCKY HISTORICAL SOCIETY REGISTER 66 (1968):147-158.

Apr 1849. Extract describing the journey from Petersburg, Kentucky, to Independence, Missouri.

RACKLEFF, WILLIAM EDWARD, 1834-1908   3159

Rackleff, Edward, ed. "A Copy of My Father's Diary." UMPQUA TRAPPER 14 (1978):31-48, 56-72, 82-86.

1849-1865 (with gaps). A brief gold rush memoir, giving way to logs and diaries of a Standish, Maine, man who settled in Coos County, Oregon; work as a farmer and boat builder with his father, William R. Rackleff; building and operating the TWIN SISTERS, KATE NOBLE and other vessels important to the lumber trade between Oregon and California as well as Coquille River boats.

RAMSAY, ALEXANDER, 1810-1901   3160

Mattes, Merrill J., ed. "Alexander Ramsay's Gold Rush Diary of 1849." PACIFIC HISTORICAL REVIEW 18 (1949):437-468.

May-Nov 1849. Journey with relatives and others from Parke County, Indiana; route from St. Joseph via the Platte to the Humboldt and unfortunate choice of Lassen's Cutoff to Feather River; good notes on provisioning, terrain, conditions, weather, illnesses, including "bloody flux" and provender for stock; a difficult but successful journey of a well-organized company that enforced Sunday layover and arrived in California with no loss of life; mining experiences in the Sacramento Valley.

REID, BERNARD JOSEPH, 1823-1904   3161

OVERLAND TO CALIFORNIA WITH THE PIONEER LINE. Edited by Mary McDougall Gordon. Stanford: Stanford University Press, 1983. 247 pp.

May-Oct 1849. Clarion, Pennsylvania, man's diary of the disastrous Pioneer Line journey under Thomas Turner, the first to transport gold seekers to California as a commercial venture; optimistic departure from near Independence giving way to cholera and scurvy, hunger, choking dust, failure of exhausted animals and eventual completion of the journey by a few survivors on foot; route via forts Kearny and Laramie, South Pass and the Humboldt; graphic descriptions throughout and notes on many fellow travelers on a journey which became "a long, dreadful dream" ending with diarist's arrival at Weber Creek in the Sacramento Valley; extracts from the diary of Niles Searls interspersed.

"Diary of B.J.R., 1850." PONY EXPRESS COURIER 4, no. 5 (1937):9-10, 13, 16.

Jan-Sep 1850. Activities in and around San Francisco; a trading venture in Stockton; in the diggings at Mormon Gulch, where he was involved in a protracted claim suit which threatened "war"; earnings and prices until "our claim is now totally abandoned as worthless"; frequent references to Robert Hawkshurst.

RICH, CHARLES COULSON   3162

In JOURNALS OF FORTY-NINERS, edited by Le Roy R. and Ann W. Hafen, pp. 181-192.

Oct. 1849-Jan 1850. Diary of one of Twelve Apostles of the Mormon Church on journey from Salt Lake City to California to manage Mormon affairs there; traveling part of the way with Jefferson Hunt wagon train; dissension with non-Mormons; arriving at Williams Ranch, visiting San Gabriel Mission and noting beautiful orchards.

ROBINSON, CHARLES, 1818-1894   3163

Barry, Louise, comp. "Charles Robinson - Yankee '49er: His Journey to California." KANSAS HISTORICAL QUARTERLY 34 (1968):179-188.

Apr-May 1849. Diary fragment by Fitchburg, Massachusetts, doctor who later became the first governor of Kansas; entries beginning at Kansas City, Missouri, thence into Kansas; conversation with Indian agent Richard Hewitt, mainly about slavery question and the agent's expulsion of missionary James Gurley for being an abolitionist; notes on mission work among the Wyandot.

In NEBRASKA AND KANSAS, by Massachusetts Emigrant Aid Company, 32 pp. passim. Boston: The Company, 1954.

May 1849, Apr 1854. Romantic and picturesque description of scenery in Kansas Territory during his gold rush journey; on return, description of Kansas City, Kansas, new settlers, their farms and language, cholera outbreak and Wyandot and Potawatomi Indians, including their chief.

ROBINSON, ZIRKLE D., 1810-1867   3164

THE ROBINSON-ROSENBERGER JOURNEY TO THE GOLD FIELDS OF CALIFORNIA. Edited by Francis Rosenberger. Iowa City: Prairie Press, 1966. 26 pp.

1849-1850 (with gaps). Gold rush journey of three men from the Shenandoah Valley, the diarist, his brother Joseph Robinson and brother-in-law Wesley Allen Rosenberger; entries beginning in Illinois; route via South Pass, with hasty notes of road conditions, scenery, land and soil, most graphic about the Humboldt; gap during most of period in the mines, with diary resuming on return aboard the MARIANA to Panama, where it ends.

SCARBOROUGH, A.   3165

Wright, Bessie L., ed. "Diary of a Member of the First Mule Pack Train to Leave Fort Smith for California in 1849." PANHANDLE-PLAINS HISTORICAL REVIEW 42 (1969):61-117. Reprint. Canyon, Tex.: Palo Duro Press, 1969? 59 pp.

Feb-May 1849. El Dorado, Arkansas, man's gold rush diary; southern route along Canadian River, Texas and New Mexico, with stops at trading posts and among Choctaw and Creek Indians; notes on buffalo hunts, terrain, grass and water, scenery, etc.; encounters with Cheyenne and other Indians; a quarrelsome journey, with breakup of original mule train in Santa Fe, before continuing into Utah and Colorado, where diary ends; several poems inspired by scenery or religious reflections.

SCHARMANN, HERMANN B., b. 1838   3166

SCHARMANN'S OVERLAND JOURNEY TO CALIFORNIA. Translated from the German by Margaret H. and Erich W. Zimmermann.

N.p., 1918. 114 pp. Reprint. Freeport, N.Y.: Books for Libraries, 1969.

1849-1851. Diary of the president of a company of Germans formed to leave New York for California gold rush; strenuous overland journey and death of his young daughter and wife; exhaustion from hard work, illness and repeated failures to find gold; disgust with greedy merchants and false reports that lured him to make the trip; details of cost of provisions, services and tools; business conditions in Marysville and Sacramento.

SEARLS, NILES, 1825-1907   **3167**

THE DIARY OF A PIONEER AND OTHER PAPERS, BEING THE DIARY KEPT BY NILES SEARLS ON HIS JOURNEY FROM INDEPENDENCE, MISSOURI, TO CALIFORNIA. San Francisco: Pernau-Walsh Printing, 1940. 90 pp.

May-Oct 1849. A rare record of a young man who paid fare for transportation to California on the Pioneer Line, one of the few commercial attempts to convey emigrants overland; careful description of organization of the company; failure of the enterprise and disaster to passengers, who suffered increasingly severe hardships from lack of provisions, accidents and illnesses, especially cholera; interesting notes on landmarks, rivers, mountains and celebrating the "glorious 4th"; a well-written, articulate diary.

SEDGLEY, JOSEPH   **3168**

OVERLAND TO CALIFORNIA IN 1849. Oakland: Butler and Bowman, 1877. 66 pp.

Mar-Sep 1849. Gold rush diary of Boston member of the Sagamore and California Mining and Trading Company of Lynn, Massachusetts; to St. Louis by several modes, including river steamer DE WITT CLINTON and the BELLE CREOLE, to Boonville, thence overland via the Sweetwater and Humboldt with L.S. Hooker as captain; cholera in the river towns and on the trail; references to other companies, graves with names, conditions and difficulties of travel; arrival at San Francisco "sick and feeble."

SHEARER, Mr.   **3169**

In THE FAR WEST AND ROCKIES: GENERAL ANALYTICAL INDEX TO THE FIFTEEN VOLUME SERIES AND SUPPLEMENT TO THE JOURNALS OF FORTYNINERS, SALT LAKE TO LOS ANGELES, prepared and edited by Le Roy R. and Ann W. Hafen, pp. 31-41. The Far West and the Rockies Historical Series, vol. 15. Glendale, Calif.: A.H. Clark, 1961.

Sep-Dec 1849. Journal of member of Gruwell-Derr party traveling from Salt Lake City to the Mohave River; notes on general appearance of country, camps, supply of water and grass, fatigued and dying oxen and lack of provisions.

SIMPSON, JAMES HERVEY, 1813-1883   **3170**

31st Cong., 1st sess., 1850, S. Exec. Doc 64, pp. 55-168.

JOURNAL OF A MILITARY RECONNAISSANCE FROM SANTA FE, NEW MEXICO TO THE NAVAJO COUNTRY. Philadelphia: Lippincott, Grambo, 1852. 140 pp.

NAVAHO EXPEDITION: JOURNAL OF A MILITARY RECONNAISSANCE FROM SANTA FE, NEW MEXICO, TO THE NAVAHO COUNTRY MADE IN 1849. Edited by Frank McNitt. American Exploration and Travel Series, 43. Norman: University of Oklahoma Press, 1964. 296 pp. Journal, pp. 5-162.

Aug-Sep 1849. Topographical engineer's official journal of Col. John Macrae Washington's expedition to subdue the Navaho; from Fort Marcy to Jemez Pueblo, with the assistance of Henry L. Dodge and his Mexican militia; exploration of Canyon de Chelly and description of ruins, inscriptions and pueblos at Chaco Canyon, El Moro, etc.; treaty negotiations with chiefs Mariano Martinez and Chapitone at Canyon de Chelly, with reports of immediate violations of the unpopular and forced treaty; notes on Navaho agriculture; references to his assistant topographers and valuable aides Edward M. and Richard Kern and Indian agent James S. Calhoun.

In REPORT OF EXPLORATIONS ACROSS THE GREAT BASIN OF THE TERRITORY OF UTAH FOR A DIRECT WAGON-ROUTE FROM CAMP FLOYD TO GENOA, IN CARSON VALLEY, IN 1859, by United States Engineer Department, pp. 41-150. Washington, D.C.: United States Government Printing Office, 1876. Reprint. Reno: University of Nevada Press, 1983.

May-Aug 1859. Journal of expedition to survey a wagon route from Utah to the Sierra Nevada and to provide scientific information; from Camp Floyd, Utah, via present Austin and Carson City to Genoa; thence to Sacramento and San Francisco to report to officials; back to Genoa by stagecoach over deplorable roads, with a drunken coachman, to rejoin his party for a return exploration over a slightly different route; daily notes of terrain, water, altitudes, temperatures, supplies, hardships, etc.; especially full and interesting notes on Digger, Shoshoni and other Indians, their customs and modes of survival; livelier and more personal than many such official journals.

Basso, Dave, ed. "Exploration Across the Great Basin of Utah." NEVADA HISTORICAL REVIEW 2 (1975):160-225. Diary, pp. 161-203.

May-Jul 1859.

SMITH, WILLIAM C.S., b. 1823   **3171**

In A HISTORY OF CALIFORNIA, by Robert G. Cleland, pp. 483-495. New York: Macmillan, 1922.

A JOURNEY TO CALIFORNIA IN 1849. Fairfield, Wash.: Ye Galleon, 1984. 75 pp.

Apr-Jun 1849. Gold rush journey of a young man who settled at Napa, California; summary of ship and overland journey from New York to Mexico, then dated entries covering harrowing trip through Baja California from San Jose del Cabo to San Diego with William F. Nye, Israel Miller and others; detailed descriptions of missions, ranches, people, terrain and the extreme hazards and discomforts of desert travel; advice and new provisions from a Portuguese landowner; activities and impressions at San Diego.

SPRAGUE, ACHSA W., 1828-1862   **3172**

Twynham, Leonard, ed. "Selections from Achsa Sprague's Diary and Journal." VERMONT HISTORY 9 (1941):132-184.

1849-1853. Extracts from the diary of a Plymouth Notch, Vermont, woman who struggled against crippling illness to become an author, lecturer, abolitionist, women's rights advocate and leader of the Spiritualist movement; her youthful years spent as a semi-invalid, seeing many doctors and consuming much medicine to no avail; enjoyment of reading, writing and horseback riding, although frequently unable to walk; deaths of several loved ones to compound her miseries; an unexplained healing which she attributed to a "Spirit Agency," enabling her to assume an active life of lecturing on Spiritualism and conducting seances throughout New England; meetings with other Spiritualists and description of a picture painted by "spirit direction."

STANSBURY, HOWARD, 1806-1863   3173

In EXPLORATION AND SURVEY OF THE VALLEY OF THE GREAT SALT LAKE OF UTAH, INCLUDING A RECONNOISSANCE OF A NEW ROUTE THROUGH THE ROCKY MOUNTAINS, by United States Army, Corps of Topographical Engineers, pp. 1-303. 32nd Cong., Spec. sess., 1851, S. Exec. Doc. 3. Philadelphia: Lippincott, Grambo, 1852.

In AN EXPEDITION TO THE VALLEY OF THE GREAT SALT LAKE OF UTAH, by United States Engineer Department, pp. 1-267. London: S. Low; Philadelphia: Lippincott, Grambo, 1852. Reprint. Ann Arbor, Mich: University Microfilms, 1966.

> 1849-1850. First survey and scientific assessment of Great Salt Lake region of Utah, made by captain in Corps of Topographical Engineers; traveling from Fort Leavenworth to Fort Kearny and Fort Laramie, seeing buffalo and noting cholera among emigrants and Indians, particularly Sioux; to Fort Bridger and on to Salt Lake; usual statistical information of weather, temperature, natural history, geology, landmarks and minerals; favorable observations on Mormon's vocational and social life after wintering among them.

"The Bannock Mountain Road." IDAHO YESTERDAYS 8, no. 1 (1964):10-15.

> Sep 1850. Extracts of exploration along the Malad River and Bannock Creek, searching for a natural wagon route from Salt Lake City to Fort Hall.

STAPLES, DAVID JACKSON, 1824-1900   3174

Taggart, Harold F., ed. "The Journal of David Jackson Staples." CALIFORNIA HISTORICAL SOCIETY QUARTERLY 22 (1943):119-150.

> Apr-Sep 1849. Gold rush journal of a member of the Boston-Newton Joint Stock Association; by train and riverboats GRIFFIN YEATMAN and BAY STATE to Independence, thence overland, suffering cholera in their own and other wagon trains during an otherwise fairly successful and uneventful journey; a buffalo hunt; a few notes on Indians; enjoyment of a stay among the Mormons at Salt Lake, with journal ending abruptly on the desert, although Staples continued to California and became a leading citizen.

STECK, AMOS, 1822-1908   3175

In AMOS STECK (1822-1908) FORTY-NINER, by Nolie Mumey, pp. 33-116. Denver: Range Press, 1981.

> May-Oct 1849. Gold rush diary of a Watertown, Wisconsin, lawyer who later became mayor and a leading citizen of Denver; full, descriptive entries on journey from Independence to Sacramento via Fort Laramie, Green River and Humboldt; references to many emigrant groups and individuals; notes on Indians; the incongruous experience of coming upon German musicians "in concert on flutes, violin and cellos" along the Humboldt trail; diary ending upon arrival in California.

STEINERT, W.   3176

Jordan, Gilbert J., trans. and ed. "W. Steinert's View of Texas in

1849." SOUTHWESTERN HISTORICAL QUARTERLY 80 (1976): 57-78, 177-200, 283-301, 399-416; 81 (1977):45-72.

> May-Jun 1849. Texas portion of a German teacher's detailed letter-diary describing a trip through the United States to consider immigration for himself and others; coastal and overland travels, particularly in the area of New Braunfels, with notes on the condition of German settlers, many of whom are mentioned by name; notes on farms, health, prosperity or lack of it, customs and adaption to American ways, markets, transportation and opportunities for education and employment; his social concern over slavery and religious and moral conditions; an interesting account of his experiences and generally unfavorable impressions of Texas as a prospect for future German settlement.

STONE, JOHN N., b. 1819?   3177

In CALIFORNIA GOLD RUSH VOYAGES, 1848-1849, edited by John E. Pomfret, pp. 99-171. San Marino, Calif.: Huntington Library, 1954. Reprint. Westport, Conn,: Greenwood, 1974.

> Feb-Aug 1849. Full, articulate account of voyage from New York to San Francisco around Cape Horn aboard the ROBERT BOWNE; weather conditions, shipboard life and poor food; celebrating Fourth of July; details of stops at Rio de Janeiro, Callao and Lima.

STOVER, SAMUEL MURRAY   3178

DIARY OF SAMUEL MURRAY STOVER, ENROUTE TO CALIFORNIA. Elizabethton, Tenn.: H.M. Folsom, 1938. 37 pp.

> May-Sep 1849. Detailed and well written emigrant diary of a Tennessee doctor's journey from Independence, Missouri, to California, traveling variously with the Tennessee Company and the Kentucky Company; the usual record of weather, water, grass, roads, landmarks, sickness, especially cholera, and death; beauty or dullness of scenery; passing and being passed by many wagon trains; mention of Pawnee, Sioux and Potowatomi Indians; stop at Fort Kearny; a buffalo hunt.

STOWELL, LEVI, 1820-1855   3179

Thorne, Marco G., ed. "Bound for the Land of Canaan, Ho!" CALIFORNIA HISTORICAL SOCIETY QUARTERLY 27 (1948):33-50, 157-164, 259-266, 361-370; 28 (1949):57-68.

> Jan-Dec 1849. Washington, D.C., carpenter's journey to California, with diary beginning at Chagres; on the CALIFORNIA to San Francisco, enduring wretched food and near mutiny among passengers; work as a mechanic in San Francisco, thence to the mines, with brief but informative notes on his life in the Stockton area; return to carpentry at San Francisco with his friend H.F. Williams; a raid on Chileans by a gang called "the Hounds," homesickness and tiring of the bachelor life; arrival of ships disgorging argonauts; local political events and his own participation in them, as well as in church and Masonic activities.

STUART, JACOB   3180

White, Kate, ed. "Diary of a 49-er." TENNESSEE HISTORICAL MAGAZINE, 2d ser. 1 (1931):279-285.

> Nov 1849-Jul 1850 (with gap). Washington County man's gold rush diary; from Knoxville with a Tennessee party under Alexander O. Anderson; notes on Santa Fe and its inhabitants,

especially the ''exceeding beautiful señoritas,'' and Spanish customs; entries ending at Albuquerque.

STUART, JOSEPH ALONZO, b. 1825   3181

MY ROVING LIFE: A DIARY OF TRAVELS AND ADVENTURES BY SEA AND LAND DURING PEACE AND WAR. Auburn, Calif., 1895. 2 vols.

1849-1853, 1864-1867. Diary of an adventurer describing with humor and detail the continually changing scene of his experiences during an overland trip to California from Lowell, Massachusetts; many mishaps, deprivations, discouraging travel conditions, cholera and uncooperative mules; miserable days in various mining camps with little profit; life as an ordinary seaman during the Civil War on the OHIO and the METACOMET taking small prizes and participating in operations at Mobile; after the war serving on the OHIO, TICONDEROGA and INDEPENDENCE, enjoying colorful and curious sights at Trieste, Venice and Jerusalem; more attempts at prospecting in California and Nevada after a discouraging illness, finally returning to Lowell after minimal success; edited for publication.

SUTHERLAND, JAMES   3182

MacShane, Frank. ''The Log of James Sutherland.'' AMERICAN NEPTUNE 18 (1958):306-314.

Aug-Sep 1849. Young Scottish immigrant's diary of passage from Liverpool to New York aboard the JOHN HANCOCK; shipboard life among first class passengers; service at captain's request as ship's doctor although ignorant of medicine; appalling conditions and illness among the mainly Irish steerage passengers.

SWAIN, WILLIAM, 1821-1904   3183

In THE WORLD RUSHED IN: THE CALIFORNIA GOLD RUSH EXPERIENCE, by J.S. Holliday, 559 pp. passim. New York: Simon and Schuster, 1981.

Apr-Oct 1849. Diary of overland trip from Youngstown, New York, to California gold diggings with Wolverine Rangers Company; hardships of travel and homesickness; good descriptions of country traveled; quotes from others' diaries and letters interpolated into Swain's account to form a very complete record of the gold rush experience.

Holliday, J.S., ed. ''An Old-Time Fourth: On the Gold Rush Trail.'' AMERICAN WEST 5, no. 4 (1968):38.

Jul 1849. Brief extracts from the diaries of forty-niners Swain, William J. Watson and William B. Lorton, showing how the Fourth of July was celebrated on the gold rush trail.

SWEENY, THOMAS WILLIAM, 1820-1892   3184

JOURNAL, 1849-1853. Edited by Arthur Woodward. Great West and Indian Series, 7. Los Angeles: Westernlore Press, 1956. 278 pp.

1849-1853. Journal of a one-armed Mexican War veteran and career soldier, the legendary ''Fighting Tom'' Sweeny, an immigrant from Ireland; narrative material giving way to dated entries beginning en route to California via Cape Horn on the EDITH; interesting notes on ports of Rio de Janeiro and Valparaiso; arrival in San Diego, thence to Fort Yuma for an extended tour of duty under Maj. Samuel Heintzelman, whom Sweeny did not admire; informative and entertaining account of life at the hot, isolated outpost; extensive notes on Yuma Indians, with inter-

views regarding their customs; marches on the Gila and in Baja California pursuing deserters lured by the gold rush; references to Capt. John W. Davidson, Lt. John D. O'Connell and others; activities at San Diego and San Francisco.

''Military Occupation of California. MILITARY SERVICE INSTITUTION OF THE UNITED STATES JOURNAL 44 (1909):276-289.

1852-1853. Extracts beginning at Yuma on the Colorado.

TAPPAN, HENRY   3185

Walters, Everett and Strother, George B., eds. ''The Gold Rush Diary of Henry Tappan.'' ANNALS OF WYOMING 25 (1953):113-139.

Apr-Sep 1849. Woodburn, Illinois, man's trip with the Jerseyville Company; route from St. Joseph via Platte, Sweetwater, South Pass, Sublette's Cutoff, Fort Hall, Humboldt Sink and Donner Pass; camping with the Hudspeth Company on August 3.

TATE, JAMES A., 1795-1849   3186

Williamson, Hugh P. ''One Who Went West.'' MISSOURI HISTORICAL REVIEW 57 (1963):369-378.

Apr-May 1849. Extracts from the diary of a Callaway County man who joined the gold rush ''to try and repair a ruined fortune'' and died in the attempt; notes covering journey to St. Joseph, where a company was organized with diarist as ''president''; remainder of diary summarized, with quotations, until his death in California; many religious reflections of a devout Presbyterian.

THORNTON, JOHN   3187

DIARY OF A TOUR THROUGH THE NORTHERN STATES OF THE UNION AND CANADA. London: F. Barker, 1850. 120 pp.

Jun-Oct 1849. Englishman's voyage to New York with visits to Tarrytown, Ithaca, Buffalo and Niagara; thence into Canada with return to New York; fairly lively touristic notes.

THURSTON, SAMUEL ROYAL, 1816-1851   3188

Himes, George H., ed. ''Diary of Samuel Royal Thurston.'' OREGON HISTORICAL QUARTERLY 15 (1914):153-205.

Nov 1849-Aug 1850. Efforts in Washington, D.C., on behalf of Oregon Territory by lawyer and first territorial delegate to Congress; interviews with President Taylor, Secretary of the Interior Thomas Ewing and others to discuss improved mail service, naval protection, land for settlement, Indian affairs, the slavery question, etc.; the diarist's opinion that Horace Greeley was ''mean, small and stinted in all his views toward Oregon''; laborious correspondence and copying of entries relating to Oregon from the journals of the House; the deliberations of Congress on Oregon and Indian matters; activities of Governor Gaines; Methodist services and views.

TINKER, CHARLES, b. 1821   3189

Roseboom, Eugene H., ed. ''Charles Tinker's Journal: A Trip to California in 1849.'' OHIO STATE ARCHAEOLOGICAL AND HISTORICAL QUARTERLY 61 (1952):64-85.

Mar-Aug 1849. Ashtabula County man's gold rush journey with a group from Kingsville led by James Haynes, with all participants listed; supplies and prices at St. Joseph; brief notes of travel with details on the assistance of the Findley-McCulloch party from Missouri in crossing of the North Platte and Green rivers in return for rescue of their drowning men; a relatively fast, successful journey ending at unspecified diggings.

TRASK, SARAH E., 1829-1892   3190

Blewett, Mary H. "I Am Doom to Disappointment: The Diaries of a Beverly, Massachusetts, Shoebinder." ESSEX INSTITUTE HISTORICAL COLLECTIONS 117 (1981):192-212. Diary, pp. 200-212.

May-Aug 1849. A young working woman's diary; doing poorly paid piecework at home for a shoe manufacturer while awaiting the return from sea of her fiancé, Luther Woodberry; boredom and uncertainty, worries about Luther's safety, sense that "I dare not speak my thoughts to anyone"; gold rush news and fears that Luther might succumb to the lure of California, which he did immediately upon his return.

May 1851. Extract of mourning Luther's death at sea during return from California and her sister's death in childbirth; the diary of a woman almost crushed by her circumstances.

UNDERHILL, GEORGE RAYMOND   3191

"Voyage to California and Return." UNDERHILL SOCIETY OF AMERICA BULLETIN (December 1980):1-52.

1849-1852 (with gaps). Gold rush journey by a member of the Greenwich and California Mining and Trading Company on the PALMETTO around Cape Horn; passenger diversions, such as Old Neptune's ceremonies, and food, which was "seasoned with dirt"; touristic notes on Rio de Janeiro and Valparaiso; mining in the Sacramento Valley and running a cloth store at Stockton, which he lost to fire; return via Panama, with later entries reminiscent.

UPHAM, SAMUEL CURTIS, 1819-1885   3192

NOTES OF A VOYAGE TO CALIFORNIA VIA CAPE HORN, TOGETHER WITH SCENES IN EL DORADO. Philadelphia: The Author, 1878. 594 pp. Diary, pp. 23-217. Reprint. New York: Arno, 1973.

Jan-Aug 1849. Philadelphia bank clerk's journal of a voyage to California on the OSCEOLA under Capt. James Fairfowl via Cape Horn, with stops at Rio De Janeiro and in Chile; lively notes on ship life, crew and passengers; his experiences in San Francisco and Sacramento.

WATSON, WILLIAM J.   3193

JOURNAL OF AN OVERLAND JOURNEY TO OREGON MADE IN THE YEAR 1849. Jacksonville: E.R. Roe, 1851. 48 pp.

May-Sep 1849. Emigrant journey from St. Joseph to Oregon City, with notes on scenery, topography, distances, etc.

WEBSTER, KIMBALL, 1828-1916   3194

THE GOLD SEEKERS OF '49. Manchester, N.H.: Standard Book, 1917. 240 pp. Diary, pp. 23-99.

Apr-Oct 1849. Pelham, New Hampshire, surveyor's gold rush journey with Granite State and California Mining and Trading Company; from Boston, by rail and steamer to Chicago and Independence, visiting Niagara Falls and Lewis Cass in Detroit on the way; fitting out, provisioning, breaking mules and suffering cholera at Independence; traveling with Mount Washington Com-

pany; through Potawatomi Indian settlement, to Fort Kearny where he "had the pleasure of beholding the 'Star Spangled Banner' floating in the breeze" at an encampment on the Fourth of July; after Fort Laramie, wandering in Rocky Mountains twelve days before recovering trail; hunting for buffalo, grouse, and deer and fishing for fresh provisions; taking Lassen's Cutoff to the Sierra Nevada and Sacramento; the usual notes of overloading, distances, camps, hardships, illnesses and discontent in company.

WHITING, WILLIAM HENRY CHASE, 1824?-1865   3195

"Whiting Diary, March From Fredericksburg to El Paso del Norte." SOUTHERN HISTORICAL ASSOCIATION PUBLICATIONS 9 (1905):361-373; 10 (1906):1-18, 78-95, 127-140.

In EXPLORING SOUTHWESTERN TRAILS, by Philip St. George Cooke, edited by Ralph P. Bieber, pp. 243-350. Glendale, Calif.: Arthur H. Clark, 1938. Reprint. Southwest Historical Series, 7. Philadelphia: Porcupine Press, 1974.

Feb-May 1849. Commander's journal of an expedition to explore feasibility of a road "for military and commercial purposes" from San Antonio to El Paso, with notes of route, terrain and camps; the usual curse of thirst and hunger for man and beast; encounters with Apaches and other Indians, with a few notes on customs and practices, including Indian use of Mexican slaves; descriptions of Mexican towns en route, as well as minerals, plants and animals; references to guide Richard A. Howard.

"Diary of a March From El Paso to San Antonio." SOUTHERN HISTORICAL ASSOCIATION PUBLICATIONS 6 (1902):283-294.

Apr 1849.

WILKINS, JAMES F., 1808?-1888   3196

AN ARTIST ON THE OVERLAND TRAIL. Edited by John F. McDermott. San Marino, Calif.: Huntington Library, 1968. 143 pp.

May-Oct 1849. Overland diary kept to accompany sketches he was making to produce an "immense moving mirror of the land route to California by the South Pass of the Rocky Mountains, embracing all the scenery from the Mississippi River to San Francisco, giving the public a pretty accurate knowledge of the difficulties our emigrant wagons have to encounter."

WILLIAMS, WILLIAM, d. 1874   3197

"Major William Williams' Journal of a Trip to Iowa in 1849." ANNALS OF IOWA, 3d ser. 12 (1915-1921):241-281.

May-Jul 1849. Guidebook type of notes of a trip from St. Louis to Fort Snelling on the riverboat KATE KARNEY; notes on towns along the Mississippi; comments on Mormons, churches and sermons; a visit with his brother, Judge Joseph Williams; cholera in river towns and on boats; return to his home in Westmoreland County, Pennsylvania.

WINDELER, ADOLPHUS   3198

THE CALIFORNIA GOLD RUSH DIARY OF A GERMAN SAILOR. Edited by W. Turrentine Jackson. Berkeley, Calif.: Howell-North Books, 1969. 236 pp.

1849-1853. Outstanding gold rush diary of a German sailor off the PROBUS, mining with his friend Carl F. Christendorff at various points on the Yuba and Feather rivers; a difficult landing at San Francisco and cargo work there; trading on the Sacramento River, then to the gold fields, with excellent technical details of mining methods; hardships of weather, discomfort, illness, discouragement, inadequate food and clothing, boredom and the wild and violent life in mining camps; the diarist's role in the hanging of David G. Brown for theft; unsuccessful prospecting and return to San Francisco to seek work; a record of profits and expenses throughout.

WISTAR, ISAAC JONES, 1827-1905   3199

AUTOBIOGRAPHY OF ISAAC JONES WISTAR. Philadelphia: Printed by the Wistar Institute of Anatomy and Biology, 1914. 2 vols. Reprint. 1937. 528 pp. New York and London: Harper & Brothers, 1938. 530 pp.

May-Aug 1849. Gold rush journey from Independence via Platte River, Fort Laramie and Humboldt River route; great problems with unbroken mules, terrain and weather, incompetent leadership and inexperienced, disorganized men; ravages of cholera in diarist's and other companies; harrassment by Pawnee and Digger Indians; terrible crossing of desert west of the Humboldt Sink; ample evidence why so many gold rush hopefuls failed to survive the overland journey.

WOODS, DANIEL B.   3200

SIXTEEN MONTHS AT THE GOLD DIGGINGS. New York: Harper, 1851. 199 pp. Diary, pp. 49-166.

Extracts in THE COURSE OF EMPIRE, compiled by Helen V. Bary pp. 134-150. PICTURES OF GOLD RUSH CALIFORNIA, edited by Milo M. Quaife, pp. 77-110, 288-295.

1849-1850. Narrative gold rush journal, probably expanded for publication, of a Philadelphia teacher who traveled to California across Mexico via Tampico and San Blas; good observations of life in Mexico and at the diggings in both northern and southern mines; processes of mining and articles of agreement of the Hart's Bar Draining and Mining Company; prospecting at Salmon Falls, Mariposa, Tuolumne, Stanislaus, etc.; opinions on amusements and the state of morals and religion in California.

YOUNG, SHELDON, 1815-1892   3201

In THE SHADOW OF THE ARROW, by Margaret Long, pp. 241-263. Caldwell, Idaho: Caxton Printers, 1941. Rev. and enl. ed., pp. 259-279. 1950.

Mar 1849-Feb 1850. Overland diary of Mormon traveling from Joliet, Illinois, to California, as a member of Jefferson Hunt wagon train from Salt Lake City to Los Angeles; first written account of Death Valley; brief notes on camps, distances, illnesses and loss of men.

Extract in "ONTO AN ALKALI VALLEY," by Elza I. Edwards, pp. 7-8. Los Angeles: Edwards and Williams, 1948.

In JOURNALS OF FORTY-NINERS, edited by Le Roy R. and Ann W. Hafen, pp. 60-66.

Jul-Oct 1849. Salt Lake City to Los Angeles.

1850

ABBEY, JAMES   3202

CALIFORNIA: A TRIP ACROSS THE PLAINS IN THE SPRING OF 1850. New Albany, Ind.: Kent & Norman, J.R. Nunemacher, 1850. 64 pp. Reprint. MAGAZINE OF HISTORY, extra no. 183, 46 (1933):107-163.

Apr-Sep 1850. New Albany, Indiana, man's gold rush diary kept for friends at home; from St. Joseph, with good notes on travel conditions, incidents and people; organization of their train under Capt. R.P. Stevens; a sense of the thousands of gold seekers on the trail in 1850 and the race to get there ahead of others: "before the sun had risen we had left some eighty teams in our rear"; contending with dust, flies, heat and cold; harrassment by Digger Indians; having to buy water at speculation prices and cutting hay for their oxen in the Humboldt; a clear, visual impression of the gold rush trail; disappointing mining on Weaver Creek.

ALEMANY, JOSE SADOC   3203

Weber, Francis J., ed. and trans. "The Long Lost Ecclesiastical Diary of Archbishop Alemany." CALIFORNIA HISTORICAL SOCIETY QUARTERLY 43 (1964):319-330.

1850-1852. Extracts from diary of Spanish archbishop of Monterey; the pope's commission to go to California, "where others are drawn by gold, you must go to carry the cross"; visiting the holy places in Rome before departure; from Paris to London, meeting with Cardinal Newman and others; to San Francisco on the COLUMBUS; church work in Los Angeles, Santa Barbara and San Francisco, with special attention to the condition of missions; pastoral visits throughout California.

BARRINGTON, ALEXANDER   3204

In A CALIFORNIA GOLD RUSH MISCELLANY, edited by Jane B. Grabhorn, pp. 3-9. San Francisco: Grabhorn Press, 1934.

Apr-Dec 1850. Gold rush journal of a man from St. Marys, Ohio, kept aboard the PAOLI, with brief notes of ship life; work and earnings in the diggings; beginning of his return on the ANTELOPE via Panama.

BEALE, JANE HOWISON, 1815-1882   3205

THE JOURNAL OF JANE HOWISON BEALE OF FREDERICKS-BURG, VIRGINIA. Fredericksburg, Va.: Historic Fredericksburg Foundation, 1979. 82 pp.

1850-1862 (with gaps). Journal begun to cope with the loss of husband and mother; grief and the solace of religious faith; domestic details and concern for her many children; notes on relatives and neighbors; war news; life under Union occupation; deprivations; death of son in battle; her views on slavery; under bombardment during battle of Fredericksburg.

BELL, WILLIAM H.   3206

Wilentz, Sean, ed. "Crime, Poverty and the Streets of New York City." HISTORY WORKSHOP 7 (1979):126-155.

1850-1851. New York policeman's diary of his duties as inspector of secondhand dealers and junk shops, as well as general police work; much petty thievery, runaway slaves and homelessness and poverty of immigrants whom he tried to assist; frequent appearances in court and at the Tombs prison, where he witnessed an execution by hanging, concluding that "It was the most sickening sight I ever beheld and God grant that I may never have an occasion to witness another execution, and that the death penalty may be abolished and imprisonment for life substituted."

BENNETT, JAMES, d. 1869   3207

OVERLAND JOURNEY TO CALIFORNIA. New Harmony, Ind.: New Harmony Times, 1906. 45 pp.

Apr-Oct 1850. Gold rush diary of a journalist and member of Robert Owen's community at New Harmony; route via St. Joseph, the Platte, Black Hills, Sweetwater, etc.; cholera, mishaps and accidents; difficulty in fording the Platte; a few notes on Sioux; having to deny entreaties of emigrants for food and the usual picture of the Humboldt strewn with carcasses of dead animals.

BROOKS, ABIEL EASTER   3208

In PICTURES OF GOLD RUSH CALIFORNIA, edited by Milo M. Quaife, pp. 330-334.

Sep 1850. Brief account of handling a case of theft in a mining camp with names of all persons involved.

BROWN, ADAM MERCER, 1826-1910   3209

Kiefer, David M., ed. "Over Barren Plains and Rock-bound Mountains." MONTANA: THE MAGAZINE OF WESTERN HISTORY 22, no. 4 (1972):16-29.

1850-1851. Extracts from the gold rush diary of a Pittsburgh member of the Harrisville California Company; notes on route and conditions of travel; a June 12 entry from the register at Fort Laramie with numbers of men, women and children registered to that date; thence to the Sweetwater, Salt Lake and the Humboldt, with detailed notes of desperate conditions there and reports of Indian depredations.

BROWN, JOHN LOWERY, 1770?-1852   3210

Wright, Muriel H. "The Journal of John Lowery Brown, of the Cherokee nation en route to California in 1850." CHRONICLES OF OKLAHOMA 12 (1934):177-213.

Apr-Nov 1850. Gold rush journey from Grand Saline in present Adair County, Oklahoma, with company largely of Cherokee Indians; route along Santa Fe Trail to Bent's Fort, thence to Salt Lake, across the desert to the Humboldt and finally to the gold camp at Weberville in the Placerville area; change of command en route from Clement McNair to Thomas Taylor; devastation of cholera; difficulties in the desert.

BROWN, WARREN, b. 1836   3211

HISTORY OF THE TOWN OF HAMPTON FALLS, NEW HAMPSHIRE. Concord, N.H.: Rumford Press, 1900. 2 vols. Diary, vol. 1, pp. 483-499.

1850-1898. Diary of life at Hampton Falls; weather, farming, public incidents, etc.

CARRINGTON, ALBERT, 1813-1889   3212

"Diary of Albert Carrington." HEART THROBS OF THE WEST 8 (1947):77-132.

1850-1855 (with gaps). Mormon leader's journey from Salt Lake to Washington, D.C., with Howard Stansbury, whom he had assisted with the Salt Lake region survey; mostly scientific notes on route, terrain, soils, minerals, etc.; references to Jim Bridger as guide; notes on Indians; from St. Louis to Washington, with detailed account of meetings with Mormon representatives and other politicians, sightseeing, attending scientific lectures and sessions of Congress and hearing Jenny Lind; spending much time making final maps of the region he had surveyed; return to Salt Lake, then work as a mineralogist with a party exploring the Sevier River region.

CHALMERS, ROBERT, 1820-1891   3213

Kelly, Charles, ed. "The Journal of Robert Chalmers." UTAH HISTORICAL QUARTERLY 20 (1952):31-55.

Apr-Sep 1850. Gold rush diary of a Scottish immigrant to Canada; journey from Haldimand County, Ontario, to Coloma, California, where he settled permanently; riverboat travel to Independence, Missouri, with notes of a fire, snags and man overboard; route via Fort Bridger, the Salt Desert and the Humboldt; distances, camps and hazards of the overland journey, including cholera.

CHANDLER, JOHN   3214

Borome, Joseph A., ed. "John Chandler's Visit to America." FRIENDS HISTORICAL ASSOCIATION BULLETIN 48, no. 1 (1959):21-62.

Jun-Sep 1850. British Quaker abolitionist's experiences in Haiti and visit to the United States and Canada, meeting with Quakers wherever he went; stay in New York, where he commended Quaker work at the Bloomingdale Lunatic Asylum; travels by stagecoach and train to Philadelphia, Ohio, Indiana, Kentucky, etc.; considerable time in Washington, where he tired of the debates in Congress; visits to churches, schools and farms; contacts with the American Anti-Slavery Society and references to Richard Mott and Elijah Coffin; voyage on the CRESCENT CITY, with vignettes of passengers.

CHRISTY, THOMAS, b. 1829?   3215

THOMAS CHRISTY'S ROAD ACROSS THE PLAINS: A GUIDE TO THE ROUTE FROM MORMON CROSSING, NOW OMAHA, NEBRASKA, TO THE CITY OF SACRAMENTO, CALIFORNIA...TOGETHER WITH HIS DIARY OF THE SAME JOURNEY. Edited by Robert H. Becker. Denver: Old West, 1969. 25, 208 pp.

Apr-Aug 1850. Gold rush diary and trail guide of Iowan from Van Buren County; departure from Council Bluffs with notes of route, camps, conditions of travel, ferries, etc.; encounters with Indians; unusual success with their oxen because they rested them every midday and were not overloaded; anger at careless emigrants who caused prairie fires; wagons and supplies littering the trail and emigrants "continually coming in starving" at the Humboldt; diarist's doubts about chances of success for many gold seekers.

CLAPP, JOHN T.   3216

A JOURNAL OF TRAVELS TO AND FROM CALIFORNIA. Kalamazoo: Geo. A. Fitch, Printer, 1851. 67 pp. Reprint. Kalamazoo: Kalamazoo Public Museum, 1977.

Mar 1850-Jan 1851. Diary of trip to visit California; joining Lake County Illinois Company at Council Bluffs; Fourth of July celebration with handkerchiefs on poles, salute of firearms and fruit cake saved for the occasion; "desolation, misery and death" of crossing the desert and Sierra Nevada; visiting mines and working as a joiner in San Francisco with information on commerce there; return to New York on sailing ship SOUTH AMERICA to Panama and aboard the PROMETHEUS to New York; meeting his wife in Pennsylvania and returning home to Kalamazoo.

COIT, JOHN SUMMERFIELD, 1829-1867   **3217**

In THE CIVIL WAR DIARIES OF JAMES B. FAULKS AND THE PERSONAL DIARIES OF JOHN SUMMERFIELD COIT, by Henry L. Lambdin, pp. 43-81 passim. Madison, N.J.: The Commission on Archives and History, Northern New Jersey Annual Conference, The United Methodist Church, 1978.

1850?-1867. Very brief extracts scattered through biography of diarist, a Methodist clergyman serving in various New Jersey pastorates and, lastly, in the Iowa Center Circuit of the Des Moines Conference; family matters, financial concerns, illnesses and remedies; a few references to the Civil War and the death of Abraham Lincoln.

CROSS, WILLIAM BERRY, d. 1891   **3218**

"The Company on the Crescent, from Salem, Mass., and an Incident of Their Voyage." NEW ENGLAND HISTORICAL AND GENEALOGICAL REGISTER 90 (1936):36-41.

Mar 1850. Brief extract from a much longer diary describing voyage of the CRESCENT from Salem to California, bound for the gold rush; attempt of the CRESCENT and CHARLES to rendezvous, resulting in danger and damage as ships were repeatedly crashed together by a rogue wind; reactions of passengers and crew in imperiled ships.

CULBERTSON, THADDEUS AINSWORTH, 1823-1850   **3219**

"Journal of an Expedition to the Mauvaises Terres and the Upper Missouri in 1850." SMITHSONIAN INSTITUTION ANNUAL REPORT 5 (1850): 84-145. Reprint. 32nd Cong., Spec. sess., 1851, S. Doc. 1, pp. 84-132. Edited by John F. McDermott. Bureau of American Ethnology Bulletin 147. Washington, D.C.: United States Government Printing Office, 1952. 164 pp.

Apr-Jul 1850. Exploring expedition made to collect specimens, including a prairie dog, buffalo head, birds, fossils and plants, for the Smithsonian Institution; customs of Gros Ventres, Assiniboins, Yanktons, Tetons, Blackfoot and Arikaras along the Missouri River; traveling on the EL PASO up the river stopping at forts Pierre, Clark, Buthold and Union and Elk Horn Prairie.

DAVIS, SARAH, 1826-1906   **3220**

In COVERED WAGON WOMEN, edited by Kenneth L. Holmes, vol. 2, pp. 171-206.

May-Oct 1850. Cass County, Michigan, Quaker's overland journey to California, settling in Nevada City; diary started after "viewing the Platte River and I think it is beautiful so I think I will write a little on the subject"; scenery, daily work, camp incidents, animals, birds, graves passed and Snake Indians.

DAVIS, STEPHEN CHAPIN, 1833-1856   **3221**

CALIFORNIA GOLD RUSH MERCHANT. Edited by Benjamin B. Richards. San Marino, Calif.: Huntington Library, 1956. 124 pp.

1850-1854. Enterprising Nashua, New Hampshire, teenager's voyage on the PHILADELPHIA with his brother Josiah to Panama, thence on the TENNESSEE to San Francisco and Long Bar on the Yuba, where the brothers operated a store and boarding house; frequent trips to San Francisco with good notes on events there, including fire of 1851; to Oregon on the MERCHANTMAN and immediate return to San Francisco; home on the OREGON, again via Panama, with account of riot at Chagres between natives and Americans; return to California with others from Nashua on the UNITED STATES and FREMONT; successful storekeeping for two years at Coulterville, with good descriptions of the area; return home on the UNCLE SAM, far richer than forty-niners who had gone for gold; an excellent diary with good descriptions of ship life, business and conditions in gold rush California by an intelligent, God-fearing and intrepid young man.

DENVER, JAMES W., 1817-1892   **3222**

Meyer, Richard E., ed. "The Denver Diary: Overland to California in 1850." ARIZONA AND THE WEST 17 (1975):35-62.

May-Sep 1850. Gold rush diary of Platte City, Missouri, lawyer traveling in the company of James M. Estill; from Fort Leavenworth via Pacific Springs and Salt Lake; route, camps and conditions of travel on a less harrowing journey than most; articulate notes on events, scenery and people, many mentioned by name, until diary ends abruptly with mention of cholera near the Humboldt Sink.

DICKINSON, ARNELL F., 1818-1867   **3223**

"Dickinson Diary." WESTCHESTER COUNTY HISTORICAL BULLETIN 24 (1948):20-29.

1850-1852. Extracts from diary of owner of large farm at Cantitoe Corners, New York; visit to niece, Hannah Frost Knapp, in Brooklyn and New York City; attendance at Friends Quarterly Meeting at Chappaqua, State Agricultural Fair at Albany, county fair at Tarrytown and fair of the Society of Agriculture and Horticulture at White Plains; honeymoon trip to Boston via New Haven and Springfield; notes on local politics, surveying equipment and farm machinery.

DUTTON, JEROME, 1826-1893   **3224**

"Across the Plains in 1850." ANNALS OF IOWA, 3d ser. 9 (1909-1910):447-483.

Mar-Sep 1850. Letters and journal of Clinton County, Iowa, man's overland journey to Sacramento; failure of Rudolphus S. Dickinson to provide enough wagons and oxen for his party, resulting in diarist and other men having to walk; departure from Scott County; notes on route and terrain.

EDMUNDSON, WILLIAM   **3225**

"Diary Kept by William Edmundson, of Oskaloosa, while Crossing the Western Plains in 1850." ANNALS OF IOWA, 3d ser. 8 (1907-1909):516-535.

May-Oct 1850. Journey to Placerville, California, via Platte River, Chimney Rock, Green River, etc.; almost entirely devoted to route, camps and distances; a brief description of Salt Lake City.

ELY, EDWARD, 1827-1858 3226

THE WANDERINGS OF EDWARD ELY, A MID-19TH CENTURY SEAFARER'S DIARY. Edited by Anthony and Allison Sirna. New York: Hastings House, 1954. 219 pp.

Extracts in A TREASURY OF THE WORLD'S GREAT DIARIES, edited by Philip Dunaway, pp. 69-71.

1850-1852. A Bucks County, Pennsylvania, physician's sea voyage aboard the DELIA MARIA, ST. THOMAS and OREGON to regain his health; in New York, with good descriptions of the Christmas season there; voyage to India, during which diarist claims to have assumed command of the ship during the captain's drunken delirium; severe storms at Cape Horn and elsewhere, with danger heightened by sickness and incompetence of crew; calls in San Francisco, Panama, Honolulu and Singapore; an interesting sea diary, but in grandiose style obviously intended for admiring readers.

EVANS, ROBERT FRANK 3227

NOTES ON LAND AND SEA. Boston: R.G. Badger, 1922. 140 pp.

Apr-Aug 1850. Shelbyville, Tennessee, man's voyage to California; by steamer down the Mississippi to New Orleans, thence to Chagres and across Panama; up the coast to San Francisco.

FAIRBANK, NATHANIEL KELLOGG, 1829-1903 3228

De Freitas, Helen, ed. "Extracts from the Journal of Nathaniel K. Fairbank." ROCHESTER HISTORY 40, no. 3 (1978):1-24.

1850-1852. A young Sodus, New York, man's journal kept while he worked for Rochester wool merchant Aaron Erickson and lived with his family; humorous, rattling notes on flirtations, social life and constant, seemingly fruitless resolves to "drop all my boyish follies" and tend strictly to business; his reactions to Rochester visits of President Fillmore, Jenny Lind, Daniel Webster and Emerson, "a perfect Bostonian as the charicaturists make them"; becoming a Mason; some sober reflections upon the deaths of his father and beloved sister; an interesting glimpse into the youth of a man who became a wealthy leading citizen of Chicago.

FLYNT, EODOCIA CARTER CONVERSE 3229

In THE YEARS AND HOURS OF EMILY DICKINSON, by Jay Leyda, 2 vols. passim. New Haven, Conn.: Yale University Press, 1960.

1850-1886. Scattered extracts mainly on social life at Amherst, Massachusetts; visits involving members of the Dickinson family, church services and deaths, including Emily Dickinson's funeral.

FRANKLIN, WILLIAM RILEY, 1825-1891 3230

Franklin, Homer, Sr., and Franklin, Homer, Jr., eds. "Journal of William Riley Franklin to California from Missouri in 1850." ANNALS OF WYOMING 46 (1974):47-74.

May?-Jul 1850. Missourian's gold rush diary, introduced by admonitions to "courteous, kind and gentle readers" and lengthy religious effusions which continue; travel with company from Clay and Clinton counties under James R. Coffman; camps, distances, route and scenery; sympathy for and desire to evangelize Indians; dated entries, but narrative, wordy style which obscures details.

FRENCH, FRANCIS ORMOND, 1837-1893 3231

EXETER AND HARVARD EIGHTY YEARS AGO: JOURNALS AND LETTERS OF F.O. FRENCH, '57. Edited by Amos T. French. Chester, N.H.: Privately printed, 1932. 174 pp.

1850-1857. School boy's diary of youthful interests; learning to ride a horse; collecting autographs and noting impressive events in Washington, D.C., such as a speech by Henry Clay, death and funeral of Zachary Taylor, the president's levee on New Year's Day, visiting the Senate, a fire in the Library of Congress and laying the cornerstone for the Capitol; attending Rittenhouse Academy in Washington and Phillips Exeter Academy in New Hampshire; studies, school ceremonies and Fourth of July celebration; admittance to Harvard as a sophomore; studies, reading, clubs, pranks, theater attendance and romance; joining Psi Upsilon Fraternity; many political notes; honors on class day; a good picture of academy and college life.

FRENCH, JOHN 3232

Dowdell, Victor L. and Everett, Helen C., eds. "California Diary of John French." MICHIGAN HISTORY 38 (1954):33-44.

Jan 1850-Sep 1851. Spring Arbor man's brief log-type diary of a gold rush voyage on the HINDOO via Cape Horn to San Francisco and then working various claims.

FRINK, MARGARET ANN ALSIP 3233

JOURNAL OF THE ADVENTURES OF A PARTY OF CALIFORNIA GOLD-SEEKERS. Oakland? Calif., 1897. 121 pp.

In COVERED WAGON WOMEN, edited by Kenneth L. Holmes, vol. 2, pp. 55-169.

Mar-Sep 1850. Martinsville, Indiana, woman's diary of emigrant journey to California in small party led by her husband, Ledyard; many comments to her in Indiana towns about the "propriety of a lady undertaking a journey of 2,000 miles"; taking advice to carry pickles and vinegar to prevent scurvy; lodging in hotels and private homes until after crossing the Missouri River; fears of possible Indian depredations; good descriptions of various conveyances seen on the plains; a buffalo chase; laying over on Sundays to repair wagons and do other necessary chores; forts Laramie and Hall, Sublette's Cutoff and Lassen's Cutoff; notes on scenery, landmarks, camps and river crossings, especially the Platte; mention of individuals or parties abandoning goods and continuing alone, hoping to travel faster; hardships and problems with worn-out wagons and animals; gratitude at finding herself "safe at the end of our long and eventful journey."

GAYLORD, ORANGE, b. 1823 3234

"Orange Gaylord." OREGON PIONEER ASSOCIATION TRANSACTIONS (1917):403-439.

1850-1851. Journey from Marshall County, Illinois, to the Carson Valley and Placerville, then to Oregon, with activities there, including much boat travel in the area; voyage down the coast to San Francisco and San Diego, across Panama and on to New York.

Mar-Aug 1853. Brief notes of a journey from Magnolia, Illinois, to Oregon City.

GLISAN, RODNEY, b. 1827   3235

JOURNAL OF ARMY LIFE. San Francisco: A.L. Bancroft, 1874. 511 pp.

1850-1858. Extracts from the journal of an assistant surgeon serving in the Washington and Oregon territorial wars; life at various Great Plains and western forts and garrisons; marches and battles, including the Rogue River campaigns; both overland and sea journeys to and from San Francisco; steamboat travel on the Columbia; some medical information, long discourses on the life of a soldier and notes on customs and nature of plains and western Indians; references to Randolph B. Marcy, R.C. Buchanan and other officers; dated but narrative entries.

GOODRIDGE, SOPHIA LOIS, 1826-1903   3236

In COVERED WAGON WOMEN, edited by Kenneth L. Holmes, vol. 2, pp. 207-235.

Jun-Oct 1850. Lunenburg, Massachusetts, Mormon's diary kept from Kanesville, Iowa, to Salt Lake City; traveling with her parents, five sisters and brother; a musician, she mentions singing and dancing; sickness and deaths from cholera in their company; notes on company organization and management and on religious instruction; meeting Sioux Indians and trading with Cheyennes; met by Mormon men sent from Salt Lake to bring provisions and a letter from Brigham Young to "cheere us on our way"; climbing Independence Rock; many names of leaders and members of various companies; a bit disappointed in appearance of Salt Lake City on first arrival.

HAILMAN, JAMES W.   3237

"A Trip from Pittsburgh to St. Louis and Return in 1850." WESTERN PENNSYLVANIA HISTORICAL MAGAZINE 23 (1940):175-181.

Jan-Feb 1850. Extract covering Pittsburgh steel manufacturer's business trip to St. Louis and return; travel on a succession of riverboats, including the NEW ENGLAND, EMPIRE STATE, SALUDA, etc., most of whose passengers and entertainments he regarded as unsavory; social and business affairs in St. Louis.

HARLAN, AARON WORD, 1811-1911   3238

"Journal of A.W. Harlan while Crossing the Plains in 1850." ANNALS OF IOWA, 3d ser. 11 (1913):32-62.

May-Sep 1850. Iowan's journey from Athens, Missouri, to the California gold fields via Council Bluffs, Platte River and Laramie; detailed notes on terrain, conditions of travel, camps and distances; great hardship for man and beast, especially on the desert, with dead animals averaging "100 to the mile"; congestion of people, wagons and stock at the Carson River.

HEINRICH, CHARLES, 1824-1856   3239

Wolf, John Quincy, ed. "Journal of Charles Heinrich." ARKANSAS HISTORICAL QUARTERLY 24 (1965):241-283.

1850-1856. Extracts covering German immigrant's settling in Batesville and establishing businesses, including a bakery, ice cream parlor and ice house, after an unsuccessful fur trading venture; sad references to loneliness compounded by chronic shyness and embarrassment over his English; membership in the singing society, with notes on its concerts, and lessons from a German music teacher; religious introspections and

Presbyterian church activities; a trip to Wolf-Bayou-Springs for his failing health; return to Batesville to endure the final stages of tuberculosis. Translated from the German.

HEWITT, HENRY LEEDS   3240

"Foundation of Bellingham." WASHINGTON HISTORICAL QUARTERLY 24 (1933):133-148.

May-Jun 1850. Journey from Vermilion, Ohio, to California, with diary ending at the Humboldt; very brief notes of camps, distances, conditions of travel, etc.

1853-1856. Trips between San Francisco and Bellingham, Washington, on schooners WILLIAM ALLEN, TARQUINA, LUCAS, etc., mainly trading in coal; brief notes of sea trip, via Panama, to New York, thence back to Vermilion; return to Bellingham, with continuous travels from there in pursuit of his coal interests.

HEYWOOD, MARTHA SPENCE, 1811-1873   3241

NOT BY BREAD ALONE. Edited by Juanita Brooks. Salt Lake City: Utah State Historical Society, 1978. 141 pp.

1850-1856. Journal of Mormon convert from Hamilton, Ontario, with entries beginning at Kanesville, Iowa; full, articulate account of journey to Utah; at Nephi, work as a milliner and teacher; social and cultural life there; plural marriage to Joseph Leland Heywood and candor about its difficulties; loneliness and management of a farm at Salt Lake during long absence of her husband; concise abstracts of Brigham Young's sermons; an intelligent and introspective journal.

HINDE, EDMUND CAVILEER, 1830-1909   3242

JOURNAL OF EDMUND CAVILEER HINDE. Edited by Jerome Peltier. Fairfield, Wash.: Ye Galleon, 1983. 82 pp.

1850-1852. Gold rush extracts from a diary covering a much longer period; from St. Louis, with notes on route via Fort Kearny, travel conditions, mileage covered and prices; the usual sufferings from hunger, thirst and extremes of weather, plus his face "swollen and festered all over" from insect bites; sporadic notes of life in San Francisco and at various diggings; return to New Orleans, where he was swindled of his gold rush earnings and unsuccessfully attempted to recover them through lawsuits.

HOLBROOK, CHARLES WILLIAM, b. 1828   3243

Hall, D.D., ed. "A Yankee Tutor in the Old South." NEW ENGLAND QUARTERLY 33 (1960):82-91.

1850-1852. Extracts from Holden, Massachusetts, student's account of his final year at Williams College, then his experiences as a tutor to the children of a Rockingham, North Carolina, planter; finding himself "much delighted with the warm-heartedness and sociability of the southerners" but distressed at seeing slavery firsthand, especially slaves being sold away from their families; his and his employers' reactions to UNCLE TOM'S CABIN.

HOLMES, HENRY MCCALL, b. 1834   3244

DIARY OF HENRY MCCALL HOLMES. State College, Miss., 1968. 99 pp. Diary, pp. 6-54.

Jul-Aug 1850. Journal, partly revised, of teenager's trip to Washington, D.C., starting from Charleston, South Carolina; by boat to Wilmington, North Carolina, and by train to Richmond and sightseeing there; by steamer MOUNT VERNON from Acquia Creek to the nation's capital; visiting the Senate, with notes on senators Foote and Benton, the Smithsonian institution, Mount Vernon, the Patent Office, Capitol and White House.

1861-1865 (with gaps). War diary, interspersed with extracts from diary of his sister Emma; service as assistant surgeon to the First Florida Cavalry; primarily a record of his unit's movements in Tennessee, Kentucky, Georgia, Alabama and North Carolina, including the battle of Chickamauga, the Atlanta campaign and the Franklin and Nashville campaign; extremely brief entries becoming a bit more descriptive by 1864; list of expenses, casualties, etc., appended.

HOUGH, WARREN   3245

"The 1850 Overland Diary of Dr. Warren Hough." ANNALS OF WYOMING 46 (1974):207-216.

Mar-Jul 1850. Doctor's journey from Deer Grove, Cook County, Illinois, to Salmon Falls, California, from which he later returned; bare notes of route, distances, deaths and Indian alarms.

HUDSON, JOHN, 1826-1850   3246

A FORTY-NINER IN UTAH: WITH THE STANSBURY EXPLORATION OF GREAT SALT LAKE: LETTERS AND JOURNALS OF JOHN HUDSON. Edited by Brigham D. Madsen. Salt Lake City: Tanner Trust Fund, University of Utah Library, 1981. 227 pp. Journal, pp. 127-192.

Apr-Jun 1850. Young English Mormon's journal of the Howard Stansbury survey, for which he was draughtsman; exploring the lake and Antelope Island, its shores and surrounding country by boat and on foot for the purpose of locating a possible rail route; excellent descriptions of wildlife, especially water birds, geology and austere beauty of the landscape; hardships and discomforts, including constant torment from gnats, borne stoically; a few notes on Digger Indians and many references to colleagues Albert Carrington and John Williams Gunnison, as well as Stansbury.

HUSE, CHARLES ENOCH, 1825-1898   3247

THE HUSE JOURNAL: SANTA BARBARA IN THE 1850s. Edited by Edith B. Conkey. Translated by Francis Price. Santa Barbara, Calif.; Santa Barbara Historical Society, 1977. 279 pp.

1850-1857 (with gaps). Harvard graduate's account of real estate and other business ventures in San Francisco and, more extensively, his life in Santa Barbara, where he served as county clerk, recorder, auditor and court interpreter for Judge Joaquin Carrillo, as well as establishing a law practice; almost encyclopedic coverage of events, people, business, shipping, legal and court matters and politics, including chicanery; references to Dr. Samuel Brinkerhoff, Vicente Deffeliz, Charles Fernald, R.G. Glenn, Augustus F. Henchman, Eugene Lies and others; descriptive notes on missions and ranches; material on newspapers; an unusually full diary by a man who functioned with ease in both the English and Spanish-speaking communities of southern California. Translated from the Spanish.

INGALLS, ELEAZER STILLMAN, 1820-1879   3248

JOURNAL OF A TRIP TO CALIFORNIA, BY THE OVERLAND ROUTE ACROSS THE PLAINS IN 1850-51. Waukegan, Ill.: Tobey & Co., Printers, 1852. 51 pp. Fairfield, Wash.: Ye Galleon, 1979. 80 pp.

1850-1851. Antioch, Illinois, lawyer's trip from Lake County, Illinois, to Hangtown, California; lengthy descriptions of Iowa City, St. Joseph and high prices charged emigrants; routes taken, road conditions, a stampede and scenery, especially the grand sight of the Rocky Mountains after crossing the desert at night; traveling or camping at different times with wagon train of Capt. William Sublette and Dr. Reed's Pennsylvania Train; lively description of Antoine Robidoux and his trading post; hardships, pickpockets, good samaritans and an account of the mines.

JAMES, SAMUEL, 1806?-1866   3249

In FROM GRAND MOUND TO SCATTER CREEK: THE HOMES OF JAMESTOWN, by David James, pp. 11-20. Olympia, Wash.: State Capitol Historical Association of Washington, 1980. 108 pp. 2d ed. 1981.

Oct 1850-Sep 1851. Diary of overland journey from Wisconsin to Oregon, wintering in Iowa; brief entries of day-by-day events, road and travel conditions, grass, water and Indians.

JAMISON, SAMUEL M., d. 1909   3250

"Diary of S.M. Jamison." NEVADA HISTORICAL SOCIETY QUARTERLY 10, no. 4 (1967):1-26.

Apr-Jul 1850. Gold rush diary of a man from Indiana, Pennsylvania, who later settled at Reno; from Independence with a horse and mule train; brief notes of route, camps and conditions of travel; Sunday rest for men and animals in spite of "a great many wagons passing"; mining at Georgetown.

KILGORE, WILLIAM H., b. 1817?   3251

THE KILGORE JOURNAL OF AN OVERLAND JOURNEY TO CALIFORNIA IN THE YEAR 1850. Edited by Joyce R. Muench. New York: Hastings House, 1949. 63 pp.

Apr-Aug 1850. Emigrant journey from Lee County, Iowa, to settle in California with his father, Matthew Kilgore, and R.D. Kepley; a prairie fire leaving the burnt corpses of many deer, buffalo and wolves; difficulties such as a ferry accident on the Platte, "alkalied" horses and deep snow in June in the Rockies; a good description of Salt Lake City and surrounding area; some Indian incidents; names on graves; desperation of hungry emigrants on the Humboldt where "we see human suffering here almost beyond description"; across the Sierra Nevada to Placerville and the Sacramento Valley, with notes on mining life there and diarist's obvious preference for its agricultural potential.

KULLGREN, CARL ALVOR, b. 1826   3252

Friman, Axel. "Two Swedes in the California Goldfields." SWEDISH AMERICAN HISTORICAL QUARTERLY 34 (1983):102-130.

1850-1856. Article summarizing and containing extracts from the diary of a Swede traveling to the gold fields and his experiences there with his friend Carl August Modh; ship life aboard the SVEA on voyage around Cape Horn to San Francisco; work in Sonoma building a bridge and other carpentry; at the gold fields at Auburn, having little luck and concluding that he must have been a madman to leave his homeland.

LAIRD, JOHN CHAMBERLAIN, 1825-1902   3253

Nute, Grace Lee. "Minnesota as Seen by Travelers: A Western Jaunt in 1850." MINNESOTA HISTORY 12 (1931):157-168.

Oct-Nov 1850. Letter-diary covering journey from Galena, Illinois, up the Mississippi on the NOMINEE under a colorful captain, Orrin Smith; notes on towns in Iowa, Illinois, Wisconsin and especially Minnesota; prospects for agriculture; prices and wages; lumbering; comments on large number of Winnebago Indians on board; return to Lafayette County, Wisconsin.

LANGWORTHY, FRANKLIN, 1798-1855?   3254

SCENERY OF THE PLAINS, MOUNTAINS AND MINES. Ogdensburgh, N.Y.: J.C. Sprague, 1855. 324 pp. Edited by Paul C. Phillips. Princeton: Princeton University Press, 1932. 292 pp.

1850-1853. Diary of overland journey from Mount Carroll, Illinois, to California via the Great Salt Lake; scientific observations; careful accounts of scenery and philosophical comments; details of Mormon life, customs and treatment of emigrants; ravages of cholera among emigrants; two years' residence in California with notes on life, customs and country; return by steamship BROTHER JONATHAN, giving lectures on scientific subjects to fellow passengers; crossing Central America and proceeding to New York on the PROMETHEUS, thence by rail, river and coach to Illinois.

LOOMIS, LEANDER VANESS, 1827-1909   3255

A JOURNAL OF THE BIRMINGHAM EMIGRATING COMPANY. Edited by Edgar M. Ledyard. Salt Lake City: Legal Printing, 1928. 198 pp. Journal, pp. 1-136.

Apr-Aug 1850. Journal of observant and uncomplaining member of gold rush company, "a jolly set," from Birmingham, Iowa, to California; camps, distances, usual trouble with horses wandering off and sickness; "a band of music" at evening camp; notes on Omaha, Pawnee and Cheyenne Indians; to Fort Laramie and via Sublette's Cutoff to Fort Hall; at Independence Rock where he "clumb to the top of this tremendous mass of stone and from here could see apparently all over creation"; noting act of kindness by a lone packer; sparse grass and dust in Humboldt region causing more suffering than all the rest of the journey; arriving in Sacramento, with description of horse market and gambling; seeing old Fort Sutter.

LOVELAND, CYRUS CLARK   3256

CALIFORNIA TRAIL HERD: THE 1850 MISSOURI-TO-CALIFORNIA JOURNAL. Edited by Richard H. Dillon. Los Gatos, Calif.: Talisman Press, 1961. 137 pp.

Mar-Sep 1850. Cowboy's journal of a cattle drive under Walter Crow to deliver beef to the gold fields; logistics and problems of herding and driving; camps, grass, water and treatment of sick cattle; considerable information on numbers, sizes and losses of trail herds; sickness and deaths from cholera among cowboys and emigrants; names on graves; "laying by" on Sunday; the agony of the Humboldt for men and stock; notes on Indians; arrival in California.

LOW, GARRETT W., 1820-1898   3257

GOLD RUSH BY SEA. Edited by Kenneth Haney. Philadelphia: University of Pennsylvania Press, 1941. 187 pp.

1850-1852 (with gaps). Fascinating journal of a young man from Erie, Pennsylvania, on a sea voyage to the California gold fields; by Lake Erie boat THE BELLE which "rides no better than a half-submerged outhouse"; from New York City on the WASHINGTON IRVING, with long, entertaining notes of the conversations, activities and intrigues of a bizarre collection of passengers, as well as Samuel Plumer, the captain, whose cruelty and madness endangered their lives; a frightful rounding of Cape Horn because of storms and disorganization of the ship; call at Valparaiso where passengers lodged complaints against Plumer at the American consulate; a severe earthquake in Chile; transfer to the JOHN BERTRAM to San Francisco; scattered but colorful notes of life in the diggings.

MCKEEBY, LEMUEL CLARKE, 1825-1915   3258

"The Memoirs of Lemuel Clarke McKeeby." CALIFORNIA HISTORICAL SOCIETY QUARTERLY 3 (1924):45-72, 126-170.

May-Aug 1850. Gold rush diary; from Council Bluffs to California via Salt Lake, with interesting notes on Mormons, including a "handsome, well educated" Mormon girl with whom he discussed polygamy; an amusing Fourth of July; discarding wagons and continuing on horseback; in the mines at Placerville; possibly expanded later.

MCKINSTRY, BYRON NATHAN, 1818-1894   3259

THE CALIFORNIA GOLD RUSH OVERLAND DIARY OF BYRON N. MCKINSTRY. Edited by Bruce L. McKinstry. American Trails Series, 10. Glendale, Calif.: A.H. Clark, 1975. 401 pp.

1850-1852. Extensive and careful gold rush diary covering journey from Illinois and experiences in the diggings; notes on terrain, conditions of travel and beauty of scenery, contrasting with such grim details as oxen dead or dying after steep ascents; route via the Platte, Fort Hall, Carson Pass and the Humboldt; successes and failures of mining in the Mokelumne Hill vicinity; voyage home via Panama.

MASON, JAMES   3260

Olson, James C., ed. "The Diary of James Mason, Ohio to California." NEBRASKA HISTORY 33 (1952):103-121.

1850-1851 (with gaps). Gold rush diary of Irish immigrant who had settled at Cambridge, Ohio; travel from Ohio by riverboat, thence overland via Salt Lake with the Cambridge-California Mining Company to Hangtown and the Rough and Ready Mine; brief notes of distances and conditions; some evidence of cholera.

MAYNARD, DAVID SWINSON, 1808-1873   3261

In DAVID S. MAYNARD AND CATHERINE T. MAYNARD: BIOGRAPHIES OF TWO OF THE OREGON IMMIGRANTS OF 1850, by Thomas W. Prosch, pp. 8-23. Seattle: Lowman & Hanford, 1906.

Prosch, Thomas W., ed. "Diary of Dr. David S. Maynard while Crossing the Plains in 1850." WASHINGTON HISTORICAL QUARTERLY 1 (1906):50-62.

Apr-Sep 1850. Doctor's journey from Lorain County, Ohio, to Oregon and the Puget Sound area; treating cholera victims en route with little success; assistance to the newly widowed Catherine Broshears, whom he later married; lack of water and grass for enfeebled oxen.

MILES, WILLIAM 3262

JOURNAL OF THE SUFFERINGS AND HARDSHIPS OF CAPT. PARKER H. FRENCH'S OVERLAND EXPEDITION TO CALIFORNIA. Chambersburg, Pa.: Printed at the Valley Spirit Office, 1851. 24 pp. Reprint. New York: Cadmus Book Shop, 1916. 26 pp. Fairfield, Wash.: Ye Galleon, 1970.

May-Dec 1850. Carlisle, Pennsylvania, man's journal and summary of the disastrous commercial gold rush journey of Parker H. French's Express Wagon Train, during which many died; succumbing to French's advertisements and guarantees at New York; voyage on the GEORGIA and FALCON to New Orleans, with roll of passengers and "compact of government" for the expedition; thence overland via Lavacca, San Antonio, El Paso, the Rio Grande and Gila River regions to San Diego; problems en route, including provision of wild rather than broken mules and the forced sale of most of the supplies because of French's bad debts.

MOORMAN, MADISON BERRYMAN, 1824-1915 3263

THE JOURNAL OF MADISON BERRYMAN MOORMAN. Edited by Irene D. Paden. California Historical Society Special Publication, no. 23. San Francisco: California Historical Society, 1948. 150 pp.

Apr 1850-Feb 1851. Overland journey from Nashville, Tennessee, to the California gold fields; by riverboat to St. Louis and Independence; thence with Havihah Company; usual landmarks and flowery descriptions of scenery; measles, cholera and other illnesses in his and other trains; Fourth of July parade and celebration; stopover for shoeing mules at Salt Lake City, where he enjoyed the hospitality of Mormon people but disliked pomposity of church dignitaries; desert crossing, encountering Indians in Humboldt region; final stage of trip on foot with five companions; mining quartz on Cosumnes River.

MORRIS, ANNA MARIA DE CAMP, 1813-1861 3264

In COVERED WAGON WOMEN, edited by Kenneth L. Holmes, vol. 2, pp. 15-43.

May-Jul 1850. Travel diary of wife of Maj. Gouverneur Morris from Fort Leavenworth to Santa Fe; traveling by carriage in comfort with maids, drivers and all services provided along with many attentions from Dr. Charles McDougal, the physician with the company; sights, incidents and accidents, storms and supplies of fresh buffalo meat; curious Indians; being entertained by Col. Edmund B. Alexander, the commandant at Las Vegas, New Mexico, and his wife; seeing ruins of old church at Pecos; finding Santa Fe "the most miserable, squalid looking place I ever beheld ... all mud."

MUNGER, JAMES F., 1830-1852 3265

TWO YEARS IN THE PACIFIC AND ARCTIC OCEANS AND CHINA, BEING A JOURNAL OF EVERY DAY LIFE ON BOARD SHIP. Vernon, N.Y.: J.R. Howlett, Printer, 1852. 79 pp. Fairfield, Wash.: Ye Galleon, 1967.

1850-1852. Journal of a young Verona, New York, man whose first whaling voyage ended when he fell from the rigging of the ANNIE BUCKNAM and drowned off Florida; mostly log entries while at sea, but interesting notes on the inhabitants of ports in China, Hawaii and on Bering Island.

NORELIUS, ERIC, 1833-1862 3266

Johnson, Emeroy, trans. "Early Life of Eric Norelius." AUGUSTANA HISTORICAL SOCIETY PUBLICATIONS 4 (1934):1-319.

1850-1854. Swedish immigrant's diary combined with memoirs; beginning with voyage to America and continuing with notes of life among the Swedes in Columbus, Ohio; attendance at Columbus College.

PANGBORN, DAVID KNAPP 3267

"A Journey from New York to San Francisco." AMERICAN HISTORICAL REVIEW 9 (1903-1904):104-115.

Jun-Aug 1850. Extracts covering a voyage from New York to San Francisco via Panama, where he was delayed; names of many ships; problems, including "cholera on shore and small pox aboard."

PARSONS, LUCENA PFUFFER, 1821-1905 3268

In COVERED WAGON WOMEN, edited by Kenneth L. Holmes, vol. 2, pp. 237-294.

Jun-Sep 1850, Jan-Jun 1851. Extracts from diary of Janesville, Wisconsin, woman accompanying her new husband, George Washington Parsons, to California; beginning at Council Bluffs crossing of the Missouri in large company soon reduced by cholera; noting numerous new graves; stopping near Fort Laramie for men to shoe the cattle whose hooves were wearing out on the rough roads; seeing many Indian huts around Fort Bridger; no entries during stop at Gardners Mills on Jordan River to rest themselves and cattle; a diatribe against the Mormons after "spending a long dreary winter among the Saints"; resuming journey on Salt Lake Road to join California Trail; trying her hand at mining in Chalk Mountains with limited success; diary ending abruptly just short of the Sierra Nevada.

PETERSON, ANDREW, 1818-1898 3269

McKnight, Roger, ed. "Andrew Peterson's Emigrant Voyage of 1850." SWEDISH PIONEER HISTORICAL QUARTERLY 31 (1980):3-11, 136.

May-Jul 1850. Brief notes of a voyage from Sweden to Boston; a terrible storm, after which the diarist helped make a new mast for the ship; even shorter entries of journey to Iowa by train, canal boat, Great Lakes steamer, etc.

Nute, Grace Lee. "The Diaries of a Swedish-American Farmer, Andrew Peterson." AMERICAN INSTITUTE OF SWEDISH ARTS, LITERATURE AND SCIENCE YEARBOOK (1945):105-132.

1855-1876 (with gaps). Extracts covering residence in a community of Swedish Baptists led by Frederik Olaus Nilsson; buying a claim at Clearwater Lake, now Waconia, Minnesota, where he cleared land and built a log cabin; sharing work with various neighbors; the development of a prosperous farm from the wilderness, producing crops of wheat and barley, dairy products, salt pork, smoked beef and maple syrup.

In BRING WARM CLOTHES: LETTERS AND PHOTOS FROM MINNESOTA'S PAST, collected by Peg Meier, pp. 56-58.

Aug-Sep 1858. Extract chiefly of farm work, often shared with neighbors, and church meetings.

McKnight, Roger. "Andrew Peterson's Journals: An Analysis." SWEDISH PIONEER HISTORICAL QUARTERLY 28 (1977):153-172.

> 1859-1895. Brief extracts revealing his life both as a farmer and eventually a Baptist minister; an important record of farming, church work, public service and immigrant pioneer life in Minnesota.

PIGMAN, WALTER GRIFFITH, 1818-1892   3270

THE JOURNAL OF WALTER GRIFFITH PIGMAN. Edited by Ulla S. Fawkes. Mexico, Mo.: Walter G. Staley, 1942. 82 pp.

> 1850-1851. Gold rush journey from Felicity, Ohio, in a company led by James Fife; traveling conditions, provisions and friendly Indian encounters; mining experiences in California; return by ship via Acapulco and Panama.

POSTON, CHARLES DEBRILLE, 1825-1902   3271

Granger, Byrd H., ed. "Southwestern Chronicle." ARIZONA QUARTERLY 13 (1957):152-163, 251-261, 353-362.

> 1850-1899 (with gaps). Journal of man considered the "father of Arizona"; from Hardin County, Kentucky, to New Orleans by riverboat OREGON, thence to Havana on the OHIO, with detailed tourist notes; on the GEORGIA to Chagres, again with good descriptions; on foot through Panama to pick up the REPUBLIC for San Francisco where he worked as chief clerk in the surveying office of the customs house; thereafter, infrequent entries summarizing his work as manager of the Sonora Exploring and Mining Company at Tubac, a term as congressman from Arizona, law practice, world travels, land office work at Florence and old age at Phoenix, where he died in poverty.

READ, GEORGE WILLIS, 1819-1880   3272

A PIONEER OF 1850. Edited by Georgia Willis Read. Boston: Little, Brown, 1927. 185 pp. Diary, pp. 17-100.

> May-Aug 1850. Diary of physician and captain of Jefferson-California Company of Greene County, Pennsylvania, on gold rush journey from Independence to Placerville; concern for health of the company, cholera and mumps; meeting discouraged returning emigrants; arbitrating dissensions; noting pioneer graves; traveling via Fort Kearny, Fort Laramie and Sublette's Cutoff, at first "getting on finely" and later having "a peep of the elephant today."

RHODES, JOSEPH, 1823-1853   3273

Mattes, Merrill. "Joseph Rhodes and the California Gold Rush of 1850." ANNALS OF WYOMING 23 (1951):52-71. Diary, pp. 61-71.

> May-Aug 1850. Brief diary of Orange County, Indiana, man; clear indication of route via the Platte, Fort Laramie, and the Green and Humboldt rivers; the usual problems of weather, terrain, cholera, violence and dissension; Indian troubles; hunger, thirst and dying animals on the Humboldt.

ROBERTSON, ELIZA MARSH   3274

Dormon, James H. "Aspects of Acadian Plantation Life in the Mid-Nineteenth Century." LOUISIANA HISTORY 16 (1975):361-370.

> 1850-1856. Article containing extracts from the diary of the mistress of an Avery Island sugar plantation, Petite Anse; social life such as visits and dances; a "blowout" for the slaves for which she prepared ginger cakes and hot whiskey.

SAWYER, LORENZO, 1820-1891   3275

WAY SKETCHES; CONTAINING INCIDENTS OF TRAVEL ACROSS THE PLAINS. Edited by Edward Eberstadt. New York: E. Eberstadt, 1926. 125 pp.

> May-Jul 1850. Lawyer's gold rush journal with entries beginning at St. Joseph; route and distances via the Platte and Sublette's Cutoff; full notes of travel conditions and events; names of emigrant parties and individuals; buffalo hunting; difficulties of the Humboldt for man and stock , with diarist's distress at seeing dead and dying animals as well as starving emigrants begging for provisions; across the Sierra Nevada with diary ending at Coloma.

SCHLIEMANN, HEINRICH, 1822-1890   3276

SCHLIEMANN'S FIRST VISIT TO AMERICA. Edited by Shirley H. Weber. American School of Classical Studies at Athens, Gennadeion Monographs, 2. Cambridge: Harvard University Press, 1942. 100 pp.

> 1850-1851. Early travel diary of the great linguist and amateur archaeologist; attempted crossing from Liverpool to New York on steamer ATLANTIC which resorted to sail and returned due to disabled engines; successful crossing on steamer AFRICA; stay at Hotel Astor, with candid notes on customs and manners of New York society; good description of train travel to Baltimore and on to Washington, where he met President Fillmore and other notables; voyage to Panama on CRESCENT CITY and arduous crossing of the Isthmus; notes on inhabitants and disastrous climate of region; to California on the OREGON; notes on San Francisco and Sacramento, with description of San Francisco fire of June 4, 1851; successful ventures in gold trading and banking; unflattering comments on Indians, Mexicans and almost everyone; return, again via the Isthmus, and thence to Europe and St. Petersburg; an entertaining, exuberant diary mostly in narrative style.

Zochert, Donald. "Heinrich Schliemann's Chicago Journal." CHICAGO HISTORY 2 (1973):173-181.

> Nov 1867. Extracts, within article, on Chicago portion of Schliemann's third American visit; excellent description of the growing city and some of its colorful inhabitants, particularly Francis A. Hoffman; visits to brewery, waterworks, grain elevators, slaughterhouse, stockyards, railroad, schools, etc., all described in considerable detail; great interest in business, earnings, wages, etc.

SCHLIEMANN IN INDIANAPOLIS. Edited by Eli Lilly. Indianapolis: Indiana Historical Society, 1961. 95 pp. Diary, pp. 11-23.

> Mar-Jul 1869. Brief stay in New York to complete naturalization as an American citizen; thence to Indianapolis to divorce his Russian wife; much on Indiana divorce laws and on proceedings of the state senate regarding them; customs, business and character of the people; accommodation at the Bates House Hotel.

Extracts in TRAVEL ACCOUNTS OF INDIANA, compiled by Shirley McCord, pp. 235-237.

> Apr-Jun 1869.

SHEPHERD, JOSEPH S.   3277

JOURNAL OF TRAVEL ACROSS THE PLAINS TO CALIFORNIA, AND GUIDE TO THE FUTURE EMIGRANT. Racine: Rebecca Shepherd, 1851. 44 pp. Reprint. Placerville? Calif., 1945.

Mar-Aug 1850. Racine, Wisconsin, doctor's gold rush journey via forts Leavenworth and Kearny and the Humboldt to Placerville; notes on availability of grass and water, scenery, conditions of road, but rather vague as to exact route; scant medical content.

SHOTTENKIRK, D.G.   **3278**

In SCENERY OF THE PLAINS, MOUNTAINS, AND MINES, by Franklin Langworthy, pp. 280-285. Ogdensburgh, N.Y.: J.C. Sprague, 1855. Princeton: Princeton University Press, 1932.

Jun-Jul 1850. Fragment of Mount Carroll, Illinois, emigrant's diary on road to California; lightening loads and abandoning wagons; making difficult crossing of the Green River.

SITGREAVES, LORENZO   **3279**

Rister, Carl Coke and Lovelace, Bryan W., eds. "A Diary Account of a Creek Boundary Survey." CHRONICLES OF OKLAHOMA 27 (1949):268-302.

Jul-Sep 1850. Topographical engineer's survey of the boundary between the Creek and Cherokee nations with a detachment from Fort Gibson; men sick with "bilious remittent fever" and diarist's study of medical books; danger from Osages, whose traditional hunting grounds were violated by the survey, and encounters with Comanches; details of life in camp and on the march; references to Lt. Israel C. Woodruff.

SMITH, CHARLES W.   **3280**

JOURNAL OF A TRIP TO CALIFORNIA ACROSS THE CONTINENT FROM WESTON, MO., TO WEBER CREEK, CAL. Edited by R.W.G. Vail. Manchester, N.H.: Standard Book, 1920. New York: Cadmus Book Shop, 1920. 79 pp. Reprint. Fairfield, Wash.: Ye Galleon, 1974.

Apr-Aug 1850. Victor, New York, printer's gold rush journey from Centerville, Indiana; on the CAMBRIA to St. Louis and PRIDE OF THE WEST to St. Joseph and Weston Ferry; overland to Pleasant Valley, Weber Creek, etc., with notes on incidents and conditions of travel and Sioux and Digger Indians.

STEELE, JOHN, 1832-1905   **3281**

ACROSS THE PLAINS IN 1850. Edited by Joseph Schafer. Chicago: Printed for the Caxton Club, 1930. 234 pp.

Mar-Sep 1850. Well written, perhaps rewritten, journal of trip from Wisconsin to California; characterizations of his traveling companions; the companies and parties he traveled with as well as their changes; encounters with cholera, mountain fever and other tragedies; hunting; a battle with Indians; grand scenic descriptions.

STIMSON, FANCHER, 1828-1902   **3282**

"Overland Journey to California by Platte River Route and South Pass in 1850." ANNALS OF IOWA, 3d ser. (1921-1923):403-440. Diary, pp. 408-423.

Apr-Jul 1850. Gold rush journey with a company outfitted at Council Bluffs, Iowa; terrain, route and difficulties of finding grass for horses and mules.

TAYLOR, CALVIN   **3283**

Williams, Burton J., ed. "Overland to the Gold Fields of California in 1850." NEBRASKA HISTORY 50 (1969):125-149.

May-Jul 1850. Nebraska portion of the gold rush journey of Calvin and Charles Wesley Taylor of Cincinnati; scenery, conditions and encounters with discouraged, returning emigrants; many pioneer graves testifying to cholera along route to Fort Laramie; long entries in a rather elevated style.

Williams, Burton J., ed. "Overland to California in 1850." UTAH HISTORICAL QUARTERLY 38 (1970):312-349.

Jul-Sep 1850. From Fort Laramie to Georgetown via South Pass, Fort Bridger and Salt Lake, with especially interesting descriptions of Utah and Nevada; no notes on California mining experiences.

TAYLOR, MARION C., d. 1871   **3284**

"Col. M.C. Taylor's Diary in Lopez Cardenas Expedition." KENTUCKY HISTORICAL SOCIETY REGISTER 19 (1921):79-89.

Apr-Jun 1850. Shelbyville lawyer's account of a filibustering expedition under Narciso Lopez to overthrow Spanish rule in Cuba; enlistment at Louisville in Jacob Allen's company and river travel to New Orleans; thence on the GEORGIANA and CREOLE to Cuba; a battle at Cardenas, with many casualties; on the CREOLE to Key West and an engagement at sea with the Spanish man-of-war PIZARRO ; some activities at Tampa and return home.

THISSELL, G.W.   **3285**

CROSSING THE PLAINS IN '49. Oakland, Calif., 1903. 176 pp.

Mar-Sep 1850. Gold rush diary of member of the Chambers train; with ox team from the Missouri River to California via the Oregon Trail; humorous events and tragedies; cholera; short tempers and quarrels as result of hardships; singing and spinning tales around the campfire; early summary of discovery of gold.

UDELL, JOHN, b. 1795   **3286**

INCIDENTS OF TRAVEL TO CALIFORNIA, ACROSS THE GREAT PLAINS: TOGETHER WITH THE RETURN TRIPS THROUGH CENTRAL AMERICA AND JAMAICA. Jefferson, Ohio: Printed for the author, at the Sentinal office, 1856. 302 pp. Diary, pp. 9-106.

1850-1855. Journey from Centerville, Iowa, with his sons; work in Placerville and Yuba; return via Panama; second trip to California in 1852, his stay there until 1854 and return; many religious reflections of a devout Baptist.

JOURNAL OF JOHN UDELL, KEPT DURING A TRIP ACROSS THE PLAINS, CONTAINING AN ACCOUNT OF THE MASSACRE OF A PORTION OF HIS PARTY BY THE MOHAVE INDIANS, IN 1859. Jefferson, Ohio: Ashtabula Sentinel Steam Press Print, 1868. 47 pp. Reprint. JOHN UDELL JOURNAL. Introduction by Lyle H. Wright. California Centennial Series, no. 3. Los Angeles: N.A. Kovach, 1946. 87 pp.

1858-1859. Elderly couple's journey from Putnam County, Missouri, with Tamerlane Davis and John Anspach; route, distances and camps via Albuquerque over Edward Beale's new road; massacre during which thirteen emigrants were wounded, eight killed and all goods taken, with graphic description of the aftermath of slaughter; return to winter in Albuquerque and notes on Catholic customs there; resumption of journey to California, traveling with Beale's road construction party as far as the Colorado; arrival of a detachment of Beale's camel corps under

Samuel Bishop; arduous mule back travel across the Mojave Sink to Los Angeles, thence by boat to San Francisco.

WILLIAMS, JOHN T., 1825-1881   **3287**

"Journal of John T. Williams." INDIANA MAGAZINE OF HISTORY 32 (1936):393-409.

Mar-Sep 1850. Gold rush journey from Clinton County to California; by riverboat from Madison to St. Louis and St. Joseph, where he provisioned; route and conditions of travel; a few notes on Indians; deaths from cholera, gun accidents, etc.; plight of those who had to continue on foot; statistics on abandoned stock and wagons strewn over the desert.

WOOD, JOHN, 1825-1896   **3288**

JOURNAL OF JOHN WOOD, AS KEPT BY HIM WHILE TRAVELING FROM CINCINNATI TO THE GOLD DIGGINGS. Chillicothe, Ohio: Press of A. Bookwalter, 1852. 76 pp. Reprint. Columbus, Ohio: Nevins & Myers, 1871. 112 pp.

Apr-Sep 1850. Greenfield, Ohio, man's gold rush journal; notes on route, hardships, difficulties, prices, etc.

WOODWARD, THOMAS, 1806-1878   **3289**

"Diary of Thomas Woodward while Crossing the Plains to California in 1850." WISCONSIN MAGAZINE OF HISTORY 17 (1933-1934):345-360, 433-446.

May-Jul 1850. Incomplete gold rush diary of English immigrant who had settled at Platteville but later became a substantial resident of Highland; route via Platte River and South Pass; camps, terrain and vicissitudes of travel; interesting notes on Indians.

1851

ANON.   **3290**

"Diary of a Fort Fillmore Dragoon." EL PALACIO 47, no. 2 (1967):42, 47-48.

Oct 1851. Brief fragment, of questioned authenticity, describing life at Fort Fillmore, New Mexico; movements of Indians, Mexicans and emigrants.

BAKER, JEAN RIO GRIFFITHS, 1810-1883   **3291**

In COVERED WAGON WOMEN, edited by Kenneth L. Holmes, vol. 3, pp. 203-281.

1851-1852 (with gaps). Diary covering the voyage from England of a Mormon widow and her seven children; from Liverpool to New Orleans on the GEORGE W. BOURNE in a Mormon company led by William Gibson; excellent descriptions of storms and calms; the death of one of her children; Mormon meetings during which some members were suspended for poor conduct; to St. Louis on the CONCORDIA, described in some detail; notes on St. Louis and outfitting for the journey to Utah; overland with comments on kindness of farm families along the way, scenery, wild flowers, many thunder storms, wagon accidents causing injuries to members of company, replacing several of her lost or exhausted oxen, gathering gooseberries or fruit to enhance camp

meals and singing around the camp fire; birth of a grandchild; a colorful procession of Shoshoni Indians in ceremonial dress on way to council of various tribes; settling briefly in Salt Lake City and then moving permanently to Ogden, Utah; a well written account.

In WOMEN'S VOICES, edited by Kenneth W. Godfrey, Audrey M. Godfrey and Jill Derr, pp. 203-221.

Jan-Apr 1851. Extract of trip from England to St. Louis.

BALLOU, MARY B.   **3292**

"I HEAR THE HOGS IN MY KITCHEN," A WOMAN'S VIEW OF THE GOLD RUSH. Cambridge?: Beinecke, 1962. 13 pp.

1851-1852 (with gaps). Brief, sporadic entries of a woman's trip to California on the ship OHIO, via the Isthmus of Panama, and difficult life in the gold fields; operating a boarding house.

In LET, THEM SPEAK FOR THEMSELVES: WOMEN IN THE AMERICAN WEST, 1849-1900, edited by Christiane Fischer, pp. 42-47.

Oct. 1852. Extract reflecting daily life in her boarding house kitchen.

BARBOUR, GEORGE W.   **3293**

Hoopes, Alban W. "The Journal of George W. Barbour." SOUTHWESTERN HISTORICAL QUARTERLY 40 (1936-1937):145-153, 247-261.

May-Oct 1851. Record of Indian affairs kept by member of a commission to formulate "a definite policy with regard to the aboriginal tribes of California"; meetings with various Indian leaders to persuade them to sign treaties and move onto reservations; names of chiefs and tribes; numbers of Indians present; summaries of some speeches; route, camps and distances.

BARNUM, CAROLINE C.   **3294**

Extracts in TRAVEL ACCOUNTS OF INDIANA, compiled by Shirley McCord, pp. 196-197.

Apr 1851. Travel from Louisville to Madison where her father, P.T. Barnum, was promoter of a concert by singer Jenny Lind; river travel aboard the BEN FRANKLIN; snobbish and hearsay reports about the audience at the concert, which she did not attend.

BLANEY, HENRY, 1822-1896   **3295**

JOURNAL OF VOYAGES TO CHINA AND RETURN. Boston: Privately printed, 1913. 134 pp.

Mar-Jun 1851, Feb-Jun 1853. Journals kept for his family by Bostonian in the employ of Wolcott, Bates and Company; voyage on the SAMUEL RUSSELL, under Captain Limeburner, from New York City to Hong Kong round the Cape of Good Hope; weather, sailing maneuvers and ship's position; birds and sea life; fellow passengers, including one who attempted suicide; diarist's activities; entertaining account of church service led by missionaries; at Anjer with notes on Malays and a short tour of Java; by steamer from Hong Kong to Canton; remarks about the city and the Chinese; return to New York City from Shanghai on the MANDARIN, captained by T.C. Stoddard, via the Cape of Good Hope with a stop at St. Helena Island; notes on other ships; amusing incidents among crew members; a vivid account of the adventure of clipper ship travel.

BOGGS, MARY JANE, b. 1833   3296

Buni, Andrew, ed. "Rambles among the Virginia Mountains." VIRGINIA MAGAZINE OF HISTORY AND BIOGRAPHY 77 (1969):78-111.

Jun 1851. A Spotsylvania County girl's trip through the Shenandoah Valley and Blue Ridge Mountains with her father, Lewis A. Boggs, and some young cousins; full and delightfully ingenuous descriptions of towns, scenes, people, social life, the logistics of wagon travel in the still backwoods area and accommodations at inns and taverns; such raptures as "Oh! If I could always behold such scenes, I think I could be better and purer - less selfish and worldly minded"; her joy marred by a "face ache" which she treated with chloroform and laudanum; a surprise meeting with Fredrika Bremer "whose writings I have so often admired."

BOOTH, WILLIAM, b. 1814   3297

In EARLY UTAH PIONEERS, LEVI HAMMON AND POLLY CHAPMAN BYBEE, compiled by Betsy R. H. Greenwell, pp. 30-50. Kaysville, Utah: Inland Printing, 196-?

Jun-Sep 1851. Journal kept by clerk of the Third Company of Ten crossing the plains under Capt. Levi Hammon, as part of the larger Mormon company under Alfred Cordon; travel conditions, settlement of disputes and references to many emigrants.

BUCKINGHAM, HARRIET TALCOTT, 1832-1890   3298

In COVERED WAGON WOMEN, edited by Kenneth L. Holmes, vol. 3, pp. 15-52.

May-Sep 1851. A young woman's emigrant trip to Oregon from Norwalk, Ohio, with her brother Henry and uncle and aunt Hiram and Hannah Smith; crossing the Platte River with help of Indians; sensitivity to scenery, wild flowers, landmarks, and geographical formations; breakfasting on trout, strawberries and cream on Fourth of July; noting Nez Percé women's costumes; references to Episcopal minister W. Richmond and newspaper editor Thomas J. Dryer after her arrival in Portland.

CARPENTER, ZACHEUS   3299

Carpenter, J. R., ed. "Zacheus Carpenter: Diary and Letter." KENTUCKY HISTORICAL SOCIETY REGISTER 50 (1952):358-369.

Jul-Aug 1851. A roundtrip journey from Shelby County, Kentucky, to Richmond, Virginia, to attend a Carpenter family gathering; travel by canal and riverboat, train and lakeboat first to New York, then to Richmond, with notes on cities and towns en route; once there, many references to members and branches of the Carpenter family; religious opinions, with comparisons between worship practices of his own group, the Disciples, and those of other persuasions.

COOL, PETER Y., 1830-1882   3300

Clebsch, William A., ed. "Goodness, Gold and God: The California Mining Career of Peter Y. Cool." PACIFIC HISTORIAN 10, no. 3 (1966):19-42.

Jun 1851-Jan 1852. A devout Methodist's account of his activities, observations and reflections in gold rush California, particularly in Amador County; attending Methodist class meetings, services and camp meetings and speaking at temperance gatherings, but equal attention to the details of gold prospecting and mining, with record of amounts of gold he "washed" and earnings; debating at the Lyceum and other efforts to educate himself; references to Isaac Owen, Milton Glover and many other ministers, missionaries and miners; activities at Volcano.

CRANSTON, SUSAN AMELIA MARSH, 1829-1857   3301

In COVERED WAGON WOMEN, edited by Kenneth L. Holmes, vol. 3, pp. 97-126.

May-Aug 1851. Matter-of-fact diary entries of Woodstock, Ohio, woman on emigrant journey from St. Joseph to Oregon; daily concerns for fuel, water and grass; graves passed; camping once with carriers of the mail traveling from Fort Kearny to Missouri; mention of Cheyenne and Sioux Indians.

CRAWFORD, P.V.   3302

"Journal of a Trip across the Plains." OREGON HISTORICAL QUARTERLY 25 (1924):136-169.

Mar-Sep 1851. Journey from Madison, Indiana, on riverboats VOLTIC and CATARACT to St. Joseph, Missouri, then overland to Oregon; constant snags and bars on the Missouri; notes on camps, sights, Indians, etc.

DAVIS, ALVAH ISAIAH, b. 1825   3303

"Diary of Alvah Isaiah Davis." OREGON PIONEER ASSOCIATION TRANSACTIONS (1909):355-381; (1910-1911):444-476.

1851-1854. Brief notes on farming and weather near Lockport, Illinois; activities at Chicago; journey via Iowa to settle in Willamette Valley; farming in Oregon, with brief notes of work, weather and prices; frequent trips to Portland where he found work at the Abrams Sawmill.

DICKINSON, LAVINIA NORCROSS, 1833-1899   3304

In THE YEARS AND HOURS OF EMILY DICKINSON, by Jay Leyda, vol. 1, pp. 191-229, 246. New Haven, Conn.: Yale University Press, 1960.

Jan 1851-Apr 1852. Extracts from a diary kept at Amherst, Massachusetts, by Emily Dickinson's sister; visits to and from relatives and friends, household chores and church-going; courtship with William Howland and parental disapproval of the relationship.

DOBLE, JOHN, 1828-1866   3305

JOURNAL AND LETTERS FROM THE MINES. Edited by Charles L. Camp. Denver: Old West, 1962. 304 pp. Journal, pp. 1-205.

1851-1854 (with gaps). Shelby County, Indiana, blacksmith's gold rush journal; detailed descriptions of voyage from New York to Nicaragua on the DANIEL WEBSTER, overland crossing of Nicaragua and remainder of journey to California on the GOLD HUNTER; in the diggings at Mokelumni Hill, Jackson, Volcano, etc., with full entries describing work, hardships, diversions and violence of miners; actions of the Vigilance Committee at Jackson; interesting notes on Indians, especially their music and methods of cooking; frequent references to his brother Abner, Doc Carpenter and others.

EVANS, JOHN   3306

In FLORIDA PLANTATION RECORDS FROM THE PAPERS OF GEORGE NOBLE JONES, by George Noble Jones, edited by Ulrich B. Phillips and James D. Glunt, pp. 339-509. St. Louis: Missouri Historical Society, 1927.

Jan-Dec 1851, Jan-Aug 1856. Overseer's daily record, compiled by Evans in 1851, A.R. McCall through June 1856 and thereafter by Benjamin S. McCall; work details at Chemonie, a plantation near Tallahassee; weather; health and discipline of the slaves.

FLINT, THOMAS, 1824-1904   3307

Westergaard, Waldemar, ed. "Diary of Dr. Thomas Flint, California to Maine and Return." HISTORICAL SOCIETY OF SOUTHERN CALIFORNIA ANNUAL PUBLICATIONS 12 (1923):53-127. Reprint. Los Angeles, 1924. 78 pp.

1851-1855 (with gaps). Gold rush and later diary of a young doctor from New Vineyard, Maine, traveling with his cousins Llewellyn and Amasa Bixby via Panama; from New York on the CRESCENT CITY; treating a man for cholera in Panama, for which his fee was $15; on the NORTHERN to San Francisco; thence to the Volcano diggings in Amador County; return by ship via Panama and depositing gold at the mint; by train to Indiana; thence to Illinois where he bought sheep and cattle to drive to California; route and camps; losses of sheep to wolves, poisonous grass, etc.; notes on Indians and Mormons, including Brigham Young; references to W. Hollister and Cyrus Burdick.

FOWLER, MATTHEW VAN BENSCHOTEN, 1814-1881   3308

Elliott, Mary Joan, ed. "The 1851 California Journal of M.V.B. Fowler." SOUTHERN CALIFORNIA QUARTERLY 50 (1968):113-160, 227-265.

Feb-May 1851. Meticulously detailed journal of a Newburgh, New York, lawyer's experiences in California during the gold rush; work as a customs inspector in San Francisco while living aboard the CURLEW and OCEAN QUEEN; murders and trials, including that of William Walker, and general lawlessness; acrimonious dealings with his superior, Thomas Butler King; seeking farm land in the Santa Clara Valley; from San Francisco to Panama on the PANAMA, with good notes on ship life and passengers.

GAY, JAMES WOODS, 1828-1903   3309

Rodman, Mary. "The 1851 Trail Diary of James Woods Gay and the Sunset Trail - Reminiscences of Martha Gay Masterson." LANE COUNTY HISTORIAN 24 (1979):3-13.

Jul-Sep 1851. Extracts, within article, of Oregon Trail diary kept by the oldest son of the thirteen-member Gay family of Springfield, Missouri; rumors of Indian attack; mostly bare notes of distances, landmarks, weather, etc.

Barton, Lois. "Further Adventures of the Martin Baker Gay Family." LANE COUNTY HISTORIAN 24 (1979):27-37. Diary, pp. 27-29.

Apr 1852, Jan-Mar 1855. Brief notes of life and work as a cabinetmaker in Lane County, Oregon; family visits, hunting and helping his father, Martin Baker Gay, with ranching.

GIBBON, LARDNER   3310

In EXPLORATION OF THE VALLEY OF THE AMAZON, MADE UNDER DIRECTION OF THE NAVY DEPARTMENT, by Wm. Lewis

Herndon and Larnder Gibbon, vol. 2. 32nd Cong., 2d sess., 1853, S. Exec Doc. 36. 33rd Cong., 1st sess., 1854, H. Exec. Doc. 53. Washington, D.C.: R. Armstrong, Public Printer, 1854.

In SOUTH FROM THE SPANISH MAIN, by Earl P. Hanson, pp. 381-391. New York: Delacorte, 1967.

Jul-Oct 1851. Notes by leader of detached party of an expedition under William L. Herndon exploring Amazon tributaries and other rivers in Brazil, Bolivia and Peru; notes on Indian customs, natural history, antiquities, mineral production, cotton manufacture, status of women, production of india-rubber and its use and the possibility of navigation and commerce; negotiating the falls and rapids of Madre de Dios and Madeira rivers.

GREENE, PAUL   3311

Sanford, Albert H., ed. "A Journey through Ohio and down the Ohio River." HISTORY TEACHER'S MAGAZINE 7 (1916):122-124.

Oct-Nov 1851. Extracts from a western New York farmer's diary of a river and canal boat journey from Buffalo to Cairo, Illinois, through Cincinnati, Louisville, Memphis, etc.; accounts of merriment on board and vignettes of passengers, from nuns to gamblers; brief descriptions of cities along the Ohio.

GUNN, ELIZABETH LE BRETON, 1811-1906   3312

In RECORDS OF A CALIFORNIA FAMILY: JOURNALS AND LETTERS OF LEWIS C. GUNN AND ELIZABETH LE BRETON GUNN, by Lewis C. Gunn, pp. 91-135. San Diego, Calif., 1928.

Feb-Aug 1851. Letter-diary kept for her Philadelphia family while making voyage with her four children around Cape Horn to join her husband in California; information on preserving food on long ocean voyages and cooking; seasickness; everyday activities of keeping the children occupied, reading, sewing and listening to sailor's work songs; comments on the captain, his wife and the one other passenger.

HADLEY, AMELIA HAMMOND, 1825-1886   3313

In COVERED WAGON WOMEN, edited by Kenneth L. Holmes, vol. 3, pp. 53-96.

May-Aug 1851. Bride's overland journey with her husband, Samuel B. Hadley, from Galesburg, Illinois to Portland, Oregon, made in record time with horses rather than oxen; cheerful entries about the "merry crowd" of emigrants which included Aaron Rose, Roseburg, Oregon settler, and the John Dennys, Puget Sound pioneers; playing her violin and accordian; noting desolate appearance of the Mormons' Winter Quarters and burying ground; visiting a Sioux camp; surprise at size of and goods available at Fort Laramie; continuing on Sublette's Cutoff; on Fourth of July "fired guns and drank toasts and had a merry time"; wounding of brother-in-law Melville Hadley by Snake Indians, requiring layover until he could travel again; a break in journal during her illness from Rocky Mountain spotted fever or Colorado tick fever which changed the tone of her last entry to relief at the "end of a long and tedious journey."

HARRIS, JEREMIAH COLLINS, 1790-1876   3314

AN OLD FIELD SCHOOL TEACHER'S DIARY. Edited by Charles W. Turner. Verona, Va.: McLure Press, 1975. 87 pp.

1851-1860. A rural Virginia teacher's diary, containing notes on school sessions, pupils and families with whom he boarded; his own farming, much of which fell to his wife and family; Baptist church activities, with record of services and preachers; local politics; trips to the University of Virginia, New York, Niagara Falls and Philadelphia; articulate and touching personal comments.

HAYES, EMILY MARTHA CHAUNCEY   3315

In PIONEER NOTES FROM THE DIARIES OF JUDGE BENJAMIN HAYES, pp. 81-86. Los Angeles: Privately printed, 1929. Reprint. New York: Arno, 1976.

Dec 1851-Feb 1852. Extracts from diary of Mrs. Benjamin Hayes on a riverboat journey from St. Louis to New Orleans, thence to Havana and Chagres and on to San Diego.

HERNDON, WILLIAM LEWIS, 1813-1857   3316

EXPLORATION OF THE VALLEY OF THE AMAZON, MADE UNDER DIRECTION OF THE NAVY DEPARTMENT, by Wm. Lewis Herndon and Lardner Gibbon. 32nd Cong., 2d sess., 1853, S. Exec Doc. 36. Washington, D.C.: R. Armstrong, Public Printer,, 1853-1854. 2 vols. 33rd Cong., 1st sess., 1854, H. Exec. Doc. 53. Washington, D.C.: R. Armstrong, Public Printer, 1854. 2 vols. Journal, vol. 1.

Extracts in SOUTH FROM THE SPANISH MAIN, by Earl P. Hanson, pp. 359-379. New York: Delacorte, 1967.

1851-1852. Journal in report of leader of a government-sponsored expedition to explore Amazon River in Peru and Brazil for navigability and commerce; traveling by canoe following main trunk of the river; overland by mules managed by undependable muleteers, lodging with missionaries at Catholic missions when possible; investigating and observing Indians and their villages, customs, dress, work of women, food and crafts; notes on mines, agriculture, plantations, game and slavery.

HICKOK, WILLIAM ALONZO, 1801-1852   3317

Harmon, Edith A., ed. "Account of a Journey on the Great Lakes." ILLINOIS STATE HISTORICAL SOCIETY JOURNAL 71 (1978):143-147.

Jul 1851. Letter-diary to his family, including his son James Butler, later to be "Wild Bill" Hickok, kept on a trip from his home in Troy Grove, Illinois, to Union, New York; by stagecoach, "such a pounding," and train, then more detailed notes of Great Lakes trip on board the VIRGINIA PURDEE; Fourth of July celebration; diary concluded before he reached destination.

HOWE, WILLIAM S.G., d. 1860   3318

In DIARY OF REV. MOSES HOW, PASTOR OF THE MIDDLE STREET CHRISTIAN CHURCH, NEW BEDFORD, by Moses How, pp. 25-29. New Bedford, Mass.: Reynolds Printing, 1932.

1851-1853. Extracts of a few important events in personal diary of New Bedford, Massachusetts, man; the launching of new ships; viewing a panorama; attending Lyceum lectures by Elizabeth Oakes Smith and Oliver Wendell Holmes; arrival of a new Chickering piano for his home and installation of gas lights for streets and Lyceum hall.

JOHNSON, JOHN LAWRENCE   3319

In WITH HER OWN WINGS, by Portland Federation of Women's Organizations, edited by Helen Krebs, pp. 47-52. Portland: Beattie, 1948.

Apr-Aug 1851. Extracts from young man's diary on Oregon Trail with incidents involving endeavors to continue with party including a Miss Harriet Jones to whom he was much attracted; their clever scheme to maintain communications with notes attached to buffalo skulls along the road when the parties were separated.

LECOUVREUR, FRANK, 1829-1901   3320

FROM EAST PRUSSIA TO THE GOLDEN GATE. Edited by Josephine R. Lecouvreur. Translated by Julius C. Behnke. New York and Los Angeles: Angelina Book Concern, 1906. 355 pp.

1851-1871. Highly narrative letter-diary of German immigrant's travels on various ships, including the VICTORIA and AURORA, and life in California as county surveyor at Los Angeles.

LOBENSTINE, WILLIAM CHRISTIAN, 1831-1918   3321

EXTRACTS FROM THE DIARY OF WILLIAM C. LOBENSTINE, New York: Privately printed, 1920. 101 pp.

1851-1858 (with gaps). German immigrant's overland trip to California and return to New York by ship via Acapulco and Panama; weather and traveling conditions; observations on life; journey to Leavenworth, Kansas, to settle.

MCKAIG, PRISCILLA ELLEN BEALL, 1810-1885   3322

THE MCKAIG JOURNAL. Edited by Hélène L. Baldwin, Michael A. Mudge and Keith W. Schlegal. Cumberland, Md.: Allegany County Historical Society, 1984. 152 pp.

1851-1866 (with gaps). Journal begun by William Wallace McKaig, Cumberland, Maryland, slaveholder and president of the Frostburg Coal Company, added to by his wife, Priscilla, and carried on by her alone after 1862; notes on significant family events; children's studies at home and costs of sons' education at Princeton, Washington College and the Virginia Military Institute; concern for sons in Confederate army, Priscilla's banishment from Maryland during Union occupation of the town and her three-month sojourn in the South Branch Valley of Virginia; household tasks, social activities, servant problems, prices, health, clothing, house renovations, etc.: visits to New York City, Baltimore and Richmond and strolls through cemeteries; sporadic entries forming a chronicle of the domestic concerns of a well-to-do family.

Baldwin, Hélène L. "'Down Street' in Cumberland." MARYLAND HISTORICAL MAGAZINE 77 (1982):222-229.

1851-1864. A few extracts in article on daily life of upper middle class women in the nineteenth-century.

MAYER, FRANCIS BLACKWELL, 1827-1899   3323

WITH PEN AND PENCIL ON THE FRONTIER IN 1851; THE DIARY AND SKETCHES OF FRANK BLACKWELL MAYER. Edited by Bertha L. Heilbron. Minnesota Historical Society Publications, Narratives and Documents, vol. 1. St. Paul: Minnesota Historical Society, 1932. 214 pp.

May-Jul 1851. Young Baltimore artist's expedition to Minnesota to observe and sketch Indians assembled for signing of treaties; travel by stagecoach and Ohio and Mississippi riverboat; stays in Cincinnati, where he met art community, Byrnham Wood, Missouri, and St. Louis; admiration of Indian life around Kaposia, Fort Snelling and Traverse des Sioux; appearance of Indians, customs, dances and religion; detailed account of a game of

Lacrosse; activities of Governor Alexander Ramsey; life at St. Paul.

OWEN, JOHN, 1818-1889   3324

THE JOURNALS AND LETTERS OF MAJOR JOHN OWEN, PIONEER OF THE NORTHWEST. Edited by Seymour Dunbar. New York: Eberstadt, 1927. 2 vols. passim.

1851-1871 (with gaps). Details of Northwest fur trade and affairs at Fort Owen, the old St. Mary's Mission, where he planted wheat and operated a grist mill and trading post; introducing agriculture to Flathead Indians; trading trips to Walla Walla, The Dalles, Fort Vancouver and Salt Lake City; trip to Fort Benton to attend Great Indian Council held by Gov. Isaac Stevens of Washington Territory, acting unofficially for Flathead Indians and later becoming their governmental representative; activities in connection with Indian War of 1858 and meeting with Spokan Gary; concern for "poor destitute Snake Indians"; frequent mention of fathers Palladino and De Smet, Jim Bridger and construction of Bridger's Road; encounters with miners on way to and from Pikes Peak, Virginia City and Deer Lodge mines; pleasant personal notes of "my old wife Nancy" and holiday celebrations; some journal entries by his brother Frank B. Owen, his assistant Thomas W. Harris or Frederick H. Burr.

PRATT, PARLEY PARKER, 1807-1857   3325

THE AUTOBIOGRAPHY OF PARLEY PARKER PRATT. Edited by his son, Parley P. Pratt. New York: Russell Brothers, 1874. Diary, pp. 414-494 passim. Chicago: Law, King & Law, 1888. 3d ed. Salt Lake City: Deseret Book, 1938.

1851-1857 (with gaps). Entries relating to missionary work by Mormon apostle; from Salt Lake City to San Francisco in an arduous wagon journey with two of his wives and other missionaries, wives and children; account of Mormon missions in San Francisco, Los Angeles, San Bernardino, etc.; defense of polygamy against attacks by local clergy; return to Utah; later train travel to New York, with Mormon work in that area.

Stanley, Reva Hollaway and Camp, Charles L., eds. "A Mormon Mission to California in 1851." CALIFORNIA HISTORICAL SOCIETY QUARTERLY 14 (1935):59-73, 175-182.

Mar-Oct 1851. Journey to California and mission work there, in slightly different form.

REYNOLDS, STEPHEN W.   3326

Ward, David A., ed. "The Old Complaint of Stephen Reynolds." HAWAIIAN JOURNAL OF HISTORY 7 (1973):87-92.

1851-1855. Extracts describing Honolulu merchant's severe recurrent illness and mental incapacity, with editor's conclusion, based on evidence in the diary, that Reynold's condition was caused by lead poisoning.

ROBE, ROBERT, 1821-1908   3327

"Robert Robe's Diary while Crossing the Plains in 1851." WASHINGTON HISTORICAL QUARTERLY 19 (1928):52-63.

Apr-Aug 1851. Brief notes of Ohio Presbyterian minister's journey to Oregon, with diary ending at Umatilla; route, camps and Indian alarms.

ROOS, ROSALIE, 1823-1898   3328

TRAVELS IN AMERICA. Edited by Sigrid Laurell. Translated by Carl L. Anderson. Carbondale: Published for Swedish Pioneer Historical Society by Southern Illinois University Press, 1982. 152 pp. Diary pp. 15-29 passim.

May-Oct 1851. Diary of young Swedish woman determined to obtain independent state following broken engagement; seasickness on voyage to South Carolina; impressions and activities of first days in Charleston; gardens, shops, food, theater, slavery, old friends and new acquaintances; traveling by train to Columbia, Chester and Limestone Springs, where she hoped to obtain employment as teacher of French, drawing and music at Female High School.

ROTCH, Mrs. BENJAMIN SMITH   3329

Lamb, Annie Lawrence. "A New Englander Looks at Louis Napoleon." NEW ENGLAND QUARTERLY 6 (1933):513-524.

1851-1853. Extracts from Paris diary kept by the daughter of Abbott Lawrence, minister to Great Britain; a fascinating picture of social functions during the Second Empire; balls, receptions, "spectacles," etc.; Paris and its aristocracy adorned for Louis Napoleon; diarist's opinion: "How shortlived has been the French Republic even in name."

TOWNSEND, EDWARD DAVIS, 1817-1893   3330

THE CALIFORNIA DIARY OF GENERAL E.D. TOWNSEND. Edited by Malcolm Edwards. Los Angeles: W. Ritchie Press, 1970. 184 pp.

1851-1856. Army officer's diary of a tour of duty on the Pacific coast; arduous ship voyage to California aboard the GEORGIA and NORTHERNER with overland crossing by muleback of Isthmus of Panama; distress over crowded and unsanitary conditions and high death rate of steerage passengers aboard ship; military and religious activities in San Francisco and Benicia, where he assisted Episcopal bishop William Kip; reports while in Washington and Oregon territories of disturbances between Indians and settlers.

WOOD, ELIZABETH   3331

"Journal of a Trip to Oregon, 1851." OREGON HISTORICAL QUARTERLY 27 (1926):192-203.

In COVERED WAGON WOMEN, edited by Kenneth L. Holmes, vol. 3, pp. 161-178.

Jun-Sep 1851. Extracts beginning at Fort Laramie of an emigrant journey from Tazewell County, Illinois; conventional notes on route, scenery, Indians, etc.

WURTS, GEORGE, 1829-1923   3332

"Journal of a Tour to Niagara Falls, Montreal, Lake Champlain, etc." NEW JERSEY HISTORICAL SOCIETY PROCEEDINGS 69 (1951):342-362.

Jul 1851. Diary of a young man from Newark; travel by train and boat, with entertaining comments on people, places and accommodations, including the Clifton House at Niagara, "a magnificent hotel commanding a full front view of the falls"; substantial, rather literary descriptions of scenes, some moving him to poetic effusions.

ZIEBER, EUGENIA, 1833-1863   3333

In COVERED WAGON WOMEN, edited by Kenneth L. Holmes, vol. 3, pp. 179-201.

Apr-Oct 1851. Diary of cheerful, adventurous teenage daughter of John Zieber family traveling from Peoria, Illinois, to Oregon City; lodging with families on early part of trip; religious homilies, long descriptions of day's travel and young folks' activities; dissension in party engendered by a Mr. Palmer; less time for journal during arduous last months of trip.

ZIEBER, JOHN SHUNK, 1803-1890   3334

"Diary of John S. Zieber." OREGON PIONEER ASSOCIATION TRANSACTIONS (1920):301-335.

Apr-Oct 1851. Emigrant journey from Peoria, Illinois, to Oregon City with notes on towns in Illinois and Iowa, conditions of travel and sights and incidents en route; names of many fellow emigrants; encounters with Indians.

1852

ANON.   3335

"A Pioneer Journal, Forsgren Company, Containing Story of the First Danish Company to Emigrate to Utah." HEART THROBS OF THE WEST 6 (1945):1-31.

Dec 1852-Sep 1853. Diary kept by a member of John E. Forsgren's Mormon emigrant company; overland journey to settle in Sanpete County.

ADAMS, CECELIA EMILY MCMILLEN, 1829-1867   3336

"Crossing the Plains in 1852." OREGON PIONEER ASSOCIATION TRANSACTIONS (1904):288-329.

May-Oct 1852. Full and articulate diary of a woman's journey from Du Page County, Illinois, to settle at Hillsboro, traveling with her husband, William Adams, and other relatives; personal, social and everyday details; some sickness and deaths en route, with numbers of graves noted; religious reflections of a cheerful nature.

AKIN, JAMES, d. 1852   3337

"Diary of James Akin, Jr." OREGON PIONEER ASSOCIATION TRANSACTIONS (1908):259-274.

THE JOURNAL OF JAMES AKIN, JR. Edited by Edward E. Dale. University of Oklahoma Bulletin, n.s., no. 172, University Studies, no. 9. Norman: University of Oklahoma Press, 1919. 32 pp. Reprint. Fairfield, Wash.: Ye Galleon, 1971.

Apr-Oct 1852. Emigrant journey, from Salem, Iowa, to Oregon, of a man who died two weeks after his arrival; travel in a company under Stuart Richey, with brief notes of route, distances, camps, trail conditions, etc.; deaths of his mother and others from cholera.

ALLEN, W.T.   3338

Thompson, Arthur T., ed. "A Massachusetts Traveler on the Florida Frontier." FLORIDA HISTORICAL QUARTERLY 38 (1959):129-141.

Mar-Apr 1852. Extract from the travel diary of a man from Leominster, Massachusetts; to Savannah on the FLORIDA; notes on Seminole prisoners at Fort Mellon and on the Seminole Wars; hunting and other activities with such New England friends as Morrill and Jeffries Wyman; good notes on Savannah, St. Augustine, etc.

ANGELL, TRUMAN O.   3339

In TREASURES OF PIONEER HISTORY, compiled by Kate B. Carter, vol. 1, pp. 460-464.

1852. Notes of architect for the Mormon church; the State House, Tabernacle, Bee Hive House, the Bowery, Social Hall, Gateway to Temple and Seventies Hall in Salt Lake City.

BAILEY, MARY STUART   3340

In HO FOR CALIFORNIA! WOMEN'S OVERLAND DIARIES FROM THE HUNTINGTON LIBRARY, edited by Sandra L. Myres, pp. 49-91.

Apr-Nov 1852. Overland diary of doctor's wife traveling from Ohio to California; chiefly weather and travel conditions, grass and water supply for the cattle; daily dreariness relieved by occasional fine scenery.

BAKER, EDWARD   3341

Hill, Helen M. "The Baker Journals: Glimpses of Daniel Webster." MANUSCRIPTS 37 (1985):195-208.

Oct-Nov 1852. Article containing brief extract from the diary of Adeline Baker describing the mourning of Marshfield, Massachusetts, for the death of its illustrious resident, Daniel Webster; longer extracts from the diary of Edward Baker of Duxbury, a worker on Webster's farm; his final illness and death; attire for burial and appearance in the coffin; distinguished people at the funeral and quotations from many public tributes; diarist's reading and analyzing of Webster's speeches for days after his death and enumerating his contributions as a statesman and thinker.

BARLOW, GEORGE   3342

"George Barlow's Diary." COWLITZ COUNTY HISTORICAL QUARTERLY 2, no. 1 (1960):15-20.

May-Jun 1852. Latter part of diary kept by Detroit man who took up a "Donation Land Claim" in Cowlitz County, Washington; diarist, possibly a doctor, treating cholera patients; description of his own sudden attack of "Singolus Opthalmie Phenomenon."

BARTON, CLARA, 1821-1912   3343

THE LIFE OF CLARA BARTON. By William Eleazar Barton. Boston and New York: Houghton Mifflin, 1922. 2 vols. passim.

1852-1911. Extracts from private, unpublished diaries sprinkled through biography to reveal her character, feelings and the difficulties of her work during the Civil War and while organizing the American Red Cross.

BASYE, LISBON, 1818-1863   3344

In THE BASYE FAMILY IN THE UNITED STATES, by Otto Basye, pp. 559-565. Kansas City, Mo., 1950.

Mar-Jun 1852. Bowling Green, Missouri, farmer's trip by wagon to Jasper County to investigate lead mining at the Center Creek diggings; conditions of travel and camping; his evaluations of farms, prairie land and towns; after observing "laborious work" at mines, concluding "it doesn't suit me at all"; returning home; complete expenses appended.

BIXBY, MARCELLUS   3345

Westergaard, Waldemar, ed. "The Diary of Marcellus Bixby from 1852 to 1856." HISTORICAL SOCIETY OF SOUTHERN CALIFORNIA ANNUAL PUBLICATIONS 13 (1924-1927): 317-333.

1852-1856. Journey of brothers Marcellus and Jotham Bixby from Norridgewock, Maine, to Amador County; brief notes of voyage from Boston on the SAMUEL APPLETON around Cape Horn to Valparaiso and San Francisco; mining at the Volcano diggings with his brother Llewellyn; weekly record of profits.

BLACK, ELIZABETH DALE, b. 1823   3346

"'Took Tea at Mrs. Lincoln's': The Diary of Mrs. William M. Black." ILLINOIS STATE HISTORICAL SOCIETY JOURNAL 48 (1955):59-64.

Jan-May 1852. Woman's diary recording frequent visits with Mary Todd Lincoln and other ladies of Springfield; attendance at First Presbyterian Church services and prayer meetings; religious quest amid sorrow over death of her baby and loneliness for her husband, who was usually away on business.

BRIGHT, HENRY ARTHUR, 1830-1884   3347

HAPPY COUNTRY THIS AMERICA. Edited by Anne H. Ehrenpreis. Columbus: Ohio State University Press, 1978. 486 pp.

May-Oct 1852. Irrepressible young Englishman's travels in America and Canada with his friend Thomas Burder; Atlantic crossing on the GREAT BRITAIN, for which he was owner's representative; social life of first class passengers and great interest in the engine room, from which he emerged "feeling very dirty and scientific"; sightseeing in New York, Boston and Concord, where he enjoyed the company of Emerson, Hawthorne, Longfellow, George Ticknor, Daniel Webster and Margaret Fuller; a meeting with President Fillmore; subsequent travels by train, stagecoach, lake and riverboat to Richmond, where he witnessed a slave auction; to St. Louis, St. Paul and Niagara Falls, with interesting notes on travels and hotels; comments on a wide spectrum of American society, customs, politics, education and religion.

Ehrenpreis, Anne H., ed. "A Victorian Englishman on Tour." VIRGINIA MAGAZINE OF HISTORY AND BIOGRAPHY 84 (1976):333-361.

Jun 1852. Extract covering stays in Washington and Richmond, his meeting with President Fillmore and other notables including William Wilson Corcoran and Daniel Webster; visit to Mount Vernon; description of a slave auction.

BROWN, JOHN W.   3348

Adams, Horace, ed. "Arkansas Traveler, 1852-1853." JOURNAL OF SOUTHERN HISTORY 4 (1938):377-383.

Aug 1852-Apr 1853. Extracts of Princeton, Arkansas, farmer's business travels; two round trips to Memphis and one to New Orleans by carriage, horseback and riverboat; inns and lodging with friends; expenses and conditions of travel during "a laborious

trip with a dull mule over bad roads in hot sickly weather"; activities and observations in New Orleans.

BURGESS, HANNAH REBECCA CROWELL   3349

In WOMEN OF THE SEA, by Edward R. Snow, pp. 137-161. New York: Dodd, Mead, 1962.

1852-1856. Diary extracts of young wife aboard clipper ships WHIRLWIND and CHALLENGER; delight in seafaring life, learning navigation and assisting her captain husband as navigator; sickness and deaths among crew, including her husband; having to assume command of ship to next port.

BUTLER, AMERICA ROLLINS   3350

Winther, Oscar O. and Galey, Rose D., eds. "Mrs. Butler's 1853 Diary of Rogue River Valley." OREGON HISTORICAL QUARTERLY 41 (1940):337-366.

1852-1854 (with gaps). Young woman's account of journey with her husband, Ashmun J. Butler, from Missouri to Yreka, California, and then to Rogue River Valley after a cold and hungry winter in Yreka; domestic chores, including "dreaded washing day"; lively social and business life of the area; her husband's farming; much on the Rogue River Indian war of 1853; brief entries with gaps during journeys but full from May-December 1853.

BYERS, WILLIAM N.   3351

Mattes, Merrill J., ed. "The Oregon Odyssey of William Byers." OVERLAND JOURNAL 1, no. 1 (1983):14-23, no. 2, 12-21; 2, no. 1 (1984):14-23, no. 2, 23-28.

May-Oct 1852. Diary, somewhat elaborated from notes, of wagon crossing from Council Bluffs, Iowa, to Oregon City via north side of the Platte River, Oregon Trail, Three Island Crossing of the Snake and Barlow Road; approximate distances, camps, terrain and availability of wood, water and grass; a fairly easy journey with reference to only one death and very little illness; summary and advice to emigrants.

Davidson, Levette J., ed. "The Early Diaries of William N. Byers." COLORADO MAGAZINE 22 (1945):145-157. Diary, pp. 155-157.

Nov-Dec 1853. Diary extract covering journey from Oregon to Muscatine, Iowa, by way of California mines and Central America; traveling by ship, train and stagecoach; brief notes of a man who was later to be prominent in the development of Denver.

CALLISON, JOHN JOSEPH, 1830-1852   3352

THE DIARY OF JOHN JOSEPH CALLISON, OREGON TRAIL, 1852. Eugene, Oreg.: Reproduced by Lane County Pioneer-Historical Society, 1959. 10 leaves.

Apr-Jun 1852. Brief notes on overland journey from Illinois to Sweetwater River; camps, distances, weather and cholera; prices of corn and hay.

CAMPBELL, LEANDER M.   3353

Extracts in TRAVEL ACCOUNTS OF INDIANA, compiled by Shirley McCord, pp. 205-207.

Apr-Jun 1852. Journey from Kentucky to settle in Indiana; work as a teacher near Brownsburg; his dislike of the local people, resulting in his move to Belleville.

CAPRON, HORACE, 1804-1885   3354

Starr, Merritt. "General Horace Capron." ILLINOIS HISTORICAL SOCIETY JOURNAL 18 (1925):259-349.

Jun-Aug 1852. Journal kept by Special Commissioner of the United States to negotiate treaties with the Texas Indians; marches out from San Antonio, with comment "the expense to the government for keeping up the army in this state is enormous"; treaty talks with Liepan and Comanche Indians and a touching description of old Chief Chequito "bent to the ground with age and trouble"; concern for the Indians' "former greatness and present poverty.

1871-1875. Extracts from his period of service as Adviser and Commissioner of Agriculture under the Japanese government; detailed notes on Japanese agriculture and his own improvements, including importation of livestock and farm implements; interesting comments on Japanese social life, culture and customs during the still feudal and aristocratic period; honors to the diarist by the emperor and exchange of speeches on several occasions.

CARTER, WILLIAM F.   3355

"Incidents from the Journal of William F. Carter." HEART THROBS OF THE WEST 4 (1943):204-220.

1852-1853 (with gaps). Mormon's account of his mission to Calcutta; departure from Utah friends and journey to San Francisco where "all manner of wickedness is carried on," thence on the MONTSOON with other missionaries to India; colorful details of his life, travels and observations there, including customs of treating the dead and the appalling condition of the Indian masses; his own sufferings as "a man too far advanced in years" to endure the heat and hardships of India; return on the JOHN GILPIN.

CASH, AZUBAH BEARSE HANDY   3356

In WOMEN OF THE SEA, by Edward R. Snow, pp. 71-85. New York: Dodd, Mead, 1962.

1852-1853. Diary extracts of captain's wife on board the whaler COLUMBIA with her two children and in port with missionaries at Hilo, Hawaii.

CLARK, JOHN HAWKINS, 1813-1900   3357

Barry, Louise, ed. "Overland to the Gold Fields in 1852." KANSAS HISTORICAL QUARTERLY 11 (1942):227-296.

Apr-Sep 1852. Diary of a Cincinnati man who formed a company with partner, Andrew Brown; steamboat travel on the Ohio and Mississippi described colorfully; thence by wagon; touching stories of deaths en route; considerable detail of daily work, social life, hardships and challenges of the overland journey: "Sometimes the wagons would take the lead and drag the teams after them until brought up by some great boulder, when wagon, oxen, women and children would tumble together in one confused mass, amid the wreck of which would soon be heard the cries of women, the screams of children and the swearing of men"; interesting observation on Mormons and Brigham Young; the horrors of the Humboldt; a descriptive and articulate diary throughout.

CLARKE, CAROLINE COWLES RICHARDS, 1842-1913   3358

DIARY OF CAROLINE COWLES RICHARDS, 1852-1872, CANAN-

DAIGUA, N.Y. Rochester? N.Y., 1908. 85 pp.

VILLAGE LIFE IN AMERICA, 1852-1872, INCLUDING THE PERIOD OF THE AMERICAN CIVIL WAR, AS TOLD IN THE DIARY OF A SCHOOLGIRL. With an introduction by Margaret E. Sangster. London: T.F. Unwin, 1912. 207 pp. New and enl. ed. New York: H. Holt, 1913. 225 pp. Reprint. Williamstown, Mass.: Corner House, 1972.

Extracts in SMALL VOICES, edited by Josef and Dorothy Berger, pp. 241-248.

1852-1872. Diary, begun at age ten, of Canandaigua, New York, girl living with her grandparents, the Thomas Beals; charming anecdotes of family and social life, school lessons with Miss Zilpha Clark and later at the Ontario Female Seminary; Congregational church and Sunday school events, including buying ten cent shares in the missionary ship MORNING STAR; hearing Charles Finney, Edward Everett and Susan B. Anthony; the hilarious antics and comments of her little sister Anna; a visit from Cyrus W. Field "because grandmother is his aunt" and excitement over his transatlantic cable; reading and her desire to be a writer; departure of Canandaigua boys for the Civil War, followed by names of casualties and account of civilian efforts, such as sewing for soldiers; war news; report of President Lincoln's assassination and description of memorial services in the village; the deaths of her grandparents; scattered entires for 1865-1872, including her marriage to E.C. Clarke.

CONDON, THOMAS, 1822-1907   3359

Gustafsen, Eric Paul, ed. "Thomas Condon's Private Log: Around the Horn, 1852-53." OREGON HISTORICAL QUARTERLY 84 (1983):229-242.

Nov 1852-Feb 1853. Voyage to Oregon of an Irish immigrant missionary on the clipper TRADE WIND under Capt. Nathaniel Webber; log items occasionally interspersed with more extended notes, particularly of a nearly disastrous fire; successful rounding of Cape Horn.

CONYERS, ENOCH W.   3360

"Diary of E.W. Conyers, A Pioneer of 1852." OREGON PIONEER ASSOCIATION TRANSACTIONS (1905):432-512.

Apr-Sep 1852. Journey to Oregon with an emigrating party from Quincy, Illinois, under John Julian; full details of hardships and dramatic moments, including difficulty in ferrying the Missouri, with two pioneers in overturned wagon rescued by Indians; Fourth of July celebration; a very entertaining and partly narrative diary of a man who settled at Clatskanie.

CORNELL, WILLIAM, 1812-1891   3361

Offen, Karen M. and Duniway, David C., eds. "William Cornell's Journal, 1852, with His Overland Guide to Oregon." OREGON HISTORICAL QUARTERLY 79 (1978): 359-393; 80 (1979):66-100.

May-Sep 1852. Journey from Licking County, Ohio, to Oregon, with diary beginning at Duncan's Ferry on the Missouri; terrain, weather, camps and condition of oxen; route via Platte, Snake and Malheur rivers; devastation of cholera and death of his brother-in-law Judson Castle; valiant attempts, with remedies at hand, to heal the sick; nursing of his cousin Bertrand Cornell through cholera and "lunacy"; dissension among the company; diarist's Methodist views, including opposition to Sunday travel; good descriptions of nature and scenery.

CUMMINGS, MARIETT FOSTER, b. 1827   **3362**

In COVERED WAGON WOMEN, edited by Kenneth L. Holmes, vol. 4, pp. 117-168.

Apr-Aug 1852. Overland journey with her husband from Plainfield, Illinois, to California with note that she wore bloomer costume "to avoid the mud" even though women in towns laughed at her; recording accommodations each night before they began camping; travel conditions, towns and villages, houses and farms, landmarks and pioneer graves; getting out her melodeon for entertainment; observing Pawnee Indians chasing the Sioux; describing home of Brigham Young in Salt Lake City and the Mormon practice of polygamy; diarist and her husband both suffering from mountain fever during last weeks of travel.

DAVID, JAMES C.   **3363**

Urbanek, Mae, ed. "1852 on the Oregon Trail." ANNALS OF WYOMING 34 (1962):52-59.

Apr-Jun 1852. Extracts recording Wisconsin man's journey to California, from which he soon returned; notes on Mormons in Iowa; much sickness and death from cholera en route; no diary after Fort Laramie, which he described.

DAVIS, JOHN SHEDDEN   **3364**

Joesting, Edward and Livingston-Little, D.E., eds. "A Scotsman Views Hawaii: An 1852 Log of a Cruise of the EMILY BOURNE." JOURNAL OF THE WEST 9 (1970):196-221.

Feb-Apr 1852. Diary kept by a passenger, probably John Shedden Davis, of a voyage from San Francisco to Hawaii to take on food for the California mines; stops at various points in the islands, where diarist made food purchases and collected botanical specimens for his private collection; overland rambles, with descriptions of natural history, scenery and Hawaiian people and their customs, which he compared disparagingly with anything British; unfavorable comments, as well, on whalers and missionaries; return to California and disappointment with profits on his food procurement venture.

DICKINSON, CHARLOTTE HUMPHREY, 1817-1893   **3365**

Lightfoot, Mary K. and Knuth, Priscilla, eds. "Diary of a Voyage to Oregon." OREGON HISTORICAL QUARTERLY 84 (1983):243-256.

Nov 1852-Jan 1853. Diary covering early part of a missionary's voyage aboard the clipper TRADE WIND with her husband, Obed Dickinson, and other missionaries; church services and Bible study for passengers and crew; excellent description of a fire aboard ship and sailors' heroism in quelling it; encounter with the NANTUCKET; much appreciation for "our indulgent captain Nathaniel Webber."

DODSON, JOHN F., 1835?-1852   **3366**

Weisel, George F., ed. "The Diary of John F. Dodson: His Journey from Illinois to His Death at Fort Owen in 1852." MONTANA MAGAZINE OF HISTORY 3, no. 2 (1953):24-33.

Apr-Sep 1852. Seventeen-year-old Pennsylvanian's terse account of travel as a herder for a wagon train assembled at Buffalo Grove, Illinois; mostly route, distances, weather and difficulties; deaths from cholera en route; employment by Frank Owen to work at Fort Owen in the Bitterroot Valley, with final entry Owen's note:

"The poor fellow was killed and scalped by Blackfeet in sight of the Fort."

DUCHOW, JOHN CHARLES, 1830-1901   **3367**

THE DUCHOW JOURNAL: A VOYAGE FROM BOSTON TO CALIFORNIA. N.p.: Mallette Dean, 1959. Unpaged.

May-Jul 1852. Young man's voyage on the clipper STAFFORDSHIRE; travel notes on seasickness, food, sights, ways to pass the time, traveling companions remarking on four women in bloomer costumes, and Old Neptune frolics; journal ending after cold and stormy rounding of Cape Horn.

EBEY, REBECCA WHITBY DAVIS, 1822-1853   **3368**

Farrar, Victor J., ed. "Diary of Colonel and Mrs. I.N. Ebey." WASHINGTON HISTORICAL QUARTERLY 7 (1916):239-246, 307-321; 8 (1917):40-62, 124-152.

1852-1853. Diary, kept mainly by Mrs. Ebey, of domestic, religious and social life on Whidbey Island; notes on Indians, settlers, such as the Crockett family, and shipping on Puget Sound; loneliness for her husband during his long absences, grief over her mother's death and worry about relatives still crossing the plains; good picture of pioneer life; report of her death in childbirth added by Colonel Ebey.

EWING, SAMUEL WILLIAM, 1818-1894   **3369**

Van Trump, James D., ed. "The Diary of Samuel W. Ewing - a Forty-Niner." WESTERN PENNSYLVANIA HISTORICAL MAGAZINE 60 (1977):73-88.

Jan-May 1852. Allegheny County man's voyage to the gold fields via Panama, thence on the ROWENA, "an awful old dirty stinking ship" on which there were many deaths; diarist's prayers for safety, longing for his family and hearty regret at having left them to seek his fortune; arrival in San Francisco.

FRIZZELL, LODISA   **3370**

Paltsits, Victor H., ed. "Across the Plains to California in 1852." NEW YORK PUBLIC LIBRARY BULLETIN 19 (1915):335-362. Reprint. New York: New York Public Library, 1915. 30 pp.

Apr-Jun 1852. Emigrant journal, written up while wintering in the Sierra Nevada, from notes taken along the trail; from Effingham County, Illinois, with her husband, Lloyd Frizzell, and George W. Elliot; by riverboat MARTHA JEWETT from St. Louis to St. Joseph; good descriptions of Indians and emigrants; crossing the Platte; admiring needlework done by Indian women; some touching and sympathetic references and occasional misgivings: "and often as I pass the freshmade graves, I have glanced at the side boards of the wagon, not knowing how soon it might serve as a coffin for some one of us."

GILLESPIE, AGNES LENORA, b. 1834?   **3371**

"On to Oregon." LANE COUNTY HISTORIAN 9 (1964):47-54.

Apr-Aug 1852. A young girl's Oregon Trail diary; travel with her father, the Rev. Jacob Gillespie, who was captain of the company, other members of her family, and her future husband, John Day; route, conditions, distances, encounters with Indians and with other emigrants; costs of ferrying wagons; typical difficulties and problems described with patience.

GREEN, JAY   **3372**

DIARY OF JAY GREEN. Stockton, Calif.: San Joaquin Pioneer and Historical Society, 1955. 20 pp.

May-Jul 1852. Emigrant journey to Placerville, California, with record beginning at Duncan's Ferry on the Missouri; distances, camps and terrain via the Platte, Sweetwater and Humboldt; an altercation resulting in murder, trial and execution, all described in detail.

HANNA, ESTHER BELLE MCMILLAN, b. 1834?   **3373**

In CANVAS CARAVANS, by Eleanor Allen, pp. 1-125 passim. Portland, Oreg.; Binfords & Mort, 1946.

Mar-Sep 1852. Journal entries, interspersed with narrative, of an eighteen-year-old bride's journey with her minister husband, Joseph A. Hanna, to establish a Presbyterian colony in Oregon; homesickness and fears of present and future dangers, but determination to be strong, for the sake of her husband's pioneer venture.

HARVEY, CHARLES H., 1825-1864   **3374**

CALIFORNIA GOLD RUSH: DIARY OF CHARLES H. HARVEY. Edited by Douglas E. Clanin. Indianapolis: Indiana Historical Society, 1983. 130 pp. passim.

Feb-Nov 1852. Ohio man's voyage around the Horn to San Francisco on the clipper GRECIAN with his brother-in-law Daniel Bonney and friend Linus A. Harrington; from Greene, Ohio, to New York City, where he saw "suffering humanity clothed in rags and filth at every nook and corner"; brief notes of voyage; in port at Rio de Janeiro and Talcahuano, Chile; problems with food and a disorderly crew afflicted with drunkenness and venereal disease; in California, hard ranch work near Marysville, mining and illness; diary ending abruptly with "what in the name of heaven will we do?"

HAYDEN, JACOB S., b. 1830?   **3375**

JOURNAL OF A TRIP ACROSS THE PLAINS TO CALIFORNIA IN 1852. Fairmont? V.VA., 1953. 70 pp.

Mar-Aug 1852. Journal of member of a well organized and congenial company from Fairmont, Virginia, bound for Rabbit Creek near Marysville; by riverboats BALTIC, GRANITE STATE, ELVIRA and HONDURAS to St. Louis and Independence; enjoyment of scenery despite delays from fires and pumps filled with mud; overland with good descriptions of camp life and entertainments, fiddling, dancing, etc; his sufferings from homesickness during night guard; the wisdom of taking it slowly across the desert and repassing all the trains that had rushed past them during the heat of the day; receiving water sent out by mule train from California to relieve emigrants; notes on Potawatomi, Snake, Sioux, Digger, and other Indians; a Fourth of July layover and its festivities; Bible reading, church services, a wedding, a funeral, in short, "a miniature of that great world we left behind us when we crossed the wilderness."

HICKMAN, RICHARD OWEN, 1831-1895   **3376**

White, Catherine M., ed. "'Dick's Works': An Overland Journey to California in 1852." FRONTIER: A MAGAZINE OF THE NORTHWEST 9 (1929):242-260. Reprint. OVERLAND JOURNEY TO

CALIFORNIA IN 1852. Sources of Northwest History, no. 6. Missoula: State University of Montana, 1929. 21 pp. FRONTIER OMNIBUS, edited by John W. Hakola, pp. 161-180.

May-Nov 1852 (with gaps). Colorful letter-diary of a journey from Independence to Nevada City, California; hardships and devastation of cholera; good description of a buffalo hunt in which the herd turned and attacked the hunters; notes on Indians; quarrels among members of his company.

HIGGINSON, HENRY LEE, 1834-1919   **3377**

LIFE AND LETTERS OF HENRY LEE HIGGINSON. By Bliss Perry. Boston: Atlantic Monthly Press, 1921. 557 pp. Diary, pp. 182-189 passim. Reprint. Freeport, N.Y.: Books for Libraries, 1972.

Jun 1852-Apr 1853, Nov 1856-May 1857. A sprinkling of extracts from European travel diaries; the opera of London, Munich and Berlin; in Switzerland, Paris and Italy.

Apr-May 1863. Extracts from war diary; service in Virginia as First Massachusetts Cavalry officer; on fringes of battle of Chancellorsville.

HOWELLS, WILLIAM DEAN, 1837-1920   **3378**

Wortham, Thomas, ed. "'The Real Diary of a Boy': Howells in Ohio." OLD NORTHWEST 10 (1984):3-40.

1852-1853 (with gaps). Young Howell's life in Columbus, working with his father on the OHIO STATE JOURNAL; visit to the Central Ohio Lunatic Asylum and his surprise to see patients "totally bereft of reason, listening like little children" as the doctor read poetry to them; rather amused picture of life in the booming town; attending the legislature for the JOURNAL, with scant respect for level of debate there; snippets of local news; the family move to Ashtabula, where he continued working for his father on the ASHTABULA SENTINAL; relocating the SENTINAL in Jefferson, with a few notes of his life there; writing and literary aspirations while chafing under his menial, ten-hour-day job in the print shop.

JACKSON, MITCHELL YOUNG, 1816-1900   **3379**

In MINNESOTA FARMERS' DIARIES. With an introduction and notes by Rodney C. Loehr, pp. 85-220. Minnesota Historical Society Publications, Narratives and Documents, vol. 3. St. Paul: Minnesota Historical Society, 1939.

Buck, Solon J., ed. "Making a Farm on the Frontier: Extracts From the Diaries of Mitchell Young Jackson." AGRICULTURAL HISTORY 4 (1930):92-120.

1852-1863. Lakeland, Minnesota, farmer's diary; fairly full notes of farming, weather, domestic, social, religious and political matters; business trips to St. Paul and Stillwater; prices, land, agricultural implements, crops and livestock; work as county commissioner for Washington County; Republican party activities; opinions on slavery and reaction to the execution of John Brown; a few personal notes, including anguish over the crippling illness of his young son.

JOHNSON, CHARLOTTE AUGUSTA PAGE, 1836-1907 **3380**

UNDER SAIL AND IN PORT IN THE GLORIOUS 1850's. With introduction and notes by Alvin Page Johnson. Salem: Peabody Museum, 1950. 88 pp. Journal, pp. 3-60.

May-Oct 1852. Journal kept by a Boston girl of sixteen sent to sea for her health; life aboard the GEORGE WASHINGTON with Capt. Josiah Sparrow Cummings and his young daughter Mary, to whom the diarist taught piano; enjoying social life at Mobile while ship loaded cotton; to Liverpool, with names of ships encountered; sightseeing and social life in England and Wales; return to New York with over seven hundred immigrants of many nationalities on board.

KERNS, JOHN T.   3381

"Journal of Crossing the Plains to Oregon in 1852." OREGON PIONEER ASSOCIATION TRANSACTIONS (1914):148-193.

Mar-Oct 1852. Young man's journey with his father and others from Rensselaer, Indiana, to settle in Portland area; route, distances and terrain; ravages of smallpox, cholera and scurvy, mainly in other emigrant trains; a count of graves en route; frequent references to James McCoy; constant complaint of ugliness of people met along the way and the hope that there would be a better-looking race to be found in Oregon.

KIRBY, GEORGIANA BRUCE, b. 1818   3382

In VICTORIAN WOMEN, edited by Erna O. Hellerstein pp. 211-213.

1852-1853. Extracts from Santa Cruz, California, woman's journal; anticipation of motherhood; depression over lack of female companionship.

LAMSON, JOSEPH   3383

ROUND CAPE HORN: VOYAGE OF THE PASSENGER SHIP JAMES W. PAIGE. Bangor, Maine: Press of O.F. & W.H. Knowles, 1878. 156 pp.

1852-1860. Bangor man's account of ship travel to San Francisco with amusing descriptions of life aboard the JAMES W. PAIGE; his experiences in San Francisco, outstanding characters there, a duel, cattle-stealing, a fandango, etc.; a trip to Yosemite.

LANE, WILLIAM CARR, 1789-1863   3384

In HISTORICAL SKETCH OF GOVERNOR WILLIAM CARR LANE, by Ralph E. Twitchell, pp. 1-62 passim. Historical Society of New Mexico Publications, no. 4. Santa Fe: Historical Society of New Mexico, 1917.

Jul-Sep 1852. Journey from St. Louis to Santa Fe.

Carson, William G.B., ed. "William Carr Lane, Diary." NEW MEXICO HISTORICAL REVIEW 39 (1964):181-234, 274-332.

Feb-Dec 1853. St. Louis physician's brief period as territorial governor of New Mexico and superintendent of Indian affairs; dealings with Navahos, Apaches and Pueblos and various opposing views of how they should be treated; boundary controversy with Mexico over the "Disputed District"; harrassment by Col. E.V. Sumner and frequent references to Indian agent E.H. Winfield, Maj. Enoch Steen and many others; unsuccessful campaign as delegate to Congress; life at Santa Fe and travels throughout the area, as well as to and from St. Louis, Santa Fe and Washington, D.C., by horseback, stagecoach and train; notes on natural history and geography of the Southwest.

LEE, AGNES, 1841-1873   3385

GROWING UP IN THE 1850s. Edited by Mary Custis Lee DeButts.

Chapel Hill: Published for the Robert E. Lee Memorial Association by the University of North Carolina Press, 1984. 151 pp.

1852-1858. Sporadic journal entries of one of Robert E. Lee's daughters, offering scenes of family and social activities and recording inchoate adolescent moods and longings; life at Arlington and the deaths of her beloved Custis grandparents; at West Point during her father's tenure as superintendent; description of the Academy, its customs and mention of many of the cadets; school days at the Virginia Female Institute in Staunton; efforts to overcome shyness and conduct herself properly in society; feelings of sinfulness and expression of religious beliefs; notes on her reading.

LIBBEY, DAVID STONE, 1828-1904   3386

In DAVID LIBBEY, PENOBSCOT WOODMAN AND RIVER-DRIVER, by Fannie H. Eckstorm, pp. 28-95 passim. Boston: American Unitarian Association, 1907.

1852-1878. Extracts containing brief, simple notes on school, hunting and timber work on the rapids of the Penobscot River; Civil War service; employment in San Francisco area as a carpenter and in a foundry.

LIPPINCOTT, SARA JANE CLARKE, 1823-1904   3387

HAPS AND MISHAPS OF A TOUR OF EUROPE, by Grace Greenwood, pseud. Boston: Ticknor, Reed and Fields, 1854. 437 pp.

1852-1853. Travel journal obviously kept for publication; aboard the steamer ATLANTIC, on which Jenny Lind was also a passenger; long, narrative entries in effusive style, describing experiences in England, Ireland and Italy.

LUCAS, GEORGE A., 1824-1909   3388

THE DIARY OF GEORGE A. LUCAS: AN AMERICAN ART AGENT IN PARIS. Transcribed and with introduction by Lilian M.C. Randall. Princeton: Princeton University Press, 1979. 2 vols.

1852-1909. Early years of work in New Haven, Connecticut, Elizabethtown, New Jersey, and New York shown in diary of a civil engineer with an avid interest in art, theater and dining out with friends; long entries of work and social life giving way to brief but regularly kept notes of his life and work as a Paris art dealer, making purchases on the Paris art market for such American collectors as William and Henry Walters, John T. Johnston, Frank Frick and William H. Vanderbilt; long association with Samuel Avery, joint buying trips and numerous purchases for him and his New York gallery; information on artists, collecting practices and prices; overseeing commissions for prominent Baltimore citizens; private life, with limited mention of his mistress Josephine Marchand; household expenditures; carefree summers at his country house in Boissise with frequent visiting artists, including James Whistler; a valuable record of the business of art in Paris and the life of American expatriates.

MCALLISTER, JOHN   3389

"Diary of Rev. John McAllister, a Pioneer of 1852." OREGON PIONEER ASSOCIATION TRANSACTIONS (1922):471-508.

Apr-Oct 1852. Emigrant journey from Louisiana, Missouri, to Oregon City via Galena, Fort Des Moines and the Platte River; mainly camps, distances and conditions, with considerable detail on terrain and vegetation, making diary almost an emigrants' guide.

MCAULEY, ELIZA ANN, 1835-1919   3390

"Across the Plains in 1852." POMONA VALLEY HISTORIAN 2 (1966):9-24, 65-72, 124-135.

In COVERED WAGON WOMEN, edited by Kenneth L. Holmes, vol. 4, pp. 33-81.

Apr-Sep 1852. Teenager's diary, an engaging description of journey of five young people from Iowa to California in company with Ezra Meeker; road, weather and camp conditions with such work as putting morning milk in a tin on wagon to churn butter for evening meal; landmarks, including Independence Rock; Pawnee Indians; the environment and the hazards of the undertaking climaxed with happy meeting with their father, James McAuley, at Little York.

MCCLUNG, ZARAH   3391

TRAVELS ACROSS THE PLAINS IN 1852. St. Louis: Chambers and Knapp, Printers, 1854. 34 pp.

Mar-Aug 1852. Diary of emigrant's trip from Putnam County, Illinois, to Sacramento; meeting Mormons at Kanesville, Iowa; accident at ferry there; encounter with Pawnee Indians; typical notes on weather, roads, grass, hunting and crossing the desert; noting rich mining area; occasional comments on companions and neighboring trains.

MCGILL, GEORGE MCCULLOCH, 1838-1867   3392

"From Allegheny to Lake Superior." MOORSFIELD ANTIQUARIAN 1 (1937-1938):256-266.

Jul-Aug 1852. Young boy's travels from present Pittsburgh with his father, Dr. Alexander T. McGill, to inspect copper mines near Ontonagon, Michigan; by train to Cleveland, then by lake steamer to Detroit, lakes St. Clair, Huron and Superior to mines operated by the Adventure Mining Company of Michigan and the Ohio Mining Company; diarist's delight with hiking on Indian trails through dense forest, exploring and fishing; a few notes on the Chippewa; on return trip, a visit to Fort Mackinaw; a happy, naive diary.

MAGOON, GEORGE D.   3393

Throne, Mildred, ed. "The California Journey of George D. Magoon." IOWA JOURNAL OF HISTORY 54 (1956):131-168.

1852-1854. Gold rush journey of several men from Muscatine, Iowa; by boat, stagecoach and train to New York, from which they sailed on the PROMETHEUS to Nicaragua; long delay there with sickness and deaths among those waiting for passage to San Francisco; finally a miserable voyage on the C.I. DOW; unsuccessful attempts at mining, but good details of activities at the mines; work as a carpenter and builder, his customary trade; return by ship via Panama.

MANIGAULT, LOUIS   3394

In LIFE AND LABOR ON ARGYLE ISLAND, edited by James M. Clifton, pp. 194-365 passim. Savannah: Beehive Press, 1978.

1852-1867. Annual entries continuing plantation journal of his father, Charles; management of sizeable rice plantations, Gowrie and East Hermitage, on Argyle Island, a few miles above Savan-

nah; difficulty with inexperienced and neglectful overseers; upheavals due to Civil War; "ingratitude" of slaves; evacuation of home; painful visit to rented plantation after the war, seeing all buildings and trees destroyed.

House, Albert V., Jr., ed. "Deterioration of a Georgia Rice Plantation during Four Years of Civil War." JOURNAL OF SOUTHERN HISTORY 9 (1943):98-113.

1861-1865. Extracts.

NEWMARK, MYER J., b. 1838?   3395

"Log around the Horn." WESTERN STATES JEWISH HISTORICAL QUARTERLY 2 (1970):227-245.

Dec 1852-Apr 1853. A fourteen-year-old's diary of a voyage from New York to San Francisco on the CARRINGTON under Capt. F.B. French, traveling with his mother and younger siblings; ship social life, including "merry tones of the pianoforte, played by the captain's daughter"; reading in English, Hebrew and French; the dinner menus, often "sumptuous" and enjoyed by the diarist with unabated appetite, in spite of others' seasickness; ships encountered.

PARMENTIER, ROSINE, b. 1829   3396

McClary, Ben H. and Graf, LeRoy P., eds. "'Vineland' in Tennessee." EAST TENNESSEE HISTORICAL SOCIETY PUBLICATIONS 31 (1959):95-111.

Oct 1852. Cultivated young Brooklyn woman's journey with her sister and brother-in-law, Adele and Edward Bayer, to visit Vineland, a tract of land which her philanthropic Catholic family owned and upon which they had settled a colony of Catholic immigrants; from New York to Savannah on the ALABAMA; by train and wagon to the Sylco Mountains settlement, with good notes on travel, various residents of Vineland and the scenery and natural history of the area; wine cultivation under manager N.E. Guerin.

PERRY, MATTHEW CALBRAITH, 1794-1858   3397

THE JAPAN EXPEDITION, 1852-1854: THE PERSONAL JOURNAL OF COMMODORE MATTHEW C. PERRY. Edited by Roger Pineau. Smithsonian Institution Publication, 4743. Washington, D.C.: Smithsonian Institution Press, 1968. 241 pp.

1852-1854. Lively personal journal of the United States Naval Expedition to Japan upon which Perry based his later official report and including much material omitted from the latter; Perry's rancor over Navy Department politics; details of life in the Chinese ports, including contrast between wealth of Chinese merchants and poverty of their sailors; Perry's protection of merchants from Taiping rebels; account of treaty negotiations to open trade with Japan; visits in Japanese homes; notes on natural history of the area.

PRATT, SARAH, b. 1832?   3398

In COVERED WAGON WOMEN, edited by Kenneth L. Holmes, vol. 4, pp. 169-207.

Apr-Dec 1852. Diary notes in fragmentary sentences of overland journey from Liberty, Michigan, to San Bernadino, California, via Mormon corridor; route and roads; lodging with farmers in Illinois; women's work of washing and cooking; noting cholera and many graves; trouble with Indians' stealing; some trading; difficult desert travel; engaged after arrival to teach school upon which she commented, "A load is from my heart."

PULSZKY, FERENCZ 3399

Extracts in TRAVEL ACCOUNTS OF INDIANA, compiled by Shirley McCord, pp. 201-205.

Feb-Mar 1852. Hungarian's travel sketches; extracts covering stay at Madison and Indianapolis; comments on his traveling companion, Louis Kossuth, and his host, Indiana governor Joseph Albert Wright; customs and manners of Hoosiers; reaction to a Methodist service.

RANDLE, WILLIAM G. 3400

"A Diary of the Travels of William G. Randle, Daguerreotypist of Henry County, Tennessee." TENNESSEE HISTORICAL MAGAZINE 9 (1925):195-208.

Jun-Aug 1852. Travels with his instructor George Street "in quest of pleasure and money," plying their trade as daguerreotypists; amusing, sometimes flippant notes on people, incidents, customs and the state of morals and religion; admiration for the work of temperance societies and Methodist churches; interest in politics.

RIKER, JOHN F. 3401

JOURNAL OF A TRIP TO CALIFORNIA. Urbana? Ohio, 1855? 32 pp.

Apr-Jul 1852. Overland journey from Cincinnati to San Francisco; description of the country, soil, climate and rivers; incidents of the trip and summary of distances.

RUDD, LYDIA ALLEN 3402

In WOMEN'S DIARIES OF THE WESTWARD JOURNEY, collected by Lillian Schlissel, pp. 187-198.

May-Oct 1852. Woman's diary of overland journey from St. Joseph, Missouri, to Oregon; usual travel and camp notes; great concern about illnesses, especially cholera, measles and dysentery, noting deaths and graves passed each day; due to lateness of season, making last leg of trip by Indian canoe down Columbia River to Salem; indication that she and her husband might not claim land as they had planned.

SAWYER, FRANCIS, b. 1831 3403

In COVERED WAGON WOMEN, edited by Kenneth L. Holmes, vol. 4, pp. 83-115.

May-Aug 1852. Cloverport, Kentucky, woman's diary of overland trip to Sacramento with her husband, Thomas, who had made two previous trips; travel by mule-drawn carriage; rain, mud, delay in crossing Missouri River due to weather and wagons ahead of them; mention of a young woman's bloomer costume, "a very appropriate dress for a trip like this"; disturbed by passing scene of bloody Sioux-Pawnee battle; noting cholera and a stampede; enjoying driving the team; having to abandon broken wagon and carriage and convert to a pack train; informative entries of people, countryside and her feelings about the trip.

SHARP, CORNELIA ANN 3404

"Diary of Mrs. Cornelia A. Sharp, Crossing the Plains from Missouri to Oregon in 1852." OREGON PIONEER ASSOCIATION TRANSACTIONS (1903):171-188.

May-Oct 1852. Emigrant journey from Jackson County, Missouri, to Oregon City with her husband, John, and their seven children, in a company under James Brown; brief notes of distances, scenery, natural history and mishaps.

SHOWERMAN, ELLEN AUGUSTA PARKER COBB, 1833-1910 3405

Showerman, Grant. "The Indian Stream Republic and Luther Parker." NEW HAMPSHIRE HISTORICAL SOCIETY COLLECTIONS 11 (1915):1-250. Diary, pp. 130-162.

1852-1857 (with gaps). Extracts from the Wisconsin pioneer diary of the daughter of Luther Parker, first permanent white settler at Muskego; attending the Teachers' Institute at Genesee; social and domestic life; teaching school, with its trials and small rewards; her father's illness and death and the death of her husband, Nathan Cobb, whom she had married in 1854.

SPENCER, LAFAYETTE 3406

"Journal of the Oregon Trail." ANNALS OF IOWA, 3d ser. 8 (1907-1909):304-310.

May-Oct 1852. Journey with emigrant train from Van Buren County to Oregon City; brief notes of distances, camps, grass, water and deaths from cholera.

STONE, FRANKLIN L., 1816-1886 3407

Stone, Lulu, ed. "Extracts from the Diaries and Letters of Franklin L. Stone." THE FRONTIER: A MAGAZINE OF THE NORTHWEST 12 (1932):375-380. Diary, pp. 375-376.

May 1852. Early diary fragment of a man who later settled at Gallatin City, Montana; train and boat trip to Detroit, presumably starting from New York, then on to Iowa.

TERRELL, JOSEPH CHRISTOPER, 1831-1909 3408

REMINISCENCES OF THE EARLY DAYS OF FORT WORTH. Fort Worth: Texas Prtg. Co., 1906. 101 pp. Diary, pp. 76-91.

May-Jul 1852. Boonville, Missouri, man's overland trip to California, with usual notes on scenery, natural history, etc.

THOMSON, ORIGEN 3409

CROSSING THE PLAINS. Greensburg, Ind.: O. Thomson, Printer, 1896. 122 pp. Fairfield, Wash.: Ye Galleon, 1983. 95 pp. Diary, pp. 16-73.

Mar-Sep 1852. Diary of a Decatur and Rush County, Indiana, emigrant with a party made up chiefly of members of Reformed Church of Springhill; to Cincinnati and down Missouri River to St. Louis and St. Joseph, where he noted many begging Indians; laying in supplies and starting for Oregon; typical travel notes of hunting for missing cattle, deaths, injuries, landmarks, Fort Kearny, Fort Laramie and Shoshone and Digger Indians around Fort Hall; matter-of-fact record of various disagreements and secessions from the company; the monotony of travel relieved by singing and by young women making garlands from wild flowers for teamsters' hats; keeping the Sabbath with preaching by James Worth or Bible reading; seeing the folly of trying to navigate the Snake River and continuing by wagon to Portland.

TURNBULL, THOMAS, 1812?-1869   3410

Paxson, Frederic L., ed. "T. Turnbull's Travels from the United States across the Plains to California." WISCONSIN HISTORICAL SOCIETY PROCEEDINGS 61 (1913):151-225.

Apr-Aug 1852. Gold rush journal of an English immigrant and longtime farmer at Glencoe, Illinois; from Chicago to Hangtown, California, via Mormon and Oregon trails; full, spontaneous notes on conditions of travel, prices of food and ferrying, encounters with Indians, violence, privation and death on the Humboldt; number of graves en route.

WALKER, WILLIAM HOLMES, b. 1820   3411

In TREASURES OF PIONEER HISTORY, compiled by Kate B. Carter, vol. 6, pp. 238-254.

1852-1857. Journal, with some later additions, of Mormon appointed to a mission in South Africa; persecution by mobs and local clergy in Cape Town for attempts to preach; winning converts in Port Elizabeth; after much opposition, gaining support to buy the ship UNITY and take new members to England, thence on the CARAVAN to New York; managing the affairs of the company and providing transportation to Salt Lake City.

WARD, JOHN   3412

Abel, Annie H., ed. "Indian Affairs in New Mexico under the Administration of William Carr Lane." NEW MEXICO HISTORICAL REVIEW 16 (1941):206-232, 328-358.

Oct 1852-Oct 1853. Official journal kept at the Superintendency of Indian Affairs at Santa Fe; feeding and housing visiting Indians, distributing presents, issuing trading licences, etc.; activities of Lane as superintendent and governor; notes on Pueblo, Apache and Navaho Indians; references to John Greiner and other officials; brief entries but revealing of Indian policy and the controversy between Lane and Col. E.V. Sumner over dealings with Navahos.

WARNER, HORATIO GATES   3413

Russell, John R., ed. "From California by Sea in 1852." UNIVERSITY OF ROCHESTER LIBRARY BULLETIN 15 (1962):1-11.

May-Jun 1852. Rochester, New York, judge's voyage from San Francisco on the PACIFIC to Nicaragua, thence on the PROMETHEUS; hasty notes of a bored and seasick passenger; description of Nicaragua.

WAYMAN, JOHN HUDSON, 1820-1867   3414

A DOCTOR ON THE CALIFORNIA TRAIL. Edited by Edgeley W. Todd. Denver: Old West Publishing, 1971. 136 pp.

Mar-Oct 1852. Cambridge City, Indiana, doctor's gold rush diary; from St. Joseph via the Sweetwater, South Pass and the Hudspeth route to Placerville, thence to the southern mines near Sonora; camps, distances, conditions of travel, with vituperation against dust, mosquitos and the stupidity of some of his fellow travelers; considerable geological but little medical information; a few notes on Indians; in the diggings in present Tuolumne County, where he seemed to mine in a rather desultory fashion.

WILLIAMS, FRANKLIN HUBBARD, 1834-1891   3415

DIARY FROM 1852 to 1891 ... AND CERTAIN PERTINENT ADDENDA. Sunderland, Mass.: Williams Family, 1975. 95 pp.

1852-1891. A Sunderland, Massachusetts, farmer's diary with a wealth of agricultural details in brief entries; courtship and marriage, church-going and attendance at public lectures; death of his eighteen-year-old son of typhoid fever; farm and social life.

WING, STEPHEN   3416

THE DAILY JOURNAL OF STEPHEN WING. Edited by Phyllis Gernes. Garden Valley, Calif.: Phyllis Gernes, 1982. 194 pp.

1852-1860. South Yarmouth, Massachusetts, man's diary of gold mining in Placer and El Dorado counties; good details of a prospector's life, including claim disputes, earnings and expenses, miners' meetings and hardships; work as a carpenter and building waterwheels for river bar companies; many references to Chinese in the diggings; activities and events in Uniontown and Coloma, including public hangings; references to Willoughby Cook and others.

WOODHAMS, WILLIAM H., 1829-1891   3417

Martin, Charles W., ed. "The Diary of William H. Woodhams: The Great Deserts or Around and Across." NEBRASKA HISTORY 61 (1980):1-101.

1852-1854. Extensive travels of a young English immigrant who had settled at Plainwell, Michigan; voyage from New York to San Francisco on the GREEN POINT under Capt. Robert McCormick, whose ignorance and crudity disgusted the diarist; good life of cabin passengers on a new and comfortable ship; reading, pranks and Old Neptune's festivities; many humorous incidents and comments; rounding Cape Horn; activities in California; return on the CORTEZ, overland via Nicaragua, thence to New York on the STAR OF THE WEST; immediately home to Michigan to prepare for overland journey back to California with horses to sell; travel with Alfred Woodhams and Joseph Chart, with colorful notes on people in Indiana and Missouri; ferrying the Missouri at St. Joseph; notes on Plains Indians and emigrants; a good description of the Humboldt; problems with keeping horses alive and well enough to sell; an excellent diary, obviously kept for the love of observing and writing.

1853

ANON.   3418

"Thirty-three Years Ago: Through Nebraska before Any Settlements." NEBRASKA STATE HISTORICAL SOCIETY TRANSACTIONS AND REPORTS 3 (1892):270-278.

Apr-Oct 1853. Extracts mainly covering Nebraska portion of a cultivated Wisconsin woman's journey with her family to California; graphic details of fording and ferrying swollen rivers, including the Platte; weather, scenery, life in camp and on the trail; description of her "rude and dreary" pioneer ranch home in Indian Valley, California, which she set about to make cheerful and comfortable.

ACTON, JOHN EMERICH EDWARD DALBERG,   **3419**
1834-1902

"Lord Acton's American Diaries." FORTNIGHTLY REVIEW 110 (1921):727-742, 914-934; 111 (1922):63-83.

ACTON IN AMERICA. Edited by Sydney W. Jackman. Shepherdstown, W. Va.: Patmos Press, 1979. 112 pp.

Jun-Jul 1853. Journal of young English Catholic, later noted historian and moralist, in America as part of Lord Ellesmere's British delegation to the New York "Crystal Palace" Exhibition; travel by rail and Hudson River steamer; visits to Niagara Falls, Boston, Cambridge, etc.; notes on faculty and curriculum of Harvard and on conversations with such writers and intellectuals as Lowell, Longfellow, Orestes Brownson and George Ticknor; a detailed and sometimes condescending observation of things American: newspapers, law, institutions, education, customs, scenery, slavery, scholarship, etc.; highly entertaining and informative.

ALLYN, HENRY   **3420**

"Journal of Henry Allyn." OREGON PIONEER ASSOCIATION TRANSACTIONS (1921):372-435.

Mar-Sep 1853. Emigrant journey from Fulton County, Illinois, to the Willamette Valley; substantial entries on topography, natural history and curiosities; names of many fellow emigrants; sicknesses and accidents en route; sympathy for displaced Indians and scathing criticism of government Indian policy; quotations from Milton and other poets; a good diary of the Oregon emigration.

In WITH HER OWN WINGS, by Portland Federation of Women's Organizations, edited by Helen Krebs, pp. 63-66. Portland: Beattie, 1948.

May, Jul 1853. Extracts; report of a murder with speedy justice to the guilty; reburying corpse at disturbed grave; making a precarious crossing of unidentified river.

ARTHUR, MALVINA, 1832-1916   **3421**

Reeves, Thomas C. "The Diaries of Malvina Arthur: Windows into the Past of Our Twenty-first President." VERMONT HISTORY 38 (1970):177-188.

1853, 1869. Article containing extracts of diaries kept by the sister of Chester A. Arthur; teaching in Cohoes, New York, at the academy of which her brother was principal; social life which she did not enjoy; at home with her parents in Hoosick, New York, where she lived in dread of her stern Baptist minister father and in despair over her rejection of his religion; later diary kept during a period of increased family discord following the death of her mother; affection for and pride in Chester; beginnings of her sister Annie's madness; a sad diary of a woman who herself died insane.

AUBRY, FRANCOIS XAVIER, 1824-1854   **3422**

In EXPLORING SOUTHWESTERN TRAILS, by Philip St. George Cooke, edited by Ralph P. Bieber, pp. 353-383. Glendale, Calif.: Arthur H. Clark, 1938. Reprint. Southwest Historical Series, 7. Philadelphia: Porcupine Press, 1974.

Jul-Sep 1853. Santa Fe trader's journal of exploring expedition for a possible wagon or rail route between New Mexico and California, largely along the thirty-fifth parallel, with notes beginning at Tejon Pass in the Sierra Nevada; eastward via the Mojave and Colorado rivers, suffering lack of water, wood and grass; Indian attacks and continuous harrassment, at one time wounding two-thirds of the party, which was saved from annihilation only by their Colt revolvers; continuing in desperate condition to Albuquerque; a good journal by a French-Canadian who became legendary during his short life in the Southwest.

Jul-Aug 1854. Second journey from California to New Mexico, this time with sixty men, including Judge José Otero, mainly over the same route as before, and with less trouble.

BALDWIN, ABIGAIL POLLARD, 1798-1876   **3423**

"Selections from the Plymouth Diary of Abigail Baldwin." VERMONT HISTORY 40 (1972):218-223.

1853-1854. Diary of a Presbyterian minister's wife, with entries beginning upon her return from a disappointing residence in Texas; many labors and cares, including deaths of numerous friends and relatives and an appalling amount of sickness in the community; destruction by wind of a new house her husband was building; religious reflections.

BALDWIN, CHARLES CANDEE, 1834-1895   **3424**

Wright, G. Frederick. "Memorial of Charles Candee Baldwin, LLD., Late President of the Western Reserve Historical Society." WESTERN RESERVE HISTORICAL SOCIETY TRACT, no. 88, 4 (1896):129-173. Diary, pp. 129-139.

1853-1856. Extracts within biography of an Elyria, Ohio, youth, later a judge in Cuyahoga County; high moral resolves and religious reflections; studies in classics, mathematics, etc., at Harvard; a poem in the meter of Longfellow's "Hiawatha."

BEALE, EDWARD FITZGERALD, 1822-1893   **3425**

In CENTRAL ROUTE TO THE PACIFIC, by Gwinn H. Heap, pp. 64-70. Philadelphia: Lippincott, Grambo, 1854.

In CENTRAL ROUTE TO THE PACIFIC: WITH RELATED MATERIAL ON RAILROAD EXPLORATIONS AND INDIAN AFFAIRS, by Gwinn H. Heap, pp. 183-191. Far West and Rockies Historical Series, vol. 7. Glendale, Calif.: Arthur H. Clark, 1957.

Jul 1853. Journal kept by California's superintendent of Indian affairs while waiting for Gwinn Harris Heap who made a side trip to get provisions and take an ailing expedition member to Taos; visiting an Indian camp, hunting with Indians and marveling at their horses and horsemanship; surviving on meat killed by their Delaware Indian guide, Dick Brown.

WAGON ROAD FROM FORT DEFIANCE TO THE COLORADO RIVER. 35th Cong., 1st sess., 1858, H. Exec. Doc. 124. Washington?, 1858. Diary, pp. 15-87.

In UNCLE SAM'S CAMELS, by May H. Stacey, pp. 144-281. Cambridge: Harvard University Press; Glorieta, N. Mex.: Rio Grande Press, 1929.

Jun 1857-Feb 1858. Commander's official journal of expediton to survey wagon route from Fort Defiance to the Colorado River and report test of camels for transportation from San Antonio to California; details of route conditions and management of camel corps; incidents with Indians.

WAGON ROAD—FORT SMITH TO COLORADO RIVER. 36th Cong., 1st sess., 1860, H. Exec. Doc. 42. Washington? 1860. 91 pp. Diary, pp. 8-53.

Oct 1858-Jun 1859. Travel, with Dick Brown, over much of the same Southwest area covered by Josiah Gregg; topographical and natural history observations; noting water, wood and grass, desirable locations for military posts, adequacy of the emigrant road, sufficient timber for building bridges, etc., on a road that would enable mail and provisions to be carried by camels; fishing and hunting bufffalo, antelope and birds; a visit to Santa Fe and old friend Kit Carson; playing ''joke'' on Indians who had killed their mule, resulting in the death of four Indians.

BECKWITH, EDWARD GRIFFIN, 1818-1881   3426

''Report of Exploration of a Route for the Pacific Railroad, near the 38th and 39th Parallels of Latitude, from the Mouth of the Kansas to Sevier River, in the Great Basin.'' In 33rd Cong., 1st sess., 1855, H. Exec. Doc. 129, pp. 1-87.

In REPORTS OF THE SECRETARY OF WAR COMMUNICATING THE SEVERAL RAILROAD EXPLORATIONS, by United States War Department, vol. 2.

Jun-Nov. 1853. Military exploration from Fort Leavenworth, across Arkansas River at mouth of Apishpa to Roubideau's Pass; to Blue River and Wasatch Pass and Sevier Lake; Cedar Springs to Great Salt Lake; sharing provisions with Colonel Burwell's party emigrating to California; extracts from diary of commander, J.W. Gunnison, who was murdered by Indians near Sevier Lake.

''Report of Explorations for the Pacific Railroad on the Line of the Forty-First Parallel of North Latitude.'' In 33rd Cong., 1st sess., 1855, H. Exec. Doc. 129, pp. 5-64.

In REPORTS OF THE SECRETARY OF WAR COMMUNICATING THE SEVERAL RAILROAD EXPLORATIONS, by United States War Department, vol. 2.

Apr-Jun 1854. Topographical information on survey of area from Salt Lake to Humboldt valley and mountains to Sacramento River.

BELSHAW, GEORGE, 1816-1893   3427

THE DIARY OF GEORGE BELSHAW (OREGON TRAIL - 1853). Eugene, Oreg.: Lane County Pioneer-Historical Society, 1960. 52 pp.

Mar-Sep 1853. English emigrant's record of a journey from Lake County, Indiana, to the Willamette Valley, kept by the captain of the wagon train; mostly logistics and conditions of travel, route, terrain, etc.; a few notes on Indians and other emigrant parties.

Castle, Gwen. ''Belshaw Journey, Oregon Trail, 1853.'' OREGON HISTORICAL QUARTERLY 32 (1931):217-239.

Mar-Sep 1853. Article containing extracts.

BELSHAW, MARIA A. PARSONS   3428

In NEW SPAIN AND THE ANGLO-AMERICAN WEST, vol. 2, pp. 215-243. Los Angeles: Privately printed, 1932.

May-Sep 1853. Record of Lake County, Indiana, woman traveling with the Parsons and Belshaw families; physical conditions and daily experiences from Council Bluffs to Oregon; weather, roads, river crossings, landmarks, water and grass.

Ellison, Joseph W. ''Diary of Maria Parsons Belshaw.'' OREGON HISTORICAL QUARTERLY 33 (1932):318-333.

Aug-Oct 1853. Extract, beginning at the Snake River; daily count of graves and dead animals along the way; prayers for the sick in her company; prices at The Dalles; steamboat voyage on the Columbia; notes on Salem and the Willamette Valley.

BETTELHEIM, BERNARD JEAN, 1811-1870   3429

Schwartz, William L., ed. ''Commodore Perry at Okinawa.'' AMERICAN HISTORICAL REVIEW 51 (1946):262-276.

May-Jul 1853, Jul 1854. Extracts from diary of a British missionary at Naha who aided Perry and the Americans in securing provisions and as an interpreter, in return for supplies needed by his family; puzzling over whether his relation to Samuel Williams, the official interpreter whose skills he questioned, was ''simple guide, or counsel, or whisperer''; enjoying, along with his delighted children, a performance of the ''Dramatic Corps'' on the MISSISSIPPI.

BLACK, READING WOOD, 1830-1867   3430

THE LIFE AND DIARY OF READING W. BLACK: A HISTORY OF EARLY UVALDE. Arranged by Ike Moore. Uvalde, Tex.: Privately printed for El Progresso Club, Austin, Texas, Calithump Press, 1934. 93 pp.

1853-1856. Texas rancher's diary; a two-month trip on a mustang chase; various business trips to Eagle Pass, San Antonio and Austin; brief notes on trade, ranching, gardening, personal affairs, visits, weather, etc.

BLAINE, DAVID EDWARDS, 1824-1900   3431

MEMOIRS OF PUGET SOUND; EARLY SEATTLE, 1853-1856: THE LETTERS OF DAVID AND CATHERINE BLAINE. Edited by Richard A. Seiber, Fairfield, Wash.: Ye Galleon, 1978. 220 pp. passim.

1853-1856. Letters and letter-diaries of a Methodist minister and his wife from Seneca Falls, New York, assigned to the Puget Sound area; on the OHIO via Panama, with good descriptions of muleback crossing of the Isthmus; thence on the PANAMA and REPUBLIC to San Francisco and on to Puget Sound on the MARY MELVILLE; experiences in Seattle, where David built a church and Catherine taught school; interesting notes of pioneer life and difficulties, including Indian unrest leading to the attack on Seattle, which the Blaines escaped by being taken aboard the DECATUR; Catherine's references to Indians as a ''degraded and abandoned race''; activities in Portland and Oregon City.

BROWN, THOMAS DUNLOP, 1807-1874   3432

Brooks, Juanita, ed. ''Indian Sketches from the Journals of T.D. Brown and Jacob Hamblin.'' UTAH HISTORICAL QUARTERLY 29 (1961):347-360.

1853-1855. Extracts within article on the activities of two Mormons engaged in the Southern Indian Mission on the Santa Clara, an important Mormon missionary effort among the Moqui and other Indians of southern Utah; notes of Thomas D. Brown, a Scottish immigrant, on healing methods of a medicine man and food preparation; Jacob Hamblin's entries on hungry Indians reduced to selling their children as slaves to ''Gentiles''; brutal Indian melees among rivals for wives; Hamblin's insistence upon peaceful, noncoercive approaches to the Indians.

JOURNAL OF THE SOUTHERN INDIAN MISSION. Edited by Juanita Brooks. Western Text Society Series, no. 4. Logan: Utah State University Press, 1972. 175 pp.

1854-1857. Brown's interesting and articulate diary; journey from Salt Lake; farming; customs and conditions of Indians and Mormon doctrines regarding them; sermons, exhortations, dreams and prophecies of various elders; arbitration of disputes and family problems in council; references to John Doyle Lee and Brigham Young; some personal details, poems and hymns of diarist.

Brooks, Juanita. "INDIAN SKETCHES FROM THE JOURNALS OF T.D. BROWN AND JACOB HAMBLIN." UTAH HISTORICAL QUARTERLY 29 (1961):346-360.

Apr-Jun 1854. Extracts within article.

BURRELL, BIRNEY, b. 1840   **3433**

Stuart, Reginald R., ed. "The Burrell Letters." CALIFORNIA HISTORICAL SOCIETY QUARTERLY 28 (1949):297-322; 29 (1950):39-59, 173-179. Diary, pp. 39-44.

Jan-Jun 1853 (with gaps). Diary fragment of a thirteen-year-old boy from Tallmadge, Ohio, arriving by ship with his mother and two sisters to join his father, Lyman J. Burrell, in California; at the ranch of J.T. Clarke near Alviso; a "strawberry hunt" in the mountains; hunting seals for blubber.

CAPRON, ELISHA SMITH, 1806-1883?   **3434**

HISTORY OF CALIFORNIA, FROM ITS DISCOVERY TO THE PRESENT TIME. Boston: J.P. Jewett; Cleveland: Jewett, Proctor and Worthington, 1854. 356 pp.

Apr-Sep 1853. Businessman's diary of steamship voyage on the PROMETHEUS from New York to Nicaragua; description of Lake Nicaragua and towns during boat and muleback trip to the west coast; continuing on overcrowded steamship BROTHER JONATHAN to San Francisco; securing commercial claims for New York businesses, gathering information on conditions of trade and returning to New York via Panama on the WINFIELD SCOTT and ILLINOIS.

CARR, WILLIAM OTIS, 1834-1904   **3435**

THE AMHERST DIARY OF WILLIAM OTIS CARR. Edited by Frank O. Spinney. Guilford, Conn.: Printed by the Shore Line Times, 1940. 30 pp.

1853-1857. Student's diary kept very sporadically at Amherst College; leaving Derry, New Hampshire, home; college traditions; religious thoughts and activities; 1855 revival among students.

CARVALHO, SOLOMON NUNES, 1815-1897   **3436**

INCIDENTS OF TRAVEL AND ADVENTURE IN THE FAR WEST. New York: Derby & Jackson, 1857. 380 pp. Centenary ed. Jacob R. Schiff Library of Jewish Contributions to American Democracy. Philadelphia: Jewish Publication Society of America, 1954. 328 pp.

Aug 1853-Jun 1854. Chiefly narrative, with some diary entries, of artist and daguerreotypist with Fremont on his fifth exploration made to survey a railroad route from New York to California; usual travel notes of scenery, water and weather; contacts with Indians and Mormons.

CIPRIANI, LEONETTO, conte, 1812-1888   **3437**

CALIFORNIA AND OVERLAND DIARIES FROM 1853 THROUGH

1861. Translated and edited by Ernest Falbo. Portland, Oreg.: Champoeg Press, 1962. 148 pp.

1853-1861. Travel diary and memoirs, written up later for his son, of the western American adventures of a Corsican aristocrat; sojourn with Mormons in Utah; a cattle drive to California; his views on Americans as barbarians, except for Mormons, whose society he admired.

CLEAVER, JOSEPH, 1833-1909   **3438**

THE DIARY OF A STUDENT AT DELAWARE COLLEGE. Edited by William D. Lewis. Baltimore: J.H. Furst, 1951. 87 pp.

Lewis, William D., ed. "Diary of a Student at Delaware College." DELAWARE NOTES, 24th ser. (1951):1-87.

Extracts in DIARY OF AMERICA, edited by Josef and Dorothy Berger, pp. 216-224.

1853-1854. A college diary showing a range of academic and social activities; admittance to and activities of literary society; debates, classes and lessons; sketch plan of college and yard; pranks of students; the sequestering of a runaway slave in the dormitory; a youthfully entertaining diary.

DINWIDDIE, DAVID   **3439**

Booth, Margaret, ed. "Overland from Indiana to Oregon: The Dinwiddie Journal." FRONTIER: A MAGAZINE OF THE NORTHWEST 8 (1928):115-130. Reprint. Sources of Northwest History, no. 2. Missoula: State University of Montana, 1928. 14 pp. FRONTIER OMNIBUS, edited by John W. Hakola, pp. 181-195.

May-Oct 1853. Porter County, Indiana, man's journey to Oregon City; notes on scenery, expenses, conditions of travel, Indian encounters on the plains and the Nez Percé in Oregon. Thought to have been written by either David or John Dinwiddie.

EARLE, STEPHEN CARPENTER, 1839-1913   **3440**

THE JOURNALS OF STEPHEN C. EARLE. Edited by Albert B. Southwick. Worcester, Mass.: Worcester Bicentennial Commission, 1976.

1853-1858. Charming journal of teenage Quaker boy living with his uncle and family in Worcester, Massachusetts; school, community and social events; significant notes on family life, abolitionists and lectures on a variety of subjects including the Kansas-Nebraska Act.

EUBANK, MARY JAMES, b. 1832   **3441**

Nunn, W.C. "A Journal of Our Trip to Texas." TEXANA 10 (1972):30-44.

Oct-Dec 1853. Diary of a journey with her family and other relatives from Glasgow, Kentucky, to the San Gabriel River at Circleville, Texas; a sad farewell to friends; traveling by wagon, stopping at Nashville, Memphis and Little Rock; passing through Dallas and Waco; looking for suitable land; the vicissitudes of travel including dust, mud, scarcity of water, losses, and accidents, road conditions and difficulty of river crossings; notes on food, prices, camping spots and description of countryside; welcome by relatives in Cameron, Texas.

GARRARD, CHARLES T. 3442

"Introduction of Imported Cattle in Kentucky." KENTUCKY STATE HISTORICAL SOCIETY REGISTER 29 (1931):400-415; 30 (1932):37-60.

Mar-Jun 1853. Substantial and interesting diary of a cattle purchasing agent from Bourbon County on a profitable buying trip to England for the North Kentucky Cattle Importing Company; from Lexington to New York by stagecoach, riverboat and train; miserable ocean crossing on the PACIFIC; travels throughout the north of England buying livestock on large estates; thorough descriptions of countryside, agriculture, antiquities, and local customs, inns etc; sightseeing in London; return on the PACIFIC, with good picture of ocean travel.

GILL, HARRIET TARLETON, 1828-1910 3443

In CALIFORNIA LETTERS OF WILLIAM GILL, edited by Eva Turner Clark, pp. 35-38. New York: Downs Print, 1922.

Apr-Jun 1853. Lexington, Missouri, woman's daily record of miles covered and camp sites established during overland journey to California.

GOLDSBOROUGH, JOHN RODGERS, 1809-1877 3444

"Commodore Perry's Landing in Japan - 1853: From the Journal of Commodore John Rodgers Goldborough, U.S.N." AMERICAN NEPTUNE 7 (1947):9-20.

Jun-Jul 1853. Notes beginning in Yedo Bay aboard the SARATOGA; assessing the military situation, including Japanese ships in the harbor and soldiers to be seen on shore; detailed account of repeated negotiations on board the SUSQUEHANNA to ensure delivery of President Fillmore's letter to the emperor and the accompanying American show of force; exchange of credentials on shore between Perry and the emperor's ambassador; reconnaissance of harbors and inlets, exchange of presents and diarist's sense of the success of the mission.

GRAVES, EBENEZER 3445

"Journal of a Peddling Trip Kept by Ebenezer Graves of Ashfield, Massachusetts." OLD-TIME NEW ENGLAND 56 (1966):81-90, 108-116.

Mar-Aug 1853. A silk peddler's record of travel, mostly on foot, and trade through New England towns, with comments on the major industries and businesses of each; visits to factories, churches, a fortune teller and a phrenologist; having a tooth filled with tin foil; a description of Siamese twins; names of families with whom he lodged.

GREGG, DAVID LAWRENCE, 1814-1868 3446

THE DIARIES OF DAVID LAWRENCE GREGG: AN AMERICAN DIPLOMAT IN HAWAII. Edited by Pauline King. Honolulu: Hawaiian Historical Society, 1982. 605 pp.

1853-1858. Personal diary of commissioner of the United States to Hawaii; sailing from Panama on the OHIO with notes on passengers, including uncomplimentary remarks about David E. Blaine's sermons and Mrs. Blaine's bloomers; political events, church and state relations, attitudes and community interest in lengthy negotiations for annexation; frequent mention of Robert C. Wyllie, Hawaiian minister of foreign relations, William Miller,

British consul general, and Louis Emile Perrin, French commissioner; character sketches of royalty and the wedding of Kamehameha IV and Emma Rooke; social life and clubs in Honolulu; arrivals and departures of mail ships; praise and criticism for American missionaries; opposition to his appointment by Richard Armstrong and Gerrit P. Judd, with eventual replacement by James W. Borden; taking position as minister of finance in Hawaiian government; a few notes on his family and visitors.

GROVER, C. 3447

In REPORTS OF EXPLORATIONS AND SURVEYS, by United States War Department, vol. 1, pp. 488-515.

Sep 1853-Feb 1854. Extracts from journal of railroad survey of the Missouri River from Fort Benton to mouth of the Milk River and from headwaters of the Missouri River to The Dalles on the Columbia River; difficult traveling with an Indian guide unacquainted with the trail when covered with snow.

HARKER, MARY HAINES 3448

"Journal of a Quaker Maid." VIRGINIA QUARTERLY REVIEW 11 (1935):61-81.

May-Dec 1853. A Quaker girl's visit to Lynchburg, with accounts of social life, horseback riding, reading of popular novels and poems; references to many local people; courtship with Jack Slaughter leading to their marriage.

HAYDEN, FERDINAND VANDIVEER, 1829-1887 3449

McLaird, James D. and Turchen, Lesta V. "Exploring the Black Hills, 1855-1875: The Scientist in Western Exploration." SOUTH DAKOTA HISTORY 4 (1974):161-197.

1853-1860. Article containing extracts from official reports and personal journals of geologist's explorations of the Black Hills, Badlands and White River region, some privately undertaken and others as a member of G.K. Warren and W.F. Raynolds expeditions; collecting and describing geological and fossil specimens; continuous quarrels with Warren who "has treated me like a dog."

HEAP, GWINN HARRIS, 1817-1887 3450

CENTRAL ROUTE TO THE PACIFIC. Philadelphia: Lippincott, Grambo, 1854. 136 pp. Diary, pp. 13-64, 71-111. Reprint. New York: Arno, 1981.

CENTRAL ROUTE TO THE PACIFIC: WITH RELATED MATERIAL ON RAILROAD EXPLORATIONS AND INDIAN AFFAIRS. Edited by Leroy R. and Ann W. Hafen. Far West and Rockies Historical Series, vol. 7. Glendale, Calif.: Arthur H. Clark, 1957. 346 pp. Diary, pp. 75-183, 192-251.

May-Aug 1853. Diary kept while accompanying Edward F. Beale, superintendent of Indian affairs in California, who was on expedition to select lands suitable for Indian reservations; route via Council Grove, Fort Atkinson, Bent's Fort, Fort Massachusetts, Green River, Cedar City and Mohave River; crossing unexplored area from Westport, now Kansas City, Missouri, to Los Angeles, which was of interest to diarist for railroad route to the Pacific; usual exploring notes on weather, grass, wood, distances, fertility of the region, traders, Mexican villages and Shawnee, Caw, Cheyenne, Arapaho, Utah and Paiute Indians; special praise for expedition's Delaware Indian guide, Dick Brown, and his hunting prowess.

HOFFMAN, WILLIAM J., b. 1801   **3451**

Taylor, Arthur S. and McKinney, William. "An Accurate Observer: William Hoffman's View of Idaho in 1853." IDAHO YESTERDAYS 8, no. 2 (1964):20-25.

Apr-Aug 1853. Article containing extracts from Oregon Trail diary of a man from Attica, Indiana; terrain, vegetation, wildlife, geological formations, minerals, etc., in a pioneer diary unusual for its attention to scientific detail; Hudspeth's Cutoff portion quoted in full.

KAUTZ, AUGUST VALENTINE, 1828-1895   **3452**

NOTHING WORTHY OF NOTE TRANSPIRED TODAY: THE NORTHWEST JOURNALS OF AUGUST V. KAUTZ. Edited by Gary Fuller Reese. Tacoma: Tacoma Public Library, 1978. 451 pp.

1853-1858. Daily life at Fort Steilacoom, Washington Territory, of German immigrant officer and quartermaster with a company of about forty men; disputes with the commanding officer of Hudson's Bay Company at Fort Nisqually; Indian encounters, including attempt to capture Chief Leschi; trips in Puget Sound as far as Vancouver Island.

"Extracts from the Diary of General A.V. Kautz." WASHINGTON HISTORIAN 1 (1900): 115-119, 181-186; 2 (1900):12-15.

Apr-Jun 1853. Extracts; visits to farms; sketches of settlers, including Colonel Ebey and "old man Crockett" on Whidbey Island; excursions throughout the Puget Sound area; notes on Indians.

Haines, Aubrey L., ed. "Mountain Challenge, 1857: Journal of Lt. Augustus V. Kautz on Mount Rainier." PACIFIC NORTHWEST QUARTERLY 48 (1957):134-138.

Jul 1857. An almost successful attempt to climb Mount Rainier; route based on information provided by Nisqually chief Leschi; food and equipment; long, difficult hike to the base of the mountain with companions Robert O. Craig and Nicholas Dogue and Indian guides; ascent up Nisqually Glacier, having to give up just short of the summit because of approaching darkness; equally difficult descent and return to the fort "much used up."

Schmitt, Martin F., ed. "From Missouri to Oregon in 1860." PACIFIC NORTHWEST QUARTERLY 37 (1946):193-230.

May-Sep 1860. Accompanying a transport of recruits under George A.H. Blake by riverboat to Fort Benton, thence over Mullan Road to join the Ninth Infantry in Oregon; from Jefferson Barracks up the Missouri on the SPREAD EAGLE, with interesting notes on travel, army personnel and civilians; shooting buffalo and wolves from the decks; activities at Fort Benton awaiting John Mullan, "quite a monomaniac about his road"; good account of journey over the road with Mullan's party in advance of Blake's; entries ending short of Walla Walla.

KETCHAM, REBECCA   **3453**

Kaiser, Leo M. and Knuth, Priscilla, eds. "From Ithaca to Clatsop Plains: Miss Ketcham's Journal of Travel." OREGON HISTORICAL QUARTERLY 62 (1961):237-287, 337-402.

May-Sep 1853. Young woman's account, kept for friends, of journey to Oregon in a small party led by William H. Gray; names of fellow emigrants and people along the way; route via Fort Kearny, forks of the Platte, Fort Laramie, Fort Boise, etc.; very detailed descriptions of terrain and conditions of travel; interactions,

some acrimonious, of members of the party; diarist's difficulties and discomforts borne with Christian fortitude.

KINGSBURY, CYRUS, 1786-1870   **3454**

"Diary of Rev. Cyrus Kingsbury." CHRONICLES OF OKLAHOMA 3 (1925):152-157.

Jan-Dec 1853. Brief extracts from journal of a Congregational missionary to the Choctaws of Oklahoma; preaching and visiting among whites, Indians and blacks; infirmities of advancing age and various medications he used.

KNIGHT, AMELIA STEWART   **3455**

"Diary of Mrs. Amelia Stewart Knight, an Oregon Pioneer of 1853." OREGON PIONEER ASSOCIATION TRANSACTIONS (1928):38-53.

Carpenter, Harold, ed. "The Oregon Trail Diary of Amelia Stewart Knight." CLARK COUNTY HISTORY 6 (1965):36-56.

Extracts in A DAY AT A TIME, edited by Margo Culley, pp. 111-124; DIARY OF AMERICA, edited by Josef and Dorothy Berger, pp. 338-339; RIVER REFLECTIONS, edited by Verne Huser, pp. 26-28; WOMEN'S DIARIES OF THE WESTWARD JOURNEY, collected by Lillian Schlissel, pp. 99-216.

Apr-Sep 1853. Emigrant journey from Iowa to near Milwaukie, Oregon, with her husband, Joel Knight, and seven children; notes on daily life, mishaps and hardships; well told, sometimes amusing incidents and unusual details, such as, "the men all have their false eyes on to keep the dust out"; races and quarrels between companies for lead position; her great sympathy for the suffering of children and animals; the accidental leaving behind of a child who was later picked up by the next wagon train; sharing and trading with Indians; the birth of her eighth child upon their arrival in Oregon; an outstanding account by an intrepid pioneer mother.

KOREN, ELSE ELISABETH HYSING, 1832-1918   **3456**

THE DIARY OF ELISABETH KOREN. Translated and edited by David T. Nelson. Northfield, Minn.: Norwegian-American Historical Association, 1955. 381 pp.

1853-1855. Trip aboard the RHEIN from Hamburg to New York with her husband, Ulrik, newly appointed Norwegian minister to a Lutheran church in Iowa; shipboard life and sights followed by wagon journey to Iowa; hospitality in meager homes of pioneers; a trip to Wisconsin; settling in Iowa parsonage.

LE VERT, OCTAVIA WALTON, 1810?-1877   **3457**

SOUVENIERS OF GRAVEL. Mobile and New York: S.H. Goetzel, 1857. 2 vols.

1853-1854? European travel journal of a young Florida aristocrat; tourist attractions and accommodations, constant society of the noble and wealthy throughout Europe; notes on music, art and architecture.

LEWIS, JOHN REDMAN COXE, 1834-1898   **3458**

Graff, Henry F., ed. "Bluejackets with Perry in Japan." NEW YORK PUBLIC LIBRARY BULLETIN 54 (1950):367-383, 429-454, 486-504; 55 (1951):3-22, 66-85, 133-147, 162-180, 225-240, 275-287, 339-344.

BLUEJACKETS WITH PERRY IN JAPAN: A DAY-BY-DAY ACCOUNT KEPT BY MASTER'S MATE JOHN R.C. LEWIS AND CABIN

BOY WILLIAM B. ALLEN. Edited by Henry F. Graff. New York: New York Public Library, 1952. 181 pp. Diary pp. 72-175.

1853-1854. Composite diary of two crewmen, Lewis on the MACEDONIAN and Allen on the VANDALIA, ships of Commodore Perry's Naval Expedition to Japan; work, interests and grumblings of the crew; sidelights on ports visited; curiosity about Japanese, the countryside and villages; weeks of boredom on board ship during lengthy negotiations for a trade agreement; Allan's detailed list of gifts sent to the Japanese emperor by the United States government.

LONG, JONATHAN DEAN, 1819-1889　　　**3459**

"A Journey from New York to San Francisco in 1853, via the Isthmus of Panama." NEW ENGLAND HISTORICAL AND GENEALOGICAL REGISTER 91 (1937):312-319.

Jul-Aug 1853. Brookline, Massachusetts, contractor's voyage on the GEORGIA with a group of passengers "not of a pleasing character"; private paid arrangement with the cook to eat separately from the "pigs"; call at Kingston, Jamaica; overland across Panama, thence to San Francisco on the OREGON; good descriptions of places and shipboard life.

LONGSWORTH, BASIL NELSON　　　**3460**

DIARY OF BASIL LONGSWORTH, Denver: D.E. Harrington, 1927. 43 pp.

THE DIARY OF BASIL N. LONGSWORTH, OREGON PIONEER. Portland: The Historical Records Survey, 1938. 68 pp.

OVERLAND JOURNEY FROM WASHINGTON, T.P. GUERNSEY CO., OHIO, TO OREGON IN THE SUMMER OF 1853. Fairfield, Wash.: Ye Galleon, 1971. 44 pp.

Mar 1853-Jan 1854. Emigrant journey of Guernsey County, Ohio, man to Alsea Valley, Oregon; by riverboat on the Ohio and Mississippi with some interesting and humorous details; overland from St. Joseph with a company of twenty-six wagons; outfitting and amounts of foodstuffs; Sunday preaching and prayer meetings in camp; Indian alarms; route, camps and good description of countryside; some religious reflections.

LOVE, HELEN MARNIE STEWART, 1835-1873　　　**3461**

DIARY OF HELEN STEWART. Eugene, Oreg.: Lane County Pioneer-Historical Society, 1961. 27 leaves.

Extract in A DAY AT A TIME, edited by Margo Culley, pp. 125-127.

Apr-Aug 1853. Diary of travel by river steamer ARCTIC from Pittsburgh to St. Louis, then on HONDURAS to St. Joseph; continuing by wagon with the usual difficulties of dusty roads and dangerous river fords; frequent notes of "romantic" scenery, storms, etc., walking ahead of train with her sister; celebrating Fourth of July with a great dance after a day of travel.

MCCAULEY, EDWARD YORKE, 1827-1894　　　**3462**

WITH PERRY IN JAPAN. Edited by Allan B. Cole. Princeton: Princeton University Press; London: H. Milford, Oxford University Press, 1942. 124 pp.

Extracts in FIFTY MAJOR DOCUMENTS OF THE TWENTIETH CENTURY, edited by Louis L. Snyder, pp. 83-86. New York: Van Nostrand, 1955.

1853-1854. Diary of naval officer with the Perry Expedition to Japan aboard the POWHATAN; port adventures and colorful descriptions of Madeira, Cape Town, Mauritius, Singapore, Labuan, Hong Kong, Yokohama, Yedo and Hakodate; visiting Chinese temple and attending opera CHIN at Celestial Opera House in Singapore; accompanying a diplomatic mission to the rajah of Brunei, Borneo, to present a treaty of commerce; missing the reception for officials and the signing of the treaty with Japan at Yokohama because of scurvy.

MCCLURE, ANDREW SAMUEL, 1829-1898　　　**3463**

THE DIARY OF ANDREW S. McCLURE. Eugene, Oreg.: Reproduced by Lane County Pioneer-Historical Society, 1973. 142 pp.

May-Oct 1853. Conventional overland diary of travel conditions on the Oregon Trail; comments on morale, food, buffalo hunts, mileage and sickness.

MATHER, GEORGIANA WOOLSON　　　**3464**

In FIVE GENERATIONS (1785-1923) BEING SCATTERED CHAPTERS FROM THE HISTORY OF THE COOPER, POMEROY, WOOLSON AND BENEDICT FAMILIES, WITH EXTRACTS FROM THEIR LETTERS AND JOURNALS, edited by Clare Benedict, vol. 1, pp. 78-84. London: Ellis, 1930?

Jun 1853. Woman's diary of a forest vacation on the Michigan shore of Lake Huron; notes on scenery, flowers and condition of Ojibwa Indians and half-breeds.

MERRIMON, AUGUSTUS SUMMERFIELD, 1830-1892　　　**3465**

Newsome, A.R., ed. "The A.S. Merrimon Journal." NORTH CAROLINA HISTORICAL REVIEW 8 (1931):300-330.

Oct 1853-Jan 1854. Asheville lawyer's diary kept on circuit; lengthy entries describing trials, court procedure and participating attorneys and judges, including Zebulon B. Vance, John Baxter and Nicholas W. Woodfin; social conditions in small towns, with special concern about drunkenness of the populace and ignorance and corruption of public officials.

MILLS, HIRAM, d. 1882　　　**3466**

"Steamboat Experiences from the Journal of Dr. Hiram Mills: The Romantic Past?" MISSOURI HISTORICAL SOCIETY BULLETIN 13 (1957):384-392.

May-Nov 1853 (with gaps). A Missouri doctor's account of travel on the Ohio and Mississippi; a trip on the ST. CLAIR to Cincinnati prompting memories of other such journeys, with amusing vignettes of gamblers, phony English nobility, greenhorns, dishonest and incompetent captains, but mostly passengers angry over delays, bad food and promises of staterooms they never got; by train from Cincinnati, where "the notorious Mrs. Bloomer came into the cars," prompting diarist's lengthy diatribe against women's rights.

MITCHELL, MARIA, 1818-1889　　　**3467**

MARIA MITCHELL, LIFE, LETTERS AND JOURNALS. Compiled by Phebe Mitchell Kendall. Boston: Lee and Shepard, 1896. 293 pp. passim.

1853-1885. Diary extracts, partially arranged topically, of astronomer, librarian and teacher; winning a gold medal from the king of Denmark for discovering a comet; making computations for American Nautical Almanac; details of trying unsuccessfully to replace wires in her transit with her own hair and then successfully with threads from a spider's cocoon; concern with developing reading habits of young patrons of Nantucket Atheneum; traveling by stagecoach to Chicago, rail to St. Louis and on the steamer MAGNOLIA, which went aground, and the WOODRUFF to New Orleans where she visited a slave market and black church; tourist attractions, including Mammoth Cave; a trip to Denver to observe solar eclipse, and to Europe to see observatories and meet with leading astronomers in England, France, Germany and Russia; meeting sculptor Harriet Hosmer and mathematician Mary Fairfax Somerville in Italy; teaching at Vassar; being elected first woman member of the American Academy of Arts and Sciences and to the American Association for the Advancement of Science and the Association for the Advancement of Women.

In GROWING UP FEMALE IN AMERICA: TEN LIVES, edited by Eve Merriam, pp. 77-90. Garden City, N.Y.: Doubleday, 1971. 308 pp. New York: Dell, 1973. 352 pp.

1853. Extracts showing her views and concerns for education of women.

MOORE, CHARLES B., 1822-1901 3468

Bowman, Larry G. and Scroggs, Jack B., eds. "A Tennessean visits Cincinnati in 1853-1854." CINCINNATI HISTORICAL SOCIETY BULLETIN 36 (1978):151-172.

Dec 1853-Jan 1854. Extract covering the sojourn of a Sumner County millwright in Cincinnati to buy and ship mill machinery; riverboat travel from Nashville to Cincinnati, where he boarded at the Jacob O. Joyce home; notes on plays, the circus, medical lectures of the Eclectic Medical Institute and church services of various kinds; visits to factories and mills; social life among fellow freethinkers and "infidels"; the Bedini Riot and subsequent trial of the German Freemen, with whom diarist sympathized.

MORROW, JAMES, 1820-1865 3469

A SCIENTIST WITH PERRY IN JAPAN. Edited by Allan B. Cole. Chapel Hill: University of North Carolina, 1947. 307 pp.

1853-1854. Diary of doctor and horticulturist on the VANDALIA with the Perry Expedition to Japan, bearing instructions to distribute plants and seeds in exchange for Asian varieties and having responsibility for farm implements designated as gifts to Japanese dignitaries; detailed observations of all cultivated plants and domestic animals seen during visits to Japanese villages; attending signing of treaty; return on the LEXINGTON with seventeen cases of plants, implements, household utensils and fabrics for the National Gallery and the Smithsonian Institution.

"Opening the Door: The Morrow Journal." AMERICAN HISTORY ILLUSTRATED 13, no. 5 (1978):40-42.

Feb-Apr 1854. Extracts describing several negotiating sessions and the signing of the treaty; delivery of gifts of seeds and agricultural implements and Japanese reaction to them; Japanese customs and diarist's characterization of the men as "gentlemanly" but "effeminate"; movements of various ships in the fleet.

MULLAN, JOHN, 1830-1909 3470

In REPORTS OF EXPLORATIONS AND SURVEYS, by United States War Department, vol. 1, pp. 301-349, 516-537.

Sep 1853. Extracts included in official report of survey exploring "routes, streams, prominent landmarks, and the characteristic features of the country passed over; noting particularly the quality of the soils, the forest trees, grasses, quality and quantity of water, and the practicability of the route for a wagon road"; from Fort Benton by southern Little Blackfoot River to St. Marys Valley.

Dec. 1853-Jan 1854. Reconnaissance from Bitter Root Valley to Fort Hall, to head of Hell Gate River and return to Bitter Root Valley; nature and character of the country and a possible route for wagon trains.

May-Oct 1854. Exploring country from Bitter Root Valley to Flathead Lake and Kootenay River; from Cantonment Stevens to Fort Dalles; aid from Indians and problems consulting with Indians and missionaries for possible wagon routes.

Clark, Pal, ed. "Journal from Fort Dalles, O.T., to Fort Wallah Wallah, W.T." FRONTIER: A MAGAZINE OF THE NORTHWEST 12 (1932):368-375. Reprint. SOURCES OF NORTHWEST HISTORY, no. 28. Missoula: State University of Montana, 1932. 11 pp. FRONTIER OMNIBUS, edited by John W. Hakola. pp. 209-218.

Jul 1858. Survey of a military road to begin campaign under Col. George White against Indians who had defeated Steptoe; historical comments, not entirely accurate, on Whitman and the Whitman massacre and on the defeat of Steptoe.

MYER, NATHANIEL, 1786-1870 3471

Ham, Edward B., ed. "Journey into Southern Oregon: Diary of a Pennsylvania Dutchman." OREGON HISTORICAL QUARTERLY 60 (1959):375-407.

Mar-Aug 1853. Elderly man's journey with his extended family from Van Buren County, Iowa, to the Rogue River area of Oregon, settling eventually at Ashland; route, camps and weather; good details of the logistics of pioneer travel; the murder of his son-in-law Fruit Walker by Griffith Johns after an unspecified quarrel.

OWEN, BENJAMIN FRANKLIN, 1828-1917 3472

MY TRIP ACROSS THE PLAINS. Lane County Pioneer-Historical Society Publications, no. 2. Eugene, Oreg.: Lane County Pioneer-Historical Society, 1959. 60 pp.

Mar-Oct 1853. Account of one of several young men who set out to get help for the "lost wagon train of 1853," which was stranded and facing starvation in the Harney-Malheur Lakes country of southeast Oregon; hunger and encounters with Indians; quarrels as to how to proceed, when wrong decisions could mean death.

PAINE, TIMOTHY OTIS, 1824-1895 3473

In THE DISCOVERY OF A GRANDMOTHER: GLIMPSES INTO THE HOMES AND LIVES OF EIGHT GENERATIONS OF AN IPSWICH-PAINE FAMILY, by Lydia A. Carter, pp. 320-325. Newtonville, Mass.: H.H. Carter, 1920. 341 pp.

1852-1895. Scattered extracts from a clergyman's diary; reflections, observations of nature and comments on poetry of Wordsworth and Holmes.

PENGRA, CHARLOTTE EMILY STEARNS, b. 1827 3474

DIARY OF MRS. BYNON J. PENGRA. Eugene, Oreg.: Lane County Pioneer-Historical Society, 1959. 60 leaves.

Apr-Aug 1853. Emigrant journey from Lysander, Illinois, to Springfield, Oregon, with her husband and three-year-old daughter; constant fatigue with concerns of baking, washing and keeping contents of wagon dry in much rainy weather; becoming separated from other members of company and traveling without female companions; frightening experience of being in a wagon with a runaway team which resulted in serious injury to her husband's ankle; in frequent demand for "packing" those who were ill; ends abruptly with entire family ill.

PIERCY, FREDERICK HAWKINS, 1830-1891   3475

ROUTE FROM LIVERPOOL TO GREAT SALT LAKE VALLEY. Edited by James Linforth. Liverpool: F.D. Richards, 1855. 120 pp. Edited by Fawn M. Brodie. Cambridge: Belknap Press of Harvard University Press, 1962. 313 pp.

1853-1854. Diary of English artist, a non-Mormon, who accompanied Mormon emigrants from Liverpool to Salt Lake as official artist and chronicler; Atlantic crossing on the JERSEY; to New Orleans, up the Mississippi and across the plains; detailed, sympathetic but dispassionate, with word pictures often as good as his sketches, and touches of humor; as edited and expanded by James Linforth, an important guide for future emigrants.

PREBLE, GEORGE HENRY, 1816-1885   3476

THE OPENING OF JAPAN: A DIARY OF DISCOVERY IN THE FAR EAST. Edited by Boleslaw Szczesniak. Norman: University of Oklahoma, 1962. 453 pp.

1853-1856. Diary of naval officer on the MACEDONIAN, one of the ships in the Naval Expedition to Japan under Commodore Perry; participating in all the important activities of the Perry mission, the treaty negotiations at Shimoda and Kanagawa and surveys of bays of Tokyo, Hakodate and Keelung, Formosa; commanding the QUEEN, chartered from the British, which had several military encounters with pirates in Chinese waters; observations on native life and customs; colorful report of American businessmen, diplomats and missionaries living in the Far East as well as candid descriptions of fellow officers and Perry.

ROBERTS, LOUISA JEWETT RAYMOND, 1819-1893   3477

BIOGRAPHICAL SKETCH OF LOUISA J. ROBERTS WITH EXTRACTS FROM HER JOURNAL AND SELECTIONS FROM HER WRITINGS. Philadelphia: A.J. Ferris, 1895. 286 pp. Journal, pp. 27-92.

1853-1892 (with gaps.) Chiefly questions, concerns and confidences of a devout Philadelphia Quaker; mourning for her mother; conversion from the Baptist church to the Society of Friends where she bore the responsibility for "First-day school" for religious instruction with her friend Jane Johnson; tragic loss in one month of three sons to diphtheria; frequent contribution to FRIENDS' INTELLIGENCER AND JOURNAL; long trips visiting isolated Friends' meetings and families including extended stay assisting missionaries at an Indian school in Nebraska; considerable thought on the "antiquity of man" in "light of scientific inquiry" and on troubling scriptures: "whatever there is in the narrative now held as Divine authority must necessarily be taken with a large allowance for the credulity that then biased the judgment of men."

SAXTON, RUFUS   3478

In REPORTS OF EXPLORATIONS AND SURVEYS, by United States War Department, vol. 1, pp. 251-269.

Jul-Oct 1853. Diary incorporated in report of railroad survey from the Columbia River to Fort Owen and Fort Benton; topographical notes; relying on Indians for transportation and provisions; comments on Palouse, Nez Percé, Spokan, Blackfoot, Gros Ventre, Salish, Arikara, Mandan and Dakota Indians with recognition of need for treaties with them.

SCHIEL, JACOB HEINRICH, b. 1813   3479

JOURNEY THROUGH THE ROCKY MOUNTAINS AND THE HUMBOLDT MOUNTAINS TO THE PACIFIC OCEAN. Translated and edited by Thomas N. Bonner. American Exploration and Travel Series, no. 27. Norman: University of Oklahoma Press, 1959. 114 pp.

1853-1854. Diary, with few dated entries, and prepared by diarist for publication, of a young German geologist for the Gunnison expedition to explore possible routes for a Pacific railroad; extensive notes on geology, plants, wildlife and topography; encounters with Indians, including the raid in which Gunnison was killed; lengthy, largely unsympathetic discourse on Mormons.

SHEPARD, GEORGE C.   3480

In THE YEARS AND HOURS OF EMILY DICKINSON, by Jay Leyda, vol. 1-2 passim. New Haven: Yale University Press, 1960.

1853-1866. Brief, sporadic extracts of minister's visits to Amherst and opinions on church affairs, especially the ministry of E.S. Dwight, probably the last clergyman heard by Emily Dickinson before her entry into seclusion at home.

SHIPLEY, CELINDA E. HINES   3481

"Diary of Celinda E. Hines, Later Mrs. H.R. Shipley." OREGON PIONEER ASSOCIATION TRANSACTIONS (1918):69-125.

DIARY OF A JOURNEY FROM N.Y. TO OREGON IN 1853. Portland, Oreg.: Portland Telegram, 1930. 12 pp.

Feb-Sep 1853. Journey with her family from Hastings, New York, to the Cascades; by train and steamboat to St. Louis and Independence; thence overland to Oregon; scenery and incidents of travel; personal, family and social notes; a pleasant diary.

STANLEY, DAVID SLOAN   3482

Shawver, Lona, ed. "Stanley Explores Oklahoma." CHRONICLES OF OKLAHOMA 22 (1944):259-270.

Jul-Sep 1853. Extracts of Oklahoma and Texas Panhandle portion of quartermaster's diary kept during Corps of Topographical Engineers survey under Lt. A.W. Whipple; departure from Fort Smith; terrain, camps, route, weather, assorted problems; notes on settlers, Indians and Mexicans.

STEWART, AGNES   3483

Churchill, Claire W., ed. "The Journey to Oregon—A Pioneer Girl's Diary." OREGON HISTORICAL QUARTERLY 29 (1928):77-98.

Mar-Aug 1853. Emigrant diary kept by an Allegheny, Pennsylvania, girl for her friend back home; delays at St. Joseph while provisioning; route via Fort Kearny, Black Hills, Malheur region, etc.; diarist's distress over the men's swearing, quarreling and insistence on Sunday travel; descriptive and charmingly sentimental.

SWETT, JOHN, 1830-1913   3484

Cluff, Will S., Jr., ed. "John Swett's Diary." CALIFORNIA HISTORICAL SOCIETY QUARTERLY 33 (1954):289-308.

Jan-Nov 1853. Diary, begun at sea on the REVERE, of a young Pittsfield, New Hampshire, teacher destined to become an outstanding California educator; unpaid farm work at Marysville for Dr. O.P. Warren, who was supposedly to teach him medicine; fruitless prospecting in the northern mines and Grass Valley, where he was "sick and without a book to read"; further efforts to find work in the San Francisco area.

THURBER, ALBERT KING, 1826-1888   3485

In TREASURES OF PIONEER HISTORY, compiled by Kate B. Carter, vol. 3, pp. 293-313.

Jul 1853. Diary of a young Mormon in the "Walker War," serving as adjutant to Maj. Stephen Markham who was defending Mormon towns against harrassment by Ute chief Walker; a comic military trial of a private accused of stealing horseshoes.

Jan-Jul 1863. Duties as bishop at Spanish Fork; meetings, marriages, preaching and counseling; work at home as a comb maker; enjoyment of local theatricals; family matters; Indian troubles.

Apr 1865-Feb 1866. Mission to England with brief notes on activities of Mormons there; church finances; enjoyment of pantomimes at Covent Garden and other theaters.

TROWBRIDGE, WILLIAM PETIT, 1828-1892   3486

Pollard, Lancaster, ed. "Journal of a Voyage on Puget Sound in 1853." PACIFIC NORTHWEST QUARTERLY 33 (1942):391-407.

Jul-Aug 1853. Canoe travel from Fort Steilacoom throughout Puget Sound of an Army Corps of Engineers lieutenant involved in the United States Coast Survey; full and interesting notes on Indians; references to his colleagues Charles H. Larned, William A. Slaughter and William A. Howard; examination of coal deposits and a few astronomical and geological observations; notes on farms, sawmills, etc.

VAN HORNE, GEORGE W., b. 1833   3487

Thorne, Mildred, ed. "The Diary of a Law Student." IOWA JOURNAL OF HISTORY 55 (1957):167-186.

1853-1855. Extracts from the diary of a young man, later a prominent Muscatine lawyer, studying first in the law offices of Charles R. Ladd and Edward B. Gillett in Chicopee, Massachusetts, and briefly in Akron, Ohio; train travel to and from Akron; notes on his reading of law books and on cases and trials in Chicopee; public indignation at the arrest in Boston and return of fugitive slave Anthony Burns; a brief sojourn at Wilbraham Academy; train travel to Muscatine; extremely florid style.

WARD, HARRIET SHERRILL, 1803-1865   3488

PRAIRE SCHOONER LADY. Great West and Indian Series, 16. Los Angeles: Westernlore Press, 1959. 180 pp.

1853-1854. Overland account from Dartford, Wisconsin, to Califor-

nia, kept for her family by a woman accustomed to comfort; adapting well to pioneer venture; acting as "doctor" with medical supplies recommended by family physician; frequent mention of flowers, games, entertainment and music in evening camp and later in Indian Valley, California, some of it provided by "gentlemen of refinement" who sang with their "guitars and voices cultivated in the Handel and Haydn Society of Boston."

WELLES, C.M.   3489

THREE YEARS' WANDERING OF A CONNECTICUT YANKEE. New York: American Subscription Publishing House, 1859. 358 pp.

THREE YEARS WANDERINGS AROUND THE WORLD. Hartford, Conn.: Hurlbut, Scranton, 1864. 358 pp.

1853-1856 (with gaps). Diary of young Hartford adventurer; starting for Australia on the clipper PEYTONA under Capt. A. Pelletier with an insubordinate crew; deplorable shipboard life with constant mismanagement by the inebriated captain; in port at Bahia; a fire and disabling of ship during a storm, necessitating diarist's transfer to the equally bad NAUTILUS; in Melbourne, then Ballerat, where many Yankees were barely making a living at mining; seeing the sights and going into a business of making coffins; on the SACUSA for Callao, Peru, upon news of gold discovery there and happy to find "decent people on a respectably managed ship"; not surprised at absence of gold in Peru; long discourse on corruption of Catholic church; a Palm Sunday procession in Lima; to Panama and San Francisco on mail ship SANTIAGO; extended notes on mining in the Carson Valley, teaching school at Petaluma, a camp meeting and the value of travel.

WENDELL, GEORGE BLUNT, 1831-1881   3490

GEORGE BLUNT WENDELL, CLIPPER SHIP MASTER. Mystic, Conn.: Marine Historical Association, 1949. 195 pp. passim.

1853-1863. Letters and diary extracts of a Portsmouth, New Hampshire, clipper captain, with entries beginning at age twenty-two during his first command, the PISCATAQUA, bound from Boston to Calcutta; log and personal notes describing a difficult voyage, with cargo of ice melting and shifting; subsequent command of the GRANADA, GANGES, BENARES and GALATEA on voyages to various Asian ports; excellent details of seamanship, crews, cargo, passengers, many of whom were missionaries, and responsibilities to his employer, ship owner William S. Bullard; marriage to Mary Elizabeth Thompson; brief indications of his devout Unitarianism; a fine record of the clipper days by an admirable Yankee captain.

WEST, CALVIN BROOKINGS, b. 1816   3491

Stuart, Reginald R. and Grace D., eds. "Calvin B. West of the Umpqua." PACIFIC HISTORIAN 4 (1960):48-57, 87-96, 112, 129-143; 5 (1961):23-46, 53-68, 86, 125-136.

1853-1854. Extracts from letters and diaries of an Oregon settler from Defiance, Ohio; brief notes of travel to the Umpqua Valley, where he became a teacher, farmer and Baptist lay preacher; people and events in Douglas County, with references to Philip Foster, Henry G. Hadley and ministers William Sperry, Thomas Stevens and Ezra Fisher; a good picture of frontier religion.

WHIPPLE, AMIEL WEEKS, 1818-1863   3492

Wright, Muriel H. and Shirk, George H. "The Journal of Lieutenant A.W. Whipple." CHRONICLES OF OKLAHOMA 28 (1950):235-283.

> Jun-Sep 1853. Field notes of topographical engineers' survey west from Fort Smith through present Oklahoma to locate the southern route for a Pacific railroad; route, topographical and geological notes; encounters with and descriptions of Choctaws, Shawnees, etc., and their customs; slaveholding practiced by Indians; many references to Indian guide Jesse Chisholm; personnel and finances of the survey.

In REPORT OF THE SECRETARY OF WAR COMMUNICATING THE SEVERAL PACIFIC RAILROAD EXPLORATIONS, by United States War Department, vol. 2.

In REPORT OF EXPLORATIONS AND SURVEYS, by United States War Department, vol. 3, pp. 1-136.

A PATHFINDER IN THE SOUTHWEST. Edited by Grant Foreman. Norman: University of Oklahoma Press, 1941. 296 pp.

> Jul 1853-Mar 1854. Official military exploration journal expanded from field notes; surveying routes in the Southwest for railroad with French Canadian guide Antoine Leroux, artist Heinrich B. Möllhausen and wagon train captain Joseph C. Ives who also conducted a detached survey party from Albuquerque to Lagunas; from Fort Smith along thirty-fifth parallel, Arkansas, Canadian and San Jose rivers, down Colorado and Chiquito to sites of present Holbrook and Flagstaff; Mojave River to Barstow, Cajon Pass to San Bernardino, Los Angeles and San Pedro; astronomical observations and geographical details; notes on game and fertile areas suitable for settlement, various Indian tribes including Choctaw, Comanche, Mohave, Pueblo, Zuni, etc., and their customs, pueblos and hospitality or hostility.

Archambeau, Ernest R., ed. "Lieutenant A.W. Whipple's Railroad Reconnaissance across the Panhandle of Texas in 1853." PANHANDLE-PLAINS HISTORICAL REVIEW 44 (1971):v-xii, 1-128. Journal, pp. 32-106.

> Jul-Oct 1853. Reprint of a segment of Whipple's official journal; mainly the Canadian River valley and exploration from Fort Smith to Albuquerque.

WHITEHEAD, LEWIS YOUNG, 1833-1908   3493

DIARY OF LEWIS YOUNG WHITEHEAD, FATHER OF THE MENOMINEE RANGE. Iron Mountain, Mich.: Mid-Peninsula Library Federation, 1976. 62 pp. Diary, pp. 22-25.

> 1853-1860 (with gaps). A few scattered dated entries, within reminiscence and genealogy, of a Vulcan, Michigan, man prominent in the development of Michigan iron mining; mostly travels to and from the Menominee area.

WILLIAMS, SAMUEL WELLS, 1812-1884   3494

Williams, F.W., ed. "A Journal of the Perry Expedition to Japan." ASIATIC SOCIETY OF JAPAN TRANSACTIONS 37 (1910):1-261.

> 1853-1854. Journal of a missionary to China who learned some Japanese from sailors and was persuaded by Commodore Perry to accompany his expedition as interpreter; sailing with the mission from Canton on the SARATOGA; details of treaty negotiations and the custom of exchanging gifts, including complete list of presents for the emperor and his dignitaries; frank and not always complimentary appraisals of Perry and his requests.

WILLIAMS, VELINA A. STEARNS   3495

"Diary of a Trip across the Plains in 1853." OREGON PIONEER ASSOCIATION TRANSACTIONS (1919):178-226.

> Apr-Sep 1853. Emigrant journey to Klamath Lake of a family from Winnebago County, Illinois; everyday life on the trail, domestic and social items, camping, fears and sickness; names of party, including her aged grandfather, the Rev. John Stearns; discord within the company leading to dismissal of William Brannan; religious reflections.

WOODWORTH, JAMES, 1829-1904   3496

DIARY OF JAMES WOODWORTH: ACROSS THE PLAINS TO CALIFORNIA IN 1853. Eugene, Oreg.: Lane County Historical Society, 1972. 61 leaves.

> Apr-Sep 1853. Diary of travel by river steamer EL PASO from St. Louis to St. Joseph, continuing overland by horse and muleback; well written entries including list of supplies, travel and camp conditions and notes on Indians; short stopover at Salt Lake City to see dentist and get provisions; descending Goose Creek Mountains by means of rope; arrival in Sacramento and San Francisco.

YOUNGS, SAMUEL   3497

Zimmer, Ethel, ed. "Colonel Samuel Youngs' Journal." NEVADA HISTORICAL SOCIETY QUARTERLY 2, no. 2 (1959):27-67.

> 1853-1866. Scattered entries of Aurora, Nevada, prospector and politician; activities at Sacramento, including "fifteen teeth and roots extracted in half an hour" and subsequent fitting of false teeth; the murder of James King by James P. Casey and his hanging by vigilantes led by William T. Coleman; the Broderick-Terry duel at San Francisco; prospecting at Washoe and Aurora; the murder of W.R. Johnson and subsequent hanging of four men; Episcopal church attendance and social life; a Fourth of July celebration; work as county commissioner of Esmeralda County, Nevada; many references to Governor Nye.

1854

ANON.   3498

MacDonnell, Anne, ed. "Fort Benton Journal." MONTANA HISTORICAL SOCIETY CONTRIBUTIONS 10 (1940):1-99.

> 1854-1856. Official record of trading at Fort Benton; a matter-of-fact daily picture of people involved in Upper Missouri fur trade and their work; numbers of robes traded; the results of hunts, provisioning the fort, etc:; frequent references to Alexander Culbertson; notes on Blackfoot Indians.

ANON.   3499

In PLANTATION AND FRONTIER DOCUMENTS: 1649-1863, by Ulrich B. Phillips, vol. 1, pp. 208-214. Documentary History of American Industrial Society, vol. 1. Cleveland, Ohio: A.H. Clark, 1909. Reprint. New York: B. Franklin, 1969.

> Jan 1854. Extracts from the journal of manager of Belmead in Powhaton County, Virginia; weather and typical week's work accomplished on a large tobacco and wheat plantation.

ANDERSON, NICHOLAS LONGWORTH, 1838-1892   3500

The LETTERS AND JOURNALS OF GENERAL NICHOLAS LONGWORTH ANDERSON. Edited by Isabel Anderson. New York: Fleming H. Revell, 1942. 320 pp. Diary, pp. 21-95 passim, 133-184.

1854-1856 (with gaps). Journals kept as a student; scattered lengthy entries describing Harvard studies and social activities, enjoyment of Boston theater, political views and concern about resisting dissipation.

1862-1863. Service as lieutenant colonel in the Sixth Ohio Volunteer Infantry, later assuming command of the regiment and being promoted to colonel; military operations in Tennessee, Mississippi, Kentucky and Georgia; battle of Shiloh and the advance to Corinth; battles of Perryville and Stones River; brief entries describing his duties and leisure activities, especially reading; much grumbling about his superior officers, conditions of soldiering and the boredom of camp life.

BELL, JAMES G., b. 1832   3501

Haley, J. Evetts, ed. "A Log of the Texas-California Cattle Trail." SOUTHWESTERN HISTORICAL QUARTERLY 35 (1931-1932):208-237, 290-316; 36 (1932-1933):47-66.

Extracts in DIARY OF AMERICA, edited by Josef and Dorothy Berger, pp. 349-358.

Jun-Nov 1854. Young "tenderfoot's" account of arduous cattle drive accompanying Texas frontiersman John James; from San Antonio via El Paso and Tucson to Los Angeles; Indian alarms; difficulties of terrain and lack of water and grass; sudden death of hundreds of cattle from eating "careless weed"; customs of California Indians; continuing alone from Los Angeles by ship AMERICA to San Francisco, thence to Sacramento.

BOARDMAN, NANCY ELLEN, 1825-1891   3502

"Diaries of Nancy Ellen Boardman." DANVERS HISTORICAL SOCIETY COLLECTIONS 29 (1941):54-74.

1854-1855. Weather, local events, social and cultural life in Putnamville, Massachusetts; very brief entries covering visits and visitors, births and deaths; attendance at Lyceum, Peabody Institute and other lectures; church services; the new railroad; her job as a teacher and marriage to Edward A. Lord.

BOWEN, CLARISSA WALTON ADGER, 1837-1915   3503

In THE DIARY OF CLARISSA ADGER BOWEN, ASHTABULA PLANTATION, by Mary Stevenson, pp. 71-81. Pendleton, S.C.: Research and Publication Committee, Foundation for Historic Restoration in Pendleton Area, 1973.

Mar-Apr 1854, May-Nov 1865. Extracts covering diarist's first visit to Pendleton, South Carolina, and the plantation and family of John C. Calhoun; life at Ashtabula near Pendleton, immediately after the Civil War; post-surrender Union depredations, baby's death, economic hardships, behavior of freedmen and Union soldiers and labor contracts with former slaves; sermons and religious reflections; notes on family affairs and medical treatment; visits to Rivoli, her parents' home; relocation to Charleston.

BURROUGHS, JOHN, 1837-1921   3504

THE HEART OF BURROUGHS'S JOURNALS. Edited by Clara Bar-

rus. Boston: Houghton Mifflin, 1928. 361 pp. Reprint. Port Washington, N.Y.: Kennikat, 1967.

1854-1921. Selected entries from copious journals of naturalist and author; reflections on literature, science, nature, philosophy and religion; wonderful descriptions of his friend Walt Whitman; tributes to Emerson, his most important mentor; comments on such acquaintances as John Muir, Theodore Roosevelt, Thomas A. Edison and Henry Ford; life on his farm at Esopus, New York; returns to his birthplace at Roxbury; deaths of his parents and brother; an adventurous old-age, despite deaths of his wife and many friends and depression over World War I; a significant journal, unusual for span of years covered.

BYRNE, J.H.   3505

In REPORT OF EXPLORATIONS OF A ROUTE FOR THE PACIFIC RAILROAD, by United States Army Corps of Topographical Engineers, pp. 66-122. 33rd Cong., 1st sess., 1855, H. Exec. Doc. 129. Washington, D.C.: 1855?

In REPORTS OF EXPLORATIONS AND SURVEYS, by United States War Department, vol. 2, pp. 51-93.

Jan-May 1854. Engineer's general diary appended to Capt. John Pope's official report of expedition to explore a route for Pacific railroad from the Red River to the Rio Grande, near the thirty-second parallel; managing mules, wagons and supplies; distances of march; camps, water and grass for animals; prairie fires; meeting or trying to avoid Indians.

CAINE, JOHN T.   3506

"Journal of John T. Caine." HEART THROBS OF THE WEST 5 (1944):217-280.

1854-1855. Mormon's diary of his mission to Hawaii; by wagon from Salt Lake to San Francisco with Brigham Young and others, noting condition of Mormon settlers en route; from San Francisco to Honolulu on the SUSAN ABIGAIL; travels throughout the islands preaching and teaching with colleagues Philip B. Lewis, William W. Cluff and I.S. Woodbury; a detailed description of a Chinese wake and funeral.

CROSBY, CHARLES A., b. 1835   3507

Crimmins, M.L., ed. "Extract from the Diary of Charles A. Crosby." WEST TEXAS HISTORICAL ASSOCIATION YEAR BOOK 17 (1941):100-107.

Oct-Nov 1854. Nineteen-year-old cavalryman's account of service in Texas under Albert Sidney Johnston; from Austin, with camps, distances and conditions of travel to forts Belknap and McKavett; Indian alerts but no action.

DAVIDSON, GREENLEE, 1834-1863   3508

CAPTAIN GREENLEE DAVIDSON, C.S.A.: DIARY AND LETTERS. Compiled by Charles W. Turner. Verona, Va.: McClure Press, 1975. 90 pp. Diary, pp. 6-20.

Nov 1854-Jan 1855. Diary kept during student days at Washington College in Lexington, Virginia; rather lengthy entries candidly relating personal, school, social and family affairs; trial of blacks charged with arson; notes on lessons, reading, his health, literary societies, young ladies, etc.

"Diaries of James D. Davidson (1836) and Greenlee Davidson (1857) during Visits to Indiana." INDIANA MAGAZINE OF HISTORY 24 (1928):130-136. Diary, pp. 134-136.

Sep 1857. Extracts from the diary of James D. Davidson's son kept on a trip through the Old Northwest after graduation from the Lexington Law School; observations from train through Ohio, Indiana and Illinois; the sights of Indianapolis, Tippecanoe battleground and Indiana countryside, "a perfect Paradise."

DE LONG, CHARLES E., 1832-1876						**3509**

Wheat, Carl I., ed. "'California's Bantam Cock': The Journals of Charles E. De Long." CALIFORNIA HISTORICAL SOCIETY QUARTERLY 8 (1929):193-215, 337-363; 9 (1930):50-80, 129-171, 243-287, 345-397; 10 (1931):40-78, 165-201, 245-297, 355-395.

1854-1863. Diary which spans gold rush mining and storekeeping to career as a self-taught lawyer and politician in California and Nevada; activities at Sacramento and in Yuba County; work as deputy sheriff collecting notorious tax on foreign miners; riverboat travel; service in California legislature; secession question in California during the Civil War; political and business activities at Virginia City, Nevada; courtship, marriage and social life.

DIMAN, JEREMIAH LEWIS, 1831-1881					**3510**

In MEMOIRS OF THE REV. J. LEWIS DIMAN, by Caroline Hazard, pp. 62-107 passim. Boston and New York: Houghton Mifflin, 1887.

1854-1855. European travel journal of Brown University graduate, a student at Andover Theological Seminary; voyage aboard the HERMAN to Bremen; five weeks with a German family in Brunswick, improving his language skills; matriculation at universities at Halle, Heidelberg and Berlin; comments on art works in Dresden and Munich; touring Switzerland and Scotland; the sights of London and Paris.

DOTY, JAMES, 1829-1857							**3511**

In REPORTS OF EXPLORATIONS AND SURVEYS, by United States War Department, vol. 1, pp. 543-565.

May-Oct 1854. Survey from Fort Benton along the base of the Rocky Mountains, "ascertaining the existence of a large body of agricultural land, the proper localities for farms, the general capabilities of the country for settlement and collecting specimens in geology, natural history and botany"; exploring the feasibility of wagon roads through Marias Pass.

JOURNAL OF OPERATIONS OF GOVERNOR ISAAC INGALLS STEVENS OF WASHINGTON TERRIORTY IN 1855. Edited by Edward J. Kowrach. Fairfield, Wash.: Ye Galleon, 1978. 116 pp.

1855-1856. Journal of secretary to Isaac Ingalls Stevens, governor of Washington Territory during negotiation of treaties with Walla Walla, Cayuse, Yakima, Nez Percé, and Blackfoot Indian nations at Walla Walla, Coeur d'Alene Mission and the council ground in Nebraska Territory; many chiefs named including Kamiakan and Spokan Garry; lengthy speeches by the chiefs and Stevens recorded; delay due to bitter winter weather in Spokane region during return trip to Olympia; learning of Yakima Indian War and murder of Indian agent Andrew J. Bolon.

EBEY, WINFIELD SCOTT							**3512**

Baydo, Gerald. "Overland from Missouri to Washington Territory in 1854." NEBRASKA HISTORY 52 (1971):65-87.

Apr-Oct 1854. Article containing diary extracts covering emigration of the large Jacob Ebey family from Plum Grove Place, Missouri, to Whidbey Island; arrival upon the scene of the Ward massacre in Idaho and burying the dead; references to cholera.

Winton, Harry N.M. "The Death of Colonel Isaac N. Ebey." PACIFIC NORTHWEST QUARTERLY 33 (1942):325-347. Diary, pp. 332-340.

Aug 1857. A long extract relating to the murder and decapitation of his brother on Whidbey Island by Indian raiders, possibly Haida, from far north of the Puget Sound area; account written three days after the event, describing the diarist's immediate arrival at the scene of the attack upon Ebey's unarmed household; the burial, care for survivors and mood of revenge in Port Townsend.

Apr 1860. Extract describing the return of Ebey's scalp, recovered from the "Northern Indians."

Winton, Harry N.M., ed. "The Powder River and John Day Mines in 1862." PACIFIC NORTHWEST QUARTERLY 33 (1942):409-437; 34 (1943):39-86.

Jun-Nov 1862. Long, articulate extracts covering gold prospecting experiences in Oregon; activities at Union Flat, Auburn, Canyon Creek, etc., with interesting details of a prospector's work, problems and diversions; the diarist's appreciation of itinerant preachers and their sermons; references to many other gold seekers, "miners' meetings," etc.

EPPES, SUSAN BRADFORD, 1845?-1942				**3513**

THROUGH SOME EVENTFUL YEARS. Macon, Ga.: Press of the J.W. Burke Co., 1926. 378 pp. Diary, pp. 46-337 passim. Reprint. Edited by Joseph D. Cushman, Jr. Gainesville, Fla.: University of Florida Press, 1968.

1854-1866. Diary claimed to have been kept through childhood and adolescence by member of prominent family but thought by the book's editor to be "a literary invention"; somewhat sporadic, lengthy entries portraying antebellum life radiating out from Pine Hill, an extensive plantation north of Tallahassee in Leon County; family matters and social activities; slaves, abolitionists and political discussions; summer retreats to North Carolina, Virginia and Tennessee; description of governesses, school work, clothes, Christmas festivities, etc.; the Union army's arrival and the departure of slaves; the social shocks of the early postwar period and preparation for marriage; notes on J.D.B. Debow, Sidney Lanier, John Yates Beall and Henry D. Capers; an interesting, romantic blend of youth and racism.

Extracts in HEROINES OF DIXIE, edited by Katharine M. Jones, pp. 4-11, 258-260, 276-277.

1861-1864. Attending the Florida secession convention and witnessing the signing of the ordinance of secession; wartime shortages; description of salt works.

ERSKINE, MICHAEL H.							**3514**

Sanderlin, Walter S., ed. "A Cattle Drive From Texas to California." SOUTHWESTERN HISTORICAL QUARTERLY 67 (1964):397-412.

Apr-Nov 1854. Extracts from a Texas cattleman's journal of a long and arduous drive to take advantage of gold rush prices in California; the usual problems of stampedes, Indian alarms, night drives to avoid desert heat, etc., but little loss of stock to thirst, poisonous plants or Indian attack, which plagued similar drives; notes on terrain, camps, fodder, prices and work of cowboys.

FOGLE, AUGUSTUS G., 1820-1897   **3515**

In HISTORY OF THE MORAVIAN MISSIONS AMONG SOUTHERN INDIAN TRIBES, by Edmund Schwarze, pp. 257-276. Moravian Historical Society Transations, Special Series, vol. 1. Bethlehem, Pa.: Times Publishing Co., Printer, 1923.

Apr-Nov 1854. Salem, North Carolina, carpenter's account of an official visitation to scattered Moravian congregations undertaken with his bishop, J.G. Herman; travel via New Salem, Illinois, as far as Indian Territory, lodging with families en route; many references to Herman, who died during the trip, and to missionary Miles Vogler, with diary of the return journey kept by Mrs. Vogler.

FORTEN, CHARLOTTE L., 1838-1914   **3516**

THE JOURNAL OF CHARLOTTE L. FORTEN. With an introduction and notes by Ray Allen Billington. New York: Dryden Press, 1953. 248 pp. Reprint. New York: Collier Books, 1967.

Extracts in DIARY OF AMERICA, edited by Josef and Dorothy Berger, pp. 402-407; WOMAN'S "TRUE" PROFESSION, by Nancy Hoffman, pp. 140-158.

1854-1864. Journal, begun at age sixteen, of a remarkable black teacher, author and abolitionist; normal school training and teaching at Epes Grammar School in Salem, Massachusetts; friendships with such abolitionist and literary figures as William Lloyd Garrison, Wendell Phillips and John Greenleaf Whittier; recovery from illness at Philadelphia; teaching of freed slaves at Port Royal and St. Helena, South Carolina, with Edward L. Pierce and Laura M. Towne; rewards and difficulties of that educational experiment; friendships with Thomas Wentworth Higginson and Mary L. Shepard; religious, literary and personal reflections, especially on her sufferings because of race; an outstanding journal.

Billington, Ray Allen, ed. "A Social Experiment." JOURNAL OF NEGRO HISTORY 35 (1950):233-264.

Oct 1862-Feb 1863. Extracts from manuscript journal; arrival at Port Royal and subsequent experiences there; praise for Thomas Wentworth Higginson and references to Gen. Rufus Saxton and Esther and John Milton Hawks; Thanksgiving celebration; appreciation of black singing and sketches of several former slaves; her account of 1863 New Year's Day ceremonies also described by Higginson in his journal.

GREGORY, HUGH McCULLOCH, 1834-1903   **3517**

THE SEA SERPENT JOURNAL: HUGH McCULLOCH GREGORY'S VOYAGE AROUND THE WORLD IN A CLIPPER SHIP. Edited by Robert H. Burgess. Museum Publications, no. 32. Charlottesville: Published for the Mariners Museum, Newport News, Virginia, by the University Press of Virginia, 1975. 142 pp.

1854-1855. Sea diary of spunky twenty-year-old college student working aboard clipper ship SEA SERPENT; good details of an ordinary sailor's work by one who took to it despite suffering from heat, cold and bad food; Cape Horn; Shanghai, where he made notes of cargo loaded; pranks he played on other sailors; tragedy of a man lost overboard; comments on the ships of the Perry Expedition to Japan.

GUERRANT, EDWARD OWINGS, 1838-1916   **3518**

In EDWARD O. GUERRANT: APOSTLE TO THE SOUTHERN HIGHLANDER, by James G. McAllister and Grace O. Guerrant, pp. 1-238 passim. Richmond, Va.: Richmond Press, 1950.

1854-1916. Brief extracts from personal diary he kept as college student, teacher, soldier, physician and, more extensively, from the many years as a Presbyterian pastor and evangelist; attending Center College, Danville, Kentucky, and teaching at Flat Creek near Sharpsburg; short term at Danville Seminary before volunteering for Confederate army and serving in the Army of Eastern Kentucky, later Army of East Tennessee; military secretary then staff officer under generals Humphrey Marshall, William E. Preston and John S. Williams and Col. Henry L. Giltner; finally, service with John H. Morgan; comments on plundering by Morgan's men at Mount Sterling and Lexington, Kentucky, and the rout at Cynthiana; attending Jefferson Medical College, Philadelphia, followed by prosperous practice at Mt. Sterling; during serious illness dedicating himself to Christian service; leaving family in Kentucky while attending Union Theological Seminary in Richmond, Virginia; holding pastorates in Kentucky and leaving First Presbyterian Church of Louisville to become evangelist of Synod of Kentucky; spending remaining years in formidable schedule of preaching, organizing churches, schools and colleges and raising money for their support in the mountains of Tennessee, Kentucky, North Carolina and Virginia, founding the Highland Orphans Home in Clay City, Kentucky, organizing the Society of Soul Winners and editing THE SOUL WINNER until his death.

THE SOUL WINNER. Lexington, Ky.: J.B. Morton, 1896. 252 pp. Diary, pp. 191-193.

Aug 1884. Extracts about preaching and organizing a new church at Hazel Green and preaching at nearby places.

HAYASHI NOBORU, DAIGAKU-NO-KAMI   **3519**

Clement, E.W., trans. "Diary of an Official of the Bakufu." ASIATIC SOCIETY OF JAPAN TRANSACTIONS, ser. 2, 7 (December 1930):98-119.

Feb-Apr 1854. Diary of Japanese official who participated in treaty negotiations with Commodore Perry; notes on movements of ships in Yedo Bay.

HOY, PHILO ROMAYNE, 1816-1892   **3520**

"Journal of an Exploration of Western Missouri in 1854." SMITHSONIAN INSTITUTION ANNUAL REPORT (1864): 431-438.

Apr-Jun 1854. Journal of a naturalist's expedition sponsored by the Smithsonian; by riverboat from Racine, Wisconsin, with sojourns on land to observe animals and birds and collect specimens; notes on terrain, streams, vegetation and wildlife of western Missouri.

JEMISON, ROBERT SEABORN, 1824-1868   **3521**

Reagan, Hugh D., ed. "Journey to Texas." ALABAMA HISTORICAL QUARTERLY 33 (1971):190-209.

Apr-May 1854. Talladega County man's trip to Texas with several relatives and friends to investigate farming possibilities there; travel by stagecoach, steamer and horseback, with comments on land quality, people and scenery en route; some colorful reactions to frontier lodgings; notes on Austin and San Antonio, with a visit to the Alamo; his sufferings from an unspecified illness and the dubious care of an Austin doctor; return to Alabama; a lively diary throughout.

JOLLY, JOHN, 1823-1899   3522

GOLD SPRING DIARY. Edited by Carlo M. De Ferrari. Sonora, Calif.: Tuolumne County Historical Society, 1966. 160 pp.

1854-1855. Englishman's diary of mining with partner Victor D. Brundage in the Gold Spring area where he later settled as a farmer; notes on mining and farming, the weather, local people and events; Masonic activities; claim disputes, violence, etc.

LAWRIE, ARTHUR S.   3523

Gibbens, V.E., ed. "Lawrie's Trip to Northeast Texas." SOUTHWEST HISTORICAL QUARTERLY 48 (1944):238-253.

Dec 1854-Jan 1855. Extracts from the diary of an Indiana farmer engaged to accompany François Cantagrel to Texas to explore possible sites for a French socialist settlement proposed by Victor Considérant, eventually the Reunion Colony near present Dallas; from Patriot, Indiana, down the Ohio and Mississippi, with a few good notes on travel and travelers; thence overland through Arkansas and Texas, with an abundance of personal and place names en route; references to Cantagrel and others.

LOMAX, ELIZABETH LINDSAY, b. 1796?   3524

LEAVES FROM AN OLD WASHINGTON DIARY. Edited by Lindsay Lomax Wood. New York: Books, 1943. 256 pp.

1854-1863. Diary kept by Virginia army officer's widow, residing with her children in Washington, D.C.; sporadic entries covering family and social activities within a circle which included many who would gain later military prominence such as Henry Wise, Rufus King, Robert E. Lee, Jeb Stuart and Raphael Semmes; the many accomplishments of her daughters, especially Victoria and Virginia; concern for her son Lindsay, first at West Point and then in frontier army service, and memories of her husband, Maj. Mann Page Lomax; financial matters, securing a clerkship at the War Department, giving music lessons, successfully petitioning for the Revolutionary War pension of her father, William Lindsay, and building a house; occasions in the capital city including the arrival of the Japanese legation and the Prince of Wales' visit; reflections on local and national events; the secession crisis, outbreak of war and her son's enlistment in the Confederate army; refugee life in Charlottesville, near Fredericksburg and in Baltimore with a brief return to her Washington home; arrest of daughters Anne, Virginia and Julia as Southern sympathizers; notes on countless social, domestic and personal interests; a good account of genteel life and the divisions wrought by war.

LYON, ALANSON FORMAN, 1798-1901   3525

Beeson, Lewis, ed. "A Trip up the Menominee River in 1854." MICHIGAN HISTORY 47 (1963):301-311.

Sep 1854. A sawmill manager's canoe trip with his son Gaius Morgan Lyon in search of lumbering possibilities; portages and camps; a few notes on Menominee Indians.

MILLWARD, BENJAMIN, d. 1904   3526

Walch, Timothy, ed. "The Voyage of an Iowa Immigrant." ANNALS

OF IOWA, 3d ser. 44 (1977-1979):137-145.

Mar-Apr 1854. Letter-diary, kept on board the CORNELIA, of an English immigrant who settled later at Decorah; departure from Liverpool; colorful notes on fellow passengers, conditions and work, some of it done by passengers; the thrashing of a stowaway; encounter with the wrecked KATE HUNTER; deaths of several children during voyage.

PARKE, JOHN GRUBB, 1827-1900   3527

REPORT OF EXPLORATIONS FOR THAT PORTION OF A RAILWAY ROUTE, NEAR THE 32D PARALLEL OF LATITUDE, LYING BETWEEN DONA ANA, ON THE RIO GRANDE, AND PIMAS VILLAGES, ON THE GILA. 33d Cong., 1st sess., 1855, H. Exec Doc. 129. Washington, D.C., 1855? 53 pp. Diary, pp. 3-24.

In REPORTS OF EXPLORATIONS AND SURVEYS, by United States War Department, vol. 2.

In REPORT OF THE SECRETARY OF WAR COMMUNICATING THE SEVERAL PACIFIC RAILROAD SURVEYS, by United States War Department, vol. 3.

Jan-Nov 1854. Military exploration for railroad route; finding Fort Wester in ashes; topographical and scientific details; noting aid of William Emory's maps.

PARKER, WILLIAM B.   3528

NOTES TAKEN DURING THE EXPEDITION COMMANDED BY CAPT. R.B. MARCY. Philadelphia: Hayes & Zell, 1856. 242 pp.

Jun-Oct 1854. Carefully detailed military exploration through Texas with Captain Marcy, surveying lands for Indian reservations from Fort Smith to Fort Washita with Delaware and Shawnee guides, hunters and interpreters; travel, weather, botanical notes, scenery and ancedotes about members of the party; into unexplored area to headwaters of Brazos River; few surveying notes but considerable information on Comanche, Wichita, Kickapoo, Cherokee and Caddo Indians; to Fort Belknap with praise for soldiers in that remote place.

"Parker's Notes Taken with Marcy: Locating the Texas Indian Reservations." WEST TEXAS HISTORICAL ASSOCIATION YEAR BOOK 1 (1925):55-72.

Aug 1854. Extract of conference with Comanches on Clear Fork of Brazos.

POCHE, FELIX PIERRE, 1836-1895   3529

Bridges, Katherine, ed. "A Louisiana Schoolboy in Kentucky." LOUISIANA STUDIES 10 (1971):187-192.

Jun 1854. Account of student life at St. Joseph's College in Bardstown, Kentucky; religious observances, leisure activities, military drill, disputes among schoolmates, etc.

A LOUISIANA CONFEDERATE. Edited by Edwin C. Bearss. Translated by Eugenie W. Somdal. Natchitoches: Louisiana Studies Institute, Northwestern State University, 1972. 352 pp.

1861-1865. War diary of Lafourche Parish lawyer, a devout Roman Catholic, who served in the commissary department as a volunteer on Col. Henry Gray's staff and later as a commander of scouts in Ascension, Livingston, St. James and St. Helena parishes; a daily record of military operations in Louisiana with excursions into Arkansas and Mississippi; battles of Sabine Cross Roads and

Pleasant Hill and other action during the Red River campaign of 1864; longing for his wife, Selima, and their daughters; some child-rearing difficulties during their reunion; religious reflections, church services and sacraments and restorative sojourns at the Jesuits' St. Charles College at Grand Coteau; description of conditions in wartime Louisiana and places visited, including Natchitoches, Washington, Monroe, Alexandria, Pointe Coupee Parish and Vermilion Bayou; mention of many persons met in his military and social lives; rather consistently inaccurate reports of war's events elsewhere; antisemitic statements; notes on Indian customs, speculators, Gen. Kirby Smith, the state insane asylum at Jackson, Louisiana, soldiers' hardships, Confederates' smuggling, pillaging by both Union and Confederate forces, etc.; an interesting account.

Sample, Wilton Wade. "A View of the Battle of Mansfield." NORTH LOUISIANA HISTORICAL ASSOCIATION JOURNAL 2 (1970):10-20.

Apr 1864. Extracts covering the battle of Mansfield or Sabine Cross Roads.

REES, WILLIAM   3530

Thornburg, Opal, ed. "Indiana to North Carolina." QUAKER HISTORY 59 (1970):67-80.

Oct-Dec 1854. Extracts within article on Indiana Quaker traveling to attend the North Carolina Yearly Meeting; by train from Richmond to Philadelphia and Baltimore, thence by Chesapeake Bay steamer, canal boat and carriage; visits to Quaker meetings along the way; notes on condition of soil and agriculture; diarist's dismay over slavery and slaveholding Quakers; concern for Quaker boarding schools; evidence of the Gurneyite-Wilburite separation.

REMEEUS, JOHANNES, b. 1815   3531

Lucas, Henry S., ed. "The Journey of an Immigrant Family from the Netherlands to Milwaukee in 1854." WISCONSIN MAGAZINE OF HISTORY 29 (1945):201-223.

In DUTCH IMMIGRANT MEMOIRS AND RELATED WRITINGS, selected by Henry S. Lucas, vol. 2, pp. 91-109. Assen, Netherlands: Van Gorcum, 1955.

May?-Jul 1854. Atlantic crossing on the FEDES KOO with other Dutch and German immigrants; quarrels between the two groups, religious services, ship discipline of crew and even of passengers, a Fourth of July celebration and other incidents aboard; from Boston by train to Chicago, where cholera was raging, thence arriving penniless in Milwaukee. Translated from the Dutch.

RICKETSON, DANIEL, 1813-1898   3532

In DANIEL RICKETSON AND HIS FRIENDS, edited by Anna and Walton Ricketson, pp. 277-332. Boston: Houghton Mifflin, 1902.

1854-1892. Extracts from the religious and intellectual diary of a New Bedford Quaker, friend of Thoreau, Emerson, Channing, the Alcotts, etc.; many walks and visits with Thoreau and correspondence and visits with most of the transcendentalists and other New England thinkers.

ROYAL, JAMES HENRY BASCOME   3533

"Journal of the Reverend James H.B. Royal at Umpqua Academy." UMPQUA TRAPPER 15 (1979):55-72.

Apr 1854-Jul 1855. Methodist minister's record of organizing the log school at Jacksonville, Oregon, and "struggling to commence a systematic and well regulated school"; list of his thirteen pupils on opening day, ranging from age five to eighteen; fees, lessons and recitations, programs, seeing a solar eclipse through smoked glass and a quite elaborate Fourth of July celebration; references to many local people, including his superior, the Rev. James Harvey Wilbur, and students.

SHOEMAKER, EMANUEL ROGER   3534

Dilla, Geraldine P., ed. "The Diary of a Late Forty-Niner." SOUTH ATLANTIC QUARTERLY 38 (1939):40-51.

Jan-Nov 1854. Extract from California portion of a young Indiana man's gold rush diary; work and life in the diggings near Downieville; church and temperance activities.

SPROSTON, JOHN GLENDY, 1828-1862   3535

A PRIVATE JOURNAL OF JOHN GLENDY SPROSTON, U.S.N. Edited by Shio Sakanishi. Monumenta Nipponica Monograph. Tokyo and Rutland, Vt.: Sophia University in cooperation with Charles E. Tuttle, 1968. 128 pp.

Feb-Aug 1854. Naval officer's diary kept on the MACEDONIAN, one of Commodore Perry's ships on his mission to Japan; events in Tokyo Bay and meetings with Japanese commissioners; many personal observations and comments.

STARLEY, JAMES, 1817-1914   3536

"Journal of James Starley." UTAH HISTORICAL QUARTERLY 9 (1941):168-176.

1854-1860 (with gaps). Brief, scattered entries of a Mormon immigrant; a few notes on activities in England, then a miserable Atlantic crossing on the CLARA WHEELER, during which many children died; from New Orleans up the Mississippi on the OCEANA; briefest of notes on overland journey to Utah.

STUART, GRANVILLE, 1834-1918   3537

FORTY YEARS ON THE FRONTIER. Edited by Paul C. Phillips. Early Western Journals, no. 2. Cleveland: Arthur H. Clark, 1925. 2 vols. Northwest Historical Series, no. 2. Glendale, Calif.: Arthur H. Clark, 1957. 2 vols. in 1.

1854-1880 (with gaps). Extracts from voluminous diary condensed by diarist in later life; frontier life in Montana before and during the gold rush, ranching, growth of cattle business, politics, Indians and Catholic Indian missions; treks to West Liberty, Iowa, to visit his parents, and other travels in the Midwest; some journals of settlement of Deer Lodge Valley kept jointly with his brother James.

DIARY SKETCHBOOK OF A JOURNEY TO "AMERICA" IN 1866. With an introduction by Carl S. Dentzel. Los Angeles: Dawson's Book Shop, 1963. 50 pp.

Jan-Jun 1866. Entertaining narrative diary and sketches of trip from Deer Lodge to Virginia City, Montana, in a snowstorm; to Salt Lake City, Fort Kearny, Atchison, where he first saw the railroad, St. Louis, Chicago, Fort Union, boyhood home in Iowa, up the Missouri River to Fort Benton and return to Montana; notes on cities and scenery.

SWINSCOE, CHARLES, b. 1833?   3538

"The Journal of a Voyage in the Clipper Ship DREADNAUGHT."
MASSACHUSETTS HISTORICAL SOCIETY PROCEEDINGS 65
(1932-1936):3-21.

Mar-May 1854. A twenty-one-year old New Yorker's voyage to
Liverpool as a stevedore on the DREADNAUGHT under Capt.
Samuel Samuels; sailing details, hard ship discipline and work;
notes on passengers; ships met and racing other clippers, particularly a rival, the FLYING SCUD.

TERWILLIGER, PHOEBE HOGEBOOM   3539

Helfrich, Devere, ed. "The Diary of Mrs. P.S. (Phoebe Hogeboom)
Terwilliger Written while Crossing the Plains in 1854." SISKIYOU
PIONEER IN FOLKLORE, FACT AND FICTION 4, no. 6 (1973):1-86.

Apr-Oct 1854. New Lebanon, Illinois, woman's journey to Shasta
Valley, California, with her husband, Sidney Terwilliger, in Willard
Stone's company of emigrants and cattle drovers; camps, con-
ditions, route and distances; encounters with Indians.

"Diary of Phoebe Hogeboom Terwilliger." SISKIYOU PIONEER IN
FOLKLORE, FACT AND FICTION 2, no. 6. (1954):16-25.

Apr-Oct 1854. Extracts.

VANDERSLICE, DANIEL, 1799-1889   3540

In VANDERSLICE AND ALLIED FAMILIES, by Howard Vanderslice,
pp. 166-186. Los Angeles: Printed by the Neuner Corp., 1931.

1854-1855. Extracts from diary of a Highland, Kansas, Indian
agent engaged in treaty negotiations involving Iowa, Sac, Fox
and Kickapoo Indians over the purchase of western tracts of land;
journey to Washington, D.C., with Indian delegates.

WALKER, CHARLES LOWELL, 1832-1904   3541

THE DIARY OF CHARLES L. WALKER. Edited by A. Karl Larson
and Katharine Miles Larson. Logan, Utah: Utah State University
Press, 1980. 2 vols.

1854-1899. English Mormon's account of life in Utah, mainly at
St. George where he was a community leader; difficult farm work;
problems of epidemics, weather and frequent flooding of Virgin
River; dissidence among the Saints; volunteer work in building
the St. George Temple; reports on sermons and testimonies of
various Mormons; frequent references to Brigham Young, James
G. Bleak, David H. and George A. Cannon, Daniel McArthur,
Erastus Snow and others; diarist's occasional verses, participation in literary and debating clubs and reaction to national and
world events; spirited defense of polygamy.

WHITE, ANDREW DICKSON, 1832-1918   3542

THE DIARIES OF ANDREW D. WHITE. Edited by Robert M. Ogden.
Ithaca, N.Y.: Cornell University Press, 1959. 500 pp.

1854-1856. Account of "Grand Tour" upon graduation from Yale,
with his friend Daniel Coit Gilman; ecstatic reactions to the historic
sites, music, art, drama, cathedrals and bookstores of London
and Paris; stagecoach journey to St. Petersburg and Moscow,
with tourist and social activities there; return through Germany
and studies in Berlin; travels in Italy, Switzerland, France and
England.

1865-1918. Record of a life of public service; presidency of Cornell University, with notes on dealings with its benefactor Ezra
Cornell, trustees and faculty; university affairs; family matters and
social and religious life of Ithaca; later diplomatic career in Germany and Russia, with further travels throughout Europe; an old
age busy with academic and civic activities, reading writing and
travel, including a voyage on the LUSITANIA; references to Andrew Carnegie, Henry Williams Sage, Willard Fiske and others.

WINDER, CHARLES SIDNEY   3543

Lloyd, Alice and Brice, Arthur T., eds. "The Wreck of the Steamer
SAN FRANCISCO." PACIFIC HISTORIAN 14, no. 1 (1970):5-8.

Jan-Jun 1854. Extracts from an artillery officer's account of the
rescue of the few survivors of the storm-wrecked SAN FRAN-
CISCO; assistance from the THREE BELLS and ANTARCTIC;
voyage to Liverpool on the ANTARCTIC under diarist's command,
thence to Boston on the AMERICA; assignment to Benicia, California, with very sketchy notes of ship voyage to San Francisco.

"Diary of a Bachelor Lieutenant at Benicia in 1854." PACIFIC
HISTORIAN 14, no. 2 (1970):77-84.

Jun 1854-May 1855. Extracts covering tour of duty at Benicia with
the Third United States Artillery Regiment; very brief notes of
travel about the area, social life, hunting, and his promotion to
captain.

WOODS, JAMES, 1815-1886   3544

Bynum, Lindley, ed. "Los Angeles in 1854-5" HISTORICAL SOCIETY
OF SOUTHERN CALIFORNIA QUARTERLY 23 (1941):65-86.

Nov 1854-Apr 1855. Extracts from the diary of a Presbyterian
minister; preaching and pastoral work; notes on trials, murders
and other evidences of lawlessness; prison visits to convicted
murderer William B. Lee and others; Spanish-Anglo relations and
customs; opinions on Catholics and Mormons; references to Benjamin Davis Wilson; much soul-searching, worry about his health
and discouragement over the low state of religion and morals in
California.

1855

ANON.   3545

Jensen, Andrew, ed. "History of the Las Vegas Mission." NEVADA
HISTORICAL SOCIETY PAPERS 5 (1925-1926):119-284.

1855-1866 (with gaps). Record, compiled from various sources,
of a Mormon mission dispatched by Brigham Young to settle at
Las Vegas; organization of mission under William Bringhurst;
journey over the Spanish Trail from Salt Lake, with route and
camps; sermons of Bringhurst and others; tasks; formation of the
Las Vegas Guards under John Steele; Fourth of July celebration; preaching to the Paiute Indians and baptizing them with
English names; traffic on the busy trade and mail route.

ANON.   3546

Langley, Wright and Parks, Arva M., eds. "Diary of an Unidentified
Land Official." TEQUESTA 43 (1983):5-24.

Jan-Feb 1855. Interesting diary of life at Key West, the Florida Keys and Miami, with descriptions of towns, people, shipping, etc.; sea voyages about the area; many references to George Washington Ferguson and his various enterprises at Miami; some extensive and sardonic observations by the diarist who was obviously an outsider, possibly British.

Mormino, Gary R., ed. '' 'The Firing of Guns and Crackers Till Light': A Diary of the Billy Bowlegs War.'' TEQUESTA 45 (1985):48-72.

Dec 1855-Feb 1856. Civilian account of war with the Seminoles in the Tampa area; hectic efforts of local leaders to raise a volunteer army and the diarist's amused reactions to the bustle, panic and heroic posturing among citizenry; hearsay account of the attack on Lt. George Hartsuff and his men near Big Cypress; references to Gen. Jesse Carter; diarist's question ''must the Indians be driven from the land and country made for them and given to them by the God of nature because the savage life is the only one adapted to the country and calculated to use the natural resources?''

ANON.   **3547**

Reese, J.W. ''OMV's Fort Henrietta: On Winter Duty.'' OREGON HISTORICAL QUARTERLY 66 (1965):133-160. Diary, pp. 143-145.

Nov 1855. Extract showing activities of Oregon Mounted Volunteers at Fort Henrietta during Yakima Indian War; defenses and alarms; the coming and going of scouting parties, with news of Indian movements.

ABBOT, HENRY LARCOM, 1831-1927   **3548**

Sawyer, Robert W. ''Abbot Railroad Surveys.'' OREGON HISTORICAL QUARTERLY 33 (1932):1-24, 115-133. Journal, pp. 14-25, 115-127.

Aug-Nov 1855. Extracts from Oregon survey journal of Corps of Topographical Engineers officer from Beverly, Massachusetts; technical notes; difficulties of terrain; lack of food and water for mules; Indian troubles; references to colleague Robert Stockton Williamson.

In EXPLORATIONS AND SURVEYS, by United States War Department, vol. 6, pp. 56-111.

Aug-Nov 1855. Includes diary notes kept by Williamson while with a detached party exploring Cascade Mountains and Willamette Valley as far as Fort Vancouver and returning to San Francisco.

BEAN, GEORGE W.   **3549**

Dees, Harry C., ed. ''The Journal of George W. Bean, Las Vegas Springs, New Mexico Territory.'' NEVADA HISTORICAL SOCIETY QUARTERLY 15, no. 3 (1972):3-29.

Apr 1855-Feb 1856. One-armed Mormon's account of a mission to the ''Lamanites''; rugged travel from Salt Lake to Las Vegas area; references to Rufus Allen, William Bringhurst, Brigham Young, James Allred and others; election as clerk and recorder of the mission; the baptism of many Indians; frequent deliveries of the California Mail.

BRAY, MARY MATTHEWS, b. 1837.   **3550**

A SEA TRIP IN CLIPPER SHIP DAYS. Boston: R.G. Badger, 1920. 164 pp.

1855?-1856? Spirited and intelligent young woman's diary of sea trip on clipper ship NATIONAL EAGLE with her sister and her father, Capt. George Matthews; learning nautical terms and geography of the sea, winds, routine of crew and passengers and dock regulations while traveling from Boston to New Orleans; visiting friends and getting acquainted with the city while the ship was loaded with cotton for Liverpool; uneventful Atlantic crossing; sightseeing and shopping in Liverpool; trip to London to buy silk, muslin and lace to sew on the ship; shipping salt to Calcutta; trip up the Ganges, taking rooms in a boarding house and being introduced to the social life of the English community; notes contrasting English section and native quarters of the city.

BROWN, HENRY BILLINGS, 1836-1913   **3551**

MEMOIR OF HENRY BILLINGS BROWN. By Charles A. Kent. New York: Duffield, 1915. 136 pp. Diary, pp. 36-72.

1855-1875. Extracts and summary of diary of a Detroit judge who later became a justice of the Supreme Court; student days at Yale, visits to Europe, reading, legal work and comments on the Civil War.

BROWN, SPENCER KELLOGG, 1842-1863   **3552**

SPENCER KELLOGG BROWN, HIS LIFE IN KANSAS AND HIS DEATH AS A SPY. Edited by George Gardner Smith. New York: D. Appleton, 1903. 380 pp. Diary, pp. 20-23, 68-155, 322-346 passim.

1855-1860, Oct 1862-May 1863. Journal kept by son of the founder of Osawatomie, Kansas; journey from New York to join his father, Orville Chester Brown, in Kansas; taken prisoner during raid by proslavery men on Osawatomie, held in comfortable circumstances in Missouri and then sent to his family in Utica, New York; return to Kansas and a visit to Missouri; notes on reading, music and love interests; religious reflections while a prisoner at Jackson, Mississippi, accused of being a Union spy; for the most part, scattered coverage of events over the years and a mixture of brief comments and longer, discursive entries; impossible to discern how heavy an editorial hand was applied to the document.

CHAMBERS, JAMES H., 1820-1866?   **3553**

MacDonnell, Anne, ed. ''Original Journal of James H. Chambers, Fort Sarpy.'' MONTANA HISTORICAL SOCIETY CONTRIBUTIONS 10 (1940):100-187.

1855-1856 (with gaps). Fur trader's journal giving a colorful and detailed picture of life at and around Fort Sarpy; trading and other business notes; social life; problems of crowding with fort frequently overrun with traders and Indians; ''Oh what a night, squaws screaming, brats bawling and dogs barking: I never saw a place completely crammed before''; notes on Crow and Sioux encamped about the fort and their intertribal warfare; hunting trips; references to Alexander Culbertson, Alfred J. Vaughn and Edwin T. Denig; frequent deletions by editor as ''too obscene to print.''

CHANDLESS, WILLIAM   **3554**

A VISIT TO SALT LAKE: BEING A JOURNEY ACROSS THE PLAINS AND A RESIDENCE IN THE MORMON SETTLEMENTS AT UTAH. London: Smith, Elder, 1857. 346 pp.

Jul 1855-Feb 1856. An Englishman's account of his journey from

Atchison, Kansas, to Salt Lake as a wagon driver, with notes on Mormons; a trip to Los Angeles via Fillmore, Cedar City, Las Vegas and San Bernardino; thence to San Francisco; entertaining, but inclined to be a travel book narrative.

CLEMENS, SAMUEL LANGHORNE, 1835-1910   **3555**

MARK TWAIN'S NOTEBOOK. Prepared for publication with comments by Albert Bigelow Paine. New York and London: Harper, 1935. 413 pp.

MARK TWAIN'S NOTEBOOKS & JOURNALS. Edited by Frederick Anderson, Michael B. Frank and Kenneth M. Sanderson. Berkeley: University of California Press, 1975-1979. 3 vols. passim.

1855-1891 (with gaps). Journals, diaries and commonplace books ranging from hastily jotted words or phrases to full, narrative entries and encompassing Twain's enormously varied travels, interests, pursuits and opinions; notes on many of the people and events of his life, and sketches which later provided material for his writings and lectures; literary, political, social and religious attitudes; reactions to specific books, newspapers, periodicals, authors, publishers, etc., with many references to William Dean Howells, Oliver Wendell Holmes, James R. Osgood, Charles L. Webster and others; his Mississippi apprenticeship under Horace Bixby on the PAUL JONES and technical details of piloting; mining experiences at Jackass Hill, California; travel to Hawaii as a correspondent for the SACRAMENTO UNION, with substantial content on his voyage on the AJAX, as well as events and people in Honolulu, including Queen Emma, Kamehameha V, Gerrit P. Judd and various missionaries; return to San Francisco; his first lecture tour; to Nicaragua on the AMERICA, with notes on voyage, passengers and Capt. Edgar Wakeman; overland across Nicaragua and continuation on the cholera-plagued SAN FRANCISCO; notes of a Mediterranean cruise on the QUAKER CITY under Capt. Charles C. Duncan, with impressions of North Africa, Europe and the Holy Land; a trip to Bermuda and extensive European travels with the Rev. Joseph Hopkins Twichell; a nostalgic return to the Mississippi; major lecture tours; his year of involvement with Webster's publishing house and resulting financial difficulties; social and literary life at his home in Hartford. The California edition is definitive, including material omitted by Paine.

Extracts in TREASURY OF THE WORLD'S GREATEST DIARIES, edited by Philip Dunaway, pp. 91-94.

Dec 1866-Jan 1867. Sailing on ship from San Francisco to New York with cholera epidemic aboard.

EGGE, HEINRICH, b. 1830   **3556**

Beinhoff, Esther, ed. and trans. "The Diary of Heinrich Egge, a German Immigrant." MISSISSIPPI VALLEY HISTORICAL REVIEW 17 (1930-1931):123-134.

May-Jun 1855. Extracts from the diary of a young German from Schleswig-Holstein who settled at Davenport, Iowa; voyage from Hamburg on the NORTH AMERICA, during which he was jolly and gregarious and, despite the seasickness of others, "well and happy, thank God"; fine picture of social life and amusements among first class passengers; a stay in New York, thence to Davenport by boat and train.

HALLIDAY, JOHN, 1815-1906   **3557**

In TREASURY OF THE WORLD'S GREAT DIARIES, edited by Philip Dunaway, pp. 43-49

1855. Extracts describing sea voyage of a Scottish immigrant to Canada and America.

HARRIS, ISAIAH MORRIS, 1819-1890   **3558**

Brodhead, Michael J. and Unruh, John D., eds. "Isaiah Harris' Minutes of a Trip to Kansas Territory in 1855." KANSAS HISTORICAL QUARTERLY 35 (1969):373-385.

Oct-Nov 1855. Clarksville, Ohio, man's journey to take a claim in Wabaunsee County, Kansas: from Cincinnati on the GRAND TURK, with interesting notes of Ohio River travel; comments on passengers, including slaveowners traveling with their slaves and diarist's opinions on the slavery question; Methodist views and interest in Methodist mission to Indians in Kansas.

HARRIS, TOWNSEND, 1804-1878   **3559**

THE COMPLETE JOURNAL OF TOWNSEND HARRIS, FIRST AMERICAN CONSUL GENERAL AND MINISTER TO JAPAN. Introduction and notes by Mario E. Cozenza. Garden City, N.Y.: Published for Japan Society, New York, by Doubleday, Doran, 1930. 616 pp. Rev. ed. Rutland, Vt.: C.E. Tuttle, 1959.

1855-1858. Travel and diplomatic journal; voyage from New York to England and France, preparing for duties in Far East; ship arrivals and departures noted at each port; to Malaysia and Ceylon; meeting friends in Bangkok, lengthy negotiations for commercial treaty with Siam, exchanges of gifts with royalty; stopover at Hong Kong, meetings with various diplomatic persons, purchasing supplies and hiring servants for his stay in Japan as first American consul general and minister to Japan; journey aboard SAN JACINTO to Shimoda; collecting natural history specimens; exasperating delays in negotiations for opening ports to American vessels and trade with Japan; discouraging lack of contact with United States; formal cavalcade to Yedo and eventual audience with the shogun, finally concluding Treaty of Amity and Commerce between the United States and Japan; serious illness; a carefully detailed, well written and valuable journal.

In TOWNSEND HARRIS, FIRST AMERICAN ENVOY IN JAPAN, by William Elliot Griffis, pp. 33-307. Boston and New York: Houghton Mifflin, 1895.

1856-1858. Japan portion of journal.

HEMBREE, WAMAN C.   **3560**

"Yakima Indian War Diary." WASHINGTON HISTORICAL QUARTERLY 16 (1925):273-283.

Oct 1855-Apr 1856. Brief notes, kept by commander's nephew, of marches and encampments of the Yamhill County Company of Oregon Mounted Volunteers, under A. J. Hembree; court-martial and hanging of an Indian spy.

HEUSKEN, HENRY CONRADUS JOANNES, 1832-1861   **3561**

JAPAN JOURNAL, 1855-1861. Translated and edited by Jeannette C. van der Corput and Robert A. Wilson. New Brunswick: Rutgers University Press, 1964. 247 pp.

1855-1861. Private journal of a Dutch immigrant who became secretary and interpreter to Townsend Harris, minister to Japan; a record of his experiences in that position from 1855 to 1858 and briefly in 1861, shortly before his death by assassination; trip out from New York via South Africa, the East Indies, Thailand, etc.; the meeting and clash of cultures as Americans negotiated the first commercial treaty with Japan; an interesting view of the last years of feudal Japan.

JAEGER, LOUIS JOHN FREDERICK   3562

Beattie, G.W., ed. "Diary of a Ferryman and Trader at Fort Yuma." HISTORICAL SOCIETY OF SOUTHERN CALIFORNIA ANNUAL PUBLICATIONS 14 (1928-1930): 89-128, 213-242.

   1855-1857 (with gaps). Diary attributed to Jaeger, a trader supplying beef and other food to the fort and river steamers, as well as ferrying emigrants and large herds of sheep across the Colorado; difficult trips to San Diego, Los Angeles, Sonora and San Bernardino; notes on emigrants, Mexicans and fort personnel; business details including prices; violence and drunkenness in frontier communities and life at a busy but isolated outpost.

JOHNSTON, ELIZA GRIFFIN   3563

Roland, Charles P. and Robbins, Richard C., eds. "The Diary of Eliza (Mrs. Albert Sidney) Johnston." SOUTHWESTERN HISTORICAL QUARTERLY 60 (1957):463-500.

   Oct 1855-May 1856. Diary kept by the wife of Col. Johnston during a march from Jefferson Barracks, Missouri, to Fort Mason, Texas, where he was assigned to command the Second Cavalry; travel with her three children on the seven hundred mile march; notes on diseases, injuries, births and deaths en route; descriptions of people and scenes in Missouri, Oklahoma and Texas; frequent pity for the hardships of cavalrymen and severity of discipline, which included whippings and being drummed out of the service; a terrible winter in Texas, with considerable loss of horses and even soldiers; notes on Indians; some amusing incidents.

Ballenger, T.L. "Colonel Albert Sidney Johnston's March through Indian Territory in 1855." CHRONICLES OF OKLAHOMA 47 (1969):132-137.

   Nov-Dec 1855. Extracts relating to Indian Territory.

JONES, ALFRED GOLDSBOROUGH, b. 1821   3564

Weaks, Mabel, ed. "Long Ago and 'Faraway': Traces of Melville in the Marquesas in the Journal of A.G. Jones." NEW YORK PUBLIC LIBRARY BULLETIN 52 (1948):362-369.

   Aug 1855. Extract covering a visit to the Marquesas while diarist was serving as a clerk to Capt. Theodorus Bailey on the warship SAINT MARY'S; notes relating to people and scenes in Melville's TYPEE; appearance and customs of the islanders, including girls similar to "Faraway"; accounts of the recently abandoned practice of cannibalism.

KELLY, PLYMPTON J., 1828-1906   3565

WE WERE NOT SUMMER SOLDIERS: THE INDIAN WAR DIARY OF PLYMPTON J. KELLY. Edited by William N. Bischoff. Tacoma: Washington State Historical Society, 1976. 191 pp. Diary, pp. 60-103.

   Nov 1855-May 1856. Military diary of an Oregon Mounted Volunteer during Yakima Indian War; brief entries on weather, terrain, privations, official bungling, casualties and scalping on both sides.

KIP, LAWRENCE, 1836-1899   3566

THE INDIAN COUNCIL IN THE VALLEY OF THE WALLA WALLA, 1855. San Francisco: Whitton, Towne, Printers, 1855. 45 pp.

MAGAZINE OF HISTORY, extra no. 39 (1915):1-45.

THE INDIAN COUNCIL AT WALLA WALLA. Sources of the History of Oregon, vol.1, pt.2. Eugene, Oreg.: Star Job Office, 1897. 28 pp.

   May-Jun 1855. Diary of a member of the military escort to assist Governor Stevens's negotiations with the Nez Percé, Cayuse and other tribes; from Vancouver on the Columbia steamer BELLE to Fort Dalles, thence overland to Fort Walla Walla, with good description of march, scenery and camp life; arrival of Indians and subsequent dances, music, horseback races, council negotiations and speeches; religious observances of Christian Nez Percé; references to Stevens, Lt. Archibald Gracie, Nez Percé chief Lawyer, etc.

ARMY LIFE ON THE PACIFIC: A JOURNAL OF THE EXPEDITION AGAINST THE NORTHERN INDIANS. New York: Redfield, 1859. 144 pp.

MAGAZINE OF HISTORY, extra no. 30 (1914):1-117.

   May-Oct 1858. Account of the expedition against the Coeur d'Alene, Palouse and Spokane Indians following the defeat of Col. Edward J. Steptoe; summary of the Steptoe battle, followed by entries describing the march from Fort Dalles to forts Walla Walla and Taylor under Col. George Wright; battle of Four Lakes against the northern Indians, including Nez Percé, with cavalry victory attributed to new long-range rifle; the battle of Spokan Plains; killing of captured Indian horses; peace negotiations with subdued Indians at Coeur d'Alene Mission.

LINES, AMELIA JANE AKEHURST, 1827?-1886   3567

TO RAISE MYSELF A LITTLE. Edited by Thomas Dyer. Athens: University of Georgia Press, 1982. 284 pp. Diary, pp. 20-253 passim.

   1855-1871 (with gaps). Diary of schoolteacher, born in England and raised in upstate New York; the infrequent pleasures and constant frustrations of teaching in Clinton, New York, and in Georgia, in Euharlee, Atlanta and Walton County and at the Southern Female Masonic College in Covington; marriage to Sylvanus Lines, a printer from Connecticut, and residence in Fayetteville, Newnan, Greenville and Atlanta, remaining in Georgia throughout the Civil War; views on the 1860 presidential election, slavery, abolitionists, emancipation and black servants; death of first child; in New Haven, Connecticut, and Macon, Georgia, after the war; religious concerns and activities, domestic affairs and social life; notes on reading, sights of Washington, D.C., dentistry, issue of prayer in school, Donati's comet, wartime prices, etc.; irregularly kept, but substantial entries filled with everyday details.

MILLER, HENRY WILLIAM   3568

Foreman, Grant, ed. "Missionaries of the Latter Day Saints Church in Indian Territory." CHRONICLES OF OKLAHOMA 13 (1935):196-213.

   1855-1859 (with gaps). Diary of Mormon missionary to the Cherokees, with apparent mission headquarters at the residence of Jacob Croft; travels and baptisms; problems with the Indian agent; published entries considerably expanded from those of manuscript.

MILLER, JOAQUIN, 1837-1913   **3569**

JOAQUIN MILLER, HIS CALIFORNIA DIARY. Edited by John S. Richards. Seattle: F. McCaffrey at his Dogwood Press, 1936. 106 pp.

SELECTED WRITINGS OF JOAQUIN MILLER. Edited by Alan Rosenus. Eugene, Oreg.: Urion Press, 1977. 268 pp. Diary, pp. 143-199.

1855-1857. Poet's diary of working mines in Squaw Town, Shasta County, California; discouragement over unsuccessful mining and subsistence living; later period at McCloud Valley living and hunting with Digger Indians; investigating Pit River massacre.

Richards, John S. "Joaquin Miller's California Diary." FRONTIER AND MIDLAND 16 (1935):35-39.

1855-1857. Extracts within article mainly showing poet's unhappy mining experiences at Shasta City and a sojourn with the Indians, during which time he had an Indian wife.

SELECTED WRITINGS OF JOAQUIN MILLER. Edited by Alan Rosenus. Eugene, Oreg.: Urion Press, 1977. 268 pp. Diary, pp. 3-24.

Aug-Sep 1870. Extracts copied from manuscript journal which Miller later "cremated"; arrival in New York to sail on EUROPA: travels in England and Scotland, with visits to Byron's and other literary sites; a stay in London to search for a publisher and hobnob with Browning, Rosetti and other luminaries; publication of his PACIFIC POEMS.

MILLS, WILLIAM G.   **3570**

In TREASURES OF PIONEER HISTORY, compiled by Kate B. Carter, vol. 5, pp. 29-37.

Apr-May 1855. Daily record of Mormon appointed historian for an English company sailing from Liverpool to Philadelphia on CHIMBORAZO: instructions for living arrangements and religious observances; sewing wagon and tent covers.

MOORE, JONATHAN L.   **3571**

"Journal of Travails on the Roade to Oregon." LANE COUNTY HISTORIAN 11 (1966):23-34.

Mar-Sep 1855. Bare notes of camps, conditions and distances "travaild"; points of departure and exact destination unclear.

MORSE, ABNER, 1819-1881   **3572**

Still, Bayrd and Herrmann, William, eds. "Abner Morse's Diary of Emigrant Travel." WISCONSIN MAGAZINE OF HISTORY 22 (1938-1939):195-212, 329-343, 427-434; 23 (1939-1940):62-88.

Dec 1855-Mar 1856. Wagon and train journey from Braintree, Vermont, to settle at River Falls, Wisconsin; extensive, literate notes on towns, agriculture, prices, people and customs; lively social comments and observations from a strong temperance perspective; lodgings in houses, inns and taverns, where "innkeepers will sell whiskey to a poor, drunken wretch, so long as he can hold a glass in one hand and a six-pence in another"; decision to "car" his team by train from Cleveland to Chicago, with good notes on Illinois as he resumed wagon travel.

1859-1861. Life as a farmer, teacher and teamster at River Falls, with interesting notes on religious revivals, social life, farming and

public lectures; circuit court and business activities at Prescott; religious and philosophical reflections of a man who was both active and introspective.

PAINTER, ROBERT MOORE, 1827-1868   **3573**

Oliphant, J. Orin, ed. "Journals of the Indian Wars of 1855-56." WASHINGTON HISTORICAL QUARTERLY 15 (1924):11-31. Journal, pp. 13-26.

Oct 1855-May 1856. Military diary kept by Oregon City private in Company D, First Regiment, of the Oregon Mounted Volunteer fighting the Yakimas and other Indians in Washington Territory; marches, distances and camps; lack of provisions, with horses "mere skeletons"; some battles and casualties, including Capt. A.J. Hembree, who was killed and scalped.

PAINTER, WILLIAM CHARLES, 1830-1900   **3574**

Oliphant, J. Orin, ed. "Journals of the Indian Wars of 1855-56." WASHINGTON HISTORICAL QUARTERLY 15 (1924):11-31. Journal, pp. 27-31.

Oct 1855-Jan 1856. Brief notes of private in Company D, First Regiment, during Oregon Mounted Volunteers' expedition against the Yakimas and other Washington Indians.

PULSIPHER, JOHN, b. 1827   **3575**

Brooks, Juanita, ed. "From the Journal of John Pulsipher." UTAH HUMANITIES REVIEW 2 (1948):351-379; WESTERN HUMANITIES REVIEW 3 (1949):38-55.

1855-1858 (with gaps). Journal of a Mormon missionary to Indians and longtime pioneer in the region of Enterprise, Utah; commissioning by Brigham Young, with text of Young's "blessing," as a missionary to the Shoshoni, with names of delegation members led by James S. Brown and later Pulsipher; notes on "Indian character"; ranching on the Green River; a dream and its interpretation; relief efforts for the disastrous Martin Handcart Company; the Utah War, activities of the Nauvoo Legion and the "Move South" of northern settlers to Mexico for safety; references to Col. Thomas L. Kane, Gov. Alfred Cumming and Gen. Albert Sidney Jonston.

In THE UTAH EXPEDITION, by LeRoy R. and Ann W. Hafen, pp. 198-219. Far West and the Rockies Historical Series, vol. 8. Glendale, Calif.: Arthur H. Clark, 1958.

1857-1858. With the Mormon army assembled to prevent government soldiers from entering Utah; daily activities until Governor Cumming arrived.

ROBBINS, HARVEY   **3576**

"Journal of the Rogue River War." OREGON HISTORICAL QUARTERLY 34 (1933):345-358.

Oct 1855-Feb 1856. Account by a Linn County man of the campaign of the Northern Battalion of Oregon Volunteers to quell an Indian uprising on the Rogue River; descriptions of Indian depredations; disagreeable marches through rain and snow of the poorly equipped and fed volunteers; references to their elected captain, Jonathan Keeney; skirmishes and news of other units.

ROBINSON, SARA TAPPAN DOOLITTLE LAWRENCE,   3577
1827-1911

KANSAS: ITS INTERIOR AND EXTERIOR LIFE. Boston: Crosby, Nichols; Cincinnati: G.S. Blanchard, 1856. 366 pp. Lawrence, Kans.: Journal Publishing Co., 1899. 438 pp. passim.

Extract in AMERICAN HISTORY TOLD BY CONTEMPORARIES, by Albert B. Hart, vol. 4, pp. 104-108.

   1855-1856. Bride's expanded diary of arrival in Kansas City from Boston with her husband, Charles; much harrassment from Missouri border people talking of driving out free-state supporters, first elections threatened by Missourians and lack of action by Governor Shannon who was in league with people in border counties; diarist's interest in Kaw and Shawnee Indians and Baptist mission to Indians; settling in Lawrence, calling on pioneers, noting scarcity of staple provisions, prevalence of cholera, prairie fires; details of newly completed house and its decor; her husband's being taken prisoner by gang of Missourians at Lexington; eloquent words for freedom.

SARGENT, EDWARD PAYSON, b. 1837   3578

Coons, Quentin L., ed. "Voyage of the Clipper Ship RINGLEADER." OLD-TIME NEW ENGLAND 63 (1972):27-32; 63 (1973):113-116; 64 (1973):22-28.

   Oct 1855-Sep 1856. Extracts from the diary of a young Salem, Massachusetts, man's voyage from Boston to London via Cape Horn, San Francisco and China; good notes of life as a "first table" passenger and detailed observations of the seamen's work, ships encountered, etc.; references to Capt. Richard Matthews; visits in San Francisco with William Quarles and other Salem folk who had settled there; to China with additional passengers, including missionary E.D. Lyle; sightseeing and visiting American people in Shangai, Hong Kong and Foo Chou Foo; books and reading of a religious and intellectual nature.

SESSIONS, JOHN, 1795-1884   3579

"Observations in California during 1855." SOCIETY OF CALIFORNIA PIONEERS QUARTERLY 5 (1928):9-29.

   Jul-Aug 1855. Extracts covering his stay in California from a Presbyterian minister's much longer travel diary; fairly detailed notes on San Francisco, Sacramento and environs, with careful descriptions of farms, orchards, business enterprises and various mining operations and methods; enjoyment of free clergy passage and stateroom on the HUNT to Sacramento; a few notes on churches and clergy as he traveled about; references to many individuals in each town.

SIMS, MARY ANN OWEN, 1830-1861?   3580

Whitman, Clifford Dale, ed. "Private Journal of Mary Ann Owen Sims." ARKANSAS HISTORICAL QUARTERLY 35 (1976):142-187, 261-291.

   1855-1861 (with gaps). Dallas county woman's journal kept for her children and begun just after the death of her husband, Dr. John D. Sims; a long retrospective account of his illness and death followed by dated entries; bereavement and sporadic consolation of religion and her relatives; the illnesses of her children, domestic chores and teaching her children at home; church and other activities at Mt. Pleasant, with mention of many local people; financial woes necessitating that she hire out her slaves; a

cathartic journal full of her struggle with sorrow.

In A DOCUMENTARY HISTORY OF ARKANSAS, edited by C. Fred Williams and others, pp. 58-59.

   May 1859. Extract deploring the near impossibility of a woman changing her position in life.

SNEDAKER, MORRIS JACKSON, 1818-1882   3581

Ferris, Norman B., ed. "The Diary of Morris J. Snedaker." SOUTHWESTERN HISTORICAL QUARTERLY 66 (1963):516-546.

   1855-1856. Mormon missionary's journey from Salt Lake to Texas, with a side trip to Louisville and Frankfort, Kentucky, to visit relatives; travel by wagon, foot and Missouri and Mississippi riverboats; missionary efforts in east Texas sometimes met with taunts, threats and physical assault; references to colleagues and to many Mormons settled in the area.

STEWART, JAMES R., 1829-1868   3582

"The Diary of James R. Stewart, Pioneer of Osage County." KANSAS HISTORICAL QUARTERLY 17 (1949):1-36, 122-175, 254-295, 360-397.

   1855-1860 (with gaps). New Castle, Pennsylvania, man's diary of settlement at Council City, later renamed Burlingame, with antislavery people of the Western Pennsylvania Kansas Company and the American Settlement Company; homesteading, organizing a Lyceum and reading to further his education in medicine and law; participation in local politics; joining the "Free-State Army" and incidents involving the Border Ruffians, including their burning of the house of John A. Wakefield and the confrontation at Lecompton; daily weather; Fourth of July observance; notes on Lotan Smith and Isaac B. Titus.

TODD, JOHN B.S., 1814-1872   3583

Mattison, Ray H., ed. "The Harney Expedition against the Sioux: The Journal of Captain John B.S. Todd." NEBRASKA HISTORY 43 (1962):89-130.

   May-Dec 1855. Extensive military, topographical and geological notes of commander of Company A of the Sixth Infantry engaged in a retaliatory campaign under William S. Harney; march from Fort Leavenworth to Fort Laramie via Fort Kearny, and the journey from Fort Laramie to Fort Pierre; camps, distances and conditions; buffalo hunting; a long description of the battle of Ash Hollow with the Brule Sioux under Little Thunder; references to Col. Philip St. George Cooke; notes on fossils in Wyoming.

WARREN, GOUVERNEUR KEMBLE, 1830-1882   3584

McLaird, James D. and Turchen, Lesta V. "Exploring the Black Hills, 1855-1875; the Dacota Explorations of Lieutenant Gouverneur Kemble Warren." SOUTH DAKOTA HISTORY 3 (1973):359-389.

   1855-1857. Article containing extracts from the official reports and unpublished personal journal kept during the Sioux Expedition of 1855; a graphic description of the battle of Ash Hollow, particularly of wounded Indian women and children; references to Gen. William S. Harney and his dealings with the Sioux; 1857 Black Hills exploration with entries on Indians, especially difficulties with Bear's Rib over results of the treaty negotiated by Harney.

In EXPLORATIONS IN THE DACOTA COUNTRY, by United States

Engineer Department, pp. 23-34. 34th Cong., 1st sess., 1856, S. Exec. Doc. 76. Washington, D.C.: A.P.O. Nicholson, Senate Printer, 1856.

Aug-Nov 1855. Report of lieutenant with F.V. Hayden and Corps of Topographical Engineers making a geological investigation between the Missouri and Platte rivers; topographical information on resources and possibilities for navigation and settlement and routes for transportation; exploring from Fort Leavenworth to Fort Laramie, Fort Pierre, Fort Kearny, Sioux City, Fort Ridgely and the Cheyenne River region.

WEIR, ROBERT, 1836-1905   **3585**

Hareven, Tamara K., ed. "The Adventures of a Haunted Whaling Man." AMERICAN HERITAGE 28, no. 5 (1977):46-65.

1855-1858. Extracts from diary of young man from Cold Spring, New York, who went whaling to atone for gambling debt; adjustment to seasickness, hard work and wretched food aboard the New Bedford whaler CLARA BELL; excellent descriptions and drawings of whaling life, with detailed and exciting accounts of whale chases; ports of call and ships encountered; homesickness, religious introspections and a prodigal son's remorse over failing his father; an outstanding diary, showing literary and artistic promise.

WELD, FRANCIS MINOT, 1840-1893   **3586**

DIARIES AND LETTERS OF FRANCIS MINOT WELD, M.D. By Sarah S. Weld Blake. Boston: Privately printed, 1925. 245 pp. Diary, pp. 11-66, 96-141, 179-206 passim.

Jan-Oct 1855. Teenager's diary of daily life in Jamaica Plains, Massachusetts; notes on weather, chores, school assignments, reading, politics, sermons, leisure activities, Louis Agassiz's lectures, the Boston Athenaeum, Fourth of July, Christmas, etc.; visit to Dalton, New Hampshire, and the White Mountains, including ascent of Mount Washington; seeing Tom Thumb and the circus; picking hops and other farm work.

Feb-Dec 1863, Jan-Jul 1865. Service in the Civil War after graduation from Harvard and training at its medical school; assistant surgeon on the ironclad NANTUCKET; a stop at New York City and then blockade duty off Savannah; assaults on Charleston; visit to Beaufort and purchase of a cotton plantation; transfer to the WABASH; switch to army due to eye problems; service as surgeon for the Twenty-seventh United States Colored Troops; successful assault on Fort Fisher and operations in North Carolina; at hospitals in Goldsboro and New Bern; Wilmington blacks' reception of Union soldiers; reaction to Lincoln's assassination; some details of medical treatment.

WOLSKI, KALIKST, b. 1816   **3587**

Coleman, Marion Moore, trans. and ed. "New Light on La Reunion: From the Pages of DO AMERYKI I W AMERYCE." ARIZONA AND THE WEST 6 (1964):41-68, 137-154. Diary, pp. 140-154.

May-Nov 1855. Polish socialist's experiences at the utopian, community La Reunion founded at Dallas by French socialist Victor Prosper Considerant; daily routine among French, Belgian, Swiss and German settlers of the colony; food, erecting buildings and farm work; problems with extreme heat, drought, poor soil and discord among colonists; comparisons with another community, the North American Phalanx; references to Considérant and his wife, Augustin Savardin, and Dallas merchant William A. Gold.

1856

ANON.   **3588**

In HANDCARTS TO ZION, by LeRoy R. and Ann W. Hafen, pp. 222-226.

Oct-Nov 1856. Account of party under Robert T. Burton dispatched from Salt Lake to rescue the fourth and fifth handcart companies stranded on the plains by an early winter; laconic notes giving little indication of dire predicament of the starving and freezing emigrants or heroism of the rescuers.

ANON.   **3589**

In YE OLDE SHAKER BELLS, by Nancy Lewis Greene, pp. 35-83. Lexington, Ky.: Transylvania Printing Co., 1930.

1856-1871 (with gaps). Sporadic entries from daily record of events in the Shaker community at Pleasant Hill, Kentucky; ordinary occurrences, weather, Shaker practices, names of persons leaving the group including those joining the army; witnessing the 1862 Confederate invasion of Kentucky and occupation of the village with notes on John H. Morgan and behavior of Southern troops; obtaining exemptions for Shakers from Union conscription; reflections on the Civil War and Lincoln's assassination.

ABBEY, CHARLES AUGUSTUS, 1841-1919   **3590**

BEFORE THE MAST IN THE CLIPPERS: COMPOSED IN LARGE PART OF THE DIARIES OF CHARLES A. ABBEY KEPT WHILE AT SEA IN THE YEARS 1856 TO 1860. By Harpur A. Gosnell. New York: Derrydale Press, 1937. 283 pp.

1856-1860. Teenage seaman's remarkable diaries kept aboard the SURPRISE, CHARMER, HENRY BRIGHAM and INTREPID; learning the ropes under a brutal mate; sickness and initial regrets at having gone to sea "to lead a dog's life"; labors, hazards, privations, monotony and occasional diversions of sailors on clippers; journeys to China, with adventures in Canton; later voyages around Cape Horn to San Francisco and Honolulu; sailors' songs, seamen's lingo and vignettes of individuals; a picture to rival Dana's of life "before the mast."

ANDERSON, WILLIAM WALLACE   **3591**

Woosley, Ann I. "Fort Burgwin's Hospital: A Surgeon's Journal and Archaeological Dig Reveal the Nature of Frontier Medicine and Healing." EL PALACIO 86, no. 1 (1980):3-7, 36-39.

1856-1861. Brief extracts from a journal containing considerable medical information within an article about the post surgeon at Cantonment Burgwin, New Mexico; description of treatments, wounds and illnesses, medicines, amputations, fees, etc., as well as military and civilian patients including Kit Carson.

BEALE, JOSEPH BOGGS, 1841-1926   **3592**

Wainwright, Nicholas B., ed. "Education of an Artist." PENNSYLVANIA MAGAZINE OF HISTORY AND BIOGRAPHY 97 (1973):485-510.

1856-1862. Extracts from the diary of the son of a cultivated Philadelphia family, showing his education and progress as an artist; visits to exhibits, art lessons and independent drawing and painting; a few family matters and local events, such as a huge mounted torchlight parade in support of Lincoln's candidacy and a later Lincoln visit to Philadelphia; Civil War news; references to many artists.

BERMINGHAM, TWISS, 1832?-1900?   3593

In THE HANDCART TRAIL, written and compiled by Eliza M. Wakefield, pp. 5-10. Arizona: Sun Valley Shopper, 1949.

Extracts in HANDCARTS TO ZION, by LeRoy R. and Ann W. Hafen, pp. 62-79 passim.

Jun-Sep 1856. Young Irish immigrant's moving account of the second Mormon handcart journey from Iowa City to Salt Lake; distances and camps; condition of men and women pulling handcarts; illnesses, exhaustion, accidents and deaths en route; graphic picture by a convert who left Mormonism the following year.

BROKMEYER, HENRY CONRAD, 1828-1906   3594

A MECHANIC'S DIARY. Washington, D.C.: E.C. Brokmeyer, 1910. 239 pp.

May-Nov 1856. Diary of a German immigrant mechanic who settled at St. Louis; natural history notes and social, political and philosophical commentary, written with much linguistic local color and dialogue.

BROWN, J. ROBERT   3595

A JOURNAL OF A TRIP ACROSS THE PLAINS OF THE U.S. FROM MISSOURI TO CALIFORNIA, IN THE YEAR 1856: GIVING A CORRECT VIEW OF THE COUNTRY, ANECDOTES, INDIAN STORIES, MOUNTAINEERS' TALES, ETC. Columbus, Ohio: The Author, 1860. 119 pp.

Apr-Oct 1856. Emigrant's colorful diary of travel from St. Louis to California with E.R. Yates and William Maunder who were transporting goods to Salt Lake City; details of forts Kearny, Laramie and Bridger; Salt Lake City, in which he was disappointed, Ogden, Carson Valley and the grandeur of the Sierra Nevada; Placerville and Sacramento; meeting Shoshone chief Wassakee; finishing last 1000 miles with greatly reduced provisions and animals after Shoshone raid; sketches of mountain men as "sociable, generous, free, frank, frolicsome and fond of fun and whiskey"; many "laughable adventures" and yarns with frequent references to food and his companionable dog Fleda.

BROWN, JOHN   3596

In A DOCUMENTARY HISTORY OF ARKANSAS. Edited by C. Fred Williams, p. 78.

Jul-Aug 1856. Extracts from diary of prominent merchant in Camden, Arkansas; forming a Fillmore club and backing the American party; reflections on survival of the Union after defeat of his candidates by Democrats.

COLT, MIRIAM DAVIS, b. 1817   3597

WENT TO KANSAS: BEING A THRILLING ACCOUNT OF AN ILL-FATED EXPEDITION TO THAT FAIRY LAND AND ITS SAD RESULTS. Watertown, N.Y.: Printed by L. Ingalls, 1862. 294 pp. Reprint. March of America Facsimile Series, no 91. Ann Arbor, Mich.,

University Microfilms, 1966.

1856-1857. Pioneer wife and mother's diary; lured by glowing description of a community to be organized by the Vegetarian Settlement Company and leaving home in Potsdam, New York, for a disappointing spot on the Neosho River in Kansas near Fort Scott; plagued by unkept promises, lack of tools, threats of Indian attack, severe illness and a hopeless economic situation in spite of backbreaking work; suffering the deaths of both her three-year-old son and husband before completing a sad return journey to New York.

Extracts in WOMEN OF THE WEST, by Cathy Luchetti, pp. 79-87.

Jan-Jul 1856.

CROWNINSHIELD, BENJAMIN WILLIAM, 1837-1892   3598

A PRIVATE JOURNAL. Cambridge: Privately printed at the Riverside Press, 1941. 153 pp.

1856-1858. Delightful journal of a Harvard student during the days when the president himself "gave me my averages for the month" and dispensed permission to leave campus for any length of time; studies in Greek, Latin, French, chemistry and physics with plenty of time left for the Hasty Pudding Club, choir, cello lessons, rowing, ice skating and almost nightly games of whist or billiards; references to faculty and many college friends; amusing incidents; social and family life with numerous relatives in Boston; attending plays, concerts, etc., and reading at the Boston Athenaeum.

DUBOIS, JOHN VAN DEUSEN, 1833-1879   3599

CAMPAIGNS IN THE WEST, 1856-1861: THE JOURNAL AND LETTERS OF COLONEL JOHN VAN DEUSEN DUBOIS. Edited by George P. Hammond. Tucson: Arizona Pioneers Historical Society, 1949. 120 pp.

1856-1861. Military diary of a young West Point graduate's experience with the Third Cavalry in the Southwest; campaigns against the Gila-Apache in 1857, the Navaho in 1859 and the Utah War with the Mormons; compassion toward Indians but decidedly anti-Mormon attitudes; a good private diary containing details and opinions often lacking in official reports.

Lobdell, Jared C., ed. "The Civil War Journal and Letters of Colonel John Van Deusen DuBois." MISSOURI HISTORICAL REVIEW 60 (1966):436-459, 61 (1966):21-50.

1861-1862. Surviving remnants of career soldier's journal interspersed with letters; on duty at Washington, D.C., after Sumter's fall, then service in Missouri as major of First Missouri Artillery, later colonel and chief of artillery on Halleck's staff; description of battle of Wilson's Creek written a couple of weeks later; critical comments about Missouri Germans and John Charles Fremont.

EBEY, ISAAC NEFF, 1818-1857   3600

Kibbe, L.A., ed. "Diary of Colonel Isaac N. and Mrs. Emily Ebey." PACIFIC NORTHWEST QUARTERLY 33 (1942):297-323.

Oct 1856-Jan 1857. Entries mainly by Colonel Ebey, with a few by his second wife, Emily Palmer Sconce Ebey, and his brother, Winfield Scott Ebey; farming on Whidbey Island and trading throughout Puget Sound; increasing antagonism between Indians and settlers, partly as a result of the attack by the MASSACHUSETTS on an Indian village.

ELKINGTON, THOMAS 3601

Elkington, J. Passmore. ''To Ohio One Hundred Years Ago.'' FRIENDS HISTORICAL ASSOCIATION BULLETIN 47, no. 1 (1958):38-45.

Sep 1856. Extracts within article describing a Quaker's train trip from Philadelphia to Somerton, Ohio, to attend the wedding of his brother Joseph S. Elkington; social life among Ohio Friends; the wedding and ''shivaree.''

FOLSOM, WILLIS F., 1825-1894 3602

Dunkle, W.F., ed. ''A Choctaw Indian's Diary.'' CHRONICLES OF OKLAHOMA 4 (1926):61-69.

1856-1894. Extracts from diary of an Indian Methodist circuit rider from Pocola; conversions and baptisms; preaching in Choctaw and English or interpreting for other missionaries; carrying on during the Civil War when many other clergy had left the Indian Mission Conference and Oklahoma circuits.

FORBUSH, EDWARD 3603

In OUR OWN DAY, by Elsie P. Mitchell, pp. 110-133. Boston: Branden Press, 1976.

Sep 1856-Mar 1857. A Boston gentleman's trip up the Nile; good descriptions of the people and scenes in Egypt, as well as logistics of boat travel on the Nile.

GALLOWAY, ANDREW 3604

''The First Handcart Company: Edmund Ellsworth, Captain of the Company.'' UTAH GENEALOGICAL AND HISTORICAL MAGAZINE 17 (1926):247-249; 18 (1927):17-21; 49-56. Reprint in HANDCARTS TO ZION, by LeRoy R. and Ann W. Hafen, pp. 199-213.

Jun-Sep 1856. Official journal kept by secretary of Edmund Ellsworth's handcart company of Mormon converts from England; matter-of-fact notes of route from Iowa City to Salt Lake; distances, camps, availability of wood, buffalo chips, water and grass; meetings and baptisms en route; a number of deaths, especially of children with whooping cough; record of those who ''backed out.''

''First Mormon Handcart Trip across Iowa.'' ANNALS OF IOWA, 3d ser. 20 (1935-1937):444-449.

Jun-Jul 1856. Segment of journey from Iowa City to Florence, Nebraska.

GOODMAN, WILLIAM JEFFERIES 3605

''A Trip to Tyler, 1856.'' CHRONICLES OF SMITH COUNTY TEXAS 5 (Spring 1966):25-29.

Mar-Apr 1856. Diary of a journey from Union District, South Carolina, to Tyler, Texas, and return; by stagecoach to Montgomery, steamer to Mobile and New Orleans, then by boat on the Mississippi and Red rivers; interesting notes on the pleasures and difficulties of travel.

HUSTON, HENRY CLAY, 1828-1899 3606

JOURNALS. Eugene, Oreg.: Lane County Pioneer-Historical Society, 1960. 59 leaves.

1856-1860 (with gaps). Diary of Oregon pioneer wounded while serving with Capt. D.W. Keith's Oregon volunteers in Rogue River Indian War; writing good word pictures of fellow officers during his recovery; attending church at pine log school house; teaching school; an extended trip from Portland by steamer to Port Townsend and Olympia, Washington, then to San Francisco, Acapulco, Panama and New York; visiting Niagara Falls and relatives in Ohio, Kentucky, Indiana and his boyhood home and parents in Linn County, Iowa, where ''nothing I could do did please my father''; returning to New York and to Oregon by ship via Panama with good descriptions of ship travel and passengers.

JACOBS, VICTORIA, 1838-1861 3607

DIARY OF A SAN DIEGO GIRL, 1856. Edited by Sylvia Arden. Santa Monica, Calif.: Norton B. Stern, 1974. 75 pp.

1856. Daily life and social activities, such as picnics, teas, dinners and balls, in small community of San Diego including the military personnel at the Mission; mention of many names, places, the regular and special arrivals of ships from San Francisco with freight and mail.

LAWRENCE, MARY CHIPMAN, 1827-1906 3608

THE CAPTAIN'S BEST MATE: THE JOURNAL OF MARY CHIPMAN LAWRENCE ON THE WHALER ADDISON. Edited by Stanton Garner. Providence: Brown University Press, 1966. 311 pp.

1856-1860. Pacific and Arctic whaling voyages as recorded by the wife of whaling captain Samuel Lawrence aboard the AD-DISON; dangers and tedium of whaling offset by cheerful piety and resourcefulness of the diarist; child-rearing aboard ship and life in ports, especially in Hawaii.

LEE, ROBERT EDWARD, 1807-1870 3609

Crimmins, M.L. ''Robert E. Lee in Texas: Letters and Diary.'' WEST TEXAS HISTORICAL ASSOCIATION YEAR BOOK 8 (1932):3-24.

1856-1861. Scattered extracts covering service in Texas while lieutenant colonel of the Second Cavalry and then in command of the Department of Texas; brief notations, mainly on his whereabouts.

LEEDS, GEORGE, 1816-1885 3610

''Diary of Rev. George Leeds, D.D., Rector of St. Peter's Church, Salem.'' ESSEX INSTITUTE HISTORICAL COLLECTIONS 90 (1954):154-166.

1856-1857 (with gaps). Clergyman's diary of pastoral duties and social life; news of parishioners, friends and family; many baptisms and funerals; clerical visits to other Massachusetts towns and churches.

MILLER, JACOB, 1835-1911 3611

JOURNAL. Prepared for publication by Joseph Royal Miller and Elna Miller. Salt Lake City: Mercury, 1967. 199 pp.

1856-1895. Farmington, Utah, Mormon's journal of his life's work; important personal or family events; farming and teaching school; at Fort Lemhi in Idaho, where he was a member of the Salmon River Mission to the Shoshoni and Bannock Indians; raising stock on islands in the Great Salt Lake; various journeys; missionary work in England and Australia, stopping at Honolulu on return voyage; sporadically kept and running to narrative except during his foreign travels.

MORSE, EDWARD SYLVESTER, 1838-1925   3612

In EDWARD SYLVESTER MORSE: A BIOGRAPHY, by Dorothy G. Wayman, pp. 1-457 passim. Cambridge: Harvard University Press, 1942.

1856-1887 (with gaps), Scattered extracts of boyhood in Portland, Maine; a dispute with his father over religion; developing interest in collecting land shells and a scientific career; studying zoology with Louis Agassiz at Harvard; disappointment at not passing physical examination for Civil War enlistment; work as director of Peabody Museum in Salem, and as curator of Japanese ceramics at Boston Museum of Fine Arts; his travels to study Oriental pottery and porcelain in China and in the museums of Europe; interesting extracts revealing his brilliance and eccentricity.

OLCOTT, EUPHEMIA MASON, 1844-1922   3613

In SMALL VOICES, edited by Josef and Dorothy Berger, pp. 53-61.

1856-1857. The largely religious diary of a lonely, scrupulous twelve-year-old girl yearning to unburden herself to her unresponsive parents; concern for the state of her soul and wish that her mother would let her join the church and take communion.

ONAHAN, WILLIAM J., 1836-1919   3614

Gallery, Mary Onahan, ed. "A Civil War Diary." MID-AMERICA 14, n.s. 3 (1931):64-72, 152-177.

Nov 1856, 1860-1864, 1866, 1872, 1874. Extracts from diary of an Irish-born Chicago resident, beginning with initial entry on his twentieth birthday; politics and the war as viewed by a Douglas Democrat with Southern sympathies; Republican National Convention of 1860, a glimpse of Lincoln, death of Douglas, honoring Col. James A. Mulligan, etc.; local events including the LADY ELGIN disaster; great involvement in Roman Catholic and Irish American activities; sermon critiques, church business affairs, items relating to the Church of the Holy Family and the Sacred Heart Convent, St. Patrick's Day festivities, etc.; concern over anti-Catholic prejudice; work as a member of the Free Library Board; an interesting document.

ORD, EDWARD OTHO CRESAP, 1818-1883   3615

THE CITY OF THE ANGELS AND THE CITY OF THE SAINTS, OR A TRIP TO LOS ANGELES AND SAN BERNARDINO IN 1856. Edited by Neal Harlow. San Marino, Calif.: Huntington Library; Los Angeles: Zamorano Club, 1978. 56 pp. Diary, pp. 19-30.

Jul-Aug 1856. Extract recording an expedition to southern California to select site for a military post near San Bernardino and determine the need for protection of settlers against Indian attack; travels in the area visiting ranchers.

PAGE, ALVIN REED, 1840-1858   3616

In UNDER SAIL AND IN PORT IN THE GLORIOUS 1850's, by Charlotte A.P. Johnson, pp. 63-79. Salem: Peabody Museum, 1950.

Sep-Dec 1856. Boston teenager's sojourn as an ordinary sailor aboard the GEORGE WASHINGTON under Capt. Josiah Sparrow Cummings, a family friend; stormy crossing to Liverpool, dur-

ing which he began to learn seamanship; fascination with England, tempting him to "turn into a John Bull"; visits to churches, castles, concerts, etc.; return, with journal ending at New Orleans.

POWELL, WILLIAM HENRY, b. 1827   3617

Pratt, Julius W., ed. "Our First 'War' In China." AMERICAN HISTORICAL REVIEW 53 (1948):776-786.

Nov-Dec 1856. Account by Williamsburgh, New York, seaman on the SAN JACINTO of hostilities at Canton and Whampoa, initially between British and Chinese, in which the United States became embroiled while trying to protect American nationals at Canton after the LORCHA ARROW incident; attacks on Chinese forts in retaliation for their firing on the PORTSMOUTH, with detailed descriptions of the forts and military action; references to Andrew H. Foote, commander of the PORTSMOUTH; reports of negotiations.

POWERS, MARY ROCKWOOD, d. 1858   3618

Thorsen, W.B., ed. "A Woman's Overland Journal to California." AMATEUR BOOK COLLECTOR 1, no. 1 (1950):1-2; no. 2 (1950):1-2; no. 3 (1950):6; no. 4 (1950):11-12; no. 5 (1951):5-6. Reprint. Fairfield, Wash.: Ye Galleon, 1985. 73 pp.

Apr-Oct 1856. Wisconsin woman's record of journey from Chicago to Sacramento with her husband, Dr. Americus Windsor Powers, and their three small children; travel through Iowa over bad roads, with lodgings at wretched houses; husband's refusal until forced by other men of the company to exchange dying horses for oxen; his continued recalcitrance and apparently declining mental health; a sojourn among the Mormons and diarist's pity for wives in polygamous marriages; great suffering of emigrants and their animals in mountains and deserts; births and deaths of her twins; a graphic and tragic account of pioneer struggle by a woman who died shortly after arrival in California.

READER, SAMUEL JAMES, 1836-1914   3619

Root, George A., ed. "The First Day's Battle at Hickory Point: From the Diary and Reminiscences of Samuel James Reader." KANSAS HISTORICAL QUARTERLY 1 (1931):28-49. Diary, pp. 30-31.

Sep 1856. Extract covering the battle of Hickory Point between free-state and proslavery forces in Kansas; diarist's participation as a member of the Second Kansas State Militia; a brief mention of Gen. James H. Lane, who led the free-state settlers.

REEDER, ANDREW HORATIO, 1807-1864   3620

In DIARY OF AMERICA, by Josef and Dorothy Berger, pp. 407-414.

May 1856. Extracts from private diary of first governor of Kansas; entries made while in hiding in Kansas City and escaping to Illinois in disguise after indictment for high treason; an entertaining account.

RUFFIN, EDMUND, 1794-1865   3621

THE DIARY OF EDMUND RUFFIN. Edited by William K. Scarborough. Baton Rouge: Louisiana State University, 1972. 2 vols.

1856-1863. A voluminous personal record begun in his "retirement" by a cultured Virginia gentleman, the pre-eminent agricultural reformer of the antebellum South, one of the foremost advocates of secession and a militant defender of slavery; his thoughts on many issues and individuals; observation of or participation in the 1858 Southern Commercial Convention in Montgomery, the execution of John Brown, the 1860 Democratic party conventions in Richmond and Baltimore and the secession conventions of South Carolina, Florida and Virginia; travel around the South, mentioning features of the countryside, people encountered and accommodations; family activities and plantation matters at Beechwood and Marlbourne; agricultural observations and work in the Virginia State Agricultural Society; his reading and religious reflections; service as a private in the Palmetto Guard, claiming to have fired the first shot at Fort Sumter, and participation in the First Bull Run campaign; the sacking of Beechwood in Prince George County; viewing the Seven Pines field of battle; notes on war's events, impact on civilians and reaction of slaves; candid sketches of Confederate political and military leaders and his views on war strategy, foreign intervention and economic conditions; assessment of Lincoln and Davis; vitriolic castigation of the North; an important chronicle of the path to civil war and its consequences.

"Extracts from the Diary of Edmund Ruffin." WILLIAM AND MARY COLLEGE QUARTERLY, 1st ser. 21 (1913):224-232; 22 (1914):258-262; 23 (1915):31-45, 154-171, 240-258.

> 1857-1865. Entries describing a severe winter storm and an 1857 visit to Washington, D.C.; his thoughts on Lincoln's war policies, prisoner of war issues, British actions affecting the Confederacy, conduct of slaves, etc.; criticism of Jefferson Davis; his reaction to Lincoln's assassination.

"Edmund Ruffin's Visit to John Tyler." WILLIAM AND MARY COLLEGE QUARTERLY, 1st ser. 14 (1906):193-211, 215.

> Nov 1857, Feb 1861. Meeting with John Tyler and a detailed account of their conversation; enunciating his decision to become a Confederate citizen and not return to Virginia as long as his native state remained in the Union.

Dodd, Dorothy, ed. "Edmund Ruffin's Account of the Florida Secession Convention." FLORIDA HISTORICAL QUARTERLY 12 (1933):67-76.

> Jan 1861. Extracts.

"The First Shot at Fort Sumter." WILLIAM AND MARY COLLEGE QUARTERLY, 1st ser. 20 (1911):69-101.

> Apr 1861. Extracts.

SAVAGE, WILLIAM, 1833-1908												3622

Harlan, Edgar R., ed. "William Savage, Iowa Pioneer, Diarist and Painter of Birds." ANNALS OF IOWA, 3d ser. 19 (1933-1935):83-114, 189-220, 470-474; 20 (1935-1937):140-150, 459-471, 535-543.

> 1856-1863. Diary of English immigrant farmer and naturalist in Van Buren County; mostly daily farming tasks, crops, livestock and prices; constant work as a tailor in his spare time; hunting; Methodist church activities, including names of people baptized, married or buried; brief but regularly kept entries showing the amazing variety of pioneer farm work.

THOMAS, ELLA GERTRUDE CLANTON, b. 1834						3623

In THE PLANTATION SOUTH, by Katharine M. Jones, pp. 191-203. Indianapolis: Bobbs Merrill, 1957.

> Jan-Jun 1856. Extracts from a journal covering forty-two years;

the domestic and social life of the mistress of Belmont near Augusta, Georgia; visits, gossip, reading, church-going, household tasks, clothes and gardening; fascinating glimpses of passion and pain within the record of ordinary events.

WALTERS, ARCHER, 1809-1856												3624

IMPROVEMENT ERA 39 (1936):483-484, 544-545, 574, 612, 635-636, 764; 40 (1937):43, 122, 154-155, 253. Extracts in HANDCARTS TO ZION, by LeRoy R. and Ann W. Hafen, pp. 56-79 passim.

> Jun-Sep 1856. Diary of an English carpenter traveling with the first Mormon handcart company; work making handcarts and coffins; sickness, hunger and deaths en route and the diarist's great distress over the suffering of his own children.

Petersen, William J. "The Handcart Expeditions, 1856." PALIMPSEST 47 (1966):368-384.

> Jun-Sep 1856. Extracts within article describing expeditions which set forth from Iowa.

WESLEY, JOHN, 1819-1900												3625

Beeson, Lewis, ed. "From England to the United States in 1856." MICHIGAN HISTORY 48 (1964):47-65.

> Jul-Sep 1856. English Methodist minister's journey with his large family to settle in Michigan; difficult voyage, with storms, sickness and hunger; landing in New York, where he found the men to be "very small, pale looking compared with Englishmen"; brief notes on train trip to Michigan.

WOLF, LAMBERT BOWMAN, 1834-1918									3626

Root, George A., ed. "Extracts from the Diary of Captain Lambert Bowman Wolf." KANSAS HISTORICAL QUARTERLY 1 (1932):195-210.

> 1856-1861 (with gaps). Experiences and observations of a cavalryman with Company K, First Cavalry, protecting Col. Joseph E. Johnston's survey of the southern boundary of Kansas, patrolling the Santa Fe Trail and guarding the mail; general notes on army life; Maj. John Sedgwick's campaign against the Kiowa and Comanche; army songs.

1857

ANON.																						3627

JOURNAL OF ANNA MAY. Edited by George W. Robinson. Cambridge, Mass.: Privately printed, 1941. 100 pp.

> Feb-Jul 1857. Diary of senior student, whose identity is concealed, at New Hampton Institution, New Hampton, New Hampshire; repetitive entries of homesickness, spiritual concern and anxiety over senior theme; good example of school life, education and graduation ceremonies.

BACON, CHARLES R.														3628

Bacon, Rosamond and Jellison, Charles A., eds. "Odyssey of a Young American." NEW ENGLAND SOCIAL STUDIES BULLETIN 15, no. 2 (1957):5-17.

1857. Extracts from the diary of a twelve-year-old boy traveling from Detroit to Vermont via Buffalo, Albany, Boston and Lowell.

BANDEL, EUGENE, 1835-1889　　　　　　　　　3629

FRONTIER LIFE IN THE ARMY, 1854-1861. Translated by Olga Bandel and Richard Jente. Edited by Ralph P. Bieber. Southwest Historical Series, no. 2. Glendale, Calif.: Arthur H. Clark, 1932. 330 pp. Reprint. Philadelphia: Porcupine Press, 1974. Diary, pp. 131-211.

May-Nov 1857. German immigrant's diary of a survey under Col. Joseph E. Johnston to establish boundary of the territory of Kansas; march from Fort Leavenworth, with fairly detailed notes of terrain, scenery, plants and animals, camp life, Kiowa Indians encountered, sufferings from heat and thirst, hunting bufffalo and other game.

BARTLETSON, JOHN　　　　　　　　　　　　　3630

In MESSAGE OF THE PRESIDENT OF THE UNITED STATES TO THE TWO HOUSES OF CONGRESS, by United States President, 1857-1861 (Buchanan), pp. 52-56. 35th Cong., 2d sess., 1858, S. Exec Doc. 1. Washington, D.C.: W.A. Harris, Printer, 1858.

Dec 1857. Diary of a trip from Fort Bridger via Bridger's Pass to Fort Laramie; road and river conditions; a few notes on soil, available grass and possibilities for bridges.

BEADLE, ERASTUS FLAVEL, 1821-1894　　　　3631

"To Nebraska in '57." NEW YORK PUBLIC LIBRARY BULLETIN 27 (1923):71-115, 171-212. Reprint. New York: New York Public Library, 1923. 89 pp.

Mar-Sep 1857. Account of a journey from Buffalo to preeempted lands near Omaha; travel by train, riverboat and stagecoach; reports of incidents with Pawnees; description of Pawnees and their chief, Corax, and conclusion that "the Indians have been greatly wronged, and as a general thing when there is Indian depredation, the whites are the first aggressors"; business and land activities at Saratoga; homesickness for his children and eventual return to New York to become publisher of Beadle's Dime Novels.

BODICHON, BARBARA LEIGH SMITH, 1827-1891　　3632

AN AMERICAN DIARY, 1857-8. Edited by Joseph W. Reed, Jr. London: Routledge & K. Paul, 1972. 198 pp. passim.

Dec 1857-Jun 1858. Vivid descriptions and lively, emphatic opinions of an emancipated Englishwoman traveling in America with her husband, Eugene Bodichon; journal and letters beginning on board the Mississippi steamer BALTIC; a long, well described stay in New Orleans, with visits to plantations, schools and churches; thence to Mobile, Montgomery, Savannah, Washington, Philadelphia and Boston, observing American customs, social life and institutions, especially slavery and its effect on both slave and master; her views on women's rights and the condition of women on all levels of society; encounters with abolitionists, women's rights advocates and intellectuals such as Lucretia Mott, Frederick Law Olmsted and Harriet Beecher Stowe; an engrossing journal.

BOZEMAN, HENRY I., b. 1837　　　　　　　　3633

Newberry, Farrar, ed. "A Clark County Plantation Journal for 1857." ARKANSAS HISTORICAL QUARTERLY 18 (1959):401-409.

Jan-Dec 1857. Extracts from the journal of plantation overseer employed by his uncle Michael Bozeman; brief notes on supervising slaves and working along with them; varied tasks of men, women and children chopping cotton, splitting rails, hoeing corn, etc.; a measles outbreak among slaves.

BROWNE, JOHN ROSS, 1817-1875　　　　　　　3634

INDIAN WAR IN OREGON AND WASHINGTON TERRITORIES. 35th Cong., 1st sess., 1858, H. Exec. Doc. 38. Washington, D.C., 1858. 62 pp.

INDIAN AFFAIRS IN THE TERRITORIES OF OREGON AND WASHINGTON. Fairfield, Wash.: Ye Galleon, 1977. 51 pp.

Aug-Sep 1857. Official report of Irish-born Treasury Department agent at Olympia; reconnaissance from Fort Steilacoom with descriptions of the fort, the Puyallup and Nisqually reservations, Kitsap, Port Townsend and other agencies; an investigation on Whidbey Island of the murder of Col. Isaac N. Ebey by northern Indians, which had occurred earlier; list of the Indian treaties negotiated by Governor Stevens and the costs of implementing them; provisions of the Medicine Creek treaty in Oregon; similar activities at Grande Ronde, Salem, etc., including grievances of chiefs at the Siletz reservation over hunger and severe breaches of treaties; investigation of charges against agent R.B. Metcalfe and references to many Indian agents, chiefs and military personnel.

CAMPBELL, HUGH　　　　　　　　　　　　　3635

Caldwell, Martha B., ed. "The Southern Kansas Boundary Survey; from the Journal of Hugh Campbell, Astronomical Computer." KANSAS HISTORICAL QUARTERLY 6 (1937):339-377.

Apr-Nov 1857. Surveyor's journal covering departure from St. Louis and return to Fort Leavenworth with the astronomical party, moving in advance of the main surveyors to establish observation stations; some contacts with Indians; astronomical and topographical notes.

CARPENTER, HELEN MCCOWEN　　　　　　　3636

In HO FOR CALIFORNIA!, edited by Sandra L. Myres, pp. 93-188.

1857. Bride's diary of a wagon trip to California from Kansas; informative, well written and often entertaining account including details of members of the train, the oxen, horses, cattle and supplies; descriptions of the wagons and how they were packed, difficult fordings, success or failure of buffalo hunts and encounters with Indians; unusual care to indicate good sources of water, wood, grass and trading posts.

CARTER, WILLIAM ALEXANDER, 1820-1881　　3637

"Diary of Judge William A. Carter Describes Life on the Trail in 1857." ANNALS OF WYOMING 11 (1939):75-110.

Sep-Nov 1857. Journey from Atchison, Kansas, to Fort Bridger in a company led by Howard Livingston; work as a sutler with Albert Sidney Johnston's forces; full entries, with many notes of social life, fellow travelers, Indians, Mormons and natural phenomena; intimations of the approaching punitive expedition against the Mormons.

CLARK, MICAJAH ADOLPHUS, 1822-1905　　　**3638**

Gregorie, Anne King, ed. "Micajah Adolphus Clark's Visit to South Carolina in 1857." SOUTH CAROLINA HISTORICAL MAGAZINE 54 (1953):15-31.

Jul-Aug 1857. Attala County, Mississippi, planter's train travel to his birthplace at Anderson, South Carolina, with entries beginning at Augusta; good notes of travel, accommodations, towns and people, with considerable lively detail on Anderson and his social life among multitudes of relatives there, as well as on nearby plantations; an entertaining picture of antebellum social life.

COWAN, ASA DOUGLAS, 1806-1857　　　**3639**

THE 1857 DIARY OF ASA DOUGLAS COWAN. Edited by Rachel Brooks. N.p., n.d. 77 pp. Diary, pp. 20-42.

1857. Farm chores and prices in Chemung County, New York; a trip to Kansas to claim land and his return to New York.

DOUGLAS, HENRY KYD, 1838-1903　　　**3640**

THE DOUGLAS DIARY: STUDENT DAYS AT FRANKLIN AND MARSHALL COLLEGE. Edited by Frederic Klein and John Carrill. Lancaster, Pa.: Franklin and Marshall College, 1973. 192 pp.

1857-1858. Entertaining diary of third year college student from Shepherdstown, Virginia; classes, recitations and pranks; activities in Diagnothian Literary Society; Lancaster community events, fairs, Fourth of July celebration, lectures and parties; notes on national affairs; attending presidential inauguration of James Buchanan with a student escort from Franklin and Marshall College, where Buchanan was president of the board of trustees.

GOTTSCHALK, LOUIS MOREAU, 1829-1869　　　**3641**

NOTES OF A PIANIST. Edited by Clara Gottschalk. Translated from the French by Robert E. Peterson. Philadelphia: J.B. Lippincott, 1881. 480 pp.

NOTES OF A PIANIST. Edited by Jeanne Behrend. New York: A.A. Knopf, 1964. 420 pp. Reprint. New York: Da Capo, 1979.

1857-1868. Lengthy diary of a composer and pianist; exhausting concert tours and music festivals in the West Indies, the United States, Panama, Mexico and South America; special fondness for New England towns; detailed impressions of places visited and people met, musicians, managers, critics, and audiences; nearly living on trains and doggedly carrying on schedule in spite of disruption of travel during Civil War; opinions on the war and Lincoln; discomforts and seasickness on journey to San Francisco via Panama; cultural scene in California and Nevada in 1865; harrowing experiences of revolution in Peru; meeting Fuegians at Punta Arenas; good descriptions of his feelings about his compositions and the audience reactions when he performed.

GOVE, JESSE A.　　　**3642**

"The Utah Expedition, 1857-1858: Letters of Capt. Jesse A. Gove." NEW HAMPSHIRE HISTORICAL SOCIETY COLLECTIONS 12 (1928):3-190.

1857-1858. Letter-diary written to his wife; the march from Fort Leavenworth, with activities at forts Bridger and Laramie, in Salt Lake City and at camps Scott and Floyd; opinions on Mormons and Mormonism; numerous references to Albert Sidney Johnston,

William S. Harney, Randolph B. Marcy, John Dunovant, Brigham Young and Governor Cumming; a full and descriptive account.

HILDT, GEORGE H., 1855-1913　　　**3643**

Caldwell, Martha B., ed. "The Diary of George H. Hildt, Pioneer of Johnson County." KANSAS HISTORICAL QUARTERLY 10 (1941):260-298.

Jun-Dec 1857. Canal Dover, Ohio, man's journey across Missouri to Johnson County, Kansas, where he took a claim on preempted Shawnee lands; farming and constant traveling about on business; interesting details of frontier life and scenes, contemporary politics, persons, settlements, etc.

HUDSON, HENRY JAMES, b. 1822　　　**3644**

Burke, Marguerette R., ed "Henry James Hudson and the Genoa Settlement." NEBRASKA HISTORY 41 (1960):201-235.

Apr-May 1857. Journal of an English immigrant and founder of the shortlived Mormon colony at Genoa, covering steamer journey on the HANNIBAL to escort settlers from St. Louis to Genoa; expenses, difficulties and sickness, including measles; notes on towns and Indians; names and activities of many Mormons, especially of Welsh descent.

IVES, JOSEPH CHRISTMAS, d. 1868　　　**3645**

In REPORT UPON THE COLORADO RIVER OF THE WEST, by United States Army Corps of Topographical Engineers, pp. 19-131. 30th Cong., 1st sess., 1859-1860, H. Exec Doc. (unnumbered). Washington, D.C.: Government Printing Office, 1861.

Abridgement. STEAMBOAT UP THE COLORADO. Edited by Alexander L. Crosby. Boston: Little, 1965. 112 pp.

Nov 1857-May 1858. Exploration of Colorado River to ascertain navigability; from San Francisco to the mouth of the river on the MONTEREY, which was carrying material and workmen to assemble boat EXPLORER for river use; traveling along the river with a pack train and Yuma runners employed to carry mail to and from San Diego; route via Fort Yuma, Black Canyon and Diamond River, examining possible connection with Mormon road; noting Heinrich Möllhausen's natural history and mineral specimens collected partly from Yuma children; concluding trip at Fort Defiance.

JOHNSTON, JOSEPH EGGLESTON, 1807-1891　　　**3646**

Miller, Nyle H., ed. "Surveying the Southern Boundary Line of Kansas: From the Private Journal of Col. Joseph E. Johnston." KANSAS HISTORICAL QUARTERLY 1 (1932):104-139.

May-Oct 1857. Survey conducted by an officer of the First Cavalry out of Fort Leavenworth; topographical notes, scenery, condition of grass and timber.

LAZELLE, HENRY M., 1832-1917　　　**3647**

Reeve, Frank D., ed. "Puritan and Apache: A Diary." NEW MEXICO HISTORICAL REVIEW 23 (1948):269-301; 24 (1949):12-53.

Apr-Jun 1857. Well educated Massachusetts officer's account of the fruitless Bonneville campaign against the Apaches; from Fort Bliss, Texas, to the Gila River in infantry attached to Company K, Regiment of Mounted Rifles, under John Van Duesen DuBois; rigors of march described with sarcastic humor, but dismay over sufferings of thirsty horses and mules and disgust with drunkenness and ribaldry of officers; notes on scenery and geology; frequent and sometimes unflattering references to Benjamin L.E. Bonneville, Dixon S. Miles, John Smith Simonson, etc., and to army policies in general; much philosophical reflection, with historical and literary allusions; glimpses of the mutual disregard between horse and foot troops; some social life at Fort Thorn.

LOWE, PERCIVAL GREEN, 1828-1908   **3648**

FIVE YEARS A DRAGOON ('49 TO '54) AND OTHER ADVENTURES ON THE GREAT PLAINS. Kansas City, Mo.: F. Hudson, 1906. 417 pp. New ed. Norman: University of Oklahoma Press, 1965. 336 pp. passim.

Jun-Sep 1857, May-Nov 1858. Journal of member of Second Dragoons in charge of transportation of supplies and mules from Fort Leavenworth to Fort Laramie for Colonel Sumner's campaign against the Cheyennes; disdain for guide's lack of knowledge of terrain; brief encounter with Cheyennes; a second trip transporting mules and supplies from Fort Leavenworth to Camp Floyd for Utah expedition, making a record round trip in severe winter weather with minimal losses.

In RELATIONS WITH THE INDIANS OF THE PLAINS, 1857-1861: A DOCUMENTARY ACCOUNT OF THE MILITARY CAMPAIGNS AND NEGOTIATIONS OF INDIAN AGENTS WITH REPORTS AND JOURNALS, edited by LeRoy R. and Ann W. Hafen, pp. 49-96. The Far West and the Rockies Historical Series, vol. 9. Glendale, Calif,; A.H. Clark, 1959.

Jun-Sep 1857.

MENEFEE, ARTHUR M.   **3649**

"Arthur M. Menefee's Travels across the Plains." NEVADA HISTORICAL SOCIETY QUARTERLY 9, no 1 (1966):1-28.

May-Oct 1857. Diary of Ralls County, Missouri, emigrant bound for California, who died at Carson City; route, camps and conditions of travel; work of both men and women pioneers; sickness of several, including the diarist; some dissension among the company; Indian alarms in Utah.

MILLER, JAMES THADEUS, 1837-1858   **3650**

In JOURNAL, by Jacob Miller, prepared for publication by Joseph Royal Miller and Elna Miller, pp. 45-47. Salt lake City: Mercury, 1967.

Oct 1857. Journey of Mormon to Fort Lemhi in Idaho to join the Salmon River Mission to the Shoshone and Bannock Indians.

MORAN, BENJAMIN, 1820-1886   **3651**

THE JOURNAL OF BENJAMIN MORAN. Edited by Sarah A. Wallace and Frances E. Gillespie. Chicago: University of Chicago Press, 1948-1949. 2 vols.

1857-1865. Voluminous personal journal of secretary at the United States legation in London; candid, often gossipy, daily entries consisting of an informative mixture of diplomatic duties, social life and personal matters; relationship with ministers George Mifflin Dallas and Charles Francis Adams and their families; antebellum diplomatic issues including British actions in Central America and right of search of American vessels; relations between the Lincoln and British governments during the Civil War;

notes on countless individuals, both the politically or socially prominent and the ordinary citizens who sought assistance at the embassy, with physical description of most, including Queen Victoria; court functions, dress and etiquette; debates in the House of Commons; the sights of London, its theater, etc.; his interest in the Atlantic and Great Western Railroad promoted by his friend James McHenry; British reaction to Lincoln's assassination; the opinions and prejudices of a staunch supporter of the Union, an ambitious and frustrated individual whose journal was his confidant.

Extracts in THE BLUE AND THE GRAY, edited by Henry S. Commager, vol. 1, pp. 535-539, vol. 2, pp. 813-314; TRAGIC YEARS, by Paul M. Angle and Earl S. Miers, vol. 1, pp. 168-170, 221.

"Extracts from the Diary of Benjamin Moran." MASSACHUSETTS HISTORICAL SOCIETY PROCEEDINGS 48 (1915):431-492.

1860-1868. Diplomatic issues of the war years, sessions of the House of Commons, the funeral of Artemus Ward, etc.

PECKHAM, EDWARD L.   **3652**

"My Journey Out West." JOURNAL OF AMERICAN HISTORY 17 (1923):225-235, 341-353; 18 (1924):39-50.

Jun 1857. Botanist's train journey from Providence, Rhode Island, to Iowa and return, with detailed, humorous notes on passengers, accommodations, meals, dangers and discomforts; comments on Chicago, "as mean a spot as I ever was in"; from Iowa City to Des Moines and various Iowa "boom towns" by stagecoach, with highly entertaining descriptions of that mode of travel, the journey and his traveling companions, including Gov. William Aiken of South Carolina; notes on Mormons encamped in Iowa; a chauvinistic New Englander's satirical reactions to the Middle West.

PHELPS, JOHN WOLCOTT, 1813-1885   **3653**

In THE UTAH EXPEDITION, by LeRoy R. and Ann W. Hafen, pp. 90-138. Far West and the Rockies Historical Series, vol. 8. Glendale, Calif.: Arthur H. Clark, 1958.

Jun-Sep 1857. Expedition from Fort Leavenworth to Utah to suppress the alleged Mormon rebellion; good descriptions of the trail, plants, animals, Platte River, his battery, camps, treatment of fellow soldiers, Fort Kearny and the Rocky Mountains.

ROBERTS, ELLEN LOIS, 1825-1908   **3654**

In ELLEN LOIS ROBERTS: LIFE AND WRITINGS, A SKETCH, by Adella P. Carpenter, pp. 1-191 passim. Chicago: Women's Missionary Society, Free Methodist Church, 1926.

1857-1908. Diary extracts within biography of the wife of B.T. Roberts, founder of the Free Methodist Church; references to her husband's activities and her own church work; spiritual struggles, especially over the ecclesiastical trial of her husband by the Methodist Church; her later years.

SANFORD, MOLLIE DORSEY, 1838?-1915   **3655**

MOLLIE: THE JOURNAL OF MOLLIE DORSEY SANFORD IN NEBRASKA AND COLORADO TERRITORIES. Introduction and notes by Donald F. Danker. Lincoln: University of Nebraska Press, 1959. 201 pp.

1857-1866. Optimistic and often humorous journal of the oldest daughter of a happy family of nine, covering the trip from Indianapolis to a homestead in Nebraska; rigorous days of establishing a farm; a parade of suitors; supplementing of meager family income by sewing; marriage to Byron Sanford and wagon trip to Denver gold mines hoping for work; several prophetic dreams related.

Sanford, Albert., ed. "Life at Camp Weld and Fort Lyon in 1861-62: An Extract from the Diary of Mrs. Byron N. Sanford." COLORADO MAGAZINE 7 (1930):132-139.

Dec 1861-Mar 1862. Travel from Camp Weld to Fort Lyon with her husband's company, the first Colorado Regiment of Volunteers; modest social life and enjoyment of her guitar and singing; agreeing to relent from her "Methodist scruples" and learn to play cards with her husband so he would not do it elsewhere; sorrow when his company was dispatched to the New Mexico campaign.

SCOTT, CHARLES A., 1830-1907   3656

Stowers, Robert E. and Ellis, John M., eds. "Charles A. Scott's Diary of the Utah Expedition, 1857-1861." UTAH HISTORICAL QUARTERLY 28 (1960):155-176, 389-402.

1857-1861 (with gaps). Entertaining account of penniless returned filibuster's stay in New York; a futile search for employment ending with enlistment in the army; by train to Fort Leavenworth, thence west with the Utah expedition under Albert Sidney Johnston; brief notes of travel conditions, especially brutal cold; some descriptions of Mormon settlements and fortifications; activities at Camp Floyd, where the population consisted of "Saints, Gentiles, Mountaineers, Greasers, Loafers, Thieves, Rumsettlers," etc.; return to Fort Leavenworth.

Ellis, John M. and Stowers, Robert E., eds. "The Nevada Uprising of 1860 as Seen By Private Charles A. Scott." ARIZONA AND THE WEST 3 (1961):355-376.

May-Oct 1860. Volunteer campaign under Stephen H. Weed to protect Pony Express and emigrants from depredations during the Nevada Indian uprising; march from Camp Floyd to Ruby Valley and Carson City along emigrant and mail routes and return; reports of attacks on mail stations; only one battle, but diarist's opinion that volunteers had largely succeeded in protecting the six hundred mile route; a few colorful notes on mining camps and emigrants.

SIMMONS, BENJAMIN FRANKLIN   3657

Colcord, Joanna C., ed. "Salvaging the Ship CRYSTAL PALACE: The Private Journals 1857-1858 of Capt. Benjamin F. Simmons and Second Officer Joshua N. Rowe." AMERICAN NEPTUNE 3 (1943):314-326; 4 (1944):31-44.

1857-1858. Extensive diary extracts from captain and second mate of a clipper ship en route from Macao to Bombay; emergency unloading and repairs when ship ran over its own anchor chain near Zamboanga, all the while holding pirates at bay; interesting for techniques of ship salvage and cargo, which included Chinese coolies who were regarded as such, and character sketches of seamen by the articulate Rowe.

STACEY, MAY HUMPHREYS, 1837-1886   3658

UNCLE SAM'S CAMELS. Cambridge: Harvard University Press;

Glorieta, New Mex.: Rio Grande Press, 1929. 298 pp. Diary, pp. 21-115.

May-Oct 1857. Travel journal of military officer; by train in Pennsylvania from Chester to Harrisburg; by packet boat, SIR WILLIAM WALLACE, to Cincinnati; by QUEEN OF THE WEST to New Orleans; navigation and notes on towns; with Lt. Edward Fitzgerald Beale's expedition determining feasibility of wagon route from Fort Defiance to the Colorado River; at San Antonio, meeting camels acquired by the government for transportation experiment; traveling west, managing mules and camels together, keeping records of weights carried and speed attained and creating great curiosity along the way.

STEVENSON, E.A.   3659

Wheeler-Voegelin, Erminie, ed. "Documents." ETHNOHISTORY 4 (1957):66-95.

Jul-Sep 1857. Letter-diary of the journey of an Indian agent at Nome Lackee Reservation in Tehama County, California, to survey numbers, condition and needs of northeastern California Indians; visits to the Achomawi, Atsugewi and Modoc during travels in Shasta and Scott valleys and Tule and Clear Lake regions; recommendation that a reservation be established in the Pit River region and that Indians of the area be supplied with goods and protection from "attempts of lawless white men to injure them."

SWIFT, ELIJAH, b. 1831   3660

Wood, Virginia Steele, ed. "Elijah Swift's Travel Journal from Massachusetts to Florida, 1857." FLORIDA HISTORICAL QUARTERLY 55 (1976):181-188.

Oct 1857. Falmouth, Massachusetts, man's exhausting train journey to Florida on business for his lumber company; arrangements with his cousin Rodolphus Swift for purchase of live oak timber lands or cutting rights in Tallahassee, St. Marks and Newport; "a most wretched stage ride" from Macon, Georgia, to Tallahassee, etc.; business dealings and Presbyterian church services in various towns.

WELD, STEPHEN MINOT, b. 1842   3661

WAR DIARY AND LETTERS OF STEPHEN MINOT WELD. Cambridge, Mass.: Privately printed? Riverside Press, 1912. 428 pp. Diary, pp. 14-394 passim.

Nov-Dec 1857, 1861-1865 (with gaps). Two brief extracts from college diary to illustrate Harvard life followed by diary and letters intertwined within narrative of war experience; civilian volunteer aboard the BALTIC and later on Horatio Wright's staff during the Port Royal expedition with descriptions of the Naval Academy, Annapolis, Fortress Monroe and sights ashore in South Carolina; lieutenant in the Eighteenth Massachusetts and appointment to Fitz-John Porter's staff and then Henry Benham's staff in the engineer corps; appointment to John Reynolds' staff and promotion; accompanying Reynolds' body to Philadelphia, thereby witnessing only a small portion of the first day at Gettysburg; visiting in Philadelphia area; on John Newton's staff; lieutenant colonel of the Fifty-sixth Massachusetts Volunteers; recruiting the regiment; in thick of battle of the Wilderness; investment of Petersburg; explosion of the mine and battle of the Crater where he was taken prisoner and witnessed killing of black prisoners; in prison at Richland Jail in Columbia, South Carolina, until exchange in December 1864; a few notes upon rejoining his regiment the first week of April 1865; long descriptive entries marking diarist's journey from jaunty, socializing staff officer to line officer beset by lice, dirt and the horrors of battle.

WHITFORD, MARIA WELLS LANGWORTHY, 1830-1861   3662

AND A WHITE VEST FOR SAM'L: AN ACOUNT OF RURAL LIFE IN WESTERN, N.Y. FROM THE DIARIES OF MARIA LANGWOR-THY WHITFORD OF ALFRED STATION, N.Y. Edited by Helene C. Whelan. Almond, N.Y.: Printed by Sun Publishing Co., 1976. 235 pp.

1857-1861. Personal diary of serious Seventh Day Baptist woman; daily and seasonal domestic chores of spinning, weaving, having yarn or cloth dyed, making clothes and rugs, occasionally to sell, butchering, baking, drying apples and making jam; adding the outdoor chores when her husband, Samuel, was ill and gratefully accepting his help with cleaning or cooking when she was sick; mention of attending singing school; little commentary but good picture of woman's farm life.

WOOD, J.C.   3663

REPORT TO HON. A.V. BROWN, POSTMASTER GENERAL, ON THE OPENING AND PRESENT CONDITION OF THE UNITED STATES OVERLAND MAIL ROUTE BETWEEN SAN ANTONIO, TEXAS AND SAN DIEGO, CALIFORNIA. Washington, D.C., 1858. 43 pp.

Jun 1857-Jan 1858. Diary kept while procuring mules and coaches and establishing a line for mail with some passenger stations from San Antonio to San Diego for John Birch, who contracted with the government to deliver semi-monthly mail; treachery of Indians and lack of cooperation by military officials to supply exchange mules; disappearance of Birch, later found to be lost in Central America, and consequent lack of funds to pay for mules and drivers.

WOODS, MARTHA J.   3664

Welsh, Donald H., ed. "Martha J. Woods Visits Missouri in 1857." MISSOURI HISTORICAL REVIEW 55 (1961):109-123.

Apr-May 1857. Extracts from the diary of a young woman who traveled from Augusta County, Virginia, to Saline County, Missouri; entries beginning at the Mississippi, with notes on scenery, terrain and people of Missouri, including "the roughest, most grotesque looking set of ruffian settlers imaginable" in the "poor hilly part of the state"; lament over the scarcity of churches; an entry for 1859 just prior to her departure from Missouri.

1858

ACKLEY, RICHARD THOMAS, 1832-1881   3665

"Across the Plains in 1858." UTAH HISTORICAL QUARTERLY 9 (1941):190-228.

Jun-Aug 1858. Camden, New Jersey, man's overland journey; departure from Sidney, Iowa, where he had been in business with Jim S. Packard, Thomas A. Atkins and Oliver Scoggins, who proved to be a "desperate character"; encounters with Indians

and cavalry; references to General Harney's movements; a conversation with Jim Bridger and notes on Fort Bridger; pioneer graves identified; later narrative material on Salt Lake, the Mormons and events in Utah.

BANKS, JOHN, 1797-1870   3666

SHORT BIOGRAPHICAL SKETCH OF THE UNDERSIGNED BY HIMSELF. Austell? Ga., 1936? 38 pp. Diary, pp. 19-38.

1858-1865. Columbus, Georgia, planter/businessman's autobiography, based on earlier diary, and sporadic diary entries covering the years of sectional conflict; major war news, prices, death of three sons in battle and suicide of fourth; desertion by his slaves after the war.

BARKER, ANSELM HOLCOMB, 1822-1895   3667

ANSELM HOLCOMB BARKER, 1822-1895:PIONEER BUILDER AND EARLY SETTLER OF AURARIA. Denver: Golden Bell Press,, 1959. 83 pp.

Sep 1858-Jul 1859. Prospector's journey from Plattsmouth, Nebraska, to Cherry Creek, now Denver, in Colorado; good description of route along Platte River, events of the day, grass, water, game, Fort Kearny and Cheyenne Indians; Cherry Creek diggings, building the first cabin there and successfully prospecting for gold; organizing Auraria Town Company.

BOLLER, HENRY A., b. 1836   3668

Mattison, Ray H., ed. "Journal of a Trip to, and Residence in, Indian Country." NORTH DAKOTA HISTORY 33 (1966):260-315.

Sep-Dec 1858. Fur trade journal of a clerk with Frost, Todd and Company at and around Fort Atkinson on the Upper Missouri; good notes on Indians with whom he lived and traded, the comings and goings of many Plains tribes, especially Sioux and Mandan, and the French traders; well described trading journeys, with danger of being caught in intertribal warfare; excellent details of work and milieu of fur trading.

BOYD, DAVID FRENCH, 1834-1899   3669

Reed, Germaine M., ed. "Journey through Southwest Arkansas." ARKANSAS HISTORICAL QUARTERLY 30 (1971):161-169.

Jul-Aug 1858. Homer, Louisiana, teacher's horseback trip through southwest Arkansas and Indian Territory, lodging with local people, most of whom he described with wry amusement, including a parson who was "fonder of good living than hard preaching"; a few notes on towns, soil, etc.; a list of expenses.

BUSHBY, ARTHUR THOMAS, b. 1835   3670

Smith, Dorothy B., ed. "The Journal of Arthur Thomas Bushby." BRITISH COLUMBIA HISTORICAL QUARTERLY 21 (1957-1958):83-198.

Nov 1858-May 1859. Journal of an Englishman in the 1858 British Columbia gold rush; voyage from England to San Francisco on the MOSES TAYLOR and SONORA, with highly entertaining notes on ship travel and passengers; "knocking about" San Francisco, with good descriptions of life and sights; on the PANAMA to British Columbia; extensive account of his experiences in the Fraser River gold region.

COOPER, DOUGLAS   **3671**

Foreman, Grant. "A Journal Kept by Douglas Cooper of an Expedition by a Company of Chickasaw in Quest of Comanche Indians." CHRONICLES OF OKLAHOMA 5 (1927):381-390.

Jul 1858. Indian agent's official expedition journal; march along Beaver Creek to Wichita village and beyond; no success in finding Comanches; return to Fort Arbuckle.

CORMANY, RACHEL BOWMAN, 1836-1899   **3672**

In THE CORMANY DIARIES, edited by James C. Mohr and Richard E. Winslow, pp. 3-382 passim. Pittsburgh: University of Pittsburgh Press, 1982.

1858-1865. Diary begun during senior year at Otterbein College in Westerville, Ohio; undergraduate life at one of the few antebellum coeducational colleges; graduation and unsuccessful job hunt in New York City; teaching at Quakertown, Pennsylvania, with discipline problems and controversy over school prayer, and at Worthington, Ohio, with the tribulations of "boarding round"; marriage to Samuel Cormany and honeymoon in Niagara Falls and Ontario, remaining in Ontario among her family because of the volatile political situation in Missouri where they had planned to farm; setting up millinery business and her own household at Elmira, then moving to Carlisle Hill; pregnancy weathered by the principles of hydropathic medicine; return to the United States, settling near the Cormany family in Chambersburg, Pennsylvania; enduring loneliness and the frustrations of unsatisfactory lodgings, financial worries, problems of child care and tightfisted in-laws while Samuel was in the Union army; Confederate occupation of Chambersburg in 1863, with scenes of looting and capturing of blacks, and burning of the town in 1864; reaction to Lincoln's assassination; notes on social activities, reading, food, household chores, clothes, dentistry, childrearing, etc.; religious activities as a member of the United Brethren in Christ and spiritual concerns; a record brimming with details of everyday life, pervaded by her evangelical faith and marriage bond; altogether, read in conjunction with her husband's diary, an exceptional chronicle of the period.

ENGLE, F.E.   **3673**

In WAGON ROAD—FORT SMITH TO COLORADO RIVER, by Edward F. Beale, pp. 76-91. 36th Cong., 1st sess., 1860, H. Exec. Doc. 42. Washington? 1860.

Foreman, Grant, ed. "Survey of a Wagon Road from Fort Smith to the Colorado River." CHRONICLES OF OKLAHOMA 12 (1934):74-96.

Oct-Dec 1858. Account of expedition under Edward F. Beale to survey from Fort Smith, Arkansas, along the Canadian River to the Colorado, as part of a series of surveys to establish route to California; topography and scenery; people met along the way; use of hired Indian hunters.

FELT, ANDREW M., 1824-1907   **3674**

"Journal of Andrew M. Felt." MICHIGAN HISTORY MAGAZINE 15 (1931):112-125.

Nov-Dec 1858. Long extract from letter-diary of Clayton man; by train to New York, steamer EMPIRE CITY to Cuba and New Orleans, across Panama, then by steamer GOLDEN AGE to San Francisco; attempt to work at mining in California cut short by illness.

FULGHUM, F. CLARKSON, d. 1904   **3675**

Thornburg, Opal, ed. "Earlham Diaries: The Diary of F. Clarkson Fulghum." FRIENDS HISTORICAL ASSOCIATION BULLETIN 36 (1947):72-75.

Oct 1858-Jan 1859. Extracts of academic, religious and social activities of a student at Friends Boarding School, later to become Earlham College; lectures, mainly in science; use of telescope; quaint and appealing.

GILLESPIE, EMILY HAWLEY   **3676**

Lensink, Judy N.; Kirkham, Christine M.,; and Witzke, Karen P. " 'My Only Confidant'—The Life and Diary of Emily Hawley Gilespie." ANNALS OF IOWA, 3d ser. 45 (1979-1981):288-312.

1858-1888. Substantial extracts, within biographical article, from diary of an Iowa farm woman; life at home in Morenci, Michigan, where she refused several suitors; move to Manchester, Iowa, to keep house for her widowed uncle; marriage to James Gillespie; a few years of relative happiness marred by her husband's ill health and mounting debts; joy in her two children, but increasing despair over conflicts in marriage, exhausting work and absence of social life; her own illness, probably dropsy, and eventual realization of her husband's insanity; a chronicle of an optimistic, promising woman worn down by loneliness, work and disappointment.

GRIMBALL, JOHN BERKLEY, 1800-1893   **3677**

"Diary of John Berkley Grimball." SOUTH CAROLINA HISTORICAL MAGAZINE 56 (1955):8-30, 92-114, 157-177; 57 (1956):28-50, 88-102.

1858-1865. Segment of Colleton District rice planter's diary covering secession and Civil War; sporadic entries on financial affairs, the concerns of an extended family and plantation matters; health of diarist and those around him; reaction to Lincoln's election and the secession of South Carolina; witnessing battle of Fort Sumter; the problems and advancement of several sons, all in Confederate service; his support of war effort including enlistment in Company E, First South Carolina Reserves; problems with his slaves; visits to Aiken and Charleston and a trip to Richmond; resettlement of his family in Spartanburg; decision to join Episcopal church; looting of one of his homes by Confederate soldiers; return of all but one son at war's end and reduced economic circumstances.

HAMILTON, JAMES B., b. 1830   **3678**

In HISTORY OF FAYETTE COUNTY, WEST VIRGINIA, by J.T. Peters and H.B. Carden, pp. 200-212. Charleston, W. Va.: Jarrett Printing Co., 1926.

Jan 1858-Jun 1859. Diary of an Ansted farmer; brief entries on religion, farm work, surveying, fishing and personal affairs.

HEINTZELMAN, SAMUEL PETER, 1805-1880   **3679**

In SAMUEL PETER HEINTZELMAN AND THE SONORA EXPLORING AND MINING COMPANY, by Diane M.T. North, pp. 47-167. Tucson: University of Arizona Press, 1980.

Aug 1858-Jan 1859. Journal of president of Sonora Exploring and Mining Company; activities as director of field operations in Arizona and New Mexico while on leave from military duties; examining mines, furnaces for smelting lead and silver, accounts and equipment; his dissatisfaction with management of mines and questionable business arrangements of Charles Debrille Poston; problems with Mexican laborers; attempts to reduce expenses and make operation profitable; notes on fiestas, particularly that of St. Augustine at Tucson; return by stagecoach to his family in Newport, Kentucky.

JACKSON, GEORGE ANDREW, 1836-1897   3680

Hafen, LeRoy R., ed. "George A. Jackson's Diary." COLORADO MAGAZINE 12 (1935):201-214.

Dec 1858-Mar 1859. Diary of a gold prospector from Glasgow, Missouri; notes on camping, hunting and prospecting around Vasquez Fork, Colorado; good picture of various prospectors and mountain men and their way of life.

JACKSON, OSCAR LAWRENCE, 1840-1920   3681

THE COLONEL'S DIARY. Sharon? Pa., 1922. 232 pp.

1858-1865. Irregular entries, some of them of a summarizing, retrospective nature, covering antebellum days at New Castle, Pennsylvania and his search for a teaching position; school and church activities in Hocking County, Ohio; debates, courtship practices, a trip on the steamboat MINERVA from Wheeling to Pittsburgh and campaigning for Lincoln; efforts to recruit a company in Pennsylvania, then in Ohio; service with the Sixty-third Ohio Volunteers as captain of Company H; action at New Madrid and Island No. 10; advance to Corinth and battles of Iuka and Corinth; General Dodge's raid into Alabama; carrying ordnance stores to Grant's army during the Vicksburg campaign; in camp at Memphis; operations in Mississippi, Tennessee and Alabama; re-enlistment, the Atlanta campaign and beginning of more or less daily entries; marching to the sea; at Savannah and Beaufort: Carolinas campaign; description of destruction by the troops, Confederates' use of primitive land mines, behavior of soldiers and slaves in Columbia and suffering of North Carolinians; reaction to the first Sherman-Johnston surrender terms; north to Richmond and Petersburg; the Grand Review; at Louisville and Camp Dennison near Cincinnati before mustering out; notes on his duties, soldiers' foraging and drinking, smuggling, black soldiers, generals including Halleck and Sherman, countryside and towns, slavery, contrabands and their treatment by Union troops.

Extract in THE BLUE AND THE GRAY, edited by Henry S. Commager, vol. 1, pp. 365-370.

Oct 1862. Battle of Corinth.

JACOBS, WILLIAM PLUMER, 1842-1917   3682

DIARY OF WILLIAM PLUMER JACOBS. Edited by Thornwall Jacobs. Oglethorpe University, Ga.: Oglethorpe University Press, 1937. 484 pp.

1858-1917. Clinton, South Carolina, clergyman's diaries beginning in his youth with studies at school and in college at Charleston; religious reflections, verses, etc.; pastoral work as a Presbyterian clergyman; philanthropic activities, including establishment of the Thornwell Orphanage and extensive notes on its history; founding of Clinton College, later named Presbyterian College of South Carolina.

KELLOGG, DAVID   3683

"Across the Plains in 1858." THE TRAIL 5, no 7 (1912):5-10; no. 8 (1913):5-12.

Sep 1858-Apr 1859. Journey from Kansas City to Pike's Peak; a long hearsay account of the battle of Black Jack and attempt of Henry Clay Pate to capture John Brown; some dissension in the group leading to election of John Price as captain; an evening of "oratory, song and jest" with Shakespearean recitations by "handsome Jim Winchester from Virginia"; good accounts of buffalo hunts; a few notes on Kiowa and Arapaho; experiences in the Colorado diggings, with entertaining anecdotes about prospectors and mountain men; return journey.

LANZIT, JACOB SAUL, 1830?-1912?   3684

In MEMOIRS OF AMERICAN JEWS, 1775-1865, by Jacob R. Marcus, vol. 3, pp. 33-37.

Extracts in DIARY OF AMERICA, edited by Josef and Dorothy Berger, pp. 240-246.

1858-1859. Tribulations of a Jewish immigrant eager to work and earn his way in America but having to contend with low wages and frequent unemployment; after various failures, establishing successful tailoring business in New York.

LINDSEY, SARAH CROSLAND, 1804-1876   3685

Jackson, Sheldon, ed. "English Quakers Tour Kansas in 1858." KANSAS HISTORICAL QUARTERLY 13 (1944):36-52

Mar-Apr 1858. Extract covering portion of a Quaker missionary's trip from St. Louis through Kansas visiting Quakers and the Friends Mission for the Shawnee Indians; notes on living conditions of settlers and Indians; difficult carriage travel and primitive lodgings borne with fortitude; activities of her husband and fellow laborer, Robert Lindsey.

Jones, Louis T., ed. "The Quakers of Iowa in 1858." IOWA JOURNAL OF HISTORY AND POLITICS 12 (1914):394-439.

Apr-Jul 1858. Extract covering travel in Iowa; report of the explosion of Mississippi steamboat FALLS CITY; travel from St. Louis on the LACLEDE and by train and stagecoach to Muscatine, Iowa City, Indianola, etc., with names of many Quakers with whom they stayed; much on her husband's preaching and on the religious condition of individuals and meetings, including the Red Cedar Quarterly Meeting.

In TRAVELS OF ROBERT AND SARAH LINDSEY, edited by One of Their Daughters, pp. 134-180. London: Harris, 1886.

1859-1861? Extract covering religious travels in California and Hawaii via Isthmus of Panama, with extensive material on Hawaii.

Jackson, Sheldon G., ed. "An English Quaker Tours California." SOUTHERN CALIFORNIA QUARTERLY 51 (1969):1-33, 153-175, 221-246.

1859-1860. Extracts of the voyage from New York on the STAR OF THE WEST via the Isthmus of Panama in order to visit Quakers and establish meetings in California, mainly in San Francisco, but with trips to Sacramento, Stockton, the Feather River mines, etc.; interesting observations on the lingering social and moral effects of the gold rush; comments on Indians and Chinese, the aftermath of the Broderick-Terry duel and the slavery question; references to James and Hannah Neal, John and Thomas Bevan and others; preaching at San Quentin Prison; throughout, concern at finding Quakerism in a distinctly unflourishing condition.

Nedry, H.S., ed. "Willamette Valley in 1859." OREGON HISTORICAL QUARTERLY 46 (1945):235-254.

Nov 1859-Jan 1860. Extract covering a sojourn in Oregon; from San Francisco on the PANAMA; notes on Portland, Salem, Corvallis, Eugene, etc., and surrounding area, where they visited Quaker and English settlers; reactions to frontier living conditions and to stagecoach travel.

MACDONALD, ALEXANDER HOLMES, 1830-1920   3686

Stuart, Reginald R. and Grace D., eds. "A Year on the Yuba." PACIFIC HISTORIAN 2, no. 1 (1950):5-6, 11-16; no. 2, 11-16; no. 3, 3, 10-12; no. 4, 13-16; 3, no. 1 (1959):17-20, 24.

Jan-Aug 1858. A Nova Scotian teacher's account of mining at Orleans Flat on the Yuba, associating there with "some of the best and perhaps most talented men as well as some of the most vicious and reckless people of this age"; interesting notes on work and hazards of mining; church activities and religious reflection amid gambling, prostitution and violence; lodge membership in the Good Templars; events in Downieville and references to many Scottish surnamed people in the area.

MCDONALD, DAVID, 1803-1869   3687

"Diaries of Judge David McDonald." INDIANA MAGAZINE OF HISTORY 28 (1932):282-306.

1858-1864 (with gaps). Indianapolis judge's various trips to Washington, D.C., traveling by train and commenting unfavorably on most of what he saw en route; wonderful description of the Supreme Court in session, each of its venerable members and some of the cases before them; the Smithsonian Institution "full of birds, quadrupeds, reptiles,corals, and the Lord knows what"; revulsion at "gaming and whoring" in the capital and its general level of humbug and pomposity; deliberations of Congress; criticism of Lincoln's appointments in Indiana and an interview with him; religious views of a Methodist who often sought out Unitarian worship; quite funny in places.

MANLY, BASIL, 1798-1868   3688

Hoole, W. Stanley, ed. "The Diary of Dr. Basil Manly." ALABAMA REVIEW 4 (1951):127-149, 221-236, 270-289; 5 (1952):61-74, 142-155.

1858-1867. Extracts from diary of influential Baptist minister, former president of the University of Alabama and founder of the Alabama Historical Society; resignation of Charleston, South Carolina, pastorate and return to Alabama as "missionary or state evangelist"; pastor of the First Baptist Church of Montgomery, 1861-1862; removal to Tuscaloosa where he attended to his large plantation in Lowndes County and occasionally preached; entries covering missionary activities, pastoral duties, family matters and business dealings; public events, such as the inauguration of Jefferson Davis at which he served as chaplain; war's effect on household and community; in Tuscaloosa during Union cavalry raid; notes on a variety of subjects, including his efforts on behalf of Alabama Central Female College; copy of contract establishing work arrangements with former slaves most of whom soon departed; interesting record of daily minutiae, recreating the reality of a past society.

MORSE, BLISS, 1837-1923   3689

CIVIL WAR DIARIES. Edited by Loren J. Morse. Pittsburg, Kans.: Pittcraft, 1964. 92 pp.

1858-1866 (with gaps). Lake County, Ohio, man's diary of peace and war; farming near Painesville and a brief stint of school teaching; notes on weather, farm tasks and social activities; serving in Company D, 105th Ohio Volunteer Infantry, in Kentucky and Tennessee; at battles of Perryville, Chickamauga, Lookout Mountain and Missionary Ridge but little or no detail; Atlanta campaign, going after Hood's army, the March to the Sea and through the Carolinas; names of owners of houses and plantations along the way; observing the war's impact on Virginia and sights in Richmond; the Grand Review and visits to the Patent Office, Smithsonian Institution and Capitol; festivities in Cleveland; postwar emigration to Missouri; brief entries tersely noting everyday activities and events.

NICAISE, AUGUSTE, 1828-1900   3690

A YEAR IN THE DESERT. Edited and translated by Edward J. Kowrach. Fairfield, Wash.: Ye Galleon, 1980. 124 pp.

1858-1859. French author's journal of travels in the United States, particularly the overland journey from St. Louis to San Francisco with trapper William Hartwood whose past heartrending adventures are quoted at length; entries in romantic style on Indians, Mormons, emigrants, scenes, etc., en route and on life in California as a prospect for future French immigration; possibly spurious.

PEABODY, GEORGE AUGUSTUS, 1831-1929   3691

SOUTH AMERICAN JOURNALS. Edited by John C. Phillips. Salem, Mass.: Peabody Museum, 1937, 209 pp.

Nov 1858-Jun 1859. Record of an ambitious hunting expedition undertaken by a resident of Salem and Danvers who traveled to South America with three companions, Robert B. Forbes, Jeffries Wyman and William G. Saltonstall; voyage on the NANKIN to Montevideo, with log entries and lengthy descriptions of life on a "hermaphrodite iron brig"; up the Plata in a small launch brought on the NANKIN; thence overland on horseback with interesting notes on gauchos, estancias, natural history and hunting adventures as they crossed the pampas and Andes from Buenos Aires to Santiago; an unusually good travel diary.

PHILLIPS, CYRUS OLIN   3692

Howay, F.W., ed. "To the Fraser River! The Diary and Letters of Cyrus Olin Phillips." CALIFORNIA HISTORICAL SOCIETY QUARTERLY 11 (1932):150-156. Diary, pp. 152-153.

Jul-Aug 1858. Brief diary of merchant supplying miners in the British Columbia gold rush; from Sacramento to San Francisco on steamer NEW WORLD; San Francisco to Victoria on the SIERRA NEVADA; thence up Fraser River on the HOPE and to Yale by canoe.

PRUDE, REUBEN H., 1836-1861   3693

Baker, Jane O.; Baker, Robert P.; and Hilburn, Iva N., eds. "Educator by Default: Problems of a Mid-nineteenth Century Southerner." LOUISIANA HISTORY 16 (1975):408-411.

1858-1860. Brief extracts from the diary of a young man teaching school in De Soto Parish; on his first day, finding "fifteen urchins to begin with, all looking smiling and saucy''; trying to do a conscientious job but finding the profession of teaching to be confining and injurious to his health.

PRUYN, JOHN VAN SCHAICK LANSING, 1811-1877   3694

Mushkat, Jerome, ed "Mineral and Timber Prospects in Upper Michigan." INLAND SEAS 30 (1974):84-94.

    Jul-Aug 1858. Extracts from diary of Albany, New York, lawyer and director of St. Mary's Falls Ship Canal Company on inspection tour of its Sault Canal and surrounding mineral lands; by boat from Albany with notes on towns and scenery en route; visits to copper and iron mines with company agent Charles Harvey; inspection of lands for further mining potential, especially in region of Ontonagon; mention of a proposal to create a new state, based on mining interests, of Upper Michigan and part of Wisconsin and Minnesota.

Mushkat, Jerome, ed. "The Impeachment of Andrew Johnson: A Contemporary View." NEW YORK HISTORY 48 (1967):275-286.

    Feb-May 1868. Extract from Albany congressman's much longer journal; events in Washington leading up to and including the impeachment of President Johnson, with references to many participants in the proceedings, especially the radical Republicans; diarist's assessment that political factors outweighed legal considerations in the outcome.

ROTH, WILLIAM, 1834-1908   3695

Roth, Britain. "Diary of a Voyage in the Clipper HESPERUS." LEHIGH COUNTY HISTORICAL SOCIETY PROCEEDINGS 17 (1949):9-27.

    1858-1859. Summary and extracts of Allentown, Pennsylvania, seaman's diary of a voyage from Boston to San Francisco and Honolulu via Cape Horn, during which he served as navigator; the miseries of two teenage boys who had gone to sea expecting "a playful jaunt with little danger, with a thrilling romantic story to tell when returning home''; a bad rounding of Cape Horn; experiences on Fanning and Jarvis islands taking on a cargo of guano.

ST. JOHN, MARY, 1838-1869   3696

Riley, Glenda, ed. "A Prairie Diary." ANNALS OF IOWA, 3d ser. 44 (1977-1979):103-117.

    Mar-Dec 1858 (with gaps). Account of Walton, New York, family's settling at Saratoga; farm work of men and domestic chores of women; church activities; some entries by her sister Esther.

SCAMMON, CHARLES MELVILLE, 1825-1911   3697

JOURNAL ABOARD THE BARK OCEAN BIRD ON A WHALING VOYAGE TO SCAMMON'S LAGOON. Edited by David A. Henderson. Baja California Travels Series, 21. Los Angeles: Dawson's Book Shop, 1970. 78 pp.

    Nov 1858-Apr 1859. Captain's journal of a whaling voyage from San Francisco to Baja California in pursuit of the Pacific gray whale; mostly log entries of weather, positions, etc., but some details of whaling; frequent references to the KATE and A.M. SIMPSON.

SELDON, JOHN ARMISTEAD, b. 1802   3698

THE WESTOVER JOURNAL OF JOHN A. SELDON. With an introduction and notes by John S. Bassett. Smith College Studies in History, vol. 6, no. 4. Northampton, Mass.: Smith College Department of History, 1921. Journal, pp. 257-330.

    1858-1864. Planter's journal kept at Westover, formerly owned by William Byrd, on the James River; plantation life, with careful attention to details of day-to-day activities of managing work; prices of goods and services; the education of his children; social life with great families of Virginia; vacationing at White Sulphur Springs; a bitter entry noting inauguration of Abraham Lincoln; effects of secession and the war; destruction and sale of Westover.

STEEDMAN, CHARLES, 1811-1890   3699

MEMOIR AND CORRESPONDENCE OF CHARLES STEEDMAN, REAR ADMIRAL, UNITED STATES NAVY, WITH HIS AUTOBIOGRAPHY AND PRIVATE JOURNALS. Edited by Amos L. Mason. Cambridge, Mass.: Privately printed at the Riverside Press, 1912. 556 pp. Journals, pp. 163-234, 447-484.

    Oct 1858-Feb 1859. Journal of commander of the brig DOLPHIN, participating in the expedition to Paraguay; from Boston to Buenos Aires and Montevideo; duties and social life ashore; up the Parana River to Rosario, Parana and Corrientes; notes on countryside, towns, Indians and hunting; a quite detailed record of his activities, problems and accomplishments with information on navigation, seamanship, crew punishments, ship movements, etc.

    Oct 1872-Sep 1873. Journal kept while in command of the South Pacific Squadron, aboard the PENSACOLA; from Panama to Payta, Concepcion and other South American ports; weather, navigation, official functions, shore excursions, etc.

TOMPKINS, SARA HAIGHT   3700

In THE RALSTON-FRY WEDDING AND THE WEDDING JOURNEY TO YOSEMITE, MAY 20, 1858, by Francis P. Farquhar, 24 pp. Bancroft Library Publications, no. 9. Berkeley: University of California, Friends of the Bancroft Library; San Francisco: Grabhorn Press, 1961.

    May 1858. Diary of a bridesmaid for San Francisco wedding of Elizabeth Fry and William C. Ralston after which the entire wedding party accompanied the newlyweds on wedding journey to Yosemite; spectacular scenery of the forest; staying at Big Trees Hotel; written in genteel and proper style.

TRACY, ALBERT H., 1818-1893   3701

Alter, J. Cecil and Dwyer, Robert J., eds. "The Utah War: Journal of Captain Albert Tracy." UTAH HISTORICAL QUARTERLY 13 (1945):1-119.

    1858-1860. Journal of commander of Company H of the Utah expedition under Albert Sidney Johnston; in winter quarters at Fort Scott, made miserable by cold, scant food and clothes, and harrassment by Mormon scouts; journey to Salt Lake City; description of and activities at Camp Floyd, followed by expedition to Provo, with trial there of John Doyle Lee and others accused of perpetrating the Mountain Meadows Massacre in 1857, and diarist's rendition of the incident; references to Maj. Edward R.S. Canby, Governor Cumming, etc.; return east by stagecoach and train, with time for expansive comments on people en route.

In AMONG THE MORMONS: HISTORIC ACCOUNTS BY CONTEM-PORARY OBSERVERS, edited by William Mulder and A. Russell Mortensen, pp. 299-302. New York: Alfred A. Knopf, 1958. Reprint. Lincoln: University of Nebraska Press, 1973.

Jun 1858. Extract covering Tenth Infantry captain's description of the march through Salt Lake City and finding it deserted, with "the rich strains of our band... wasted somewhat except to our own ears."

Irwin, Ray W., ed. "Missouri in Crisis." MISSOURI HISTORICAL REVIEW 51 (1956):8-21, 151-164, 270-283.

Feb-Nov 1861. Extracts covering service in Missouri; working under Capt. Nathaniel Lyon in defense of United States arsenal in St. Louis; in command of the magazine near Jefferson Barracks; appointed mustering officer in St. Louis and then to Fremont's staff; campaigning in southwest Missouri; confiscating property of secessionists; removal of Fremont from command; lengthy, nicely descriptive entries.

Wayland, Francis F., ed. "Fremont's Pursuit of Jackson in the Shenandoah Valley." VIRGINIA MAGAZINE OF HISTORY AND BIOGRAPHY 70 (1962):165-193, 332-354.

Mar, May-Jul 1862. Service on Fremont's staff during the Valley campaign, for which he was breveted lieutenant colonel; preparations for the campaign; the condition of the army; from New Creek to Strasburg and Harrisonburg; battle of Cross Keys; return down the Valley; resignation of Fremont and diarist's return to Wheeling and New York City; notes on military operations, camp life, destruction of civilian property at Franklin, foreign-born Union troops, supply problems, political influences on the army, etc.; references to many individuals including Cyrus Hamlin, Leonidas Haskell, Irvin McDowell and George Ward Nichols; long entries in a mostly daily record.

UPSON, THEODORE FRELINGHUYSEN, 1845-1919   3702

WITH SHERMAN TO THE SEA. Edited by Oscar O. Winther. Baton Rouge: Louisiana State University Press, 1943. 181 pp. Reprint. Bloomington: Indiana University Press, 1958.

Extracts in THE BLUE AND THE GRAY, edited by Henry S. Commager, vol. 1, pp. 39-40; NORTH CAROLINA CIVIL WAR DOCUMENTARY, pp. 336-337; TRAGIC YEARS, by Paul M. Angle and Earl S. Miers, vol. 2, pp. 973-974; TREASURY OF THE WORLD'S GREAT DIARIES, edited by Philip Dunaway, pp. 258-259.

1858-1865. Hoosier farm boy's record, rewritten from diaries, journals and letters; lengthy single entries for 1858-1860 concerning slavery controversy; homefront patriotism around Lima, now Howe, and enlistment in Company C, 100th Indiana Infantry Volunteers; service in Indiana, Kentucky, Tennessee, Mississippi and Alabama; Vicksburg campaign, inside the surrendered city and the battle of Jackson; Missionary Ridge, the Atlanta campaign and Sherman's marches through Georgia and the Carolinas; fall of Savannah, burning of Columbia, celebrating Lee's surrender, soldiers' desire to avenge Lincoln's death, sightseeing in Washington, D.C., and the Grand Review; notes on military duties, camp life, Irish and black soldiers, Fourth of July celebration, religion, foraging, destruction, freed slaves following in the army's wake, Sherman, Grant, etc.; a lively account but impossible to sort out original diary or journal entries from the reworked material.

VOORHEES, AUGUSTUS, 1828-1905   3703

Hafen, LeRoy, ed. "The Voorhees Diary of the Lawrence Party's Trip to Pikes Peak." COLORADO MAGAZINE 12 (1935):41-50.

In PIKE'S PEAK GOLD RUSH GUIDEBOOKS OF 1859, edited by LeRoy R. Hafen, pp. 336-346. Southwest Historical Series, 9. Glendale, Calif.: Arthur H. Clark, 1941.

Jun-Jul 1858. Journey to the Colorado gold fields with a group from Lawrence, Kansas; joining the party at Bluff Creek; distances, camps and conditions of travel; provisioning with buffalo, deer, etc., hunted en route; barter with Indians; arrival at Jim's Camp.

WAY, PHOCION R., 1827-1898   3704

Duffen, William A., ed. "Overland via 'Jackass Mail' in 1858." ARIZONA AND THE WEST 2 (1960):35-53, 147-164, 279-292, 353-370.

May-Oct 1858. Journey to Arizona of an agent for the Santa Rita Mining Company in Tubac; from his home in Cincinnati by riverboats to New Orleans, by steamer to Indianola, Texas, thence overland by stagecoach, mainly on the San Antonio-San Diego Mail Line, with well armed drivers, guards and passengers; very colorful and extensive details of travel and accommodation in the Southwest; stays at Tucson and Tubac, with notes on Indians in a starved and declining condition, miners, emigrants and traders; a footrace between suitors for "the only virgin in the place"; Catholic festivals, etc.; an interesting diary.

Eaton, W. Clement. "Frontier Life in Southern Arizona, 1858-1861." SOUTHWESTERN HISTORICAL QUARTERLY 36 (1932):173-192. Diary, pp. 180-188.

Jun 1858. Extract within article.

WEBSTER, JOHN BROWN, 1822-1864   3705

Lale, Max S. and Campbell, Randolph B., eds. "The Plantation Journal of John B. Webster." SOUTHWESTERN HISTORICAL QUARTERLY 84 (1980):49-79.

1858-1859. Extracts from the journal of a Harrison County, Texas, planter; daily notes on the tasks, health and productivity of individual slaves; reference to his wife's newborn baby being nursed by a slave; a useful picture of variety of work, crops and livestock on a prosperous plantation.

WILLIAMS, ELIZA AZELIA GRISWOLD   3706

In ONE WHALING FAMILY, edited by Harold Williams. Boston: Houghton Mifflin, 1964.

Extracts in AMERICAN HERITAGE 15, no. 4 (1964):64-79.

1858-1861. Diary of the wife of New Bedford whaling captain Thomas W. Williams, kept on a thirty-eight month voyage of the FLORIDA during which she gave birth to two children; quite meticulous descriptions of whaling work and processes, the excitement of lowering boats for the chase and the dirty, malodorous tasks of cutting up whales and rendering their oil; the bizarre experience of going inside a whale's mouth when the head had been brought on deck; notes on various ports of call in New Zealand, Asia, etc., and in San Francisco; ships encountered and exchanges of pleasantries with captains; a very interesting but discrete diary with few strictly personal details.

WILSON, CHARLES WILLIAM, Sir, 1836-1905　　3707

MAPPING THE FRONTIER: CHARLES WILSON'S DIARY OF THE SURVEY OF THE 49TH PARALLEL. Edited by George F.G. Stanley. Seattle: University of Washington Press; Toronto: Macmillan of Canada, 1970. 182 pp.

1858-1862. Journal of the levelheaded young secretary of the British Boundary Commission sent to assist the United States in establishing the border with Canada at British Columbia; a chronicle of endurance and leadership, both physical and psychological, as the surveyors contended with forests, mountains, wild rivers and extremes of weather; hardships lightened by the frontier social life of Victoria and Walla Walla; an entertaining and substantial journal rich in scientific and personal detail.

1859

BAKER, HOZIAL H., b. 1789　　3708

OVERLAND JOURNEY TO CARSON VALLEY, UTAH. Seneca Falls, N.Y.: F.M. Baker, 1861. 38 pp.

OVERLAND JOURNEY TO CARSON VALLEY & CALIFORNIA. San Francisco: Book Club of California, 1973. 91 pp.

Mar 1859-Jan 1860. Western diary of an incredibly hardy seventy-year-old man from Seneca Falls, New York; from Manchester, Michigan, intending to go to Pikes Peak; train travel during which he helped to raise railroad cars onto tracks sinking in mud and quicksand in Illinois; provisioning at St. Joseph, then by riverboat, with good descriptions of population, towns and farm land along the Missouri; overland journey, often walking ahead of teams; after Fort Kearny meeting disillusioned emigrants returning from Pikes Peak and changing his destination to California; good notes on weather, birds, wildlife, etc.; a feeling at Salt Lake that "a general apathy seems to prevail on inhabitants"; meeting and sometimes trading with Shoshoni, Snake and Paiute Indians; camping on Carson River, prospecting and working briefly for miners because he was out of provisions; concern about lawlessness in the Nevada mines; crossing the Sierra Nevada alone and on foot; nearly freezing until rescued by Simon Shouf and Charles Honeywell and aided to San Francisco where he took steerage passage on the CHAMPION to Panama and NORTHERN LIGHT to New York, arriving home acknowledging "a particular Providence over me throughout my journey."

BATES, EDWARD, 1793-1869　　3709

THE DIARY OF EDWARD BATES. Edited by Howard K. Beale. American Historical Association Annual Report, 1930, vol. 4. Washington, D.C.: United States Government Printing Office, 1933. 685 pp. Reprint. New York: Da Capo, 1971.

1859-1866. Diary of Missouri lawyer, former state legislator and Whig leader, who became Lincoln's attorney general; sporadic entries interspersed among newspaper articles, letters, diarist's opinions read to the cabinet and miscellaneous documents; coverage of state and federal government, politics and legal issues as well as aspects of his personal life; the escalating sectional crisis; the Prince of Wales' visit to St. Louis; diarist's candidacy for the 1860 Republican presidential nomination; the Republican convention, presidential campaign and secession; the

events and issues of the Civil War; reports of cabinet meetings; comments about Lincoln, fellow cabinet members, especially Stanton, Seward and Chase, and military leaders including Scott, Fremont, McClellan, Halleck, Butler, Grant and Sherman; the presidential campaign of 1864; his resignation from office, return to St. Louis and conflict with radical Republicans in Missouri; notes on many persons, among them Andrew Johnson, Lewis Cass, John Brown, Millard Fillmore, James B. Eads and Roger B. Taney; his opinions on slavery, black Union soldiers, emancipation, black suffrage, confiscation of Southern property, Reconstruction, the Supreme Court, the Freedmen's Bureau, etc.; a valuable record.

Extracts in TRAGIC YEARS, by Paul M. Angle and Earl S. Miers, vol. 2, pp. 828-829.

Jun 1864. Comments about the National Union Convention in Baltimore.

BISHOP, ROBERT　　3710

Weatherford, John, ed. "School and Other Days, 1859: Selections from the Diaries of Robert and Sylvester Bishop." OHIO HISTORICAL QUARTERLY 70 (1961):58-63.

Jan-May 1859. Interspersed extracts from the diaries of eleven and nine-year-old brothers, sons of Robert Hamilton Bishop II, Latin professor at Miami University; mostly school notes in which classroom disorder and beatings of various students predominate; death of a sister and a little brother's resolve to "be a good boy so I can meet her in heaven"; a Washington's birthday celebration that turned into something of a riot.

BOLTON, CHARLES EDWARD, b. 1840?　　3711

Bolton, Charles K., ed. "A Journey to Maine in 1859." NEW ENGLAND QUARTERLY 9 (1936):119-131.

Aug 1859. Brief journey from South Hadley Falls, Massachusetts, to Maine; sightseeing in Augusta and Boston, with great interest in libraries, museums, paper and saw mills, etc.; return to Boston on the EASTERN QUEEN; prayers and gratitude for safe travel throughout diary.

BOOTY, JAMES HORATIO　　3712

THREE MONTHS IN CANADA AND THE UNITED STATES. London: Printed by the author, 1862. 94 pp.

May-Jul 1859. An English tourist's observations of New York, Niagara Falls, Philadelphia, Washington, Chicago, St. Louis, etc.; notes on stagecoach and riverboat travel; amused comments on Americans and their ways, as well as a gruesome description of processes at the pig slaughterhouse in Cincinnati.

BOWER, EDWIN A., d. 1900　　3713

Smith, Duane A., ed. "Pikes Peak Fifty-Niner." COLORADO MAGAZINE 47 (1970):269-311.

Feb-Oct 1859. Colorado gold rush diary of a man from La Salle, Illinois; route, camps, organization and officers of the company; good description of a buffalo hunt; work, mainly operating a sluice, at the Gregory diggings and notes on John Gregory; life in Denver.

BROWN, JAMES BERRY, b. 1837　　3714

JOURNAL OF A JOURNEY ACROSS THE PLAINS IN 1859. Edited

by George R. Stewart. Book Club of California Publication, no. 135. San Francisco: Book Club of California, 1970. 72 pp.

May-Sep 1859. Young Cincinnati, Iowa, teacher's emigrant journey with his brother Jesse to settle at Eureka, California; wagon travel via the newly opened Lander's Cutoff; intention originally to go to Pikes Peak gold fields discouraged by numbers returning disillusioned and penniless; detailed notes on terrain, roads, emigrants, hunting, etc., during a relatively trouble-free crossing; a well described buffalo hunt; meeting train escorting children who had survived Mountain Meadows Massacre; arrival at Inskip to prospect.

CAMP, JOSEPH, 1834-1916?   **3715**

Camp, Truman W., ed. "The Journal of Joseph Camp." NEBRASKA HISTORY 46 (1965):29-38.

May-Jul 1859. Extract of Hartford, Connecticut, farmer's journal covering travel from Durant, Iowa, to Omaha; by river steamer WILLIAM B. EWING to Hannibal, Missouri, and train and steamer to St. Joseph, "The muddiest, nastiest border ruffian town on the earth," and by wagon to Omaha and Council Bluffs, with description of Fourth of July celebration there.

CARDON, THOMAS   **3716**

Cardon, A.F. "Mountain Meadows Burial Detachment." UTAH HISTORICAL QUARTERLY 35 (1967):143-146.

Apr-May 1859. Bare notes of a French immigrant working at Camp Floyd; camps and distances on march to bury victims of the Mountain Meadows Massacre; brief description of the "men's grave" and "women's grave."

CASLER, MELYER, d. 1862   **3717**

A JOURNAL GIVING THE INCIDENTS OF A JOURNEY TO CALIFORNIA IN THE SUMMER OF 1859 BY THE OVERLAND ROUTE. Toledo: Commercial Steam Book and Job Office, 1863. 48 pp. Reprint. Fairfield, Wash.: Ye Galleon, 1969. 62 pp.

Mar-Sep 1859. Overland journey from Delta, Ohio, over South Pass to Salt Lake City and along Humboldt to Placerville, California; many names of companions and persons visited in Illinois and Iowa; good details of repairing wagons; fishing, hunting, including buffalo hunt, and trading with Indians along Platte River; sightseeing and selling traps in Salt Lake City; brief prospecting in Nevada.

CLARK, CALVIN PERRY, 1835?-1907   **3718**

TWO DIARIES. Denver: Denver Public Library, 1962. 91 pp.

Mar 1859-Feb 1860 (with gaps). Overland journey from Plano, Illinois, to Denver via Santa Fe Trail; route, mileage, water, grass, hunting buffalo and antelope and warding off wolves; eloquent descriptions of mountain scenery; securing mining claims; a rugged life of enduring cold and wet weather and trying to make a living by mining and hunting; good description of life in early Denver and settling on a ranch.

CLOPPER, EDWARD NICHOLAS, 1840-1880   **3719**

AN AMERICAN FAMILY: ITS UPS AND DOWNS THROUGH EIGHT GENERATIONS. Huntington, W. Va.: Printed by Standard Printing & Publishing, 1950. 624 pp. Diary, pp. 501-507.

Jan-Nov 1859. Student activities and studies while attending Miami University at Oxford, Ohio.

CORMANY, SAMUEL E., 1838-1921   **3720**

In THE CORMANY DIARIES, edited by James C. Mohr and Richard E. Winslow, pp. 24-581 passim. Pittsburgh: University of Pittsburgh Press, 1982.

1859-1865. Diary begun while attending Otterbein College in Westerville, Ohio; starting a farm in Macon County, Missouri; marriage to Rachel Bowman and honeymoon trip to Niagara Falls and Ontario where they decided to settle among the Bowman family at Elmira and later at Carlisle Hill because of the political turmoil in Missouri; work as store clerk, singing master and seller of books on hydropathy and phrenology; notes on social life, religious activities as member of the United Brethren in Christ, spiritual concerns and happiness in his marriage; intimations of Rachel's desire to limit childbearing; explicit description of daughter's birth and hydropathic postpartum treatment of wife and child; return to the United States, stopping in New York City before leaving Rachel in Chambersburg, Pennsylvania, near his family, and joining the Sixteenth Pennsylvania Volunteer Cavalry; the excitement, hardships and temptations of soldiering with advancement from Company H clerk to commander of Company I and adjutant of the regiment; camp life, duties, illness and remedies, drinking in the army and remorse over his own indulgences, pleasures of visits home, interactions with Southerners and acquiring "souvenirs"; substantial, vivid descriptions of cavalry action; Chancellorsville and Gettysburg campaigns, noting Confederate acts against civilians in the North; Bristoe and Mine Run campaigns; Sheridan's Richmond and Trevilian raids; the siege of Petersburg; pursuing Lee's army to Appomattox; service in occupation force at Lynchburg, Virginia, until mustered out in August; a record pervaded by his evangelical faith and love for wife and child which, accompanied by Rachel's diary, forms a chronicle extraordinarily rich in the matters of everyday life and human concerns.

DAVIS, SYLVESTER, b. 1839?   **3721**

Walter, Paul A. F., ed. "Diary of Sylvester Davis." NEW MEXICO HISTORICAL REVIEW 6 (1931):383-416.

Apr-Oct 1859. Young man's Colorado gold rush journey from Iowa to Denver; information on provisions, prices, hunting, food, camps, route, etc.; Sunday observance to rest men and animals; mining in the Pikes Peak country; "Rules and Laws" drawn up to govern the Missouri Gulch Mining District, of which the diarist was secretary.

DOEDERLEIN, PAUL THEODOR KARL FERDINAND,   **3722**
1835-1915

Moldenhauer, Roger. "The Doederlein Diary." CONCORDIA HISTORICAL INSTITUTE QUARTERLY 51, no. 3 (1978):99-136.

May 1859-Feb 1860 (with gaps). Young German immigrant's diary of a Lutheran missionary expedition to the Crow Indians; brief stay at Dubuque, Iowa, upon arrival from Germany, and departure from Wartburg Seminary; route along Platte River Road; problems with sickness, oxen, supplies, etc.; diarist's extreme homesickness, discouragement and sense of being miscast as a missionary; encounters with Dakota Indians, but failure to meet the Crow; invaluable help of Upper Platte Indian agent Thomas

S. Twiss; Doederlein's agonized decision to return to Iowa and miserable horseback journey back; a stay at Fort Des Moines, where his preaching proved by his own admission, a "disaster." Translated from the German.

EDMONDS, AMANDA VIRGINIA, 1839-1921   3723

JOURNALS OF AMANDA VIRGINIA EDMONDS. Edited by Nancy C. Baird. Delaplane, Va.: N.C. Baird, 1984. 282 pp.

1859-1867. Journal kept sporadically at Belle Grove, near Paris, Virginia; death of father and sale of their slaves; report of John Brown's execution; the war in Fauquier County as troops of both armies passed through or occupied the area; conversing with enemy soldiers and accounts of their depredations; behavior of slaves; providing hospitality for Confederate soldiers and housing some of Mosby's men; civilian births and deaths and casualties among friends and acquaintances in the military; description of many weddings; the end of the Confederacy; her approval of Lincoln's assassination; social life after the war; notes on sermons and preachers, reading, dentistry, games, clothing, visits, visitors and celebration of Christmas, Valentine's Day and April Fool's Day; much discussion of various men to whom she was attracted.

"Helping Mosby's Men." In THE YEARS OF ANGUISH, compiled by Emily G. Ramey, pp. 73-77.

Feb-Mar 1864. Extracts describing Union raid on Belle Grove, which flushed out some of Mosby's men housed there, and recounting incident in which Mosby's horse was taken by escaping Union prisoner.

FAULKS, JAMES B., 1838-1920   3724

In THE CIVIL WAR DIARIES OF JAMES B. FAULKS AND THE PERSONAL DIARIES OF JOHN SUMMERFIELD COIT, by Henry L. Lambdin, pp. 1-42 passim. Madison, N.J.: The Commission on Archives and History, Northern New Jersey Annual Conference, The United Methodist Church, 1978.

1859-1864. Extracts from diary of Methodist minister from Newark, New Jersey, within biography which summarizes the diary's content; student days at the Methodist General Biblical Institute at Concord, New Hampshire; pastorates at Lempster, New Hampshire, and Millstone, New Jersey; notes on his reading, health and various trips; activities while serving as United States Christian Commission delegate in Maryland, Virginia, Alabama and Tennessee; notes on soldiers, refugees, Union troops' pillaging, Southerners' views, a plantation worked by freedmen and his friend James M. Buckley.

FONTAINE, WILLIAM WINSTON   3725

"Diary of Col. William Winston Fontaine." WILLIAM AND MARY COLLEGE QUARTERLY, 1st ser. 16 (1907-1908):157-161.

Feb 1859. Account of a visit to William and Mary College; meeting with former president Tyler and Tyler's account of his father's description of Patrick Henry's delivery of "Give Me Liberty" speech; attendance at a "dinner given to the alumni and invited guests of William and Mary by the fair and accomplished ladies of Williamsburg," with more anecdotes by the "bland and courteous" Tyler.

GANSEVOORT, CATHERINE   3726

Kenney, Alice P. "Kate Gansevoort's Grand Tour." NEW YORK HISTORY 47 (1966):343-356.

1859-1860. Article containing a few extracts from the extensive travel diary of an Albany debutante and Herman Melville's cousin, who completed her education by touring Europe with her family.

GASS, A.M.   3727

In OVERLAND ROUTES TO THE GOLD FIELDS, edited by LeRoy R. Hafen, pp. 218-231.

Apr-Jun 1859. Travel from Bonham, Texas, to a few miles from Pikes Peak and the gold diggings; good water and grass on route; abundance of buffalo, deer, turkeys, antelope, fish and turtles; annoyance of many mosquitoes; discouraging reports from gold seekers returning empty-handed from the mines.

GERRISH, BENJAMIN   3728

Baldwin, Carolyn W. "The Dawn of the Republican Party in New Hampshire." HISTORICAL NEW HAMPSHIRE 30 (1975):21-32.

Jan-Mar 1859. Extracts from storekeeper's diary; entertaining accounts of characters who regularly gathered around the stove in the rear of his Dover store to discuss politics, religion and local affairs; details of meeting place and conduct of both Republican and Democratic rallies and conventions; Lyceum speakers, ministers, local entertainments, traveling salesmen, biases and prejudices against increasing numbers of Irish immigrants, all receiving colorful treatment in the diary; mention of a number of local political figures.

HALL, SUSAN MITCHELL   3729

Harvey, Genevieve. "The Diary of a Trip from Ione to Nevada in 1859." CALIFORNIA HISTORICAL SOCIETY QUARTERLY 17 (1938):75-80.

Sep 1859. Pleasant carriage trip from Ione, California, to Nevada; through Sierra Nevada to Lake Tahoe, Carson City, Virginia City, etc.; visits to mines; great enjoyment of scenery and comfortable lodgings.

HASKELL, THALES HASTINGS, 1834-1909   3730

Brooks, Juanita, ed. "Journal of Thales L. Haskell." UTAH HISTORICAL QUARTERLY 12 (1944):69-98.

Oct 1859-Mar 1860. Diary kept by a participant in the second Mormon mission to the Hopi Indians of northern Arizona; details of journey from Utah, including ferrying the Colorado; life at the Oraibi village with notes on customs and ceremonies; learning the Hopi language and teaching them the "Deseret Alphabet"; frequent references to Jacob Hamblin, leader of the mission, fellow missionaries and settlers.

HUNT, ELLEN ELIZABETH KELLOGG, 1835-1880   3731

Hafen, LeRoy, ed. "Diary of Mrs. A.C. Hunt," COLORADO MAGAZINE 21 (1944):161-170.

Apr-Sep 1859 (with gaps). Monroe, Michigan, woman's account of the Pikes Peak gold rush on which she accompanied her husband, Alexander Cameron Hunt; difficulties of travel with two small children and contending with her own chronic illness; operating a boarding house, with "weary days of labor and pain"; the beginning of a trip home.

KENNICOTT, ROBERT, 1835-1866   3732

In TRANSACTIONS OF THE CHICAGO ACADEMY OF SCIENCES, vol. 1, pp. 146-214. Chicago, 1869.

In THE FIRST SCIENTIFIC EXPLORATION OF RUSSIAN AMERICA AND THE PURCHASE OF ALASKA, by James Alton James, pp. 46-135. Northwestern University Studies in the Social Sciences, no. 4. Evanston and Chicago: Northwestern University, 1942.

1859-1862. Naturalist's journal of a scientific expedition sponsored by the Smithsonian Institution and Audubon Club of Chicago; from Fort William to Lake Winnepeg by canoe; details of construction and maneuvering of canoes by Iroquois voyageurs; negotiating rapids and portages on Winnipeg, Clearwater, Elk and MacKenzie rivers; travel by snowshoe and dogsled; the hospitality of Hudson's Bay posts, Norway House, where he met Governor Simpson, forts Alexander, Simpson, Resolution and Yukon and mission of the English Church Missionary Society; regular notation of camp management, geography, plant and animal life, insects and birds; customs of Yellow Knife and Yukon Indians.

KINGMAN, ROMANZO S.   3733

Millsap, Kenneth F., ed. "Romanzo Kingman's Pike's Peak Journal." IOWA JOURNAL OF HISTORY 48 (1950):55-85.

Mar-Jul 1859. Colorado gold rush journey from Sparta, Wisconsin, to the vicinity of Central City; route, conditions of travel and distances; brief stay at the diggings, with quick decision to sell his claim and return home.

MANWARING, JOSHUA, d. 1903   3734

Warner, Robert M. "Journal of a Fifty-Niner." COLORADO MAGAZINE 36 (1959):161-173.

Jun-Sep 1859. Extracts from the Colorado gold rush journal of a lumberman from Lapeer County, Michigan; route, distances, etc.; a prospecting tour in Colorado with John Morey as guide; sickness with "bilious fever"; trying his luck with a claim and at various diggings; return to Michigan.

MURAGAKI, NORIMASA, 1813-1880   3735

In THE FIRST JAPANESE EMBASSY TO THE UNITED STATES OF AMERICA, by America-Japan Society, pp. 1-312. Tokyo: America-Japan Society, 1920. Reprint. 1977.

KOKAI NIKKI: THE DIARY OF THE FIRST JAPANESE EMBASSY TO THE UNITED STATES OF AMERICA. Tokyo: Foreign Affairs Association of Japan, 1958. 209 pp. Diary, pp. 1-181.

"Kokai Nikki: The Diary of the First Japanese Envoy to the United States of America." CONTEMPORARY JAPAN 22 (1953-1954):288-319, 502-532, 679-705; 23 (1954-1955):147-188, 342-391.

1859-1860. Voyage from Japan to San Francisco on the POWHATAN with a Japanese delegation escorted by Commodore Josiah Tattnall; detailed notes on ship travel; consular activities in San Francisco characterized by long speeches and champagne bottles opened "like a volly of pistol shots"; to Panama on the POWHATAN, then overland to the ROANOKE for remainder of

the voyage to Washington, D.C., where delegation received a clamorous public welcome; opening the Japanese embassy and enduring a whirlwind of receptions, balls and interviews; meetings with Secretary of State Lewis Cass and President Buchanan described in detail, with great attention to the etiquette of the occasions; his difficulties in adjusting to American customs and food; train travel to Baltimore, Philadelphia and New York, where the "Japanese Treaty Box" was displayed in an elaborate procession; references to his escort Capt. Samuel Francis Du Pont; on the NIAGARA for the return to Japan, with a lengthy account of the voyage.

PALMER, ALONZO BENJAMIN, 1815-1887   3736

In MEMORIAL OF ALONZO BENJAMIN PALMER, by Love M.R. Palmer, pp. 21-126. Cambridge, Mass.: Printed at the Riverside Press, 1890.

Apr-Oct 1859. Physician's diary of a trip to England and Scotland, visiting hospitals and attending lectures; tourist notes on monuments, galleries, etc.; some social views.

PATTERSON, E.H.N., 1829-1880   3737

In OVERLAND ROUTES TO THE GOLD FIELDS, edited by LeRoy R. Hafen, pp. 65-197.

Mar-Jun 1859. Journalist's full account, written for OHIO SPECTATOR, of travel from Oquawka, Illinois, to the Pikes Peak gold fields and Boulder City, Colorado, via the Platte River route; notes of scenery, animals, camping and first gold panning; brief descriptions of various mining localities.

PEASE, EDWIN R.   3738

In OVERLAND ROUTES TO THE GOLD FIELDS, edited by LeRoy R. Hafen, pp. 203-213.

Apr-May 1859. Teacher's travel diary from northeast Illinois to St. Joseph and on to Fort Kearny, never reaching goal of Pikes Peak gold fields; conditions of prairie travel.

POST, CHARLES C., 1831-1906   3739

In OVERLAND ROUTES TO THE GOLD FIELDS, edited by LeRoy R. Hafen, pp. 19-55.

May-Jun 1859. Lawyer's travel diary of conditions, sights, distances and difficulties from Decatur, Illinois, via Missouri riverboat and through Kansas to Denver and Pikes Peak diggings; description of a wind-powered wagon on trail.

PUTNAM, THEODORE L.   3740

Miller, Ernest C., ed. "Down the Rivers: A Rafting Journal of 1859." WESTERN PENNSYLVANIA HISTORICAL MAGAZINE 40 (1957):149-162.

Mar-Apr 1859. Journey from Warren, Pennsylvania, to Louisville, Kentucky, as a worker on the largest lumber raft ever to go down the Allegheny and Ohio rivers; problems with the rivers, snags, winds, etc., and diarist's regret that "I ever started from home on this trip"; comments on steamboats they passed.

RANKIN, ALEXANDER TAYLOR, 1803-1885   3741

ALEXANDER TAYLOR RANKIN, 1803-1885, HIS DIARY AND LET-

TERS. Edited by Nolie Mumey. Boulder, Colo.: Johnson, 1966. 188 pp.

1859-1861. Western missionary sojourn of a Presbyterian minister from Buffalo, New York; visiting settlers, preaching and establishing churches in eastern Kansas; by stagecoach to Denver with similar work there during lawless Jefferson Territory period; preaching to receptive and growing congregations and founding of the First Presbyterian Church of Denver; religious work in mining camps; notes on settlers, gold-seekers, Indians and outlaws; sorrow over many deaths, including "the murderer and the murdered lying side by side"; efforts to comfort and convert young murderer James A. Gordon before hanging; brief notes of journey home to Buffalo, thence to Baltimore, where he preached in many churches.

RAVENEL, HENRY WILLIAM, 1814-1887   3742

THE PRIVATE JOURNAL OF HENRY WILLIAM RAVENEL. Edited by Arney R. Childs. Columbia: University of South Carolina Press, 1947. 428 pp.

1859-1887. Extracts from diary kept by internationally known botanist at Hampton Hill, his plantation near Aiken, South Carolina, and at Pooshee, his father's plantation in Berkeley County; a prewar trip to New York City, attending a church service for the deaf conducted by Thomas Gallaudet; war news, especially events at Charleston; prices and shortages; weighing the merits of executing the Andersonville prisoners to protect the civilian population; depredations committed by the Twenty-first Colored Troops at Pooshee and pillaging of Hampton Hill by confederate soldiers; approval of murdering black agitators in order to control the freedmen; pondering taking the oath of allegiance; establishing new labor arrangements with former slaves; reestablishing contact with Northern scientific colleagues; his reduced financial circumstances and multitudinous efforts to make a living; a scientific expedition to investigate cattle disease in Texas; the effects of Reconstruction policies on blacks and whites; concern for his father, Henry Ravenel, and other family members; much meditation on secession, slavery, the Confederacy's defeat, emancipation and black suffrage, all reconciled according to his firm religious beliefs; notes on brief trips, illnesses and remedies, his hearing loss and celebrations of Christmas and the Fourth of July, etc.; substantial entries covering his scientific pursuits, plantation matters and the historical events which drastically altered a way of life.

Extracts in THE BLUE AND THE GRAY, edited by Henry S. Commager, vol. 1, pp. 60-61, 519.

Apr-May 1861. Exposition of secessionist position and his expectation of foreign intervention on behalf of the Confederacy.

RAYNOLDS, WILLIAM FRANKLIN, 1820-1894   3743

McLaird, James D. and Turchen, Lesta V. "Exploring the Black Hills, 1855-1875: The Explorations of Captain William Franklin Raynolds." SOUTH DAKOTA HISTORY 4 (1973):18-62.

1859-1860. Extracts, within article, from the official reports and unpublished field journals of the commander of an expedition to the Black Hills; entries relating to his delivery of overdue goods promised to the Sioux as a condition of peace and to camps, distances, terrain and exploration details.

In EXPLORING THE NORTHERN PLAINS, edited by Lloyd McFarling, pp. 243-263.

Jul-Aug 1859. Extracts covering expedition along the Powder River to the Yellowstone with Jim Bridger as guide; route, terrain and topographical details; buffalo hunting; notes on Crow Indians and their customs; the effective oratory of Chief Red Bear.

In REPORT ON THE EXPLORATION OF THE YELLOWSTONE RIVER, by United States Army Corps of Engineers, pp. 18-127. 40th Cong., 2d sess., 1868, S. Exec. Doc. 77. Washington, D.C.: Government Printing Office, 1868.

Jun-Oct 1860. Exploration of area drained by upper Missouri and Yellowstone rivers; descriptions of the rivers, their tributaries, navigable streams, possible wagon and rail routes, mineral products and agricultural prospects; notes on Dakota and Crow Indians.

RICHARDSON, ALBERT D.   3744

In OVERLAND ROUTES TO THE GOLD FIELDS, edited by LeRoy R. Hafen, pp. 240-262.

May-Jun 1859. Journalist's travel diary to the Colorado gold fields from Leavenworth via the Leavenworth and Pikes Peak Express route; passing hundreds of wagons stalled in mud; St. Marys Catholic mission; joined by Horace Greeley at Manhattan; mention of vast buffalo herds; service at stage stations for overnight stops; Indians and emigrants passed on road.

SALISBURY, WILLIAM W.   3745

Lindsey, David, ed. "The Journal of an 1859 Pike's Peak Gold Seeker." KANSAS HISTORICAL QUARTERLY 22 (1956):321-341.

Apr-Sep 1859. Colorado gold rush journey of a young Cleveland man; brief notes of camps, route, weather and conditions of travel; life and work of a prospector and miner; the return journey as far as Kansas.

SEARS, MARY E., 1838-1863   3746

Jones, Daryl E. and Pickering, James H., eds. "A Young Woman in the Midwest." OHIO HISTORY 82 (1973):215-234.

1859-1860. Extracts from the diary of a young Greenwich, Massachusetts, woman struggling to support herself as a teacher in Rochester, Ohio, with a crowded classroom of "trying" students; some satisfaction in religious consolation and family life with her sister and brother-in-law, Carrie and Oscar Clark; a visit to Columbus, with sightseeing and social life; hearing the Spiritualist lecturer Emma Hardinge Britten; move to Amboy, Illinois, to live with other relatives, but enjoyment of church, social and family life there impaired by her ill health; a heartrending description of the death of her sister Eliza Powers and her husband shortly after, leaving their baby in diarist's care; a visit to friends at Pana, Illinois, where she was offended by dirty and primitive conditions; a sad diary of a young woman burdened with worries and work beyond her strength.

SMITH, ELIAS, 1804-1888   3747

Mortensen, A.R., ed. "Elias Smith: Journal of a Pioneer Editor." UTAH HISTORICAL QUARTERLY 29 (1953):1-24, 137-168, 237-266, 331-360.

1859-1863. Long extract from the journal of prominent Mormon judge and editor of the DESERET NEWS; notes on trials and cases in his own and other courts, including murder, theft, grave robbing and a surprising number of divorces; local events and people, especially Brigham Young, Governor Cumming and the unpopular judge John Cradlebaugh; news dispatches arriving by Pony Express and the Eastern Mail; a record of a busy man juggling newspaper and judicial duties, as well as church activities and responsibilities of a large polygamous family; distress over growing awareness of Brigham Young's dissatisfaction with his work, leading to dismissal from the paper.

SNOW, TAYLOR N., d. 1859?   **3748**

Hays, Arthur H. "Diary of Taylor N. Snow, Hoosier Fifty-Niner." INDIANA MAGAZINE OF HISTORY 28 (1932):193-208.

May-Aug 1859. Overland journey from Des Moines with the Kiplinger party; enjoyment of music and dancing in camp; burying dead and rescuing wounded after Indian attack on another wagon train; the hanging of a seventeen-year-boy for murder; a Fourth of July celebration with two hundred people, a brass band and "toast drinkers."

SPAIN, DAVID F.   **3749**

Morrison, John D., ed. "The Diary of David F. Spain: Gregory's Grubstakes at the Diggings." COLORADO MAGAZINE 35 (1958):11-34.

Mar-Jul 1859. Colorado gold rush diary of a young man from South Bend, Indiana; difficulty crossing the infamous Skunk Bottoms in Iowa; discouraging news en route from people returning; hard but fairly profitable work at Gregory's diggings; a visit from Horace Greeley; return to Indiana.

STEELE, EDWARD DUNSHA, 1829-1865   **3750**

"In the Pikes Peak Gold Rush of 1859." COLORADO MAGAZINE 29 (1952):299-309.

May-Aug 1859. Journey from Arena, Wisconsin, with Samuel F. and John Steele, Charles and Solomon Hatch and others; route, camps and conditions of travel; discouraging reports from many returning from Colorado convinced that "Pikes Peak gold is a humbug"; taking a claim at Gold Hill.

SUCKLEY, GEORGE, d. 1869   **3751**

Beidleman, Richard G., ed. "The 1859 Overland Journal of Naturalist George Suckley." ANNALS OF WYOMING 28 (1956):68-79.

Jun-Aug 1859. Nature observations of an army surgeon accompanying recruits from Fort Leavenworth to Utah; collecting specimens for Spencer F. Baird of the Smithsonian; notes on wildlife, especially birds, and vegetation; list of birds, eggs and nests appended.

THIBODO, AUGUSTUS J., b. 1834?   **3752**

Brode, Howard S., ed. "Diary of Dr. Augustus J. Thibodo of the Northwest Exploring Expedition." PACIFIC NORTHWEST QUARTERLY 31 (1940):287-347.

Jun 1859-Feb 1860. Diary of adventurous Canadian-born doctor on an expedition under W.H. Noble to locate a road from St. Paul to Walla Walla via Canada; route, distances and camps; extreme problems with roads, weather, fording of rivers, accidents, thirst, etc.; notes on other members of the party, including Charles L. Anderson, who was collecting minerals for the Smithsonian, and

on Indians; an amazingly detailed diary kept under adverse circumstances.

TRAVER, MILES E.   **3753**

Boney, F.N., ed. "Southern Sojourn: A Yankee Salesman in Ante-Bellum Alabama." ALABAMA REVIEW 20 (1967):142-154.

1859-1861 (with gaps). Diary of a young traveling salesman from Minnesota selling lightning rods in Alabama; by wagon through small towns, with notes on roads, difficulties, people, sales or lack thereof, curiosities, a circus, etc.; lodgings in homes; interesting notes on people along the way.

Jan 1868. In port in Savannah during a business trip from California to New York by ship; a brief but good picture of the economic and social difficulties of the postbellum city.

TUTTLE, CHARLES M., d. 1906   **3754**

"California Diary of Charles M. Tuttle." WISCONSIN MAGAZINE OF HISTORY 15 (1931-1932):69-85, 219-233.

Apr-Aug 1859. Rock County farmer's journey to Salt Lake City; thence to California by the risky southern route of James H. Simpson, who recommended it to the Tuttle party; camps, route and distances, with diary ending at Neill Creek; a lecture by Horace Greeley at Fort Laramie.

VESSEY, JOHN HENRY, 1827-1887   **3755**

MR. VESSEY OF ENGLAND, BEING THE INCIDENTS AND REMINISCENCES OF TRAVEL IN A TWELVE-WEEKS TOUR THROUGH THE UNITED STATES AND CANADA. Edited by Brian Waters. New York: G.P. Putnam's Sons, 1956. 184 pp.

Mar-May 1859. Travel diary of a young Tory landowner; Atlantic crossing on the PERSIA; agricultural notes; meeting with President Buchanan; manners and mores of Americans; extensive travels in the South for firsthand observation of slavery, of which he formed a rather favorable opinion; slave auctions, including catalog of a sale in Savannah of slaves belonging to the Pierce Butler plantation; experiences in Chicago, Detroit and New York; notes on train travel and hotels.

WILLARD, FRANCES ELIZABETH, 1839-1898   **3756**

GLIMPSES OF FIFTY YEARS: THE AUTOBIOGRAPHY OF AN AMERICAN WOMAN. Introduction by Hannah Whitall Smith. Chicago: Woman's Temperance Publication Association, 1889. 698 pp. passim.

MY HAPPY HALF-CENTURY: THE AUTOBIOGRAPHY OF AN AMERICAN WOMAN. Edited by Frances E. Cook. London: Ward, Lock & Bowden, 1894. 392 pp. passim.

1859-1870. Autobiography, containing diary extracts of the founder of the Women's Christian Temperance Union; school days and years of teaching, including presidency of Evanston College for Ladies; death of her sister; reading; trip to Europe and Middle East; beginnings of her concern for women's suffrage and temperance; religious introspections.

WILLING, GEORGE M.   **3757**

Bieber, Ralph P., ed. "Diary of a Journey to the Pike's Peak Gold Mines in 1859." MISSISSIPPI VALLEY HISTORICAL REVIEW 14 (1927-1928):360-378.

May-Jun 1859. St. Louis doctor's letter-diary to his wife describing a journey to the Colorado gold rush via the Santa Fe Trail to Bent's Fort and Pueblo, where he continued on the Cherokee Trail to the Goose Pasture diggings; concern en route for hardships of men, women and unshod oxen; good descriptions of country, people and mining, with occasional wry humor.

YOUNG, JOHN EDWARD, 1824-1904 3758

"An Illinois Farmer during the Civil War." ILLINOIS STATE HISTORICAL SOCIETY JOURNAL 26 (1933):70-135.

1859-1865. Extracts from diary of a Republican farmer in Menard County near Athens; discussion of weather, crops and livestock; prices, business transactions and general economic conditions; commencement exercises at North Sangamon Academy and other local festivities; detailed descriptions of Republican rallies for Lincoln at Athens and Springfield; war news, support for volunteers and the Union cause and celebration of Fourth of July; journey to be with sick soldier and remarks on Louisville, slavery, war's impact on Kentucky and Tennessee, Nashville sights, including Mount Olivet Cemetery, and the Illinois countryside; trip to the 106th Illinois Infantry at Pine Bluff, Arkansas, to visit county men in Company K with notes on hardships of travel and various places along the way, including Cairo, Memphis and Little Rock; reaction to Lincoln's assassination and funeral in Springfield; a splendid account.

1860

ANON. 3759

Schmandt, Raymond H. and Schulte, Josephine H., eds. "Spring Hill College Diary." ALABAMA REVIEW 15 (1962):213-226.

1860-1865. Extracts from official diary, supposedly kept by the vice president of the college, at that time a boarding school offering courses at the secondary and college levels; effects of the war on the Catholic institution, a few miles west of Mobile, Alabama; brief entries detailing enrollment fluctuations, discipline problems, efforts to prevent conscription of lay brothers, arrival of Union soldiers, etc.; war news; names of students who came and went.

ANON. 3760

In FAMOUS ADVENTURES AND PRISON ESCAPES OF THE CIVIL WAR, pp. 1-82. New York: Century, 1893, 1898, 1915. London: T.F. Unwin, 1894.

1860-1863. Sporadic diary entries of Louisiana unionist; the passions of the first months of secession and war in New Orleans; marriage and her new home in Arkansas; flooded out by the rising Mississippi; difficult journey, to Chickasaw Bayou by way of Steele's Bayou and the Yazoo River, eased by hospitality along the way; the turbulence of wartime Jackson, Mississippi; in Vicksburg to avoid husband's conscription; shortages and the pitiful condition of Confederate soldiers; seeking shelter in caves, cellars and churches from the constant shelling; notes on slavery, form and content of Vicksburg's DAILY CITIZEN and illiteracy of Southern soldiers; criticism of Pemberton; arrival of Union fleet and troops; death of her newborn baby.

In CIVIL WAR EYEWITNESS REPORTS, edited by Harold E. Straubing, pp. 181-202.

Cable, George W., ed. "A Woman's Diary of the Siege of Vicksburg under Fire from the Gunboats." CENTURY ILLUSTRATED MAGAZINE 8 (1885):767-775.

Jan-Jul 1863. Extracts.

Extracts in THE BLUE AND THE GRAY, edited by Henry S. Commager, vol. 2, pp. 662-668; TRAGIC YEARS, by Paul M. Angle and Earl S. Miers, vol. 2, pp. 618-621.

ANON. 3761

"The Diary of a Public Man." NORTH AMERICAN REVIEW 129 (1879): 125-140, 259-273, 375-388, 484-496.

THE DIARY OF A PUBLIC MAN. Prefatory notes by F. Lauriston Bullard. Chicago: Privately printed for the Abraham Lincoln Book Shop, 1945. 117 pp. Diary, pp. 29-110. New Brunswick, N.J.: Rutgers University Press, 1946, 1980.

In THE MYSTERY OF "A PUBLIC MAN," by Frank Maloy Anderson, pp. 189-249. Minneapolis: University of Minnesota Press, 1948.

Dec 1860-Mar 1861. Diary extracts recording conversations with and opinions about major political figures in the secession crisis, including Lincoln, Douglas, Buchanan, Seward, Stanton and the Blairs; discussion of the Fort Sumter situation with James L. Orr and Judah P. Benjamin, with reports on developments at Montgomery and Major Anderson's loyalty; notes on secession's effects on business; the issue of Lincoln's cabinet and Charles Sumner's opposition to the inclusion of Simon Cameron; dismay at Lincoln's surreptitious entry into Washington; description of the inauguration ceremonies, the inaugural ball and Mrs. Lincoln; various assessments of the new president; attributed to Sam Ward, a prominent New Yorker of many talents.

Extracts in THE BLUE AND THE GRAY, edited by Henry S. Commager, vol. 1, pp. 15-16.

Mar 1861. Lincoln's inauguration.

ANON. 3762

Schultz, Charles R., ed. "New Orleans in December 1860." LOUISIANA HISTORY 9 (1968):53-61.

Dec 1860-Jan 1861. Extracts from journal of consumptive seventeen-year-old son of an owner of the WESTON MERRIT, on board in hopes that a sea voyage would restore his health; description of the Mississippi River and its delta and the sights of New Orleans, with notes on increasing secession sentiment.

ADAMS, CHARLES FRANCIS, 1835-1915 3763

Blegen, Theodore C. "Minnesota as Seen by Travelers: Campaigning with Seward in 1860." MINNESOTA HISTORY 8 (1927):150-171. Diary, pp. 165-171.

Extracts in DIARY OF AMERICA, edited by Josef and Dorothy Berger, pp. 485-487.

Sep 1860. Extracts describing William H. Seward's campaign for Lincoln in Minnesota; travel with a large party which included his father, Charles Francis Adams; interesting sketches of members of the party, especially the eccentric judge, Aaron Goodrich; by Mississippi steamboat MILWAUKEE to St. Paul, which impressed diarist with its prospects for development; Seward's political activities; return on the ALHAMBRA.

ANTHONY, WEBSTER D., b. 1838   3764

"Journal of a Trip from Denver to Oro City in 1860." COLORADO MAGAZINE 11 (1934):228-237.

Jul 1860. Wagon journey from Denver freighting goods to Oro City, now Leadville, over primitive and dangerous mountain roads; appreciation of scenery, which often inspired him to poetry; notes on mining towns and diggings.

BANCROFT, ALBERT LITTLE, b. 1841   3765

Wagner, Henry R., ed. "Albert Little Bancroft: His Diaries, Account Books, Card String of Events, and Other Papers." CALIFORNIA HISTORICAL SOCIETY QUARTERLY 29 (1950):97-128, 217-227, 357-367. Diary, pp. 97-128.

1860-1862. Brief, often amusing, entries of the younger brother of Hubert H. Bancroft, bookkeeper and man-of-all-work in his brother's publishing and book business in San Francisco; family and social life in the Bancroft household; business details including ship arrivals and delays crucial to profits; Presbyterian church activities, with many references to the Rev. William A. Scott; attending concerts and lectures; an interesting picture of the work and fortunes of the Bancroft book empire and of a lively young man chafing under a boring job and straightlaced domesticity.

BARRY, JAMES BUCKNER, 1821-1906   3766

Greer, James K., ed. "The Diary of James Buckner Barry." SOUTHWESTERN HISTORICAL QUARTERLY 36 (1932):144-162.

1860-1862 (with gaps). Portion of diary kept by Texas pioneer who settled in Bosque County, farming and raising stock; notes on work, hunting, slaves, religious activities, visitors, crimes and punishments; authorized to raise a company to patrol frontier against Indian attacks and depredations; assisting in the takeover of United States military posts in Texas; mustered into Confederate service, again patrolling the frontier.

BOND, J. HARMAN   3767

Moehlman, Arthur H., ed. "A Journey to the Forks of the Red River of the North." NORTH DAKOTA HISTORICAL QUARTERLY 6 (1932):231-238.

Jul 1860. Diary of a journey taken for the Hudson's Bay Company by an ensign with the Royal Canadian Rifles; by train from Kingston, Ontario, to Prairie de Chien, Wisconsin, then by river steamer SUCKER STATE to St. Paul and by stagecoach, wagon and riverboat ANSON NORTHRUP to Fort Garry; notes on route, countryside, settlements, etc.; a good picture of difficulties and varieties of transportation of the time.

BREWER, WILLIAM HENRY, 1828-1910   3768

UP AND DOWN CALIFORNIA IN 1860-64. Edited by Francis Farquhar. New Haven: Yale University Press, 1930. 601 pp. 2d ed. Berkeley: University of California Press, 1949. 3d ed., 1966.

1860-1864. Letter-diaries kept while Brewer was plant specialist with the California State Geological Survey and affording a panoramic view of post-gold rush California; voyage to San Fran-

cisco via Panama on the NORTH STAR; stagecoach travel within the state; excellent notes on vegetation, wildlife, geology, fossils, mines and mining methods, the climbing of Mount Shasta and other mountains, Indian life and the sad condition of gold rush die-hards; many references to his colleagues Josiah Whitney, Charles F. Hoffman, Clarence King and James T. Gardiner; appointment as professor of agriculture at Yale.

Extracts in DIARY OF AMERICA, edited by Josef and Dorothy Berger, pp. 372-380.

1862-1864. Extracts describing conditions of several former and present major mining areas.

BROWN, BENJAMIN, b. 1831   3769

THE DIARY OF BEN BROWN. Supplement to History of Union County, no. 7. Union County, Oregon: Union County Historical Society, n.d. Diary, pp. 1-27.

1860-1862. English immigrant's journey from Michigan to Oregon; homesteading and freight hauling in the Grande Ronde area; local people and events in Union County, including trial of Henry Leasy for maltreatment and neglect of his family.

BURGES, SAMUEL EDWARD, 1832-1916   3770

Chadwick, Thomas W., ed. "The Diary of Samuel Edward Burges." South Carolina Historical and Genealogical Magazine 48 (1947):63-75, 141-163, 206-218.

1860-1862 (with gaps). Diary of Charlestonian, a traveling collector for the CHARLESTON MERCURY; business trips around the state, recording modes of travel, distances covered, traveling companions, sights and events; activities at his farm near Cheraw; service with the Moultrie Guards in Charleston and vicinity, observing Fort Sumter's fall from Sullivan's Island; notes on horse races at Pineville, capture of runaway slave and December 1861 Charleston fire.

BURTON, RICHARD FRANCIS, 1821-1890   3771

THE CITY OF THE SAINTS, AND ACROSS THE ROCKY MOUNTAINS TO CALIFORNIA. London: Longman, Green, Longman, and Roberts, 1861. 707 pp. Reprint. New York: Harper & Brothers, 1862. 574 pp.; Edited by Fawn M. Brodie. New York: Alfred A. Knopf, 1963. 654 pp. Diary, pp. 16-103, 145-223.

Aug-Oct 1860. Travel diary of renowned English author and adventurer; dated but narrative entries covering journey from St. Joseph, Missouri, by mail coach; extensive descriptions and comments on people and places, particularly Utah and the Mormons.

THE LOOK OF THE WEST, 1860: ACROSS THE PLAINS TO CALIFORNIA. Foreword by Robert G. Athearn. Lincoln: University of Nebraska Press, 1963. 333 pp.

Aug-Oct 1860. Extract containing much of the original travel but omitting portions which Burton devoted to description of Utah and Mormonism.

In AMONG THE MORMONS: HISTORIC ACCOUNTS BY CONTEMPORARY OBSERVERS, edited by William M. and A. Russell Mortensen, pp. 328-333. New York: Alfred A. Knopf, 1958. Reprint. Lincoln: University of Nebraska Press, 1973.

Aug-Sep 1860. Extracts describing Salt Lake City.

"City of the Saints." NEVADA HISTORICAL SOCIETY QUARTERLY 3, no. 2 (1960):7-35.

Oct 1860. Extracts relating to Burton's description of the Overland Mail and rival Pony Express stations in Utah and Nevada; detailed notes on route, life and dangers of Pony Express riders; comments on Mormons, Indians, stagecoach travel and such colorful stations as Butte Station at Robber's Roost Ridge.

CAMP, WILLIAM JOSEPH 3772

Snell, William R., ed. "From Tennessee to Texas through Alabama." ALABAMA HISTORICAL QUARTERLY 44 (1982):92-108.

Sep-Nov 1860. A youth's record of an emigrant journey of a group of families from Bradley County, Tennessee, to resettle in Grayson County, Texas; articulate notes of route, camps, roads, towns, incidents of travel, scenes and people encountered.

CAMPBELL, ZOE J., 1841?-1866 3773

Doyle, Elizabeth J., ed. "Zoé Campbell: A Southern Lady Travels North." LOUISIANA STUDIES 13 (1974):313-344.

July-Oct 1860. New Orleans woman on luxurious tour with her uncle Samuel Jarvis Peters and family, with whom she lived, to New York; visiting Niagara Falls with notes on hotels, food and tourist attractions such as tightrope walkers Blondin and Farini; by train and riverboat ISAAC NEWTON, "a floating paradise," to New York City; shopping, sightseeing, visiting and meeting other New Orleans tourists; notes on all churches and priests where they attended mass.

CISNE, JONAH GIRARD, 1834-1877 3774

"Across the Plains and in Nevada City." COLORADO MAGAZINE 27 (1950):49-57.

1860-1863 (with gaps). Zenia, Illinois, farmer's Colorado gold rush notes; route, expenses, purchase and sale of claims.

CLARK, GEORGE T., 1837-1888 3775

"Across the Plains and in Denver, 1860: Portion of the Diary of George T. Clark." COLORADO MAGAZINE 6 (1929):131-140.

May-Jun 1860. Diary segment covering journey from Iowa to the Pikes Peak area; a few notes on the gold diggings and life in Denver; a hanging for murder with "a great crowd and a good many ladies present."

CLARK, HELEN E. 3776

In TWO DIARIES, by Calvin P. Clark, pp. 1-44. Denver: Denver Public Library, 1962.

Apr-Jun 1860. Young woman's diary of overland journey from Plano, Illinois, to Denver via Platte River route; astonished comments on an Indian woman laughing at her bloomer costume; descriptive notes on towns and villages; music and dancing at evening camps; sad separation of company at Fort Kearny for California or Denver; many instances of Indians begging food, wanting to trade or wanting to buy her! joy of joining her father and brother in Denver on a ranch and immediately setting about cleaning and making a home.

COWELL, EMILIE MARGUERITE EBSWORTH, b. 1818 3777

THE COWELLS IN AMERICA. Edited by M. Willson Disher. London: Oxford University Press, H. Milford, 1934. 426 pp.

1860-1861. Private diary of the wife of Sam Cowell, English "king of comic song," kept during a profitless concert tour in the United States and Canada; references to many actors, actresses, agents, vaudeville performers, plays, operas and songs with some extended criticism; travel to, theaters in and box office receipts in major cities including New York, Boston, Portland, Worcester, Baltimore, Atlanta, New Orleans, Philadelphia, Pittsburgh, St. Louis, Montreal and Toronto; frequent pawning of watches and jewelry to pay bills; her husband's illness and excessive drinking; observations on many aspects of American life including manners, overheated homes, hotels and saloons; New York celebrations and parades on Fourth of July and St. Patrick's Day; opinions on slavery, election and inauguration of Lincoln, onset of the Civil War; an optimistic diary, despite their financial straits, and a valuable source on theater history.

CRARY, JERRY, 1842-1936 3778

JERRY CRARY, 1842-1936: TEACHER, SOLDIER, INDUSTRIALIST. Warren, Pa.: Newell Press, 1960. 142 pp. Diary, pp. 19-62.

1860-1865 (with gap). Brief entries covering activities while teaching in Angola, Indiana, and then serving as sergeant with Company H. 143d Regiment, New York Volunteers, in Virginia, Tennessee and Georgia; camp life, food and prices, duties, foraging, correspondence and a Christmas celebration; battles of Lookout Mountain and Missionary Ridge; conditions and treatment at hospitals in Nashville and Jeffersonville, Indiana, after being wounded at battle of Resaca.

CURD, SAM, 1835?-1919 3779

SAM CURD'S DIARY. Edited by Susan S. Arpad. Athens: Ohio University Press, 1984. 172 pp. Diary, pp. 43-151.

1860-1863 (with gap). Diary covering woman's life from marriage to the death of her husband, Thomas, a well-to-do merchant; retrospective account of wedding trip through Northern states mentioning the sights of Philadelphia, New York City and Niagara Falls, including cemeteries; settling down in Fulton, Missouri; trip home to Richmond, Virginia, against the background of secession and war preparations; return to Fulton and the tensions of the border state situation for a Southern sympathizer; birth of daughter and child's subsequent development; notes on local events, weather, church activities, family and friends, visits and visitors, health of diarist and others, domestic tasks, etc.; homesickness and religious reflections; an interesting record of ordinary middle-class female concerns and experiences.

EDMONDSTON, CATHERINE ANN DEVEREAUX, 3780
1823-1875

"JOURNAL OF A SECESH LADY." Edited by Beth G. Crabtree and James W. Patton. Raleigh, N.C.: Division of Archives and History, Department of Cultural Resources, 1979. 850 pp.

1860-1866. Diary kept by mistress of Looking Glass, on the Roanoke River, and Hascosea, a summer home, both in Halifax County, North Carolina; sporadic but generally substantial entries focusing on war news, with her partisan commentary on events, but also concerning plantation management and war's effect on diarist and the extended Devereaux and Edmondston families; details of domestic tasks and her garden, especially fruit trees and dahlias; reflections on her relationship with her husband, Patrick Muir Edmondston, and her childless state; ardent support of the Confederate cause except for impressment; prices, shortages and improvisations; defense of slavery and stories told to illustrate the nature of blacks; anecdotes about Lincoln; selections from her poetry; thoughts on diary-keeping; reports of enemy depredations and outrages; the behavior and departure of former slaves and the financial impact of defeat; views on secession, Union and Confederate leaders, emancipation and the Freedmen's Bureau; notes on medical treatments, war work, refugees and visits to Richmond, Raleigh and her father's nearby plantation, Conneconara; a forthright and engrossing record of both everyday duties and pleasures and the passions and excitements of war.

JOURNAL, 1860-1866. Edited by Margaret Mackay Jones. N.p., 1954. 111 pp.

1860-1865. Extracts.

In TRUE TALES OF THE SOUTH AT WAR, edited by Clarence H. Poe, pp. 101-140.

1860-1865. Extracts.

FEILNER, JOHN   **3781**

"Exploration in Upper California in 1860." SMITHSONIAN INSTITUTION ANNUAL REPORT (1864):421-430. Diary, pp. 421-424.

May 1860. Dragoon's journal and report of expedition sponsored by the Smithsonian to collect birds, eggs and nests near Rhett and Klamath lakes; traveling and camping in rough country with his assistant Alexander Guise; help from various Indians but an attack by others, during which many of his specimens were lost.

FERRIS, ANNA M., 1815-1890   **3782**

Hancock, Harold B., ed. "The Civil War Diaries of Anna M. Ferris." DELAWARE HISTORY 9 (1961):221-264.

1860-1865. Extracts from Wilmington Quaker's diary giving her Republican, abolitionist reactions to political and military events of the war, including the presidential elections of 1860 and 1864, major battles, McClellan's removal from command and the Emancipation Proclamation; notes on Southern sympathizers in Baltimore, visits to Philadelphia and its Sanitary Commission fair, celebrating the fall of Vicksburg in Wilmington, Frederick Douglass, British antislavery orator George Thompson, black soldiers, Lincoln's assassination and the funeral procession through Philadelphia; religious reflections and differing Quaker views on the war.

FIELDS, ANNIE ADAMS, 1834-1915   **3783**

In MEMORIES OF A HOSTESS, by Mark A. de Wolfe Howe, pp. 1-312 passim. Boston: Atlantic Monthly Press, 1922.

1860-1876 (with gaps). Extracts arranged in topical order from the journal of the prominent Boston hostess and wife of publisher James T. Fields; personal impressions from her "journal of literary events and glimpses of interesting people" who included Oliver Wendell Holmes, Hawthorne, Henry and Alice James, Emerson, Whittier, Lowell, Longfellow, Harte, Twain and Dickens, a frequent guest during his visit to America, Thomas Bailey Aldrich, actors Edwin Booth and Joseph Jefferson and national figures Charles Sumner and Henry Ward Beecher.

Howe, M. A. DeWolfe, ed. "Bret Harte and Mark Twain in the 'Seventies.'" ATLANTIC MONTHLY 130 (1922):341-348.

1871-1876. Extracts including character sketches and anecdotes of the young authors who frequented her salon; their literary and political opinions, jokes, conversations and western lore; a few of her own observations on their wives and family life.

FLEET, BENJAMIN ROBERT, 1846-1864   **3784**

GREEN MOUNT: A VIRGINIA PLANTATION FAMILY DURING THE CIVIL WAR. Edited by Betsy Fleet and John D.P. Fuller. Lexington: University of Kentucky Press, 1962. 374 pp. Diary, pp. 3-310 passim. Reprint. Charlottesville: University Press of Virginia, 1977.

1860-1864. Teenager's journal, interspersed among family letters, recording life at Green Mount in King and Queen County, Virginia; studies at nearby Aberdeen Academy and chores at home; attending the 1860 Whig convention at Richmond; the progression to war and the close of the school; supporting the Confederate cause; resumption of studies at Stevensville Academy; Union raids in the county; serving in the home guard; visit to his brother in camp at Charleston; preparing to join Mosby's partisans; notes on social activities, Baptist church services, crops, hunting, neighborhood events, a circus, visits to Richmond, shortages, prices, his physician father's practice, war news, etc.; a nicely detailed account of a boy's enjoyments and the responsibilities of a plantation having some 3000 acres and about fifty slaves.

GREEN, WILLIAM MERCER, 1798-1887   **3785**

Capers, Charlotte, ed. "The Civil War Journal of Bishop William Mercer Green." JOURNAL OF MISSISSIPPI HISTORY 8 (1946):136-145.

1860-1864. Extracts from journal kept by Mississippi's first Episcopal bishop; trips around the state carrying out his clerical duties; baptisms and confirmations of whites and blacks, preaching, ordinations, etc.; visits to Vicksburg under fire and under occupation; pillaging of his home in Jackson and flight to Demopolis, Alabama; probably written up somewhat after the fact.

HAWLEY, H.J.   **3786**

Perrigo, Lynn I., ed. "H.J. Hawley's Diary, Russell Gulch in 1860." COLORADO MAGAZINE 30 (1953):133-149.

Mar-Dec 1860. Extracts covering Colorado gold rush experiences of a young man from Argyle, Wisconsin, who later settled at Central City and became a successful merchant; a few details of the journey with his uncle Lewis Sargent; hardships and dangers both en route and at the diggings; the shift from placer to deep mining.

Perrigo, Lynn I., ed. "Hawley's Diary of His Trip across the Plains in 1860." WISCONSIN MAGAZINE OF HISTORY 19 (1936):319-342.

Apr-May 1860. Extensive extract covering the journey from Argyle to Colorado; notes on route, distances, camps and encounters with "thousands" of other gold seekers; a May snowstorm and other problems; mining near Central City, his future home.

HOLMAN, JAMES H., 1836-1910 3787

Rees, Beatrice Milhaus and Alderson, William T., eds. "A Tennesseean, Texas and Camels." TENNESSEE HISTORICAL QUARTERLY 16 (1957):250-261.

Jun-Aug 1860. Record of a military escort accompanying a topographical mapping expedition from Fort Hudson to Fort Davis to locate site for a military post on the Rio Grande; loss of precious water when some camels fell during steep ascent out of Pecos River canyon; grueling march on reduced water with men and mules who "gave out" left on the trail; recuperation at Fort Davis and continuing on the San Carlos trail; interesting for comparison of camels and mules as pack animals and as a record of human and animal endurance.

HUTTON, J.D. 3788

In REPORT ON THE EXPLORATION OF THE YELLOWSTONE RIVER, by United States Army Corps of Engineers, pp. 170-174. 40th Cong., 2d sess., 1868, S. Exec. Doc. 77. Washington, D.C.: Government Printing Office, 1868.

Mar-Apr 1860. Record kept by a member of detached party with the Raynolds exploration expedition; reconnaissance for a wagon road from Platte to Powder River.

LATHAM, MILTON SLOCUM, 1827-1882 3789

Robinson, Edgar, ed. "The Day Journal of Milton S. Latham." CALIFORNIA HISTORICAL SOCIETY QUARTERLY 11 (1932):3-28.

Jan-May 1860. Political notes of a California lawyer who was briefly governor, then senator upon the death of David C. Broderick; political life in Washington, D.C., with notes on Stephen A. Douglas, William M. Gwinn and others; Douglas's anger over Latham's "Labor and Capital" speech.

LEWIS, EDWARD J., 1828-1907 3790

Pratt, Harry E., ed. "Diary of a Pike's Peak Gold Seeker in 1860." COLORADO MAGAZINE 14 (1937):201-219; 15 (1938):20-33.

Mar-Sep 1860. Colorado gold rush diary of a newspaper editor and others from Bloomington, Illinois; suffering from unseasonably cold and snowy weather; notes on Indians and on other gold seekers en route; a stay in Denver, then unprofitable mining at Iowa Gulch, California Gulch and Tennessee Gulch, where he described gambling, camp life and fare; return to Bloomington.

LYNN, WILLIAM 3791

"Touring Virginia." NATIONAL HISTORICAL MAGAZINE 73, no. 11 (1939):54-57.

Jul 1860. Diary of a trip with his wife, Ellen Taylor Lynn, from Zanesville, Ohio, to visit friends and "drink water" at various medicinal springs in Virginia; sightseeing in Harpers Ferry, including the cemetery, and hearing campaign speeches at Woodstock in favor of the nomination of John C. Breckinridge over Stephen A. Douglas; thence to Wardensville; travel by carriage, stage and railroad but with scant information on the experience.

MCBETH, SUE L. 3792

Lewis, Anna, ed. "Diary of Sue McBeth, A Missionary to the Choctaws." CHRONICLES OF OKLAHOMA 17 (1939):428-447; 21 (1943):186-195.

1860-1861 (with gaps). Missionary's diary kept mostly at the Goodwater Mission; stagecoach travel to Indian Territory with interesting descriptions of station accommodations and personnel; visit to the mission school at Wapanucka, the Bennington Mission, etc.; notes on her Choctaw and halfbreed students and her work as a teacher; Choctaw customs, beliefs, language and adaptation to Christianity; references to other missionaries, particularly the Rev. Charles C. Copeland, and Choctaw preachers, including the Rev. Pliny Fiske.

MACE, RUSSELL PERRY, b. 1820 3793

Sweet, Nathan C., ed. "Placer Mining on the San Joaquin River." MADERA COUNTY HISTORIAN 4, no. 3 (1964):1-8.

Jul-Dec 1860. Brief notes of a mining venture undertaken by a resident of Millerton, later of Madera, and several partners; mainly a record of "dirt washed" and earnings.

MCLEAN, MARGARET SUMNER, d. 1905 3794

"When the States Seceded." HARPER'S MONTHLY MAGAZINE 128 (1914):282-288.

Extracts in LADIES OF RICHMOND, edited by Katharine M. Jones, pp. 20-22, 29-30, 33-36, 50-56.

Nov 1860-Feb, Apr 1861. Extracts from diary of Massachusetts woman, daughter of Union general E.V. Sumner, who would follow her husband, Eugene McLean, to the Confederate side; the disintegration of the Union as witnessed in Washington, D.C.; observations from the Senate gallery of Jefferson Davis, Stephen Douglas, William H. Seward, John J. Crittenden and Andrew Johnson; arrival of Lincoln and his inauguration; notes on friends Varina Davis and Mrs. Joseph E. Johnston; effects on social life and the pain of severed relationships.

"A Northern Woman in the Confederacy." HARPER'S MONTHLY MAGAZINE 128 (1914):440-451.

Apr?-Jul 1861. Undated entries covering early days of the Confederate nation at Montgomery, Richmond and Memphis; trip to Manassas with Mrs. Joseph E. Johnston immediately after the battle, describing the suffering of the wounded; on boat under fire near Columbus, Kentucky; caring for the Belmont wounded and describing the distorted countenances of the dead; notes on Varina Davis.

MATTHEWS, JAMES WASHINGTON, 1798-1880 3795

In THE CIVIL WAR IN MAURY COUNTY, TENNESSEE, by Jill K. Garrett and Marise P. Lightfoot, pp. 123-137.

1860-1866. Extracts from teacher/surveyor's diary; very brief entries reflecting war's impact on his family and neighbors; prewar politics; three sons in the Confederate army; imprisonment for supposedly helping Southern guerillas and release upon taking oath of allegiance though "in my heart I am far, very far, from being a Yankee"; providing Confederate soldiers with food and lodging, for most of which he was reimbursed; problems with slaves and meting out punishment; Confederate impressment and Union foraging.

MAYNADIER, HENRY E.   **3796**

In REPORT ON THE EXPLORATION OF THE YELLOWSTONE RIVER, by United States Engineer Department, pp. 134-154. 40th Cong., 2nd sess., 1868, S. Exec. Doc. 77. Washington, D.C.: Government Printing Office, 1868.

May-Oct 1860. Journal of the commander of detached party of the Raynolds exploration expedition; reconnaissance of country between Yellowstone and Platte rivers.

"The Journal of H.E. Maynadier: a Boat Trip from Fort Union to Omaha in 1860." NORTH DAKOTA HISTORY 1, no. 2 (1927):41-51.

Jul-Oct 1860.

MULLINS, JOHN   **3797**

In REPORT ON THE EXPLORATION OF THE YELLOWSTONE RIVER, by United States Army Corps of Engineers, pp. 162-170. 40th Cong., 2d sess., 1868, S. Exec. Doc. 77. Washington, D.C.: Government Printing Office, 1868.

Jul-Aug 1860. Member of detached party with the Raynolds expedition; topographical examination of country from Fort Benton to Fort Union between Missouri and Yellowstone rivers.

OVERTON, WALTER ALEXANDER, b. 1830   **3798**

Price, Beulah M.D., ed. "Excerpts from the Diary of Walter Alexander Overton." JOURNAL OF MISSISSIPPI HISTORY 17 (1955):191-204.

1860-1862. Extracts from diary of Corinth resident, a graduate of Mercer University, who followed several occupations including those of brickmason and magistrate; work and leisure pursuits against the background of secession and war; notes on presidential campaign of 1860, activities of his slave John, prices and financial matters, damage to his property by Confederate soldiers, etc.; relocating his family in West, Mississippi, while he remained at Corinth as the Union army approached; a few entries by his wife, Mary Beazley Overton, while he was serving with Southern forces in Kentucky.

RIDGELY, ANNA, 1841-1926   **3799**

Corneau, Octavia R. and Osborne, Georgia L., eds. "A Girl in the Sixties." ILLINOIS STATE HISTORICAL SOCIETY JOURNAL 22 (1929):401-446.

1860, 1863-1865. Extracts from diary of daughter of prominent Springfield banker; local events and social activities; religious reflections; the pleasures and hardships of travel, visiting Fayette, Missouri, Chicago, New York City, Galena, Illinois, and Washington, D.C., where she attended a White House reception and found the Smithsonian Institution boring; thoughts about the war and death of friends; description of celebrations of Lincoln's 1860 nomination and election and his funeral in Springfield; notes on reading, Christmas festivities, John Hay, death of Governor Bissell, burglary of family's home, weddings and refugees from Missouri and Arkansas; an interesting account of a young woman's concerns and perceptions.

ROBERTSON, MARTHA WAYLES, 1812-1867   **3800**

"A Prayer for the Spirit of Acceptance." HISTORICAL MAGAZINE OF THE PROTESTANT EPISCOPAL CHURCH 46 (1977):399-408.

1860-1866. Extracts illustrating summary of the journal of a pious, educated Episcopalian, living at Hollywood, Chesterfield County, Virginia, just north of Petersburg; prayers and supplications; concern for sons in Confederate service; trying to reconcile war's events with her religious faith; servant problems at war's end.

SANTMYER, CHARLES A.   **3801**

In "THE CANNONEER." RECOLLECTIONS OF SERVICE IN THE ARMY OF THE POTOMAC, by Augustus Buell, pp. 398-400. Washington, D.C.: National Tribune, 1890.

Jul-Aug 1860. Extracts from sergeant's diary of action with Battery B, Fourth Artillery, then mounted as cavalry, against hostile Indians between Camp Floyd and Carson Valley; Shoshoni decoration and dancing; a "ball" at the emigrant camp with comments on the ladies; a fight at Egan Canyon; destruction and plundering in Indian village; making peace with the Goshantes.

SNOW, J.E.   **3802**

Snow, Charles J., ed. "An 1860 Vacation Jaunt." INLAND SEAS 6 (1950):177-184.

Aug 1860. Diary of a Great Lakes boat excursion taken by members of the West Andover, Ohio, Brass Band, aboard the steamer IRON CITY; great delight with everything; towns, scenery, the boat and its crew, many of them escaped slaves, whose freedom the diarist applauded; notes on other passengers, including "the celebrated Mr. Dodsworth ... leader of the largest band in the United States."

SNOWDEN, J. HUDSON   **3803**

In REPORT ON THE EXPLORATION OF THE YELLOWSTONE RIVER, by United States Army Corps of Engineers, pp. 154-161. 40th Cong., 2d sess., 1868, S. Exec. Doc. 77. Washington, D.C.: Government Printing Office, 1868.

Apr-Oct 1860. Journal of topographer with detached party of the Raynold's expedition.

SPOONER, JOHN PITCHER   **3804**

"Commencement of the Seafaring Life of John P. Spooner." PACIFIC HISTORIAN 14, no. 3 (1970):26-30.

1860-1862. Brief extracts from the whaling diary of a New Bedford lad who became an early Stockton, California, photographer; on the RAINBOW, with notes on ports and whaling; return because of sickness, or possibly homesickness, via Cape Horn on the MOUNT WELLESTON.

Scribner, Sarah, ed. "More Concerning the Life of John Spooner." PACIFIC HISTORIAN 14, no. 4 (1970):86-89.

Nov 1863-Apr 1864. Voyage from New Bedford to San Francisco as a seaman on the JAMES R. KELLER on which "the officers are all pleasant and no profane language is allowed"; notes on his nineteenth birthday, homesickness, dismay at loss of a man overboard; arrival at San Francisco, "where ends my sailor life, I hope forever."

STRONG, GEORGE TEMPLETON, 1820-1875   **3805**

DIARY. Edited by Allan Nevins and Milton H. Thomas. New York: Macmillan, 1952. 4 vols. Civil War diary, vol. 3. Reprint. New York: Octagon Books, 1974.

DIARY OF THE CIVIL WAR. Edited by Allan Nevins. New York: Macmillan, 1962. 664 pp.

1860-1865. Diary of New York lawyer, member of the city's elite and conscientious public servant; reports of and his commentary on the events of the secession crisis and Civil War; formation of the United States Sanitary Commission and his indefatigable efforts on its behalf; serving as the Commission's treasurer, organizing materials and volunteers, visiting army camps and battlefields, confronting the ineptitude of the United States Army Medical Department, meeting with political and military leaders, supporting Frederick Law Olmsted, chief executive officer of the Commission, and Surgeon-General William A. Hammond and encountering the hostility of Secretary of War Stanton; continuing his labors as Columbia College trustee and Trinity Church vestryman; founding the Union League Club of New York; observing the New York draft riots; growing admiration for Lincoln, phonetic transcription of the president's speech in conversations and description of his funeral; references to numerous significant persons of the period; an engagingly written, extraordinary, invaluable account of the Union home front.

STUART, JAMES EWELL BROWN, 1833-1864   **3806**

Robinson, W. Stitt, ed. "The Kiowa and Comanche Campaign of 1860 as Recorded in the Personal Diary of J.E.B. Stuart." KANSAS HISTORICAL QUARTERLY 23 (1957):382-400.

In RELATIONS WITH THE INDIANS OF THE PLAINS, 1857-1861, edited by LeRoy R. Hafen and Ann W., Hafen, pp. 215-244. The Far West and the Rockies Historical Series, vol. 9. Glendale, Calif.: A.H. Clark, 1959.

May-Aug 1860. Jeb Stuart's personal account of the First Cavalry's expedition under Maj. John Sedgwick against the Kiowa and Comanche; march from Fort Riley, with route, camps, terrain; little contact with Indians during period recorded in the diary.

TALLACK, WILLIAM, 1831-1908   **3807**

"The California Overland Express: the Longest Stage Ride in the World." LEISURE HOUR (1865):11-15, 21-23, 43-45, 60-64.

1860. Englishman's twenty-three day journey from San Francisco to the Pacific Railroad terminus near St. Louis on the mail stage, with around-the-clock travel allowing stops only twice a day for food; narrative descriptions of terrain, vegetation, people, settlements and stage stations along the Butterfield route through California, Utah, Arizona, Texas, Indian Territory, Arkansas and Missouri; a graphic picture of hardships of western stage travel, including frequent walking to spare the jaded horses; notes on Indians, with opinion that all land once belonging to them should be given over to "superior races."

Franks, Kenney A., ed. "The California Overland Express Through Indian Territory and Western Arkansas." ARKANSAS HISTORICAL QUARTERLY 33 (1974):70-81.

Jul 1860. Oklahoma and Arkansas segment of the journey; discursive notes on Choctaws and other tribes in Indian Territory, settlers with whom the travelers took meals, American manners,

mores, politics, scenery and slavery; the discomforts of day and night stagecoach travel borne somewhat stoically.

TALLMAN, CORNELIA AUGUSTA, b. 1838?   **3808**

Salisbury, Rachel. "1860—the Last Year of Peace." WISCONSIN MAGAZINE OF HISTORY 44 (1960-1961):85-94.

Jan-Dec 1860. Extracts from diary of daughter of prominent Janesville businessman and abolitionist, selected to illustrate the narrative summary of the document's contents; notes on weather, clothing, social life, courtship, presidential campaign of 1860, etc.

TUTTLE, JOHN WILLIAM, 1837-1927   **3809**

THE UNION, THE CIVIL WAR AND JOHN W. TUTTLE. Edited by Hambleton Tapp and James C. Klotter. Frankfort: Kentucky Historical Society, 1980. 298 pp.

1860-1866 (with gaps). Condensation of diary of Wayne County lawyer, a graduate of the University of Louisville; his work and social life in Monticello; Union service as captain, Company G, Third Kentucky Infantry; campaigning in Kentucky and Tennessee and noting pillaging by Union troops; in Stevenson, Alabama, and Nashville hospitals after breaking his leg; watching the battles for Chattanooga; on light duty in Nashville before rejoining his regiment at Loudon; daily, detailed account of the Atlanta campaign; resignation from army in September 1864; business and social affairs as he settled into civilian life back in Monticello; notes on reading, military duties, correspondence, hardships of wartime travel, climbing Lookout Mountain, the presidential election of 1864, visits to Lexington and Louisville, numerous drinking and gambling sprees, etc.; mention of many friends and acquaintances, especially members of the Hardin and Milton families; a candid and interesting record.

WARD, LESTER FRANK, 1841-1913   **3810**

YOUNG WARD'S DIARY. Edited by Bernhard J. Stern. New York: G.P. Putnam's Sons, 1935. 321 pp.

1860-1869 (with gap). Diary of ambitious, intelligent young man who would later become an eminent sociologist; work as laborer, student and teacher in Bradford County, Pennsylvania; academic tasks at the Susquehanna Collegiate Institute; his passionate attraction to Lizzie Vought, their marriage and his departure for war; recovering from wounds at home; in charge of ward at Fairfax Seminary Hospital; service in the Invalid Corps, Second Battery, Eighty-sixth Company, Veteran Reserve Corps; discharge and lengthy effort to secure a position in government service, finally obtaining a clerkship in the Treasury Department and later transferring to the Bureau of Statistics; independent study and at Columbian College; sporadic entries, originally written in French and covering, with unusual frankness, the diarist's domestic, social and intellectual lives; family matters including health of diarist and his wife, birth control and abortion, household duties, furnishings, clothing, income and expenses, etc.; visits to New York City and Philadelphia; intellectual and cultural events in Washington, D.C.; the issues and politics of Reconstruction; celebration of Christmas, April Fool's Day and Decoration Day; notes on Howard University, Lincoln's funeral, classroom discipline, playing with a ouija board and other leisure activities; an informative record of antebellum rural life, especially economic and social customs, in and around Towanda, Pennsylvania, and the postwar scene in the nation's capital.

Extracts in DIARY OF AMERICA, edited by Josef and Dorothy Berger, pp. 247-250.

1860-1862. Courtship and marriage.

WILLARD, MARY E., 1843-1862   3811

In NINETEEN BEAUTIFUL YEARS, by Frances E. Willard. New York: Harper & Brothers, 1864. Chicago: Women's Temperance Publication Association, 1886. New and revised edition, pp. 43-153. New York: Fleming H. Revell, 1889.

1860-1862. Young woman's personal diary in a quaint and pious style; student days at Northwestern Female College, Evanston, Illinois; contentment with quiet, uneventful life; much reflection on religious matters and death, books and reading; a few entries during the invalid months just before her death; interesting for references to her sister, temperance leader Frances E. Willard.

WILLIAMSON, JOHN COFFEE, 1833-1898   3812

McClary, Ben H., ed. "The Education of a Southern Mind." EAST TENNESSEE HISTORICAL SOCIETY PUBLICATIONS, no. 32 (1960):94-105.

Nov 1860-Jan 1861. Extracts from Old Fort, Tennessee, teacher's diary; student pranks and other school matters; law studies; comments on presidential election, other political events and the probability of civil war.

Williamson, J.C., ed. "The Civil War Diary of John Coffee Williamson." TENNESSEE HISTORICAL QUARTERLY 15 (1956):61-74.

Aug-Oct 1864. Record of raid into Tennessee penned while commissary sergeant, Fifth Tennessee Cavalry; military maneuvers and visits with friends in Georgia and Tennessee; support and non-support from civilians; destruction wrought by both sides; problems of securing food and forage; notes on deserters and Champ Ferguson; return to Georgia, connecting with Hood's army.

WISE, HENRY AUGUSTUS, b. 1819   3813

Cole, Allan B., ed. "Private Journal of Henry A. Wise, U.S.N. on Board Frigate NIAGARA." PACIFIC HISTORICAL REVIEW 11 (1942):319-329.

Jul-Nov 1860. Journal of a voyage to transport members of the Japanese embassy back to Japan, with disrespectful and humorous notes on those distinguished gentlemen; log and sailing details from New York to Japan; reveries of diarist.

WOODWARD, WILLIAM   3814

Beal, M.D. "Cache Valley Pioneers: The Founding of Franklin in 1860." IDAHO YESTERDAYS 4, no. 1 (1960):2-7.

Apr-Oct 1860. Brief entries of Mormon pioneer's migration from Utah to Idaho and the founding of Franklin, described in article as Idaho's oldest town.

YANAGAWA, MASAKIYO KANESABURO   3815

THE FIRST JAPANESE MISSION TO AMERICA. Translated by Junichi Fukuyama and Roderick H. Jackson. Edited by M.G. Mori. Kobi: J.L. Thompson, 1937. 85 pp. Reprint. Wilmington, Del.: Scholarly Resources, 1973.

Jan-Sep 1860. Diary of a member of the Japanese Embassy, a

retainer for the Japanese High Commissioner for Foreign Affairs and head of the deputation to Washington, D.C.; stormy Pacific voyage on the POWHATAN, with stop at Honolulu; first impressions of America at San Francisco while ship was being repaired; to Panama, where he crossed the Isthmus by train; experiences in Washington and other cities, with quaint, detailed descriptions of people, hotels, banquets and enthusiastic reception by Americans; official meeting with President Buchanan; ratifying treaty of commerce; sightseeing in Baltimore, Philadelphia and New York; return on the NIAGARA to Japan; a valuable foreign view of America.

1861

ANON.   3816

"A Sketch of 12 Months Service in the Mobile Rifle Co." ALABAMA HISTORICAL QUARTERLY 25 (1963):149-189.

Apr-Oct 1861, Feb-Jul 1862. Company I, Third Alabama Infantry, member's war diary; enthusiastic send-off from Montgomery, somewhat hostile reception in Tennessee and a rousing welcome in Lynchburg and Petersburg, Virginia; stationed at Norfolk; monotony of camp life alleviated by observing duels between shore batteries and Union ships and running picket lines to enjoy social life in the city; making maps of the area and planning winter encampment; a visit to the navy yard and the MERRIMAC; battle of Fair Oaks; Seven Days' battles; mixed-up arrangement of dated entries.

ANON.   3817

THREE MONTHS IN CAMP AND FIELD: DIARY OF AN OHIO VOLUNTEER. By a Musician. Cleveland: The Author, 1861. 63 pp.

May-Aug 1861. Account of three months' tour of duty by a musician in Company H, Nineteenth Regiment, Ohio Volunteer State Militia; events and conditions at camps in Cleveland and Zanesville, Ohio, and in western Virginia; daily weather reports; description of battle of Rich Mountain; return to Ohio for mustering out.

ANON.   3818

"Fremont's Hundred Days in Missouri." ATLANTIC MONTHLY 9 (1862):115-125.

Sep-Oct 1861. Extracts from journal kept by one of General Fremont's staff officers, describing march from St. Louis to Springfield; an enthusiastic welcome from the German residents of Hermann; notes on military operations, camps, civilian loyalties, General Sigel, etc.

ANON.   3819

In A HISTORY OF THE EIGHTH REGIMENT OF NEW HAMPSHIRE VOLUNTEERS, by John M. Stanyan, pp. 33-37, 41-42, 48-49.

Oct 1861-Feb 1862. Diary extracts containing soldier's spritely account of early army days in camp at Manchester, New Hampshire; ceremonies, quality of food and clothing, drills, drinking, etc.

ANON.   **3820**

"A College Magazine of 1861." INDIANA MAGAZINE OF HISTORY 26 (1930):307-316. Diary, pp. 308-309.

Nov 1861. Journal describing Thanksgiving kept by a student at Wabash College; metaphoric references to the Civil War: "the national bird is sick—diseased in one wing"; much purple prose and diarist's intention to finish off the day by having a "high old time."

ADAMS, JACOB, b. 1842   **3821**

"Diary of Jacob Adams." OHIO ARCHEOLOGICAL AND HISTORICAL QUARTERLY 38 (1929):627-721. Diary, pp. 632-721 passim. Reprint. Columbus, Ohio: F.J. Heer, 1930. 99 pp.

1861-1865 (with gaps). Record of private, Company F, Twenty-first Ohio Volunteer Infantry, compiled in 1924 from wartime diary and letters; operations in Tennessee, including battle of Stones River and the Tullahoma campaign; wounding at Chickamauga and treatment afterwards; in camp at Chattanooga; veteran furlough at home near Findlay; the Atlanta campaign and pursuit of Hood in northern Georgia; the March to the Sea, Carolinas campaign and battle of Bentonville; reaction to Lincoln's assassination; march to Washington, D.C., the Grand Review and sightseeing in the city; unpleasant trip to Louisville and in camp there until mustered out; return home.

ALISON, JOSEPH DILL, 1828-1905   **3822**

"War Diary of Dr. Joseph Dill Alison of Carlowville, Alabama." ALABAMA HISTORICAL REVIEW 9 (1947):384-398.

1861-1863 (with gaps). Generally sporadic entries covering Confederate physician's war experience; stationed at Pensacola; notes on bugs and military operations; at Corinth and battle of Shiloh; Union assault on Chickasaw Bluffs and conditions, hopes and morale in beseiged Vicksburg; brief mention of medical situation at Corinth and Vicksburg.

"Eyewitness Account of Pensacola and Shiloh." CIVIL WAR TIMES ILLUSTRATED 5, no. 10 (1967):40-46.

May 1861-Apr 1862. Extracts dealing with service at Pensacola and Corinth; battle of Shiloh.

"With a Confederate Surgeon at Vicksburg." AMERICAN HISTORY ILLUSTRATED 3, no. 4 (1968):31-33.

May-Jul 1863. Extracts reporting on the siege of Vicksburg.

ALLEN, MICHAEL M., b. 1830   **3823**

De Sola Pool, D., ed. "The Diary of Chaplain Michael M. Allen." AMERICAN JEWISH HISTORICAL SOCIETY RECORDS 39 (1949):177-182.

Sep 1861. Diary kept while he was serving as chaplain of the Cameron Dragoons in camp near Washington, D.C.; attending synagogue services in the city; weather and war news; appointment as regimental postmaster and resignation as chaplain.

ALLEY, CHARLES   **3824**

Exell, John S., ed. "Exerpts from the Civil War Diary of Lieutenant Charles Alley." IOWA JOURNAL OF HISTORY 49 (1951):241-256.

Oct 1861-Mar. 1862. Extracts from diary of well-educated,

deeply religious Irish immigrant, a resident of Nebraska Territory; record of private's early service with Company C, Fifth Iowa Cavalry; journey from Omaha to St. Louis; notes on weather and activities at Benton Barracks; commentary on the wickedness in the camp and the arrogance of officers; into Tennessee, description of Fort Henry and battle of Fort Donelson; foraging expeditions and brief picture of countryside and its inhabitants; a skirmish at Paris, Tennessee.

ANDREWS, W.H.   **3825**

DIARY OF W.H. ANDREWS. N.p., 1891. 16 pp.

1861-1865. Occasional brief entries of sergeant, Company M, First Georgia Regulars, recording significant events in the regiment's military career; service in Virginia, Florida, Georgia, South and North Carolina; Peninsular campaign, Seven Days' battles, Second Bull Run and Antietam; opposing Sherman in the Carolinas campaign; notes on black Union troops.

BANCROFT, ALBERT H., d. 1864   **3826**

In ANNUAL REPORT, 5th, by New York State Bureau of Military Statistics, pp. 575-612.

1861-1864. Corporal's diary of service in Company B, Eighty-fifth New York Volunteers, at first only sporadically kept but with terse daily entries commencing in December 1862 and becoming more fulsome in 1864; Peninsular campaign; weather, duties, military operations and leisure activities, including New Year's Day celebration, in North Carolina; a few notes on conditions during imprisonment at Andersonville.

BARNES, JOHN SANFORD, 1836-1911   **3827**

Hayes, John D. and O'Brien, Lillian, eds. "The Early Blockade and the Capture of the Hatteras Forts." NEW YORK HISTORICAL SOCIETY QUARTERLY 46 (1962):60-85.

Jul-Sep 1861. Extracts from journal of United States Naval Academy graduate, acting lieutenant on the steam frigate WABASH; on blockade duty off South Carolina and his opinion of the blockade's effectiveness; collision with steam gunboat SEMINOLE and criticism of her commander Edward R. Thomson; taking prizes; the expedition to Hatteras Inlet and a full description of the battle; reactions of men under fire; strong condemnation of performance of Commodore Stringham and General Butler.

Hayes, John D., ed. "The Battle of Port Royal, S.C." NEW YORK HISTORICAL SOCIETY QUARTERLY 45 (1961):365-395.

Oct-Nov 1861. Extracts from journal kept on the WABASH, now Du Pont's flagship; description of the fleet setting forth from Hampton Roads; storms and damage en route to South Carolina; a lengthy account of the action at Port Royal Sound.

Hayes, John D. and O'Brien, Lillian. "The Battle of Port Royal Ferry, S.C." NEW YORK HISTORICAL SOCIETY QUARTERLY 47 (1963):109-136. Diary, pp. 117-121.

Jan 1862. Extract describing the initial stages of the assault on Confederate fortifications during which diarist was in command of the gunboat E.B. HALE.

BARNES, RICHARD T., b. 1844?   **3828**

In BEFORE THE REBEL FLAG FELL, edited by Thomas C. Parramore and others, pp. 11-14. Murfreesboro, N.C.: Johnson, 1965.

Jun 1861. Extract from diary of young enlistee in the Hertford County Volunteers; a lighthearted description of the festivities surrounding the company's departure from Murfreesboro, North Carolina, and their journey to Ocracoke.

BARROW, WILLIE MICAJAH, 1843-1863   **3829**

Stephenson, Wendell Holmes and Davis, Edwin Adams, eds. "The Civil War Diary of Willie Micajah Barrow." LOUISIANA HISTORICAL QUARTERLY 17 (1934):436-451, 712-731.

Extracts in OUR SOLDIERS SPEAK, by William Matthews and Dixon Wecter, pp. 175-182; TRAGIC YEARS, by Paul M. Angle and Earl S. Miers, vol. 2, pp. 734-737.

Sep 1861-Jul 1862. Private's experiences while in Company F, Fourth Louisiana Infantry; duties and leisure pursuits in Mississippi and Louisiana camps; visit home to West Baton Rouge Parish; into Tennessee and capture at Shiloh; conditions at Camp Douglas; notes on weather, reading, punishment of slaves and some good meals; interesting record of everyday life in the ranks.

BARTLETT, WILLIAM FRANCIS, 1840-1876   **3830**

MEMOIR OF WILLIAM FRANCIS BARTLETT. By Francis Winthrop Palfrey. Boston: Houghton, Osgood, 1878. 309 pp. Diary, pp. 2-276 passim.

1861-1866, 1875-1876. Extracts from journal of a Harvard graduate from Winthrop, Massachusetts; a captain in the Twentieth Massachusetts until loss of his leg at Yorktown; colonel of the Forty-ninth Massachusetts, campaigning in Louisiana; colonel of the Fifty-seventh Massachusetts, wounded in the Wilderness; brigadier general, First Brigade, Ledlie's Division, Ninth Corps, under constant fire at Petersburg and captured during the battle of the Crater; prisoner of war at Danville, in the prisoner's hospital there and at Libby Prison; conditions, prices, food, games, reading and other activities; the problems of exchange; recuperating after his release; a visit with Garibaldi during postwar European honeymoon; opinions on blacks and the politics of Reconstruction; notes on his several war wounds and his declining health.

BEATTY, JOHN, 1828-1914   **3831**

THE CITIZEN-SOLDIER: OR MEMOIRS OF A VOLUNTEER. Cincinnati: Wilstach, Baldwin, 1879. 401 pp. Reprint. Alexandria, Va.: Time-Life Books, 1983.

MEMOIRS OF A VOLUNTEER. Edited by Harvey S. Ford. New York: W.W. Norton, 1946. 317 pp.

Extracts in THE BLUE AND THE GRAY, edited by Henry S. Commager, vol. 1, pp. 308-310, 881; TREASURY OF THE WORLD'S GREAT DIARIES, edited by Philip Dunaway, pp. 272-274.

1861-1864. War diary of Cardington, Ohio, banker, later congressman and novelist; service as lieutenant colonel and colonel of the Third Ohio Volunteer Infantry; campaigning in western Virginia; stationed in Kentucky, Tennessee and Alabama; battles of Perryville and Stones River; wintering near Murfreesboro and promotion to brigadier general; Tullahoma campaign; battle of Chickamauga; Chattanooga campaign; notes on drinking, maintaining discipline, Southern civilians, Copperheads, emancipation, foraging, destruction perpetrated by Union soldiers, etc.;

problem of contrabands, their treatment and anecdotes portraying their behavior; description of people and surroundings encountered; candid opinions about fellow officers and superiors, including Rutherford B. Hayes, James A. Garfield, Robert B. Mitchell, Jacob Ammen, James S. Negley, James A. Connolly and Alexander McCook; dispute with Rosencrans satisfactorily resolved; a critical assessment of Confederate William H.F. Lee; a fulsome account of camp life, military operations and the demands of leadership.

Ford, Harvey S., ed. "The Diary of John Beatty." OHIO STATE ARCHAEOLOGICAL AND HISTORICAL QUARTERLY 58 (1949):119-151, 390-427; 59 (1950):58-91, 165-195.

Jan-Jun 1884. Diary of a prominent Columbus banker, politician and civic leader; much on local and national politics, including Henry B. Payne's senatorial campaign, with references to Governor George Hoadly, Congressman Joseph Warren Keiffer, Senator John Sherman, Joseph Benson Foraker and others; the Republican national convention at Chicago, described in some detail; arguments for free trade, civil rights and prison reform; concern about growing corruption in politics, as evidenced by the Boynton case, and increasing ability of the rich to influence votes; religious reflections, with notes on the sermons of his pastor, Washington Gladden; hearing and giving many speeches, with comments on the art of oratory; reading interests.

BENSON, WALLACE P.   **3832**

A SOLDIER'S DIARY. Algonquin, 1919. 31 pp.

1861-1863. Service record of member of Company H, Thirty-sixth Illinois Volunteers; operations in Missouri, Arkansas, Mississippi and Kentucky; battles of Pea Ridge and Perryville; wounding at latter engagement and subsequent medical discharge; notes on countryside.

BERKELEY, HENRY ROBINSON, 1840-1918   **3833**

FOUR YEARS IN THE CONFEDERATE ARTILLERY. Edited by William H. Runge. Chapel Hill: Published for the Virginia Historical Society by University of North Carolina Press, 1961. 156 pp.

1861-1865. Rewritten version of artilleryman's diary; with the Hanover Artillery, later disbanded and absorbed into Ewell's Second Corps of the Army of Northern Virginia; military duties and events from the Peninsular campaign to Early's Washington raid and Sheridan's Shenandoah Valley campaign; Yorktown, Seven Days' battles, Fredericksburg, Gettysburg, Mine Run, the Wilderness, Spotsylvania, Cold Harbor, Kernstown, Fishers Hill and Cedar Creek; capture during battle of Waynesboro; hardships of journey to Fort Delaware and conditions there; release after war's end and journey home; notes on camp life, unit's movements, leadership problems, gruesome sights and appropriation of Union goods on the field of battle, pleasant times in winter camp, visits home to Hanover County and execution of a deserter; growing feeling of hopelessness as Southern forces are ground down in the last year of war; Lincoln's assassination; uncertainty about taking the oath of allegiance; substantial, detailed entries.

BETTS, ALEXANDER DAVIS, 1832-1918   **3834**

EXPERIENCE OF A CONFEDERATE CHAPLAIN. Edited by William Archibald Betts. Greenville? S.C., 19--? 103 pp. Diary, pp. 6-79.

1861-1865. Diary of chaplain's service with the Thirtieth North Carolina; Antietam and Gettysburg campaigns, Early's Washington raid and the 1864 Shenandoah Valley campaign; brief entries recording, but giving scant details of, his clerical activities; visiting hospitals, preaching, prayer meetings, etc.; notes on his health, casualties, deaths, Weir's Cave, Methodist conferences, his family, furloughs to North Carolina, especially in the Chapel Hill area, and the many persons encountered during the war years; enhancement of some entries in 1890s.

BILLINGSLEY, AMOS S., 1818-1897　　　3835

Danker, Donald F. and Riley, Paul D., eds. ''The Journal of Amos S. Billingsley, a Missionary in the Colorado Gold Fields, 1861-1862, and Chaplain of the House of Representatives.'' COLORADO MAGAZINE 40 (1963):241-270.

1861-1862. Presbyterian minister's work as an itinerant missionary among the Colorado miners and prospectors; services and prayer meetings in Denver and in the mining camps; many funerals of those who met violent deaths; organization of churches in Denver and Montgomery; references to Governor Gilpin and John M. Chivington; much soul searching and introspection.

BIRCH, THOMAS STEWART, 1840?-1862　　　3836

In AMERICAN PATRIOTISM, by Leonard Brown, pp. 69-74.

Nov 1861-Jul 1862. Extracts from diary of soldier in Company D, Second Iowa Infantry Volunteers; at St. Louis, noting secessionist sympathies among citizenry; successful assault on Fort Donelson; battle of Shiloh; Confederate evacuation of Corinth.

BLACKFORD, WILLIAM M.　　　3837

In MEMOIRS OF LIFE IN AND OUT OF THE ARMY IN VIRGINIA, compiled by Susan Leigh Colston Blackford, edited by Charles Minor Blackford, vol. 1, pp. 20-292 passim, vol. 2, pp. 2-216 passim. Lynchburg, Va.; J.P. Bell Co., Printers, 1894-1896.

1861-1864. Extracts from diary of Lynchburg, Virginia, banker whose five sons served in the Confederate army; war news and his commentary on it; the activities of his sons and other members of the Blackford and Minor families; notes on weather, church services, business affairs, friends, casualties, deaths and funerals; visits to Richmond and Charlottesville; criticism of Jefferson Davis and praise for Stonewall Jackson whose body he accompanied to Lexington; description of the Fredericksburg battlefield and destruction in the town; an evening of conversation with Vallandigham.

In LETTERS FROM LEE'S ARMY, compiled by Susan Leigh Colston Blackford, edited and abridged by Charles Minor Blackford III, pp. 53-54, 58-59, 70, 152-153, 229-230. New York: C. Scribner's Sons, 1947. Reprint. New York: A.S. Barnes, 1962.

Nov 1861, Dec 1862, Nov-Dec 1863. Extracts covering a wartime journey to Manassas, a peek at Jeb Stuart's headquarters and diarist's comments on Union war spirit and the Confederate cause.

BOMBAUGH, CHARLES C.　　　3838

''Extracts from a Journal Kept during the Earlier Campaigns of the Army of the Potomac.'' MARYLAND MAGAZINE OF HISTORY 5 (1910):301-326.

Sep 1861-Jun 1862. Extracts from diary of surgeon with the Irish Regiment raised by Sen. Edward D. Baker which became the Sixty-ninth Pennsylvania Volunteers; on the sidelines at Ball's Bluff and defending the actions of Baker and Gen. Charles P. Stone afterwards; the Peninsular campaign, with observations on McClellan and notes on damage done by Confederate land mines; amputating O.O. Howard's arm at Fair Oaks; praise for the enlisted man and recognition that the Army of the Potomac was losing strength.

BOYD, CYRUS F., b. 1837?　　　3839

Throne, Mildred, ed. ''The Civil War Diary of C.F. Boyd.'' IOWA JOURNAL OF HISTORY 50 (1952):47-82, 155-184, 239-270, 345-378. Reprint. THE CIVIL WAR DIARY OF CYRUS F. BOYD. Edited by Mildred Throne. New introduction by E.B. Long. Millwood, N.Y.: Kraus Reprint, 1977. 135 pp.

1861-1863. Diary of Warren County sergeant with Company G, Fifteenth Iowa, rewritten after the war; frank, sometimes humorous account of war in the western theater; getting organized in Keokuk; at Benton Barracks, St. Louis; vivid description of Shiloh, possibly enhanced retrospectively; operations in Mississippi and Tennessee; sacking of Holly Springs; at Lake Providence, Louisiana, as Grant's army tries to find a way to Vicksburg; notes on duties, social activities, foraging, slaves, contrabands and race relations, troop transport and reviews, soldiers' morale, drinking and escapades, illness, the battlefield of Iuka, a Southern family burying ground, politics, etc.; comments on leadership problems, blame for Grant after Shiloh and praise for Lt. Col. William K. Belknap throughout.

BRADFORD, RUTH　　　3840

''MASKEE!'': THE JOURNAL AND LETTERS OF RUTH BRADFORD. Hartford, Conn.: Prospect Press, 1938. 162 pp.

1861-1864. Spirited, independent young woman's diary of journey to China with her father and brother aboard the JULIA S. TYLER; shipboard life, passengers, everyday activities, seasickness, food, water, storms; arriving and living at Amoy where her father was consul for a year; social life chiefly with English community; return to New York on the ST. PAUL.

BROWN, JOHN HENRY　　　3841

Lemke, W.J., ed. '' 'The Paths of Glory—': The War-Time Diary of Maj. John Henry Brown, C.S.A.'' ARKANSAS HISTORICAL QUARTERLY 15 (1956):344-359.

Nov 1861-Apr 1862. Extracts from diary of publisher of THE WAR BULLETIN, Fayetteville, Arkansas, and close friend of Confederate brigadier general Ben McCulloch; various entries concerning defense of the general's reputation; troop movements prior to and a brief account of the battle of Pea Ridge; thirty-three day journey with McCulloch's body from the battlefield to Austin, Texas; notes on disposition of the general's belongings and receptions or ceremonies along the way.

BROWN, JOHN MASON, 1837-1890　　　3842

Brown, John Mason, ed. ''A Trip to the Northwest in 1861.'' FILSON CLUB HISTORICAL QUARTERLY 24 (1850):103-135, 246-275.

May-Nov 1861. Travel diary of Frankfort, Kentucky, lawyer and historian; travel from St. Louis, where he was currently practicing law, on the SPREAD EAGLE and CHIPPEWA to Fort Benton, thence by wagon, on foot and horseback and by Overland Mail stage, before returning, largely by train, to St. Louis; good description of travel on Mullan Road to Walla Walla, with notes on Catholic missions and Indian reservations; activities and observations in Portland, San Francisco, Sacramento and Salt Lake; an interesting and detailed picture of travel, scenes, forts, Indian customs, events, etc., in somewhat the manner of Francis Parkman.

BUCK, LUCY REBECCA, 1842-1918   **3843**

DIARY OF LUCY REBECCA BUCK. Edited by L. Neville Buck. N.p., 1940. 240 leaves.

1861-1865. Diary kept at Bel Air, just east of Front Royal, Virginia, where diarist's father was a merchant and leading citizen; family and social life; Union occupations of Front Royal and the destruction wrought; occupation of Bel Air by Gen. Nathan Kimball, staff and troops; anger and contempt for Northerners, verbal duels with them and the discomfort of having to admit some were gentlemen; Confederate liberations of the area and support for the Southern troops passing through; providing hospitality for Longstreet and Lee; departure of servants; anxiety for brothers, relatives and friends in the army and deaths of loved ones; notes on domestic activities, reading, songs, games, her garden, prices, shortages, visits to relatives' homes, military action at Front Royal during Jackson's Valley campaign, war news, reports of Union depredations and atrocities, Belle Boyd, etc.; lengthy, daily entries becoming irregular and generally shorter as the war progressed; a valuable record of the everyday life of an extensive, prosperous family and the tumult in which civilians lived in the war-torn Shenandoah Valley.

SAD EARTH, SWEET HEAVEN: THE DIARY OF LUCY REBECCA BUCK DURING THE WAR BETWEEN THE STATES. Birmingham, Ala.: Cornerstone, 1973. 304 pp.

1861-1865. A more polished edition, easier to follow because of editorial notes but, unfortunately, deleting some passages from the 1940 edition which are not exciting but which do provide information on people, Lucy's reading and the tenor of everyday activities.

BURGE, LOUISIANA, 1844-1863   **3844**

Harwell, Richard B., ed. "Louisiana Burge: The Diary of a Confederate College Girl." GEORGIA HISTORICAL QUARTERLY 36 (1952):144-163. Diary, pp. 151-160.

1861-1862. Diary kept by Dolly Burge's step-daughter; school days at Wesleyan Female College in Macon; celebrating Georgia's secession; return to her home in Newton County; war news and patriotic sentiments; notes on friends; a lively record of a young woman's concerns and opinions.

BURNS, AMANDA MCDOWELL, b. 1839   **3845**

FIDDLES IN THE CUMBERLAND. By Amanda McDowell and Lela McDowell Blankenship. New York: Richard R. Smith, 1943. 310 pp. Diary, pp. 45-303 passim.

1861-1866 (with gaps). Diary kept at Cumberland Institute, founded by her father, Curtis McDowell, in White County, Tennessee, where she taught; sporadic entries some of which were later excised by the diarist; her thoughts on the war; religious reflections; concern for brothers Lafayette and Jackson, who chose the Con-

federate and Union causes respectively, and her father and sister Mary; discussion of local events and the divided sympathies and guerilla activities in the area; notes on domestic tasks, dentistry, illnesses and romantic involvements.

BURRAGE, HENRY S.   **3846**

" 'Tis Fifty Years Since." BROWN ALUMNI MONTHLY 11 (1911):221-226.

Apr 1861. Extracts from diary of Brown University senior, reporting events at Charleston, South Carolina, and the patriotic response of students, faculty and the citizens of Providence; raising the United States flag over University Hall; ceremonies marking the departure of Rhode Island troops for Washington, D.C.; praise for Governor Sprague.

BUTTERFIELD, IRA H.   **3847**

In COVERED WAGON DAYS, by Albert J. Dickson, edited by Arthur J. Dickson, pp. 125-129. Cleveland: Arthur H. Clark, 1929.

Jul 1861. Extracts of travel over Lander's Road driving purebred Shorthorn and Devon cattle and Merino sheep to California from Nebraska, having been shipped there from Wisconsin; a daring undertaking successfully accomplished.

BUZHARDT, BEAUFORT SIMPSON, 1838-1862   **3848**

BEAUFORT SIMPSON BUZHARDT. Newberry, S.C.: Printed for private destribution, 1916? 73 pp.

1861-1862. Diary kept by enlisted man, Company E, Third South Carolina Volunteers; service in Virginia, including battle of First Bull Run, the Peninsular campaign, battle of Fair Oaks and the Seven Days' battles during which diarist was killed; a pleasant record of the soldier's life; duties, weather, new sights and experiences; notes on troop reviews, packages received, election of officers, relations between picket lines, the regimental flag, winter quarters, furlough home to Newberry, South Carolina, deaths, etc.; account of the problem of holding twelve-month men at the front during the Peninsular campaign after their enlistments had expired; glimpses of Jefferson Davis and generals Beauregard, Van Dorn, Kershaw and Magruder.

CAMM, WILLIAM, 1837-1906   **3849**

Haskell, Fritz, ed. "Diary of Colonel William Camm." ILLINOIS STATE HISTORICAL SOCIETY JOURNAL 18 (1926):793-969.

1861-1863, Jan-Jun 1865. War diary of Illinois schoolteacher, born in England; service in Missouri as captain, Company K, Fourteenth Illinois Infantry and quick promotion to lieutenant colonel of the regiment; roaming the gory battlefield after the surrender of Fort Donelson; extensive account of battle of Shiloh and the advance to Corinth; subsequent military operations in Mississippi and Tennessee and the Vicksburg campaign; at Benton Barracks after furlough home to Scott County; return to regiment in Mississippi; enlistment in Hancock's Veteran Corps; stationed in Virginia; coverage of duties, responsibilities, decisions, illnesses and adventures; notes on camp life, selection of officers and relationship with enlisted men, leisure activities, sightseeing in Washington, D.C., and the Grand Review; disapproval of Union soldiers' depredations; interactions with Southern civilians and blacks; thoughts on war and the Union cause; a record, kept daily with few lapses, providing a wealth of descriptive detail, amusing incident and thoughtful reaction to people and events.

CAMPBELL, ANDREW JACKSON, 1834-1863   3850

CIVIL WAR DIARY. Edited by Jill K. Garrett. Columbia, Tenn., 1965. 132 pp. Diary, pp. 1-119.

1861-1863. Diary of officer serving with the Forty-eighth Tennessee Volunteers; lengthy description of battles of Fort Henry and Fort Donelson; capture and transport to Camp Chase; prison conditions there and at Johnson's Island; south to Vicksburg and exchange in September 1862; in various Mississippi camps; overcoming obstacles to furlough travel to Tennessee; being sick at Port Hudson, inadequate care and grueling trip back to Tennessee; comments on Southern sympathizers and unionists in border states, contrabands, shortages and prices and war and political news as reported in various newspapers North and South; Union insults and atrocities witnessed in prison or said to have occurred elsewhere.

CAMPBELL, CHARLES LEWIS   3851

In ON TO GRAFTON, by William Thompson Price, pp. 47-56. Marlington, West Va., 1901.

Apr-Oct 1861. Highland County soldier's diary of operations in western Virginia: with the "Highlanders" until marching proved too much for him, then transfer to the "Wild Horse" cavalry; notes on enthusiastic civilian support.

CASTLEMAN, ALFRED LEWIS, 1809-1877   3852

ARMY OF THE POTOMAC. BEHIND THE SCENES. A DIARY OF UNWRITTEN HISTORY. Milwaukee: Strickland, 1863. 288 pp.

1861-1863. Journal of surgeon with the Fifth Regiment Wisconsin Volunteers, bearing a lengthy critique of the management of medical services and McClellan's leadership of the Army of the Potomac; harsh words for his brigadier general Winfield Scott Hancock; descriptions of camp hygiene, a regimental hospital, Fort McHenry, Hampton, Virginia, an eighteenth-century church near Stafford Court House, etc.; notes on medical theories and treatments, female nurses, New Year's Day celebration, McClellan-Pope rivalry and Union soldiers' vandalism; praise for the Sanitary Commission; the Peninsular campaign and the battle of Williamsburg; the Seven Days' battles, Second Bull Run, Antietam and Fredericksburg; his resignation from the service.

CHASE, CHARLES MONROE, 1829-1902   3853

Welsh, Donald H., ed. "A Union Band Director Views Camp Rolla." MISSOURI HISTORICAL REVIEW 55 (1961):307-343.

Jul-Oct 1861. Diary kept by Dartmouth graduate, a Sycamore, Illinois, lawyer, newspaper editor and brass band leader, during special three-month enlistment as director of sixteen-piece band with the Thirteenth Illinois Infantry; conditions, duties and events at Rolla, Missouri; detailed descriptions of band's performances; problem of getting band members to practice; notes on war news, camp life, refugees, foraging, Sabbath-keeping, treatment of wounded, divided sympathies of the area, etc.; a few forays out of camp.

CHASE, JULIA   3854

"Record of the Various Occupations of Winchester by Federal and Confederate Forces during the Civil War as Set Down in the Diary

of Miss Julia Chase." WINCHESTER-FREDERICK COUNTY HISTORICAL SOCIETY PAPERS 3 (1955):9-13.

1861-1865. Record extracted from day-by-day account of troop movements.

CHASE, SALMON PORTLAND, 1808-1873   3855

INSIDE LINCOLN'S CABINET. Edited by David Donald. New York: Longmans, Green, 1954. 342 pp. Reprint. New York: Kraus, 1970.

1861-1865 (with gaps). Record of war events, issues and personalities; cabinet meetings, the business of the Treasury Department and the conduct of the war; a steady stream of visitors and their requests, reports, opinions, etc.; his views on many issues including the TRENT affair, emancipation and regulation of trade in occupied territory; problems of patronage; dissatisfaction with McClellan, and Hooker's thoughts on the subject; much armchair generalship; presidential aspirations and the 1864 campaign; resignation from the Treasury and summary of his accomplishments in office; travel in New England and the Midwest; work as chief justice; receiving news of attacks on Lincoln and the Sewards; administering oath of office to Johnson; urging the new president to promote black suffrage.

In THE LIFE AND PUBLIC SERVICES OF SALMON PORTLAND CHASE, by Jacob W. Schuckers, pp. 436-519 passim. New York: D. Appleton, 1874.

Jun-Sep 1862, Jul 1864, Apr 1865. Extracts.

DIARY AND CORRESPONDENCE OF SALMON P. CHASE. American Historical Association Annual Report for the Year 1902, vol. 2. Washington, D.C.: Government Printing Office, 1903. 527 pp. Diary, vol. 2, pp. 45-106. Reprint. New York: Da Capo, 1971.

Jul-Oct 1862. Extracts.

Extracts in THE BLUE AND THE GRAY, edited by Henry S. Commager, vol. 2, pp. 1088-1090; TRAGIC YEARS, by Paul M. Angle and Earl S. Miers, vol. 1, pp. 397-400.

CHASE, THOMAS E.   3856

In HISTORY OF THE FIFTH MASSACHUSETTS BATTERY, by Massachusetts Artillery, 5th Battery, pp. 100-686 passim.

1861-1863. Extracts from corporal's diary covering the battery's activities, including the Peninsular campaign, Seven Days' battles, Second Bull Run campaign, battle of Fredericksburg, Burnside's "Mud March" and the Chancellorsville campaign; wounding at Gettysburg; journey to Philadelphia and in hospital there.

CHERRY, AMOS R.   3857

"Iowa Troops in the Sully Campaigns." IOWA JOURNAL OF HISTORY AND POLITICS 20 (1922):364-443. Diary, pp. 374-412, 418-440.

Nov-Dec 1861, Jul-Nov 1864. Diary kept by sergeant, Company B, Fourteenth Iowa Volunteers; the march from Iowa City to Fort Randall, on the Missouri River near the present Nebraska-South Dakota border; food shortages and foraging, leisure activities, bad weather; description of countryside and towns; arrival at Fort Randall and a summary of its attractions; Sully's campaign against the Sioux; encounter with Indians and destruction of their property; daily entries providing flavor of frontier soldiering; 1861 portion obviously rewritten later.

CHESNUT, MARY BOYKIN MILLER, 1823-1886   **3858**

A DIARY FROM DIXIE. Edited by Isabella D. Martin and Myrta L. Avary. New York: D. Appleton, 1905. 424 pp. Reprint. New York: Peter Smith, 1929. 423 pp. Gloucester, Mass.: Peter Smith, 1961. Edited by Ben Ames Williams. Boston: Houghton Mifflin, 1949. 572 pp. Reprint. Cambridge: Harvard University Press, 1980.

MARY CHESNUT'S CIVIL WAR. Edited by C. Vann Woodward. New Haven: Yale University Press, 1981. 886 pp.

Widely extracted. See, for instance, in THE BLUE AND THE GRAY, edited by Henry S. Commager, vol. 1, pp. 31-35: DIARY OF AMERICA, edited by Josef and Dorothy Berger, pp. 458-468; LADIES OF RICHMOND, pp. 65-69, 162-164, 194-198, 303-305; TREASURY OF THE WORLD'S GREAT DIARIES, edited by Philip Dunaway, pp. 239-257.

  1861-1865. The most famous of Civil War diaries, now known to be more literary masterpiece than artles contemporary commentary; the disintegrating world of the Southern aristocracy portrayed by one of its own, the intelligent, socially adept and well connected, outspoken and independent wife of Southern gentleman and public servant, James Chesnut, Jr.; government and politics of the Confederacy from its inception and the attack on Fort Sumter until after the surrender of its armies; society in Montgomery, Charleston, Columbia and Richmond; plantation life at Mulberry and Sandy Hill, near Camden, South Carolina; gossip, war news and prices; friendships, flirtations and frictions; views on slavery and the status of women; notes on many individuals, including Jefferson and Varina Davis, Lewis Wigfall, John L. Manning, John Bell Hood and various members of the Chesnut, Boykin, Williams and Preston families. The definitive edition is MARY CHESNUT'S CIVIL WAR, the "simulated diary" composed in the 1880's through which Woodward has threaded extracts from the actual wartime diaries.

THE PRIVATE MARY CHESNUT. Edited by C. Vann Woodward and Elisabeth Muhlenfeld. New York: Oxford University Press, 1984. 292 pp.

  Feb-Dec 1861. Jan?-Feb, May-Jun 1865. The surviving, original, wartime diaries on which Chesnut based her later work; coverage of the same social, political and personal worlds but with even more candor and personal revelation.

CHITTENDEN, LUCIUS EUGENE, 1824-1900   **3859**

INVISIBLE SIEGE. San Diego, Calif.: Americana Exchange Press, 1969. 133 pp.

  Apr-Jul 1861. Diary of Vermont Republican lawyer and bank president, appointed register of the Treasury by Lincoln; life in Washington, D.C., including rumors and news, patriotism, morale, fears and local defense measures; weather and his health; interactions with Salmon P. Chase; notes on his work, reading, sermons, Georgetown Cemetery, Ellsworth's Zouaves, Caleb Cushing and Dorothea Dix; reports of capture of Alexandria, the death of Ellsworth and the battle of Big Bethel.

CILLEY, DANIEL P.   **3860**

In A HISTORY OF THE EIGHTH REGIMENT OF NEW HAMPSHIRE VOLUNTEERS, by John M. Stanyan, pp. 42-488 passim.

  1861-1864 (with gaps). Bits of chaplain's diary; notes on duties,

deaths, etc.; Bank's accusations concerning Franklin at the battle of Sabine Cross Roads.

CLARKE, Miss   **3861**

Gemmill, Chalmers L., ed. "Midway Hospital." ALBEMARLE COUNTY HISTORICAL SOCIETY MAGAZINE 22 (1963-1964):161-189.

  1961-1863. South Carolina woman's diary kept while she was nursing in Charlottesville, Virginia; brief notes primarily covering social activities with relatively few details of hospital life; weather, deaths, correspondence, war news, etc.; interesting account of sightseeing and collecting "relicks" at Monticello.

COLLIER, ELIZABETH   **3862**

In NORTH CAROLINA CIVIL WAR DOCUMENTARY, edited by W. Buck Yearns and John G. Barrett, pp. 31-32. Chapel Hill: University of North Carolina Press, 1980.

  Aug-Sep 1861. Extracts from diary of Everettsville, North Carolina, teenager; histrionic response to capture of Confederate defenses at Hatteras by Union forces.

In WHEN SHERMAN CAME, edited by Katharine M. Jones, pp. 289, 292-294, 323-324.

  Mar-Apr 1865. The final days of war in North Carolina; Union soldiers' plundering; sentiments on hearing of Johnston's surrender.

COOK, ANNA MARIA GREEN, 1844-1936   **3863**

THE JOURNAL OF A MILLEDGEVILLE GIRL. Edited by James C. Bonner. University of Georgia Libraries Miscellaneous Publications, no. 4. Athens: University of Georgia Press, 1964. 131 pp.

  1861-1867. A journal of anxiety about love and religion, kept by the daughter of the superintendent of the Georgia Lunatic Asylum at Midway near Milledgeville; sporadic entries focusing on religious doubts, spiritual well-being and her feelings about various men, written against the background of secession, war and its aftermath; notes on reading, sermons, family relationships, visits and visitors and the passage of Sherman's soldiers; concern about her idleness, self improvement and "air-castle building."

Extracts in WHEN SHERMAN CAME, edited by Katharine M. Jones, pp. 27-32.

  Nov 1864. Occupation of Milledgeville.

COOK, FREDERICK N.   **3864**

COOK'S WAR JOURNAL. New York, 1861? 32 pp.

  Apr-Aug 1861. New Yorker's account of service with the Seventy-first New York infantry; on the R.R. CUYLER to Washington, D.C.; billeted at the navy yard; much talk of food, including his cooking duties; consoling himself with liquor and cigars amidst the deprivations of army life; battle of Bull Run; self-consciously humorous journal, apparently directed to a friend.

CRACROFT, SOPHIA, 1816-1892   **3865**

In THE VICTORIAN VISITORS:AN ACCOUNT OF THE HAWAIIAN KINGDOM, 1861-1866, by Alfons L. Korn, pp. 25-273 passim. Honolulu: University of Hawaii Press, 1958.

Apr-Jun 1861. Diary of niece of Sir John Franklin and companion to Lady Franklin on pleasure trip to Hawaii; impressions of American missionaries and the "lower class"; staying with Robert C. Wyllie, English minister of foreign affairs; notes on history of the Islands, the eloquent and remarkable Kamehameha IV and shy, gracious Queen Emma; enjoying Mauna Loa and beautiful scenery.

LADY FRANKLIN VISITS SITKA, ALASKA, 1870: THE JOURNAL OF SOPHIA CRACROFT, SIR JOHN FRANKLIN'S NIECE. Edited by R.N. DeArmond. Anchorage: Alaska Historical Society, 1981. 134 pp.

May-Jun 1970. A one-month stay in Sitka, Alaska, hoping Sir John Franklin's papers might have reached the old capital; arrival in ship NEWBERN: description of the layout of the town; condescending sketches of American, Russian and Indian inhabitants, their language and customs; agreeable walks and explorations of Indian villages and trading settlements; keen interest in history and economic conditions; hospitality of "Army ladies" and a ball; bargaining for reduction of exhorbitant prices of lodging and travel.

CRENSHAW, EDWARD, 1842-1911   3866

"Diary of Captain Edward Crenshaw." ALABAMA HISTORICAL QUARTERLY 1 (1930):261-270, 438-452; 2 (1940):52-71, 221-238, 365-385, 465-482.

1861-1865. Alabama officer's account; narrative, probably composed from war diary, of service with Company K, Seventeenth Alabama, until the battle of Chickamauga in which diarist was severely wounded; transfer to position as lieutenant of marines and commencement of daily record, with some gaps and later enhancements added; from Richmond to Wilmington and monotony of camp life there; on the TALLAHASSEE, raiding Union shipping along the North Atlantic coast; back on duty near Richmond, assigned to the ironclad VIRGINIA; destruction of the James River fleet and evacuation of Richmond; in army brigade commanded by Raphael Semmes in defense of Danville; retreat into North Carolina, surrender and journey home with Semmes across South Carolina and Georgia; early postwar days in Alabama, freedmen and labor contracts; notes on weather, reading, social life, politics, Confederate officials Stephen Mallory, John A. Campbell and Judah P. Benjamin, Northern propaganda, black prisoners of war, Johnston's removal from command, peace "feelers," etc.

CRIPPEN, EDWARD W., d. 1863   3867

Kenner, Robert J., ed. "The Diary of Edward W. Crippen." ILLINOIS STATE HISTORICAL SOCIETY PUBLICATIONS, no. 14 (1909):220-282.

1861-1863. Record of the Twenty-seventh Illinois Volunteer Infantry penned by Company C private and at least two others; events and routines at camps in Sangamon and Morgan counties and then at Cairo; battle of Belmont, occupation of Columbus, Kentucky, and operations around Island No. 10; the advance to Corinth; stationed in Mississippi and Tennessee; the Stones River and Chickamauga campaigns; notes on regimental matters including an abortive rebellion among the officers, drunken soldiers, etc.; references to hardships borne by Southern civilians.

CROSSLEY, WILLIAM J.   3868

EXTRACTS FROM MY DIARY, AND FROM MY EXPERIENCES WHILE BOARDING WITH JEFFERSON DAVIS IN THREE OF HIS NOTORIOUS HOTELS, Personal Narratives of Events in the War of the Rebellion, Being Papers Read before the Rhode Island Soldiers and Sailors Historical Society, ser. 6, no. 4. Providence: The Society, 1903. 49 pp. passim.

Jul 1861-May 1862. Diary quotations peppered through humorous narrative of member of Company C, Second Rhode Island Infantry Volunteers, who was wounded and taken prisoner at Bull Run; conditions at Libby Prison and military prisons at Tuscaloosa, Alabama, and Salisbury, North Carolina; parole and voyage home; notes on jailor Wirz.

DALY, MARIA LYDIG, 1824-1894   3869

DIARY OF A UNION LADY. Edited by Harold Earl Hammond. New York: Funk & Wagnalls, 1962. 396 pp.

1861-1865. Diary of well-to-do woman, a member of old New York families and wife of noted Irish-American judge, Charles P. Daly; commentary, laced with cattiness and gossip, by a Democrat and unionist on the New York City social scene, the Civil War, the Lincoln administration and the 1864 presidential campaign; disparaging remarks about the president and his wife; support for the Irish Brigade, especially the Sixty-ninth New York, leaders Michael Corcoran and Thomas F. Meagher and chaplain Bernard O'Reilly; events in New York City including the draft riots, Sanitary Commission fair, visit of the Russian fleet and postwar reception for General and Mrs. Grant; economic effects of the war; local and state politics; Lydig family matters; diarist's reflections on her marriage and her childless state; Irish-American concerns; Episcopalianism and Roman Catholicism; diarist's feelings about slavery and blacks; the assassination of Lincoln; trips to Washington, D.C., Boston and Bedford Springs, Pennsylvania; notes on a multitude of prominent persons, including civilians Adam Gurowski, Townsend Harris, Albert Bierstadt, Edwin Booth, George Bancroft, Frank Leslie, James T. Brady, George T. Davis, John A. Dix, Jessie Fremont and Edwards Pierrepont, military figures Adam Badeau, Francis Barlow, John C. Fremont, George B. McClellan, Winfield Scott, Ambrose Burnside, Benjamin Butler and James Shields and foreign diplomats Baron Friedrich Von Gerolt and Valdemar Rudolf Raasloff.

Extract in CIVIL WAR EYEWITNESS REPORTS, edited by Harold E. Straubing, pp. 220-224.

Jul 1863. New York City draft riots.

DARDEN, ANNIE B. DILLARD, 1812-1883   3870

In BEFORE THE REBEL FLAG FELL, edited by Thomas C. Parramore and others, pp. E-10. Murfreesboro, N.C.: Johnson, 1965.

Jul-Oct 1861. Buckhorn, Hertford County, North Carolina, housewife's diary describing local events and support of war effort.

DAVIS, NICHOLAS A., 1824-1894   3871

CHAPLAIN DAVIS AND HOOD'S TEXAS BRIGADE. Edited by Donald E. Everett. San Antonio: Principia Press of Trinity University, 1962. 234 pp. Diary, pp. 1-14 passim.

Sep 1861-Jan? 1862. A few undated extracts amidst editor's summary of diary kept by Presbyterian clergyman, chaplain of the

Fourth Texas; clerical duties in camp near Richmond; notes on train accidents, military punishment, John Bell Hood and the death of G.W Cross, the brigade surgeon and brother of Gen. Louis T. Wigfall.

DAVIS, WILLIAM P. 3872

Harrison, Lowell H. "A Confederate View of Southern Kentucky, 1861." KENTUCKY HISTORICAL SOCIETY REGISTER 70 (1972):163-178.

May-Dec 1861. Extracts embedded in narrative summary of diary of lieutenant from Enterprise, Mississippi, serving in Company B, Fourteenth Mississippi; military operations in Mississippi, Tennessee and southern Kentucky.

DAY, DAVID L. 3873

MY DIARY OF RAMBLES WITH THE 25th MASSACHUSETTS VOLUNTEER INFANTRY. Milford, Mass.: King & Billings. Printers, 1884. 153 pp.

1861-1864. Enlisted man's diary, no doubt embellished after the fact, with long anecdotal entries attempting a humorous viewpoint; hospitality for the soldier in New York City and Philadelphia; in camp near Annapolis with visits to town and to the naval academy; a stormy sea journey to North Carolina on the NEW YORK, the assault on Roanoke Island and observations on captured Confederates; battle at New Bern, occupation of the town and slaves' rejoicing; Fourth of July celebration; in camp and on the march in North Carolina; duties and sightseeing around Williamsburg, Virginia, while resisting appeals for reenlistment; in hospital, return to New Bern and discharge from service; a proud Yankee's opinions on Southerners, black and white, and their ways.

DODD, JAMES MCKEE, 1840-1862 3874

"Civil War Diary of James M. Dodd of the 'Cooper Guards.' " KENTUCKY HISTORICAL SOCIETY REGISTER 59 (1961):343-349.

Jul-Nov 1861. Very brief entries reporting events and hardships in a Confederate soldier's life; journey from Mississippi through Tennessee to Virginia; service in western Virginia, Tennessee and Kentucky.

DOWNING, ALEXANDER G., b. 1842 3875

DOWNING'S CIVIL WAR DIARY. Des Moines: Historical Department of Iowa, 1916. 325 pp.

1861-1865. Diary, rewritten for publication, of sergeant, Company E, Eleventh Iowa Infantry; early military days at Davenport and Tipton; down the Mississippi to Benton Barracks, St. Louis; operations in Missouri, Mississippi and Tennessee, including Shiloh, the advance to Corinth and battles of Iuka and Corinth; the Vicksburg campaign, with expeditions to Jackson, Mississippi, and Monroe, Louisiana; occupation duty at Vicksburg; reenlistment; the Meridian campaign; furlough home to Cedar County, in camp at Cairo, Illinois, and journey south to Huntsville, Alabama; the Atlanta campaign and hospitalization at Rome, Georgia; pursuing Hood's forces north of Atlanta; the March to the Sea; at Savannah and then by ship to Beaufort, South Carolina; the Carolinas campaign; marching to Washington, D.C., the Grand Review and sightseeing; trip to Louisville, Kentucky, remaining in camp there until mustering out; return home to work on the harvest; notes on weather, camp life, activities as cook for officers' mess, foraging, pillaging and destruction by Union

soldiers, atrocities attributed to Confederates in South Carolina, the Sanitary Commission, black troops, refugee camp for freedmen in Louisiana, gambling, the countryside and towns through which he passed, Sherman's farewell to the Army of the Tennessee, etc.; a matter-of-fact, low-key but interesting account of life in the ranks.

EAGLETON, ETHLINDA M. FOUTE, b. 1835 3876

Skipper, Elvie E. and Gove, Ruth, eds. " 'Stray Thoughts.' " EAST TENNESSEE HISTORICAL SOCIETY PUBLICATIONS, no. 40 (1968):128-137; no. 41 (1969):116-128.

1861-1865, 1867. Extracts from diary kept sporadically by Presbyterian minister's wife, experiencing the vicissitudes of Union occupation, largely in absence of her husband; harrassment by Tennessee unionists in New Market; depredations by Union soldiers; hardships endured by her children; postwar journey to new pastorate in Mount Holly, Arkansas.

EDWARDS, MARY T. HUNLEY HUDGINS 3877

In ECHOES OF HAPPY VALLEY, by Thomas F. Hickerson, pp. 62-63.

1861-1864. Extracts from widow's diary, describing depredations by Union soldiers and forced removal of slaves on Gwynn Island, Mathews County, Virginia.

ELY, ALFRED, 1815-1892 3878

JOURNAL OF ALFRED ELY. Edited by Charles Lanman. New York: D. Appleton, 1862. 359 pp. Diary, pp. 7-239.

Jul-Nov 1861. Journal kept by New York Republican congressman, captured at Bull Run, while imprisoned at Richmond with Union officers in a tobacco warehouse; generally lengthy entries covering his visitors, conditions at the prison and the inaccurate newspaper reports on his capture and present state of mind; activities, including presidency of the Richmond Prisoners Association; discussion of problems of exchange; importance of newspapers and letters to the prisoners; the illness, death and burial of colleague Calvin Huson, Jr.; lists of prisoners and copies of letters; notes on escape attempts, religious services, Quaker peace testimony, medical care and many individuals, including John H. Winder, Robert Tyler, Lewis Wigfall, Elizabeth Van Lew, John C. Breckinridge and Col. Michael Corcoran.

ELY, RALPH, 1819-1883 3879

THE DIARY OF CAPTAIN RALPH ELY. Edited by George M. Blackburn. Mount Pleasant: Central Michigan University Press, 1965. 73 pp.

1861-1864. Officer's diary of service with the Eighth Michigan; generally brief entries covering participation in the seizure of Port Royal Sound and military operations in South Carolina, Virginia, Kentucky, Mississippi and Tennessee; battles of Antietam and Fredericksburg; sieges of Vicksburg and Knoxville; notes on weather, health, duties, social and leisure activities, sightseeing in Washington, D.C., etc.

FAIRCHILD, CHARLES BRYANT, b. 1842 3880

In HISTORY OF THE 27th REGIMENT N.Y. VOLS., pp. 183-230 Binghamton, N.Y.: Carl & Matthews, Printers, 1888.

Jul 1861-May 1862. Diary entries, possibly rewritten, within narrative of imprisonment at Richmond in what would be known as Libby Prison, at New Orleans in Parish Prison and finally, before parole, at Salisbury, North Carolina; rations, illness, worship services, etc.; volunteer nursing of sick and wounded prisoners.

FAVILL, JOSIAH MARSHALL   3881

THE DIARY OF A YOUNG OFFICER. Chicago: R.R. Donnelley & Sons, 1909. 298 pp.

1861-1864. Record of Civil War service; private in Company C, Seventy-first New York; on the R.R. CUYLER to Annapolis; on foot and by train to camp at the navy yard in Washington, D.C.; battle of Bull Run; discharge and efforts to raise a company and gain a commission; advancement from lieutenant to brevet major with the Fifty-seventh New York; the Peninsular campaign, Fair Oaks and the Seven Days' battles; Second Bull Run, Antietam, Fredericksburg, Chancellorville and Gettysburg; appointed judge advocate of the division; Bristoe and Mine Run campaigns; winter camp at Stevensburg, enjoying ladies' visits; the Wilderness and Spotsylvania; very full entries running into narrative, with lengthy descriptions of military events, camp life and his surroundings; notes on many officers including McClellan, E.V. Sumner and Samuel K. Zook.

Extracts in THE BLUE AND THE GRAY, edited by Henry S. Commager, vol. 1, pp. 72-73; TRAGIC YEARS, by Paul M. Angle and Earl S. Miers, vol. 1, pp. 104-107.

FLETCHER, CALVIN, 1798-1866   3882

THE DIARY OF CALVIN FLETCHER. Edited by Gayle Thornbrough. Indianapolis: Indiana Historical Society, 1972-1983. 9 vols. Civil War diary, vols. 7-9.

1861-1866. Leading Indianapolis citizen, lawyer, banker and farmer's voluminous record of family, business, local and national affairs; reports of war news and his commentary on it; concern for his soldier sons Stephen and William; much public service, supporting Indiana troops, the Sanitary Commission and the Freedmen's Aid Commission and advising Gov. Oliver P. Morton on various matters; views on slavery and emancipation and advocacy of enlistment of blacks in the Union armies; summer sojourns in New England and a trip to Washington, D.C., meeting briefly with Lincoln; reaction to the assassination, local memorial service and the mourning crowds which gathered to meet the funeral train as it passed from Ohio to Indianapolis; diarist's thoughts on the initial Sherman-Johnston surrender terms; postwar business and civic activities; good description of Indianapolis reception for Sherman; notes on his religious beliefs, reading, affairs of the Indianapolis Branch Banking Company, his agricultural interests with frequent mention of birds, flowers and ripening fruits and vegetables, holiday celebrations, etc.; a detailed, engrossing picture of the home front Union and a major source for Indiana history.

FLETCHER, WILLIAM B., 1837-1907   3883

Brigham, Loriman S., ed. "The Civil War Journal of William B. Fletcher." INDIANA MAGAZINE OF HISTORY 57 (1961):41-76.

Jun 1861. Fragmentary journal kept by Indianapolis physician, son of Calvin Fletcher and brother of Stephen Keyes Fletcher, enlisted in the Sixth Indiana Volunteers; civilian response during regiment's journey through Indiana and Ohio; operations in what is now West Virginia; a scouting mission to sketch the

enemy's fortifications at Laurel Hill; description of Indiana senator John Peter Cleaver Shanks; account written up somewhat after events occurred and illustrated by diarist's sketches.

FONTAINE, EDWARD   3884

In MISSISSIPPI IN THE CONFEDERACY, edited by John K. Bettersworth and James W. Silver, vol. 1, pp. 41-122 passim, 285.

1861-1864. Extracts from diary of Episcopal rector, planter, Confederate army officer and father of legendary Confederate hero Lamar Fontaine; regret for dissolution of the Union; reports of Sumter's fall and war preparations; prayers for peace; decision to accept command of Burt Rifles; ideas for ordnance and strategy for meeting the union invasion of Mississippi; criticism of Gen. John C. Pemberton; an 1864 plantation dinner menu.

Baylen, Joseph O. and Moore, Glover, eds. "Notes & Documents: Edward Fontaine and the Emperor Dom Pedro II." JOURNAL OF MISSISSIPPI HISTORY 22 (1960):239-248.

May-Jun 1876. Extracts covering an erudite Episcopal rector's interview with the Brazilian emperor during his visit to the United States; mostly conversation about education and science and a detailed description of the emperor's appearance and manner.

FROST, GRIFFIN, b. 1833   3885

CAMP AND PRISON JOURNAL. Quincy, Ill: Printed at the Quincy Herald Book and Job Office, 1867. 303. pp. Journal, pp. 1-245.

1861-1865. Marion County man's journal of service as captain in the Missouri State Guard in Missouri, Arkansas and Mississippi and experiences as a prisoner of war; capture in Missouri in November 1862; held at Springfield, the Gratiot Street Prison in St. Louis, briefly at Fort Delaware and aboard the STATE OF MAINE; exchange through City Point, Virginia, to Demopolis, Alabama, parole camp; journey west, noting war's ravaging of Mississippi; battle of Helena; unsuccessful recruiting effort, with description of areas passed through, including Arkansas Post and Little Rock, and refugees heading for Texas; much derogatory commentary about Arkansas residents; problem of Confederate deserters; immediate capture after entering Missouri in October 1863; imprisoned briefly at Macon City and then at the Gratiot Street Prison and at Alton, Illinois; prison conditions, incidents and prisoners, Catholic priests, etc.; support from ladies of St. Louis and elsewhere; notes on Wilson's Creek battlefield, blacks, jayhawkers, bushwhackers and members of his family loyal to the Union; references to "miscegenation photographs" and fellow prisoner "feminine Joe"; long, detailed entries.

FUSZ, LOUIS   3886

Billings, Elden E. "Letters & Diaries." CIVIL WAR TIMES ILLUSTRATED 2, no. 3 (1963):38-40.

May 1861. Extract from diary of German-American resident of St. Louis, a Southern sympathizer; diarist's eyewitness account of St. Louis riots following Nathaniel Lyons's capture of Fort Jackson, recorded one year later.

GARRETT, HENRY A.   3887

In MISSISSIPPI IN THE CONFEDERACY, edited by John K. Bettersworth and James W. Silver, vol. 1, pp. 46-48.

Mar-Jun 1861. Extract from University of Mississippi law student's diary; reaction to events leading to war; joining the Adams Troop and the pain of leaving loved ones.

GEER, ALLEN MORGAN, 1840-1926   3888

THE CIVIL WAR DIARY OF ALLEN MORGAN GEER. Edited by Mary Ann Andersen. Denver: R.C. Appleman, 1977. 306 pp.

1861-1865 (with gap). Diary of service with the Twentieth Illinois, recording everyday activities and the events of war; capture of Fort Henry and Fort Donelson, battle of Shiloh and occupation of Corinth; at Jackson, Tennessee, under the command of John A. Logan; the Vicksburg campaign; wounding at Raymond, capture and parole; life as paroled prisoner at Benton Barracks near St. Louis and visiting the city; return to regiment near Vicksburg; assignment to provost guard of Third Division, Seventeenth Army Corps, following decimation of diarist's regiment during the Atlanta campaign; Sherman's flanking movement near Jonesboro, operations in northwest Georgia, the March to the Sea and the Carolinas campaign; final days of war, Lincoln's assassination and the Grand Review; journey home to Lexington, Illinois, and civilian life; notes on duties, illnesses, correspondence, visits and visitors, prices, war, rumors and news, Emancipation Proclamation, presidential politics, foraging and Savannah; sightseeing in Washington, D.C., and Indianapolis; description of areas traveled through; comments on drunkenness among officers and in the ranks and soldiers' pillaging; the record of an active and creative intellect seen in his prodigious reading, writing of articles, poems and songs, Lyceum participation, French and Latin studies, etc.

GIESECKE, JULIUS, b. 1838   3889

CIVIL WAR DIARY OF CAPTAIN JULIUS GIESECKE. Translated by Oscar Haas. N.p., 19--. 44 leaves.

Haas, Oscar, trans. "The Diary of Julius Giesecke." TEXAS MILITARY HISTORY 3 (1963):228-242; 4 (1964):27-54.

Oct 1861-Jul 1862, Apr-Jul, Oct 1863-Jul 1864, Mar 1865. German-American officer's record of service with Company G, Fourth Texas Cavalry; with Sibley's unsuccessful effort to expel Union forces from New Mexico Territory; engagement at Valverde and Battle of La Glorieta Pass; problems securing water and food; return to Fort Bliss and San Antonio; taken prisoner during spring 1863 Bayou Teche campaign and imprisoned at New Orleans; escape when prisoners seize the MAPLE LEAF on the way to Fort Delaware; return across the lower South to Louisiana; the second Bayou Teche campaign; Red River campaign of 1864 including the battle of Sabine Cross Roads; in Texas; somewhat irregular entries, extremely brief at first but becoming more substantial by 1863.

GILBERT, ALFRED WEST, 1816-1900   3890

COLONEL A.W. GILBERT, CITIZEN-SOLDIER OF CINCINNATI. Edited by William E. Smith and Ophia D. Smith. Cincinnati: Historical and Philosophical Society of Ohio, 1934. 122 pp. Diary, pp. 50-117.

1861-1862. War diary of Cincinnati civil engineer, lieutenant colonel of the Thirty-ninth Ohio Volunteer Infantry; in camp and on the march in Missouri, Tennessee and Mississippi; taking Island No. 10 and the battles of Shiloh, Iuka and Corinth where

the diarist was disabled by a fall from his horse; notes on his support for the employment of contrabands by the Union army and for James H. Lane's policy of firm treatment of Missouri secessionists.

GILLASPIE, IRA MYRON BAILEY, 1837-1897   3891

THE DIARY OF IRA GILLASPIE OF THE ELEVENTH MICHIGAN INFANTRY. Edited by Daniel B. Weber. Mount Pleasant: Central Michigan University Press, 1965. 51 pp.

1861-1863. Detailed record of army service of farmer and small businessman from Sturgis, Michigan; taking leave of family and urging friends to volunteer; early days in camp in Michigan; chasing Morgan's cavalry in Kentucky and Tennessee; illnesses, deaths, desertions, duties, foraging for food, etc.; battle of Stones River; substantial entries presenting both military life's everyday activities and moments of intense action as viewed by an unlettered corporal and natural storyteller.

GLAZIER, WILLARD WORCESTER, 1841-1905   3892

THREE YEARS IN THE FEDERAL CAVALRY. New York: R.H. Ferguson, 1870. 347 pp. Diary, pp. 24-342 passim.

1861-1863. Much amplified diary entries scattered through and difficult to distinguish from narrative detailing the history of the Harris Light or Second New York Cavalry; service in the ranks and later as lieutenant; operations in Virginia, including Stoneman's raid; the Gettysburg campaign; notes on bad weather and its consequences, April Fool's Day, punishment of deserters, cavalryman's regard for his horse, etc.

THE CAPTURE, THE PRISON PEN AND THE ESCAPE. New York: United States Publishing, 1865. 422 pp. Diary, pp. 31-314 passim. Hartford, Conn.: H.E. Goodwin, 1868. 400 pp.

1863-1865. Diary entries, again much enhanced, within narrative; capture by Stuart's troopers near Warrenton, Virginia; incarceration at Libby Prison and then at Danville, Macon, Savannah, Charleston and Columbia; escape and efforts to catch up with Sherman's army; assistance from many blacks; recapture twenty miles from Savannah; successful escape, reaching Savannah on Christmas eve; by sea to New York City and the exultation of freedom; notes on prison conditions, Confederates, unionist sentiment in Charlotte, North Carolina, the Sanitary Commission, cavalry leaders Morgan, Mosby and Wheeler, prisoners' presidential election vote, etc.; list of fellow prisoners.

OCEAN TO OCEAN ON HORSEBACK. Philadelphia: Hubbard Publishing, 1896. 543 pp.

May-Nov 1876. Account of travel from Boston to San Francisco by horseback; lecturing in northeastern cities on his Civil War experiences and visiting old war comrades; longer stopovers in Albany, Rochester, Buffalo, Cleveland, Toledo, Detroit, Chicago, Davenport and Omaha where he included detailed descriptions and historical notes on each city; exchanging his old horse for a mustang in Omaha for the long rides westward which he summarized in a narrative; entertaining and informative travelog.

Petersen, William J., ed. "Down the Great River." PALIMPSEST 51 (1970):353-416.

Sep 1881. Extract covering Iowa portion of Captain Glazier's canoe voyage down the entire length of the Mississippi; long historical anecdotes relating to regions and towns; notes on scenery, Dubuque, Davenport, Burlington, Keokuk, etc.; according to editor, some inaccuracies; highly florid style.

GLOVER, AMOS, 1832-1890   **3893**

Carman, Harry J., ed. "Diary of Amos Glover." OHIO STATE AR-CHAEOLOGICAL AND HISTORICAL QUARTERLY 44 (1935):258-272.

Sep 1861-May 1862, May-Jul 1863. Brief daily entries penned by captain, Company F, Fifteenth Ohio Volunteer Infantry; weather, duties, deaths, etc.; service in Kentucky and Tennessee, including the battle of Shiloh.

GOODMAN, RICHARD FRENCH, 1841?-1915   **3894**

Plumb, Robert J. "Yankee Paymaster." UNITED STATES NAVAL INSTITUTE PROCEEDINGS 103, no. 10 (1977):50-57.

1861-1865. Undated extracts from journal illustrating biography of Hartford, Connecticut, youth; comments on political and military events; observing work at navy yard and other sights of Washington, D.C.; appointment as acting assistant paymaster in February 1864; voyage to Pensacola on the ADMIRAL; brief service on the NIGHTINGALE and then on the MIAMI stationed in Virginia waters; notes on naval activities, his work, various vessels, Gideon Welles, Benjamin Butler, celebration of Lee's surrender, etc.; the record of an observant individual which deserves publication in its entirety.

GOULD, JOHN MEAD, b. 1839   **3895**

HISTORY OF THE FIRST—TENTH—TWENTY-NINTH MAINE REGI-MENT. Portland, Maine: S. Berry, 1871. 709 pp. Diary, pp. 20-308, 387-601 passim.

1861-1865. Extracts from Maine soldier's diary; ninety-day service in Company C, First Maine; getting started at home, hospitality in Philadelphia en route to camp and sightseeing in Washington, D.C.; sergeant major of reorganized unit, the Tenth Maine; operations against Jackson in the Shenandoah Valley; Second Bull Run and Antietam campaigns; Burnside's "Mud March," wintering at Stafford Court House and Lincoln's review of troops; Portland's welcome home for the regiment when its enlistment expired; reenlistment as Twenty-ninth Veteran Regiment; receiving an officer's commission; the Red River expedition, including battle of Sabine Cross Roads; operations countering Early's Washington raid and the 1864 Shenandoah Valley campaign, with notes on Phil Sheridan; winter service in the Valley; participation in the Grand Review; garrison duty in South Carolina, with observations on both Southerners and freedom.

GRABILL, JOHN H.   **3896**

DIARY OF A SOLDIER OF THE STONEWALL BRIGADE. Woodstock, Va.: Press of the Shenandoah Herald, 1909. 20 pp.

1861-1862. Daily record of Dickinson College graduate, a resident of Woodstock, Virginia; service as lieutenant, Company C, Thirty-third Virginia Volunteers; Jackson's farewell to his brigade; military operations in the Shenandoah Valley; battle of First Bull Run; Jackson's Shenandoah Valley campaign and the battle of First Kernstown; generally brief entries covering camp life, duties, sermons, visits with the ladies, etc.

GRISCOM, GEORGE L., 1837-1901   **3897**

FIGHTING WITH ROSS' TEXAS CAVALRY BRIGADE, C.S.A. Edited by Homer L. Kerr. Hillsboro, Tex.: Hill Junior College Press, 1976. 255 pp.

1861-1864. Ninth Texas Cavalry adjutant's record of military activities, replete with statistics and detailing cavalry movements, skirmishes and engagements in a terse, telegraphic style; fighting alongside and against factions of the divided Five Civilized Tribes in engagements of Round Creek Mountain and Bird Creek and battle of Pea Ridge; to Mississippi and the battles of Iuka and Corinth; participation in Van Dorn's raids on Holly Springs and Thompson's Station; the murder of Van Dorn; carrying out guerilla actions against Grant's forces until the fall of Vicksburg; across Alabama to Georgia; the Atlanta campaign, including the battles of Atlanta and Jonesboro; the Franklin and Nashville campaign; retreat into Alabama.

GROWS, DAVID HENRY   **3898**

In HISTORY OF THE FIFTH MASSACHUSETTS BATTERY, by Massachusetts Artillery, 5th Battery, pp. 97-417 passim.

Dec 1861-Aug 1862. Substantial extracts from private's diary; an artilleryman's life in action and in camp; journey from Massachusetts to Washington, D.C., and the sights of the nation's capital; operations in Virginia including the Peninsular campaign and Seven Days' battles; in Philadelphia hospital; descriptions of the workings of an artillery battery and discussion of ammunition and horses; notes on weather, food, leisure activities, a funeral, the MONITOR, etc.; an informative account.

GUILD, AMASA   **3899**

"War Diary Kept by Amasa Guild in 1861." DEDHAM HISTORICAL REGISTER 13 (1902):41-47.

Aug-Nov 1861. Diary of Dedham, Massachusetts, resident serving in Company F, Eighteenth Massachusetts; generally brief entries describing journey south to Washington, D.C., and duty in that area.

GULICK, WILLIAM O., 1842?-1863   **3900**

Guyer, Max H., ed. "The Journal and Letters of Corporal William O. Gulick." IOWA JOURNAL OF HISTORY AND POLITICS 28 (1930):194-267, 390-455, 543-603.

Dec 1861-Nov 1862. Trooper's journal of service with Company M, First Iowa Cavalry Volunteers, interspersed with letters; dullness of life in camp at St. Louis at the fairground adjoining Benton Barracks; notes on weather, duties, food, activities, celebrations for the fall of Fort Donelson and for Washington's birthday, soldiers' misdemeanors and punishments; operations against guerilas, ranging out from the Cavalry's headquarters at Clinton, Missouri; scouting, skirmishing and foraging; description of the destroyed towns of Papinsville and Osceola; a brief foray into Arkansas.

GUROWSKI, ADAM, 1805-1866   **3901**

DIARY. Boston: Lee and Shepard; New York: Carleton; Washington, D.C.: W.H. & O.H. Morrison, 1862-1866. 3 vols. Reprint. New York: B. Franklin, 1968.

1861-1866 (with gaps). Diary of Polish political refugee, a translator at the State Department; what may have been monthly entries or summary of more frequent entries through the summer of 1862, an almost daily record through 1864 and spotty thereafter; commentary on political and military events and the Union's foreign policy; his support of emancipation, enlistment of blacks in the army and racial equality; his opinions about Lincoln and most Union leaders in and out of uniform; fervent denunciation of Seward, Halleck, McClellan and Meade; praise for Stanton, Butler, Grant, Sherman and James S. Wadsworth; observations on the progress of the presidential campaign of 1864; notes on Thurlow Weed's activities, biases of various newspapers, the Sanitary Commission, Lincoln's assassination, Grant's report on the last campaigns of the war, postbellum efforts to deny freedmen their rights, etc.; a highly opinionated, entertaining and unreliable record.

Extracts in THE BLUE AND THE GRAY, edited by Henry S. Commager, vol. 1, pp. 552-554.

Dec 1862-Apr 1863.

HALL, JAMES EDMOND, 1841-1915   **3902**

DIARY OF A CONFEDERATE SOLDIER. Edited by Ruth W. Dayton. Lewisburg, W. Va., 1961. 141 pp.

1861-1865. Account of service in Company H, Thirty-first Virginia Infantry; action in western Virginia and the Shenandoah Valley; battle of Fredericksburg; Gettysburg campaign, wounding in the battle and later capture; poor treatment during transport to Fort Delaware; transfer to Point Lookout and conditions there; exchange and furlough; in the defenses of Petersburg during the final days of the siege and the Appomattox campaign; the surrender and return home to Barbour County; notes on prices, the refuse of a battlefield, black prison guards, etc.; irregular entries suffused with the complaints and depression of a man who hated being in the army.

HAMILTON, JAMES ALLEN, 1842-1864   **3903**

Barr, Alwyn, ed. "The Civil War Diary of James Allen Hamilton." TEXANA 2 (1964):132-145.

1861-1864. Navarro County soldier's service with Company E, Thirteenth Texas Infantry, on the Texas coast and with Company G, Fifteenth Texas Infantry, in Arkansas, Indian Territory and Louisiana; the Red River campaign with notes on battles of Sabine Cross Roads and Pleasant Hill; very brief, sporadic entries, focusing on regiment's movements.

HANEY, JOSEPH HANCOCK, b. 1835?   **3904**

Taylor, Orville W. "Joseph H. Haney, an Arkansas Engineer in the Civil War: The First Phase." ARKANSAS HISTORICAL QUARTERLY 14 (1955):62-71.

Jul-Sep 1861. Summary of content of diary of civil engineer, dealing with secession of Arkansas and his first military experiences; a few extracts covering state service with the Third Arkansas Volunteers, including the battle of Wilson's Creek and celebration in Van Buren after his discharge.

Steely, Will F. and Taylor, Orville W., eds. "Bragg's Kentucky Campaign: A Confederate Soldier's Account." KENTUCKY HISTORICAL SOCIETY REGISTER 57 (1959):49-55.

Aug-Oct 1862. Diary covering service as private in the Fifth Company of the Washington Artillery; march through Tennessee and operations in Kentucky; the taking of Munfordville and the battle of Perryville; very brief entries, mainly noting route of march and

distances covered, but with some detail of military and personal activities.

HANLEITER, CORNELIUS REDDING, 1815-1897   **3905**

"Extracts from the Diary of C.R. Hanleiter." ATLANTA HISTORICAL BULLETIN 1, no. 4 (1930):39-43.

Nov 1861. Reprinted in article below.

"Extracts from the Diary of C.R. Hanleiter." ATLANTA HISTORICAL BULLETIN 14, no. 3 (1969):8-101; no. 4, 52-99; 15, no. 1 (1970):59-86; no. 2, 47-84; no. 3, 53-94.

1861-1865 (with gaps). Diary of pioneer Atlanta printer and publisher, kept while he was captain of the Jo Thompson Artillery; journey from Atlanta to Savannah amidst cheers and bouquets but in cold open stock cars; stationed between Savannah and the sea, guarding the coast and water approaches to the city, and then at Beaulieu, the estate of John Schley, on the Vernon River; long daily entries through 1862, thereafter becoming shorter and sporadic; his duties, problems of drill, drinking, discipline and sickness in his company, inefficiency and ineptitude among officers and securing proper guns and accoutrements; deaths from disease, with description of many deathbeds and funeral arrangements; conflict with Lt. Elijah P. Craven, resulting in courtsmartial; social life, enjoying "clever" people and his family; notes on food, prices, sexual frustration, runaway slaves, Lewis J. Parr, military punishments, etc.; trips to Augusta, Atlanta and Rome; evacuation of Savannah; near Pocotaligo and Green Pond, South Carolina, then James Island at Charleston; last weeks of war in North Carolina and observations on residents and countryside.

HARASZTHY, AGOSTON, 1812-1869   **3906**

GRAPE CULTURE, WINES AND WINE-MAKING. New York: Harper, 1862. 120 pp.

FATHER OF CALIFORNIA WINE, AGOSTON HARASZTHY: INCLUDING GRAPE CULTURE, WINES & WINE-MAKING. Edited by Theodore Schoenman. Santa Barbara, Calif.: Capra Press, 1979. 126 pp.

Aug-Sep 1861. Hungarian-born vintner's trip, commissioned by the California legislature, to gather information on wine-making methods in Europe; visiting wineries in France, Germany, Italy, Spain and Switzerland, analyzing soil, climate and varieties of grapes, as well as gathering cuttings for his winery in Sonoma County; dated but highly narrative entries with much technical detail.

HARLAND, W.D.   **3907**

In GENEALOGICAL RECORDS, by Daughters of the American Revolution, Illinois, vol. 3, pp. 268-284. N.p., 1941?

Jul 1861-Apr 1862 (with gap). Diary kept by Harland, a lieutenant in Company H, Eighteenth Illinois Volunteers, and Thomas C. Watkins, orderly sergeant in the same company; camp life at Bird's Point, Missouri, and Cairo, Illinois; operations in Missouri and Kentucky; capturing Fort Henry and Fort Donelson; at Savannah, Tennessee, commenting on its cemetery, "a beautiful place"; the battle of Shiloh; notes on deaths in the regiment, military punishments, foraging, drunkenness, accidents, sutlers, etc.: substantial entries.

HARRINGTON, LEONARD ELSWORTH, 1816-1883   3908

"Journal of Leonard E. Harrington." UTAH HISTORICAL QUARTERLY 8 (1940):3-64.

1861?-1881 (with gaps). Mormon bishop's autobiography merging into scattered dated entries; involvement in Utah's quest for statehood, service in territorial legislature and as longtime mayor of American Fork; preaching of Brigham Young, the diarist and others at the Salt Lake tabernacle; attending lectures on "scientific, historical and practical subjects"; much on the activities of Young, Heber C. Kimball, etc; social life and a few family notes; many births, deaths, including that of Brigham Young, weddings and baptisms; political travel throughout Utah and to Washington, D.C.

HARRIS, JAMES S.   3909

HISTORICAL SKETCHES OF THE SEVENTH REGIMENT NORTH CAROLINA TROOPS. Mooresville, N.C.: Mooresville Printing Co., 1893. 70 pp.

1861-1865. History of the regiment's service including what appear to be original and reworked entries from diary of officer in Company B, organized as Young's Company in Cabarrus County; in camp on Bogue Island and in action at the battle of New Bern; Seven Days' battles; Second Bull Run campaign; capture of Harpers Ferry and the last hours of Antietam; battles of Fredericksburg and Chancellorsville; Gettysburg campaign and the retreat into Virginia; Bristoe campaign; from the Wilderness to the siege of Petersburg; final days of the war in North Carolina; primarily a record of military operations but also mention of black Union soldiers, the execution of deserters and the soldiers' vote for North Carolina governor in 1864.

HARRISON, SAMUEL ALEXANDER, b. 1822   3910

Wagandt, Charles L., ed. "The Civil War Journal of Dr. Samuel A. Harrison." CIVIL WAR HISTORY 13 (1967):131-146.

1861-1865. Diary of physician, a slaveholder, loyal to the Union, pursuing his agricultural and literary interests in Talbot County, Maryland; lengthy entries ruminating on slavery and emancipation and considering political, economic and social aspects of these issues in Maryland; notes on pro-Southern feelings in his state, the 1864 presidential election, Gov. Thomas H. Hicks, Lincoln's assassination, black Union soldiers and suffrage, etc.; an interesting combination of a gentleman's antislavery, humanitarian and racist sentiments.

HAY, JOHN, 1838-1905   3911

LETTERS OF JOHN HAY AND EXTRACTS FROM DIARY. Selected by Henry Adams. Edited by Mrs. Hay. Washington, D.C., 1908. 3 vols. Diary, vol. 1, pp. 8-384 passim, vol. 3, p. 350. Reprint. New York: Gordian Press, 1969.

1861-1869, 1905. Extracts from diary begun six weeks after taking up duties as assistant to John G. Nicolay, Lincoln's private secretary; an insider's view of the Lincoln administration and commentary on the Union's military and political leaders; social and political notes during postwar diplomatic service as secretary of the legation in Paris and in Madrid and charge d'affaires at Vienna; a visit to England; a single entry made shortly before his death, reflecting on his life and accomplishments. This edition suffers from the editorial hand of Mrs. Hay who operated without suffi-

cient historical objectivity and also reduced all proper names to initials.

LINCOLN AND THE CIVIL WAR IN THE DIARIES AND LETTERS OF JOHN HAY. Selected and with an introduction by Tyler Dennett. New York: Dodd, Mead, 1939. 348 pp. Diary, pp. 1-292 passim. Reprint. Westport, Conn.: Negro Universities Press, 1972.

1861-1868. Diary extracts selected because of the light they shed on Abraham Lincoln, the war and the politics of the Reconstruction period; the wartime capital and the process of organizing a government and army; border state tensions; war aims, the Emancipation Proclamation and plans for reconstruction of the Union; Lincoln, his words and actions; trips to Point Lookout Prison, the South Carolina coast and Florida to offer oath of allegiance under the Proclamation of Amnesty and Reconstruction; Northern politics and the 1864 presidential election; postwar diplomatic service interspersed with visits to Washington, D.C.; descriptive notes and commentary on most Union leaders including Jim Lane, Carl Schurz, Elmer Ellsworth, Seward, McClellan, Chase, Hooker, Montgomery Blair, Sickles, Meade, Rosencrans, Grant, Butler and Charles Sumner. Working from the original papers, but including many of the entries contained in the 1908 edition, Dennett both deletes from and adds to the record compiled by Mrs. Hay.

Thayer, William Roscoe, ed. "Lincoln and Some Union Generals." HARPER'S MAGAZINE 130 (1914-1915):93-100.

1861-1864. Extracts from manuscript diary, reporting the diarist's and Lincoln's interactions with generals McClellan, Halleck, Hooker, Meade, Butler and Grant.

Extracts in THE BLUE AND THE GRAY, edited by Henry S. Commager, vol. 2, pp. 1083-1085, 1093-1096; TRAGIC YEARS, by Paul M. Angle and Earl S. Miers, vol. 1, pp. 83-84, vol. 2, pp. 851, 920-922; TREASURY OF THE WORLD'S GREAT DIARIES, edited by Philip Dunaway, pp. 278-280.

HEARTSILL, WILLIAM WILLISTON, 1839-1916   3912

FOURTEEN HUNDRED AND 91 DAYS IN THE CONFEDERATE ARMY. Marshall, Tex.: W.W. Heartsill, 1876. 264 pp. Edited by Bell I. Wiley. Jackson, Tenn.: McCowat-Mercer Press, 1953. 332 pp.

1861-1865. Diary, revised for publication, of Tennessean who had moved to Texas in 1859; service with the W.P. Lane Rangers, or Company F, Second Texas Cavalry; patrol duty on the Texas frontier, providing protection from Indians; notes on fauna, flora, Mexicans and rancher J.D. Westfall; promotion to sergeant; capture at the battle of Arkansas Post; hardships of imprisonment at Camp Butler near Springfield, Illinois, until exchange some four months later; brief service guarding Richmond from Stoneman's cavalry during Chancellorsville campaign and comment on Virginians' reaction to Jackson's death; sent to Bragg's army at Tullahoma, Tennessee, and gathered with other cavalry remnants into an infantry unit, Company L, R.Q. Mills's regiment, the Arkansas Post Brigade; low morale due to having to serve as foot soldiers under officers not of their choosing while their old company operated west of the Mississippi; the battle of Chickamauga; decision to leave upon receipt of order dispersing remaining members of Company L through the regiment; surreptitious six weeks journey with three friends on foot across the Confederacy to Texas; once more in the Texas cavalry, Company I of Morgan's Battalion; guarding prisoners at Camp Ford, followed by assignments in Louisiana, Arkansas and Texas; a veritable history of his unit, recording names of those present at various times, the sick, wounded, killed and those on furlough; description of countryside, civilian support, camp life, deserters, visits home to Marshall, etc.; appendices containing the unrevised manuscript versions of Chickamauga and flight from the Army of Tennessee.

HOLMES, EMMA, 1838-1910   3913

THE DIARY OF MISS EMMA HOLMES. Edited by John F. Marszalek. Baton Rouge: Louisiana State University Press, 1979. 496 pp.

1861-1866. The war and its aftermath as seen by intelligent, aristocratic Charlestonian within the social network of the Holmes, De Saussure and Gibbes families and their friends; events at Charleston including the taking of Fort Sumter, the destructive December 1861 fire and the bombardment of the city in July 1863; reports, often distorted, of war's progress; refugee life at Camden, South Carolina; the satisfactions and frustrations of teaching; description of depredations as Union troops pass through and comments on miscegenation; hardships endured as servants depart, black troops arrive and economic recovery is sought; details of family and social life, ceremonies at the Citadel, reading, religion, clothing, visits to the dentist, etc.; lengthy entries expressing the partisan viewpoint of an ardent Confederate who hated the North and unquestioningly accepted slavery.

In DIARY OF HENRY MCCALL HOLMES, by Henry McCall Holmes, pp. 13-35 passim. State College, Miss., 1968.

1861-1865. Extracts containing news of family and conditions in the Confederate army transmitted in letters from her brother Henry.

Marszalek, John F., Jr., ed. "The Charleston Fire of 1861 as Described in the Emma E. Holmes Diary." SOUTH CAROLINA HISTORICAL MAGAZINE 76 (1975):60-67.

Dec 1861. Extracts describing the conflagration which consumed many significant public buildings as well as private residences, including the home of the diarist's family; detailed record of damage and property losses.

Extracts in HEROINES OF DIXIE, edited by Katharine M. Jones, pp. 4, 17-22; TRAGIC YEARS, by Paul M. Angle and Earl S. Miers, vol. 1, pp. 56-57, 59-60.

HOLMES, OLIVER WENDELL, 1841-1935   3914

TOUCHED WITH FIRE; CIVIL WAR LETTERS AND DIARY OF OLIVER WENDELL HOLMES, JR. Edited by Mark De Wolf Howe. Cambridge: Harvard University Press, 1946. 158 pp. Diary, pp. 23-33, 101-152 passim. Reprint. New York: Da Capo, 1969.

Oct 1861, May-Jul 1864. Future eminent jurist's record of combat; retrospective account of his wounding at Ball's Bluff while serving in the Twentieth Massachusetts; the last two months of his active duty as aide-de-camp on Gen. Horatio G. Wright's staff; the Wilderness, Spotsylvania campaign and Cold Harbor.

Extracts in THE MILITARY IN AMERICA, edited by Peter Karsten, pp. 184-185. New York: Free Press, 1980; TREASURY OF THE WORLD'S GREAT DIARIES, edited by Philip Dunaway, pp. 268-271.

Oct 1861. Ball's Bluff.

HOLMES, SARAH KATHERINE STONE, 1841-1907   3915

BROKENBURN; THE JOURNAL OF KATE STONE. Edited by John Q. Anderson. Baton Rouge: Louisiana State University Press, 1955, 1972. 400 pp.

Extracts in THE CONFEDERACY, edited by Albert D. Kirwan, pp. 90-92, 289-290. New York: Meridian Books, 1959; TRAGIC YEARS, by Paul M. Angle and Earl S. Miers, vol. 2, pp. 571-573.

1861-1865, Sep 1867, Sep 1868. Journal recording young woman's days at Brokenburn, a large Louisiana cotton plantation, thirty miles northeast of Vicksburg, and refugee life in Texas; family and social life in Madison Parish; domestic tasks, visits and visitors, slaves' behavior, plantation management and concern for her brothers and others in Confederate service; Union operations on the Mississippi and depredations of enemy and blacks; family's flight west preceded by their slaves; stopping near Monroe and Trenton, Louisiana, and then traveling by buggy to Lamar County, Texas; commentary on rough frontier conditions and unionist sentiments there; move to Tyler, Texas, reunion with Louisiana friends and encountering local prejudice against refugees; a long visit near Oak Ridge, Louisiana, and return to Tyler; social activities, deprivations, deaths of friends and loved ones, reaction to Lincoln's assassination, the pain of defeat and, above all, the indomitable spirit of the diarist's mother, Amanda Ragan Stone; return to Brokenburn; long entries, sporadically penned, with annual postwar summaries as the family tries to rebuild their lives; a richly detailed portrait.

HOTZE, HENRY, 1834-1887   3916

THREE MONTHS IN THE CONFEDERATE ARMY. With an introduction and notes by Richard B. Harwell. University: University of Alabama Press, 1952. 38 pp. Diary, pp. 14-28.

Apr-May 1861. First appearing in the Swiss-born Hotze's London newspaper, THE INDEX, and no doubt polished up for publication, a diary of service with the Mobile Cadets, a company in the Third Alabama; journey to Virginia; conditions of transport aboard the ST. NICHOLAS en route to Montgomery from Mobile and in cattle cars north from Dalton, Georgia; enthusiasm and generosity of citizens along the way, especially at Montgomery, Knoxville and Lynchburg; notes on unionist sympathies in eastern Tennessee and Parson Brownlow; glimpse of Andrew Johnson; election of officers and the politics involved; camp life at Lynchburg and Norfolk.

HOWE, HENRY WARREN, b. 1841   3917

PASSAGES FROM THE LIFE OF HENRY WARREN HOWE. Lowell, Mass.: Courier-Citizen Co., Printers, 1899. 211 pp. Diary, pp. 9-84.

1861-1865 (with gaps). Diary of Civil War service; enlistment in the Richardson's Light Guard, or Seventh Battery, Massachusetts Light Artillery; events at and around Fortress Monroe; detailed as orderly to Ben Butler; a visit to Baltimore; expedition to Hatteras Inlet; recruiting back home in Lowell and becoming quartermaster sergeant of the Thirtieth Massachusetts; to Ship Island, New Orleans and Baton Rouge; promotion to second lieutenant for bravery at battle of Baton Rouge; in camp near New Orleans, then at Baton Rouge before and after assaults on Port Hudson; expedition to Sabine Pass; operations in Louisiana; regimental reenlistment as veteran volunteers and subsequent furlough; voyage back to New Orleans and assignment at Morganza; countering Early's Washington raid, participation in Sheridan's Shenandoah Valley campaign and return home; notes on duties, leisure activities, reading, drinking in the army, foraging, Lincoln, Sheridan, Butler, Simon Cameron, Col. Nathan Dudley, etc.; long, somewhat scattered entries at first, becoming daily but shorter.

HUBBERT, MIKE M., 1838?-1863   3918

Fisher, John E., ed. "The Travels of the 13th Mississippi Regiment." JOURNAL OF MISSISSIPPI HISTORY 45 (1983):288-313.

Sep-Dec 1861, Mar-Dec 1862. Diary of enlisted man from Attala County; journey back to regiment in Virginia; battle of Ball's Bluff; in camp near Leesburg; battle of Fair Oaks; Seven Days' battles; crossing the Potomac to a disappointing civilian response in Maryland; successful investment of Harpers Ferry and battle of Antietam; battle of Fredericksburg; notes on weather, military action, destruction by Union forces, etc.

HUNDLEY, DANIEL ROBINSON, 1832-1899   3919

PRISON ECHOES OF THE GREAT REBELLION. New York: S.W. Green, Printer, 1874. 235 pp. Diary, pp. 7-13, 75-196.

Apr-May 1861, Jun-Dec 1864. Extracts from diary of Alabama officer; trip to Chicago at war's outbreak to settle his affairs, with notes on public temper there and in Louisville; later internment at Johnson's Island after capture during the Atlanta campaign; prison facilities, routines and regulations; notes on escape attempts, rat hunts, Masonic assistance to inmates, demoralization of fellow prisoners, etc.; lengthy reports and commentary on political and war news; thoughts on Yankees, their religion and their leaders, educated man's articulate account of coping with confinement and harsh conditions until his escape.

HUPP, ORMAND   3920

MY DIARY. Odessa, Mo.: Ewing Printers, 1923. 107 pp.

1861-1864. Record of member of Fifth Battery, Indiana Light Artillery; narrative of events from enlistment until March 1863, then commencing dated entries; nursing duties at New Albany, Indiana, hospital while recovering from wounds suffered at the battle of Perryville; weather, war news, correspondence, his health, Fourth of July ceremonies and celebration of Vicksburg's surrender, furlough with family near La Porte, social life, cemetery strolls and other leisure pursuits; return to the battery at Cleveland, Tennessee; the Atlanta campaign, with notes on military action, campaign conditions and the Georgia countryside.

ICKES, ALONZO FERDINAND, 1836-1917   3921

BLOODY TRAILS ALONG THE RIO GRANDE. By Nolie Mumey. Denver: Old West, 1958. 123 pp. Diary, pp. 47-105.

1861-1863. Diary of gold miner who enlisted in Company B, Second Colorado Volunteers; march from Canon City, Colorado, through the Sangre de Cristo Pass into the San Luis Valley to Fort Garland; march to Fort Marcy at Santa Fe and then on through Albuquerque and along the Rio Grande to Fort Craig; battle of Valverde; following Sibley, dull days at Fort Craig and return to Santa Fe; at Fort Scott, Kansas; description of countryside and settlements; mention of soldiers' drinking, gambling and fighting, prostitution and venereal disease; anti-Mexican comments; notes on Col. Edward Canby, Capt. James Graydon and Kit Carson; a candid look at army life.

JAMES, WESTWOOD WALLACE, d. 1868   3922

Musick, Michael, ed. " 'This is War—Glorious War.' " CIVIL WAR TIMES ILLUSTRATED 17, No. 6 (1978):34-42.

Apr, Nov-Dec 1861, Jan 1862. Physician's diary; treating wounded

from Bull Run at a Charlottesville hospital and reflecting on the human cost of war; campaigning in Kentucky as corporal, Company I, Sixteenth Alabama Volunteer Infantry.

JAQUES, JOHN WESLEY   3923

THREE YEAR'S CAMPAIGN OF THE NINTH. New York: Hilton, 1865. 199 pp.

1861-1864. Diary of soldier in Company D, Ninth New York, obviously reworked and augmented for publication, often lapsing into narrative; primarily a record of the regiment's marches, encampments and engagements; operations in Maryland and the Shenandoah Valley; Second Bull Run campaign and battles of Antietam, Fredericksburg, Chancellorsville, Gettysburg, Mine Run, the Wilderness, Spotsylvania and Cold Harbor; notes on accidents, casualties, a soldier's suicide, Burnside's "Mud March," etc.

JAY, CORNELIA, 1839-1907   3924

THE DIARY OF CORNELIA JAY. Rye, N.Y.: Published for private circulation, 1924. 228 pp.

1861-1866, 1868-1873. Diary of John Jay's great granddaughter; social life in New York City and at family estate in Rye, New York; war news and women's efforts to support the soldiers; notes on family and friends, especially members of the Van Rensselaer and Prime families; voyage on the HENRY HILL to Marseilles, sojourning there and subsequently at Nice, Lausanne and Paris; notes on reading, New York City's celebration of Lincoln's second inauguration, the black pianist Blind Tom, Wendell Phillips, George B. McClellan, Fourth of July and Christmas festivities, a vacation in New Hampshire, Japanese visitors, her church work, etc.; long but sporadic entries.

JEFFRIES, LEMUEL, 1839?-1909   3925

Silverman, Jason H., ed. " 'The Excitement Had Begun!' " MANUSCRIPTS 30 (1978):265-278.

1861-1863. Extracts from diary of Wayne County, Ohio, newspaper editor, a member of Company E, Fourth Ohio Volunteer Infantry; action in western Virginia; description of the Army of the Potomac in the wake of the Seven Days' battles; soldiers' reaction to McClellan's dismissal; battle of Fredericksburg; winter camp at Falmouth, conversing with Confederates across the Rappahannock; battle of Chancellorsville; passing over the Second Bull Run battlefield on the way to Pennsylvania; battle of Gettysburg; in New York City after the draft riots and return to Virginia; gruesome execution of two deserters; a well-written account.

JOHNSON, CHARLES F., b. 1843   3926

THE LONG ROLL. Duluth ed. East Aurora, N.Y.: Roycrofters, 1911. 241 pp.

1861-1863. Diary of Swedish-born member of Hawkin's Zouaves, Company I, Ninth New York volunteers, kept somewhat irregularly; starting out at Castle Garden and Rikers Island camps; military duties in Virginia, at and near Newport News, and at Hatteras Inlet, noting Union naval actions at both places; first battle experience at Roanoke Island and the grim sights of the field afterwards; stationed on Roanoke with expeditions to Winton and Elizabeth City; in Virginia, near Fredericksburg and Acquia Creek;

a glimpse of Lincoln while in hospital at Frederick, Maryland, recovering from wound received at Antietam; in convalescent camp at Alexandria, sightseeing in Washington, D.C. and return to regiment; stationed at Newport News and in Suffolk area until expiration of enlistment; nice descriptions of countryside, towns, forts, fauna and flora; the enjoyment he found in his sketches, many of which illustrate the diary; concern and frustration with inept officers but praise for Gen. Ambrose Burnside, Lt. Col. Victor De Monteuil, Lt. Col. Edgar A. Kimball and Col. Rush C. Hawkins; notes on his uniform, baseball, reading and other leisure activities, Fourth of July and Saint Patrick's Day celebrations, contrabands, hospitals and treatment of the wounded, Union troops' plundering and destruction, etc.; lengthy, detailed entries, no doubt revised after the fact, providing a richly textured picture of life in camp and on the field of battle.

Extracts in THE BLUE AND THE GRAY, edited by Henry S. Commager, vol. 1, pp. 489-490, vol. 2, pp. 798-802.

Oct 1861, Feb 1862. Forcing the resignation of an undesirable officer; battle of Roanoke Island.

JOHNSTON, ADAM S.   3927

THE SOLDIER BOY'S DIARY BOOK. Pittsburg, Pa., 1866. 139 pp.

1861-1864. Account of service with Company D, Seventy-ninth Pennsylvania Volunteers, campaigning in Kentucky, Tennessee and Alabama; regiment's movements and distances covered; wounding in the battle of Perryville and medical treatment; description of unionist refugees; duties, activities and events in camp; witnessing executions; battle of Chickamauga and capture; a hard journey to Libby Prison and conditions there; transfer to prison and hospital at Danville; exchange, in hospital at Annapolis and recuperating in Philadelphia until discharged; home to Turtle Creek, Pennsylvania; generally notes on weather and rations, with much lamenting, obviously reworked for publication.

JONES, JOHN BEAUCHAMP, 1810-1866   3928

A REBEL WAR CLERK'S DIARY AT THE CONFEDERATE STATES CAPITAL. Philadelphia: J.B. Lippincott, 1866. 2 vols. New and enl. ed. Edited by Howard Swiggett. New York: Old Hickory Bookshop, 1935. 2 vols. Abr. ed. Edited by Earl S. Miers. New York: Sagamore Press, 1958. 545 pp.

Widely extracted. See, for instance, in THE ALABAMA CONFEDERATE READER, edited by Malcolm M. McMillan, pp. 65-70. THE BLUE AND THE GRAY, edited by Henry S. Commager, vol. 1, pp. 25-27, vol. 2, 744-749; TRAGIC YEARS, by Paul M. Angle and Earl S. Miers, vol. 1, pp. 69-70, 282-284, 323-324, 522-523, 526-528, vol. 2, p. 601; TREASURY OF THE WORLD'S GREAT DIARIES, edited by Philip Dunaway, pp. 275-277.

1861-1865. Chronicle of the Confederacy as seen from Richmond compiled, and later reworked, by author/editor who sought and obtained government clerkship necessary to the keeping of a full diary of events; service under six secretaries of war; observations on many politicians and generals; commentary on political wrangling within and against the administration of Jefferson Davis and problems of military manpower, supplies and security; fulminations about speculators, profiteers and, especially, Winder's martial law in the city; his patriotic, proslavery and anti-Semitic views and suspicions of highly placed Confederates of Northern origin; record of prices; notes on Emancipation Proclamation's effects, Southern conscription and its evasion, Jackson's funeral, economic hardships, debate over Confederate army's use of black

soldiers, various peace plans including a communication with Vallandigham, evacuation and occupation of Richmond, Lincoln's assassination, etc.; mostly reports of, and his reactions to, the official and unofficial correspondence passing under his purview at the War Department but with occasional warm glimpses of family life and the joys of his garden.

KEAN, ROBERT GARLICK HILL, 1828-1898   3929

INSIDE THE CONFEDERATE GOVERNMENT. Edited by Edward Younger. New York: Oxford University Press, 1957. 241 pp. Reprint. Westport, Conn.: Greenwood, 1973.

Extracts in TRAGIC YEARS, by Paul M. Angle and Earl S. Miers, vol. 1, pp. 205-206.

1861-1865 (with gaps). Diary of Lynchburg, Virginia, lawyer, appointed head of the Bureau of War after brief service with Company G, Eleventh Virginia Infantry; war news, gossip and full commentary on military and diplomatic events; working under secretaries of war George W. Randolph, James A. Seddon and John C. Breckinridge, and admiration for his immediate superior, John A. Campbell, assistant secretary of war; evaluation of leading political and military figures including Jefferson Davis, Jeb Stuart, Stonewall Jackson, Judah P. Benjamin, Braxton Bragg, Joseph E. Johnston and Robert E. Lee; discussion of government finances, administration of the War Department, shortages and prices, legality of Union recruitment of Southern blacks, use of slaves in the Confederate armies, the Hampton Roads Peace Conference, constitutional violations of Reconstruction government and the consequences of emancipation, etc.; notes on the military commission prosecuting Wirz before which the diarist was summoned to testify; in the main, views of conflict and incompetence within the Confederate leadership penned by a staunch believer in the Southern cause.

KELLAM, C.F.   3930

In A DOCUMENTARY HISTORY OF ARKANSAS, edited by Fred C. Williams and others, pp. 103-104.

Oct-Nov 1861. Extracts from Camden, Arkansas, merchant's diary, reflecting war's effect on business transactions and the economy.

KIENE, FRANCIS A., 1839-1924   3931

A CIVIL WAR DIARY. Compiled by Ralph E. Kiene, Jr. Shawnee Mission, Kan.: R.E. Kiene, 1974. 372 pp.

1861-1864 (with gap). Pandora, Ohio, resident's account of service with Company I, Forty-ninth Ohio Volunteers; getting organized at Tiffin, Ohio; routines at Camp Denison near Cincinnati; camp life and provost guard duties in Kentucky, near Elizabeth Town and Munfordsville on the Green River; battle of Shiloh and the sights of the battlefield afterwards; the advance on Corinth and a tour of the evacuated city; passing through Iuka, Florence and Huntsville; battle of Stones River; Chickamauga and Chattanooga campaigns; transfer to Sixty-eighth Indiana because he would not reenlist as veteran, then back to the Forty-ninth; the Atlanta campaign until wounding at Pickett's Mill; long daily entries recording work and other activities, revealing the tenor of life in the ranks; notes on slavery, foraging, pillaging, the Perryville battlefield, exploring caves in Kentucky, military punishments, drinking in the army, his health and that of others, debates, etc.; description of countryside through which he passed.

KINGSBURY, ALLEN ALONZO, 1840-1862   3932

THE HERO OF MEDFIELD. Edited by E.A. Johnson. Boston: J.M. Hewes, Printer, 1862. 144 pp. Journal, pp. 7-21, 43-50.

Jun 1861-Mar 1862 (with gap). Journal of bugler in Company H, Chelsea Volunteers, First Massachusetts, who was killed in April 1862 near Yorktown; in camp near Washington, D.C., and sightseeing in the city; duties, weather, rations, etc.; battle of Bull Run; journey home and return; in Maryland camp.

KIRCHER, HENRY ADOLPH, 1841-1908   3933

A GERMAN IN THE YANKEE FATHERLAND. Edited by Earl J. Hess. Kent, Ohio: Kent State University Pres, 1983. 169 pp. Diary pp. 7-153 passim.

1861-1863. Scattered extracts from and summary of contents of diary used to provide chronological framework for war letters of German-American machinist from Belleville, Illinois; service as officer with the Twelfth Missouri Infantry; operations in Missouri and Arkansas; Vicksburg and Chattanooga campaigns.

KITTINGER, JOSEPH, b. 1839   3934

DIARY 1861-1865. Buffalo, N.Y.: Kittinger Co., 1979? 213 pp.

1861-1865. Diary of member of the Twenty-third Independent Battery, New York Volunteer Light Artillery; getting organized at Albany; stationed at Washington, D.C.; extensive sightseeing, attending Senate sessions and one of President Lincoln's levees, Washington's birthday celebration and a view of Dorothea Dix while in hospital; description of Fortress Monroe, the MONITOR and other ironclads; by ship to New Bern; military operations in North Carolina, based at New Bern, Carolina City, Morehead City and Washington and participating in various expeditions; furlough home to Niagara County and visits to Gettysburg, Norfolk, New York City, Petersburg, Richmond and the University of North Carolina at Chapel Hill; religious concerns; patriotic sentiments; sketches of comrades; notes on church services, reading, target practice, camp life, illnesses, foraging, soldiers' drinking, reenlistment, etc.; lengthy, detailed entries.

LATHAM, HENRY C., 1837-1917   3935

"A Young Man's View of Lincoln and Douglas in 1861." ABRAHAM LINCOLN ASSOCIATION BULLETIN, no. 52 (June 1938):7-9.

Jan-Mar, Jun 1861. Extracts from Springfield, Illinois, resident's diary; making New Year's Day calls; witnessing Lincoln's departure for Washington, D.C.; diarist's thoughts on the day of the inauguration; public reaction to Lincoln's inaugural speech and his cabinet choices; words of praise for the recently deceased Stephen A. Douglas.

LAW, J.G.   3936

"Diary of J.G. Law." SOUTHERN HISTORICAL SOCIETY PAPERS 11 (1883):175-181, 297-303, 460-465; 12 (1884):22-28, 215-219, 390-395, 538-543.

Nov 1861-Sep 1862. Daily record of soldier's life in the 154th Tennessee; battle of Belmont; work at hospitals in Memphis; return to active duty; evacuation of Columbus; battle of Shiloh and retreat from Corinth; advance into Kentucky, battle of Richmond and warm reception from Southern sympathizers in Lexington; details

of marches, duties, food, health, reading and other leisure activities, camp rumors, etc.

LENOIR, WALTER W.   3937

In ECHOES OF HAPPY VALLEY, by Thomas F. Hickerson, pp. 78-88.

1861-1863. Extracts from soldier's diary of service with the Twenty-fifth North Carolina Volunteers and the Thirty-seventh North Carolina Troops; sporadic, lengthy entries, summarizing and reflecting upon events of past few weeks or months; Second Bull Run campaign, wounding and treatment; belief in eventual Southern victory; concern about his ability to be an officer and his spiritual condition; description of his feelings in battle and hardships of soldiering; an informative, introspective account of the war experience.

LEON, LOUIS, 1841-1919   3938

DIARY OF A TAR HEEL CONFEDERATE SOLDIER. Charlotte, N.C.: Stone, 1913. 87 pp. Diary , pp. 1-71.

Extracts in MEMOIRS OF AMERICAN JEWS, 1775-1865, by Jacob R. Marcus, vol. 3, pp. 197-225; A DOCUMENTARY HISTORY OF THE JEWS IN THE U.S., 1654-1875, 3d ed., by Morris U. Schappes, pp. 481-491. New York: Schocken Books, 1971.

1861-1865. Generally sporadic entries, with some evidence of later reworking, in Jewish private's diary; service in the Charlotte Grays, Company C, First North Carolina, and the battle of Big Bethel; with the Fifty-third North Carolina, campaigning in their home state and in Virginia; battle of Gettysburg, especially action at Culp's Hill, and the carnage of the battlefield; in rear guard as the Confederates retreat; Mine Run campaign; the Wilderness and capture; prison conditions at Point Lookout and Elmira and feelings about black Union guards; primarily description of military action but also notes on General Lee, foraging and the ladies.

LITTLE, LEWIS HENRY, 1817-1862   3939

Castel, Albert, ed. "The Diary of General Henry Little, C.S.A." CIVIL WAR TIMES ILLUSTRATED 11, no. 6 (1972):4-11, 41-47.

Mar-Jun 1861, Apr-May, Jul-Sep 1862. Extracts from Marylander's diary; trip from Fort Smith, Arkansas, to new post at St. Louis; agonizing decision to resign from United States Army and join the Confederate cause; service as assistant adjutant general to Sterling Price, at that time commander of the Missouri State Guard; in Mississippi, leading the First Missouri Brigade; war news and brief comment on Confederate strategy; notes on illnesses and expressions of longing for his wife and child; events leading up to the battle of Iuka in which he was killed.

LURIA, ALBERT MOSES, 1843-1862   3940

"Albert Moses Luria: Gallant Young Confederate." AMERICAN JEWISH ARCHIVES 7 (1955): 90-103.

Aug 1861-Jan 1862. Extracts from diary of lieutenant in Company I, Twenty-third North Carolina Volunteers; scenes of home in Columbus, Georgia, and of camp; the gory battlefield of First Bull Run; love for cousin Eliza Moses and reflections on the admirable character of her sister Alice; opinion concerning theory that the Confederates should have pursued the Union army after Bull Run and belief that the Confederacy should fight a defensive rather than offensive war.

MCCLURE, THOMAS D.   **3941**

In THE REBELLION RECORD, edited by Frank Moore, vol. 3, pp. 79-83.

Sep 1861. Siege and surrender of Lexington, Missouri, as described in the diary of lieutenant, Company D, Twenty-third Illinois Volunteers.

MCCONNELL, WILLIAM, 1840-1865   **3942**

DIARY OF WILLIAM MCCONNELL. Tiro, Ohio: Chas. McConnell, 1899. 198 pp. Diary, pp. 3-147.

1861-1865. Extracts from diary of private, Company I, Fifteenth Ohio Volunteer Infantry; short, unemotional daily entries becoming longer and more responsive late in the war and afterwards; service in Kentucky, Tennessee and Alabama, including Shiloh, the advance to Corinth, Stones River, where he was wounded, captured and quickly paroled, and the Chattanooga campaign; veteran furlough home to Crawford County, Ohio; the Atlanta campaign; assignment as clerk in mustering office at division headquarters; Franklin and Nashville campaign; stationed in Alabama and Green Lake, Texas, where he died suddenly; notes on weather, duties, camp routines, photography atop Lookout Mountain and reaction to Lincoln's assassination.

MCDONALD, ANDREW YOUNG   **3943**

PERSONAL CIVIL WAR DIARY OF ANDREW YOUNG MCDONALD. Dubuque, 1956. 24 pp.

Apr-Sep 1861. A daily account of service by enlisted man in the Governor Grays of Dubuque, First Iowa; in camp at Davenport and Keokuk; journey to Missouri and operations there, including the battle of Wilson's Creek in which he was wounded; recovering at Springfield and trip home; notes on activities, correspondence, miles covered, prices, discipline problems, civilian support, etc.

MCGUIRE, JUDITH WHITE BROCKENBROUGH,   **3944**
1812-1896

DIARY OF A SOUTHERN REFUGEE DURING THE WAR. New York: E.J. Hale & Son, 1867. 360 pp. Reprint. New York: Arno, 1972. 2d ed. 1868. 3d. ed. Richmond, Va.: J.W. Randolph & English, 1889. 372 pp.

Widely extracted. See, for instance, in HEROINES OF DIXIE, edited by Katharine M. Jones, pp. 24-26, 31-42, 302-304, 355-356, 383-385, 397-402; LADIES OF RICHMOND, edited by Katharine M. Jones, pp. 100-107, 109-110, 112-114, 123-125, 150-152, 191-194, 289-291; TRUE TALES OF THE SOUTH AT WAR, edited by Clarence H. Poe, pp. 148-184; WOMEN OF THE SOUTH IN WARTIME, compiled by Matthew Page Andrews, pp. 71-104, 155-189, 372-397, 405-412.

1861-1865. Diary kept by Virginian, wife of the Rev. John P. McGuire, principal of the Episcopal High School near Alexandria; thoughts on the war and preparations for invasion; Union occupation of Alexandria and flight to various locations, including Chantilly, the Shenandoah Valley and, finally, Richmond, where her husband secured a clerkship in the Post Office Department, and nearby Ashland; the hardships of refugee life, especially finding lodgings; war news, deaths of friends and loved ones and sacrifices made for the cause; nursing duties and her clerkship in the Commissary Department; reports of Union cruelties and depredations; her concern for departing slaves; coping with short-

ages and inflation; notes on Robert E. Lee and his wife, Jeb Stuart, Stonewall Jackson, Jefferson and Varina Davis and prominent Episcopal clergymen; the fall of Richmond and the Confederacy; a staunch Confederate portrait of war's impact on civilians, particularly women.

MCKINLEY, WILLIAM, 1843-1901   **3945**

Morgan, H. Wayne, ed. "A Civil War Diary of William McKinley." OHIO HISTORICAL QUARTERLY 69 (1960):272-290.

Jun-Sep, Nov 1861. Future president's diary of service with Company E, Twenty-third Ohio Volunteer Infantry; at Camp Chase, with notes on camp routines, duties, celebration of the Fourth of July, prayer meetings and religious services, sightseeing in Columbus, etc.; operations in western Virginia and the hardships of campaigning; patriotic and religious declarations.

MACKLEY, JOHN, b. 1831?   **3946**

Throne, Mildred, ed. "The Civil War Diary of John Mackley." IOWA JOURNAL OF HISTORY 48 (1950):141-168.

Apr 1861-Mar 1862. Keokuk soldier's record; transformation of Keokuk Guards into Union Guards and then into Company A, Second Iowa Volunteer Infantry; service in Missouri and briefly at Fort Jefferson, Kentucky; guarding Confederate prisoners at St. Louis, with names of prominent Confederates among the captives; battle of Fort Donelson; down the Tennessee River to Pittsburgh Landing.

MARCHAND, JOHN BONNET, b. 1808   **3947**

CHARLESTON BLOCKADE. Edited by Craig L. Symonds. Newport, R.I.: Naval War College Press, 1976. 287 pp.

Sep 1861-Aug 1862. Extracts from diary of captain of the Union side-wheel steamer JAMES ADGER, embedded in editor's narrative of events involving diarist; training crew at New York City; trying to intercept the NASHVILLE which supposedly was transporting Mason and Slidell to Great Britain; in pursuit of the GLADIATOR and a stop at Fayal Island; joining Du Pont's command at Port Royal; stationed off Georgetown, South Carolina, and Savannah; expedition to Fernandina, Florida, and description of the abandoned town; senior officer in charge of the South Atlantic Blockading Squadron off Charleston; the monotony of blockade duty punctuated by false alarms and jolly times with friends; the pressures of his position and concern with making a reputation for himself; problems of organizing the blockade, obtaining supplies, keeping ships repaired, dealing with British and French warships, intercepting blockade runners and dispatching prizes; leading a reconnaissance of the Stono River; notes on weather, his work and responsibilities, relations with Du Pont, contrabands; mention of many ships and naval officers.

In OFFICIAL RECORDS OF THE UNION AND CONFEDERATE NAVIES IN THE WAR OF THE REBELLION, ser. 1, vol. 21, pp. 809-823.

Mar-Oct 1864. Extracts from journal while in command of the steam sloop LACKAWANNA and the Third Division of the West Gulf Blockading Squadron along the Texas coast; events in the blockade of Galveston; names of Southern deserters who repaired to Union vessels; movements of various ships within the squadron; orders to relinquish division command and bring the LACKAWANNA to Mobile; description of battle of Mobile Bay, including capture of the Confederate ram TENNESSEE; surrender of Fort

Gaines; bombardment of Fort Morgan and its surrender; detailed military notes and several lists of Union vessels and their commanders.

MATHEWS, ALFRED EDWARD, 1831-1874   3948

INTERESTING NARRATIVE: BEING A JOURNAL OF THE FLIGHT OF ALFRED E. MATHEWS, OF STARK CO., OHIO, FROM THE STATE OF TEXAS. N.p., 1861. Civil War Centennial Issue. Denver: N. Mumey, 1961. 34 pp.

Apr-May 1861. Record of Northern man who had been teaching school in Tuscaloosa County, Alabama, when war came; journey on foot from Carthage, Texas, through Louisiana, Arkansas and Missouri to Ohio; description of countryside and settlements, including soil, timber and crops, and emphasizing the inhabitants' poor standard of living and noting many encounters with Southerners who preferred the Union; physical hardships of the journey and a couple of threatening situations with secessionists; assessment of Confederate soldiers.

MAUPIN, SOCRATES, 1808-1871   3949

"Socrates Maupin's Journal as Chairman of the Faculty, University of Virginia." ALBEMARLE COUNTY HISTORICAL SOCIETY PAPERS 3 (1942-1943):56-69.

1861-1864. Official journal reflecting war's impact on the University in its record of the steady stream of students withdrawing to join the military, temporary troop encampments on campus, housing wounded in university buildings, etc.

MAURY, BETTY HERNDON MAURY, 1835-1903   3950

THE CONFEDERATE DIARY OF BETTY HERNDON MAURY. Edited by Alice Maury Parmelee. Washington, D.C.: Privately printed, 1938. 102 pp.

Extracts in HEROINES OF DIXIE, edited by Katharine M. Jones, pp. 42-55, 117-121, 150-153, 197-198, 207-209.

1861-1863. War diary of Matthew Fontaine Maury's daughter; difficulties of passing through the lines from Washington, D.C., to Fredericksburg; reports of capture of the ST. NICHOLAS and an unsuccessful naval venture undertaken by her father; Union occupation of Fredericksburg; problems of refugee life in the country near Fredericksburg and in Richmond; frequent reference to her father and expression of her frustration over the Confederate government's apparent lack of appreciation of his abilities; concern about her relationship with her husband and the fragility of her daughter; mention of many relatives including members of the Minor family; war news; notes on prices, shortages and increasing problems with slaves; comparison of Confederate and Union soldiers; report of destruction sustained in the town during the battle of Fredericksburg.

MEANS, ALEXANDER, 1801-1883   3951

DIARY FOR 1861. Edited by Ross H. McLean. Emory University Publications, Sources & Reprints, ser. 6, no. 1. Atlanta: The Library, Emory University, 1949. 46 pp.

Jan-Dec 1861. Diary of noted scientist, educator and licensed Methodist exhorter living in Oxford, Georgia, but frequently visiting nearby Covington and Atlanta; business, family and farming concerns; preaching and other church activities; lectures at Atlanta Medical College and Emory; delegate to state convention which voted for secession and to second session in Savannah at which the Confederate constitution was adopted; war fervor and his patriotic support; trip to Richmond, sightseeing there and visit with soldier son near Manassas; notes on health, slaves, prices, a new process for making soap, etc.

MEIGS, MONTGOMERY CUNNINGHAM, 1816-1892   3952

"General M.C. Meigs on the Conduct of the Civil War." AMERICAN HISTORICAL REVIEW 26 (1921):285-303. Diary, pp. 299-303.

Mar-Apr 1861, Jan 1862. Extracts from diaries kept by the Union's quartermaster-general of the army; substantial entries describing his contribution to the efforts of Lincoln and Seward to reinforce Fort Pickens; brief jottings covering White House council meetings aimed at getting McClellan to activate the army.

MELVIN, SAMUEL, 1844-1864   3953

In THE MELVIN MEMORIAL, by Alfred Seelye Roe, pp. 77-133. Cambridge, Mass.: Privately printed at the Riverside Press, 1910.

1861-1864. Extracts from diary of soldier, Company K, First Massachusetts Heavy Artillery; sightseeing in Washington, D.C., and operations in Virginia; stationed at forts Craig and Tillinghast; buying books, electroplating various objects and longing to be out of the army; capture at Harris' Farm; journey to Georgia, reporting treatment, rations and a train accident; the horrible conditions at Andersonville, gradually wearing him down; notes on food, prices, weather, the "raiders," deaths, etc.; thoughts of friends and home; a poignant record of a young man's dreams smashed by the war.

MOORE, JOSEPHUS C., 1842-1865   3954

Bowman, Larry G. and Scroggs, Jack B., eds. "Diary of a Confederate Soldier." MILITARY REVIEW 62, no. 2 (1982):20-34.

1861-1862 (with gap). Diary of Bedford County native, a member of Company F, Eighteenth Tennessee, stationed in his home state; enjoying furloughs; capture at Fort Donelson; monotony and loneliness of prison life at Camp Butler near Springfield, Illinois; deaths of comrades; taking oath of allegiance to secure release.

MOORE, NANCY E., 1807-1889   3955

JOURNAL OF ELDRESS NANCY. Edited by Mary Julia Neal. Nashville: Parthenon, 1963. 256 pp.

1861-1864. Journal kept by Shaker eldress, apparently an official record of the colony at South Union, Kentucky; the tribulations of pacifists in an area of divided loyalties; behavior and depredations of Union and Confederate troops; the colony's business matters; local events and activities of fellow Shakers; notes on weather, refugees, guerillas, war news, etc.; description of dreams.

MOORE, ROBERT AUGUSTUS, 1838-1863   3956

Silver, James W., ed. "Robert A. Moore: The Diary of a Confederate Private." LOUISIANA HISTORICAL QUARTERLY 39 (1956):235-374.

A LIFE FOR THE CONFEDERACY. Edited by James W. Silver. Jackson, Tenn.: McCowat-Mercer, 1959. 182 pp.

1861-1863 (with gap). Patriotic young Holly Springs farmer's record as private, corporal and lieutenant, Company G, Seventeenth Mississippi; organization of the regiment at Corinth and journey to join the Army of Northern Virginia; battles of Bull Run, Ball's Bluff, Fredericksburg, Chancellorsville and Gettysburg; movement of army through Carolinas and Georgia to Chickamauga where Moore was killed; candid notes on army life in Virginia; camp activities and entertainments; weather, sickness, boredom and drinking; religious conversion; circuitous furlough trip to Holly Springs by train and steamboat SOUTHERN REPUBLIC; mention of unionist or disloyal sentiments in eastern Tennessee and Raleigh, North Carolina.

MOOREHEAD, JAMES W.   3957

In MISSISSIPPI IN THE CONFEDERACY, edited by John K. Bettersworth and James W. Silver, vol. 1, pp. 60-61.

Jul 1861. Extract from diary of a captain from Brooksville, Mississippi; marching to Bull Run and description of battlefield after the clash of arms.

MORGAN, GEORGE P., 1820-1861   3958

Moore, George E., ed. "A Confederate Journal." WEST VIRGINIA HISTORY 22 (1961):201-216. Diary, pp. 202-206.

Jul-Sep 1861. Journal kept by Marion County soldier; engagement at Laurel Hill and retreat to Monterey in Highland County; ill with measles; in Pocahontas County camp, waiting for action; journal continued by nephew Stephen A. Morgan after his uncle's capture.

MORGAN, STEPHEN A., 1835-1911   3959

Moore, George E., ed. "A Confederate Journal." WEST VIRGINIA HISTORY 22 (1961):201-216. Diary, pp. 207-216.

Oct-Dec 1861. Marion County lawyer's continuation of the journal of his uncle George P. Morgan after the latter's capture; election to membership in the Virginia state convention; journey to Richmond, noting places and people along the way; at the convention and some of the matters considered; return to camp.

MORSE, W.E.H.   3960

In THE NATIONAL TRIBUNE SCRAP BOOK, no. 3, pp. 33-101. Washington, D.C.: National Tribune, 1909?

1861-1865. Diary kept by member of Company E and the color guard, Fifth Maine; rain, mud, duties, hardships and pleasures; notes on military punishments, soldiers' gear and habitations, pillaging, foraging and grisly sights at various battlefields; participation in Peninsular campaign and battles of Fair Oaks, Gaines's Mill, Fredericksburg, Chancellorsville, Gettysburg, the Wilderness, Spotsylvania and Cold Harbor; reenlistment, furlough home to Minot, Maine, and reassignment to Company B, Sixth Maine, and then reorganization into First Maine Veteran Volunteers; service around Harpers Ferry and campaigning in the Shenandoah Valley; pursuing Lee's army to Appomattox; a visit to Richmond before mustering out; detailed, candid, witty at times, providing an interesting view of a world of inexplicable orders, rumors and satisfaction in small comforts.

NASON, ELIAS, 1811-1887   3961

BRIEF RECORD OF EVENTS IN EXETER, N.H. DURING THE YEAR 1861. Exeter: Fogg & Fellowes, 1862. 16 pp.

Jan-Dec 1861. Extracts from daily record of weather, local events, marriages, deaths, etc.

BRIEF RECORD OF EVENTS IN EXETER, N.H. DURING THE YEAR 1862. Exeter: Fogg & Fellowes, 1863. 20 pp.

Jan-Dec 1862. Extracts noting weather, cloud formations and the night sky, local and national events, women's war work, etc.

BRIEF RECORD OF EVENTS IN EXETER, N.H. DURING THE YEAR 1863. Exeter: Fogg & Fellowes, 1864. 17 pp.

Jan-Dec 1863. Extracts describing local activities and incidents; civilian efforts in support of the Civil War; names of Exeter soldiers and those citizens who paid a commutation fee, hired a substitute or were drafted; meteorological observations taken for the Smithsonian Institution.

NEESE, GEORGE MICHAEL, b. 1839   3962

THREE YEARS IN THE CONFEDERATE HORSE ARTILLERY. New York and Washington, D.C.: Neale, 1911. 362 pp.

1861-1865. Gunner's diary, probably rewritten after the war; service with Capt. R.P. Chew's battery, Stuart's Horse Artillery, Army of Northern Virginia; battle of Kernstown and Jackson's Shenandoah Valley campaign, including battle of Cross Keys and Port Republic and battle of Cedar Mountain; Antietam campaign; battle of Brandy Station; Gettysburg campaign and retreat into Virginia; Mine Run, Wilderness, Spotsylvania and Petersburg campaigns; capture in the Shenandoah Valley in October 1864; conditions at Point Lookout Prison until release at war's end; observing Turner Ashby, Fitzhugh Lee, Jeb Stuart, R.E. Lee and Phil Sheridan; focus on military operations with some notes on countryside, Weir's Cave, Edmund Ruffin's home and the Second Bull Run battlefield.

NORTON, REUBEN S.   3963

Aycock, Roger. "The Diary of Reuben S. Norton Records What Happened in Rome from 1861 to 1865." GEORGIA LIFE 3, no. 4 (1977):18-19, 36.

1861-1864, 1867. A few extracts from Rome, Georgia, merchant's diary within article; burning of town by Union troops; a postwar note summarizing conditions in the town.

ONDERDONK, JAMES H., 1845-1863   3964

Fabris, Dino. "A Civil War Diary." NEW YORK HISTORY 49 (1968):76-89.

1861-1863. Extracts selected to illustrate an analysis of what the diary reveals about its author, a Rockland County youth; activities at home before enlistment in a New York regiment; voyage to Louisiana and service there before being hospitalized with dysentery which proved fatal.

ORR, HENRY GOODLOE, b. 1837?   3965

In CAMPAIGNING WITH PARSONS' TEXAS CAVALRY BRIGADE, CSA; THE WAR JOURNALS AND LETTERS OF THE FOUR ORR BROTHERS, edited by John Q. Anderson, pp. 1-47 passim, 130. Hillsboro, Tex.: Hill Junior College Press, 1967.

Oct 1861-May 1862, Mar 1864. Nicely descriptive entries extracted from journal kept by farmer turned soldier with the Ellis County Rangers, Twelfth Texas Cavalry; in camp and on the march through Texas; a visit to Houston; Christmas in the army; details of regimental drill and review; war news; in Arkansas; brief notes on whereabouts during previous month entered while on furlough in 1864.

PARKER, FRANCIS LEJAU, 1836-1913　　　3966

"The Battle of Fort Sumter as Seen from Morris Island." SOUTH CAROLINA HISTORICAL MAGAZINE 62 (1961):65-71.

Apr 1861. Diary of South Carolinian, an assistant surgeon stationed at Morris Island; description of military operations as observed from his position and the emotional response of the Confederate troops when Sumter fell.

PATTERSON, EDMUND DEWITT, b. 1842　　　3967

YANKEE REBEL. Edited by John G. Barrett. Chapel Hill: University of North Carolina Press, 1966. 207 pp.

1861-1865. Diary of Ohioan who, after residing less than two years in the South, joined Company D, Ninth Alabama; generally sporadic but substantial entries with vivid descriptions of combat; the Peninsular campaign and his baptism of fire at Williamburg; the battle of Fair Oaks, the Seven Days' battles and his wounding at Frayser's Farm; recuperating at Richmond and Inglewood near Gordonsville; furlough home to Lauderdale County, Alabama; promotion to lieutenant; battle of Fredericksburg and the Chancellorsville campaign; capture at Gettysburg; briefly at Fort Delaware and then imprisonment at Johnson's Island until parole in March 1865; notes on duties, First Bull Run battlefield, soldiers' hardships, Union depredations, prison conditions and war news; comments concerning various Confederate government leaders and generals, including Jefferson Davis and Alexander Stephens; viewing war trophies at the Virginia State Library; estrangement from his Ohio family and strong advocacy of Confederate cause.

Barrett, John G. "Edmund Dewitt Patterson: Yankee Rebel." ALABAMA REVIEW 28 (1975):32-47.

1861-1865. Scattered extracts illustrating summary of diary's contents.

PEARL, LOUISA BROWN, 1810-1886　　　3968

Hoobler, James A., ed. "The Civil War Diary of Louisa Brown Pearl." TENNESSEE HISTORICAL QUARTERLY 38 (1979):308-321.

Sep 1861-Mar 1862. Sporadic entries comprising diary of Massachusetts woman, wife of Joshua Fenton Pearl, Nashville's first superintendent of schools; loneliness and anxiety of staying in Nashville to protect their home after her unionist husband and daughters moved to Detroit and her son joined the Confederate army; managing a house full of boarders and servants; threats of destruction as Confederate forces evacuate Nashville and the Union army occupies the city.

PEIRSON, CHARLES LAWRENCE, 1834-1920　　　3969

...BALL'S BLUFF. Salem, Mass.: Privately printed by the Salem Press, 1913. 54 pp. Diary, pp 43-54.

Nov 1861-Jan 1862. Prison diary of adjutant of the Twentieth Massachusetts, captured at Ball's Bluff and incarcerated at Libby Prison; sporadic entries covering his reflections on the war and the boredom of prison life; description of his efforts to secure the release of his superior officers, held at Henrico County Jail, while in Richmond and, after his exchange, in Washington, D.C.

PHILLIPS, CHARLES A., d. 1876　　　3970

In HISTORY OF THE FIFTH MASSACHUSETTS BATTERY, by Massachusetts Artillery, 5th Battery, pp. 36-958 passim.

1861-1865. A scattering of brief entries extracted from officer's diary covering organizational matters and the battery's operations in Virginia.

PICKERING, EDWARD CHARLES, 1846-1919　　　3971

Plotkin, Howard, ed. "Edward C. Pickering's Diary of a Visit to the Harvard College Observatory." HARVARD LIBRARY BULLETIN 28 (1980):282-290.

Nov 1861. Account by a fifteen-year-old boy, later to become an astronomer and longtime director of the Harvard College Observatory; a sophisticated bit of scientific reporting, with detailed description of the "Great Refractor," astronomical observations and explanations by director George Phillips Bond.

Plotkin, Howard, ed. "Edward Charles Pickering's Diary of a Trip to Pasadena to Attend Meeting of Solar Union." SOUTHERN CALIFORNIA QUARTERLY 60 (1978):29-44.

Aug-Sep 1910. Harvard astronomer's train journey to attend an international meeting at Mount Wilson Observatory; travel via Chicago and the Grand Canyon with notes on scenery and stops, as well conversations with colleagues accompanying him; at Mount Wilson, describing distinguished participants and the sessions; visits to San Francisco and the University of California at Berkeley.

POOLE, CHARLES A.　　　3972

"Three Years on Board the KEARSARGE." NEW ENGLAND HISTORICAL AND GENEALOGICAL REGISTER 35 (1881):341-343.

1861-1864. Extracts from diary of Brunswick, Maine, resident, serving as engineer in the United States Navy; getting the ship ready at Portsmouth, New Hampshire, navy yard; duty off Spain and the Azores; sinking the ALABAMA.

PORTER, WILLIAM CLENDENIN, 1832-1867　　　3973

Frederick, J.V., ed. "War Diary of W.C. Porter." ARKANSAS HISTORICAL QUARTERLY 11 (1952):286-314.

Jul 1861, 1862-1863. Confederate soldier's diary; early service with the militia in Arkansas and Missouri; at home in Johnson County near Pittsburg; service with the Tenth Arkansas; maneuvers in Arkansas and Mississippi; engagements at Iuka and Corinth; seige of Port Hudson; brief entries noting everyday happenings, military events and his anxieties.

PRETZ, ALFRED C., b. 1840　　　3974

Ettinger, Amos A. "An Allentonian in Florida during the Civil War." LEHIGH COUNTY HISTORICAL SOCIETY PROCEEDINGS 12 (1939):50-80. Diary, pp. 50-56.

1861-1862. Extracts from Allentown, Pennsylvania, resident's diary within narrative summary of his war experience; the war spirit and social life in the town; a visit to army camp at Chambersburg.

REESE, GEORGE W. 3975

In SEMI-HISTORY OF A BOY-VETERAN OF THE TWENTY-EIGHTH REGIMENT ILLINOIS INFANTRY VOLUNTEERS, by Edwin L. Hobart, pp. 4-17. Denver? 1909.

1861-1864 (with gaps). Record of the regiment's service as seen by member of Company H; in camp at Bird's Point, Missouri; Fort Henry, Fort Donelson, Shiloh and the advance to Corinth; operations in Tennessee; the Vicksburg campaign; expedition to Jackson, then stationed at Natchez; notes on slaves' response to the Union army and the lack of patriotism observed in Illinois on his return after discharge.

REICHARDT, THEODORE 3976

DIARY OF BATTERY A, FIRST REGIMENT RHODE ISLAND LIGHT ARTILLERY. Providence: N.B. Williams, 1865. 153 pp.

1861-1864. Diary kept by private in the field but obviously enhanced for publication; trip south to Washington, D.C., camp; battle of First Bull Run; service under Banks in Maryland and Virginia; the Peninsular campaign and battle of Fair Oaks; the Seven Days' battles; the Antietam campaign; the battles of Fredericksburg, Chancellorsville, Gettysburg and Bristoe Station; the Mine Run campaign; the Wilderness, Spotsylvania and Cold Harbor; expiration of enlistment and journey home; brief daily entries describing the battery's part in military actions, with notes on weather, marches, camp locations and casualties.

RILEY, JAMES WESLEY, b.1843 3977

CIVIL WAR DIARY OF JAMES WESLEY RILEY. Washington, D.C.?: C.W. Denslinger, 1960. 108 leaves.

1861-1865. Diary of resident of Dowagiac, Michigan, serving with Company E, Forty-second Illinois Infantry; military operations and camp life in Missouri, Kentucky, Tennessee and Mississippi; with the fleet shelling Island No. 10; in Halleck's advance to Corinth after Shiloh; battles of Stones River, Chickamauga and Missionary Ridge; the Atlanta campaign, including battles of Resaca, Peach Tree Creek and Jonesboro; battles of Franklin and Nashville and operations in Alabama; notes on weather, unit's movements, duties and amusements, 1864 presidential election, Lincoln's assassination, dodging pickets to visit the ladies, his disobediences and punishments, etc.; candid, interesting account by a high-spirited, patriotic young soldier.

ROBERTS, BENJAMIN TITUS, 1823-1893 3978

In BENJAMIN TITUS ROBERTS: LATE GENERAL SUPERINTENDENT OF THE FREE METHODIST CHURCH, by Benson Roberts, 570 pp., passim. North Chili, N.Y.: The Earnest Christian, 1900.

1861-1874. Biography, containing extensive diary extracts, of the founder of the Free Methodist church; work in early years of the denomination; defense of women as church workers and preachers; camp meeting and revival experiences; writing and editing.

ROBERTSON, ORRIN WOOD, b. 1849? 3979

Cunningham, Mary E., ed. "The Background of an American." NEW YORK HISTORY 27 (1946):76-87, 213-223.

Apr 1861-Mar 1862. Extracts from boy's diary kept at his parents' behest; life on a hill farm near Ithaca; chores, farm tasks and leisure pursuits; school days; the ague and treatment; visitors and activities of parents and relatives.

ROBERTSON, ROBERT STODDARD, 1839-1906 3980

DIARY OF THE WAR. Edited by Charles N. Walker and Rosemary Walker. Old Fort News, vol. 28, nos. 1-4. Fort Wayne, Ind.: Allen County-Fort Wayne Historical Society, 1965. 4 vols. in 1. 232 pp.

1861-1864. Washington County, New York, lawyer's account of service as officer in Company I, Ninety-third New York Volunteers and on staff of Col. Nelson A. Miles, rewritten and obviously supplemented after the war; getting underway at Albany and New York City; noting Philadelphia's hospitality on trip south; the Peninsular campaign, including the battle of Williamsburg; regiment detached to serve as provost and depot guards; touring the Custis home at White House Landing; destruction of the house and also that of Edmund Ruffin; detailed as headquarters guard, Army of the Potomac, and from that position witnessing the battles of South Mountain, Antietam and Fredericksburg; Burnside's "Mud March"; operations at Fredericksburg during the Chancellorsville campaign; Gettysburg campaign but not at the battle; operations in Virginia and appointment to Miles's brigade staff in Hancock's Second Corps; battle of the Wilderness; Spotsylvania campaign during which he won the Congressional Medal of Honor; action at North Anna River and Totopotomoy Creek, where he was severely wounded; treatment in the field and in Washington, D.C., and subsequent medical discharge; notes on daily events and activities, gruesome sights of the Williamsburg and Gettysburg battlefields, plundering at Fredericksburg, execution of a spy, etc.; comments regarding McClellan, Burnside and Meade.

ROBINSON, OLIVER, 1839-1863 3981

THE DIARY AND LETTERS OF OLIVER S. ROBINSON. Edited by Opal Hanson. Kensington, Md.: Village Press, 1968. 86, 21 leaves.

1861-1863. Diary of young man from Vernon County, Wisconsin, member of Company H, Eleventh Wisconsin Volunteers; in camp at Madison, Wisconsin, and then based at Sulphur Springs, Missouri, with subsequent operations in that state and in Arkansas and Mississippi; back in southeastern Missouri and then to Milliken's Bend; the Vicksburg campaign; very brief daily entries, recording activities and news of the day, interspersed with several letters and editor's voluminous background notes.

ROBINSON, SAMUEL, 1825-1907 3982

Altshuler, Constance Wynn, ed. "Arizona in 1861." JOURNAL OF ARIZONA HISTORY 25 (1984):21-76.

Apr-Aug 1861. Diary kept by accountant for the Santa Rita Mining Company during a period of great peril from the Apaches; death of mine manager Horace C. Grosvenor in an Apache raid on a mine supply wagon and the constant state of alert and tension that followed; attempts to get help from Fort Buchanan, itself under duress, leading to eventual abandonment of forts Buchanan and Breckinridge; report of a stagecoach robbery and murder of passengers, this time believed to be by "Americans from the Pino Alto Mines"; a manhunt for outlaw Bill Ake; continued Apache depredations and removal to Tubac, which, in turn, became unsafe; diarist's intermittent illness with "fever and ague"; references to Raphael Pumpelly, Charles D. Poston and many others.

ROSS, CHARLES, b. 1838?   3983

"Diary of Charles Ross." VERMONT HISTORY 29 (1961):65-78; 30 (1962):85-148; 31 (1963):4-64.

1861-1863. Extracts from diary of farmer and teacher turned soldier; chores, social activities and family events in Lower Waterford, Vermont; the vicissitudes of teaching and diptheria epidemic in Lyndon, Vermont; notes on medications, expenses, sermon texts and making maple syrup; service as corporal, later sergeant, Company A, Eleventh Vermont Infantry; in camp near Washington, D.C.; weather, military duties, his illnesses, correspondence and sightseeing.

Destler, C.M., ed. "An Andersonville Prison Diary." GEORGIA HISTORICAL QUARTERLY 24 (1940):56-76.

Destler, C.M., ed. "A Vermonter in Andersonville." VERMONT HISTORY 25 (1957):229-245.

Jun-Nov 1864. Diary covering experiences as prisoner of war; capture near Petersburg; hardships of journey south by train; observations of Libby Prison during brief stay there; conditions at Andersonville; sickness, deaths, rumors of exchange, 1864 presidential election, longing for true Sabbaths, etc.; in hospital with rheumatism; train journey to Savannah, then on board Union transport, eating well.

Destler, Charles M., ed. "A Vermonter Returns from Andersonville." VERMONT HISTORY 25 (1957):344-351.

Nov-Dec 1864. Last of journey to Annapolis, regaining his strength at United States Hospital there and return home.

RUDISILL, ABRAHAM, 1811-1899   3984

In THE DAY OF OUR ABRAHAM, by James Jefferson Rudisill, pp. 73-490 passim. York, Pa.: York Printing, 1936.

1861-1865. War diary, interspersed with letters, of tailor, publisher of THE MONTHLY FRIEND and fervent member of the United Brethren in Christ; service with Battery G, First Pennsylvania Light Artillery; battles of Second Bull Run, Fredericksburg and Gettysburg; Mine Run campaign; battles of the Wilderness, Spotsylvania and Cold Harbor; siege of Petersburg; long entries devoted to family concerns, prayers and religious thoughts; notes on reading, a visit to the MONITOR and life in various camps; at home in York, Pennsylvania, at war's end.

RUSSELL, WILLIAM HOWARD, 1820-1907   3985

MY DIARY NORTH AND SOUTH. Boston: T.O.H.P. Burnham; New York: O.S. Felt, 1863. 602 pp. London: Bradbury and Evans, 1863. 2 vols. New York: Harper & Brothers, 1863. 225 pp.

MY DIARY, NORTH AND SOUTH. Edited and introduced by Fletcher Pratt. Gloucester, Mass.: P. Smith, 1969. 268 pp.

Widely extracted. See, for instance, in THE ALABAMA CONFEDERATE READER, edited by Malcolm C. McMillan, pp. 70-75; THE BLUE AND THE GRAY, edited by Henry S. Commager, vol. 1, pp. 106-112; DIARY OF AMERICA, edited by Josef and Dorothy Berger, pp. 421-426.

1861-1862. Noted LONDON TIMES war correspondent's observations as Americans separated and the Civil War ensued; meetings with the Lincolns, various cabinet members, the Southern commissioners and people of note in Washington, D.C.; by train to Charleston, following the fall of Fort Sumter; planta-

tion life in South Carolina and Southern rationales for slavery; to Montgomery, where the Confederacy was being formed, with stops at Savannah and Macon, Georgia; down the Alabama River on the SOUTHERN REPUBLIC to Mobile and forts Gaines and Morgan; at Braxton Bragg's Pensacola headquarters and Fort Pickens; from Mobile to New Orleans and up the Mississippi to Vicksburg, stopping at sugar plantations on the way, then on to Jackson, Mississippi, and Memphis; inspecting Fort Randolph with General Pillow; return to Washington, D.C., because of the blockade's endangering overseas correspondence, via Cairo, Illinois, Chicago, Niagara Falls and New York City; visits to army camps at Arlington and Fortress Monroe; the retreat from Bull Run and Northern anger over his reporting; trip to Pittsburgh and Chicago before return to England when access to the war front was denied him; notes on countryside, accommodations, drinking, dueling, tobacco chewing, etc.; evaluation of many political personalities, including William Seward, Gov. Francis Pickens, Jefferson Davis, Louis Wigfall, Judah Benjamin, Robert Toombs and John Slidell, and of military figures such as McDowell, Winfield Scott, Beauregard, Butler, Fremont and McClellan; assessment of public attitudes and military abilities, North and South; his evolving views on slavery; long, detailed, perceptive entries, later amplified for publication.

SALISBURY, AUGUSTUS HARRISON, b. 1841?   3986

In PAGES FROM THE DIARIES OF DE WITT CLINTON SALISBURY, edited by Mildred H. Osgood, pp. 8-9, 34, 52-59. Wauwatosa, Wis.: M.H. Osgood, 1974.

Dec 1861, Jun-Jul 1864. Extracts from diary of brother of De Witt Clinton Salisbury; notes on farm work, events of the first year of the war and service with Company G, Fortieth Wisconsin Volunteers, near Memphis; mention of duties, food, former slaves and black soldiers.

SALISBURY, DE WITT CLINTON, 1843?-1915   3987

PAGES FROM THE DIARIES OF DE WITT CLINTON SALISBURY. Edited by Mildred H. Osgood. Wauwatosa, Wis.: M.H. Osgood, 1974. 123 pp. Diary, pp. 8-114 passim.

1861-1914. Diary extracts sprinkled through biography of citizen of Oregon, Wisconsin; farm and social activities and student days at the University of Wisconsin; enlistment in August 1864 and service in Virginia near Washington, D.C.; teaching experiences and a description of his school at Fitchburgh; marriage, family life and deaths of children; notes on Fourth of July celebrations, support of Lincoln in 1860, exploring a deserted spa on Lake Monona, Lincoln's assassination, World's Columbian Exposition, etc.; tantalizing extracts, unfortunately neither selected nor arranged to provide the type of eyewitness account which would effectively communicate the spirit of the times.

SANDERS, RICHARD A., 1834-1862   3988

"Civil War Diary of Richard Sanders." NOW AND THEN 4 (1931-1932):232-234, 276-277, 302-303; 13 (1961-1962):36-43, 151-162.

Dec 1861-Aug 1862. Former schoolteacher's record of service as sergeant, Company K, 106th Pennsylvania Volunteers, in Virginia; journey home to recruit in Hughesville, Pennsylvania, area; trip back to Virginia, sighting the MONITOR near Fortress Monroe; the Peninsular campaign and description of the abandoned Confederate works at Yorktown; battle of Fair Oaks and the Seven Days' battles; lengthy entries with notes on camp life, hardships, leisure activities, prices, the Virginia countryside and drinking in the army.

SANGSTON, LAWRENCE   3989

THE BASTILES OF THE NORTH. Baltimore: Kelly, Hedian & Piet, 1863. 136 pp.

PERSONAL JOURNAL OF A "PRISONER OF STATE" IN FORTS MCHENRY, MONROE, LAFAYETTE AND WARREN. N.p., 1863?

Sep 1861-Jan 1862. Journal written by member of Maryland legislature while imprisoned at Fort McHenry, Fortress Monroe, Fort Lafayette and Fort Warren; character and behavior of guards; physical environment; provisions ranging from champagne to tadpoles in the drinking water; daily activities, interaction with fellow prisoners including Mason and Sidell; commentary on war news, Union government policies, etc.; release and return home to Baltimore.

SCHILLICH, JOHN W., 1843-1873   3990

Parsons, Phyllis Vibbard, ed. "The Schillich Diary." MONTGOMERY COUNTY HISTORICAL SOCIETY BULLETIN 21 (1979):326-357.

1861-1864. Diary of drummer from East Vincent, Pennsylvania, serving in Company A, Fifty-first Pennsylvania; Burnside's expedition to North Carolina and subsequent military operations there; brief entries, mostly noting unit's movements but with scant details of participation in battles of Second Bull Run, South Mountain, Antietam and Fredericksburg, the Vicksburg campaign or the sieges of Jackson, Mississippi, and Knoxville.

SCOFIELD, WALTER KEELER   3991

Schellings, William J., ed. "On Blockade Duty in Florida Waters." TEQUESTA 15 (1955):55-72.

1861-1863. Extracts from diary of Connecticut physician, assistant surgeon aboard the SAGAMORE, a gunboat in the East Coast Blockading Squadron; service along east and west coasts of Florida; descriptions of Key West and Apalachicola; attacks on Tampa and Smyrna and destruction of salt works at St. Andrew Bay; notes on blockade operations, contrabands, refugees, food supplies, mosquitoes, etc.

SEATON, BENJAMIN M.   3992

THE BUGLE SOFTLY BLOWS. Edited by Harold B. Simpson. Waco, Tex.: Texian, 1965. 117 pp.

1861-1865 (with gaps). Untutored westerner's diary of Confederate service with the Tenth Texas Infantry; movement through Texas and action in Arkansas; execution of deserters; battle of Arkansas Post; train journey from Baltimore to Tennessee; battles of Chickamauga, Missionary Ridge and Lookout Mountain; the Atlanta campaign and battle of Jonesboro; in hospital and then back on active duty in war's last days; mainly record of duties, routes of travel and distances covered, war news and rumors; personal reaction to events but no mention of family, friends, etc.

SEMMES, RAPHAEL, 1809-1877   3993

THE CRUISE OF THE "ALABAMA" AND THE "SUMTER." Lon-

don: Saunders, Otley, 1864. 2 vols. New York: Carleton, 1864. 2 vols. in 1. 328 pp. Diary, pp. 11-231 passim.

THE LOG OF THE "ALABAMA" AND THE "SUMTER." Abr. from the library ed. London: Saunders, Otley, 1865. 297 pp. Diary, pp. 5-252 passim.

1861-1864. Extracts from Confederate captain's private journals; the cruise of the SUMTER; at Maranham, Brazil, in shipping lanes between New York and San Roque and at Martinique, Cadiz and Gibralter; preparing the ALABAMA at Terceira Island; at work in the Caribbean and Gulf of Mexico; visiting South Africa; in the Indian Ocean and China Sea, stopping at various ports; readying to meet the KEARSARGE off Cherbourg; notes on weather and navigation; the logistics of coaling, provisioning and making repairs; chasing ships and taking prizes and the difficulties of interpreting neutrality restrictions; good descriptions of places visited; problems with crew about drink, discipline, desertion and protection given by United States counsels; comments on Mason-Slidell affair, race relations in other countries and the Confederate cause. In the preface to SERVICE AFLOAT, Semmes repudiated these versions of the history of the Confederate cruisers.

In OFFICIAL RECORDS OF THE UNION AND CONFEDERATE NAVIES IN THE WAR OF THE REBELLION, ser. 1, vol. 1, pp. 691-744.

May 1861-Apr 1862. Extracts from the journal kept while he was commander of the SUMTER; outfitting in New Orleans, with a green crew and apprehensive pilots; running the blockade and eluding the BROOKLYN; capturing Union merchant vessels in the Caribbean; along the northern coast of South America; getting away from the IROQUOIS at Martinique; across the Atlantic to Cadiz and Gibralter; arrival of the KEARSARGE and TUSCARORA and decision to leave the SUMTER at Gibralter, the crew returning to the Confederacy; notes on reception, legal disputes and racial matters at various neutral ports; weather conditions and navigational data, discipline and desertions; comments on war news and aims, Northerners and blacks.

In OFFICIAL RECORDS OF THE UNION AND CONFEDERATE NAVIES IN THE WAR OF THE REBELLION, ser. 1, vol. 1, pp. 783-817; vol. 2, pp. 720-807; vol. 3, pp. 669-677.

1862-1864. Extracts; taking charge of the new Confederate cruiser ALABAMA at Terceira Island and the problems of assembling a crew; capturing merchant vessels and whalers in the Atlantic; the legalities of neutrality and what constitutes enemy cargo; to Martinique and Dominica; what to do with too many prisoners; sinking of the Union gunboat HATTERAS off Galveston; in port at Bahia, Brazil, with the GEORGIA; meeting the TUSCALOOSA off South Africa; around the Cape of Good Hope to the Indian Ocean and China Sea; comparison of slavery in this area and in the Confederacy; anti-British comments; around the Cape of Good Hope to the Atlantic; at Cherbourg, preparing to engage the KEARSARGE.

SERVICE AFLOAT. Baltimore: Baltimore Publishing, 1887. 833 pp. New York: P.J. Kenedy, 1903. Diary, pp. 103-322 passim.

May 1861-Jan 1862. Extracts.

Hoole, W.Stanley, ed. "Admiral on Horseback." ALABAMA REVIEW 28 (1975):129-150.

Feb-May 1865. Aboard the landlocked ironclad VIRGINIA, commanding the James River squadron until ordered to destroy the fleet and withdraw to Danville, Virginia, where he and his sailors became an artillery brigade for defense of the new Confederate capital; retreat to Greensboro, North Carolina; surrender and parole; description of countryside and inhabitants on journey through the Carolinas and Georgia to his home at Mobile.

Bethel, Elizabeth, ed. "The Prison Diary of Raphael Semmes." JOURNAL OF SOUTHERN HISTORY 22 (1956):498-509.

Dec 1865-Mar 1866. Arrest at his home and journey to the Marine Barracks at Washington, D.C., meeting with prominent ex-Confederates along the way; prison conditions and his daily routine; actions of President Johnson and Secretary Welles regarding his imprisonment and prosecution.

SILL, EDWARD ROWLAND, 1841-1886   3994

AROUND THE HORN. Edited by Stanley T. Williams and Barbara D. Simison. New Haven: Yale University Press; London: H. Milford, Oxford University Press, 1944. 79 pp.

Dec 1861-Mar 1862. A gentleman's trip, perhaps in search of better health, aboard the clipper SIERRA NEVADA from New York to San Francisco around Cape Horn; regular descriptions of weather, locations, sea life, fish, birds, butterflies, etc.; names of ships met.

SMITH, BENJAMIN T., 1844-1908   3995

PRIVATE SMITH'S JOURNAL. Edited by Clyde C. Walton. Chicago: R.R. Donnelly & Sons, 1963. 253 pp.

1861-1865. Kankakee, Illinois, resident's diary; member of Company C, Fifty-first Illinois, at Camp Douglas; New Madrid and Island No. 10 campaign and Halleck's advance to Corinth; service with Powell's Scouts, an irregular mounted infantry unit commanded by Capt. Frank Powell, in Nashville area; diarist's duties as escort and orderly at Second Division headquarters, Army of the Cumberland, and operations in Tennessee, Alabama and Georgia; battle of Chickamauga; Chattanooga, Atlanta, Franklin and Nashville campaigns; occupaton duty in Nashville; notes on the Hermitage, execution of a bounty jumper and of Confederate guerilla Champ Ferguson, Louisville theater, black soldiers, Lincoln's assassination and viewing his body in Chicago; furlough visits to Lookout Mountain, New York City, Boston, Chicago and Providence, Rhode Island.

SMITH, ISAAC NOYES, b. 1831?   3996

Childers, William C., ed. "A Virginian's Dilemma." WEST VIRGINIA HISTORY 27 (1966):173-200.

Sep-Nov 1861. Diary of Charles Town lawyer, a major in the Twenty-second Virginia Volunteers; military operations in western Virginia; concern for unionist father Benjamin Harrison Smith; defection of his slave Mike; a fulsome sketch of Lee upon his arrival at their camp; hardships of army life including the actions of John B. Floyd which negatively affected the regiment; his resignation after a final insult from Floyd which the diarist was "obliged to notice" and a threatening interview with the general; apprehension about Union tolerance of his residence in Charles Town without taking the oath of allegiance; lengthy entries describing military operations and revealing the pressures of politics, ambition and divided families.

SPERRY, KATE, b. 1843?   3997

In ECHOES OF HAPPY VALLEY, by Thomas F. Hickerson, pp. 88-95.

1861-1865. Extracts from diary of spirited young resident of Winchester, Virginia; social life and flirtations; notes on Belle Boyd and Stonewall Jackson; denying charge of being a Confederate spy; marriage to Dr. E.N. Hunt and visiting his family in North Carolina.

STEELE, NIMROD HUNTER, 1839-1861   3998

"The Nimrod Hunter Steele Diary and Letters." WINCHESTER-FREDERICK COUNTY HISTORICAL SOCIETY PAPERS 3 (1955):48-61.

Jun-Oct 1861. Newtown Artillery lieutenant's diary; battle of Bull Run and Confederate soldiers' appropriation of Union equipment and provisions left behind by owners; a pleasant, youthful account of camp life in Virginia early in the war.

STICHTER, VALENTINE   3999

In THE LOGAN GUARDS OF LEWISTOWN, PENNSYLVANIA, by Willis R. Copeland, pp. 28-29. Lewistown: Mifflin County Historical Society, 1962.

Apr 1861. Extracts from diary of sergeant in the Washington Artillerists; in camp at Washington, D.C.; duties, events and sightseeing.

STORY, JAMES OSGOOD ANDREW, 1843-1862   4000

Friend, Llerena, ed. "Pocket Diary for 1861." ALABAMA HISTORICAL QUARTERLY 28 (1966):51-121. Diary, pp. 62-121.

Jan-Dec 1861. College student's diary, commencing on the day Alabama seceded from the Union; assignments, the Belles Lettres Society and social life at Southern University in Greensboro, Alabama; conversion and religious activities; political and war news; exodus of students from the school to the army; summer vacation with family near Tuskegee, teaching younger siblings and going back to old home at Cotton Valley in southern Macon County; notes on reading, correspondence and celebration of George Washington's birthday.

STOWE, JONATHAN PERLEY, 1832-1862   4001

"Life with the 15th Mass." CIVIL WAR TIMES ILLUSTRATED 11, no. 5 (1972):4-11, 48-55.

Oct-Dec 1861, Feb-Sep 1862. Extracts from diary of sergeant, Company G, Fifteenth Massachusetts Infantry; battle of Ball's Bluff and imprisonment at Libby; exchange and furlough; Peninsular campaign; battle of Fair Oaks; the Seven Days' battles; glimpses of McClellan; lying wounded on Antietam battlefield; graphic, wrenching description of field hospital conditions as diarist slips toward death.

THOMPSON, SAMUEL A., d. 1908   4002

In DOUGLAS'S TEXAS BATTERY, by James Douglas, edited by Lucia R. Douglas, pp. 170-201. Tyler, Tex.: Smith County Historical Society, 1966.

Sep 1861-Aug 1862. Sporadic, often lengthy, entries in diary of private with the First Texas Battery; camp life in Arkansas; battle of Pea Ridge, with critique of Confederate generalship in that engagement; operations in Mississippi, Tennessee and Kentucky.

VEDDER, CHARLES STUART, 1826-1917   **4003**

Wight, Willard E., ed. ''The Diary of the Reverend Charles S. Vedder.'' GEORGIA HISTORICAL QUARTERLY 39 (1955):68-90.

May-Jul 1861. Diary kept during a visit to Monticello, Georgia, by Presbyterian clergyman, a New Yorker who chose to remain in the Confederacy; daily record focusing on religious matters; church services, Sunday school, interdenominational relationships, critiques of other preachers including blacks, sermon topics, etc.; notes on activities and health of his wife, Helen Scovel Vedder, and his sister-in-law Harriet Scovel White; war support efforts in the town; decision to accept call to Summerville Presbyterian Church, Berkeley County, South Carolina.

WADDELL, JOSEPH ADDISON   **4004**

ANNALS OF AUGUSTA COUNTY, VIRGINIA. Richmond: W.E. Jones, 1886. Diary, pp. 285-342.

1861-1865. Substantial diary extracts, contained within explanatory narrative, presenting Staunton civilian's view of the war; notes on troop movements, prices, and shortages; reports of war news and local military activities, reflecting preponderance of rumors and inaccurate information; life in the occupied town after the Confederacy's defeat.

WAGNER, AUGUST, b. 1826?   **4005**

Frese, Hans, ed. ''A Soldier's Diary.'' AMERICAN-GERMAN REVIEW 28, no. 1 (1961):17-19, 38.

Apr-Jul 1861. Extracts from diary of Eighth New York musician; on duty near Washington, D.C.; battle of Bull Run; lengthy entries apparently rewritten later.

WAINWRIGHT, CHARLES SHIELS, 1826-1907   **4006**

A DIARY OF BATTLE. Edited by Allan Nevins. New York: Harcourt, Brace & World, 1962. 549 pp.

1861-1865. Diary of a Hudson Valley aristocrat, a conscientious soldier who distinguished himself in many of the Army of the Potomac's engagements; major in the First New York Artillery, then Chief of Artillery for Hooker's division and, subsequently, the First and Fifth Corps, advancing in rank from colonel to brigadier general; detailed observations on the Peninsular campaign, Fair Oaks, Antietam, Fredericksburg, Chancellorsville, Gettysburg, the Wilderness, Spotsylvania, Cold Harbor, siege of Petersburg and the battle of the Crater, the Appomattox campaign and smaller actions including Burnside's ''Mud March''; a thorough resume of the Grand Review; a conservative Democrat's commentary on Lincoln and his administration; evaluations of his superior officers and colleagues such as McClellan, Burnside, Hooker, Meade, Grant, Doubleday, Reynolds, Newton, Hunt, Warren, Sickles, Sumner, Kearny and Butterfield; mention of friends and acquaintances including Marsena Patrick and J.M. Sanderson; his duties and efforts to reorganize the artillery; the frustrations of acquiring good servants, especially cooks, and concern for creature comforts, particularly of the table; the behavior of men in battle and his own feelings under fire; description of villages, towns and countryside; comments on the work of the Sanitary Commission and its 1864 Metropolitan Fair in New York City, the Congressional Committee on the Conduct of the War, blacks and emancipation, gam-

bling and drinking in the army, etc.; an immensely rich record of military action, personalities and life in camp and field.

Nevins, Allan, ed. '' 'So Ends the Great Rebel Army...' '' AMERICAN HERITAGE 13, no. 6. (1962):33-47.

Jun 1864-Apr 1865. Extracts.

WAITZ, JULIA ELLEN LEGRAND, 1829-1881   **4007**

THE JOURNAL OF JULIA LEGRAND. Edited by Kate M. Rowland and Mrs. Morris L. Croxall. Richmond, Va.: Everett Waddey, 1911. 318 pp.

1861-1863. Remnants of journal kept by genteel lady for her niece, mostly covering January through April 1863; very long entries, detailing Southerner's hardships in Union-occupied New Orleans; behavior of servants, the unsettled situation of the city's black population and her racist observations; praise for Vallandigham; critical comments on Jefferson Davis and General Beauregard; her thoughts on the war and her religious views; living with friends and desiring privacy amidst constant flow of visitors.

WATSON, ROBERT   **4008**

In KINFOLKS, A GENEALOGICAL AND BIOGRAPHICAL RECORD, prepared by William Curry Harllee, vol. 2, pp. 1889-1904. New Orleans: Printed by Searcy & Pfaff, 1934-1937.

1861-1865. Extracts from Key West resident's diary of service with Company K, Seventh Florida Infantry, and in the Confederate navy; battles of Chickamauga, Lookout Mountain and Missionary Ridge; opposing Sherman's advance at Dalton; transfer to navy and duty aboard the ram SAVANNAH until she was destroyed to prevent Union capture; battle of Fort Fisher and evacuation of Wilmington; with Semmes's unit retreating with Lee from Richmond; capture and parole to Washington, D.C.; refusal to take oath of allegiance; finding his way back home; notes on military punishments, treatment while a prisoner and Lincoln's assassination.

Still, William N., Jr. '' 'Yankees Were Landing below Us.' '' CIVIL WAR TIMES ILLUSTRATED 15, no. 1 (1976):12-21.

Dec 1864-Apr 1865. Extracts covering journey through South Carolina after destruction of the SAVANNAH; at Charleston, Wilmington and Drewry's Bluff; retreating with the Army of Northern Virginia; capture, parole, refusal to take oath and securing passage home at New York City; notes on shortages and prices, foraging, duties, hardships of troop transport, etc.; complaints about drunken, inept and unjust officers; brief mention of mourning and funeral observances for Lincoln.

WAYLAND, MRS. JOHN WESLEY   **4009**

In A HISTORY OF SHENANDOAH COUNTY, VIRGINIA, by John Walter Wayland, pp. 297-306. Strasburg, Va.: Shenandoah Publishing House, 1927. 2d. augm. ed., 1969. Reprint. Baltimore: Regional Publishing, 1980.

1861-1865. Extracts from diary kept at Woodlawn, three miles north of Mount Jackson; very brief entries reporting domestic tasks and war's impact; the ebb and flow of the contending armies through the Shenandoah Valley; the sounds of battle and deaths of local residents; prices; Union depredations.

WEBBER, THOMAS B. 4010

In MISSISSIPPI IN THE CONFEDERACY, edited by John K. Bettersworth and James W. Silver, vol. 1, pp. 65, 252-254.

Jan-Oct 1861. Extracts from diary of storekeeper turned soldier; business problems and preparation for war in Byhalia, Mississippi; boredom of army life at Camp Esau near Pensacola.

WHITE, THOMAS BENTON, 1843-1922 4011

Williams, Charles G., ed. "Down the Rivers." KENTUCKY HISTORICAL SOCIETY REGISTER 67 (1969):134-174.

1861-1862. Diary of apprentice printer from Ashland, Ohio, serving in Company H, Forty-second Ohio Volunteer Infantry; early days in Camp Chase; operations in Kentucky and, briefly, in western Virginia; participation in the Vicksburg campaign; very short daily entries covering duties, leisure activities, bad weather and the hardships of military life.

WHITE, WILLIAM S. 4012

In CONTRIBUTIONS TO A HISTORY OF THE RICHMOND HOWITZER BATTALION, by Virginia Artillery, Richmond Howitzers, no. 2, pp. 89-286, no. 3, pp. 61-62.

1861-1865. Diary of member of the Third Company, First Virginia Artillery; military operations and personal adventures; battles of Big Bethel, Seven Days', Fredericksburg, Chancellorsville, Gettysburg and Spotsylvania; long entries indicating much later enhancement.

"Stray Leaves from a Soldier's Journal." SOUTHERN HISTORICAL SOCIETY PAPERS 11 (1883):552-559.

Apr. 1865. Extracts covering the final days of the Army of Northern Virginia; evacuating Richmond, searching for an escape route and surrendering at Appomattox.

WHITMAN, GEORGE WASHINGTON, 1829-1901 4013

CIVIL WAR LETTERS OF GEORGE WASHINGTON WHITMAN. Edited by Jerome M. Loving. Durham, N.C.: Duke University Press, 1975. 173 pp. Diary, pp. 137-160.

1861-1863. War diary of Walt Whitman's younger brother, much of which seems to have been written somewhat after events occurred; service in Company G, Fifty-first New York Volunteers; Burnside's expedition to North Carolina, the capture of Roanoke Island and New Bern; Second Bull Run and Antietam campaigns; battle of Fredericksburg; train transport through Pennsylvania and Ohio; in Kentucky; the Vicksburg campaign; operations in Mississippi, including capture of Jackson; return to Kentucky.

WIENEKE, HENRY J., 1837-1923 4014

Throne, Mildred, ed. "Iowa Troops in Dakota Territory." IOWA JOURNAL OF HISTORY 57 (1959):97-190.

1861-1864. Extracts from diary of drummer, Company B, Fourteenth Iowa, interspersed with letters of diarist and of other members of the regiment; hardships of journey from Iowa City to Fort Randall, on the Missouri River near present Nebraska-South Dakota border; service on the frontier in regiment which was subsequently reorganized into the Forty-first Iowa Infantry Battalion and then into the Seventh Iowa Cavalry; notes on cooking duties of the diarist, a former baker, bad weather and the

beauties of the countryside; friendly and hostile encounters with Indians, including expedition to rescue prisoners of the Santees and Sully's expedition against the Sioux.

"Iowa Troops in the Sully Campaigns." IOWA JOURNAL OF HISTORY AND POLITICS 20 (1922):364-443. Diary, pp. 366-374.

Jun-Aug 1864. Substantially revised diary extracts from diary covering activities of Company L, Seventh Iowa Cavalry.

WILLOUGHBY, CHARLES H., b. 1842? 4015

In ANNUAL REPORT, 5th, by New York State Bureau of Military Statistics, pp. 473-543.

1861-1863. Extracts from journal of private, Company C, Thirty-fourth New York Volunteers; stationed in Maryland, guarding the Chesapeake and Ohio Canal; military operations in Virginia, including duty at Harpers Ferry and in the Shenandoah Valley; Peninsular campaign and the battle of Fair Oaks; wounding at Antietam and several months' recuperation in Baltimore hospital before discharge; notes on weather, camp life, daily events, sickness, deaths, mud, war rumors, drinking and its consequences, military punishments, medical treatment, McClellan, etc.; informative record of life in the ranks.

WILSON, OSBORNE 4016

In ON TO GRAFTON, by William Thompson Price, pp. 34-47. Marlington, W. Va., 1901.

May-Aug 1861. Monterey, Virginia, resident's daily account of service with Company E, Thirty-first Virginia; organizing the unit and enjoying the civilian enthusiasm; hard marching and the adjustment to army life; operations in western Virginia.

WINFIELD, JOHN QUINCY, 1822-1892 4017

In VIRGINIA VALLEY RECORDS, edited by John W. Wayland, pp. 238-240. Baltimore: Genealogical Publishing, 1965.

Mar-May 1861. Extracts from notes taken by Virginia physician on trip to Texas, recounting public sentiments on secession and Northerners; his observations of the region's martial spirit.

WISTER, SARAH BUTLER, b. 1835 4018

Wister, Fanny Kemble, ed. "Sarah Butler Wister's Civil War Diary." PENNSYLVANIA MAGAZINE OF HISTORY AND BIOGRAPHY 102 (1978):271-327.

In THAT I MAY TELL YOU: JOURNALS AND LETTERS OF THE OWEN WISTER FAMILY, edited by Fanny K. Wister, pp. 23-68. Wayne, Pa.: Haverford House, 1979.

Apr-Sep 1861. Extracts from diary of accomplished, well-to-do Philadelphian, reflecting the turmoil of the times and the complexity of loyalties between family, state and nation; substantial entries covering her daily life; social engagements, cultural pursuits and domestic tasks including care of her young son Owen; relationships with her parents, Fanny Kemble and Pierce Butler, and her younger sister Fanny; reaction in Philadelphia to news of Sumter's surrender, the thirst for war and women's efforts to aid the soldiers; her commentary on war news; concern for her father imprisoned at Fort Lafayette; critical or admiring remarks about many friends and acquaintances; notes on weather, servant problems, music, reading, trips to Atlantic City and Lenox, Massachusetts, etc.; description of her mother reading

Shakespeare; a fascinating account of family ties and frustrations, the impact of the Civil War on many lives and, not least, a candid, richly detailed view of a woman's world.

WITHERS, ANITA DWYER, b. 1839   **4019**

In LADIES OF RICHMOND, by Katharine M. Jones, pp. 76-78, 156-157, 173-174, 188-189, 210-211, 296-297.

    1861-1865. Extracts from diary of devout Catholic, wife of John Withers, assistant adjutant general in Richmond; notes on social activities; death of first child and birth of second; journey home to San Antonio, Texas.

WITHERS, JOHN, b. 1827   **4020**

Sterkx, H.E. and Trapp, L.Y., eds. "One Year of the War." ALABAMA HISTORICAL QUARTERLY 29 (1967):133-184.

    1861-1862. Sporadic diary entries of West Point graduate, assistant in the United States Adjutant General's Department and then assistant adjutant general for the Confederate army; enjoying social life among the prominent in Washington, D.C., Montgomery and Richmond; diarist's health and that of his wife, Anita; death of young son; notes on personal finance, weather and Roman Catholic church services; no details of his work.

WOMACK, JAMES J., 1834-1922   **4021**

THE CIVIL WAR DIARY OF CAPT. J.J. WOMACK. McMinnville, Tenn.: Womack Printing, 1961. 115 pp.

    1861-1863. Account of Warren County resident's service with the Sixteenth Tennessee Volunteers; elected captain of Company E; operations in Tennessee, under Lee in western Virginia, in South Carolina near Pocotaligo, retreat from Corinth, Mississippi, in Tennessee near Chattanooga and with Bragg in Kentucky; battle of Perryville and march to Tullahoma; wounded at Stones River and taken prisoner as Confederates leave Murfreesboro; journey to exchange at City Point, Virginia, noting Southern sympathizers in Louisville, Cincinnati and Baltimore; back in Tennessee; resignation from command because of disability; civilian life as Union forces invade; notes on weather, company's health, camp life, prices, reading, duties, drinking in the army, correspondence and his financial matters; visits to Jefferson's Monticello, Charleston and Savannah; furloughs home to McMinnville.

WOOLWINE, RUFUS J., 1840-1908   **4022**

Manarin, Louis H., ed. "The Civil War Diary of Rufus J. Woolwine." VIRGINIA MAGAZINE OF HISTORY AND BIOGRAPHY 71 (1963):416-448.

    1861-1865. Patrick County, Virginia, saddler's diary, written up shortly after war's end from wartime notebooks; service with the Fifty-first Virginia Infantry, first as noncommissioned officer in Company C and, after May 1862, as lieutenant in Company D; operations in western Virginia; defense of Fort Donelson; stationed in western and southwestern Virginia and eastern Tennessee; in the Shenandoah Valley under Breckinridge; battle of Cold Harbor; Early's invasion of the North; promotion to captain and capture at Waynesboro, Virginia; imprisonment at Fort Delaware; very brief entries, noting his duties and the regiment's movements, military action and casualties.

WRIGHT, MARCUS JOSEPH, 1831-1922   **4023**

"Diary of Brigadier-General Marcus Joseph Wrigtht, C.S.A." WILLIAM AND MARY COLLEGE QUARTERLY, 2d ser. 15 (1935):88-95.

DIARY OF BRIGADIER-GENERAL MARCUS J. WRIGHT, C.S.A. N.p., 193-? 8 pp.

    1861-1863. Sporadic entries, which apparently were written at least somewhat later, by prominent Confederate, serving as lieutenant colonel of the 154th Tennessee Volunteers; scant details of military operations in the western theater; battles of Belmont, Shiloh and Perryville.

YANCY, WILLIAM LOWNDES, 1814-1863   **4024**

Hoole, W. Stanley, ed. "William L. Yancey's European Diary." ALABAMA REVIEW 25 (1972):134-142.

    Mar-Jun 1861. Brief, sketchy diary entries covering part of the period during which this Southern "fire-eater" was one of the special commissioners assigned to explain the Confederacy's actions to European leaders and secure recognition of its independence; journey from Montgomery to London via New Orleans, Havana and St. Thomas, noting expenses and people he met; interviews with Lord John Russell and other British politicians; visit to Paris and Confederates there.

1862

ANON., b. 1798   **4025**

HARRISONBURG, VIRGINIA: A DIARY OF A CITIZEN FROM MAY 9, 1862-AUGUST 22, 1864. Harrisonburg: E.R.G. Heneberger, 1961. 200 pp.

    1862-1864. Confederate's brief entries forming daily record of local events; weather, births, deaths from sickness and wounds and marriages; church, social and household activities; war news and the passage of army units and Union prisoners through the town; sketchy jottings of barest detail, the sum of which communicates the life of a community.

ANON.   **4026**

In HISTORY OF THE 103d REGIMENT, PENNSYLVANIA VETERAN VOLUNTEERS, by Luther S. Dickey, pp. 122-130.

    1862-1864. Diary recording the marches and major events in which Gen. H.W. Wessells' brigade participated in Virginia and North Carolina; supposedly published in pamphlet form during the war.

ANON.   **4027**

Ingersoll, Paul B., ed. "They Also Marched." MISSISSIPPI VALLEY HISTORICAL REVIEW 16 (1929):223-236.

    1862-1863. Extracts from Company E, Seventeenth Ohio, member's diary, reflecting the hard lot of the Civil War infantryman; service in Kentucky, Tennessee, Mississippi and Alabama, including the battle of Stones River; brief entries noting distances marched, foraging, Fourth of July observation, punishment of a deserter, etc.

ANON.   4028

In THE REBELLION RECORD, edited by Frank Moore, vol. 5, pp. 278-281.

> May-Jul 1862. Confederate soldier's account of successful efforts to turn back a Union advance on the defenses of Charleston.

ANON.   4029

In THE REBELLION RECORD, edited by Frank Moore, suppl., pp. 660-662.

> Aug 1862. Diary entries providing evocative descriptions of the Army of Northern Virginia as it moved toward Second Bull Run; notes on engagements with the enemy and the execution of Confederate deserters and a Union spy.

ANON.   4030

"A Young Lady's Diary." OUR LIVING AND OUR DEAD 1 (1874-1875):42-44, 220-221, 336-337; 4, no. 1 (1876):97-100.

> Sep 1862-May 1863 (with gaps). Confederate woman's diary reporting the war news; no personal or local items.

ANON.   4031

Vaught, Elsa, ed. "Diary of an Unknown Soldier." ARKANSAS HISTORICAL QUARTERLY 18 (1959):50-89.

THE DIARY OF AN UNKNOWN SOLDIER. Edited by Elsa Vaught. Van Buren, Ark.: Press-Argus Print, 1959. 45 pp.

> Sep-Dec 1862. Part of a diary, belonging to a member of the Nineteenth Iowa, found on a battlefield, probably that of Prairie Grove; uncomfortable voyage down the Mississippi to St. Louis and Benton Barracks; diarist's evaluation of regiment's officers; comments on troop train accommodations to Rolla, Missouri; notes on hardships endured and evidence of war's devastation observed while on the move to Springfield, Missouri; into Arkansas, a visit to the Pea Ridge battlefield and back to Missouri; sniping from houses and soldiers' retaliation; in camp at Wilson's Creek and notes on the battlefield; the forced march to Prairie Grove and the beginning of battle; an interesting, irreverent, often sarcastic, view of military operations from the ranks.

ANON.   4032

In THE CAMPAIGNS OF THE FIFTY-SECOND REGIMENT, PENNSYLVANIA VOLUNTEER INFANTRY, FIRST KNOWN AS "THE LUZERNE REGIMENT," Pennsylvania Infantry, 52d Regiment, pp. 108-114. Philadelphia: J.B. Lippincott, 1911.

> Dec 1862-Feb, Apr 1863. Extracts from soldier's diary; regiment's journey aboard the GEORGIA and the EXPOUNDER from Yorktown to St. Helena Island with a stop at Carolina City, North Carolina; on the MILTON to Port Royal; service along the South Carolina coast; notes on rough seas and collisions.

AMBLER, LUCY JOHNSTON, 1800-1888   4033

In THE YEARS OF ANGUISH, FAUQUIER COUNTY, VIRGINIA, compiled by Emily G. Ramey and John K. Gott, pp. 104-109.

> Feb 1862, Jul-Aug 1863. Details of depredations of Union soldiers at the plantation, Morven, and reports of losses by neighbors.

ANDREWS, ELLIE M. BUTZ, b. 1835   4034

ELLIE'S BOOK. Transcribed and annotated by Ann Campbell MacBryde. Davidson, N.C.: Briarpatch, 1984. 147 pp. Diary, pp. 27-132.

> 1862-1865. Diary kept by woman from Easton, Pennsylvania, who, before the war, married a North Carolinian and moved to Statesville, North Carolina; long initial entry summarizing events from January to August 1862 followed by sporadic entries covering the war years in Iredell County; social life, family matters, domestic tasks and Presbyterian church activities; news from her husband, Clinton, commanding the Nineteenth North Carolina, and general war news; visits to Davidson College and Asheboro, North Carolina; communication with her family in Pennsylvania; illnesses, deaths, weddings and births; efforts to find teaching position after death of husband in battle, finally locating at Mill Grove in Harnett County; Union raiding parties and a visit to the Averasboro battlefield; notes on food, clothing, particularly a mourning wardrobe, prices, Concord Female College and her son Clarence.

AREHART W.H.   4035

"W.H. Arehart's War Diary, 1862." ROCKINGHAM RECORDER 1 (1946-1948):111-133, 195-215, 271-282; 2, no. 1 (1954):23-31; no. 2 (1958):30-37; no. 3 (1959):145-160; no. 4 (1961):221-235.

> 1862-1864. Confederate cavalryman's daily but generally sparse notes; mostly record of military activities in Virginia, tightly focused on the particular duties, movements, actions, etc., that he was involved in with little or no mention of major battles or the wider war; some details of life at home in Rockingham County, Virginia.

ARMS, FRANK H.   4036

Henwood, James N.J. "A Cruise on the U.S.S. SABINE." AMERICAN NEPTUNE 29 (1969):102-105.

> Nov 1862-Feb 1863. Extracts from diary of paymaster's clerk, illustrating life aboard a sailing frigate searching for the Confederate cruiser ALABAMA in the Atlantic; a storm; crew members' offenses and the punishments meted out; a patriotic moment at sea; articulate, nicely detailed description.

BAER, CHARLES A., 1831-1863   4037

Bryan, Kirke, ed. "The Diary of Charles A. Baer." HISTORICAL SOCIETY OF MONTGOMERY COUNTY BULLETIN 7 (1950):101-126, 197-212.

> 1862-1863. Extracts from Norristown, Pennsylvania, minister's diary; his work as pastor of Trinity Lutheran Church; sermons, visits, singing school, statistics of church attendance, preparations for a new building, etc.; local travel and longer journeys; to Washington, D.C., visiting his brother in the 122d Pennsylvania and the Cliffburne Hospital near the city; following the regiment to Harpers Ferry, with remarks on the Antietam battlefield and the destruction in Sharpsburg; stopping at Baltimore; to synod meeting at Reading; to Gettysburg, shortly after the battle, for meeting of the Lutheran Theological Seminary's board of directors; viewing the battlefield and a hospital there; supporting the war effort, especially the Fifty-first Pennsylvania; notes on war developments and the response to calls for militia when Pennsylvania is threatened by Lee's army.

BAIRD, GEORGE W.   4038

In OFFICIAL RECORDS OF THE UNION AND CONFEDERATE
NAVIES IN THE WAR OF THE REBELLION, ser. 1, vol. 19, pp.
331-333, 394, 519-520; vol. 20, pp. 113, 137-138, 154.

Oct-Dec 1862, Jan, Mar-Apr 1863. Extracts from diary kept by
assistant engineer; aboard the CALHOUN in Atchafalaya Bay and
Bayou Teche, dueling with the Confederate gunboat J.A. COT-
TON; aboard the DIANA, capturing the steamboats SOUTHERN
MERCHANT and NANIOPE; on the CALHOUN in Bayou Teche,
under attack from Confederates in onshore rifle pits, and aground
off Bayou Sorrel; destruction of QUEEN OF THE WEST; capture
of Fort Burton at Butte-à-la-Rose, Louisiana.

BARDEEN, CHARLES WILLIAM, 1847-1924   4039

A LITTLE FIFER'S WAR DIARY. Syracuse, N.Y.: C.W. Bardeen,
1910. 320 pp.

Extracts in OUR SOLDIERS SPEAK, by William Matthews and Dixon Wecter, pp. 213-225 passim.

1862-1864. Extracts from diary, threaded through reminiscences,
of teenage musician in Company D, First Massachusetts Infantry; very brief entries, mainly recording conditions and events of
camp life in Virginia; participation in Fredericksburg, the "Mud
March," Chancellorsville and Gettysburg campaigns and the
battle of the Wilderness, but few military details; in New York
City in wake of draft riots; notes on leisure activities and
marches.

BARKSDALE, WILLIAM HENRY, 1827-1904   4040

Baker, Russell P., ed. "The Reverend William Henry Barksdale."
PHILLIPS COUNTY HISTORICAL QUARTERLY 15 (December
1976):34-46.

1862-1865 (with gaps). Pages torn out of a lost diary of Baptist
clergyman in Helena, Arkansas; destruction of his property by
flood and Union soldiers; having to take the oath of allegiance.

BARR, HENRIETTA FITZHUGH, 1825?-1893?   4041

THE CIVIL WAR DIARY OF MRS. HENRIETTA FITZHUGH BARR
(BARRE). Edited by Sallie Kiger Winn. Marietta, Ohio: Marietta College, 1963. 32 pp.

1862-1863. Diary kept by Confederate woman staying with her
parents in Ravenswood, West Virginia; irregular entries recounting family activities, war news and insults and depredations suffered at the hands of Union soldiers or unionist neighbors; trip
to Cincinnati and Louisville, remarking on Southern sympathizers
there; a civilian's view of local military operations.

BARR, JAMES W., 1837-1899   4042

"Diary of James W. Barr." WINCHESTER-FREDERICK COUNTY
HISTORICAL SOCIETY PAPERS 3 (1955):129-133.

Aug-Nov 1862. Winchester resident's diary kept while member
of Company G, Twenty-fifth Battalion, Local Defense, Virginia Infantry, responsible for providing cavalry with horses and forage;
capture, parole to Winchester and imprisonment at Washington,
D.C., until exchange in early October; in camp at Culpeper and
en route to Fredericksburg.

BEALL, JOHN YATES, 1835-1865   4043

MEMOIR OF JOHN YATES BEALL: HIS LIFE; TRIAL; COR-
RESPONDENCE; DIARY. By Daniel B. Lucas. Montreal: Printed by
J. Lovell, 1865. 297 pp. Diary, pp. 51-55, 224-297.

Jul 1862-Jan 1863, Aug, Dec 1864-Jan 1865. Virginian's diary
kept between periods of Confederate military service; sporadic
entries bearing lengthy reviews of military and political news; diary
first kept at Dubuque, where he managed a mill, and Cascade,
Iowa, and then at Dundas, Ontario, where he fled when his
Southern sympathies were discovered; a few entries from prison
cell in New York City police headquarters before his trial and execution for espionage and guerilla activities.

"Last Days of John Yates Beall." CONFEDERATE VETERAN 30
(1922):426-428.

In REBELS ON LAKE ERIE, by Charles E. Frohman, pp. 106-109.
Columbus: Ohio Historical Society, 1965.

Dec 1864-Jan 1865. Extracts covering imprisonment.

BEAN, STEPHEN S., 1829-1863   4044

In AMERICAN PATRIOTISM, by Leonard Brown, pp. 172-175.

1862-1863. Extracts from diary of private serving with Company
A, Tenth Iowa Infantry Volunteers; unit's movements in Tennessee
and Mississippi; battles of Iuka and Corinth.

BELL, GEORGE, 1821-1869   4045

Bell, Whitfield J., Jr., ed. "A Record of Captivity in a Federal Military
Prison." GEORGIA HISTORICAL QUARTERLY 22 (1938):169-184.

Apr-Aug 1862. Diary of naturalized citizen, an immigrant from
Ireland, captured at fall of Fort Pulaski; transport north by ship
and imprisonment at Governor's Island in New York Harbor and,
for a brief period, at Fort Delaware before exchange; notes on
weather, war news, food and events such as the New York Yacht
Club's annual regatta.

BELL, HENRY H.   4046

In OFFICIAL RECORDS OF THE UNION AND CONFEDERATE
NAVIES IN THE WAR OF THE REBELLION, ser. 1, vol. 18, pp.
682-716; vol. 19, pp. 711-747; vol. 20, pp. 753-763.

1862-1863. Private diary of Union naval officer; mainly log-like
record of fleet operations; ship movements; decision-making process within Farragut's command; occasional notes of non-military
nature and descriptions of significant events including raising of
United States flag above the New Orleans custom house and
removal of state flag from the city hall; scenes along the Mississippi; perils of navigating the river and efforts to extricate the HART-
FORD which had run aground; skirmishes with Confederates in
occupied Baton Rouge; disputes over launching assault on
Vicksburg and details of the attack; orders to relieve Captain
Craven of command of the BROOKLYN; contending with the Confederate ram ARKANSAS: return to New Orleans for repairs;
report detailing the sinking of the ARKANSAS; blockade duty at
Mobile Bay; to Galveston Bay to restore Union control after
Magruder's attack and the capture of the HARRIET LANE; sinking of the HATTERAS and events along the Texas coast; concern for United States-Mexico relations; return to New Orleans
to assume new command.

BENSELL, ROYAL AUGUSTUS, 1838-1921   **4047**

ALL QUIET ON THE YAMHILL. Edited by Gunter Barth. Eugene: University of Oregon Books, 1959. 226 pp. Diary, pp. 3-182.

1862-1864. Corporal's diary of service with Company D, Fourth California Infantry, at Fort Yamhill, Fort Hoskins and Siletz Blockhouse in western Oregon; a daily record of generally monotonous military life; routine duties and poor rations; unjust regulations and punishments meted out by commissioned officers; description of towns and countryside; military duties on the Coast Reservation, Indian-white relations, Indian language and customs; denunciation of officers and Indian agents; notes on weather, leisure activities, soldiers' drinking, religious services, war news, etc.; celebration of Fourth of July, April Fool's Day and Thanksgiving; a candid, interesting account of a frustrating term of service.

BENSON, CHARLES A., 1830-1881   **4048**

Richardson, Katherine W., ed. "The Travels and Tribulations of Charles Benson, Steward on the GLIDE." ESSEX INSTITUTE HISTORICAL COLLECTIONS 120 (1984):73-109.

1862-1880. Extracts from the logs and diaries of a black resident of Salem who served as steward on various Salem vessels, particularly his experiences on the GLIDE involved in trade with Zanzibar; his duties and notes on work of other crewmen; activities on ship and ashore; quarrels and violence, especially brutal beating of the cabin boy by captain William Beadle; constant homesickness for his wife and children; ship's fare; illnesses, including his own sufferings from rheumatism; a few notes on Arab customs at Zanzibar.

BERRY, JOHN GREEN, 1840-1924   **4049**

Berry, Charles R. "A Prospecting Trip to Idaho." IDAHO YESTERDAYS 24, no. 3 (1980):2-22.

Jan-Sep 1862. Harrison County, Kentucky, man's mining venture in the Salmon River area, with entries beginning at Santa Clara, California; travel with his uncle George P. Swinford and Robert Reyburn from San Francisco to Portland on the BROTHER JONATHAN; outfitting; travel on the Columbia, thence overland to Florence and Elk City, with notes on prospecting in the gulches; return to Portland.

Berry, Charles R., ed. "Prospecting in the Reese River Mines of Nevada in 1864." NEVADA HISTORICAL SOCIETY QUARTERLY 24 (1981):51-78.

Apr-Sep 1864. Silver prospecting activities in the Austin area; travel from Santa Clara, California, with notes of route and camps; references to many people; some doggerel verse.

BIGGERT, FLORENCE C., d. 1910   **4050**

Beck, Harry R., ed. "Some Leaves from a Civil War Diary." WESTERN PENNSYLVANIA HISTORICAL MAGAZINE 42 (1959):363-382.

Sep 1862, Jun-Aug 1863. Diary of Pittsburgh resident, a corporal in Company D, Fifteenth Regiment of Pennsylvania Militia, called to active service during Confederate invasions of Maryland and Pennsylvania; in camp at Harrisburg and Chambersburg; arriving at Antietam after the battle, describing the dead and debris of the struggle and quickly returning to Harrisburg; garrisoning the defenses of Pittsburgh during the Gettysburg campaign;

resigning from his company and joining an artillery unit at Hancock, Maryland.

BILLENSTEIN, J.T.   **4051**

In MISSISSIPPI IN THE CONFEDERACY, edited by John K. Bettersworth and James W. Silver, vol. 1, pp. 89-92.

Jul 1862. Extracts from journal kept aboard the U.S.S. BROOKLYN; naval operations at Vicksburg; attack on Confederate ram ARKANSAS by the gunboat ESSEX.

BIRCHER, WILLIAM, b. 1846   **4052**

A DRUMMER-BOY'S DIARY. St. Paul, Minn.: St. Paul Book and Stationary, 1889. 199 pp.

1862-1865. Record kept by drummer boy of Company K, Second Minnesota; narrative covering first year or so of service followed by diary of mostly brief entries, obviously rewritten for publication; campaigning in Kentucky and Tennessee; battles of Perryville, Chickamauga, Lookout Mountain and Missionary Ridge; furlough home to St. Paul when regiment reenlists; the Atlanta campaign and the March to the Sea; touring Savannah; through the Carolinas to Richmond and seeing the sights there and at the Wilderness battlefield; the Grand Review and more sightseeing in Washington, D.C.; return to Minnesota; notes on weather, his unit's movements and foraging.

BLANC, SAMUEL P.   **4053**

In OFFICIAL RECORDS OF THE UNION AND CONFEDERATE NAVIES IN THE WAR OF THE REBELLION, ser. 1, vol. 17, pp. 700-702.

May 1862. Extract from diary of Confederate passed midshipman, listing members of expedition launched from the CHATTAHOOCHEE against Union forces in St. George Sound, Florida.

BLOOMER, SAM, b. 1837?   **4054**

In BRING WARM CLOTHES, collected by Peg Meier, pp. 84, 86.

Sep-Dec 1862. Extracts from diary of Stillwater, Minnesota, resident, member of Company B, First Minnesota Volunteer Infantry; battle of Antietam; lying wounded on the battlefield and recuperating from leg amputation.

BOIES, ANDREW J., b. 1836   **4055**

RECORD OF THE THIRTY-THIRD MASSACHUSETTS VOLUNTEER INFANTRY. Fitchburg: Sentinel Printing, 1880. 168 pp. Diary, pp. 7-136.

1862-1865. Company E enlisted man's diary, amended to some extent for publication; stationed in Virginia; passing over Bull Run battlefields; Burnside's "Mud March"; detached service as mule driver in ammunition train; reaction of Marylanders as Union army moves north to Gettysburg; the battle; transfer to pioneer corps and sent to the Army of the Cumberland at Bridgeport, Alabama; Chattanooga and Knoxville campaigns; the view from Lookout Mountain; driving mules in the Third Division's supply train as the Atlanta campaign commences; return to regiment and battle of Kenesaw Mountain; patrol duty in Atlanta and the burning of the city; the March to the Sea, noting foraging, destruction, Millen Prison and soldiers' behavior at Milledgeville; occupied Savannah; the Carolinas campaign, the burning of Columbia and battles of Kinston and Bentonville; celebrating the surrenders; descriptions of Raleigh, the Grand Review, Washington, D.C., and welcome home to Boston; notes on camp life, contrabands and Southern women; praise for Joseph Hooker and evaluations of Meade, Burnside, Slocum and other prominent generals.

BOND, SAMUEL R.   **4056**

In EXPEDITION FROM FORT ABERCROMBIE TO FORT BENTON, by James Liberty Fisk, pp. 4-28. 37th Cong., 3rd sess., 1863, H. Exec. Doc. 80. Washington, D.C.; Govt. Print. Off., 1863.

In IDAHO: HER GOLD FIELDS AND THE ROUTES TO THEM, A HANDBOOK FOR EMIGRANTS, by James Liberty Fisk, pp. 25-89. New York: John A. Gray, Printer, 1863.

Jun-Nov 1862. Condensed summary and extracts of journal kept by secretary of Fisk's expedition from St. Paul to Walla Walla to escort first emigrant train on the northern route explored by Isaac Stevens, and accompanied by Stevens's guide, Pierre Bottineau, from Fort Abercrombie to Fort Union, with admiration for Minnesota lumbermen who built bridges; killing buffalo to feed visiting Assiniboin; notes on Crow, Gros Ventre and Blackfoot Indians; accounts of personal interest such as observance of Sabbath, birth of a baby, a wedding; end of government assignment at Fort Benton and summary of travel over Mullan Road.

BOOTH, GEORGE W.   **4057**

"Running the Inland Blockade." CIVIL WAR TIMES ILLUSTRATED 11, no. 3 (1972):12-19.

Feb 1862. Journal of trip from Henderson, Kentucky, to New Orleans, written up in April of that year by an Englishman, a hat manufacturer in Newark, New Jersey; by carriage, stage and train; notes on travel conditions and people, including General Beauregard, encountered along the way; description of countryside, the towns of Hopkinsville, Kentucky, and Clarksville, Tennessee, and war conditions in the Confederacy; lengthy, richly detailed entries.

" 'We've Played Cards and Lost.' " CIVIL WAR TIMES ILLUSTRATED 11, no. 9 (1973):16-24.

Apr 1862. Events leading up to the occupation of New Orleans; the conflagration of burning cotton; conditions in the city; surrender negotiations; murder of a unionist; substantial, nicely descriptive entries.

BORTON, DAVID   **4058**

In HISTORY OF THE MEN OF COMPANY F, by New Jersey Infantry, 12th Regiment, pp. 20-28. Camden, N.J.: C.S. Magrath, 1897.

Dec 1862-Apr 1863. Extracts from war diary of soldier in the Twelfth New Jersey Volunteers; trip from Ellicott Mills, Maryland, through Washington, D.C., arriving at Fredericksburg just after the battle; in camp near Fredericksburg and moving towards Chancellorsville.

BOSTON, WILLIAM, 1837-1915   **4059**

THE CIVIL WAR DIARY OF WILLIAM BOSTON. Ann Arbor, Mich., 1937. 96 leaves.

1862-1865. Diary kept by corporal, Company H, Twentieth Michigan Volunteer Infantry, detailing a soldier's everyday experiences; journey from Michigan to Maryland; operations there

and in Virginia; battle of Fredericksburg; service in Kentucky and Tennessee; description of Todd Cave in Adair County; taken out of action by illness in Mississippi and Tennessee; battle of the Wilderness; ill again, then taking care of wounded at Fredericksburg, White House Landing and City Point; siege of Petersburg; stationed at Washington, D.C., after Lee's surrender; the Grand Review.

BOWERS, STEPHEN C., 1832-1907   **4060**

Schroeder, Glenna R., ed. "The Civil War Diary of Chaplain Stephen C. Bowers." INDIANA MAGAZINE OF HISTORY 79 (1983):167-185.

Aug-Sep 1862. Extracts from diary of Methodist clergyman; service as lieutenant, Company K, Sixty-seventh Indiana Volunteer Infantry, and then as regimental chaplain; operations in Kentucky; trip back to Indiana on military business; battle of Munfordville; briefly a prisoner; list of casualties.

BOYER, SAMUEL PELLMAN, 1839-1875   **4061**

NAVAL SURGEON. Edited by Elinor Barnes and James A. Barnes. Bloomington: Indiana University Press, 1963. 2 vols.

1862-1866. Diary of physician from Berks County, Pennsylvania, a graduate of the University of Pennsylvania; service as acting assistant surgeon aboard the FERNANDINA; boring blockade duty off the South Carolina and Georgia coasts; at Port Royal and Doboy Sound; foraging and sightseeing excursions ashore; descriptions of plantations and diarist's acquisition of books from abandoned dwellings; scenes of plundering by the First South Carolina Volunteers at St. Simons Island and the burning of Darien; voyage to New England and return south to Sapelo and St. Catherines sounds; capturing a prize at long last; transfer to the MATTABESETT; operations in Albemarle Sound including engagement with the ALBEMARLE; postwar service as acting passed assistant surgeon on the supply steamer NEWBERN along the Atlantic and Gulf coasts; detailed information on patients and treatments; comments about freedmen and black Union soldiers; mention of many ships and naval officers; notes on food, reading, prices, songs, weather and celebrations of April Fool's Day, Thanksgiving and Christmas; daily record through 1864 with erratic entries 1865-1866.

1868-1869. From New York to Panama on the HENRY CHAUNCEY, across the Isthmus, to San Francisco on the CONSTITUTION and to China on the GREAT REPUBLIC; traveling companions, other ships, expenses and colorful shipboard social life; assignment on the IROQUOIS at Yokohama; activities of his daily life; medical duties, including prescriptions and treatments, especially for venereal disease; personal expenses and prices of oriental gifts; obtaining food, china and service for the wardroom mess; notes on Japanese Civil War, complex political situations, social customs, status of women, living conditions, clothing, housing and food; excursions into the countryside around Hyogo, Osaka, Nagasaki and Hakadate, visiting temples, shrines and festivals; escorted to Kyoto to treat a prince and royally feted upon his recovery; shocking judicial methods sanctioned by the American consul; visiting Shanghai and other ports; assigned to the ASHUELOT and return home on the JAPAN.

BRADY, JOHN J., b. 1843?   **4062**

In ANNUAL REPORT, 5th, by New York State Bureau of Military Statistics, pp. 438-473.

Jun-Sep 1862. Journal of Twelfth New York's color corporal; record of service in Company K from mustering in to return to New York City after engagement at Maryland Heights during the Antietam campaign; Philadelphia hospitality for soldiers on way to Ft. McHenry; sightseeing in Baltimore; description of countryside passed through on way to Harpers Ferry; in camp at nearby Bolivar and expeditions to Shepherdstown and Winchester; officers' efforts to persuade regiment, whose enlistment was up, to remain in place to meet Confederate invasion; accusations of commanders' treachery and cowardice when their position is surrendered; notes on weather, food, pranks, altercations, Fourth of July celebration and Stonewall Jackson; an account rich in the details of army life and expression of soldiers' feelings; some evidence of later polishing.

BRECKINRIDGE, LUCY GILMER, 1834-1865   4063

LUCY BRECKINRIDGE OF GROVE HILL. Edited by Mary D. Robertson. Kent, Ohio: Kent State University Press, 1979. 235 pp.

1862-1864. Confidential diary of member of prominent family residing at Grove Hill plantation near Fincastle, Botetourt County, Virginia; thoughts on love, marriage, the nature of man and woman, slavery, the war, etc.; church services and religious reflections; mourning death of favorite brother and concern for other brothers in Confederate service; visits to the Burwell family at Avenal, Bedford County, and Soldier's Joy, the home of a Gilmer uncle in Nelson County; notes on reading, suitors, many friends and relatives; insults and looting when Union soldiers arrive at her home; the hopes, pleasures, sorrows, fears and doubts of a young woman's coming of age in wartime and a candid view of family and social life in the Confederacy.

In OUR WOMEN IN THE WAR, pp. 385-389 passim.

Robertson, Mary D., ed. "The Dusky Wings of War." CIVIL WAR HISTORY 23 (1977):26-51.

1862-1864. Extracts.

BROADDUS, WILLIAM F., 1801-1876   4064

Griffith, Lucille, ed. "Fredericksburg's Political Hostages." VIRGINIA MAGAZINE OF HISTORY AND BIOGRAPHY 72 (1964):395-429. Diary, pp. 405-429 passim.

Jul-Sep 1862. Extracts from prison diary kept by pastor of the Fredericksburg Baptist Church who also conducted the Broaddus Female Institute; conditions and events at Old Capitol Prison where he was imprisoned in retaliation for incarceration of fellow townsmen of purportedly unionist persuasion by Confederate authorities; meeting with Belle Boyd, also a prisoner; frustrated mission to Richmond to secure release of the Fredericksburg prisoners and George Rowe's subsequent successful endeavor.

BROWN, JOHN   4065

Beattie, G.W., ed. "The Diary of John Brown." HISTORICAL SOCIETY OF SOUTHERN CALIFORNIA ANNUAL PUBLICATIONS 13 (1927):360-364.

Jun-Jul 1862. Extract from the diary of a San Bernardino toll road owner covering his first journey from San Bernardino to his ferry at Fort Mojave on the Colorado; brief notes and camps and conditions of travel, especially on the Mojave Desert.

BROWN, NATHAN, 1807-1886   4066

Brown, N. Worth and Downes, Randolph C., eds. "A Conference with Abraham Lincoln." NORTHWEST OHIO QUARTERLY 24 (1950):48-63. Diary, pp. 56-62.

Dec 1862. Extracts from diary of Baptist minister, editor of anti-slavery magazine THE AMERICAN BAPTIST AND FREEMAN; account of meeting with the president at which diarist and fellow clergymen George B. Cheever and William Goodell presented a petition from New York City and Brooklyn churches urging the complete abolition of slavery in the United States; interesting description of Lincoln's appearance, ways of dealing with people and thoughts on emancipation; text of petition included.

BRUCE, DANIEL E., 1836-1920   4067

Bruce, Foster and Lynch William O. "Daniel E. Bruce: Civil War Teamster." INDIANA MAGAZINE OF HISTORY 33 (1937):187-198.

1862-1865. Scattered extracts within narrative summary of diary kept by Indiana farmer, a member of Company E, Eighty-seventh Indiana, but assigned to duty as a teamster; service in Kentucky and Tennessee; the Atlanta and Carolinas campaigns; everyday affairs and ordinary routines; an interesting diary which should have been published in full.

BURGESS, E.G.   4068

In THE SOLDIER OF INDIANA IN THE WAR FOR THE UNION, by Catharine Merrill, vol. 2, pp. 256-262.

Dec 1862-Jan 1863. Extracts from the diary of a private in the Eighth Indiana; camp life, duties and bad weather in Missouri.

BURKE, CURTIS R., b. 1842   4069

Bennett, Pamela J., ed. "Curtis R. Burke's Civil War Journal." INDIANA MAGAZINE OF HISTORY 65 (1969):283-327; 66 (1970):110-172, 318-361; 67 (1971):129-170.

1862-1865. Extracts from daily record prepared in 1914 from wartime notes by member of Company B, Fourteenth Kentucky Cavalry; taken prisoner while escorting ladies to Murfreesboro under flag of truce and held there and at Nashville and Louisville until exchange through Virginia; participation in Morgan's July 1863 raid through Indiana and Ohio and capture at Buffington Island, Ohio; incarcerated briefly at Camp Morton, and then at Camp Douglas; prison conditions and events; notes on activities, food, price of gold and other items, sutlers, weather, Fourth of July and Christmas celebrations, confinement in the smallpox hospital, medical treatments, Prisoners Masonic Association, etc.; exchange through Richmond in March 1865; inspection of Libby Prison, Castle Thunder and other sights of the city; furlough to Abbeville, South Carolina; at Danville, Virginia, and in North Carolina as the Confederacy crumbles; reactions to Lincoln's death; travel around the South with stops at Atlanta and Memphis, finally returning to Lexington, Kentucky; a fulsome, engaging account but very difficult to determine the merging point between contemporary notes and memory.

Extracts in TRAVEL ACCOUNTS OF INDIANA, compiled by Shirley S. McCord, pp. 216-222.

Jul 1863. The raid through southern Indiana.

BURTON, ROBERT T.   4070

In TREASURES OF PIONEER HISTORY, compiled by Kate E. Carter, vol. 5, pp. 376-389.

Apr-May 1862. Record kept by captain of volunteers from Utah called to protect mail route from Indians and renegades; gathering mail from abandoned mail stations from Green River to Deer Creek and returning it to La Prele to be sent East; returning by partially different route collecting mail for the West, finding much thievery and vandalism.

CAMPBELL, HENRY, 1846?-1915   4071

"Campbell Diary." CIVIL WAR TIMES ILLUSTRATED 2, no. 7 (1963):26-29; 2, no. 9 (1964):42-45; 3, no. 2 (1964):34-37; 3, no. 5 (1964):46-48; 3, no. 6 (1964):46-48; 3, no. 9 (1965):36-39.

1862-1866. Extracts from diary of Eighteenth Indiana Artillery Battery's bugler, a teenager from Crawfordsville; campaigning in Kentucky and Tennessee; advance from Murfreesboro to Chattanooga; battle of Chickamauga; pursuing Wheeler's cavalry; a welcome from unionists in Shelbyville, Tennessee; admiring the attractions of Huntsville, Alabama; action in eastern Tennessee; the Atlanta campaign and touring the fallen city; commissioned second lieutenant, 101st United States Colored Infantry; assigned to guard the Louisville and Nashville Railroad; focus on military action but also notes on hardships of marches, foraging, drinking, his captain Eli Lilly, and execution of Confederate guerilla Champ Ferguson; generally long, articulate passages indicating later rewriting.

CANNON, J.P.   4072

INSIDE OF REBELDOM: THE DAILY LIFE OF A PRIVATE IN THE CONFEDERATE ARMY. Washington, D.C.: National Tribune, 1900. 288 pp. Diary, pp. 73-269.

1862-1864. Chatty, somewhat anecdotal diary kept by private in Company C, Twenty-seventh Alabama; duties, poor rations, sickness, etc., at Port Hudson; in camp and on the march in Mississippi; notes on developments at Vicksburg, foraging adventures and improved rations, revivals, punishment of deserters, military performances for the ladies, Christmas celebrations, etc.; retreat into Alabama; furlough home to Gravelly Springs; unionist sentiments and Yankee depredations in that region; the Atlanta campaign; comments on death of Leonidas Polk, Johnston's removal from command and Sherman's order to evacuate Atlanta; the battles of Franklin and Nashville and the consequent demise of his regiment; home on furlough; a substantial, entertaining account.

CANSDELL, HENRY W., 1808-1869   4073

"Journal of Dr. Henry W. Cansdell." VINELAND HISTORICAL MAGAZINE 7 (1922):55-60; 8 (1923):72-76, 92-97, 111-114, 135-138.

Jan-Aug, Dec 1862. Diary of surgeon, an immigrant from England, serving with the Third Wisconsin Battery of Artillery and the Twenty-second Wisconsin Infantry; in Wisconsin camp and then in Tennessee, Mississippi and Alabama; brief, choppy entries covering family and social activities, food and his health with scant mention of medical duties; notes on Tom Thumb, Wisconsin legislation on pay of officers and surgeons and the drowning of Wisconsin governor Harvey.

CARY, HARRIETTE   4074

"Diary of Miss Harriette Cary." TYLER'S QUARTERLY HISTORICAL AND GENEALOGICAL MAGAZINE 9 (1927-1928):104-115; 12 (1930-1931):160-173.

May-Jul 1862. Diary covering life in occupied Williamsburg, Virginia; the strength of the Union forces, their depredations and treatment of Confederate wounded; constant inaccurate news of Peninsular campaign; supplications for God's help; the support of friendship and clandestine religious services; notes on reading, contrabands, social life and deaths.

CHADICK, MARY IONE COOK   4075

"Civil War Days in Huntsville." ALABAMA HISTORICAL QUARTERLY 9 (1947):195-333.

1862-1865 (with gaps). Journal of Northern-born Huntsville matron, wife of Presbyterian minister, a Confederate army officer; conditions in the occupied city and stories of Southern pluck and civility during encounters with Union soldiers; threats of Confederate and Union raids; a short experience as a refugee to Warrenton; brief reunions with husband as opportunity allowed; Yankee cruelties and kindnesses, stealing and destruction; confiscation of slaves and later departures of servants; notes on reading, clothes, friends, neighbors, April Fool's Day, prices, shortages, regulations, etc.; distorted war news; reaction to black Union soldiers, events of surrender, Lincoln's assassination and returning soldiers.

Extracts in THE ALABAMA CONFEDERATE READER, edited by Malcolm C. McMillan, pp. 154-172.

Apr-Aug 1862. First Union occupation of Huntsville and its effect on slaves; notes on Union generals Ormsby M. Mitchel and Lovell H. Rousseau.

CHAMBERS, HENRY ALEXANDER, 1841-1925 4076

DIARY OF HENRY A. CHAMBERS. Edited by T.H. Pearce. Wendell, N.C.: Broadfoot's Bookmark, 1983. 290 pp.

1862-1865. Record of Iredell County resident who left his studies at Davidson College to join Company C, Fourth North Carolina State Troops; detached service as member of the provost marshal's police guard, Army of Northern Virginia, near Manassas and south along the Orange and Alexandria Railroad; visits to Richmond; glimpses of Jackson and Lee; captain of Company C, Forty-ninth North Carolina; battle of Fredericksburg; stationed at various locations in eastern North Carolina and southeastern Virginia; battle of Drewry's Bluff; siege of Petersburg including battle of the Crater and service on court martial; wounding at Five Forks, last days of war and the surrender at Appomattox; coverage of duties, reading, camp life, prices, theater, correspondence, church attendance, war news and rumors, train travel home on furloughs, social life and the ladies, an execution, Christmas celebrations, etc.; description of Henry A. Wise; reaction to black Union soldiers.

CHAMBERS, WILLIAM PITT, 1839-1916   4077

Polk, Ruth, ed. "My Journal." MISSISSIPPI HISTORICAL SOCIETY PUBLICATIONS, Centenary ser. 5 (1925):221-386.

1862-1865. Diary of member of Company B, Forty-sixth Mississippi Infantry Volunteers; sporadic, lengthy entries, with some parts of the record, revised by the author in 1891, in purely narrative form; service in Mississippi, Alabama and Georgia, including the battle of Port Gibson, the siege of Vicksburg and the Atlanta campaign; notes on reading, religion, visits to cemeteries, morale and desertions, Jefferson Davis, Joseph E. Johnston and many locations including Meridian, Mississippi, Mobile and Pollard, Alabama; dealing with defeat.

CHURCHILL, LEE   4078

In ANNUAL REPORT, 5TH, by New York State Bureau of Military Statistics, pp. 559-568.

1862-1864. Extracts from captain's diary of service with the 125th New York Volunteers; battle and surrender at Harpers Ferry during Antietam campaign; description of Stonewall Jackson and reflections on Confederate soldiers' determination; journey to parole camp in Maryland and then Camp Douglas; civilian support shown along the way; question of propriety of drill under terms of parole; sketchy notes on military operations in Virginia after his exchange.

CLARK, JAMES H.   4079

THE IRON HEARTED REGIMENT. Albany, N.Y.: J. Munsell, 1865. 337 pp. Journal, pp. 4-144 passim.

1862-1864. What appear to be actual entries scattered within narrative based on entire wartime diary of officer in Company H, 115th New York Volunteers; action in western Virginia; events at Yorktown, Virginia, Beaufort and Hilton Head, South Carolina, Jacksonville and Palatka, Florida; operations along the Chickahominy River and siege of Petersburg; donations from the Christian Commission and the Sanitary Commission.

CLARK, LEANDER   4080

In ANNUAL REPORT, 5TH, by New York State Bureau of Military Statistics, pp. 568-575.

Dec 1862. Extracts from diary of captain, Company I, 124th New York, focusing on his official activities at camp near Falmouth, Virginia; dissatisfaction with medical facilities; names of company members on sick list and assigned to specific duties; last entry ending abruptly with order to cross the Rappahannock to Fredericksburg.

CLEVELAND, EDMUND J., 1842-1902   4081

Cleveland, Edmund J., Jr., ed. "The Early Campaigns in North Carolina." NEW JERSEY HISTORICAL SOCIETY PROCEEDINGS 68 (1950):119-161, 216-266; 69 (1951):143-167, 248-273, 362-386; 70 (1952):61-65, 137-140, 278-283; 71 (1953):62-64, 136-141, 204-209.

1862-1864. Extracts from diary of Elizabeth soldier, a private in Company K, Ninth New Jersey Volunteers; in camp at Alexandria; in North Carolina near Bogue Sound, with retrospective account of the December 1862 Goldsboro expedition, including engagements at Kinston and Whitehall; more than a week on board transports before going to Port Royal; in camp on St. Helena Island and Union soldiers' plundering of blacks homes there; expedition to Edisto Island and return to North Carolina; garrison duty at Carolina City and various military operations in the state; at Newport News; controversy over regimental reenlistment; furlough home with a brief stop at Princeton and an unsuccessful attempt to get a commission; notes on many events and subjects, including food, games, prices, foraging, Gen. Benjamin Butler, fellow soldiers, physical surroundings, black troops, a black church service, holiday celebrations, etc.; an interesting, quite readable description of camp life and military action.

Cleveland, Edmund J., Jr., ed. "The Campaign of Promise and Disappointment." NEW JERSEY HISTORICAL SOCIETY PROCEEDINGS 67 (1949):218-240, 308-328.

Mar-May 1864. Extracts covering the unsuccessful campaign of the Army of the James against Richmond; daily entries describing military operations, including an expedition up the James and Chuckatuck rivers to Cherry Grove plantation and Smithfield; notes on camp life, games, celebration of Saint Patrick's and April Fool's days, prices, chores, a soldier's suicide, illness, a military funeral, a black wedding procession, troop transport, black Union soldiers, etc.

Cleveland, Edmund J., Jr., ed. "The Second Battle of Cold Harbor." NEW JERSEY HISTORICAL SOCIETY PROCEEDINGS 66 (1948):25-37.

Jun 1864. Substantial entries extracted from diary dealing with his participation in events at Cold Harbor; delays in transport of the regiment; arrival at the battlefield after the disastrous June third assault; life in the rifle pits; religious reflections; a hard march to White House and by crowded boat to Bermuda Hundred.

Cleveland, Edmund J., Jr., ed. "The Siege of Petersburg." NEW JERSEY HISTORICAL SOCIETY PROCEEDINGS 66 (1948):76-96, 176-196.

Jun-Sep 1864. Extracts describing military and leisure activities during the investment of Petersburg; much time spent in hospital and convalescent camp; notes on food, close calls, casualties, a revival, black Union troops, relations with Confederate soldiers, the Sanitary and Christian commissions, etc.; a glimpse of Grant; sightseeing around the fortifications; beginning of journey to North Carolina.

COE, HAMLIN ALEXANDER, 1840-1899   4082

MINE EYES HAVE SEEN THE GLORY. Edited by David Coe. Rutherford, N.J.: Fairleigh Dickinson University Press, 1975. 240 pp.

1862-1865. Elkhart, Michigan, wagon maker's war diary; service with Company E, Ninteenth Michigan Volunteer Infantry in Ohio, Kentucky and Tennessee; capture near Franklin, journey to Richmond and brief detention at Libby before exchange; in hospital at Annapolis; action of the Atlanta campaign; in hospital in Georgia and Nashville; discharge and return home; description of countryside, towns and cities, including Covington, Paris, Louisville and Nicholasville, Kentucky, McMinnville, Tennessee, and Columbus, Ohio; negative feelings about freedmen; notes on camp life, foraging, drinking in the army, women snuff dippers, Confederate deserters, Chickamauga battlefield, black Union soldiers, casualties, duties, theater in Nashville, the Christian Commission and Lincoln's assassination.

COGSHALL, ISRAEL   **4083**

Byrd, Cecil K., ed. "Journal of Israel Cogshall." INDIANA MAGA-
ZINE OF HISTORY 42 (1946):69-87.

Oct 1862-Sep 1863. Methodist minister's diary of service with
the Nineteenth Michigan Volunteer Infantry; military operations
in Kentucky and Tennessee, including battle of Thompson's Station; taken prisoner in Tennessee and transported around the
South to release at Vicksburg; journey up the Mississippi to Cairo
and then home to Coldwater, Michigan; back in Tennessee from
June until resignation accepted in September; activities as
chaplain and as person in charge of staff mess; notes on illnesses.

COLTON, MATTHIAS BALDWIN, 1839-1915   **4084**

In COLUMN SOUTH, compiled by Suzanne Colton Wilson, edited
by J. Ferrell Colton and Antoinette G. Smith, pp. 32-323 passim.
Flagstaff, Ariz.: J.F. Colton, 1960.

1862-1865. Extracts from chatty, candid journal of Philadelphian,
a Fifteenth Pennsylvania Cavalry trooper, brother of William Francis Colton; operations in Kentucky; a potential regimental mutiny;
capture, imprisonment and waiting for exchange at Camp Chase;
return to regiment in Tennessee; Tullahoma campaign,
Chickamauga and the Chattanooga, Franklin and Nashville campaigns; service in Alabama, Tennessee and North Carolina; a
glimpse of Sherman; notes on many aspects of camp life, including the regiment's 1864 presidential vote and April Fool's Day
observance.

THE CIVIL WAR JOURNAL AND CORRESPONDENCE OF MAT-
THIAS BALDWIN COLTON. Edited by Jessie S. Colton. Philadelphia:
Macrae-Smith, 1931. Journal, pp. 3-49.

Aug 1862-Feb 1863. Extracts; duties, events and leisure activities
in camp at Carlisle; on the fringe of battle of Antietam; journey
from Pennsylvania to Kentucky; battle of Stones River, capture
and circuitous trip to Richmond with notes on scenery, treatment,
food, prices, etc.; early parole to camp near Annapolis; sightseeing in Washington, D.C.; some nice descriptive details.

COLTON, WILLIAM FRANCIS, 1841-1921   **4085**

In COLUMN SOUTH, compiled by Suzanne Colton Wilson, edited
by J. Ferrell Colton and Antoinette G. Smith, pp. 2-313 passim.
Flagstaff, Ariz.: J.F. Colton, 1960.

1862-1865. Extracts from diary of Fifteenth Pennsylvania Cavalry
officer, brother of Matthias Baldwin Colton; leaving friends in
Philadelphia; in camp at Carlisle; the Antietam campaign; stationed at Louisville; threat of a regimental mutiny; operations in
Tennessee including the Franklin and Nashville campaign; service in Alabama, Tennessee, the Carolinas, Virginia and Georgia;
many details of army life in camp and in the field; notes on
furloughs home, a visit to Atlantic City, the Chickamauga battlefield, April Fool's observance, etc.

COOKE, JOHN ESTEN, 1830-1886   **4086**

Hubbell, Jay B., ed. "The War Diary of John Esten Cooke." JOUR-
NAL OF SOUTHERN HISTORY 7 (1941):526-540.

1862-1865. Extracts from diary of noted author, a Virginian serving on Jeb Stuart's staff; Stuart's ride around McClellan's army
and the Seven Days' battles; conversations with Stuart; diarist's
regard for Stonewall Jackson, Lee and Lee's family; references
to his uncle, Union general Philip St. George Cooke; his daily
routine, responsibilities, feelings under fire and philosophy of life;
an intriguing glimpse of the writer's first impressions of an experience he later recorded in biography, autobiography and
fiction.

CORT, CHARLES EDWIN, 1841-1903   **4087**

"DEAR FRIENDS"; THE CIVIL WAR LETTERS AND DIARY OF
CHARLES EDWIN CORT. Compiled and edited by Helyn W. Tomlinson. N.p., 1962. 194 pp. Diary, pp. 7-192 passim.

1862-1865. Extracts from Ninety-second Illinois Volunteer Infantry member's diary; service in Kentucky and Tennessee, the regiment becoming a mounted infantry unit in July 1863; battle of
Chickamauga; picket duty and scouting in Alabama; attached to
Kilpatrick's cavalry corps; the Atlanta campaign, March to the
Sea and through the Carolinas; journey to Chicago after the surrender and activities there; brief entries focusing on military operations, but with an occasional nice bit of description.

COWELL, CHARLES   **4088**

"An Infantryman at Corinth." CIVIL WAR TIMES ILLUSTRATED 13,
no. 7 (1974):10-14.

Oct 1862. Two long entries extracted from diary of member of
Company I, Ninth Illinois Infantry; diarist's efforts to keep the
troops supplied and cared for during the battle of Corinth; his
dislike of sutlers; description of Gen. Thomas A. Davies in action.

CROSBY, CLARA SNOW, 1838-1899   **4089**

"Early Orleans, Mass., Almanacs." NEW ENGLAND HISTORICAL
AND GENEALOGICAL REGISTER 102 (1948):281-290.

1862-1899. Brief entries of events, chiefly births, marriages,
deaths, in Orleans, Massachusetts; mainly of interest to
genealogists.

CROSSLEY, MARTHA JANE, 1831-1898   **4090**

Sterkx, H.E., ed. "A Patriotic Confederate Woman's War Diary."
ALABAMA HISTORICAL QUARTERLY 20 (1958):611-617.

Aug-Dec 1862. Extracts, grouped by subject, from diary of Perote,
Alabama, resident; spinning and knitting for Confederate soldiers'
needs; hardships created by conscription; concern about her
slaves and their souls; friend's description of authoress Augusta
Jane Evans.

CUMMING, KATE, 1835-1909   **4091**

A JOURNAL OF HOSPITAL LIFE IN THE CONFEDERATE ARMY

OF TENNESSEE. Louisville: John P. Morgan; New Orleans: W. Evelyn, 1866. 199 pp.

KATE: THE JOURNAL OF A CONFEDERATE NURSE. Edited by Richard B. Harwell. Baton Rouge: Louisiana State University Press, 1959. 321 pp. Savannah, Ga.: Beehive, 1975. 288 pp.

Extracts in THE ALABAMA CONFEDERATE READER, edited by Malcolm C. McMillan, pp. 132-138; HEROINES OF DIXIE, edited by Katharine M. Jones, pp. 107-117, 325-329.

> 1862-1865. Journal of Mobile, Alabama, lady, a matron in Army of Tennessee hospitals at Corinth, Chattanooga, Cherokee Springs, Kingston, Newnan and Griffin; description of hospitals, her work and patients; coping with shortages and prejudice toward female nurses; trip home to Mobile with several stops in Georgia, Tennessee, Mississippi and Alabama; nursing the wounded near Chickamauga; treatment of Union wounded, tales of Andersonville and reports of Union depredations; wild rumors as the Confederacy crumbles; difficult journey from Newnan, Georgia, to Montgomery with Laetitia Nutt, her husband and daughters; early postwar days in Mobile, behavior of freedmen and Yankees' treatment of them; reflections on the war, slavery and reasons for the South's defeat; pride in her Scots heritage; portraits of Confederate notables such as generals Price, Morgan, Hardee and Hindman and clergyman Charles Quintard; praise for Confederate physicians, hospital attendants and the Sisters of Charity; criticism of Southern women who were not working actively in support of the army; concern for soldiers' religious state; very long, informative entries providing a realistic account of Confederate medical care and the experiences of a pioneer in women's nursing.

CUNNINGHAM, DAVID, 1837-1917   4092

Cometti, Elizabeth, ed. "Major Cunningham's Journal." WEST VIRGINIA HISTORY 34 (1973):187-211.

> Jan-Dec 1862. Extracts from daily journal of Franklin College graduate, lawyer and captain of Company B, Thirtieth Ohio Volunteer Infantry; service in western Virginia; Second Bull Run and Antietam campaigns; description of Lincoln reviewing the army at Antietam; back on duty in western Virginia.

CUNNINGHAM, JOHN LOVELL, b. 1840   4093

THREE YEARS WITH THE ADIRONDACK REGIMENT. Norwood, Mass.: Plimpton, 1920. 286 pp. Diary, pp. 34-166 passim.

> 1862-1865. Extracts from officer's diary running through narrative of service with Company F, 118th New York Volunteer Infantry; campaigning in Virginia; battles of Drewry's Bluff and Cold Harbor; siege of Petersburg.

DANIELS, JAMES   4094

In A HISTORY OF THE FIFTH REGIMENT, NEW HAMPSHIRE VOLUNTEERS, by William Child, pp. 87-88, 93, 149-150, 170-176, 192-193. Bristol, N.H.: R.W. Musgrove, Printer, 1893.

Extracts in TRAGIC YEARS 1860-1865, by Paul M. Angle and Earl S. Miers, vol. 2, pp. 724-725.

> 1862-1863. Extracts from daily diary of noncommissioned officer; notes on weather and camp life; brief mention of battles of Fair Oaks, Fredericksburg and Chancellorsville.

DAVIDSON, W.J.   4095

In THE ANNALS OF THE ARMY OF TENNESSEE, edited by Edwin L. Drake, pp. 16-369 passim. Nashville, Tenn.: Printed by A.E. Haynes, 1878.

> Dec 1862-Sep 1863. Diary of private in Company C, Forty-first Tennessee; defending Vicksburg; Mississippi River journey to Port Hudson and smallpox quarantine confinement there; assistant ship's carpenter aboard the DR. BEATTY on expedition to eliminate the Union gunboat INDIANOLA; additional naval operations on the Mississippi and Red rivers; summary of events mid-March to mid-May including occurrences at Port Hudson and engagements at Jackson and Raymond; summary of events mid-August to early October including battle of Chickamauga; in camp near Chattanooga; long entries covering military action, food and foraging, drinking sprees and the monotony of camp life; occasional comments on scenery and notes on desertion from both armies.

DAVIS, CHARLES H.   4096

In OFFICIAL RECORDS OF THE UNION AND CONFEDERATE NAVIES IN THE WAR OF THE REBELLION, ser. 1, vol. 23, pp. 52-54, 270-272.

> May-Aug 1862. Extracts from diary of naval captain in command of the Western Flotilla, preparing to attack Fort Pillow; reasons for abandoning Vicksburg campaign of that year.

DAWES, RUFUS R., 1838-1899   4097

SERVICE WITH THE SIXTH WISCONSIN VOLUNTEERS. Marietta, Ohio: E.R. Alderman & Sons, 1890. 330 pp. Diary, pp. 34-52, 134-140 passim. Edited by Alan T. Nolan. Madison: State Historical Society of Wisconsin for Wisconsin Civil War Centennial Commission, 1962. 336 pp. Diary, pp. 34-52, 134-140 passim.

> Feb-Jul 1862, Apr-May 1863. Extracts from officer's journal; activities while in camp near Washington, D.C.; on the march in Virginia; chasing Stonewall Jackson in the Shenandoah Valley; Chancellorsville campaign; notes on congressional investigating committee, consequences of whiskey ration, counterfeit Confederate currency, choosing officers of the regiment, John Pope, a mutiny in the Twenty-fourth New York, etc.

DAWSON, SARAH MORGAN, 1842-1909   4098

A CONFEDERATE GIRL'S DIARY. Boston and New York: Houghton Mifflin, 1913. 439 pp. Edited by James I. Robertson, Jr. Bloomington:

Indiana University Press, 1960. 473 pp. Reprint. Westport, Conn.: Greenwood, 1972.

Frequently extracted. See, for instance, in THE BLUE AND THE GRAY, edited by Henry S. Commager, vol. 1, pp. 500-503, vol. 2, pp. 758-759; HEROINES OF DIXIE, edited by Katharine M. Jones, pp. 121-123, 128-138, 168-171; TREASURY OF THE WORLD'S GREAT DIARIES, edited by Philip Dunaway, pp. 264-267; WOMEN OF THE SOUTH IN WARTIME, compiled by Matthew Page Andrews, pp. 344-352.

1862-1865. A convinced, but level-headed, upper-class Confederate's chronicle of civilian life in wartime; Union occupation of Baton Rouge and the sacking of the Morgan home; refugee life with her mother and sisters, primarily at Clinton, Louisiana, and Gen. A.G. Carter's plantation, Linwood, near Port Hudson; notes on family, friends and suitors, social life, shortages and servants; witnessing the destruction of the ARKANSAS; commentary on Union soldiers, bad and good, and the excessive patriotism of some Confederate women; concern for her brother James Morris Morgan, serving in the Confederate navy; the carriage accident that left her a semi-invalid; the agony of having to take oath of allegiance in order to seek refuge with her unionist brother Philip Hickey Morgan in New Orleans and the deaths of two brothers in the Confederate army; reaction to Lincoln's assassination; a diary kept to give vent to her feelings, its lengthy entries candidly presenting war's human suffering and material devastation.

DEARBORN, SAMUEL Q.   **4099**

In HISTORY OF THE EIGHTEENTH NEW HAMPSHIRE VOLUNTEERS, by Thomas L. Livermore, pp. 27-28. Boston: Fort Hill Press, 1904.

Sep-Oct 1862. Diary extracts providing brief notes on new soldier's journey from Concord, New Hampshire, to City Point, Virginia.

DE BOW, JAMES DUNWODY BROWNSON, 1820-1867   **4100**

"Journal of the War." DE BOW'S REVIEW 33 (1862):81-89; n.s. 1 (1866):646-656; n.s. 2 (1866):57-70, 189-201, 322-331, 430-446, 537-557, 649-661; n.s. 3 (1867):95-108, 199-213, 319-331.

1862-1863. Brief journal entries, interspersed with public documents, tracking war's progress; much news and rumor but also diarist's experience of war at New Orleans, Jackson and Mobile, and during travels across the South with stops including Charleston, Richmond and Demopolis, Alabama; view of a population in motion, soldiers and refugees, and the conditions of railroad transportation; notes on many topics such as hospitals, prices, trade with the enemy, morale, destructiveness of Grierson's raid, Benjamin Butler and McClellan.

DELANY, JOHN O'FALLON, d. 1930   **4101**

Sunder, John E., ed. "Up the Missouri to the Montana Mines." MISSOURI HISTORICAL SOCIETY BULLETIN 19 (1962-1963):3-22, 127-149.

May-Oct 1862. Journey of young scion of a wealthy St. Louis family; on the SPREAD EAGLE with Father De Smet, whom he assisted at Mass; brief but interesting references to sights en route, passengers, who wantonly killed buffalo and set fire to the prairie, and Indians; on horseback from Fort Benton over Mullan Road with a party bound for the gold fields; the death of his friend J.P. Lyons in a gun accident; trading among the miners in Deer Lodge Valley and Gold Creek area; return overland and by river boats.

DEWOLF, CHARLES WESLEY, 1834-1927?   **4102**

Monnett, Howard N., ed. "A Yankee Cavalryman Views the Battle of Prairie Grove." ARKANSAS HISTORICAL QUARTERLY 21 (1962):289-304.

Dec 1862. Extract from diary kept by schoolteacher from Saline County, Missouri, a lieutenant in Company E, Seventh Missouri Volunteer Cavalry; suffering from acute dysentery and struggling to keep up with his unit as it moves into Arkansas; the battle and the horrible sights left in its wake; articulate, realistic description.

Wright, Thomas E., ed. "The Capture of Van Buren, Arkansas during the Civil War." ARKANSAS HISTORICAL QUARTERLY 38 (1979):72-89.

Dec 1862-Jan 1863. Extracts covering advance from Prairie Grove to Van Buren, engaging Confederates and inspecting the captured town; official admonitions against pillaging; notes on camp life, duties, Christmas and New Year's Day festivities, etc.

DIBB, WILLIAM DENTON   **4103**

In HO! FOR THE GOLD FIELDS, edited by Helen M. White, pp. 51-72, 85-98.

Jun-Nov 1862. Diary of expedition's physician, an English immigrant, with James L. Fisk's company from Minnesota to the Montana gold fields; journey over Isaac I. Stevens' route and Mullan Road; good details of terrain, conditions and camp life; exciting buffalo hunts described with enthusiasm; cursory mention of medical duties; interactions of company with various Indian chiefs.

Jun-Sep 1863. Fisk's second expedition; brief notes on gold diggings at Virginia City, Bannack and at mines along Alder Creek; wagon journey from Bannack to Salt Lake City, then miserable return east by stagecoach.

DICKSON, JAMES, 1836-1878   **4104**

Durham, Roger S., ed. "Voyage of Fear and Profit." CIVIL WAR TIMES ILLUSTRATED 18, no. 7 (1879):14-19; no. 8, 30-36.

Feb-Mar 1862. Diary of Georgia-born blockade runner; voyage of the STANDARD from Nova Scotia with a cargo of groceries, medicines, dry goods, ammunition, etc.; storms, vermin, short rations and colorful sailors; aground off St. Catherines Island, exploration of the island and successful evasion of Union blockading vessels; long, nicely descriptive entries.

DIMON, THEODORE, 1816-1889 4105

Robertson, James I., Jr. "A Federal Surgeon at Sharpsburg." CIVIL WAR HISTORY 6 (1960):134-151.

Sep 1862. Extracts from diary of Auburn, New York, physician, acting surgeon, Second Maryland Regiment; heading toward Sharpsburg with the Union army; watching the action at Burnside's bridge, treating casulties and organizing care of the wounded; notes on General Burnside.

DODD, EPHRAIM SHELBY, d. 1864 4106

DIARY OF EPHRAIM SHELBY DODD. Austin: Press of E.L. Steck, 1914. 32 pp.

1862-1864. Diary kept by member of Company D, Terry's Texas Rangers, or the Eighth Texas Cavalry; operations in Tennessee, Georgia and Kentucky; battle of Stones River; notes on reading and social life; capture and execution as a spy, supposedly on the evidence of this diary found in his pocket.

DOOLEY, JOHN EDWARD, 1842-1873 4107

JOHN DOOLEY, CONFEDERATE SOLDIER. Edited by Joseph T. Durkin. Washington, D.C.: Georgetown University Press, 1945. 244 pp. Notre Dame, Ind.: Notre Dame University Press, 1963.

Extracts in THE BLUE AND THE GRAY, edited by Henry S. Commager, vol. 1, pp. 304, 510-511; THE TRAGIC YEARS 1860-1865, by Paul M. Angle and Earl S. Miers, vol. 1, pp. 341-343, vol. 2, pp. 637-638, 658, 661-662.

1862-1865. War diary, kept by member of prominent Irish-American, Richmond family; service with the First Virginia, for a time as lieutenant of Company C; entries, often undated, covering the campaigns of Second Bull Run, Antietam, Fredericksburg and Gettysburg; wounding and capture in Pickett's charge; suffering of the wounded after the battle; imprisonment at Fort McHenry, mainly in the hospital; impressions of Pittsburgh en route to Johnson's Island; prison conditions, events, escape attempts, reading, dramatics and other diversions; parole and return to Richmond in early March, 1865; wandering in the wake of the Confederate government to Danville and North Carolina; decision to enter the priesthood and his return home; richly detailed description but difficult to distinguish between firsthand reporting and later ruminations and elaborations.

DORITY, ORIN G., b. 1845 4108

"The Civil War Diary of Orin G. Dority." NORTHWEST OHIO QUARTERLY 37 (1964-1965):7-26, 104-115.

1862-1865. Scattered entries made by member of Battery H, First Ohio Light Artillery; battles of Fredericksburg, Chancellorsville, Gettysburg and Cold Harbor; Burnside's "Mud March"; siege of Petersburg and battle of the Crater; march north through Virginia after Appomattox and welcome home in Toledo; notes on

Chancellorsville battlefield, Mount Vernon and the execution of a black soldier.

DOUD, GEORGE W. 4109

"The Doud Diary." SOUTH DAKOTA HISTORICAL COLLECTIONS 9 (1918):471-474.

1862-1863. A few extracts within article summarizing the diary of a young Dakota County farmer, a private in Company F, Eighth Minnesota Volunteers, engaged in protecting frontier residents from Indians; the town of New Ulm in the wake of the massacre; "Maj. Brown's famous steam wagon" and conditions at Fort Wadsworth.

DRAKE, A.F. 4110

In MISSISSIPPI IN THE CONFEDERACY, edited by John K. Bettersworth and James W. Silver, vol. 1, pp. 196-197, 346-348.

Jun-Dec 1862, Dec 1863. Extract from diary of soldier in the Jefferson Artillery, detailing his Sabbath activities and his dismay at the lack of proper observance of Christmas in camp.

DULANY, IDA, b. 1837? 4111

In SCRAPS OF PAPER, by Marietta Minnigerode Andrews, pp. 15-82. New York: E.P. Dutton, 1929.

Extracts in THE YEARS OF ANGUISH, FAUQUIER COUNTY, VIRGINIA, compiled by Emily G. Ramey and John K. Gott, pp. 62-73.

Jun-Dec 1862, May-Jul 1863. Extracts from Virginia matron's diary of war as experienced at Oakley near Upperville; anxiety for husband and others in the army and frustration concerning unreliable news sources; management of plantation and dealing with foragers; watching a nearby battle; providing for Confederate soldiers as they pass through, boarding some of Mosby's men and regretting the loss of family privacy; notes on shortages, prices, deaths, rebellious slaves, Union plunderers, diptheria epidemic, Turner Ashby, Fitzhugh Lee, etc.

DURGIN, HENRY J. 4112

In A HISTORY OF THE EIGHTH REGIMENT OF NEW HAMPSHIRE VOLUNTEERS, by John M. Stanyan, pp. 59-532 passim.

Feb-May 1862, Jan-Dec 1864. Extracts from musician's diary; voyage to Ship Island; duties in Mississippi and Louisiana; the Red River campaign; battle of Pleasant Hill; prisoner of war in Camp Ford near Tyler, Texas; exchange and return to regiment.

DYE, HENRY L. 4113

Elsas, Frederick J., "The Journal of Henry L. Dye, Confederate Surgeon." SURGERY 63 (1968):352-362.

1862-1864. Extracts from journal of Plano, Texas, physician, an 1861 graduate of Jefferson Medical College, who served with Capt. A. Johnson's "Spy" Company and then at several hospitals in Arkansas; a record of patients' conditions, both wounds and disease, and his treatments.

ELDER, WILLIAM HENRY, 1819-1904 4114

CIVIL WAR DIARY (1862-1865) OF BISHOP WILLIAM HENRY ELDER, BISHOP OF NATCHEZ. Natchez? Miss.: R.O. Gerow, Bishop of Natchez-Jackson, 1960? 125 pp.

1862-1865. Roman Catholic bishop's record of war's impact in Mississippi and Louisiana; church administration and finances; his priestly functions for soldiers, civilians and freedmen; visits to Port Hudson, Port Gibson, Yazoo City, Jackson, Canton and Vicksburg; notes on many persons; content of sermons; debris in the wake of battle of Port Gibson; destruction and plundering by Union forces; cooperation received from generals Grant and McPherson after Vicksburg's fall; situation of former slaves; brief exile to Vidalia, due to diarist's refusal to include the prayer for the President of the United States in his service.

ELLIS, JASON L., 1843?-1863					**4115**

In AMERICAN PATRIOTISM, by Leonard Brown, pp. 245-248.

Jul 1862-Feb 1863. Extracts from soldier's diary; service with Company I, Eighteenth Iowa Infantry Volunteers, in Missouri with a brief foray into Arkansas.

ESTES, WILLIAM KENNEDY, 1843-1863				**4116**

In THE CIVIL WAR IN MAURY COUNTY, TENNESSEE, by Jill K. Garrett and Marise P. Lightfoot, pp. 1-8.

1862-1863. Extracts from Confederate soldier's diary of service in Mississippi, Tennessee and Kentucky with Company E, Forty-eighth Tennessee Infantry; notes on duties, prices, expenses, miles covered and revival of religion among the soldiers; very brief entry concerning the battle of Perryville.

EYRE, DAVID WILSON, 1832-1896					**4117**

In HISTORY OF THE ONE HUNDRED AND TWENTY-FOURTH REGIMENT, PENNSYLVANIA VOLUNTEERS, by Pennsylvania Infantry, 124th Regiment, p. 271.

Sep 1862. Brief extract from diary of corporal in Company D describing battle in cornfield at Antietam.

FAUNTLEROY, JAMES HENRY, 1842-1864				**4118**

Calkin, Homer L., ed. "Elk Horn to Vicksburg." CIVIL WAR HISTORY 2 (1956):7-43.

1862-1863. Diary of Buchanan County, Missouri, farmer, a member of Company E, First Missouri Cavalry; retrospective summary of service in Arkansas, including the battle of Pea Ridge, then brief, fairly regular entries covering operations in Mississippi; at Memphis and Corinth and the evacuation of the latter; battles of Iuka and Corinth; capture during Vicksburg campaign and imprisonment at Fort Delaware where last entry was written; Fourth of July speech by Sterling Price; an enlisted man's view of camp life and the hardships of campaigning.

FINK, ROBERT H., 1836-1863						**4119**

In AMERICAN PATRIOTISM, by Leonard Brown, pp. 319-320.

Aug-Nov 1862. Extracts from journal of soldier with Company E. Twenty-third Iowa Infantry Volunteers; various Sabbath thoughts with notes on religious life in camp.

FISHER, CHARLES BENNETT, 1840?-1903				**4120**

DIARY OF CHARLES B. FISHER. Edited by Paul E. Sluby, Sr. and Stanton L. Wormley. Washington, D.C.: Columbian Harmony Society, 1983. 106 leaves.

1862-1864. Diary kept by black crew member of the KEARSARGE; across the Atlantic to Cadiz; blockading the SUMTER at Gibralter; cruising in the Mediterranean, to Madeira, around the Azores and Canary Islands and in the English Channel; ashore at Tangiers, several Spanish and English ports, London, Ostend, Brest, Boulougne, Cherbourg and Flushing; battle with the ALABAMA and assisting the Confederate survivors; voyage to Boston via Fernando de Noronha, Barbados and St. Thomas; notes on the KEARSARGE's operations, diarist's duties as steward, leisure activities, minstrel shows, a masquerade ball at Cadiz, drinking and other misbehavior among the crew, a shark attack, sea chanteys, burial at sea, shipmates, observations on and relations with foreign populations, etc.; ruminations on war; nice descriptions of places visited and life aboard ship.

FISKE, GEORGE M., 1842-1933						**4121**

CIVIL WAR JOURNAL OF PVT. GEORGE M. FISKE. Edited by Richard A. Atkins and Helen Fiske Atkins. Syracuse, N.Y.: R.A. Atkins, 1962. 59 leaves.

Nov 1862-Feb 1863. Medfield, Massachusetts, soldier's record of service with the Forty-second Massachusetts; by train and boat from New England to New York City; a storm and seasickness aboard the steamer SAXON bound for Galveston; lengthy description of the battle of Galveston and the capture of the HARRIET LANE, with notes on the performance of various officers; surrender and incarceration at Houston; comments on the general friendliness of captors and civilians and Southern women's swearing; good description of long train trip to Beaumont and on to Vicksburg via the Neches and Sabine rivers on the ROE BUCK and then overland to Alexandria, Louisiana; down the Mississippi, noting war's effect on plantations along the river, to Baton Rouge, the Union lines and parole camp at New Orleans; a most readable, informative account, but some uncertainty about how much is the editors' work.

FLETCHER, STEPHEN KEYES, 1840-1897				**4122**

McCandless, Perry, ed. "The Civil War Journal of Stephen Keyes Fletcher." INDIANA MAGAZINE OF HISTORY 54 (1958):141-190.

Mar-Oct 1862. Account of service with Company E, Thirty-third Indiana Volunteer Infantry, penned by Indianapolis resident, son of Calvin Fletcher and brother of William B. Fletcher; narrative of events from enlistment in October 1961 followed by occasional lengthy entries; military operations in Kentucky and Tennessee; occupation and evacuation of Cumberland Gap; a detailed, vivid account of campaigning and army life.

FOREMAN, SUSAN E.							**4123**

Finley, Linda. "Notes from the Diary of Susan E. Foreman." CHRONICLES OF OKLAHOMA 47 (1969-1970):388-397.

Apr 1862-Dec 1863 (with gaps). Diary of a young teacher at the Webber Falls School for Cherokee Indians; great loneliness and longing for letters from her family and sweetheart at Park Hill; trouble with school discipline and sporadic attendance; Civil War news and fears for the life of her father, the Rev. Stephen Foreman; eventual flight, apparently in advance of Union troops; a sad diary.

FREEMAN, JULIA SUSAN WHEELOCK, 1833-1900   4124

THE BOYS IN WHITE. New York: Printed by Lange & Hillman, 1870. 274 pp. passim.

   1862-1865. Narrative containing scattered extracts, doubtless reworked for publication, from journal of Ionia, Michigan, schoolteacher, serving as an agent for the Michigan Soldiers' Relief Association; visiting soldiers of her home state in the hospitals of Alexandria, Washington, D.C., and Baltimore and at Fredericksburg during the Spotsylvania campaign; an outing to Mount Vernon; reaction to Lincoln's assassination.

Kincaid, Robert L. "Julia Susan Wheelock: The Florence Nightingale of Michigan during the Civil War." LINCOLN HERALD 46, no. 3 (1944):42-46.

   Mar-Apr 1863, Jun 1864, Apr-May 1865. Extracts from manuscript diary; a visit to Washington, D.C., listening to speakers in the House of Representatives and observing Lincoln; a meeting with Grant at City Point; report of the assassination and description of the president lying in state; watching the Grand Review; attending the trial of Booth's alleged accomplices and noting their appearance.

FRENCH, SAMUEL GIBBS, 1818-1910   4125

TWO WARS: AN AUTOBIOGRAPHY OF GENERAL SAMUEL G. FRENCH. Nashville, Tenn.: Confederate Veteran, 1901. 404 pp. Diary, pp. 152-292 passim.

   1862-1864. Extracts from diary of New Jersey-born Confederate general, a West Point graduate; operations in North Carolina, with Longstreet in Virginia and with Johnston's forces in final days of Vicksburg campaign; depredations by Union troops at his Mississippi home and elsewhere; retreat from Jackson into Alabama; the Atlanta campaign; Franklin and Nashville campaign; military details and assessment of fellow officers including Polk, Johnston and Hood.

"Kennesaw Mountain." SOUTHERN BIVOUAC, old ser. 1 (1883):273-280.

In NEW JERSEY AND THE CIVIL WAR, edited by Earl S. Miers, pp. 84-90. New Jersey Historical Series, vol. 2. Princeton: Van Nostrand, 1964.

In TRAGIC YEARS, by Paul M. Angle and Earl S. Miers, vol. 2, pp. 834-838.

   Jun 1864. Battle of Kenesaw Mountain.

FULLAM, GEORGE TOWNLEY, 1841-1879   4126

THE CRUISE OF THE "ALABAMA." By an Officer on Board. Liverpool: Lee and Nightingale, W.H. Peat, 1863. 48 pp. N.p., 1864. 56 pp.

OUR CRUISE ON THE CONFEDERATE STATES' STEAMER ALABAMA. London: Printed by A. Schulze, 1863? 64 pp.

THE JOURNAL OF GEORGE TOWNLEY FULLAM, BOARDING OFFICER OF THE CONFEDERATE SEA RAIDER "ALABAMA." Edited and annotated by Charles G. Summersell. University: Published for the Friends of the Mobile Library by University of Alabama Press, 1973. 229 pp.

   1862-1864. Almost daily entries in journal of Britisher, acting master's mate and principal boarding officer of the ALABAMA, providing details of the career of the Confederacy's most famous war cruiser from the time Semmes took command at Terceira

until just before her destruction by the KEARSARGE; neutral ships encountered and prizes taken as they prowled the Atlantic and Indian oceans and the China Sea; sinking of the HATTERAS; notes on weather, neutral ports, desertions, insubordination and courts-martial. The 1973 edition, heavily annotated and including diarist's statistical appendices and navigational log, is the only complete version.

GAILOR, FRANK M., 1833-1862   4127

Cleveland, Charlotte and Daniel, Robert, eds. "The Diary of a Confederate Quartermaster." TENNESSEE HISTORICAL QUARTERLY 11 (1952):78-85.

   Sep-Oct 1862. Record of Bragg's Kentucky campaign, commencing three days after the surrender of Munfordville; problems encountered as quartermaster serving under General S.A.M. Wood, Fourth Brigade, Third Division, Army of Mississippi; notes on military operations and encounters with civilians; brief discussion of likelihood of foreign intervention.

GARDNER, HENRY RUFUS, 1842-1913   4128

Shewmaker, Kenneth E. and Prinz, Andrew K., eds. "A Yankee in Louisiana." LOUISIANA HISTORY 5 (1964):271-295.

   1862-1865. Extracts from diary and letters of private, Eighteenth New York Independent Battery Light Artillery, who later served as lieutenant, Company G, Tenth United States Colored Heavy Artillery; the Port Hudson campaign and conversation with the surrendered enemy; notes on a variety of topics, including Grant's strategy in Virginia, Southern women, blacks, cotton speculation, Confederate attitudes in occupied New Orleans and wartime reconstruction efforts in Louisiana.

GAULT, WILLIAM PERRYANDER, b. 1843   4129

In ROSTER OF THE REGIMENTAL ASSOCIATION, by Ohio Veteran Volunteer Infantry, 78th Regiment, pp. 2-22. N.p., 1901.

   1862-1865. Diary of Company F sergeant, recording the movements of the Seventy-eighth Ohio; service in Tennessee and Mississippi; the Vicksburg and Atlanta campaigns and the march through Georgia and the Carolinas; the Grand Review; notes on distances covered, campsites and engagements, but no battle details.

GEDNEY, JOHN, 1834-1922   4130

"John Gedney, 1834-1922: Civil War Soldier from White Plains." WESTCHESTER COUNTY HISTORICAL BULLETIN 26 (1950):111-117.

   1862-1865. Extracts from 135th New York member's diary; journey from Yonkers to Baltimore via hospitable Philadelphia; an expedition into Pennsylvania to head off Jeb Stuart raid; evacuation of Harpers Ferry during Gettysburg campaign; the Wilderness and Spotsylvania campaigns; explosion of the Petersburg mine; battle of Cedar Creek; last days of the war; very brief entries seemingly rewritten in a narrative type form.

GORDON, MARQUIS LAFAYETTE, 1843-1900   4131

M.L. GORDON'S EXPERIENCES IN THE CIVIL WAR FROM HIS NARRATIVE, LETTERS AND DIARY. Edited by Donald Gordon. Boston: Privately printed, 1922. Diary, pp. 52-66.

Nov 1862-Aug 1863, Apr-Jun 1864. Enlisted man's diary, kept while serving in the Eighty-fifth Regiment, Pennsylvania Volunteers; on foot and by gunboat from Suffolk, Virginia, to New Bern, North Carolina; skirmishing and battle of Kinston; to islands off Charleston; assaults on Fort Wagner; return to Virginia and duty with the Army of the James.

GORGAS, JOSIAH, 1818-1883   4132

THE CIVIL WAR DIARY OF GENERAL JOSIAH GORGAS. Edited by Frank E. Vandiver. University: University of Alabama Press, 1947. 208 pp.

1862-1865. War years portion of diary kept from 1857 to 1877 for the enjoyment of the diarist's family, principally his eldest son William; substantial, although somewhat sporadic, entries focusing on war news, with commentary on events and individuals, and presenting a broad panorama of Confederate military operations; few details of work as Confederacy's chief of ordnance; glimpses of family and social life in Richmond; observations, often critical, on his friend Jefferson Davis; notes on prices; thoughts on army's use of slaves within its ranks; flight from Richmond and last days of the war.

GOULD, JANE AUGUSTA HOLBROOK, b. 1833   4133

Lack, Philip K., ed. "Iowa to California in 1862." ANNALS OF IOWA 3d ser. 37 (1963-1965):460-476, 544-559, 623-640; 38 (1965-1967):68-75.

Extracts in WOMEN'S DIARIES OF THE WESTWARD JOURNEY, collected by Lillian Schlissel, pp. 217-231.

Apr-Oct 1862. Mitchell County woman's journey with her family and other emigrants to settle in California; route via Platte River; camps, scenery, conditions of travel, her own chores of cooking, washing and caring for her sick son en route; notes on Indians; notice of graves along the way; accidents and illnesses of emigrants.

GOVE, GEORGE S.   4134

In A HISTORY OF THE FIFTH REGIMENT, NEW HAMPSHIRE VOLUNTEERS, by William Child, pp. 45-177 passim. Bristol, N.H.: R.W. Musgrove, Printer, 1893.

1862-1863. Scattered extracts from soldier's diary; participation in battles of Fair Oaks, Fredericksburg and Chancellorsville.

GRAY, RICHARD L., 1832-1915   4135

"Prison Diary of Lieutenant Richard L. Gray." WINCHESTER-FREDERICK COUNTY HISTORICAL SOCIETY PAPERS 3 (1955):30-45.

Jul-Sep 1862. Diary kept by lieutenant of Company C, Thirty-first Virginia Infantry, while imprisoned at Johnson's Island; some notes on prisoners' activities but mainly dealing with the contents of his correspondence, especially with his wife in Winchester; by train to Cairo, down the Mississippi on Union steamer UNIVERSE and exchange at Vicksburg; a brief stay in Jackson and by rail to Virginia.

GRAYSON, WILLIAM JOHN, 1788-1863   4136

Puryear, Elmer L., ed. "The Confederate Diary of William John Grayson." SOUTH CAROLINA HISTORICAL MAGAZINE 63 (1962):137-149, 214-226.

May-Nov 1862. Diary of former state legislator and congressman, a poet whose work included "The Hireling and the Slave," and owner of Fair Lawn, a plantation near Charleston; lengthy commentary on the events of the Civil War; notes on prices, depredations by Confederate troops, military operations around Charleston, prospects of European intervention, visit to Columbia and northern area of the state, blockade runners, salt-making, Judge Mitchell King, etc.

GREENHOW, ROSE O'NEAL, 1815?-1864   4137

MY IMPRISONMENT AND THE FIRST YEAR OF ABOLITION RULE AT WASHINGTON. London: R. Bentley, 1863. 352 pp. Diary, pp. 215-218, 260-315 passim.

Extracts in DIARY OF AMERICA, edited by Josef and Dorothy Berger, pp. 426-430.

Mar-May 1862. Extracts from diary of Washington, D.C., political hostess and Confederate spy while she and her eight-year-old daughter Rose were confined in Old Capitol Prison; interrogation on treason charges; prison conditions and confrontations with guards and Union officers.

GREER, GEORGE H.T.   4138

" 'All Thoughts Are Absorbed in the War.' " CIVIL WAR TIMES ILLUSTRATED 17, no. 8 (1978):30-35.

Nov-Dec 1862. Diary kept by North Carolina teenager, a clerk and courier on Jubal Early's staff; enjoying civilian hospitality in Virginia but receiving poor fare at Madison's Montpelier; battle of Fredericksburg; an evening of entertainment in Richmond; Christmas Day reflections at home in Rocky Mount.

GUY, JOHN HENRY   4139

Cooling, B. Franklin, ed. "A Virginian at Fort Donelson." TENNESSEE HISTORICAL QUARTERLY 27 (1968):176-190.

Apr-May 1862. Extracts from journal of Richmond, Virginia, captain, a battery commander of the Goochland Light Artillery, written while imprisoned at Camp Chase and Johnson's Island after capture at Fort Donelson; lengthy entries describing events during the investment of Fort Donelson, analyzing decisions made and assigning blame for the debacle; notes on generals John B. Floyd, Gideon Pillow and Bushrod Johnson; brief mention of prison conditions.

HACKETT, BENJAMIN FRANKLIN, 1826-1905   4140

Zeilinger, Elna R. and Schweikart, Larry, eds. " 'They Also Serve...' " VERMONT HISTORY 51 (1983):89-97.

Sep 1862-May 1863. Extracts from diary of sergeant, Company F, Twelfth Vermont Volunteers, selected to illustrate the Civil War soldier's life when not in combat; in Vermont, Washington, D.C., and Virginia camps; notes on accidents, disease, food, contrabands and a visit to the Capitol.

HAINES, WILLIAM K., 1842-1916   4141

DIARY OF SERGEANT WILLIAM K. HAINES. Prepared by Mary F.B. Hewitt. N.p., 1966. 83 leaves.

1862-1864. Burlington County, New Jersey, soldier's experiences with Company I, Fifth New Jersey, rewritten several years later; the Peninsular campaign and gruesome sights at the battle of

Williamsburg; Seven Days' battles; his unit's drunken spree upon return to Alexandria; destruction of Union supply train at Manassas; lengthy descriptions of battles of Fredericksburg, Chancellorsville and Gettysburg; securing medical treatment and food after being wounded on second day of Gettysburg; in hospitals until discharge home to Vincentown; notes on duties, weather, Charles City Court House, foraging, camp life, soldier suicides, amusements, McClellan's dismissal, Dan Sickles, etc.; candid, graphic, somewhat bragging account.

HALEY, JOHN WEST, 1840-1921   **4142**

THE REBEL YELL AND THE YANKEE HURRAH. Edited by Ruth L. Silliker. Camden, Maine: Down East Books, 1985. 311 pp.

1862-1865. Expanded field diary kept by member of Company I, Seventeenth Maine, written up many years after the war; early days in camp near Portland; troop transport by train and boat; first stationed at Fort Stanton overlooking Washington, D.C., then in Maryland and Virginia; battle of Fredericksburg, the "Mud March," and Chancellorsville; Gettysburg, Mine Run, Wilderness and Spotsylvania campaigns; Cold Harbor; siege of Petersburg and battle of the Crater; trading and conversing with Confederates and the hazards of life in the trenches; Appomattox campaign and the day of surrender; through ruined Richmond to the nation's capital and to Portland for mustering out; notes on camp life, leisure activities, the Christian Commission, Southern civilians, foraging, an April Fool's prank, executions of deserters, nurse Anna Etheridge, hospitality at Philadelphia's Cooper Shop, reaction to Lincoln's assassination, etc.; description of Union depredations and destructive impact of war on Virginia; critical view of officers' leadership and perquisites in general and specific criticism of generals George W. West and William H. French, among many others, but praise for generals Hiram Berry, Daniel Sickles and Winfield Hancock; views on the Irish and the equality of blacks; objection to Grant's surrender terms; company roster with diarist's opinion of each man; an interesting, candid account of life in the ranks, but obviously reworked to a considerable extent.

HAND, GEORGE O., 1830-1887   **4143**

Carmony, Neil B., ed. "The California Column Occupies Tucson." JOURNAL OF ARIZONA HISTORY 26 (1985):11-40.

Aug-Dec 1862. Extracts from diary of forty-niner from Oneida County, New York, serving as sergeant, Company G, First Infantry Regiment, California Volunteers; hard march from Fort Yuma across the Sonoran Desert; occupation of Tucson; notes on local agriculture, the Mission of San Xavier, a Catholic festival, Indian alarms, Pima and Apache Indians, drunken soldiers, etc.; his attitude toward Mexicans and blacks; fulminations about unjust treatment of enlisted men by officers; sketches of officers of the California Column.

HARDING, GEORGE ALBERT, 1843-1926   **4144**

Tanasoca, Steven, and Sudduth, Susan, eds. "A Journal Kept by George A. Harding." OREGON HISTORICAL QUARTERLY 79 (1978):172-202.

May-Oct 1862. Young Australian immigrant's journal of a brief sojourn in the gold camps of Idaho, mostly as a builder, painter and paperhanger; horseback and riverboat travel from his home in Oregon City with his brother and stepfather, Charles E. Mur-

ray; route and camps, exasperating problems with horses; work at Elk City, Idaho, on stores, houses and the saloon; a trial and unsuccessful hanging after which the convicted man was released; other rough, violent or amusing incidents; return to Oregon.

HARKNESS, JAMES   **4145**

"Diary of James Harkness, of the Firm of La Barge, Harkness and Company." MONTANA HISTORICAL SOCIETY CONTRIBUTIONS 2 (1896):343-361.

May-Oct 1862. Diary of a trader in business with Joseph and John La Barge; travel on the Missouri with goods for Indians and miners; descriptions of farms, towns, villages, scenery; notes on timber and having to cut wood for boats EMILIE and SHREVEPORT; stops at forts Pierre and Clark, which was abandoned by Indians because of smallpox, and Benton and Union; building a trading post named Fort La Barge near Fort Benton; news of gold dust; a trading journey to Deer Lodge Valley made more difficult by washouts on the Mullan Road; prospecting on rivers and creeks with little success; encounters with hostile Indians at Fort Union; building a boat for return trip to Omaha and St. Louis.

HARLAN, EDWARD T.   **4146**

In HISTORY OF THE ONE HUNDRED AND TWENTY-FOURTH REGIMENT, PENNSYLVANIA VOLUNTEERS, by Pennsylvania Infantry, 124th Regiment, pp. 129-144.

Aug 1862-May 1863. Extracts from diary of private, later captain's clerk, in Company E; enlistment and first days in service; battle of Antietam and description of the resulting gore of the battlefield; camp life and duty in Virginia; battle of Chancellorsville.

HARRIS, EMILY JANE LYLES, 1827-1899   **4147**

Racine, Philip N. "Emily Lyles Harris: A Piedmont Farmer during the Civil War." SOUTH ATLANTIC QUARTERLY 79 (1980):386-397.

1862-1865. Extracts amidst summary of diary kept by wife of South Carolina farmer David Harris as a continuation of his diary after he entered the Confederate army; her feelings as she dealt with problems of managing a one-hundred-acre farm, ten slaves and seven children near Spartanburg.

HARRIS, JOHN H., 1827-1864   **4148**

In CONFEDERATE STAMPS, OLD LETTERS AND HISTORY, by Raynor Hubbell, app., pp. 2-13. Griffin, Ga., n.d.

1862-1863, Feb-Mar 1864. Diary of former cotton buyer now captain, Company I, Forty-fourth Georgia; organization of volunteers from Morgan and Henry counties; transport to Goldsboro, North Carolina, and, shortly thereafter, to Virginia; operations there, including the battle of Fair Oaks, the Seven Days' battles and the Antietam, Chancellorsville and Gettysburg campaigns; focus on military details.

HARTSOCK, ANDREW JACKSON, 1832-1909   **4149**

SOLDIER OF THE CROSS: THE CIVIL WAR DIARY AND CORRESPONDENCE OF REV. ANDREW JACKSON HARTSOCK. Edited by James C. and Eleanor A. Duram. Manhattan, Kans.: Military Affairs/Aerospace Historian, 1979. 264 pp. Diary, pp. 13-140.

1862-1863. Clergyman's diary; service as chaplain, 133d Pennsylvania Volunteers; at Sharpsburg after the battle of Antietam, holding worship services, visiting hospitals and the battlefield and noting damage in the town; into the Loudon Valley and in Falmouth camp assisting soldiers in getting discharges, pay, etc.; substantial description of the battle of Fredericksburg; battle of Chancellorsville; notes on generals McClellan and Fitz-John Porter, conditions in various camps and on the march, inadequate physicians and officers, slaves' reaction to the Union army, drunken officers and the evils of whiskey rations for the troops, etc.; pastor of the Johnstown, Pennsylvania, United Brethren in Christ Church; pastoral duties, sermons and reading; political disputes in the town; militia preparations for meeting threat of Gettysburg campaign; an account permeated by the diarist's religious faith and practice.

HAVILAND, THOMAS P.   4150

"A Brief Diary of Imprisonment." VIRGINIA MAGAZINE OF HISTORY AND BIOGRAPHY 50 (1942):230-237.

Aug-Sep 1862. Twelfth Massachusetts officer's account of prison life after capture at Second Bull Run; treatment during journey to Richmond; prices, food, fellow prisoners, activities, etc.

HAWKS, ESTHER HILL, 1833-1906   4151

A WOMAN DOCTOR'S CIVIL WAR. Edited by Gerald Schwartz. Columbia: University of South Carolina Press, 1984. 301 pp.

1862-1866 (with gap). Diary of physician, a graduate of the New England Female Medical College, working as a teacher for the National Freedmen's Relief Association; narrative summary, most likely reworked diary entries, of events from October 1862 to February 1864; description of Beaufort, South Carolina, the destruction by Union troops and their brutal treatment of freedmen; characteristics and behavior of former slaves; teaching and nursing members of the First South Carolina Volunteers and other black troops; expedition to Jacksonville, caring for the wounded from the battle of Olustee and establishing the first free, racially integrated school in Florida; continued service there and at Hilton Head; in Charleston as war ends; commemoration of the anniversary of Anderson's raising the flag over Fort Sumter; reactions to Lincoln's assassination; celebration of Decoration Day and Fourth of July; conditions in the freedmen's camps near the city; various excursions, including trips to St. Augustine, Tallahassee and Volusia, Florida; voyages along the coast; slave narratives, among them that of a woman claiming to be Winfield Scott's daughter; notes on a black praise meeting, prejudice and race relations, Florida "crackers," social activities, etc.; mention of many persons, especially her husband, John Milton Hawks, James Redpath, Henry O. Marcy and James C. Beecher; an interesting, detailed and straightforward account.

HAYNES, DRAUGHTON STITH, 1837-1879   4152

THE FIELD DIARY OF A CONFEDERATE SOLDIER. Ashantilly Leaflet, ser. 2: Regional History, no. 3. Darien, Ga.: Ashantilly Press, 1963. 44 pp.

1862-1863 (with gaps). Diary kept by sergeant, later lieutenant, in Company I, Forty-ninth Regiment, Georgia Volunteer Infantry; battles of Fair Oaks, Harpers Ferry and Gettysburg; awful sights on field of battle after Second Bull Run and Chancellorsville; a very readable, engaging account, sometimes written while in line of battle.

HELMAN, HOWARD, 1844-1886   4153

Thurner, Arthur W., ed. "A Young Soldier in the Army of the Potomac." PENNSYLVANIA MAGAZINE OF HISTORY AND BIOGRAPHY 87 (1963):139-155.

Sep-Dec 1862. Mifflin County printer's diary of service in Company K, 131st Pennsylvania Volunteers; summary of events since August enlistment; dull days in Maryland camp; stationed in Virginia; battle of Fredericksburg; notes on food, prices and camp routines.

HERMAN, LINA   4154

In MY JOURNAL, by James M. Carselowey, pp. 42-43. Adair, Okla., 1962.

Nov 1862. Extracts from woman's diary of incidents along the Arkansas-Indian Territory border during the Civil War; overrunning of her farm by Hindman's Confederate troops; trying to save enough food for her children from soldiers' depredations; regretting that she must leave her "beautiful piano" as she prepares to abandon her home.

HERMANN, KAROLINA   4155

Evans, Clarence, ed. and trans. "Memoirs, Letters and Diary Entries of German Settlers in Northwest Arkansas." ARKANSAS HISTORICAL QUARTERLY 6 (1947):225-249. Diary, pp. 234-239.

Nov-Dec 1862. Extract from diary kept at Hermannsburg by Mrs. Karl Fredrich Hermann, a slaveholder but anti-secessionist; constant harrassment by both Union and Confederate soldiers seeking food, horses and clothing.

HERMANN, NANI   4156

Evans, Clarence, ed. and trans. "Memoirs, Letters and Diary Entries of German Settlers in Northwest Arkansas." ARKANSAS HISTORICAL QUARTERLY 6 (1947):225-249. Diary, pp. 242-247.

Nov-Dec 1862. Extract from diary kept at Hermannsburg by Mrs. Johann Heinrich Hermann; cooking alternately for Northern and Southern soldiers encamped in the area, and the pilfering of food and clothing by both, leaving her family destitute; flight to relative safety at Washington, Missouri.

HEWITT, CLARICE   4157

DIARY OF A REFUGEE. Edited by Frances Hewitt Fearn. New York: Moffatt, Yard, 1910. 149 pp.

1862-1867. Sporadic diary entries with evidence of later rewriting by diarist or editor; the life of a wealthy Southern planter's family in the Civil War and Reconstruction; the happy circumstances of slavery at Crescent Plantation near Donaldsonville, Louisiana; flight to Alexandria, Louisiana, and then on to a ranch near Fairfield, Texas; journey from San Antonio to Bagdad, Mexico, with stops at Laredo and Matamoras; voyage to Havana and on the ST. THOMAS to Liverpool; settling in Paris and social life there; return to New York City at war's end and rebuilding in New Orleans; notes on Gen. Richard Taylor's family, Gen. William Preston, Ulysses Grant, Swedish prima donna Christine Nilsson, Napoleon III and his empress Eugénie; discussion of Lincoln's assassination and concern for emancipation's effect on blacks.

HEWITT, RANDALL HENRY, 1840-1891   **4158**

NOTES BY THE WAY: MEMORANDA OF A JOURNEY ACROSS THE PLAINS, FROM DUNDEE, ILL., TO OLYMPIA, W.T. Olympia: Printed at the office of the Washington Standard, 1863. Seattle: F. McCaffrey, 1955. 79 pp. Version expanded by the diarist. ACROSS THE PLAINS AND OVER THE DIVIDE: A MULE TRAIN JOURNEY FROM EAST TO WEST. New York: Broadway, 1906. Reprint. Argosy-Antiquarian, 1964. 521 pp.

> May-Nov 1862. Seneca County, New York, man's articulate account of his emigrant journey; notes of camps, conditions, difficulties, availability of water and grass, layovers for recuperation of animals and to wash, bake, mend, etc., other wagon trains encountered and "disgraceful" incidents as members became fatigued; comments on Beaverhead mines, Deer Lodge Prairie, Coeur d' Alene mission and Walla Walla, where the "principle business is gambling and charging exhorbitant prices for everything"; by steamboat down the Columbia to Portland with portage at The Dalles.

HOGE, JOHN MILTON, 1844-1912   **4159**

A JOURNAL. Cincinnati: M.H. Bruce, 1961. 43 leaves.

> 1862-1865 (with gaps). Cavalryman's journal of events while serving in Company F, Eighth Virginia Cavalry, written up shortly after war's end; movements of diarist and his troop in Virginia and West Virginia; Knoxville campaign; burning of Chambersburg; opposing Sheridan in the Shenandoah Valley; battle of Cedar Creek; dissension over unit's transfer to another brigade.

HOLLISTER, OVANDO JAMES, 1834-1892   **4160**

BOLDLY THEY RODE: A HISTORY OF THE FIRST COLORADO REGIMENT OF VOLUNTEERS. With an introduction by William M. Raine. Lakewood, Colo.: Golden Press, 1949. 190 pp. Diary, pp. 45-144 passim.

> Mar-Sep 1862. Diary kept by cavalryman, Company F, First Colorado Volunteers, during the campaign against Sibley's Confederate forces; march south to Fort Union; joining up with Canby's troops at Carnuel Pass; battle of Peralta; following the retreating Confederates along the Rio Grande; at Fort Craig; journey to Santa Fe and Fort Union and a foray out from the latter; description of countryside and settlements passed through; frustration with officers; thoughts on Southern attitudes, slavery and Mexicans; criticism of General Canby; a very readable account but with entries obviously added to later.

HOLMES, JAMES TAYLOR, 1837-1916   **4161**

52d O.V.I. THEN AND NOW. Columbus, Ohio: Berlin Printing, 1898. 285 pp. Journal, pp. 1-38.

> 1862-1865. War journal of officer with the Fifty-second Ohio Volunteer Infantry; recruiting a company; capture in Kentucky, parole to Ohio and exchange; military operations in Tennessee and Alabama; assuming command of the regiment; battles of Chickamauga and Missionary Ridge; Knoxville and Atlanta campaigns; expedition into Alabama to intercept Forrest; the March to the Sea and Carolinas campaign; Lincoln's assassination; the Grand Review and journey home; brief notes but with some longer entries beginning in February 1865.

HOLMES, ROBERT MASTEN, 1844-1864   **4162**

KEMPER COUNTY REBEL. Edited by Frank Allen Dennis. Jackson: University and College Press of Mississippi, 1973. 115 pp.

> Nov 1862-May 1863. Private's account of soldiering in Tennessee with Company I, Twenty-fourth Mississippi Volunteers; weather, marches and camp life; duties, chores, rations, drills and reviews, military punishments, rumors, mail and homesickness; battle of Stones River.

HOLTON, WILLIAM C.   **4163**

CRUISE OF THE U.S. FLAGSHIP HARTFORD. By B.S. Osbon. New York: L.W. Paine, Printer, 1863. 84 pp. Reprint. Tarrytown, N.Y.: William Abbatt, 1922. 100 pp. MAGAZINE OF HISTORY, extra no. 87.

> 1862-1863 (with gap). Journal kept aboard the screw sloop HARTFORD, flagship of the Western Gulf Blockading Squadron; naval operations on the Mississippi, including action at forts Jackson and St. Philip and the siege of Port Hudson; notes on weather, other vessels, contrabands, casualties, etc.; reworked to some extent for publication.

HONEYMAN, ROBERT R., 1836-1873   **4164**

"Colonel Honeyman and His War Journal." OUR HOME AND FIRESIDE MAGAZINE 1 (1873):347-353, 396-399, 463-467, 499-503, 545-550.

> Sep 1862-May 1863. Account of service with the Thirty-first New Jersey by resident of New Germantown, Hunterdon County; in camp at Washington, D.C., and Belle Plain, Virginia, advancing from captain of Company A to lieutenant colonel in command of the regiment; activities of his unit and his pride in the men; visiting Fredericksburg the day before the battle; Burnside's "Mud March"; the Chancellorsville campaign; notes on camp life; critical remarks about Col. A.P. Berthoud and Gen. James Wadsworth; praise for Gen. Gabriel Paul; long, descriptive entries, many of which originally were sent as letters to a friend.

HOSMER, JAMES KENDALL, b. 1834   **4165**

THE COLOR-GUARD: BEING A CORPORAL'S NOTES ON MILITARY SERVICE IN THE NINETEENTH ARMY CORPS. Boston: Walker, Wise, 1864. 244 pp.

> Nov 1862-Jul 1863. Diary-letters, revised for publication, of minister who served as one of the color guards in the Fifty-second Regiment Massachusetts Volunteers; well-developed description of facilities and a dress parade at Jamaica, Long Island camp, quarters aboard troop transports ILLINOIS and ST. MARY'S, a plundered plantation and military hospitals; on the march through Louisiana; bayous Lafourche, Bouef and Teche; notes on Nathaniel Banks, New Orleans, Baton Rouge, the tedium of army life, foraging, nursing and the hardships of marching; assault on Port Hudson and a ramble around the surrendered defenses.

HOTCHKISS, JEDEDIAH, 1828-1899   **4166**

MAKE ME A MAP OF THE VALLEY; THE CIVIL WAR JOURNAL OF STONEWALL JACKSON'S TOPOGRAPHER. Edited by Archie P. McDonald. Dallas: Southern Methodist University Press, 1973. 352 pp.

> 1862-1865. Portion of diary kept by teacher and engineer during most of his adult life; long, detailed entries, supplemented in the

earlier part of the record by copies of letters and commentary obviously added later; acting as topographer and staff officer under Jackson, Ewell and Early; Jackson's Shenandoah Valley campaign; battle of Cedar Mountain and the Second Bull Run campaign; crossing into Maryland, Antietam and the retreat into Virginia; battle of Fredericksburg and the destruction left in its wake; Chancellorsville and the wounding and death of Jackson; the Gettysburg, Wilderness and Spotsylvania campaigns; with Early on the Washington Raid and in the Shenandoah Valley; the last days of war; notes on duties, sermons, visits to his home near Churchville, Virginia, and on many prominent members of the Army of Northern Virginia, including Stonewall Jackson as living general and fallen hero; an important record of the war in Virginia by a man of many talents, providing a fascinating view of the role of cartography in Civil War military operations.

"Letters & Diaries." CIVIL WAR TIMES ILLUSTRATED 1, no. 5 (1962):24-25.

Sep 1862. Extracts covering the Antietam campaign.

HOUGLAND, JAMES H., b. 1836 4167

CIVIL WAR DIARY FOR THE YEAR 1862. Edited by Oscar F. Curtis. Bloomington, Ind.: Monroe County Civil War Centennial Commission, 1962. 40 leaves.

Jan-Dec 1862. Boonville, Indiana, soldier's view of service in Company G, First Indiana Cavalry; brief, choppy, daily entries giving a picture of life in camp and on the move in Missouri, Arkansas and Mississippi.

HOUSEHOLDER, JOHN, 1824-1887 4168

In CEMETERY TALES AND CIVIL WAR DIARY, by George Stragand, pp. 53-74. Scottsdale, Pa.: Laurel Group, 1978. 91 pp.

1862-1863. Private's brief diary entries written while serving in Company G, 101st Pennsylvania Volunteers; in camp at Harrisburg and a visit home to Elizabeth, Pennsylvania; sightseeing in Washington, D.C.; the Peninsular campaign; battle of Fair Oaks; campaigning in North Carolina; court martial and punishment; notes on weather, duties, Fourth of July celebration, etc.; last six months of record in monthly condensations.

HOWE, HENRY 4169

Lee, D. Collins. "The Ramparts of the Three Cities." HISTORICAL AND PHILOSOPHICAL SOCIETY OF OHIO BULLETIN 4, no. 1 (1946):5-11. Diary, pp. 8-10.

Sep 1862. Extracts from Cincinnati man's diary describing defensive measures taken when Confederate invasion threatened the city; among untried soldiers stationed in earthworks at Covington, Kentucky.

HUBBELL, FINLEY L., 1830-1863 4170

"Diary of Lieut. Col. Hubbell, of 3d Regiment Missouri Infantry, C.S.A." THE LAND WE LOVE 6 (1868):97-105.

1862-1863. Extracts covering operations in Mississippi; battles of Iuka and Corinth; the Vicksburg campaign; comment on Union army's destructiveness and their treatment of blacks; mourning deaths of comrades and friends.

HUGHES, FRANK, d. 1864 4171

Niccum, Norman, ed. "Diary of Lieutenant Frank Hughes." INDIANA MAGAZINE OF HISTORY 45 (1949):275-284.

May-Jul 1862. Diary of officer from Adams, Indiana, serving in Company E, Thirty-seventh Indiana; military activities prior to capture at Elk River engagement near Athens, Alabama; march through Moulton to Tuscaloosa and from there to Montgomery via the Tombigbee and Alabama rivers; incarceration at Macon and Madison, Georgia; description of countryside passed through and prison conditions at all locations; notes on war news, deaths, escape attempts, etc.

HUNGERFORD, BENJAMIN FRANKLIN, 1825-1916 4172

Birdwhistell, Jack. "Extracts from the Diary of B.F. Hungerford." BAPTIST HISTORY AND HERITAGE 14 (1979):24-31.

1862-1866. Extracts, arranged by topic, from diary of Shelby County, Kentucky, pastor, a Democrat and staunch unionist; pastoral activities; depredations of Confederate guerillas and Union soldiers; diarist's fear of the draft; reaction to war news, Confederacy's defeat and Lincoln's assassination.

HUNTER, WILLIAM W. 4173

In OFFICIAL RECORDS OF THE UNION AND CONFEDERATE NAVIES IN THE WAR OF THE REBELLION, ser. 1, vol. 16, pp. 485-488; vol. 19, pp. 813-817.

Dec 1862-Feb 1863, Apr 1863, Dec 1864. Extracts from journal of Confederate naval officer; commanding group assigned to obstruct and defend the Trinity River in eastern Texas; serving as flag officer aboard the SAMPSON, opposing Sherman's forces; engagements on the Savannah River; proceeding up the river to Augusta after loss of Savannah.

HYATT, A.W. 4174

In MILITARY RECORD OF LOUISIANA, by Bartlett Napier, part 3, pp. 1-14. New Orleans: L. Graham & Co., Printers, 1875. Reprint. Baton Rouge: Louisiana State University Press, 1964.

1862-1864. Scattered extracts from journal of lieutenant colonel of the Crescent City Regiment; brief entries recording military operations in Louisiana, including the battle of Sabine Cross Roads; notes on ladies' hospitality, a lieutenant's suicide, etc.

IBBETSON, WILLIAM H.H., 1840-1883 4175

"Diary of William H.H. Ibbetson, Chesterfield, Illinois." ILLINOIS STATE HISTORICAL LIBRARY PUBLICATIONS, no. 37 (1930):235-273.

1862-1864 (with gaps). Company D, 122d Illinois Infantry, corporal's account, obviously rewritten, of service in Tennessee, Mississippi, Alabama, Kentucky and Georgia; notes on military operations, including the battle of Tupelo, foraging, depredations of Union troops, Southern women, etc.; description of areas passed through; company muster roll appended.

INZER, JOHN WASHINGTON, 1834-1928 4176

THE DIARY OF A CONFEDERATE SOLDIER. Edited by Mattie Lou Teague Crow. Huntsville, Ala.: Strode, 1977. 191 pp. Diary, pp. 21-147.

1862-1865 (with gaps). War experiences of Ashville, Alabama, lawyer; private, Fifth Alabama Battalion, in the retreat from Shiloh, suffering from rain, mud and the effects of his first hard march; officer in the Eighteenth Alabama Infantry, reorganized as the Ninth Alabama Battalion; stationed in Mississippi and his home state, experiencing the discomforts of public transportation where "everything stinks on the boats and cars"; lieutenant colonel of the Fifty-eighth Alabama Infantry at the battles of Lookout Mountain and Missionary Ridge, surrendering at the latter; held at Chattanooga for several weeks; journey to Johnson's Island, mentioning food and moral support provided by Louisville ladies; prison conditions, weather, food, purchases, correspondence, war news, his health and that of fellow prisoners, gifts received from friends and relatives, gold prices, prisoner exchange issue, hopes for McClellan's election, etc.; prayers, patriotic sentiments and increasing bitterness; stops and expenses during journey home after war's end.

JACKSON, LUTHER WASHINGTON, 1822?-1862　　　4177

"A Prisoner of War." ANNALS OF IOWA, ser. 3, 19 (1933):23-41.

Apr-Jun 1862. Prison diary of lieutenant, Company H, Twelfth Iowa Infantry, captured during battle of Shiloh; journey through Mississippi to Montgomery, Alabama, and incarceration in cotton shed; notes on conditions, war news and rumors of exchange; longing for preaching and his wife; angry words for Southerners, treatment of prisoners and inaction of Union government concerning their imprisoned soldiers; transfer to Macon, Georgia, where conditions were better, shortly before his death.

JACKSON, SAMUEL MCCARTNEY, 1833-1906　　　4178

DIARY OF GENERAL S.M. JACKSON FOR THE YEAR 1862. Apollo? Pa., pref. 1925. 64 pp.

Jan-Dec 1862. Diary of lieutenant colonel of the Fortieth Pennsylvania Infantry, brother of J. Thompson Jackson; military operations in Virginia; battle of Gaines's Mill and capture; incarceration at Libby with mention of religious services, reading and conditions there; exchange and participation in the battles of Second Bull Run, Antietam and Fredericksburg; notes on weather, activities, health, war and family news; furlough home to Apollo, Pennsylvania.

JOHNSON, FRANCIS MARION　　　　　　　　　4179

Hough, Granville W., ed. "Diary of a Soldier in Grant's Rear Guard." JOURNAL OF MISSISSIPPI HISTORY 45 (1983):194-214.

May 1862-Feb 1863. Diary of "principal musician," Thirty-second Illinois Infantry, from Alton, Illinois; journey to rejoin regiment near Corinth, passing by the Shiloh battlefield; advancing to and taking Corinth; subsequent operations in Mississippi and Tennessee and meeting civilians professing unionist sentiments in the former state; notes on weather, hardships, Fourth of July festivities, foraging and confiscation; brief mention of duties.

JOHNSON, JONATHAN HUNTINGTON, 1815?-1863

THE LETTERS AND DIARY OF CAPTAIN JONATHAN HUNTINGTON JOHNSON. Collected and compiled by Alden Chase Brett. N.p., 1961. 166 leaves. Diary, pp. 3-163 passim.

Nov 1862-Jun 1863. Diary entries interspersed among letters of Deerfield, New Hampshire, shoemaker and farmer, captain of Company D, Fifteenth New Hampshire Volunteers; transport by sea from New York City to New Orleans, observing sights along the way; in camp at Carrollton, Louisiana; notes on weather, expenses, drills and duties, deaths; lengthy description of assault on Port Hudson.

JONES, JENKINS LLOYD, 1843-1918　　　　　　4181

AN ARTILLERYMAN'S DIARY. Madison: Wisconsin History Commission, 1914. 395 pp.

Extracts in THE BLUE AND THE GRAY, edited by Henry S. Commager, vol. 1, pp. 411-414, vol. 2, pp. 898-902.

1862-1865. Welsh-American's diary of service with the Sixth Wisconsin Battery; in camp in Mississippi; operations in Tennessee; the Vicksburg and Chattanooga campaigns; stationed in Alabama, primarily at Huntsville; at Kingston and Etowah Bridge as Sherman moves toward and takes Atlanta; guarding Nashville as Hood's army approaches but kept in reserve during the battle; in camp at Chattanooga; home to Spring Green, Wisconsin, after mustering out; notes on his health and that of others, prices, foraging, cemetery visits, military transportation, duties, medical treatments, April Fool's Day, military funerals, General McPherson, the presidential election of 1864, Mother Bickerdyke, the Sanitary and Christian commissions, theater in Nashville, games, entertainments and other leisure activities; occasional descriptions of the countryside especially in comparison to Northern agricultural areas; excursion to the top of Lookout Mountain, where he was photographed; observations concerning Confederate soldiers, Southern civilians, slavery and freedmen; a Unitarian's view of Episcopal and black church services and witnessing ecstatic religious expression near Chickamauga Creek; remarks on the monotony of camp life, officers' efforts to achieve discipline, methods of outwitting the system, the prevalence of drinking and other vices and the importance of mail and reading materials; a rich account of a soldier's everyday activities and the conditions under which he labored, longing for home but willing to do his duty.

JONES, SAMUEL CALVIN, b. 1838　　　　　　　4182

REMINISCENCES OF THE TWENTY-SECOND IOWA VOLUNTEER INFANTRY... AS TAKEN FROM THE DIARY OF LIEUTENANT S.C. JONES OF COMPANY A. Iowa City, Iowa, 1907. 164 pp.

1862-1865. Diary entries mixed with narrative; from Iowa through Missouri to St. Genevieve and then down the Mississippi to near Vicksburg; comments on different allegiances among Missourians; battle of Port Gibson; siege of Vicksburg; in Louisiana and Texas; by steamer from New Orleans to Virginia; military action in lower Shenandoah Valley; confinement at Libby Prison; recovery at the United States Hospital in Annapolis and home to Iowa; return to Annapolis, visiting relatives at his birthplace, Ebensburg, Pennsylvania, on the way; reaction to Lincoln's assassination; from Savannah to Augusta, noting devastation of the country and destitution of the population; guard detail aboard the LEESBURG on the Savannah River; an adventurous journey from Augusta to Savannah to be mustered out; by steamer to Baltimore and by train through the Midwest to welcome in Iowa.

JORDAN, STEPHEN A., b. 1823?　　　　　　　4183

In THE CIVIL WAR IN MAURY COUNTY, TENNESSEE, by Jill K. Garrett and Marise P. Lightfoot, pp. 15-44.

1862-1865. Confederate private's diary of service with Company G, Ninth Tennessee Cavalry, also known as the Nineteenth or Biffle's Regiment; operations in Tennessee, North Carolina, Georgia, Alabama and Mississippi; the Atlanta campaign and Hood's Tennessee campaign; notes on weather, health and miles covered; company roster.

JOSSELYN, FRANCIS   **4184**

Taylor, John M. "Francis Josselyn: A Gunboat Captain's Diary." MANUSCRIPTS 33 (1981):113-122.

Apr-May, Aug 1862, Apr 1863. A few extracts from Maine native's diary, describing patrol duty of the fourth-class steamer RELIANCE, part of the Potomac Flotilla, in Virginia waters; rescuing survivors of the WEST POINT and GEORGE PEABODY collision; commanding the side-wheeler COMMODORE HULL during the siege of Washington, North Carolina; firing on the Confederate ram ALBEMARLE.

KASSLER, GEORGE W., 1836-1890   **4185**

Alexander, Philip K., ed. "George W. Kassler: Colorado Pioneer." COLORADO MAGAZINE 39 (1962):29-45, 137-144. Diary, pp. 131-138.

Jun-Sep 1862. Army paymaster clerk's journey from Denver to Valverde and Fort Craig, New Mexico, with Major John S. Fillmore, paymaster; carrying pay to Union troops stationed there; brief notes of route, camps, Indian alarms.

KEEGAN, PETER, 1833-1904   **4186**

THE DIARIES OF PETER KEEGAN. Edited by Dwight Reynolds. Indianapolis, 1930. 33 pp.

1862-1863 (with gaps). War diary of Peru, Indiana, cobbler who emigrated from Ireland in 1851 and served as a sergeant in Company C, Eighty-seventh Indiana; military operations in Kentucky, Tennessee and Dade County, Georgia; lengthy description of battle of Chickamauga; notes on weather, his health, miles marched, countryside and towns, Nashville, sermons, soldiers' drinking, Gov. Andrew Johnson, etc.

KELSEY, ALBERT WARREN, b. 1840   **4187**

AUTOBIOGRAPHICAL NOTES AND MEMORANDA. Baltimore: Munder-Thomsen, 1911. 129 pp. Diary, pp. 44-47.

Mar 1862. Extracts from diary of New Englander serving as acting assistant paymaster aboard the HENRY ANDREWS in the Union blockade; brief description of expedition to find blockade runner near Smyrna, Florida, and the aftermath of his being wounded.

KINSMAN, ABBOTT, 1844-1864   **4188**

"Excerpts from the Diary and the Letters of Abbott Kinsman." ESSEX INSTITUTE HISTORICAL COLLECTIONS 89 (1953):72-93. Diary, pp. 72-80, 86-88.

Aug 1862-Jul 1863. Diary kept during a voyage aboard the SHIRLEY; notes on New York, San Francisco, Hong Kong; pleasant, youthful account of life aboard ship and in port.

KITTS, JOHN HOWARD, 1842-1870   **4189**

"The Civil War Diary of John Howard Kitts." KANSAS STATE HISTORICAL SOCIETY COLLECTIONS 14 (1918):318-332.

Aug-Dec 1862, Oct 1864. Diary kept by member of Company E, Eleventh Kansas Volunteers, a printer from Lyon County; marching distances and camps in Kansas; military operations in Missouri and Arkansas; notes on Union acts of destruction in the latter state.

KYGER, TILMON D., d. 1876   **4190**

In A HISTORY OF THE SEVENTY-THIRD REGIMENT OF ILLINOIS INFANTRY VOLUNTEERS, by Illinois Infantry, 73d Regiment, pp. 69-531 passim.

1862-1865. Extracts from diary of captain of Company C; action in Kentucky, Tennessee, Georgia and Alabama; battles of Stones River, Chickamauga, and Missionary Ridge; Atlanta campaign and visit to the conquered city; battle of Franklin; notes on execution of deserters; regiment's return to Illinois at war's end.

LANE, DAVID   **4191**

A SOLDIER'S DIARY. Jackson, Mich., 1905. 270 pp.

1862-1865. Company G member's account of service in the Seventeenth Michigan Volunteer Infantry, probably reworked somewhat for publication; at Fort Baker near Washington, D.C.; the Antietam campaign; stationed in Virginia and Kentucky; on the fringes of the Vicksburg siege; expedition to Jackson, Mississippi; return to Kentucky; siege of Knoxville and conditions of hospital there in which he served as a nurse; battle of the Wilderness, captured with the wounded and immediately paroled; his efforts to maintain the integrity of his parole; siege of Petersburg; working for the Christian Commission; glimpses of Lincoln; notes on duties, camp life, surroundings, gun accidents, supply problems, the Sanitary Commission, the Michigan Soldiers' Relief Association and Julia Wheelock Freeman, contrabands, the presidential election of 1864 and Lincoln's assassination; diarist's opinion of Parson Brownlow, Salmon P. Chase and McClellan; love and concern for his wife, homesickness and his thoughts on the war's progress; substantial entries revealing how one soldier dealt with the loneliness and hardships of army life.

LATHROP, DAVID   **4192**

In A HISTORY OF THE FIFTY-NINTH REGIMENT ILLINOIS VOLUNTEERS, pp. 180-187. Indianapolis: Hall & Hutchinson, Printers, 1865.

Dec 1862. Extracts surviving within diary-based narrative; in camp near Nashville; notes on weather, foraging and punishments.

LE DUC, WILLIAM GATES, 1823-1917   **4193**

RECOLLECTIONS OF A CIVIL WAR QUARTERMASTER. St. Paul, Minn.: North Central, 1963. 167 pp. Diary, pp. 76-77, 79-80, 90-92.

Jun-Jul 1862. Extracts from diary of Hastings, Minnesota, resident, quartermaster of the Third Brigade, Third Division, Second Corps, Army of the Potomac; his work and conditions in Virginia.

LEE, MARY CHARLTON GREENHOW, 1819-1906   **4194**

Hopkins, C.A. Porter, ed. "An Extract from the Journal of Mrs. Hugh H. Lee of Winchester, Va." MARYLAND HISTORICAL MAGAZINE 53 (1958):380-393.

> May 1862. Widow's description of the occupation and evacuation of Winchester by Jackson's troops during the Shenandoah Valley campaign; providing hospitality and nursing for Confederate soldiers; praise for Randolph McKim; civilians' fears of Union retaliation.

LUCAS, DANIEL R.   **4195**

HISTORY OF THE 99TH INDIANA INFANTRY. Lafayette, Ind.: Rosser & Spring, Book and Job Printers, 1865. 179 pp. Diary, pp. 9-81.

> 1862-1865. Chaplain's record of the regiment's marches and movements in Tennessee, the Atlanta campaign and with Sherman through Georgia and the Carolinas; bare facts with no personal details or color; entries apparently reworked and later commentary added.

LUCAS, THOMAS O.   **4196**

A DIARY. FOUR MONTH'S PRISON LIFE OF FIRST MARYLAND REGIMENT AT LYNCHBURG AND RICHMOND. Baltimore: Printed by Sherwood, 1862. 24 pp.

> May-Sep 1862. Prison diary, supposedly kept by sergeant, Company A, first Maryland Volunteers; a hard trek from Front Royal to Lynchburg and conditions of confinement there and at Belle Isle; inadequacies of food and medical treatment; hostility of civilians; names of many of those who died as prisoners; exchanged to parole camp at Annapolis.

In HISTORICAL RECORD OF THE FIRST REGIMENT MARYLAND INFANTRY, compiled by Charles Camper and J.W. Kirkley, pp. 51-79. Washington, D.C.: Gibson Brothers, Printers, 1871.

> Jun-Sep 1862. Takes up the journey to Lynchburg prison at Waynesboro, Virginia; account possibly supplemented by compilers.

LYNCH, CHARLES H., b. 1845   **4197**

THE CIVIL WAR DIARY, 1862-1865, OF CHARLES H. LYNCH, 18TH CONN. VOLS. Hartford, Conn.: Privately printed by the Case, Lockwood & Brainard Co., 1915. 163 pp.

> 1862-1865. Company C member's account of life in the regiment's color company; the sendoff from Norwich; at Fort McHenry and then service in the Shenandoah Valley; Gettysburg campaign, not at the battle but involved in the skirmishing of Lee's retreat; in the Valley under Sigel, Hunter, Crook and Sheridan; battles of Piedmont, Cedar Creek and Opequon; regimental furlough home to vote and transport to New Haven in anticipation of antiwar disturbances; in camp at Halltown and Martinsburg; notes on destruction at Staunton and Lexington, execution of a deserter, celebrating the surrender and mourning Lincoln; back to Connecticut; considerable evidence of later rewriting.

LYON, ADELIA C.   **4198**

In REMINISCENCES OF THE CIVIL WAR, by William Penn Lyon, pp. 73-96, 134-219 passim. San Jose, Calif.: Press of Muirson & Wright, 1907.

> 1862-1865. Extracts from diary of wife of William Penn Lyon, colonel of the Thirteenth Wisconsin; with the regiment at Fort Henry, Fort Donelson, Nashville, Huntsville, Alabama; and various Tennessee locations including New Market; notes on freedmen, Southern women chewing tobacco and dipping snuff, train and boat travel, Jackson's Hermitage, Nashville accommodations and her husband's election to Wisconsin judgeship.

MCADAMS, FRANCIS MARION   **4199**

EVERYDAY SOLDIER LIFE, OR A HISTORY OF THE ONE HUNDRED AND THIRTEENTH OHIO VOLUNTEER INFANTRY. Columbus: C.M. Cott, Printers, 1884. 400 pp. Diary, pp. 5-171.

> 1862-1865. Daily entries of enlisted man in Company E, later revised and supplemented for publication; getting used to army life at camp in Ohio; transport on the steamer SUPERIOR to Kentucky and on the ST. PATRICK to Nashville; battles of Chickamauga and Missionary Ridge; dull days in Tennessee; the Atlanta campaign; promotion to sergeant; pursuing Hood northward; the March to the Sea; the Carolinas campaign; march north and the Grand Review; in camp in Kentucky, mustering out and home; remarks on foraging and other evidences of soldierly ingenuity, camp regulations, Sanitary Commission provisions, Lincoln's assassination and Sherman's farewell to the Second Division.

MCCOMAS, EVANS SMITH, 1839-1911   **4200**

A JOURNAL OF TRAVEL. Edited by Martin Schmitt. Portland, Oreg.: Champoeg Press, 1954. 84 pp.

> 1862-1867. Emigrant journey from Iowa City to Oregon of a man who came west to avoid service in the Civil War and settled in the gold mining region at Powder River; notes on mining; work as a teacher and newspaper publisher; Civil War songs, ballads, comic pieces and pen sketches of mining life appended.

MCCOY, JAMES   **4201**

In ANNUAL REPORT, 5TH, by New York State Bureau of Military Statistics, pp. 544-559.

> 1862-1863. Extracts from journal of captain, Twenty-second New York Volunteers; military operations in Virginia; Second Bull Run, Antietam and Chancellorsville; notes on weather, hard marches, duties, First Bull Run battlefield, etc.; glimpses of McDowell and McClellan.

MCCREARY, JAMES BENNETT, 1838-1918   **4202**

"The Journal of My Soldier life." KENTUCKY STATE HISTORICAL SOCIETY REGISTER 33 (1935):97-117, 191-211.

> 1862-1864 (with gaps). War diary of lawyer, major and then lieutenant colonel of the Eleventh Kentucky Cavalry and future governor of Kentucky; military operations in Kentucky and Tennessee; participation in Morgan's July 1863 raid into Indiana and Ohio and capture at Buffington Island; incarceration at Columbus, Ohio, penitentary; transfer on the CRESCENT to Morris Island; imprisonment there and at Fort Pulaski; notes on engagement at Hartsville, ladies encountered, various locations including Knoxville, Murfreesboro, Lebanon and Albany, prison conditions and punishments and reaction to news of Morgan's death; account marred by occasional overblown prose.

Extracts in THE BLUE AND THE GRAY, edited by Henry S. Commager, vol. 2, pp. 681-684.

July 1863. Morgan's raid.

MCDONALD, CORNELIA PEAKE, 1822-1909   4203

A DIARY WITH REMINISCENCES OF THE WAR AND REFUGEE LIFE IN THE SHENANDOAH VALLEY. Nashville: Cullom & Ghertner, 1935. 540 pp. Diary, pp. 40-176.

Mar 1862-Jun 1863. Record kept by cultivated Virginia woman for her husband, Angus W. McDonald, in Confederate service; with her small children in Union-occupied Lexington, trying to defend her property from pillaging enemy soldiers; caring for wounded while the town is in Confederate hands; a successful interview with General Milroy, allowing her to remain in her home; mourning the death of her youngest child; notes on war news, deaths, her slaves, destruction of trees by the foraging Union troops, etc.; diary partially written up after the war.

Extracts in HEROINES OF DIXIE, edited by Katharine M. Jones, pp. 94-106, 140-145.

Mar, May 1862.

MCGEHEE, VALENTINE MERRIWETHER, d. 1876   4204

"Captain Valentine Merriwether McGehee." ARKANSAS HISTORICAL ASSOCIATION PUBLICATIONS 4 (1917):140-151.

Dec 1862, Mar-Apr 1863. Diary letters of commander of Company G, Second Arkansas Infantry; battle of Stones River; notes on members of his company; thoughts on the winning of the war.

MCINTYRE, BENJAMIN FRANKLIN, b. 1827   4205

FEDERALS ON THE FRONTIER. Edited by Nannie M. Tilley. Austin: University of Texas Press, 1963. 429 pp.

1862-1864. Detailed, objective, sometimes flowery account of the war in the West by Iowa carpenter serving as sergeant, then lieutenant, with Company A, Nineteenth Iowa Infantry; camps and marches in Missouri and Arkansas; battle of Prairie Grove; siege of Vicksburg, sights in the fallen city and respect for its defenders; operations along the Mississippi and in camp at Yazoo City, Mississippi, and Carrollton, Louisiana; action at Stirling Farm; to Texas aboard the GENERAL BANKS; activities and observations at Brownsville; return to Carrollton; notes on weather, food, foraging, execution of deserter, Fourth of July celebration, illnesses and deaths; description of countryside, towns, including Van Buren and Fayetteville, Arkansas, and Matamoros, Mexico, and battlefields of Pea Ridge and Wilson's Creek; comments on generals Schofield and Dana and other commanders, Southern blacks and the Corps d'Afrique, refugees, drunkenness in the army, Mexicans and Mexican politics, Roman Catholicism, etc.

MCKIM, RANDOLPH HARRISON, 1842-1920   4206

A SOLDIER'S RECOLLECTIONS. New York: Longmans, Green, 1910. 362 pp. Diary, pp. 51-241 passim. Reprint. Washington, D.C.: Zenger, 1983; Alexandria, Va.: Time-Life Books, 1984.

1862-1864. A sprinkling of extracts from wartime diaries of Baltimore youth, a graduate of the University of Virginia; service in the ranks of the First Maryland, as officer on staff of George H. Steuart and, after ordination as Episcopal priest, as chaplain of the Second Virginia Cavalry; Jackson's Shenandoah Valley campaign; the Gettysburg campaign; notes on reading, hardships of army life and activities of chaplaincy.

Extracts in THE BLUE AND THE GRAY, edited by Henry S. Commager, vol. 2, pp. 621-623.

Jul 1863. Gettysburg.

MCMYNN, Mrs. JOHN GIBSON   4207

In WAR PAPERS, by Military Order of the Loyal Legion of the United States, Wisconsin Commandery, pp. 455-467. Milwaukee: Burdick, Armitage & Allen, 1914.

Aug-Oct 1862. Diary of Tenth Wisconsin Infantry officer's wife; roundtrip train journey to be with her husband at Larkinsville, Alabama; menace of guerillas and under enemy fire; accommodations; regimental activities and a glimpse of Don Carlos Buell; stops at Nashville, Stevenson, Alabama, and Bowling Green, Kentucky; interaction with Southern civilians; negative reaction to Halleck's order ejecting blacks without free papers from Union camps; hospitalized for typhoid in Louisville.

MAFFITT, JOHN NEWLAND, 1819-1886   4208

In OFFICIAL RECORDS OF THE UNION AND CONFEDERATE NAVIES IN THE WAR OF THE REBELLION, ser. 1, vol. 1, pp. 763-769; vol. 2, pp. 667-673.

May 1862-Apr 1863. Extracts from journal of lieutenant commanding the FLORIDA; summary of legal battle in the Bahamas to secure the gunboat ORETO for the Confederacy and yellow fever epidemic aboard the ship which was renamed the FLORIDA; eluding Union ships to reach Cárdenas and Havana; a harrowing run through the blockade into Mobile; assembling a crew and almost losing his command; into the Gulf of Mexico and capture of Yankee merchant vessels; coaling and problems of neutrality at Havana, Nassau and Bridgetown.

MALLORY, MARY ALICE SHUTES, 1849-1939   4209

DIARY: 800 MILES IN THIRTY-SIX DAYS. Bloomington, Ill.: L.L. Shutes, 1967. 45 1eaves.

Riley, Glenda, ed. "Pioneer Migration: The Diary of Mary Alice Shutes." ANNALS OF IOWA, 3d ser. 43 (1975-1977):487-514, 566-592.

May-Jun 1862. Thirteen-year-old girl's diary of wagon and horseback journey with family and friends from Marseilles, Wyandot County, Ohio, to Jasper Township, Carroll County, Iowa; departure from relatives, home and possessions; distances as determined by her father's pedometer; riding her horse "straddle"; detailed description of crossing the Mississippi by steam ferry at Muscatine; purchase of a farm and log cabin by her father, G. Hiram Shutes, with gold brought from Ohio; an interesting account occasionally supplemented or rewritten en route by her stepmother, Ann Drown Shutes.

MALONE, BARTLETT YANCEY, 1838-1890   4210

Pierson, William W., Jr., ed. "The Diary of Bartlett Yancey Malone." JAMES SPRUNT HISTORICAL PUBLICATIONS 16 (1919):3-59.

WHIPT 'EM EVERYTIME; THE DIARY OF BARTLETT YANCEY MALONE. Edited by William W. Pierson, Jr. Jackson, Tenn.; McCowat-Mercer, 1960. 131 pp.

Extracts in OUR SOLDIERS SPEAK, by William Matthews and Dixon Wecter, pp. 207-213 passim.

1862-1865. Diary of North Carolina farmer who rose from private to sergeant in the Sixth North Carolina Infantry, was captured at Rappahannock Station in November 1863 and imprisoned until parole in February 1865; terse, unemotional view from the ranks of the Army of Northern Virginia's battles and campaigns, including Gettysburg; routine reports of weather and sermons; prison life at Point Lookout where the guard included black soldiers; interesting phonetic spellings.

Extracts in POINT LOOKOUT PRISON CAMP FOR CONFEDERATES, by Edwin W. Beitzell, pp. 55-65. Abell, Md., 1972.

1863-1865.

MARKELL, CATHERINE SUSANNAH, 1828-1900   4211

Bardsley, Virginia O., ed. "Frederick Diary: September 5-14, 1862." MARYLAND HISTORICAL MAGAZINE 60 (1965):132-138.

Sep 1862. Extracts from diary of Southern sympathizer, a woman of social prominence; entertaining Confederate generals and other officers as the Army of Northern Virginia passes through Frederick; notes on Stuart, Jackson and Lee; reference to an incident which may be basis for Barbara Fritchie episode.

MARSHALL, JOHN WESLEY, 1834-1922   4212

CIVIL WAR JOURNAL OF JOHN WESLEY MARSHALL. N.p., 1958. 373 leaves.

1862-1865. Diary of Muskingum County resident enlisted in the Ninety-seventh Ohio Volunteer Infantry; service as ordnance sergeant, Company K, and then as lieutenant, Company G; campaigning in Kentucky and Tennessee; the battles of Stones River and Chickamauga; the Chattanooga and Atlanta campaigns; operations in northern Georgia and Alabama; the Franklin and Nashville campaign; duty at Huntsville, Alabama, and in eastern Tennessee; an almost daily record, primarily of military matters but also describing activities and events which reveal the tenor of a soldier's life.

MARSHALL, JOSEPH K., 1841-1919   4213

CIVIL WAR DIARY OF JOSEPH K. MARSHALL. Columbus, Ohio: W.L. Phillips, 1982. 1 vol., various pagings.

1862-1864. Very brief entries covering service with Company E, Ninetieth Ohio Volunteer Infantry; record of unit's travels in Kentucky and Tennessee with scant notes concerning battles of Perryville, Stones River and Chickamauga; in Bridgeport, Alabama; somewhat more substantial entries covering the Atlanta campaign.

MAXFIELD, ALBERT   4214

In THE STORY OF ONE REGIMENT, by Maine Infantry, 11th Regiment, pp. 24-162 passim. New York: Press of J.J. Little, 1896.

1862-1864. Scattered extracts from diary of noncommissioned officer, later commissioned officer; Peninsular campaign and Seven Days' battles; in Virginia camps; operations at Charleston; high regard for Gen. Henry M. Naglee; small bits of information.

MENDENHALL, WILLARD HALL, 1832-1910   4215

Frazier, Margaret M. and Goodrich, James W., eds. " 'Life Is Uncertain.' " MISSOURI HISTORICAL REVIEW 78 (1984):428-452; 79 (1984):65-88.

Jan-Dec 1862. Extracts from diary of Lexington carriage-maker and farmer, a Southern sympathizer, reflecting the impact of the Civil War on Lafayette County; substantial entries describing incidents of confiscation, looting, destruction and harrassment inflicted by Union soldiers on the diarist and others; notes on farm operations.

MERVINE, CHARLES K., 1847?-1865   4216

Packard, Kent, ed. "Jottings by the Way." PENNSYLVANIA MAGAZINE OF HISTORY AND BIOGRAPHY 71 (1947):121-151, 242-282.

1862-1864. Diary of Philadelphian who entered the navy as a "second class boy," serving on the steam frigate POWHATAN; on duty in the South Atlantic blockade; naval assaults on Charleston; in port at Philadelphia; West Indies cruise with stops including Haiti, Cuba, St. Thomas, Curacao and Key West but no land tours; routines and events aboard ship; accidents, casualties, a suicide and an attempted suicide; names of the many ships encountered; notes on blacks, sailors' vote for president, drinking, etc.

MERZ, LOUIS, 1833-1862   4217

"Diary of Private Louis Merz." CHATTAHOOCHIE VALLEY HISTORICAL SOCIETY BULLETIN, no. 4 (1959):18-43.

Jan-Jul 1862. Account by Bavarian-born resident of West Point, Georgia, a member of the West Point Guards; incidents and routines in camp near Norfolk, witnessing the MERRIMAC's activities, including the destruction of the CUMBERLAND and the CONGRESS; notes on military punishments, election of company officers, etc.; march to Richmond area and a visit to the city.

MILLER, EDWARD GEE, 1840-1906   4218

.CAPTAIN EDWARD GEE MILLER OF THE 20TH WISCONSIN. Edited by Walter J. Lemke. Booklet Series of the Washington County Historical Society, no. 37. Fayetteville, Ark.: Washington County Historical Society, 1960. 42 pp.

1862-1865. Diary of Company G's captain, lately a student at the University of Wisconsin; in camp and on the move in Missouri and Arkansas; battle of Prairie Grove; fall of Vicksburg; duty in Louisiana, Mississippi, Brownsville, Texas and and Alabama; assault on Fort Morgan and fall of Mobile; to Texas to be mustered out and then home to Wisconsin; administrative notes with few details of battle and portions apparently rewritten later.

MILLINGTON, ADA, 1849-1930   4219

Clarke, Charles G., ed. "Journal Kept while Crossing the Plains." SOUTHERN CALIFORNIA QUARTERLY 59 (1977):13-48, 139-184, 251-269.

Apr-Sep 1862. Emigrant journey of a girl from Keosaukua, Iowa, to Santa Rosa, California, with her father, Seth Millington, and other friends and relatives; route via Platte Bridge, Salt Lake and a newly opened route across central Nevada; full and interesting notes of travel and sights, Indians, Mormons, emigrants, cavalry, ranches and stagecoach stations; some Indian alarms during a dangerous year; an excellent description of getting wagons across a river; touching personal details, such as joyous reunion with their long lost dog; her thirteenth birthday; the death of her baby brother and sending the body on by stage for burial at Carson City; outstanding account by a very young diarist who rewrote it somewhat at age nineteen.

MONIER, HENRY D.   4220

In MILITARY RECORD OF LOUISIANA, by Napier Bartlett, part I, pp. 30-32, 44-56. New Orleans: L. Graham & Co., Printers, 1875. Reprint. Baton Rouge: Louisiana State University Press, 1964.

1862-1865. Diary of officer in the Tenth Louisiana, tracing the regiment's participation in the operations of the Army of Northern Virginia; battles of Antietam, Chancellorsville, Gettysburg and the Wilderness; action in the Shenandoah Valley, including the battle of Winchester; in the Petersburg fortifications; retreat to surrender at Appomattox; brief entries, obviously embellished later.

MORTON, ELIAS P.   4221

In THE STORY OF ONE REGIMENT, by Maine Infantry, 11th Regiment, pp. 72-161 passim. New York: Press of J.J. Little, 1896.

1862-1863. Scattered extracts from noncommissioned officer's diary; Peninsular campaign; stationed in Virginia and at Fernandina, Florida, and Charleston; snippets of information.

MOSEY, ALBERT WASHINGTON, 1843-1895   4222

A UNION SOLDIER'S DIARY. Mansfield, Ohio: Mansfield City Board of Education, 1967? 1 vol. unpaged.

1862-1865. Brief sporadic entries in diary of member of Company C, Forty-fourth Regiment, Ohio Volunteer Infantry, and Company C, Eighth Regiment, Ohio Volunteer Cavalry; military movements and action, mainly in Kentucky, Tennessee, West Virginia and the Shenandoah Valley.

MOSMAN, CHESLEY A., b. 1844?   4223

In EPISODES OF THE CIVIL WAR, by George W. Herr, pp. 361-397. San Francisco: Bancroft, 1890.

Jan-Dec 1862. Fast-paced account by Missourian serving with Company D, Fifty-ninth Illinois; operations in Missouri, Arkansas, Tennessee and Mississippi; notes on the countryside, foraging, punishments for thievery, etc.

MOSS, A. HUGH, b. 1844?   4224

THE DIARY OF A. HUGH MOSS. Lake Charles? La., 1948. 56 pp. Diary, pp. 18-56.

Jun 1862, Mar-Jul 1863. Record of siege penned by one of Vicksburg's defenders, a young artilleryman from Coulie Croche, St. Landry Parish, Louisiana; military operations, rumors and hopes for reinforcements; parole and journey home through scenes of devastation; views on slavery.

NELSON, SOLOMON, 1826-1882   4225

In HISTORY OF THE FIFTIETH REGIMENT OF INFANTRY, MASSACHUSETTS VOLUNTEER MILITIA, by William Burnham Stevens, pp. 10-224 passim.

Nov 1862-Aug 1863. Extracts from diary kept by Company K sergeant; early days in camp and sightseeing in New York City; voyage on the JERSEY BLUE to Baton Rouge and camp life there; expeditions to Winter's Plantation and White's Bayou; siege of Port Hudson; regiment's decision to extend their nine-month enlistment until Port Hudson is taken; surrender of the city; diarist's assignment to retrieve regiment's belongings from Baton Rouge and place markers on graves of company members buried there; monotony of waiting at Port Hudson to go home; an irreverent, humorous and nicely descriptive account which deserves publication in its entirety.

NEWCOMB, WILLIAM H., d 1878   4226

In THE STORY OF ONE REGIMENT, by Maine Infantry, 11th Regiment pp. 25-198 passim. New York: Press of J.J. Little, 1896.

1862-1864. Scattered extracts from enlisted man's diary, noting regiment's involvement in the Peninsular campaign and Seven Days' battles; subsequent operations at Fernandina, Florida, Charleston and in Virginia.

NEWSOME, EDMUND   4227

EXPERIENCE IN THE WAR OF THE GREAT REBELLION. Carbondale, Ill.: E. Newsome, 1879. 137 pp.

1862-1865. Diary of captain, Company B, Eighty-first Illinois, enhanced for publication; in camp at Cairo and operations in Tennessee and Mississippi; at Lake Providence, Louisiana; the Vicksburg campaign, siege and surrender; expedition into Louisiana; furlough home to Union County, Illinois, then stationed at Vicksburg; the Red River campaign of 1864; in Tennessee and Mississippi again; battle of Brice's Cross Roads; capture and treatment en route to Macon, Georgia, prison; conditions there and at Savannah, Charleston and Columbia; transfer to North Carolina, exchange and stay in parole camp at Benton Barracks, St. Louis; some postwar duties; mostly a narrative record during imprisonment.

NEWTON, M.   4228

In DIARY OF A SOUTHERN REFUGEE, by Judith White Brockenbrough McGuire, 2d ed., pp. 134-149. New York: E.J. Hale & Son, 1868.

May-Jul 1862. Diary kept by sister of Judith McGuire and copied in the latter's diary; events in Union-occupied Hanover County, Virginia; outwitting the enemy and helping Confederate soldiers; depredations by Union soldiers.

NICHOLS, NORMAN K., 1835?-1915   4229

Williams, T. Harry, ed. "The Reluctant Warrior." CIVIL WAR HISTORY 3 (1957):17-39.

Feb-Oct 1862. Extracts from diary of private, Company K, 101st New York, from Chitenango, New York: in camp near Syracuse and at Washington, D.C., Alexandria and Harrison's Landing, Virginia; sightseeing in the nation's capital; the Seven Days' battles and Second Bull Run; work as cook and ambulance driver; brief entries recording weather and camp routines, candidly noting his acts of theft, pillaging and straggling.

NIXON, LIBERTY INDEPENDENCE, b. 1824?   4230

Bailey, Hugh C., ed. "An Alabamian at Shiloh." ALABAMA REVIEW 11 (1958):144-155.

Feb-Apr 1862. Limestone County man's record of service with the Twenty-sixth Alabama; journey to Mobile to enlist and in camp at Corinth; events and new acquaintances; moving north to Shiloh; the battle and his religious convictions which supported him through first war experience.

NOURSE, MARGARET TILLOSTON KEMBLE, 1830?-1883   4231

Campbell, Edward D.C., Jr. " 'Strangers and Pilgrims.' " VIRGINIA MAGAZINE OF HISTORY AND BIOGRAPHY 91 (1983):440-508.

Apr-Nov 1862. Diary of Washington, D.C., resident, a New York native, kept during sojourn with her husband, Charles, and child at Weston, their 468 acre farm near Warrenton in Fauquier County; a difficult wagon journey into Virginia; frequent substantial entries describing daily life under the pressures of war; domestic and farm tasks, shortages and prices, illnesses and deaths; relationships with neighbors and servants; husband's activities, concern for his welfare and for the proper upbringing of their son; having to feed Union soldiers and notes on their depredations in the area; feelings about the war and emancipation; her strong religious faith; a keen but gentle detailing of people's foibles.

PAINE, HALBERT ELEAZER, 1826-1905   4232

In A HISTORY OF THE EIGHTH REGIMENT OF NEW HAMPSHIRE VOLUNTEERS, by John M. Stanyan, pp. 95-280 passim.

May-Jun 1862, Jan-Jun 1863. Extracts from brigadier general's record of military operations in Louisiana and Mississippi; the capture of New Orleans; mostly brief notes on troop movements, actions and duties but also including a letter-diary bearing his impressions of Louisiana and of black soldiers.

In HISTORY OF THE FIFTIETH REGIMENT OF INFANTRY, MASSACHUSETTS VOLUNTEER MILITIA, by William Burnham Stevens, pp. 144-146, 178.

May-Jun 1863. Extracts describing assaults on Port Hudson obviously written up or supplemented after the fact.

PATON, JAMES E.   4233

"Civil War Journal of James E. Paton." KENTUCKY HISTORICAL SOCIETY REGISTER 61 (1963):220-231.

Jul-Aug 1862. Prison diary of member of Second Kentucky; lengthy retrospective account of battle of Fort Donelson at which he was captured; conditions at Camp Morton, Indiana.

PATRICK, MARSENA RUDOLPH, 1811-1888   4234

INSIDE LINCOLN'S ARMY. Edited by David S. Sparks. New York: T. Yoseloff, 1964. 536 pp.

1862-1865. War diary of West Point graduate; in Washington, D.C., seeking an appointment and eliciting the aid of Preston King; service as brigadier general in McDowell's First Corps and as military governor of Fredericksburg; the Shenandoah and Second Bull Run campaigns; the battle of Antietam; appointed provost marshal general of the Army of the Potomac; removal of McClellan; Fredericksburg campaign and the sacking of the ci-

ty; Chancellorsville, Gettysburg, Bristoe and Mine Run campaigns; from the Wilderness to Petersburg; observations on the battle of the Crater; operations around Petersburg; appointed provost marshal of the armies operating against Richmond, incurring Meade's wrath; at City Point until war's end, then in command of the District of Henrico, with headquarters at Richmond, dealing with Confederates, freedmen and Northern tourists; resignation in June 1865; an almost daily record of his activities in the various positions held, giving a unique view of the internal workings, frictions and problems of the Union army; dealing with stragglers, pillagers, rapists, obscene publications, liquor, prisoners, the Christian Commission, etc.; his concern over discipline of Union troops and his efforts to ameliorate Southern civilian hardships; much discussion regarding dissension and jockeying for position within the military and political leadership; his opinion of or reports of interaction with many individuals, including Rufus King, Daniel Butterfield, Burnside, Hooker, Grant, Stanton, "Baldy" Smith, Ben Butler, Sickles, Halleck and Lincoln; thoughts on the 1864 presidential contest and his reasons for supporting McClellan; reaction to the initial Sherman-Johnston negotiations; some personal notes expunged by diarist or family and routine notes deleted by the editor.

PATRICK, ROBERT, 1835-1866   4235

RELUCTANT REBEL: THE SECRET DIARY OF ROBERT PATRICK. Edited by F. Jay Taylor. Baton Rouge: Louisiana State University Press, 1959. 271 pp. Diary, pp. 46-255.

1862-1865 (with gaps). Diary of member of the Fourth Louisiana, serving as clerk in the commissary and quartermaster departments, transcribed from shorthand notebooks to his ledger as time allowed; stationed at Port Hudson; description of enemy fleet's attempt to pass the batteries and destruction of the Union's MISSISSIPPI; with Johnston's forces, hoping to relieve Vicksburg, and the harsh march of retreat after its capitulation; at Mobile and Pollard, Alabama; journey to Resaca and the Atlanta campaign; fall of Atlanta; moving north with Hood to attack Sherman's communication lines; at Aberdeen and Columbus, Mississippi; weather, reading, war rumors and news; his health, romances and drinking problems; visits home to Clinton; learning phonography; notes on conditions of soldiers and civilians, desertion and pillaging; criticism of Bragg and Hood; lengthy entries, often uninhibited, sometimes anecdotal and embroidered with dialog.

PAXSON, LEWIS C., b. 1836   4236

"Diary Kept by Lewis C. Paxson." NORTH DAKOTA STATE HISTORICAL SOCIETY COLLECTIONS 2, part 2, app. (1908):102-163.

1862-1865. Account of service in Company G, Eighth Minnesota Infantry; stationed at forts Abercrombie and Ripley, guarding against Indians in Minnesota; the Sibley-Sully expedition into Dakota Territory; march back to Minnesota; Franklin and Nashville campaign; seeing the sights in Washington, D.C.; operations in North Carolina; troops's reception in St. Paul and return to Lake City; expenses, duties, collecting Indian skulls and other relics; sermons, correspondence and his myriad activities; brief, choppy daily entries nicely communicating the soldier's milieu.

PEARSON, BENJAMIN FRANKLIN, 1815-1883   4237

"Benjamin F. Pearson's War Diary." ANNALS OF IOWA 15

(1925):83-129, 194-222, 281-305, 377-389, 433-463, 507-535.

1862-1865. Lieutenant's record of service with Company G, Thirty-sixth Iowa; recruiting efforts and church activities around Centerville; in camp at Keokuk and at Benton Barracks, St. Louis; in the lower Mississippi Valley, based at Helena and Little Rock; operations at Yazoo Pass, Coldwater and Tallahatchie rivers; battle of Marks' Mill; furloughs home to Keosauqua; a trip to Chicago to receive deacon's orders in the Methodist church; substantial entries covering daily events, both military and personal, and bristling with the names of friends, family and acquaintances; emphasis on religious activities but also notes on military movements and duties, his illnesses and remedies, service on court-martial, slavery, politics, weather, food and places visited such as Arkadelphia and Camden, Arkansas, New Orleans, Vicksburg and Memphis; lists of marriages performed; attendance at a black Methodist church and interracial socializing.

Harlan, E.R., ed. "A Trip to Kansas and Return." ANNALS OF IOWA, 3d ser. 20 (1935-1937):207-218.

May-Jun 1872. Extract covering wagon trip from Keosauqua, Iowa; visits with Civil War companions, ministers and relatives en route; camps, weather, scenery, towns and churches; lively interest in religious matters of all kinds; abundance of personal and place names.

PEHRSON, IMMANUEL C., b. 1848   **4238**

Kieffer, Elizabeth C., ed. "A Lancaster Schoolboy Views the Civil War." LANCASTER COUNTY HISTORICAL SOCIETY PAPERS 54 (1950):17-39.

1862-1863. Extracts from diary of orphan residing with the widow of Frederic J. Kramph on a small farm just outside Lancaster, Pennsylvania; the incidents and entertainments of an energetic teenager's days; chores and farm matters; school work, especially science experiments, and a school picnic; war news and enlistment of friends; a letter from Lincoln to Mrs. Krampf relating to the Home for Friendless Children in Lancaster; Fourth of July and Christmas celebrations; a delightful, informative record.

PELLET, ELIAS PORTER, b. 1837   **4239**

In HISTORY OF THE 114TH REGIMENT, NEW YORK STATE VOLUNTEERS, pp. 36-44, 172-238. Norwich, N.Y.: Telegraph & Chronicle Power Press Print, 1866.

Dec 1862-Jan 1863, Mar-May 1864. Extracts from officer's diary, not easily distinguishable from his memoir; troop transport from Port Royal to the Mississippi; a burial at sea, the Red River campaign; marching through Louisiana, noting the war's effects and Union sympathies among residents; battles of Sabine Cross Roads and Pleasant Hill; retreat of Union army and destruction of Confederate resources.

PENNINGTON, GEORGE W., 1841?-1864   **4240**

Billings, Elden E. "Letters & Diaries." CIVIL WAR TIMES ILLUSTRATED 1, no. 6 (1962):40-41.

1862-1864. Extracts from diary of corporal, Company K, 141st Pennsylvania Volunteers; brief note on Chancellorsville; on duty in Virginia; the Wilderness and Spotsylvania campaign.

PETER, FRANCES DALLAM, 1843-1864   **4241**

WINDOW ON THE WAR. Edited by John David Smith and William

Cooper, Jr. Lexington, Ky.: Lexington-Fayette County Historic Commission, 1976. 53 pp.

1862-1864. Extracts from diary kept by daughter of prominent family in Lexington, reflecting the conflicting loyalties of border states; views of a staunch unionist, recording war news, experiencing Confederate occupation of the city and reporting enemy's acts of destruction; derogatory remarks about Confederate soldiers and blacks; frequent mention of Henrietta Morgan, mother of John Hunt Morgan, and her family; notes on social events, politics and prices.

PETICOLAS, ALFRED BROWN, 1838-1915   **4242**

REBELS ON THE RIO GRANDE. Edited by Don E. Alberts. Albuquerque: University of New Mexico Press, 1984. 187 pp.

Feb-Jun 1862. Victoria, Texas, lawyer's diary of the Confederate invasion of New Mexico; service as sergeant, Company C, Fourth Texas Mounted Volunteers, part of Sibley's brigade; battles of Valverde and Glorieta; hard marches, especially the grueling retreat to El Paso; substantial entries containing arresting word images of the campaign and diarist's sketches of what he saw; notes on countryside and settlements, Mexicans, Santa Fe, reading, his comrades, etc.; praise of officers James Reily and Bethel Coopwood and criticism of Sibley; reference to and brief quotes from prewar diary kept in Amherst County, Virginia, within editor's biography of the diarist.

PETTIT, IRA S., 1841-1864   **4243**

THE DIARY OF A DEAD MAN. Compiled by Jean P. Ray. N.p., 1969. 203 pp. Diary, pp. 1-167 passim. 1972. 262 pp. 1976. 430 pp. Diary, pp. 1-173 passim.

1862-1863. Interwoven diary and letters; farm chores and weather near Wilson, New York, before enlistment in the Eleventh Infantry Regiment, United States Army; drills, duties, events and activities in camps at Fort Independence, Boston, and near Falmouth, Virginia; brief notes on Christmas festivities and review of the army by Lincoln; battle of Chancellorsville; on the march to Pennsylvania, the battle of Gettysburg and following Lee's forces back into Virginia; on leave in New York City; campaigning in Virginia.

PITTS, FLORISON   **4244**

Kaiser, Lee M., ed. "The Civil War Diary of Florison D. Pitts." MID-AMERICA 40 (1958):22-63.

1862-1865 (with gap). Extracts from diary of Illinois bugler, serving with the Chicago Mercantile Battery; various military operations along the Mississippi from Memphis to New Orleans; battles of Chickasaw Bluffs and Arkansas Post; the Vicksburg campaign and the battles of Port Gibson and Champion's Hill; expedition to Matagorda Bay, Texas; Red River campaign and battle of Sabine Cross Roads; battery's refusal to serve as infantry at Camp Parapet, New Orleans; good-natured view of the soldier's everyday life; amusements, housing, food and foraging, the diversions of music and reading, drinking among the troops, sightseeing in New Orleans, Sanitary Commission's distributions, army slang, etc.

In TRAGIC YEARS, by Paul M. Angle and Earl S. Miers, vol. 2, pp. 725-726.

Nov 1863. Louisiana camp life described in additional extracts from original manuscript.

PITTS, JOSEPH J.   4245

Martin, John M., ed. "A Methodist Circuit Rider between the Lines." TENNESSEE HISTORICAL QUARTERLY 19 (1960):252-269.

1862-1864. Diary of Methodist clergyman on Smith's Fork Circuit of the Tennessee Conference, some fifty miles east of Nashville; primarily a record of his clerical activities but reflecting war's impact on the area and on his work; shortages and disruption of attendance at church services; destruction and depredations by Union soldiers; having to take oath of allegiance in order to stay on the circuit; teaching at the New Middleton Male and Female Institute with mention of discipline problems, curriculum and prices.

POE, JAMES T., 1829-1913   4246

THE RAVING FOE: THE CIVIL WAR DIARY OF MAJOR JAMES T. POE. C.S.A. Compiled and edited by J.C. Poe. Eastland, Texas: Printed by the Longhorn Press, 1967. 72, 56 pp. Diary, pp. 42-51.

Jul-Aug 1862. Summary of the organization and activities of the Eleventh Arkansas followed by brief prison diary; conditions at Johnson's Island; war news and rumors of pending exchange.

POLIGNAC, CAMILLE ARMAND JULES MARIE,   4247
prince de, 1832-1913

"Camille Polignac's Service." CIVIL WAR TIMES ILLUSTRATED 19 (August 1980):8-18; (October 1980):34-41.

Apr-Oct 1862. Diary of French aristocrat, Crimean War veteran, who became a Confederate major general; lieutenant colonel on Beauregard's staff; at Corinth and retreating to Tupelo; participation in Kirby Smith's invasions of Kentucky as staff officer and as lieutenant colonel of the Fifth Tennessee at the battle of Richmond; a warm reception from citizens of Lexington; intrigues of fellow officers leading to his resignation from the regiment and return to Smith's staff; text of his farewell address; frustration with the unruliness and democratic ways of the American soldier; his efforts to secure rank of brigadier general; notes on Butler's General Order No. 28, Bragg, Beauregard and Confederate strategy; a record of his activities and motivations, reflecting a considerable ego and intense ambition.

POMEROY, FERNANDO E., b. 1837   4248

Downes, Randolph C., ed. "The Civil War Diary of Fernando E. Pomeroy," NORTHWEST OHIO QUARTERLY 19 (1947):129-156.

1862-1865. Extracts from diary of Lambertville, Michigan, resident, serving in the Eighteenth Michigan Infantry; early days in camp at Hillsdale; hospital duty in Lexington, Kentucky; captured near Danville, Kentucky, and confined to Camp Chase on parole; patrol duty and guarding Confederate and Union prisoners at Nashville; based at Decatur, Alabama, protecting lines of communication between Nashville and Union armies in Georgia and eastern Tennessee; stationed at Huntsville; return home and mustering out; notes on food, work, camp life, a slave sale in Lexington, contrabands, Lincoln's assassination, etc.

POWELL, MILDRED ELIZABETH, 1842?-1877   4249

In REMINISCENCES OF THE WOMEN OF MISSOURI DURING THE SIXTIES, by United Daughters of the Confederacy, Missouri Division, pp. 148-183. Jefferson City, Mo.: Hugh Stephens Printing, 192-?.

Sep 1862-Feb 1863. Extracts from journal of fiery, outspoken Confederate sympathizer; arrest at Palmyra, Missouri, by Union soldiers; sufferings of imprisonment there and at Mexico and Hannibal; retaliatory execution of ten Southern men at Palmyra; cruelties of her captors and support and kindnesses of family, friends and strangers; expressions of Southern patriotism.

POWER, ELLEN LOUISE   4250

"Excerpts from the Diary of Ellen Louise Power." UNITED DAUGHTERS OF THE CONFEDERACY MAGAZINE 11, no. 12 (1948):11.

1862-1863. Diary kept at West Feliciana, Louisiana, plantation; local war news concerning Jackson, Clinton, Port Hudson, etc.; a Yankee raid on diarist's larder; dates mixed up.

PRESSLEY, JOHN G.   4251

"Extracts from the Diary of Lieutenant-Colonel John G. Pressley, of the Twenty-fifth South Carolina Volunteers." SOUTHERN HISTORICAL SOCIETY PAPERS 14 (1886):35-62.

1862-1863. Diary extracts obviously written up some time later and expanded upon; operations at Charleston; an expedition to Pocataligo and two expeditions to Wilmington; special assignment to board evaluating officers and a court-martial; command of regiment; military operations at Charleston; opinions on state legislature's involvement in military reorganization; notes on camp life, discipline, sickness, casualties, troop reviews, Sabbath observance, speculators, etc.

"The Wee Nee Volunteers of Williamsburg District, South Carolina; in the first (Hagood's) Regiment." SOUTHERN HISTORICAL SOCIETY PAPERS 16 (1888):116-194. Diary, pp. 135-189 passim.

1862-1864. What appear to be diary extracts embedded in reminiscences; engagements at Charleston; transfer of the Twenty-fifth South Carolina Volunteers to Virginia where diarist was wounded.

PRESTON, MARGARET JUNKIN, 1820-1897   4252

In THE LIFE AND LETTERS OF MARGARET JUNKIN PRESTON, by Elizabeth R. Allan, pp. 134-208 passim. Boston and New York: Houghton Mifflin, 1903.

1862-1865. Extracts from diary of poetess, raised in Pennsylvania, wife of Virginia Military Institute professor; wartime conditions and family matters in Lexington; war news, prices and shortages; casualties including her stepsons; fears for husband serving with the Confederate forces; hardship of separation from her family in the North; funeral of Stonewall Jackson whose first wife was the diarist's sister; pillaging of her home and destruction in the town; saving Jackson's sword; notes on slaves' behavior during war and afterwards; description of children's war games.

QUINCY, SAMUEL MILLER, 1833-1887   4253

HISTORY OF THE SECOND MASSACHUSETTS REGIMENT OF INFANTRY. A PRISONER'S DIARY. Boston: G.H. Ellis, Printer, 1882. 24 pp.

Aug-Oct 1862. Extracts from officer's diary; prisoner of war in hospital at Staunton, Virginia, and at Libby Prison; long, sporadic entries summarizing events from his wounding and capture at Cedar Mountain to his arrival at Washington, D.C., upon being paroled; notes on hospital and prison conditions; commentary on differing attitudes of Confederate soldiers and Staunton civilians towards Union prisoners.

RATHBUN, ISAAC R.   4254

Cavanaugh, Lawrence R., ed. "A Civil War Diary." NEW YORK HISTORY 36 (1955):336-345.

Aug 1862-Jan 1863. Company D, Eighty-sixth New York Volunteers, member's experiences after being wounded at Second Bull Run; treatment on the field, chatting with enemy soldiers while in Confederate hands and journey to Harwood Hospital in Washington, D.C.; a very rough voyage on the DANIEL WEBSTER; service as nurse at the United States Army Hospital, Central Park, until discharged; a train accident on his way home to Steuben.

READY, ALICE   4255

In HEROINES OF DIXIE, edited by Katharine M. Jones, pp. 83-93.

Mar 1862. Extracts from diary of young lady of Murfreesboro, Tennessee, whose sister, Mattie, would marry John Hunt Morgan; socializing with Confederate officers, including General Hardee; Morgan's exploits; anxiety for brothers and friends.

RHODES, SAMUEL, 1841-1864   4256

Horst, Samuel L., ed. "The Journal of a Refugee." MENNONITE HISTORICAL REVIEW 54 (1980):280-304.

1862-1864. Journal kept by Rockingham County, Virginia, Mennonite forced to leave his home to avoid conscription into Confederate service; summary of events leading up to arrival in Maryland; clusters of brief daily notations and more summarizing entries covering work in Frederick County, Maryland, and Altoona, Pennsylvania, journey to Iowa and work there in a wagon-making shop; evidence that most, if not all, of this record composed somewhat after the fact.

RICHARDS, LOUIS, 1842-1924   4257

ELEVEN DAYS IN THE MILITIA DURING THE WAR OF THE REBELLION. By a militiaman. Philadelphia: Collins, Printer, 1883. 58 pp.

Sep 1862. Personal journal, much rewritten years later, giving account of tour of duty with Company G, Second Regiment, Pennsylvania Militia, in response to threat posed by Lee's invasion of Maryland; formation of unit in Reading; in camp at Harrisburg, Chambersburg and Hagerstown.

ROE, FRANCIS A.   4258

In OFFICIAL RECORDS OF THE UNION AND CONFEDERATE NAVIES IN THE WAR OF THE REBELLION, ser. 1, vol. 18, pp. 765-773; vol. 19, pp. 770-779.

Apr-May, Jul-Oct, Dec 1862. Extracts from Union naval lieutenant's diary; commanding the PENSACOLA in attack on the Mississippi River forts Jackson and St. Philip; the fall of New Orleans; detailed notes on preparing ships for battle, the engagements, the forts' defenses and civilian behavior; commanding the KATAHDIN on duty between New Orleans and Baton Rouge; destruction of the Confederate ram ARKANSAS; being fired upon by various small Southern units along the river; military events at Baton Rouge and Donaldsonville; eyeing Port

Hudson's defenses; criticism of Farragut; notes on activities of other Union ships.

ROGERS, SARAH ELIZABETH, b. 1843   4259

Clopper, E.N. ed. "Country Life during the Civil War." HISTORICAL AND PHILOSOPHICAL SOCIETY OF OHIO BULLETIN 9 (1951):171-196.

1862-1864. Extracts from the diary of a young woman living in Fairfield Township, Butler County; bible reading, domestic tasks and social activities; the nearby town of Hamilton and assignments at the academy she attended there; her support of Clement Vallandigham and the Peace Democrats; notes on friends, family members, her music teacher and her future husband, Union soldier Henry Moser.

ROHRER, JEREMIAH   4260

In HISTORY OF THE 127th REGIMENT, PENNSYLVANIA VOLUNTEERS, FAMILIARLY KNOWN AS THE "DAUPHIN COUNTY REGIMENT," by Pennsylvania Infantry, 127th Regiment, pp. 267-298. Lebanon, Pa.: Press of Report Publishing, 1902?

Dec 1862-May 1863. Extracts from major's diary with perhaps some later additions; weather, duties and amusements in Virginia; celebration of St. Patrick's Day in Meagher's Irish Brigade.

ROPES, HANNAH ANDERSON CHANDLER, 1809-1863   4261

CIVIL WAR NURSE: THE DIARY AND LETTERS OF HANNAH ROPES. Edited by John R. Brumgardt. Knoxville: University of Tennessee Press, 1980. 149 pp. Diary, pp. 71-119 passim.

Oct-Dec 1862. Diary kept, with a view to future publication, by Bedford, Massachusetts reformer, abolitionist, Swedenborgian and authoress, now matron of the Union Hotel Hospital, Georgetown, D.C.; conflict with head surgeon and the hospital steward over treatment of the wounded; successful appeal to Secretary Stanton after rebuff from Surgeon General William A. Hammond; hospital conditions, her work and regard for patients; deathbed scenes; notes on the Sanitary Commission, gathering a Thanksgiving feast and soldiers' drinking and tobacco chewing; comments about members of her staff, including Louisa May Alcott in whose HOSPITAL SKETCHES the diarist was praised; a much too brief view of a strong, caring personality.

ROSE, ALEXANDER GRANT, 1838-1920   4262

THE CIVIL WAR DIARIES OF ALEXANDER GRANT ROSE. Edited by Alexander G. Rose III. Baltimore: A.G. Rose III, 1974. 110 leaves. Diary, pp. 1-84.

Oct 1862-Sep 1863, Aug 1864-Jun 1865. Record of Albany, New York, clerk's experiences as an enlisted man, first with Company B, 177th New York Volunteers, and in 1864 with Company C, Eleventh Regiment, New York Independent Battery, Light Artillery; aboard the steamer MERRIMACK from New York City to the Mississippi with a stop at Hilton Head, South Carolina; service as clerk in brigade quartermaster's department on the outer defense perimeter of New Orleans; sightseeing in that city; serving as courier during expedition to capture Port Hudson; journey up the Mississippi and collision with another vessel; homecoming festivities at Buffalo and Albany; in camp near New York City; good transport accommodations by sea to City Point, going directly into the lines at Petersburg; pressing Lee toward Appomattox; notes on election day celebrations, Lincoln's assassination and sightseeing in Washington, D.C.

ROWE, GEORGE HENRY CLAY, 1830-1878   4263

Griffith, Lucille, ed. "Fredericksburg's Political Hostages." VIRGINIA MAGAZINE OF HISTORY AND BIOGRAPHY 72 (1964):395-429. Diary, pp. 399-429.

Aug-Sep 1862. Prison diary of Fredericksburg resident, a lawyer and newspaperman; arrest with eleven other citizens in retaliation for incarceration of several supposedly unionist townspeople by Confederate authorities; hospitable reception from Burnside at Chatham; transport to Old Capitol Prison at Washington, D.C.; conditions there; the intriguing prisoner Belle Boyd; jokes and pranks; sketches of fellow prisoners from Fredericksburg, including Mayor Montgomery Slaughter, John Coakley, John H. Roberts, Michael Ames and Abraham Cox; good times with fellow inmate John C. Hunter; the Reverend Broaddus's unsuccessful mission to Richmond to arrange an exchange; the beginning of diarist's journey through devastated Virginia to reopen negotiations; lengthy entries presenting a vivid, well-written account.

ROWLAND, KATE MASON   4264

In LADIES OF RICHMOND, by Katharine M. Jones, pp. 145-148, 165-168, 172-173, 235-236.

1862-1864. Extracts from diary of young refugee from Alexandria; war news; observation of Confederate Congress in session; nursing at Camp Winder Hospital; funeral services for Stonewall Jackson; Richmond social life; soldiers' hardships.

RUMLEY, CHARLES, 1824-1897   4265

Howard, Helen Addison, ed. "Diary of Charles Rumley from St. Louis to Portland." FRONTIER AND MIDLAND 19 (1939):190-200. Reprint. Sources of Northwest History, no. 28. Missoula: State University of Montana, 1939. 11 pp. FRONTIER OMNIBUS, edited by John W. Hakola, pp. 230-242.

May-Oct 1862. Brief notes of travel by Missouri steamboat EMILIE from St. Louis to Fort Benton, with nonchalant references to shooting buffalo trying to swim the river; overland across Montana with a bit of prospecting en route; to Walla Walla on Mullan Road, giving a table of distances and campgrounds available to travelers; a few notes of expenses.

RUMPEL, JOHN WESLEY, 1844-1910   4266

Rosenberger, H.E., ed. "Ohiowa Soldier." ANNALS OF IOWA, 3d ser. 36 (1961):111-148.

Jun 1862, Apr-May, Sep-Dec 1863. A few extracts from Fifty-fifth Ohio Infantry private's diary; operations in the Shenandoah Valley and the battle of Cross Keys; Chancellorsville; journey from Virginia to Alabama and the Chattanooga campaign.

SAUNDERS, ELLEN VIRGINIA, b. 1848?   4267

"War-time Journal of a 'Little Rebel.'" CONFEDERATE VETERAN 27 (1919):451-452; 28 (1920):11-12.

1862-1864. Extracts from teenager's journal kept at Rocky Hill, near Courtland, Alabama, as a refugee in Huntsville and in Tuscaloosa where she attended the Tuscaloosa Female College; activities, family concerns and her social life which included prom-

inent generals and other Confederate officers; patriotic sentiments; notes on Nathan B. Forrest.

SESSIONS, JAMES OLIVER HAZARD PERRY   4268

Fike, Claude E., ed. "Diary of James Oliver Hazard Perry Sessions of Rokeby Plantation on the Yazoo." JOURNAL OF MISSISSIPPI HISTORY 39 (1977):239-254.

1862-1863. Extracts from Mississippi planter's diary embedded in editor's summary of the document's contents; an account of life on a modest plantation, reflecting the problems of weather, disease and war; a flood engulfing crops and livestock; illnesses of whites and blacks; depredations by soldiers of both armies; departure of many slaves after Vicksburg's fall.

SEXTON, FRANKLIN BARLOW, b. 1828   4269

Estill, Mary S., ed. "Diary of a Confederate Congressman." SOUTHWESTERN HISTORICAL QUARTERLY 38 (1935):270-301; 39 (1935):33-65.

Jul 1862-May 1863. San Augustine, Texas, lawyer's diary covering part of his tenure in the congress of the Confederate States of America; journey to Richmond; the issues before the congress, such as conscription, taxation, appropriations, limiting cotton production, waging offensive versus defensive war, increasing pay of soldiers and government employees, martial law and the currency; his opinions and votes on these matters; his efforts on behalf of constituents and individual soldiers; appraisal of colleagues including Henry S. Foote and Louis T. Wigfall; notes on social life, sermons, health, war news, hunger riot in Richmond, etc.; a candid, interesting account.

SHATTUCK, TYLER M.   4270

In A HISTORY OF THE EIGHTH REGIMENT OF NEW HAMPSHIRE VOLUNTEERS, by John M. Stanyan, pp. 38-140, 404-462 passim.

Jan-Jul, Oct 1862, Apr-May 1864. Extracts from diary of noncommissioned officer later promoted to lieutenant; commissary duties; events during voyage to Ship Island, Mississippi; action in Louisiana including battle of Sabine Cross Roads; retreat from the Red River campaign.

SHEERAN, JAMES B., 1819-1881   4271

CONFEDERATE CHAPLAIN, A WAR JOURNAL. Edited by Joseph T. Durkin. Milwaukee: Bruce, 1960. 168 pp.

1862-1865 (with gaps). Extracts from record kept by Irish immigrant, former resident of the North, now a fiery Southern patriot; service as Catholic chaplain of the Fourteenth Louisiana but with a seemingly wide-ranging arena of concern and activity; celebrating the Mass, administering sacraments and caring for the wounded; conversing with and chastising prisoners of war; discouraging drinking, gambling and profanity and rebuking officers for immoral conduct; miliatry action at Cedar Mountain, Second Bull Run, Antietam, Gettysburg and the Wilderness and the grisly sights of the Chancellorsville and Spotsylvania battlefields; notes on soldiers' behavior, morale, straggling and desertion; an interview with Lee and visits with General Ewell and his wife; stopping at Frederick, Maryland, travel through Georgia and delivering a sermon under fire in Charleston; with Early's Washington raid; crossing enemy lines to be with Confederate wounded at Winchester; imprisoned there and at Baltimore and Fort McHenry;

dismal prison conditions and his efforts to improve inmates' behavior; interview with Sheridan, securing a parole; horseback journey up the devastated Shenandoah Valley; return to his Redemptorist brethren at New Orleans at war's end; a somewhat jumbled and incomplete text but, nevertheless, a compelling account of the experiences and perceptions of a strong-minded, resolute and outspoken, yet essentially humble, man of integrity.

SHOTWELL, RANDOLPH ABBOTT, 1844-1885   4272

THE PAPERS OF RANDOLPH ABBOTT SHOTWELL. Edited by J.G. de Roulhac Hamilton. Raleigh: North Carolina Historical Commission, 1929-1936. 3 vols. Diary, vol. 1, pp. 153-171, 366-501 passim, vol. 2, pp. 33-202, 493-556 passim, vol. 3, pp. 1-429 passim.

1862-1865, 1871-1873. Extracts from diary strung through narrative of his war and prison experiences; serving with the Eighth Virginia in North Carolina and Virginia; lengthy commentary on war's progress and the Confederate government; denunciation of Winder's rule in Richmond; account of march to Gettysburg and retreat to the Rapidan but not the battle; prison conditions and incidents at Fort Delaware after capture near Cold Harbor; notes on prices, black Union soldiers, death of Jeb Stuart, Lincoln's assassination, etc.; postwar imprisonment for alleged Ku Klux Klan activities in North Carolina; in jail at Rutherfordton, Marion and Raleigh; sentenced to six years in the federal penitentiary at Albany; conditions of confinement, physical suffering, the political issues of his situation, support from friends, family and colleagues, etc.; pardon from President Grant; lengthy entries of impassioned opinion.

Extracts in THE BLUE AND THE GRAY, edited by Henry S. Commager, vol. 2, pp. 697-700.

Jul-Aug, Oct 1864. Awful conditions at Fort Delaware.

SLIFER, ELI   4274

Oliphant, James O., ed. "Newly Accessible Papers Offer Glimpses of Civil War's Impact on Life in Susquehanna Valley." PENNSYLVANIA DEPARTMENT OF INTERNAL AFFAIRS MONTHLY BULLETIN 23, no. 5 (1955):19-22, 27; no. 6, 12-15, 18-22. Diary, no. 6, pp. 13-15, 18, 21-22.

Jan-Dec 1862, Jan-Jul 1865. Extracts from diary together with letters of Pennsylvania's secretary of the commonwealth; very brief entries, noting work at Harrisburg, the comings and goings of Governor Curtin and matters at diarist's farm near Lewisburg; militia response during the Antietam campaign; passage of Lincoln's funeral train through Harrisburg; attendance at the Grand Review.

SMITH, ROBERT DAVIS, 1842-1910   4275

CONFEDERATE DIARY OF ROBERT D. SMITH. Transcribed by Jill K. Garrett. Columbia, Tenn.: Captain James Madison Sparkman Chapter, United Daughters of the Confederacy, 1975. 88 pp.

1862-1863, Feb-Jul, Oct 1864. Columbia, Tennessee, youth's account of war service; member of Company B, Second Tennessee Infantry, the Maury Rifles; a precarious train trip from Chattanooga to Huntsville and on to Corinth; battle of Shiloh and evacuation of Corinth; in Tupelo; to eastern Tennessee via Mobile and Atlanta; appointed ordnance officer for Cleburne's command; Kentucky campaign, including the battles of Richmond and Perryville and noting pro-Southern enthusiasm in Lexington and pro-Union sentiment in Barbourville; return to Tennessee and appointment as

ordnance officer for Leonidas Polk's brigade; battle of Stones River; the Atlanta campaign; retreat to Alabama; notes on duties and his accomplishments, social activities, camp life, reading, food, his illnesses, prices, execution of deserters, battlefield booty, killing a black soldier, Tennessee unionists, etc.; references to his father, the Rev. Franklin Gillette Smith, head of the Atheneum in Columbia, his brother William Austin Smith and Confederate generals Kirby Smith, Bragg, Hardee and, especially, Patrick Cleburne.

SMITH, THOMAS CRUTCHER, 1843-1913   4276

HERE'S YER MULE. Waco: Little Texas Press, W.M. Morrison Pub., 1958. 40 pp.

Mar-Dec 1862. Diary kept by Confederate sergeant, Company G, Wood's Regiment, Thirty-second Texas Cavalry; description of countryside passed through from home in Clinton to San Antonio, noting lack of patriotism in the latter city; stationed near San Marcos, at Fredericksburg and Fort Clark, Brackettville, in Kinney County; notes on fellow company members, execution of traitors or bushwhackers, food, gambling, profanity and a dream; rules of debating society; record of expenses.

SOUTHWICK, THOMAS PAINE, 1837-1892   4277

A DURYEE ZOUAVE. Washington, D.C.: Acme Printing, 1930. 119 pp. Diary, pp. 91-119.

Oct 1862-May 1863. Extracts from war diary seemingly left intact at end of memoir of service in the Fifth New York Volunteers; notes on campaigning in Virginia; soldiers' enthusiasm for McClellan and Gouverneur K. Warren; long description of battle of Fredericksburg.

SPEER, WILLIAM HENRY ASBURY, d. 1864   4278

Murphy, James B., ed. "A Confederate Soldier's View of Johnson's Island Prison." OHIO HISTORY 79 (1970):101-111.

May-Aug 1862. Extracts from diary of Yadkin County soldier, a captain in the Twenty-eighth North Carolina Volunteers, apparently written up a bit after the fact; reaction of Union soldiers as Confederate prisoners were marched from capture at Hanover Court House to White House Landing; imprisoned at Governor's Island in New York harbor and then at Johnson's Island; receiving help from Northern Masons; notes on the pastimes of prisoners and prison conditions; an account interestingly flavored by the reactions, assessments and spellings of the diarist.

SPRENGER, GEORGE F.   4279

CONCISE HISTORY OF THE CAMP AND FIELD LIFE OF THE 122d REGIMENT, PENN'A VOLUNTEERS. Lancaster, Pa.: New Era Steam Book Print, 1885. 372 pp.

Aug 1862-May 1863. Diary, obviously reworked and expanded, kept by sergeant in Company K; in camp and action in Virginia; weather, duties, illness, deaths, hardships, amusements, Christmas celebrations, provisions, foraging, etc.; drills, dress parades and reviews; battles of Second Bull Run, Fredericksburg and Chancellorsville; mustering out and welcome home in Lancaster.

SPRINGER, AUSTIN D.   4280

In THE SOLDIER OF INDIANA IN THE WAR FOR THE UNION, by

Catharine Merrill, vol. 1, pp. 473-476.

> Jun 1862. Prisoner of war experience of drummer, Company F, Seventh Indians; capture at Port Republic; rigors of journey to Lynchburg and imprisonment there.

STAGER, HENRY J.   4281

In HISTORY OF THE ONE HUNDRED AND TWENTY-FOURTH REGIMENT, PENNSYLVANIA VOLUNTEERS, by Pennsylvania Infantry, 124th Regiment, pp. 150-190 passim.

> Aug 1862-May 1863. Extracts from diary of sergeant of Company G, interspersed with other documents; first days in the army; battle of Antietam; in camp and on duty at Maryland Heights, Loudon Valley, Stafford Court House and Aquia Creek; battle of Chancellorsville.

STAMPER, ISSAC J.   4282

THE CIVIL WAR DIARY OF ISSAC J. STAMPER. Cleveland, Tenn.: Cleveland Public Library, 1970. 82 leaves.

> 1862-1863. Account of enlisted man, later lieutenant, serving with the Forty-third Tennessee; campaigning in Kentucky, in camp in Tennessee and furlough home to Bradley County; transfer to Vicksburg and the siege; parole, trip home and exchange; siege of Knoxville; nicely descriptive entries covering events and activities of camp life, food, marches and military operations, punishments and executions, etc.

STAUFFER, NELSON   4283

CIVIL WAR DIARY. American Classics Facsimile Series - 4. Northridge: California State University, Northridge Libraries, 1976. ca. 150 pp.

> 1862-1865. Brief daily entries, with occasional longer anecdotal or "poetical" passages apparently added later, detailing a soldier's life in Company A, Sixty-third Illinois Infantry; early days in camp at Bird's Point, Missouri, and then into Kentucky, Tennessee, Mississippi, Louisiana and Alabama; Missionary Ridge and the dreadful sights of the battlefield; marching through Georgia with Sherman to Savannah; by steamer to Beaufort, South Carolina; entry into Columbia, jubilation of the slaves and the fire; through North Carolina to Raleigh, noting friendliness of that city's inhabitants, and Virginia, then to Washington, D.C., and the Grand Review; commentary on the Sanitary Commission's neglect of the western army; sightseeing at the Smithsonian Institution and the Patent Office; on the Baltimore and Ohio Railroad and down the Ohio to Louisville, attendance at Campbellite church service; mustering out and journey home; statistical account of his duties, pay and miles covered; list of his company's dead.

STEELE, JOHN MAGILL, 1853-1936   4284

"Diary of John Magill Steele and Sarah Eliza Steele," WINCHESTER-FREDERICK COUNTY HISTORICAL SOCIETY PAPERS 3 (1955):61-94.

> May 1862, 1863-1864. Diary kept, in Newtown, Virginia, with their mother's help, by younger siblings of Nimrod Hunter Steele; a single 1862 entry followed by daily recording of events; household tasks and family activities; local and war news; constant traffic of Confederate and Union soldiers through the town; refugees

and wounded taken into their home; deaths of father and sister; a matter-of-fact, engrossing account.

STEINER, LEWIS HENRY   4285

REPORT OF LEWIS H. STEINER, M.D., INSPECTOR OF THE SANITARY COMMISSION. New York: D.F. Randolph, 1862. 43 pp. Diary, pp. 5-28.

Extracts in THE UNION READER, edited by Richard B. Harwell, pp. 156-174. New York: Longmans, Green, 1958.

> Sep 1862. Diary contained within report to the Sanitary Commission's secretary, Frederick L. Olmsted, concerning events in Frederick, Maryland, while it was occupied by Confederate troops; appearance and behavior of soldiers; blacks serving in the Confederate army; unionist and secessionist support in the town; some anecdotes possibly used as basis for Barbara Fritchie story; notes on Stonewall Jackson, Howell Cobb and Jeb Stuart.

STOCKTON, JOSEPH, 1833-1907   4286

WAR DIARY (1862-5) OF BREVET BRIGADIER GENERAL JOSEPH STOCKTON. Chicago: 1910. 35 pp.

> 1862-1865 (with gaps). Chicagoan's record of service with the Seventy-second Illinois Infantry, advancing in rank from lieutenant in Company A to lieutenant colonel of the regiment; in camp at Cairo; operations in Kentucky, Tennessee and Mississippi; the Vicksburg campaign; refusing appointment to Grant's staff; military details, including mention of the Indian sharpshooters of the Fourteenth Wisconsin; interaction with Confederate prisoners after the surrender; expedition to Louisiana, confiscating provisions and liberating blacks; stationed at Vicksburg; wounding at battle of Franklin; in terrible camp near New Orleans; investing Spanish Fort at Mobile; reaction to news of Lincoln's assassination; final days in uniform before August discharge; notes on drinking and religion in the army, contrabands, University of Mississippi, etc.; diary rewritten and supplemented by letters.

STONE, E. WYMAN, b. 1831?   4287

Mariani, Paul, ed. "From the Civil War Diary and Letters of Corporal E.W. Stone, 21st Massachusetts." MASSACHUSETTS REVIEW 16 (1975):759-780. Diary, pp. 772-779.

> Mar-Apr 1862. Extracts from diary of resident of the Otter River district of Templeton, Massachusetts; conditions aboard the NORTHERNER off Roanoke Island; wounded at battle of New Bern; stoically suffering in New Bern hospital until amputation of his foot.

STONER, GEORGE W., 1830-1912   4288

"Diary of George W. Stoner." WISCONSIN MAGAZINE OF HISTORY 21 (1937-1938):194-212, 322-336, 420-431; 22 (1938):74-89.

> Jan-Dec 1862. Record of daily activities of Madison, Wisconsin, resident, a state government clerk; work, leisure, weather and household chores; local, state and war events; brief notes on many individuals; death of Governor Harvey.

STOOKEY, JAMES M.   4289

In EPISODES OF THE CIVIL WAR, by George W. Herr, pp. 371-374. San Francisco: Bancroft, 1890.

Apr-May 1862. Extracts from diary kept by captain, Company E, Fifty-ninth Illinois; mostly regiment's movements in Missouri and Arkansas.

STRANG, ELLEN   4290

Greene, Lida L., ed. "Diary of a Young Girl: Grundy County to Correctionville, 1862." ANNALS OF IOWA, 3d ser. 36 (1961-1963):437-457.

Nov 1862-Apr 1863. Quaker girl's account of a visit to her married sister Sarah Ann Kellogg; farm work and household chores, hearing her nieces' lessons; mention of various travelers and Union soldiers lodging with the family; a spotted fever epidemic and nursing of the sick, including her sister, who eventually died, whereupon diarist assumed all housework and child care.

STRATTON, EDWARD L.   4291

In HISTORY OF THE MEN OF COMPANY F, by New Jersey Infantry, 12th Regiment, pp. 29-36. Camden, N.J.: C.S. McGrath, Printer, 1897.

Sep 1862-May 1863. Extracts from diary of officer with the Twelfth New Jersey; moving to the front from Ellicott Mill, Maryland, with a stop in Washington, D.C., to Falmouth, Virginia; marching towards Chancellorsville where the diarist lost a leg.

STRIBLING, MARY CARY AMBLER, 1835-1868   4292

In THE YEARS OF ANGUISH, FAUQUIER COUNTY, VIRGINIA, compiled by Emily G. Ramey and John K. Gott, pp. 109-138.

Apr-May 1862. Extracts from journal kept by Lucy Johnston Ambler's daughter at Morven for the dual purpose of recording events and self-examination; long narrative-type entries reflecting diarist's efforts to come to terms with the war, Union occupation, departure of slaves and submission to God's will; description of plundering of Morven; notes on differences of opinion within her family over war issues and interaction with Yankees.

STROTHER, DAVID HUNTER, 1816-1888   4293

A VIRGINIA YANKEE IN THE CIVIL WAR. Edited by Cecil D. Eby, Jr. Chapel Hill: University of North Carolina Press, 1961. 294 pp.

1862-1864 (with gap). Extracts from diary of "Porte Crayon," noted writer and artist, a native of Berkeley County, who chose the Union cause; serving on the staffs of Banks, Pope, McClellan, Kelley, Sigel and Hunter; participating in the Shenandoah Valley campaign of 1862, Cedar Mountain, the Second Bull Run campaign and Antietam; with Banks in New Orleans, commenting on Butler's regime there; the 1863 Red River campaign and return to Washington, D.C., via Havana; the battle of New Market; destruction and pillaging in the Shenandoah Valley and diarist's justification of the burning of the Virginia Military Institute; Early's raid and the diarist's resignation from the army; notes on his topographical and other duties; details of family rifts and reunions; his opinion of his commanders and other military figures, including Hooker, Farragut, Heintzelman, Schurz and Fitz-John Porter, and of Lincoln; his views on blacks and slavery; interviews with Stanton and Arthur I. Boreman, governor of West Virginia; lengthy, interesting, daily entries describing military operations and reflecting the divided loyalties of western Virginia.

Eby, Cecil B., ed. "With Sigel at New Market." CIVIL WAR HISTORY 6 (1960):73-83.

May 1864. Extracts.

SWAN, JAMES GILCHRIST, 1818-1900   4294

In SWAN AMONG THE INDIANS: LIFE OF JAMES G. SWAN, 1818-1900, by Lucile McDonald, pp. 1-233 passim. Portland, Oreg.: Binfords & Mort, 1972.

In WINTER BROTHERS: A SEASON AT THE EDGE OF AMERICA, by Ivan Doig, pp. 1-252 passim. New York: Harcourt Brace Jovanovich, 1980.

1862-1890. Two books which quote extensively from the diaries of Bostonian who became a self-taught anthropologist, writer, teacher, artist and longtime friend of Northwest coastal Indians; teaching on the Makah Reservation at Neah Bay, Washington; travels about the Olympic Peninsula collecting Indian arts and crafts and preparing ethnographic reports for the Smithsonian and other institutions; working with Gov. Isaac Stevens on Indian treaties.

TAYLOR, B.F.   4295

In THE WAR OF THE 'SIXTIES, compiled by Edward R. Hutchins, pp. 36-51. New York: Neale, 1912.

Oct-Nov 1862. Union soldier's diary entries with much material reworked or added at a later date; on the march in the Fredericksburg campaign; supply problems; arrival opposite Fredericksburg.

TAYLOR, ISAAC LYMAN, 1837-1863   4296

Wolf, Hazel C., ed. "Campaigning with the First Minnesota." MINNESOTA HISTORY 25 (1944):11-39, 117-152, 224-257, 342-361.

1862-1863. Diary of private, formerly teacher in Fulton County, Illinois, now serving in Company E; at Edward's Ferry, Maryland, Harpers Ferry and Berryville, Virginia; seeing the sights of Washington, D.C., and Alexandria; the Peninsular campaign, battle of Fair Oaks and capture at Savage's Station when he and brother Henry voluntarily remained with the wounded; prison conditions at Richmond and Belle Isle; parole to Annapolis and later return to regiment at Harpers Ferry; advance to Fredericksburg, the battle and the ruined city; duty at Fredericksburg during the Chancellorsville campaign; march to Gettysburg and death in the regiment's charge on the second day of battle; notes on weather, camp life, duties, reading, foraging, drinking among the soldiers, deserters, war and political news, contrabands, military punishments, tombstone inscriptions, celebrating St. Patrick's Day, etc.; glimpses of McClellan, Burnside, Hooker, Lincoln and Meagher; reactions to the Army of the Potomac's command changes.

Extracts in BRING WARM CLOTHES, collected by Peg Meier, pp. 92, 94.

Jun-Jul 1863. Gettysburg campaign; comments on replacement of Hooker with Meade.

TAYLOR, ROBERT BELT, 1831-1888   4297

Tapp, Hambleton, ed. "The Battle of Perryville." KENTUCKY HISTORICAL SOCIETY REGISTER 60 (1962):255-292.

Oct 1862. Extracts from diary of Frankfort resident, serving in Union army as captain of Company I, Twenty-second Kentucky; hardships of the march from Brunerstown in pursuit of Bragg's forces; visiting along the way; remarks on cemetery at Bloomfield; notes on Gen. William R. Terrill; the battle of Perryville; treatment of his wounds while the army moves on to Bardstown; lengthy, nicely descriptive entries.

TEAL, JOHN W., 1828?-1880   4298

Walker, Henry P., ed. "Soldier in the California Column." ARIZONA AND THE WEST 13 (1971):33-82.

1862-1864 (with gaps). War diary of Canadian who had emigrated to California; service as private, Company B, Second California Volunteer Cavalry; operations in California, Arizona and New Mexico; encounters with hostile Indians; notes on duties, marches, events of the day, etc.; journey from San Francisco to Ontario via the Isthmus of Panama, with sightseeing in New York City.

THIEL, WILLIAM, b. 1837   4299

"Diary of William Thiel of Oregon." UMPQUA TRAPPER 12 (1976):83-94; 13 (1977):17-23, 30-47.

1862-1867. Diary of a German immigrant who farmed for many years in Douglas County; freight-hauling journeys in the area; farming for himself and others, with notes on crop yields and tasks; references to many local people.

THOBURN, THOMAS CRAWFORD, 1829-1911   4300

MY EXPERIENCES DURING THE CIVIL WAR. By Lyle Thoburn. Cleveland? 1963. 197 pp.

1862-1865 (with gap). Journal of enlisted member of Company F, Fiftieth Ohio, later an officer; campaigning in Kentucky, with a view of the field after the battle of Perryville; furlough home to Belmont County to vote in the effort to defeat Vallandigham; promotion to lieutenant while stationed near Knoxville; the Atlanta campaign and description of the fallen city; operations against Hood in Georgia, Alabama and Tennessee, including battles of Franklin and Nashville; the comforts of camp life at Washington, D.C., and sightseeing in the city; by sea to North Carolina; description of Fort Anderson, Wilmington and Union prisoners released from Salisbury; promotion to major, transfer to the 196th Ohio in the Shenandoah Valley and service as president of general court-martial, Hancock's Veteran Reserve Corps; comments on drinking, profanity and cardplaying among the troops, Copperheads, Tennessee women chewing tobacco, refugees and a Catholic mass; notes on duties, foraging, religious activities, the Christian Commission, exploring Kentucky caves, Southern countryside and agricultural practices, slaves' reaction to Union presence, etc.; substantial entries with later additions.

THOMPSON, JOSEPH DIMMIT, b. 1825   4301

Biel, John G., ed. "The Battle of Shiloh: From the Letters and Diary of Joseph Dimmit Thompson." TENNESSEE HISTORICAL QUARTERLY 17 (1958):250-274. Diary, pp. 255-261.

Apr 1862. Extracts from diary of member of Company B, Thirty-eighth Tennessee, recording the action and carnage of the battle.

Biel, John G., ed. "The Evacuation of Corinth." JOURNAL OF MISSISSIPPI HISTORY 24 (1962):40-56. Diary, pp. 47-52.

May-Jun 1862. Extracts describing evacuation of Corinth in the face of Halleck's advancing force.

TOOTLE, ELLEN BELL, d. 1904   4302

"The Diary of Mrs. Thomas E. Tootle: Journey to Denver." MUSEUM GRAPHIC 13, no. 2 (1961):3-19.

May-Aug 1862. Honeymoon diary, with entries beginning at Plattsmouth, Nebraska; notes on the area and their preparations for overland journey; thence by wagon to Denver, with notes on wagon trains bound for Pikes Peak, California or Washington; descriptions of Indians; observations on silver, gold and copper mining in the Central City, Colorado City and Pikes Peak areas; brief notes of return journey.

TORREY, RODNEY WEBSTER, b. 1836   4303

WAR DIARY OF RODNEY W. TORREY. N.p., 19--. 93 pp. Diary, pp. 5-73.

Oct 1862-Aug 1863. Company K, Forty-ninth Massachusetts, member's diary; last days at home near Windsor, Massachusetts; daily report of activities and weather; in camp at Pittsfield and on Long Island; sea voyage to New Orleans; at Carrollton and Baton Rouge; assaults on Port Hudson; talking with the enemy after the surrender and swapping food; journey up the Mississippi and then by train to Massachusetts; notes on military punishments, Southern crops and flora, Confederate deserters, foraging, etc.

TOWNE, LAURA MATILDA, 1825-1901   4304

LETTERS AND DIARY OF LAURA M. TOWNE: WRITTEN FROM THE SEA ISLANDS OF SOUTH CAROLINA. Edited by Rupert S. Holland, Cambridge, Mass.: Printed at the Riverside Press, 1912. Reprint. New York: Negro Universities Press, 1969. 310 pp. Diary, pp. 1-137.

1862-1884 (with gaps). Diary of a Northern woman who went, under auspices of the Port Royal Relief Committee of Philadelphia, as an agent of the federal government to assist freed slaves who had fled the plantations of the Sea Islands; enthusiastic and perceptive record of her activities as a teacher at Penn School, social and health worker, particularly in treating and preventing smallpox and malaria.

Extracts in WOMAN'S "TRUE" PROFESSION, by Nancy Hoffman, pp. 170-183.

1862-1877.

Extracts in IN THE CAGE: EYEWITNESS ACCOUNTS OF THE FREED NEGRO IN SOUTHERN SOCIETY, compiled by Alton Hornsby, pp. 17-20, 235-240. Chicago: Quadrangle Books, 1971.

1877-1879. Closing activities at Penn School; election in Georgia, especially defeat of Robert Smalls.

TRACY, CARLOS   4305

"Operations before Charleston in May and July 1862." SOUTHERN HISTORICAL SOCIETY PAPERS 8 (1880):541-547.

May-Jul 1862. Diary kept by colonel on Gen. States Rights Gist's staff; record of troop, gunboat and artillery encounters.

TRIMBLE, ISAAC RIDGEWAY, 1802-1888   4306

"The Civil War Diary of General Isaac Ridgeway Trimble." MARYLAND HISTORICAL MAGAZINE 17 (1922):1-20.

1862-1863. Irregularly kept record of Confederate general, a West Point graduate; Second Bull Run campaign and months spent recovering from wound; Gettysburg campaign and amputation of leg; in hospitals at Gettysburg and Baltimore, then imprisoned at Fort McHenry and Johnson's Island; prison conditions; opinions on Southern strategy at Gettysburg; reflections on the war addressed to Northerners.

TRIPLETT, JOE F.   **4307**

"The Scout's Story: From the Journal of a Cattleman." ATLANTIC MONTHLY 135 (January-June, 1925):493-500.

Patterson, Edna B., ed. "The Diary of Joe F. Triplett." NEVADA HISTORICAL SOCIETY QUARTERLY 2, no. 1 (1959):3-14.

May-Jun 1862. Colorful account of a mounted expedition of cattle owners from Carson City to recover a large herd presumably stolen by Paiute Indians; travel through the Carson, Truckee and Humboldt river areas and "other portions of this ill-begotten, God-forsaken, sagebrush, alkali, sand, lice and mosquito country"; route, difficulties with heat, lack of water, etc.; record of cattle rounded up from place to place; many references to J.B. Winters, captain of the group.

TUCKER, JOHN S., b. 1834   **4308**

Wilson, Gary, ed. "The Diary of John S. Tucker." ALABAMA HISTORICAL QUARTERLY 43 (1981):5-33.

1862-1863, May 1864-Feb 1865. Extracts from Greensboro, Alabama, resident's war diary; hardships of journey to Richmond with Company D, Fifth Alabama; Peninsular campaign including evacuation of Yorktown and battle of Williamsburg; battle of Fair Oaks; appointment as commissary sergeant, removing him from line of battle; observing stragglers and war's destruction as the army moved north in the Antietam campaign; description of half-buried dead at Cedar Mountain battlefield; condition of Fredericksburg in wake of the battle; Chancellorsville and Gettysburg campaigns; death of brother at Gettysburg; return to Virginia; the Wilderness, Spotsylvania campaign and Cold Harbor; siege of Petersburg; short entries with notes on drinking and profanity among the troops, the election of officers, pro-Southern feeling in Maryland, etc.

TURNER, EDWARD CARTER, 1816-1891   **4309**

In THE YEARS OF ANGUISH, FAUQUIER COUNTY, VIRGINIA, compiled by Emily G. Ramey and John K. Gott, pp. 15-44.

Aug-Dec 1862, Apr-May 1863. Diary of owner of Kinloch, chronicling war's effect on civilians as both Confederate and Union forces occupy the area; notes on weather, farm and business matters, General Ewell, Confederate stragglers and deserters, emancipation, plundering and cruelty; opinions about soldiers of both sides; death of son, one of Mosby's Rangers.

Sanford, Orlin M. "A Virginian's Diary in Civil War Days." AMERICANA 18 (Oct 1924):353-368.

Aug-Dec 1862. An abbreviated and somewhat paraphrased version.

VAN ALSTYNE, LAWRENCE, b. 1839   **4310**

DIARY OF AN ENLISTED MAN. New Haven, Conn.: Tuttle, Morehouse & Taylor, 1910. 348 pp.

Extracts in THE BLUE AND THE GRAY, edited by Henry S. Commager, vol. 1, pp. 270-271, 397-400; TRAGIC YEARS, by Paul M. Angle and Earl S. Miers, vol. 2, pp. 777-778, TREASURY OF THE WORLD'S GREAT DIARIES, edited by Philip Dunaway, pp. 285-288.

1862-1864. Diary of member of Company B, "Bostwick's Tigers," 128th New York Volunteers; social activities before taking leave of Dutchess County home; early military days at Hudson; service in Maryland and Pennsylvania; in Baltimore hospital; aboard the ARAGO off Newport News and Fortress Monroe and voyage to Louisiana; in camps near New Orleans and in hospital again; siege of Port Hudson and the regiment's baptism of fire; service in Louisiana at Baton Rouge, Donaldsonville and other locations; commissioned lieutenant, Company D, Ninetieth United States Colored Infantry; at Pilottown, New Orleans and Brashear City; furlough voyage home on the CREOLE and dangerous return on the MCCLELLAN, dealing with a mob of deserters, conscripts and bounty jumpers and enduring a storm at sea; coaling at Key West; return to regiment at New Orleans; the ill-fated Red River campaign, aboard the LAUREL HILL AND JENNIE ROGERS, burning of Alexandria and the retreat; an extremely detailed record of a soldier's life; food, housing, clothing, duties, dentistry, disease, death, funerals, troop transport, differing conditions for officers and enlisted men, leisure activities, etc.; the burden of heat, lice, mosquitoes and snakes; reflections on diary-keeping; perceptive observations of people and surroundings; candid sketches of fellow officers; conversing with Confederate prisoners and receiving both Southern hospitality and scorn; words of sympathy for suffering enemies; much information concerning the transformation of newly freed slaves into Union soldiers with notes on their abilities and customs; an engrossing account by an honest, sensitive and articulate individual.

VAN LEW, ELIZABETH, 1818-1900   **4311**

In LADIES OF RICHMOND, by Katharine M. Jones, pp. 118-120, 184-185, 198-199, 201-203, 216-217, 278-280.

Jun 1862, 1864, Apr 1865. Extracts from a generally circumspect journal kept by prosperous Richmond spinster, abolitionist and Union spy; suspicions and threats of Confederate authorities, excitement of war and hunger in the city; mass escape of Libby prisoners in February 1864; war news; the fall of the Confederate capital.

WADLEY, SARAH L., b. 1845?   **4312**

In HEROINES OF DIXIE, edited by Katharine M. Jones, pp. 195-197.

Dec 1862. Extracts from diary of daughter of William Morrill Wadley, prominent railroad president, penned while at Oakland, near Monroe, Louisiana; approach of Union forces; notes on slaves' Christmas celebration.

WALDROP, JOHN   **4313**

In CONTRIBUTIONS TO A HISTORY OF THE RICHMOND HOWITZER BATTALION, by Virginia Artillery, Richmond Howitzers, no.3, pp. 35-57.

1862-1865. Combined entries from the diaries of Waldrop and William Y. Mordecai, enlisted men in the Second Company; the Peninsular campaign and Seven Days' battles; service in the Shenandoah Valley; winter camp at Bowling Green; battles of Gettysburg and Spotsylvania; operations in the Valley, around Petersburg and the retreat to Appomattox; extremely brief notes, mainly relating weather and their unit's movements.

**WALKER, GEORGIANA FREEMAN GHOLSON, 4314
1833-1904**

PRIVATE JOURNAL, 1862-1865, WITH SELECTIONS FROM THE POST-WAR YEARS, 1865-1876. Edited by Dwight F. Henderson. Tuscaloosa, Ala.: Confederate Publishing, 1963. 148 pp.

1862-1876. Diary of Virginia woman of prominent family, begun in Richmond and kept irregularly through the war years; at St. George's Island, Bermuda, and Halifax, Nova Scotia, where her husband, Norman Stewart Walker, served as an agent of the Confederate government; voyage to England aboard the INDEX, wartime sojourn in London and Leamington, Warwick County, and a visit to Paris; postwar residence in Leamington and Liverpool and a visit to White Sulphur Springs, West Virginia; focus on family concerns and social life but much mention of blockade runners and their fates; notes on prices in Richmond during the war, behavior of blacks in Bermuda, Rose Greenhow, Varina Davis, diarist's father, Thomas Saunders Gholson, and Bermuda governor Harry St. George Ord and his wife.

WALKER, SUSAN, 1811-1887 4315

Sherwood, Henry Noble, ed. "Journal of Miss Susan Walker." HISTORICAL AND PHILOSOPHICAL SOCIETY OF OHIO QUARTERLY PUBLICATIONS 7 (1912):3-47.

Mar-Jun 1862. New England abolitionist's diary of the Port Royal experiment for care and education of freed slaves at Port Royal and the South Carolina Sea Islands; teaching Sunday school and reading, visiting plantations to assist black women, distributing food and clothes; notes on employment of blacks to bring in the abandoned cotton crop, black and white religious services and the evident confusion and demoralization of newly freed slaves.

WALLACE, MARY AUSTIN, 1837?-1921 4316

MARY AUSTIN WALLACE: A MICHIGAN SOLDIER'S WIFE RUNS THEIR FARM. Edited by Julia McCune. Lansing: Michigan Civil War Centennial Observance Commission, 1963. 18 pp.

Aug-Dec 1862. Account kept while her husband, Robert Bruce Wallace, was serving in Company C, Nineteenth Michigan Volunteer Infantry; the multitudinous tasks of managing a 160 acre farm in Calhoun County, Michigan; overseeing the building of a new house; expenses and financial transactions; a visit to her husband in camp at Dowagiac.

WELLES, GIDEON, 1802-1878 4317

DIARY OF GIDEON WELLES. With an introduction by John T. Morse, Jr. Boston: Houghton Mifflin, 1911. 3 vols.

DIARY. Edited by Howard K. Beale. New York: W.W. Norton, 1960. 3 vols.

Extracts in THE BLUE AND THE GRAY, edited by Henry S. Commager, vol. 1, pp. 193-194, vol. 2, pp. 1101-1104; DIARY OF AMERICA, edited by Josef and Dorothy Berger, pp. 450-455; TRAGIC YEARS, by Paul M. Angle and Earl S. Miers, vol. 2, p. 847; TREASURY OF THE WORLD'S GREAT DIARIES, edited by Philip Dunaway, pp. 289-291.

1862-1869. Diary of secretary of the navy during the Lincoln and Johnson administrations; a few notes on family matters but mainly a record of the great variety of naval affairs, cabinet meetings, foreign relations, legal questions, interdepartmental squabbles, the conduct of the war and the issues and politics of Reconstruction; assessment of naval personnel, military leaders, politicians and fellow cabinet members, including Wilkes, Du Pont, D.D. Porter, Dahlgren, Foote, Farragut, Fox, Banks, Halleck, McClellan, Scott, Hooker, Meade, Sherman, Pope, Bates, Fessenden, McCulloch, Speed, Montgomery Blair, John P. Hale, Preston King, Thurlow Weed, Sumner and Stevens; discussion of many issues and events such as emancipation, Connecticut and national politics, Congress, the integrity of the blockade, privateers and letters of marque, Fort Pillow massacre, 1864 presidential campaign, currency and finance, Sherman's original surrender terms, prisoner Jefferson Davis, Freedman's Bureau bill and other postwar legislation, Johnson's impeachment trial, black suffrage and blacks in public office; description of Johnson's behavior at Lincoln's second inauguration; Lincoln's assassination and funeral; Grant's inaugural; remarks concerning the two presidents he served and their administrative style; conflicts with and particularly negative assessments of Seward, Stanton, Chase and Grant; mention of the diaries of Adam Gurowski and John Wilkes Booth; a rich, opinionated, extremely valuable account of the personal and political dynamics of the Civil War and Reconstruction; diarist's revisions shown in the Beale edition.

"The Diary of Gideon Welles." ATLANTIC MONTHLY 103 (1909)-104 (1909):passim.

1862-1865. Extracts.

"A Diary of the Reconstruction Period." ATLANTIC MONTHLY 105 (1910)-107 (1911):passim.

1865-1869. Extracts.

WELLS, SETH JAMES, 1842-1864 4318

THE SIEGE OF VICKSBURG. Detroit, Mich.: W.H. Rowe, 1915. 101 pp.

Nov 1862-Jul 1863. Extracts from diary kept by member of Company K, Seventeenth Illinois; journey south to Louisiana; duties, marches and foraging; comments on devastation of the countryside and creation of black army units; besieging Vicksburg; under fire and out picking berries; surrender of the city; conversation with and respect for the enemy.

WENTWORTH, HEBRON M. 4319

In HISTORY OF THE FOURTH MAINE BATTERY, LIGHT ARTILLERY IN THE CIVIL WAR, by Maine Artillery, 4th Battery, pp. 123-141. Augusta, Maine: Burleigh & Flynt, Printers, 1905.

1862-1864. Extracts from bugler's diary; at camp in and near Washington, D.C.; with Sigel's command in the Shenandoah Valley and military operations in northern Virginia; battle of Antietam and the gruesome sights afterwards; stationed at Harpers Ferry, Maryland Heights and Virginia locations; siege of Petersburg; discharge due to illness in August 1864; mainly military information with a few notes on food, duties and Lincoln's visit to the army after Antietam.

WEST, BECKWITH 4320

EXPERIENCE OF A CONFEDERATE STATES PRISONER. Richmond, Va.: West & Johnston, 1862. 64 pp.

May-Aug 1862. Confederate officer's account of capture near Front Royal and imprisonment in Old Capitol Prison and Fort Delaware; notes on prison conditions, war news, fellow inmates, visitors, civilian support, Belle Boyd, etc.; reports of Union depredations; many extracts from Northern newspapers.

WHETTEN, HARRIET DOUGLAS   4321

Hass, Paul H., ed. "A Volunteer Nurse in the Civil War." WISCONSIN MAGAZINE OF HISTORY 48 (1965):205-221.

Jul-Aug 1862. Diary kept by well-bred and educated New York woman working in the hospital transport service of the Sanitary Commission; caring for wounded aboard the steamer SPAULDING; leisure activities and teaching contrabands; visiting Satterlee Hospital, Fourth and George Street Hospital, the Burd Orphan Asylum and the Episcopal Asylum in Philadelphia; destruction of Edmund Ruffin's home; awful conditions in hospital at Harrison's Landing, Virginia; praise for wounded soldiers and complaints about co-workers.

WHIPPLE, ALPHONZO, b. 1842   4322

THE DIARY OF ALPHONZO WHIPPLE. St. Louis: Skaer Print, 1922. 64 pp.

1862-1864. Private's record of service with Company A, Fifteenth Illinois Volunteer Infantry; Shiloh and the advance to Corinth; operations in Tennessee and Mississippi; the Vicksburg and Meridian campaigns; notes on weather, correspondence, camp life, theater in Memphis, furlough at home near Woodstock, incidents concerning the "Dead Rabbits" mess, etc.

WHITE, KATHERINE   4323

Overton, Marion F. "Wintertime in Old Brooklyn." LONG ISLAND FORUM 11 (1948):23, 37.

Jan-Mar, Nov-Dec 1862. Article containing extracts from the diary of a sixteen-year-old girl relating her ice skating experiences with her friends on the ponds of Brooklyn.

WILCOX, CHARLES EDWARDS, 1839-1931   4324

Erickson, Edgar L., ed. "Hunting for Cotton in Dixie." JOURNAL OF SOUTHERN HISTORY 4 (1938):493-513.

Jul-Oct 1862. Extracts from diary kept by Illinois schoolteacher, a member of Company A, Thirty-third Illinois Volunteer Infantry, to provide news for family back home; expeditions to find and confiscate cotton in Arkansas and Mississippi; down the Mississippi to Eustice, Arkansas, venturing as far as fifteen miles inland; a stop at Memphis before returning to Ironton, Missouri; description of Western Mississippi River Flotilla; notes on reading, foraging, slaves, engagements with Confederate troops, the burning of Prentiss, Mississippi, illnesses, casualties and deaths.

Erickson, Edgar L., ed. "With Grant at Vicksburg." ILLINOIS STATE HISTORICAL SOCIETY JOURNAL 30 (1938):441-503.

Extracts in THE BLUE AND THE GRAY, edited by Henry S. Commager, vol. 2, pp. 649-656.

Mar-Jul 1863. Daily account of the Vicksburg campaign; from St. Genevieve down the Mississippi to Milliken's Bend; promotion to sergeant major of the regiment and getting used to his new role; working on canal connecting Duckport and New Carthage; advancing on Vicksburg, battle of Port Gibson, the siege and sur-

render; touring the fallen city; pursuit of Johnston's army and occupation of Jackson; considering a commission as officer in black regiment; notes on military action and tasks, reading, correspondence, foraging, surroundings, drinking, making salt, illness, casualties, food, etc.; a substantial record.

WILKINS, WILLIAM D., d. 1882   4325

"Forgotten in the 'Black Hole.' " CIVIL WAR TIMES ILLUSTRATED 15, no. 3 (1976):36-44.

Aug-Sep 1862. Prison diary of Detroit resident, assistant adjutant general on Gen. Alpheus S. Williams's staff; capture at battle of Cedar Mountain; journey to Richmond amidst civilian antipathy; conditions at Libby; overcrowding, poor food, cruel guards, horrible odors and ways of coping; diarist's perception that Pope's officers were receiving particularly harsh treatment and that their government was neglecting them; mention of prison commander Henry Wirz; parole and journey north to Baltimore.

WILKINSON, DAVID S.   4326

In HISTORY OF THE ONE HUNDRED AND TWENTY-FOURTH REGIMENT, PENNSYLVANIA VOLUNTEERS, By Pennsylvania Infantry, 124th Regiment, pp. 110-111.

Sep, Nov 1862. Extracts from diary of corporal in company A; description of march from Fort Blenker, in Virginia, to Antietam, with attention centered on food and its acquisition; diarist's advance into battle and wounding.

WILLIAMS, JOHN C., b. 1843   4327

LIFE IN CAMP: A HISTORY OF THE NINE MONTHS' SERVICE OF THE FOURTEENTH VERMONT REGIMENT. Claremont, N.H.: For the author, by the Claremont Manufacturing Co., 1864. 167 pp.

Oct 1862-Jul 1863. Soldier's diary; ill treatment of troops passing through New York City; duties near Washington, D.C., and in Virginia; sightseeing in the nation's capital and a visit to the Chantilly battlefield; opinions on emancipation, secessionist sympathies in the North and leadership of the Army of the Potomac; battle of Gettysburg.

WILSON, JOHN, 1842-1910   4328

Frederick, J.V., ed. "An Illinois Soldier in North Mississippi." JOURNAL OF MISSISSIPPI HISTORY 1 (1939):182-194.

Feb-Dec 1862. War diary of Illinois schoolteacher, a member of Company H, Fifty-sixth Illinois Volunteer Infantry; routines at Shawneetown, Illinois, camp; service as ordnance department clerk at Paducah, Kentucky; advancing on Corinth; operations in northern Mississippi; the battle of Corinth; at Memphis; notes on foraging, contrabands, the Shiloh battlefield and soldiers' response to emancipation as a war aim.

WILSON, WILLIAM LYNE, 1843-1900   4329

A BORDERLAND CONFEDERATE. Edited by Festus P. Summers. Pittsburgh: University of Pittsburgh Press, 1962. 138 pp.

1862-1865, 1896-1897 (with gaps). War diary, interspersed with letters to his mother, of Charles Town, West Virginia, resident, a graduate of Columbian College; service with Company B, Twelfth Virginia Cavalry; Jackson's Shenandoah Valley campaign; death of Turner Ashby and a lengthy appreciation of the man;

a prisoner at Fort McHenry, quickly exchanged; a brief stay in Richmond; winter camp and picket duty in the Valley; "Grumble" Jones's raid across the Alleghenies in the spring of 1863 with commentary on towns, countryside and inhabitants; reviews by Stuart and Lee and the battle of Brandy Station; in the Valley under Rosser in January 1865; trip to King and Queen County; efforts to rejoin brigade as the Confederacy collapses; witnessing the flight of government from Richmond; battle of Sayler's Creek; the many army stragglers, confusion and panic of the last days; scattered extracts, touching on Civil War experiences, from later diary.

THE CABINET DIARY OF WILLIAM L. WILSON. Edited by Festus P. Summers. Chapel Hill: University of North Carolina Press, 1957. 276 pp.

    1896-1897. Diary kept while serving as President Cleveland's postmaster general, personal friend and confidant privy to discussion far beyond the scope of his own department; issues relating to the Cuban question, free silver, Populism, growth of trusts, etc., described from the perspective of a conservative Cleveland Democrat; speaking engagements; accounts and analysis of cabinet meetings; references to John G. Carlisle, Hilary A. Herbert, William Jennings Bryan, etc.; quite a few family items and references to his wife, Nanny Judson Wilson.

WINGFIELD, HENRY WYATT, 1829-1902   4330

Scott, W.W., ed. "Two Confederate Items." VIRGINIA LIBRARY BULLETIN 16, nos. 2-3 (1927):5-76. Diary, pp. 5-47. Reprint. In TWO CONFEDERATE ITEMS, edited by W.W. Scott. Richmond: D. Bottom, 1927. 76 pp.

    1862-1864. Captain's diary, omitting what the editor considered personal, non-historical material; service with the Fifty-eighth Virginia Infantry; Jackson's Valley campaign and the Seven Days' battles; battles of Second Bull Run, Antietam, Fredericksburg, and the Wilderness; operations in the Shenandoah Valley before capture at Winchester; notes on General Ewell and "Extra Billy" Smith.

WOOD, RICHARD DAVIS   4331

"Richard Davis Wood: Extracts from His Journal." VINELAND HISTORICAL MAGAZINE 24 (1939):239-245.

    1862-1869. Brief extracts covering constant train trips between Millville and Vineland on various forms of business, including land transactions with Charles K. Landis and timber sales.

WORTHINGTON, THOMAS, 1807-1884   4332

EXTRACTS FROM A DIARY OF THE TENNESSEE EXPEDITION, 1862. N.p., n.d. 8 pp. Diary, pp. 1-2.

In ABSTRACT OF EVIDENCE, &C, IN THE PROCEEDINGS OF THE COURT MARTIAL FOR THE TRIAL OF COL. T. WORTHINGTON, pp. 2-3. N.p., 1862.

    Mar-Apr 1862. Extracts from diary of colonel of the Forty-sixth Ohio Volunteer Infantry, covering the days before Shiloh; his predictions of an imminent Confederate attack and concern about the Union forces' unpreparedness; accusations of incompetence, improvidence and negligence on the part of Union generals, especially William T. Sherman.

WYETH, JOHN JASPER, b. 1841?   4333

LEAVES FROM A DIARY. Boston: L.F. Lawrence, 1878. 76 pp. Diary, pp. 5-54.

    Aug 1862-Jun 1863. Account of service of the Forty-fourth Massachusetts in North Carolina written by member of Company E; the reality of army life first encountered at camp; transport on the steamer MERRIMAC to New Bern; operations in the area, including an engagement at Rawle's Mill, the burning of Hamilton and an expedition to Plymouth on the NORTHERNER; besieged at Washington; return to New Bern; home to Massachusetts; notes on Thanksgiving celebration and other entertainments; lengthy entries describing conditions in camp and field, apparently rewritten for publication.

YOST, GEORGE, b. 1848?   4334

"Resurrection of an Ironclad." LIFE, 12 February 1965, pp. 41-44. Diary, p. 44.

    Jan-Aug, Dec 1862. Extracts from cabin boy's diary giving a picture of life aboard the Union gunboat CAIRO and describing the destruction of the vessel by an underwater mine in the Yazoo River.

1863

ANON.   4335

In OPDYCKE TIGERS, 125th O.V.I., A HISTORY OF THE REGIMENT, by Charles T. Clark, pp. 17-421 passim. Columbus, Ohio: Spahr & Glenn, 1895.

    1863-1865. Extracts from diaries of unidentified regiment members; early days of a new regiment; military training, troop transport and foraging; operations in Tennessee and the Atlanta campaign; preparing to fight Hood's forces at Nashville; the last months of the war in Alabama and Tennessee; grand review at Nashville; postwar duty in Texas; return home to Ohio.

ANON.   4336

In OFFICIAL RECORDS OF THE UNION AND CONFEDERATE NAVIES IN THE WAR OF THE REBELLION, ser. 1, vol. 24, pp. 492-496.

    Mar 1863. Extracts from journal of officer aboard the CINCINNATI during expedition to Steele's Bayou, Mississippi, in hopes of opening an entrance into the Yazoo River; cutting a path through dense vegetation; foraging and exchanging fire with Confederates; observations on slaves' reactions to the Union advance.

ANON.   4337

In THE REBELLION RECORD, edited by Frank Moore, vol. 7, pp. 165-170.

    May-Jul 1863. Citizen's diary of events during the siege of Vicksburg; military clashes and bombardment of the city; indications of later rewriting.

ANON. 4338

"Vicksburg in 1863." CONFEDERATE VETERAN 36 (1928):424-425.

May-Jun 1863. Extracts from diary of woman resident of Vicksburg; view of Confederate army entering the city after defeat at Champion's Hill; life under bombardment and her aversion to the caves; notes on generals Stephen Lee and John Pemberton whom she entertained.

ANON. 4339

In TWO LADIES AT GETTYSBURG, edited by Paul Dean Robinson, 15 leaves, unpaged. Kensington, Md.: Village Press, 1973.

Jul 1863. What appear to be lengthy diary entries of a Philadelphia woman who journeyed to Gettysburg to aid the wounded; good account of conditions in the wake of the battle, her work and the organization and dispensation of supplies and services.

ANON. 4340

In THE REBELLION RECORD, edited by Frank Moore, vol. 7, pp. 594-596.

Extracts in THE BLUE AND THE GRAY, edited by Henry S. Commager, vol. 2, pp. 688-690.

Sep-Oct 1863. Account of hardships endured after being wounded and captured at Chickamauga; confinement at Atlanta, Libby Prison and the Alabama Hospital until exchanged.

ADAMS, R.L. 4341

In THE STAR CORPS; OR, NOTES OF AN ARMY CHAPLAIN, by George S. Bradley, pp. 48-52. Milwaukee: Jermain & Brightman, Printers, 1865.

Mar-Apr 1863. What appear to be diary extracts, perhaps written or amended later, describing journey of Union soldier to Libby Prison after capture in Tennessee by Forrest's cavalry; notes on treatment by captors and on unionist sentiments in Farmington, Tennessee.

AFFELD, CHARLES E., 1843-1934 4342

Bearss, Edwin C., ed. "From Milliken's Bend to Vicksburg with Private Affeld." LOUISIANA STUDIES 6 (1967):203-265.

Apr-May 1863. Extracts from diary of Chicagoan, born in Prussia, who like his twin brother Frank Otto Affeld, was a member of Battery B, First Illinois Light Artillery; stationed in Louisiana opposite Vicksburg, noting the vessels running past the Confederate guns; operations in Mississippi, stopping at deserted, pillaged plantations and occupied Raymond; assaults on Vicksburg's fortifications and the toll taken by enemy sharpshooters; good description of his cannoneer duties and other military matters as well as of everyday activities, making his one of the best diaries of the Vicksburg campaign.

Bearss, Edwin C., ed. "Pvt. Charles E. Affeld Describes the Mechanicsburg Expeditions." ILLINOIS STATE HISTORICAL SOCIETY 56 (1963):233-256.

May-Jun 1863. Extracts covering operations in the "Mechanicsburg Corridor," trying to monitor Johnston's activities while Grant invested Vicksburg; much criticism of Gen. Nathan Kimball's leadership; activities of the diarist and his brother; description of countryside, towns and plantations; notes on forag-

ing and meals; an informative and engaging record of life in camp and field.

Bearss, Edwin C., ed. "Pvt. Charles E. Affeld Reports Action West of the Mississippi." ILLINOIS STATE HISTORICAL SOCIETY JOURNAL 60 (1967):267-296.

Jun-Jul 1863. Extracts describing participation in operations on the Louisiana side of the Mississippi, reinforcing Union positions there; in camp at Young's Point and firing on Vicksburg from DeSoto on the west bank; acquiring books, china and other items from deserted plantation and perusing the owner's family letters; visit to Union fortifications at Chickasaw Bayou; surrender of the besieged city; notes on military activities, reading, food, etc.

ALLEN, LUCY E., 1830-1908 4343

"Diary of Miss Lucy Allen of 'Clifton.'" CLARKE COUNTY HISTORICAL ASSOCIATION PROCEEDINGS 9 (1949):26-35.

Mar-May 1863. Diary kept at Clifton, near Berryville, Virginia; weather, war news and neighbors' activities; life in occupied territory, with notes on behavior of Union soldiers and defecting servants; concern for friends in the Confederate army.

ALLSTON, ELIZABETH WATIES, 1845-1921 4344

In OUR WOMEN IN THE WAR, pp. 354-363.

Extracts in HEROINES OF DIXIE, edited by Katharine M. Jones, pp. 237-239; WHEN SHERMAN CAME, edited by Katharine M. Jones, pp. 250-256, 261-263.

May-Jul 1863, Feb-Oct 1864, Jan-Apr 1865. Extracts from diary of South Carolina planter's daughter; rough fare at school in Plantersville; a dance at Fort Sumter before leaving Charleston home and establishing residence elsewhere in the state; prices and dance styles encountered during Wilmington visit; food and clothing shortages; burying valuables in anticipation of invasion; looting and destruction at family's South and North Carolina properties; reaction of blacks to Union army's passage. See also Pringle, Elizabeth Waties Allston.

ALSTON, Lt. Col. 4345

In THE REBELLION RECORD, edited by Frank Moore, vol. 7. pp. 358-360.

Extracts in THE BLUE AND THE GRAY, edited by Henry S. Commager, vol. 2, pp. 678-681.

Jul 1863. Diary kept by John Morgan's chief of staff during raid through Kentucky; action including engagement at Lebanon; death of Morgan's brother Thomas; officers' futile efforts to prevent plundering; taken to Lexington after capture by Union troops.

ANDERSON, SAMUEL THOMPSON, 1838-1894 4346

In CLAIM OF CERTAIN CONFEDERATE OFFICERS, by United States Congress, House, Committee on War Claims, pp. 23-30. Washington, D.C.: Government Printing Office, 1914.

1863-1865. Prison diary of lieutenant, Company D, First South Carolina Cavalry, captured near Martinsburg, West Virginia, during Lee's retreat from Pennsylvania; sporadic entries describing kind treatment while ill at Wheeling and detailing his subsequent imprisonment at Camp Chase, Johnson's Island, Point Lookout, Fort Delaware, Morris Island and Fort Pulaski.

ANDREWS, GILMAN A.   4347

In HISTORY OF THE FIFTIETH REGIMENT OF INFANTRY, MASSACHUSETTS VOLUNTEER MILITIA, by William Burnham Stevens, pp. 103-105.

> May 1863. Extracts from Company A corporal's journal; operations at White's Bayou, during the campaign against Port Hudson; notes on contrabands.

APPLETON, NATHAN   4348

In HISTORY OF THE FIFTH MASSACHUSETTS BATTERY, by Massachusetts Artillery, 5th Battery, pp. 21-839 passim.

> Sep-Nov 1863, May 1864. Extracts from lieutenant's diary covering operations in Virginia; the Spotsylvania campaign; brief note on the brigade badge; some entries possibly rewritten later.

ASTON, HOWARD   4349

In HISTORY AND ROSTER OF THE FOURTH AND FIFTH INDEPENDENT BATTALIONS AND THIRTEENTH REGIMENT OHIO CAVALRY VOLUNTEERS, pp. 5-34, 39-51. Columbus, Ohio: Press of F.J. Heer, 1902.

> 1863-1865. Sporadic entries in cavalryman's diary; action and foraging in Kentucky; reenlistment and furlough in Ohio; infantry service in Virginia; trench life at Petersburg and then action in that area as remounted cavalry; donations of Christian Commission; postwar duty in Virginia.

ATKINS, MARY, 1819-1882   4350

THE DIARY OF MARY ATKINS, A SABBATICAL IN THE EIGHTEEN SIXTIES. Mills College, Calif.: Eucalyptus Press, 1937. 46 pp.

> Nov 1863-Mar 1864. Pleasant diary of a sailing ship voyage by the principal of Young Ladies Seminary, Benicia, California, aboard the ADVANCE during her sabbatical; shipboard life, scenery, people, Thanksgiving Day services and a concert at Fort Street Church, Honolulu; observances of the death of Kamehameha IV; visiting Yokohama and Shanghai; daily record of weather and latitude.

AYERS, JAMES T., 1805-1865   4351

THE DIARY OF JAMES T. AYERS, CIVIL WAR RECRUITER. Edited by John Hope Franklin. Illinois Historical Society Publications, no. 20, Occasional Publications, no. 50. Springfield: Printed by authority of the state of Illinois, 1947. 138 pp.

Extracts in THE BLUE AND THE GRAY, edited by Henry S. Commager, vol. 1, pp. 76-79.

> 1863-1865 (with gaps). Methodist preacher's war diary kept while in Company E, 129th Illinois Infantry, and on detached service recruiting freedmen for the Union army; recruiting adventures in Alabama, primarily around Huntsville, discouragement with task and his resignation; at Chattanooga and home to McLean County, Illinois; uncomfortable roundabout journey to rejoin regiment at Savannah; the Carolinas campaign, in hospital at Savannah and on to Washington, D.C., at war's end; discussions of his work, slavery, freedmen and the war; description of countryside, Savannah and Charleston; notes on miscegenation, raising the United States flag over Fort Sumter and Lincoln's assassination; vitriolic passage on Jefferson Davis; sporadic, long, sometimes rambling

entries; appendices containing verse and newspaper clippings around which diary entries were originally penned.

BACON, CYRUS, d. 1868   4352

Whitehouse, Frank, Jr. and Whitehouse, Walter M., eds. "A Michigan Surgeon at Chancellorsville One Hundred Years Ago." UNIVERSITY OF MICHIGAN MEDICAL BULLETIN 29 (1963):315-331.

> Apr-May 1863. Extracts from diary of assistant surgeon of the Seventh Michigan Volunteers, a graduate of the National Medical College at Washington, D.C.; experiencing the hardships of march to Chancellorsville; operating in field hosptial, transporting wounded and remaining behind with patients who could not be moved; praise for fellow surgeon John Shaw Billings; behavior of Confederates while he and Union stores were in their hands; notes on stragglers, the significant number of back wounds and treatment of various cases.

BARNETT, JOHN LYMPUS, d. 1865   4353

Barnett, James, ed. "Some Civil War Letters and Diary of John Lympus Barnett." INDIANA MAGAZINE OF HISTORY 37 (1941):162-173. Diary, pp. 172-173.

> Feb 1863. Company B, Thirty-ninth Indiana, enlisted man's brief diary kept while in Nashville hospital; personal matters.

BELL, JOHN N., b. 1834?   4354

Bearss, Edwin C., ed. "Diary of Captain John N. Bell." IOWA JOURNAL OF HISTORY 59 (1961):181-221.

> Apr-Jul 1863. Informative daily record of Vicksburg campaign penned by captain, company E, Twenty-fifth Iowa Infantry; Steele's Greenville expedition; following the advance from Milliken's Bend to Vicksburg; the siege and surrender; details of military operations; notes on plantations, slaves, foraging, looting and destruction; discussion of formation of regiments of former slaves for Union service and praise for black soldiers.

BENDER, FLORA ISABELLE, b. 1848   4355

"Memoranda of a Journey Across the Plains." NEVADA HISTORICAL SOCIETY QUARTERLY 1 (1953):144-174.

> May-Aug 1863. Teenager's record of a journey with her family from Washington County, Nebraska, to Virginia City, falling in with other emigrants en route; candid remarks about quarrelsome members of the company and on Mormons; report of Indian attacks; the usual notes on conditions of travel enlivened by a romantic eye for scenery, moonlight and young men.

BENNETT, HENRY   4356

In THE YEARS OF ANGUISH, FAUQUIER COUNTY, VIRGINIA, compiled by Emily G. Ramey and John K. Gott, pp. 44-52.

> 1863-1864. Record of marches and camp life in Virginia with commentary on countryside through which diarist passed; notes on military punishments; transfer to North Carolina and operations there; return home to Virginia on furlough.

BERNARD, GEORGE S., 1837-1912   4357

In WAR TALKS OF CONFEDERATE VETERANS, edited by George S. Bernard, pp. 64-93, 278-284 passim. Petersburg, Va.: Fenn & Owen, 1892.

May 1863, May 1864, Apr 1865. Extracts from diary of soldier in the Twelfth Virginia Regiment; battles of Chancellorsville and the Wilderness; last days of the war and false hopes that the Confederacy was not at an end.

BIGELOW, EDWIN BURNHAM, 1838-1916   4358

Klement, Frank L., ed. "Edwin B. Bigelow: A Michigan Sergeant in the Civil War." MICHIGAN HISTORY 38 (1954):193-252.

1863-1864. Dairy of Oakland County resident serving in Company B, Fifth Michigan Cavalry; in camp near Washington, D.C., seeing the sights of the capital; forays into Virginia and mention of Col. Freeman Norvell's drunkenness; the Gettysburg campaign and subsequent engagements in Maryland and Virginia; capture at Buckland Mills in October 1863; the journey to Belle Isle and conditions there; weather, rations, monotony, exchange hopes and visits of Gen. Neal Dow; escape in North Carolina while being transported to Georgia; recaptured and imprisoned at Asheville, Camp Vance near Morgantown and Salisbury; escape from train, again while en route to Georgia; arrival in Union occupied territory at Strawberry Plains, Tennessee; a daily record composed of short entries except for what appear to be the editor's deletions.

BLAIR, JOHN INSLEY, b. 1802   4359

Cassen, Anthony L., ed. "Surveying the First Railroad Across Iowa." ANNALS OF IOWA, 3d ser. 35 (1959-1961):321-362.

Jun-Jul 1863. Record of a survey conducted for the Cedar Rapids and Missouri River Railroad; departure from Boonsboro with a sizable party; route and distances; interesting notes on people, hotels and private lodgings in Carroll County, Denison, Onawa, Iowa, and Decatur, Fremont and Omaha, Nebraska; some financial details; surveying along the Platte River, with comments on Indians, settlers and emigrant parties, especially Mormons; an abundance of personal names.

BODMAN, ALBERT HOLMES, 1826?-1885   4360

Kaiser, Leo M., ed. " 'In Sight of Vicksburg': Private Diary of a Northern War Correspondent." HISTORICAL BULLETIN 34 (1956):202-221.

Feb-Mar 1863. Private diary of war correspondent of the CHICAGO TRIBUNE, kept at urging of the secretary of the Chicago Historical Society; long entries discussing military activities and persons; negative comments about generals S.A. Hurlbut and J.B. McPherson and praise of Gen. John A. Logan; conditions in Memphis hospitals, the good work of Cordelia Harvey and the Sanitary Commission and criticism of some medical administrators; canal building efforts viewed from Young's Point and Lake Providence and the beauties of the latter area; connecting the Mississippi River with Lake Providence and consequent flooding; notes on cotton speculators, Copperheads, miscegenation, Spanish moss and Andrew Jackson Donelson.

BOSWELL, JAMES KEITH, 1839?-1863   4361

"The Diary of a Confederate Staff Officer." CIVIL WAR TIMES ILLUSTRATED 15, no. 1 (1976):30-38.

Jan-Apr 1863. Diary of Stonewall Jackson's topographical engineer, later killed by the same volley which fatally wounded the general; military matters; unsuccessful courtship of Sophie Carter at Glen Welby in Fauquier County and suicide of another unhappy suitor; socializing in Richmond; notes on Jackson, D.H. Hill and A.P. Hill.

BREIDENTHAL, H.   4362

In THE REBELLION RECORD, edited by Frank Moore, suppl., pp. 337-350.

Apr-May 1863. Streight's raid to Rome, Georgia, as recorded in the diary of sergeant, Company A, Third Ohio Volunteer Infantry; from Murfreesboro, Tennessee, into Alabama; marches, foraging and military operations; surrender to Forrest near Rome; observations on conditions in the Confederacy as prisoners were transported through Rome, Atlanta, Dalton, Knoxville and Lynchburg to Belle Isle from which they were soon paroled; notes on food, prices, Southern soldiers and civilians, attitudes toward blacks, Copperheads, crops, etc.; long entries blending straightforward account of events with patriotic sentiments, literary allusions and sometimes ornate prose.

BRINKERHOFF, ARCH M.   4363

Bearss, Edwin C., ed. "The Civil War Diary of an Iowa Soldier at Vicksburg." IOWA JOURNAL OF HISTORY 59 (1961):222-237.

May-Jul 1863. Daily entries of private, Company H, Fourth Iowa Infantry, during the siege of Vicksburg; an interesting view from the ranks of life in the trenches; work and leisure activities.

BRINTON, DANIEL GARRISON, 1837-1899   4364

Thompson, D.G. Brinton, ed. "From Chancellorsville to Gettysburg." PENNSYLVANIA MAGAZINE OF HISTORY AND BIOGRAPHY 89 (1965):292-315.

Apr-Jul 1863. Diary of Pennsylvania physician, surgeon-in-chief of division, Eleventh Corps of the Army of the Potomac; getting his things together and visiting the surgeon general's office in Washington, D.C.; rout of the corps at Chancellorsville and a glimpse of Hooker retreating across the Rappahannock; description of surroundings on the march to Pennsylvania; arduous duty during battle of Gettysburg and afterwards; notes on reading, food and his accommodations; brief mention of Confederate general Lewis A. Armistead.

Thompson, D.G. Brinton, ed. "Dr. Daniel Garrison Brinton with the Army of the Cumberland." PENNSYLVANIA MAGAZINE OF HISTORY AND BIOGRAPHY 90 (1966):466-490.

Oct-Dec 1863. Diary covering experiences while medical director of the Eleventh Corps; briefly in Washington, D.C., to ascertain location of the corps; journey to Bridgeport, Alabama, with comments on countryside of Ohio, Indiana and Tennessee and the cities of Columbus and Nashville; description of Tennessee civilians, Chattanooga, Cleveland and other Tennessee settlements; observing the battles of Lookout Mountain and Missionary Ridge; with the corps command between Chattanooga and Nashville; notes on conditions of soldiers and depredations by Sherman's men.

BROADHEAD, SALLIE ROBBINS   4365

In GETTYSBURG, edited by Earl S. Miers and Richard A. Brown, pp. 7-282 passim. New Brunswick, N.J.: Rutgers University Press, 1948.

Jul 1863. Extracts from Gettysburg schoolteacher's diary; rumors and fears as the Army of Northern Virginia advances; civilian life during the battle; appearance and behavior of Confederates; the horrible sights after the battle; caring for the wounded through July 14.

In THE UNION READER, edited by Richard B. Harwell, pp. 224-236. New York: Longmans, Green, 1958.

Jul 1863. Similar content using slightly different extracts and ending on July 5.

Extracts in TRAGIC YEARS, by Paul M. Angle and Earl S. Miers, vol. 2, pp. 634, 664.

BULLARD, WILLIAM J. 4366

In A HISTORY OF THE SEVENTY-THIRD REGIMENT OF ILLINOIS INFANTRY VOLUNTEERS, by Illinois Infantry, 73d Regiment, pp. 598-601.

Dec 1863-Jan 1864. Account of convalescent soldiers' march to Knoxville and an engagement with Wheeler's cavalry.

BURTON, ANTHONY B. 4367

Bearss, Edwin C., ed. "Lt. Anthony Burton's Account of the Activities of the 5th Battery, Ohio Light Artillery, at Vicksburg." LOUISIANA STUDIES 10 (1971):274-330.

May-Jul 1863. Battery commander's diary; down the Mississippi from Memphis to the Yazoo River, within sight of Vicksburg; fine substantial entries providing detailed account of activities of the artillery unit during the siege; comments on generals Lauman, Grant, McClernand and Ord; notes on various weapons and ammunition; description of surrender, Confederate soldiers and a portion of the captured works.

BYNUM, G.W. 4368

Love, W.A. "Forward and Back." CONFEDERATE VETERAN 33 (1925):9-10.

Jun 1863. Extract from diary of private, Company A, Second Mississippi; at Fredericksburg and Falmouth, Virginia; on the march to Gettysburg.

CABOT, STEPHEN, 1826-1906 4369

REPORT OF THE "DRAFT RIOT" IN BOSTON, JULY 14, 1863. Boston, 1902. 11 pp. New ed. 1906.

Jul 1863. Extract from diary of major, First Battery, Massachusetts Heavy Artillery, stationed at Fort Warren; in command of the armory on Cooper Street during the disturbance; what appears to be an official report of his actions in quelling the riot, including firing canister into the mob.

CAMPBELL, JOHN Q.A. 4370

Bearss, Edwin C., ed. "The Civil War Diary of Lt. John Q.A. Campbell." ANNALS OF IOWA 39 (1969):519-541.

May-Jun 1863. The siege of Vicksburg as seen by officer in Company B, Fifth Iowa Infantry; substantial entries of an intelligent observer, describing developments along the siege lines; a few notations on weather, etc., but primarily a record of military activities.

CARPENTER, CAROLINE 4371

Thornburg, Opal, ed. "Earlham Diaries: The Diary of Caroline Carpenter." FRIENDS HISTORICAL ASSOCIATION BULLETIN 36 (1947):76-77.

Jul-Aug 1863. A few extracts from diary of a Quaker girl at Earlham College in Richmond, Indiana; religious and academic notes; news and fright about Morgan's Ohio raid.

CHAPIN, JAMES W., 1825?-1906 4372

Reynolds, Donald E. and Kele, Max H., eds. "With the Army of the Cumberland in the Chickamauga Campaign." GEORGIA HISTORICAL QUARTERLY 59 (1975):223-242.

Jun-Nov 1863. War diary of Indianapolis clerk, serving as a lieutenant with the Thirty-ninth Indiana Mounted Infantry; daily record of campaign life in Tennessee and Georgia; battle of Chickamauga; notes on weather, duties, correspondence, etc.

Reynolds, Donald E. and Kele, Max H., eds. "A Yank in the Carolinas Campaign." NORTH CAROLINA HISTORICAL REVIEW 46 (1969):42-57.

Jan-Mar 1865. Record of service as adjutant of Eighth Indiana Cavalry with Kilpatrick's division, operating on the left wing of Sherman's army as it pushed from Savannah to near Goldsboro, North Carolina; brief entries, mainly recording route and distances covered, prisoners taken, casualties suffered, etc.; burning of Barnwell Court House, South Carolina; allegations of murder of prisoners of war by Wheeler's cavalry; battle of Averasboro.

CLANDENING, WILLIAM H., 1834-1914 4373

"Across the Plains in 1863-1865." NORTH DAKOTA HISTORY 2 (1928):247-272.

1863-1865 (with gaps). Canadian mining engineer's journey from Walkerton, Ontario, to the Montana gold fields as a member of the Fisk company, which he joined in Minnesota; descriptions of country people, travel conditions and route, partly along Sibley's road; buffalo hunting; once in Montana, a graphic depiction of violent life there, with several murders, hasty trials and hangings; brief notes of mining in the gulches around Virginia City and return home.

CLARK, GEORGE MUNFORD 4374

"A Journal." UMPQUA TRAPPER 14 (1978):87-96; 15 (1979):4-7.

1863-1876. Extracts from rancher's diary; burning of houses by Civil War secessionists near Healdsburg, California; cattle drive into Oregon and return to San Francisco on the SIERRA NEVADA; service in the California Militia; marriage to Nancy M. Miller; ranching; move to Douglas County, Oregon, thence to Linn County; ranch chores and sawmill business.

COIT, JOSEPH HOWLAND, 1831-1906 4375

McLachlan, James, ed. "The Civil War Diary of Joseph H. Coit." MARYLAND HISTORICAL MAGAZINE 60 (1965):245-260.

Jan-Jul 1863. Extracts from diary of Episcopal priest, an instructor at the College of St. James, six miles south of Hagerstown, Maryland; concern for school and students as Lee's army passes through to Pennsylvania; visits from alumni in Confederate service; efforts of some students to join the Southern troops; behavior of Confederate soldiers and reclamation of runaway slaves; the college faculty's successful endeavor to transport students home to their parents.

COOKE, Mrs. GEORGE, b. 1808?   4376

"Mrs. Cooke's Civil War Diary for 1863-1864." VERMONT HISTORY 25 (1957):56-65.

1863-1864. Extracts from account kept by Corinth, Vermont, farmer's wife; tasks, visitors, weather and entertainments; deaths, mainly from diptheria; a few references to the war and the 1864 presidential election.

CORBIN, HENRY   4377

"Diary of a Virginian Cavalry Man." HISTORICAL MAGAZINE, 3d ser. 2 (1873):210-215.

1863-1864. Diary found on the battlefield of Fisher's Hill, thought to be the work of a sergeant in Company B, Eighteenth Virginia Cavalry; very brief entries concerning military movements; invasion of Pennsylvania and acting as rear guard for Lee's retreating army; action in the Shenandoah Valley.

COWDIN, WILLIAM H., d. 1895   4378

Wilson, Gary, E., ed. "Diary of a Union Prisoner in Texas." SOUTHERN STUDIES 23 (1984):103-119.

Jan-Dec 1863. Account believed to be the work of Company D lieutenant, Forty-second Massachusetts; wounding and capture at the battle of Galveston; taken to Houston hospital, then imprisoned at Huntsville, Camp Groce near Hempstead and, finally, Camp Ford near Tyler; notes on Sam Houston, a visitor to the Union prisoners.

CUMINGS, HENRY HARRISON, 1840-1913   4379

In IN MEMORIAM HENRY HARRISON CUMINGS, CHARLOTTE J. CUMINGS, by Jason N. Fradenburgh, pp. 35-163 passim. Oil City, Pa.: Derrick, 1913.

1863-1865. Extracts from war diary of officer, Company D, 103th Ohio; military operations in Tennessee, including the pillaging of Tullahoma; battles of Chickamauga, Lookout Mountain and Missionary Ridge; the Atlanta campaign; marching across Georgia and the Carolinas; notes on reading, foraging, slavery, women's rights, Southern women, conscription, unionist sentiment in the South, inaccurate newspaper accounts, generals Rosencrans and Kilpatrick, etc.; references to conflict among the regiment's officers and the waning of military spirit in the army; mixed emotions concerning Union destruction at Atlanta, Milledgeville and elsewhere; mention of Union soldiers' treatment of blacks; his reaction to the surrender and Lincoln's assassination; long, detailed entries, possibly revised later.

In THE STORY OF A THOUSAND, by Albion W. Tourgee, pp. 310-313.

Aug 1864. On the skirmish line during the Atlanta campaign.

DAHLGREN, JOHN A.   4380

In OFFICIAL RECORDS OF THE UNION AND CONFEDERATE NAVIES IN THE WAR OF THE REBELLION, ser. 1, vol. 14, pp. 325-326, 366-367, 394, 472-473, 507, 566-567, 635-636; vol. 15, pp. 18-19, 84-86, 123-124; vol. 16, pp. 357-374.

Jul-Nov 1863, Oct 1864-Jun 1865. Extracts from diary of Union admiral, commanding the South Atlantic Blockading Squadron; overseeing operations against the Confederate defenses at Charleston; coordinating the sea and land offensives with General Gillmore against forts Wagner, Gregg, Sumter and Moultrie; movements of the ironclads and monitors; evacuation of Wagner and Gregg, delivering Morris Island into Union hands; attack of "David," Confederate torpedo boat, on the IRONSIDES; differences of opinion on strategy between military commanders and Secretary of War Stanton; operations on the Broad River; meeting Sherman at Savannah; inspection of Fort McAllister, remarking on ingenuity of the defenses, including primitive mines, and both the quantity and quality of obstructions in the waters around Savannah; planning assault on Charleston; conferring with Sherman; moving into evacuated Charleston and appraisal of Confederate defenses there; ceremony of raising the United States flag at Fort Sumter; last day of command.

DANIELS, ARTHUR M.   4381

A JOURNAL OF SIBLEY'S INDIAN EXPEDITION DURING THE SUMMER OF 1863. Minneapolis: James D. Thueson, 1980. 154 pp.

Jun-Aug 1863. A journal of Gen. Henry H. Sibley's punitive campaign against the Sioux, kept by a young soldier in Company H, Sixth Regiment; long, hot marches across the Dakota prairies in pursuit of Indians.

DICKINSON, ALBERT   4382

In TRAGIC YEARS, by Paul M. Angle and Earl S. Miers, vol. 2, p. 725.

Oct-Nov 1863. Routine military operations in northern Alabama as reflected in extracts from diary of member of Taylor's Battery, Illinois Light Artillery.

DOUGHERTY, MICHAEL, b. 1846?   4383

PRISON DIARY OF MICHAEL DOUGHERTY. Bristol, Pa.: C.A. Dougherty, Printer, 1908. 75 pp.

DIARY OF A CIVIL WAR HERO. With a pictorial history of the war by James Boylan. New York: Pyramid Books, 1960. 128 pp. Diary, pp. 7-47, 81-125.

1863-1865 (with gap). Prison experiences of Irish immigrant, Congressional Medal of Honor recipient, member of the Thirteenth Pennsylvania Cavalry, taken prisoner in the Shenandoah Valley and held at Libby, Pemberton, Belle Isle and Andersonville; conditions which grew progressively worse as the diarist was moved from one prison to another; hardships and cruelties; rations, getting extras, rate of currency exchange, vermin, deaths resulting from forced vaccination, etc.; notes on the "raiders," mock presidential election, Captain Wirz and Father Hamilton at Andersonville; prisoners' feelings of abandonment by Union government; release and journey home to Bristol, Pennsylvania, surviving the wreck of the SULTANA; detailed description of prisons added later, rendering the work dubious and bringing charges of plagiarism.

DOW, NEAL, 1804?-1897   4384

Byrne, Frank L., ed. "A General behind Bars: Neal Dow in Libby Prison." CIVIL WAR HISTORY 8 (1962):164-183.

Dec 1863-Mar 1864. Prison diary of Portland, Maine, temperance and abolition advocate, a brigadier general captured near Port

Hudson; daily entries detailing conditions at Libby; weather, rations, accommodations, regulations, etc.; prices and exchange rates; guards' thefts and cruelty; reports of conditions at Belle Isle; rumor that powder had been placed under the prison to destroy it in the event of invasion; contributions of the Sanitary Commission; harsher treatment of black soldiers and their officers.

DRIPS, JOSEPH H., b. 1828?   4385

THREE YEARS AMONG THE INDIANS IN DAKOTA. Kimball, S.D.: Brule Index, 1894. 139 pp. Reprint. With a new introduction by John M. Carroll. New York: S. Lewis, 1974.

1863-1865 (with gaps). Diary, rewritten while in winter quarters, of sergeant, Company L, Sixth Iowa Cavalry; march from Davenport, Iowa, to Fort Randall, on the Missouri River near present Nebraska-South Dakota border; military operations in Dakota Territory, including expeditions led by Gen. Alfred Sully; minor and major engagements with Indians; journey back to Iowa home; good descriptions of countryside, forts and other settlements; details of weather, distances and routes of march and availability of water, grass and wood; notes on hardships, duties, casualties, desertions, military punishments, etc.

DYER, JOHN E.   4386

In HISTORY OF THE FIFTH MASSACHUSETTS BATTERY, by Massachusetts Artillery, 5th Battery, pp. 526-893 passim.

1863-1864. Extracts from private's diary covering operations of the battery; Burnside's "Mud March"; the Chancellorsville campaign; battle of Gettysburg; the Petersburg campaign.

EDGAR, HENRY   4387

"Journal of Henry Edgar." MONTANA HISTORICAL SOCIETY CONTRIBUTIONS 3 (1900):124-142.

Feb-Jun 1863. Prospector's journal of an expedition from Bannack to the Yellowstone River area; trouble with straying and stampeding horses, getting lost, frustrating attempt to rendezvous with James Stuart; capture by Indians, with good account of captivity; release, but continuing danger from Indians; prospecting in Madison River area and mention of gold discovery at Alder Gulch, with subsequent gold rush to the area.

ELVIDGE, FRANK H.   4388

In HISTORY OF THE ONE HUNDRED AND FIFTIETH REGIMENT, PENNSYLVANIA VOLUNTEERS, SECOND REGIMENT, BUCKTAIL BRIGADE, by Thomas Chamberlin, pp. 207-264 passim. Philadelphia: J.B. Lippincott, 1895. Rev. and enl. ed., pp. 253-311 passim. Philadelphia: F. McManus, Jr., Printers, 1905.

1863-1865. Extracts from pocket diary of a soldier in Company A; experiences as a prisoner of war, captured at Gettysburg and marched shoeless to Staunton, Virginia, held at Belle Isle and paroled in September 1863; notes on military action in Virginia with occasional personal comments; Petersburg campaign.

EVERETT, EBEN   4389

Lindgren, Raymond E., ed. "A Diary of Kit Carson's Navaho Campaign." NEW MEXICO HISTORICAL REVIEW 21 (1946):226-246.

Aug 1863. A march of the First New Mexico Volunteers to pursue a "scorched earth" policy against the Navahos, killing all

livestock and burning corn fields, driving Indians to seek refuge in Canyon de Chelly; route and conditions of travel; skirmishes and casualties; diarist's alarm over the scalping of Indians by troops; references to Capt. Albert H. Pfeiffer and Maj. Joseph Cummings. Usually attributed to Eben Everett.

EXEL, CHRISTIAN   4390

Rothfuss, Hermann. "German Witnesses of the Sioux Campaign." NORTH DAKOTA HISTORY 25 (1958):123-133.

Jun-Jul 1863. German immigrant newspaper publisher's account of service with the Sixth Minnesota Infantry Regiment as part of Gen. Henry H. Sibley's campaign aganist the Sioux; activities at Fort Abercrombie; marches made unbearable by the hot, dry summer. Translated from the German.

FALLIS, LEROY   4391

In THE SOLDIER OF INDIANA IN THE WAR FOR THE UNION, by Catharine Merrill, vol. 2, pp. 451-452.

Oct 1863. Brief notes from diary of member of Eighth Indiana Cavalry on camp conditions and military movements in Tennessee's Sequatchie Valley; comment on troops transferred from eastern army.

FERGUS, JAMES   4392

"A Leaf from the Diary of James Fergus Relative to the Fisk Emigration Party of 1862, and Early Mining Life at Bannack, 1863." MONTANA HISTORICAL SOCIETY CONTRIBUTIONS. 2 (1896):252-254.

Jan 1863. Extract from memorandum kept by a man who had come to Montana in James L. Fisk's party; work as a carpenter at Bannack, busy making coffins for victims of the violent life there; a massacre by whites of Indians in their lodges nearby, with the murderers apparently going unpunished; diarist's reflections on the unstable nature of Bannack society, including activities of the outlaw Henry Plummer.

FLAKE, LUCY HANNAH WHITE   4393

In JAMES MADISON FLAKE, PIONEER, LEADER AND MISSIONARY, compiled by S. Eugene Flake, pp. 66-74. Bountiful, Utah: Wasatch Press, 1970.

1863-1890? Extracts from the diary of a Mormon ranch wife in Snowflake, Arizona; cattle drives, household chores, busy, happy family life; interest in women's suffrage.

Extracts in WITH THESE HANDS, by Joan M. Jensen, pp. 136-140. Old Westbury, New York: Feminist Press; New York: McGraw-Hill, 1981.

1896-1898.

FORREST, DOUGLAS FRENCH, 1837-1902   4394

ODYSSEY IN GRAY. Edited by William N. Still, Jr. Richmond: Virginia State Library, 1979. 352 pp.

1863-1865 (with gaps). Diary of Virginia lawyer, Yale graduate, who had served in the army at First Bull Run, now an officer in the Confederate navy; running the Charleston blockade in the MARGARET & JESSIE, fired on by the enemy and forced to abandon ship in the Bahamas; at Nassau, Havana and St. Thomas before securing passage to England; seeing the sights of that country and Scotland while awaiting assignment; appointed paymaster of the commerce raider RAPPAHANNOCK at Calais; duties of his position and considerable social life; visits to Paris; French efforts to keep the Confederate ship in port; touring Germany, Switzerland and Italy; return to the Confederacy, running the blockade at Galveston; rejoining the army in Texas, a member of Gen. John G. Walker's staff; a scheme to go to Mexico after the surrender foiled by his illness; lengthy entries detailing his activities, the people he met and the sights he saw; much discussion of the young ladies; good travel descriptions; notes on food, foreign customs, prostitutes, Tom Thumb and his family, fellow officers, proper behavior, etc.; religious sentiments; bitter feelings towards Northerners; an informative account, particularly in terms of the manners and mores of the period.

"An Odyssey in Gray." VIRGINIA CAVALCADE 29, no. 3 (1980):124-129.

1863-1865. Extracts.

FREMANTLE, Sir ARTHUR JAMES LYON, 1835-1901   4395

THREE MONTHS IN THE SOUTHERN STATES. Edinburgh and London: W. Blackwood and Sons, 1863. 316 pp. Reprint. Alexandria, Va.: Time-Life Books, 1984. 316, 19 pp. Mobile, Ala.: S.H. Goetzel, 1864. 158 pp. New York: J. Bradburn, 1864. 309 pp. Reprint. Westport, Conn.: Negro Universities Press, 1970.

THE FREMANTLE DIARY. Edited by Walter Lord. Boston: Little Brown, 1954; London: A. Deutsch, 1956. 304 pp.

Widely extracted. See, for instance, in THE BLUE AND THE GRAY, edited by Henry S. Commager, vol. 2, pp. 636-638; DIARY OF AMERICA, edited by Josef and Dorothy Berger, pp. 431-435; TRAGIC YEARS, by Paul M. Angle and Earl S. Miers, vol. 2, pp. 647-648.

Mar-Jul 1863. The South at war as seen by an Englishman, a lieutenant colonel on leave from the Coldstream Guards, a lively gadabout, quickly accepted into Southern society and the company of generals, a fine diarist with a keen eye for people, places and events; travel across the Confederacy with stops including Brownsville, San Antonio, Houston, Galveston, Natchez, Jackson, Mobile and Shelbyville; description of frontier conditions in Texas, transportation, accommodations and countryside; observations of slavery; enjoying the hospitality of John B. Magruder, Kirby Smith, Leonidas Polk, Joe Johnston, Dabney H. Maury and Braxton Bragg; meeting with Beauregard at Charleston and inspecting the city's defenses; interviews with Jefferson Davis, Judah P. Benjamin and James Seddon at Richmond; notes on hardships of railroad travel, destruction in the South, the Vicksburg campaign, the Union blockade, Sam Houston, Stonewall Jackson, St. Leger Grenfell, Clement Vallandigham, etc.; accompanying the Army of Northern Virginia as it advanced into Pennsylvania; occupation of Chambersburg; with the First Corps during the battle of Gettysburg, observing Lee, Longstreet and many of their subordinates in action; retreat to Hagerstown; through the lines to New York City; noting Northern prosperity and witnessing the draft riots; pro-Southern assessment of the opposing armies and leadership.

"The Battle of Gettysburg and the Campaign in Pennsylvania." BLACKWOOD'S MAGAZINE 94 (1863):365-394.

Jun-Jul 1863. Extracts.

In TWO VIEWS OF GETTYSBURG, by Sir Arthur J.L. Fremantle and Frank A. Haskell, edited by Richard Harwell, pp. 3-92. Chicago: Lakeside, 1964.

Jun-Jul 1863. Extracts.

FRENCH, LUCY VIRGINIA SMITH, 1825-1881   4396

Gower, Herschell, ed. "The Beersheba Diary of L. Virginia French." EAST TENNESSEE HISTORICAL SOCIETY PUBLICATIONS, nos. 52 and 53 (1980-1981):89-107. To be continued in a subsequent number.

May-Dec 1863. Extracts from diary kept at Beersheba Springs, Grundy County, by the wife of wealthy landowner and horsebreeder, John Hopkins French, of Forest Home near McMinnville; efforts to restore her health and find a situation conducive to her work as an author defeated by visitations of Union troops and local bushwackers; description of depredations; notes on her health and emotions.

FURNAS, ROBERT W.   4397

Rowan, Richard D., ed. "The Second Nebraska's Campaign against the Sioux." NEBRASKA HISTORY 44 (1963):3-53. Journal, pp. 6-25.

Jun-Sep 1863. Official military journal of commander of the Second Nebraska Volunteer Cavalry, with reports by Sergeant Smith G. Ward interspersed; route and camps; difficulty in maintaining cavalry during terribly hot, dry weather; references to Gen. Alfred Sully; a monotonous, uneventful campaign except for the battle of Whitestone Hill, during which the Nebraska Second attacked and killed a large number of Sioux already "in full retreat."

GRAHAM, ZIBA B., b. 1839   4398

In WAR PAPERS, by Military Order of the Loyal Legion of the United States, Michigan Commandery, vol. 1, pp. 3-16. Detroit: Ostler Printing, 1888.

ON TO GETTYSBURG. Detroit: Winn & Hammond, Printers, 1893. 16 pp.

Extract in TRAGIC YEARS, by Paul M. Angle and Earl S. Miers, vol. 2, pp. 653-654.

Jun-Jul 1863. Officer's diary extracts describing the march of the Sixteenth Michigan to Gettysburg and its costly participation in the battle; comments on frequent changes of command in the Army of the Potomac, patriotism of Marylanders and soliders' regard for McClellan; some evidence of later embellishment.

GRANNIS, JOHN W.   4399

In A SUNDAY BETWEEN WARS, by Ben Maddow, pp. 90-96.

1863-1865. Account of a difficult lonely and dangerous life mining for gold in Colorado and Nevada after being divorced by his wife.

GRAY, VIRGINIA DAVIS, 1834-1886   4400

Moneyhon, Carl H., ed. "Life in Confederate Arkansas." ARKANSAS HISTORICAL QUARTERLY 42 (1983):47-85, 134-169.

1863-1866. Diary of Maine native who moved to Arkansas in 1858, remaining there during the war, a staunch supporter of the Confederate cause; social and religious activities in Princeton and surrounding area; the passage of troops of both sides through the town; missing her husband, the former principal of the Princeton Female Academy, serving in the Confederate army; mention of many friends and neighbors; notes on reading, a

Christmas celebration, conscripts, deaths, marriages, etc.

Extract in A DOCUMENTARY HISTORY OF ARKANSAS, edited by C. Fred Williams and others, pp. 105-106.

Dec 1863. A single long entry describing Union raid; notes on losses in the fighting, behavior of Union soldiers and exodus of slaves.

GRAYSON, SPENCE M.   4401

In RECOLLECTIONS OF A MARYLAND CONFEDERATE SOLDIER AND STAFF OFFICER, by McHenry Howard, pp. 222-223, 233-234. Baltimore: Williams & Wilkins, 1914.

Jul-Aug, Oct 1863. Extracts from diary of private, Company A, Second Maryland Battalion, Steuart's Brigade; very brief entries recording the march back from Gettysburg and subsequent movements of his unit in Virginia.

GREEN, ISAAC   4402

In EVERYDAY SOLDIER LIFE, OR A HISTORY OF THE ONE HUNDRED AND THIRTEENTH OHIO VOLUNTEER INFANTRY, by Francis M. McAdams, pp. 30-148 passim. Columbus: C.M. Cott, 1884.

Jun-Jul 1863. Extracts from Company E private's diary, tracing regiment's movements between Triune and Shelbyville and describing other events in Tennessee; notes on the Christian Commission, a visit to Atlanta, an incident while marching through Georgia and a military execution.

GREEN, J.E.   4403

"As a North Carolina Lieutenant Saw Gettysburg." CIVIL WAR TIMES ILLUSTRATED 3, no. 5 (1964):30.

Jul 1863. Extract from diary of Union County man, lieutenant with the Fifty-third North Carolina; substantial entries covering all three days of battle and evaluating outcome.

HABERSHAM, JOSEPHINE CLAY HABERSHAM, 1821-1893   4404

EBB TIDE; AS SEEN THROUGH THE DIARY OF JOSEPHINE CLAY HABERSHAM. By Spencer B. King, Jr. Athens: University of Georgia Press, 1958. 129 pp.

Jun-Nov 1863. Diary kept by member of prominent Georgia family, mother of Anna Wylly Habersham; social and leisure activities at Avon, summer retreat at White Bluff on the Vernon River near Savannah; maternal joys and worries, particularly relating to eldest son in army and youngest son in diapers; notes on religious concerns, enjoyment of music and literature, war rumors and news, prices, deaths, etc.; return to Savannah home; meeting with Jefferson Davis; a vivid portrait of family life within the Southern aristocracy.

HAGADORN, HENRY J., 1832-1903   4405

Pritchett, John P., ed. "On the March with Sibley in 1863." NORTH DAKOTA HISTORICAL QUARTERLY 5 (1931):103-129.

Jan-Aug 1863. Diary of a private with Company H of the Seventh Minnesota engaged in Gen. Henry H. Sibley's campaign against the Sioux; in quarters at Mankato, then on march to Devil's Lake, with camps, distances and reports of Indian movements; the diarist's suffering from illness as well as the usual discomforts

of heat, thirst and dust; Civil War news, including the "glorious news" of Union victory at Vicksburg; disgust with the "wickedness and depravity of man" evident in the military; notes on the beauty and agricultural potential of the region.

HALL, JOHN C.   4406

In SERVICE WITH THE SIXTH WISCONSIN VOLUNTEERS, by Rufus R. Dawes, p. 148. Marietta, Ohio: E.R. Alderman & Sons, 1890; edited by Alan T. Nolan, p. 148. Madison: State Historical Society of Wisconsin for Wisconsin Civil War Centennial Commission, 1962.

Jun 1863. Three diary extracts reflecting soldier's opinion of Joe Hooker after Chancellorsville.

HANDER, CHRISTIAN WILHELM, b. 1834   4407

Plummer, Leonard B., ed. "Excerpts from the Hander Diary." JOURNAL OF MISSISSIPPI HISTORY 26 (1964):141-149.

May-Jul 1863. Extracts from diary of Danish immigrant to Texas, a Confederate soldier defending Vicksburg; conditions under the siege and hopes of rescue by Johnston's forces; treatment after the surrender; noting war's destruction in Louisiana on his way home after being paroled.

HANDY, ISAAC WILLIAM KER, 1815-1878   4408

UNITED STATES BONDS. Baltimore: Turnbull Brothers, 1874. 670 pp. Diary, pp. 1-603.

1863-1864. Portsmouth, Virginia, Presbyterian minister's prison diary; arrest while visiting Delaware and incarceration as a political prisoner at Fort Delaware; long daily entries covering conditions and events; cruelties and kindnesses of captors; notes on filth, bugs, sickness, medical care, rations, prisoners' pastimes, escape attempts, deaths, punishments, exchange problems, sermons, the Christian Commission, April Fool's Day and Fourth of July celebrations, etc.; receipt of boxes of food and other comforts; conducting worship services, visiting the sick and counseling individuals; concern about drinking, gambling and other vices of inmates and the effect of his religious activities on their behavior; defending his Southern views with commentary on taking oath of allegiance and "galvanized Confederates"; mention of many fellow prisoners, visitors, Union officers and friends, including Col. Basil Duke, Capt. Charlton H. Morgan and Gen. Albin Schoepf, the prison commander.

HARRISON, MARY DOUGLASS WARING, b. 1845   4409

MISS WARING'S JOURNAL. Edited by Thad Holt, Jr. Chicago: Wyvern Press of S.F.E., 1964. 17 pp.

Jul-Aug 1863, Mar-Sep 1865. Diary kept by young Mobile woman as means of self-improvement; social life and a boat trip to Bladon Springs; a civilian's view of the Mobile campaign; work of the Soldier's Hope Society; fall of Spanish Fort and farewells to brothers and soldier friends; Union occupation of Mobile and observations on enemy soldiers.

Extracts in HEROINES OF DIXIE, edited by Katharine M. Jones, pp. 385-389.

Mar-Apr 1865. Fall of Mobile and its occupation.

HASKINS, NANNIE E., b. 1846?   4410

Underwood, Betsy Swint. "War Seen through a Teen-ager's Eyes." TENNESSEE HISTORICAL QUARTERLY 20 (1961):177-187.

Feb-Oct 1863. Extracts, generally undated, from diary of Clarksville, Tennessee, adolescent, reflecting life under Union occupation and the undependable nature of reports of war's events; feelings toward the enemy, contempt for Southern men not in the army and her anguish about having to take oath of allegiance.

HAWK, ELLEN MARIA MILLER, b. 1846   4411

In MY MOTHER'S DIARY AND I, by Philip B. Hawk, pp. 1-46 passim. Miami Beach? Fla., 1951.

1863-1879 (with gaps). Extracts from East Branch, New York, woman's diary; teenage days of school at Walton Academy, Walton, New York; teaching in village school there; returning home to care for sick brothers and sisters and to get away from teaching which she disliked; reluctantly marrying; confidences in diary revealing happier days after births of children; a pleasant trip to Centennial Exposition in Philadelphia.

HAWKES, GEORGE P.   4412

IN HISTORY OF THE TWENTY-FIRST REGIMENT, MASSACHUSETTS VOLUNTEERS, by Charles F. Walcott, pp. 286-290, 297.

Nov-Dec 1863. Extracts from diary of regiment's commander, covering the siege of Knoxville and afterwards; military action, lack of provisions and regimental reenlistments.

HAZARD, SARAH CONGDON HAZARD, b. 1831   4413

Hart, Helen Hazard, ed. "Around the Horn: Journal of the Captain's Wife." NEWPORT HISTORY 38 (1965):131-149.

Jul-Nov 1863. Journal kept at sea by the wife of Newport ship captain Lewis Ludlam Hazard on the LANCASHIRE en route from New York to San Francisco; terrors of the Horn and admiration of her husband's seamanship; a seminarrative journal in rather elevated style.

HEGEMAN, GEORGE W., b. 1845   4414

Heslin, James J., ed. "The Diary of a Union Soldier in Confederate Prisons." NEW YORK HISTORICAL SOCIETY QUARTERLY 41 (1957):233-278.

1863-1865. Diary of member of Company B, Fifty-second New York; wounding and capture during the Bristoe campaign; treatment during transport to Richmond; imprisonment at Belle Isle; visit from Neal Dow, fights among prisoners and a dog for dinner; observations on South Carolina and Georgia en route to Andersonville; descriptions of the horrible situation there, behavior of Henry Wirz and kind treatment from Confederate physician; shifted to Charleston, Savannah, Jefferson County, Florida, and back to Charleston; escape and recapture; prisoners' presidential vote at Florence and another foiled escape; conditions at each prison, with notes on weather, rations, prices, his health, war news, deaths, etc.

HIGHT, JOHN J., 1834-1886   4415

HISTORY OF THE FIFTY-EIGHTH REGIMENT OF INDIANA VOLUNTEER INFANTRY. Compiled by Gilbert R. Stormont. Princeton, Ind: Press of the Clarion, 1895. 577 pp. Diary, pp. 122-540 passim.

1863-1865. Entries from diary of Methodist minister, chaplain of the Fifty-eighth Indiana, merging into narrative, condensed by the compiler for publication; campaigning in Tennessee, including the battles of Chickamauga, Lookout Mountain and Missionary Ridge and the Knoxville campaign; at Chattanooga; regiment's reenlistment as veteran volunteers, at Nashville and assignment as pontoniers in the Pioneer corps; the Atlanta campaign and the March to the Sea; condemnation of Gen. Jefferson C. Davis's abandonment of contrabands at Buck Head Creek; at Savannah and then through the Carolinas; mustering out in Indiana; description of and opinions on military matters; duties of his chaplaincy, including sermons, prayer meetings and work among the wounded; notes on towns and countryside, destruction in the South and soldiers' drinking and on many individuals, including generals John A. Logan, Judson Kilpatrick, James Morgan and Sherman; his abolitionist sentiments on slavery, contrabands and black Union soldiers.

HINTON, W.J., b. 1837   4416

"Diary of Lt. W.J. Hinton of Richmond, Arkansas." COWLITZ COUNTY HISTORICAL QUARTERLY 3, no. 1 (1961):11-17; no. 2, 20-27; no. 4 (1962):19-21.

Mar-Aug 1863. Account of Confederate soldier, Company H, Twelfth Arkansas Infantry, at Port Hudson; military and leisure activities; the siege, casualties and surrender; description of countryside, Northern civilians, reaction to prisoners on way to Johnson's Island and early days of imprisonment there.

HOAG, LEVI L., b. 1831   4417

Bearss, Edwin C., ed. "The Civil War Diary of Sgt. Levi L. Hoag." ANNALS OF IOWA, ser. 3 39 (1968):168-193.

Apr-Jul 1863. Record of the Vicksburg campaign by Cedar County farmer, a sergeant in Company H, Twenty-fourth Ohio; the battles of Port Gibson and Champion's Hill; besieging Vicksburg until its surrender; notes on weather, unit's movements, foraging and everyday activities and events.

HOPKINS, OWEN JOHNSTON, 1844-1902   4418

UNDER THE FLAG OF NATION. Edited by Otto F. Bond. Columbus: Ohio State University Press for the Ohio Historical Society, 1961. 308 pp. Diary, pp. 54-81, 93-186.

Apr-Aug 1863, Jan-Nov 1864. Pocket diaries of member of Company K, Forty-second Ohio Volunteer Infantry, occasionally interspersed with letters and extracts from later manuscript narrative; the Vicksburg campaign, describing bombardment of Grand Gulf, battle of Port Gibson and the siege of Vicksburg; subsequent operations in Mississippi; stationed at Plaquemine and Baton Rouge, Louisiana; assisting Banks's retreating forces in the Red River campaign; dull times at camp at Morganza, Louisiana, and at the mouth of the White River in Arkansas; mustering out of service, return home to Ohio, appointment as regimental quartermaster of the 182d Ohio Volunteer Infantry and journey to new post at Nashville; notes on foraging, reading, weather, correspondence, river traffic, news from eastern theater, etc.

HOPPER, SILAS L.   4419

''Diary of Silas L. Hopper, Blandinsville, Illinois.'' ANNALS OF WYOMING 3 (1925):117-126.

Apr-Aug 1863. Journey from Nebraska City to San Francisco, thence to Panama on the steamer CONSTITUTION and to New York on the OCEAN QUEEN; very brief notes of overland trip; camp, route, costs of hay, ferrying, etc., and fewer details of ship travel.

HOWARD, HARLAN SMITH, b. 1842?   4420

Jennings, Warren A., ed. ''Prisoner of the Confederacy.'' WEST VIRGINIA HISTORY 36 (1975):309-323.

Sep-Dec 1863. Diary of Cottage Grove, Wisconsin, resident, a member of the Badger Battery, Third Wisconsin Light Artillery; battle of Chickamauga and capture; journey through Georgia and the Carolinas to Richmond prison; notes on rations, lice, activities, etc.; transferred to Danville and escape from there; journey to West Virginia assisted by blacks; reunion with family.

HOWARD, MCHENRY, 1838-1923   4421

RECOLLECTIONS OF A MARYLAND CONFEDERATE SOLDIER AND STAFF OFFICER. Baltimore: Williams & Wilkins, 1914. 423 pp. Diary, pp. 195-222 passim.

Jan-Sep 1863. Officer's diary; trip from Richmond, through Lynchburg, to Montgomery Sulphur Springs, seeking renewed health; appointment to Gen. Isaac Trimble's staff; journey down the Shenandoah Valley, trying to catch up with the army on its way to Pennsylvania but missing the battle; retreat to Virginia; in camp at Montpelier, serving on Gen. George H. Steuart's staff.

HOWE, DANIEL WAIT, 1839-1920   4422

CIVIL WAR TIMES, 1861-1865. Indianapolis: Bowen-Merrill, 1902. 421 pp. Diary, pp. 139-155, 250-267.

Jan-Jun 1863, Nov 1863-Apr 1864. Extracts from diary kept by member of Company I, Seventy-ninth Indiana; activities and conditions of camp life at Murfreesboro, Tennessee; assessment of Union soldiers' attitudes toward abolition of slavery; war news and commentary on it; hardships of campaigning in east Tennessee; notes on weather, food, reading, etc.

HOWE, JAMES   4423

In HISTORY OF THE FIFTIETH REGIMENT OF INFANTRY, MASSACHUSETTS VOLUNTEER MILITIA, by William Burnham Stevens, pp. 136-137.

May 1863. Extract from journal of Company F private; assault on Port Hudson.

HUSE, EVERETT B.   4424

In HISTORY OF THE FIFTEENTH REGIMENT, NEW HAMPSHIRE VOLUNTEERS, by Charles McGregor, pp. 406-409. Concord, N.H.: I.C. Evans, 1900.

May 1863. Extracts from diary of member of Company C on detached service as clerk in quartermaster's department, Gen. T.W. Sherman's Second Division, Nineteenth Corps; with the army by ship to Baton Rouge and wagon train to Port Hudson; eavesdropping on generals in strategy sessions; report on assault of Confederate fortifications and consequent casualties.

HUTT, WARREN B.   4425

''An Interesting Human Document.'' CONFEDERATE VETERAN 36 (1928): 36-38.

Jul 1863-May 1864. A Virginian's prison diary kept at Point Lookout; brief entries, noting food, correspondence, deaths, prices, activities, etc.; comments on black Union guards.

INGERSOLL, E.J.   4426

In A HISTORY OF THE SEVENTY-THIRD REGIMENT OF ILLINOIS INFANTRY VOLUNTEERS, by Illinois Infantry, 73d Regiment, pp. 595-597.

Dec 1863-Jan 1864. Captain's memoranda of convalescent soldiers' march to Knoxville and an engagement with Wheeler's cavalry.

INGRAHAM, ELIZABETH MARY MEADE, b. 1806   4427

In RECOLLECTIONS OF HENRY WATKINS ALLEN, by Sarah A. Dorsey, pp. 397-420. New York: M. Doolady; New Orleans: J.A. Gresham, 1866.

Darst, W. Maury, ed. ''The Vicksburg Diary of Mrs. Alfred Ingraham.'' JOURNAL OF MISSISSIPPI HISTORY 44 (1982):148-179.

May-Jun 1863. Extracts from diary kept by older sister of Union general George Meade, residing at Ashwood, a plantation in Claiborne County, Mississippi, eight miles from Grand Gulf and thirty miles below Vicksburg; extensive pillaging of her home by successive waves of Union troops and by her own slaves; reports of depredations elsewhere; mourning the loss of cherished personal possessions; cleaning up and listening to distant cannonading; depending on the charity of a few faithful servants and living in fear of retaliation by others; news of son's death in Confederate service.

IRWIN, SAMUEL S.   4428

Monahan, James, ed. ''Excerpts from the Diary of Samuel S. Irwin.'' JOURNAL OF MISSISSIPPI HISTORY 27 (1965):390-394.

Jul 1863. Extracts from diary of lieutenant, Company I, Second Illinois Cavalry, covering Sherman's advance on Johnston's forces at Jackson; very brief note on the Champion's Hill battlefield; mention of Confederate use of land mines; Union sacking of the town.

JACKSON, J. THOMPSON, 1838-1892   4429

DIARY. McKeesport, Pa., 1954. 33 leaves.

1863-1865. Diary kept by brother of Samuel M. Jackson, serving with the Fortieth Pennsylvania Infantry; wounding and capture in the battle of Fredericksburg; briefly at Libby Prison; in hospital at Annapolis, suffering from wound and low spirits; daily report on his wound and on entertainments at hospital in Philadelphia; furlough home to Armstrong County; battle of Gettysburg; following Lee through the rain and mud; days in Virginia where entries usually note that nothing new or important has occurred.

JOHNSON, ANDREW JACKSON, 1841-1916   **4430**

CIVIL WAR DIARY OF ANDREW J. JOHNSON. Greenwood, Ind., 1961. 20 leaves.

> 1863-1865. Carpenter/farmer's diary of service with Company I, Seventieth Indiana Volunteers; daily activities in Tennessee, including making wreaths; the Atlanta campaign, especially the battle of Peach Tree Creek; battle of Nashville; by boat on the Cumberland and Ohio rivers, train to Alexandria, Virginia, and ship to North Carolina; campaigning there in the last days of the war; looking around Raleigh; the march north and the Grand Review; sightseeing in Washington, D.C.; journey home to Indiana; brief notes, covering a variety of subjects.

JOHNSON, HANNIBAL AUGUSTUS, b. 1841   **4431**

THE SWORD OF HONOR. Personal Narratives of Events in the War of the Rebellion, Being Papers Read before the Rhode Island Soldiers and Sailors Historical Society, ser. 6, no. 6. Providence: The Society, 1903. 72 pp. Diary, pp. 18-46. Hallowell, Maine: Register Printing House, 1905. 97 pp. Diary, pp. 22-42.

> Sep 1863-Jan 1864. Third Maine Infantry member's diary describing his imprisonment at Charleston, under bombardment by Union forces, and at Columbia; escape to Knoxville, aided by slaves and Southern unionists.

JOHNSON, HENRY H.   **4432**

In HISTORY OF THE FIFTIETH REGIMENT OF INFANTRY, MASSACHUSETTS VOLUNTEER MILITIA, by William Burnham Stevens, pp. 168-169, 214-215.

> Jun-Jul 1863. Extracts from Company F corporal's diary; siege of Port Hudson; death of a comrade; guarding Confederate officers being transported to New Orleans after the surrender.

JOHNSON, W.L., b. 1844   **4333**

In ANNUAL REPORT, 5th, by New York State Bureau of Military Statistics, pp. 682-714.

> 1863-1864. Sergeant's diary kept while in Company C, Thirty-third Ohio; capture during battle of Chickamauga and transport via Atlanta, Charlotte and Raleigh to Belle Isle; criticism of his division commander, General Baird, and comments on Confederate soldiers; transfer to Smith's tobacco factory in Richmond, then to Danville and finally Andersonville; prison conditions and activities, including reading and debates; notes on weather, rations, illness, escape attempts, exchange hopes and execution of "raiders"; glimpses of Wirz.

JOHNSON, WELCOME A.   **4434**

In SABRES AND SPURS: THE FIRST RHODE ISLAND CAVALRY IN THE CIVIL WAR, by Frederic Denison, pp. 259-270. Central Falls, R.I.: First Rhode Island Cavalry Veteran Association, 1876.

> Jun-Jul 1863. Trooper's account, possibly written or rewritten later, of prisoner of war experience; treatment of captives on march through the Shenandoah Valley; conditions at Belle Isle; exchange by way of City Point to Annapolis.

JOHNSTON, LEWIS SAURIN   **4435**

"Excerpts from the Diary of a Soldier Wounded in the Battle of Get-

tysburg." FLINT GENEALOGICAL QUARTERLY 3, no. 3 (1961):37.

> Jul 1863. Extracts from Sixteenth Michigan soldier's diary, briefly describing events of July 2 during which he was wounded and the hardships suffered by him and others in the days following the battle.

JOHNSTON, THOMAS W.   **4436**

In A HUNDRED BATTLES IN THE WEST, by Marshall P. Thatcher, pp. 359-364. Detroit: The Author, 1884.

> 1863-1865. Extracts from Second Michigan Cavalry officer's diary; wounding near Dandridge, Virginia, and grueling trip through Tennessee, Alabama and Kentucky home to Marshall, Michigan; in Georgia at war's end, noting presence of paroled Confederate soldiers.

KENNEDY, JOHN A.   **4437**

In THE REBELLION RECORD, edited by Frank Moore, vol. 7, pp. 267-269.

> May-Jun 1863. Diary of soldier, Company H, First Alabama, under siege at Port Hudson.

KEY, THOMAS J., 1831-1908   **4438**

In TWO SOLDIERS, edited by Wirt A. Cate, pp. 3-217. Chapel Hill: University of North Carolina Press, 1938.

Extract in TRAGIC YEARS 1860-1865, by Paul M. Angle and Earl S. Miers, vol. 2, pp. 851-852, 854-855, 880-881.

> 1863-1865. Diary kept by former Arkansas state legislator and newspaper publisher, battery captain in artillery battalion attached to Cleburne's division, Army of Tennessee; winter quarters at Tunnel Hill, Georgia; journey to family in Helena, Arkansas, and dodging Union soldiers while there; the Atlanta campaign; in command of the battalion during battle of Atlanta; reunion with old friends in Tuscumbia, Alabama; the Franklin and Nashville campaign; in Mississippi, Alabama and Macon, Georgia; imprisoned at Chattanooga and forced to take oath of allegiance at Nashville while trying to reach home at war's end; daily entries, with a few gaps, covering military operations and providing information on the environment of soldiering as well as wartime social and economic conditions; camp life, prices, reading, songs, religion, sexual conduct, deserters, celebration of Christmas and April Fool's Day, etc.; views on leadership of Johnston and Hood; discussion of Cleburne's recommendation that slaves be allowed to fight for their freedom in the Confederate armies; report of pillaging of his home and description of destruction in Georgia and Alabama; attending Georgia state legislature and assessment of Governor Brown; notes on 1864 presidential campaign and peace negotiations; bitter remarks about Union soldiers and leaders.

KILLGORE, GABRIEL M., 1825-1863   **4439**

Maynard, Douglas, ed. "Vicksburg Diary." CIVIL WAR HISTORY 10 (1964):33-53.

> Feb-Jul 1863. Daily record of Vicksburg campaign kept by Claiborne Parish, Louisiana, planter, captain of Company H, Seventeenth Louisiana Infantry; difficult journey from Minden, Louisiana, to Vicksburg; notes on prices of gold, cotton and food; the Confederate retreat into Vicksburg and the siege; conditions under fire, rations, casualties and waiting for Johnston; in hospital after the surrender, dying of disease on way home.

LABADIE, CECELIA, 1839-1873   4440

Williams, Marjorie L., ed. "Cecelia Labadie: Diary Fragment." TEX-ANA 10 (1972):273-283. Diary, pp. 279-281.

Jan-Feb 1863. Daily activities in Galveston; under fire from Union ships; noting movements of the blockading vessels.

LEE, FLORIDE CLEMSON, 1842-1871   4441

A REBEL CAME HOME; THE DIARY OF FLORIDE CLEMSON. Edited by Charles M. McGee, Jr. and Ernest M. Lander, Jr. Columbia: University of South Carolina Press, 1961. 153 pp.

1863-1866. Diary of John C. Calhoun's granddaughter, brimming with notes on a wide circle of family, friends and acquaintances; details of her everyday life and social activities in Bladensburg and Beltsville, Maryland; trips to Niagara Falls, Long Beach, New Jersey, and Lancaster, Pennsylvania, where she visited with Harriet Lane and James Buchanan; the war news as received by a Southern sympathizer; return to South Carolina and her maternal grandmother's home, Mi Casa, at Pendleton in December 1864; fears, rumors and conditions there as the war ends; her brother John Calhoun Clemson's report of his imprisonment at Johnson's Island; routine mention of her own and others' illnesses, medical treatments and a graphic account of Floride Calhoun's death from cancer; inheritance of Fort Hill; a listing of her jewelry; description of a celebration honoring the Confederate dead.

LENNON, MARTIN, d. 1864   4442

In ANNUAL REPORT, 5th, by New York State Bureau of Military Statistics, pp. 731-756.

1863-1864. Extracts from diary of schoolteacher now captain, Company I, Seventy-seventh New York Volunteers; Burnside's "Mud March"; Chancellorsville campaign; following Lee north but not at Gettysburg; the Wilderness, Spotsylvania, Cold Harbor and the beginning of the siege of Petersburg; between Washington, D.C., and the Shenandoah Valley, countering Early's threat; Sheridan's Valley campaign; fairly brief entries focused on military movements but with some comments providing a nice sense of his perspective on campaigning.

LIGHTNER, MARY ELIZABETH ROLLINS,   4443
1818-1913

"Mary Elizabeth Lightner Rollins." UTAH GENEALOGICAL AND HISTORICAL MAGAZINE 17 (1926):193-205, 250-260. Diary, pp. 252-260.

May-Sep 1863. Mormon woman's diary of a journey by riverboat from Stillwater, Minnesota, thence overland to Salt Lake with a group of Mormon immigrants from various countries; chores en route and complaint that "the Danes are at prayers by themselves...while I, poor sinner, am baking bread"; care for her sick children.

LODGE, GEORGE R., 1827-1911   4444

Tusken, Roger, ed. " 'In the Bastile of the Rebels.' " ILLINOIS STATE HISTORICAL SOCIETY JOURNAL 56 (1963):316-339.

Jul 1863-May 1864. Extracts from diary of lieutenant, Company G, Fifty-third Illinois Infantry, kept for his wife during confinement

in Libby Prison; description of the prison; notes on prices, rations, amusements and treatment of prisoners, including blacks and their officers; a visit by generals John H. Morgan and A.P. Hill; controversies among prisoners; the mass escape of February 1864; substantial entries providing an articulate, candid and angry record.

LORD, Mrs. W.W.   4445

In TRAGIC YEARS, by Paul M. Angle and Earl S. Miers, vol. 2, pp. 621-622.

1863. Brief extract from Vicksburg woman's diary telling of the cave where she and her children sought refuge from the Union bombardment.

MCCABE, WILLIAM GORDON, 1841-1920   4446

In MEMORIES AND MEMORIALS OF WILLIAM GORDON MCCABE, by Armistead C. Gordon, vol. 1, pp. 129-156, 163-167, 252-273. Richmond, Va.: Old Dominion, 1925.

Aug-Oct 1863, Mar-Apr 1865, Jul-Sep 1866. Diaries kept during Confederate service and a postwar European tour; assistant adjutant general with the forces under bombardment at Charleston; visits to forts Sumter and Wagner, description of artillery duels and copies of dispatches concerning Union assaults on the batteries defending the city; meeting poet Henry Timrod; serving as Col. William J. Pegram's adjutant; battle of Five Forks and death of Pegram; escape through enemy lines to Beauregard's headquarters in North Carolina; voyage to England and notes on sights seen, especially Eton and Oxford; comments on Spurgeon in his tabernacle; at Paris and through France, Switzerland and Germany; socializing with ex-Confederates; a rough voyage home.

Extracts in THE BLUE AND THE GRAY, edited by Henry S. Commager, vol. 2, pp. 1125-1126.

Apr 1865. Pegram's death.

MACY, WILLIAM MADISON, 1833-1926   4447

"The Civil War Diary of William M. Macy." INDIANA MAGAZINE OF HISTORY 30 (1934):181-197.

1863-1865. Extracts from diary of member of Company I, Ninety-fourth Illinois Volunteers; moving around Missouri and Arkansas; down the Mississippi to the siege of Vicksburg; relations between Union and Confederate soldiers after the surrender; stationed at Yazoo City, Vicksburg, Port Hudson, Carrollton and Brownsville; at Mobile, participating in assaults on Fort Morgan. Spanish Fort and Fort Blakely and noting torpedoes planted along roads by Confederates; mourning for Lincoln; return to Texas before mustering out.

MAYFIELD, LEROY S., b. 1841   4448

Barnhart, John D., ed. "A Hoosier Invades the Confederacy." INDIANA MAGAZINE OF HISTORY 39 (1943):144-191. Diary, pp. 156-191.

Aug-Dec 1863, Mar-Jun 1864. Diary of Twenty-second Indiana officer; daily entries, mostly recording military operations; stationed near Stevenson, Alabama, campaigning in Tennessee and viewing the battle of Chickamauga from Lookout Mountain's summit; the Chattanooga campaign; wounding at Missionary Ridge and afterwards visiting Confederate fortifications there and at Lookout Mountain; return from Indiana visit, traveling by train to Nashville and on foot to Chattanooga via Bridgeport, Alabama; in camp at Lee and Gordon Mills; the Atlanta campaign and wounding at the battle of Kenesaw Mountain; notes on countryside, execution of deserters, the Christian Commission, etc.

MEHRING, MAGGIE, b. 1850?   **4449**

In JUST SOUTH OF GETTYSBURG: CARROLL COUNTY, MARYLAND, IN THE CIVIL WAR, edited by Frederic S. Klein, pp. 211-216. Westminster, Md.: Newman, 1963.

Jun-Jul 1863. Portion of thirteen-year-old's journal describing passage of Union army units through New Windsor, Maryland, before and after the clash at Gettysburg; inaccurate reports of the battle.

MERRICK, LAURA   **4450**

In OLD TIMES IN DIXIE LAND, by Caroline E.T. Merrick, pp. 37-43, 51-52. New York: Grafton, 1901.

May-Jun 1863. Extracts from Southerner's diary; Union occupation of family's Louisiana plantation, depredations and the slaves' reactions.

MERRILIES, JOHN   **4451**

In TRAGIC YEARS, by Paul M. Angle and Earl S. Miers, vol. 2, pp. 723-724, 831-834.

Dec 1863, Jun 1864. Extracts from diary of lieutenant, Battery E, Illinois Light Artillery; skirmishes in Tennessee; clash at Brice's Cross Roads with Nathan B. Forrest and retreat of Union troops; praise for the performance of black soldiers of the Fifty-ninth United States Colored Troops.

MERRITT, E.A.   **4452**

In ANNUAL REPORT, 5TH, by New York State Bureau of Military Statistics, pp. 84-87.

May 1863. Extracts from journal of Sixtieth New York's quartermaster describing action seen by the regiment at Chancellorsville.

MINOR, HUBBARD TAYLOR, 1845-1874?   **4453**

"'I Am Getting a Good Education...'" CIVIL WAR TIMES ILLUSTRATED 13, no. 7 (1974):24-32, no. 8, 24-36.

Aug-Dec 1863, May, Jun, Dec 1864-Apr 1865. Extracts from the diary of midshipman in training at the Confederate Naval Academy located aboard the PATRICK HENRY, a converted man-of-war anchored off Drewry's Bluff; assigned to active duty on the SAVANNAH at Savannah; expedition resulting in capture of the WATER WITCH; return to the academy after Savannah's fall; following the Confederate government to Danville and Charlotte despite severe dysentery; routines of duty and study; church attendance and social activities in Richmond and Savannah; entries sometimes penned in batches.

MITCHELL, CHARLES D.   **4454**

In SKETCHES OF WAR HISTORY, by Military Order of the Loyal Legion of the United States, Ohio Commandery, vol. 6, pp. 174-194, 238-251. Cincinnati: R. Clarke, 1883-1908.

Jun 1863. Seventh Ohio Volunteer Cavalry lieutenant's account of cavalry raid led by Gen. William P. Sanders; military action and daily events.

Mar-Apr 1865. Account of Wilson's raid to Selma, Alabama; notes on military action, countryside, towns and cities, especially Montgomery; burning of Columbus, former slaves' enthusiasm for joining Union army.

MORGAN, JOHN S., 1841-1874   **4455**

"Diary of John S. Morgan." ANNALS OF IOWA, ser. 3 13 (1923):483-508, 570-610.

Feb-Dec 1863, Jan-Aug 1865. Diary of service with Company G, Thirty-third Iowa Infantry; military operations from bases at Helena and Little Rock, Arkansas; promotion to lieutenant and transfer of regiment to Mobile; investing Spanish Fort and Confederate evacuation of Mobile; reaction to Lincoln's assassination; waiting for all Southern armies to surrender; service along the Rio Grande until mustered out in July; journey home to Pella, Iowa; very brief entries except while at Mobile; notes on weather, duties, troop movements and demeanor of defeated Confederates; war news, mostly inaccurate.

MORROW, HENRY ANDREW, d. 1891   **4456**

"To Chancellorsville with the Iron Brigade." CIVIL WAR TIMES ILLUSTRATED 14, no. 9 (1976):12-22.

"The Last of the Iron Brigade." CIVIL WAR TIMES ILLUSTRATED 14, no. 10 (1976):10-22.

Jan-May 1863, Nov 1864-Feb 1865. Extracts from diary of Wayne County judge, the colonel commanding the Twenty-fourth Michigan Infantry, part of the Iron Brigade; Burnside's "Mud March"; operations at Fredericksburg during the Chancellorsville campaign; the siege of Petersburg; breveted brigadier general and temporarily placed in command of his division's Third Brigade; conversations with generals Hooker, Meade and Gouverneur K. Warren; reports of praise for his actions; Solomon Meredith's views on blacks and diarist's assessment of soldiers' support of emancipation as war aim; his negative opinion of Phil Sheridan and Edward S. Bragg, the last commander of the Iron Brigade; lamenting the destruction of civilian property and instances of rape during raid on the Weldon railroad; notes on army politics, troop reviews and use of substitutes; an interesting perspective on the Army of the Potomac's leadership.

MOYER, LYCURGUS ROSE, 1848-1917   **4457**

Bray, Edmund C. "Surveying the Seasons on the Minnesota Prairies." MINNESOTA HISTORY 48 (1982):72-82.

1863-1884 (with gaps). Article containing extracts from the few surviving portions of a self-taught botanist's diary; thirty years as county surveyor at Montevideo, Minnesota, which enabled him to observe and describe the seasons and changing vegetation of the prairie; civic and Congregational Church activities; contributing articles and reports to botanical and horticultural journals, speaking at learned societies and collecting specimens for herbaria; a lifelong concern for preservation of the prairie ecosystem.

MUMFORD, WILLIAM TAYLOR, 1841?-1901   **4458**

"Diary of the Vicksburg Siege." AMERICAN HISTORY ILLUSTRATED 12, no. 8 (1977):46-48.

Mar-Jul 1863. Extracts from diary of officer in the First Louisiana Artillery; enemy activity on the Mississippi and artillery operations along the river at Vicksburg; notes on morale and rations.

NASH, WILLIAM H. 4459

In HISTORY OF THE FIFTIETH REGIMENT OF INFANTRY, MASSACHUSETTS VOLUNTEER MILITIA, by William Burnham Stevens, pp. 35-42.

Jan 1863. Extracts from diary of Company D corporal detailing company's voyage on the MONTEBELLO from Fortress Monroe to Louisiana; quarantined for smallpox below New Orleans; sights and occurrences in new camp; notes on contrabands; proceeding to Baton Rouge.

NORTON, HENRY 4460

DEEDS OF DARING, OR, HISTORY OF THE EIGHTH N.Y. VOLUNTEER CAVALRY. Norwich, N.Y.: Chenango Telegraph Printing House, 1889. 184 pp. Diary, pp. 62-121.

1863-1865 (with gaps). Regiment's action record in Virginia, supposedly the wartime diary of member of Company H but bearing signs of later composition; generally brief entries of unit's movements with some longer summaries of major engagements; few details of participation in battles of Chancellorsville, Gettysburg and Sheridan's Valley campaign; notes on George A. Custer.

NUTT, LAETITIA LAFON ASHMORE, b. 1835 4461

COURAGEOUS JOURNEY. Edited by Florence Ashmore C.H. Martin. Miami, Florida: E.A. Seeman, 1975. 88 pp.

Oct 1863-Aug 1864. Journal kept at husband's request, recounting experiences as she and their three small daughters left home in Shreveport and tried to stay close to him while he served with Cleburne's Second Division, I Corps, Army of Tennessee; at Ringgold, Georgia, and then moving south, finally to Newnan, as the Confederate forces fell back towards Atlanta; much plaintive moaning over the absence of and the dangers confronting her husband but also some nice scenes of family life surviving war's upheaval.

O'BLENESS, JAMES, 1823-1863 4462

In AMERICAN PATRIOTISM, by Leonard Brown, pp. 292-294.

May-Jun 1863. Extracts from diary of sergeant in Company C, Twenty-third Iowa Infantry Volunteers; operations in Mississippi; battle of Port Gibson; transporting Confederate prisoners up the Mississippi.

O'BRIEN, GEORGE W., 1833-1909 4463

Ragan, Cooper K., ed. "The Diary of Captain George W. O'Brien." SOUTHWESTERN HISTORICAL QUARTERLY 67 (1963-1964): 26-54, 235-246, 413-433.

May-Dec 1863. Diary of Beaumont, Texas, lawyer, captain of Company E, Eleventh Battalion of Texas Volunteers; march to Louisiana and campaigning there; death of brother-in-law George Henry Rowley; battle of Bayou Fordache or Stirling's Plantation; on the way back to Texas.

ODEN, JOHN PINEY, b. 1823 4464

Barton, Michael, ed. "The End of Oden's War." ALABAMA HISTORICAL REVIEW 43 (1981):73-98.

Apr-Jun 1863. Account of wounded captain's efforts to get back to active duty; journey from Alabama to rejoin Company K, Tenth Alabama; stops in Selma, Montgomery, Knoxville and Richmond; days in camp; observing battle of Chancellorsville from the sidelines and touring the battlefield afterwards; unsuccessful effort to secure position as quartermaster to Talladega County; near Banks's Ford and at Richmond; resignation from army and journey home via Wilmington and Augusta; notes on camp life, sermons, soldiers' activities and news from home and of the war.

O'HAGEN, JOSEPH B., 1826-1878 4465

Lacey, William L., ed. "The Diary of Joseph B. O'Hagen, S.J., Chaplain of the Excelsior Brigade." CIVIL WAR HISTORY 6 (1960):402-409.

Feb 1863. Brief record of Irish Jesuit, chaplain of Dan Sickles's brigade, in winter quarters at Falmouth, Virginia; his work and social calls; notes on weather, camp life, Confederate women, collecting fossils, etc.; disgust with some military leaders and the conduct of the war; visit to Washington, D.C., and a short retreat at Georgetown College.

OLDROYD, OSBORN HAMLINE, 1842-1930 4466

A SOLDIER'S STORY OF THE SIEGE OF VICKSBURG. Springfield, Ill.: For the author, 1885. 200 pp. Diary, pp. 3-75.

Extracts in MISSISSIPPI IN THE CONFEDERACY, edited by John K. Bettersworth and James W. Silvers, vol. 1, pp. 126-128.

May-Jul 1863. Company E, Twentieth Ohio, sergeant's diary of the siege of Vicksburg from the landing at Bruinsburg to the surrender; engagement at Raymond and battle of Champion's Hill; investing the city and forays out to protect the army's rear; coverage of military operations and a variety of other subjects including foraging, chaplains, contrabands, newspapers, morale, food, treatment of slaves and the peace party; notes on generals Logan, McPherson and Grant and the regiment's colonel M.F. Force; long descriptive entries supposedly written on the spot but obviously with an eye toward publication.

OWEN, EDWARD 4467

In IN CAMP AND BATTLE WITH THE WASHINGTON ARTILLERY, by William Miller Owen, pp. 228-229. Boston: Ticknor, 1885.

May 1863. Extracts from diary of lieutenant, First Company, Washington Artillery; captured at Marye's Heights during Chancellorsville engagement; briefly at Old Capitol Prison; critiquing Northern newspaper accounts of the action in which he was taken prisoner; back in Richmond.

PARK, ROBERT EMORY, b. 1843? 4468

"War Diary of Capt. Robert Emory Park." SOUTHERN HISTORICAL SOCIETY PAPERS 26 (1898):1-31.

1863-1864 (with gaps). Company F, Twelfth Alabama captain's record of military action and social life; stationed near Richmond and enjoying theater in the city; battle of Chancellorsville; invasion of Pennsylvania and the battle of Gettysburg; furlough home to Greenville, Georgia; operations in Virginia, including battle of Bristoe Station and the Mine Run campaign; notes on duties, casualties, songs, train fares and sutler's prices, execution of a deserter, visit to Madison's Montpelier, religious activities in the army, etc.

"Diary of Robert E. Park." SOUTHERN HISTORICAL SOCIETY PAPERS 1 (1876):370-386, 430-437; 2 (1876):25-31, 78-85, 172-180, 232-239, 306-315; 3 (1877):43-46, 55-61, 123-127, 183-189, 244-254.

1864-1865. In hospital at Lynchburg; with Early's forces to the outskirts of Washington, D.C.; departure of his "faithful" slave; action in the Shenandoah Valley and comments on Union destructiveness there; seriously wounded at battle of Winchester, receiving assistance from Mrs. Hugh Lee and other ladies of the town; cruel treatment at West's Building Prison Hospital in Baltimore; guarded by black soldiers at Point Lookout; transferred to Old Capitol Prison, then to Fort Delaware and terrible conditions at the latter; reaction to news of Lee's surrender and Lincoln's assassination; names of forty prisoners steadfastly refusing to take oath of allegiance until after Edmund Kirby Smith's surrender; notes on reading, deaths of comrades, fellow prisoners of war, civilian supporters in border states, etc.

Extracts in POINT LOOKOUT PRISON CAMP FOR CONFEDERATES, by Edwin W. Beitzell, pp. 99-101. Abell, Md., 1972.

Dec 1864.

PATTERSON, WILLIAM T.   4469

In RECORD OF THE ONE HUNDRED AND SIXTEENTH REGIMENT, OHIO INFANTRY VOLUNTEERS, by Thomas F. Wildes, pp. 73-74. Sandusky: F. Mack & Brothers, Printers, 1884.

Aug 1863. Extracts from diary of soldier sick with fever in Martinsburg, Virginia, being won over by the kindness of the wife and daughter of a Confederate named Faulkner.

PATTISON, JOHN J.   4470

"With the U.S. Army along the Oregon Trail." NEBRASKA HISTORY 15 (1935):79-93.

1863-1866 (with gaps). Cavalryman's diary of marches on the plains with the Seventh Iowa and activities at Fort Laramie, with brief notes on Indians in the area; the battle of Horse Creek and escorting Indian prisoners to Fort Kearny; other skirmishes and Indian attacks on emigrants; erection of Fort Heath.

PIERCE, HENRY A.   4471

Rowan, Richard D., ed. "The Second Nebraska's Campaign against the Sioux." NEBRASKA HISTORY 44 (1963):3-53. Diary, pp. 25-50.

Jun-Sep 1863. Record of a hot, monotonous march to Fort Pierce and north, with notes on camps and routines; some dissension and leadership problems; the battle of Whitestone Hill graphically described; "never was a tribe of Indians so completely cut up"; taking of prisoners and spoils by the volunteers and the burning of Indians' supply of food and equipment.

PIERCE, NATHAN FRANK   4472

Kirk, Russell, ed. "A Michigan Soldier's Diary." MICHIGAN HISTORY 28 (1944):231-245.

1863-1864. Extracts from diary of Leonidas farmer and mail carrier who enlisted as hospital attendant, Company K, First Regi-

ment, United States Sanitary Service; battle of Gettysburg and following the Confederates back into Virginia; Mine Run campaign; from the Wilderness through Spotsylvania to Petersburg; notes on correspondence, his work, casualties, officers' drinking and the execution of a deserter; a spare but interesting account of a soldier's life.

PIKE, JAMES SHEPHERD, 1811-1882   4473

Davis, Harold, ed. "Dickens, Carlyle and Tennyson." ATLANTIC MONTHLY 164 (1939):810-819.

1863-1866. Extracts from journal of noted member of NEW YORK TRIBUNE editorial staff, a Republican leader from Calais, Maine, serving as United States minister to the Netherlands; in England, enjoying Dickens reading from his works, once with Thomas Carlyle in the audience; visits with Carlyle and the latter's opinions on various topics; calling on Tennyson, a celebrity beset by tourists; detailed descriptions of all three authors; a few remarks on the Civil War.

Davis, Harold A., ed. "From the Diaries of a Diplomat." NEW ENGLAND QUARTERLY 14 (1941):83-112.

1864-1872. Diary extracts interspersed among letters; diplomatic service with notes on European royalty; a French view of the Civil War; political and social activities in Washington, D.C., during Reconstruction; description of William M. Stewart addressing the Senate; postwar tales about Lincoln; conversations with generals Rosencrans and Butler; some curious proposals concerning women's suffrage.

POST, CHARLES A., b. 1844?   4474

"A Diary of the Blockade in 1863." UNITED STATES NAVAL INSTITUTE PROCEEDINGS 44, no. 10 (1918):2333-2350; 44, no. 11 (1918):2567-2594. Reprint. A DIARY OF THE BLOCKADE IN 1863. Annapolis, Md., 1918?

Mar-Jun 1863. New Yorker's account of service aboard the sidewheeler FLORIDA, acting as clerk and personal aide to her commander John P. Bankhead; the monotony of duty off the Atlantic coast occasionally spiced with the prospect of pursuing a blockade runner or some daring duels with the shore batteries; comments on officers and sailors; capture of the CALYPSO and a stormy passage taking the prize north; notes on reading, fishing, Beaufort, South Carolina, Newport News and the desolated Virginia village of Hampton, German troops in the Union army, British snobbery, etc.; a delightfully irreverent view, edited for publication by the diarist.

PRINGLE, CYRUS GUERNSEY, 1838-1911   4475

"The United States versus Pringle." ATLANTIC MONTHLY 3, no. 2 (1913):145-162.

THE RECORD OF A QUAKER CONSCIENCE. New York: Macmillan, 1918. 93 pp. Diary, pp. 23-93.

THE CIVIL WAR DIARY OF CYRUS PRINGLE. Pendle Hill Pamphlet 122. Wallingford, Pa.: Pendle Hill, 1962. 39 pp.

Extracts in CIVIL WAR EYEWITNESS REPORTS, edited by Harold E. Straubing, pp. 12-33.

Aug-Nov 1863. Diary kept by drafted Quaker from East Charlotte, Vermont, during his struggle to be released from the military, refusing to pay the commutation fine or take up alternative service; in camps at Brattleboro and on Long Island in Boston harbor; relations with soldiers; officers' efforts to persuade him to serve; by sea to Virginia where he was assigned to the Fourth Vermont and forced to carry arms; physical punishments for his refusal to comply with orders; support of other Quakers but conflicting views about acceptability of service in hospitals or with contrabands; doubts and faith; in Washington, D.C., where through the intercession of Isaac Newton, commissioner of agriculture, the diarist was paroled by Lincoln.

In LIFE AND WORK OF CYRUS GUERNSEY PRINGLE, by Helen B. Davis, pp. 19-252. Burlington: University of Vermont, 1936. 756 pp.

1885-1909 (with gaps). Botanical expeditions to Mexico undertaken by distinguished botanist and horticulturalist; mostly notes of itinerary and botanical samples collected for the Gray Herbarium at Harvard.

RANSOM, JOHN L., 1843-1919   **4476**

ANDERSONVILLE DIARY. Auburn, N.Y.: The Author, 1881. 304 pp. Philadelphia: Douglass Brothers, 1883. 381 pp. Reprint. New York: Haskell House, 1974. 381 pp.

JOHN RANSOM'S DIARY. New York: P.S. Eriksson, 1963. 281 pp.

Extracts in DIARY OF AMERICA, edited by Josef Berger and Dorothy Berger, pp. 435-450.

1863-1864. Prisoner of war experiences of brigade quartermaster sergeant of the Ninth Michigan Cavalry, a printer from Jackson, Michigan, captured near Rogersville, Tennessee; incarceration at Belle Isle and the Pemberton Building in Richmond and then six months at Andersonville under steadily worsening conditions; transfer to Marine Hospital, Savannah, and Millen Prison; escape and recapture while being transported away from advancing Union forces and successful escape with David and Eli Buck while en route to Charleston prison; assistance from slaves and Southern unionists; description of conditions at all places of imprisonment, emphasizing food and health; at Andersonville, notes on Henry Wirz, the "raiders" and execution of some of their leaders, escape attempts and punishments, setting up a laundry and barber shop and other means of obtaining small comforts; comments on Union's refusal to exchange prisoners; mention of friends and acquaintances, especially the daring George W. Hendryx and the staunch Battese, a Minnesota Indian; a gripping, evenhanded record of one man's capacity to endure and survive, with help from his friends, appalling abuse of mind and body.

RAYNOR, WILLIAM H., 1834-1912   **4477**

Bearss, Edwin C., ed. "The Civil War Diary of Colonel William H. Raynor during the Vicksburg Campaign." LOUISIANA STUDIES 9 (1970):243-300.

Apr-Jul 1863. Diary kept by colonel commanding the Fifty-sixth Ohio; the march from Milliken's Bend, observing devastation of plantations by Union troops; engaging the enemy at Grand Gulf, Port Gibson and Champion's Hill; siege of Vicksburg with interesting notes on relations with Confederates along the fortifications; excellent account of the campaign, encompassing military details, camp life, effects of heat and rain, etc.

REED, ANNA MORRISON, 1849-1921   **4478**

ANNA MORRISON REED, 1849-1921. Edited by John E. Keller. Lafayette, Calif.: J.E. Keller, 1979. 285 pp., passim.

1863-1920. Extensive extracts from the diary of a remarkable California lecturer and journalist; as a teenager, supporting her destitute parents by writing and lecturing in opposition to women's suffrage, traveling on foot, by stagecoach or horseback, often with a younger child in tow; later as a widow, working as a journalist for several northern California newspapers and lecturing, eventually in support of suffrage, as well as temperance; attending the 1893 Columbian Expositon at Chicago as editor of the SONOMA COUNTY INDEPENDENT; speeches, articles and poems included.

RIDLEY, REBECCAH CROSTHWAITE   **4479**

Trimble, Sarah Ridley, ed. "Behind the Lines in Middle Tennessee." TENNESSEE HISTORICAL QUARTERLY 12 (1953):48-80.

1863-1865. Diary begun by Bettie Ridley Blackmore in Union-occupied Tennessee, consisting mainly of bimonthly entries for 1864, noting her health, teaching, family matters, black Union soldiers, war news, etc; continued in four lengthy entries penned by Rebeccah Ridley after her daughter's death, covering the burning of their home, Fair Mont, near Murfreesboro and other depredations by Union soldiers, visits from her son Bromfield during the Franklin and Nashville campaign and problems with slaves.

Extracts in HEROINES OF DIXIE, edited by Katharine M. Jones, pp. 349-351.

Dec 1864. From Rebeccah's portion of the diary.

RILEY, F.L.   **4480**

Love, W.A. "Forward and Back." CONFEDERATE VETERAN 33 (1925):9-10.

Jun 1863. Extract from diary of private, Sixteenth Mississippi, giving daily route of march to and from Gettysburg but no battle details.

ROEDEL, JOSEPHINE FORNEY, 1825-1904   **4481**

Singmaster, Elsie, ed. "The Diary of Josephine Forney Roedel." PENNSYLVANIA MAGAZINE OF HISTORY AND BIOGRAPHY 67 (1943):390-411.

Oct 1863-Jul 1864. Diary kept by Pennsylvanian, a resident of Wytheville, Virginia, during journey to visit her parents in Gettysburg; difficulties of crossing through the lines of both armies, preventing her reaching her destination before her mother's death; description of the dedication of the national cemetery at Gettysburg, hearing "the brief dedication by the President" and noting the popular support for Lincoln; visiting family, in-laws and friends in Lebanon, Lancaster and Philadelphia and in Maryland; again in Gettysburg, nursing her father and seeing the inadequate interment of the Confederate dead; in Washington, D.C., meeting with Thaddeus Stevens and Secretary Stanton to secure a pass back through the lines and touring the Smithsonian; waiting in Baltimore and then going west where she encountered Wythe County soldiers taking part in Early's raid; journey back to her sorely missed husband, the Rev. William D. Roedel, president of the Wytheville Female Seminary; a good example of the hardships of family separation brought by the Civil War.

ROOT, WILLIAM H., b. 1842?   **4482**

Root, L. Carroll, ed. "The Experiences of a Federal Soldier in Louisiana in 1863." LOUISIANA HISTORICAL QUARTERLY 19 (1936):633-667.

Apr-Jun 1863. Farmer's journal of service as lieutenant with the Seventy-fifth New York Infantry; on the march from Brashear City, Louisiana, up the Teche to Alexandria, engaging Confederates along the way; assault on Port Hudson; criticism of Banks's regulations protecting Southern property; praise for Godfrey Weitzel; long entries covering military activities, personal concerns, casualties, crops, plantations and countryside; observations of effect of Union invasion on slaves and their understanding of freedom.

Extracts in THE BLUE AND THE GRAY, edited by Henry S. Commager, vol. 2, pp. 673-675.

Jun 1863. Port Hudson assault.

ROSS, R.D.   **4483**

"Journal of R.D. Ross, across the Plains in 1863." NORTH DAKOTA HISTORICAL SOCIETY COLLECTIONS 2 (1908):219-231.

Jun-Sep 1863. Overland journey from Council Bluffs, Iowa, to Oregon; a "legend" about origin of the name of Rawhide Creek, which claimed a young emigrant was skinned alive for wantonly murdering an Indian woman; camps, terrain, distances and "the monotony of the dusty road without any incident of interest" except occasional encounters with cavalry, other emigrant trains and Indians; names on recent graves; frequent references to his companion L.R. Holmes and to the freighters Ed and James Creighton.

RUPERT, JOHN F.   **4484**

In HISTORY OF THE 103rd REGIMENT, PENNSYLVANIA VETERAN VOLUNTEER INFANTRY, by Luther S. Dickey, pp. 55-59.

May-Dec 1863. Extracts from Company A corporal's diary recording events while stationed at Fort Williams, Plymouth, North Carolina; camp life and military operations.

RUSSELL, ELIZABETH ANN BARTLETT, 1834-1877   **4485**

Williams, T.R., Jr. "A Ouachita Family's Texas Sojourn." NORTH LOUISIANA HISTORICAL ASSOCIATION JOURNAL 15 (1984):167-172.

1863-1865, 1867. Extracts from random entries made in diary of Ouachita Parish woman during wartime residence in Upshur County, Texas; expressions of great homesickness; mention of farm and business matters and the whereabouts of her husband, Augustus Dunreth Russell; postwar return to Louisiana.

SATTENWHITE, JOHN W.   **4486**

In THE REBELLION RECORD, edited by Frank Moore, vol. 7, pp. 170-173.

May-Jul 1863. Siege of Vicksburg described in diary of member of Company A, Sixth Missouri Volunteers; military events, ferocity of Union bombardment, meager rations, casualties and surrender.

SCHURICHT, HERMANN   **4487**

"Jenkin's Brigade in the Gettysburg Campaign." SOUTHERN HISTORICAL SOCIETY PAPERS 24 (1896):339-350.

Jun-Jul 1863. Extracts from Company D, Fourteenth Virginia Cavalry, lieutenant's diary, originally written in German, translated by diarist for publication and obviously rewritten to some extent; a view of cavalry operations during the Gettysburg campaign; reconnoitering, skirmishing, destroying communications and appropriating horses and mules; civilian reaction in Pennsylvania and Maryland; occupation of Chambersburg and Mechanicsburg, coming within sight of Harrisburg; the battle and the retreat into Virginia.

SCOTT, HENRY D.   **4488**

In HISTORY OF THE FIFTH MASSACHUSETTS BATTERY, by Massachusetts Artillery, 5th Battery, pp. 550-753 passim.

Jan-Dec 1863. A few extracts from lieutenant's diary covering battery's operations in Virginia; Chancellorsville and Gettysburg campaigns.

SEAMAN, HENRY I., 1840?-1863   **4489**

Poole, Miriam and Hoffsommer, Robert, eds. "Henry Seaman's Vicksburg Diary." CIVIL WAR TIMES ILLUSTRATED 22, no. 5 (1983):18-31.

May-Jul 1863. Extracts from diary of Northville farmer, a member of Company E, Thirteenth Illinois Infantry; substantial daily entries focusing on military details and covering the Vicksburg campaign from Milliken's Bend to the surrender of the besieged city; weather reports; notes on looting in Raymond by Union soldiers and Southern civilians, Mechanicsburg expedition, generals Steele and Sherman, relations with Confederate soldiers, etc.

SEISER, AUGUST FRIEDERICH, 1823-1904   **4490**

In ROCHESTER IN THE CIVIL WAR, edited by Blake McKelvey, pp. 174-198. Rochester Historical Society Publication Fund Series, vol. 22. Rochester, N.Y.: The Society, 1944.

Sep-Dec 1863, Apr-June 1864. Partial account of mason contractor's service as a private in Company B, 140th New York; weather and hardships; the Bristoe campaign; visit to Second Bull Run battlefield; the Mine Run campaign; battle of Wilderness; in the rifle pits at Petersburg.

SHACKLEY, JONAS   **4491**

In HISTORY OF THE FIFTH MASSACHUSETTS BATTERY, by Massachusetts Artillery, 5th Battery, pp. 710-909 passim.

Sep-Oct 1863, May-Sep 1864. A few extracts from corporal's diary covering the activities of the battery in Virginia; the Wilderness and the Spotsylvania and Petersburg campaigns; brief note on the battle of the Crater.

SHAFFNER, JOHN FRANCIS   **4492**

DIARY OF DR. J.F. SHAFFNER, SR. Edited by Caroline Lizetta Shaffner. Winston Salem, N.C.: Privately printed, 1936. 67 pp.

1863-1865. Fourth North Carolina surgeon's account of army life; journey back to Virginia from North Carolina home; stationed along the Rapidan and in the Shenandoah Valley; pushed up the

Valley by Sheridan; battles of Winchester, Cedar Creek, Fisher's Hill and a tour of Weir's Cave; at Petersburg; daily record except for May-June 1864; weather, correspondence, medical duties, reading, servants, etc.; entries include copies of documents for his defense plea when brought before court-martial, a graphic tetanus case history and diarist's charges against one of Early's couriers.

SHAW, WILLIAM H., b. 1833 4493

A DIARY AS KEPT BY WM. H. SHAW DURING THE GREAT CIVIL WAR. N.p., n.d. 76 pp.

1863-1865. Diary, rewritten in 1904, of sergeant, Company D, Thirty-seventh Massachusetts; summary of military service from 1861 to early 1863 when what appear to be the original, extremely brief daily entries begin, supplemented by many later remarks; Chancellorsville and Gettysburg campaigns; duty in New York City after draft riots; Mine Run campaign; the Wilderness, Spotsylvania and Cold Harbor; siege of Petersburg; transfer to Maryland in response to Early's raid, in hospital and return to Petersburg; Appomattox campaign and completion of service after war's end; notes on military and leisure activities and the weather.

SHELDON, OTIS E. 4494

In HISTORY OF THE FIFTIETH REGIMENT OF INFANTRY, MASSACHUSETTS VOLUNTEER MILITIA, by William Burnham Stevens, p. 105.

May 1863. Extracts from Company F corporal's journal describing operations at White's Bayou.

SHOOK, HEZEKIAH 4495

In THE SOLDIER OF INDIANA IN THE WAR FOR THE UNION, by Catharine Merrill, vol. 2. pp. 186-187.

Jan-Feb 1863. Extracts from diary of captain, Thirty-seventh Indiana; notes on Stones River battlefield and home front politics.

SHULTZ, JOHN A., b. 1839 4496

ONE YEAR AT WAR. Edited by Hobart L. Morris, Jr. New York: Vantage, 1968. 111 pp.

1863-1864. Diary of Vermilion County, Illinois, farmer serving as private with Company E, Seventy-third Illinois Infantry, in Tennessee and Alabama; in various hospitals for seven months, suffering from chronic diarrhea and scrofula; duties as member of pioneer and pontoon corps; the Atlanta campaign; return to Chattanooga to serve in the First Veteran Engineer Regiment; terse entries.

SIMONS, MAURICE KAVANAUGH, 1824-1867 4497

Mays, Walter H., ed. "The Vicksburg Diary of M.K. Simons." TEXAS MILITARY HISTORY 5 (1965):21-38.

Apr-Oct 1863. Diary kept by major of the Second Texas Infantry, now brigade quartermaster, who had lost his leg during Mexican War service; reports of military action as Grant pushes the Confederates inside Vicksburg's defenses; constant bombardment and dwindling supplies; morale and hopes of reinforcement; taunting the enemy; surrender, fraternizing between Union and Confederate soldiers and the wealth of the Union commissary; angry comments about black Union soldiers and racial equality; criticism

of Pemberton; parole and journey home to Texana on furlough; daily entries through July 11, with extracts from subsequent months' record.

SIMPSON, S.R. 4498

IN PEN AND SWORD, by Randal W. McGavock, pp. 85-86. Nashville: Tennessee Historical Commission, 1959.

May 1863. Extracts from diary of Confederate captain, assistant quartermaster of the Thirtieth Tennessee, describing march from Port Hudson to Jackson, Mississippi.

SLACK, COMFORT I. 4499

Anderson, Charles A. "Journal of Comfort Slack." PRESBYTERIAN HISTORICAL SOCIETY JOURNAL 35 (1957):229-248.

1863-1864. Diary of new graduate of Auburn Theological Seminary, establishing himself in Newton, Iowa, under the auspices of the New School Presbyterian Home Missions; installation as minister of Westminster Church; sermons, funerals and other clerical activities; marriage to Sophie Ransom of Clinton County, New York, and return to Newton.

SMEDLEY, CHARLES, 1836-1864 4500

. LIFE IN SOUTHERN PRISONS. Lancaster? Pa: Ladies' and Gentleman's Fulton Aid Society, 1865. 60 pp.

Jun-Jul 1863, May-Oct 1864. Portions of corporal's diary of service with Company G, Ninetieth Pennsylvania Volunteers and imprisonment at Andersonville and Florence; marching to Gettysburg and description of diarist's part of the battle; capture in the battle of the Wilderness; transport by train to Georgia in packed stock cars; daily activities, events, rations, cooking, prices, illness, etc; a detailed record, surprising in its lack of protest or bitterness.

SMITH, HARRIET AMELIA, 1841-1923 4501

Fraker, Fleming, Jr., ed. "To Pikes Peak by Ox Wagon." ANNALS OF IOWA, 3d ser. 35 (1959-1961):113-148.

Jul-Sep 1863. Warren County woman's journey in the party of her uncle Porter T. Hinman, from Polk County to Colorado; much on the varied work of men and domestic chores of women en route and in camp, especially cooking for the company; encounters with Indians.

SMITH, JAMES WEST, 1830-1863 4502

"A Confederate Soldier's Dairy." SOUTHWEST REVIEW 28 (1943):293-327.

May-Jul 1863. Diary kept by Company H, Thirty-seventh Mississippi member, a former dentist and schoolteacher, during the siege of Vicksburg; summary of events during later half of May; in the trenches under fire of sharpshooters and artillery; conversing between enemy soldiers; longing to be clean again; in hospital and reports of regiment's activities in his absence; notes on rations; Union soldiers' treatment of Confederates after the surrender of the city; homeward trek after parole.

SMITH, WILLIAM WRENSHALL, b. 1830 4503

"Holocaust Holiday." CIVIL WAR TIMES ILLUSTRATED 18, no. 6 (1979):28-40.

Nov 1863. Diary kept by Washington, Pennsylvania, businessman, Julia Grant's cousin and the general's friend; journey from Nashville to Chattanooga via Bridgeport, Alabama; visiting with Grant and observing the battles of Lookout Mountain and Missionary Ridge and subsequent operations in north Georgia.

SPAWR, VALENTINE   **4504**

DIARY OF THE LATE REBELLION. Lexington, Ill.: Unit Pub. Co., Printers, 1892. 42 pp.

Jun-Sep 1863. Long, descriptive entries penned by member of Company C, Fourteenth Regiment, Iowa Infantry Volunteers; stationed near Columbus, Kentucky; weather, sickness, funerals, sermons, punishments and a hanging, reading, military and leisure activities, rumors and alarms, etc.; attitude toward blacks.

STEARNS, AMOS EDWARD, 1833-1912   **4505**

THE CIVIL WAR DIARY OF AMOS E. STEARNS. Edited by Leon Basile. Rutherford, N.J.: Fairleigh Dickinson University Press; London: Associated University Presses, 1981. 127 pp.

1863-1865 (with gap). Diary of Worcester, Massachusetts, machinist serving with the Twenty-fifth Massachusetts in North Carolina and later reassigned to the 139th New York; journey to Virginia and operations there; notes on duties, chores, health, correspondence, leisure activities and celebration of St. Patrick's Day; capture at Drewry's Bluff; briefly in Libby and more than three months at Andersonville; transfer to Charleston, then Florence as Union forces advance; conditions and activities at all prisons, including illnesses, deaths, hopes of exchange and, especially, the inadequate rations; mention of Andersonville "raiders" and "galvanized Yankees" at Florence; prisoners' presidential election; longing for his sweetheart Lydia Maria Fisher; solace of religion; short, daily entries, notably lacking in bitterness.

STEVENSON, WILLIAM GRAFTON, d. 1910   **4506**

Stevenson, Carl R., ed. "Diary of William Grafton Stevenson, Captain, C.S.A." ALABAMA HISTORICAL QUARTERLY 23 (1961):45-72.

Aug 1863-Apr 1864 (with gaps). Seventeenth South Carolina Infantry captain's record of happenings at Charleston; duties, bombardments, weather, military punishments, reading, hospitalization, furloughs and train breakdowns; transfer to Green Pond, South Carolina, and then Wilmington, Tarboro and Wilson, North Carolina, guarding Union prisoners.

STEWART, CHARLES   **4507**

In HISTORY OF THE ONE HUNDRED AND TWENTY-FOURTH REGIMENT, N.Y.S.V., by Charles H. Weygant, pp. 247-250.

Dec 1863. Extracts from officer's diary; life in camp at Brandy Station, Virginia.

STODDARD, GEORGE N.   **4508**

"The 100th Regiment on Folly Island." NIAGARA FRONTIER 1 (1954):77-81, 113-116.

May-Jul 1863. Diary of private, Company H, 100th Regiment, New York Volunteers, stationed at Folly Island, South Carolina; military events at Charleston harbor; the monotony of camp life enlivened by ocean bathing and fishing; afflictions of homesickness, poor

rations and drunken Colonel Dandy; detailed to quartermaster's department.

STOKES, MISSOURI   **4509**

In HEROINES OF DIXIE, edited by Katharine M. Jones, pp. 209-211.

Mar, May-Jun 1863. Extract from diary of young teacher in Decatur, Georgia, half-sister of author Mary Ann Harris Gay; account of hardships suffered by her soldier brother, Thomie, exchanged from Camp Chase military prison.

STRICKLER, SARAH ANN, b. 1845   **4510**

Freudenberg, Anne. "Sheridan's Raid." ALBEMARLE COUNTY HISTORICAL SOCIETY MAGAZINE 22 (1963-1964):56-65.

Jul 1863, Mar 1865. Extracts from schoolgirl's diary; description of Jubal Early whom the diarist met when he made his headquarters at her family's home in 1863; account of Sheridan's raid on Charlottesville where she was a student at the Albemarle Female Institute.

SWAN, SAMUEL ALEXANDER RAMSEY, 1826-1913   **4511**

Osborn, George C., ed. "A Tennessean at the Siege of Vicksburg." TENNESSEE HISTORICAL QUARTERLY 14 (1955):353-372.

Apr-Jul 1863. Diary of schoolteacher serving in the quartermaster corps attached to Stephen D. Lee's brigade; summary of events leading up to the investment of Vicksburg, then daily record of situation in the city; military action across the trenches and on the Mississippi River; conditions during the siege, including morale, supplies and health of the troops; rumors and hopes of rescue; surrender and parole with remarks on friendly relations between Union and Confederate soldiers and on the Union army's actions regarding blacks; notes on Lamar Fontaine and Pemberton; religious reflections.

TALBOT, JOSEPH CRUICKSHANK, 1816-1863   **4512**

Jenkins, Thomas, ed. "Journal of the First Bishop of the Northwest." HISTORICAL MAGAZINE OF THE PROTESTANT EPISCOPAL CHURCH 17 (1948):60-105.

May-Dec 1863. Bishop's diary of missionary travels in Nebraska, Colorado, New Mexico, Utah and Nevada.

TAYLOR, THOMAS JONES, 1829-1894   **4513**

Wall, Lillian T. and McBride, Robert M., eds. " 'An Extraordinary Perseverance.' " TENNESSEE HISTORICAL QUARTERLY 31 (1972):328-359.

1863-1865 (with gaps). Company K, Forth-ninth Alabama, captain's record more than half of which is retrospective summary of soldiering from Shiloh to the siege of Port Hudson, his journey to prison and conditions at Johnson's Island; sporadic but lengthy journal entries, commencing in November 1863 and covering prison events and hardships, the weather, Northern politics, war news, etc.

THOMPSON, HENRY YATES, 1838-1928   **4514**

AN ENGLISHMAN IN THE AMERICAN CIVIL WAR. Edited by Sir Christopher Chancellor. London: Sidgwick and Jackson, 1971; New York: New York University Press, 1971. 185 pp.

Jul-Dec 1863. Diary, interspersed with letters, of Cambridge graduate, holding antislavery views and sympathetic to the Union's cause; travel through the country, North and South, informing himself about the conditions of slavery and the war; guest of Edward Everett in Boston where he met such other notables as Oliver Wendell Holmes, Charles Eliot Norton, Nathaniel Hawthorne, Ralph Waldo Emerson and Wendell Phillips; an itinerary which included stops at Keene, New Hampshire, Syracuse, New Haven, New York City, Oyster Bay, Philadelphia, Baltimore and Washington, D.C.; journey through the Ohio Valley to Detroit and Ann Arbor, then Chicago and St. Louis; a visit with Mrs. James Knox Polk in Nashville; observing the battles around Chattanooga from Fort Wood and Grant's demeanor during the conflict; working among the wounded with the Sanitary Commission; return to New York City via Munfordville, Kentucky, and Cincinnati; notes on slavery in eastern Maryland, the Christian Commission, appearance of Confederate soldiers, traveling conditions, etc.

TORRENCE, LEONIDAS, d. 1863   **4515**

Monroe, Haskell, ed. "The Road to Gettysburg." NORTH CAROLINA HISTORICAL REVIEW 36 (1959):476-517. Diary, pp. 509-514.

Jun-Jul 1863. Diary of corporal from Gaston County, a member of Company H, Thirteenth North Carolina; the northward progress of Lee's army; brief daily entries sketching route of march and events of battle of Gettysburg during which he was mortally wounded.

TOURGEE, ALBION W., 1838-1905   **4516**

Keller, Dean H. "A Civil War Diary of Albion W. Tourgée." OHIO HISTORY 74 (1965):99-131.

May-Nov 1863. Diary of future novelist, a lieutenant in Company G, 105th Ohio Volunteer Infantry, begun on the day of his marriage to Emma Kilbourne; attending the theater in Louisville and Nashville on his way to regiment near Murfreesboro; the Tullahoma campaign; battle of Chickamauga; stationed at Chattanooga; notes on duties, military action, correspondence, etc.; support of Capt. Byron W. Canfield by regiment's line officers; brought before a court-martial and sitting as judge advocate on another; many thoughts of his wife; the record of an observant individualist.

TURCHIN, NADINE, 1826-1904   **4517**

McElligott, Mary Ellen, ed. " 'A Monotony Full of Sadness.' " ILLINOIS STATE HISTORICAL SOCIETY JOURNAL 70 (1977):27-89.

May 1863-Apr 1864. Diary of Russian émigré, wife of Army of the Cumberland brigadier general John Basil Turchin, originally written in French so that she would not forget the language; dull days at Murfreesboro and other Tennessee camps, Huntsville, Alabama, near Chattanooga and, finally, at Ringgold, Georgia, trying to stay close to her husband; extensive criticism of Union political and military leadership with praise for few individuals; negative opinion of Grant, regular army officers, agents of the Sanitary Commission and French-Americans; reflections on religion, woman's role and the ways in which the social order in the North fell short of democratic ideals; admiration for common volunteer soldier; commentary on war events including Chickamauga and the battles for Chattanooga; description of Tennessee countryside; her antislavery views and concern for treatment of freedmen; quite lengthy entries used as a means of

releasing her passionate feelings about the war, its prosecution and the lack of appreciation for her husband's abilities.

TURNER, WILLIAM H., 1834?-1900   **4518**

"Diary of W.H. Turner, M.D." IOWA JOURNAL OF HISTORY 48 (1950):267-282.

Mar-May 1863. Record of service aboard hospital steamer written by Iowa Medical College graduate, an army surgeon; journey from Memphis to Young's Point, describing sights along the way; duties aboard the CITY OF MEMPHIS, transporting the sick and wounded to the hospital steamboat NASHVILLE and to St. Louis and Memphis; ward management, medical treatment and dealing with malingerers; notes on leisure activities, manners, surgeons' drinking, unhealthy conditions, etc.

VAUGHN, TURNER   **4519**

"Diary of Turner Vaughn." ALABAMA HISTORICAL QUARTERLY 18 (1956):573-604.

Mar-Nov 1863, Jan-Feb 1864. Diary kept by officer, Company C, Fourth Alabama; service in Virginia; the Gettysburg campaign; company's casualties at Chickamauga; summary of Knoxville campaign; notes on duties, visits to Richmond and Petersburg, prices, foraging and religion in the army.

WALLACE, ELIZABETH MCINTOSH CURTIS,   **4520**
1816-1866

GLENCOE DIARY. Edited by Eleanor P. Cross and Charles B. Cross, Jr. Chesapeake, Va.: Norfolk County Historical Society, 1968. 156 pp.

1863-1864. Plantation mistress's wartime diary; notes on weather, domestic chores, family, friends, prices, religious beliefs, illnesses and remedies, war news, etc.; increased hardships for those at Glencoe in Norfolk County, Virginia, after slaves' departure and Union occupation; concern for sons in Confederate army; imprisonment of husband in Norfolk; feelings toward black Union troops; agonizing over taking oath of allegiance to avoid property loss; exchanging civilities with enemy officers and reports of Yankee depredations and cruelties; death of one son and journey through the lines to be with second wounded son in Louisa County; a few extracts from prewar journals included in editor's introduction.

WALLSH, THOMAS F.   **4521**

"Gettysburg, 1863: Two Intimate Accounts." ARLINGTON HISTORICAL MAGAZINE 2, no. 2 (1962):43-52. Diary, pp. 48-52.

Jun-Jul 1863. Fragment of diary kept by noncombatant clerk in the Seventy-fourth New York Infantry; reception by civilian population as the Union army moves through Maryland; the battle of Gettysburg and the devastation left in its wake.

WARD, JOSEPH RICHARDSON, 1838-1912   **4522**

AN ENLISTED SOLDIER'S VIEW OF THE CIVIL WAR. Edited by D. Duane Cummins and Darryl Hohweiler. West Lafayette, Ind.: Belle Publications, 1981. 271 pp. Diary, pp. 46-248 passim.

Sep 1863-Jan 1964, Jan-Jul 1865. Farmer's diary-letters while serving in Company G, Thirty-ninth Illinois Volunteer Infantry; quite detailed record of military activities at Charleston, including the capture of Morris Island; description of forts Wagner and Gregg;

in Virginia with the Army of the James; postwar days at Petersburg and Richmond; notes on duties, casualties, emancipation, Libby Prison, Drewry's Bluff battlefield, Virginia crops, Epps Island and the Sea Islands.

WARMOTH, HENRY CLAY, b. 1842   4523

Hass, Paul H., ed. "The Vicksburg Diary of Henry Clay Warmoth." JOURNAL OF MISSISSIPPI HISTORY 31 (1969):334-347; 32 (1970):60-74.

Apr-May 1863. Extracts from wartime diary of future notorious Reconstruction governor of Louisiana; commissioned a lieutenant colonel, serving on General McClernand's staff during the Vicksburg campaign; a lively and articulate account of military operations and personal activities; an expedition with generals McClernand and Osterhaus and his relationship with the former; interactions with Southern women; General A.J. Smith's views on arming blacks; diarist's wounding during assault on the Vicksburg works.

WASH, W.A.   4524

CAMP, FIELD AND PRISON LIFE. Saint Louis: Southwestern Book, 1870. 382 pp. Diary, pp. 158-176.

Aug 1863. Extracts from Confederate officer's diary preserved within his narrative of experiences at Johnson's Island; regulations and routines of imprisonment; commentary on Northern politics and the Union cause.

WEBSTER, N.H.   4525

"Journal of N.H. Webster." MONTANA HISTORICAL SOCIETY CONTRIBUTIONS 3 (1900):300-330.

Aug-Nov 1863. Wagon driver's journal of a freighting trip from Central City, Colorado, to Bannack; route and conditions of travel via Fort Bridger; references to fellow teamster Ben Dittes; work as a glove maker at Bannack and vicinity, with interesting notes on people and events there, including a meeting with the notorious Henry Plummer who "appears to be a very nice man."

WESCOAT, ARTHUR BRAILSFORD, 1848-1941   4526

"Journal of Arthur Brailsford Wescoat." SOUTH CAROLINA HISTORICAL MAGAZINE 55 (1954):71-102.

1863-1864. Teenager's record of his activities in and around Pinopolis, Berkley County, where his refugee family acquired California, a small plantation; visits with his brother Jabez R. Wescoat, Jr., a member of the Third South Carolina Cavalry, in camp at Adams Run and Johns Island; trips to Charleston, Wadamalaw Island and the family's home on Edisto Island; news of military operations, especially in the Charleston area; school days; casualties among family and friends.

WESCOAT, JOSEPH JULIUS, 1842-1908   4527

Gregorie, Anne King, ed. "Diary of Captain Joseph Julius Wescoat." SOUTH CAROLINA HISTORICAL MAGAZINE 59 (1958):11-23, 84-95.

1863-1865 (with gaps). Record kept by captain, Company B, Eleventh South Carolina Volunteers; stationed at James Island, with description of situation at Charleston and its harbor; campaigning in Florida, noting civilian support at Madison and poor

accommodations at Lake City; return to Charleston; transfer to Virginia and action at Drewry's Bluff and Petersburg; captured while defending Wilmington; confined briefly at Old Capitol Prison and then sent to Fort Delaware; frustrations of imprisonment; reaction to Lincoln's assassination; refusal to take oath of allegiance.

WEST, JOHN CAMDEN, b. 1834   4528

A TEXAN IN SEARCH OF A FIGHT. Waco, Tex.: Press of J.S. Hill, 1901. 180, 8 pp. Reprint. Waco, Tex.: Texian, 1969. 189 pp. Diary, pp. 13-60, 143-160.

Apr-Jun 1863, Feb-Apr 1864. War diary of Waco, Texas, lawyer; journey by stage, boat and train to Virginia to join Company E, Fourth Texas Volunteer Infantry; travel delays at Marshall and Shreveport; visiting with friends and relatives in Columbia, South Carolina; socializing in Richmond with Mary Chesnut and others; a glimpse of Jeb Stuart; finding his regiment on the Rapidan near Raccoon Ford; duties, a division review and the monotony of camp life; heading north as the Gettysburg campaign begins; returning home by train, boat, horseback and on foot after discharge from the army; from eastern Tennessee to Texas, again stopping to be with loved ones in Columbia and Camden, South Carolina; notes on his reading, the trials of wartime travel, the towns and countryside through which he passed and the many persons encountered along the way.

WHITE, HENRY   4529

In HISTORY OF THE TWENTY-FIRST REGIMENT, MASSACHUSETTS VOLUNTEERS, by Charles F. Walcott, pp. 294-297.

Dec 1863. Extracts from sergeant's diary, describing life under siege at Knoxville and his reenlistment afterwards.

WILCOX, ALFRED G.   4530

In THE STORY OF A THOUSAND, by Albion W. Tourgée, pp. 257-265.

Sep-Nov 1863. Extracts from diary of Oberlin graduate, an officer in Company F, 105th Ohio Volunteer Infantry; life under siege at Chattanooga; commentary on Rosencrans, Thomas and the battle of Chickamauga.

WILLIAMS, L.L., 1831-1881   4531

Abdill, G.B., ed. "The Pathfinders: Report of L.L. Williams of the Exploration of the Country from the Mines on the North Umpqua to the 'Dalles & California Trail.'" UMPQUA TRAPPER 1, no. 4 (1965):15-20, 2, no. 1 (1966):22-24, no. 2, 21-24, no. 3, 21-24.

Sep-Oct 1863. Douglas County man's expedition to determine feasibility of a new road in the area, with much of the route along old Indian trails; notes on terrain and geology; many references to the long illness en route of his colleague Jesse Davenport.

WILLIAMSON, JAMES JOSEPH, 1834-1915   4532

PRISON LIFE IN THE OLD CAPITOL AND REMINISCENCES OF THE CIVIL WAR. West Orange, N.J., 1911. 162 pp. Diary, pp. 25-119.

Feb-Apr 1863. Diary, sometimes indistinguishable from reminiscences, of Washington, D.C., civilian of Southern sympathies who, refusing to take oath of allegiance, was imprisoned at Old Capitol Prison; conditions, routines and ill treatment; exchange and detention at parole camp near Petersburg; journey to Upperville to join Mosby.

WILSON, JAMES H.   4533

"A Staff-Officer's Journal of the Vicksburg Campaign." MILITARY SERVICE INSTITUTION OF THE UNITED STATES JOURNAL 43 (1908):93-109, 261-275.

> May-Jul 1863. Lieutenant colonel's record of military operations, perhaps kept as part of his duties as inspector-general on Grant's staff; especially interesting indications of how information was gathered from blacks, Southern civilians, Confederate prisoners and deserters, etc.

WINNE, PETER   4534

Athearn, Robert G., ed. "Across the Plains in 1863." IOWA JOURNAL OF HISTORY 49 (1951):221-240.

> Apr-Jun 1863. Extracts from Wisconsin man's diary of a journey with his family to settle in Colorado; route, conditions of travel, especially difficult in Skunk River "bottoms" in Iowa; humorous as well as violent incidents; Civil War news.

WORD, SAMUEL   4535

"Diary of Colonel Samuel Word." MONTANA HISTORICAL SOCIETY CONTRIBUTIONS 8 (1917):37-92.

> May-Oct 1863. Expedition from St. Joseph, Missouri, to open up a more direct road to Virginia City; encounter with Indians demanding that they go back or risk death, with resultant detour via Fort Bridger and Salt Lake City; notes on Brigham Young and work in progress on the Mormon Temple; diarist's loneliness for his wife and little son and distress over Sunday travel; excellent details on many aspects of journey, including decision-making processes, especially after threat by Indians; notes on Indian disposal of the dead; eventual arrival at Bannack with intention to move on to Virginia City.

WRIGHT, JOHN P.   4536

Rea, Ralph R., ed. "Diary of Private John P. Wright, U.S.A." ARKANSAS HISTORICAL QUARTERLY 16 (1957):304-318.

> 1863-1864. Numerous extracts from diary of member of Company F, Twenty-ninth Iowa Infantry embedded in editor's narrative summary; down the Mississippi from Columbus, Kentucky, to Helena, Arkansas; foray up the White River and operations around Yazoo Pass and on the Tallahatchie River; battle of Helena; expedition south to Duvall's Bluff, Little Rock, Arkadelphia, Prairie DeAnn and Camden; retreat to Little Rock.

YAGER, JAMES PRESSLEY, b. 1834   4537

Harris, Everett W., ed. "The Yager Journals: Diary of a Journey across the Plains." NEVADA HISTORICAL SOCIETY QUARTERLY 13, no. 1 (1970):3-19, no. 2, 19-39, no. 3, 27-48, no. 4, 25-52; 14, no. 1 (1971):27-54, no. 2, 33-54.

> Apr 1863-Dec 1864. Emigrant journey from Kentucky to Nevada with his cousin Michael L. Yager; initially by train and Missouri riverboat; thence overland with a wagon train; unusually detailed descriptions of people, terrain, scenery, camps, condition of roads, etc., and a clearly identified route; references to telegraph stations and the news of Indian troubles received by telegraph; the preaching of the Rev. John Duncan during Sunday "layovers" and the identity of Lucinda Duncan, occupant of the "Maiden's Grave" near Beowave; a few references to Salt Lake and the Mormons and difficulties at the Humboldt.

1864

ANON.   4538

Smith, Sara Trainer, ed. "Notes on Satterlee Military Hospital." AMERICAN CATHOLIC HISTORICAL SOCIETY RECORDS 8 (1897):399-449. Diary, pp. 409-449.

> 1864-1865. Long, narrative passages extracted from journal kept by a Sister of Charity, serving in a large Philadelphia hospital; mainly description of deathbed reformations and conversions with some notes on medical matters and hospital arrangements; interesting vignette of laundresses' party.

ANON.   4539

In THE REBELLION RECORD, edited by Frank Moore, vol. 11, pp. 479-481.

> May 1864. Confederate officer's diary recording artillery operations in the fury of Spotsylvania.

ANON.   4540

In HISTORY OF THE ONE HUNDRED AND TWENTY-FOURTH REGIMENT, N.Y.S.V., by Charles H. Weygant, pp. 357-359.

> Jul 1864. Extracts from diary of enlisted man in the 124th New York Volunteers; picket duty and fortifying earthworks at Petersburg.

ANON.   4541

In IN AND OUT OF THE LINES, by Frances Thomas Howard, pp. 179-186, 191-228. New York and Washington, D.C.: Neale, 1905.

Extracts in WHEN SHERMAN CAME, edited by Katharine M. Jones, pp. 85-92, 103-105.

> Dec 1864-May 1865. Diary of a Georgia woman, a refugee in Savannah; Confederate army's evacuation of the city and arrival of Union forces; conditions under occupation and after Appomattox; examples of enemy cruelty and kindness and the spirit of Southern women; notes on generals Barnum and Howard, Jewish customs, behavior of blacks, a munitions fire, a meningitis epidemic and the ejection of wives of Confederate officers from the city; supposedly fictitious names for real persons.

ABBOTT, LEMUEL ABIJAH, b. 1842   4542

PERSONAL RECOLLECTIONS AND CIVIL WAR DIARY. Burlington, Vt.: Free Press Printing Co., Printers, 1908. 296 pp. Diary, pp. 1-246.

> Jan-Dec 1864. Diary of former teacher, now an officer with the Tenth Vermont; life in winter quarters near Brandy Station, Virginia; a trip to Washington, D.C., in an unsuccessful attempt to secure position as field officer with black regiment; a view of Lincoln and the theater in the capital city; the Wilderness; Spotsylvania and the gory battlefield left in its wake; Cold Harbor; siege of Petersburg; travel to Maryland to counter Early's raid; wounding at the battle of Monocacy; parading up Pennsylvania Avenue and receiving the thanks of Washington, D.C., residents; service in the Shenandoah Valley; home in Vermont recovering from wound suffered during battle of Winchester; return to duty in Virginia; notes on weather, duties, social activities, generals Grant, Custer and Butler, black troops, Confederate deserters, etc.; the excitement and carnage of battle and the dullness of camp life;

considerable later supplementing of his description of Monocacy and Winchester; a basically good document rather spoiled by diarist's need for recognition.

AGNEW, SAMUEL A.   4543

"Extracts from the Daily Journal of Rev. Samuel A. Agnew." THE SOUTHERN BIVOUAC, old ser. 1 (1883):356-365.

Jun 1864. Diary extracts pertaining to battle of Brice's Cross Roads; civilian's view of conflict waged around his home; destruction of property and attempts to make claims on Confederate army for damage suffered; killing of black Union soldiers; the stench of improperly buried bodies; notes on Union and Confederate soldiers, books picked up on the battlefield and Nathan B. Forrest; other war news; lengthy entries making an absorbing account.

AMES, AMOS W., 1840-1913   4544

"A Diary of Prison Life in Southern Prisons." ANNALS OF IOWA 40 (1969):1-19.

Aug 1864-Apr 1865. Diary of corporal in the Fourth Iowa, captured after the battle of Jonesboro and held at Macon, Millen and Andersonville; weather and prison conditions; constant rumors of exchange; presidential vote among prisoners at Millen; Wirz's orders; shifting of prisoners to various locations during final days of war; journey to exchange at Jacksonville, Florida.

ANDERSON, JAMES W., b. 1835   4545

Osborn, George C. "A Confederate Prisoner at Camp Chase." OHIO STATE ARCHAELOGICAL AND HISTORICAL QUARTERLY 59 (1950):38-57.

Dec 1864-Jan 1865. Extracts within narrative summary of prison diary of Confederate private arrested by Union troops while home on furlough in McNairy County, Tennessee; prison conditions, weather and food.

ANDREWS, ELIZA FRANCES, b. 1840   4546

THE WAR-TIME JOURNAL OF A GEORGIA GIRL. New York: D. Appleton, 1908. 387 pp. Edited by Spencer B. King, Jr. Macon, Ga.: Ardivan, 1960. 396 pp.

Extracts in THE BLUE AND THE GRAY, edited by Henry S. Commager, vol. 2, pp. 690-692, 958-959, 1145-1147; A DAY AT A TIME, edited by Margo Culley, pp. 128-142; HEROINES OF DIXIE, edited by Katharine M. Jones, pp. 405-409; WHEN SHERMAN CAME, edited by Katharine M. Jones, pp. 76-81.

Dec 1864-Aug 1865. Privileged young woman's account of the last months of war and early postwar period, kept to cultivate composition skills and revised for publication; difficult trek across the wake of Sherman's march to her sister's plantation, Pine Bluff, between Albany and Thomasville; sojourning there in fear of Union raids and retribution but enjoying social life and appreciating the natural beauty of the environment; recurring guilt and rationalization about conditions at Andersonville; journey to Haywood, her home in Washington, Georgia, by way of Cuthbert and Macon, getting caught up in the flood of refugees as Union forces advance; the disheartening spectacle of confusion, plunder and demoralization as the Southern nation crumbles and the last remnants of government and army pass through Washington; in the midst of ruin, the enjoyment of parties and meeting a variety of

people thrown together by circumstance; condemnation of emancipation and a catalog of privations endured and abuses suffered from Union soldiers and freedmen; the everyday activities of a well-to-do family, including clothes, medicine, dances, food and religion; notes on such prominent Confederates as generals Arnold Elzey and John B. Gordon, Varina Davis and Gov. Joseph E. Brown; a glimpse of Sidney Lanier; interesting description of slave praise meeting and examples of spirituals; distress over continued opposition to secession and allegiance to the Union of her father Judge Garnett Andrews; long narrative type entries, replete with class consciousness and racist commentary, effectively revealing a part of the world of the slaveholding aristocracy.

ARNOLD, JOSEPH WARREN, 1841-1903   4547

Martin, Charles W., ed. "Joseph Warren Arnold's Journal of His Trip to and from Montana." NEBRASKA HISTORY 55 (1974):463-552.

1864-1866 (with gaps). Galena, Illinois, man's journey to Montana gold fields with John S. Collins and James McNear; across Iowa for outfitting and departure at Council Bluffs with wagons carrying goods to open a store; from Omaha with a train under Isaac Evans and William Prowse; route, distances, camps; difficulties with rivers, including ferries at the Loup and Snake; notes on Sioux and Pawnee Indians; colorful and violent life of miners in Nevada City and Virginia City; a trial and hanging of Jim Brady; prospecting at Pioneer and Ophir gulches, with rugged travels in the area; journey to Fort Benton made dangerous by Indians; by riverboat to St. Louis and Kentucky.

ASHLEY, W.   4548

In THE REBELLION RECORD, edited by Frank Moore, vol. 11, pp. 153-157.

Jul-Sep 1864. Diary of lieutenant in John C. Vaughn's brigade; Early's raid through Maryland to the outskirts of Washington, D.C.; hunger and the desire for soap and clean clothes; record of military operations in the Shenandoah Valley until the day before his death in the battle of Winchester.

AUBERY, JAMES MADISON, b. 1843   4549

THE THIRTY-SIXTH WISCONSIN VOLUNTEER INFANTRY...WITH REMINISCENCES FROM THE AUTHOR'S PRIVATE JOURNAL. Milwaukee?, 1900. 430 pp. Journal, pp. 160-250 passim.

Sep 1864-Jun 1865. A smattering of entries in officer's journal interspersed with other documents within narrative; siege of Petersburg; pursuing Lee's army to Appomattox; soldiers' reaction to news of Lincoln's assassination; visit to Bull Run battlefield.

BAKER, I. NORVAL, 1844-1924   4550

"Diary and Recollections of I. Norval Baker." WINCHESTER-FREDERICK COUNTY HISTORICAL SOCIETY PAPERS 3 (1955):96-128. Diary. pp. 107-117.

Sep-Oct 1864. Diary extracts embedded in recollections of Frederick County resident, serving as private in Company F, Eighteenth Virginia Cavalry; military activities in the Shenandoah Valley.

BARTLESON, FREDERICK A., 1833-1864   4551

LETTERS FROM LIBBY PRISON. Edited by Margaret W. Peelle. New

York: Greenwich Book Publishers, 1956. 95 pp. Diary, pp. 15-55, 74-83.

Jan-Mar 1864. Diary kept by Joliet, Illinois, lawyer and colonel of the 100th Illinois Volunteers, captured at Chickamauga, for the purpose of later observing how he changed during his imprisonment; events and conditions at Libby, especially escape attempts and guards pilfering from boxes sent to prisoners; reflections on a variety of topics such as political life, newspapers, foreign policy, decision-making and the virtue of common sense; analysis of problems involved in prisoner exchange; return home by way of Washington, D.C.

BEDFORD, A.M.   4552

In THE IMMORTAL SIX HUNDRED, by John Ogden Murray, pp. 250-318. Roanoke, Va.: Stone Printing and Manufacturing, 1911.

Aug 1864-May 1865. Diary of Confederate officer in the Third Missouri Cavalry, a prisoner at Morris Island, Fort Pulaski, Hilton Head and Fort Delaware; prison conditions, focusing on quantity and quality of rations; notes on weather, illness, black soldiers guarding the prisoners, prices, war news, artillery action at Charleston, sea transport between prisons, reaction to Lincoln's assassination, etc.

BENEDICT, GILBERT   4553

In HO! FOR THE GOLD FIELDS, edited by Helen M. White, pp. 119-131.

Apr-Oct 1864. Terse account of a journey from Shakopee, Minnesota, to Helena, during Montana gold rush, in Thomas A. Holmes' company under military escort of Gen. Alfred Sully; replacement of Holmes with Oliver D. Keep as captain; constant harrassment by Indians; news of Indian ambush of Fisk's expedition; nearly disastrous crossing of the Badlands.

BENEFIEL, JOHN K.   4554

DIARY OF JOHN K. BENEFIEL FOR THE YEAR 1864. Lompoc, Calif.: Mrs. R.Q. McKinney, 1972. 27 leaves.

Jan-Dec 1864 (with gap). Record of Pulaski County soldier, a member of the Forty-sixth Indiana Volunteers; in camp at Indianapolis; journey south; stationed in vicinity of New Orleans; notes on duties, reading, correspondence, etc.; use of Christian Commission services; ill at home; return to regiment in Kentucky.

BENSON, WILLIAM C., d. 1865   4555

"Civil War Diary of William C. Benson." INDIANA MAGAZINE OF HISTORY 23 (1927):333-364. Diary, pp. 333-356.

1864-1865 (with gap). Very brief entries covering Owensville, Indiana, soldier's service with the 120th Indiana Volunteers; at Camp Knox, Vincennes, Indiana, and then south to Tennessee; the Atlanta campaign; in hospitals at Allatoona, Marietta and Knoxville; the Franklin and Nashville campaign; from Tennessee to Washington, D.C., and on to North Carolina where diarist was mortally wounded during battle of Kinston.

BERRY, CARRIE, b. 1854?   4556

In TRAGIC YEARS, 1860-1865, by Paul M. Angle and Earl S. Miers, vol. 2, pp. 882-883, 888-889, 928.

Sep 1864. Diary extracts providing a child's view of the fall of

Atlanta, life under Union occupation and the burning of the city.

BETZ, AUGUST, 1841-1919   4557

In FINDING THE GRAIN: PIONEER JOURNALS, FRANCONIAN FOLKTALES, ANCESTRAL POEMS, by Norbert Krapf, pp. 35-46. Jasper, Ind.: Dubois County Historical Society and Herald Printing, 1977.

1864-1890. A few personal entries about birth of his children; chiefly folk remedies and recipes of an Indiana farmer, son of a German immigrant. Translated from the German.

BONEBRAKE, HENRY G., b. 1838   4558

In HISTORY OF THE SEVENTEENTH REGIMENT PENNSYLVANIA VOLUNTEER CAVALRY, by Pennsylvania Cavalry, 17th Regiment, pp. 135-154. Lebanon, Pa.: Sowers Printing, 1911.

Sep 1864-Apr 1865. Extracts from diary of lieutenant, Company G, awarded the Medal of Honor for bravery in battle of Five Forks; patrolling against Mosby's querillas in the Shenandoah Valley around Winchester and Martinsburg; ravaging the Loudon Valley; raid on Gordonsville; to the James River; closing in on Lee's forces; in Washington, D.C., after Lincoln's assassination.

BOOTH, BENJAMIN F., b. 1837?   4559

DARK DAYS OF THE REBELLION, OR, LIFE IN SOUTHERN MILITARY PRISONS. Indianola, Iowa: Booth Publishing, 1897. 375 pp. Diary, pp. 57-343.

Oct 1864-Mar 1865. Prison diary kept by member of Company I, Twenty-second Iowa Infantry, after capture at Cedar Creek; briefly at Libby Prison and then at Salisbury, North Carolina; conditions at both places but emphasizing the terrible treatment received at the latter; rations, vermin, filth, cruel guards, sickness, deaths and stealing among prisoners; bartering, the solace of tobacco, ways of passing the time, rumors of exchange and remedies for illness; escape attempts and an unsuccessful insurrection; effort to recruit prisoners for Confederate service; harsher treatment of black Union prisoners; notes on celebrating Lincoln's reelection, the assistance of Masons and Oddfellows, his suffering and the supportive friendship of David W. Connely; release to Wilmington and by boat to Annapolis; long entries, rewritten and embellished after the war.

BOYKIN, LAURA JOSEPHINE NISBET, b. 1834?   4560

SHINPLASTERS AND HOMESPUN. Edited by Mary Wright Stock. Rockville, Md.: Printex, 1975. 76 pp.

Aug-Oct 1864, May-Jul 1865. Diary containing long, confiding entries made by wife of Baptist minister, editor and publisher in Macon, Georgia; social life, hospital work and domestic duties; her pleasures in music and other cultural activities; irritations, flirtations and boredom; hatred for Yankees; content of sermons and her religious beliefs; notes on Jefferson Davis's visits to Macon as president and prisoner and on her father, Eugenius Aristides Nisbet, former United States congressman and author of Georgia's ordinance of secession; adjustment to postwar world without slavery and beginning of social engagements with Union officials; for the most part, a record of vanity and self-indulgence.

BOYLE, FRANCIS ATHERTON, 1838-1907   4561

Thornton, Mary Lindsay, ed. "The Prison Diary of Adjutant Francis

Atherton Boyle.'' NORTH CAROLINA HISTORICAL REVIEW 39 (1962):58-84.

1864-1865. Military action during battle of the Wilderness and Spotsylvania campaign recorded by officer from Plymouth, North Carolina, serving with the Thirty-second North Carolina Infantry until his capture on May 10; sporadic, lengthy entries describing and comparing conditions of imprisonment at Point Lookout and Fort Delaware; notes on reading, prices, religious services, rations, the hospital, war news and rumors of exchange; comments on the monotony of prison life and the support afforded by his extensive correspondence; establishment of the Christian Association among the prisoners and praise for the leadership of the Rev. Isaac W.K. Handy; effects of Lincoln's assassination on treatment of prisoners; waiting for release after war's end.

BRADLEY, GEORGE S. 4562

THE STAR CORPS; OR, NOTES OF AN ARMY CHAPLAIN. Milwaukee: Jermain & Brightman, Printers, 1865. 304 pp. Journal, pp. 181-209, 252-261.

Nov 1864-Feb 1865. Diary of Twenty-second Wisconsin's chaplain, appearing originally in newspapers, of Sherman's march through Georgia and South Carolina; notes on countryside and settlements, destruction of resources, foraging and pillaging, spirit or temper of the troops, resistance of Confederates and slaves helping and joining the Union cavalcade; at Milledgeville; visit to Millen Prison; conversations with civilians.

BRAWLEY, WILLIAM HIRAM, 1841-1916 4563

THE JOURNAL OF WILLIAM H. BRAWLEY. Edited by Francis Roe Brawley. Charlottesville, Va., 1970. 263 pp.

Jun 1864-Mar 1865 (with gaps). Travel diary kept by South Carolinian who, having lost his left arm at the battle of Fair Oaks, set forth on a European tour, studying law and literature, and perhaps carrying on some business for the Confederacy; touring England and France and socializing with prominent Confederates such as James M. Mason; sojourning in London and seeing its sights, including the British Museum, National Gallery, Madame Tussaud's, Spurgeon's tabernacle, the Crystal Palace and Hyde Park with comments on theater, opera and Haymarket prostitutes; living in the Paris Latin Quarter, learning French and finding the city delightful and wicked; people-watching on the boulevards and notes on theater, opera, Adelina Patti and gothic architecture; visits to Dieppe, Chartres, LeMans, Angers and a Benedictine monastery; observations on and comparisons between the English and French cultures; fulsome descriptions of what a well-to-do, intelligent, sensitive, young American experienced abroad.

BROTHER, CHARLES 4564

In TWO NAVAL JOURNALS, edited by C. Carter Smith, Jr., pp. 18-45. Chicago: Wyvern Press of S.F.E., 1964.

In CIVIL WAR NAVAL CHRONOLOGY, 1861-1865, by United States Naval History Division, part IV, pp. 47-83. Washington, D.C.: United States Government Printing Office, 1861-1866.

Mar-Aug 1864. Journal of a marine private from Bath, New York, serving on the Union sloop-of-war HARTFORD, Farragut's flagship; routines of ship life at Pensacola; duties, chores and food; description of uniforms required at various times; mention of vessels arriving and departing while at Pensacola and on blockade off Mobile; the battle of Mobile Bay.

BROWN, AUGUSTUS CLEVELAND, 1839-1915 4565

THE DIARY OF A LINE OFFICER. New York, 1906? 117 pp.

Extracts in THE BLUE AND THE GRAY, edited by Henry S. Commager, vol. 2, pp. 791-792, 1013-1016; TREASURY OF THE WORLD'S GREAT DIARIES, edited by Philip Dunaway, pp. 281-282.

Mar-Aug, Dec 1864. ''An elaboration of a daily record, kept at the time,'' by the captain of Company H, Fourth New York Heavy Artillery; garrisoning Fort Marcy, part of the defenses of Washington, D.C.; assigned to infantry duty in support of batteries already in the field with the Second Corps and then the Fifth Corps of the Army of the Potomac; protesting the injustice of being recruited for the artillery but having to serve as infantry; in camp at Stevensburg, enduring rain and mud, and at Culpeper, serving on examination board screening candidates for commissions in black regiments; battle of the Wilderness, Spotsylvania campaign, action at the North Anna River and Cold Harbor; an artillery duty assignment, at last, for the siege of Petersburg; the battle of the Crater and criticism of the high command's management of the assault; sunstroke and subsequent medical discharge; gripping descriptions of battle and treatment of the wounded; scenes of camp life and the soldier's everyday hardships and small pleasures; notes on Southern civilians, Confederate soldiers, artillery operations, his comrades, General Meade, etc.; a first-rate account.

BUHRER, GEORGE W., b. 1835? 4566

Billings, E.E. ''Letters & Diaries.'' CIVIL WAR TIMES ILLUSTRATED 1, no. 1 (1962):16, 18.

Jan-Feb, Mar-Oct 1864. Extracts from diary of farmer, an immigrant from Germany, serving in Company E, Second Massachusetts Cavalry; actions involving Mosby's Rangers and Early's troops; battle of Cedar Creek.

BURDICK, JOHN M., d. 1865 4567

Futch, Ovid L., ed. ''The Andersonville Journal of Sergeant J.M. Burdick.'' GEORGIA HISTORICAL QUARTERLY 45 (1961):287-294.

Jun-Oct 1864. Prison diary of trooper, Company I, Twenty-first New York Cavalry, from Greenwich, New York; very brief entries made during confinement at Lynchburg, Danville, Andersonville, Charleston and Florence.

BURNHAM, FRANKLIN J. 4568

In HISTORY OF THE NINTH REGIMENT, NEW HAMPSHIRE VOLUNTEERS, edited by Edward O. Lord, pp. 459-464, 490-493. Concord: Republican Press Association, 1895.

Jun-Jul 1864. Extracts from sergeant's diary; life in the trenches during siege of Petersburg; a duel with a Confederate sharpshooter; ''luxuries'' acquired from the Sanitary Commission and the Christian Commission; explosion of the mine and battle of the Crater.

BURTON, ELIJAH P. 4569

DIARY OF E.P. BURTON. Prepared by the Historical Records Survey, Division of Professional and Service Projects, Works Projects Administration. Des Moines, Iowa: Historical Records Survey, 1939. 92 pp.

1864-1865. Diary of surgeon assigned first to the Seventh Illinois and later to the Twelfth Illinois; activity and monotony of camp life in Tennessee and Alabama; emphasis on personal matters rather than professional duties; homesickness, correspondence, sermons and his illnesses; comments on contrabands and drunkenness in the army; the Atlanta campaign; marching through Georgia and the Carolinas; notes on countryside, people and destruction; burning of Columbia, South Carolina; north to Wasington, D.C., the Grand Review and sightseeing in the capital city; tranfer to Louisville, Kentucky, awaiting discharge.

BUSTER, SAMUEL R., b. 1845 4570

"The Bold Guerilla Boy." THE SOUTHERN BIVOUAC 2 (1883):180-566 passim; 3 (1884):35-372 passim.

Jan-Apr, Jul-Oct 1864. Adventures, comedy and romance of young guerila serving in Captain Jumper's company; authenticity questioned.

CAMPBELL, ROBERT J., 1837-1927 4571

In TWO SOLDIERS, edited by Wirt A. Cate, pp. 221-258. Chapel Hill: University of North Carolina Press, 1938.

Jan-Jul 1864. Diary of captain, Company E, Third Iowa; brief daily entries except during April furlough at home in Nevada, Iowa; the Meridian campaign; detached duty in rear of Sherman's forces until the battles around Atlanta during which diarist was captured; notes on activities and correspondence.

CAPERS, ELLISON, 1837-1908 4572

In CONFEDERATE STAMPS, OLD LETTERS AND HISTORY, by Raynor Hubbell, pp. 47-48. Griffin, Ga., n.d.

Sep-Dec 1864. Diary of Hood's campaign into Tennessee written by colonel of the Twenty-fourth South Carolina Volunteers; very brief entries, mainly noting route of march; wounding at battle of Franklin and journey home to Charleston.

CARPENTER, WALTER TOTTEN, 1811-1910 4573

Levstik, Frank R., ed. "A Journey among the Contrabands." INDIANA MAGAZINE OF HISTORY 73 (1977):204-222.

Jan-Mar 1864. Extracts from diary kept by superintendent of Earlham College when sent by Indiana Yearly Meeting of the Society of Friends to aid the freedmen; visiting hospitals and contraband camps in middle Tennessee and northern Alabama; notes on number of contrabands, their condition and assistance provided by the military, Friends and other groups.

CARY, CLARENCE FAIRFAX, b. 1845 4574

Thompson, Brooks and Owsley, Frank Lawrence, Jr., eds. "The War Journal of Midshipman Cary." CIVIL WAR HISTORY 9 (1963):187-202.

Sep 1864-Mar 1865 (with gaps). Record of service aboard the commerce raider CHICKAMAUGA; preparing for sea, waiting for adequate conditions for running the blockade at Wilmington; going to theater in the city; seizing prizes along the Atlantic coast and a stop at Bermuda; return to Wilmington, manning a battery in defense of Fort Fisher during Butler's unsuccessful assault; notes on collecting coal "tithes" from blockade runners; diary used as evidence in the ALABAMA claims.

In OFFICIAL RECORDS OF THE UNION AND CONFEDERATE NAVIES IN THE WAR OF THE REBELLION, ser. 1, vol. 3, pp. 710-714; vol. 11, pp. 375-378.

"Journal of a Confederate Midshipman." ALL HANDS, no. 472 (June 1956):59-63.

Sep-Dec 1864. Extracts.

CHAPIN, ARTHUR T., b. 1844? 4575

Longacre, Edward G., ed. "From the Wilderness to Cold Harbor in the Union Artillery." MANUSCRIPTS 35 (1983):202-213.

May-Jun 1864. Diary of private in the Fourth Maine Battery; daily account of Grant's campaign; movements of his battery and care of horses; foraging and destruction by Union soldiers; praise for John Sedgwick; good description with some interesting details.

CHURCH, FRANK L., 1842-1910 4576

CIVIL WAR MARINE. Edited by James P. Jones and Edward F. Keuchel. Washington, D.C.: History and Museums Division, Headquarters, United States Marine Corps, 1975. 89 pp. Diary, pp. 29-59.

Feb-May 1864. Diary of lieutenant from prominent Chicago family, commanding the marine guard on the BLACK HAWK and CRICKET, D.D. Porter's flagships in the Mississippi squadron and the Red River campaign, respectively; down the Mississippi from Cairo to the mouth of the Red River; up the latter with stops at Alexandria and Grand Encore; military operations and social activities; visiting with Southerners; many references to other ships and officers of the fleet; the retreat and return north; notes on his duties, celebrating April Fool's Day, foraging, acts of destruction and preventing such acts.

CLAIBORNE, WILLIS H., d. 1869 4577

Billings, Elden E. "Letters & Diaries." CIVIL WAR TIMES ILLUSTRATED 2, no. 5 (1963):20-21.

Mar 1864. Extract from Mississippi officer's diary; entries summarizing Confederate defeat at Missionary Ridge, retreat into Georgia and improved conditions after Bragg is replaced by Johnston.

CLARK, CHARLES A. 4578

In WAR SKETCHES AND INCIDENTS, by Military Order of the Loyal Legion of the United States, Iowa Commandery, vol. 2, pp. 389-439. Des Moines: Kenyon Press, 1898. Diary, pp. 438-439.

Jun, Sep, Oct 1864. Extracts from Sixth Maine officer's diary referring to Gen. Hiram Burnham, formerly lieutenant colonel of the regiment; description of his death in battle during the charge on Fort Harrison at Petersburg and his funeral at Cherryfield, Maine.

CLARK, WALTER AUGUSTUS 4579

UNDER THE STARS AND BARS. Augusta, Ga.: Chronicle Printing, 1900. 239 pp. Diary, pp. 98-102.

May-Jun 1864. Condensed extracts from war diary of soldier in the Oglethorpe Infantry, First Georgia Volunteer Regiment, covering the Atlanta campaign; very brief notes on unit's movements and casualties; battles of Resaca and Kenesaw Mountain.

CLARKE, JOHN T., 1843-1922   **4580**

"With Sherman in Georgia." MISSOURI HISTORICAL SOCIETY BULLETIN 8 (1952):356-370.

> May-Aug 1864. Company J, Thirty-first Missouri Infantry, member's diary; journey from Missouri to the brigade at Ayersville, Georgia, with brief notes on Kentucky and Tennessee; short daily entries covering the Atlanta campaign; return to Missouri.

CLAY-CLOPTON, VIRGINIA TUNSTALL, 1825-1915   **4581**

In LADIES OF RICHMOND, edited by Katharine M. Jones, pp. 211-212.

> Apr-May 1864. A scrap from diary of Clement C. Clay's wife, bemoaning her husband's absence on diplomatic mission; flight from Petersburg when Union forces threatened.

COHEN, FANNY YATES, 1840-1938   **4582**

King, Spencer B., Jr., ed. "Fanny Cohen's Journal of Sherman's Occupation of Savannah." GEORGIA HISTORICAL QUARTERLY 41 (1957):407-416.

Extracts in WHEN SHERMAN CAME, edited by Katharine M. Jones, pp. 92-96.

> Dec 1864-Jan 1865. Brief diary kept by fiercely Confederate daughter of Octavus Cohen, commission merchant and cotton exporter; behavior of Union soldiers, father's efforts to avoid receiving them in their home but ultimately having to provide rooms for Gen. William B. Hazen; pleasure of gathering with Confederate friends and her successful snubbing of the enemy; effect of occupation on blacks.

CONNOLLY, JAMES AUSTIN, 1843-1914   **4583**

"Three Years in the Army of the Cumberland." ILLINOIS STATE HISTORICAL SOCIETY PUBLICATIONS, no. 35 (1928):215-438. Diary, pp. 384-438.

THREE YEARS IN THE ARMY OF THE CUMBERLAND; THE LETTERS AND DIARY OF MAJOR JAMES A. CONNOLLY. Edited by Paul M. Angle. Bloomington: Indiana University Press, 1959. 399 pp. Diary, pp. 267-369.

Extracts in TRAGIC YEARS, by Paul M. Angle and Earl S. Miers, vol. 2, pp. 928-929, 936-937.

> Oct-Dec 1864. Diary of military operations in Georgia, kept by lawyer, formerly major in the 123d Illinois Infantry, now serving as staff officer in the Army of the Cumberland; marches and bivouacs as Union forces pursue Hood's army north and west of Atlanta; diarist's enthusiastic anticipation of proposed march through Georgia and disgust for fears of fellow officers; notes on Georgia towns, crops, countryside and colonial history; foraging and property destruction; burning of Acworth, part of Marietta and Atlanta; plundering of state library at Milledgeville; encounters with civilians; description of slaves and treatment of contrabands; a diversionary move toward Augusta and skirmishes with the enemy; disparaging remarks about the cavalry and a concise portrait of its commander Hugh Judson Kilpatrick; admiration for Sherman; arrival at Savannah and capitulation of the city.

Extracts in SHERMAN IN GEORGIA, edited by Edgar L. McCormick and others, pp. 33-56. Boston: Heath, 1961.

> Nov-Dec 1864.

COOK, F.A.   **4584**

Reeve, Frank D., ed. "War and Peace: Two Arizona Diaries." NEW MEXICO HISTORICAL REVIEW 24 (1949):95-129. Diary, pp. 95-120.

> Aug 1864. Diary of a member of King S. Woolsey's 1864 punitive expedition against the Indians; route, distances, terrain and camps.

COOK, SUSAN, d. 1912   **4585**

Faust, Betty M., ed. "Diary of Susan Cook." PHILLIPS COUNTY HISTORICAL QUARTERLY 4 (December 1965):29-42.

> Jan-Apr 1864. Diary kept by young woman in the Barton area of Phillips County, Arkansas; weather, visitors and visiting, reading, April Fool's Day, etc.; local events including Union searches for hidden Confederate soldiers; war news and hopes; departure of one of the family's slaves; frequent mention of Ed Hicks whom she would later marry.

COOKE, GILES BUCKNER, 1838-1937   **4586**

"Rev.-Maj. Giles Buckner Cooke." TYLER'S QUARTERLY HISTORICAL AND GENEALOGICAL MAGAZINE 19 (1937):1-10, 87-94.

> Jun, Aug 1864, Mar-Apr 1865. Extracts from diary of assistant adjutant and inspector general on Beauregard's staff and then on Lee's; under attack at Petersburg and dispatched to Lee for reinforcements; the siege; breaking of the Confederate lines, the Appomattox campaign and Lee's farewell to the Army of Northern Virginia.

COOKE, PHILIP, b. 1845   **4587**

In CHRONICLES OF THE ONE HUNDRED AND FIFTY-FIRST REGIMENT NEW YORK STATE VOLUNTEER INFANTRY, compiled by Helena A. Howell, pp. 65-68, 73-79. Albion, N.Y.: A.M. Eddy, Printer, 1911.

> May 1864. Extracts from diary of English-born corporal, Company F, describing his unit's participation in the Spotsylvania campaign and operations at North Anna River and Totopotomoy Creek.

CORNWELL, LOUISE CAROLINE REESE   **4588**

In WHEN SHERMAN CAME, edited by Katharine M. Jones, pp. 19-24.

> Nov 1864. Extract from Hillsborough, Georgia, resident's diary, describing the town's occupation by Union troops; taking tea with Gen. O.O. Howard and his staff; examples of enemy soldiers' behavior, mostly negative, and slaves' loyalty and disloyalty.

COX, JABEZ T.   **4589**

"Civil War Diary of Jabez T. Cox." INDIANA MAGAZINE OF HISTORY 28 (1932):40-54.

Extracts in TRAVEL ACCOUNTS OF INDIANA, compiled by Shirley S. McCord, pp. 222-226.

> May-Aug 1864. Extracts from diary of Hamilton County resident, enlisted in the 136th Indiana for one hundred days service; at Camp Carrington, Indianapolis; a send-off speech from Governor Morton; journey from Louisville on the Ohio and Cumberland rivers to Nashville, with good description of sights along the way;

stationed near Nashville; notes on camp life, contrabands, black Union soldiers, the Christian Commission, etc.; return to Indianapolis; interesting details and pleasant writing style.

CRAIG, J.M.   4590

Kendall, John S. "The Diary of Surgeon Craig." LOUISIANA HISTORICAL QUARTERLY 8 (1925):53-70.

Sep 1864-Feb 1865. Regimental surgeon's record of Fourth Louisiana remnant's service, following the decimating losses at the battle of Jonesboro; retreat to Florence, Alabama, and advance into Tennessee; march through Mississippi to New Orleans; brief entries, focusing on route and length of marches but with some more substantial notes on the battle of Nashville; list of regiment's killed, wounded and captured.

CUTLER, NATHAN F., b. 1841   4591

In HISTORY OF THE FIRST REGIMENT OF HEAVY ARTILLERY, MASSACHUSETTS VOLUNTEERS, FORMERLY THE FOURTEENTH REGIMENT OF INFANTRY, by Alfred Seelye Roe and Charles Nutt, p. 156-183 passim. Worcester and Boston: Regimental Association, 1917.

May-Jun 1864. Extracts from Company D member's diary covering action from Spotsylvania to Petersburg.

DAVIS, CREED T.   4592

In CONTRIBUTIONS TO A HISTORY OF THE RICHMOND HOWITZER BATTALION, by Virginia Artillery, Richmond Howitzers, no. 3, pp. 9-35; no. 4, pp. 3-28.

1864-1865. Diary, containing some nice details, of private serving with the Second Company; battle of Spotsylvania; military operations in the Shenandoah Valley; retreat from Richmond and capture before the surrender; prison conditions at Newport News until release in late June; comments on Lincoln's assassination, cruelty of black guards, Yankee preachers, abolition of slavery, etc.

DAVIS, WILLIAM   4593

In THE SOLDIER OF INDIANA IN THE WAR FOR THE UNION, by Catharine Merrill, vol. 2, pp. 651-660.

Jun-Jul 1864. Account of escape from convalescent hospital near Lynchburg, Virginia, by severely wounded lieutenant, Company F, Seventh Indiana, captured at battle of the Wilderness; assistance provided by unionists as diarist and comrade search for Union forces; hardships endured during Hunter's retreat into West Virginia; return home to Indiana.

DELOACH, OLIVIA HILL   4594

Holden, John A., ed. "Journey of a Confederate Mother." WEST TENNESSEE HISTORICAL SOCIETY PAPERS, no. 19 (1965):36-57.

Jun-Sep 1864. Diary kept by Collierville, Tennessee, woman on trip taken with her husband to visit their sons in the Confederate army; the hazards, delays and roundabout ways of wartime travel by freight and passenger trains and various types of boats and horse-drawn vehicles; meeting one son in Montgomery, then going on alone to Richmond to see other son; journey south, reunion with husband in Georgia and on to Alabama; notes on prices, war news, people met along the way and various places

including Jackson and Oxford, Mississippi, Augusta, Georgia, Mobile and Richmond; description of Robert E. Lee.

DENZER, VALENTINE   4595

Denzer, Betty Sue and Cummings, Warren D. "Valentine Denzer: He Made Circus History." NEW JERSEY HISTORY 85 (1967):138-144.

1864-1865. Interesting extracts within an article about an acrobat and trapeze artist with the Great National Circus; notes on New Jersey towns, circus life and fortunes.

DICKINSON, HENRY CLAY, 1830-1871   4596

DIARY OF CAPT. HENRY C. DICKINSON, C.S.A. Denver: Press of Williamson-Haffner, 191-. 189 pp.

Sep 1964-May 1865. Diary of imprisonment written by lawyer, a captain in the Second Virginia Cavalry; long summary of events of capture in May 1864, detention at Point Lookout and Fort Delaware and journey to Morris Island; prison life and captors' cruelties at Morris Island and Fort Pulaski; contempt for black Union soldiers and hatred of Yankees; rations, prices and eating cats; sickness, deaths and escape attempts; journey to Fort Delaware and resistance to taking oath of allegiance until last hopes of Confederacy's survival are dashed.

DONAGHY, JOHN, b. 1837   4597

ARMY EXPERIENCE OF CAPTAIN JOHN DONAGHY, DeLand, Fla.: E.O. Painter Printing, 1926. 244 pp. Diary, pp. 192-239.

Oct-Nov 1864. Diary, with some later amplification, of escape from imprisonment near Columbia, South Carolina, by officer of the 103d Pennsylvania Volunteers; first breakout and recapture; second escape and journey down the Congaree and South Santee rivers by boat, dodging detection and receiving assistance from slaves, to Cedar Island and rescue by Union blockade ship.

DOUGHERTY, WILLIAM THOMPSON   4598

Coan, Donald J., ed. "Civil War Diary of an Ohio Volunteer." WESTERN PENNSYLVANIA HISTORICAL MAGAZINE 50 (1967):171-186.

Jan-May, Nov-Dec 1864. Extracts from diary of Greentown, Ohio, schoolteacher; work and social life in the small town; enlistment in Company B, 104th Ohio Volunteer Infantry; stationed in Tennessee; the Atlanta campaign; the Franklin and Nashville campaign.

DOUGLAS, JAMES POSTELL, 1836-1901   4599

DOUGLAS'S TEXAS BATTERY, CSA. Edited by Lucia R. Douglas. Tyler, Tex.: Smith County Historical Society, 1966. 238 pp. Diary, pp. 202-214.

Jul-Dec 1864. Officer's brief entries recording activities of the First Texas Battery on the march and in action; battles of Atlanta, Jonesboro, Franklin and Nashville; capture of the battery's guns while covering Hood's retreat from Tennessee.

DOYLE, JAMES M., 1839-1909   4600

Jacobsen, Jerome V., ed. "The Diary of James M. Doyle." MID-AMERICA 20 (1938):273-283.

Aug-Dec 1864. Extracts from war diary of Irish-born Chicago resident, a member of the Twenty-third Illinois, Mulligan's Brigade, serving as a clerk in the quartermaster's department; operations in Maryland and in the Shenandoah Valley.

DOZER, JESSE L., b. 1845   4601

Black, Wilfred W., ed. "Marching with Sherman through Georgia and the Carolinas." GEORGIA HISTORICAL QUARTERLY 52 (1968):308-336, 451-479.

1864-1865. War diary of carpenter from Stoverton, Muskingum County, Ohio, serving in Company A, Twenty-sixth Illinois Infantry; daily entries covering new recruit's journey to Georgia, the Atlanta campaign, the March to the Sea and the Carolinas campaign with the Fifteenth Corps in Howard's wing; weather reports and description of military operations as seen from the ranks; notes or foraging, destruction of Columbia, South Carolina, battle of Bentonville, etc.

DRAKE, JOHN M., 1830-1913   4602

Knuth, Priscilla, ed. "Cavalry in the Indian Country." OREGON HISTORICAL QUARTERLY 65 (1964):5-118.

Apr-Oct 1864. Commander's private diary of an expedition against the Snake Indians by several companies of the First Oregon Volunteer Cavalry assigned to protect travel along the Canyon City road; route from Fort Dalles via Crooked River; diarist's complaints about poor equipment, raw recruits, inept officers and foolish orders from his superior, General Benjamin Alvord; vexing delays in getting to Indian country because of breakdowns, overloading, etc., eulogy for Chief Stockwhitley, "the noblest Indian I ever knew," killed in battle against the Snake; reports of smallpox epidemic in Oregon towns; rendezvous with George B. Currey and continuing under his command; notes on John F. Noble; diarist's reading and intellectual interests, reflections on Civil War news, disillusionment with his own expedition.

DUNLAP, KATE, 1834-1901   4603

THE MONTANA GOLD RUSH DIARY OF KATE DUNLAP. Edited by J. Lyman Tyler. University of Utah Western History Center Publications, vol. 1. Denver: F.A. Rosenstock Old West Publishing, 1969. A-15, B-43, C-15 pp. Diary pp. B-1-43.

May-Aug 1864. Keokuk, Iowa, woman's diary, with entries beginning at Omaha; notes of distances, camps, land suitable for development, emigrants and freighters encountered, Sioux Indians on the move, graves with names; a woman's work in camp and during layovers for rest; cooking, washing, mending, etc.; difficult travel over Lander's Cutoff and in Bear River Mountains region; illnesses, especially mountain fever; references to Bannock chief George Krokokee, who traveled with them for some days; a good, detailed diary of the difficulties, hardships and eventual reward of the journey.

DUNNING, EDWIN P.   4604

In THE NINTH NEW YORK HEAVY ARTILLERY, by Alfred Seelye Roe, pp. 310-314. Worcester, Mass.: The Author, 1899.

Jul-Oct 1864. Brief entries in diary kept by member of Company D while a prisoner at Danville, Virginia; the journey south to prison, conditions there and eventual exchange.

DUVERGIER DE HAURANNE, ERNEST, 1843-1877   4605

Robbins, Suzanne, trans. "Political Rally at Galena in 1864." ILLINOIS STATE HISTORICAL SOCIETY JOURNAL 45 (1952):76-79.

Sep 1864. Extract, from Frenchman's travel journal, giving a wonderful description of colorful campaign oratory of Richard J. Oglesby and Clark E. Carr in support of Lincoln's bid for reelection; reaction of the audience.

Spencer, Ivor D., ed. "Chicago Helps to Reelect Lincoln." ILLINOIS STATE HISTORICAL SOCIETY JOURNAL 63 (1970):167-179.

Nov 1864. Extract relating to Lincoln's campaign and that of his opponent, George B. McClellan; amusing accounts of the political oratory of Richard Yates, Salmon P. Chase, John Wentworth and others; parades, fights, etc.; reports of a Confederate plot to free prisoners from Camp Douglas in order to sack Chicago, and diarist's visit to the camp; the "fraud, lies and violence" which he perceived in the election process; betting on election day; ease of aliens voting with no checks on identity; Lincoln's victory; amused, rather affectionate comments on American customs and character. Translated from the French.

EBERHART, JAMES W.   4606

McLaughlin, Florence C., ed. "Diary of Salisbury Prison." WESTERN PENNSYLVANIA HISTORICAL MAGAZINE 56 (1973):211-251.

Aug 1864-Mar 1865. Extracts from diary of sergeant, Company G, Eighth Pennsylvania Reserve Volunteer Corps, 191st Pennsylvania Veteran Volunteers; capture near Petersburg; briefly at Libby before imprisonment at Belle Isle; transport to Salisbury in October and unsuccessful mass escape attempt there; notes on prison conditions, weather, food and its procurement, etc.; exchange through Wilmington to Annapolis.

EDDY, VALORA D., b. 1840?   4607

In ANNUAL REPORT, 5th, by New York State Bureau of Military Statistics, pp. 631-661.

1864-1865. Corporal's diary; service with Company A, Forty-fourth New York; through the Wilderness, Spotsylvania and Cold Harbor; capture, a brief stop at Libby Prison and transport to Andersonville; commentary on countryside and crops along the way; prison conditions including weather, lack of shelter, rations, trading, execution of "raiders," escape attempts, deaths, rumors of war's progress and hopes of exchange; transfer to Florence, South Carolina, prison; comments on "galvanized Yanks"; mock presidential election among prisoners; exchange after nearly nine months of imprisonment.

EDMONDSON, BELLE   4608

In HEROINES OF DIXIE, edited by Katharine M. Jones, pp. 270-275.

Mar-Apr 1864. Diary extracts describing young woman's adventures while smuggling contraband goods between Union-occupied Memphis and her family's plantation near Nonconnah in Shelby County, Tennessee.

EGGLESTON, EDMUND T.   4609

Noyes, Edward, ed. "Excerpts from the Civil War Diary of E.T. Eggleston," TENNESSEE HISTORICAL QUARTERLY 17 (1958):336-358.

Feb-Dec 1864. Extracts from diary of sergeant, Company G, First Mississippi Regiment of Artillery; operations in Mississippi and Alabama during Sherman's Meridian campaign; the Atlanta campaign; the Franklin and Nashvile campaign; mainly description of military action.

ELLIS, JOB B., b. 1829   4610

"Job B. Ellis." VINELAND HISTORICAL MAGAZINE 19 (1934) - 22 (1937) passim.

Sep 1864-Aug 1865. Extracts from journal interspersed among letters of New York schoolteacher serving aboard the steam frigate SUSQUEHANNA; duties, his health, weather and ship's location; capture of Fort Fisher; transfer to the "School Ship SAVANNA"; return to Potsdam, New York, after the war and then settling in Newfield, New Jersey.

ELLZEY, FRANCES WESTWOOD, b. 1846   4611

In SCRAPS OF PAPER, by Marietta Minnigerode Andrews, pp. 216-222. New York: E.P. Dutton, 1929.

Jan 1864. Extracts from diary of Leesburg, Virginia, resident on a short visit to Middleburg, Virginia; solace of religious faith; inspiration of romantic reading; deeds of Mosby and his men.

ELY, ROBERT B., b. 1841?   4612

" 'This Filthy Ironpot.' " AMERICAN HERITAGE 19 (1968):46-51, 108-111.

Jul-Aug 1864. Extracts from diary kept by lieutenant aboard the MANHATTAN; voyage to Mobile with stops at Key West and Pensacola: at anchor outside Mobile Bay and then the battle; surrender of the Confederate ram TENNESSEE; attacks on Fort Morgan and its capitulation; an engaging, good-humored and detailed account of the constant discomfort of life on a monitor.

FERGUSON, LEONARD C., 1839-1873   4613

Hunter, William A., ed. "The Civil War Diaries of Leonard C. Ferguson." PENNSYLVANIA MAGAZINE OF HISTORY AND BIOGRAPHY 14 (1947):196-224, 289-313.

1864-1865. Diary of private, Company B, Fifty-seventh Pennsylvania Volunteer Infantry; extremely short, repetitious entries while in camp near Philadelphia; Spotsylvania and Petersburg campaigns; capture, brief stay at Libby before transport south; at Andersonville and Florence; entries routinely recording weather and rations with occasional notes on events, rumors or his health; member of camp police at Florence, receiving extra rations, but no description of duties; exchange through Wilmington to Annapolis; at Camp Curtin near Harrisburg until discharge.

FLEHARTY, STEPHEN F.   4614

In OUR REGIMENT. A HISTORY OF THE 102d ILLINOIS INFANTRY VOLUNTEERS, pp. 108-124. Chicago: Brewster & Hanscom, Printers, 1865.

Nov-Dec 1864. Noncommissioned officer's diary transcribed for publication "with but slight alterations" from the original; from Atlanta to the outskirts of Savannah; the scourging of the earth, foraging and pillaging and the flocking of contrabands to the army; a visit to Milledgeville and observance of vandalism there;

report of conditions at Millen Prison; sense of glory in the march but also sympathy for innocent suffering.

FORBES, EUGENE, 1833?-1865   4615

DIARY OF A SOLDIER, AND PRISONER OF WAR IN THE REBEL PRISONS. Trenton, N.J.: Murphy & Bechtel, Printers, 1865. 68 pp.

Mar 1864-Feb 1865. Prison diary of soldier of the Fourth New Jersey Volunteers; capture in battle of the Wilderness; journey south to Andersonville, trading personal items for food; arrival at the prison and comments on appearance and spirit of the men who had been there for some months and on the presence of blacks and Indians among the prisoners; daily events with notes on weather, rations, escape attempts, punishments, prices, gambling, news of the regiment, peddlers, etc.; description of the prison, death statistics and graphic details of conditions and suffering of the inmates; praise for Wirz's execution of the "raiders"; approval of Lincoln's refusal to meet Confederate exchange terms; transfer to Florence, South Carolina; retaliation against prisoners taking Confederate oath of allegiance, black labor pace and a work song, prisoners' preference in the 1864 presidential election etc.; straightforward, detailed, substantial account with last entry made two days before death.

FORMAN, GEORGE   4616

Larson, T.A., ed. "Across the Plains in 1864 with George Forman." ANNALS OF WYOMING 40 (1968):5-21, 267-281.

Jun-Sep 1864. Ontario man's journey to the gold fields of Montana; discovery of bodies of emigrants killed by Indians and news of other depredations; conditions at the Montana mines and boom towns, especially Virginia City, where diarist was unsuccessful in his mining ventures.

Davis, William E., ed. "George Forman, the Great Pedestrian." IDAHO YESTERDAYS 10, no. 1 (1966):2-11.

Sep 1864-Aug 1865. Rambles in Idaho in search of gold, with entertaining observations of life in the Boise Basin; mining experience and earnings; the burning of Idaho City by robbers and "about fifty murders while I was there and not a single case of the murderers being punished."

FOSTER, SAMUEL T.   4617

ONE OF CLEBURNE'S COMMAND: THE CIVIL WAR REMINISCENCES AND DIARY OF CAPT. SAMUEL T. FOSTER, GRANBURY'S TEXAS BRIGADE, CSA. Edited by Norman D. Brown. Austin: University of Texas Press, 1980. 192 pp. Diary, pp. 73-186.

1864-1865. War diary of lawyer and judge, the commander of Company H, Twenty-fourth Texas Cavalry, a dismounted unit; the Atlanta campaign and the battles of New Hope Church, Peach Tree Creek, Atlanta and Jonesboro; return to Tennessee and the battles of Franklin and Nashville; duties, chores, rations and rumors; the carnage of the battlefield and the primitive treatment available for the wounded; commentary on removal of Johnston and condemnation of Hood after the Tennessee campaign; the pain of defeat and the journey home to Texas; interesting opinions on slavery, loss of Lincoln, future race relations and possible retribution toward Confederate veterans.

GARNETT, JAMES MERCER   4618

"Diary of Captain James M. Garnett." SOUTHERN HISTORICAL SOCIETY PAPERS 27 (1899):1-76.

Aug-Nov 1864. Military operations in the Shenandoah Valley as seen by ordnance officer, Rode's Division, Second Corps, Army of Northern Virginia; retreating from Winchester to Staunton with Early's forces; the task of trying to supply sufficient arms and complete the reports of his office; battles of Winchester, Fishers Hill and Cedar Creek.

GIBSON, WILLIAM J.   **4619**

In THE STORY OF A THOUSAND, by Albion W. Tourgée, pp. 333-346.

Nov-Dec 1864. Commissary sergeant's letter-journal; with the 105th Ohio Volunteer Infantry from Kingston, Georgia, through Milledgeville to the sea; foraging, destruction, food, reading, sights, etc.; entry into Savannah.

GILLET, ORVILLE   **4620**

Worley, Ted R., ed. "Diary of Lieutenant Orville Gillet, U.S.A." ARKANSAS HISTORICAL QUARTERLY 17 (1958):164-204.

1864-1865. Union trooper's diary of service as sergeant with Company I, Third Michigan Volunteer Cavalry, and as lieutenant with Company G, Third Arkansas Cavalry; stationed at Duvall's Bluff, Cadron Mills and Lewisburg, Arkansas; very brief entries covering duties, activities, correspondence, deaths, prices, Fourth of July celebration and military engagements; getting settled in Portland, Arkansas, after discharge.

GRAYSON, D.C.   **4621**

In CLAIM OF CERTAIN CONFEDERATE OFFICERS, by United States Congress, House, Committee on War Claims, pp. 32-42. Washington, D.C.: Government Printing Office, 1914.

Aug 1864-Mar 1865. Confederate soldier's account of imprisonment aboard the CRESCENT en route to Morris Island; conditions there and at Fort Pulaski; rations and rumors of exchange; humiliation of being guarded by black Union soldiers; almost daily entries during 1864 with monthly summaries thereafter.

HABERSHAM, ANNA WYLLY, b. 1849   **4622**

JOURNAL. New ed. The Ashantilly Leaflets, ser. 2: Regional History, no. 2. Darien, Ga.: Ashantilly Press, 1961. 23 pp.

Aug-Oct 1864. Brief diary kept at Avon on the Vernon River near Savannah by Josephine Habersham's teenage daughter; courtship of diarist by Johnie Scharf; activities with family members and friends; remembering brother Willie and another soldier killed in Confederate service.

HALL, SETH M., d. 1864   **4623**

In ANNUAL REPORT 5TH, by New York State Bureau of Military Statistics, pp. 613-617.

Sep-Dec 1864. Leighton, Michigan, man's diary of service with the Twenty-second New York Cavalry; first days in the military and operations in the Shenandoah Valley; capture and journey south; brief stay at Pemberton Prison, Richmond, then transfer to Salisbury, North Carolina; conditions of imprisonment; diarist's will.

HARRIS, BENJAMIN R., 1801-1888   **4624**

In THE CIVIL WAR IN MAURY COUNTY, TENNESSEE, by Jill K. Garrett and Marise P. Lightfoot, pp. 165-168.

Oct 1864-Jan 1865, Apr-May 1865. Extracts from diary of Tennessean living just north of Mt. Pleasant; terse entries of weather and work raising cotton and livestock; civilian's view of Hood's Tennessee campaign; an earthquake; Union foraging and destruction.

HATFIELD, ROBERT MILLER   **4625**

"In Meade's Camp." ILLINOIS STATE HISTORICAL SOCIETY JOURNAL 12 (1920):515-531.

Feb-Mar 1864. Diary kept by pastor of the Fleet Street Methodist Episcopal Church in Brooklyn while an agent of the Christian Commission with the Army of the Potomac; notes on his work, interesting people, freedmen, Gen. Marsena Patrick, the spiritual condition of soldiers, etc.; his opinion that the Sanitary Commission exaggerated the soldiers' need for the materials it supplied.

HEINEMANN, F.   **4626**

"The Federal Occupation of Camden as Set Forth in the Diary of a Union Officer." ARKANSAS HISTORICAL QUARTERLY 9 (1950):214-219.

Apr 1864. Extracts from candid and humorous captain's diary; brief notes on the town and its inhabitants, enemy ambushes and criticism of West Pointers; apprehension concerning advance of Confederate forces and preparation for retreat.

HEMPSTEAD, JUNIUS LACKLAND, 1844?-1920   **4627**

Beatty, Bess and Caprio, Judy, eds. " 'How Long Will This Misery Continue.' " CIVIL WAR TIMES ILLUSTRATED 19, no. 10 (1981):20-23.

Sep-Oct 1864. Diary kept by one of the six hundred Confederate officers sent from Fort Delaware to Morris Island where the prisoners were held under fire of Charleston's guns; mainly a record of his awful rations.

HILLEARY, WILLIAM M., 1840-1917?   **4628**

A WEBFOOT VOLUNTEER. Edited by Herbert B. Nelson and Preston E. Onstad. Oregon State Monographs, Studies in History, no. 5 Corvallis: Oregon State University Press, 1965. 240 pp. Diary, pp. 31-214.

1864-1866. Diary of corporal, an Iowa native, recently a schoolteacher in Linn county, Oregon, kept for fiancée Irene L. Cornelius; service with Company F, First Oregon Volunteer Infantry, stationed at forts Hoskins, Vancouver, Walla Walla and Boise; expeditions into eastern Oregon; daily entries covering duties, military operations and camp life; concern with constructive use of leisure time; notes on weather, misbehavior and punishment, a visit to Portland, soldiers' drinking, Indian language, celebration of Fourth of July, Indian-white relations, etc.; much mention of food and supplementing rations by hunting and fishing; nice descriptions of natural surroundings.

HINSON, WILLIAM GODBER, 1838-1919   **4629**

Waring, Joseph Ioor, ed. "The Diary of William G. Hinson during the War of Secession." SOUTH CAROLINA HISTORICAL MAGAZINE 75 (1974):14-23, 111-120.

1864-1865 (with gap). War diary of officer in the Seventh South Carolina Cavalry; brief history of his unit; journey to Virginia, receiving support of patriotic ladies; service in vicinity of Richmond; furlough home to Charleston, burying family valuables before returning to Virginia; his reaction to James Longstreet; evacuation of Richmond, the Appomattox campaign, surrender and the agony of defeat; observing war's impact on his way back home.

HITCHCOCK, GEORGE A.   4630

In HISTORY OF THE TWENTY-FIRST REGIMENT, MASSACHUSETTS VOLUNTEERS, by Charles F. Walcott, pp. 401-426.

Jun-Dec 1864. Private's daily diary kept while prisoner of war, with some later additions; at Andersonville until November; the horror of the place, with notes on weather, rations, shelter, illnesses, escape attempts, execution of "raiders," Fourth of July celebration, Captain Wirz, etc.; brief stays at Millen and Florence; exchange through Charleston.

HITCHCOCK, HENRY, 1829-1902   4631

MARCHING WITH SHERMAN. Edited by M.A. De Wolfe Howe. New Haven: Yale University Press; London: H. Milford, Oxford University Press, 1927. 332 pp. Diary, pp. 49-181, 223-244, 247-262.

Nov 1864-Feb 1865. The March to the Sea and into South Carolina as witnessed by prominent St. Louis lawyer, nephew of Gen. Ethan Allen Hitchcock, newly embarked on military service as member of Sherman's staff; campaign diary, written for the benefit of wife and friends when communication by letters was impossible; long, detailed entries, describing Union progress through Confederate territory with commentary on Sherman; dismay at destruction of private property in spite of official orders joined with rationalization of soldiers' behavior; conversations with Southerners and slaves; notes on countryside, foraging, burning of Marietta and Atlanta, Howell Cobb's plantation, Millen Prison, newspaper leaks and Confederate lies, various officers including George Ward Nichols and O.O. Howard, etc.

HORTON, DEXTER, b. 1835?   4632

Eaton, Clement, ed. "Diary of an Officer in Sherman's Army Marching through the Carolinas." JOURNAL OF SOUTHERN HISTORY 9 (1943):238-254.

Jan-May 1864. Daily record, with a few gaps, kept by commissary captain from Fentonville, Michigan, traveling with the army's left wing under Slocum; conditions of the march from Savannah to Virginia; notes on leisure activities, foraging, destruction, Southern women, blacks, towns and the countryside.

HOWE, HENRY, 1811-1868   4633

THE DIARY OF A CIRCUIT RIDER. Edited by Jessie H. Nebelthau. Minneapolis: Voyageur Press, 1933. 144 pp.

1864-1868. Short diary entries of Disciples of Christ itinerant preacher in southern Wisconsin; places where he preached, sometimes with his text or a comment on listeners' reception; income and expenses; planting and harvesting on his farm; health and illnesses; reading and books he wished to acquire.

HULL, LEWIS BYRAM, 1841-1902   4634

Hull, Myra E., ed. "Soldering on the High Plains." KANSAS HISTORICAL QUARTERLY 7 (1938):3-53.

1864-1866. Greenfield, Ohio, trooper's diary of service with the Eleventh Ohio Cavalry protecting mail, stage, telegraph and emigrant routes chiefly in Wyoming; by train from Cincinnati to Fort Leavenforth, with complaints about filthy barracks en route; thence on foot to forts Kearny and Laramie during which "whiskey in the ascendant" and "beans and dirt for breakfast"; the Tongue River and Powder River expeditions and other scouts and campaigns against several Plains tribes engaged in constant pressure against travel and settlement; garrison social life and duties at forts Laramie and Halleck; Civil War news and the report of Lincoln's assassination, which erroneously listed Seward as also dead.

HULTS, ELLSWORTH H.   4635

"Aboard the GALENA at Mobile." CIVIL WAR TIMES ILLUSTRATED 10, no. 1 (1971):12-21; no. 2, 28-40.

Apr-Nov 1864. Extracts from diary of paymaster's clerk aboard the Union ironclad GALENA; reception received by ship and its crew at Nassau; war's damage observed at Pensacola; joining the fleet off Mobile; naval operations climaxing in the battle of Mobile Bay; gathering souvenirs from the captured Confederate ram TENNESSEE; assaults on and surrender of Fort Morgan; party on the GALENA at the Dry Tortugas for Fort Jefferson's officers and ladies; voyage to Philadelphia; notes on duties, the monotony of blockade life, hot weather's effects, fleet's observation of Fourth of July, etc.; list of personal property drawn up the night before battle; vivid, detailed description of places and events.

HUTT, CHARLES WARREN, 1842-1906   4636

In POINT LOOKOUT PRISON CAMP FOR CONFEDERATES, by Edwin W. Beitzell, pp. 65-87. Abell, Md., 1972.

Jan-Dec 1864. Account of prison life by private from Westmoreland County, Virginia, who served in Company K, Fortieth Infantry, Virginia Volunteers; notes on weather, food, reading, sickness, deaths, correspondence, blacks in Union army, war news, little enjoyments, etc.

IMLER, GEORGE R., b. 1841?-   4637

1864 POCKET DIARY OF PVT. GEORGE R. IMLER. Edited by Richard A. Gray, Jr. N.p., 1963. 102 leaves.

1864-1865. Experiences of member of Company E, 138th Regiment, Pennsylvania Volunteers; in camp near Brandy Station, Virginia, where times were good, and then near Culpeper; notes on weather, duties, activities and, especially, food; battles of the Wilderness, Spotsylvania and Cold Harbor; in the Petersburg lines; marching as prisoner of war to Winchester, up the Shenandoah Valley and over to Danville; notes on rations, prices, health and the lonesomeness and dullness of prison days; exchange and home to St. Clairsville.

JAMES, FREDERIC AUGUSTUS, 1832-1864   4638

CIVIL WAR DIARY. Edited by Jefferson J. Hammer. Rutherford, N.J.: Fairleigh Dickinson University, 1973. 153 pp.

Feb-Aug 1864. Prison diary of Massachusetts carpenter and ship-joiner who enlisted in the United States Navy in 1862, was captured in an abortive raid on Fort Sumter in September 1863 and died at Andersonville a year later; conditions at Salisbury, North Carolina, prison and at Andersonville; notes on weather, rations, prices, reading, correspondence, religion, chores, illnesses, deaths, camp events and war news; a matter-of-fact account by an intelligent, generous, persevering individual, an admirable man.

JAMISON, MATTHEW H., b. 1840   **4639**

RECOLLECTIONS OF PIONEER AND ARMY LIFE. Kansas City: Hudson, 1911. 363 pp. Diary, pp. 230-341.

Apr 1864-Jun 1865. Diary kept by lieutenant from Monmouth, Illinois, serving in Company E, Tenth Illinois Veteran Volunteer Infantry; the Atlanta campaign from Rossville to the city's fall; in command of Company F as the army marches to Savannah and of Company G during the Carolinas campaign; the conflagration in Columbia; reaction to Lincoln's assassination; seeing the sights of Richmond and Fredericksburg on the way to the Grand Review; a visit to the White House; journey to Louisville camp; notes on military action, casualties, contrabands, reading and other leisure activities; glimpses of Sherman, Kilpatrick and other generals; foraging and efforts to discourage pillaging; an almost daily record of choppy notes with some lengthy entries, obviously touched up for publication.

JOHN, ENOCH D.   **4640**

Scott, Paul, ed. "On the Road to the Sea." CIVIL WAR TIMES ILLUSTRATED 22, no. 9 (1983):26-29.

Nov-Dec 1864. Extracts from private's diary included in a letter to his parents; service with Shannon's Scouts, Company C, Eighth Texas Cavalry, shadowing Sherman's forces through Georgia and engaging small parties of the enemy.

JOHNSON, HATTIE CARTER   **4641**

Carmichael, Eleanor J., ed. "The Birthday Book of Hattie Carter Johnson, Mooresville, Indiana." INDIANA HISTORY BULLETIN 55 (1978):103-115.

1864-1883. Quaker woman's annual diary, kept only on her birthday and beginning with the eleventh; events of each year, mostly family news, studies, reflections of girlhood, courtship, marriage and births of children.

JOHNSON, JOHN, 1814-1897   **4642**

Johnson, Emeroy, ed. "Jonas Jonsson-John Johnson: Pages from a Diary." SWEDISH PIONEER HISTORICAL QUARTERLY 28 (1977):7-26.

1864-1895. Extracts from Swedish farmer's diary begun in Sweden with brief farm and family notes; immigration on the MONTREAL; thence to settle at Hastings, Minnesota, with short account of farming, family and church activities there; references to many other Swedish immigrants in the area.

JONES, MARY SHARPE JONES, 1808-1869   **4643**

In YANKEES A 'COMING, by Mary Sharpe Jones and Mary Jones Mallard, edited by Haskell Monroe, pp. 33-84 passim. Tuscaloosa, Ala.: Confederate Publishing, 1959.

Dec 1864-Jan 1865. Extracts from the diary of widow of Charles Colcock Jones, noted Presbyterian clergyman, interspersed with extracts from the diary of her daughter Mary Mallard, with no indication of authorship of specific entries; coverage of same events, within identified time period, as in the Myers editions.

In THE CHILDREN OF PRIDE, edited by Robert M. Myers, pp. 1227-1248 passim, 1427-1429. New Haven: Yale University Press, 1972.

Dec 1864-Jan 1865, Mar 1865, Dec 1867. Extracts describing the disintegration of a Southern family's domain; the pillaging of Montevideo, one of their three Liberty County, Georgia, plantations; the support of their religious faith in the face of enemy threats and depredations; belief in the inferiority of blacks and defense of slavery; confinement of daughter and birth of granddaughter as Union troops gathered outside the house; postwar thoughts of the world that was lost.

In THE CHILDREN OF PRIDE, by Robert M. Myers, new abr. ed., pp. 509-530 passim. New Haven: Yale University Press, 1984.

Dec 1864-Jan 1865. Extracts.

JONES, ROBERT ELAM   **4644**

In MISSISSIPPI IN THE CONFEDERACY, edited by John K. Bettersworth and James W. Silver, vol. 1, pp. 194-196.

Jan-Feb 1864. Extracts from diary detailing entertainments enjoyed by a Mississippi soldier.

JUDD, A.N.   **4645**

CAMPAIGNING AGAINST THE SIOUX. Watsonville, Calif.: Press of the Daily Pajaronian, 1906. 45 pp. Reprint with a new introduction by John M. Carroll. New York: Sol Lewis, 1973.

1864-1865. Extracts expanded from the diaries of a Sixth Iowa cavalryman in Sully's campaign with entries starting in June 1864 when the expedition from Fort Randall "began to get interesting"; exciting yarns of Indian fighting and buffalo hunting during march to the Yellowstone region; canoe travel on the Missouri and its tributaries; notes on Sioux customs, especially hard work of women and the lofty position held by men; interesting description of a Mandan drinking orgy using home brew; a diatribe against fur companies' exploitation of Indians and the practice of halfbreed traders inciting them against settlers; a few notes on Shoshoni and Flathead Indians.

KEILEY, ANTHONY M.   **4646**

PRISONER OF WAR, OR FIVE MONTHS AMONG THE YANKEES. Richmond, Va.: West & Johnson, 1865. 120 pp. Diary, pp. 49-115.

IN VINCULIS; OR, THE PRISONER OF WAR. Petersburg, Va.: "Daily Index" Office, 1866. 216 pp. Diary, pp. 84-116, 151-209.

Jun-Nov 1864. Confederate soldier's diary extracts within narrative of experiences at Point Lookout and Elmira; prison conditions and regulations; war rumors and news; commentary on black soldiers serving as guards.

KELLY, SETH, 1836-1868   **4647**

Hemphill, Anne E., ed. "The 1864 Diary of Cpl. Seth Kelly." KANSAS HISTORY 1 (1978):189-210.

Jan-Dec 1864. Diary kept by Ohio native, alumnus of Antioch College, a resident of Douglas County; service with Company B, Ninth Kansas Volunteer Cavalry; in Lawrence camp, finding time for visits home; military operations in Missouri and Arkansas with description of towns and countryside; up the Mississippi to Fort Leavenworth and back at his farm; notes on reading, duties, etc.

KLOCK, JACOB C., 1836?-1864   4648

In ANNUAL REPORT, 5TH, by New York State Bureau of Military Statistics, pp. 672-677.

Jul-Sep 1864. Extracts from diary of major with the 153d New York Volunteers; march from Washington, D.C., to the Shenandoah Valley and military activities there.

KOEMPEL, PHILIP, b. 1840   4649

PHIL KOEMPEL'S DIARY. N.p., 192-. 53 pp.

Mar 1864-Feb 1865. Diary kept by German immigrant, sergeant in Company B, First Connecticut Cavalry; Sheridan's Richmond raid including battle of Yellow Tavern; captured during engagement at Ream's Station and held at Andersonville, Charleston and Florence; notes on weather, prison conditions, rations, prices, activities, "galvanized Yankees," soldiers' vote for Lincoln, etc.; distorted war news and fluctuating hopes of exchange; trip north for exchange through Richmond.

LADD, JAMES ROYAL, b. 1836?   4650

"From Atlanta to the Sea." AMERICAN HERITAGE 30 (Dec 1978):4-11.

Nov-Dec 1864. Sherman's march as recorded by 113th Ohio adjutant, written up for his wife just before Savannah's fall; starting off from Cartersville; burning of Atlanta, Milledgeville, Sandersville and other towns and Howell Cobb's plantation; foraging; help from slaves; encounters with Confederate troops; an account of acts of destruction obviously relished by the diarist.

LAMB, WILLIAM   4651

In OFFICIAL RECORDS OF THE UNION AND CONFEDERATE NAVIES IN THE WAR OF THE REBELLION, ser. 1, vol. 11, pp. 90, 245, 371-372, 596, 740-747.

Oct 1864-Jan 1865. Extracts from the official diary of army colonel in command of the defenses at Federal Point, North Carolina; record of military operations, ships running the blockade and unsuccessful December attack on Fort Fisher; a few personal items and notes on minor military details; mention of disposition of the drowned Rose Greenhow's property.

LARNED, WILLIAM L.   4652

Mattison, Ray H., ed. "The Fisk Expedition of 1864." NORTH DAKOTA HISTORY 36 (1969):209-274.

1864-1866 (with gaps). Anoka, Minnesota, merchant's diary of emigrant journey to Idaho and Montana gold fields under James Fisk; route via Fort Ridgely and the Yellowstone, terrain, camps, conditions of travel, problems of scant grass and water; repeated harrassment by Sioux culminating in a siege during which the emigrants defended themselves behind earth barracades while awaiting relief from Fort Rice; a number of casualties, including diarist's employee, Thomas Jefferson Dilts, for whom the site was later named Fort Dilts; "laying over" at Fort Rice for some months,

engaging in business; notes on weather, troop movements and Indian activities; news from the mines and of Indian attacks.

LAWTON, SARAH ALEXANDER   4653

In HEROINES OF DIXIE, edited by Katharine M. Jones, pp. 298-302.

May-Jun 1864. Diary extracts sent from Richmond as letters to family members in Georgia by wife of Alexander Lawton, Confederate quartermaster-general; war news, rumors, prices and fears.

LAY, HENRY C.   4654

"Sherman in Georgia." ATLANTIC MONTHLY 149 (1932):166-172.

Sep-Oct 1864. Extracts from diary of Arkansas clergyman, acting as missionary bishop to the Army of Tennessee; stopping in occupied Atlanta on way through the Union lines to Huntsville, Alabama; dinner and an extended conversation with Sherman; text apparently written or rewritten somewhat after events occurred.

"Grant before Appomattox." ATLANTIC MONTHLY 149 (1932):333-340.

Nov 1864. Report of more conversation with Sherman, including the latter's ideas about how to deal with freedmen; at City Point, discussing various subjects with Grant and chatting briefly with Meade before passing through the Union lines to Richmond; summary of his observations while traveling through Union territory, reinforcing his support for the Southern cause.

LECONTE, EMMA, b. 1847   4655

WHEN THE WORLD ENDED. Edited by Earl S. Miers. New York: Oxford University Press, 1957. 124 pp.

Extracts in HEROINES OF DIXIE, edited by Katharine M. Jones, pp. 360-370; TRAGIC YEARS, by Paul M. Angle and Earl S. Miers, vol. 2, p. 1050; WHEN SHERMAN CAME, edited by Katharine M. Jones, pp. 180-183.

Dec 1864-Aug 1865. Diary kept by teenager at Columbia, on the campus of South Carolina College; anxious times as Sherman's forces advance from Savannah; concern for her father Joseph LeConte as he tries to rescue relatives and evade capture; Union bombardment, the arrival of enemy troops and the conflagration which consumed Columbia; reports of Union depredations and description of the runied city; hardships endured in the wake of Sherman's passing; agonizing over the Confederacy's demise and exulting over Lincoln's assassination; life under Union occupation and acknowledgment that there are some good Yankees; notes on social life, shortages and prices, reading war news and rumors, behavior of servants, family matters, freedmen's celebration of Fourth of July, etc.; a fervent, bitter account.

Stephens, Lester D., ed. "A Righteous Aim: Emma LeConte Furman's 1918 Diary." GEORGIA HISTORICAL QUARTERLY 62 (1978):213-224.

Jan-Aug 1918. Extracts from the diary of elderly Macon, Georgia, resident; World War I home front activities, including volunteer Red Cross work; reactions to war news; the death of a Macon soldier, Henry Lee Jewitt Williams; interest in the progress of women's suffrage; the Liberty Loan drive.

LECONTE, JOSEPH, 1823-1901 4656

THE AUTOBIOGRAPHY OF JOSEPH LECONTE. Edited by William D. Armes. New York: D. Appleton, 1903. 337 pp. Diary condensed in chaps. 7-8.

'WARE SHERMAN, A JOURNAL OF THREE MONTHS' PERSONAL EXPERIENCE IN THE LAST DAYS OF THE CONFEDERACY. With an introductory reminiscence by Caroline LeConte. Berkeley: University of California Press, 1937. 146 pp.

Dec 1864-Feb 1865. Adventures and dangers experienced by former professor at South Carolina College, now a chemist with the Confederate States Nitre and Mining Bureau; dodging Union troops while evacuating his sister, nieces and one of his daughters from the family plantation south of Savannah near Walthourville; return to Columbia; evacuation of the Bureau's chemical laboratory as Sherman's forces approached; days of hiding in the woods while Columbia burned and the Union army moved north; descriptions of pillaging; racist, paternalistic remarks about blacks.

A JOURNAL OF RAMBLINGS THROUGH THE HIGH SIERRAS OF CALIFORNIA BY THE "UNIVERSITY EXCURSION PARTY." San Francisco: Francis & Valentine, 1875. 103 pp. Reprint. San Francisco: The Sierra Club, 1930, 152 pp.; 1960, 148 pp.

"Ramblings through the High Sierra." SIERRA CLUB BULLETIN, 3, no. 1 (1900):1-107.

Jul-Aug 1870. Journal of geologist and university professor joining University of California students on camping trip in High Sierras and Yosemite; weather, scenery, animals and many geological notes; partly in company with John Muir.

In JOHN MUIR: TO YOSEMITE AND BEYOND, by John Muir, edited by Robert Engberg and Donald Wesling, pp. 94-96. Madison: University of Wisconsin Press, 1980.

In A TREASURY OF THE SIERRA NEVADA, edited by Robert L. Reid, pp. 177-183.

Aug 1870. Extract relating to Yosemite and John Muir.

LEE, CHARLES, 1844?-1865 4657

Helmreich, Paul C., ed. "The Diary of Charles G. Lee in the Andersonville and Florence Prison Camps." CONNECTICUT HISTORICAL SOCIETY BULLETIN 41 (1976):12-28.

Jan-Dec 1864. Extracts, primarily from May through September, within narrative summary of the experiences of a Guilford soldier, Company B, Sixteenth Connecticut Volunteers; capture at surrender of Plymouth, North Carolina, garrison; description of the Andersonville stockade and inmates upon his arrival there; notes on prison conditions, food, illness and treatment, "raiders" and execution of their leaders, escape plans, etc.; coping with the situation through activity, religion and friends; transfer to Charleston, then to Florence; mention of "galvanized Yankees" and mock presidential election at Florence.

LETTEER, ALFRED W. 4658

"Andersonville." HISTORICAL MAGAZINE, 2d ser. 9 (1871):1-7.

Jun-Sep 1864. Diary attributed to sergeant major of a Pennsylvania regiment; notes on prison conditions, food, prices, "raiders," rumors, weather, activities, etc.; efforts to send petition to Lincoln concerning prisoner exchange.

LEVY, EUGENE HENRY, 1840-1921 4659

In MEMOIRS OF AMERICAN JEWS, 1775-1865, by Jacob R. Marcus, vol. 3, pp. 299-323.

1864-1865. Diary of cultured southern Jew before and after Appomattox; in prison for a short time and return to home in New Orleans.

LEWIS, WHITSEL 4660

A UNION SOLDIER'S DIARY. Edited, printed and published by Donald Lewis Osborn. Independence, Mo., 1964. 11 leaves.

Jul-Sep 1864. With Sherman's forces from Marietta to Atlanta; daily report of military action; sightseeing in Jonesboro and Atlanta.

LINDSLEY, MARGARET LAWRENCE, 1840-1922 4661

"MAGGIE!" MAGGIE LINDSLEY'S JOURNAL. Southbury, Conn.: Muriel Davies Mackenzie. Privately printed, 1977. 129 pp.

Oct 1864-May 1865. Lively, sentimental journal of a young Nashville lady of a prominent Union family; social life in Nashville and Washington, D.C.; visits of Union officers; opinions about the war, slavery, family matters, books; various flirtations and romances; Lincoln's assassination.

LINING, CHARLES E. 4662

In A CALENDAR OF CONFEDERATE PAPERS, by Confederate Memorial Literary Society, pp. 126-163. Richmond, Va.: Confederate Museum, 1908.

1864-1865. Abstracts of daily entries in journal of Confederate naval surgeon, formerly of the United States Navy; cruise of the SHENANDOAH; record of ship's position and destruction of Northern commercial vessels; events on board; ashore at Melbourne, Australia and Ascension Island; news of surrender and dissension over where to take the ship; arrival at Liverpool.

LYBARGER, EDWIN L. 4663

LEAVES FROM MY DIARY. Coshocton? Ohio, 1910. 13 pp.

Nov 1864-Jul 1865. Account kept by the commander of Company A, Forty-third Ohio Volunteer Infantry; a daily record of the March to the Sea and the Carolinas campaign; sightseeing in Richmond and at Mount Vernon on the way to Washington, D.C.; the Grand Review; in Louisville camp until mustered out; return home to Millwood, Ohio.

MCCAIN, G.S., 1836-1885 4664

"A Trip from Atchison, Kansas, to Laurette, Colorado." COLORADO MAGAZINE 27 (1950):95-102.

Sep-Nov 1864 or 1865. Diary of a wagon train journey with many problems driving "wild cattle" on bad roads; constant repairing of wagons.

MCCALLUM, H.B. 4665

In HISTORY OF THE FIRST - TENTH - TWENTY-NINTH MAINE REGIMENT, by John Mead Gould, p. 522. Portland: S. Berry, 1871.

Oct 1864. Brief diary notes made during the Shenandoah Valley campaign by a member of the Fifteenth South Carolina Volunteers and found by Union officer on the Cedar Creek battlefield.

MCCLATCHEY, MINERVA LEAH ROWLES, 1820-1880   4666

Bryan, T. Conn, ed. "A Georgia Woman's Civil War Diary." GEORGIA HISTORICAL QUARTERLY 51 (1967):197-216.

1864-1865. Sporadic entries, mostly monthly summaries, describing events at the diarist's farm near Marietta as the Union army advances through Georgia; under fire in their home as Confederate forces retreat; receiving both harsh and kind treatment from Union soldiers as some robbed and others gave provisions; a conversation with Joe Hooker; the actions of the Eighth Indiana Cavalry; the burning of Marietta; mourning her eldest son; support of religious faith through the harrowing times; behavior of freed blacks; an engrossing, well-expressed account.

MCKELL, WILLIAM JAMES, d. 1864   4667

Marchman, Watt P., ed. "The Journal of Sergt. Wm. J. McKell." CIVIL WAR HISTORY 3 (1957):315-339.

Apr-May 1864. Account of imprisonment by member of Company D, Eighty-ninth Ohio; escape attempts from and rumors of exchange at Danville prison; transfer to Andersonville and the situation there; notes on McClellan and other Union leaders and on Forrest's capture of Fort Pillow.

MACKEY, JAMES F., b. 1821   4668

In HISTORY OF THE 103rd REGIMENT, PENNSYLVANIA VETERAN VOLUNTEER INFANTRY, by Luther S. Dickey, pp. 314-340.

1864-1865. Officer's diary of daily events; weather, duties, prices and leisure activities while stationed at Plymouth, North Carolina; capture with nine of the regiment's companies at the battle of Plymouth; march to Wilmington and by train to Macon, Georgia; imprisonment there and, subsequently, at Savannah, Charleston, in woods near Columbia and at that city's insane asylum; escape, blacks' help and betrayal, recapture and exchange through Wilmington to Annapolis; notes on prison conditions and activities, weather, his health, food, prices, solace of religion, Fourth of July celebration, prisoners' presidential vote, etc.

MCMICHAEL, JAMES ROBERT, 1835-1893   4669

DIARY OF CAPTAIN J.R. MCMICHAEL. Atlanta? 194-? 34 leaves. Diary, pp. 1-18.

Aug 1864-Jun 1865. Diary kept by captain, Company K, Twelfth Georgia Volunteer Infantry, while imprisoned at Fort Delaware, aboard the steamer CRESCENT, at Morris Island, Fort Pulaski and, again, at Fort Delaware; notes on weather, prison conditions, correspondence, war news, religious beliefs, health, hunger, artillery duels at Charleston harbor, etc.; decision to take oath of allegiance; journey home, mentioning warm reception in Louisville.

MCVICAR, CHARLES W.   4670

"Chew's Battery." SOUTHERN HISTORICAL SOCIETY PAPERS 18 (1890):281-286.

Nov 1864-Apr 1865. Brief notes of captain in the Stuart Horse

Artillery; military events in Virginia and disbanding of Confederate troops.

MALLARD, MARY JONES, 1835-1889   4671

In YANKEES A 'COMING, by Mary Sharpe Jones and Mary Jones Mallard, edited by Haskell Monroe, pp. 33-84 passim. Tuscaloosa, Ala.: Confederate Publishing, 1959.

Dec 1864-Jan 1865. Extracts from diary of Charles Colcock Jones's daughter, interspersed with extracts from diary of her mother, Mary Jones, with no indication of authorship of specific entries; coverage of same events as in Myers editions.

In THE CHILDREN OF PRIDE, edited by Robert M. Myers, pp. 1221-1238 passim. New Haven: Yale University Press, 1972; new abr. ed., pp. 502-520 passim. New Haven: Yale University Press, 1984.

Dec 1864-Jan 1865. Extracts giving an account of the despoliation of Montevideo, one of the family's three Liberty County, Georgia, plantations; Union cruelties toward her family and their servants; staunch demeanor of her mother in the face of soldiers' threats.

Extracts in WHEN SHERMAN CAME, edited by Katharine M. Jones, pp. 61-67.

Dec 1864.

MALLORY, SAMUEL, 1823-1883   4672

Spring, Agnes Wright. "Samuel Mallory, Hat King in the West." MONTANA: THE MAGAZINE OF WESTERN HISTORY 15, no. 2 (1965):24-37; no. 3, 68-79.

Mar-May 1864. Unfinished diary of Danbury, Connecticut, hat maker who became a Ruby Valley rancher; a wagon trip from Denver to the Bannack Mines, with notes on camps and terrain along route via Salt Lake.

Jul-Aug 1864. Extracts from diary covering a journey from Virginia City, Montana, to Fort Benton, thence aboard the BENTON from Fort Union to St. Louis, with notes on forts and sights along the Missouri; part of a longer journey to Connecticut to oversee his interests in the Mallory Hat Company.

MANN, NEHEMIAH HALLECK, d. 1864   4673

In ANNUAL REPORT, 5TH, by New York State Bureau of Military Statistics, pp. 617-631.

Feb-Aug 1864. Extracts from diary of captain, Company M, Fourth New York State Volunteer Cavalry; operations in Virginia; notes on military and leisure activities, the joys of furlough and his horse Trotty.

MANSUR, W.H., b. 1840   4674

"Diary of Lieutenant W.H. Mansur." UNITED DAUGHTERS OF THE CONFEDERACY MAGAZINE 11, no. 12 (1948):9-10.

Oct-Dec 1864. Pocket diary of Ray County, Missouri, soldier serving in Company C, Third Missouri Infantry; operations in Georgia and Alabama; wounding and capture at battle of Franklin.

MATTHEWS, JAMES LOUIS, 1839-1924   4675

Hackett, Roger C., ed. "Civil War Diary of Sergeant James Louis Matthews." INDIANA MAGAZINE OF HISTORY 24 (1928):306-318.

Dec 1864-Jul 1865. Diary of Newburgh, Indiana, soldier, serving in Company F, Twelfth Indiana Infantry; very brief, almost daily entries, primarily recording distances covered by the regiment; travel through Kentucky and Tennessee and then to New York for voyage to Beaufort, South Carolina; participation in the Carolinas campaign including the assault at Columbia and the battle of Bentonville; march through Virginia and the Grand Review; in camp near Louisville where diarist was "consolidated" into the Fifty-ninth Indiana and assigned to Company E; trip home after mustering out.

MECHLING, WILLIAM THOMPSON, d. 1898   4676

Barr, Alwyn, ed. "William T. Mechling's Journal of the Red River Campaign." TEXANA 1 (1963):363-379.

Apr-May 1864. Account by West Point graduate, lately a farmer near San Antonio, now acting assistant adjutant general of cavalry division under Hamilton P. Bee; military details of the campaign, including battle of Pleasant Hill and action at Monett's Ferry.

MEDFORD, HARVEY C., 1831-1902   4677

Smith, Rebecca W. and Mullins, Marion, eds. "The Diary of H.C. Medford, Confederate Soldier." SOUTHWESTERN HISTORICAL QUARTERLY 34 (1930-1931):106-140, 203-230.

Jan-Apr 1864. Diary of Canton schoolteacher serving as private in Lane's Texas Cavalry; camp life at Houston and Galveston and a description of the latter and its defenses; march to Louisiana; battles of Sabine Cross Roads and Pleasant Hill; notes on meals, hours of sleep, expenses, reading and other leisure activities, countryside and towns and on generals John B. Magruder, Richard Taylor, Alfred Mouton and Hamilton Bee; the record of a lively, observant individual.

MELLETTE, ARTHUR CALVIN, 1842-1896   4678

Wolff, Gerald W., ed. "The Civil War Diary of Arthur Calvin Mellette." SOUTH DAKOTA HISTORICAL COLLECTIONS 37 (1974):344-407.

Oct 1864-Jun 1865. Edition based on inaccurate transcription of the original diary.

THE CIVIL WAR DIARY OF ARTHUR CALVIN MELLETTE. Rev. ed. Edited by Gerald W. Wolff and Joanita Kant. Watertown, S.D.: Codington County Historical Society, Kampeska Heritage Museum, 1983. 97 pp.

Oct 1864-Jun 1865. War diary of Henry County youth, an Indiana University graduate who would later be the last governor of Dakota Territory and the first governor of South Dakota; service in Company H, Ninth Indiana Volunteers; in Indianapolis camp; troop train to Tennessee; at Dalton, Georgia, mostly in hospital where he also served as nurse; stationed at various locations in Tennessee after rejoining his regiment; a daily record of homesickness, hunger, religious reflections and fears that he might die of disease; notes on camp life, cemeteries, military punishments, medical treatments, deaths at the hospital, the Christian and Sanitary commissions, etc.; description of Tennessee surroundings; many thoughts of his sweetheart, Margaret Wylie, whom he would later wed.

MILLER, ALONZO   4679

DIARIES AND LETTERS. Prescott? Wis., 1958. 122 leaves. Diary, pp. 65-122.

1864-1865. Private's experiences with the Twelfth Wisconsin Infantry; work, social and church activities around Prescott, Wisconsin, before leaving for war; in camp at Vicksburg and Cairo and on the march in Alabama; the Atlanta campaign; following Hood north; the March to the Sea, the Carolinas campaign and on to Washington, D.C., for the Grand Review; at Kentucky camp until mustering out and return home; brief notations on many things, including duties, activities, chores, amusements, distances covered, foraging and burning, Sanitary Commission provisions, sightseeing in the nation's capital, etc., but with great emphasis on food.

MILLER, JAMES KNOX POLK, 1845-1891   4680

THE ROAD TO VIRGINIA CITY. Edited by Andrew F. Rolle. American Exploration and Travel Series, 30. Norman: University of Oklahoma, 1960. 143 pp.

1864-1867. Detailed and personally revealing diary of a young adventure seeker's travels from Chicago to Salt Lake City and Virginia City, Montana, and return to New York; interesting account of Mormon life from a "gentile" perspective and of mining and frontier society at Virginia City, with not only its violence and debauchery, but also churches, schools, musicals and literary societies; notes on his reading, from a personal library he managed to transport by stagecoach and riverboat during his travels.

MILLER, JAMES NEWTON   4681

THE STORY OF ANDERSONVILLE AND FLORENCE. Des Moines, Iowa: Welch, the Printer, 1901. 47 pp. Diary, pp. 45-47.

May-Nov 1864. Extracts from diary kept by member of Company A, Twelfth West Virginia Infantry, during his confinement at Andersonville and Florence; brief entries noting prison conditions and events.

MOCKETT, RICHARD H., 1838-1935   4682

Sellers, James L., ed. "The Richard H. Mockett Diary." MISSISSIPPI VALLEY HISTORICAL REVIEW 26 (1939):233-240.

Nov 1864-Jan 1865. Diary of "fife major," Forty-third Wisconsin Volunteers; campaigning in Virginia; bushwhackers and destruction by Union soldiers; note on the regiment's presidential vote; obviously written or rewritten some time after the events.

MORDECAI, EMMA   4683

In LADIES OF RICHMOND, by Katharine M. Jones, pp. 228-230.

Jun 1864. Extracts from Virginia woman's diary; visits to Camp Winder Hospital; food prices; distribution of food, etc., to soldiers applying for aid at Rosewood, the family's plantation outside of Richmond.

In MEMOIRS OF AMERICAN JEWS, 1775-1865, by Jacob Marcus, vol. 3, pp. 324-348.

Apr-May 1865. Events at Rosewood after fall of Richmond; difficulties with Yankee marauders and freedmen; servant problems; accepting a new life.

In TRUE TALES OF THE SOUTH AT WAR, edited by Clarence H. Poe, pp. 196-198.

Apr-May 1865. Homecoming of nephews from Confederate service and departure of former slaves from Rosewood.

MORRILL, JAMES   **4684**

In THE EARLY HISTORY OF WILMOT, NEW HAMPSHIRE, by Caspar L. LeVarn, pp. 125-131. Concord, N.H.: Evans Printing, 1957.

1864-1865. Scattered extracts from soldier's diary of Civil War service in Virginia; wounding near Petersburg and recovery at Mount Pleasant Hospital, Washington, D.C., and Chestnut Hill Hospital, Philadelphia.

MYERS, JOHN C.   **4685**

A DAILY JOURNAL OF THE 192d REG'T PENN'A VOLUNTEERS. Philadelphia: Crissy & Markley, Printers, 1864. 203 pp.

Jul-Nov 1864. Account of regiment's 100-day tour of duty by member of Company E, probably enlarged upon after the fact; rallying to the colors in Pennsylvania and in camp at Fort McHenry, Maryland; transfer west to Gallipolis, Ohio, with a brief stop at Johnson's Island; camp life in Ohio; notes on weather, regimental activities, 1864 presidential contest, emancipation, Irish antipathy towards blacks, etc.; return to Baltimore for discharge, observing Sheridan's supply base at Martinsburg, West Virginia, along the way.

NELSON, HORATIO, 1844-1864   **4686**

"IF I AM KILLED ON THIS TRIP, I WANT MY HORSE KEPT FOR MY BROTHER." Edited by Harold E. Howard. Manassas, Va.: Manassas Chapter United Daughters of the Confederacy, 1980. 23 pp.

Jan, Apr-Jun 1864. Young Confederate's diary of last few weeks of his service with Company A, Fourth Virginia Cavalry; brief entries, embedded in editor's explanatory narrative, relating military actions in Virginia.

NEWCOMB, SAMUEL P., d. 1869   **4687**

In INTERWOVEN: A PIONEER CHRONICLE, by Sallie R. Matthews, pp. 195-209. El Paso, Tex.: C. Hertzog, 1958; Houston, Tex.: Anson Jones, 1936.

Feb-Apr 1864. Texas pioneer's journey from Clear Fork to the San Saba River to retrieve horses stolen by Indians; detention at Camp San Saba by the commander who mistook him as the thief; camping, hunting, stopping at remote cattle ranches, visiting ruins of an old Spanish fort and considering areas for future ranches.

NICHOLS, GEORGE WARD, 1837-1885   **4688**

THE STORY OF THE GREAT MARCH. New York: Harper & Brothers, 1865. 394 pp. passim. London: Sampson Low, Son, & Marston, 1865. 288 pp. passim.

Extracts in THE BLUE AND THE GRAY, edited by Henry S. Commager, vol. 1, pp. 417-421, 964-965; TRAGIC YEARS, by Paul M. Angle and Earl S. Miers vol. 2, pp. 938-939, 995-997, 1004.

Sep 1864-Apr 1865. Extracts from diary kept by one of Sherman's staff officers, forming core of memoir of the March to the Sea

and Carolinas campaign; discussion of military strategy and events along the way, pointing out the evils of slavery and inferiority of Southerners; description of destruction, including burning of Atlanta and Columbia, but emphasizing official efforts to preserve private property; portraits of various Union officers including, of course, William Tecumseh Sherman, especially his military acumen and his interactions with freed blacks; evaluation of Confederate generals Johnston and Hood; notes on countryside and cities of Savannah and Fayetteville, Millen Prison, Howell Cobb's plantation, "bummers," surrender negotiations between Sherman and Johnston, etc.

Extracts in SHERMAN IN GEORGIA, edited by Edgar L. McCormick and others, pp. 30-32. Boston: Heath, 1961.

Nov 1864. The burning of Atlanta.

NICHOLSON, ALEX C.   **4689**

In A HISTORY OF THE SEVENTY-THIRD REGIMENT OF ILLINOIS INFANTRY VOLUNTEERS, by Illinois Infantry, 73d Regiment, pp. 425-428

Nov 1864. Extracts from sergeant's diary; location, movements and duties of the regiment in Tennessee just prior to the battle of Franklin; participation in the battle.

NORTHROP, JOHN WORRELL   **4690**

CHRONICLES FROM THE DIARY OF A WAR PRISONER IN ANDERSONVILLE AND OTHER MILITARY PRISONS OF THE SOUTH IN 1864. Wichita, Kans.: The Author, 1904. 228 pp. Diary, pp. 22-196.

May-Dec 1864. Prisoner's diary kept as a means of coping with his confinement; very lengthy entries and poetry, reworked after the war; with the Seventy-sixth New York at the Wilderness, capture and glimpses of Lee and Longstreet; hardships during journey south with stops at Lynchburg, Danville, Greensboro, Augusta and Macon; description of Andersonville and a catalog of its horrors; notes on food, disease, medical care, deaths, effects of weather, the "raiders" and execution of some of their number, prices, punishments, escape attempts, reading and other activities; discussion of treatment of black Union soldiers and their white officers and its effect on the exchange situation; condemnation of Henry Wirz and Lieutenant Barrett, the officer in charge of prisoners at Florence, where diarist was imprisoned from September to December; conditions at Florence, pressure to take oath of allegiance and prisoners' presidential election; exchange through Charleston, taking the CRESCENT north; notes on the Confederacy's dependence on black labor, Union sympathizers, Northern politics and war news; talking with Southerners about politics and slavery and reproduction of Southern dialect in recorded conversations.

O'CONNELL, JOHN CHARLES, b. 1837   **4691**

In TWO NAVAL JOURNALS, edited by C. Carter Smith, Jr., pp. 1-17. Chicago: Wyvern Press of S.F.E., 1964.

May 1864-Mar 1865. Sporadic entries in journal kept by second assistant engineer aboard the Confederate ram TENNESSEE; preparing the vessel for encounter with Union fleet; monotonous wait for Farragut's attack; battle of Mobile Bay, wounding of diarist and surrender of the ram; conditions in Union hospital at Pensacola, in military prison at 151 Common Street, New Orleans, and on Ship Island; exchange and return to Mobile.

OWEN, THOMAS JAMES, b. 1842?   4692

"DEAR FRIENDS AT HOME..." Edited by Dale E. Floyd. Engineer Historical Studies, no. 4. Washington, D.C.; Historical Division, Office of Administration Services, Office of the Chief of Engineers, 1985. 124 pp. Diary, pp. 111-114.

Apr-May 1864. Brief daily entries from diary of lieutenant, Company I, Fiftieth New York Engineers Regiment; activities of combat engineering unit during the battle of the Wilderness and the Spotsylvania campaign.

OWENS, IRA S.   4693

GREENE COUNTY IN THE WAR. Xenia, Ohio: Torchlight Job Rooms, 1872. 196 pp. Diary, pp. 56-129 passim.

GREENE COUNTY SOLDIERS IN THE LATE WAR. Dayton, Ohio: Christian Publishing House, 1884. 294 pp. Diary, pp. 66-109 passim.

1864-1865. Extracts from war journal of enlisted man with the Seventy-fourth Ohio; the Atlanta campaign; marching north after Hood's army and then with Sherman to the sea and through the Carolinas and Virginia to Washington, D.C.; brief entries noting military action, the unit's route of march and distances covered; sometimes difficult to discern where contemporary journal ends and his historical narrative begins.

PAGE, RICHARD CHANNING MOORE, 1841-1898   4694

"Diary of Major R.C.M. Page, Chief of Confederate States Artillery." SOUTHERN HISTORICAL SOCIETY PAPERS 16 (1888):58-68. Reprint. DIARY OF MAJOR R.C.M. PAGE, CHIEF OF CONFEDERATE STATES ARTILLERY, DEPARTMENT OF SOUTHWEST VIRGINIA AND EAST TENNESSEE, FROM OCTOBER 1864, TO MAY, 1865. New York, 1888. 12 pp.

Oct 1864-Apr 1865. Sporadic entries; inventory and deployment of artillery; fighting in eastern Tennessee; operations against Stoneman in southwestern Virginia; last days of the Confederate forces in Virginia; evidence of later rewriting.

PATTEN, JAMES COMFORT, 1826-1903   4695

Athearn, Robert G., ed. "An Indiana Doctor Marches with Sherman." INDIANA MAGAZINE OF HISTORY 49 (1953):405-422.

Jul-Dec 1864. Extracts from diary of resident of Princeton, Indiana, assistant surgeon of the Fifty-eighth Indiana; with Sherman's army from Marietta to Atlanta; entering the fallen city; hunger among civilians and attitudes of women; delight that "traitors" back home are caught in the draft; notes on camp comforts, muscadine pie, conscripts, destruction, drinking, etc.; criticism of Col. George P. Buell, the regiment's commander; the March to the Sea; condemnation of Gen. Jefferson C. Davis' abandonment of blacks at Buck Head Creek; expression of vengeance to be wrought on South Carolina; in Savannah; substantial entries containing interesting observations of the campaigns but no medical information.

PHILLIPS, JOHN WILSON, 1837-1896   4696

Athearn, Robert G., ed. "The Civil War Diary of John Wilson Phillips." VIRGINIA MAGAZINE OF HISTORY AND BIOGRAPHY 62 (1954):95-123.

Feb-Dec 1864 (with gaps). Diary of Watertown, Tennessee, native, a graduate of Allegheny College, who chose the Union cause,

serving as an officer in the Eighteenth Pennsylvania Volunteer Cavalry; Kilpatrick-Dahlgren raid to Richmond; the Wilderness and Spotsylvania campaign; stationed near Washington D.C., and in the Shenandoah Valley; taken prisoner by General Rosser during the Valley campaign of 1864 and confined at Libby; prison conditions and thoughts of his wife.

PIERSON, MARSHALL SAMUEL, b. 1838   4697

Delaney, Norman C. "The Diary and Memoirs of Marshall Samuel Pierson." MILITARY HISTORY OF TEXAS AND THE SOUTHWEST 13, no. 3 (1976-1977):23-38.

Apr-May 1864. Diary entries embedded in memoir; New Salem, Texas, schoolteacher's account of service as officer in Company C, Seventeenth Texas Cavalry; operations in Louisiana; battle of Sabine Cross Roads, description of which was later expanded; journey home to recover from wound; return to duty.

PINCKNEY, WILLIAM H.H.   4698

In THE HISTORY OF THE FIGHTING FOURTEENTH, by C.V. Tevis, pp. 171-182. Brooklyn: Brooklyn Eagle, 1911?

May-Aug 1864. Extracts from diary of soldier in Company C, Fourteenth New York Infantry, and then Company H, Fifth Veteran Infantry; compaigning in Virginia and the siege of Petersburg; capture and transport to Libby Prison; notes on conditions in Petersburg as diarist passed through as a Confederate prisoner.

POOLE, THEODORE L.   4699

In HISTORY OF ONONDAGA COUNTY, NEW YORK, by W. Woodford Clayton, pp. 111-115. Syracuse, N.Y.: D. Mason, 1878. Reprint. New Berlin, N.Y.: Molly Yes, 1980.

Extracts in RUGGLES' REGIMENT, by David B. Swinfen, pp. 35-41 passim. Hanover, N.H.: University Press of New England, 1982.

May 1864. Extracts from officer's diary, possibly rewritten later, describing experience of the 122d New York Volunteers from the Wilderness to Cold Harbor.

PORTER, NIMROD   4700

In THE CIVIL WAR IN MAURY COUNTY, TENNESSEE, by Jill K. Garrett and Marise P. Lightfoot, pp. 168-171.

Dec 1864-Jan 1865. Diary extracts detailing the plundering of diarist's plantation by both Confederate and Union troops during Hood's Tennessee campaign; condition of retreating Confederates; an earthquake.

POWERS, ELVIRA J.   4701

HOSPITAL PENCILLINGS. Boston: E.L. Mitchell, 1866. 211 pp.

1864-1865. Massachusetts woman's diary of nursing activities; journey down Ohio River on the GENERAL BUELL to Louisville and by train to Nashville, meeting Joseph R. Underwood and commenting on slavery's effect as witnessed by the countryside's appearance in Kentucky and Tennessee; visiting hospitals and sightseeing in and around Nashville and meeting with Mrs. James Knox Polk; appointment to Small Pox Hospital and teaching in school for former slaves; escorting sick friend home to western Illinois on the VICTORY and the WARSAW via the Cumberland, Ohio and Mississippi rivers; inability to secure permanent position at Nashville and acceptance of appointment as ward matron at Jefferson General Hospital, a pavilion hospital in Jefferson, Indiana, and work there until discharge; long entries replete with anecdotes of hospital life and deathbed scenes; duties, treatments, abuses and unselfish deeds in various hospitals; attendance at black church and discussion of freedmen's capabilities; comments on "poor white" Southern refugees, prejudices against Universalist Church, physicians, misdiagnoses of measles for smallpox, Lincoln's assassination, injustices suffered by female nurses, etc.; praise for the Christian Commission; reproduction of Southern dialect in recorded conversations; transcription of some Confederate love letters.

PRICE, WILLIAM NEWTON, 1831-1905   4702

ONE YEAR IN THE CIVIL WAR. N.p., 190-? 59 pp.

1864-1865. Diary of Union soldier, Company D, Sixth Tennessee; in camps in Tennessee; reception at Knoxville and march into Georgia; the Atlanta campaign; service in Alabama; in camp at Johnsonville, Tennessee, and in hospital at Nashville; battle of Nashville; stationed at Camp Stoneman overlooking Washington, D.C., and at Alexandria; a stormy voyage to North Carolina for a brief stay before return to Tennessee for mustering out; religious thoughts, concerns and activities; notes on weather, marches, duties, military routines and operations, correspondence, the Christian and Sanitary commissions, casualties and his health; criticism of the regiment's physician; disapproval of theater, gambling and profanity; daily entries of varying length.

QUINTARD, CHARLES TODD   4703

In HISTORY OF MAURY COUNTY, TENNESSEE, by Willam Bruce Turner, pp. 216-224. Nashville: Parthenon Press, 1955.

Extracts in THE ROMANCE OF THE EPISCOPAL CHURCH IN WEST TENNESSEE, by Ellen Davies Rodgers, pp. 128-129. Brunswick, Tenn.: Plantation Press, 1964.

Extracts in THE CIVIL WAR IN MAURY COUNTY, TENNESSEE, by Jill K. Garrett and Marise P. Lightfoot, pp. 171-174.

Nov-Dec 1864. Extracts from diary of future Episcopal bishop of Tennessee; socializing with Confederate officers during Franklin and Nashville campaign; visiting the wounded; a meeting with Hood before the battle of Franklin and officiating afterwards at the funerals of Strahl, Granbury, Cleburne and others at Columbia.

RANLETT, MRS. CHARLES E.   4704

In A TOWN THAT WENT TO SEA, by Aubigne L. Packard, pp. 283-302. Portland, Maine: Falmouth Publishing House, 1950.

1864-1865. Extracts from diary kept by Thomaston, Maine, woman who with her two children accompanied her husband on a trading voyage aboard his barque SUNBEAM; to Australia, the Chinchas off Peru, Ireland, Cadiz, Boston and home; brief entries mostly about weather with a few notes on ships met and sightseeing in London.

RATHBONE, THOMAS W., b. 1825?   4705

Bartlett, Louis, ed. "Captain T.W. Rathbone's 'Brief Diary of Imprisonment.' " OHIO HISTORY 71 (1962):33-56.

Jul-Nov 1864. Diary of Amelia, Ohio, man serving 100-day enlistment as a captain in the 153d Ohio Volunteer Infantry; capture near North River Mills, West Virginia, during a scout up the north

fork of the Big Cacapon River; conditions of imprisonment as he was moved south, especially at Lynchburg; confined at Camp Oglethorpe near Macon, Georgia; in Roper Hospital at Charleston; escape with others en route to Columbia; capture and confinement at Columbia; escape again, with others, receiving aid from blacks; rescued by the Union blockading fleet and treated royally at Hilton Head; journey home; notes on food, prices, weather, etc.; most of the document obviously written or rewritten somewhat after the fact.

RAWSON, MARY   4706

In HEROINES OF DIXIE, edited by Katharine M. Jones, pp. 335-341.

Aug-Sep 1864. Extracts from war diary kept by daughter of a member of Atlanta's city council; Confederate abandonment of the city and burning of the military stores; Union occupation; trying to cope with Sherman's order for civilian evacuation of Atlanta.

In TRAGIC YEARS, by Paul M. Angle and Earl S. Miers, vol. 2, pp. 883, 886-887.

Sep 1864. Extracts describing Union occupation of Atlanta and effect of Sherman's evacuation order on diarist and her family.

RICHARDS, DAVID ALLEN, 1820-1893   4707

Williams, Frederick D., ed. "The Civil War Diary of David Allen Richards." MICHIGAN HISTORY 39 (1955):183-220.

Sep 1864-Jan 1865. Diary kept by Methodist clergyman enlisted in the Thirteenth Battery, Michigan Light Artillery; briefly in Jackson, Michigan, camp before transfer to Washington, D.C.; illness and assignment as nurse at forts Sumner and Reno; remarks on profanity and other vices, deploring the spiritial condition of the soldiers; description of Acqueduct Bridge spanning the Potomac River; notes on duties, religious activities and thoughts, correspondence, the Christian and Sanitary commissions, sights of nation's capital, Lincoln's inauguration, assassination and aftermath and watching the Grand Review; welcoming festivities in Detroit and Jackson for the returning troops.

RIDGEWAY, FRANK, 1840-1911   4708

Heslin, James J. "From the Wilderness to Petersburg." NEW YORK HISTORICAL SOCIETY QUARTERLY 45 (1961):113-140.

Jan, May-Jul 1864. Extracts from diary of Seventy-fourth New York Volunteers' surgeon sprinkled through narrative summary of the document's contents; military action and medical matters; notes on Chancellorsville battlefield, a spy, General Grant, black soldiers at Petersburg, etc.

RILEY, FRANK M.   4709

In HISTORY OF THE MEN OF CO. F, by New Jersey Infantry, 12th Regiment, p. 247. Camden, N.J.: C.S. Magrath, Printer, 1897.

Aug 1864. Extract from diary of officer captured while serving with the Twelfth New Jersey; first day's experience at Libby Prison.

ROBERTS, JAMES WALTER, 1839-1912   4710

"The Wilderness and Spotsylvania." FLORIDA HISTORICAL QUARTERLY 11 (1932):58-76.

May 1864. Diary of member of Company L, Sixth Alabama, covering the battles of the Wilderness and Spotsylvania; probably written up shortly after the events occurred.

ROBERTSON, MELVILLE COX, 1840-1865   4711

"Journal of Melville Cox Robertson." INDIANA MAGAZINE OF HISTORY 28 (1932):116-137.

1864-1865 (with gap). War diary of Indiana University law student from Deputy, serving in Company E, Ninety-third Indiana; journey from Indianapolis to Memphis; reflections on monotony of camp life, the ensuing drinking and fighting and his declaration of temperance; notes on military punishments; expedition into Mississippi and capture at battle of Brice's Cross Roads; sent to Mobile to nurse Union wounded and then imprisoned in Castle Morgan at Cahaba; varied conditions and lack of kindred spirits while confined; at Selma after parole.

ROGAN, LAFAYETTE, 1830-1906   4712

Hauberg, John H., ed. "A Confederate Prisoner at Rock Island." ILLINOIS STATE HISTORICAL SOCIETY JOURNAL 34 (1941):26-49.

Jan-May, Aug-Dec 1864. Extracts from Mississippi soldier's diary; notes on weather, food, activities, escape attempts and his health; much reporting of war news; longing for home; justification for working as clerk for the prison administration which took him outside the barracks for a time; donations to prisoners from Northern civilians; dismay at the number of prisoners joining Union army to secure release.

RYAN, BENJAMIN WILLIAMS, 1826-1898   4713

"The Bozeman Trail to Virginia City, Montana." ANNALS OF WYOMING 19 (1947):77-104.

Apr-Dec 1864. Journey from Sheffield, Illinois, to Virginia City gold fields; route via Platte and Yellowstone; camps, prices of provisions; fight with Indians and fatalities; mining and other ventures; profits and expenses.

RZIHA, JOHN   4714

De Laubenfels, David J., ed. "With Sherman through Georgia." GEORGIA HISTORICAL QUARTERLY 41 (1957):288-300.

Nov-Dec 1864. Brief journal kept by the Fourteenth Corps's Austrian-born chief topographical engineer; diarist's view of the army's progress from Atlanta to Louisville, Georgia; condemnation of Union soldiers' destruction; list of buildings included on his detailed sketch maps of the route from near Covington to Milledgeville and the present condition of these structures.

SALTER, WILLIAM, b. 1821   4715

Jordan, Philip D., ed. "Forty Days with the Christian Commission." IOWA JOURNAL OF HISTORY AND POLITICS 33 (1935):123-154.

Jul-Aug 1864. Record of Burlington clergyman's service as a "delegate to the field"; journey to Nashville by way of Chicago, Indianapolis and Louisville; his work at Murfreesboro and Chattanooga, Tennessee, Stevenson, Alabama, Marietta, Georgia, and near Atlanta; notes on conditions, people met, freedmen, Copperheads, refugees, miscegenation, drinking among surgeons, expenses, prices, Dwight L. Moody, etc.; briefly set down, but some nice details.

SAYR, HAL   4716

Perrigo, Lynn I. "Major Hal Sayr's Diary of the Sand Creek Campaign." COLORADO MAGAZINE 15 (1938):41-57. Diary, pp. 48-57.

Aug-Dec 1864. Participant's brief account of the Sand Creek campaign and massacre; recruiting of volunteers to form the Third Colorado Cavalry; activities at Fort Lupton; J.M. Chivington's assumption of command amid "pretty general dissatisfaction"; surprise attack on Cheyennes, who had been led to believe they were under government protection at Sand Creek, with "nearly 400 Indians killed to a loss of only eight volunteers"; no mention of the mutilations which occurred.

SCOTT, JEFFERSON K.   4717

THE 1864 DIARY OF LT. COL. JEFFERSON K. SCOTT, 59th INDIANA VOLUNTEER INFANTRY. Transcribed...and with an introduction by H. Engerud. Bloomington, Ind.: Monroe County Civil War Centennial Commission and Monroe County Historical Society, 1962. 54 leaves.

Jan-Dec 1864. Martinsville, Indiana, resident's account of army life; stationed at Huntsville, Alabama; regiment's furlough as reward for reenlistment, festivities in Indianapolis and unsuccessful recruiting efforts at home; return to Huntsville, shortly joined by wife and daughter; transfer to Kingston, Georgia, remaining there, with the exception of an expedition into Tennessee in pursuit of Wheeler's cavalry, until setting forth to the sea; observations while on the march; in occupied Savannah; daily entries detailing administrative duties and leisure activities.

SCROGGS, JOSEPH J., d. 1876   4718

Synnestvedt, Sig, ed. " 'The Earth Shook and Quivered.' " CIVIL WAR TIMES ILLUSTRATED 11, no. 8 (1972):30-37.

Jul, Sep 1864. Two lengthy entries extracted from diary of Columbiana County, Ohio, farmer, serving as lieutenant, Company H, Fifth Regiment, Union Infantry of African Descent; description of battle of the Crater, feeling that someone in the high command should be punished for criminal negligence; fighting for Fort Gilmer at New Market Heights.

SEDGWICK, ARTHUR G., 1844-1914   4719

Armstrong, William M. "Libby Prison." VIRGINIA MAGAZINE OF HISTORY AND BIOGRAPHY 71 (1963):449-460.

Jul-Sep 1864. Extracts from diary of recent Harvard graduate, who served briefly as lieutenant with the Twentieth Massachusetts before being captured and imprisoned at Libby; notes on the prison, food, prices, his health, hopes of exchange, fellow prisoner Gen. William F. Bartlett and treatment of officers of black regiments.

SHATZEL, ALBERT HARRY, 1843?-1908   4720

Danker, Donald F., ed. "Imprisoned at Andersonville." NEBRASKA HISTORY 38 (1957):81-125.

May-Sep 1864. Extracts from diary of private, Company A, First Vermont Cavalry; capture during battle of the Wilderness; treatment at various locations, including Danville, Virginia, on the way to Georgia; mention of Confederate soldiers and supplies at railway depots; description of Andersonville on his arrival; prison conditions, rations, weather, lack of clothing, escape attempts, war news, the "raiders" and execution of their leaders, etc.; note on situation of black Union prisoners; en route to Charleston prison, commenting on fields of dried-up crops and families living in train cars; an observant daily record.

SHELDON, CHARLES LEROY, 1840-1925   4721

Melton, John L., ed. "The Diary of a Drummer." MICHIGAN HISTORY 43 (1959):315-348.

Oct 1864-Jun 1865, Jan-Feb 1867. Extracts from lively, daily diary of band member, Second Brigade, Fourth Division, Twenty-third Army Corps; leaving home in Fenton, Michigan; getting outfitted and enjoying time with the ladies of Detroit; by boat from Cincinnati to Louisville; accommodations there and at Nashville; stationed at Knoxville; participation in Tenth Michigan Cavalry raid on local distilleries in Union County; expeditions into North Carolina; service in that state and in Tennessee after war's end; notes on duties, leisure activities, dissension within the band, drinking, pillaging in North Carolina, the Sanitary Commission, socializing with Southern civilians and reaction to news of Lincoln's assassination; a few postwar entries expressing religious concerns.

SMALL, ABNER RALPH, 1836-1910   4722

THE ROAD TO RICHMOND. Edited by Harold Adams Small, pp. 205-260. Berkeley: University of California Press, 1939. Diary, pp. 205-260.

Aug 1864-Feb 1865. Conditions in Libby Prison and military prisons at Salisbury, North Carolina, and Danville, Virginia, as seen by officer of the Sixteenth Maine Volunteers; prison occurrences; his reading; focus on food or lack of same; prices and rates of exchange with a record of accounts; disgust with selfishness and thievery among prisoners; Bible quotations and thoughts on Calvinist doctrine.

SMITH, JOHN HENRY, b. 1827   4723

Smith, David M., ed. "The Civil War Diary of Colonel John Henry Smith." IOWA JOURNAL OF HISTORY 47 (1949):140-170.

Apr-Nov 1864. Clinton County Republican farmer's diary of service as captain of Company A, Sixteenth Iowa Volunteer Infantry, during the Atlanta campaign and experiences as a prisoner of war; marching through Alabama to Rome, Georgia, and the fighting from above Marietta until his capture on July 22; notes on weather and duties while in the field and conditions, prices, activities and rumors of exchange while incarcerated at Macon, Charleston and Columbia; comments on Union exchange policy, Copperheads, Charlestonians and General George Stoneman; escape from Columbia prison; assisted by blacks down the Congaree and Santee rivers to the ocean and the hospitality of the Union blockade.

SMITH, WILLIAM AUSTIN, 1845-1922   4724

In CONFEDERATE DIARY OF ROBERT D. SMITH. Transcribed by Jill K. Garrett, pp. 78-88. Columbia, Tenn.: Captain James Madison Sparkman Chapter, United Daughters of the Confederacy, 1975.

Oct-Nov 1864, Feb-Mar 1865. Fragments of diary kept by younger brother of Robert Davis Smith, also serving with Company B, Second Tennessee Infantry; through Alabama into Tennessee, then back to Alabama and on to Georgia and the Carolinas with obser-

vations along the way; notes on duties, reading, food, military action, Raleigh, etc.

SNOWDEN, GEORGE RANDOLPH, 1842?-1932   4725

Ness, Charles H., ed. "Home to Franklin!" WESTERN PENNSYLVANIA HISTORICAL MAGAZINE 54 (1971):158-166.

Apr-May 1864. Diary extracts covering captain's journey from Washington, D.C., after discharge from the 142d Pennsylvania Volunteers; discussing war with friends and relatives in Philadelphia and touring the monitor SAUGUS; stopping to visit various family members, with notes on Hogestown, Harrisburg, Pittsburgh, Freeport and Butler.

STANFIELD, HOWARD STILLWELL, 1846-1923   4726

DIARY OF HOWARD STILLWELL STANFIELD: OVERLAND TRIP FROM INDIANA TO CALIFORNIA. Edited by Jack J. Detzler. Indiana University Social Science Series, no. 25. Bloomington: Indiana University Press, 1969. 232 pp.

Mar 1864-May 1865. Diary of a sickly seventeen-year-old South Bend, Indiana, boy's wagon and stagecoach journey to California "in quest of health and adventure"; notes on life at Virginia City, Montana, Salt Lake City and San Francisco; return, after eight months, on the MOSES TAYLOR via Panama, with good notes on the voyage; references to his twenty-one-year old traveling companion William S. Bartlett; a charming and ingenuous diary revealing many hardships and occasional rewards of overland and ship travel of the period.

STARR, DARIUS, 1842-1864   4727

Coulter, E. Merton, ed. "From Spotsylvania Courthouse to Andersonville." GEORGIA HISTORICAL QUARTERLY 41 (1957):176-190.

Jan-Mar, May-Aug 1864. Diary of sergeant, Company F, Second Regiment, United States Sharpshooters; army life in Virginia; in home state of Massachusetts; battles of the Wilderness and Spotsylvania, considering the escape offered by a self-inflicted wound; capture and transport on foot and by train to Andersonville; conditions en route and in prison; notes on weather, rations, activities, execution of "raiders," illnesses, etc.; brief entries matter-of-factly recording the brutal circumstances endured.

STEARNS, AUSTIN C., 1835-1924   4728

THREE YEARS WITH COMPANY K. Edited by Arthur A. Kent. Rutherford, N.J.: Fairleigh Dickinson University Press, 1976. 346 pp. Diary, pp. 257-311 passim.

May-Jul 1864. Daily diary entries within reminiscences; with the Thirteenth Massachusetts Infantry in Virginia; battles of the Wilderness, Spotsylvania and Cold Harbor; siege of Petersburg; sightseeing in Washington, D.C.

STEPHEN, ASBERRY C., 1839-1929   4729

THE CIVIL WAR DIARY OF ASBERRY C. STEPHEN. Edited by Oscar F. Curtis. Bloomington, Ind.: Monroe County Indiana Historical Society, 1973. 50 pp.

May 1864-Apr 1865. Diary of Ohio tobacconist, serving as private in Company H, 116th Infantry Division, Ohio Volunteers, wounded and captured at the battle of Piedmont; somewhat cryptic and many undated entries; notes on conditions and his activities at several Confederate prisons including Andersonville.

TAFT, THOMAS   4730

In HISTORY OF THE ONE HUNDRED AND TWENTY-FOURTH REGIMENT, N.Y.S.V., by Charles H. Weygant, pp. 250-253, 264-265.

Jan-Mar 1864. Extracts from Company C sergeant's diary; moving camp from Brandy Station to Culpeper, Virginia; weather and activities in winter quarters.

TARBELL, ELI M.   4731

Rausch, David A., ed. "Civil War Medicine: A Patient's Account." PENNSYLVANIA FOLKLIFE 26 (1977):46-48.

May-Jun 1864. Extracts from Company C, Nineteenth United States Infantry, sergeant's diary covering his experiences after being wounded during the Atlanta campaign; grueling transport from field hospital near Dallas, Georgia, to Chattanooga; enduring pain and loneliness at Cumberland Hospital in Nashville; fighting gangrene there and at Browns United States General Hospital at Louisville.

TARR, H.H.   4732

In THE TWENTIETH CONNECTICUT, by John W. Storrs, pp. 148-156. Ansonia, Conn.: Press of the Naugatuck Valley Sentinel, 1886.

Nov-Dec 1864. Extracts from officer's diary, containing substantial descriptive entries; burning of Atlanta; with Sherman to the sea; foraging and destruction of property; pillaging in Milledgeville; assistance of slaves who then joined the army's entourage; visit to Millen Prison; arrival at Savannah.

TAYLOR, JAMES   4733

Skoch, George F., ed. "With a Special in the Shenandoah." CIVIL WAR TIMES ILLUSTRATED 21, no. 2 (1982):32-43.

Sep 1864. Extracts from artist's diary, kept while he was sketching events in Sheridan's Valley campaign; surveying the battlefield of Bunker Hill and observing the battles of Winchester and Fishers Hill; description of arresting scenes, including appearance of the dead.

THOMAS, ANNA HASELL, 1828-1908   4734

Thomas, Charles E., ed. "The Dairy of Anna Hasell Thomas." SOUTH CAROLINA HISTORICAL MAGAZINE 74 (1973):128-143.

Dec 1864-May 1865. Account of journey of South Carolinian, a New York City resident, and her mother, to their native state in a futile effort to restore her sister's health; crossing the lines into Charleston; traveling to Columbia and on to Ridgeway to bury her sister; enemy's plundering of Mount Hope, her aunt Henrietta's home, taking belongings of white and black alike; behavior of Union soldiers and slaves; return to Charleston, noting the destruction wrought by Sherman's troops.

Extracts in WHEN SHERMAN CAME, edited by Katharine M. Jones, pp. 211-217.

Feb 1865. Pillaging of Mount Hope.

THOMPSON, HEBER SAMUEL, 1840-1911   4735

DIARY OF CAPTAIN HEBER S. THOMPSON, N.p., 1911? 32 pp.

May-Dec 1864. Diary of officer with the Seventh Pennsylvania Volunteer Cavalry; notes on action seen in the Union advance through northern Georgia; capture near Jonesboro; imprisonment in Charleston hospital, nursing wounded comrade; arrival of Andersonville inmates and deteriorating conditions at the hospital while waiting for exchange.

THOMPSON, HENRY ALLEN, 1846-1939   4736

Heinritz, Stuart F., ed. "The Life of a Vermont Farmer and Lumberman." VERMONT HISTORY 42 (1974):89-139.

1864-1933. Extracts within article from long but laconic diaries of a Vermont farmer and lumberman; mainly work at Grafton and Saxtons River, but an interlude in Iowa and in the Colorado gold rush; interest in reading, the Lyceum, national and local politics; little family or personal information; some prices.

THOMPSON, JOHN R.   4737

"From the Diary of John R. Thompson." CONFEDERATE VETERAN 37 (1929):98-100.

1864-1866. Extracts from diary of Virginian, who held an "editorial position" on THE INDEX and, after its demise, worked for other newspapers before returning to the United States in September 1866; brief entries covering events and prices in Richmond prior to diarist's making his way through the blockade from Wilmington to London in July 1864; social life in London; a church service in Kingussie, Scotland; visits with Carlyle and the latter's opinions on Lee, Davis and other topics; a visit to Paris; reaction in London to Lincoln's assassination.

TURNER, HENRY M.   4738

Redkey, Edwin S., ed. " 'Rocked in the Cradle of Consternation.' " AMERICAN HERITAGE 31, no. 6 (1980):70-79.

Dec 1864. Extracts from diary kept by the first black army chaplain; with the First Regiment, United States Colored Troops during Butler's unsuccessful assault on Fort Fisher; setting forth from Virginia; uncomfortable quarters aboard the HERMON LIVINGSTON; lying off the North Carolina coast; weathering a storm at sea, the battle and return to Virginia.

TYLER, MASON WHITING, 1840-1907   4739

RECOLLECTIONS OF THE CIVIL WAR. Edited by William S. Tyler. New York and London: G.P. Putnam's Sons, 1912. 379 pp. Diary, pp. 135-136, 226-343 passim.

1864-1865. Entries, probably revised, extracted from diary of officer, an Amherst College graduate, serving with the Thirty-seventh Massachusetts; a few personal notes but mainly a record of military activities; the siege of Petersburg; the defense of Washington, D.C., when threatened by Early; Sheridan's Shenandoah Valley campaign including the battle of Winchester; back at Petersburg; return of the regiment to Massachusetts at war's end.

VAN DUZER, JOHN **4740**

"The John Van Duzer Diary of Sherman's March from Atlanta to Hilton Head." GEORGIA HISTORICAL QUARTERLY 53 (1969):220-240.

Nov-Dec 1864. Letter-diary written to unidentified captain by the chief telegrapher in the Military Division of Tennessee, describing events on the March to the Sea; military operations and signal corps activities; notes on destruction at Atlanta, Howell Cobb's plantation and elsewhere, the countryside and its inhabitants, Sherman, the pleasures of foraging, etc.; assault on Fort McAllister and Confederate use of land mines on the roads approaching the fort; comments about possible consequences of letting Hardee's army escape; an interesting perspective on the campaign.

VINTER, THOMAS H., 1841-1923 **4741**

MEMOIRS OF THOMAS H. VINTER. Edited by Emma Vintner Jenkins. Philadelphia: W.H. Jenkins, 1926. 97 pp. Diary, pp. 24-78, 81-83.

Jan-Dec 1864, Mar-Dec 1865. Diary of English-born resident of Suspension Bridge, New York, near Niagara Falls; member of Company F, Tenth New York Cavalry, mostly on detached service in charge of his division's cattle herd during the Spotsylvania and Petersburg campaigns; with his regiment during the Appomattox campaign; the Grand Review; postwar service in Virginia and in Syracuse, New York, camp; notes on duties, religious concerns, correspondence, reading and other leisure activities; studies at Eastman Business College in Poughkeepsie after return to civilian life.

WALKER, EZRA L. **4742**

In RECORD OF THE ONE HUNDRED AND SIXTEENTH REGIMENT, OHIO INFANTRY VOLUNTEERS, by Thomas F. Wildes, pp. 118, 156, 188-189. Sandusky: F. Mack & Brothers, Printers, 1884.

Jun, Aug, Sep 1864. Extracts from diary of quartermaster sergeant, describing foraging activities in the Shenandoah Valley.

WASHINGTON, ELLA MORE BASSETT, d. 1898 **4743**

Hall, James O., ed. " 'An Army of Devils.' " CIVIL WAR TIMES ILLUSTRATED 16, no. 10 (1978):18-25.

May-Jun 1864. Diary kept by wife of Confederate colonel Lewis Washington at her parents' estate, Clover Lea, in Hanover County, Virginia; looting of their property by Union soldiers; assistance from a few of the enemy, especially Gen. George A. Custer; an unkind description of Gen. William F. Smith.

WEIMER, JOHN, b. 1836 **4744**

THE DIARY OF A UNION SOLDIER. Edited by Walter Rankins. Frankfort, Ky.: Roberts Printing, 1952. 34 pp.

1864-1865. Diary kept by naval crewman from Augusta, Kentucky; service aboard the Union gunboat NYMPH on the lower Mississippi; off-duty activities; funeral observances for Lincoln at Baton Rouge.

WILEY, HARVEY WASHINGTON, 1844-1930 **4745**

Fox, William L., ed. "Corporal Harvey W. Wiley's Civil War Diary." INDIANA MAGAZINE OF HISTORY 51 (1955):139-162.

May-Sep 1864. Record of future chief of the Bureau of Chemistry, United States Department of Education, the man largely responsible for passage of the Pure Food and Drugs Act, who interrupted his studies at Hanover College for a 100-day enlistment in Company I, 137th Indiana Volunteer Infantry; conditions and monotony at Camp Carrington, Indianapolis; journey south, observing the countryside and the military build-up at Nashville; stationed at Tullahoma; notes on duties, food, flora, black soldiers and leisure activities; substantial entries penned by a good-natured, observant young man.

Anderson, Oscar E., ed. "Harvey Wiley Spends the Christmas Holidays in the Miami Valley." HISTORICAL AND PHILOSOPHICAL SOCIETY OF OHIO BULLETIN 12 (1954):209-217.

Dec 1865-Jan 1866. Spending Christmas vacation from Hanover College at the home of his classmate Frederick Thomin, near Venice; "villainous cold" in Cincinnati and environs; social life in the area and his surprise that "where there is so much wealth and nothing to hinder the progress of education, the people as a whole should be so ignorant."

WILLS, CHARLES WRIGHT, 1840-1883 **4746**

In REMINISCENCES OF THE CIVIL WAR FROM THE DIARIES OF MEMBERS OF THE 103d ILLINOIS VOLUNTEER INFANTRY, by Illinois Infantry, 103d Regiment, pp. 44-221. Chicago: Press of J.F. Leaming, 1904.

ARMY LIFE OF AN ILLINOIS SOLDIER. Compiled by Mary E. Kellogg. Washington, D.C.: Globe Printing, 1906. 383 pp. Diary, pp. 234-383.

1864-1865. Officer's diary-letters, providing substantial, interesting descriptions of both military operations and the soldier's life; the difficult Atlanta campaign, including battles of Kenesaw Mountain, Atlanta and Ezra Chapel; expedition north and into Alabama, tracking the Confederates after fall of Atlanta; the holiday atmosphere of the March to the Sea and the Carolinas campaign; foraging, destruction and admonitions against both; journey through Virginia, remarking on the devastation there and visiting the Petersburg battlefields; notes on military operations, generals Logan and Thomas, the countryside, chiggers, ticks and other pests, the heartlessness of soldiers' humor, the army's morale and confidence in Sherman, slaves' reaction to Union invasion, civilian attitudes toward the Union, the burning of Columbia, Lincoln's assassination, etc.; apprehensions about returning to civilian life; comments on the initial Sherman-Johnson surrender terms.

1865

ANON. **4747**

In NORTH CAROLINA CIVIL WAR DOCUMENTARY, edited by W. Buck Yearns and John G. Barrett, pp. 334-335. Chapel Hill: University of North Carolina Press, 1980.

Mar-Apr 1865. Extract from diary of one of Gen. A.P. Stewart's aides; notes on Joseph E. Johnston, Bentonville engagement and condition of the Army of Tennessee.

ANON. **4748**

"A Memory: Lincoln's Body Comes to Albany." NEW YORK HISTORY 46 (1965):187-188.

Apr 1865. A Fulton County girl's account of the news of Lincoln's assassination and viewing the funeral train during its stop in Albany.

AGASSIZ, LOUIS, 1807-1873   4749

A JOURNEY IN BRAZIL. By Professor and Mrs. Louis Agassiz. Boston: Ticknor and Fields, 1868. 540 pp. Frequently reprinted, most recently A JOURNEY IN BRAZIL. By Louis and Elizabeth Agassiz. New York: Praeger, 1969.

Apr 1865-Jun 1866. Largely a scientific diary devoted to activities and observations of the great naturalist as recorded mainly by his wife and intended for publication; voyage from New York to Rio de Janeiro; lectures and scientific work; notes on flora, fauna and geology of the Amazon Basin; social conditions, customs, races, slavery, intellectual life, etc., of Brazil.

AGGENS, STEFFEN HEINRICH   4750

Farr, William E., ed. "Germans in the Montana Gold Camps." MONTANA: THE MAGAZINE OF WESTERN HISTORY 32, no. 4 (1982):58-73.

1865-1868. Diary of a German who later immigrated to the United States; mining experiences in Virginia City, the Kootenay mines and travels between; taking and selling a claim; references to other Germans in the area; return to Germany on the HAMMONIA.

AMES, MARY, 1831-1903   4751

FROM A NEW ENGLAND WOMAN'S DIARY IN DIXIE IN 1865. Norwood and Springfield, Mass.: Plimpton, 1906. 125 pp. Diary, pp. 6-92. Reprint. New York: Negro Universities Press, 1969.

Extracts in WOMAN'S "TRUE" PROFESSION, by Nancy Hoffman, pp. 134-139.

1865-1866. Diary of Springfield, Massachusetts, woman, serving as teacher with the Freedman's Bureau on Edisto Island, South Carolina; settling into a dilapidated plantation house with her colleague, Emily Bliss; the growing school and its problems; dealing with heat, snakes and shortages; evening school for adults; using donated clothing for barter; a praise meeting and black singing; stories of life in slavery; claiming a deserted beach home for summer vacation; informative description of conditions among the newly freed slaves.

AMORY, CHARLES BEAN, b. 1841   4752

A BRIEF RECORD OF THE ARMY LIFE OF CHARLES B. AMORY, Boston?: Privately printed, 1902. 43 pp. Diary, pp. 31-38.

Feb-Mar 1865. Daily diary kept by Union officer, formerly of Company F, Twenty-fourth Massachusetts Volunteers, then member of Gen. W.F. Bartlett's staff, captured during the battle of the Crater; escape from Charlotte, North Carolina, prison camp with Captain Hoppin of the Second Massachusetts Heavy Artillery; hiding from Confederates with help of slaves and free blacks; journey over the Blue Ridge and Allegheny mountains, reaching Thomas's army at Greenville, Tennessee.

ARNOLD, MARY ELLEN LYMAN APPLETON   4753

In HEROINES OF DIXIE, edited by Katharine M. Jones, pp. 351-352.

Feb 1865. Journal extracts describing her experiences running

the Union blockade from Wilmington, North Carolina, to the Bahamas aboard the steamer HANSA.

BAKER, NATHAN ADDISON, 1843-1934   4754

In NATHAN ADDISON BAKER, by Nolie Mumey, pp. 27-93. Denver, Colo.: Old West Publishing, 1965.

1865-1867. Extracts from the diary of a pioneer journalist and civic leader in Colorado and Wyoming; brief notes of newspaper work as business manager for the ROCKY MOUNTAIN NEWS in Denver; social life, local events, church activities, occasional plays, etc.; his courtship and marriage to Clarissa Moyn; prices and personal accounts; a job with his in-laws for the "planing mill, sash, door and blind factory business," then work on the ROCKY MOUNTAIN HERALD and ROCKY MOUNTAIN ADVERTISER; move to Cheyenne, where he established the CHEYENNE LEADER.

BANNISTER, HENRY MARTYN, 1844-1920   4755

In FIRST SCIENTIFIC EXPLORATION OF RUSSIAN AMERICA AND THE PURCHASE OF ALASKA, by James A. James, pp. 137-264. Northwestern University Studies in the Social Sciences, no. 4. Evanston and Chicago: Northwestern University, 1942.

1865-1867. Diary of a doctor and assistant at Smithsonian Institution on Russian American expedition sponsored by Western Union Telegraph Company and Chicago Academy of Sciences; travel from New York to Nicaragua on steamship GOLDEN RULE, crossing Isthmus, exploring lagoons and rivers; on the AMERICA to San Francisco; receiving news of the capture of Richmond and assassination of President Lincoln while at sea; excursions on Columbia and Willamette rivers; to British Columbia on SIERRA NEVADA; dull routine at New Westminster waiting for assignment; on MILTON BADGER to "detestable raining at Sitka"; caring for supplies, making observations on climate and tides, collecting fossils while with Robert Kennicott's party at Fort St. Michaels; returning to New York via Petropaulski, San Francisco and Isthmus of Panama.

BARNARD, DANIEL PADDOCK, d. 1908   4756

Billings, E.E. "Letters & Diaries." CIVIL WAR HISTORY ILLUSTRATED 1, no. 3 (1962):22-23.

Apr 1865. Extract from diary of Brooklyn lawyer, a captain in the 139th New York Infantry, detached for service on General Gibbon's staff; the Appomattox campaign.

BATTIN, C. MILTON, 1839?-1920?   4757

"Diary of C. Milton Battin." NOW AND THEN 7 (1942-1945):106-110.

Jan-Nov 1865. Extracts from diary of Union soldier from a Quaker family, begun at Cuyler Hospital, Philadelphia, while he was recovering from dysentery and continued after return home to Fox Township, Sullivan County, Pennsylvania; social activities, courtship and marriage; events and tasks on his farm; notes on prices.

BEAULIEU, SARAH E.   4758

In WOMEN IN THE AMERICAN ECONOMY, by W. Elliot Brownlee, pp. 126-130.

Mar-Apr 1865. Extracts from nineteen-year-old Wisconsin farm girl's diary of cleaning, washing, sitting up with the sick and farm chores, including sugaring; getting a license to teach and starting a school while her father was off to war; concluding with "O, the bad news, our President is killed."

BEAUMONT, JOHN C.   4759

In OFFICIAL RECORDS OF THE UNION AND CONFEDERATE NAVIES IN THE WAR OF THE REBELLION, ser. 1, vol. 12, pp. 32-33.

Feb 1865. Extracts from diary of officer commanding the U.S.S. MACKINAW; details of involvement in naval operations on the Cape Fear River; shelling of Fort Anderson.

BOOTH, JOHN WILKES, 1838-1865   4760

"From Diary of John Wilkes Booth." CONFEDERATE VETERAN 18 (1910):403.

Apr 1865. Two long entries for April 14 and 21, copied from what is purported to be a memorandum book found on Booth's body, justifying his assassination of Lincoln.

In DIARY OF AMERICA, edited by Josef and Dorothy Berger, pp. 456-458.

Apr 1865. Justification of the assassination.

BROWNE, THOMAS M.   4761

In HISTORY OF THE SEVENTH INDIANA CAVALRY VOLUNTEERS, by Thomas S. Cogley, pp. 167-176. Laporte, Ind.: Herald Co., Printers, 1876.

Aug 1865. Portion of officer's journal, likely written up or rewritten later; on the march from Alexandria, Louisiana, to Hempstead, Texas; hardships of the journey; notes on countryside and settlements.

BULCK, LUTHER E.   4762

Longacre, Edward G., ed. "With Lincoln on His Last Journey." LINCOLN HERALD 84 (1982):239-241.

Apr-May 1865. Extracts from diary of sergeant, Company E, Ninth Regiment, United States Veteran Reserve Corps, a member of the honor guard accompanying Lincoln's remains from Washington to Springfield; good description of crowds and ceremonies.

CARY, WILSON MILES, 1835-1914   4763

"From the Diary of Wilson Miles Cary." TYLER'S QUARTERLY HISTORICAL AND GENEALOGICAL MAGAZINE 24 (1942):106-109.

Apr 1865. Extract from diary of assistant to Lee's chief quartermaster; description of evacuation of Richmond.

COLFAX, SCHUYLER, 1823-1885   4764

"Hon. Schuyler Colfax's Journey from the Missouri River to California." TULLIDGE'S MONTHLY MAGAZINE-THE WESTERN GALAXY 1 (1888):32-41, 233-251, 349-357.

May-Jul 1865. Western journey of Indiana speaker of the house; of particular interest for his stay in Salt Lake City as guest of the Common Council; meetings with Brigham Young and discussions of polygamy; attendance at Mormon services; visits to mines; death and funeral of Gov. James D. Doty.

CONKLIN, MELVIN MOTT, b. 1844   4765

In CHRONICLES OF THE ONE HUNDRED AND FIFTY-FIRST REGIMENT NEW YORK STATE VOLUNTEER INFANTRY, compiled by Helena A. Howell, pp. 108-110. Albion, N.Y.: A.M. Eddy, Printer, 1911.

Apr-Jun 1865. Extracts from Company A private's diary covering the fall of Petersburg, the Appomattox campaign and soldiers' response to news of Lee's surrender and Lincoln's assassination.

COOKE, JAY, 1821-1905   4766

THE JOURNAL OF JAY COOKE: OR, THE GIBRALTER RECORDS. By James E. Pollard. Columbus, Ohio: Ohio State University Press, 1935. 359 pp.

1865-1905. Wealthy Ohio banker's record of life on Gibralter, his island retreat in Lake Erie, where he fished and enjoyed a constant parade of guests, many of them Protestant clergymen; his efforts to build and sustain an Episcopal church and Sunday school on Gibralter; curious juxtaposition of religious activities and attitudes with fishing achievements; some entries inserted by family members and guests.

CORTAZZO, EMMA CULLUM HUIDEKOPER, 1842-1918   4767

EMMA CULLUM CORTAZZO. Meadville, Pa.: Printed by E.H. Shartle, 1919. 307 pp.

1865-1880. Well-to-do woman's journal of frequent trips to Europe and extended periods living in France; sightseeing, shopping, theater, artist's studios; annoyance over delays in transportation during Franco-Prussian War.

COX, ABNER R.   4768

Shingleton, Royce G., ed. "South from Appomattox." SOUTH CAROLINA HISTORICAL MAGAZINE 75 (1974):238-244.

Apr 1865. Diary of lieutenant commanding Company L of the Palmetto Sharpshooters, Bratton's Brigade, Field's Division, Longstreet's First Corps; surrender at Appomattox; journey home to Anderson County, South Carolina; notes on food, depredations by Confederate soldiers, countryside and towns; garbled report of Lincoln's assassination.

CRAVEN, JOHN J.   4769

PRISON LIFE OF JEFFERSON DAVIS. New York: Carleton, 1866. 377 pp.

May-Nov 1865. Diary entries, obviously expanded upon later, penned by Union army physician who cared for Jefferson Davis during his incarceration at Fortress Monroe; a record of Davis's health, behavior and his observations on many subjects including disease, natural history and the issues of war and reconstruction; reports of conversations in which Davis aired his views on blacks and race relations, miscegenation, the economic recovery of the South, Mexico, woman's role, etc.; the former president's opinions of his cabinet officers, Confederate generals, especially Jackson, Pemberton, Bragg and A.S. Johnston, Lincoln, McClellan, Grant, Johnson and other Union leaders; discussion of the first Sherman-Johnston surrender terms; letters to diarist from Varina Davis; description of prison conditions and mention of patient's physical symptoms and treatment prescribed.

CURREY, MARY ELIZA, b. 1849? 4770

Yeatman, Ted, ed. " 'What an Awful and Grand Spectacle It is!' " CIVIL WAR TIMES ILLUSTRATED 22 (1984):41-43.

Apr 1865. Teenager's diary entries describing Stoneman's occupation of Salisbury, North Carolina, and looting by the Union troopers.

DILL, SAMUEL PHILLIPS 4771

JOURNAL OF THE ESCAPE AND RE-CAPTURE OF SAMUEL P. DILL. Brooklyn: J.H. Broach & Bro., Printers, 1867. 23 pp.

Mar-Jun 1865. Daily account of escape of 173d New York officer and two other prisoners from Camp Ford, near Tyler, Texas; assistance from blacks; recapture at Sabine Pass, return to Camp Ford and release because war was over; traveling to New Orleans; return to New York.

ELLIOTT, FERGUS 4772

"Fergus Elliott's Savannah." CIVIL WAR TIMES ILLUSTRATED 14, no. 3 (1975):10-16.

Jan 1865. Extracts from diary of sergeant, Company G, 109th Pennsylvania Veteran Volunteers, covering occupation of Savannah; notes on need to regulate prices in the occupied city; short rations and troop reviews; concern about rumors that the 109th would be merged with another regiment; thoughts on slavery, officers, religion and the temptations of a soldier's life.

ELLIS, E. JOHN, 1841-1889 4773

Buck, Martina. "A Louisiana Prisoner-of-War on Johnson's Island." LOUISIANA HISTORY 4 (1963):233-242.

Feb-Jul 1865. Extracts within narrative summary of diary of Sixteenth Louisiana lieutenant held at Johnson's Island; notes on correspondence, chores, vermin, rumors, the Confederate cause, Lincoln and his inauguration.

ELLIS, EMILY CAROLINE SEARSON, b. 1838 4774

THE FLIGHT OF THE CLAN; A DIARY OF 1865; BEING AN ACCOUNT OF HOW THE ELLIS FAMILY OF SOUTH CAROLINA, TOGETHER WITH THEIR KINSMEN, THE DE LOACHES, HAYS, AND FRAMPTONS FLED BEFORE SHERMAN'S RAIDERS. Introduction and historical notes by Frampton Erroll Ellis. Atlanta, 1954. 14 pp.

Feb 1865. Account of hardships suffered while trying unsuccessfully to outrun Sherman's advance through South Carolina; from near Orangeburg to Columbia and then Camden; invasion of Camden by Union forces and reports of pillaging.

EMMA I, 1836-1885, Queen of the Hawaiian Islands 4775

In THE VICTORIAN VISITORS: AN ACCOUNT OF THE HAWAIIAN KINGDOM, 1861-1866, by Alfons L. Korn, pp. 230-233. Honolulu: University of Hawaii Press, 1958.

Jul-Aug 1865. Occasional notes of Hawaiian queen during a trip to England; visiting and receiving visitors, sightseeing incognito, annoyance over delays and service and irksomeness of her lady-in-waiting.

ENNIS, WILLIAM H. 4776

Taggart, Harold F., ed. "Journal of William H. Ennis, Member, Russian-American Telegraph Exploring Expedition." CALIFORNIA HISTORICAL SOCIETY QUARTERLY 33 (1954):1-12, 147-168.

Jul 1865-Feb 1866 (with gaps). Journal of travel from San Francisco to Sitka on the GOLDEN GATE with Major Robert Kennicott's "Russian-American" division of the Western Union Telegraph Company's unsuccessful expedition to span the world; life and diversions on board ship; notes on Sitka and its Russian and Indian inhabitants; difficult coastal and Bering Sea travel; activities in the Norton Bay area, with good notes on work, dangers, dog sled travel and Eskimo customs; references to colleagues Charles M. Scammon and Charles S. Bulkley.

FALCONER, KINLOCH, d. 1878 4777

"Diary of Maj. Kinloch Falconer." CONFEDERATE VETERAN 9 (1901):408-410, 450-453.

May-Jun 1865. Diary of Confederate officer, lately assistant adjutant general on Johnston's staff, covering the diarist's homeward journey from near Greensboro, North Carolina, to near Bridgeville, Mississippi; traveling with other Confederate officers, using mule-drawn wagons; drawing rations from Union commissaries until insulted; description of countryside, residents and many places passed through, including Charlotte, Abbeville and Tuskeegee; observing hunger among North Carolina civilians, praising South Carolina hospitality, signposts and milestones and condemning Georgians' selfishness; notes on destruction wrought by Wilson's April raid; angry feelings toward Northerners and comments about freedmen.

FLEMING, ROBERT H., 1846-1922? 4778

Herndon, G. Melvin, ed. "The Confederate Naval Cadets and the Confederate Treasure." GEORGIA HISTORICAL QUARTERLY 50 (1966):207-216.

Mar-May 1865. Diary of midshipman, a cadet in the Confederate States Naval Academy; in Richmond after the academy's home, the PATRICK HENRY, is ordered to be scuttled; with other cadets selected as military escort for Confederate archives and specie being shipped south; evacuation of the burning capital city; journey by train to Chester, South Carolina, and by wagon to Augusta and, finally, Washington, Georgia; furlough and journey home to Monterey, Virginia.

GALLAGHER, WILLIAM HOUSTON, d. 1874 4779

Moss, James E., ed. "Ho! For the Gold Mines of Montana: Up the Missouri in 1865." MISSOURI HISTORICAL REVIEW 57 (1963):156-183, 261-284.

Apr-Oct 1865. Journey on the ST. JOHNS from St. Joseph to Fort Benton, then by wagon to Gallatin, where he took out a claim and promptly sold it; good picture of river travel and difficulties, especially snags and sandbars and the need for passengers to chop wood, hunt for food and help pull boat over rapids; notes on other steamers; Indian alarms and the arming of passengers; shooting buffalo from the boat; many references to his friend Bud Audrain and a few notes on his life in the Gallatin area.

GAYLE, RICHARD H., b. 1831?   **4780**

Vandiver, Frank E., ed. "Extracts from the Diary of Richard H. Gayle, Confederate States Navy." TYLER'S QUARTERLY HISTORICAL AND GENEALOGICAL MAGAZINE 30 (1948):86-92.

Jan-Apr 1865. Naval lieutenant's prisoner of war diary; good treatment aboard OSCEOLA after capture of diarist's ship, the blockade runner STAG, at Wilmington; accommodations at Fort Warren, hopes of exchange, reports of war and political news, correspondence and amusements.

GRAY, SAMUEL HOWARD, 1846-1885   **4781**

A CONFEDERATE DIARY OF THE RETREAT FROM PETERSBURG. Edited by Richard B. Harwell. Emory University Publications, Sources and Reprints, ser. 8, no. 1. Atlanta: The Library, Emory University, 1953. 23 pp.

Apr 1865. Confederate signalman's candid, sometimes humorous, view of the retreat of the Army of Northern Virginia from Petersburg to Amelia, Farmville and, finally, Appomattox; effective description of the crushing exhaustion of the march; non-participant's view of the battle of Saylor's Creek; post-surrender journey to Halifax County and search for acceptable food and shelter along the way; distorted report of Lincoln's assassination; use of army slang; authorship uncertain but attributed to Gray.

GWYN, JAMES   **4782**

In ECHOES OF HAPPY VALLEY, by Thomas F. Hickerson, pp. 105-106, 122-123.

1865-1880, 1883-1884. Extracts from North Carolinian's diary containing items about Gwyn, Lenoir and Hickerson family members.

HAMILTON, EDWARD JOHN, 1834-1918   **4783**

Mooney, Chase C., ed. "A Union Chaplain's Diary." NEW JERSEY HISTORICAL SOCIETY PROCEEDINGS 75 (1957):1-17.

Mar-Jul 1865. Diary of Presbyterian clergyman, born in Ireland, a graduate of Hanover College and Princeton Theological Seminary, serving as chaplain of the Seventh New Jersey Volunteers; last days of the siege of Petersburg and the Appomattox campaign; return to Petersburg and brief description of its fortifications; march through Richmond and on to Washington, D.C.; notes on military operations and Virginia countryside; reactions of soldiers, Southern civilians and, especially, newly freed slaves to war's end; a richly descriptive and compelling account.

HANDY, MOSES PURNELL, 1847-1897   **4784**

"The Fall of Richmond in 1865." THE AMERICAN MAGAZINE AND HISTORICAL CHRONICLE 1, no. 2 (1985-1986):2-21.

Apr 1865. Extracts from the rewritten and augmented war diary of the Rev. Isaac Handy's son, a lieutenant and courier on the staff of Gen. Walter H. Stevens; a detailed and vivid description of the collapse of Lee's defenses, the evacuation of Richmond and the plundering of government stores and private businesses by Confederate soldiers and civilians.

HERNDON, SARAH RAYMOND   **4785**

DAYS ON THE ROAD: CROSSING THE PLAINS IN 1865. New York: Burr Printing House, 1902. 270 pp.

In OVERLAND DAYS TO MONTANA IN 1865: THE DIARY OF SARAH RAYMOND AND JOURNAL OF DR. WAID HOWARD, Edited by Raymond W. and Mary L. Settle, pp. 37-177. American Trail Series, 8. Glendale, Calif.: A.H. Clark, 1971.

May-Sep 1865. Richly detailed diary in somewhat novelistic style of wagon journey from Missouri to Virginia City, Montana, kept to send to friends back home; sunrise to nightfall account of route and camps, labors, events, scenes, vignettes of people; enthusiasms of young diarist whose mother exempted her from evening work in order to keep the diary; opinions on Indians and Mormons, mournful attention to deaths en route and graves along the way.

HIGGINSON, IDA AGASSIZ   **4786**

In LIFE AND LETTERS OF HENRY LEE HIGGINSON, edited by Bliss Perry, pp. 244-266 passim. Boston: Atlantic Monthly, 1921. Reprint. Freeport, N.Y.: Books for Libraries, 1972.

Apr, Jul 1865, Feb 1866-May 1867. Extracts from diary of daughter of Louis Agassiz and wife of Henry Lee Higginson; domestic life at Duck Creek, near Caldwell, Ohio; frustrating relations with freedmen at Cottonham, a Georgia cotton plantation; labor contracts, wages and reflections on blacks' behavior.

HOBSON, WILLIAM, 1820-1891   **4787**

Young, F. Harold, ed. "William Hobson, Quaker Missionary." OREGON HISTORICAL QUARTERLY 34 (1933):134-143.

1865-1891. Extracts relating to Marshall County, Iowa, Quaker's interest and eventual settlement in Oregon; a sojourn in California, thence to Yamhill County, where he established Quaker meetings at Dayton and Newberg; active interest in the Friends Pacific Academy and the temperance movement.

HODGES, HENRY H., b. 1829   **4788**

In ANTIETAM TO APPOMATTOX, by Pennsylvania Infantry, 118th Regiment, pp. 602-604. Philadelphia: J.L. Smith, 1892.

May 1865. Extract from enlisted man's diary recounting the march of the 118th Pennsylvania Volunteers through Virginia to Washington, D.C.

HOSMER, JOHN ALLEN, 1850-1907   **4789**

Duncan, Edith M., ed. "A Trip to the States in 1865." FRONTIER: A MAGAZINE OF THE NORTHWEST 12 (1932):149-172. Sources of Northwest History, no. 17. Missoula: State University of Montana, 1932. 27 pp. FRONTIER OMNIBUS, edited by John W. Hakola, pp. 290-317.

Sep-Nov 1865. Diary of a trip, with relatives and others, from Virginia City, Montana, to Detroit via the Yellowstone and Missouri rivers; a week by stage to the Yellowstone and forty-four days' boating to Iowa; notes on boats, campgrounds, difficult traveling conditions and natural beauty.

HOWARD, WAID, 1822-1885   **4790**

In OVERLAND DAYS TO MONTANA IN 1865: THE DIARY OF SARAH RAYMOND AND JOURNAL OF DR. WAID HOWARD, edited by Raymond W. and Mary L. Settle, pp. 183-217. American Trail Series, 8. Glendale, Calif.: A.H. Clark, 1971.

Apr-Sep 1865. A physician's travel from Tipton, Missouri, with the Clinton Wing party bound for Montana gold fields; entertaining narrative entries, edited for publication, describing pelting hailstorm, mosquitoes, heat and dust of the desert and difficult ascents and descents in the Rockies, with some wagons giving out before reaching Fort Bridger; such diversions as serenading a young lady in an adjoining camp; entries ending before he reached Virginia City.

HULBERT, ERI BAKER 4791

Kibby, Leo P., ed. "The Civil War Diary of a Christian Minister." JOURNAL OF THE WEST 3 (1964):221-232.

Mar-Apr 1865. Diary extracts within article about Hamilton, New York, man's experience as a Christian Commission delegate assigned to the Army of the James; reception of antislavery views in Baltimore; Lincoln's inauguration; mules and mud in Virginia; description of wretched condition of Union soldiers released from Salisbury prison compared with "fat & hearty, strong and active" Confederates to be exchanged from Elmira; witnessing an amputation; description of Grant; in occupied Richmond with a brief note on Belle Isle; glimpses of the Commission's work.

HUNT, FRANCES CALDERN DE LA BARCA, b. 1851 4792

"The Last Days of Richmond." CIVIL WAR TIMES ILLUSTRATED 12, no. 10 (1974):20-22.

Apr 1865. Extracts from teenager's diary, describing the fall of Richmond; fire's destruction and behavior of Union soldiers.

INGALLS, WILLIAM BOWERS BOURN, 1853-1922 4793

Hayne, F. Bourn, ed. "A Boy's Voyage to San Francisco." CALIFORNIA HISTORICAL SOCIETY QUARTERLY 36 (1957):205-212, 293-306.

Oct 1865-Jul 1866. Brooklyn boy's diary of a trip with his mother to visit her brother, William Bowers Bourn, in San Francisco; on the NEW YORK to Panama, then on the COLORADO to San Francisco; entertaining notes on sightseeing, music lessons, family and social life, rather sporadic school attendance, Sunday school and church activities, a baseball club; many references to family friend W.G. Badger; return home on the GOLDEN AGE to Panama, continuing on the NORTHERN LIGHT.

JERVEY, SUSAN RAVENEL, b. 1840 4794

IN TWO DIARIES FROM MIDDLE ST. JOHN'S, pp. 3-26. Pinopolis, S.C.: St. John's Hunting Club, 1921.

Feb-May 1865. Extracts from diary of a cousin of Charlotte Ravenel, chronicling the arrival of the enemy at Northampton plantation and reporting the sufferings of relatives and friends in Berkeley County; behavior of servants and fear of black Union soldiers and freed slaves; events involving Union troops, Confederate guerillas and various members of the Ravenel, Jervey, Porcher, White, Snowden and other local families; destruction and pillaging at plantations including Cedar Grove, Pooshee, Somerset and Mexico.

JULIAN, GEORGE W., 1817-1899 4795

"George W. Julian's Journal." INDIANA MAGAZINE OF HISTORY 11 (1915):324-337.

Jan-Apr 1865. Substantial entries selected from journal of Indiana congressman, a Radical Republican; legislative matters, including passage by the House of the Thirteenth Amendment; work of the Committee on the Conduct of the War of which he was a member; congress-executive branch conflicts; New York City's celebration of Richmond's fall and a visit with Jessie Fremont; touring Richmond and Point Lookout Prison; assassination of Lincoln, the funeral and his thoughts about the slain president; dismay at lenient treatment of Confederates; efforts to influence Johnson's policies and appointments.

KIMBALL, GORHAM GATES, 1838-1904 4796

Wentworth, Edward N., ed. "Trailing Sheep from California to Idaho in 1865," AGRICULTURAL HISTORY 53 (1954):49-83.

White, Loring, ed. "Sheep Drive: The Journal of Gorham Gates Kimball," MODOC COUNTY HISTORICAL SOCIETY JOURNAL 9 (1980):1-27.

Jun-Aug 1865. Substantial account of a sheep drive from Tehama County, California, to Idaho; route, distances, camps and terrain; discomforts from dust, heat, flies and lack of water; dangers of passing through Indian areas in California and Nevada; predation of sheep by coyotes.

KINGMAN, SAMUEL A., 1818-1904 4797

"Diary of Samuel A. Kingman at Indian Treaty in 1865." KANSAS HISTORICAL QUARTERLY 1 (1932):442-450.

Sep-Oct 1865. Atchison lawyer's experiences as a member of delegation to negotiate a peace treaty with the Cheyenne, Arapaho, Apache, Kiowa and Comanche; references to Black Kettle's moving speech about the Sand Creek massacre; the return of prisoners held by the Indians; the destitute and demoralized condition of "refugee" Indians; interesting and sometimes ironic ruminations of an articulate diarist.

KNOWLTON, ELEANOR FITZGERALD BRITTAIN, 4798
1834-1907

In VICTORIAN WOMEN, edited by Erna O. Hellerstein, pp. 266-269, 488-489.

1865-1870. Extracts from Lakeport, California, pioneer woman's journal; death of her husband; surviving as widow with three young daughters; teaching school at Morgan Valley.

1883-1893. Day work, nursing, cannery work at Lakeport and San Jose to support herself and fourth daughter after separating from her second husband.

LEIGHTON, CAROLINE C., b. 1838 4799

LIFE AT PUGET SOUND WITH SKETCHES OF TRAVEL IN WASHINGTON TERRITORY, BRITISH COLUMBIA, OREGON & CALIFORNIA. Boston: Lee & Shepard, 1884. 139 pp. Fairfield, Wash.: Ye Galleon, 1980.

1865-1879. Long but sporadically kept entries covering sea voyage to San Francisco on the AMERICA, during which they were rescued from shipwreck; thence to settle at Port Townsend, Washington, with a good account of life there; travels to Port Angeles, Seattle, Olympia, Portland, etc., with her husband Rufus Leighton, a Treasury Department employee; notes on Indians and their customs; move to San Francisco, where she was equally observant of life, scenes and customs; especially interesting for descriptions of Chinese and Spanish in California.

Adams, Glen. "A Lady Travels Our Region: The Northwest in 1865." PACIFIC NORTHWESTERNER 24 (1980):33-40.

1865-1868. Extracts, mainly from 1865, within article.

LOVELL, SAMUEL C.   4800

Buck, Stuart H., ed. "With Lee after Appomattox." CIVIL WAR TIMES ILLUSTRATED 17, no. 7 (1978):38-43.

Mar-Apr 1865. Extracts from diary of lieutenant, Company F, Fourth Massachusetts Cavalry, covering the last three weeks of war in Virginia; the Appomattox campaign; in command of escort for Lee and his staff, feeling "a deep sympathy for the broken-down old man."

MCCALL, JOHN MARSHALL   4801

Merriam, L.C., ed. "The First Oregon Cavalry and the Oregon Central Military Road Survey of 1865." OREGON HISTORICAL QUARTERLY 60 (1959):89-124.

Jul-Sep 1865. Official journal kept by commander of a military escort protecting the survey of a road from Eugene across the Cascades to the southeast boundary of Oregon; route, camps, distances; loss of mules and supplies over dangerous terrain; references to superintendent of construction, Byron J. Pengra, especially his negotiations with Paulina and other chiefs; arrival at Fort Klamath.

MCCORMICK, HENRY, 1831-1900   4802

ACROSS THE CONTINENT IN 1865. Harrisburg, Pa.: Printed for private distribution, the Patriot Co., 1937. 49 pp.

Jun-Nov 1865. Extracts embedded in narrative summary of the diary of Harrisburg resident; trip with two friends from Atchison, Kansas; travel by stage to Denver and Salt Lake City; following the Oregon Trail through Idaho to Portland; by steamer to Victoria and San Francisco; trips to Sacramento, Virginia City, Stockton and southern California; return to New York via the Isthmus of Panama; mining prospects in various places; notes on countryside, prices, Indian threats, Oregon weather, the sequoias, etc.

MCCORMICK, MARGARET HUNT   4803

Tessman, Norm, ed. "The Personal Journal and Arizona Letters of Margaret Hunt McCormick." JOURNAL OF ARIZONA HISTORY 26, no. 1 (1985):41-52.

1865-1866. Brief entries by the young wife of Richard C. McCormick, secretary of Arizona Territory; voyage from New York to San Francisco; some social life in California, then to Prescott, Arizona, with short, amusing notes of the trip.

MCDIARMID, JOEL CALVIN, 1836-1900   4804

In THE ALABAMA CONFEDERATE READER, edited by Malcolm C. McMillan, pp. 428-432.

Apr-Jun 1865. Extract from diary of private, Company D, Fifth Alabama Infantry; capture at Petersburg and transport to Point Lookout; narrative of conditions and events at the prison; release after taking oath of allegiance.

MARCY, HENRY ORLANDO, 1837-1924   4805

Leland, Harriott C. and Greene, Harlan, eds. " 'Robbing the Owner or Saving the Property from Destruction.' " SOUTH CAROLINA HISTORICAL MAGAZINE 78 (1977):92-103. Diary, pp. 93-96.

Feb, Jun 1865. Extracts from diary of medical director on Sherman's staff; description of the plundering and burning of Middleton Place on the Ashley River, the home of Williams Middleton, a signer of the South Carolina ordinance of secession; diarist's plea to Fifty-sixth New York Volunteers officer to spare the Middleton library, his acquisition of a "few small" paintings and a later trip to retrieve library books hidden in the woods.

MATHEWS, G.H.   4806

DIARY OF A SUMMER IN EUROPE, 1865, by Porte, pseud. New York: Marsh's Printer, 1866. 110 pp.

1865. Travel diary; by steamship to Europe, during which he helped rescue passengers from a burned ship; arriving at Havre and sightseeing in France, Germany, Switzerland, Belgium, England and Scotland; patriotic tributes and pious comments on return to America.

MELLETTE, MARGARET WYLIE, 1843-1938   4807

MAGGIE: THE CIVIL WAR DIARY OF MARGARET WYLIE MELLETTE. Edited by Joanita Kant. Watertown, S.D.: Codington County Historical Society, 1983. 70 pp.

1865-1866 (with gaps). Diary kept by Indiana University professor's daughter, reflecting life on the home front during the final months of war and first year of peace; social activities, church attendance and domestic tasks; mention of a number of Bloomfield residents; recording lurid details of the attacks on Lincoln and Seward; reactions to the president's death and the local memorial service; her thoughts on the initial Sherman-Johnston surrender terms; her love for Arthur Calvin Mellette, fears for his safety while a soldier and joy at his homecoming; notes on her dreams, the Christian Commission, a wedding ceremony, illnesses, etc.; concern over relationship with her mother, frustrated creative impulses and religion; marriage and removal to Muncie.

MINOR, JOHN BARBEE, 1813-1895   4808

Freudenberg, Anne and Casten, John, eds. "John B. Minor's Civil War Diary." ALBEMARLE COUNTY HISTORICAL SOCIETY MAGAZINE 22 (1963-1964):45-55.

Feb-Mar 1865. University of Virginia professor's account of Sheridan's raid on Charlottesville and his efforts to guard university property from destruction.

PALMER, H.E.   4809

In CIVIL WAR SKETCHES AND INCIDENTS, by Military Order of the Loyal Legion of the United States, Nebraska Commandery, vol. 1. pp. 59-109. Omaha: The Commandery, 1902.

Aug-Sep 1865. Diary kept by a captain in the Eleventh Cavalry serving in the Powder River Indian expedition under Gen. Patrick E. Connor in a major campaign against Cheyenne, Arapaho and Sioux; difficulties with bad weather, troop morale, loss of horses to thirst and starvation and severe privations suffered by soldiers; assistance by Pawnee scouts, with descriptions of their war dance, holding scalps aloft, "the most savage scene I had ever witnessed''; marches and scouts in the Bighorn Mountain area and into Montana; attack on a huge Arapaho village on the Tongue River and the bloody battle which ensued; a graphic description of cavalry warfare and casualties; news from scouts of the discovery of hundreds of dead horses belonging to Col. Nelson Cole's column and the diarist's assumption that the expedition ''must end disastrously''; finding the starving survivors of Cole's command.

PARKER, N. ADDISON   **4810**

In HISTORY OF THE EIGHTEENTH NEW HAMPSHIRE VOLUNTEERS, by Thomas L. Livermore, p. 64. Boston: Fort Hill Press, 1904.

Mar-Apr 1865. Diary extracts containing Company B member's brief notes on last days of the siege of Petersburg.

PENDLETON, WILLIAM FREDERIC, 1845-1927   **4811**

CONFEDERATE DIARY. Bryn Athyn, Pa., 1957. 21 pp.

Jan-Apr 1865. The final months of war as seen by captain of Company B, Fiftieth Georgia; stationed in Virginia near Richmond; home on furlough to Tebeauville, now Waycross, Georgia; return journey interrupted by news of Richmond's fall and Lee's surrender; trying to report for duty at whatever remained of the Confederate States of America.

PENNOCK, JAKE   **4812**

''Diary of Jake Pennock.'' ANNALS OF WYOMING 23, no. 2 (1951):4-29.

May-Sep 1865. Diary of a cavalryman with Company L of the Eleventh Kansas Cavalry on an expedition to protect stage and telegraph stations from continuous Indian harrassment; news of attack on Rocky Ridge Station and depredations along emigrant route; subsequent skirmishes and casualties of the consistently outnumbered cavalry and gruesome atrocities against soldiers and station operators; refusal of troops to go in suicidally small numbers to repair telegraph at Sweetwater, but diarist's volunteering to lead a larger company which then suffered a massive attack; the tension of waiting, surrounded by Indians, for message to come over the telegraph that reinforcements were on the way; relief by the Thirty-sixth Michigan and return to Fort Kearny, with notes on march and camps; a harrowing picture of cavalry life during western Indian campaigns with, in addition to fighting Indians, a drunken brawl between rival cavalry units over jurisdiction to grant camping rights to emigrants.

POPPENHEIM, MARY ELINOR BOUKNIGHT   **4813**

In SOUTH CAROLINA WOMEN IN THE CONFEDERACY, by United Daughters of the Confederacy, South Carolina Division, edited by Mrs. Thomas Taylor and others, vol. 1, pp. 254-261. Columbia, S.C.: State, 1903.

Extracts in WHEN SHERMAN CAME, edited by Katharine M. Jones, pp. 243-246.

Feb-Mar 1865. Flight from Sherman's army across South Carolina, through Florence, Kingville and Camden to Liberty Hill; plundering by Union soldiers; using ''the Masonic sign of distress'' to save her husband.

In WOMEN OF THE SOUTH IN WAR TIMES, compiled by Matthew Page Andrews, pp. 246-256.

Feb 1865. Flight to Liberty Hill; Union soldiers' depredations.

PORCHER, EMMA   **4814**

In OUR WOMEN IN THE WAR, pp. 212-218 passim.

Mar-Jun 1865. Extracts from young Charlestonian's diary within narrative of hardships experienced by South Carolina civilians; description of raids on plantation in the low country; behavior of slaves and black Union soldiers.

PORTER, GEORGE LORING, 1838-1919   **4815**

In THE SURGEON IN CHARGE, by Mary Abbie Walker Porter, pp. 5-48 passim. Alstead? N.H.: Rumford, 1949.

Apr-Jul 1865, Jul-Aug 1867. Extracts from army physician's diary kept while medical officer at Washington Arsenal Post; report of Lincoln's assassination but no mention of diarist's role in the secret burial of Booth or his activities as physician for the accused and convicted accomplices during their imprisonment in Washington, D.C.; the Grand Review, noting ''spat'' between Sherman and Stanton; journey on the FLORIDA, transporting Mudd, Arnold, O'Laughlin and Spangler to Fort Jefferson in the Dry Tortugas; visiting Port Royal and Key West; three brief later entries concerning Indian threat at his new post in Montana Territory.

RAE, GEORGE, b. 1840   **4816**

Birch, Brian P., ed. ''Seeking a Prairie Farm: A Scotsman's Search through Missouri and Iowa in 1865.'' ANNALS OF IOWA, 3d ser. 46 (1982):198-219.

Apr-Dec 1865. Young Scottish immigrant's journey by Mississippi riverboat and on foot to settle eventually in Crawford County; descriptions of farms, with names of their owners, boarding house and private accommodations; conditions and conviviality on board riverboats; systematic inquiries everywhere about land and prices; jobs he took along the way; great interest in people, schools and Sunday schools; employment as a teacher in Denison; a short but articulate diary.

RAUDABAUGH, SAMUEL B.   **4817**

In DIARY OF WILLIAM MCCONNELL, by William McConnell, p. 147. Tiro, Ohio: Chas. McConnell, 1899.

Aug 1865. Two brief entries from diary of soldier, Company I, Fifteenth Ohio, from Auburn Township, reporting the sudden death and burial of William McConnell while stationed at Green Lake, Texas.

RAVENEL, CHARLOTTE ST. JULIEN   **4818**

In TWO DIARIES FROM MIDDLE ST. JOHNS, pp. 27-45. Pinopolis, S.C.: St. John's Hunting Club, 1921.

Feb-Apr 1865. Diary-letter written by daughter of Henry William Ravenel, describing the Union invasion of South Carolina as seen from Pooshee, a plantation in Berkeley County; description of events involving members of the Ravenel, Jervey, Stevens, Snowden, White and other local families; pillaging by black Union soldiers and conduct of enemy officers; behavior of newly freed slaves and retaliation of Confederate guerillas; a record of depredations suffered by relatives and friends.

Extracts in HEROINES OF DIXIE, edited by Katharine M. Jones, pp. 370-374.

Mar 1865.

RIDLEY, BROMFIELD L.   4819

''Journal of B.L. Ridley.'' CONFEDERATE VETERAN 3 (1893):20, 36-37, 70-71, 99, 134-135, 184-185, 203-205, 234-235, 260-261, 308-309, 328-329, 366-367.

In BATTLES AND SKETCHES OF THE ARMY OF TENNESSEE, pp. 452-483. Mexico, Mo.: Missouri Printing & Publishing Co., 1906. Reprint. Dayton, Ohio: Press of the Morningside Bookshop, 1978.

Mar-Jun 1865. Journal kept by Rebeccah Ridley's son, aide-de-camp of Gen. A.P. Stewart, accompanied by postwar notes; details of combat with Sherman's forces in North Carolina; visit to Raleigh; a view of Joe Johnston; notes on controversy over Hood's report of operations while in command of the Army of Tennessee; a review of the decimated, tattered ranks of the army; effect of news of Lee's surrender and Lincoln's assassination; negotiations and terms of surrender of Johnston's forces; a listing of army nicknames, banter, slang, etc., probably added later; dealing with defeat; hardship and hospitality on the journey home through South Carolina and Georgia to Tennessee.

Extracts in TENNESSEE'S WAR: 1861-1865, edited by Stanley F. Horn, pp. 353-362. Nashville: Tennessee Civil War Centennial Commission, 1965.

Apr-Jan 1865.

ROCKAFELLOW, B.F., b. 1835   4820

In POWDER RIVER CAMPAIGNS AND SAWYERS EXPEDITION OF 1865, edited by LeRoy R. Hafen and Ann W. Hafen, pp. 153-203. The Far West and the Rockies Historical Series, vol. 12. Glendale, Calif.: A.H. Clark, 1961.

Jun-Nov 1865. Military diary of officer of Sixth Michigan Cavalry on the Powder River expedition sent to stop Sioux, Cheyenne and Arapaho raids and open a road to the Montana gold fields; descriptions of weather, roads, water, camps, marches and encounters with settlers and Indians, from Fort Leavenworth to Julesburg.

ROWE, MARY   4821

''A Southern Girl's Diary.'' CONFEDERATE VETERAN 40 (1932):264-265, 300-302.

Extracts in WHEN SHERMAN CAME, edited by Katharine M. Jones, pp. 139-140, 165-166, 191-193.

Feb, May-Jun 1865. Flight from Orangeburg to Columbia; the destruction of South Carolina's capital; journey back home; black Union soldiers, defecting servants and other trials of the postwar world.

SALTER, FRANCIS   4822

In THE REBELLION RECORD, edited by Frank Moore, vol. 11, pp. 704-708.

Extracts in THE ALABAMA CONFEDERATE READER, by Malcolm C. McMillan, pp. 406-412.

Mar-Apr 1865. Daily record of Wilson's raid through Alabama and Georgia penned by medical director and seemingly part of the official report; weather, military movements, description of countryside and towns; capture and burning of Columbus, Georgia; little information about medical concerns.

SEIXAS, ELEANOR H. COHEN, 1839?-1874?   4823

IN MEMOIRS OF AMERICAN JEWS, 1775-1865, by Jacob R. Marcus, vol. 3, pp. 357-374.

Feb 1865-Jan 1866. Fiercely patriotic diary of Confederate Jewish woman from Columbia and Charleston, South Carolina; romantic and emotional entries of fleeing her home, anxiously waiting for word of her betrothed; marriage and removal to New York and a new life with her husband's family.

SEWARD, FRANCES ADELINE   4824

Johnson, Patricia C., ed. I Have Supped Full on Horrors. AMERICAN HERITAGE 10, no. 6 (1959):59-65, 96-101.

Apr 1865. Extracts from a diary kept from 1858 to just before her death in 1866 by the daughter of William Henry Seward; her account of the fateful Victory Fortnight of the North during which Lincoln was assassinated and her father suffered an assassination attempt; a few days of reporting on his gradual recovery from an illness, then, in great detail, the events of the night on which Lewis Powell entered his sickroom and stabbed him; the diarist's discovery of her severely wounded father and a vivid, breathless account of getting help and the confused events of the next hours; the arrival and assistance of Secretary Stanton and fears for his safety as well; receiving the news of Lincoln's death.

SHAW, JAMES, b. 1830   4825

OUR LAST CAMPAIGN AND SUBSEQUENT SERVICE IN TEXAS. Personal Narratives of Events in the War of the Rebellion, Being Papers Read before the Rhode Island Soldiers and Sailors Historical Society, ser. 6, no. 9. Providence: The Society, 1903. 52 pp. Diary, pp. 17-31.

Apr 1865. Extracts from diary of commander of the black troops of the First Brigade, Second Division, Twenty-fifth Army Corps; movements of diarist's unit during the last days of war in Virginia; march from Appomattox to Richmond after the surrender; news of Lincoln's assassination.

SIMMONS, Mrs. WILLIAM A.   4826

In LADIES OF RICHMOND, by Katharine M. Jones, pp. 264-265, 269-270.

Mar-Apr 1865. Diary extracts describing last days of the Confederate capital as experienced by Georgia woman whose husband was serving with Longstreet's corps in the trenches below Richmond; prices and scarcity of food for civilians and soldiers; events of the day when it was decided to evacuate the city.

SMILLIE, JAMES DAVID, 1833-1909   4827

Schneider, Rona. ''The Career of James David Smillie.'' AMERICAN ART JOURNAL 16, no. 1 (1984):4-33.

1865-1904 (with gaps). A few extracts from journal within article on an artist's life and work in New York and Poughkeepsie; exhibitions, activities in American Water Color Society, National Academy of Design and New York Etching Club; views of the New York art scene.

SPENCER, CORNELIA PHILLIPS, 1825-1908   **4828**

In OLD DAYS IN CHAPEL HILL, BEING THE LIFE AND LETTERS OF CORNELIA PHILLIPS SPENCER, edited by Hope Chamberlain, pp. 1-325, passim. Chapel Hill: University of North Carolina Press, 1926. Reprint. Raleigh: North Carolina State University Print Shop, 1966.

> 1865-1907. Diary and letters of a cultivated woman influential in the reopening the University of North Carolina after the Civil War; a picture spanning many years of family, social, religious and intellectual life in Chapel Hill; her marriage and early widowhood, strong Confederate sympathies, reactions to war news and effects of Civil War on civilians; literary efforts including advocacy of the university through her columns in the RALEIGH SENTINAL; references to Gov. William W. Holden.

STEPHENS, ALEXANDER HAMILTON, 1812-1883   **4829**

"Prison Life of Vice President Stephens." CONFEDERATE VETERAN 14 (1906):169-173.

> May, Oct 1865. Extracts from diary kept by the vice president of the Confederate States of America; lengthy entries detailing arrest at his home in Crawfordville, Georgia; journey north via Atlanta, Augusta and Hilton Head and aboard the CLYDE to Hampton Roads; hardships, food, and accommodations of the journey; notes on other prisoners, including Jefferson Davis and his family, Clement Clay, his wife and J.H. Reagan, and treatment of black servants; behavior of Union officers, particularly General Upton at Atlanta and Captain Fraley of the TUSCARORA; conditions at Fort Warren; longing for home and loved ones; defense of his actions; religious reflections.

STEVENS, EDWARD L., 1844?-1865   **4830**

Moore, John Hammond, ed. "The Last Officer - April 1865." SOUTH CAROLINA HISTORICAL MAGAZINE 67 (1966):1-14.

> Apr 1865. Diary kept by recent Harvard graduate, a lieutenant in the Fifty-fourth Massachusetts Infantry, perhaps the last Union officer to be killed in action; an expedition, commanded by General Potter, to destroy railroad communication between Camden and Florence; details of military operations; looting of towns by Union troops; description of newly liberated blacks flocking to the army as it moved along.

THOMAS, MARTHA CAREY, 1857-1935   **4831**

THE MAKING OF A FEMINIST: EARLY JOURNALS AND LETTERS OF M. CAREY THOMAS. Edited by Marjorie H. Dobkin. Kent, Ohio: Kent State University Press, 1979. 314 pp.

> 1865-1879. Diary beginning with childhood entries dictated to her mother during painful recovery from serious burn and continuing with school life, vacations, friends, youthful pranks and daily life in her substantial Quaker family; early desire for education equal to that of her brothers; attending Howland Institute and graduating from Cornell University; being admitted to Johns Hopkins University graduate school but only for tutoring as no woman was allowed to attend classes; going to Europe to study at Leipzig and receiving doctorate from University of Zurich and later an appointment as first woman dean at Bryn Mawr College; a view of a sprightly child, persistent young woman and intelligent educator; extract from journal of Mary Whitall Thomas, her mother, describing the accident that caused her daughter's burn.

TILGHMAN, TENCH FRANCIS, 1833-1867   **4832**

Hanna, A.J., ed. "The Confederate Baggage and Treasure Train Ends Its Flight in Florida." FLORIDA HISTORICAL QUARTERLY 17 (1939):158-180.

> May 1865. Extracts from diary of Maryland engineer in charge of Jefferson Davis's private baggage wagon as the remnants of the Confederate government fled southward; traveling through Florida to a point southwest of Gainesville where they were informed of Johnston's capitulation and the capture of Davis; preparing to surrender.

TOMPKINS, CHRISTOPHER QUARLES, 1813-1877   **4833**

Rachal, William M.E., ed. "The Occupation of Richmond." VIRGINIA MAGAZINE OF HISTORY AND BIOGRAPHY 73 (1965):189-198.

> Apr-May 1865. Diary of West Point graduate whose skills as a mining engineer and foundry operator were utilized in the Confederate war effort; at the Dover coal pits in Goochland County, learning of Richmond's evacuation and assisting refugees from the fallen capital, including Gov. William Smith; desertion of Virginia soldiers, disappearance of black workers and looting by white workers; a visit to occupied Richmond; notes on Union troops' behavior, black Union soldiers, Gen. E.O.C. Ord and Lincoln's assassination; speculations as to what the future would bring.

TOWNSEND, HARRY C.   **4834**

"Townsend's Diary." SOUTHERN HISTORICAL SOCIETY PAPERS 34 (1906):99-127. Reprint. TOWNSEND'S DIARY. Richmond: W.E. Ellis, Book and Job Printer, 1907. 31 pp.

> Jan-May 1865. Diary of corporal, First Company, Richmond Howitzers; in camp at Petersburg; march to Appomattox, last resistance and news of Lee's surrender; decision to join Johnston's army and small party's subsequent walk of 455 miles to North Carolina, via the Blue Ridge Mountains; hospitality and provisions along the way; arrival at Lincolnton and news that the Confederate army no longer existed east of the Mississippi; decision to accept parole and return to Richmond.

TRENHOLM, ANNA HELEN HOLMES   **4835**

In LADIES OF RICHMOND, by Katharine M. Jones, pp. 273-274.

> Apr 1865. A scrap from diary of wife of the Confederate secretary of the treasury; flight from Richmond to Danville with Jefferson Davis and his cabinet.

TYLER, JOHN GARDINER   **4836**

"Diary for 1865." TYLER'S QUARTERLY HISTORICAL AND GENEALOGICAL MAGAZINE 30 (1948/49):251-255.

> Mar-Apr, Aug 1865. Brief diary of Confederate artilleryman with the Rockbridge Battery; last days of Army of Northern Virginia; at Lexington after the surrender amidst rumors of foreign intervention, assassination of Lincoln and others, etc.; later in Charles County.

VANMETER, ABEL J., 1834-1920   **4837**

Hamilton, Jean Tyree, ed. "Abel J. Vanmeter, His Park and His Diary." MISSOURI HISTORICAL SOCIETY BULLETIN 28 (1971):3-37.

Mar-Jun 1865. Saline County cattleman's travel on the Missouri River to Montana gold fields aboard the DEER LODGE with his partner, N.M. Hallaway; problems with bars, snags and April snowstorms; frequent hunting en route, including killing twenty buffalo as they swam the river; arrival at Fort Benton.

WARING, MALVINA SARAH BLACK   4838

In SOUTH CAROLINA WOMEN IN THE CONFEDERACY, by United Daughters of the Confederacy, South Carolina Division, edited by Mrs. Thomas Taylor and others, vol. 1, pp. 272-288. Columbia, S.C.: State, 1903.

Extracts in HEROINES OF DIXIE, edited by Katharine M. Jones, pp. 356-360, 376-383.

Feb-Jun 1865. Interesting account of last days of the Confederacy written by employee of the Treasury Department; clothes, lessons and fears of Sherman in Columbia; evacuation of diarist and fellow employees to Richmond; gay social life and the pinch of hunger; flight from the beleagured Confederate capital while suffering from typhoid fever; return home to Columbia and first sight of the ruined city; some nice bits amidst sophomoric wisdom and romantic style.

WEAND, HENRY K.   4839

In COLUMN SOUTH, compiled by Suzanne Colton Wilson, edited by J. Ferrell Colton and Antoinette G. Smith, pp. 277-322 passim. Flagstaff, Ariz.: J.F. Colton, 1960.

Mar-May 1865. Extracts from diary of captain, Company H, Fifteenth Pennsylvania Cavalry; expedition from Tennessee into North Carolina and Virginia; pursuing Jefferson Davis through South Carolina and Georgia; capture of Braxton Bragg; military details and description of countryside and settlements.

WEBB, LOUIS H.   4840

In WAR TALKS OF CONFEDERATE VETERANS, edited by George S. Bernard, pp. 290-291, 293-294, 296. Petersburg, Va.: Fenn & Owen, 1892.

Apr 1865. Captain's diary extracts covering activities of Thirteenth Battalion, North Carolina Light Artillery during the last days of war in North Carolina; vacillation among officers about whether or not to surrender after hearing news of Appomattox.

WEBBER, EMMA   4841

Foll, Llewellyn E. "Emma Webber's Diary: Window into Early Battle Creek." ADVENTIST HERITAGE 7 (1982):53-64.

1865-1874. Article containing extracts from the diary of a Michigan Seventh-day Adventist, a single woman who had lost her fiancé in the Civil War; teaching school in Burlington, where she became interested in Adventist doctrines; a move to Battle Creek to do domestic work for several families and to enjoy the thriving Adventist community there; housekeeping for Uriah and Harriet Smith and then working as a typesetter for Smith's REVIEW AND HERALD; return to her parents' farm at Union City for several unhappy years; some schooling at Albion College; Adventist camp meetings; sermons and influence of James and Ellen White, Joseph Bates and others; diarist's self-condemnation for her weak

character, pride and envy, as well as her inability to "witness" to friends and strangers about her faith; a rather troubled and unsettled life.

WHITING, FRED S.   4842

In WAR SKETCHES AND INCIDENTS, by Military Order of the Loyal Legion of the United States, Iowa Commandery, vol. 1, pp. 89-104. Des Moines: Press of P.C. Kenyon, 1893. Diary, pp. 98-104.

Apr 1865. Captain's diary extracts, within narrative, detailing participation of the Fourth Iowa Cavalry in James H. Wilson's raid through Alabama and Georgia; rumors of Lee's surrender and Lincoln's assassination; search of entire corps and seizure of stolen or contraband goods by provost marshal near Macon, Georgia.

WIRZ, HENRY, 1823?-1865   4844

In PRISON LIFE IN THE OLD CAPITOL AND REMINISCENCES OF THE CIVIL WAR, by James J. Williamson, pp. 147-151. West Orange, N.J., 1911.

Oct 1865. Extracts from diary kept at Old Capitol Prison while diarist was on trial for his activities at Andersonville; prayers, assertions of his innocence and unjust treatment received.

WOOD, GEORGE GLENN, b. 1848   4845

"Diary of a Muncy Boy Kept while Attending the West Branch High School in Jersey Shore." NOW AND THEN 5 (1936):42-53.

Jan-Apr 1865, Oct 1865-Jan 1866. Life at school in Pennsylvania, recorded by Muncy, Pennsylvania, teenager; notes on food, classmates, dormitory conditions, prices, misbehavior and discipline; celebrating the fall of Richmond and Lee's surrender; mourning Abraham Lincoln; a visit to Lock Haven; grievances against principal F. Donleavy Long; decision to leave school and return home.

WOODRUFF, MATHEW   4846

A UNION SOLDIER IN THE LAND OF THE VANQUISHED. Edited and annotated by F.N. Boney. Southern Historical Society Publications, no. 13. University: University of Alabama Press, 1969. 103 pp.

Jun-Dec 1865. Life in army of occupation as recorded by sergeant in the Twenty-first Missouri Volunteer Infantry; return from furlough in Clark County, passing through Vicksburg, where diarist noted lack of proper Fourth of July observances, New Orleans and Mobile; service at Pascagoula, Mississippi, and later in Mobile; the paperwork and tedium of desk duty; continual problems of drinking and brawling among the men, most notably violent clashes between members of the Twenty-first and of the Fifteenth United States Infantry; various entertainments including dances, fishing, swimming, ball games, the circus and theater; comments concerning soldiers of the Eighty-sixth and Ninety-sixth United States Colored Infantry; notes on the behavior and politics of the former Confederates.

YOUNG, FRANCIS CRISSEY, b. 1844   4847

ACROSS THE PLAINS IN '65: A YOUNGSTER'S JOURNAL FROM "GOTHAM" TO "PIKE'S PEAK." Denver: Lanning Brothers, 1905. 224 pp. Diary, pp. 43-224.

Mar-Apr 1865. Colorado gold rush journey on foot with several other young New Yorkers; from Atchison to Denver via Fort Kearny in company with various wagon trains; descriptions of camps, terrain, ranches, forts, graves, overland traffic, an April snowstorm; historical digressions, including many narratives of past Indian raids; news of Lincoln's assassination received by telegraph at a ranch; daily notes "smoothed down" for publication.

YOUNG, WILL H.   **4848**

"Journals of Travel of Will H. Young." ANNALS OF WYOMING 7 (1930):378-382.

May-Dec 1865. Brief extracts from a young Missourian's journal of work as clerk for the post trader, Mr. Ward, at Fort Laramie; officers, traders, soldiers and Indians in and out of the fort; news of Indian disturbances and return of the Powder River expedition; some surprisingly sumptuous dining at officers' mess.

1866

ADAMS, GEORGE RUSSELL, 1845-1938   **4849**

Taggart, Harold F., ed. "Journal of George Russell Adams, Member, Exploring Expedition in Russian America." CALIFORNIA HISTORICAL SOCIETY QUARTERLY 35 (1956):291-307.

Dec 1866-Jul 1867. Extensive extract from longer manuscript diaries, with entries beginning in Unanacklet and Nulato areas of Alaska during the second year of an expedition to establish Western Union telegraph lines through Canada, "Russian-America" and Siberia; a good picture of the cold, danger, tedium and privations of the undertaking and especially the work of road-building and telegraph installation under Arctic conditions; references to William Ennis and Jay B. Chappel.

ALEXANDER, EVELINE THROOP MARTIN, 1843-1922   **4850**

THE DIARY OF EVELINE M. ALEXANDER. Edited by Sandra L. Myers. College Station: Texas A&M University Press, 1976. 175 pp.

1866-1867. Army wife's lively diary of trip from New York to Fort Smith to meet her husband, Gen. Andrew Jonathan Alexander; obvious enjoyment of the adventure of marching with Third Cavalry across prairie to Fort Union; frequent amusing incidents, a storm, buffalo stampedes; her husband's assuming command of Fort Stevens; entertaining Gen. William Tecumseh Sherman during his inspection of western United States; skirmish with Ute Indians; being stationed at forts Garland, Union and Bascom; conversations with Kit Carson; visiting Taos, Santa Fe and neighboring pueblos and ruins; descriptions of Navaho life on reservation near Fort Sumner.

ANDERSON, JOHN C., d. 1913   **4851**

MACKINAWS DOWN THE MISSOURI. Edited by Glen Barrett. Logan, Utah: Western Text Society, 1973. 105 pp.

1866. Journal of a trip from St. Louis, Missouri, to Virginia City, Montana, and return.

BURGESS, PERRY A.   **4852**

Athearn, Robert G., ed. "From Illinois to Montana in 1866." PACIFIC NORTHWEST QUARTERLY 41 (1950):43-65.

Mar-Sep 1866. Lena, Illinois, man's Montana gold rush journey via Iowa, Nebraska and the Bozeman Trail with his uncles Lewis, Lyman and Mansel Cheney, driving cattle bought at Plattsmouth; an ambush by Indians, during which Mansel was killed, and other Indian incidents; employment herding cattle at Gallatin.

Jul 1868. Return to "the states" on Missouri steamer URILDA.

CANFIELD, SARAH ELIZABETH HAAS, 1840-1932   **4853**

Mattison, Ray H., ed. "An Army Wife on the Upper Missouri." NORTH DAKOTA HISTORY 20 (1953):191-220.

1866-1868 (with gaps). Marshalltown, Iowa, woman's account of joining her officer husband, Andrew Nahum Canfield, at Fort Berthold and Camp Cooke; up the Missouri on the DEER LODGE, with interesting notes of river travel; extensive observations of "friendly" Indians, especially Mandans, assembled at Fort Berthold; reference to Father De Smet; on the LUELLA to Camp Cooke, with notes of troop movements and constant fear of Indian attack.

CONANT, ROGER, 1833-1915   **4854**

MERCER'S BELLES: THE JOURNAL OF A REPORTER. Edited by Lenna A. Deutsch. Seattle: University of Washington Press, 1960. 190 pp.

Jan-Jun 1866. Private diaries, discovered and published long after his death, of young NEW YORK TIMES reporter's sea voyage accompanying the famous Mercer Girls from New England to Seattle; life aboard the steamship CONTINENTAL; ports of call; the Strait of Magellan; character and foibles of Asa Mercer and his passengers; the diarist's escapades and disappointed attempts at courtship; highly entertaining, with more details and self-revelation than Conant's originally published newspaper stories.

CREIGH, THOMAS ALFRED, b. 1840   **4855**

Olson, James C., ed. "From Nebraska City to Montana." NEBRASKA HISTORY 29 (1948):208-237.

May-Oct 1866. Diary of a freighting expedition taking boilers and quartz stamping machinery to the Montana mines; from Nebraska City to Virginia City via Fort Kearny, Fort Laramie and the Bozeman Trail; difficulties of travel; some Indian scares during a period of considerable danger; books read en route.

CROMMELIN, CLAUDE AUGUST   **4856**

Hidy, Muriel E., ed. and Poatgieter, A. Hermina, trans. "A Dutch Investor in Minnesota." MINNESOTA HISTORY 37 (1960):152-160.

Jun 1866. Extract covering Minnesota segment of Dutch railroad investor's Canadian and American tour; on the riverboat KEY CITY to St. Paul; business dealings with Hermann Trott of the First Division of the St. Paul and Pacific Railroad Company; a train trip as guest of the company and extensive comments on its progress and prospects; notes on Dutch financial interests in the region.

DAWSON, WILLIAM HARRISON, 1841-1908   **4857**

"THE LIFE BEAUTIFUL". Owensboro, Ky.: Messenger Job Printing, 1908. 157 pp. Diary, pp. 1-92.

1866-1908. Extracts from Kentucky Baptist minister's brief diary; churches served and preaching; marriages, funerals, baptisms with names; a few personal and family notes.

DRIVER, WILLIAM, 1837-1920   **4858**

Reeve, Frank Driver, ed. "London to Salt Lake City." NEW MEXICO HISTORICAL REVIEW 17 (1942):37-63.

May-Sep 1866. Diary of English Mormon's immigration to Utah; Atlantic crossing on the CAROLINE; attending his sick wife and son, with eventual death of the son and several others at sea; storms and privations of a miserable voyage; overland from New York by train and wagon with a company of Mormons; some Indian alarms and more deaths from sickness.

DUFFIELD, GEORGE C., 1824-1908   **4859**

Baldwin, W.W., ed. "Driving Cattle from Texas to Iowa." ANNALS OF IOWA, 3d ser. 14 (1923-1924):241-262.

Extracts in THE FRONTIER EXPERIENCE, by Robert V. Hine, pp. 244-249; TREASURY OF THE WORLD'S GREAT DIARIES, edited by Philip Dunaway, pp. 72-76.

Feb-Oct 1866. Cattle drive by partners George C. Duffield and Harvey Ray; trip from Keosauqua, Iowa, to Texas by train, riverboat and stagecoach; purchase and branding of a thousand cattle; brief notes of subsequent harrowing drive; route, camps, terrain; problems with storms and stampedes; encounters with Indians.

"An 1885 Excursion From Keosauqua to Storm Lake." ANNALS OF IOWA, 3d ser. 41 (1971-1973):867-874.

Oct-Nov 1885. Deer hunting trip in area of Des Monies, Coon and Boyer rivers; camps and lodgings; brief details of a successful hunt to provide meat for the table and hides for sale.

FISK, ANDREW J.   **4860**

In HO! FOR THE GOLD FIELDS, edited by Helen M. White, pp. 214-235.

Sep-Dec 1866. Account, kept by a brother of James L. Fisk, of travel from Sun River to Helena during the last leg of Fisk's expedition; description of gold rush, Helena and life there; prices; extensive and colorful details of gold prospecting at various claims.

FISK, ROBERT EMMET   **4861**

In HO! FOR THE GOLD FIELDS, edited by Helen M. White, pp. 194-214.

Jun-Sep 1866. Diary, kept by a brother, of James L. Fisk of his fourth expedition from Minnesota to Montana; notes on people in large train emigrants bound for the gold fields; route, distances, terrain, grass and water; wasteful slaughter of buffalo; suffering of people and cattle from heat; peaceful encounters with Indians.

FLETCHER, ELLEN GORDON, b. 1841   **4862**

A BRIDE ON THE BOZEMAN TRAIL: THE LETTERS AND DIARY OF ELLEN GORDON FLETCHER. Edited by Francis D. Haines, Jr. Medford, Oreg.: Grandee Printing Center, 1970. 139 pp. Diary, pp. 94-123.

Apr-Nov 1866. Diary expanded in letters to her family in Rushford, New York; from Bellevue, Nebraska, via forts Laramie and Kearny and the Bozeman Trail to Virginia City, Montana; description of wagons and provisions for travel, scenery, flowers, landmarks, camps, weather, wood, cooking, washing and the company of other wagon trains; details of Sioux costumes and ornaments; Indians gathered at Fort Laramie for treaty council; noting Arapaho and Cheyenne Indians met on the trail; settling at Summit City, near Virginia City, with notes on size and furnishings of pioneer homes and social life in a mountain mining town.

FOX, GEORGE W.   **4863**

"George W. Fox Diary." ANNALS OF WYOMING 8 (1932):580-601.

Jan-Sep 1866. Great Plains and Wyoming segment of a longer diary kept by prominent resident of Laramie; from Davis County, Iowa, to Virginia City, Montana, route via Platte, Black Hills and Bighorns; work as camp cook; endless problems with straying cattle and incompetent, dissatisfied greenhorns; worries about Indians; hunting of buffalo, antelope, etc.; diarist's intention to take up interest in the store at Fort Cassiday.

GILCHRIST, LEONARD WHITING, 1831-1891   **4864**

Potter, James E., ed. "The Missouri River Journal of Leonard W. Gilchrist." NEBRASKA HISTORY 58 (1977):267-300.

May-Jun 1866. Nebraska City man's steamboat voyage aboard the AGNES to Fort Benton, with description of difficult Missouri River navigation, scenes, towns, forts and riverboats; a good account of his first buffalo hunt, "a signal failure"; entries ending just short of Fort Benton.

GOODNOUGH, ELLEN SAXTON   **4865**

In THE ONEIDAS, by Julia K. Bloomfield, pp. 254-284. New York: Alden Brothers, 1907.

1866-1869 (with gaps). Missionary diary of Episcopal work among the Oneida Indians after their removal from New York to Wisconsin; customs, smallpox epidemic, mission church and school; strenuous efforts to spare Oneidas further removal and even threat of extinction.

HARLAN, WILSON BARBER, 1848-1935   **4866**

Harlan, Gilbert Drake, ed. "The Diary of Wilson Barber Harlan." JOURNAL OF THE WEST 3 (1964):141-162, 291-312, 501-516.

1866-1868. Montana gold rush diary of an eighteen-year-old Civil War veteran traveling on foot with Robert E. Fisk's last wagon train from St. Cloud, Minnesota, to Helena, Montana; route via Fort Abercrombie, with distances, terrain, wildlife, including "thousands of buffalo," hunting, etc; prospecting and sluice mining in the Helena area gulches, with references to people and events; later narrative covering farming in the Bitteroot area in 1877.

HARRSION, CONSTANCE CARY   **4867**

In RECOLLECTIONS GRAVE AND GAY, by Constance Cary Harrison, pp. 251-259, 353-355. New York: Charles Scribner's Sons, 1911.

1866 or 1867. Undated extracts from diary kept while sojourning in Paris; cultural events and socializing with royalty and ex-Confederates; notes on Adelina Patti, Napoléon III and the empress Eugénie.

188? Undated extracts from journal, describing the publication and reaction to her novel THE ANGLOMANIACS.

JACKSON, WILLIAM HENRY, 1843-1942   4868

THE DIARIES OF WILLIAM HENRY JACKSON, FRONTIER PHOTOGRAPHER. Edited by LeRoy R. Hafen and Ann W. Hafen. The Far West and the Rockies Historical Series, vol. 10. Glendale, Calif.: A.H. Clark, 1959. 345 pp.

1866-1867. Western diaries of a painter and photographer; journey from Nebraska to California over the heavily used "Steam Wagon Road"; humorous descriptions of his work as a "bull whacker," camping, cooking, daily routines, etc.; good notes on scenery; anxiety for letters from home; leaving train at Ham's Fork, first walking, then hiring on as a teamster for a hay contractor to Fort Bridger; at one point, suffering frozen feet; work for a Mormon, then continuing to California, often starting ahead of the train to make sketches; return to Omaha to work as a painter.

May-Sep 1873. Work as an unpaid photographer with the Colorado division of Ferdinand Hayden's United States Geological and Geographical Survey of the Territories; interesting notes on photography of scenic and geological features including the first photograph of Mount of the Holy Cross; repairing equipment; making difficult climbs and river crossings to get pictures.

Jun-Oct 1874. Continued work as Hayden's photographer in western Colorado; notes on pleasure campers in mountains and at lakes near Los Pinos Indian Agency; in addition to scenery, photographing Ute Indians, including Chief Ouray, assembled at the Pinos Agency to draw rations of food and supplies; Indian belief that photographing of women and children would cause them harm, but willingness of men to be photographed; descriptions of cliff dwellings of Mesa Verde region; collecting pottery and shards; a fascinating account of remarkable achievements.

"The Most Important Nebraska Highway: Nebraska City-Fort Kearny-Denver Trail." NEBRASKA HISTORY 13 (1932):137-159.

Jun-Aug 1866. Extracts including humorous details of travel and his work as a bull whacker, camping, cooking, etc.; difficulties of the Platte and other river crossings.

"A Visit to the Los Pinos Indian Agency in 1874." COLORADO MAGAZINE 15 (1938):201-209.

Aug 1874. Extracts relating mainly to Chief Ouray and other Utes assembled at the Pinos agency and Indian beliefs about the dangers of photography.

JONSSON, PETER JOHAN, 1835-1914   4869

Swanson, Alan, trans. and ed. " 'Some Cried and Some Sang'...The Emigrant Journal of Peter Johan Jonsson." SWEDISH PIONEER HISTORICAL QUARTERLY 26 (1975):157-183.

May-Aug 1866. Record of Swedish immigrant's voyage on the ARGO HULL as leader of a group of family and friends; concerns for the health, moral and religious condition of his group; several deaths from cholera including his little son's; bereavement, prayers and religious reflections; upon arrival in New York, con-

tinued problems with illness and poverty, with near despair over sense of betrayal by the "so-called Scandinavian Union"; entries ending at Chicago.

KEAYS, ELIZABETH PARKE, 1830-1922   4870

In THE SAGA OF "AUNTIE" STONE AND HER CABIN, by Nolie Mumey, pp. 51-93. Boulder, Colo.: Johnson Publishing, 1964.

Apr-Jun 1866. Diary of a Bloomington, Illinois, widow with ten year old son Wilbur Parke Keays; traveling by train to St. Joseph to join the Wiliamsburg, Ohio, company of H.C. Peterson bound for Fort Collins, Colorado; cheerful relation of daily scenery, especially flowers, and traveling companions and conditions which she regarded as enjoyable and less arduous than expected; notes on stage stations, forts and availability of supplies; happy to settle with her aunt Elizabeth Stone and eventually become first teacher in Fort Collins.

"Across the Plains in a Prairie Schooner: From the Diary of Elizabeth Keyes." COLORADO MAGAZINE 10 (1933):71-78.

Apr-Jun 1866. Extract.

LATHAM, HENRY, 1828?-1871   4871

BLACK AND WHITE: A JOURNAL OF A THREE MONTHS' TOUR IN THE UNITED STATES. London: Macmillan, 1867. Reprint. New York: Negro Universities Press, 1969. 304 pp.

Dec 1866-Mar 1867. Englishman's American travel diary; observations on the two races in New York, Philadelphia, Baltimore, Washington, Richmond, Atlanta, New Orleans and Boston; extensive entries on transportation, hotels, economics, business, commerce, free education, penal system, rebuilding of southern cities and problems of operating large plantations following the Civil War; Creole society in Louisiana, comparison of Cuban slavery while in Havana with what he had been told about American slavery; entertaining report of ingenious sales techniques of newsboys on the train; the unforgettable majesty of Niagara Falls; attending New Year's Day open reception by President Johnson, visiting Louis Agassiz and seeing the specimens he collected on his Brazilian expedition up the Amazon and discussing international copyright law with Longfellow; an informative diary polished for publication.

LESTER, GURDON P.   4872

Martin, Charles W., ed. "A Round Trip to the Montana Mines: The 1866 Travel Journal of Gurdon P. Lester." NEBRASKA HISTORY 46 (1965):273-313.

May-Oct 1866. Journey from Lodomillo, Iowa, mostly by the Overland Stage, with detailed and colorful descriptions of stagecoach travel, stations, accommodations, discomforts, expenses and dangers; a stopover at Salt Lake, thence to Virginia City and Helena, with descriptions of both; to Fort Benton and down the Missouri on the LUELLA to Sioux City; reports of Indian depredations along the river; notes on Fort Berthold and Indians encamped in that area; references to the JENNIE BROWN and other riverboats.

MCKAY, WILLIAM CAMERON   4873

Clark, Keith and Clark, Donna. "William McKay's Journal, 1866-67; Indian Scouts." OREGON HISTORICAL QUARTERLY 79 (1978):121-171, 269-333. Diary, 141-171, 269-305.

Nov 1866-Nov 1867. Military journal kept by Warm Springs Indian Reservation doctor appointed commander of a unit of Indian scouts, part of Gen. George Crook's campaign; activities at The Dalles; forays into Oregon Snake country; camps, weather, route, condition of horses; raids and casualties, including some scalping by troops; prisoners taken; references to fellow commander, John Darragh, and to Snake chief Paulina.

MUZZALL, THOMAS ABRAM, 1834-1915   **4874**

Shirk, George A. "The Lost Colonel: Thomas A. Muzzall's Memoranda of a Trip across the Plains in 1866." CHRONICLES OF OKLAHOMA 35 (1957):180-193. Diary, pp. 182-191.

"Across the Plains in 1866." NEW MEXICO HISTORICAL REVIEW 32 (1957):246-258.

Jun-Oct 1866. Brief notes of an English immigrant serving as hospital steward with the Fifty-seventh Colored Infantry under Paul Harwood; difficult march across Indian Territory; diarist's treatment of hernia, sunstroke, pneumonia, dropsy, etc., among the troops; Colonel Harwood's disappearance while on a buffalo hunt, with subsequent searches and fears for his safety, his eventual escape from Indians and return to the company; trip from Fort Union to Fort Stanton, New Mexico, via Bosque Rodonda, with "orders to kill all male Indians we meet" after leaving Fort Sumner; notes on plants and animals.

OSTRANDER, A.B.   **4875**

"Diary of A.B. Ostrander." ANNALS OF WYOMING 2, no. 1 (1924):27-32.

Oct 1866-May 1867. Very brief entries of cavalry movements on the plains; forts McPherson, Laramie, Phil Kearny, Reno, etc.; narrative report of handling the mail at Fort Reno and a longer diary extract of a cavalry march from Fort Reno to Fort Phil Kearny in brutally cold February weather.

REAGLES, JAMES   **4876**

Roberson, Jere W., ed. "A View from Oklahoma." RED RIVER VALLEY HISTORICAL REVIEW 3, no. 4 (1978):19-46. Diary, pp. 23-39.

1866-1868. Extract from diary of surgeon with the Tenth Cavalry; interesting notes on Indians of various tribes in Oklahoma Indian Territory and during his march from Fort Gibson to Fort Arbuckle; some reports of depredations and captivities; few medical details except mention of deaths from dysentery and cholera and one successful childbirth upon which the diarist "immediately drank the health of the brat in whiskey"; activities at Fort Sill.

SHAFFNER, CARRIE FRIES, 1839-1922   **4877**

In VICTORIAN WOMEN, edited by Erna O. Hellerstein, pp. 252-254.

Dec 1866, Sep 1867. Extracts from diary of a mother anguished over death of her infant daughter.

STEVENS, HARRIET F.   **4878**

"One of the Mercer Girls: A Journal of Life on the Steamer CONTINENTAL." ANNALS OF WYOMING 35 (1963):213-228.

Jan-Apr 1866. A participant's journal, somewhat written up for newspaper publication, of Asa Mercer's second expedition bringing marriageable women from New England to Seattle; notes on

crew, passengers and Mercer; colorful description of Rio de Janeiro; studying navigation with the captain; a stormy passage through the Strait of Magellan; ports of call along the west coast of South America; very spritely and loquacious account, but a bit coy in places.

THOMPSON, RODIE, b. 1847?   **4879**

In AN ENGLISHMAN IN THE AMERICAN CIVIL WAR, edited by Sir Christopher Chancellor, pp. 3-4. London: Sidgwick and Jackson, 1971; New York: New York University Press, 1971.

Apr 1866. Extract from diary of Englishman, younger brother of Henry Yates Thompson; record of after dinner conversation of Ulysses Grant at home of Rhode Island senator Sprague; the general's opinion of various comrades and opponents during the Civil War.

TOBEY, WARREN P.   **4880**

THE CABIN BOY'S LOG: SCENES AND INCIDENTS ON A NEW BEDFORD WHALER. Boston: Meador, 1932. 163 pp.

1866-1869. Diary, partly written up later, of a boy who went to sea at age fifteen on an unnamed whaler; good details of whaling life and work as well as experiences of the hapless lad who was the brunt of the captain's sadistic temper; rebellion of the crew over severe discipline and meager rations; ships encountered in the Indian and Pacific oceans.

URBINO, LEVINA BUONCUORE   **4881**

AN AMERICAN WOMAN IN EUROPE: THE JOURNAL OF TWO YEARS AND A HALF SOJOURN IN GERMANY, SWITZERLAND, FRANCE AND ITALY. Boston: Lee and Shepard, 1869. 338 pp.

1866-1868. A Boston woman's extended travels in Europe, with detailed, fairly spontaneous notes on scenes, people, customs, accommodations, etc., providing a good picture of the pleasures and problems of being a nineteenth century tourist.

WAGNER, GEORGE, 1841-1906   **4882**

Campbell, William A., ed. "A Freedmen's Bureau Diary by George Wagner." GEORGIA HISTORICAL QUARTERLY 48 (1964):196-214, 333-360.

1866-1868. Philadelphian's tour of duty as a lieutenant in the Veteran Reserve Corps serving in the Freedmen's Bureau at Macon, Augusta and Americus; brief notes of weather, his whereabouts, office work and reports; letters to and from home; occasional mention of settlement of disputes between planters and freedmen; efforts toward getting a school for children of freedmen; Masonic and church activities.

WESTON, DANIEL H., b. 1835   **4883**

Silliman, Lee. " 'Up This Great River': Daniel Weston's Missouri Steamboat Diary." MONTANA: THE MAGAZINE OF WESTERN HISTORY 30, no. 3 (1980):32-41.

May-Jun 1866. Extracts within article describing a trip on the LILLIE MARTIN from Sioux City to Fort Benton; notes on scenery and wildlife, including buffalo shot from the boat; troubles with sandbars, weather, etc.; interesting account by a Helena settler.

1867

AMBERLEY, JOHN RUSSELL, 1842-1876   **4884**

THE AMBERLEY PAPERS: THE LETTERS AND DIARIES OF LORD AND LADY AMBERLEY. Edited by Bertrand and Patricia Russell. London: L. & Virginia Woolf at the Hogarth Press, 1937. New York: W.W. Norton, 1937. 2 vols. American diaries, vol. 2, pp. 49-82.

Aug 1867-Jan 1868. Travels in America of Bertrand Russell's freethinking parents with entries from the diaries of both Viscount John and Lady Katharine Amberley; impressions of post-Civil War conditions and institutions, as they visited schools, prisons, hospitals, etc. and conversed with people ranging from New England intellectuals to former slaves; very candid opinions on Emerson, Bronson, Alcott, Harriet Beecher Stowe, Laura Bridgman, etc.; detailed description of a seance; approving notes on Oberlin College.

BARNITZ, ALBERT, d. 1912   **4885**

LIFE IN CUSTER'S CAVALRY: DIARIES AND LETTERS OF ALBERT AND JENNIE BARNITZ. Edited by Robert M. Utley. Yale Western Americana Series, 31. New Haven: Yale University Press, 1977. 302 pp. passim.

1867-1868. Extracts from the diaries and letters of a cavalry officer and his wife; garrison life and marches with Custer's Seventh Cavalry during Gen. Winfield Scott Hanock's expedition against the Sioux and Cheyenne; many complaints against Custer's severe and capricious discipline and prediction that he would "come to grief as a result of his tyrannical behavior"; march with a military escort accompanying a railroad survey under W.W. Wright from Big Creek Camp, Kansas, to Fort Lyon, Colorado; activities at Fort Wallace, Kansas; references to many officers including Frederick Benteen, Joel Elliott, Alfred Gibbs, etc.; the Sully expedition; battle of Washita, during which Albert was severely wounded; Jennie's interesting notes on garrison social life; concern about drunkenness of General Gibbs.

Utley, Robert M., ed. "Campaigning with Custer." AMERICAN WEST 14, no. 4 (1977):4-9, 58-60.

Apr-Jun 1867. Extracts mainly covering Albert's criticism of Custer, particularly for his punishment of men "perfectly crazy for canned fruit or fresh vegetables" because of scurvy, who left post without permission to get fruit; Jennie's notes of camp life.

BRAINERD, C.N.   **4886**

MY DIARY: OR THREE WEEKS ON THE WING. New York: Egbert, Bourne & Company, Printers, 1868. 45 pp.

Jul-Aug 1867. New Yorker's effusive account of travel to the "Great West," which, in his case, meant Wisconsin and Minnesota; travel by train, river and lake boats; hotels at which he "put up."

BROWN, JABEZ   **4887**

In TRAVEL ACCOUNTS OF INDIANA, compiled by Shirley McCord, pp. 226-227.

Mar 1867. Diary extracts covering Sauk County, Wisconsin, Quaker's train journey to Richmond, Indiana, to enter his son Alonzo in Earlham College; mostly expenses en route.

DERBY, EMMA C., b. 1848?   **4888**

"Diary of Emma C. Derby: Bancroft's Niece Keeps a Record of European Tour." CALIFORNIA HISTORICAL SOCIETY QUARTERLY 31 (1952):219-228, 355-374; 32 (1953):65-80.

Mar, Aug 1867. Article containing extracts of a diary kept by Hubert H. Bancroft's nineteen-year-old niece; travel with the Bancrofts on a tour of Europe to collect material related to his historical research and to buy art and furnishings for their home in San Francisco; sightseeing and social life in Paris, Brussels, Amsterdam, London, etc.; enjoyment of the Paris Exhibition of 1867, the Alps and everything in London; extensive notes on services in English-speaking churches throughout Europe, with a good description of the usual visit to Spurgeon's tabernacle in London; a good diary of a young lady's "Grand Tour" and of Bancroft's book and art collecting activities.

DEVOL, WILLIAM DUDLEY, 1834-1906   **4889**

Jones, Robert Leslie, ed. "Flatboating down the Ohio and Mississippi." OHIO STATE ARCHAEOLOGICAL AND HISTORICAL QUARTERLY 59 (1950):287-309, 385-418.

1867-1873. Extracts from the diaries of Washington County farmer and his wife, Bitha Marshall Devol, illustrative of flatboating as a means of getting farm produce to market; William's diaries of winter runs down the ice choked rivers shipping apples, potatoes and other produce to large cities on the Mississippi; Bitha's of life and work on their farm; four such difficult and non-too-profitable ventures common to the period before increased railroads made flatboating unnecessary.

FARRAGUT, DAVID GLASGOW, 1801-1870   **4890**

In THE LIFE OF DAVID GLASGOW FARRAGUT, by Loyall Farragut, pp. 485-510. New York: D. Appleton, 1879, 1882, 1907.

Jun-Oct 1867. Diary extracts concerning admiral's cruise aboard the FRANKLIN, his flagship, while in command of the European squadron; a blend of official social events, naval duties and sightseeing; in port at Cherbourg, Cronstadt, Waxholm, Gravesend, Portsmouth, Plymouth and Lisbon; visits to Paris, St. Petersburg, Moscow, Copenhagen and London; inspection of dockyards, ironclads, military installations, weaponry, etc.

HALL, CHRISTOPHER NEWMAN, 1816-1902   **4891**

FROM LIVERPOOL TO ST. LOUIS. London and New York: George Routledge and Sons, 1870. 294 pp. Diary, pp. 1-23.

Aug 1867. English clergyman's ship diary, followed by narrative of his travels in America; Atlantic crossing on the CUBA with colorful and detailed notes of ship life, passengers, crew and religious services on board.

HASKELL, RACHEL MITCHELL CLARK, 1829-1900   **4892**

Lillard, Richard G., ed. "A Literate Woman in the Mines: The Diary of Rachel Haskell." MISSISSIPPI VALLEY HISTORICAL REVIEW 31 (1944-1945):81-98.

In LET THEM SPEAK FOR THEMSELVES, WOMEN IN THE AMERICAN WEST, 1849-1900, edited by Christiane Fischer, pp. 58-71. New York: Archon Books, 1977.

Mar-Apr 1867. Fragment of a lost diary kept by the wife of the toll-keeper at Aurora, Nevada; domestic chores and care of children interspersed with reading of a wide variety of books and magazines; a constant parade of lodgers, a few of whom could discuss literature with her and her husband; her own and her children's illness compounded by severely cold weather; a good picture of frontier family life in a cultivated home.

HOWELL, CHARLES W. 4893

Johnson, Leland R., ed. "An Army Engineer on the Missouri in 1867." NEBRASKA HISTORY 53 (1972):253-291.

"Report of a Steamboat Trip on the MINER from Sioux City, Iowa, to Fort Benton and Return." NORTH DAKOTA HISTORICAL SOCIETY COLLECTIONS 2 (1980):392-415.

Jun-Sep 1867. Engineer's diary of his survey of the upper Missouri authorized to improve navigation; descriptions of Omaha and Sioux City; thence upriver on the Northwest Fur Company steamer MINER under Capt. Alpheus F. Hawley, to study the river and its banks, depths, snags, sandbars, etc.; notes on forts along the river, passengers and crew; shooting buffalo swimming the river; a few notes on Crow Indians, including a delegation of chiefs aboard the MINER after a disappointed effort to hold a council with Gen. Alfred Sully.

KEYES, JENNIE RUTLEDGE, 1852-1879 4894

Brannon, Peter A. "Southern Emigration to Brazil." ALABAMA HISTORICAL QUARTERLY 1 (1930):280-305, 467-488.

1867-1869 (with gaps). Diary kept by Julia Keyes's teenaged daughter during the family's sojourn in Brazil; living at Lake Juparena in the Rio Doce Colony about 300 miles north of Rio de Janeiro, the Isle of Rebeira in the Bay of Rio, Capt. James Johnston's plantation, Pao Grande, and San Domingos, a village near Rio de Janeiro; daily routines of washing, cooking, etc., reading, visitors; notes on scenery, suitors, friendship with Lizzie Freligh, her emotions; sightseeing in Rio de Janeiro and the Carnival; loneliness of life in the country, desire to live in the city and homesickness for Montgomery, Alabama; some of her poetry.

KEYES, JULIA LOUISA 4895

Brannon, Peter A. "Southern Emigration to Brazil." ALABAMA HISTORICAL QUARTERLY 1, no. 2 (1930):74-95. Diary, pp. 91-95.

Apr, Oct 1867. Two long, basically retrospective entries from diary of Alabama dentist's wife, mother of Jennie Rutledge Keyes, describing sea voyage to Brazil on the emigrant ship MARMION and getting settled in Brazil.

KEYES FAMILY 4896

"Our Life in Brazil." ALABAMA HISTORICAL QUARTERLY 28 (1966): 125-339. Diary, pp. 146-339 passim.

1867-1870. Extracts from the journals kept by Jennie and some of the other children of Julia and John W. Keyes during the family's years in Brazil; from arrival in Rio de Janeiro, during residence at several sites to homeward journey on the WAVELET; primitive conditions at Lake Juparena; learning new foods and new ways of doing things; coping with insects, malaria and Brazil's slower pace; social life within the American colony; aversion to the Brazilians; life on the Isle of Rebeira, nicknamed Dixie Island, the plantation Pao Grande and San Domingos; notes on domestic activities, natural surroundings, black servants, Rio de Janeiro

and the Carnival; journey back to Montgomery, Alabama, with a stop for shopping in the Barbados; a revealing view of the pioneering life attempted by some former Confederates.

LAWRENCE, JOHN, 1835-1908 4897

"John Lawrence, 'Father of Saguache': Memorandum." COLORADO MAGAZINE 38 (1961):53-64, 123-130, 195-200; 39 (1962):63-68.

Feb-Nov 1867; April 1868. Rancher's diary of a cattle drive from Conejos to Saguache, where he settled; building a house and daily notes of ranch work; references to many other ranchers and settlers, especially his partner, J.B. Woodson, and José Antonio Moran.

LEE, WILLIAM WALLACE, 1836-1911 4898

"A Mississippian Moves to Franklin Parish." NORTH LOUISIANA HISTORICAL ASSOCIATION JOURNAL 6 (1975):154-163.

Sep-Oct 1867. Account of physician's move from Ludlow, Mississippi, to Gilbert, Louisiana; bad roads, weather and menace of strangers along the way; first month in Gilbert; land values, beginning practice, fishing, scarcity of eligible women, etc.; enthusiasm for new location mixed with bouts of homesickness.

LUEG, HENRY, b. 1830 4899

Kingston, C.S. "The Northern Overland Route in 1867." PACIFIC NORTHWEST QUARTERLY 41 (1950):234-253.

Jun-Nov 1867. Brief extracts within article describing a German immigrant's journey with a wagon train from Minnesota to the Montana gold fields, then settling at Portland.

MUIR, JOHN, 1838-1914 4900

JOHN OF THE MOUNTAINS: THE UNPUBLISHED JOURNALS OF JOHN MUIR. Edited by Linnie Marsh Wolfe. Boston: Houghton Mifflin, 1938. 459 pp. Reprint. Madison: University of Wisconsin Press, 1979.

1867-1899. Important journal of Scottish-American naturalist, mountaineer and champion of wilderness preservation; scientific exploration of Sierra Nevada, Yosemite Valley and Alaska; extensive notes on plants, trees, wildlife, geological features, particularly glaciers and their effects; trip aboard the CORWIN with John Burroughs on the Harriman-Alaska Expedition; philosophical musings throughout; an outstanding journal, both as natural history and literature.

TO YOSEMITE AND BEYOND: WRITINGS FROM THE YEARS 1863-1875. Edited by Robert Engberg and Donald Wesling. Madison: University of Wisconsin Press, 1980. 192 pp. Diary, pp. 46-63.

1868-1870. Extracts from the Sierra Nevada and Yosemite.

RICHARDS, S.P. 4901

Garrett, Franklin M. "Atlanta and Environs." ATLANTA HISTORICAL BULLETIN 16, no. 1 (1971):68-113. Diary, pp. 108-109.

Feb-Dec 1867. Extracts selected to provide picture of life in Atlanta; notes on a Sunday school excursion to Kenesaw Mountain, black votes, celebration of Fourth of July, etc.

SIMONIN, LOUIS LAURENT, 1830-1886   4902

Clough, Wilson O., trans. and ed. "Fort Russell and the Fort Laramie Peace Commission in 1867." FRONTIER: A MAGAZINE OF THE NORTHWEST 11 (1931):3-12. Reprint. Sources of Northwest History, no. 14. FRONTIER OMNIBUS, edited by John W. Hakola, pp. 319-333.

Nov 1867. Frenchman's account of journeys with the Indian Peace Commission of 1867; mores of American officers and soldiers and good picture of transport of army and equipment; scenes and terrain; council with Crow Indians.

TROBRIAND, PHILIPPE REGIS DENIS DE KEREDERN,   4903
comte de, 1816-1897

ARMY LIFE IN DAKOTA. Translated from the French by George F. Will; edited by Milo M. Quaife. Lakeside Classics, 39. Chicago: Lakeside Press, 1941. 387 pp.

MILITARY LIFE IN DAKOTA. Translated and edited from the French by Lucile M. Kane. Mississippi Valley Historical Association, Clarence Walworth Alvord Memorial Commission Publication, vol. 2. St. Paul: Alvord Memorial Commission, 1951. 395 pp. Reprint. Lincoln: University of Nebraska, 1982.

1867-1869. Journal of commander of military posts in Upper Missouri and North Dakota region in period before the Sioux wars; trip from Chicago to Fort Stevenson, learning as much as possible about country and especially Indians; building and administering the fort; full description of daily life with extensive information about Indian life and government relations; in fine literary style.

1868

BARD, ISAAC NEWTON, b. 1842   4904

"Isaac Newton Bard Dug Potatoes, Not Gold." COLORADO MAGAZINE 33 (1956):161-176.

Aug-Dec 1868. Extract covering journey from his home in Polk City, Iowa, to Oro City, Colorado; travel by train and on foot; in Colorado, mostly doing ranch work for his brother Andrew Bard.

BUNYARD, HARRIET, 1849-1900   4905

Cooney, Percival, ed. "Diary of Miss Harriet Bunyard from Texas to California in 1868." HISTORICAL SOCIETY OF SOUTHERN CALIFORNIA ANNUAL PUBLICATIONS 13 (1924-1927):92-124.

In HO FOR CALIFORNIA! edited by Sandra L. Myres, pp. 199-252.

Apr-Oct 1868. Record of journey with her family from Collin County, Texas, to settle in El Monte, California; some Indian alarms and taking her turn standing guard at night; a description of Fort Griffin and activities there; camps, terrain and scenery, mainly along the stagecoach route; trouble crossing the Pecos.

CHISHOLM, JAMES, 1838-1903   4906

SOUTH PASS, 1868: JAMES CHISHOLM'S JOURNAL OF THE WYOMING GOLD RUSH. Introduced and edited by Lola M. Hom-

sher. The Pioneer Heritage Series, vol. 3. Lincoln: University of Nebraska Press, 1960. 244 pp.

Sep 1868. Dated entries, within a longer narrative journal, recounting experiences of Scottish-born reporter for the CHICAGO TRIBUNE; a rainy, miserable trip from Green River to South Pass City with companion A.L. Houghton; on to Miner's Delight diggings, where he stayed with Maj. Patrick A. Gallagher; life among the miners entertainingly described, with diarist's opinion that most gold prospectors should have remained in their former occupations.

COOK, JOSEPH WITHERSPOON, 1836-1902   4907

DIARY AND LETTERS OF THE REVEREND JOSEPH W. COOK, MISSIONARY TO CHEYENNE. Arranged by N.S. Thomas. Laramie, Wy.: Laramie Republican Company, Printers, 1919. 137 pp. passim

1868-1869 (with gaps). Diary of a hard-working Episcopal missionary and founder of the church at Cheyenne, who considered St. Paul's policies for "licentious Corinth" appropriate for the frontier town; tireless pastoral visiting, help to sick and destitute; concerns about the family and marital upheavals, drunkenness, etc., among settlers and military personnel; preaching to responsive congregations, but trouble with getting vestrymen to perform their duties; establishing a Sunday school and parish school; acquiring land and materials and overseeing the building of the church; quiet pleasures, including his garden.

CRANE, JAMES   4908

In TREASURES OF PIONEER HISTORY, compiled by Kate B. Carter, vol. 2, pp. 398-399.

1868-1869. Scattered notes of a Mormon working on the railroad being built in Utah; composing a railroad song "Echo Canyon" and buying musical instruments.

DAVIS, MARK S., d. 1893   4909

"By Spring-Wagon to Missouri and Kansas." INDIANA MAGAZINE OF HISTORY 29 (1933):48-65.

May-Jun 1868. Wabash, Indiana, Quaker's journey with three other men to State Line City, Missouri; camping or sleeping in barns; notes on towns and countryside en route; visit to Lincoln's tomb in Springfield, Illinois; visit to Blind, Deaf and Dumb Asylum at Jacksonville; great admiration for Illinois farm land and prosperity; taking a claim and starting a Sabbath school in Missouri, from which diarist later returned to settle at Indianapolis.

GALPIN, CHARLES   4910

Garraghan, Gilbert J., ed. "Father De Smet's Sioux Peace Mission of 1868 and the Journal of Charles Galpin." MID-AMERICA 13 (1930):141-163.

Pfaller, Louis, ed. "The Galpin Journal: Dramatic Record of an Odyssey for Peace." MONTANA: THE MAGAZINE OF WESTERN HISTORY 18, no. 2 (1968):2-23.

Jun 1868. Journal of a trader at Fort Rice and interpreter for Father De Smet on his journey to the Powder River as a member of the Indian Peace Commission of 1868; from Fort Rice with an escort of Indian allies from various tribes; good descriptions of camps, travel and incidents en route; speeches of Sitting Bull and other chiefs, as well as De Smet.

HARVEY, WINFIELD SCOTT, 1848-1931 4911

Shirk, George H. "Campaigning with Sheridan: A Farriers' Diary." CHRONICLES OF OKLAHOMA 37 (1959):68-105.

Sep 1868-Mar 1869. That portion of diary of blacksmith in Troop K, Seventh Cavalry, covering the Indian War of 1868-1869; operations in Kansas and the Indian Territory with Alfred Sully and George Custer; notes on weather, duties, health, countryside, availability of wood and water, troop losses, Indian raids and cavalry engagements; battle of the Washita; opinions on Capt. Robert M. West and on land ownership in the Indian Territory.

HOPKINS, MARCUS STERLING, 1840-1914 4912

Mugleston, William F., ed. "The Freedmen's Bureau and Reconstruction in Virginia." VIRGINIA MAGAZINE OF HISTORY AND BIOGRAPHY 86 (1978):45-102.

Jan-Dec 1868. Diary kept by Union veteran from Berlin Heights, Ohio, of his work and impressions as head of the Freedmen's Bureau at Gordonsville serving Orange and Louisa counties; frank accounts of violence and harrassment against blacks, as well as murders, rapes, etc., unrelated to race; reactions to national and local political issues; pessimism over prospects for educating newly freed slaves to self-sufficiency; doubts over effectiveness of Bureau's temperance policy; references to many Bureau personnel, including such Northern teachers as Jane Hosmer, and a few local people; enjoyment of wide reading and following newspaper accounts of impeachment proceedings against Andrew Johnson.

HOWELL, SAUL SYLVESTER, 1841-1879 4913

Kuhns, Frederick J., ed. "Diary of S.S. Howell." IOWA JOURNAL OF HISTORY 49 (1951):143-167.

Jan-Jun 1868. Extract from the diary of a young classics professor at the State University of Iowa at Iowa City; teaching and administrative work; faculty social life; home chores and family life; much Baptist church activity, with reflections on sermons and lessons; hearing traveling lecturers of amazing variety; seriousness about teaching; "how lofty the occupation to be moulding immortal minds"; declining health, leading to decision to move to California.

JERNEGAN, LAURA, b. 1862 4914

In WHALING WIVES, by Emma M. Whiting and Henry B. Hough, pp. 127-133. Boston: Houghton Mifflin, 1953.

Extracts in DIARY OF AMERICA, edited by Josef and Dorothy Berger, pp. 491-493; SMALL VOICES, edited by Josef and Dorothy Berger, pp. 191-199.

1868-1871. Extracts from diary of a very young daughter of whaling captain Jared Jernegan, accompanying him on the ROMAN during a voyage from New Bedford around Cape Horn; lessons, meals, whales taken and a child's view of the processes of whaling; ships encountered, weather, family activities; such homey details as the condition of mama's laying hens.

Jernegan, Marcus Wilson, ed. "A Child's Diary of a Whaling Voyage." NEW ENGLAND QUARTERLY 2 (1929):130-139.

1868-1869. Extracts.

JOHNSTON, JOHN TAYLOR, 1820-1893 4915

Baetjer, Katharine, ed. "Extracts from the Paris Journal of John Taylor Johnston: First President of the Metropolitan Museum." APOLLO, n.s. 114 (1981):410-417.

Oct-Nov 1868. Art collector's trip to Europe with his family; life in the American community in Paris, sightseeing, attending opera, theater, etc.; visiting galleries and studios, often with dealer George A. Lucas; purchases; personal comments on French art.

LANDIS, CHARLES KLINE, b. 1833 4916

"Journal of Charles K. Landis, Founder of Vineland." VINELAND HISTORICAL MAGAZINE 1 (1916)-43 (1964) passim.

1868-1900. Journal of a Philadelphian who purchased a 16,000 acre tract of New Jersey land for development; land sales and prices, with many sales to immigrants as well as Americans; encouragement of business, small industry, agriculture and railroad development, including his own Vineland Railroad; all sorts of business and social dealings, including visits with many of his settlers, in whom he showed a paternal interest, but contempt for speculators; local and New Jersey politics; a vigorous intellectual life, with much reading and reflection; enjoyment of his family, playing with and reading to his children; frequent train trips for business in Camden, Philadelphia and New York.

"European Journal of Charles K. Landis." VINELAND HISTORICAL MAGAZINE 5 (1920)-12 (1927) passim.

Jul-Dec 1874. European trip undertaken to improve his health, to investigate architecture, housing, sanitation, civic and social institutions in order to get ideas for improvement of his beloved Vineland and to promote European immigration; tourist notes and business in England, Scotland, France, Germany and the Tyrolean Alps; enjoying plays in London; impression of Edinburgh: "Why can we not have the same clean streets, cab conveniences and good government in our American cities?" but conclusion that laboring classes much better off in the United States.

"Florida Journal of Charles K. Landis." VINELAND HISTORICAL MAGAZINE 26 (1941):255-260; 27 (1942):277-285.

Nov 1883. Trip by steamer NACHACHEE from New York to Savannah; thence by train, with visits to orange groves and other fruit-growing enterprises.

Dec 1884-Jan 1885. A train trip to Florida, where he investigated Leesburg and the land development there, with notes on prices; thence to New Orleans for business and sightseeing; interesting notes on people.

"Foreign Journal of Charles K. Landis." VINELAND HISTORICAL MAGAZINE 27 (1942)-38 (1953) passim.

Dec 1889-May 1890. Journey to Europe and Egypt to "investigate sea defenses with a view to the protection of Sea Isle City"; Atlantic crossing on the French steamer GASCOYNE; in Holland for inspection of the dikes, but also vast enjoyment of people, towns, scenery, villages, hotels, art, music and appreciation of Dutch institutions; briefly through Germany, where he was guest of a consul from Vineland, Edward Johnson; then extended stay in Italy, with excellent notes far surpassing most travel journals; rambles in the country, as well as taking advantage of seemingly all that Rome and Florence could offer, with contempt for tourists who spend their time in first class hotels and associate only with other Americans; references to many people, including expatriate artist Charles C. Coleman; finally, travels throughout

Egypt seeing all the tourist attractions, but, as was the case in Holland and Italy, with even more interest in people; unselfconscious notes in which the colors, sounds and smells of Egypt are vivid to the reader.

"A Fragment of the 1884 Mexican Journal of Charles K. Landis." VINELAND HISTORICAL MAGAZINE 42 (1957):345-351.

Mar 1894. Notes taken mainly at Tampico, with scenes, activities, people, etc.; a mention of his "European emigration plan" to bring into Mexico twenty thousand new immigrants yearly.

"Jamaica Journal of Charles K. Landis." VINELAND HISTORICAL MAGAZINE 43 (1964).

Feb 1900. By steamer SAMPSON to Jamaica for his health; visits to pineapple and sugar plantations; notes on people, with interest in the racial mixture.

MATTHEWS, WASHINGTON, 1843-1905   4917

Mattison, Ray H., ed. "The Diary of Surgeon Washington Matthews, Fort Rice, D.T." NORTH DAKOTA HISTORY 21 (1954):5-74.

1868-1869. Irish immigrant's diary which he kept while post surgeon at Fort Rice; numbers of sick and their "prevailing diseases," plus daily weather; arrivals of Missouri River steamers; a few notes on Indians of the area; botanical studies and collecting; little on medical treatments except the vaccinating of some men.

MATTSON, HANS   4918

Ljungmark, Lars-Olov. "Notes from a Travel Diary." SWEDISH PIONEER HISTORICAL QUARTERLY 9 (1960):108-115.

Dec 1868. Extracts within article on journey to Sweden undertaken by an immigrant who was commissioner of emigration for Minnesota, land agent for the St. Paul and Pacific Railroad and prominent resident of Red Wing; observing on his arrival at the Malmo, Sweden railroad station "how badly the lower classes and the poor are treated in comparison with the upper classes"; enjoyment of seeing old friends after many years.

PEIRCE, CLOTHIER   4919

In WHALING, by Charles B. Hawes, pp. 239-257. Garden City, N.Y.: Doubleday, Page, 1924.

In DIARY OF AMERICA, edited by Josef and Dorothy Berger, pp. 487-491.

1868-1870. Extracts from logs of the captain of New Bedford whaler MINNESOTA, selected to show his deteriorating mental condition; little luck in spotting whales and less in holding them; stormy relations with the crew; captain's conviction that "the Lord's power and vengeance is against the Peirce family."

RICHARDS, ELLEN HENRIETTA SWALLOW, 1842-1911   4920

In THE LIFE OF ELLEN H. RICHARDS, by Caroline L. Hunt, pp. 40-79, Boston: Whitcomb & Barrows, 1912. Centennial ed. Washington, D.C.: American Home Economics Association, 1942.

1868-1870. The weekly record of schedules and studies while a student at Vassar; comments on women's education and her work with Maria Mitchell.

RICHMOND, REBECCA, 1840-1925   4921

Millbrook, Minnie Dubbs, ed., "Rebecca Visits Kansas and the Custers." KANSAS HISTORICAL QUARTERLY 42 (1976):366-402.

Jan-Apr 1868, Feb-Mar 1870. Visits to Topeka and Fort Leavenworth of Elizabeth Custer's cousin from Grand Rapids, Michigan; a rather good picture of cavalry and Kansas social life with the Custers and the diarist's sister and brother-in-law, Mary and Charles Kendall, and others; Episcopal services with special comments on music; items relating obliquely to court-martial charges against Custer.

ROOSEVELT, THEODORE, 1858-1919   4922

THEODORE ROOSEVELT'S DIARIES OF BOYHOOD AND YOUTH. Edited by Mrs. Douglas Robinson. New York and London: C. Scribner's Sons, 1928. 365 pp.

1868-1877. Youthful diaries of the future president; childhood adventures at home and in Europe; visits to zoos, museums, historic and literary sites dutifully and consistently recorded; delightfully frank and naive notes on people, his family and friends, games and romps in hotels; later trip to Egypt, Jerusalem, etc.; interest in birds and animals throughout; a fine record of an affluent childhood at home and abroad.

Extracts in SMALL VOICES, edited by Josef and Dorothy Berger, pp. 80-86.

May-Sep 1869. Travels in Europe with his family.

"Theodore Roosevelt's Diaries." PERSONALITY: A MAGAZINE OF BIOGRAPHY 1, no. 6 (1928):3-33; 2, no. 1 (1928):69-82, no. 2, 54-62, no. 3, 65-72.

1868-1877. Extracts from childhood and teenage diaries.

Apr-Jul 1898. A brief diary of his Spanish-American War experience and attitudes while serving as a lieutenant colonel with the First Volunteer Cavalry, his famous Rough Riders; impatience with the "delays and stupidity" of the Ordnance Department, "idiotic" orders from some of his superiors and problems of getting to and underway from Tampa Bay.

Jan-Feb 1901. Hasty notes of a western hunting trip undertaken while he was vice president; hunting couger, lynx, etc.

Apr-May 1905. Western hunting diary kept while he was president; using dogs to track bears in the Rockies; hard going on horseback through snow and rugged terrain.

SCHLESINGER, SIGMUND, 1848-1928   4923

Mattes, Merrill J. "The Beecher Island Battlefield Diary of Sigmund Schlesinger." COLORADO MAGAZINE 29 (1952):161-169. Diary, pp. 168-169.

Aug-Sep 1868. Hungarian Jewish immigrant's account of the battle of Beecher Island during which he was a volunteer scout with George E. Forsyth's expedition to protect Oregon wagon trains; besieged on a small sand island at the Arikaree Fork of the Republican River, holding off Cheyennes during several days of fighting, virtually without food and water; eventual victory of the badly outnumbered scouts.

SHUTE, HENRY AUGUSTUS, 1856-1943   4924

THE REAL DIARY OF A REAL BOY. Boston: Everett, 1902, 135 pp. Frequently reprinted.

Extracts in SMALL VOICES, edited by Josef and Dorothy Berger, pp. 260-265.

> Jan-Apr 1868. Exeter, New Hampshire, boy's diary; cutting up in school; folk treatment for warts.

SMITH, SALLIE DIANA, b. 1849　　　　　　　4925

Jensen, Mrs. Dana O., ed. "The Journal of Sallie D. Smith." MISSOURI HISTORICAL SOCIETY BULLETIN 20 (1964):124-143.

> Jun-Oct 1868. Extracts of Howard County girl's journey with friends to visit relatives in Kentucky; travel by riverboat; a visit to Shaw's Garden in St. Louis; thence to Cairo on the PARAGON, with detailed description of her stateroom and sumptuous fare; to Louisville on other less prepossessing boats; social life among numerous relatives, with her obvious enjoyment of being "the pretty cousin from Missouri"; a Fourth of July celebration and visits to Mammoth Cave, a fair and the Union cemetery at Cave Hill.

SPOTTS, DAVID L., b. 1848　　　　　　　　4926

CAMPAIGNING WITH CUSTER AND THE NINETEENTH KANSAS VOLUNTEER CAVALRY ON THE WASHITA CAMPAIGN. Edited by E.A. Brininstool. Los Angeles: Wetzel, 1928. 215 pp.

> Oct 1868-Apr 1869. Campaign against the Cheyennes, Kiowas and Comanches through Kansas and Oklahoma Indian Territory to protect settlers, stage route and railroad; diarist's enlistment at Springhill, Kansas, motivated by desire for adventure and to open the frontier to land claims; choice of Charles H. Finch as captain of L Troop; march from Topeka under Samuel J. Crawford, governor of Kansas and colonel of the Nineteenth Kansas Volunteer Cavalry; joining up with Custer's Seventh Cavalry and diarist's eagerness to get a look at the great Indian fighter; report of the battle of Washita against Black Kettle and the death of Maj. Joel Elliott and his nineteen troopers; a circuitous march via Wichita and Fort Cobb into Texas and return to forts Dodge and Hays; negotiations of Kiowa chief Santanta with Custer and Gen. Philip H. Sheridan; reports of Custer's visitation of "all the tribes that have not come in yet" to the reservations; release of captives Anna Belle Morgan and Sarah C. White; many references to Lt. Winfield S. Tilton, Sgt. William W. Mather, Lt. Henry E. Stoddard and his friend George Vann; an unusually full, unselfconscious diary of a volunteer Indian fighter's life in camp and on the march.

VOGDES, ADA ADAMS　　　　　　　　　　4927

Adams, Donald K., ed. "The Journal of Ada A. Vogdes." MONTANA: THE MAGAZINE OF WESTERN HISTORY 13, no. 3 (1963):2-17.

> 1868-1871. Extracts from diary kept by the wife of Lt. Anthony Wayne Vogdes at forts Laramie and Fetterman; fort theatricals with names of plays, Christmas celebrations, social life; extensive notes on Indians, including minute descriptions of physiques, garb and face painting of Chief Red Cloud and others whom she frequently entertained at lunch; Sioux and Cheyenne councils and negotiations at forts; descriptions of the women and their habits, which disgusted her, but sympathy for their hard work; Indian dancing; a visit to a teepee.

WHITNEY, CHAUNCEY BELDEN, 1842-1873　　　4928

"Diary of Chauncey B. Whitney, a Scout with Forsyth at Beecher Island." KANSAS STATE HISTORICAL SOCIETY COLLECTIONS 12 (1911-1912):296-299.

> Aug-Sep 1868. Brief diary of a scout at the battle of Beecher Island; march from Fort Hays, with camps and distances; good account of sudden attack by Indians on the Arikaree Fork of the Republican River, with besieged troops holding off Indians and reduced to eating putrid horsemeat; many dead or wounded, including Lt. Fred H. Beecher; rescue by Louis H. Carpenter's Tenth Cavalry and return to Fort Wallace.

1869

BAILEY, MARY ELLEN JACKSON, 1847-1915　　　4929

Spring, Agnes W., ed. "The Diary of Mary Ellen Jackson Bailey." DENVER WESTERNERS BRAND BOOK 18 (1962).

> Jan-Dec 1869. Diary of ranch wife at Latham, Colorado, an important station on the Overland State route and stopping point for weary emigrants fed and tended by diarist, who also taught school and accommodated early Colorado court in her log home; household chores, guests, reports of Indian raids, delight in mail and affection for her husband; some loneliness.

BAKER, J.H., b. 1832　　　　　　　　　　4930

Ritchie, E.B. "A Trail Driver Who Kept a Diary; Daily Events on Trail, Palo Pinto to Abilene." THE CATTLEMAN 19, no. 3 (1932):14-20.

> Sep-Nov 1869. Record of a cattle drive led by the Rev. G.W. Slaughter; route, grass, weather; such hazards as swimming cattle across rivers and fleeing prairie fire; losses en route, but successful conclusion of the tedious and exhausting venture, with sale of diarist's portion of the cattle for $4,664.

BECKLEY, LEVI　　　　　　　　　　　　4931

"Levi Beckley's Book." UMPQUA TRAPPER 15 (1979):8-24.

> 1869-1872. Mainly a work diary; odd jobs from Knob Noster, Missouri, to Denver, traveling by train and stopping off to work en route; wages, prices, hotels and lodgings; thence to Cheyenne, with reports on brawls, fights and drunkenness observed there; ranch work; church attendance; to San Francisco by train and then to Oregon, where diarist began ranching in Douglas County; much train lore and fact throughout diary.

BRACKETT, ALBERT GALLATIN　　　　　　4932

"A Trip through the Rocky Mountains," MONTANA HISTORICAL SOCIETY CONTRIBUTIONS 8 (1917):329-344.

> May-Jul 1869. Commanding officer's journal of a march of the Second Cavalry from Carter's Station, Wyoming, to Fort Ellis, Montana, to protect settlers in the Gallatin Valley; route, camps, terrain, difficulties of a grueling march; a list of officers and companies; encounters and councils with Bannock Indians; references to Mormons; optimistic prediction for Montana's growth and prosperity.

Peters, Joseph P. "Montana Battalion, 1869: The 437-Mile Cavalry Trek, Delineated by Its Commander." MONTANA: THE MAGAZINE OF WESTERN HISTORY 15, no. 2 (1965):38-51.

May-Jul 1869. A few extracts within article, mainly describing mud and rain, tensions with Indians at Fort Ellis and encounters with "Morrisite" apostate Mormons.

BRADLEY, GEORGE YOUNG, 1836-1885   **4933**

Darrah, William Culp, ed. "George Y. Bradley's Journal." UTAH HISTORICAL QUARTERLY 15 (1947):1-72. Journal, pp. 31-72.

May-Aug 1869. Detailed account, by a member of the expedition, of John Wesley Powells' first exploration of the Green and Colorado rivers and geological survey of the area, running rapids and portaging around those that were impassable; geological reconnoiters with Powell; dangers and near starvation; excellent descriptions of canyons and mountains; his lifesaving assistance to the one-armed Powell while scaling a canyon wall; introspections.

BRALY, SUSANNAH HYDE, 1805-1897   **4934**

In VICTORIAN WOMEN, edited by Erna O. Hellerstein, pp. 486-488.

1869. Extracts from journal of Presbyterian minister's wife at Lawrence Station, California, near San Jose; cares and anxieties of old age; concern for her children and unhappiness at separating from them.

CAMPBELL, JOHN A., b. 1835   **4935**

"Diary of John A. Campbell." ANNALS OF WYOMING 10 (1938):5-11, 59-78, 120-143, 155-185.

1869-1875. Territorial governor's brief notes of political activities, travels, social life and speaking engagements; stagecoach and train travel throughout the West; a trip to Washington, D.C., to confer on Indian matters and other territorial business; Presbyterian church work; a busy public life very briefly noted.

COOK, CHARLES W., 1839-1927   **4936**

THE VALLEY OF THE UPPER YELLOWSTONE: AN EXPLORATION OF THE HEADWATERS OF THE YELLOWSTONE RIVER IN THE YEAR 1869 AS RECORDED BY CHARLES W. COOK, DAVID E. FOLSOM, AND WILLIAM PETERSON. Edited by Aubrey L. Haines. American Exploration and Travel Series, no. 47. Norman: University of Oklahoma Press, 1965. 70 pp.

Sep 1869. Reconstructed composite diary of the first exploration of the area later to become Yellowstone Park; good description of the spectacular geological and scenic features of the region.

HILL, PAUL   **4937**

Hill, Mabel. "Paul Hill: Railroad Builder." NEBRASKA HISTORY 18 (1937):21-38. Diary, pp. 24-26.

1869-1872. Brief extracts from diary and letters of a Lowell, Massachusetts, engineer, recording his work as a construction engineer building the extension of the Burlington and Missouri Railroad from Plattsmouth to Fort Kearny.

KOCH, PETER, 1844-1917   **4938**

Koch, Elers, ed. "Journal of Peter Koch." FRONTIER: A MAGAZINE OF THE NORTHWEST 9 (1929):148-160. Reprint. Sources of Northwest History, no. 5. FRONTIER OMNIBUS, edited by John W. Hakola, pp. 334-345.

1869-1870 (with gaps). Danish immigrant's experiences at Fort Musselshell on the Missouri and on a trip to Fort Ellis; work at the trading post and cutting wood for the steamboats, "twenty-five years old and poor as a rat yet"; hunting and trapping; mention of boat arrivals and departures; a few notes on Indians.

LARGE, SAMUEL POLLOCK, d. 1912   **4939**

Bothwell, Margaret, ed. "Samuel Pollock Large's Diary of 1869." WESTERN PENNSYLVANIA HISTORICAL MAGAZINE 47 (1964):111-124.

Jan-Dec 1869. Extracts from diary of an Elizabeth boatbuilder in partnership with his brother Isaac Newton Large; brief notes of tasks and expenses; a few items of family and local news, including several deaths.

MCQUIG, JOHN   **4940**

Patterson, Edna E., ed. "John McQuig Diary." NEVADA HISTORICAL SOCIETY QUARTERLY 6, no. 2 (1963):1-27.

Feb-Jul 1869. Account of a prospecting trip in Nevada; mining at Treasure City, with forays to Elko, Hamilton and Shermantown; notes on Irish miners; reports of murders and hangings; snow storms in May; mine accidents, etc; concern over lack of observance of Catholic holy days; a good picture of rowdy mining life.

NEWBERRY, JULIA ROSA, 1853-1876   **4941**

JULIA NEWBERRY'S DIARY. With an introduction by Margaret A. Barnes and Janet A. Fairbank. New York: Norton, 1933. 176 pp.

Extracts in DIARY OF AMERICA, edited by Josef and Dorothy Berger, pp. 510-515.

1869-1871. Diary of the teenage daughter of Walter L. and Julia Butler Newberry; social life of a wealthy Chicago belle, with trips to resorts, flirtations, parties, books and reading; at Miss Haines' School in New York; her increasing illness and parents' search for cure involving trips to St. Augustine, Florida, and Europe, where the family stayed for extended periods in France, Italy and Switzerland; Julia's homesickness, especially for her house, one of the great Chicago mansions, and dismay upon learning of its destruction in the Chicago Fire.

NORTH, FRANK JOSHUA, 1840-1885   **4942**

Danker, Donald F., ed. "The Journal of an Indian Fighter." NEBRASKA HISTORY 39 (1958):87-177.

Jan-Dec 1869. Journal of captain of Pawnee scouts in the service of government forces during the Republic River Expedition under generals E.A. Carr and Thomas Duncan; skirmishes, including destruction of the Cheyenne village at Summit Springs; activities at Columbus and Kearney and trips to Omaha; evidence of the impact of the new Union Pacific Railroad; buffalo hunting; references to Buffalo Bill Cody, who was later his partner in ranching and Cody's wild west show.

PAXSON, JOSEPH ARMITAGE, 1842-1888   **4943**

Sellus, James L., ed. "Diary of Joseph A. Paxson, Physician to the Winnebago Indians." NEBRASKA HISTORY 27 (1946):143-204, 244-275.

Jul 1869-Jun 1870. Diary of a Quaker doctor working at the Winnebago Indian Agency; notes on illnesses afflicting the Indians, some customs still practiced and the work of teachers and missionaries; diarist's visits to Omaha and the agency there; an eclipse of the sun; references to agents Howard White, E. Painter and others, and to Dr. E.G. Shortledge; little specific medical information except the vaccination of many children, some of whom died.

POWELL, JOHN WESLEY, 1834-1902   4944

EXPLORATION OF THE COLORADO RIVER OF THE WEST AND ITS TRIBUTARIES. Explored in 1869, 1870, 1871, and 1872. Under the direction of the secretary of the Smithsonian Institution. Washington, D.C.: Government Printing Office, 1875. 291 pp. passim.

Reprint of narrative portion. THE EXPLORATION OF THE COLORADO RIVER. New York: Anchor Books, 1961.

Republication with additional chapters. CANYONS OF THE COLORADO. Meadville, Pa.: Flood & Vincent, 1985. 400 pp. Reprint. New York: Dover, 1961.

Abridgement. THE EXPLORATION OF THE COLORADO RIVER. With an introduction by Wallace Stegner. Chicago: University of Chicago Press, 1957. 137 pp.

Abridgement. DOWN THE COLORADO: DIARY OF THE FIRST TRIP THROUGH THE GRAND CANYON, 1869. Photos and epilogue by Eliot Porter. Foreword and notes by Don D. Fowler. New York: E.P. Dutton, 1969. 168 pp.

May-Sep 1869. Official journal of Major Powell's first expedition to explore the Green and Colorado rivers and geological survey of the area; from Green River Station, Wyoming, down the Green through Utah, joining the Colorado and continuing through the Grand Canyon; geological and scenic descriptions; logistics of exploration and survival; the loss of four of eleven men and two of four boats; an important scientific and geographic achievement of a one-armed Civil War veteran and professor of geology at Illinois State Normal University.

"Down the Colorado." AMERICAN HERITAGE 20, no. 6 (1969):52-61, 83.

May-Sep 1869. Extracts.

In THE FRONTIER EXPERIENCE, by Robert V. Hine, pp. 395-400.

Aug 1869. Extracts.

Darrah, William Culp, ed. "Major Powell's Journal, July 2-Aug 28, 1869." UTAH HISTORICAL QUARTERLY 15 (1947):125-131.

Jul-Aug 1869. Extracts.

Fowler, Don D. and Fowler, Catherine S., eds. "John Wesley Powell's Journal." THE SMITHSONIAN JOURNAL OF HISTORY 3, no. 2 (1968):1-44.

May-Oct, 1871, Aug-Sep 1872. Powell's second expedition down the Green and Colorado and geological survey of the area from Green River, Wyoming, to Kanab Creek; scientific notes and logistics of river exploration through the Grand Canyon, Marble Canyon, etc.; dealings with Jacob Hamblin; original photographs by E.O. Beaman.

PRICE, MORGAN PHILIPS, b. 1885   4945

AMERICA AFTER SIXTY YEARS: THE TRAVEL DIARIES OF TWO

GENERATIONS OF ENGLISHMEN. Edited by W.E. Price. London: George Allen & Unwin, 1936. 235 pp.

1869, 1878, 1934. Appealing diaries of father's and son's cross-country travels in the United States, edited in undated form by the son, William E. Price; notes of two trips by the elder Price and his companions, all members of the House of Commons and among the first to cross the United States by train; the son's 1934 traverse of the same route, pursuing interests in agriculture, economic and social conditions, etc., particularly the effects of the Depression and New Deal.

PUTNAM, GEORGE PALMER, 1814-1872   4946

Myerson, Joel, ed. "George Palmer Putnam: Literary London in 1869." MANUSCRIPTS 38 (1986):155-160.

Mar 1869. Brief letter-diary kept by publisher, head of the firm G.P. Putnam, on a business trip to London; escorted by Queen Victoria herself on her yacht ALBERT, "very considerate of H.M."; a round of social life and meetings with publishers; hearing Charles Spurgeon preach with ten thousand people in attendance.

SMITH, LUCY P. VINCENT, 1842-1933   4947

In TWELVE WORKS OF NAIVE GENIUS, edited by Walter M. Teller, pp. 240-254. New York: Harcourt, Brace, Jovanovich, 1972.

1869-1874. Extracts from the diary of a whaling captain's wife; life aboard the NAUTILUS for over four years with her husband, George A. Smith, and son who was three at outset of the voyage from New Bedford, Massachusetts; sewing and caring for family; loneliness and tedium, especially when left in Hawaii while the ship went to the Arctic; notes on difficulty with crew and first mate.

SUMNER, JOHN COLTON, 1840-1907   4948

Marston, O. Dock, ed. "The Lost Journal of John Colton Sumner." UTAH HISTORICAL QUARTERLY 37 (1969):173-189.

Extracts in RIVER REFLECTIONS, edited by Verne Huser, pp. 37-42.

May-Jun 1869. Journal of Powell's lead boatman on the first Colorado River expedition and geological survey of the area; from Green River, Wyoming, to the Uinta basin, with notes of distances, portages, rapids, surrounding terrain, discomforts and dangers; good descriptions of scenery and exhilaration of the adventure: "We plunge along singing, yelling like drunken sailors, all feeling that such rides do not come everyday"; the activities of Powell, referred to as "the Professor."

Darrah, William Culp, ed. "J.C. Sumner's Journal." UTAH HISTORICAL QUARTERLY 15 (1947):109-124.

Jul-Aug 1869. Continuing down the Colorado through the Grand Canyon.

WHITWORTH, JAMES EDWIN   4949

McDonald, Lucile. "On the Duwamish Route to Lake Washington." SEA CHEST 9 (1976):152-159.

Jan-Jun 1869. Extracts from brief diaries and logs of five scow trips on the Duwamish River of a barge skipper working for his father, the Rev. George Whitworth, part owner of the Lake Washington Coal Company.

WILEY, CALVIN HENDERSON   **4950**

Wiley, Mary M., ed. "With Calvin H. Wiley in Tennessee, through Unpublished Letters." NORTH CAROLINA HISTORICAL REVIEW 36 (1959):72-95.

 1869-1874. Diary and letter extracts, within article describing Raleigh, North Carolina, educator's period of duty as superintendent of the American Bible Society for middle and east Tennessee; travels on horseback, with a good picture of post-Civil War disarray in which he found the area; a cholera epidemic in 1873; activities at Knoxville.

WOOLLEY, EDWIN GORDON, 1844-1930   **4951**

Crampton, C. Gregory and Miller, David E., eds. "Journal of Two Campaigns by the Utah Territorial Militia against the Navajo Indians." UTAH HISTORICAL QUARTERLY 29 (1961):148-176.

 Feb-May, Nov 1869. March from St. George under Capt. Willis Copelan in southern Utah and northern Arizona; terrain, camps, conditions, etc.; evidences of and encounters with Indians; fording the Colorado at Crossing of the Fathers; November expedition to Kanab under Col. James Andrus; little action in the campaigns, part of the broader Mormon-Navaho War.

1870

ARNY, WILLIAM FREDERICK MILTON, 1813-1881   **4952**

INDIAN AGENT IN NEW MEXICO: THE JOURNAL OF SPECIAL AGENT W.F.M. ARNY. Edited by Lawrence R. Murphy. Southwestern Series, no. 5. Santa Fe: Stagecoach Press, 1967. 60 pp.

 May-Nov 1870. Travels throughout New Mexico to conduct a census of Indians, examine land titles, settle reservation disputes and assess English literacy of Indians as a special agent for President Grant's new Indian "peace policy"; good descriptions of terrain and scenery; considerable information on villages, especially Apache and Ute, as well as individuals whom he interviewed, from an apparent sympathetic and enlightened viewpoint; census statistics appended.

BISHOP, FRANCIS MARION, 1843-1933   **4953**

Kelly, Charles, ed. "Captain Francis Marion Bishop's Journal." UTAH HISTORICAL QUARTERLY 15 (1947):155-238.

 1870-1872 (with gaps). Journal of Powell's scholarly Mormon topographer on his second Colorado River expedition and geological survey of the area; preparations; departure from Green River; the usual notes of terrain, camps, rapids and portages, but quite full and interesting on the activities of various members of the expedition and on geological and biological features of the Green and Colorado canyons and surroundings.

BOYES, CHARLES   **4954**

Meamber, Bernice Soule. "A Rancher's Life - In Charles Boyes' Day." SISKIYOU PIONEER IN FOLKLORE, FACT AND FICTION. 4, no. 10 (1977):102-111.

 1870-1890. Extracts within article describing life of a Butte Valley, California, rancher; work, vicissitudes and profits of cattle and horse breeding; a few notes of family and social life, with references to local people.

BRIGHT, ABBIE, 1848-1926   **4955**

Snell, Joseph W., ed. "Roughing It on Her Kansas Claim." KANSAS HISTORICAL QUARTERLY 37 (1971):233-268, 394-428.

 1870-1871. Lively Pennsylvania girl's visit with her brother Hiram's family at Red Oak Shelter, Indiana, where she enjoyed farm and social life, as well as teaching school; then by train and stagecoach to join her brother Philip on his claim in Kansas; excellent account of stagecoach travel, hotels and adventures of a circumspect young lady traveling alone; keeping house for her brother while suffering with "fever and ague"; battling such hazards as snakes, prairie fires and stampeding Texas longhorns; eventually taking out her own claim on Osage Indian land before returning to Indiana; a good picture of homesteading life by an observant and articulate diarist.

BRYCE, JAMES BRYCE, 1838-1922   **4956**

Lefcowitz, Allen B. and Barbara F. "James Bryce's First Visit to America: The New England Sections of His 1870 Journal and Related Correspondence." NEW ENGLAND QUARTERLY 50 (1977):314-331.

 Sep 1870. Extracts from American travel journal of an English intellectual, later author of THE AMERICAN COMMONWEALTH and ambassador to the United States; experiences mainly in the Boston area discussing literature and ideas with Longfellow, Lowell, Emerson, etc., and establishing friendships with Oliver Wendell Holmes, Jr., and Charles William Eliot; hiking in the White Mountains, with good descriptions of scenery, and traveling about New England by stagecoach and train; some evidence of post-Civil War Anglo-American attitudes and relations.

BUCKLEY, MICHAEL BERNARD, 1831-1872   **4957**

DIARY OF A TOUR IN AMERICA. Edited by Kate Buckley. Dublin: Sealy, Bryers & Walker, 1886. 384 pp.

 1870-1871. Irish priest's diary of a tour to raise funds for completion of Cork Cathedral; on the CHINA to New York, with entertaining notes on the voyage and social life among his fellow cabin passengers; tourist experiences and fund-raising in New York, thence to Niagara and Canada; in Boston, "the Athens of America," expressing concern for difficulties of the Irish there and the "changes wrought in their manners by settlement in this country"; a visit to Cooperstown, New York, and "Leatherstocking's Land"; frank opinions throughout on American mores and customs; references to many priests, Irish immigrants and donors to his cause.

CONGER, CLARA, 1853?-1879   **4958**

Conger, Roger N. "The Emigration of the N.H. Conger Family from Oneida, Illinois, to Waco, Texas." SOUTHWESTERN HISTORICAL QUARTERLY 64 (1960):80-91.

 Sep-Oct 1870. Extracts from the diary of the seventeen-year-old daughter of Norman H. Conger kept during the extended family's trip to settle in Texas; wagon route through Missouri and Kansas; camps, meals, scenery and people en route; some problems, especially illness of several in the party.

COOK, CHARLES H.   4959

Anderson, Charles A., ed. ''Day Book of Rev. Charles H. Cook.'' PRESBYTERIAN HISTORICAL SOCIETY JOURNAL 37 (1959):104-121.

Sep 1870-Feb 1871. Missionary diary of a German immigrant Methodist minister who later became a Presbyterian; train travel from Illinois to Colorado, then by stagecoach and wagon to Arizona to take a teaching post at the government Pima agency; preaching en route to finance his journey; notes on towns, forts, countryside, etc.; at Pima, starting his school; studies of Pima language and missionary work, with instruction in Christianity part of the school lessons.

DOANE, GUSTAVUS CHEYNEY, 1840-1892   4960

In BATTLE DRUMS AND GEYSERS: THE LIFE AND JOURNALS OF LT. GUSTAVUS CHEYNEY DOANE, SOLDIER AND EXPLORER OF THE YELLOWSTONE AND SNAKE RIVER REGIONS, by Orrin H. and Lorraine Bonney, pp. 215-574 passim. Chicago: Sage Books, 1970.

Aug-Sep 1870. Official journal of the Washburn-Doane scientific expedition to explore the area later to become Yellowstone National Park; route from Fort Ellis, Montana, along Yellowstone River with Henry Washburn, Nathaniel Langford and six others; daily temperature, barometric reading and elevation; notes on terrain, scenery, wildlife and fantastic geological features of the area; fears of Indian attack; great problems with one member, Jacob Smith; the rescue of Truman C. Everts, lost for over a month from his colleagues.

Oct-Dec 1876. Official report of early winter exploration of Snake River by boat, which was dismantled for portaging and reassembled; departure from Fort Ellis through Yellowstone region to the Snake with eight well chosen men; constant dangers and obstacles, combined with difficulties of winter survival; ingenious solutions to some problems, others proving almost calamitous; valuable assistance from trapper John Pierce at Jackson Hole; period of near starvation followed by recuperation at Keenan City, Idaho.

Bonney, Orrin H. and Bonney, Lorraine, eds. ''Lieutenant G.C. Doane: His Yellowstone Exploration Journal.'' JOURNAL OF THE WEST 9 (1970):222-239.

Aug-Sep 1870. Extracts, beginning at Fort Ellis; detailed description of the mud springs of Yellowstone; a few notes on Indians.

''Gustavus C. Doane's Military Expedition to Cariboo Mountain.'' IDAHO YESTERDAYS 19, no. 4 (1976):25-27.

Dec 1876. Extract covering a side trip to the Cariboo Mountains on his way from Fort Ellis to Fort Hall; description of Keenan City and some of the miners in the area.

EDMONDS, JOSEPH A., 1837-1913   4961

Moffitt, James W., ed. ''Diary of Joseph A. Edmonds.'' CHRONICLES OF OKLAHOMA 17 (1939):309-314.

Nov 1870. Extract relating to Oklahoma of horseback journey from Lexington, Missouri, to Texas, through Indian Territory; camps, distances, scenery; encounters with cattle drives coming up from Texas and with United States marshals controlling liquor traffic.

GERITY, WILL S.   4962

Wisbey, Herbert A., ed. ''Camping on Keuka Lake.'' YORK STATE TRADITION 27, no. 4 (1973):36-42; 28, no. 1 (1974):40-52.

Jul-Aug 1870. Extracts from the diary of a young Elmira, New York, druggist; an account of camping and fishing with the Minisink Magnolia Fishing Club, a group of young men from Elmira and Waverly, all named in the diary; setting up a cozy camp by the lake, but relying on nearby farm produce to vary the diet of fish; prayers and Bible reading.

GILLETTE, WARREN C., 1832-1918   4963

Cockhill, Brian, ed. ''The Quest of Warren Gillette.'' MONTANA: THE MAGAZINE OF WESTERN HISTORY 22, no. 3 (1972):12-30.

Aug-Sep 1870. Helena merchant's account of the Washburn-Doane expedition to explore the Yellowstone region; good details of the incidents and members of the expedition; notes on hot springs, geysers and geological features; camps and difficulties of terrain; lengthy, ultimately successful, search for Truman Everts, who had become separated from the group.

HUGGINS, EDWARD   4964

''Journal of Occurrences at Nisqually in 1870.'' WASHINGTON HISTORICAL QUARTERLY 25 (1934):60-64.

May-Jun 1870. Hudson's Bay Company official's record continued after he acquired the old Fort Nisqually as a homestead when the Company ceased operations there; farming, fur trading, a few business details; references to activities of William F. Tolmie.

LANE, EMMA DURANT, 1852-1922   4965

THE DIARIES AND MEMOIRS OF EMMA (DURANT) LANE. Edited by Alexander G. Rose. Family Document Series, 20. Baltimore: Rose, 1978. 163 leaves passim.

1870-1922. Mostly narrative memoirs with a few dated entries increasing from 1916; life of a teacher in various midwestern towns including St. Charles, Illinois; a happy marriage of less than two years to Dr. Larmon B. Lane, some thirty years her senior, with a long description of his fatal illness; later teaching and travels to Biloxi, Mississippi, New Orleans and Santa Barbara, California; vacations at Madeline Island, Wisconsin; much family information of possible genealogical interest.

LANGFORD, NATHANIEL PITT, 1832-1911   4966

DIARY OF THE WASHBURN EXPEDITION TO THE YELLOWSTONE AND FIREHOLE RIVERS IN THE YEAR 1870. St. Paul? Minn.: N.p., 1905. 122 pp. Reprint. THE DISCOVERY OF YELLOWSTONE PARK: JOURNAL OF THE WASHBURN EXPEDITION TO THE YELLOWSTONE AND FIREHOLE RIVERS IN THE YEAR 1870. Lincoln: University of Nebraska Press, 1972. 125 pp.

THE DISCOVERY OF YELLOWSTONE PARK. 2d ed. Approved by the National Park Service. St. Paul: J.E. Haynes, 1923. 188 pp.

Aug-Sep 1870. Diary of organizer and member of Yellowstone exploraton expedition led by Henry D. Washburn and Gustavus Doane; detailed descriptions of mountains, geysers, hot springs, waterfalls, etc., by the future first superintendent of Yellowstone National Park; comments on fear of Indians, hazards of weather and terrain; humorous incidents of camp life.

OLNHAUSEN, MARY PHINNEY, von, 1818-1902   **4967**

ADVENTURES OF AN ARMY NURSE IN TWO WARS. By James Phinney Munroe. Boston: Little, Brown, 1904. Diary, pp. 225-236, 265-280.

Nov-Dec 1870, Mar-Apr 1871. Diary of American widow, former Civil War nurse, now volunteering in the Franco-Prussian War; frustration at inability to serve fully because of uncooperative officials and German nurses; condemnation of hospital conditions and medical procedures which compared unfavorably with those of her Civil War experience; disparaging remarks concerning the French; war's destruction and suffering; transporting wounded through France to Germany; notes on Lagny, Blois, Orleans, Tours, Vendome and Corbeil, France, and Munich and Nuremberg, Germany.

ROBERTS, ANNIE GIBSON, 1849-1914   **4968**

In A SUMMER ON THE PLAINS, by Brian Pohanka, pp. 22-65. Mattituck, N.Y.: J.M. Carroll, 1983.

Jun-Sep 1870. Young woman's visit to her aunt and uncle, Maj. George Gibson, commander at Fort Hays; the beginning of a lifelong friendship with Elizabeth Custer; parties and dances, frequently escorted by Capt. George W. Yates, her future husband and one of many admirers; walks and horseback rides including a ''grand buffalo hunt'' in which she made a kill; return by train to her home in St. Louis with happy memories of frontier garrison social life.

SCOTT, P.G.   **4969**

''Diary of a Freighting Trip from Kit Carson to Trinidad in 1870.'' COLORADO MAGAZINE 8 (1931):146-154.

Aug-Sep 1870. Canadian's record of work as a teamster for a Mexican freight wagon train; interesting but none too favorable notes on Mexican ways; subsisting at times on bad water and prairie dog meat; suffering from a chest illness, possibly tuberculosis, and sad yearnings for his home and family in Canada; good descriptions of southern Colorado towns and terrain.

SEWARD, WILLIAM HENRY, 1801-1872   **4970**

WILLIAM H. SEWARD'S TRAVELS AROUND THE WORLD. Edited by Olive R. Seward. New York: D. Appleton, 1873. 730 pp.

1870-1871. A full and exotic travel diary of Lincoln's former secretary of state and instigator of Alaska purchase; an incredible catalog of places and experiences, from Mormon Utah to Chinese opium dens, palaces of Indian maharajas, Egyptian pyramids, the Nile, partly finished Suez Canal, Palestine, Europe, etc.; an audience with Pope Pius IX; many modes of travel, from steamers COLORADO, TRAVANCORE, ALASKA, etc., to camelback, cheerfully endured by the sixty-nine year old diarist, who was treated variously as an American dignitary and an inconsequential tourist.

SHRODE, MARIA HARGRAVE, b. 1826   **4971**

''Overland by Ox Train in 1870.'' HISTORICAL SOCIETY OF SOUTHERN CALIFORNIA QUARTERLY 26 (1944):9-37.

In HO FOR CALIFORNIA!, edited by Sandra L. Myres, pp. 255-295.

May-Dec 1870. Journal of overland trip from Texas to California via Southwest; travel and camp conditions, health problems and

children's activities; descriptions of the countryside, especially Mexican farms.

VAN OSTRAND, FERDINAND, 1848-1873   **4972**

Reid, Russell, ed. ''Diary of Ferdinand A. Van Ostrand.'' NORTH DAKOTA HISTORICAL QUARTERLY 9 (1942):219-242; 10 (1943):3-46, 83-124.

1870-1872 (with gaps). Dakota fur trader's diary beginning during a visit home in Marion, New York; retrospective account of journey from Fort Berthold and his stay at Marion; dated entries covering return by train and stagecoach to clerk in the store at Fort Sully; a journey to Fort Rice; activities at Fort Berthold, with references there to traders, military personnel, Indians and some unsavory western characters; Missouri steamboat arrivals; a plague of grasshoppers; a good picture of fur trading life.

1871

ANON.   **4973**

DIARY OF THE JESUIT RESIDENCE OF OUR LADY OF GUADALUPE PARISH, CONEJOS, COLORADO. Edited by Marianne L. Stoller and Thomas J. Steele. Translated by Jose B. Fernandez. Colorado College Studies, no. 19. Colorado Springs: Colorado College, 1982. 227 pp.

1871-1875. Church activities and pastoral work as recorded by several Jesuit missionary priests serving a Spanish parish in the San Luis Valley of southern Colorado; visiting remote members and trying to reunite a previously neglected and schismatic congregation, including Penitentes; references to many landowners and others over a wide area; yearly statistics of baptisms, marriages and funerals. A work in progress expected to publish the complete diaries to 1886 and extracts thereafter.

AVERY, SAMUEL PUTNAM, 1822-1904   **4974**

THE DIARIES, 1871-1882, OF SAMUEL P. AVERY, ART DEALER. Edited by Madeleine F. Beaufort, Herbert L. Kleinfield and Jeanne K. Welcher. New York: Arno, 1979. 936 pp. Diary, pp. 1-730.

1871-1882. The business diary of an art dealer and associate of George A. Lucas in France, England, Holland, Germany and Belgium; purchases and commissions for American collectors William H. Huntington, John T. Johnston, William H. Stewart, George Whitney, William T. Walters, Cornelius and William H. Vanderbuilt and the Metropolitan Museum of Art; transactions with numerous dealers and auction houses; a record of style and taste of the period with hundreds of artists and their works named.

BALTZLY, BENJAMIN, 1835-1883   **4975**

BENJAMIN BALTZLY: PHOTOGRAPHS AND JOURNAL OF AN EXPEDITION THROUGH BRITISH COLUMBIA. Edited by Andrew Birrell. Toronto: Coach House Press, 1978. 159 pp. Journal, pp. 107-159.

Jun-Dec 1871. Journal of Ohio photographer who was member of Geological Survey of Canada expedition; train travel from Michigan to California, noting scenery and emigrant trains that were ''wending their way along the dusty plains toward the far west''; by steamer JOHN L. STEVENS from San Francisco to

Portland and stagecoach to points in Washington Territory; describing and photographing Victoria, Indians and villages along the rivers, lakes and scenic spots in the Canadian Rockies until difficult mountain terrain and snow forced their return; loss of some goods and animals and less photographic success than expected.

DEADY, MATTHEW PAUL, 1824-1893   4976

PHARISEE AMONG PHILISTINES. Edited by Malcolm Clark, Jr. Portland: Oregon Historical Society, 1975. 2 vols.

1871-1892. Well kept diary of busy, civic-minded man, federal district court judge, member of the board of regents of University of Oregon and vestryman of Trinity Episcopal Church, Portland; notes on many legal cases and decisions; social, cultural and political affairs of the city and state; literary opinions on a broad range of reading and on professional and amateur entertainers; many names of friends and associates in law, business and city affairs; trips to San Francisco where he presided over the Ninth Circuit Court; fund raising and support of the Library Association of Portland; comments on clergy and sermons at Trinity Church; indefatigable committee work; personal and family finances.

FLETCHER, ROBERT, 1847-1936   4978

Richardson, Leon B. "A Hanover Diary." DARTMOUTH ALUMNI MAGAZINE 40, no. 4 (1948):16-19; no. 6, 17-20.

1871-1934. Article containing extracts from Dartmouth Thayer School of Engineering professor's lifelong diary, recording his methodical daily regimen and events at the college and in Hanover; social life, student disorders and local customs; weather, from the ordinary to such dramatic events as blizzards, floods and heat waves; accidents, fires and epidemics; diarist's attendance at public lectures but avoidance of theater because of Baptist scruples; opinions, mostly of a Republican bent, on local and national politics; volunteer civic work, including holding many city offices and planning and installing the town water system; church and temperance activities, with notes on liquor raids during Prohibition; reaction to Dwight L. Moody's preaching in Hanover; a few notes on his own family life, as well as improvements to the old house in which he lived for sixty-four years.

HART, WILLIAM JEREMIAH, 1843-1921   4979

Turner, Charles W., ed. "A Virginia Small Farmer's Life after the Civil War." VIRGINIA MAGAZINE OF HISTORY AND BIOGRAPHY 63 (1955):286-305.

1871-1873. Extracts from diary of a Louisa County farmer, with mainly brief notes of his own agricultural tasks and those of his hired black workers, indicating a wide variety of crops and livestock; visits among friends and relatives and activities at the Elk Creek Baptist Church.

HILLERS, JOHN K., 1843-1925   4980

"PHOTOGRAPHED ALL THE BEST SCENERY": JACK HILLER'S DIARY OF THE POWELL EXPEDITIONS. Edited by Don D. Fowler. University of Utah Publications in the American West, vol. 9. Salt Lake City: University of Utah Press, 1972. 225 pp.

1871-1875 (with gaps). Record of a boatman with Powell's second Colorado River expedition and photographer for his Rocky

Mountain survey; running rapids, portaging, fishing, hunting; repairing boats and making moccasins; camping activities on Fourth of July; serving as photographer with Powell's Geological and Geographical Survey of the Rocky Mountain Region and in Utah and Nevada where Powell was investigating Indian problems as special commissioner of Indian affairs; photographing southern Paiute Indians and Indians in Oklahoma for Centennial Exposition for Smithsonian and Bureau of Indian Affairs exhibits.

JAMES, CHARLES ALBERT, 1841-1875   4981

James, Fleming H., ed. "Excerpts from the Mexican Diary of Charles Albert James." NEW MEXICO HISTORICAL REVIEW 30 (1955):44-71.

Aug 1871-Jun 1872. Extracts of tubercular Texan's search for improved health in northern Mexico; interesting description of a huge ranch, Hacienda San Blas, at which he stayed, contrasting its appearance with milieu of southern plantations; a celebration at Santa Rosa; evidences of insurrection in progress and rumors of Juárez's victories; a battle at Monclova; celebrations, social life, military activities and rumors at Saltillo; full and interesting descriptions of Mexican customs.

JONES, STEPHEN VANDIVER, 1840-1920   4982

Gregory, Herbert E., ed. "The Journal of Stephen Vandiver Jones." UTAH HISTORICAL QUARTERLY 16-17 (1948-1949):11-174.

1871-1872. Meticulous journal of Washburn, Illinois, teacher and self-taught scientist who was assistant topographer for Powell's second Colorado River expedition; daily activities of Powell and his colleagues; notes on geology, topography, fossils, scenery, etc.; an important document in the exploration of Utah, the Colorado and Green rivers and their canyons.

MANDELBAUM, L.   4983

"Texas Merchants after the Civil War." AMERICAN JEWISH ARCHIVES 12 (1960):71-74.

Feb 1871. Extracts from report of New Haven, Connecticut, man's visit to merchant relatives, Asher and Philip Mandelbaum, in Bremond and Kosse, Texas; minute descriptions of stores and merchandise, from clothing to pistols; favorable impression of local people and modes of doing business.

POWELL, WALTER CLEMENT, 1850-1883   4984

Kelly, Charles, ed. "Journal of W.C. Powell." UTAH HISTORICAL QUARTERLY 16-17 (1948-1949):253-478.

1871-1872. Engaging journal of John Wesley Powell's young cousin from Naperville, Illinois, and member of the second Powell expedition down the Green and Colorado rivers and geological survey of the area; good details of rapids, portages and climbs; notes on Indians; frequent references to his brother Morris for whom he kept the journal; reading in the small library carried with the expedition; "cleaned my gun inside and out and read Shakespeare nearly all day"; studying photography; valuable for the personal aspects of the undertaking and the diarist's candid opinions of events and people.

RICKETSON, ANNIE HOLMES, b. 1841?   4985

THE JOURNAL OF ANNIE HOLMES RICKETSON ON THE

WHALESHIP A.R. TUCKER. New Bedford, Mass.: Old Dartmouth Historical Society, 1958. 79 pp.

1871-1874. Diary of the wife of whaling captain Daniel Lake Ricketson, kept while she accompanied her husband on a whaling voyage in the Atlantic and Indian oceans; ports of call in Azores and Canary islands, Ternate, New Guinea, etc.; the birth and death of her baby; excellent details of work of whalers, both the routine and excitement, and social life in ports.

Extract in A DAY AT A TIME, edited by Margo Culley, pp. 143-148.

Aug-Oct 1871. Storms at sea; in port for birth and death of her first baby.

ROSSER, THOMAS LAFAYETTE, 1836-1910   4986

Hoyt, William D., ed. "Rosser's Journal, Northern Pacific Railroad Survey, September, 1871." NORTH DAKOTA HISTORICAL QUARTERLY 10 (1943):47-51.

Sep 1871. Engineer's account of a segment of a railroad survey along the Heart River to the Badlands; conditions for laying railroad bed; difficulties with wagons and with Indians burning the prairie.

SCHENCK, ANNIE B.   4987

Filipiak, Jack D., ed. "Camping Vacation, 1871," COLORADO MAGAZINE 42 (1965):185-215.

Aug 1871. Young woman's account of a wagon trip to Twin Lakes area with her uncle, George Dwight, and his family; list of supplies, food and equipment; enjoyment of Rocky Mountain scenery and solitude; notes on campsites, ranches and mining settlements, including South Park, Montgomery, Montezuma, Georgetown, Fairplay, etc.; excitement of climbing Silver Heel Mountain; a happy and adventurous vacation.

SHERMAN, WILLIAM TECUMSEH   4988

"General Sherman's Tour of Europe." CENTURY ILLUSTRATED MAGAZINE 57 (November 1898-April 1899):729-740.

Dec 1871-Apr 1872. Diary extracts describing famous general's journey through Europe, accompanied by President Grant's son Fred; Gibralter, Spain, France, Italy, Egypt, Turkey and Russia; description of various sights; social engagements with diplomats, military men and Americans living abroad; meetings with political leaders and royalty including the Pope, the Khedive Ismail and Sultan Abdul-Aziz; criticism of Prince Frederick Charles of Prussia; an American view of European notions of hierarchy.

"General Sherman in Russia." CENTURY ILLUSTRATED MAGAZINE 57 (November 1898-Apr 1899):866-875.

Apr-May 1872. Extracts covering continuation of European tour; travel through the Caucasus and visits to Moscow and St. Petersburg among other stops; conversations with Czar Alexander II and members of his family; notes on Russian railroads, cossacks, etc.

"Sherman on Franco-Prussian Battlefields." CENTURY IL-LUSTRATED MAGAZINE 58 (May-Oct 1899):278-287.

Jun-Sep 1872. Extracts dealing with final segment of European tour; sizing up Gen. Helmuth C. B. von Moltke in Berlin; watching Eduard Strauss conduct in Vienna; diarist's commentary on various sites of the Franco-Prussian War; his thoughts on British-

United States relations during the Civil War and current war claims disputes; more meetings with European political leaders and royalty including the British royal family at Cowes.

SHIPP, ELLIS REYNOLDS, 1847-1939   4989

THE EARLY AUTOBIOGRAPHY AND DIARY OF ELLIS REYNOLDS SHIPP. Edited by Ellis Musser. Salt Lake City?, 1962. 292 pp. Diary pp. 69-276.

1871-1878. Young Salt Lake City Mormon woman's diary; early days of marriage to Milford Bard Shipp and dutiful acceptance of his other wives; devotion to her children; longing for learning; traveling to Philadelphia alone and studying medicine at Women's Medical College; homesickness and loneliness during long months of study and living under spartan conditions; greatly enjoying a visit of her husband and their pleasant trip to Washington, D.C., and Mount Vernon; returning to Salt Lake City and later, with her infant daughter, resuming her studies in Philadelphia until graduation.

SJOBORG, SOFIA CHARLOTTA, b. 1805?   4990

Westerberg, Wesley M., trans. "Journey to Florida." SWEDISH PIONEER HISTORICAL QUARTERLY 26 (1975):24-45.

Apr-May 1871. A sixty-six-year-old woman's journey on the ANGLIA with a large group of Swedish immigrants; good notes of ship travel, consoling herself for its difficulties by prayer, Bible reading and companionship of relatives and friends; from New York to Savannah, thence to settle at Lake Jessup, Florida, where the diary ends with the immigrants living in tents and beginning "work on our new settlement" under August Henschen.

SLAUGHTER, B.F.   4991

"Portions of the Diary of Dr. B.F. Slaughter, Dakota Territory." NORTH DAKOTA HISTORY 1, no. 2 (1927):36-40.

Jun-Aug 1871. A diary kept at Fort Rice by assistant surgeon for the Seventeenth Infantry; a Sioux raid on cattle belonging to the fort; an insertion by his wife complaining that the diary is too bare a record of army events.

STEWARD, JOHN F., 1841-1915   4992

Darrah, William Culp, ed. "Journal of John F. Steward." UTAH HISTORICAL QUARTERLY 16-17 (1948-1949):175-251.

Mar-Nov 1871. Journal of a serious amateur geologist from Plano, Illinois, who was Powell's assistant on his second expedition down the Green and Colorado rivers; important technical notes, especially on geology, fossils and logistics of the enterprise, but of less historical value because of later editing; curious details, such as "rested poorly on account of having been kept awake by the splashing of beavers"; inabiltiy to complete the voyage because of aggravation of an old Civil War wound.

THOMPSON, ALMON HARRIS, 1839-1906   4993

Gregory, Herbert E., ed. "Diary of Almon Harris Thompson, Geographer, Exploration of the Colorado River of the West and Its Tributaries." UTAH HISTORICAL QUARTERLY 7 (1939):3-139. Diary, pp. 11-128.

1871-1875. Important account by geographer and cartographer for Powell's second expedition and subsequent mapping of much of Utah; notes on terrain, wildlife and geological features; astronomical observations; brief but interesting notes on expedition members and their interactions; encounters with Indians; dealings with Jacob Hamblin.

WARNER, LUNA E.   4994

Bivans, Venola Lewis, ed. "The Diary of Luna E. Warner, a Kansas Teenager of the Early 1870s." KANSAS HISTORICAL QUARTERLY 35 (1969):276-311, 411-441.

1871-1874. Barre, Massachusetts, girl's journey by train with her family to homestead in Kansas; good details of building and furnishing a house, farming and gardening; her delight in wildflowers and animals of the prairie, family and social life, dances and other activities at Cawker; books read aloud in the home and playing the piano; problems, including rattlesnakes, prairie fires, malaria and an uncle's drinking and delirium tremens; buffalo hunts reported secondhand.

YOUNG, MARY ELIZA WILLARD   4995

McDonough, Marian McIntyre. "Quest for Health Not Wealth." MONTANA: THE MAGAZINE OF WESTERN HISTORY 14, no. 1 (1964):25-37.

Jun-Oct 1871. Extracts within article about a Chicago woman's move to Colorado seeking a cure for consumption; wagon travel from Fort Leavenworth with a party consisting of her husband William Bangs Young, their children, Dr. Henry Gatschell and several friends; route along the Kansas Pacific railroad and through towns to Colorado Springs, where her husband became a prominent banker.

1872

BEALS, ELLA AMANDA, b. 1857?   4996

Clark, R.C., ed. "Oregon to California by Wagon." OREGON HISTORICAL QUARTERLY 38 (1937):109-114.

Aug-Sep 1872. A fifteen-year-old girl's account of a journey with her family from Day Creek, Oregon, to Marysville, California; mostly route, distances and camps, including one they called flea camp, "as the fleas bothered us considerable."

BREWSTER, WILLIAM, 1851-1919   4997

OCTOBER FARM, FROM THE CONCORD JOURNALS AND DIARIES. With an introduction by Daniel C. French. Cambridge: Harvard University Press, 1936, 285 pp.

1872-1919. Eminent ornithologist's nature diary, mainly of bird and animal life near Concord, Massachusetts; delightful style in the Thoreau manner.

"The Birds of the Lake Umbagog Region of Maine." HARVARD MUSEUM OF COMPARATIVE ZOOLOGY BULLETIN 66 (1924):1-209.

1876-1909 (with gaps). Extracts from ornithologist's journal of collecting and observing expeditions in Maine and New Hampshire; birds observed, dates and weather conditions.

CONCORD RIVER. Edited by Smith O. Dexter. Cambridge: Harvard University Press, 1937. 258 pp. passim.

1879-1919. Extracts arranged topically according to birds observed, overlooking no detail of appearance, song or habit; sensitive, unadorned nature, notes made at various seasons of the year on the Concord River; valuable to the specialist and engaging for the general reader.

Simpson, Marcus B., ed. "William Brewster's Exploraton of the Southern Appalchian Mountains." NORTH CAROLINA HISTORICAL REVIEW 57 (1980):43-77.

May-Jun 1885. Search for little-known species of birds in the mountains around Asheville and in the Highlands area; train travel in North Carolina, with forays on foot and horseback to observe birds and collect specimens; scientific notes on dozens of birds and other wildlife still abundant in the virgin forests.

In FRANK M. CHAPMAN IN FLORIDA: HIS JOURNALS & LETTERS, by Frank A. Chapman, pp. 100-117. Gainesville: University of Florida Press, 1967.

Mar-Apr 1890. Journal of first ornithological exploration of the Suwannee River, made with Frank M. Chapman; natural history observations and listing of birds seen and collected.

FUNK, JOHN F.   4998

Schnell, Kempes, ed. "John F. Funk's Land Inspection Trips as Recorded in His Diaries." MENNONITE QUARTERLY REVIEW 24 (1950):295-311.

Sep-Oct 1872, Jun-Jul 1873. Extracts covering quest of a Mennonite minister and editor of the HERALD OF TRUTH in Elkhart, Indiana, for land on which to settle Mennonite immigrants escaping persecution in Russia; with Bernard Warkentin, a Russian, through Minnesota and eastern Dakotas as guest of the Northern Pacific Railroad; descriptions of farms, land and water quality and condition of people; concern for plight of Indians; second trip through Manitoba, Minnesota, Dakotas, Iowa and Missouri with a larger delegation of Mennonites seeking prospects for immigration; travel by riverboat, train and wagon; during both trips, many settlers mentioned by name.

HAMP, SIDFORD 1855-1919   4999

Brayer, Herbert Oliver, ed. "Exploring the Yellowstone with Hayden." ANNALS OF WYOMING 14 (1942):253-298.

Extracts in DIARY OF AMERICA, edited by Josef and Dorothy Berger, pp. 515-519.

May-Nov 1872. English teenager's delightful diary of the 1872 Geological Survey Expedition under Ferdinand V. Hayden; uneventful ocean crossing and visits to New York, Washington, D.C., and Niagara Falls, then by train to Salt Lake City; by horseback to Yellowstone, where he worked as a "topographical assistant" to the expedition; ascent of Grand Teton by James Stevenson and Nathaniel P. Langford; enthusiastic descriptions, especially of geysers and hot springs; camp life, conversations, food, etc; admiration for work of photographer William Henry Jackson; return to Salt Lake by stagecoach and robbery by "highwaymen"; amusing chauvinisms, but basic approval of American ways, by one who later immigrated and became a journalist at Colorado Springs.

HANCOCK, EDWIN B., b. 1856?   5000

Dixon, Ford, ed. "The Diary of Edwin B. Hancock." TEXANA 3 (1965):297-320.

Nov 1872-Apr 1873. Diary of a sixteen-year-old Austin schoolboy, later a prominent lawyer, kept while he was living with the family of John C. Raymond; activities at the Austin Normal School and frequent references to its principal S.G. Sneed; hunting and games with his friends and cousins; local events and weather.

HART, H. MARTYN   5001

Arps, Louisa Ward, ed. "Dean Hart Pre-Views His Wilderness: Excerpts from the 1872 Diary of H. Martyn Hart." COLORADO MAGAZINE 36 (1959):23-26.

Dec 1872. Highly narrative entries by an English clergyman, later dean of St. John's Cathedral in Denver, on a western trip for his health; from Kansas City by train; buffalo hunting with guide Jerry Gardner, a rather wild individual; concern over massive slaughter of buffalo; descriptions of Denver, with analysis of western character and customs, especially its lawlessness.

HUDDLESTON, DAVID, 1801-1890   5002

Thornburg, Opal. "David Huddleston: A Plain Friend and His Journal." FRIENDS HISTORICAL ASSOCIATION BULLETIN 38 (1949):75-91.

1872-1890. Undated journal extracts within article on elderly Quaker nurseryman at Dublin, Indiana; attempts to preserve the quiet "Inward Light" tradition of Quakerism against evangelical and holiness influences; opposition to paid ministry, "loud singing" and "boistrous discourse," revival meetings and organ music.

Thornburg, Opal, ed. "Earlham Diaries: A Visit to Earlham in 1884." FRIENDS HISTORICAL ASSOCIATION BULLETIN 36 (1947):72-79.

Dec 1884. Aged Quaker's visit to Richmond, Indiana, and Earlham College; detailed description of Earlham Meeting; objections to such innovations as hired ministry and instrumental music.

KELLOGG, MINER KILBOURNE, 1814-1889   5003

TEXAS JOURNAL. Edited by Llerena Friend. Austin and London: University of Texas Press, 1967. 183 pp. Journal, pp. 59-163.

May-Oct 1872. Journal of a distinguished artist and world traveler employed by the Texas Land and Copper Association as artist for its exploration of the inhospitable Llano Estacado region of northern Texas; encampment and preparations in Indian Territory and Kellogg's assessment that "matters in camp disorganized - or rather in disorder - entire lack of discipline - boding no good to the Expedition"; from Sherman to the Red River region and beyond to the Llano; horrible suffering from heat, insects, bad water and inedible food; his almost fatal illness; nevertheless, hasty but descriptive notes on weather, terrain, scenery, ranches, settlements, buffalo herds and other wildlife, flowers, various ores found and the changing colors and moods of the vast landscape; cattle drives encountered; frequent references to company personnel including Anton R. Roessler, W.C. McCarty, Lucius H. Chandler and Oscar Loew.

MATTHEWS, WILLIAM EDWARD   5004

Koster, John, ed. "The Forty-Day Scout." AMERICAN HERITAGE 31, no. 4 (1980):99-107.

Aug-Sep 1872. Letter-diary, one of many sent to his family in Maryland, of homesick young cavalryman under Col. John Irvin Gregg on retaliatory campaign against Kiowas and Comanches; departure from Fort Bascom, New Mexico; camp routine and humorous complaints about food; a surprise attack by Indians, with subsequent chases and encounters described in full and fascinating detail; buffalo hunt; an outstanding diary probably worthy of publication in its entirety.

RAYMOND, HENRY HUBERT, 1848-1936   5005

Snell, Joseph W., ed. "Diary of a Dodge City Buffalo Hunter." KANSAS HISTORICAL QUARTERLY 31 (1965):345-395.

Nov 1872-Nov 1873. Brief notes kept in the Dodge City area during the first year of the town's existence; hunting buffalo with the Masterson brothers, with numbers of buffalo and wolves killed and hides traded; notes on Indians and their ways; references to his sometime employer Thomas C. Nixon; a gun fight; diarist's love for playing his fiddle; occasional entries in German.

SAWYER, OTIS   5006

McCool, Elsie A., comp. "Gleanings from Sabbathday Lake Church Journals." SHAKER QUARTERLY 6 (1966):103-112, 124-134.

1872-1884. Extracts from official journals kept for the Shaker Church Family at Sabbathday Lake, Maine, by Elder Otis Sawyer; notes on Shaker farming and enterprises, such as preparing pickles and applesauce for market, brickmaking, etc.; notes on worship services open to the public, attracting hundreds of visitors; records of Shaker discussions and decision making on matters affecting their community, such as purchase of land and a possible move to New York state, and practices regarding tobacco and beards; the visit of author Charles Nordoff to gather material for a book; daily routines of the largely self-sufficient community; diarist's illness, with final entries by Eldress Mary Ann Gillespie recording his death.

SEGALE, BLANDINA, Sister, 1850-1941   5007

AT THE END OF THE SANTA FE TRAIL. Columbus, Ohio: Columbian Press, 1932. 347 pp. Milwaukee: Bruce, 1948. 298 pp.

1872-1892. Journal of a Sister of Charity sent from Steubenville, Ohio, on her first mission, to Trinidad, Colorado; establishing a school and hospital and doing charitable work in the frontier town; meeting Billy the Kid, whose respect she commanded, and later taking him food and comfort in jail in Santa Fe; opening a school and convent in Albuquerque, gaining the admiration and appreciation of territorial governor Lew Wallace.

SUSSMAN, EMILIE WORMSER   5008

MY TRIP TO YOSEMITE FROM THE JOURNAL OF EMILIE SUSSMAN. San Francisco: Grabhorn Press, 1939. 7 pp.

Jul 1872. Young woman's scenic excursion with friends, first by train and wagon from San Francisco to Merced, then by horseback, the women wearing bloomer costumes, to Yosemite Valley; noting well known places, especially El Capitan, Bower's Cave, Mirror Lake and Hutching's Hotel where the party stayed.

TUNSTALL, JOHN HENRY, 1853-1878   5009

THE LIFE & DEATH OF JOHN HENRY TUNSTALL: THE LETTERS, DIARIES & ADVENTURES OF AN ITINERANT ENGLISHMAN. Albuquerque: University of New Mexico Press, 1965. 480 pp. passim.

1872-1876 (with gaps). Diary intermingled with letters of an English fortune-seeker's experiences in America; travel from London to New York, where he enjoyed the service, food and amenities of the Hotel St. Nicholas; by rail to San Francisco; by packet boat to Victoria, British Columbia, to look after family business; settling in New Mexico where he took up sheep ranching during the turbulent days of the Lincoln County War.

WATSON, JOHN   5010

SOUVENIR TOUR OF THE UNITED STATES OF AMERICA AND CANADA. Glasgow: Printed for private circulation, 1872. 91 pp.

Extracts in PRAIRIE STATE, by Paul M. Angle, pp. 379-389. Chicago: University of Chicago Press, 1968.

Sep 1872. Scottish visitor's favorable impressions of Chicago rebuilding after the great fire; notes on grain elevators, loading of railroad cars, Union Stock Yards; to Quincy to take riverboat to St. Louis; prices and productivity.

1873

COE, HARVEY, 1807-1879   5011

Dale, Porter H., ed. "A Doctor's Life in Island Pond." VERMONT HISTORY 42 (1974):36-43. Diary, pp. 37-39.

Jan-Dec 1873. Brief extracts from the diary of a Vermont doctor; illnesses, injuries and a few treatments.

DAWSON, GEORGE MERCER, 1849-1901   5012

Turner, Allan R., ed. "Surveying the International Boundary." SASKATCHEWAN HISTORY 21 (1968):1-23.

Sep-Oct 1873. Canadian geologist's journal of the joint British and American boundary survey of the Great Plains portion of the forty-ninth parallel; route mainly through the Souris River valley in present Manitoba, Saskatchewan and North Dakota, with notes on topography, natural history, camps, traveling conditions, blizzards and a prairie fire; descriptions of Indians and Métis.

DIER, W. ARTHUR, 1850-1925   5013

"W. Arthur Dier, Pioneer Teacher and Lawyer." COLORADO MAGAZINE 34 (1957):213-225, 294-299.

1873-1875. Extracts covering life at Cheyenne where he clerked in a store; work on a surveying crew which was attacked by Indians; teaching school at Ralston Creek near Golden, Colorado, where he settled eventually, and at Georgetown; beginnings of law studies and legal work; some entries sent as articles to his home newspaper at Forreston, Illinois.

HUNTON, JOHN, 1839-1928   5014

DIARY. Lingle, Wyo., 1956. 6 vols.

Mar-May 1873, 1875-1888. Daily record penned by former Confederate soldier, a Wyoming pioneer and last post trader at Fort Laramie; the activities of his everyday life; work, leisure, friends, etc.; trips back home to Madison, Virginia; information on the cattle industry, agriculture, Indians, transportation and politics; short entries interspersed with editor's explanatory notes.

KENNEY, JAMES   5015

In A HISTORY OF ROCKINGHAM COUNTY, by John Walter Wayland, pp. 168-171, 173-174, 231, 239. Dayton, Va.: Ruebush-Elkins, 1912.

1873, 1875-1880. Extracts from diary of a prominent citizen of Rockingham County, Virginia; notes on local events and residents, a Confederate memorial and the presidential election of 1876.

MAGHEE, THOMAS G., 1842-1927   5016

Lindsay, Charles, ed. "The Diary of Dr. Thomas G. Maghee." NEBRASKA HISTORY 12 (1929):247-304.

1873-1875. Warrentown, Indiana, army surgeon's diary kept while he was serving at forts in Nebraska and Wyoming and as member of military escort on Professor O.C. Marsh's Niobrara expedition to collect fossils; later travel from Fort McPherson to Old Camp Brown, or Fort Washakie, where he was stationed for many years; reconnoiters in Wyoming under A.E. Bates; notes on Indians and skirmishes, including Bates' Battle; reference to Buffalo Bill Cody; a good picture of military and social life of frontier forts and the practice of medicine, with details of treating military and civilian patients for a variety of ills and injuries, including a long description of an amputation with anesthetic and removal of live larvae from a man's ear.

MILLER, GEORGE   5017

"Ranching in Chicorica Park." COLORADO MAGAZINE 33 (1956):52-66.

Oct 1873-Apr 1874. Diary of an English immigrant rancher in Colfax County, New Mexico, later prominent in Denver real estate; bare notes of trip from England to Trinidad, Colorado, with references to business activities and people there; beginnings of ranch work and building a frame house; loneliness for wife and children still in England; constant mention of mail, newspapers and magazines received.

PAGE, ANNE NELSON, 1855-1936   5018

Brydon, Anne Page, ed. "Diary of a Young Girl in Albemarle." ALBEMARLE COUNTY HISTORICAL SOCIETY MAGAZINE 20 (1961-1962):5-73.

Jan-Dec 1873. Sprightly diary of young Virginia girl, beginning with a visit to her uncle, the Rev. Cleland Kinloch Nelson, president of St. John's College in Annapolis; shopping, theater in Baltimore and social activities with young folks from the college; teaching school for a term at Culpeper; returning home to Millward near Cobham; a pleasant time of visiting, games and reading mostly women's novels; going to Scottsberg to teach the children of Mr. John Clark in a jolly household with horseback riding and many evenings of games and dancing.

RICHARDS, W.A.   5019

"Diary Kept by W.A. Richards in Summer of 1873." ANNALS OF WYOMING 7 (1931):467-482; 8 (1931):492-505.

May-Nov 1873. Diary of a survey of the southern boundary of Wyoming, kept by brother and assistant to A.V. Richards; full notes on terrain, route, astronomical observations and encounters with cattle drives; much hunting to provision crew; good picture of camp life.

SAVAGE, LEVI MATHERS, 1851-1935   5020

Peterson, Charles S., ed. " 'Book A-Levi Mathers Savage': The Look of Utah in 1873." UTAH HISTORICAL QUARTERLY 41 (1973):4-22.

Jul-Nov 1873. Extracts of young Mormon's observations as he traveled from his home in Toquerville to Salt Lake and while working in a sawmill at Kamas; notes on towns and ranches and, in places, criticism of residents as lazy and irreligious; discomforts of living in a tent; reports on effects in Utah of the Panic of 1873.

TSCHETTER, PAUL, 1842-1919   5021

Hofer, J.M., trans. and ed. "The Diary of Paul Tschetter." MENNONITE QUARTERLY REVIEW 5 (1931):112-127, 198-218.

Apr-Jul 1873. Russian Hutterite minister's account of a journey to America with other German-speaking Russian Hutterites and Mennonites to investigate immigration prospects; by train to Hamburg, thence on an unnamed ship to Hoboken and from there by train to Elkhart, Indiana, with substantial notes on travel experiences, fellow travelers and others encountered; customs and attitudes of American Mennonites; travels in Illinois, Minnesota, Dakotas, Manitoba, etc., with notes on land and agricultural prospects; writing a petition to the President asking that his people be guaranteed exemption from military service.

WYANT, ALEXANDER HELWIG, 1836-1892   5022

Dawdy, Doris Ostrander, ed. "The Wyant Diary: An Artist with the Wheeler Survey in Arizona." ARIZONA AND THE WEST 22 (1980):255-278.

Aug-Nov 1873 (with gaps). Diary of a New York artist with George M. Wheeler's Geographical Surveys West of the One Hundredth Meridian; train and stagecoach journey to join a contingent under civilian photographer Timothy H. O'Sullivan; from Fort Defiance to Canyon de Chelly and Canyon Bonita, with notes on terrain, ruins and Indians; then a harrowing search for a crossing of the San Juan, with privations leading to ruin of the diarist's health; return to Fort Defiance.

1874

ADAIR, CORNELIA WADSWORTH RITCHIE, 1838-1921   5023

MY DIARY. Bath: Fyson & Company, Printers, 1918. 125 pp.

MY DIARY. Introduction by Montagu K. Brown. Austin: University of Texas Press, 1965. 125 pp.

Aug-Nov 1874. Travel diary of adventurous daughter of pioneer Genesee Valley, New York, family and wife of English gentleman John Adair; voyage from England to New York on the CUBA; impatience with inconveniences of travel; comments on society, politics and American character; luxurious train trip to Lake Superior; sightseeing in Chicago; visiting sawmills and iron mines near Lake Michigan; glowing description of scenery along Mississippi River on steamboat trip from St. Paul to Clinton; train trip to Omaha and Sydney Barracks and with sportsmen's hunting party across prairie to Denver; council with Chief Two-Lance, hunting antelope, buffalo and small game, camping along Platte River and old emigrant trail and generally enjoying wild, uncivilized prairie.

ANDREWS, EMILY KEMBLE OLIVER BROWN   5024

Myres, Sandra L., ed. "A Woman's View of the Texas Frontier." SOUTHWESTERN HISTORICAL QUARTERLY 86 (1982):49-80.

Aug-Sep 1874. Pleasant letter-diary of a journey with her husband, Col. George Lippitt Andrews, to take up his post as commander at Fort Davis; notes beginning en route along Austin-Fredericksburg road and continuing along the San Antonio-El Paso military road; obvious enjoyment of sights and experiences of the journey, including camp life; descriptions of towns, forts, ranches, stagecoach stations, etc.

BORLASE, WILLIAM COPELAND, 1849-1899   5025

SUNWAYS: A RECORD OF RAMBLES IN MANY LANDS. Plymouth: W. Borendon, 1878. 484 pp.

Oct 1874-Sep 1875. Dated but narrative-style journal of an English traveler's impressions and experiences in the United States; travels by train and stagecoach, noting people, customs and events in such cities as Boston, New York, Philadelphia, Washington, Cincinnati, Louisville, New Orleans, St. Louis, Chicago, Denver, Salt Lake City, San Francisco, etc.; scenic attractions including Niagara Falls and Yosemite; comments on Indians, Mormons, blacks and women; after-the-fact accounts of the New Orleans Riot of September, 1874, Chicago Fire of 1871, Civil War and Reconstruction; mainly a picture of American social life and mores.

BULLENE, THOMAS B.   5026

Wilson, William H., ed. "The Diary of a Kansas City Merchant." MISSOURI HISTORICAL SOCIETY BULLETIN 19 (1963):247-259.

1874-1880. Extracts from prosperous merchant's diary; opening a large retail store in which he installed a steam elevator; visits to the store of various personages, including Mrs. U.S. Grant, who "was pleased to say many complimentary things" about it; the Kansas City Industrial Exposition; a plague of grasshoppers upon the area; personal interests, such as reading, book collecting, with purchase of a Breeches Bible from England, amateur theatricals, etc., and emphatic opinions on many items in the news.

CALHOUN, JAMES, 1845-1876   5027

WITH CUSTER IN '74: JAMES CALHOUN'S DIARY OF THE BLACK HILLS EXPEDITION. Edited by Lawrence A. Frost. Provo, Utah: Brigham Young University Press, 1979. 140 pp.

Jun-Aug 1874. Official log, supplemented by personal observations and comments, of Custer's brother-in-law and acting assistant adjutant general during the Seventh Cavalry's controversial reconnaissance of the Black Hills, land granted to the Sioux by treaty; camps, terrain, route, supplies; activities and reports of General Custer; a tirade against budgetary restrictions hampering military operations; praise for career soldiers opening the West for settlement and much philosophizing in an elevated style.

CAMPBELL, JOHN FRANCIS, 1822-1885   5028

MY CIRCULAR NOTES: EXTRACTS FROM JOURNALS, LETTERS SENT HOME, GEOLOGICAL AND OTHER NOTES, WRITTEN WHILE TRAVELING WESTWARD ROUND THE WORLD. London: Macmillan, 1876. 2 vols. American diary, v. 1 passim.

1874-1875. Notes on the geology, landscape, people, especially Indians, of the American West by a prodigious Scottish traveler.

CURTISS, ROSWELL C.   5029

"A Trip up the Lakes in 1874." INLAND SEAS 29 (1973):163-169.

Aug 1874. Medina, Ohio, lawyer's Great Lakes vacation trip on steamers R.N. RICE, ST. PAUL, PACIFIC and ANNIE L. CRAIG; pleasant notes on life on board, islands, towns en route, with leisure to stroll about and dine; much interest in rocks and minerals; expense account appended.

DUFFERIN AND AVA, HARIOT GEORGINA HAMILTON-   5030
TEMPLE-BLACKWOOD, marchioness of

MY CANADIAN JOURNAL. New York: D. Appleton, 1891. 456 pp. passim.

1874-1877 (with gaps). Diary of various visits to United States made with her husband who was governor-general of Canada; official reception in Chicago with complimentary remarks about the service at the Palmer House; in New York, where she enjoyed shopping, theater, opera, Central Park, etc., and admired ladies' attire; attending church and complaining of "little service and much sermon"; a western trip to Omaha, Cheyenne, the Rocky Mountains, Ogden, Salt Lake City and the Mormon tabernacle, San Francisco and Chinese theater in Chinatown; visits to St. Paul, Minneapolis and the Falls of St. Anthony; curious zigzag travel on the Red River.

LUDLOW, WILLIAM, 1843-1901   5031

In REPORT OF A RECONNAISSANCE OF THE BLACK HILLS OF DAKOTA, by United States Army Corps of Engineers, pp. 7-19. Washington, D.C.: Government Printing Office, 1875.

McAndrews, Eugene V., ed. "An Army Engineer's Journal of Custer's Black Hills Expedition." JOURNAL OF THE WEST 13, no. 1 (1974):78-85.

Jul-Aug 1874. Army engineer's journal within official report of Custer's Black Hills expedition; route from Fort Abraham Lincoln, to area secured by Sioux but desired for future military posts, settlement and gold mining; exploration along Belle Fourche River, South Fork of the Cheyenne, at Bear Butte, etc., with topographical and natural history information; a disappointing search for gold; conclusion that the area would be promising for settlement but that the Indians would tolerate no incursion into their Black Hills sanctuary.

McLaird, James D. and Turchen, Lesta V. "Exploring the Black Hills." SOUTH DAKOTA HISTORY 4 (1974):281-319.

1874. Undated extracts within article.

In EXPLORING THE NORTHERN PLAINS, edited by Lloyd McFarling, pp. 289-299.

Jul 1874. Extracts covering exploration from Fort Abraham Lincoln to the Black Hills.

In REPORT OF A RECONNAISSANCE FROM CARROLL, MONTANA TERRITORY, ON THE UPPER MISSOURI, TO THE YELLOWSTONE NATIONAL PARK, AND RETURN, by United States Army Corps of Engineers, pp. 9-37. Washington, D.C.: Government Printing Office, 1876.

Jul-Sep 1875. From Bismarck on steamer JOSEPHINE to forts Stevenson, Berthold and Buford, continuing on KEY WEST to Fort Peck and Carroll, terminus of the road from Helena and point where freight was transferred to Missouri riverboats; determining need for additional military posts and defense; overland to Judith Basin, etc., and Yellowstone, where he noted "pictorial splendors," which met the "two requisites of majesty and beauty," of the major points which are now tourist attractions, complained of vandalism and destruction by visitors and recommended mounted police for Yellowstone.

MCFADDEN, THOMPSON   5032

Carriker, Robert C., ed. "Thompson McFadden's Diary of an Indian Campaign." SOUTHWESTERN HISTORICAL QUARTERLY 75 (1971):198-232.

Aug-Dec 1874. A scout's account of the Indian Territory expedition as a member of Lt. Frank D. Baldwin's unit of guides during the Red River War; marches, camps and scenery from Fort Dodge; excellent description of fights with Kiowas, Comanches and Cheyennes united to resist cavalry attempts to drive them onto reservations; problems with lack of water and transport; heroism of several, including Wyllys Lyman and his badly outnumbered troops saving supply train from Indian attack; the rescue of captive white children; references to Col. Nelson A. Miles and other soldiers and scouts.

MIDDLETON, THOMAS COOKE, 1842-1923   5033

Tourscher, Francis E. "Fr. Thomas Cooke Middleton, D.D., O.S.A." AMERICAN CATHOLIC HISTORICAL SOCIETY OF PHILADELPHIA RECORDS 35 (1924):20-32.

1874-1899. Extracts within article on priest who was for many years an administrator at Villanova; brief notes of university events and people,.

MILLER, GEORGINA   5034

"Ranching in Chicorica Park." COLORADO MAGAZINE 33 (1956):133-148.

Apr 1874-Jan 1875. Extract covering English woman's trip to join her husband, George Miller, ranching in Colfax County, New Mexico; travel with her three small children and her brother, Arthur Marsland; enjoyment of social life on board the CITY OF BRUSSELS; by train and wagon from New York to New Mexico where she "set to work in earnest"; good details of ranch life, with many notes on local people in an apparently thriving community in and around Trinidad, Colorado.

PARKERSON, JULIA ETTA, 1853-1889   5035

Paullin, Ellen Payne, ed. "Etta's Journal." KANSAS HISTORY 3 (1980):201-219, 255-278.

    1874-1875. Journal of a young woman working as housekeeper for her uncle William E. Goodnow at Manhattan; very personal notes of exhausting domestic tasks, prayers, religious reflection, introspections about the effects of her hunchbacked condition on her life; observations on people, social life and church activities; a semester at Kansas State Agricultural College, which she had to abandon for lack of money; patient courtship by Alvin Reynolds, thirty years her senior, whom she eventually married; attempts to get a job as a teacher; a very cathartic diary of a girl who, at times, felt she was "born to sorrow and woe."

POYNEER, GEORGE E.   5036

Harlan, James R., ed. "The Iowa Game Book of George E. Poyneer." ANNALS OF IOWA, 3d ser. 23 (1941-1942):189-212.

    1874-1877. Iowa portion of hunting diary kept by Clinton sportsman; numbers and kinds of game killed, including now extinct passenger pigeons and other presently rare birds; hunting methods and the performance of his various dogs.

SANFORD, WILMOT P.   5037

Innis, Ben, ed. "The Fort Buford Diary of Private Wilmot P. Sanford." NORTH DAKOTA HISTORY 33 (1966):335-378.

    Sep 1874-May 1875. Hudson, New Hampshire, private's diary kept at Fort Buford during a relatively peaceful period; marches, drills, meals, escapades of soldiers, tasks, weather, etc.; his sick headaches, possibly caused by filthy, poorly ventilated quarters; frequent reference to books from post library and eventually serving as librarian.

THOMAS, CYNTHIA   5038

Raper, Horace W., ed. "Accounts of Moravian Mountain Excursions of a Hundred Years Ago." NORTH CAROLINA HISTORICAL REVIEW 4 (1970):281-316.

    1874-1880 (with gaps). A young woman's account of four summer camping expeditions of the "Rough and Ready Mountain Club" of Salem Moravians led by Augustus Gottlieb Fogle; travel of some by horseback and others in carriages; detailed notes on people and places en route to the mountains of western North Carolina and Virginia; scenery, especially of Mount Mitchell and the Black Mountains; occasional hazards and illnesses; camp routines, hymn-singing and prayers; good food enjoyed with hearty appetites.

WELLS, EMMELINE B. WOODWARD, 1828-1921   5039

In WOMEN'S VOICES, edited by Kenneth Godfrey, Audrey Godfrey and Jill Derr, pp. 294-306.

    Aug 1874-Apr 1875. Extracts from the long diaries of an intellectual Mormon woman, kept during a period of tension between domestic cares and growing literary interests; loneliness of a plural wife whose husband, Daniel H. Wells, always stayed at "the other house"; worries about her children and her own poor health; moments of respite from house and church work to write poetry, help with the WOMAN'S EXPONENT, of which she soon became editor, and became a leader in the women's suffrage movement.

WILLIAMS, ESPY, 1852-1908   5040

Nolan, Paul T. "The Journal of a Young Southern Playwright, Espy Williams of New Orleans." LOUISIANA STUDIES 1, no. 3 (1962):30-50; no. 4 (1962):33-54.

    1874-1875 (with gaps). Journal of a New Orleans banker whose chief interest was literature and only ambition was for literary fame, kept "not for common events, but for a record of books read and other things which appertain to literature"; thoughts suggested by reading, subjects for research, discourses on authors, especially poets and dramatists; theater events in New Orleans with special praise for Tomasso Salvini, Italian actor; negotiating with Edwin Adams to get his plays performed, particularly ARAM; having some of his poems published, but never reaching his longed for goal.

1875

BRADLEY, EDWARD E., 1857-1938   5041

"Before the Mast on the Clipper Ship MARY WHITRIDGE of Baltimore." LOG OF MYSTIC SEAPORT 31 (1979):79-90, 130-133.

    1875-1876. Stonington, Connecticut, seaman's narrative and diary of serving under Capt. Benjamin F. Cutler on a voyage to Hong Kong; good sailing details; vivid description of a severe gale; ships encountered.

DANA, RICHARD HENRY, 1851-1931   5042

HOSPITABLE ENGLAND IN THE SEVENTIES: THE DIARY OF A YOUNG AMERICAN. Boston and New York: Houghton Mifflin, 1921. 378 pp.

    1875-1876. Pleasant, leisurely and informative diary of young Dana's "Grand Tour" in England and the Continent with access to the great houses and influential people on the strength of his father's literary fame and past visits; social and political life in England; attention to nuance and detail of customs, particularly in contrast with American practices; conversations with and speeches of Gladstone and others; notes on English theater, music, universities of Oxford and Cambridge, courts, etc.; English attitudes toward the United States; travels in France, where he enjoyed Paris social life and theater, lived with a French family and, again, noted differences in custom, particularly distinguished Frenchmen discussing their mistresses "with the frankness and simplicity which we should use in talking of rare books or beautiful bindings"; travel to Rome and Cairo, with experiences and observations there.

ENGLISH, LYDIA E.   5043

Snell, Joseph W., ed. "By Wagon from Kansas to Arizona in 1875: The Travel Diary of Lydia English." KANSAS HISTORICAL QUARTERLY 36 (1970):369-389.

    Sep-Dec 1875. Diary sent in installments to the CONCORDIA EMPIRE of emigrant journey from Concordia, Kansas, with her husband, William K. English, and sons; route mainly along the Santa Fe Trail; terrain, scenery, vegetation, evidence of past Indian attacks, settlements and ranches; rather wistful notes on agricultural potential by a homesick woman who had left a promising farm because of her husband's wanderlust; a few references to Mexicans and their way of life.

GLOVER, ELI SHELDON, 1845-1919   5044

THE DIARY OF ELI SHELDON GLOVER. Transcribed from the original by the Oregon Historical Records Survey Project, Division of Professional and Service Projects, Work Projects Administration. Sponsored by the University of Oregon. Portland: Oregon Historical Records Survey Project, 1939. 41 pp.

Oct-Dec 1875. Journey by horseback, railroad and steamship from Missoula County, Montana, through Idaho and Washington Territory to Portland, Oregon, and the lower Willamette Valley; comments on the government road built by Lt. John Mullan and Indian trails; overnight stays with ranchers or in vacant houses; the old Jesuit Mission at Coeur d'Alene, Idaho; a country fair at Walla Walla, Washington; good weather and terrain of Willamette Valley.

HAYES, RUTHERFORD BIRCHARD, 1822-1893   5045

HAYES: THE DIARY OF A PRESIDENT. Edited by T. Harry Williams. New York: David McKay, 1964. 329 pp.

1875-1881. The segment of Hayes' lifelong diaries covering his nomination, the campaign of 1876 and disputed election, the end of Reconstruction and beginnings of the civil service; the major events and figures of his administration, with substantial references to Roscoe Conkling, William M. Evarts, Ulysses S. Grant, John Sherman and others; presidential travels and White House family and social life, all quite simple and modest by present standards.

In IN THE CAGE: EYEWITNESS ACCOUNTS OF THE FREED NEGRO IN SOUTHERN SOCIETY, compiled by Alton Hornsby, pp. 241-244. Chicago: Quadrangle Books, 1971.

1877-1878. Extracts regarding the political situation for freed slaves.

JONES, BENJAMIN FRANKLIN, b. 1824   5046

In A SUNDAY BETWEEN WARS, by Ben Maddow, pp. 117-126.

1875-1879. Notes of expanding business of Jones & Laughlin Company's iron furnaces and rolling mill; production, wages, strikes, riots; a visit to the mill by President Rutherford B. Hayes.

LUMBARD, GILES BARTON, d. 1935   5047

"By Train from Omaha to Sacramento One Hundred Years Ago." AMERICAN WEST 12 (1975):14-17.

Apr-May 1875. Young Iowa City man's train journey via North Platte, Nebraska, Green River, Wyoming, and Elko, Nevada; descriptions of scenery and anecdotes on passengers, a jolly bunch whose "lively time is from supper time until bed time"; Indians begging at the stations in Nevada; entries ending in San Francisco.

NEWTON, HENRY, 1845-1877   5048

McLaird, James D. and Turchen, Lesta V. "Exploring the Black Hills, 1855-1875: The Scientists' Search for Gold." SOUTH DAKOTA HISTORY 4 (1974):404-438.

1875. Undated extracts, within article, of a government sponsored expedition led by geologists Walter P. Jenney and Henry Newton to determine the extend of gold deposits in the Black Hills; entries from official report of the scientists and news dispatches, memoirs, etc., of others.

RONEY, FRANK, 1841-1925   5049

Shumsky, Neil L., ed. "Frank Roney's San Francisco." LABOR HISTORY 17 (1976):245-265.

Apr 1875-Mar 1876. Diary of an Irish immigrant iron molder who later became a California labor leader; entries covering a stressful time of poverty, short-term jobs and long periods of unemployment brought on by the effects of nation-wide depression on San Francisco; diarist's difficulties of maintaining his self-respect and keeping his family fed and clothed; worries about his health; constant preoccupation with money, noting rent, prices and earnings.

STRONG, WILLIAM EMERSON, 1840-1891   5050

A TRIP TO THE YELLOWSTONE NATIONAL PARK. Washington, D.C., 1876. 143 pp.

Aug-Sep 1875. General Strong's account of journey with group led by Gen. W.W. Belknap, the secretary of war; pleasant train trip from Chicago to Salt Lake City; comments on Mormons; travel through Utah and Idaho by stagecoach, with excellent account of the journey and route to Virginia City, Montana, and Yellowstone; thence by horseback; descriptive notes on Yellowstone area; geysers, plant and animal life.

STURM, JACOB J.   5051

Wallace, Ernest, ed. "The Journal of Ranald S. MacKenzie's Messenger to the Kwahadi Comanches." RED RIVER VALLEY HISTORICAL REVIEW 3 (1978):227-246.

Apr-May 1875. Diary of physician and interpreter dispatched to take a message to Chief Quanah Parker and his Kwahadi Comanches with Mackenzie's ultimatum that they surrender and come to the reservation at Fort Sill; travel through Oklahoma and Texas to their encampments; summaries of conversations and negotiations with Quanah and Ishatai, an influential medicine man; full notes of travel on the Staked Plains, buffalo hunting, etc.; a journal which fills a gap in the history of the Red River War.

TRUE, THEODORE E.   5052

Olson, Gary D., ed. "Relief for Nebraska Grasshopper Victims: The Official Journal of Lieutenant Theodore E. True." NEBRASKA HISTORY 48 (1967):119-140.

Jan-Mar? 1875. Record of Army aid to settlers made destitute by the grasshopper plague of 1874; supervision of relief effort in Dawson County, where the people of Plum Creek and Cozad were in "pitiable condition" from cold and hunger; efforts hampered by blizzards; references to Everard S. Childs, chairman of a local relief committee, and diarist's immediate superior, John F. Trout.

UDALL, DAVID KING, 1829-1910   5053

ARIZONA PIONEER MORMON: DAVID KING UDALL, HIS STORY AND HIS FAMILY. Tucson: Arizona Silhouettes, 1959. 304 pp. Diary, pp. 275-286.

1875-1885. Extracts from the diary of an English Mormon; mission to England in 1875-1876, farming in Arizona and Mormon activities there, including bishopric at St. Johns; plural marriage, which he considered his duty, and his imprisonment for polygamy in Detroit.

WHITNEY, CLARA A., b. 1860?   5054

CLARA'S DIARY: AN AMERICAN GIRL IN MEIJI JAPAN. Edited by M. William Steele and Tamika Ichimata. Tokyo and New York: Kodansha International, 1979. 353 pp.

1875-1884. Engaging diary, begun at age fifteen, of an American girl in Japan, where her father administered a business college and she and her mother did missionary work and enjoyed international social life; Japanese mores, events, and holidays at a time of transition from traditional to somewhat Western ways, growth of diarist from adolescence to womanhood, moving from American chauvinism to admiration for Japanese life.

1876

ATKINS, BENJAMIN ELBERFIELD, 1848-1909   5055

EXTRACTS FROM THE DIARY OF BENJAMIN ELBERFIELD ATKINS, "A TEACHER OF THE OLD SCHOOL." Gastonia, N.C.: Privately published, 1947. 97 pp.

1876-1909. Extracts from the diary of a beloved teacher who served the Asheville Female Academy in Asheville, North Carolina, Pryor Institute in Jasper, Tennessee, Oakland High School in Gastonia, North Carolina, Athens Female College in Athens, Tennessee, Martin College in Pulaski, Tennessee, and Logan College for Young Ladies in Russellville, Kentucky; notes on students, teaching, school activities of many kinds, Methodist church work, including lay preaching; purchase and management of the GASTONIA GAZETTE; financial and other difficulties borne with faith and fortitude.

BAGLEY, SARAH   5056

In THE HISTORY OF A HOUSE, ITS FOUNDER, FAMILY AND GUESTS, by Mary H.B. Longyear, pp. 46-58. Brookline, Mass.: Zion Research Foundation, 1925. 69 pp. 2d ed., rev. Longyear Foundation, 1947. 70 pp.

1876-1877. Diary of a Christian Science healer and friend of Mary Baker Eddy in Amesbury, Massachusetts; religious reflections; treating of the sick in her home.

BERENSON, MARY SMITH COSTELLOE, 1864-1945   5057

MARY BERENSON: A SELF-PORTRAIT FROM HER LETTERS & DIARIES. Edited by Barbara Strachey and Jayne Samuels. New York: Norton, 1984. 336 pp. passim.

1876-1937. Extracts from diaries of a talented woman who early in life displayed signs of an independent, dominant personality; breaking from her Philadelphia Quaker background and marrying Frank Costelloe, a Catholic London barrister; soon finding the demands of household and children in conflict with her desire for education and freedom; meeting and moving to Italy with Bernard Berenson, whom she married when her husband died; editing his work, becoming an art expert in her own right, managing their villa and gardens and entertaining a steady flow of guests

at I Tatti; a picture of a fascinating, but selfish woman in a stormy but interesting marriage and a life of wealth, art and famous people.

Gilmore, Myron P. "The Berensons and Villa I Tatti." AMERICAN PHILOSOPHICAL SOCIETY PROCEEDINGS 120 (1976):7-12.

Sep 1903-Apr 1904. Article containing extracts from a diary kept during a trip to America with her husband and fellow art historian, Bernard Berenson, to promote interest in Italian painting; entertainment by the rich of Newport, Boston and Chicago, whose artistic taste and knowledge she did not admire but whose good will she continued to cultivate in case they might prove to be potential benefactors; visits with their former professors at Harvard and Bryn Mawr and with the Berenson and Smith families before return to Florence.

BRADLEY, JAMES H., 1844-1877   5058

"Journal of the Sioux Campaign of 1876." MONTANA HISTORICAL SOCIETY CONTRIBUTIONS 2 (1896):140-228. Reprint. THE MARCH OF THE MONTANA COLUMN. Edited by Edgar I. Stewart. American Exploration and Travel Series, no. 32. Norman: University of Oklahoma Press, 1961. 182 pp.

Extracts in DIARIES OF THE LITTLE BIG HORN, by Michael J. Koury, pp. 55-56 passim; EXPLORING THE NORTHERN PLAINS, edited by Lloyd McFarling, pp. 373-397; LITTLE BIG HORN DIARY, by James Willert, pp. 1-427 passim.

Mar-Jun 1876. Important diary of John Gibbon's chief of scouts with the Seventh Infantry of the Montana Column, one of three units involved in the Sioux expedition; march from Fort Shaw to join companies of the Second Cavalry at Fort Ellis, suffering and recovering from snow blindness en route; down valley of the Yellowstone for the intended rendezvous with Custer's Seventh Cavalry, Dakota Column, but diarist's assertion that "it is understood that if Custer arrives first, he is at liberty to attack at once if he deems prudent"; a council with Crow Indians, including speeches and negotiations between Gibbon and chiefs; diarist's appointment as commander of Crow scouts and subsequent reconnoiters; difficult forced march, floundering in total darkness the night of June 25, to try to meet Custer as planned; first news of the annihilation of Custer's command; astounded and incredulous reaction of officers; throughout diary, extensive information on Crow customs and history, possibly expanded from original notes, and references to Capt. H.B. Freeman, Gen. Alfred Terry and Gibbon; letter appended describing the burial of Custer's dead.

BRANDRETH, HELEN WARD, 1862-1905   5059

In A DAY AT A TIME, edited by Margo Culley, pp. 149-164.

1876-1885 (with gaps.) The love life of an Ossining, New York, girl; courting, a broken engagement, suffering over unrequited love, a second engagement "not at all romantic" and concluding her journal by signing her "dear new name."

BRODERICK, JAMES LONSDALE, 1841-1886   5060

THE CHARACTER OF THE COUNTRY: THE IOWA DIARY OF JAMES L. BRODERICK. Edited by Loren N. Horton. Iowa City: Iowa State Historical Department, 1976. 136 pp.

Oct 1876-May 1877. English land agent's visit to Dubuque and other parts of Iowa, staying with Yorkshire immigrants who had settled there; transatlantic crossing on the BRITANNIC in seven days, "the quickest trip on record"; sightseeing in New York, Niagara Falls, the Philadelphia Centennial Exposition; train trip to Dubuque with a stop in Chicago, where he attended a revival meeting of Dwight L. Moody and Ira Sankey; interesting picture of Dubuque and its surroundings, with notes on many people, including fellow Yorkshireman James Woodward, with whom he traveled, and his landlady, Mrs. Anna Marsh; comparisons between American and British politics, customs, articulture, prices and wages; the horrors of a slaughterhouse described in detail; a visit to New Mellaray Monastery; church attendance of an ecumenical nature; a public lecture by Edith O'Gorman, "the escaped nun"; return to England on the ALBERIA; an entertaining and informative diary.

Horton, Loren N., ed. "The Character of the Country: Excerpts." PALIMPSEST 57 (1976):157-160; 61 (1980):130-137.

Dec 1876-Mar 1877. Extracts of period spent in Dubuque.

BRYAN, JERRY   5061

AN ILLINOIS GOLD HUNTER IN THE BLACK HILLS. Edited by Clyde C. Walton. Illinois State Historical Society Pamphlet Series, no. 2. Springfield: Illinois State Historical Society, 1960. 40 pp.

Mar-Aug 1876. Cordova, Illinois, man's Black Hills gold rush diary; by train, then wagon via Cheyenne with hundreds of others flocking into the area; jaunty notes on life in the boom towns of Custer and Deadwood and the mining gulches; fears of Sioux attack during the summer of Custer's defeat; the murder in Deadwood of Wild Bill Hickok by Jack McCall; diarist's discouragement with lack of success and return to Cordova.

CARROLL, MATTHEW   5062

"Diary of Matthew Carroll, Master in Charge of Transportation for Colonel John Gibbon's Expedition against the Sioux Indians." MONTANA HISTORICAL SOCIETY CONTRIBUTIONS 2 (1896):229-240.

Extracts in DIARIES OF THE LITTLE BIG HORN, by Michael J. Koury, pp. 71-74 passim.

May-Sep 1876. Diary of a noncombatant in charge of Diamond R supply wagons during the Montana Column's march from the Yellowstone River; route, conditions, bad weather, with snow in June; details of provisions, wagons, loads per team, etc.; news from Crow scouts that there had been "a big fight on the Little Big Horn and Custer badly whipped"; hearsay report of Custer's final battle; coming upon and burying the dead; removing the wounded survivors of Reno's battle and siege.

COFFMAN, JOHN S., 1848-1899   5063

Coffman, Barbara F. "Extracts from J.S. Coffman's Diaries." MENNONITE QUARTERLY REVIEW 23 (1949):147-160.

1876-1896. Extracts relating to his ministry from diaries of an itinerant Mennonite clergyman; in the Shenandoah Valley; assistant editor of the HERALD OF TRUTH in Elkhart, Indiana; continuing pastoral and evangelistic work there and in travels to Pennsylvania, Iowa, Kansas, etc., to conduct meetings; texts and substance of sermons; references to many congregations and individuals during itinerations.

COLEMAN, THOMAS W., 1849-1921   5064

I BURIED CUSTER: THE DIARY OF PVT. THOMAS W. COLEMAN. Edited by Bruce R. Liddic. College Station, Tex.: Creative Pub., 1979. 210 pp. Diary, pp. 8-27.

Jun-Jul 1876. Terse daily account by a soldier with B Comapny of Seventh Cavalry; march and camps mainly with the rear guard pack train under Capt. Thomas McDougall; mention of Custer "highly pleased" to hear scouts' report of a large village ahead; Custer's battle plan and division of companies; Company B under "murderous fire" with Marcus Reno's and Frederick Benteen's companies, initially unaware of Custer's predicament; digging holes with hunting knives and enduring twenty-two hours without water until cessation of fire; carrying out wounded to the riverboat FAR WEST; working as part of the detail that buried Custer and his troops, with graphic descriptions of the dead; an especially vivid account of action and its aftermath from June 25 through 28.

CREW, HENRY, 1859-1953   5065

Crew, William H., ed. "Centennial Notes." PENNSYLVANIA MAGAZINE OF HISTORY AND BIOGRAPHY 100 (1976):406-413.

Jun-Jul 1876. Richmond, Ohio, boy's trip to Philadelphia to see the Centennial Exposition, where he enjoyed most the "furs from the north, the firearms from different nations and the Chinese work"; visit to Independence Hall, the zoo and other attractions.

CUSHMAN, MARY AMES   5066

SHE WROTE IT ALL DOWN. New York and London: C. Scribner's Sons, 1936. 226 pp. passim.

1876-1880. Charming, unselfconscious diary and letters of a St. Louis girl from age eleven to fifteen, traveling in Europe in the grand manner with her mother, sister, two brothers and governess; lively reports on tourist attractions, accommodations, boarding schools and a trip to St. Petersburg; worries about her lapses of goodness; beginnings of teenage interest in romance; an expatriate childhood in the Jamesian tradition.

DEWOLF, JAMES M., d. 1876   5067

Luce, Edward S., ed. "The Diary and Letters of Dr. James M. DeWolf, Acting Assistant Surgeon, U.S. Army." NORTH DAKOTA HISTORY 25 (1958):33-81. Diary, pp. 35-41. Reprint. Bismarck, N.D.: State Historical Society, 1958?

Extracts in DIARIES OF THE LITTLE BIG HORN, by Michael J. Koury, pp. 19-22 passim.

Mar-Jun 1876. Diary of a contract surgeon with the Dakota Column; march from Fort Abraham Lincoln during which time he treated troops suffering from frostbite and frozen feet; notes on route, camps, difficulties of terrain; references to generals George Custer and Alfred Terry, as well as assistant surgeon John W. Williams; participation in Maj. Marcus Reno's scout and his subsequent battle on June 25, which the diarist did not survive.

FREEMAN, HENRY BLANCHARD, 1837-1915   5068

THE FREEMAN JOURNAL: THE INFANTRY IN THE SIOUX CAMPAIGN OF 1876. Edited by George A. Schneider. San Rafael, Calif.: Presidio Press, 1977. 104 pp.

Mar-Oct 1876. Journal of commander of Seventh Infantry during march of the Montana Column from Fort Shaw, events at the

Little Bighorn and return; receiving command when Capt. Charles C. Rawn was incapacitated by snow blindness; distances and conditions of march; concern over incidents of drunkenness, lack of cooperation between various columns of the Sioux campaign and rivalry between cavalry and infantry; contending with his own illness and severe toothaches; relations with Gibbon and Terry; complaints against Capt. James M.J. Sanno; report of Gibbon's council with the Crow; learning of Custer's debacle from Crow scouts, and seeing smoke in the distance, but Gibbon's reaction that "it was all right, Custer had the village and Indians were burning it for themselves" and offering $200 to any trooper who could get a message through to Custer; graphic details of the Custer and Reno battlefields, with all bodies "more or less mutilated" except Custer's and the terrible stench of dead men and horses; making litters and carrying out Reno's wounded; diarist's retrospective summary of Custer's march from the mouth of the Rosebud and events of June 22 through 25; return march, with mention of Reno's arrest.

FREW, JAMES BARCUS   5069

Hedren, Paul L., ed. "Campaigning with the 5th Cavalry: Private James B. Frew's Diary and Letters from the Great Sioux War of 1876." NEBRASKA HISTORY 65 (1984):443-466.

Jul-Nov 1876. Missouri enlisted man's account of Gen. George Crook's campaign against the Sioux and their allies; clash with the Northern Cheyenne at Warbonnet Creek, Nebraska, during which Buffalo Bill Cody killed and scalped Yellow Hair; brief notes of subsequent marches and conditions, including joining of Crook's forces with Terry's, then breaking off of Crook's Bighorn and Yellowstone expedition and the "Starvation March" during which troops suffered from cold, rain, mud and such hunger that they eventually were reduced to eating their horses; the Battle of Slim Buttes; references to Cole Wesley Merritt.

GODFREY, EDWARD SETTLE, 1843-1932   5070

THE FIELD DIARY OF LT. EDWARD SETTLE GODFREY. Edited by Edgar I. Stewart and Jane R. Stewart. Portland, Oreg.: Champoeg Press, 1957. 74 pp.

Extracts in THE CUSTER TRAIL, by Frank L. Anders, edited by John M. Carroll, pp. 76-123 passim. Hidden Springs of Custeriana, 8. Glendale, Calif.: Arthur H. Clark, 1983.

Extracts in DIARIES OF THE LITTLE BIG HORN, by Michael J. Koury, pp. 9-14 passim; LITTLE BIG HORN DIARY, by James Willert, pp. 1-427 passim.

May-Sep 1876. Diary of commander of Company K, Seventh Cavalry; march from Fort Abraham Lincoln with Custer's Dakota Column accompanied partway by Custer's immediate superior, Gen. Alfred Terry, who is mentioned frequently in the diary; attached to Frederick Benteen's detail and with him on the "scout to the left," ordered by Custer, during which they floundered in ravines and encountered no Indians; catching up with Maj. Marcus Reno's detail, also separated from the main command by Custer, in time to assist him in battle and siege of June 25 and 26, during which they were unaware of Custer's exact location; suffering from thirst, hunger and exhaustion while pinned down by Sioux; diarist's contempt for Reno's performance under fire; awareness of Custer's whereabouts upon hearing occasional shots and concluding "the fight was over" and there was nothing

to do but "go up and congratulate the others & help destroy plunder"; upon arrival of the Montana Column, learning from Lt. James H. Bradley of Custer's defeat: "I was dumbfounded"; going to scene of the battle and burying the dead.

GRAY, KATHIE, b. 1864   5071

In KATHIE'S DIARY: LEAVES FROM AN OLD, OLD DIARY, edited by Margaret W. Eggleston, pp. 1-339. New York: George H. Doran, 1926.

Extracts in HEART SONGS: THE INTIMATE DIARIES OF YOUNG GIRLS, selected by Laurel Holliday, pp. 35-69. Guerneville, Calif.: Bluestocking Books, 1978; New York: Methuen, 1980.

1876-1878. Diary, kept from age twelve through fourteen, of an Ohio girl who recorded affectionate family life, small adventures with her dear friend Jessie, school outings, a dramatic boating accident, joys and sorrows, including a funeral for a tree that had been cut down; a charming and ingenuous diary.

HAWKES, EDWARD, 1837-1902   5072

Paine, Clarence S., ed. "The Diaries of a Nebraska Farmer." AGRICULTURAL HISTORY 22 (1948):1-31.

1876-1877. Brief entries kept by English immigrant farming near Fairbury; routine farm work, hunting and trapping; Lyceum debates and grange activities, including a grange "trial"; crops, prices and wages; Jefferson county politics, trials and lawsuits; battle against a plague of grasshoppers; diarist's great suffering with rheumatism.

HUGHES, RICHARD B., 1856-1930   5073

PIONEER YEARS IN THE BLACK HILLS. Edited by Agnes W. Spring. Western Frontiersmen Series, 6. Glendale, Calif.: Arthur H. Clark, 1957. 366 pp. Diary, pp. 323-335.

1876-1877. Brief entries of a young man in the Black Hills gold rush; hunting, camping and prospecting, which gave way to newspaper reporting for the DEADWOOD WEEKLY PIONEER.

HUNNIUS, CARL JULIUS ADOLPH, b. 1842   5074

Mothershead, Harmon, ed. "The Journal of Ado Hunnius, Indian Territory." CHRONICLES OF OKLAHOMA 51 (1973-1974):451-472.

Jan 1876. Journal of a German immigrant conducting a federal government survey in Indian Territory; good notes on terrain, wildlife, geological features, settlements, ranches, stage stations, etc.; visit with Indian agent John D. Miles and at the agency school at Darlington; extensive notes on settlers and Indians.

JACKSON, WILLIAM EMSLEY, 1858-1945   5075

Oliphant, Orin and Kingston, C.S., eds. "William Emsley Jackson's Diary of a Cattle Drive from La Grande, Oregon, to Cheyenne, Wyoming, in 1876." AGRICULTURAL HISTORY 23 (1949):260-273.

WILLIAM EMSLEY JACKSON'S DIARY OF A CATTLE DRIVE FROM LA GRANDE, OREGON, TO CHEYENNE, WYOMING, in 1876. Edited by J. Orin Oliphant. Fairfield, Wash.: Ye Galleon, 1983. 38 pp.

Jun-Sep 1876. A seventeen-year-old boy's account of cattle drive; route, mainly along Overland Trail, terrain, camps, water and grass; sufferings from mosquitoes; encounters with wagon trains bound for Oregon and Washington; Mormon settlements; graves, including that of Nancy J. Hill; interest in the American Centennial; wages of $145 for the summer's work; a detailed and entertaining diary.

KELLOGG, MARK, d. 1876 5076

"Notes of the Little Big Horn Expedition under General Custer." MONTANA HISTORICAL SOCIETY CONTRIBUTIONS 9 (1923):213-222.

"Mark Kellogg's Diary." NORTH DAKOTA HISTORY 17 (1950):164-176.

In CUSTER'S "MYSTERIOUS MR. KELLOGG" AND THE DIARY OF MARK KELLOGG, by John C. Hixson, pp. 1-34. Bismarck: North Dakota Historical Society, 1950.

In THE CUSTER TRAIL, by Frank L. Anders, edited by John M. Carroll, pp. 29-123 passim. Hidden Springs of Custeriana, 8. Glendale, Calif.: Arthur H. Clark, 1983.

Extracts in DIARIES OF THE LITTLE BIG HORN, by Michael J. Koury, pp. 23-27 passim.

May-Jun 1876. Diary, found on his body after the battle of the Little Bighorn, of a BISMARCK TRIBUNE reporter sent to cover the march of the Dakota Column; brief notes of route, availability of grass and water; references to Gen. Alfred Terry and obvious admiration for Custer; entries made after June 9 not found.

MCCLERNAND, EDWARD JOHN, 1848-1926 5077

In CUSTER'S LAST BATTLE ON THE LITTLE BIG HORN, MONTANA TERRITORY, by Charles F. Roe ... MARCH OF THE "MONTANA COLUMN" DOWN THE YELLOWSTONE RIVER AND THROUGH THE BIG HORN REGION, by Edward J. McClernand, pp. 17-32. New York: R. Bruce, 1927.

Extracts in DIARIES OF THE LITTLE BIG HORN, by Michael J. Koury, pp. 59-62 passim.

Apr-Oct 1876. Sioux War journal of a lieutenant in the Second Cavalry who was acting engineer in John Gibbon's Seventh Infantry; march from Fort Shaw to Fort Ellis with the Montana Column over "frightful roads," then along the Yellowstone to intended rendezvous with Custer's Dakota Column; notes on scenery, soil, geology, etc.; difficulty fording many streams; the arrival of Gen. Alfred H. Terry on the steamboat FAR WEST; soon thereafter, "a big dust is seen in the direction of Big Wolf Mountains, and soon General Custer's long line of cavalry comes in sight"; hot, thirsty march of the Twenty-fifth impeded by Gatling guns; the difficult all night march ordered by Terry, followed by morning arrival of scout James H. Bradley with word that two of Custer's Crow scouts report the annihilation of Custer's detail; but, "report of the Crows not being generally believed," resumption of march along the Little Bighorn until sighting "something on the hill to the left resembling buffalo lying down" and concluding that "Custer has not been entirely successful"; on June 28, burying Custer's and Reno's dead and transporting Reno's wounded to the FAR WEST; march to the mouth of the Rosebud, where Gen. George Crook's arrival announced by Buffalo Bill Cody; combined movements of several commands following Sioux from Big Bend of the Rosebud across Tongue and Powder rivers to the Yellowstone.

MCGILLYCUDDY, VALENTINE T. 5078

Spring, Agnes Wright, ed. "Dr. McGillycuddy's Diary," DENVER

WESTERNERS' BRAND BOOK 9 (1953):277-307.

May 1876-Apr 1877. Diary of the Yellowstone and Bighorn expedition under Gen. George Crook during the Sioux War of 1876; his journey from Washington, D.C., then marches in Wyoming, Montana, the Dakotas and Nebraska.

MULFORD, AMI FRANK, 1854-1901 5079

FIGHTING INDIANS IN THE 7TH UNITED STATES CAVALRY, CUSTER'S FAVORITE REGIMENT. Corning, N.Y.: Lee & A.E. Mulford, 1878. 223 pp. 2d ed., rev. Corning, N.Y.: Paul L. Mulford, 1879. 155 pp. Reprint. Bellevue, Neb.: Old Army Press, 1970. Fairfield, Wash.: Ye Galleon, 1972.

1876-1877. Corning, New York, enlisted man's diary entries amid narrative of Nelson A. Miles's campaign against Chief Joseph; activities at and around Fort Rice, with notes on Indians; summary of battle against the Nez Percé and surrender of Joseph.

REYNOLDS, CHARLIE, d. 1876 5080

In DIARIES OF THE LITTLE BIG HORN, by Michael J. Koury, pp. 27-37 passim.

May-Jun 1876. Civilian scout's diary of the march with the Dakota Column, with entries ending on June 22; diary found on his body after he was killed on June 25 in Maj. Marcus Reno's desperate cavalry charge after his initial disastrous engagement; sporadically continued by Alexander Brown.

SMITH, OSCAR B., d. 1916 5081

Bowen, Dana Thomas, ed. "The Schooner LA PETITE." INLAND SEAS 26 (1970):102-117, 129, 198-214, 223-228, 275-292.

1876-1878. Diary of a Great Lakes ship owner and captain from Huron, Ohio, transporting cargoes of coal, Italian marble, cement, grain, etc.; details of navigation, business and social life in ports; great enjoyment of his two small daughters frequently on board, but grief over one who had died; trip to Washington, D.C., New York and other eastern cities, where he appreciated the sights and good dining; prayers for safe journeys and the health of his family; a good picture of Great Lakes shipping, entrepreneurship and an unusual family life.

Bowen, Dana Thomas, ed. "The Schooner D.K. CLINT." INLAND SEAS 33 (1977):22-29, 43, 121-127, 215-218, 227-232.

1889-1890. Command of the D.K. CLINT, a combination steamer and sailing vessel, sometimes towed behind other steamers; his young son frequently on board, getting "very dirty, but as happy as ever a boy was"; letters and news from home; cargoes of ore and coal; much on other ships and activities in many lake ports; severe storms, including one in which the COMRADE was lost, with all hands; a good diary of a jolly captain, wonderful family man and a great eater of oysters!

STANTON, WILLIAM SANFORD 5082

In EXPLORING THE NORTHERN PLAINS, edited by Lloyd McFarling, pp. 355-372.

May-Jun 1876. Extract from army engineer's report of a march of an expeditionary force under George Crook from Fort Fetterman to the Rosebud; route and terrain through the Powder River Valley; brief account of battles with the Sioux under Crazy Horse at Goose Creek.

TANNER, MARY JANE MOUNT, 1837-1890   5083

In WOMEN'S VOICES, edited by Kenneth Godfrey, Audrey Godfrey and Jill Derr, pp. 309-324.

In A FRAGMENT: THE AUTOBIOGRAPHY OF MARY JANE MOUNT TANNER, edited by Margery W. Ward, pp. 3-19. Salt Lake City: Tanner Trust Fund, University of Utah Library, 1980.

> 1876-1878. Extracts from the diary of a Mormon wife, mother and writer; domestic life and work alongside presidency of the Relief Society, writing poetry and contributing articles to the WOMAN'S EXPONENT; references to her husband, Myron Tanner, whom she shared with his second wife, Ann Crosby Tanner; problems with frequent headaches and being "tired and nervous."

TERRY, ALFRED HOWE, 1827-1890   5084

THE FIELD DIARY OF GENERAL ALFRED H. TERRY: THE YELLOWSTONE EXPEDITION, 1876. Bellevue, Neb.: Old Army Press, 1969. 32 pp. 2d ed., 1970. 37 pp.

Extracts in DIARIES OF THE LITTLE BIG HORN, by Michael J. Koury, pp. 1-6 passim; LITTLE BIG HORN DIARY, by James Willert, pp. 1-427 passim.

> May-Aug 1876. Brief technical notes of Custer's commander; on march with the Dakota Column, then joining John Gibbon's Montana Column on the Yellowstone; difficulties of moving troops and artillery over rough terrain; the desperate night march of June 25; no personal reactions, even to the loss of Custer and his detail.

1877

BERRY, MARIA GOVE   5085

In KATIE-SAN: FROM MAINE PASTURES TO JAPAN SHORES, by Katherine F. Berry, pp. 1-285 passim. Cambridge, Mass.: Dresser, Chapman & Grimes, 1962.

> 1877-1893. Extract from Maine woman's diary about missionary life in Japan with her husband, John C. Berry; her children's "sayings and doings," first words, childhood illnesses, play activities and learning to read.

BISCHOFF, HERMAN   5086

Waldo, Edna Le Moore, trans. "Deadwood to the Big Horns." ANNALS OF WYOMING 9 (1933):19-34.

> Jul-Sep 1877. German immigrant merchant's journey from Deadwood, South Dakota, to the Bighorn Mountains as outfitter and leader of an international company of gold seekers, among them "a number of rough and desperate looking men"; murder by Indians of young brother and sister traveling together and other Indian alarms; dissatisfaction among his "passengers," who gradually deserted the company; site of Custer battlefield strewn with bones apparently dug up by wolves; unsuccessful attempt to find gold upon arrival.

CARPENTER, WILSON HOWELL   5087

Mahrer, Douglas L., ed. "The Diary of Wilson Howell Carpenter: An Account of the 1877 Railroad Riots." WESTERN PENNSYLVANIA HISTORICAL MAGAZINE 60 (1977):305-313.

> Jul 1877. Long narrative extract describing the railroad strike and riot; incident at Pittsburgh in which Philadelphia National Guard fired upon and killed a number of strikers and sympathizers; withdrawal of troops to the roundhouse, where they were besieged by the armed mob until forced to flee from the burning building and railroad yard with further casualties on both sides; continued looting, destruction and burning of trains and stations of the Pennsylvania Railroad.

CROMBIE, HELEN ELIZABETH, 1862-1950   5088

Crombie, John Newell, ed. "Account of the Pennsylvania Railroad Riots: From a Young Girl's Diary." WESTERN PENNSYLVANIA HISTORICAL MAGAZINE 54 (1971):385-389.

> Jul 1877. Extracts from the diary of a Beaver Falls girl who reported the riots while visiting her aunt, Rachel Jane Henry McKee, in Old Allegheny; a "war" between strikers and Philadelphia National Guard which had been called in to aid local police; burning and lootings, with people "carrying ham, bacon, tobacco, ... plunder from the cars"; violence and destruction in Pittsburgh.

FISHER, S.G.   5089

"Journal of S.G. Fisher, Chief of Scouts to General O.O. Howard during the Campaign against the Nez Percé Indians, 1877." MONTANA HISTORICAL SOCIETY CONTRIBUTIONS 2 (1896):269-282.

> Aug-Sep 1877. Recruiting Bannock Indians, for which he was hired as "Chief of scouts, wages not stated"; scouting from Fort Hall ahead of the main command over difficult terrain; a few skirmishes, then a major battle on Canyon Creek involving Colonel Sturgis's cavalry; a detailed description of the battle and diarist's part in it; criticism of Sturgis's tactics and admiration for Robert Fletcher.

HARLAN, JOHN MARSHALL, 1833-1911   5090

Farrelly, David G., ed. "John M. Harlan's One-Day Diary, August 21, 1877: An Interpretation of the Harlan-Bristow Controversy." FILSON CLUB HISTORICAL QUARTERLY 24 (1950):158-168.

> Aug 1877. Kentucky lawyer's "one-day diary" kept two months before his appointment to the Supreme Court by President Hayes, which chronicles deteriorating relations with his friend and law partner, Benjamin H. Bristow, both under consideration for the post; summary of July political activities in Kentucky and Washington; then a record of "sundry matters which have transpired in reference to Col. Bristow and myself and which have disturbed perhaps permanently the very pleasant and confidential relations which have existed between us for more than ten years."

HILL, ERASTUS G.   5091

"A Florida Settler of 1877." FLORIDA HISTORICAL QUARTERLY 28 (1950):271-294.

> Jan-Feb 1877. Chicago man's train trip to settle in Florida; observations of and opinions on the South, including the detrimental effects of carpetbaggers; long, descriptive notes on Jacksonville; Fernandina, Gainesville, etc.; ancedotes on people; prospects for business and farming, especially orange growing; eventual purchase of land at Lawtey; a garrulous, run-on style.

JAMES, FRANK LOWBER, 1841-1907   5092

YEARS OF DISCONTENT: DR. FRANK L. JAMES IN ARKANSAS.
Edited by W. David Baird. Memphis: Memphis State University Press,
1977. 84 pp.

Sep 1877-Apr 1878. Diary of an intellectual physician from Memphis, suffering in the small town atmosphere of Osceola, Arkansas; notes on medical treatments; comments on local religion, especially Baptists; strong personal opinions on literature, politics, economics, opera, drama, religion; exploring mounds in surrounding area and sending Indian artifacts to Smithsonian; many names of Osceola persons and friends in and around Memphis.

KEELER, MARY FERGUSON, 1856-1927   5093

Keeler, Ruth, ed. "A Much Travelled Young Lady." WESTCHESTER HISTORIAN 26 (1950): 3-28.

1877-1880. Extracts from travel diaries of a wealthy young Westchester woman accompanying her father, Yates Ferguson; train travel to San Francisco, where she enjoyed social life, theater and Episcopal church services; briefly to Seattle, a "wild place" where "the people are mostly freethinkers"; European tour with both Atlantic crossings on the BOTHNIA; a mad whirl of tourist attractions in London, Paris, Berlin, Vienna, etc., with some ingenuous notes of luxury travel; summary of a third trip through New England and eastern Canada.

MAGUIRE, DON, 1852-1933   5094

Topping, Gary, ed. "A Trader in the Rocky Mountains." IDAHO YESTERDAYS 27, no. 2 (1983): 2-12.

Aug-Dec 1877. Peddler's diary kept on trips through Utah, Idaho and Montana; from Ogden, Utah, by wagon, carrying "one thousand dollars worth of silks, poplins, linens and embroidery" to trade in towns, mining camps and Indian reservations; notes on Mormons, Indians and various settlers, towns of Boise and Atlanta, Idaho, and lodgings; cursing his lot in life while reading Byron and the SPECTATOR; scattered bits of information on the recent Bannock and Nez Percé wars.

MAYER, FREDERICK   5095

Brimlow, George F., ed. "Nez Percé War Diary." IDAHO STATE HISTORICAL SOCIETY, 17th Biennial Report, 1939-1940. Boise, 1940. Pp. 27-31.

Jun-Sep 1877. Diary of a German immigrant private in Troop L, First Cavalry, on marches from Fort Walla Walla to Indian Valley, Oregon, then to the "seat of war" in Idaho; on June 28 at White Bird Canyon, where they buried remains of F and H troops who had been killed on the 15th, "the most sickening sight I ever seen"; an ambush of advance guard at Craigs Mountain, with all killed including commander Lt. Sevier Rains; subsequent engagements in the Cottonwood and Clearwater areas until the Nez Percé "crossed the Clearwater and started for Montana on the Lo Lo Trail."

Brimlow, George F., ed. "Two Cavalrymen's Diaries of the Bannock War." OREGON HISTORICAL QUARTERLY 68 (1967): 293-316.

Jun-Oct 1878. Diary of Oregon campaign against Bannock and Paiute Indians; bare notes of route, marches and camps.

MOXLEY, LYDIA DART   5096

Sanders, James, ed. "Times Hard But Grit Good." ANNALS OF IOWA 47 (1984): 270-290.

Jan-Dec 1877. A farm wife's diary of domestic chores, farm and social life near Grinnell, with most entries beginning: "I did up work"; prices for crops and livestock; farm work done by her husband, Anson Moxley; a good picture of the enormous and exhausting range of tasks for both husband and wife on a prosperous farm of the period.

NOLAN, NICHOLAS   5097

Carroll, H. Bailey, ed. "Nolan's 'Lost Nigger' Expedition of 1877." SOUTHWESTERN HISTORICAL QUARTERLY 44 (1940): 55-75.

Jul-Aug 1877. Captain's report of punitive expedition from Fort Concho against Comanches undertaken by Company A, Tenth Cavalry, a black unit, and a group of buffalo hunters under James Harvey; a waterless march on the Llano Estacado during which many men died of thirst, particularly in the area later named "Nigger Hill," and survivors were reduced to drinking the blood and urine of horses.

ROBSON, WALTER, 1842-1929   5098

AN ENGLISH VIEW OF AMERICAN QUAKERISM: THE JOURNAL OF WALTER ROBSON. Edited by Edwin B. Bronner. Memoirs of the American Philosophical Society, vol. 79. Philadelphia: American Philosophical Society, 1970. 162 pp.

Aug-Nov 1877. Journal of an English Quaker minister's arduous sojourn to visit American Friends and attend their yearly meetings in various locations; detailed notes on dissension, revivals, camp meetings, policies, sermons, testimonies of believers, hymns, etc.; tourist diversion of Niagara Falls; interesting account of transatlantic crossings, including the shipwreck of the OASIS, which collided with his ship, the PENNSYLVANIA; amusing incident of preaching while clinging to a pillar during a storm.

SELBY, THOMAS GUNN, 1846-1910   5099

Welland, Dennis, ed. "Across the Continent 1877-78." BRITISH ASSOCIATION FOR AMERICAN STUDIES BULLETIN 9 (December 1964): 56-68.

Dec 1877-Jan 1878. American travels of an English missionary en route to resume his work in China; to New York on the ALGERIA, "a perfect pandemonium of gambling and blasphemy"; tourist sites and a lecture by Henry Ward Beecher in New York; Niagara Falls, train travel to Chicago, Salt Lake and San Francisco; comments on Indians and Chinese.

WEIKERT, ANDREW J.   5100

"Journal of the Tour through the Yellowstone National Park in August and September, 1877, the Nez Percé's Raid." MONTANA HISTORICAL SOCIETY CONTRIBUTIONS 3 (1900): 153-174.

Aug-Sep 1877. Horseback journey with Richard Dietrich, Fred Pfister, Joe Roberts and others "to see the wonders of the Northwest," described with detail and enthusiasm until party surprised by Nez Percé, who plundered their camp and killed or wounded several of the men; narrative account of escape and subsequent difficulties in finding the missing and recovering dead and wounded.

WISE, ISAAC MAYER, 1819-1900   5101

Kramer, William M., ed. "The Western Journal of Isaac Mayer Wise." WESTERN STATES JEWISH HISTORICAL QUARTERLY 4 (1972):150-167, 202-227; 5 (1973):40-56, 117-134.

> Jul-Aug 1877. Diary, originally kept for his newspaper, AMERICAN ISRAELITE, of a Cincinnati rabbi, a Bohemian immigrant; summary of a journey to Salt Lake, with notes on cities, newspapers and Jewish residents en route; Salt Lake City described in some detail, with a few comments on Mormons; dated entries covering travel to Eureka, Nevada, where he preached to a Jewish congregation in a Methodist church and described Jewish, Indian and Chinese residents; extensive notes on San Francisco, with attention to Jewish residents to whom he often preached; race and labor relations between white and Chinese and economic problems of the city; a visit to Santa Cruz and the "big trees"; speeches on behalf of his Hebrew Union College.

"Rabbi Wise: by Parlor Car across the Great American Desert." PACIFIC HISTORIAN 11, no. 4 (1967):17-27.

> Jul 1877. Extracts.

"Rabbi Wise sees San Francisco." PACIFIC HISTORIAN 11, no. 3 (1967):10-25.

> Jul-Aug 1877. Extracts.

1878

ANDREWS, WILLIAM ALBERT   5102

A DARING VOYAGE ACROSS THE ATLANTIC OCEAN BY TWO AMERICANS. Introduction and notes by Dr. Macaulay. New York: E.P. Dutton, 1880, 151 pp.

DANGEROUS VOYAGES OF CAPTAIN WILLIAM ANDREWS. Compilation and commentary by Richard Henderson. New York: Abercrombie & Fitch; Ann Arbor: University Microfilms, 1966. 394 pp. Diary, pp. 100-174.

> Jun-Aug 1878. Beverly, Massachusetts, yachtsman's log and diary of his daring crossing of the Atlantic with his brother Asa Walter Andrews, on the nineteen foot schooner NAUTILUS from Boston to Le Havre; names of ships encountered and cheers of the passengers for their well publicized voyage; weather, problems and dangers, including the proximity of curious whales; an unexplained apparition of some sort of sea monster.

COLUMBUS OUTDONE: AN EXACT NARRATIVE OF THE VOYAGE OF THE YANKEE SKIPPER, CAPT. WM. A. ANDREWS. Compiled by Artemas Ward. New York: Enoch Morgan's Sons, 1893. 198 pp.

DANGEROUS VOYAGES OF CAPTAIN WILLIAM ANDREWS, pp. 214-356.

> Jul-Sep 1892. His solo voyage on the SAPOLIO from Atlantic City, New Jersey, to Palos, Spain, Columbus's departure point; satisfaction that the SAPOLIO was "the smallest and fastest seagoing yacht in the world"; some "glorious days" interspersed with storms and sleepless nights; throwing bottles with notes in them overboard; having to pull his own tooth; ingenious methods of staying alive and reasonably comfortable.

BERRELL, GEORGE BARTON, b. 1849   5103

Carlander, Harriet Bell and Kenneth D., eds. "George Barton Berrell's Piscatorial Summer of 1878." MISSOURI HISTORICAL SOCIETY BULLETIN 7 (1951):413-439.

> Mar-Jul 1878. St. Louis actor's diaries of fishing trips, mostly on the Illinois side of the Mississippi, in creeks and "river bottom lakes" which no longer exist; logistics of expeditions with his companions from De Bar's Opera House; baits used, sizes, kinds and numbers of catch.

BROWN, WILLIAM CAREY   5104

Brimlow, George F., ed. "Two Cavalrymen's Diaries of the Bannock War, 1878." OREGON HISTORICAL QUARTERLY 68 (1967):221-258.

> Jun-Oct 1878. Military diary of officer in the First Cavalry, Company L, under Gen. Oliver O. Howard during the Bannock-Paiute campaign; departure from Fort Walla Walla; distances and route, mainly quartering at ranches in Oregon; problems with horses "giving out"; occasional skirmishes; arrival of Paiute princess Sarah Winnemucca.

BUTLER, SARAH ELIZABETH, 1857-1931   5105

"An Oregon Trail Story." CLARK COUNTY HISTORY 15 (1974):358-381.

> Apr-Jul 1878. Young Missouri woman's lively account of driving a covered wagon to settle at Vancouver, Washington; departure from Carthage, Missouri; route; vivid descriptions of scenery and incidents; alarm of company over reports of massacres in Oregon; her enjoyment of Portland and Vancouver.

GOODALE, EPHRAIM, 1806-1887   5106

Goodale, Roy, ed. "A Civilian at Fort Leavenworth and Fort Hays." KANSAS HISTORICAL QUARTERLY 33 (1967):138-155.

> 1878-1879. Orrington, Maine, farmer's diary extracts of later years spent on the frontier; brief notes of life at forts Leavenworth and Hays, where his son Greenleaf Goodale was stationed; social life, church services, daily weather, troop movements.

Goodale, Roy, ed. "A Civilian at Old Fort Bayard." NEW MEXICO HISTORICAL REVIEW 25 (1950):296-304.

> 1881-1883. Brief extracts; some Indian alarms; the death of his daughter-in-law Fidelia Beach Goodale.

HARDESTY, GEORGE WASHINGTON, 1850-1926   5107

Louden, Richard H., ed. "Diary of George W. Hardesty." COLORADO MAGAZINE 38 (1961):174-187.

> 1878-1879 (with gaps). Trip from Germantown, Missouri, to Colorado; work on the Atchison, Topeka and Santa Fe Railroad and hauling freight by wagon; rambles about Colorado, New Mexico and Oklahoma Indian Territory before settling at Folsom, New Mexico, to begin ranching; notes on towns and settlements, but mostly a rugged outdoor life.

IDE, LUCY A.   5108

Oliphant, J. Orin, ed. "In a Prairie Schooner, 1878." WASHINGTON HISTORICAL QUARTERLY 18 (1927):122-131, 191-198, 277-288.

May-Sep 1878. Woman's journey with others from Mondovi, Wisconsin, to settle at Dayton, Washington; pleasant, articulate notes of scenery, weather, domestic chores, people, towns and settlements en route; fears generated by news of Bannock uprising; diarist's sympathy for Mormon wives.

JAMES, HENRY, 1843-1916   5109

THE NOTEBOOKS OF HENRY JAMES. Edited by F.O. Matthiessen and Kenneth B. Murdock. New York: Oxford University Press, 1947. 425 pp. Reprint. New York: George Braziller, 1955. Phoenix ed. Chicago: University of Chicago Press, 1981.

1878-1911. Mainly a daybook of ideas for stories, some of which never saw print but which were no less interesting for that; few events but references to Alice and William James and friends such as the aged Fanny Kemble and Mrs. Ritchie, daughter of Thackeray, both of whom were frequent sources of story ideas; a fascinating record of the creative processes of a writer wholly absorbed in his craft.

Extracts in TREASURY OF THE WORLD'S GREAT DIARIES, edited by Philip Dunaway, pp. 477-480.

1881-1882. Impressions of Boston, New York and Cambridge; the death of his mother.

LEE, FRANCIS HENRY, 1836-1913   5110

"Forty Years Ago in Salem." ESSEX INSTITUTE HISTORICAL COLLECTIONS 59 (1923):102-104, 359-360; 60 (1924):75-80; 61 (1925):396-400.

Jan-Jul 1878. Extracts from diary of a Salem man with interests in books, choral society, violin lessons and the collecting of antiques and art, with many examples described in the diary; Salem anecdotes, historical tidbits, social life and individuals; the beginnings of philanthropic and civic endeavors, especially for the Essex Institute, of which he was eventually a director.

MCNAUGHT, JOHN S., 1843-1914   5111

Schneider, George A., ed. "A Border Incident of 1878: From the Journal of Captain John S. McNaught." SOUTHWESTERN HISTORICAL QUARTERLY 70 (1966):314-320.

Jun 1878. An expedition under William R. Shafter from Fort Clark, Texas, into Mexico against Indians who had killed settlers and fled across the Rio Grande; skirmishes mainly with Mexicans determined to oppose repeated United States incursion into Mexican soil in pursuit of Indians and bandits.

MORAN, GEORGE HENRY ROBERTS, b. 1840   5112

Hagemann, E.R., ed. "Arizona Territory 1878: The Diary of George H. Moran, Contract Surgeon." ARIZONA AND THE WEST 5 (1963):249-267.

Feb-Sep 1878. Army surgeon's brief notes of train travel from Baltimore to San Francisco, then to Yuma, where he was stationed at Camp Bowie and accompanied patrols into areas held by Chiricahuas; sketchy notes on distances, water, camps and stopovers at ranches; reports of mail riders killed by Indians; little medical information.

MUDGE, SARAH W.   5113

"From the Diary of Sarah W. Mudge." DANVERS HISTORICAL SOCIETY COLLECTIONS 41 (1961):30.

Feb, Apr 1878. Extracts from travel diary; description of "a lady of the Harem" and her attendants in Cairo; celebrating the anniversary of Greek independence in Athens and glimpses of that country's royal family.

PALMER, HORACE L.   5114

Palmer, Virginia A., ed. "A Wisconsin Whaler: The Letters and Diaries of Horace L. Palmer." WISCONSIN MAGAZINE OF HISTORY 54 (1970-1971):87-118.

1878-1880 (with gaps). Well-educated Milwaukee man's adventures as a common seaman aboard the New Bedford whaling ship WANDERER on a South Atlantic voyage; long, detailed descriptions of whaling, with initial enthusiasm tempered by the realities of danger, overwork and inadequate food, especially the "miserable stinginess" of the owners and Capt. Andrew R. Heyer; a dismal Christmas; in port at St. Helena.

PETROFF, IVAN, b. 1842   5115

Hinckley, Theodore C. and Caryl, eds. "Ivan Petroff's Journal of a Trip to Alaska in 1878." JOURNAL OF THE WEST 5 (1966):25-70. Diary, pp. 43-66.

Jul-Oct 1878. Russian immigrant's journal of travels in Alaska to translate Russian documents and interview Russian residents for the Bancroft Library and Hubert H. Bancroft's HISTORY OF ALASKA; on the RICHARD RUSH under Capt. Lewis W. Bailey, with notes on Indians and scenes along the inland channel; in Alaska, visits to missions, schools, Russian settlements, Aleut villages and various business enterprises, with many references to the Alaska Commercial Company; ethnographic notes on Aleuts and Russians; an interesting and unusual diary recording one episode of a long and controversial career in Alaska affairs marred later by suspician of imposture and forgery.

SMITH, GEORGE WATSON   5116

Parker, Watson, ed. "An Illinois Greenhorn in Bismarck, D.T." NORTH DAKOTA HISTORY 35, no. 1 (1968):21-27.

May 1878. Young Evanston banker's trip to consider farm loans and investment opportunities; description of Bismarck and its prospects for growth; a land deal at Brainerd, Minnesota.

WOOD, CHARLES ERSKINE SCOTT   5117

"Private Journal, 1878," OREGON HISTORICAL QUARTERLY 70 (1969):5-38.

Jun-Aug 1878. Cavalryman's Bannock War journal; trip from Portland to Wallula on Columbia River steamer WIDE WEST enlivened by troupe of Rose Manning Opera Bouffe and flirtations of actresses; overland to Idaho with Gen. Oliver O. Howard; Paiute princess Sarah Winnemucca's moving plea for her people; amusing encounter with eccentric Joseph Magone; discoveries of killed and mutilated settlers; the battle of Birch Creek; ruminations on death, frontiersmen and Indians; Paiute customs described by Sarah Winnemucca.

"Private Journal, 1879." OREGON HISTORICAL QUARTERLY 70 (1969):139-170.

Feb-May 1879 (with gaps). Wintering at Goldendale, Washington; clever vignettes of local characters; boredom and meager social life; move to Yakima Indian Agency where Wood recorded an extensive interview between himself, Chief Moses and Indian agent James H. Wilbur over removal of Indians to the reservation; references to General Howard; hostility of local settlers against Moses; negotiations with Chief Homily.

1879

BRIDGES, F.D.   5118

JOURNAL OF A LADY'S TRAVELS ROUND THE WORLD. London: John Murray, 1883. 413 pp. American journal, pp. 336-413.

Jun-Aug 1879. English traveler's journal of visit to San Francisco and Portland, Oregon, by steamer and Yosemite Valley, Tahoe, Salt Lake, Denver and Chicago by railroad while on trip around the world; comments on character of each place, the hotels, service, food, shopping, American customs.

BROSS, WILLIAM, 1813-1890   5119

Destler, Chester, ed. "Diary of a Journey into the Valleys of the Red River of the North and the Upper Missouri." MISSISSIPPI VALLEY HISTORICAL REVIEW 33 (1946-1947):425-442.

May-Jun 1879. Travel diary of retired publisher of the CHICAGO TRIBUNE, kept on a journey to assess potential for further railroad development of the northern plains; by train and riverboat to Winnipeg and Bismarck; thence on the DAKOTA up the Missouri; comments on weather, country and Indians, which he found "horrid looking ... treacherous and murderous"; great interest in geological feature and agricultural potential of Minnesota, the Dakotas and Montana.

DE LONG, GEORGE WASHINGTON, 1844-1881   5120

THE VOYAGE OF THE JEANNETTE. Edited by Emma De Long. Boston and New York: Houghton Mifflin, 1883. 2 vols.

1879-1881. Journal of the commander of the JEANNETTE, a ship privately fitted by James Bennett for the United States Navy's American Arctic Expedition in a search for the North Pole via Bering Straits; San Francisco to St. Lawrence Bay; drifting in ice off Herald Island; winter conditions and routines while frozen fast in the ice; leak in and eventual breakup of the ship with escape in three small boats; separation of boats, landing in Siberia and futile attempt to survive the Arctic cold along the Lena River.

In OUR LOST EXPLORERS, by Richard W. Bliss, edited by Raymond L. Newcomb, pp. 262-269, 379-392. Hartford; American Publishing, 1882; San Francisco: A.L. Bancroft, 1888.

May-Oct 1881. Extract covering struggle across pack ice and open water to the Lena.

DRINKWATER, SUMNER PIERCE, b. 1859   5121

Freehand, Julianna. A SEAFARING LEGACY: THE PHOTOGRAPHS, DIARIES, LETTERS AND MEMORABILIA OF A MAINE SEA CAPTAIN AND HIS WIFE. New York: Random House, 1981. Diaries, pp. 35-141 passim.

1879-1901. Extracts from logs and diaries of a Yarmouth, Maine, ship captain and his wife, Alice Gray Drinkwater; early married life on board coasting schooners GRACE CUSHING and BRAMHILL, followed by his first "deepwater" command on a voyage of the GRACE DEERING from New York to Australia; longer entries by his wife from 1898-1901 while aboard the DEERING; fascinating details of seafaring life during the waning days of sail; notes on Singapore and other ports; a wealth of photographs and letters as well as diaries.

DRUMMOND, HENRY, 1851-1897   5122

THE LIFE OF HENRY DRUMMOND. New York: Doubleday & McClure, 1898. 541 pp. London: Hodder and Stoughton, 1899. 506 pp.

Sep 1879. Autobiography containing diary of a scientific expedition to the Rocky Mountains with geologists from Edinburgh University, an early event in the life of popular Scottish evangelist and theological writer; geological and topographical notes, with special attention to geysers of Yellowstone.

DUVAL, BURR G., d. 1893   5123

Woolford, Sam, ed. "The Burr G. Duval Diary." SOUTHWESTERN HISTORICAL QUARTERLY 65 (1962):487-511.

Dec 1879-Apr 1880. Extracts from diary of an exploring expedition organized by the Galveston, Houston & San Antonio Railroad, the International & Great Northern Railroad and the Texas & Pacific Railroad to search for gold, silver and other minerals in the Rio Grande area; wagon travel from San Antonio to the Chinati Mountains with a party of railroad men under military escort from Fort Clark led by Lt. John L. Bullis; camps, ranches, conditions of travel, hunting; reports of past Indian atrocities; colorful notes on others in the party, including B.A. Fessenden, Duval West and E.S. Niccolls, whose apparently poor leadership caused dissension; diarist's pessimism about prospects for success of the expedition; return to San Antonio.

HEWARD, TEANCUM WILLIAM, 1854-1915   5124

Buice, David. "Excerpts from the Diary of Teancum William Heward." GEORGIA HISTORICAL QUARTERLY 64 (1980):317-325.

1879-1880. Mormon missionary's itineration through Georgia, preaching in homes and schoolhouses, especially in Union, Fannin and White counties; opposition by local Baptists and threats of ruffians; some conversions, including that of Baptist minister Willis King.

JACOBSEN, JAMES ROBERT, 1857-1885   5125

Jackson, John C., ed. "A Wild Mustang Campaign of 1879 in Pumpkin Valley." NEBRASKA HISTORY 57 (1976):315-330.

Mar-Sep 1879. Extracts from Saline County cowboy's diary; riding herd at night guarding freighters' oxen along the Sidney-Deadwood trail; wild horse roundups with three other "stout hearted frontiersmen," capturing and running horses into Sidney to sell.

PARSONS, GEORGE WHITWELL, 1850-1933   5126

THE PRIVATE JOURNAL OF GEORGE WHITWELL PARSONS. Prepared by Arizona Statewide Archival and Records Project, Division of Professional and Service Projects, Work Projects Administration. Phoenix: Arizona Statewide Archival and Records Project, 1939. 333 pp.

1879-1882. Personal journal of an agreeable man in San Francisco who tried, not always successfully, to combine earning a living with a busy social life of balls, opera, theater and visiting friends in the city and Oakland; an unsettling experience at a seance; studying German with a private tutor; long notes on events such as the departure of the JEANETTE on a polar expedition and arrival of President Grant on the CITY OF TOKIO, both amid great fanfare; serving at the California Wire Works Company display at the Fourteenth Industrial Fair; references to a family intrigue in veiled language; removing to Tombstone, Arizona, and establishing Parsons and Redfern Mining Company; good descriptions of the country, including a visit to the mission church San Xavier; work and life of miners; primitive living conditions of the rough mining town; incidents of mine jumping, hotly contested local political campaigns, a fire in which he was seriously injured and affairs involving the Earp brothers; complicated business dealings resulting in a long court case and problems with his alcoholic partner; references to a literary society, books read and churches.

RANOUS, DORA KNOWLTON THOMPSON, 1859-1916   5127

DIARY OF A DALY DEBUTANTE. New York: Duffield, 1910. 249 pp. Reprint. New York: B. Blom, 1972.

1879-1880. Actress's youthful and enthusiastic descriptions of plays, performers and theaters during a winter season at Augustin Daly's Theater in New York and a summer tour of Philadelphia, Newport, Boston, Portsmouth, Portland, Providence, Hartford, Albany, Rochester, Detroit, Milwaukee and Chicago; rigid deportment required of all actresses in the company; complete casts of all productions.

SHEARER, MARY HALLOCK, 1843-1917   5128

JOURNAL: EARLY HISTORY FROM SOUTHEASTERN ILLINOIS' WABASH COUNTY. Edited by Clara Pixley. St. Louis?, 1967. 169 pp. Journal, pp. xi-xiv, 163-169.

1879-1905 (with gaps). Extracts from woman's diary of rural family life, daily home duties, children and grandchildren; love of reading, desire for learning, attending the literary society and Lyceum lectures, enjoying writing her "Recollections"; recounting the happy times such as a great family celebration of her eighty-one year old father's birthday and the sad times, "the new, strange, incomprehensible, and sometimes bitter grief that fills my heart" as she records the deaths of her husband and only daughter.

STACEY, MARY BANKS, 1846-1918   5129

Myres, Sandra L., ed. "An Arizona Camping Trip." ARIZONA AND THE WEST 23 (1981):53-64.

Aug 1879. Lively letter-diary of an army wife whose husband, Col. Stacey, was stationed at Camp Thomas; bumping along in an ambulance with her children, camping at Mount Graham and visiting Camp Grant, where she considered the officers' wives to be stupid and boring; a bout of malaria.

TAYLOR, CORA BEST, 1860-1924   5130

Flanders, Bert H., ed. "The Diary of Cora Best Taylor." ATLANTA HISTORICAL BULLETIN 16, no. 2 (1971):47-59.

Mar-Apr 1879. Young woman's diary of a visit with her friend Nannie Outland, in Scarboro, Georgia; social life and her love for fiance Jesse Parker Williams; return home to Rosedale, South Carolina, engagement and plans for the future; a pleasant diary of youthful spirits, apprehension and resolve.

TREXLER, FRANK MATTERN, 1861-1947   5131

THE DIARY OF JUDGE FRANK M. TREXLER. Edited by Edwin R. Baldridge. Lehigh County Historical Society Proceedings, vol. 35. Allentown, Pa.: Lehigh County Historical Society, 1982. 400 pp. Diary, pp. 15-304.

1879-1891. Diary of an Allentown lawyer and judge beginning just after his graduation from Muhlenberg College; law studies, business and social life, squiring an amazing number of girls to dances, parties, church functions, sleigh rides, etc.; local events, politics, people, with many marriages and funerals reported; legal work and court cases, including descriptions of specific suits and trials; trips to Philadelphia, Niagara Falls, Canada, etc.; courtship and marriage to Jennie R. Shelling; a full and varied source on Allentown people, events and social life.

TUGGLE, WILLIAM ORRIE, 1841-1884   5132

SHEM HAM & JAPHETH: THE PAPERS OF W.O. TUGGLE, COMPRISING HIS INDIAN DIARY, SKETCHES & OBSERVATIONS. Edited by Eugene Current-Garcia with Dorothy B. Hatfield. Athens: University of Georgia Press, 1973. 361 pp. Diary, pp. 29-113, 178-272.

Aug-Oct 1879. Record of Georgian appointed agent for the Creek Nation; travel to Indian Territory, noting wealth and farming methods of Midwest; meeting frontier characters and Indian officials, including Hepsey Leeder, Osceola's sister; addressing the House of Warriors on Creek Orphan Claim; much on Creek tribal law, customs, games and medicine; making manuscript collection of Creek myths; digging in mounds near Arkansas and Grand rivers; attending camp meetings and visiting Asbury and Tallahassee missions.

1880-1882. In Washington promoting the Creek Orphan Claim and lobbying for Choctaws and Chickasaws; notes on leading political issues of the day and prominent individuals involved, including election of Alexander H. Stephens as governor of Georgia; Star Route scandals; Washington gossip and social life; his irritation with delays and congressional inefficiency.

1880

ABBOTT, ETHEL B.   5133

A DIARY OF A TOUR THROUGH CANADA AND THE UNITED STATES. London, 1882. 63 pp.

Aug-Oct 1880? An English girl's trip with her affluent family; Atlantic crossing on the SARMATIAN; tour through eastern Canada, then to Chicago, St. Louis, New York, Boston and Philadelphia, mainly by train; constant unfavorable comparisons with things British.

**BANDELIER, ADOLPH FRANCIS ALPHONSE,   5134
1840-1914**

THE SOUTHWEST JOURNALS OF ADOLF F. BANDELIER. Edited
by Charles H. Lange and Carroll L. Riley. Albuquerque: University
of New Mexico Press, 1966-1984. 4 vols.

> 1880-1892. Extensive diaries and field notes of Swiss-born ar-
> chaeologist studying Pueblo culture in Arizona and New Mex-
> ico; important pioneering efforts in archaeology, ethnology and
> Indian history conducted with insatiable curiosity but, according
> to some successors, inadequate methodology; Pueblo customs,
> conditions of living, work, artifacts, etc., observed in situ and
> studied in local Spanish archives; mention of many names and
> places, reading and wide intellectual interests; correspondence
> with Francis Parkman and Charles Eliot Norton; personal material.

BRIGGS, LLOYD VERNON, b. 1863   5135

AROUND THE HORN TO HONOLULU ON THE BARK "AMY
TURNER." Boston: Charles E. Lauriat, 1926. 186 pp.

> Jul-Dec 1880. Diary of a sixteen-year-old Bostonian sent to sea
> to cure his tuberculosis, sailing as the only passenger on the AMY
> TURNER under Capt. Albert W. Newell; unusually interesting
> notes on the voyage, with the sharp diarist missing little from his
> deck chair, including the captain's adroit handling of a near mutiny
> caused by the brutality of first mate Arthur Lewis; contrast be-
> tween cabin food and that of the crew; King Neptune's festivities,
> sailors' songs, ships encountered; the beauties of sea and sky;
> "grand" storms, including the usual gales of the Horn; notes on
> Honolulu sights, people and customs; social life of the New
> England community, with vignettes of Joseph O. Carter and
> others; diarist's satisfaction with his improved health.

EXPERIENCES OF A MEDICAL STUDENT IN HAWAII. Boston:
David D. Nickerson, 1926. 251 pp.

> 1880-1881. Adventures in Honolulu studying medicine with and
> assisting Dr. John S. McGrew; a smallpox epidemic and govern-
> ment efforts to control its spread, including hiring the seventeen-
> year-old diarist as "deputy vaccinating officer"; his sometimes
> dangerous horseback travels around Oahu, vaccinating the un-
> willing residents; social life in Honolulu, where he was evidently
> a great favorite; staying with the families of the Rev. Samuel M.
> Damon and Joseph O. Carter; a relapse of his tuberculosis, dur-
> ing which he was nursed by the Damons; full, entertaining notes.

CALIFORNIA AND THE WEST, 1881 AND LATER. Boston: Privately printed by Wright and Potter, 1931. 214 pp. passim.

> 1881-1882. Tourist entries scattered throughout reminiscent nar-
> rative of travels in California; extensive comment on the sights
> in California; San Francisco, including Chinatown, Los Angeles,
> with notes on Samuel Henry Kent, Santa Monica, etc.; itinerary
> and hotels.

> 1921-1923 (with gaps). Train trip with his wife, Mary Cabot Briggs,
> from Boston to Lake Tahoe, Mono Lake, Yosemite, etc., with
> chauffeured automobile travel throughout the area; return via the
> Grand Canyon.

ARIZONA AND NEW MEXICO, 1882, CALIFORNIA, 1886, MEXICO,
1891. Boston: Privately printed, 1932. 282 pp. passim.

> 1882-1891 (with gaps). Diary entries scattered throughout nar-
> rative of events, travels, scenery, cities, people, etc., through the
> West; snatches of hearsay and history, material on Indians, in-

cluding Geronimo; an especially gruesome public hanging in
California; an interesting picture of train travel of the time.

CATTELL, JAMES MCKEAN, 1860-1944   5136

AN EDUCATION IN PSYCHOLOGY: JAMES MCKEAN CATTELL'S
JOURNAL AND LETTERS FROM GERMANY AND ENGLAND.
Edited by Michael M. Sokal. Cambridge: MIT Press, 1981. 372 pp.
Journal, pp. 23-275.

> 1880-1887 (with gaps). Extracts showing personal and profes-
> sional growth of a scientist and his development of experimen-
> tal psychology; student years as a tourist and scholar in Germany
> and England studying under Wilhelm Wundt at the University of
> Leipzig and as fellow-commoner of St. John's College, Cam-
> bridge; experimenting with hashish, writing scientific papers and
> accepting an appointment as lecturer at the University of
> Pennsylvania.

FERGUSON, ROBERT, 1855-1935   5137

HARPOONER: A FOUR-YEAR VOYAGE ON THE BARQUE
KATHLEEN. Edited by Leslie D. Stair. Philadelphia: University of
Pennsylvania Press, 1936. 310 pp.

> 1880-1884. Whaling diary of a Scottish immigrant who was har-
> pooner on the KATHLEEN of New Bedford; excellent descriptions
> of whale chases, storms and the hazards and work of whaling;
> sailors' activities such as scrimshaw, singing and dancing; their
> humor and superstitions; studying navigation and teaching Ger-
> man and Portuguese crewmen to read and write; ships en-
> countered; ports of call at Azores, Tristan da Cunha, African ports
> and St. Helena, where he enjoyed social life with Highland Scots
> settled there; fierce battles at sea with Malay pirates and Arab
> slave traders; from St. Helena to Boston as captain of the mer-
> chant ship DAYLIGHT; return to the KATHLEEN; an outstanding
> whaling diary by a young man of great natural ability and staunch
> Presbyterian principles.

HARRISON, WILLIAM GREGORY, 1855-1882   5138

Miller, Roger G., ed. "Chronicles of Upper Burnet." INDIANA
MAGAZINE OF HISTORY 74 (1978):316-363; 75 (1979):147-210.

> Oct 1880-May 1881. Pleasant journal of well-educated young
> Morgan County farmer; a thorough and varied picture of work,
> crops and general farm life; family matters, social and Methodist
> activities in a seemingly populous and interesting community, with
> many personal names identified by the editor; a description of
> "sugaring"; diarist's recurrent suffering with toothache and
> abcessed jaw; touches of wry humor; some private material in
> code.

HUNT, EMMETT, d. 1933   5139

McDonald, Lucile. "Emmett Hunt Diaries." SEA CHEST 6
(1972-1973):47-57, 98-107, 133-144; 7 (1973-1974):26-33.

> 1880-1907. Article containing summary and extracts of
> voluminous diaries of an Artondale, Washington, teacher and
> Puget Sound boatman; carrying mail, freight and passengers in-
> itially by small sailboat, later by a succession of steamboats, many
> of which he built himself; problems with inspectors and malfunc-
> tions of his boats, weather, drunken engineeers, etc.; interesting
> notes on Puget Sound ports and maritime activities.

LOWENSTEIN, EMANUEL, 1857-1939   5140

In MANNIE'S CROWD, EMANUEL LOWENSTEIN, COLORFUL CHARACTER OF OLD LOS ANGELES, by Norton B. Stern, pp. 95-122. California Jewish History, 3. Glendale: Arthur H. Clark, 1970.

> May 1880. Diary kept by merchant's clerk, later a prominent Los Angeles figure; family and social life among Jewish residents; preparations to leave for Tucson with his father; train trip with entertaining notes on journey and passengers.

> 1883. A brief note after "I took a rest for a few years" describing Tucson and its Jewish community.

PAXSON, MARY SCARBOROUGH, 1872-1948   5141

In SMALL VOICES, edited by Josef and Dorothy Berger, pp. 11-15.

> 1880-1884. Diary extracts containing the engaging, thoughtful experiences, and spellings, of an eight-to-eleven-year-old girl; a charming diary.

STANTON, ELIZABETH CADY, 1815-1902   5142

ELIZABETH CADY STANTON AS REVEALED IN HER LETTERS, DIARY AND REMINISCENCES. Edited by Theodore Stanton and Harriot Stanton Blatch. New York and London: Harper & Brothers, 1922. 2 vol. Reprint. New York: Arno, 1969. Diary, vol. 2, pp. 175-369.

> 1880-1902. A record of her work on HISTORY OF WOMAN SUFFRAGE, speeches, reading, letter writing and meetings with major figures at home and abroad, both for and against her cause; views on marriage, women, the church; events and people such as Lucretia Mott, Susan B. Anthony, Matilda J. Gage and President and Mrs. Hayes.

In THE OVEN BIRDS: AMERICAN WOMEN ON WOMANHOOD, 1820-1920, compiled by Gail Parker, pp. 267-275. Garden City, N.Y.: Anchor Books, 1972.

> 1881-1895 (with gaps). Extracts on her reading, speeches, the direction of the women's suffrage movement and her vision for it; the death of Frederick Douglass.

WISE, LEWIS LOVATT ASHFORD   5143

Lott, Howard B., ed. "Diary of Major Wise, an Englishman, Recites Details of Hunting Trip in Powder River Country in 1880." ANNALS OF WYOMING 12 (1940): 85-118.

> Aug-Nov 1880. Extract from diary of adventurous English sportsman on a journey around the world; from Fort Fetterman to Cheyenne with hunting party, whose game included buffalo, mountain sheep, deer, bear, etc.; hospitality of English rancher Moreton Frewen of Powder River Cattle Company; mauling of his American guide Oliver P. Hanna by a grizzly bear; a fairly exciting hunting diary.

WITHERLE, GEORGE H.   5144

EXPLORATIONS WEST AND NORTHWEST OF KATAHDIN IN THE LATE NINETEENTH CENTURY. 2d ed. Augusta: Maine Appalachian Trail Club, 1950. 5 leaves.

> 1880-1886, 1895, 1898-1899, 1901. Castine, Maine, resident's journals reporting his hiking trips in the Katahdin region of central Maine; notes on weather, distances and scenery; some parts in narrative form.

1881

AMBLER, JAMES MARKHAM, d. 1881   5145

Gatewood, J.D., ed. "The Private Journal of James Markham Ambler, M.D." UNITED STATES NAVAL MEDICAL BULLETIN 11 (1917):183-218. Journal, pp. 191-215.

> Jun-Oct 1881. Journal of assistant surgeon on the JEANNETTE, of the navy's American Arctic Expedition, which had drifted helplessly in the pack ice for almost two years until finally crushed north of Siberia; entries beginning "Camp on ice floe"; medical notes on his care of the men left to struggle across ice and open ocean laboriously hauling their boats, sleds and supplies; accidental separation of two boats during a storm and diarist's continuation with the small group under Lt. George W. De Long; notes on conditions, morale, disheartening progress; dwindling food supplemented with occasional seal, walrus, deer and finally sled dogs; diarist's struggle to save the badly infected eye of one man, but need to amputate the gangrenous foot of another; finally landing at the Lena River delta but without food; two sent ahead for help but diarist turning down the opportunity to accompany them because of his duty to care for survivors, all of whom perished except the two sent ahead; a document of quiet heroism.

BARTON, HARRY SCOTT, b. 1862   5146

WHAT I DID IN "THE LONG": JOURNALS HOME DURING A TOUR THROUGH THE UNITED STATES AND CANADA IN THE LONG VACATION OF 1881. London: Edward Stanford, Printer, 1881? 91 pp.

> Jul-Oct 1881. Letter-journal of an Oxford student's travels in North America with two friends; Atlantic crossing on the steamship SCYTHIA, followed by rattling notes on Lake George, Boston, Harvard, "one of their universities on this side," Newport, where they enjoyed the casino and social life, the White Mountains, Quebec, St. Paul, Chicago, with the usual visit to slaughterhouse, "great corn elevators," etc.

BENTON, VIRGINIA BELLE   5147

"The Spears of Sheridan County." ANNALS OF WYOMING 14 (1942):98-127. Diary, pp. 108-120.

> Jun-Oct 1881. Seventeen-year-old girl's account of a journey from Kansas to Wyoming with her family; Baptist services conducted at settlements en route by her father, the Rev. George W. Benton; pleasant notes on people and events of journey; much on fellow settlers in northern Wyoming; reactions to books.

BIGELOW, ELIAKIM, 1831-1915   5148

Bigelow, Edwin L. "Eliakim Bigelow: A Stowe Farmer." VERMONT HISTORY 31 (1963):253-271.

> 1881-1892. Article containing brief extracts from a farmer's diary; laconic notes of chores, livestock sales and purchases, sugaring, road maintenance, logging and ice operations, all in the course of Vermont "hill farming."

CHASE, JOSEPHINE STREEPER, 1835-1894   5149

Dix, Fae, ed. "The Josephine Diaries: Glimpses of the Life of Josephine Streeper Chase." UTAH HISTORICAL QUARTERLY 46 (1978):167-183.

1881-1894. Extracts, within article, from the diary of a Mormon woman, polygamous second wife of George Ogden Chase and mother of fifteen children; family and church life at Centerville; a record of unrelenting work and occasional protest: "Pa and all men folks can go to bed at ten and rest and sit and read all evening, but woman, poor woman, must iron, sew, bake, dust, tend babies ..."; grieving the deaths of several of her children; hurried notes on activities of husband and children, her religious reflections and yearning for books.

GARFIELD, JAMES RUDOLPH   5150

In MOLLIE GARFIELD IN THE WHITE HOUSE, by Ruth Stanley-Brown Feis, pp. 80-90 passim.

Jul-Aug 1881. Extracts from diary of James Garfield's son covering day of assassination and period immediately following. Edited for children.

HYATT, ALPHEUS, 1838-1902   5151

Burbank, Jeanne B. and Dexter, Ralph W., eds. "Excerpts from Alpheus Hyatt's Log of the ARETHUSA." ESSEX INSTITUTE HISTORICAL COLLECTIONS 90 (1954):229-260.

Jun-Aug 1881. Naturalist's log of a marine biology research voyage, with five students and three crew, from Annisquam Seaside Laboratory to Anticosti and Mingan islands, Labrador, collecting fossils, insects, birds, eggs, plants and animals; ship routine and humorous incidents.

Jul-Aug 1885. Extracts from a similar voyage to Newfoundland and Labrador, again on the ARETHUSA under Capt. Gilbert Davis.

JONES, THOMAS JEFFERSON, 1838-1914   5152

In OUR FAMILY, THE JONES'S, by Mary C.J. Beatty, pp. 10-41. Los Angeles: Wetzel, 1950.

1881-1882. Diary of Mormon bishop in Washington County, Utah; church duties, farm work, the business of Z.C.R.V Manufacturing Company and the Mohave Stock Company.

KALAKAUA, DAVID, King of Hawaii, 1836-1891   5153

Marumoto, Masaji. "Vignette of Early Hawaii-Japan Relations: Highlights of King Kalakaua's Sojourn in Japan on His Trip around the World." HAWAIIAN JOURNAL OF HISTORY 10 (1976):52-63.

Mar-Oct 1881. Extracts within article describing Japanese segment of Hawaiian king's journey around the world with his chamberlain, Charles H. Judd, and Attorney General William N. Armstrong; meetings with Emperor Mutsuhito with descriptions of him, his imperial household, ceremonies and receptions; enjoyment of Japan and its "kind and hospitable inhabitants."

LINGREN, JOHN, 1844-1915   5154

In TREASURES OF PIONEER HISTORY, compiled by Kate B. Carter, vol. 1, pp. 233-272 passim.

1881-1912 (with gaps). Journal entries in autobiography of Swedish immigrant; from Malmo, Sweden, on the PATRIOT to England and on the ARIZONA to New York; joining Mormon church in 1890; doing home missionary work; dreams, family and church affairs.

LOGAN, ALGERNON SYDNEY, 1849-1925   5155

VISTAS FROM THE STREAM. Philadelphia: National, 1934. 2 vols.

1881-1925. Philadelphia author's reflections on events, people, his reading, politics and news; his life as an active gentleman farmer on his properites at Goshenville, Pennsylvania, and Jones' Neck, Delaware; extensive notes on travels to England and the Continent; hobbies of photography, woodworking and music, including violin collecting; enjoyment of concerts and musical evenings; disillusioned reactions to American politics and foreign policy and to involvement in World War I, a "banker's and broker's war."

LOMAX, VIRGINIA   5156

In LEAVES FROM AN OLD WASHINGTON DIARY, by Elizabeth Lindsay Lomax, edited by Lindsay Lomax Wood, pp. 243-252. New York: Books, 1943.

Jan-Mar 1881. Extracts from diary kept by daughter of Elizabeth Lindsay Lomax at Warrenton, Virginia; notes on weather, family, visitors and her writing, but essentially a record of mourning the death of her sister Victoria; the solace of flowers and friends.

McCONNELL, ROBERT, b. 1828   5157

Brown, John A., ed. "Businessman's Search: Pacific Northwest." OREGON HISTORICAL QUARTERLY 71 (1970):5-25.

Mar-Jul 1881. Xenia, Illinois, merchant's trip on the new transcontinental railroad to seek business opportunities; from Illinois to California, with brief notes on fares and scenery; from San Francisco to Portland on the steamer COLUMBIA; visits to Vancouver, Tacoma, Seattle and Kalama, Washington; return to Portland and Eugene; thence to Moscow, Idaho; notes on fares, hotels, prices and business prospects.

MARTIN, CHALMERS, 1859-1934   5158

Anderson, Charles A., ed. "Journal of My Summer in Dakota." PRESBYTERIAN HISTORICAL SOCIETY JOURNAL 23 (1945):86-118.

May-Sep 1881. Princeton Theological Seminary student's account of work under the Presbyterian Board of Home Missions helping to organize churches among Dakota settlers; departure from Princeton, with a happy visit among friends and relatives at Washington, D.C.; good descriptions of his continuing train journey via Chicago, with full notes on sights and visits there; preaching at Huron and Chamberlain and itineration by bicycle; interesting notes on various families with whom he boarded; observations of social life, religion and hardships of prairie agriculture; trainloads of new arrivals, many of them European immigrants; a pleasant, observant journal.

MAYNE, ISABELLA MAUD RITTENHOUSE, b. 1864   5159

MAUD. Edited by Richard L. Strout. New York: Macmillan, 1939. 593 pp.

1881-1895. Spritely diary of the popular young daughter of a commission grain merchant of Cairo, Illinois, with entries up to the time of her marriage to Dr. Earl Mayne; school events, escorts and admirers, clothes, girl friends, balls, opening of the opera house, Fourth of July celebrations, traveling to Chicago for World's Columbian Exposition; moving to St. Louis to attend Mrs. Cuthbert's Young Ladies Seminary and St. Louis School of Fine Arts at Washington University; returning to Cairo, writing stories for GODEY'S LADY'S MAGAZINE and other women's magazines, publishing a novel, teaching school and experiencing an embarrassing broken engagement.

MUNROE, KIRK, 1850-1930   5160

Leonard, Irving A., ed. "A Lost 'PSYCHE': Kirk Munroe's Log of a 1,600 Mile Cruise in Florida Waters." TEQUESTA 28 (1968):63-89.

Nov 1881-Mar 1882. Journal of a writer and canoe enthusiast of his expedition in a decked sailing canoe; navigating the Suwannee and Caloosahatchee rivers and Lake Okeechobee, with complicated and dangerous adventures trying to find the mouth of the Kissimmee River; references to local people and fellow sportsmen.

SAUNDERS, FRANK M.   5161

McDonald, Lucile. "Rock Creek Shepherd." OREGON HISTORICAL QUARTERLY 81 (1980):261-280.

Jan-Sep 1881. Twenty-year-old youth's cryptic entries of work on a sheep ranch in present Gilliam County; desperately cold weather; problems in collecting pay from the bankrupt ranching company; spring planting, haying and other chores; trips to The Dalles; references to his employers Thomas Lang and James A. Varney; difficulties with his improvident father.

SIMMONS, RACHEL EMMA WOOLLEY, 1836-1926   5162

"Journal of Rachel Emma Woolley Simmons." HEART THROBS OF THE WEST 11 (1950):153-208.

1881-1891. Mormon midwife's diary; family activities, household routine, church attendance, attitudes toward antipolygamy actions of the federal government.

STANLEY-BROWN, MARY GARFIELD, b. 1867   5163

In MOLLIE GARFIELD IN THE WHITE HOUSE, by Ruth Stanley-Brown Feis, pp. 86-89, 94-96, 99-110. Chicago: Rand McNally, 1963.

1881-1882. Extracts from diary of teenage daughter of President Garfield; family life, the tragic days following her father's assassination, details of the funeral day and adjusting to life without her "dear Papa"; falling in love. Edited for children.

Extracts in SMALL VOICES, edited by Josef and Dorothy Berger, pp. 148-151.

Jul-Sep 1881. Assassination of her father.

STETSON, CHARLES WALTER, 1858-1911   5164

ENDURE: THE DIARIES OF CHARLES WALTER STETSON. Edited by Mary A. Hill. Philadelphia: Temple University Press, 1985. 373 pp.

1881-1888. Extracts from an artist's diary; personal details of his relationship with radical feminist Charlotte Perkins Gilman and the severe depression she suffered during their marriage; trying to earn a living as an artist but often unable to afford models; notes on patrons Mr. and Mrs. George V. Cresson and John H. Mason; artistic commitment, religious concerns and need for love and friendship.

STONE, STEPHEN   5165

Gaither, Gerald and Finger, John R., eds. "A Journey of Stephen Stone: Observations on Kansas in 1881." KANSAS HISTORICAL QUARTERLY 37 (1971):148-152.

Mar 1881. Extract covering part of a Wisconsin man's train journey to Arizona; good notes on Kansas City, Missouri, where he stopped over for several days before continuing to Topeka, etc.; brief comments on agriculture and mining along the way.

STOREY, GEORGE C.   5166

"My Trip West in 1881." COLORADO MAGAZINE 49 (1972):314-324.

Feb-Sep 1881. Very brief notes of prospector's unprofitable travels through the Colorado gold camps with his brother Myles Storey.

TODD, MABEL LOOMIS, 1856-1932   5167

In THE YEARS AND HOURS OF EMILY DICKINSON, by Jay Leyda, vol. 2 passim. New Haven: Yale University Press, 1960.

1881-1886. Scattered extracts from the diary of a young newcomer to Amherst who, after Emily Dickinson's death, was to become editor of her poems and their rescuer from private obscurity; friendship with the Dickinson family and reactions of their unusual household, where she was one of the few visitors Emily would receive or to whom she showed poems.

WEBBER, ANNA, 1860-1948   5168

Scrimsher, Lila Gravatt, ed. "The Diary of Anna Webber: Early Day Teacher in Mitchell County." KANSAS HISTORICAL QUARTERLY 38 (1972):320-337.

May-Jul 1881. Record of a three-month term in a school with three windows and four seats, two boards placed on rocks; her desire to improve as a teacher in spite of lack of books, blackboard and other necessities; fluctuating attendance; touching, amusing or disruptive behavior of some of her students; occasional discouragement: "Oh, dear, this is a hard place to live, this Kansas is."

1882

BENT, LEVANCIA   5169

Herrington, George Squires, ed. "Levancia Bent's Diary of a Sheep Drive, Evanston, Wyoming, to Kearney, Nebraska." ANNALS OF WYOMING 24 (1952):24-51.

Jul-Oct 1882. Aurora, Illinois, woman's diary extract of a sheep drive with her brother-in-law, George Jackson Squires; encampment on Bear River near Evanston; domestic details in camps; attempts to pursue her hobby of painting; traveling with other women in a large carriage; difficulty of sheep fording rivers; encounters with many emigrant trains.

DAVIES, WILLIAM GILBERT   5170

Proctor, Samuel, ed. "Leaves from a Travel Diary: A Visit to Augusta and Savannah." GEORGIA HISTORICAL QUARTERLY 41 (1957):309-315.

Jan 1882. Extract of New York lawyer's diary covering travels in Georgia; good details of Augusta and accommodation at the Planters' Hotel; inconvenient train travel to Savannah; on steamer CITY OF BRIDGETON to Fernandina, Florida, during which his wife "had one of her nervous fits... lest we might be going to the bottom" and his daughter's stomach proved "unreliable."

**DAVIS, CHARLES K.									5171**

"A Colony in Kansas: They Worry Me to Death." AMERICAN JEWISH ARCHIVES 17 (1965):114-139.

Jul-Aug 1882. Extracts from diary kept by young Cincinnati man sent by Moritz Loth of the Hebrew Union Agricultural Society to settle immigrant Jews from eastern Europe on farms in Kansas; inspecting land at Ellsworth; trying to secure supplies and worrying about the pilfering of colony goods by some of the young immigrants; trying, with little success, to get jobs for them and to counteract antagonism of local gentiles; concern about mounting expenses of the venture; eventually choosing a site twenty-six miles from Cimarron and establishing the short-lived colony of Beersheba.

**EVANS, HARTMAN K.									5172**

Burns, Robert H., ed. "Sheep Trailing from Oregon to Wyoming." MISSISSIPPI VALLEY HISTORICAL REVIEW 28 (1941-1942):581-582. Reprint. ANNALS OF WYOMING 23 (1951):77-96.

May-Sep 1882. Record of a drive of 23,000 sheep from Pendleton, Oregon, to Laramie, Wyoming; financial accounts; camps, route, problems of grass and water; defection of many sheepherders; dogs troubled with sore feet and exhaustion; nevertheless, a profitable venture for diarist and his partner Robert H. Homer.

**GILBOY, BERNARD, b. 1852									5173**

VOYAGE OF THE BOAT "PACIFIC," FROM SAN FRANCISCO TO AUSTRALIA. Sydney, Australia: J.G. O'Connor, Printer, 1883. 37 pp.

A VOYAGE OF PLEASURE: THE LOG OF BERNARD GILBOY'S TRANSPACIFIC CRUISE IN THE BOAT "PACIFIC." Edited by John Tompkins. Cambridge, Md.: Cornell Maritime Press, 1956. 64 pp.

Aug 1882-Apr 1883. A Buffalo, New York, man's log of solo voyage from San Francisco to Australia on an eighteen-foot boat built to specifications of the diarist; weather, course and distances sailed; birds, fish and ships sighted; capsizing in high seas, righting the boat and continuing with sextant and patent log, his only remaining instruments; surviving on limited provisions, flying fish that landed on board in the night and an occasional bird until being rescued near Australia by Captain Boor and the ALFRED VITTERY; recovering from near exhaustion in Maryborough.

**NAPTON, WILLIAM BARCLAY, 1808-1883					5174**

"The Jackson Resolutions of 1849." MISSOURI HISTORICAL SOCIETY BULLETIN 5 (1948):50-54.

Jan-Apr 1882. Diary extracts concerning the diarist's much earlier writing of resolutions relating to the slavery question, which had been introduced into the Missouri State Senate by Claiborne F. Jackson; unflattering references to abolitionist T.T. Gantt and to

Thomas Hart Benton, who was "kicked out of the Senate by reason of his refusing to comply" with the resolutions.

**PRATT, TEANCUM, 1851-1900									5175**

Romano, Edna, ed. "Teancum Pratt, Founder of Helper." UTAH HISTORICAL QUARTERLY 48 (1980):328-365.

1882-1900 (with gaps). Mormon's diary covering his life in Castle Valley and the settling of Helper; struggle to support his large polygamous family while "my children were small and numerous and my crops poor"; supplementing his income with occasional outside work and hunting; ordination to the "Seventy" and concern that many of the Mormon leaders were "sodden with tobacco and careless with the holy word of wisdom"; imprisonment for polygamy.

**PRICE, GEORGE MOSES, 1864-1942							5176**

Shpall, Loe, ed. "The Diary of Dr. George M. Price." AMERICAN JEWISH HISTORICAL SOCIETY PUBLICATIONS 40 (1950):173-181.

May-Jul 1882. Jewish youth's account of his immigration to the United States from Poltava, Russia; bitter dissatisfaction with conditions for Jews in Russia and his own personal circumstances; delay among thousands of Jews lodged in factories and stables under deplorable conditions while awaiting passage to New York; wretched crossing from Hamburg aboard the AUSTRALIA. Translated from the Russian.

**UDALL, IDA FRANCES HUNT									5177**

In ARIZONA PIONEER MORMON, by David K. Udall, pp. 102-109. Tucson: Arizona Silhouettes, 1959.

1882-1885. Extracts from diary of a plural wife of David Udall; temple wedding, feelings for her husband and desire to be friends with his first wife; persecutions for polygamy, including imprisonment of her husband; a touching diary.

**ZEHME, FRIEDRICH WILHELM HEINRICH, 1840-1895		5178**

DIARY OF FRIEDRICH WILHELM HEINRICH ZEHME, A PERSPECTIVE OF AMERICA. Translated by David D. Clement. Eureka, Calif.: Clement, 1976. 98 pp.

May-Jul 1882. German immigrant's diary; ocean crossing, then train trip from New York to Chicago where he worked in steel and lumber industries; interest in agriculture and technology; enthusiasm for America.

1883

**BRADFORD, GAMALIEL, 1863-1932							5179**

THE JOURNAL OF GAMALIEL BRADFORD. Edited by Van Wyck Brooks. Boston and New York: Houghton Mifflin, 1933. 560 pp.

1883-1932. Substantial extracts from the massive diary of a biographer and man of letters; quiet, reclusive life in Wellesley Hills, Massachusetts; visits to Boston Athenaeum, Boston Symphony rehearsals and concerts, occasional baseball games; an ambivalent fascination with movies; passionate love of reading and book collecting, with special interest in diaries and letters;

early failures as a novelist and poet, but discovery in midlife of his vocation as a biographer and writer of ''psychographs''; chronic ill health and depression, occasionally eased by the consolations of music, nature and books; vivid descriptions of his recurring attacks of vertigo, leading to invalidism.

''The Journal of a Man of Letters.'' HARPERS 166 (1933):419-429, 609-619.

1916-1928. Extracts.

FEDDE, ELIZABETH, 1850-1921 5180

Folkedahl, Beulah, trans. and ed. ''Elizabeth Fedde's Diary.'' NORWEGIAN-AMERICAN STUDIES AND RECORDS 20 (1959):170-196.

1883-1888. Diary of Norwegian deaconess and nurse who established the Norwegian Lutheran Deaconesses' Home and Hospital in Brooklyn, later to become the Lutheran Medical Center; a record of nursing and social work among destitute Norwegian immigrants; an exhausting daily round of home visits, hospital work and difficult board meetings; Sunday school work and assistance to local pastors; organizing charities and training other deaconesses; entries ending before her return to Norway.

FRIES, CHRISTINA, 1867-1945 5181

Yothers, Jean and Wehr, Paul W., eds.; Miller, Margareta, trans. ''Diary of Kena Fries.'' FLORIDA HISTORICAL QUARTERLY 62 (1984):339-351.

1883-1936 (with gaps). Swedish immigrant's diary kept regularly at Oviedo, then sporadically thereafter; home, school, domestic chores, social life, etc., of a teenager; discontent over her mother's taking in boarders who usurped the parlor; move to Orlando, with later occasional entries of adult life with her parents; Swedish customs in both areas.

GARRISON, FRANCIS JACKSON, b. 1848 5182

Seckinger, Katherine Villard, ed. ''The Great Railroad Celebration.'' MONTANA: THE MAGAZINE OF WESTERN HISTORY 33, no. 3 (1983):12-24.

Aug-Sep 1883. Extracts from a diary kept by the brother-in-law of Henry Villard, president of the Northern Pacific Railroad, and describing celebration of its completion; travel in a caravan of special cars carrying international guests, reporters and such dignitaries as Ulysses S. Grant, George Mortimer Pullman and Carl Schurz for festivities in towns along the route from Minneapolis to the ''last spike'' at Gold Creek, Montana; crowds, speeches, decorations and clamorous reception in St. Paul, Fargo and Bismarck, where Sitting Bull attended the celebration and met important guests; an embarrassing and dangerous accident, which sobered the travelers' mood.

HEALY, MARY JANE ROACH 5183

Apostol, Jane. ''Sailing with the Ruler of the Arctic Sea.'' PACIFIC NORTHWEST QUARTERLY 72 (1981):146-156 passim.

1883-1891. Article containing extracts from diaries of the wife, Mary Jane, and teenage son, Fred, of Michael A. Healy of the United States Revenue Marine, kept on board two of his ships, the CORWIN and the BEAR in Alaskan waters; notes on Kodiak and St. Paul islands; Eskimo customs, including the killing of old people and the activities of a shaman; a graphic description of the CORWIN's struggle against enclosure in the ice pack; references to Sheldon Jackson and the transport of reindeer from Siberia to Alaska.

MASTON, GEORGE A., 1849-1913 5184

Scrimsher, Lila Gravatt, ed. ''The Diaries and Writings of George A. Maston, Black Citizen of Lincoln, Nebraska.'' NEBRASKA HISTORY 52 (1971): 133-168. Diary, pp. 145-164.

Jan-Jun 1883. Extracts from the diary of a black teacher, barber and Methodist minister in Union, Missouri, who later settled in Lincoln, Nebraska; notes on teaching school and Sunday school and preaching. Republican party activities, wide reading and contributing to local newspapers; experiences of discrimination in almost every sphere of life; the trial of a white man for murder of a black, with predictable results; notes on friends and family; temporary discouragements but underlying confidence that ''the Negro is irrepressible and bound to come to the top.''

MEAD, SOLOMON, 1808-1897 5185

NOTES OF TWO TRIPS TO CALIFORNIA AND RETURN. Greenwich?, 189-? 144 pp.

May-Jun 1883, Dec 1886-May 1887. Greenwich, Connecticut, resident's tour with Cook and Sons' Continental Excursion Party; the sights of Washington, D.C., and a visit to Kentucky's Mammoth Cave; by train through Illinois, Missouri, Kansas, Colorado, New Mexico and Arizona with special mention of Santa Fe; in California, seeing Los Angeles, Yosemite, the sequoias, the Monterey area, San Francisco and Sacramento; return through Nevada and Utah to Chicago and on to New York via Canada; notes on Chinese, Indians, Mormons, Salt Lake City, a synagogue service, church services, etc.; later trip on the COLON from New York City to Aspinwall, by train to Panama City and on the COLIMA to San Francisco, stopping at Aculpulco, Manzanillo, San Blas and Mazatlan; on the ANCON to Los Angeles; a protracted visit in the San Jacinto area where his son farmed and he owned property; return home by train; substantial, quite descriptive entries.

RUSSELL, CHARLES RUSSELL, 1832-1900 5186

DIARY OF A VISIT TO THE UNITED STATES OF AMERICA IN THE YEAR 1883. Edited by Charles Herbermann. New York: United States Catholic Historical Society, 1910. 235 pp.

Aug-Oct 1883. Prominent Irish Catholic lawyer's Atlantic crossing on the CELTIC to New York and travel about the United States by train, stagecoach and horseback, with notes on experiences in the East, plains states, including a sojourn with the Crow Indians, Rocky Mountains and west coast from California to Washington; concern for the condition of Irish immigrants and Indians; comments on scenery, American mores, institutions, politics and Catholicism; a visit to his sister, Mother Baptist Russell, of St. Mary's Hospital, San Francisco; a few notes on Mormons.

SPEAR, WILLIS, b. 1862 5187

''The Spears of Sheridan County.'' ANNALS OF WYOMING 14 (1942):98-127. Diary, pp. 102-108.

Aug-Sep 1883. Journey from New Chicago, Montana, to take up ranching in Wyoming; herding cattle en route; the loss of many horses drowned while crossing the Yellowstone; visit to Custer battlefield.

YOUNG, JANETTE LEWIS   **5188**

In AN OREGON IDYL, by Nellie May Young, pp. 1-111 passim. Glendale, Calif.: A.H. Clark, 1961.

1883-1884. Extensive diary extracts of young Presbyterian missionary couple's journey to Oregon; entertaining details of early transcontinental train travel, itineration to establish or strengthen Oregon churches, domestic chores, diarist's struggle against tuberculosis, of which she died at age twenty-nine; a pleasant, feminine diary and cheerful, despite illness.

1884

ANON.   **5189**

"Diary of a Young Oil Speculator." WESTERN PENNSYLVANIA HISTORICAL MAGAZINE 1 (1918):37-45, 97-105.

Apr 1884-Feb 1885 (with gaps). Diary of a young man engaged in speculation on the Pittsburgh Petroleum Exchanges suffering "days of mental anguish and nights of feverish slumber" over his financial risks; reports of each day's trading and its effects on his fortune; becoming a "Broker in Petroleum" and his determination to be ethical in his dealings; continued worry, making him irritable at home; his final resolution to withdraw altogether from oil speculation.

BOURKE, JOHN GREGORY, 1843-1896   **5190**

Casanova, Frank E., ed. "General Crook Visits the Supais as Reported by John G. Bourke." ARIZONA AND THE WEST 10 (1968):253-276.

Nov 1884. Extract covering aide-de-camp's journey with Crook and others of the "Department of Arizona" to investigate the Havasupai Indians of Havasu Canyon; good notes of the journey and geological features en route, with excellent descriptions of canyon country; detailed account of Havasupai life; food, clothing, dwellings, etc., of an apparently thriving people; conversations between Crook and Chief Navajo.

Buechler, John, ed. "Two Excursions on Lake Champlain in the 1890's: Excerpts from the Diaries of Capt. John G. Bourke." VERMONT HISTORY 39 (1971):62-71.

Jun 1895. Excursion, with other officers at Fort Ethan Allen, on the OLEATIC from Burlington to Vergennes, evoking ecstatic description of scenery and amenities.

Feb 1896. Across the lake by sleigh with Capt. Francis H. Hardie to Plattsburgh, New York, to inspect the garrison and enjoy food and society there; return in a blizzard.

BOWEN, ORSAMUS ALLAN, 1823-1886   **5191**

In THE DIARY OF CLARISSA ADGER BOWEN, ASHTABULA PLANTATION, by Mary Stevenson, pp. 84-86. Pendleton, S.C.: Research and Publication Committee, Foundation for Historic Preservation in Pendleton Area, 1973.

Nov-Dec 1884, Oct 1886. Extracts from diary of Clarissa Adger Bowen's husband; moving into Rivoli near Pendleton, South Carolina; plantation tasks.

BREMNER, JOHN   **5192**

In SHORES AND ALPS OF ALASKA, by Heywood W. Seton-Karr, pp. 202-221. London: S. Low, Marston, Searl & Rivington, 1887.

Sep 1884-Feb 1885. Diary of prospector and trader on Copper River; descriptions of river and mountains; Mount Wrangell, which was erupting with volcanic plumes and rock; hunting, fishing, camping along the river, building a cabin for the winter; an unsuccessful attempt to climb the mountain; visits from Indians who regarded him as "boss medicine man"; information on their customs; waiting for them to guide him out of the area but mistrusting them and doubting their estimates of distances.

FLAKE, WILLIAM JORDAN, b. 1839   **5193**

Boone, David and Flake, Chad J., eds. "The Prison Diary of William Jordan Flake." JOURNAL OF ARIZONA HISTORY 24 (1983):145-170.

Dec 1884-Jan 1885. Extracts from the diary of an Arizona Mormon convicted of polygamy at Prescott and transported to the Yuma Territorial Penitentiary; description of prison, rules, conditions, fellow inmates of all kinds; some diversions including convict concerts; the encouragement of letters from home, visits by such Mormon leaders as Francis M. Lyman and Christopher Layton, as well as companionship of James N. Skousen, also in prison for polygamy.

GOSSE, Sir EDMUND WILLIAM, 1849-1928   **5194**

AMERICA: THE DIARY OF A VISIT. Edited by Robert L. Peters and David G. Halliburton. English Literature in Transition: 1880-1920. Special series, no. 2. Lafayette, Ind.: Purdue University, 1966. 30 pp. Diary, pp. 1-14.

Nov 1884-Jan 1885. American lecture tour, arranged by William Dean Howells, of English poet and critic; lectures at the Lowell Institute and Johns Hopkins University; a constant round of social life among the literary and intellectual elite of New York, Boston, Philadelphia, etc.; hasty notes on Oliver Wendell Holmes, Walt Whitman and others.

HARTMANN, J.A.H.   **5195**

In REPORT ON EDUCATION IN ALASKA, by Sheldon Jackson for United States Office of Education, pp. 55-75. Washington, D.C.: Government Printing Office, 1886.

Apr-Aug 1884. Diary of a Moravian sent from Bethlehem, Pennsylvania, with companion W.H. Weinland to explore western Alaska for possible locations for a mission and school; obtaining equipment and supplies including photographic apparatus in San Francisco along with letters of introduction to Alaska Commercial Company agents who were supportive of the undertaking; by ship CORWIN to Unalaska; meeting with Orthodox priest and determining not to settle in Nushagak and Togiak districts regarded as his parish; exploring up Kuskokwim River to trading posts; learning Eskimo beliefs and customs and appreciating their friendliness and honesty; finding no suitable site for a mission and returning the people to be to Unalaska.

QUIN, AH 5196

Griego, Andrew, ed. "Rebuilding the California Southern Railroad: The Personal Account of a Chinese Labor Contractor." JOURNAL OF SAN DIEGO HISTORY 25 (1979):324-337. Diary, pp. 330-334.

Jan-Dec 1884. Extract from diaries of a Chinese immigrant and San Diego merchant who acted as a labor recruiter and manager for the California Southern Railroad; entries covering his travels to Los Angeles, Riverside and San Francisco trying to persuade laborers who had recently completed the railroad to return to the job because of severe damage storms had caused to the roadbed; rebuilding track in the Oceanside and Temecula Valley areas; provisioning; settling disputes.

STEWART, HELEN JANE WISER, 1854-1926 5197

In WOMEN OF THE WEST, by Cathy Luchetti, pp. 151-159.

1884-1899. Extracts from brief journal entries interspersed with letters of the widow of a successful Nevada land and cattle dealer murdered by a disgruntled ranch hand; taking up unaccustomed work of managing legal affairs and the ranch; concern for her children and their education.

STODDARD, CHARLES WARREN, 1843-1909 5198

CHARLES WARREN STODDARD'S DIARY OF A VISIT TO MOLOKAI IN 1884. Introduction by Oscar Lewis. San Francisco: The Book Club of California, 1933. 52 pp.

Oct 1884. California author's diary of his second trip to Molokai, with notes on Father Damien and the leper colony; graphic descriptions of the ravages of leprosy on its victims; conversations with Father Damien, masses, meals, etc.; rambles about the island; a letter from Father Damien appended.

TROWBRIDGE, ROBERTSON 5199

FORTY-EIGHT YEARS: ANECDOTES AND OTHER ODDMENTS COLLECTED FROM ORIGINAL SOURCES, 1884-1932. New York: Privately printed, 1937. 363 pp. passim.

1884-1932. A New Yorker's extensive notes on his reading and plays and concerts attended; humorous anecdotes from European travels, newspapers, hearsay and family lore going back several generations; a leisurely and pleasant miscellany.

WOODS, GEORGE W. 5200

Swartout, Robert R. and Bohm, Fred C. "An American Naval Officer in 19th Century Korea." JOURNAL OF SOCIAL SCIENCE AND HUMANITIES 52 (December 1980):18-30 passim.

Feb-May 1884. Article describing and containing extracts from the journal of ship's surgeon aboard the JUNIATA, part of the navy's Asiatic Squadron; difficult survey of the Korean coast, with chain men up to their waist in water and annoyed with "the bothersome curiosity of the local populous"; extended trips ashore, with largely approving comments on scenery, people and their homes, crafts and customs; interesting notes on Seoul.

WOODWARD, MARY DODGE, 1826-1890 5201

THE CHECKERED YEARS. Edited by Mary B. Cowdrey. Caldwell, Idaho: Caxton, 1937. 265 pp.

1884-1889. Diary of a widow farming with her grown children on a Dakota bonanza farm near Fargo and Mapleton; a good picture of life on the prairie; hard work, diversions and particular beauty of each season; isolation and bitter cold of winter but company of her diary, allowing her to "do all the talking"; reading and playing checkers; occasional visits from neighbors; memories of happy and sad times.

1885

BUCKLE, CHARLES M. 5202

Birch, Brian P. "A Victorian Englishman's View of the West." ANNALS OF WYOMING 54, no. 1 (1982):2-9 passim.

1885. Undated extracts within article describing a train trip from New York to Yellowstone and back.

CORNELL, ROBERT, 1822-1909 5203

Gibson, William and Rudoff, Andrew E., eds. "The Diaries of Robert Cornell." WESTERN PENNSYLVANIA HISTORICAL MAGAZINE 63 (1980):265-272.

1885-1887 (with gaps). Sporadic entries by a Scottish immigrant employed by the Southwest Coal and Coke Company of Westmoreland City; work apparently as a mining engineer; brief mention of wages and subsequent strikes during which the diarist represented management.

DURANT, FRANK ROSS, 1866-1934 5204

THE 1885 MORRISTOWN, NEW JERSEY, DIARY OF FRANK ROSS DURANT. Edited by Alexander Grant Rose. Baltimore: Rose, 1976. Diary, pp. 1-39.

Jan-Dec 1885. Diary kept while attending Morris Academy and living with his brother William, pastor of the First Presbyterian Church; extremely brief, sketchy entries noting his church, school and social activities; trips to New York City, New York state, Illinois and Wisconsin.

EDISON, THOMAS ALVA, 1847-1931 5205

THE DIARY AND SUNDRY OBSERVATIONS OF THOMAS ALVA EDISON. Edited by Dagobert D. Runes. New York: Philosophical Library, 1948. Reprint. Greenwood Press, 1968. 181 pp. Diary, pp. 3-38.

THE DIARY OF THOMAS A. EDISON. Introduction by Kathleen L. McGuirk. Old Greenwich, Conn.: Chatham Press, 1971. 71 pp.

Extracts in DIARY OF AMERICA, edited by Josef and Dorothy Berger, pp. 521-522; TREASURY OF THE WORLD'S GREAT DIARIES, edited by Philip Dunaway, pp. 481-483.

Jul 1885. Brief diary kept at Menlo Park, New Jersey, and Woodside Villa, Massachusetts; amusing comments on reading, acquaintances, children, flirtation with his future second wife; little to indicate the great inventor's scientific work or interests.

"His Diary Reveals an Unsuspected Mr. Edison." AMERICAN HERITAGE 22, no. 1 (1970):68-74.

Jul 1885. Extracts.

FRANKLIN, GEORGE WASHINGTON   **5206**

Koch, William E., ed. ''Farm Building on the Nebraska High Plains.'' JOURNAL OF THE WEST 16, no. 1 (1977):37-39.

> 1885-1892. Brief extracts from a much longer diary of a Perkins County, Nebraska, farmer; early years on his claim, with notes on building a house and barn, digging a well and growing various crops.

GILPIN, Mrs. JOHN R.   **5207**

Gilpin, Vincent, ed. ''Diary of a West Coast Sailing Expedition.'' TEQUESTA 7 (1947):44-64.

> Jan-Mar 1885. Extract covering a couple's hunting, fishing and exploring expedition as guests of Joseph Willcox, a Philadelphia naturalist; from Homosassa River to Key West, with notes on weather, route, sailing conditions, game, accommodations on shore and the general pleasures and discomforts of the expedition; the death from rattlesnake bite of a member of another party, despite efforts to save him.

HERREN, MARY E. LACEY, 1858-1887   **5208**

Hood, Brenda, ed. '' 'This Worry I Have': Mary Herren Journal.'' OREGON HISTORICAL QUARTERLY 80 (1979):229-257.

> Sep 1885-May 1886. Courageous young mother's struggle with tuberculosis; wagon trip from Yamhill County, Oregon, to Pasadena, California, in futile attempt to recover health; notes on Siskiyou Mountains, Oregon and California towns, camping experiences, activities of her husband and children; her own pain and fatigue; appreciation for kindnesses; return home on ship YAQUINA; entries sporadic for 1886.

ORLOV, VASILII   **5209**

Shalkop, Antoinette. ''The Travel Journal of Vasilii Orlov.'' PACIFIC NORTHWEST QUARTERLY 68 (1977):131-140.

> Dec 1885-Jan 1886. Report to his superiors of an Orthodox missionary's dogsled journey from the Nushagak Mission along the Kuskokwim River; preaching in Eskimo villages; evaluation of Kolmakovski Redoubt as a site for a mission station; a brief but interesting picture of Russian religious activity in Alaska. Translated from the Russian.

PENROSE, CHARLES W., 1832-1925   **5210**

Seifrit, William C., ed. '' 'To Get Utah in the Union': Diary of a Failed Mission.'' UTAH HISTORICAL QUARTERLY 51 (1983):358-381.

> Jan-Feb 1885. English-born Mormon leader's diary kept during an expedition to Washington, D.C., and New York to lobby for Utah statehood; travels with Brigham Young, Jr., all the while dodging United States Marshal E.A. Ireland, intent on indicting him for polygamy; by train to Niagara Falls and New York City, where he saw a number of plays, heard Henry Ward Beecher preach, conferred with New York Mormons and met frequently with a mysterious Mr. Miller to promote Utah interests; hectic activities in Washington, including attendance at Supreme Court to hear arguments on the Utah Commission and other cases; meetings with John T. Caine, Utah's delegate to Congress, and lobbying among a number of influential people; more sightseeing, theater and meetings with Miller, who attempted to defraud

the delegation of $20,000 in church funds; continuing, all the while, to submit articles to the DESERET NEWS, of which he was editor; learning of his assignment to a mission in England.

WISTER, OWEN, 1860-1938   **5211**

OWEN WISTER OUT WEST: HIS JOURNALS AND LETTERS. Edited by Fanny K. Wister. Chicago: University of Chicago Press, 1958. 269 pp., passim.

> 1885-1895. Diaries of young Philadelphia blueblood, later to be author of THE VIRGINIAN and other popular western fiction, who spent many summers roughing it in Wyoming and other states; travels by horseback, with stays at ranches and army outposts, and by train; much cowboy lore and other material and experiences important to his personal well-being and development as a writer.

Wister, Fanny K., ed. ''Owen Wister's West: The Unpublished Journals.'' ATLANTIC MONTHLY 195 (May, 1955):29-35; (June 1955): 52-57.

> 1885-1894. Extracts.

In THAT I MAY TELL YOU: JOURNALS AND LETTERS OF THE OWEN WISTER FAMILY, edited by Fanny K. Wister, pp. 229-268. Wayne, Pa.: Haverford House, 1979.

> 1914-1915. Struggles with depression after the death of his wife; business and social life of Philadelphia; care of his children; a therapautic trip to Europe on the MINNEAPOLIS; travels there and meeting with Henry James in London; resumption of life at home, with writing for the ATLANTIC MONTHLY and speaking engagements.

1886

ABER, MARTHA WILSON MCGREGOR, 1861-1932   **5212**

Westermeier, Clifford P. ''Our Western Journey.'' ANNALS OF WYOMING 22 (1950):90-100.

> Jun-Sep 1886. Brief notes of a journey from Aurora, Nebraska, to settle at Wolf Creek, Wyoming; camps, route, distances.

BOAS, FRANZ, 1858-1942   **5213**

THE ETHNOGRAPHY OF FRANZ BOAS. Edited by Ronald P. Rohner; translated by Hedy Parker. Chicago: University of Chicago Press, 1969. 331 pp. passim.

> 1886-1931 (with gaps). Letters and diaries of German anthropologist studying Indians of the Pacific Northwest coast, principally the Kwakiutl, but also Haida and Tsimshian; field work in British Columbia, Washington and Oregon, with special interest in Indian languages, mythology, folklore, art, dances and religions; collecting linguistic material on vocabulary and grammar and recording anthropometric measurements for the British Association for the Advancement of Science.

BROWN, WILLIAM HARVEY, d. 1913   **5214**

Peterson, John M., ed. ''Buffalo Hunting in Montana in 1886.'' MONTANA: THE MAGAZINE OF WESTERN HISTORY 31, no. 4 (1981):2-13.

Sep-Dec 1886. Extracts from the diary of a University of Kansas student assisting taxidermist William T. Hornaday on a Smithsonian expedition to obtain skins and skeletons of buffalo; by train from Washington, D.C., to Miles City, thence, accompanied by two soldiers and two cowboys, to hunt the few remaining buffalo in Montana; skinning and "skeletonizing" specimens; a few notes on camp life and cowboy humor.

CHAPMAN, FRANK MICHLER, 1864-1945   **5215**

FRANK M. CHAPMAN IN FLORIDA: HIS JOURNALS & LETTERS. Compiled and edited by Elizabeth S. Austin. Gainesville: University of Florida Press, 1967. 228 pp. Journal, pp. 5-34, 122-138, 158-173.

1886-1888, 1891-1892, 1932-1934. Ornithologist's journal of first winter in Gainesville, Florida, watching and collecting birds, with lists and locations of birds observed; return trips noting changes in lakes and marshes, renewing acquaintances; trips to Corpus Christi, Texas, and Cuba always noting and collecting birds and some small mammals for the American Museum of Natural History in New York.

DE COTTON, L.   **5216**

Joyaux, Georges J., trans. "A Frenchman's Visit to Chicago in 1886." ILLINOIS STATE HISTORICAL SOCIETY JOURNAL 47 (1954):45-56.

Jul-Aug 1886. Dated, but long narrative extracts from Frenchman's travel account; complaints of heat and industrial air pollution, but admiration for Chicago's size and progressiveness; delight with Lincoln Park gardens and zoo; a ghastly visit to stockyards and slaughterhouse.

GIBSON, WALTER MURRAY, 1822-1888   **5217**

THE DIARIES OF WALTER MURRAY GIBSON. Edited by Jacob Adler and Gwynn Barrett. Honolulu: University of Hawaii Press, 1973. 199 pp.

1886-1887. Brief daily entries by an English immigrant and excommunicated Mormon turned Catholic who became the controversial prime minister of Hawaii under King Kalakaua and architect of the ill-fated "primacy of the Pacific" policy; stormy meetings of cabinet and legislature, dealings with sugar tycoon Claus Spreckels, quarrels with colleagues; constant social life with nuns at the Convent of Sisters of St. Francis, including a rebuffed infatuation with the mother superior; visits to the leper colony at Kakaako and opinions on Father Damien; his final illness.

KELLOGG, DAVID SHERWOOD, 1847-1909   **5218**

A DOCTOR AT ALL HOURS: THE PRIVATE JOURNAL OF A SMALL-TOWN DOCTOR'S VARIED LIFE. Edited by Allen S. Everest. Brattleboro, Vt.: Stephen Greene Press, 1970. 228 pp.

1886-1909. Fine diary of a devoted doctor serving a large practice in Plattsburgh, New York, and surrounding Clinton County villages and farms; house calls by sleigh or buggy in all weathers, with notes on his patients, including the poor, whom he treated for little or nothing; references to many people and incidents, including President McKinley's several vacations at the Hotel Champlain; effects of the Spanish-American War on Plattsburgh, where the Twenty-first Infantry was stationed, and diarist's service as post surgeon; wide literary, historical and intellectual interests; appreciation of nature during his country rounds; hob-

bies of book collecting, visiting forts and other historic sites, garnering folklore, local and personal history from old-timers, collecting Indian relics and studying the archaeology of Champlain Valley; a brief, treasured acquaintance with William Dean Howells; national and local political news reported from the diarist's Republican perspective; raising of a large family.

LORD, HERBERT W., b. 1870   **5219**

Davison, Stanley R., ed. " 'We Done the Chores and Set by the Fire.' " MONTANA: THE MAGAZINE OF WESTERN HISTORY 33, no. 4 (1983):40-51.

1886-1887 (with gaps). Diary of a sixteen-year-old in thinly settled Bitterroot Valley; hunting, fishing and trapping with a few relatives and friends, taking a variety of animals including elk, moose, mountain lions, lynx, marten, coyotes, mink, beaver and wolverine; record of temperatures during the hard winter of that year; travels on snowshoe; enjoyment of photography.

MERRILL, MARRINER WOOD, 1832-1906   **5220**

In UTAH PIONEER AND APOSTLE: MARRINER WOOD MERRILL AND HIS FAMILY, by Melvin C. Merrill, pp. 94-294. Salt Lake City: Deseret News, 1937.

1886-1906. Extracts from diaries of Mormon leader, businessman and farmer; a few family matters in a large polygamous household, but mostly brief notes of business, farming, prices, etc., and Logan Temple events during his tenure as president; prosecution and imprisonment of various Mormon men for polygamy; references to many local people.

SMITH, JULINA LAMBSON, 1849-1936   **5221**

In WOMEN'S VOICES, edited by Kenneth Godfrey, Audrey Godfrey and Jill Derr, pp. 345-357.

Jan-Mar 1886. Extract from the diary of a Mormon woman accompanying her husband, Joseph F. Smith, on a mission to Hawaii; cooking, sewing and other communally shared chores among the mission women; tending her baby and missing her five older children at home in Utah; language study; serving as midwife.

WESTFALL, EDWARD DIXON, 1820-1897   **5222**

Sexton, Kathryn and Sexton, Irwin, eds. "Edward Dixon Westfall, Early Texas Climatologist, Philosopher and Philanthropist." SOUTHWESTERN HISTORICAL QUARTERLY 68 (1964):1-13.

1886-1897. Brief extracts, within article, from a journal kept in old age by an Elmendorf farmer and avid reader who willed his estate to establish a public library in San Antonio; although journal itself mainly concerned with weather, extracts selected to indicate reading interests and homespun philosophy of Westfall.

WOOD, LEONARD, 1860-1927   **5223**

CHASING GERONIMO. Edited by Jack C. Lane. Albuquerque: University of New Mexico Press, 1970. 152 pp.

May-Sep 1886. Indian campaign journal of a young assistant surgeon in the Army Medical Corps serving with Troop B, Fourth Cavalry, under Capt. Henry Lawton, for whom he was principal aide; marches from Fort Huachuca against the elusive Apaches through difficult terrain in Arizona and the Sierra Madre of Mexico; diarist's recovery from a poorly tended tarantula bite; his dangerous negotiations with a band of Mexican irregulars also pursuing Geronimo; frequent references to Lt. Charles Gatewood, Gen. Nelson Miles and Maj. George Crook and the controversy over credit for Geronimo's surrender; an articulate account of the campaign and cavalry life by a young soldier who went on to a distinguished military career.

YOUNG, HIRAM H., 1842-1919 5224

Moore, Powell, ed. "A Hoosier in Kansas." KANSAS HISTORICAL QUARTERLY 14 (1946):166-212, 297-352, 414-446; 15 (1947):42-80, 151-185.

1886-1895. Diary of a prominent Cloud County farmer, originally from Wolf Lake, Indiana, to which he later returned; farm work, weather, crops, prices; participation in local politics as a member of Farmers' Alliance and the Populist party; activities at Concordia; suffering from rheumatism; reference to illnesses and injuries of other members of his large family; dealings with many local people.

1887

BEADLE, CHARLES 5225

A TRIP TO THE UNITED STATES IN 1887. London: Printed for private circulation by J.S. Virtue, 1887. 210 pp.

Mar-Jun 1887. British gentleman's travel diary of steamer voyage to United States with his son; interest in government, business, agriculture and industry; railroad trip to Niagara; visiting ironworks, steel mills, gold mining in Colorado, lumber industry in the Pacific Northwest; details of watching baseball game in Kansas City; distress over conditions in Chinatown in San Francisco.

BRUCE, MAZIE, b. 1864? 5226

Baldwin, Hélène, L. " 'Down Street' in Cumberland." MARYLAND HISTORICAL MAGAZINE 77 (1982):222-229.

1887-1888. A few extracts from diary of unmarried woman living in Cumberland, Maryland, selected to depict the everyday life of upper middle-class women of the period.

FLOOK, SAM G. 5227

Holden, W.C., ed. "A Spur Ranch Diary." WEST TEXAS HISTORICAL ASSOCIATION YEAR BOOK 7 (1931):68-94.

Jan-Dec 1887. Record kept by an office employee of the Spur Ranch at Spur, Texas; bookkeeping, checks written, correspondence; tasks of ranch hands; weather and its effects on ranching; reference to visitors and neighboring ranchers; arrival of the "report of meeting of shareholders in London"; frequent trips to Dockums.

LESLIE, HYDE 5228

In THE DIARIES OF SALLY AND PAMELA BROWN, by Sally E. Brown, 176 pp. passim. Springfield, Vt.: William L. Bryant Foundation, 1970.

Apr-Dec 1887. Farming notes of a hired man at Plymouth Notch, Vermont; weather, crops, livestock, etc.

OLIVEIRA, JOÃO BAPTISTA D' 5229

Canario, Lucille de Silva, trans. "Destination Sandwich Islands." HAWAIIAN JOURNAL OF HISTORY 4 (1970):3-52.

Nov 1887-Apr 1888. Journal kept by Oliveira and Vicente d'Ornellas of a voyage on the THOMAS BELL from Funchal, Madeira, to Hawaii with a large group of Portuguese immigrants; colorful and entertaining descriptions of voyage and passengers; quarrels; music and festivals, including Portuguese Christmas celebration; births, illnesses and deaths aboard ship; terrors of the Horn; survival on reduced rations, leading to passenger protests.

ROSE, FOREST 5230

"The Diary of Forest Rose." THE HIGH COUNTRY, no. 21 (Summer 1972):24-30.

Nov 1887. Extract from a young woman's diary of train travel with her father, C.H.P. Rose, from their home at Carthage, Missouri, to San Diego: enthusiastic descriptions of scenery, towns and Indians seen en route.

WILSON, DELMER, 1873-1961 5231

Johnson, Theodore E., ed. "The Diary of a Maine Shaker Boy." SHAKER QUARTERLY 8, no. 1 (1968):3-22. Reprint. NEW ENGLAND SOCIAL STUDIES BULLETIN 31, no. 1 (1974):52-70.

Jan-Aug 1887. The first entries from a diary kept faithfully from 1887 to 1961; pleasant, naive notes of a thirteen-year-old boy and good picture of life at the Sabbathday Lake Shaker community; tending newborn calves and rejoicing that "the calf I was learning to drink will drink good now"; school work, Shaker meetings, such additional chores as cutting ice, hauling wood, sugaring and gardening; leisure diversions of "us boys"; resisting his mother's efforts to remove him from the community; references to many individuals.

1888

ANDERSON, LARZ, 1866-1937 5232

LARZ ANDERSON: LETTERS AND JOURNALS OF A DIPLOMAT. Edited by Isabel Anderson. New York and London: Fleming H. Revell, 1940. 672 pp. passim.

1888-1937. Extracts beginning with his "Grand Tour" upon graduation from Harvard; from San Francisco on the CITY OF PEKING with his friend Malcolm Thomas for a voyage around the world; notes on diplomatic service in Belgium and Japan and the social life of London, Paris, Brussels and Tokyo; long periods in Boston enjoying an affluent, cultivated life with his wife, Isabel Perkins Anderson; automobile journeys in the United States, Canada and Mexico during the early 1900's with good notes of travel experiences and sights, including the Grand Canyon, "a deep, cruel wound in Mother Nature's side."

BROKE, HORATIO GEORGE   5233

WITH SACK AND STOCK IN ALASKA. London: Longmans, Green, 1891. 158 pp. Diary, pp. 37-158.

Jul-Aug 1888. Englishman's account of a mountaineering expedition to Mount St. Elias; feats of canoeing, hiking, packing and climbing, with the help of local Indians; customs of Indians at Yakutat, including the potlatch.

BRUNDAGE, THEODORE, 1839-1907   5234

Lander, Richard N., ed. "Theodore Brundage, 1839-1907, North Castle Farmer." WESTCHESTER COUNTY HISTORICAL BULLETIN 25 (1949):23-28.

Jan-Dec 1888. Very brief, sporadic entries noting farm, social and church activities; prices of goods and services.

CANNON, GEORGE QUAYLE, 1827-1901   5235

Cannon, M. Hamlin, ed. "The Prison Diary of a Mormon Apostle." PACIFIC HISTORICAL REVIEW 16 (1947):393-409.

Sep-Dec 1888. Diary of an English immigrant, Mormon leader and former congressman imprisoned for polygamy at the Utah penitentiary; prison life and routines, with considerable freedom to write, study and conduct classes for fellow Mormon inmates; a stream of visitors to his cell "which has seemed a heavenly place and I feel that angels have been there"; references to many other people.

"Excerpts from the Journal of George Q. Cannon." IMPROVEMENT ERA 53 (1950):623-624, 672, 674.

Dec 1900-Jan 1901. Extracts covering meeting with former Queen Liliuokalani and other incidents of his Hawaiian mission.

CARBUTT, MARY RHODES   5236

FIVE MONTHS' FINE WEATHER IN CANADA, WESTERN U.S. AND MEXICO. London: Low, Marston, Searle & Rivington, 1889. 243 pp. American diary, pp. 1-152.

Aug 1888-Jan 1889. Englishwoman's travel diary; arriving on UMBRIA in New York, visiting Montreal and Niagara Falls; by train to see the Armour "stock killing establishment" at Chicago and the Pillsbury Company in Minneapolis; Yellowstone Park, mines in Helena, Montana, the Columbia River, Tacoma, Washington, and San Francisco, noting there the cable cars, the Presidio, Golden Gate Park and anti-Chinese sentiments; Yosemite Valley, Monterey, Palo Alto with Senator Stanford's "horse breeding establishment"; southern California fruit ranches, Nevada silver mines, Mormon buildings in Salt Lake City and health resorts in Colorado; observations on food, hotels, service, servants, business, wages, working conditions and hours, which she felt were too long to "allow an interest in music, literature, politics and science."

CREEMER, WILLIAM HENRY, 1829-1900   5237

Lander, Richard N., ed. "William Henry Creemer." WESTCHESTER COUNTY HISTORICAL BULLETIN. 28 (1952):6-11, 53-59, 82-88, 116-122.

Jan-Dec 1888. Extracts from Westchester County, New York, farmer's diary; tasks at Green Valley Farm; weather, especially blizzard in March; notes on reading, prices, politics, family, community and church activities, Thanksgiving, Christmas cards and air pollution from cities; preserving North Castle's town records; brief entries but rich in the details of everyday life.

DALLY, BENJAMIN HART, 1865-1946   5238

A MILWAUKEE, WISCONSIN DIARY (FOR THE YEAR 1888) OF BENJAMIN HART DALLY. Edited by Alexander G. Rose. Baltimore, Md.: Rose, 1974. 80 pp.

1888. Diary of freight agent for Star Union National and Green Lines, a Pennsylvania Railroad affiliate; daily work at the office, afternoons off, evening and weekend activities of visiting and "declaring his intentions" to Myra Rose; calling on friends, drill night with the Wisconsin National Guard, social life at the Armory and Commercial Club, attending Presbyterian church; political participation in Republican party and campaign for Benjamin Harrison; evenings at home reading, tobogganing in winter, swimming and rowing at the lake in summer at the summer place of Alexander G. Rose, plays, concerts and lectures; a view of a young man's life.

ELLIOTT, CHARLES BURKE, 1861-1935   5239

Elliott, Charles W., ed. "The University of Minnesota's First Doctor of Philosophy." MINNESOTA HISTORY 18 (1937):121-151.

Jan-Jun 1888. Extracts from Minneapolis lawyer's diary covering a busy legal practice mixed with preparation for his doctoral examination in history, which he passed "with credit"; comments on professor and friend Harry Pratt Judson; specific books read for examination; family responsibilities and struggle with Minnesota winter.

LUKENS, MATILDA BARNS   5240

INLAND PASSAGE. N.p., 1889. 84 pp.

Jun 1888? Eastern woman's trip from Tacoma, Washington, up the inland passage to Chilikat and back aboard the CORONA; brief stops at Seattle, Port Townsend and Victoria; visiting Sheldon Jackson's mission at Sitka and other Presbyterian missions at Juneau and Wrangell; notes on Russian palace of the governors and church in Sitka, Indians of Alaska, Northwest scenery including whales, icebergs and glaciers.

MOORE, FRANK LINCOLN, 1866-1935   5241

SOULS AND SADDLEBAGS: THE DIARIES AND CORRESPONDENCE OF FRANK L. MOORE. Edited by Austin L. Moore. Denver: Big Mountain Press, 1962. 207 pp. Diary, pp. 21-155.

1888-1891. Diary of Presbyterian missionary and circuit rider in Wyoming and northern Colorado; descriptions of territory, ranches and settlers; discovery that the area was a difficult one for missionary work because of rough pioneer life and lawlessness, but some success in starting Sunday school and singing school; love of scenery, outdoors, fishing, etc.; brief interlude for education at University of Michigan terminated by lack of money; marriage to Coral E. Leigh; return to Wyoming as a circuit rider in the Bighorn Basin.

Moore, Austin L., ed. "Fossil Hunting in the Big Horn Basin." ANNALS OF WYOMING 36 (1964):22-33.

Jul-Aug 1899. Minister's account of a geological expedition with Dr. F.W. Sardeson of the University of Minnesota; finding fossils of many prehistoric creatures; hospitality of Brown's Ranch and others; preaching on Sundays.

**OGDEN, ANNA FREDERIKE LUISE HARDER,   5242
1867-1960**

In WOMEN OF THE WEST, by Cathy Luchetti, pp. 193-198.

1888-1895. Diary of chambermaid in a succession of California cities and resorts; unsuccessful attempt to learn telegraphing; much berating of herself and acquaintances; worry over debts which she finally paid.

PARKER, OCTAVIUS   5243

Sunder, John E., ed. "The Reverend Octavius Parker's 'Journey from San Francisco to Anvik, Alaska, Taken at a Time When a Direct Journey was Impracticable.'" HISTORICAL MAGAZINE OF THE PROTESTANT EPISCOPAL CHURCH 34 (1965):333-348.

Aug-Oct 1888. Episcopal priest's ship travel to Alaska; activities and observations in the Kuskokwin and Yukon river areas, with interesting notes on Indians, Moravians, Russians, Roman Catholics and Episcopalians; visits to missions; problems with food and illness on the sometimes dangerous trip.

PARRISH, HELEN, 1859-1942   5244

Davis, Allen F. and Sutherland, John F., eds. "Reform and Uplift among Philadelphia Negroes." PENNSYLVANIA MAGAZINE OF HISTORY AND BIOGRAPHY 94 (1970):496-517.

Jul-Nov 1888. Extracts from the diary of a Philadelphia philanthropist and housing reformer employing methods developed by Octavia Hill in London; overseeing properties bought to rent at low rates to the poorest of slum blacks; attempts to raise standard of living by improved housing and urging cleanliness, sobriety and thrift; much on her tenants' personal lives and problems and her efforts to secure health care, clothing and food for many families; some stormy encounters over rents and other matters; references to her friend and colleague Hannah Fox.

PEABODY, MARIAN LAWRENCE, b. 1875   5245

TO BE YOUNG WAS VERY HEAVEN. Boston: Houghton Mifflin, 1967. 366 pp. passim.

1888-1906. Personal diary of school days in Cambridge and Boston with vacations in Bar Harbor, Maine; genteel social life in Boston; travel to Europe with her father, dean of the Episcopal Theological School in Cambridge, and visiting Archbishop of Canterbury Davidson and his wife who returned to visit and attended the General Convention of the Protestant Episcopal Church in 1904; charity work, especially for Sailors' Haven in Charlestown; attending art school; visiting the Chicago Exposition in 1893; marriage to Harold Peabody.

PERKINS, DANIEL M., 1844-1904   5246

Sherman, Rexford B. "One Year on a New Hampshire Farm." HISTORICAL NEW HAMPSHIRE 32 (1977):1-17.

Jan-Dec 1888. Brief extracts from Newbury, farmer's diary of daily activities; plowing, planting, harvesting corn, potatoes, cabbages, oats and barley; tapping trees for maple syrup; community affairs and Masonic meetings.

PHILIPSON, DAVID, 1862-1948   5247

"Strangers to a Strange Land." AMERICAN JEWISH ARCHIVES 18 (1966):133-138.

1888-1905. A few substantial extracts from voluminous diaries of the American Reform rabbi of Cincinnati's Bene Israel Temple; chiefly the "Jewish Russian problem" and "how can we Americanize them?"; concern about the "fanatic and ignorant zeal" of the older immigrants, yet equal worry that the younger generation would throw aside all religion; reports on the persecution driving more and more Jews from Russia; opening a school for their children and organizing Society for Ameliorating the Condition of Russian Immigrants.

SMITH, TELAMON CRUGER CUYLER, 1873-1951   5248

Moore, John Hammond, ed. "Telamon Cuyler's Diary: To Texas in 1888." SOUTHWESTERN HISTORICAL QUARTERLY 70 (1967):474-488.

Oct 1888. Fifteen-year-old Atlanta boy's letter-diary of a trip to Texas with Henry W. Grady, editor of the ATLANTA CONSTITUTION, and his son, Henry Jr., the diarist's friend; travel in a private railroad car with a large party; good, sometimes humorous, descriptions of train travel, scenery, people and countryside; a stop in Memphis with sights and activities there; towns in Texas, where Grady and others made speeches; an exposition at Dallas; thence to Austin and San Antonio, with a visit to the Alamo.

TRAUBEL, HORACE, 1858-1919   5249

WITH WALT WHITMAN IN CAMDEN. Boston: Small, Maynard, 1906-14. 3 vols.

1888-1890. Voluminous notes kept by Whitman's friend and literary executor of conversations about people and literature, the state of Whitman's health and visitors, distinguished and otherwise; frequent references to Richard Bucke, John Burroughs, Emerson, Thomas B. Harned, William Douglas O'Connor, John Herbert Clifford, Herbert Gilchrist, David McKay and other friends, past and present; an encyclopedic coverage of Whitman's contacts, interests and memories during his last years.

In WALT WHITMAN'S CAMDEN CONVERSATIONS, by Walt Whitman, selected and arranged by Walter Teller, pp. 1-215 passim. New Brunswick, N.J.: Rutgers University Press, 1973.

1888-1890. A dated but topical rather than chronological arrangement of Whitman's conversations as recorded by Horace Traubel in Camden.

WATSON, WALTER A.   5250

"Notes on Southside Virginia." VIRGINIA STATE LIBRARY BULLETIN 15, no. 2-4 (1925):201-263.

1888-1909 (with gaps). Diary of a judge and politician; social life, fox hunting, church activities, etc., in rural and small-town Virginia near Richmond; local events, deaths, funerals, marraiges and notes on numerous people in Nottoway, Amelia, Powhatan and Dinwiddie counties; service as a delegate to the Virginia Constitutional Convention of 1901-1902, with much information on the debates over black suffrage, poll tax, etc., and the positions of various delegates; apparently as circuit judge, convening courts in many towns, with description of various cases; an attack of malaria; Civil War reminiscences and vignettes of Confederate leaders.

WOODMAN, ABBY JOHNSON, b. 1828   5251

PICTURESQUE ALASKA: A JOURNAL OF A TOUR AMONG THE MOUNTAINS, SEAS AND ISLANDS OF THE NORTHWEST FROM SAN FRANCISCO TO SITKA. Boston: Houghton, Mifflin, 1889. 212 pp.

Apr-May 1888. Travel journal of tourist trip by train and ship from San Francisco through Oregon, Washington, British Columbia and Alaska; scenic beauty of Mount Hood and Mount Shasta; the character of the cities and villages; interest in Indian artifacts and missionary work.

1889

BANTA, JOHN JACKSON   5252

Alcorn, Rowena L. and Alcorn, Gordon D. "Evergreen on the Queets." OREGON HISTORICAL QUARTERLY 74 (1973):5-33 passim.

1889-1891. Substantial extracts within article on founder of settlement in the Queets River area of the Olympic Peninsula; trip from Tacoma, Washington, with his partner S. Price Sharp aboard the STATE OF WASHINGTON, POINT ARENA and EVANGEL, then on foot with Charles A. Gilman; help from Indians and settlers with guiding, food and shelter; return to Tacoma; later journeys bringing more people, some aboard the LUCY LOWE and MISCHIEF, dangerous and difficult life in the Queets Corridor, eventually part of Olympic National Park.

BOND, J.H.   5253

Bond, I.W., comp. "Old Trails in Reverse: Journal of J.H. Bond and Family from the San Luis Valley, Colorado, to Graham, Missouri." COLORADO MAGAZINE 32 (1955):225-233.

Aug-Oct 1889. Journey of a family giving up Colorado homesteading to return to Missouri; route, distances, camps; comments on ranches, farms, towns and settlements; encounters with westbound emigrants.

BUTLER, JULIA COLT, b. 1872   5254

Wensel, Melissa A. "The Diary of Julia Colt Butler." RUTGERS UNIVERSITY LIBRARY JOURNAL 46 (1984):47-57.

1889-1890. Article containing a few extracts from the diary of a wealthy Paterson, New Jersey, girl; social life in Paterson and her experiences as a conventional and well-supervised tourist in Europe; some indication of a lighthearted girl eager for adventure but thwarted by her circumstances.

CARROLL, LEN F.   5255

In A SUNDAY BETWEEN WARS, by Ben Maddow, pp. 149-152.

1889-1890. Extracts from Newkirk, Oklahoma, farmer's diary; daily work and illness of his wife.

ECKSTORM, FANNY PEARSON HARDY, 1865-1946   5256

Hatch, Benton L., ed. "Down the West Branch of the Penobscot." APPALACHIA 15 (1949):480-498.

Extracts in A DAY AT A TIME, edited by Margo Culley, pp. 179-183.

Aug 1889. Observations during a canoe trip on the Penobscot; good natural history notes.

FLAKE, JAMES MADISON, 1859-1946   5257

JAMES MADISON FLAKE, PIONEER, LEADER, MISSIONARY. Compiled by S. Eugene Flake. Bountiful, Utah: Wasatch Press, 1970. 284 pp. Diary, pp. 47-65.

May-Dec 1889. Extracts from diary of a Mormon's mission to England, condensed and summarized in places; side trip to Paris to attend World's Fair of 1889; in England, Mormon meetings, conversions and baptisms; return voyage, during which he was in charge of the Mormon immigrants on board; return to ranching in Snowflake, Arizona; a pleasant, unselfconscious diary.

GREEN, ALFRED JOHN, 1851-1926   5258

JOTTINGS FROM A CRUISE. Seattle, Wash.: Kelly Printing, 1944. 451 pp., passim.

Feb 1889-Jan 1890. Maritime diary, letters and memoirs of an English ship captain who immigrated to the Puget Sound area of Washington; voyage of the sailing vessel MERTOLA, involving ports in Florida and California.

JAMES, ALICE, 1848-1892   5259

ALICE JAMES, HER BROTHERS — HER JOURNAL. Edited by Anna R. Burr. New York: Dodd, Mead; London: Macmillan, 1934. Reprint. Boston: Milford House, 1972. 252 pp.

THE DIARY OF ALICE JAMES. Edited by Leon Edel. New York: Dodd, Mead, 1964. Reprint. Harmondsworth, Middlesex, and New York: Penguin Books, 1982. 241 pp.

Extracts in REVELATIONS: DIARIES OF WOMEN, compiled by Mary J. Moffat, pp. 192-205.

1889-1892. Private diary of Henry and William James' invalid sister who presided over an unusual salon attracting an endless assortment of literary and leisured English people whose comments afforded much material for her sometimes caustic diary; residence in London and Leamington; musings on reading, English manners and mores, her childhood, politics, illness and death, including suicide; frequent references to her brothers and to her tireless companion Katharine Peabody Loring; a candid, self-revealing diary of literary and psychological interest.

JONES, BURTON RENSSELAER, b. 1845   5260

INCIDENTS IN THE LIFE AND LABORS OF BURTON RENSSELAER JONES. Chicago: Free Methodist Publishing House, 1909. 316 pp. passim.

1889-1898. Scattered extracts from the diary of a Free Methodist circuit preacher, mainly in the Michigan Conference; activities at Spring Arbor and Jackson; preaching services, love feasts and quarterly meetings; later travels throughout the United States as general superintendent of the church and editor of the FREE METHODIST.

KENDRICK, FRANK CLARENCE, b. 1852   **5261**

Stiles, Helen J., ed. "Down the Colorado in 1889." COLORADO MAGAZINE 41 (1964):225-246.

Mar-May 1889. Denver mining engineer's survey of the Colorado River route envisioned for the Denver, Colorado Canyon and Pacific Railroad, part of a larger survey under its president, Frank M. Brown, who perished in the process; difficulties of navigating the Colorado and Green rivers; scenery and surveying details.

MODJESKA, HELENA, 1840-1909   **5262**

In MODJESKA: HER LIFE AND LOVES, by Antoni Gronowicz, pp. 167-179. New York: T. Yoseloff, 1956.

Apr-May 1889. Extracts from diary of Polish Shakespearean actress on tour with Edwin Booth to Milwaukee, Cedar Rapids, Davenport, Peoria, Decatur, Bloomington, Indianapolis, Vincennes, Louisville, Dayton, Zanesville and Wheeling; notes on the towns, audiences, her feelings about the performances and Booth's after-performance conversations.

NIMS, FRANKLIN A.   **5263**

THE PHOTOGRAPHER AND THE RIVER, 1889-1890: THE COLORADO CANYON DIARY OF FRANKLIN A. NIMS WITH THE BROWN-STANTON RAILROAD SURVEY. Edited by Dwight L. Smith. Santa Fe, N.M.: Stagecoach Press, 1967. 75 pp.

May-Jul, Nov 1889-Jan 1890. Diary of a survey undertaken by the short-lived Denver, Colorado Canyon and Pacific Railroad Company to determine feasibility of a railway along the Colorado River from the Rocky Mountains to the Pacific; hazardous river travel down the Green and Colorado in an expedition under Frank M. Brown and Robert B. Stanton; dangerous rapids and laborious portages; frequent spills ruining food and supplies; diarist's struggles to preserve his photographs and equipment; the drowning of Brown, P.M. Hansbrough and H.C. Richards and return of survivors to Denver; further exploration with a reorganized company under Stanton.

SYDENHAM, ALVIN H., d. 1893   **5264**

"The Daily Journal of Alvin H. Sydenham." NEW YORK PUBLIC LIBRARY BULLETIN 44 (1940):113-116, 326-330, 405-409, 529-536.

1889-1890. Young cavalryman's record of marches, campaigns, scouts and garrison life from Fort Kearny to Fort Robinson and covering most of his tour of duty at Fort Keogh, Montana; expedition with ranchers to "clean out the Indian village that had been scaring settlers" only to discover that the supposed teepees were conical sand formations; passion for hunting; social life among military personnel and ranch folk; a meeting with Frederic Remington.

TAYLOR, EMMA CATHERINE HARD, 1845-1926   **5265**

In THE DIARY OF CLARISSA ADGER BOWEN, ASHTABULA PLANTATION, by Mary Stevenson, pp. 86-87. Pendleton, S.C.: Research and Publication Committee, Foundation of Historic Preservation in Pendleton Area, 1973.

Summer 1889. Extracts from combination diary and guest book kept by Emma and husband, George Edwyn Taylor, in-laws of eldest son of Clarissa and Orsamus Bowen, at Mountain View

farm near Pendleton, South Carolina; business and social activities.

WHIPPLE, CHARLES W.   **5266**

Wright, Muriel H. "Captain Charles W. Whipple's Notebook: The Week of the Run into Oklahoma in 1889." CHRONICLES OF OKLAHOMA 48 (1970):146-154.

Apr 1889. Army ordnance officer's account of the opening of Unassigned Lands in Indian Territory to settlement; from Fort Leavenworth to the Cherokee Strip with his commander Wesley Merritt; maintaining order among thousands of settlers arriving to race for claims; events at present Oklahoma City, Kingfisher and Fort Reno.

WILLIAMS, NANCY ABIGAIL CLEMENT   **5267**

In WOMEN'S VOICES, edited by Kenneth Godfrey, Audrey Godfrey and Jill Derr, p. 359-372.

1889-1891. Extracts from the diary of a Mormon plural wife of Fredrick Granger Williams after the practice had been outlawed; participating in baptism for the dead and other temple ordinances at Manti; visits to relatives and friends in prison for polygamy; attending school at Ephraim Academy while secretly married; move with her husband and his family from Fairview, Utah, to Colonia Dublan, Mexico, to avoid his arrest.

1890

ANON.   **5268**

Wolkovich-Valkavicius, William, ed. "Lithuanian Immigrant's Diary - A Rarity." LITUANUS 27, no. 1 (1981):39-48.

1890?-1907. Lithuanian immigrant's largely undated entries recounting immigration first to England and then to the United States; mostly a discouraging search for work in the Boston area and Brockton, Massachusetts, where he eventually settled; work in a shoe factory with enough income to enable the purchase of a house for his growing family; references to other Lithuanians in the area.

ANON.   **5269**

Wagner, Dorothy, ed. "The Varsity Whirl." PALIMPSEST 10 (1929):109-126.

1890-1899. Anonymous diary extracts, apparently from the pens of several students, giving the flavor of social and fraternity life of the Gay Nineties at University of Iowa; games, banquets, dances, pranks and, for the last big university party of the century, the Armory decorated to "a maze of color, a veritable dreamland of ecstasy."

BERRY, KATHERINE FISKE, b. 1877   **5270**

KATIE-SAN: FROM MAINE PASTURES TO JAPAN SHORES. Cambridge, Mass.: Dresser, Chapman & Grimes, 1962. 285 pp. passim.

1890-1893. Diary of missionary's daughter growing up in Japan and keeping a "jernal"; home schooling, books read, Bible verses learned, music lessons and "great fun" or "jolly times" with her sister, brother and friends; observing local Japanese customs; markets, festivals and entertainments; visiting temples.

BROWN, LEO G. 5271

In THE PHOTOGRAPHER AND THE RIVER, by Franklin A. Nims, edited by Dwight L. Smith, pp. 63-64. Santa Fe, N.M.: Stagecoach Press, 1967.

Jan 1890. Brief account of a fall and injuries suffered by Franklin A. Nims, photographer for the Brown-Stanton Railway Survey Expedition down the Green and Colorado rivers; a serious fall from the cliffs above the Colorado while trying to position himself for photographs; Brown and others carrying him with great difficulty to Lees Ferry.

DORIAN, LYDIA G. HALEY, 1866-1926 5272

Seligmann, G.L., ed. "North to New Mexico." RED RIVER VALLEY HISTORICAL REVIEW 1 (1974):165-177, 281-293.

May, 1890-Feb 1891. Texas woman's diary of a wagon journey with her husband, Samuel M. Dorian, and their two children through western Texas and the Panhandle to settle in Colfax County, New Mexico; full, engaging details of travel and camping; such difficulties as fording streams, keeping a herd of pigs alive on the trail and contending with "ruff roads"; notes on ranches and settlers en route; joining her parents, the Robert K. Haleys, and establishing a home and ranch, with many cheerful domestic details; concluding that "I like our place splendid."

FITZMAURICE, MARY L., d. 1892 5273

Donnell, Eileen H., ed. "Rowe Creek, 1890-91: Mary L. Fitzmaurice Diary." OREGON HISTORICAL QUARTERLY 83 (1982):171-194, 288-310.

1890-1891. Irish immigrant's account of homesteading in Wheeler County with her son, Maurice Fitzmaurice, and his large family; gardening, domestic chores, nursing of the sick; difficulties of sheep and cattle ranching; brief but telling notes of family and social life among Irish settlers in the area; visit to land office at The Dalles; a sensitive diary.

JACKSON, NANNIE STILLWELL 5274

VINEGAR PIE AND CHICKEN BREAD: A WOMAN'S DIARY OF LIFE IN THE RURAL SOUTH. Edited by Margaret Bolsterli. Fayetteville: University of Arkansas Press, 1982. 108 pp.

Jun 1890-Apr 1891. Tedious daily routine on a farm near Watson in Desha County, Arkansas; washing, cooking, sewing, caring for the sick and visiting neighbor women; a good view of life on a small cotton farm, the women's social network and mutual support.

Bolsterli, Margaret J. " 'It Seems to Help Me Bear It Better When She Knows About It.' " SOUTHERN EXPOSURE 11 (March/April 1983):58-61.

Jun 1890-Apr 1891. Extracts selected to illustrate the importance of friendship and emotional support among hardworking and isolated rural Arkansas women.

PATTERSON, SAM L. 5275

In ECHOES OF HAPPY VALLEY, by Thomas F. Hickerson, p. 121.

Jul 1890. Brief diary extract recording diarist's tribute to Walter N. Lenoir.

STEVENSON, FANNY VAN DE GRIFT, 1840-1914 5276

OUR SAMOAN ADVENTURE. By Fanny and Robert Louis Stevenson; edited by Charles Neider. New York: Harper, 1955. 264 pp. passim. London: Weidenfeld and Nicolson, 1956. 287 pp. passim.

1890-1893. Journal, interspersed with Stevenson's letters, of his American wife, kept during their last years in Samoa; building a house and gardening; nursing her frail husband and contending with her own illnesses; variety of experiences with Samoan employees; notes on local lore and superstitions, political affairs and war; honest feelings of depression and moments of humor in an entertaining narrative.

WILSON, ELIZABETH RUFFNER, b. 1810 5277

Trotter, Margaret G. "A Glimpse of Charleston in the 1890's: From a Contemporary Diary." WEST VIRGINIA HISTORY 35 (1973-1974):131-144.

1890-1892. A few extracts within article about the diary of an elderly Charleston woman living with her daughter, Mrs. Charles C. Lewis, and their large, prosperous family; local events and social life.

WRIGHT, LOUISA STEPHENS, b. 1871 5278

GOLDEN ADVENTURE. Pasadena, Calif.: San Pasqual Books, 1941. 198 pp.

1890-1891. Travel diary of voyage around the world on ships UMBRIA and OCEANIC; sightseeing in Ireland and England where she heard Spurgeon preach, Paderewski play the piano and Patti sing; visiting places of tourist interest in Germany, Greece, Italy, Egypt, India and Japan.

1891

BARRON, CLARENCE WALKER, 1855-1928 5279

MORE THEY TOLD BARRON: CONVERSATIONS AND REVELATIONS OF AN AMERICAN PEPYS IN WALL STREET. Edited by Arthur Pound and Samuel T. Moore. New York and London: Harper, 1931, 334 pp.

1891-1928. Diaries of a financier with eventual connections to the WALL STREET JOURNAL, BARRON'S and the Dow, Jones Company; conversations, gossip, speculations, etc., about development of international oil, railroads, investments, the stock market and financial activities of F.H. Prince, John D. Rockefeller, Charles M. Schwab and others; references to Woodrow Wilson; the diarist's life in Boston and during European travels, both dominated by financial interests.

Extracts in DIARY OF AMERICA, edited by Josef and Dorothy Berger, pp. 525-534.

1892-1928. Notes on talks with and about industrialists and businessmen such as George Westinghouse, etc.

THEY TOLD BARRON. Edited by Arthur Pound and Samuel T. Moore. New York and London: Harper, 1930. 372 pp.

1918-1928. Conversations with and notes on a host of financiers, industrialists and political leaders, including presidents Coolidge, Wilson, Harding and Hoover, J.P. Morgan, Harry F. Sinclair, Henry Ford and Edward L. Doheny; the development of the chain store phenomenon, General Motors and other major companies; almost every aspect of big business, finance and investment of the period; Wall Street gossip and anecdotes.

BULLOCK, STANLEY HENRY, 1866-1934   **5280**

Dodson, Pat, ed. "Cruise of the MINNEHAHA." FLORIDA HISTORICAL QUARTERLY 50 (1972): 385-413.

Nov 1891-Feb 1892. An English immigrant's log and diary of a round trip cruise on his thirty-foot sloop from Narcoossee, his home, down the Kissimmee River to Lake Okeechobee and out to the Gulf of Mexico, via the Caloosahatchee River; difficulties of river and canal navigation; notes on boats encountered, villages, vegetation and wildlife; unsuccessful attempt to communicate with Seminoles by using words from Longfellow's "Hiawatha."

CRAWFORD, FLORENCE   **5281**

Socolofsky, Homer E., ed. "The Private Journals of Florence Crawford and Arthur Capper." Kansas Historical Quarterly 30 (1964):15-61, 163-208.

Jun 1891-Feb 1892. Interspersed entries of a young engaged couple's journals kept during a lonely and prolonged absence from each other, Florence Crawford, the governor's daughter, at home in Topeka, and Arthur Capper, a journalist and future governor of Kansas, working for the NEW YORK TRIBUNE and WASHINGTON CAPITAL; Florence's hectic and exhausting social schedule; train trip and family vacation at Nantucket, with a good picture of fashionable resort life there; Arthur's train travel, interesting reporting assignments and much on New York, Washington, D.C., and Boston.

EVANS, ROBLEY DUNGLISON, 1846-1912   **5282**

A SAILOR'S LOG; RECOLLECTIONS OF FORTY YEARS OF NAVAL LIFE. New York: D. Appleton, 1901. 407 pp. Diary, pp. 221-407.

1891-1898. Dated entries within a much longer memoir of navy captain whose career spanned the Civil War to Spanish-American War; diary covering commands of SARATOGA and YORKTOWN; tense relations with Chile, especially over incident at Valparaiso involving the BALTIMORE, under Winfield S. Schley, while Evans was stationed there; later calls at Mare Island, California, Port Townsend, Washington, and Unalaska; commands of INDIANA and IOWA just before and during war with Spain; later portion mainly narrative.

JACKSON, SHELDON, 1834-1909   **5283**

Anderson, Charles A., ed. "Exploring for Reindeer in Siberia, Being the Journal of the Cruise of the U.S. Revenue Steamer BEAR." PRESBYTERIAN HISTORICAL SOCIETY JOURNAL 31 (1953):1-24, 87-112.

May-Oct 1891. First expedition of Presbyterian missionary and educator to transport Siberian reindeer to Alaska to alleviate starvation of native population; from Port Townsend, Washington, with a party from the United States Geological and Geographical Survey and the National Geographic Society intent upon explor-

ing Mount St. Elias; drowning of a number of this expedition when their small boat capsized; inspection of missions and schools at Sitka and other ports; across Holy Cross Bay to Siberia amid floating ice and treacherous waves, arranging at villages for the purchase of reindeer; further cruise of the BEAR among islands and inlets, often serving as hospital ship; return to trade for deer and transport a small herd to Unalaska Island; the assistance throughout of officers of the BEAR, Captain M.A. Healy, D.H. Jarvis and S.J. Call; notes on Indian and Eskimo customs.

KRISTIANSEN, SOREN, d. 1932   **5284**

DIARY OF CAPTAIN SOREN KRISTIANSEN, LAKE MICHIGAN SCHOONER CAPTAIN. Iron Mountain, Michigan: Mid-Peninsula Library Cooperative, 1981. 82 pp.

1891-1893. Norwegian immigrant's diary as captain of the MISHICOFF, mainly in the wood and bark trade; much on weather and shipping, with names of vessels in and out of such ports as Onekama and Sheboygan.

MUNRO, GEORGE C.   **5285**

Shelmidine, Lyle S. "The Early History of Midway Island." AMERICAN NEPTUNE 8 (1948):179-195. Diary extracts, pp. 186-191.

Jul 1891. Voyage to Midway by scientist with Rothschild Expedition aboard the KAALOKAI; information on his captain, F.D. Walker, who had survived the wreck of his previous ship, the WANDERING MINSTREL, and mystery and possible foul play surrounding the entire incident; remains of another wreck, the GENERAL SIEGAL; notes on gooney birds and other wildlife and desolate scenery of the islands.

PAGE, THOMAS NELSON, 1853-1922   **5286**

Holman, Harriet R., ed. "The Kentucky Journal of Thomas Nelson Page." KENTUCKY HISTORICAL SOCIETY REGISTER 68 (1970):1-16.

1891-1892. Extracts, with most dates removed, from the journal of a Richmond, Virginia, lawyer and author on a nostalgic visit to friends and relatives at Louisville; a round of social and speaking engagements; amusing gossip and anecdotes, including some secondhand about Grant and Lincoln; admiring references to his frequent host, the Rev. John A. Broadus, and his family, as well as other prominent people.

PEABODY, JOSEPHINE PRESTON, 1874-1922   **5287**

DIARY AND LETTERS OF JOSEPHINE PRESTON PEABODY. Edited by Christina H. Baker. Boston and New York: Houghton Mifflin, 1925. 346 pp.

1891-1921. Personal diary of poet, playright and lecturer at Wellesley College; sympathy for labor causes, suffrage and peace; criticisms of Professor Francis J. Child and her first editor, Horace Scudder of ATLANTIC MONTHLY; marriage to Lionel S. Marks; delight in birth of first child; battling a crippling disease; a record of the intellectual and artistic tastes, ambitions and joys of a creative spirit.

PEARY, JOSEPHINE DIEBITSCH   **5288**

MY ARCTIC JOURNAL. New York and Philadelphia: Contemporary Publishing, 1893. 240 pp. Reprint. New York: AMS Press, 1975.

1891-1892. Diary, enlarged for publication, kept by Robert E. Peary's wife while accompanying him on his North Greenland Expedition; sailing on the whaler KITE, with a stop at Duck Islands to gather eggs and eiderdown for winter; pushing through ice pack in Melville Bay to McCormick Bay; Peary's accident and broken leg on ship; building a house and preparing for winter, with assistance of Eskimos, particularly women chewing skins to make fur outfits; housekeeping with limited equipment and furniture; waiting while Peary was exploring the island ice; useful for early ethnological information on Eskimos.

ROCKHILL, WILLIAM WOODVILLE, 1854-1914   5289

DIARY OF A JOURNEY THROUGH MONGOLIA AND TIBET IN 1891 AND 1892. Washington, D.C.: Smithsonian Institution, 1894. 412 pp.

Nov 1891-Oct 1892. Geographer's diary of an expedition to Mongolia and Tibet sponsored by the Smithsonian; condition, occupations, languages and customs of the people; climate, geology, plants and animals of the region; the logistics and hardships of exploration; an interesting diary full of exotic details, illustrated with photographs and sketches.

STEPHEN, ALEXANDER M., d. 1894   5290

HOPI JOURNAL OF ALEXANDER STEPHEN. Edited by Elsie C. Parsons. Columbia University Contributions to Anthropology, vol. 23. New York: Columbia University Press, 1936. 2 vols. Reprint. New York: AMS Press, 1969.

1891-1894. Diary of an Indian trader in Arizona; learning Navaho language; recording ceremonial and daily life of Hopi Indians, chiefly at First Mesa; relations between Navaho and Hopi Indians; some information on population and economics. This edition has all entries for a specific ceremony arranged together.

SULLIVAN, THOMAS RUSSELL, 1849-1916   5291

PASSAGES FROM THE JOURNAL OF THOMAS RUSSELL SULLIVAN. Boston and New York: Houghton Mifflin, 1917. 252 pp. passim.

1891-1903 (with gaps). Bostonian's notes on theater and performances by Richard Mansfield, Alessandro and Tommaso Salvini; events at the Tavern Club; art activities and purchases at Boston Museum of Fine Arts; reading and literary interests.

WOOD, WILL   5292

Henrickson, Wilma, ed. "Summer Escapes." HISTORICAL SOCIETY OF MICHIGAN CHRONICLE 20 (1984):6-9.

1891-1893. Diary kept by cabin boy aboard the steam yacht UARDA owned by wealthy Detroit land developer Cameron D. Waterman; successive summers of Waterman family tours on the Great Lakes and entertaining friends at parties aboard the yacht.

1892

BROWN, JOSEPHINE EDITH   5293

Hopkins, Vivian C., ed. "Diary of an Iowa Farm Girl." ANNALS OF IOWA, 3d ser. 42 (1973-1975):126-146.

1892-1901. Delightful and unselfconscious record of farm, school and social life of a Shelby girl; good details of school subjects and lessons; a hilarious account of "Professor Sangerman's Lecture on Voice Culture"; Methodist church activities and the Epworth League; love of parties, clothes and clubs; the beginning of her own teaching career at age eighteen; a few entries from college days at Iowa State.

MCGAVRAN, MARY THEODORA, 1869-1923   5294

Kaiser, Robert M. and others, eds. "A Philadelphia Medical Student of the 1890s." PENNSYLVANIA MAGAZINE OF HISTORY AND BIOGRAPHY 108 (1984):217-236.

1892-1896. Extracts from the diary of a student at the Women's Medical College of Pennsylvania; interesting notes on lectures, laboratory and dissecting sessions, clinical work, fellow students and faculty members, including her favorite, Dr. Anna Broomall; enthusiasm for her studies and plans to be a medical missionary; test anxieties; a few leisure diversions; additional clinical work at Dr. John S. Pyle's Private Hospital in Canton, Ohio, and visit to her home in Columbiana County; return to Philadelphia for further training leading to her graduation.

MOORE, EALY, b. 1866   5295

Haley, J. Evetts, ed. "A Log of the Montana Trail as Kept by Ealy Moore." PANHANDLE-PLAINS HISTORICAL REVIEW 5 (1932):44-56.

Apr-Jul 1892. Cowboy's brief entries of a major cattle drive from Channing, Texas, to Cedar Creek, Montana; mostly camps and route; supplies, expenses, salaries and losses appended.

MOSES, WALLACE R.   5296

Marchman, Watt P., ed. "The Ingraham Everglades Exploring Expedition." TEQUESTA 7 (1947):3-43.

Mar-Apr 1892. Journal kept by the secretary of James E. Ingraham's expedition for the South Florida Railroad Company; exploration on foot of the Everglades south of Lake Okeechobee; the organization and duties of expedition members; route through snake infested bogs, with a short respite at Miami; natural history of the area; conversations with the aged widow of Chief Osceola and other Indians; assessment that some of the area could be drained for agriculture but would be impractical for a railroad.

SLEMMONS, JOHN W., 1841-1901   5297

Grant, H. Roger, ed. "Terrace Mound Farm: The 1892 Diary of John W. Slemmons." ANNALS OF IOWA, 3d ser. 45 (1979-1981):620-644.

Jan-Dec 1892. Extracts from diary of a Johnson County farmer; daily work and routine on a diversified and prosperous farm; crops, livestock, prices; Presbyterian church functions; showing of his pigs at the Iowa State Fair.

1893

DAWES, CHARLES GATES, 1865-1951   5298

A JOURNAL OF THE MCKINLEY YEARS. Edited by Bascom N. Timmons, Chicago: H.R. Donnelley & Sons, 1950. 458 pp.

1893-1908. Rising political career of young lawyer and banker of Lincoln, Nebraska, and later Chicago; friendships with William Jennings Bryan, John J. Pershing and John R. Walsh; his role in the Republican national conventions of 1896, 1900 and 1908 and in the election of McKinley; the McKinley and Bryan campaigns; the work of Marcus A. Hanna; service as comptroller of the Treasury under McKinley and extensive notes on his presidency; banking and financial activities, especially with establishment of his Central Trust Company of Illinois; the panics of 1893 and 1907; the assassination of McKinley; notes on Theodore Roosevelt and on the Spanish-American War; encyclopedic in its coverage of people, events and issues.

JOURNAL OF THE GREAT WAR. Boston and New York: Houghton Mifflin, 1921. 2 vols.

1917-1919. Service in France as chief of supply procurement of the American Expeditionary Force; work toward unification of supply activity resulting eventually in the Military Board of Allied Supply; much frustration over fragmented conduct of the war, with effectiveness and safety of troops hampered by the chaotic supply situation; extensive notes on Pershing, whom he admired greatly; visits to England.

A JOURNAL OF REPARATIONS. New York: Macmillan, 1939. 527 pp. Journal, pp. 1-235.

Jan-Jul 1924. Journal kept while Dawes was chairman of the First Committee of Experts, Reparations Commission, negotiating the settlement of German reparations after World War I and working to "balance the budget" and "stabilize the currency" of Germany; development of the Dawes Plan; much on Owen D. Young, the other American member of the international committee.

NOTES AS VICE PRESIDENT. Boston: Little, Brown, 1935. 329 pp.

Jun 1928-Mar 1929. Political and personal diary of vice president under Coolidge; candid notes on leaders and activities of government; constant deploring of "obstructionism," special interests and lack of disinterested statesmanship in the Senate; activities in Chicago and at his home in Evanston, Illinois; Washington social life; advance planning for Chicago World's Fair of 1933, for which his brother, Rufus C. Dawes, was president of trustees.

JOURNAL AS AMBASSADOR TO GREAT BRITAIN. New York: Macmillan, 1939. 442 pp.

1929-1932. Diplomatic journal; recounting, on board the S.S. OLYMPIC, his recent financing of the "doomed" Chicago World's Fair, the Century of Progress; in England, travels, speaking engagements, official diplomatic and social functions in London; England's attempt to retain the gold standard and evidence of the effect of worldwide depression; notes on activities and attitudes of prime minister J. Ramsay MacDonald, President Hoover, Dwight W. Morrow, Henry L. Stimson, etc.; minute analysis of the Naval Conference of 1930; comments on Manchuria Crisis.

GILMAN, JAMES F.   **5299**

RECOLLECTIONS OF MARY BAKER EDDY, DISCOVERER AND FOUNDER OF CHRISTIAN SCIENCE. Rumford, R.I., 1935. New York: Distributed by Rare Book Company, n.d. 92 pp.

Mar 1893-Jan 1894, Aug 1895. Diary kept by a Boston area artist and Christian Science disciple of Mary Baker Eddy while he was illustrating her CHRIST AND CHRISTMAS, photographing

her house and performing other frequently unpaid artistic chores; much on Mrs. Eddy's teachings and personal counsel; the diarist's frequent anguish of spirit and struggles against the "claims of the material" and "malicious animal magnetism"; a vague but protracted quarrel with Ebenezer J. Foster Eddy and references to Calvin A. Frye; evidence of Mrs. Eddy's compelling personality and of the diarist's willing but occasionally ambivalent subjection to her regimen.

RUSSELL, MARION B.   **5300**

"Our Trip to Mount Hood, 1893." OREGON HISTORICAL QUARTERLY 79 (1978):203-210.

Jul 1893. Woman's account of a jolly excursion of fifteen people by train along the Columbia from Portland to Hood River, thence by stagecoach to Cloud Cap Inn; enthusiasm for scenery and good meals; hikes and climbs attired in the "shortest skirts, thick books, gaiters and caps with "gauze veils"; Fourth of July celebration; games and ghost stories at night around the fire; delightful.

SLOANE, FLORENCE ADELE, 1873-1960   **5301**

MAVERICK IN MAUVE: THE DIARY OF A ROMANTIC AGE. With a commentary by Louis Auchincloss. Garden City, N.Y.: Doubleday, 1983. 227 pp.

1893-1896. Personal diary of great granddaughter of Cornelius Vanderbilt, her loves, travels and social life in New York and the family's other home, Elm Court, in Lenox, Massachusetts; visits and house parties with cousins ranging from Bar Harbor, Maine, and Newport, Rhode Island, to Asheville, North Carolina; suffering over the attentions or inattentions of beaux Worthington Whitehouse, Creighton Webb, Harry Payne Whitney and James Abercrombie Burden, Jr., her successful suitor; trips to Europe, where she especially enjoyed the opera and theater in Paris, and to the Columbian Exposition in Chicago; her wedding day and, after a gap, two sorrowful entries on the death of their first child, a daughter, at the age of three months; an inside picture of aristocratic life.

WOOD, ANNA S. PROUTY, 1844-1926   **5302**

Ragland, H.D. "The Diary of Mrs. Anna S. Wood: Trip to the Opening of the Cherokee Outlet in 1893." CHRONICLES OF OKLAHOMA 50 (1972):307-325.

Sep-Nov 1893. Covered wagon trip from Denver with her grown son Clarence and others to take claims in Oklahoma; camps and domestic chores en route; homesteading in Alfalfa County.

WOOD, ERSKINE   **5303**

"Diary of a Fourteen Year Old Boy's Days With Chief Joseph." OREGON HISTORICAL QUARTERLY 51 (1950):71-94.

DAYS WITH CHIEF JOSEPH: DIARY, RECOLLECTIONS AND PHOTOS. Portland: Binfords & Mort, 19--. 26 pp. Rev. ed. Oregon Historical Society, 1970. 40 pp.

Sep-Dec 1893. Fourteen-year-old Portland boy's account of life among the remnant of Nez Percé at Nespelem, Washington; a fine picture of Chief Joseph, in whose family the diarist lived; trapping and fishing with other young men; the fall hunt led by Joseph; a glimpse of Indians during period of transition.

1894

ELLIOTT, MAUD HOWE, b. 1854 5304

ROMA BEATA: LETTERS FROM THE ETERNAL CITY. Boston: Little, Brown, 1904. 362 pp.

1894-1900. Letter-diary of an American writer living in Rome; effusively descriptive but interesting.

ENGLISH, JAMES DOUGLASS, 1858-1929 5305

Thornbrough, Gayle, ed. "To the West in 1894: Travel Journal of Dr. James Douglass English of Worthington, Indiana." INDIANA HISTORICAL SOCIETY PUBLICATIONS 25, no. 3 (1977):1-98.

Jun-Aug 1894. An Indiana dentist's adventurous trip through the western United States to Mexico, Hawaii and British Columbia with his friend Eugene Byrd Squire; overland by train and on the S.S. AUSTRALIA to Honolulu; interesting for arrangements and logistics of travel, with first class hotel, train and ship accommodations; colorful notes on cities, sights, people and amusing incidents; especially good details on San Francisco Chinatown and Hawaii.

FOOTE, ARTHUR 5306

Foote, Mary Hallock. "The Harshaw Bride." IDAHO YESTERDAYS 20, no. 2 (1976):18-32. Diary, pp. 18-19.

Sep 1894. Brief notes, kept by popular author's husband, of a wagon trip which later provided source material for her story, "The Harshaw Bride"; from Boise to Thousand Springs to investigate the possibility of using springs to produce electricity for the Trade Dollar Mine at Silver City; bad roads; good description of countryside.

FOX, RUTH MAY, 1853-1967 5307

Thatcher, Linda, ed. " 'I Care Nothing for Politics': Ruth May Fox, Forgotten Suffragist." UTAH HISTORICAL QUARTERLY 49 (1981):239-253.

In WOMEN'S VOICES, edited by Kenneth Godfrey, Audrey Godfrey and Jill Derr, pp. 375-386.

Dec 1894-Nov 1895. Extracts from the diary of incredibly long-lived and active Mormon mother of twelve, an English immigrant with little formal education, who became a hymn writer, leader in Mormon women's organizations and a suffragette; work to get women's suffrage attached to the statehood issue; suffrage, press club, literary society and Republican party meetings; the visits of Susan B. Anthony and Anna Howard Shaw.

HOWARD OF GLOSSOP, WINIFRED MARY DE LISLE 5308
HOWARD, baroness, 1861-1909

JOURNAL OF A TOUR IN THE UNITED STATES, CANADA AND MEXICO. London: Sampson Low, Marston, 1897. 355 pp.

1894-1895. Lady Howard's journal of her first class travels throughout the United States, with particular comments on New York, Boston, Washington, D.C., the South, Chicago, Denver, Rocky Mountains, Salt Lake City, California, etc.; extensive notes on art museums, scenery, train and steamship people; observa-

tions on people, mostly compared unfavorably with the British; comments on Mormons.

LONDON, JACK, 1876-1916 5309

JACK LONDON ON THE ROAD: THE TRAMP DIARY AND OTHER HOBO WRITING. Edited by Richard W. Etulain. Logan: Utah State University Press, 1979. 209 pp. Diary, pp. 29-60.

Briggs, John E., ed. "Tramping with Kelly through Iowa: A Jack London Diary." PALIMPSEST 52 (1971):316-352. Diary, pp. 316-346.

Apr-May 1894. Jack London's transcontinental hobo journey from San Francisco with Charles T. Kelly's "Industrial Army" of some 1500 men thrown out of work by the Panic of 1893; traveling in boxcars and riding the rails; townspeoples' assistance with food and shelter; travel through Iowa on foot, aided by farmers' wagons for supplies and the sick, when Iowa railroads refused any form of transport; "Kelly's Navy" of makeshift flatboats on the Des Moines River; diary later revised and published as his THE ROAD.

REDFEARN, GERTRUDE VANSANT, 1873-1968 5310

Larson, Velma E. "Dairy of the Trip to Texas: A Journey to the Far West." PANHANDLE-PLAINS HISTORICAL REVIEW 43 (1970):21-36.

Apr-May 1894. Young woman's wagon journey with a party of fourteen relatives from Ben Franklin to settle at Canyon; a few notes on ranches where they camped and bought food; problems with weather, sick children and lost cattle; dissatisfaction with Amarillo, where diary ends.

WILDER, LAURA INGALLS, 1867-1957 5311

ON THE WAY HOME: THE DIARY OF A TRIP FROM SOUTH DAKOTA TO MANSFIELD, MISSOURI. New York: Harper & Row, 1962. 101 pp.

Jul 1894. The beloved children's author's diary of a family move from South Dakota because of drought and economic depression to take up farming in the Ozarks; by covered wagon, with descriptions of countryside and other people on the move; notes on crops and the unbearable summer heat.

1895

ABERDEEN AND TEMAIR, ISHBEL MARIA 5312
MARJORIBANKS GORDON, marchioness of, 1857-1939

THE CANADIAN JOURNAL OF LADY ABERDEEN. Edited by John T. Saywell. Publications of the Champlain Society, 38. Toronto: Champlain Society, 1960. 517 pp. American journal, pp. 201-208; 382-392.

Feb 1895, Feb 1897. Extracts from personal diary of wife of governor general of Canada; some American content with generally unfavorable comments about Americans; staying at the British Embassy in Washington while attending National Council of Women of the United States, including a tea for Susan B. Anthony; visiting Chicago and President Harper of Chicago University where she was to be convocation orator, noting that students and faculty included both men and women; a wedding in Nashville; visiting William Hicks Jackson and his famous Belle

Meade farm; attending Congress and official functions in Washington, D.C.

BOWERS, CLAUDE GERNADE, 1879-1958   5313

INDIANAPOLIS IN THE "GAY NINETIES": HIGH SCHOOL DIARIES OF CLAUDE G. BOWERS. Edited by Holman Hamilton and Gayle Thornbrough. Indianapolis: Indiana Historical Society, 1964. 241 pp.

  1895-1899. Diary of student at Indianapolis High School; studies, clubs, contests, interest in oratory, many hours spent with good friend George Langsdale, often reading some great author such as Edmund Burke; frequent mention of friends Paxton P. Hibben, Myla Jo Closser, Frank Tarkington Baker and Abraham Cronbach; theater attendance with details of performances by Sir Henry Irving, Ellen Terry, Robert Downing and Sarah Bernhardt; following events of political conventions and disgust at nomination of McKinley, admiration for William J. Bryan and Albert J. Beveridge; insight into influences and early education of an orator, editor, politician and diplomat.

MACE, REBECCA ELIZABETH HOWELL, 1833-1917   5314

In WOMEN'S VOICES, edited by Kenneth Godfrey, Audrey Godfrey and Jill Derr, pp. 389-396.

  1895-1896. Extracts from English Mormon's diary; social life and church meetings in Kanab, Utah; proclamation of Utah statehood and the celebration which followed.

SPRUNGER, DAVID, 1857-1933   5315

Sprunger, Milton F. "Courtship and Marriage." MENNONITE LIFE 3, no. 2 (1976):13-16.

  1895? Article containing diary extracts describing Indiana Mennonite farmer's courtship of Caroline Tschantz, whom he married as a second wife and stepmother to his seven children.

1896

ANDREWS, ELLEN MIRIAM GIBSON, 1849-1921   5316

HUDSON DIARY. Edited by Willis Harry Miller. Hudson, Wis.: Star-Observer Printer, 1968. 51 pp.

  1896-1900. Devoted Baptist woman's personal diary of family, community and church events in Hudson, Wisconsin.

BEECHER, WILLARD C.   5317

Miner, Ward L. and Miner, Thelma S., eds. "Gold Prospecting on the Cook Inlet in 1896: The Diary of a Failure." PACIFIC NORTH-WEST QUARTERLY 64 (1973):97-111.

  Apr-Nov 1896. Extracts of Reed City, Michigan, man's Alaska gold rush experiences; outfitting in Seattle; transport on the CITY OF TOPEKA and the BERTHA to Cook Inlet, with good descriptions of the struggle for survival there and the work of prospecting; travels throughout the area and problems ranging from snow blindness to mosquitoes; notes on fellow gold seekers.

BUTCHER, THOMAS, 1850-1935   5318

Littleton, Betty, ed. "Touring the Southeast Kansas Area in 1896." KANSAS HISTORICAL QUARTERLY 35 (1969):143-154.

  Jan-Jul 1896. Diary of an Englishman who had farmed for some years in Barber County, but was seeking better land elsewhere in Kansas, Missouri and Oklahoma; good notes on towns, crops, livestock, land and farming methods; description of the Indian school at Chilocco, Oklahoma.

CHITTENDEN, HIRAM MARTIN, 1858-1917   5319

H.M. CHITTENDEN: A WESTERN EPIC, BEING A SELECTION FROM HIS UNPUBLISHED JOURNALS, DIARIES AND REPORTS. Edited by Bruce Le Roy. Tacoma: Washington State Historical Society, 1961. 136 pp. Diary, pp. 22-61.

  Dec 1896. Train trip of army engineer and historian to the Pacific coast to attend Irrigation Congress in Phoenix and visit irrigation projects and dams in other western states, particularly California.

  May 1897. Train trip to Wyoming and Colorado; conversations with local people about disposition of public lands; inspection of reservoirs, etc.; travels by horseback and stagecoach, staying at ranches, including that of intellectual rancher Albert J. Bothwell.

  Aug 1897. Travel to Jackson Hole and Idaho; by horseback through the area.

  Apr-May 1903. Extracts covering President Theodore Roosevelt's visit to Yellowstone while diarist was engaged in road building there; interesting character sketch of Roosevelt.

HAGUE, JAMES D.   5320

Smith, Duane A. " 'At This Altitude One Gets Weary Very Soon.' " HUNTINGTON LIBRARY QUARTERLY 44 (1981):173-187.

  Nov 1896, Jul 1897, Jul 1898. Extracts within article relating to mining engineer's experiences at the Tomboy Mine at Telluride, Colorado, evaluating mine for potential buyers; effects of exertion at 12,000 feet altitude on the sixty-year-old diarist; returns to Tomboy as president and principal stockholder of the prosperous company, which became a major gold producer.

HOPPIN, BENJAMIN, 1851-1923   5321

A DIARY KEPT WHILE WITH THE PEARY ARCTIC EXPEDITION OF 1896. New Haven? Conn., 1897? 80 pp.

  Jul-Sep 1896. Diary of a mineralogist with Robert E. Peary on a summer expedition to Greenland to obtain a meteorite known since 1816; on the HOPE from Sydney, Nova Scotia, sighting icebergs and noting birds; descriptions in Greenland of fossils, animals, rocks and minerals; details of Eskimo life including villages, sleds, dogs, kayaks and dwellings; failed attempt to move meteorite to the ship.

LANE, HORACE GREELEY, b. 1861   5322

"The Travel Journal of Horace Greeley Lane." WASHINGTON HERITAGE 2 (1984):140-150.

  May-Sep 1896. Diary of a wagon journey from Clarks, Nebraska, to Seattle with family and friends; itinerary via Wyoming, Montana and Idaho traveling along the Northern Pacific Railroad as much as possible; camps and weather; the death of his wife, possibly from malaria; setting up house in Seattle with his children and doing many domestic chores, including making their clothes.

LAPHAM, FANNIE CROSLEY   5323

"Journey from Montana to Western Washington Told in Diary of 1896." COWLITZ COUNTY HISTORICAL QUARTERLY 9, no. 3 (1967):3-16.

Aug-Oct 1896. Letter-diary of a wagon journey with her husband, Nelson Lapham, partly in the company of Seventh-day Adventists, whose proselytizing she did not appreciate; difficult travel, often using railroad bed as road; enthusiastic description of Portland; tearful reunion with her daughter.

NOLAND, JAMES F.   5324

McDonald, Lucile, ed. "A Puget Sound Sealer's Log." SEA CHEST 17 (1983):1-6, 46-55.

Mar-Sep 1896. Log, with diary content, of a sealer aboard the M.M. MORRILL under Capt. Edward Cantillion; following seal herds from the coast of Japan to the Pribilof Islands; other sealing ships encountered, with numbers of skins on board; discouragement over decline of catches; in port at Unalaska.

VAN BUSKIRK, PHILIP CLAYTON, b. 1834   5325

Monroe, Robert D., ed. "An Excursion to Wrangell." PACIFIC NORTHWEST QUARTERLY 50 (1959):48-52.

Aug 1896. Entertaining extract covering Alaska boat trip of a Snohomish Valley, Washington, bachelor farmer on a quest to find a wife; from Seattle on the AL-KI, where he enjoyed the company of Tlingit chief Kadashan and his family; notes on Indian villages en route; social life at Wrangell, but no prospects of matrimony.

1897

BANON, EDWARD MAGAWLY, 1867-1944   5327

THE DIARY OF EDWARD MAGAWLY BANON, KLONDIKE, BRITISH YUKON. Compiled by Mrs. Edward M. Banon. Newport, R.I.: Privately printed by Ward Printing Company, 1948. 20 pp.

May-Jun 1897. Full, interesting entries of the Klondike gold rush by a young Irishman who became an explorer of the Yukon and Alaska and a well-known mining engineer; activities at Dyea, the rigors of hauling supplies over Chilkoot Pass in the Elias Range; good details of the logistics and hazards of the undertaking.

BARTINE, MARY OAKLEY   5328

Roach, Martha. "The Diary of Mary Oakley Bartine." RUTGERS UNIVERSITY LIBRARY JOURNAL 46 (1984):84-90.

Feb-Mar 1897. Article containing extracts from the diary of a seventeen-year-old Somerville, New Jersey, girl in "comfortable circumstances"; enjoyment of her girls' club but mixed reaction to other social life; a few domestic notes and church activities.

BASI, WILHELM, 1869-1951   5329

WILHELM BASI DIARY ON 1898 YUKON RESCUE. Finnish American Historical Society of the West Historical Tract, vol. 6, no. 4. Portland, Oreg.: Finnish American Historical Society of the West, 1971. 27 pp.

1897-1947 (with gaps). Diary of a Finnish-speaking Norwegian recruited to help herd reindeer originally intended for relief of Yukon gold rushers, but being brought to Alaska by the United States government to improve Eskimo livelihood; transport of reindeer and their Finnish, Norwegian and Lapp herdsmen and families on the MANITOBA from Norway to New York, then by rail to Seattle and by ship to Haines, Alaska, with many reindeer perishing for lack of moss to eat; later scattered notes of his move to Eaton, Alaska, and building a house; filing a claim at Anvil City and successful gold mining; a bout of typhoid; marrying; farming in various locations in Oregon and Washington; faithful support of the Finnish Apostolic Lutheran Church, once as pastor at Quincy, Oregon.

COHEN, MORRIS RAPHAEL, 1880-1947   5330

In PORTRAIT OF A PHILOSOPHER, by Leonora D.C. Rosenfield, pp. 1-461 passim. New York: Harcourt, Brace & World, 1962.

1897-? Biography containing brief diary extracts and much more extensive letters of a Russian Jewish immigrant who became an eminent philosopher, professor and legal theorist; engaging diaries of his student days at Harvard, the "Journal of a boy philosopher, the thoughts and acts of a vain fool trying to learn how to be wise"; teaching at City College of New York, University of Chicago and Harvard; reflections on a vast range of topics.

HARRISON, THOMAS SKELTON, 1837-1919   5331

THE HOMELY DIARY OF A DIPLOMAT IN THE EAST. Boston and New York: Houghton Mifflin, 1917. 364 pp.

1897-1899. Experiences and work of consul general and diplomatic agent to Cairo; being presented to and officially received by Abbas II, Khedive of Egypt; attending a reception for the entire diplomatic corps given by the King of Siam during his visit to the Khedive; frequent social events with Lord Cromer, the British ambassador; extensive details on the redecorating of the reception rooms of the agency; successfully securing positions for representative judges from the United States to the Cairo and Alexandria Mixed Tribunals; securing permission for the American Exploration Society to excavate at Tunis; active social life, including frequent opera attendance and much entertaining with his wife, an admired hostess.

MOSIER, CHARLES   5332

Warner, Iris, ed. "Klondike Diaries." NORTH (September/October, 1976):40-55.

Mar-May 1897. Extracts from the gold rush diary of a man with a group from Byron and Caledonia, New York, including Bert Bower, John G. McJury, H.H. Scott and Alden R. Smith; hauling their supplies, camping and mining in the Dyea area.

NICHOLS, LORA WEBB   5333

Anderson, Nancy. "Diary of a Pioneer Teenager." IN WYOMING 11, no. 1 (1978):36-39.

1897-1899. Extracts within article about a ranch girl's life on a homestead near Grand Encampment; her love of horseback riding and hobby of photography; domestic and ranch chores, as well as family and social life; delight at getting her first bustle "to improve the shape of my gable end, so to speak"; an interesting segment from a lifelong diary.

PATTERSON, CARL, 1873-1942   **5334**

CARL PATTERSON: A BIOGRAPHY. N.p., 1949. 86 pp. Diary, pp. 28-29.

1897-1898. Extracts from spiritual diary of a Quaker in Chesterhill, Ohio, concerning his speaking in meeting for worship.

POSEY, ALEXANDER LAWRENCE, 1873-1908   **5335**

Dale, Edward Everett, ed. "The Journal of Alexander Lawrence Posey." CHRONICLES OF OKLAHOMA 45 (1967-1968):393-432.

Jan-Sep 1897. Half-breed Creek Indian's journals kept while he served as superintendent of the Creek Indian Orphanage at Okmulgee; orphanage administration and care of children; activities at Eufaula; notes of reading, especially the classics, and writing poetry.

"Journal of Creek Enrollment Field Party, 1905." CHRONICLES OF OKLAHOMA 46 (1968):2-19.

Aug 1905-Mar 1906. Journal of work as clerk and interpreter of the Commission to the Five Civilized Tribes seeking to identify Creek Indians entitled to land allocations; travel with Drennan C. Skaggs from headquarters at Muskogee; interviews with Indians, with notes on their homes and lives; attempts to conciliate the followers of Crazy Snake, who were opposed to relinquishment of tribal authority; a scattered nature diary appended.

ROMIG, EMILY CRAIG, b. 1871   **5336**

THE LIFE AND TRAVELS OF A PIONEER WOMAN IN ALASKA. Colorado Springs: Privately printed, 1945. 136 pp. passim.

A PIONEER WOMAN IN ALASKA. Caldwell, Idaho: Caxton, 1948. 140 pp. passim.

1897-1944 (with gaps). Scattered entries of trip from Chicago to Klondike during the gold rush; across Canada, down Athabasca River, wintering at Great Slave Lake where the manager of the loosely organized company absconded with all the funds; travel by dog sled and riverboat to Dawson; little success at mining there or later at Shushana; making ends meet by cooking for miners; good narrative of rugged pioneer life.

SLAYDEN, ELLEN MAURY, 1860-1926   **5337**

WASHINGTON WIFE: JOURNAL OF ELLEN MAURY SLAYDEN. New York: Harper & Row, 1963. 385 pp.

1897-1919. Personal diary of wife of Texas congressman, James Luther Slayden, edited by the diarist for publication before her death; the Washington, D.C., social scene and major historical events; numerous political figures in official and unofficial settings, including Charles Francis Adams, Jr., Joseph W. Bailey, William Jennings Bryan, Albert S. Burleson, Joseph G. Cannon, Andrew Carnegie, James B. Clark, Edward Everett Hale, William McKinley, Zelia Nuttall; Jeanette Rankin, Theodore Roosevelt, William Howard Taft and Woodrow Wilson; impressions of Porfirio Días while attending Mexican Centennial; meetings of Inter-

parliamentary Union for the Promotion of Peace by Arbitration; race problems; woman's suffrage; disapproval of vote to go to war in 1917; scorn at Washington socialites' ideas of wartime domestic economies; her husband's defeat in election and their permanent return to Texas.

Webb, Walter P., ed. "Washington Wife: From the Journal of Ellen Maury Slayden." SOUTHWEST REVIEW 48 (1963):1-14.

1897-1917. Extracts beginning in San Antonio, with an interesting account of entertaining William Jennings Bryan; vignettes of Bryan, former governor James Stephen Hogg and her husband; social and political life in Washington, with some spirited opinions on people and events there; references to Gertrude Atherton; a Confederate reunion at Kerrville in 1907.

WELLS, EDMOND HAZARD   **5338**

In MAGNIFICENCE AND MISERY: A FIRSTHAND ACCOUNT OF THE 1897 KLONDIKE GOLD RUSH, edited by Randall M. Dodd, pp. 1-254 passim. Garden City, N.Y.: Doubleday, 1984.

Jul 1897-Feb 1898 (with gaps). Journalist's hazardous travel by horseback and boat via White Pass to Lake Bennett and Yukon River to Dawson during severe winter weather; exorbitant prices for scant provisions; organizing a press club; observations on old-timers and enterprising new arrivals, some suffering from scurvy; the Catholic Hospital; Protestant services by Presbyterian missionary J. Hall Young; a summary of his diary kept on a confidential mission by dog sled and boat to General Merriam at Vancouver Barracks, carrying government dispatches regarding the scarcities at Fort Yukon, continuing to Washington, D.C., and personally reporting the dangerous situation to Secretary of War Russell Alexander Alger.

1898

ANON.   **5339**

Alcorn, Rowena L. and Alcorn, Gordon. "Tacoma Seaman's Rest: Waterfront Mission, 1897-1903." OREGON HISTORICAL QUARTERLY 66 (1965):101-131. Diary, pp. 115-119.

Aug-Nov 1898. Diary of an English sailor off the CHARLES NELSON while in port at Tacoma, Washington; frequent and grateful references to the Seaman's Rest Mission, kept by Brigitte Funnemark and her daughter Christine, with whom he corresponded; a brief but good picture of a sailor's work, diversions and problems in various Puget Sound ports; a sense of failure and disgust with seafaring life in a diary which ends as a suicide note.

CROSS, R.   **5340**

THE VOYAGE OF THE OREGON FROM SAN FRANCISCO TO SANTIAGO IN 1898, AS TOLD BY ONE OF THE CREW. Boston: Privately printed, The Merrymount Press, 1908. 34 pp.

Extracts in OUR SOLDIERS SPEAK, by William Matthews and Dixon Wecter, pp. 239-248.

Mar-Jul 1898. Journal of navy crewman on first class battleship; speedy, uneventful cruise along coast keeping sharp lookout for Spanish torpedo boats; coaling at Callao, Peru, and Sandy Point,

Chile; through the Strait of Magellan escorted by the MARIET-TA; eagerness for battle fulfilled at Guantanamo Bay.

CURTIN, WALTER RUSSELL   5341

YUKON VOYAGE: UNOFFICIAL LOG OF THE STEAMER YUKONER. Caldwell, Idaho: Caxton, 1938. 299 pp. Diary, pp. 40-272.

Sep 1898-Jul 1899. Diary of the Pat Galvin expedition to Dawson; work on the YUKONER during Klondike gold rush for his father, John, who was general manager for Galvin's North British American Trading and Transportation Company transporting merchandise and supplies for miners and large companies; mishaps on the river culminating in their being frozen in for the winter before reaching Dawson; cutting wood, learning to ski and visiting other stranded boats and parties; two women from the YUKONER going on to Dawson by dog sled, one "looking trim and neat in her bloomers"; spring thaw and finally arriving in Dawson, only to be met by British soldiers and discover Galvin's company in receivership; a venture which made little money for the diarist, "but the fun I had while earning it was worth it."

CURTIS, ASAHEL, 1874-1941   5342

Frederick, Richard. "Asahel Curtis and the Klondike Stampede." ALASKA JOURNAL 13 (1983):113-121.

Nov 1898-Jan 1899. Article containing extracts from the diary of a young Seattle photographer sent to Dawson and the Klondike gold rush to take photographs for his brother, the famous photographer Edward Curtis, during an expedition underwritten by Edward Curtis's studio; taking out a claim with Charles G. Ainsworth, with good notes on mining.

EINSTEIN, ALFRED, 1880-1952   5343

Fink, Michael and Hieronymus, Bess. "The Autobiography and Early Diary of Alfred Einstein." MUSICAL QUARTERLY 66 (1980):361-377 passim.

1898-1899. Article containing extracts from the first years of the lifelong diary of German-born musicologist; mostly depressive mood swings added to the normal trauma of youthful self-discovery and doubt; feelings that he was suffering "like no one ever before me" alternating with a sense of progress in becoming a "real human being"; brief reactions to a few concerts.

GARLAND, HAMLIN, 1860-1940   5344

DIARIES. Edited by Donald Pizer. San Marino, California: Huntington Library, 1968. 281 pp.

1898-1940. Author's diary, arranged topically rather than chronologically, although dates are given for each entry; social and literary experiences; family matters; political and literary figures and events; the flavor of midwestern life; satisfactions of a varied public career, but personal disappointments.

GODDARD, ROBERT HUTCHINGS, 1882-1945   5345

THE PAPERS OF ROBERT H. GODDARD. Edited by Esther C. Goddard. New York: McGraw-Hill, 1970. 3 vols. passim.

1898-1945. Diary of physicist who laid ground work for rocket research and space flight; early entries recording teenage school activities, reading, writing, first scientific experiments, intense interest in electricity and space navigation; later selections from

meticulously kept records regarding his research supported by Clark University, the Smithsonian Institution and the Daniel and Florence Guggenheim Foundation; frequent references to Smithsonian Secretary Charles G. Abbot, his instrument maker Henry Sachs and the interest and support of Charles Lindbergh.

GOODALE, I. PRESTON   5346

Mudge, Florence A., ed. "Diary of I. Preston Goodale, a Klondike Prospector of 1898." DANVERS HISTORICAL SOCIETY COLLECTIONS 25 (1937):4-12.

Feb-Jul 1898. Brief diary of a young Danvers, Massachusetts, man who, with Danvers resident Frank Purdy, joined the gold rush "mushing in" from Skagway to the gold fields; winter camp on Windy Arm of Tagish Lake; the arrival of spring and on to the Stewart River; notes on tasks, transportation, weather, natural surroundings, etc.

GRINNELL, JOSEPH, 1877-1939   5347

GOLD HUNTING IN ALASKA. Edited by Elizabeth Grinnell. Elgin, Ill.: David C. Cook, 1901. 96 pp. Reprint. Anchorage: Alaska Northwest, 1983. ALASKA JOURNAL 13 (1983):33-111.

1898-1899. Long, narrative entries describing Alaska gold rush journey and experiences as a member of the Long Beach and Alaska Mining and Trading Company; from San Francisco to Kotzebue Sound on the PENELOPE, describing ship life, food, passengers and crew; at crowded Kotsebue; inland on the Kobuk River, with entertaining notes on prospecting, working as camp cook and activities of such local characters as Carl Knobelsdorff, the "Flying Dutchman," who skated the frozen Kobuk to deliver mail and relay news of gold discoveries; establishment of church services in their camp; notes on missionaries and their activities; prospecting in the Nome area, where some succeeded, others failed tragically, and lawlessness was rampant; descriptions of Indian and Eskimo customs; bird collecting by the diarist, who became an eminent zoologist.

HUISH, ORSON PRATT   5348

Groesbeck, Kathryn D. "A Southwest Photographic Expedition." UTAH HISTORICAL QUARTERLY 34 (1966):191-201.

Jul 1898-Jul 1899. Brief notes kept by Orson P. Huish and Thomas E. Hinshaw of a commercial photography trip by wagon from Payson through parts of Utah, Colorado, New Mexico and Arizona, photographing scenes and people; mostly route, expenses and earnings.

JARVIS, JOSEPH RUSSELL, 1874-1906   5349

Probert, Alan, ed. "The Cape Nome Gold Rush." JOURNAL OF THE WEST 9 (1970):153-195.

Jul 1898-Jun 1899. Young Californian's account of the Alaska gold rush; voyage from Portland with his father, Francis Carr Jarvis, two brothers and a friend on the NATIONAL CITY, with dated entries beginning during a long delay at St. Michael awaiting passage up the Yukon River; building a cabin and staking claims on the Fish River, with good details of hunting, fishing, trapping, hauling wood, etc. but mainly efforts at surviving the winter and nursing his ailing father; trips to Council City; a few notes on Eskimos.

JOHNSON, WILLIAM R., 1881-1952   **5350**

Carmony, Donald F. and Tannenbaum, Karen, eds. "Three Years in the Orient." INDIANA MAGAZINE OF HISTORY 63 (1967):268-298.

1898-1902. Franklin, Indiana, volunteer's tour of duty during Philippine Insurrection after the Spanish-American War; assignment to Company K of the Twenty-second Infantry; departure from San Francisco on the SENATOR amid cheering crowds and brass bands; notes on Manila; marches, skirmishes and ambushes; horrible conditions of hunger, sickness and fatigue borne stoically by diarist; return on the KILPATRICK.

KIRBY, ALBERT   **5351**

Kirby, Dale A., ed. "Without Purse or Scrip: A Missionary in the Territory." CHRONICLES OF OKLAHOMA 60 (1982-1983):388-399.

1898-1900. Extracts from Mormon elder's journal covering his mission to Oklahoma; lodging with local families, white, Indian and black; travels on foot with his missionary companion James M. Anderson, preaching to all three races and holding "gospel conversations"; return to his home at Hyde Park, Utah.

LONGDEN, CHARLES E.   **5352**

Agnew, James B. "Private Longden and the Medical Corps of 1898." MILITARY REVIEW 59, no. 7 (1979):11-21.

May-Sep 1898. Article containing extracts from the Spanish-American War diaries of a pharmacist with the First California Volunteer Regiment serving in the Philippines as a medic; complaints of ration deficiencies on board the CITY OF PEKING and in the Philippines, which led to the "Canned Beef Scandal"; work as a combat medical corpsman, pharmacist and field hospital nurse, attending patients with typhoid, malaria and smallpox; a disheartening picture of the state of military medicine.

MARSH, MARVIN SANFORD, b. 1854   **5353**

Petrone, Gerard S. "An Iowan in the Klondike Gold Rush." BRAND BOOK 6 (1979):119-130.

Feb-Oct 1898. Extracts from Iowa man's diary of seeking gold in Klondike with Iowa-Alaska Gold Mining Company; by train to Seattle and by steamer CLEVELAND to Skagway; difficulties of transporting provisions and equipment, setting up a sawmill and building the IOWA, a boat to go down river to Dawson; growing suspicions among members and eventual break up of company; disappointing results of mining endeavors and eagerness to return home even without expected wealth.

PENNELL, ELIZABETH ROBINS, 1855-1936   **5354**

THE WHISTLER JOURNAL, by E.R. & J. Pennell. Philadelphia: J.B. Lippincott, 1921. 339 pp.

1898-1903. Specialized diary notes kept by the Pennells with the purpose of incorporating the material in a biography after Whistler's death; anecdotes, conversations at parties, critics' comments, other artists' opinions and the function of International Society of Sculptors, Printers and Engravers.

REID, WHITELAW, 1837-1912   **5355**

MAKING PEACE WITH SPAIN: THE DIARY OF WHITELAW REID. Edited by H. Wayne Morgan. Austin: University of Texas Press, 1965. 276 pp.

Sep-Dec 1898. Diplomatic diary of minister to France and member of United States commission in Paris, negotiating peace following the Spanish-American War; notes on activities and opinions of members of both the American and Spanish commissions, as well as senators George Gray and William P. Frye and President William McKinley; discussions on the fate of Cuba and the Philippines; references to the NEW YORK TRIBUNE of which diarist was longtime managing editor; some personal matters, including coping with asthma attacks; an important document for the 1898 Treaty of Paris.

ROBERTS, WILLIAM RANSOM, b. 1879   **5356**

"Under fire in Cuba; A Volunteer's Eyewitness Account of the War with Spain." AMERICAN HERITAGE 29, no. 1 (1977):78-91.

Jun-Jul 1898. Extracts from record by Traverse City, Michigan, man of service with Hannah's Rifles; to Cuba on troopship HARVARD; description of Siboney and its people; grueling marches and awareness of inadequate training for march or combat; long description of battle of San Juan Hill; sufferings from heat, insects, terrible food and fatigue in addition to almost incessant combat; a full and articulate diary.

SCOTT, JAMES FOSTER   **5357**

In SOURDOUGH GOLD: THE LOG OF A YUKON ADVENTURE, by Mary Lee C. Davis, pp. 1-351 passim. Boston: W.A. Wilde, 1933.

1898-1899. Brief diary jottings which provide the basis for a physician's tale of his medical practice in Dawson at the height of the gold rush; notes on the town, social life and its inhabitants, especially William H. Judge and the Catholic priest; cold, dark winter followed by breakup of ice on the Yukon River; a solo trip on the river with a few notes on settlements.

SMITH, JOHN   **5358**

"Record of a Trip to Dawson." BRITISH COLUMBIA HISTORICAL QUARTERLY 16 (1952):67-97.

Mar-Jun 1898. Englishman's journey to the Klondike with a few notes on Wrangell, Alaska, "a dreadful place," and arduous journey along the Stikine and Teslin route.

TILESTON, ELEANOR BOIES, 1886-1912   **5359**

ELEANOR BOIES TILESTON. Norwood, Mass.: Norwood Press, 1915. 283 pp.

1898-1911. A Boston girl's various European trips over several years; notes on art galleries, concerts, Oberammergau Passion Play, bookbinding lessons in Paris and mountain climbing in Cortina; return to Boston to enter School of Social Work.

WEBB, BEATRICE POTTER, 1858-1943   **5360**

BEATRICE WEBB'S AMERICAN DIARY. Edited by David A. Shannon. Madison: University of Wisconsin Press, 1963. 181 pp.

Mar-Jul 1898. The 1898 American portion of the massive lifelong diary of British intellectual, economist, political scientist and wife of Sidney Webb, co-founder of the Fabian Society; entries beginning at sea en route to America and ending at Honolulu; keen observations of society and conditions in New York, Washington, Boston, Philadelphia, Chicago, Denver, Salt Lake City, San Francisco and other cities, with notes on city government, public and private institutions, politics, people and mores; interviews with Theodore Roosevelt, Woodrow Wilson, Jane Addams, Lillian Wald, ''Czar'' Reed and others; emphatic opinions and witty, sometimes arch, style which exhibit Mrs. Webb's sense of herself as a very clever citizen of ''the cleverest nation in the world.''

1899

BROWN, JOHN CLIFFORD, 1872-1901   5361

DIARY OF A SOLDIER IN THE PHILIPPINES. Portland, Me.: Privately printed by the Lakeside Press, 1901. 248 pp.

1899-1900. Engineer in Company B, Engineer Battalion, United States Army; travel to Philippines with stops at San Francisco and Honolulu; great detail of everyday work and boredom in Philippines, making maps with an advance command during the Insurrection, noting the countryside, people, and customs; superintending the building of a bridge at Paranaque.

CARSON, CARRIE MCKINLEY   5362

Carson, Clifford M., ed. ''A Summer at Lake Okoboji: Excerpts from a Vacation Diary.'' PALIMPSEST 57 (1976):86-95.

Jul-Aug 1899. Marengo, Iowa, woman's account of a family vacation at ''a summer resort in the north''; by train to Arnolds Park, then across the lake on the MANHATTAN, with many subsequent trips on it to The Inn, focal point of lake activity, and to the once elegant, but partly demolished Hotel Orleans; enjoyment of fishing, ''bathing'' and lake scenery.

GILLESPIE, ANNA ELIZA COOK   5363

''Coxville, Nebraska, to Fay, Oklahoma, by Wagon.'' NEBRASKA HISTORY 65 (1984):344-365.

Aug-Oct 1899. Woman's diary of a wagon journey with her husband, Josiah B. Gillespie, her children and other families to move from Nebraska to Oklahoma; travel conditions, with some roads nothing but cattle trails; suffering from wind, dust and insects; deaths of many of the large herd of horses they were driving; condition of farms and crops en route.

HADLEY, MARTHA E., 1852-1915   5364

THE ALASKAN DIARY OF A PIONEER QUAKER MISSIONARY. Mt. Dora, Fla.: Loren S. Hadley, 1969. 210 pp.

1899-1903. Traveling from her home in Wilmington, Ohio, to Los Angeles by train, to Cape Prince of Wales, Alaska, by ship and finally to Kotzebue where she served the community as both teacher and ''doctor''; customs, weather and rigorous pioneer life; an interesting diary which includes photographs she took and developed.

HAYES, WEBB C.   5365

In UNCOMMON VALOR, edited by James M. Merrill, pp. 244-248.

Nov 1899. Extracts from diary of lieutenant colonel of the Thirty-first Volunteer Infantry, son of Rutherford B. Hayes; events and problems aboard a transport en route to Manila to suppress Philippine insurgents; storm at sea.

LACEY, EDWIN M.   5366

Tingley, Donald F. ''The Cuban Diary of Edwin M. Lacey.'' ILLINOIS STATE HISTORICAL SOCIETY JOURNAL 56 (1963):20-35.

Jan-May 1899. Experiences of a signal corps man from Neoga, Illinois, serving with the Fourth Illinois Volunteer Infantry Regiment in Cuba immediately after the Spanish-American War; transport to Cuba on the MANITOBA; installing telegraph lines in difficult terrain; hard work on hopelessly inadequate rations; delight when his tour of duty was over.

1900

BAINBRIDGE, Mrs. WILLIAMS E.   5367

Borzo, Henry, ed. ''Diary of an Iowan under Fire in Peking.'' ANNALS OF IOWA, 3rd ser. 36 (1961-1963):613-640.

May-Aug 1900. Account of the siege of Peking during Boxer Rebellion kept by Council Bluffs woman who was wife of secretary of the American legation; sheltering of missionaries and other foreigners within the legation compound; reports of torture and atrocities; shelling and burning of buildings; casualties among American, German, British, French and Japanese soldiers; references to American minister to China, Edwin Hurd Conger; heroism of Calvin Pearl Titus of Clinton, Iowa.

HOWE, HENRY R., d. 1951   5368

Alcorn, Rowena L. and Alcorn, Gordon D., eds. ''Voyage of the CABUL.'' SEA CHEST 17 (1984):137-146.

Oct 1900-Mar 1901. Weekly letter-diary from English first mate aboard the CABUL to Christine Funnemark of the Seaman's Rest Mission at Tacoma, Washington; a long and difficult voyage from Tacoma to Dublin via Cape Horn with a cargo of wheat; storms and calms, crew incidents and idiosyncrasies.

KREHBEIL, C.E.   5369

''The Passion Play at Oberammergau.'' MENNONITE LIFE 35 (1980):4-9.

Aug 1900. Mennonite seminarian's account of the Oberammergau Passion Play, the behavior of the audience and quality of the acting.

WILLIAMS, DANIEL RODERICK, 1871-1931   5370

THE ODYSSEY OF THE PHILIPPINE COMMISSION. Chicago: A.C. McClurg, 1913. 362 pp.

1900-1901. Letter-diary of the secretary to a commission sent by President McKinley to govern the Philippines during the Philippine Insurrection; attempts ''to convince an embittered, suspicious and beaten race that we are sincere in our desire to help them and have no purpose in our hearts save their highest good''; references to work and attitudes of commission members William H. Taft, Bernard Moses, etc.; travels in the islands, with notes on various peoples and their customs and attitudes; American social life; voyages on the HANCOCK and SUMNER.

YOUNGER, MAUD, 1870-1936   5371

"The Diary of an Amateur Waitress: An Industrial Problem from the Workers' Point of View." MCCLURE'S MAGAZINE 28 (1907):543-552, 665-677.

May 1900. Diary of a San Francisco socialite turned women's suffragist and eventually labor union leader; the rounds of trying to get a job in New York as a waitress; learning the work, suffering humiliations from some bosses and customers, but enjoying the kindness of others; hard work at very low wages; discussions with co-workers about unionization; dated entries, but written up in fictional style.

1901

ANON.   5372

"Diary of a Prospecting Trip." UMPQUA TRAPPER 15 (1980):88-91.

Apr 1901. Brief account of a prospecting journey to Camas Valley; leading pack donkeys over difficult terrain; concluding that "there is no place like home," but failing to specify its location.

CHAMBERS, JOHN WHITECLAY   5373

Chambers, John W., II. "Under Steam for the Gold Rush." AMERICAN WEST 11, no. 5 (1974):30-39.

May-Jun 1901. Article containing diary extracts of young Pennsylvania Quaker's voyage on the RUTH from San Francisco to Nome, Alaska; impatience with slow progress through the pack ice until ship was severely damaged; anger at passengers' wanton shooting of walruses; in Nome, with notes on people, prices, scenes, but nothing on mining experiences; on return, brief notes on Seattle.

FIFE, WILLIAM J.   5374

In TREASURES OF PIONEER HISTORY, compiled by Kate B. Carter, vol. 1, pp. 304-308.

1901-1903. Brief notes of Mormon farmer at Dempsey, Idaho, present Lava Hot Springs; missionary work in Portland, Oregon, area and Washington cities; names of Mormon families with whom he lodged.

MACLANE, MARY, 1881-1929   5375

THE STORY OF MARY MACLANE. Chicago: H.S. Stone, 1902. 322 pp. New ed. New York: Duffield, 1911. 354 pp.

Extracts in A DAY AT A TIME, edited by Margo Culley, pp. 187-203.

Jan-Oct 1901. Personal diary of lonely, unhappy, bitter, nineteen-year-old girl in Butte, Montana; long imagined conversations with the devil; introspections comparing herself with Marie Bashkirtseff.

I, MARY MACLANE: A DIARY OF HUMAN DAYS. New York: Frederick A. Stokes., 1917. 317 pp.

1915? Personal feelings, daydreams, monotony of friendless existence, questioning life; notes of reading and writing, especially poetry, and admiration of Keats.

MAHONEY, MARY MANION, 1874-1964   5376

Mahoney, Donald, ed. "End of an Era: The Travel Journey of Mary Mahoney." NEBRASKA HISTORY 47 (1966):329-338.

May 1901. Covered wagon journey of seven families from Alliance seeking better farm land in Colorado; constant problems of finding enough food at scattered ranches, bad roads, keeping horses adequately fed and watered.

MUSSER, BENJAMIN, 1889-1951   5377

DIARY OF A TWELVE-YEAR-OLD. Caldwell, Idaho: Caxton, 1932. 88 pp.

Extract in SMALL VOICES, edited by Josef and Dorothy Berger, pp. 118-127.

Oct-Dec 1901. School activities, pranks and home theatricals of boy who became a very prolific but little read poet.

OGILVIE, CHRISTOPHER TINSLEY, d. 1904   5378

Ogilvie, Craig, ed. "A Preacher's Diary." INDEPENDENCE COUNTY CHRONICLE 8, no. 1 (1966):18-26.

Jan-Dec 1901. Diary kept by the pastor of the Cumberland Presbyterian Church at Batesville, Arkansas; move from Spencer, Indiana, to Batesville for a one-year preaching assignment; parish visits, weddings and funerals; concerns about his health.

TWIFORD, ORMOND H.   5379

Brown, Walter L., ed. "Life of an Arkansas Logger in 1901." ARKANSAS HISTORICAL QUARTERLY 21 (1962):44-74.

Feb-Aug 1901. Colorful extract covering Ray County, Missouri, farmer's sojourn as a logger near Mena, Arkansas; arrival by train in time to see the body of a Negro just lynched by a mob; work at Ellis Short's sawmill and logging operation at Cove with George Anderson, Spence Logan, Boone Dale and others, mostly Mormons; drinking, card playing and visiting the "quarters of the scarlet women"; some surprisingly erudite reading, including Ingersoll's lectures.

WICKERSHAM, JAMES, b. 1857   5380

OLD YUKON: TALES — TRAILS — AND TRIALS. Washington, D.C.: Washington Law Book Company, 1938. 514 pp. Diary, pp. 62-77.

Feb-Mar 1901. Diary of a United States District Court judge of Eagle, Alaska, on trip to mines at Rampart to settle disputes between mine owners and alleged jumpers; case of Allen vs. Myers involving a rich claim; details of daily travel, frequently walking ahead of dog sled to break trail; treatment of blistered feet with coal oil; lodgings; inspecting a mildly productive gold mine; seeing mammoth tusks and horns of extinct Alaska buffalo.

YESCALIS, JOSEPHINE KONCAVAGE, 1886-1956   5381

Duffy, Joseph W. "A Lithuanian Grandmother: Triumph of Spirit over Circumstances." LITUANUS 29, no. 3 (1983):26-34.

1901 - ? Article containing extracts from a Lithuanian immigrant's diary, with entries beginning upon her marriage at age sixteen to William Yescalis, a miner at Shenandoah, Pennsylvania; births of sixteen children and deaths of many; deaths of her father and then her husband in mine accidents; extracts selected to show the unusual amount of tragedy in her life and the courage with which she transcended it.

1902

DREISER, THEODORE, 1871-1945   5382

AMERICAN DIARIES, 1902-1926. Edited by Thomas P. Riggio, James L.W. West III and Neda M. Westlake. Philadelphia: University of Pennsylvania Press, 1982. 471 pp.

1902-1926. Novelist's diary; repetitious and self-absorbed, but quite revealing of various states of mental health, including a nervous breakdown, which he recorded for his doctor; relations with such literary friends as H.L. Mencken, Ludwig Lewisohn and Hapgood Hutchins; affairs of varying lengths and intensities with many women, including Helen Richardson, whom he eventually married; the struggle to support himself as a writer and discouragement over poor reception of his work until the success of AN AMERICAN TRAGEDY; life in Philadelphia, Greenwich Village and Hollywood; visits to Florida, Savannah and particularly to his hometown of Warsaw, Indiana; reactions to books; a few notes and story ideas for his work, but little that is truly revealing of Dreiser as a writer.

FIELDING, FIDELIA A. H., 1827-1908   5383

In NATIVE TRIBES AND DIALECTS OF CONNECTICUT, by Frank Speck, pp. 229-251. United States Bureau of American Ethnology, 43d Annual Report, 1925/26. Washington, D.C., 1928.

1902-1905 (with gaps). Diary of a Connecticut Mohegan Indian woman, the last native speaker of Mohegan-Pequot language; weather, nature, frequent praise to God and thanks for his gifts of strength and food; Mohegan-Pequot and English translation on facing pages.

1903

CH'I-CH'AO, LIANG, 1873-1929   5384

Lo, Jung-pang. "Chinese Reform in Idaho." IDAHO YESTERDAYS 5, no. 3 (1961):20-21.

Aug 1903. Extract within article about journey of a Chinese scholar through western states to arouse support for the Chinese Reform Association; brief notes on numbers of Chinese and activities of the Association in Pocatello and other Idaho towns.

COMER, GEORGE, 1858-1937   5385

AN ARCTIC WHALING DIARY. Edited by W. Gillies Ross. Toronto: University of Toronto Press, 1984. 271 pp.

1903-1905. Log and diary kept by East Haddam, Connceticut, captain of the New Bedford whaler ERA operating in Hudson Bay during a period of strained relations with Canada over maritime sovereignty in Arctic waters; interactions with staff of Canadian vessels NEPTUNE and ARCTIC sent to observe ERA's activities; interesting details of whaling, as well as hunting and trading with

Eskimos for game, furs and skins; references to Dr. Lorris E. Borden and medical aspects of the voyage; extensive information on Eskimos and their customs, modes of survival and precarious existence.

GEORGE, THOMAS BLADEN, b. 1826   5386

DIARY OF MY ITINERARY OF SIXTY DAYS ACROSS THE WATER. St. Augustine, Fla.: Record, 1904. 43 pp.

Oct-Nov 1903. Florida man's travel diary to England and France; by ship ETRURIA from New York to Liverpool, sightseeing in begrimed city; train to Caerleon, Monmouthshire, long description of Pontypool and its cheerless working people; disappointing search for ancient Roman relics; usual London tourist attractions, concerts and entertainments during wet, depressing weather; one night of luxury for an "ordinary Florida cracker" in Paris, followed by sightseeing.

GREGORIE, ANNE KING, 1887-1960   5387

In ANNE KING GREGORIE, by Flora B. Surles, pp. 1-218 passim. Columbia, S.C.: Printed for the author by R.L. Bryan Company, 1968.

1903-? Biography which quotes extensively from diaries of a teacher, historian and professor at various South Carolina colleges and the University of South Carolina from which she received her doctorate; trips to Berkeley, Wisconsin and Scotland; work for Works Projects Administration; interesting opinions and reflections, including satisfactions of academic life.

KNICKERBOCKER, FRANCES WENTWORTH CUTLER,   5388
1887-1973

THE MINISTER'S DAUGHTER: A TIME-EXPOSURE PHOTOGRAPH OF THE YEARS 1903-4. Edited by Charles H. Knickerbocker. Philadelphia: Dorrance, 1974. 148 pp.

1903-1904. The religious reflections, lessons, parties, vacations and happy home life of a teenager in Bangor, Maine; a record of her reading, love of her family and candid opinions on friends and teachers; experiences at school and at the Maine Music Festival.

PRINGLE, ELIZABETH WATIES ALLSTON, 1845-1921   5389

A WOMAN RICE PLANTER. By Patience Pennington, pseud. Edited by Cornelius O. Cathey. Cambridge: Belknap Press of Harvard University, 1961. 446 pp.

Extracts in WOMEN IN THE AMERICAN ECONOMY, by W. Elliot Brownlee, pp. 98-110.

1903-1905. Daily and seasonal hard work of woman who owned two plantations near Georgetown, South Carolina, during period before storms destroyed the banks and flood gates, eliminating rice as an agricultural product; managing production; personal interactions with family, friends, black employees and renters; amusing stories; a picture of a sympathetic, industrious woman and the difficulties of blacks trying to establish themselves as free workers among white land owners. See also Allston, Elizabeth Waties

1904

GREW, JOSEPH CLARK, 1880-1965   5390

TURBULENT ERA: A DIPLOMATIC RECORD OF FORTY YEARS. Edited by Walter Johnson. Boston: Houghton-Mifflin, 1952. 2 vols, passim.

> 1904-1945. Copious diary extracts within autobiography of a distinguished life in diplomatic service; the years in Europe, including Berlin at the outset of World War I, ambassadorships to Turkey and Japan, involvement in the diplomatic aspects of both world wars and events leading up to them; work as special assistant to Secretary of State Cordell Hull; frequent references to James W. Gerard, Charles Evans Hughes, Frank Kellogg and American presidents, particularly Wilson, Roosevelt and Truman.

TEN YEARS IN JAPAN: A CONTEMPORARY RECORD DRAWN FROM THE DIARIES AND PRIVATE AND OFFICIAL PAPERS. New York: Simon and Schuster, 1944. 554 pp. passim.

> 1932-1942. Significant portions of ambassador's diary revealing military extremists and a Japanese sector that realized the futility of war; daily round of work, official receptions and speeches; press relations, visits to factories, temples, parks; formal and informal events, theater, Fourth of July; assassinations and revolutions.

SNOW, FRANCIS HUNTINGTON, 1840-1908   5391

Peterson, John M., ed. "The Diaries of Francis H. Snow." KANSAS HISTORY 1 (1978):101-132.

> 1904-1907. Diary kept by a natural history professor and administrator at the University of Kansas; brief notes of social, religious and academic life in Lawrence and his entomological expeditions in the Southwest; his work as curator of the natural history museum; books and reading, particularly popular novels of the time; reactions to lectures, concerts, sermons, etc.; reference to many university faculty and Lawrence residents.

ULRICH, MABEL S.   5392

" 'Men Are Queer That Way': Extracts from the Diary of an Apostate Woman Physician." SCRIBNER'S 93 (1933):365-369. Reprint. "A Doctor's Diary." MS. 1, no. 1 (1972):11-14.

> 1904-1924 (with gaps). Diary of a woman doctor whose husband, also a physician, agreed intellectually but not emotionally that her career was equal in importance to his; in the early years of her practice, discovering that both patients and colleagues doubted the skills of women doctors; motherhood; World War I work as a health director for the Red Cross; travels and lectures; postwar public health work, during which she was paid less than men in similar work and constantly battled the male medical establishment.

1905

CULMER, HENRY LAVENDER ADOLPHUS, 1854-1914   5393

Steen, Charlie R. "The Natural Bridges of White Canyon." UTAH HISTORICAL QUARTERLY 40 (1972):55-87.

> Apr 1905. Diary of an English immigrant who had settled in Salt Lake and become a newspaper publisher and artist; notes on a horseback expedition with Samuel T. Whitaker and Carleton W. Holmes to explore, sketch and photograph the part of San Juan County which later became Natural Bridges National Monument; weather, route, terrain and detailed descriptions of scenic and geological wonders of the area; interesting notes on a few residents of Moab, Monticello and Bluff.

LEAPHART, C.W., d. 1978   5394

Leaphart, Susan, ed. "Wheelmen in Yellowstone." MONTANA: THE MAGAZINE OF WESTERN HISTORY 31, no. 4 (1981):46-53.

> Jul-Aug 1905. Extracts from the diary a young man kept of his bicycle trip through Yellowstone with several friends; by train from Cameron, Missouri, with full, humorous notes on passengers and travel; then on their bicycles, recounting mechanical problems, steep climbs, camping, food, scenery, inns, etc.; help from strangers; amusing incidents with local people and tourists.

McCLAY, PAULINE OELO, 1864-1950   5395

Rickard, Aileen B., ed. "My Trip to the Fair." OREGON HISTORICAL QUARTERLY 80 (1979):51-65.

> Sep-Oct 1905. Coos County woman's journey by horseback, stagecoach and train to the Lewis and Clark Exposition in Portland; sights at the fair, including baby incubators, forestry building, museum of arts, balloon ascensions, arcades and games; the marvels of Portland; library, zoo, electric lights and streetcars; a lecture by Mary Baker Eddy and a Catholic mass; visits to orphanages seeking a child to adopt; return by coastal steamer, ALLIANCE, and Coos River stern-wheeler, ALERT; complete list of expenses; engaging and unselfconscious.

SCOFIELD, ANNIE W.   5396

MY FIRST TRIP ABROAD. Stamford, Conn.: R.H. Cunningham, 1906. 64 pp.

> Jul-Aug 1905? European trip of a first class tourist; Atlantic crossing on the AMERIKA to Plymouth, England, then to the Continent, with rather typical travelogue notes and many facts and figures; return on the OCEANIC.

1906

DUNN, ROBERT STEED, b. 1877   5397

THE SHAMELESS DIARY OF AN EXPLORER. New York: Outing Publishing, 1907. 297 pp.

> Jun-Sep 1906. Geologist's diary of an unsuccessful attempt to climb Mount McKinley with an exploring party led by Frederick A. Cook, whose inexperience contributed to failure of the effort; route from Tyroneck on Cook Inlet, along Keechatna River to Kuskokwim River and across the rugged Brooks Range; notes on camps, terrain, problems of managing horses and keeping dry; complaints about poor organization of the expedition; a record which purports to expose Cook's claim to have made the ascent of McKinley.

MIDDLETON, GEORGE WILLIAM, b. 1866   5398

DIARY OF A TRIP TO ROME. Salt Lake City: Deseret News, 1908. 132 pp.

Nov 1906-Mar 1907. A Salt Lake City physician's trip to Europe; from New York to Gibraltar on the steamship CANOPIC; long but conventional tourist notes on Pompeii, Rome, Venice, Berne, Paris and the Louvre, London, etc.

SLOAN, JOHN, 1871-1951   5399

JOHN SLOAN'S NEW YORK SCENE. Edited by Bruce St. John. New York: Harper & Row, 1965. 658 pp.

1906-1913. Artist's diary of daily life and professional struggle; associations with many artists, editors, critics and patrons including Jerome Myers, Rockwell Kent, James B. Moore, Mary Fanton Roberts and John Butler Yeats; exhibitions with "The Eight," led by Robert Henri, at the Macbeth Gallery, the Independent Artists Exhibition and the Armory Show; notes on his own work, illustrations, the Puzzle Series for the PHILADELPHIA PRESS, etchings and paintings; interest in and support of socialism; frequent mention of his wife Dolly and her work, especially arranging for care of children of Lawrence, Massachusetts, woolen mill strikers; a good view of artists' lives, New York and the subjects of his painting.

WHITELEY, OPAL STANLEY   5400

"The Story of Opal." ATLANTIC MONTHLY 125 (1920):289-298, 445-455, 639-650, 772-782; 126 (1920):56-66, 201-213.

THE STORY OF OPAL: THE JOURNAL OF AN UNDERSTANDING HEART. Boston: Atlantic Monthly Press, 283 pp.

THE DIARY OF OPAL WHITELEY. London: Putnam, 1920. 311 pp.

Extracts in SMALL VOICES, edited by Josef and Dorothy Berger.

In OPAL WHITELEY: THE UNSOLVED MYSTERY, TOGETHER WITH OPAL WHITELEY'S DIARY, by Elizabeth S. Bradburne. London: Putnam, 1962. 293 pp.

Verse adaptation. OPAL: THE JOURNAL OF AN UNDERSTANDING HEART. Adapted by Jane Boulton. New York: Macmillan, 1976. Palo Alto, Calif.: Tioga, 1984. 190 pp. Extracts in MS. 3, no. 10 (1975):55-58.

1906?-? A famous and puzzling diary begun by a girl possibly as young as six, an orphan raised by foster parents in logging camps of Oregon; wistful memories of her "Angel Mother" and "Angel Father"; conversations with farm animals and woodland creatures whom she named after figures in classical antiquity; evident knowledge of European place-names and French which added to the mystery of her origins; a mixture of naivete and creative imagination in such passages as "and I did have meditations about what things the eyes of potatoes do see there in the ground"; an interesting diary which created both sensation and skepticism upon publication and continues to fascinate readers.

WHYTE, JOHN, 1887-1952   5401

JOHN WHYTE: HIS LIFE AND THOUGHT. Edited by William R. Gaede and Daniel Coogan. Brooklyn: Brooklyn College Press, 1954. 183 pp. Diary, pp. 5-43.

Jan-Nov 1906, 1908-1909. Diary of serious University of Wisconsin student revealing a strict religious conscience, worry over thesis

and great pleasure in orchestra in which he played violin; study in Germany, chiefly at University of Leipzig, after winning Ottendorfer Memorial Fellowship; impressions of German politics, student life, plays and concerts; discouragement over studies and differences with his major professor; struggle with choice between music and German linguistics as a career.

1907

EVARTS, JEAN   5402

In THE DIARY OF JEAN EVARTS, by Charles F. Stocking, pp. 1-352. Freeport, Ill.: Standard, 1912.

May 1907? Daily record of recovery from tuberculosis; spiritual birth through Christian Science as revealed to her by her lifelong admirer and future husband, Charles Stocking.

MONAHAN, ELMER PERRY, 1874-1964   5403

Sokolovsky, Homer, ed. "A Scientific Expedition to Idaho's Shining Mountains." IDAHO YESTERDAYS 14, no. 4 (1970):18-35.

Jun-Sep 1907. Idaho segment of a biology professor's journey to the Pacific Northwest to bring back specimens for the museum of Baker University at Baldwin, Kansas; wagon travel over rough roads; camping and fishing; notes on birds, eggs and mammals taken; references to student assistant William D. Green and Idahoan Thomas C. Bacon, also a student at Baker.

1908

DUNCAN, SINCLAIR THOMSON   5404

FROM SHETLAND TO BRITISH COLUMBIA, ALASKA AND THE UNITED STATES. Lerwick: Charles J. Duncan, 1911. 282 pp. American diary, pp. 140-160, 191-198.

Sep-Oct 1908. Diary of an elderly Shetland gentleman visiting family members in Canada and making a trip to the Treadmill Gold Mines in Juneau, Alaska, with good descriptions of the city, assay office and refining process.

ELWELL, ALCOTT FARRAR, 1886-1962   5405

"Alcott Farrar Elwell; His Diary, Wyoming 1908, as Camp Cook, United States Geodetic Survey, Roosevelt Lignite Conservation." ANNALS OF WYOMING 38 (1966):143-172.

Jul-Oct 1908. Extracts covering Cambridge, Massachusetts, man's train trip to Wyoming and work for the Geodetic Survey as cook, a skill he had to learn on the job; horseback travel, with camping and stays at ranches, mostly in Buffalo area; many amusing mishaps, but little information about the survey.

GAG, WANDA, 1893-1940   5406

GROWING PAINS: DIARIES AND DRAWINGS FOR THE YEARS 1908-1917. New York: Coward-McCann, 1940. 479 pp. Reprint. St. Paul: Minnesota Historical Society, 1984.

Extracts in TREASURY OF THE WORLD'S GREAT DIARIES, edited by Philip Dunaway, pp. 130-138; YESTERDAY'S AUTHORS OF BOOKS FOR CHILDREN, edited by Anne Commire, vol. 1, pp. 136-141. Detroit: Gale Research, 1977.

1908-1917. Adolescence and youth of renowned author and illustrator, especially of children's books; early years in New Ulm, Minnesota, dominated by poverty and hard work as eldest of a large, fatherless family; love of school, drawing and reading; a difficult year of teaching a country school; several years at art schools in Minneapolis and St. Paul on a scholarship; the normal ups and downs of youth combined with the struggles of an artist, especially to overcome the misunderstanding of relatives and neighbors who wanted her to do something "useful"; an excellent diary.

HILL, JOHN ENSIGN, 1887-1950　　　　**5407**

DIARIES AND BIOGRAPHICAL MATERIAL. Edited by Ivy H.B. Hill. Logan, Utah: J.P. Smith, 1962. 213 pp. Diary pp. 19-82.

1908-1911. Diary of first Mormon missionary to preach in the Hungarian language, translator of Book of Mormon into Hungarian, and President of Hungarian Conference, 1911; language lessons, tourist and cultural attractions of Budapest; work establishing Mormon community; God's providences.

PERKINS, EDITH FORBES, 1843-1925　　　　**5408**

LETTERS AND JOURNAL OF EDITH FORBES PERKINS. Cambridge, Mass.: Printed at the Riverside Press for private distribution, 1931. 4 vols. passim.

1908-1925. Journal of widow of Charles Elliott Perkins, president of Chicago, Burlington and Quincy Railroad; comfortable, elegant life, chiefly at The Apple Trees, a farm at Burlington, Iowa, with periods in Cincinnati, Boston, Westwood, Massachusetts, and Santa Barbara, California; the happy, sad, and amusing times with her extended family; an impressive entertainment of the Italian War Commission at The Apple Trees, other volunteer activities and anxiety for her grandchildren serving in World War I; travels in her private railroad car with family and friends to Yellowstone, Glacier, Mount Rainier, Carmel, California, and the Pendeleton Roundup in Oregon, always receiving generous treatment from her husband's friends and colleagues; late in life building her dream cottage on the beach at Santa Barbara; many tributes to her husband; excellent picture of the privileged style of life of a grand dame.

TOMLINSON, AMBROSE JESSUP, 1865-1943　　　　**5409**

DIARY OF A.J. TOMLINSON. Edited by Homer A. Tomlinson. New York: Church of God, World Headquarters, 1949. 3 vols.

1908-1943. Church of God founder's diary beginning with his "baptism of the Holy Spirit as they received Him on the day of Pentecost"; travels to establish the church, with preaching, tent and cottage meetings, camp meetings, revivals, etc., including the "Great 1908 Revival" in Cleveland, Tennessee; speaking in tongues and other ecstatic manifestations; schism and court action leading to reestablishment of his group with new headquarters in New York; references to the continuing rise of other Pentecostal sects and leaders, including Aimee Semple McPherson; diarist's old age and the increasing leadership of his son Homer A. Tomlinson.

WIER, JEANNE ELIZABETH, 1870-1950　　　　**5410**

Miller, William C., ed. "Diary, Jeanne Eliz. Wier." NEVADA HISTORICAL SOCIETY QUARTERLY 4, no.1 (1961):5-21.

Jul-Oct 1908. University of Nevada professor's hot, uncomfortable train trip from Reno to Las Vegas, where she visited Helen Wiser Stewart at her historic ranch and gathered material for the Nevada Historical Society; further train and stagecoach travel to Caliente, Rhyolite and to numerous mines and mining sites; interesting notes on a variety of lodgings, from incommodious hotels to ranch houses; references to many prominent Nevada people; a good picture of historical field work.

1909

ANGLE, HELEN M. BLONDEL, b. 1871　　　　**5411**

THE LOG OR DIARY OF OUR AUTOMOBILE VOYAGE THROUGH MAINE AND THE WHITE MOUNTAINS. Stamford, Conn.: R.H. Cunningham, 1910. 91 pp.

Sep 1909? Daughter's humorous diary of vacation trip with her father and mother in their new automobile; from a "town among the Connecticut hills" to Boston and as far as Portland, Maine; finding hotels and after an accident, a hospitable farmer and his spinster sister; chiefly the innumerable breakdowns and repairs needed for the auto identified only as "Billie."

FISH, Mrs. HARVEY J.　　　　**5412**

"Automobile Trip of Mrs. Harvey V. Fish." WESTCHESTER COUNTY HISTORICAL BULLETIN 25 (1949):43-45.

Nov 1909. Mount Kisco, New York, woman's travel diary; by Stoddard-Dayton automobile with four other persons to Mount Dora, Florida; route through Pennsylvania, Maryland and the Shenandoah Valley, visiting Gettysburg, Antietam, the Luray Caverns and the Natural Bridge; on to Lexington and Charlotte, North Carolina, Spartanburg and Greenville, South Carolina. Atlanta and Macon, Georgia; having to ship car from latter city to Gainesville, Florida, because of inadequate roads; drive from Gainesville to Mount Dora via Ocala; notes on repairs, road conditions, sights, accomodations, changing license for the different states, costs; encounters with horsedrawn vehicles; brief but fascinating glimpse of the beginning of a new era of transportation.

STONE, JULIUS FREDERICK　　　　**5413**

CANYON COUNTRY: THE ROMANCE OF A DROP OF WATER AND A GRAIN OF SAND. New York and London: G.P. Putnam's Sons, 1932. 442 pp. Journal, pp. 43-107.

Sep-Nov 1909. Journal of a trip through the canyons of the Green and Colorado rivers with companions Charles C. Sharp, R.A. Coggswell, Nathan T. Galloway and S.S. Dubendorff; preparing and loading the boats, negotiating difficult rapids and portages; taking photographs; keeping detailed notes on geology; surviving accidents and maintaining high spirit of adventure; many references to John Wesley Powell's earlier trip.

1910

ASHURST, HENRY FOUNTAIN, 1874-1962   **5414**

A MANY-COLORED TOGA: THE DIARY OF HENRY FOUNTAIN
ASHURST. Edited by George F. Sparks. Tucson: University of
Arizona Press, 1962. 416 pp.

> 1910-1937. Appealing diary of a largely self-educated lawyer and
> Democratic senator from Arizona; political career in Washington,
> D.C., spanning the administrations of Taft, Wilson, Harding,
> Coolidge, Hoover and Roosevelt; admission of Arizona to
> statehood; notes on issues before the Senate, committee work,
> Washington social life and a host of government personages;
> World War I, the League of Nations, the Depression and New
> Deal measures; trips home to Flagstaff, Arizona, to England and
> Europe.

Sparks, George F., ed. "Three Years of the Diary of Henry Fountain Ashurst." ARIZONA AND THE WEST 3 (1961):7-38.

> 1910-1913. Extracts covering activities at Prescott prior to his elec-
> tion as senator and his first months in the Senate; speaking
> engagements, social life, work as a lawyer; colorful notes on local
> people; much that sheds light on events leading to Arizona
> statehood.

BANCROFT, FREDERIC   **5415**

Cooke, Jacob E. "Chats with Henry Adams." AMERICAN HERITAGE
7, no. 1 (1955):42-45.

> 1910-1914. Extracts within article about sporadic visits with the
> elderly Adams over several years; his opinions on many subjects,
> ranging from taxes to the Civil War, as well as his appearance,
> manner and idiosyncrasies.

FLAHERTY, ROBERT JOSEPH, 1884-1951   **5416**

In THE WORLD OF ROBERT FLAHERTY, by Richard Griffith, pp.
3-43. New York: Duell, Sloan and Pearce; Boston: Little Brown, 1953.

> 1910-1912, 1920 (with gaps). Diary extracts and narrative material
> from papers of distinguished author and maker of such documen-
> tary films as NANOOK OF THE NORTH; diary portions mainly
> covering sojourns among Canadian Eskimos; travelling by dog
> sled, hunting and living in igloos with them; an interesting sup-
> plement to his books and films.

MARQUISS, OLLIE HATIE, 1880-1917   **5417**

DIARY OF A STUDENT NURSE: THE DIARY OF OLLIE MARQUISS.
Edited by Philip Mulkey Hunt. N.p., Hunt, Marquis, Mulkey Family
Association, 1978. 102 pp.

> 1910-1913. Diary of a nurse's life and training at Good Samaritan
> Hospital in Portland, Oregon; a busy routine with lectures, surgery,
> obstetrics and work in the wards; notes on patients and their
> ailments; outings with her sister Florence and other nurses.

PATTON, GEORGE SMITH, 1885-1945   **5418**

In THE PATTON PAPERS, by Martin Blumenson, 2 vols. passim.
Boston: Houghton Mifflin, 1974.

> 1910?-1945. Diary entries within collected papers of "Old Blood
> and Guts" Patton, revealing much of the outwardly confident
> general's fears and self-doubts as well as his brilliant military
> career; West Point days; World War I service under Pershing,
> with considerable information on cavalry and tank operations;
> World War II and military operations in North Africa, Sicily, France
> and Germany; the slapping incident which delayed his promo-
> tion; the Normandy invasion, Lorraine and Saar campaigns, battle
> of the Bulge, etc.; copious references to generals John J. Per-
> shing, Samuel D. Rockenbach, Omar N. Bradley, Mark W. Clark,
> Dwight D. Eisenhower, George C. Marshall and others.

1911

BLATCHLEY, WILLIS STANLEY, 1859-1940   **5419**

IN DAYS AGONE: NOTES ON THE FAUNA AND FLORA OF SUB-
TROPICAL FLORIDA IN THE DAYS WHEN MOST OF ITS AREA
WAS A PRIMEVAL WILDERNESS. Indianapolis: Nature, 1932. 338
pp.

> 1911-1922 (with gaps). A "roving naturalist's" diaries of six trips
> to southern Florida to observe and record locations of plants and
> animals, but particularly insects, of which he identified many new
> species; detailed notes of camping trips in the Florida Keys,
> Okeechobee Wilderness, the dune region, Dunedin, etc., and
> steamer trips on the Kissimmee and Caloosahatchee rivers;
> references to his son Ralph and Judge Lucius M. Hubbard, who
> often accompanied him.

SOUTH AMERICA AS I SAW IT. Indianapolis: Nature, 1934. 391 pp.

> Nov 1933-Mar 1934. Indianapolis man's "diary of the more im-
> portant things I saw and the thoughts that they engendered" on
> a South American trip; shipboard routine, passengers and Nep-
> tune Day on VESTRIS; trains, hotels, museums, parks, living con-
> ditions and products in Brazil, Argentina, Chile and Peru; meeting
> naturalists and collecting insects; returning on EBRO.

DOS PASSOS, JOHN RODERIGO, 1896-1970   **5420**

THE FOURTEENTH CHRONICLE: LETTERS AND DIARIES OF
JOHN DOS PASSOS. Edited by Townsend Ludington. Boston: Gam-
bit, 1973. 644 pp. Diary, pp. 1-237 passim.

> 1911-1918. Novelist's diary, begun with a flourish at age fifteen;
> studies at Choate School and Harvard; travels in Europe, especial-
> ly Spain, followed by service with the Norton-Harjes Ambulance
> Corps, with war experience, mainly in France and Italy, reveal-
> ed as formative to his early writing and Socialist politics; notes
> on his reading and reactions to books.

FRANKFURTER, FELIX, 1882-1965   **5421**

FROM THE DIARIES OF FELIX FRANKFURTER. With a biographical
essay and notes by Joseph P. Lash. New York: Norton, 1975. 366 pp.

> 1911-1948 (with gaps). Extracts from diaries of a Jewish immigrant
> who became a law professor at Harvard and influential justice
> of the Supreme Court; administrations of Taft, Roosevelt and
> Truman; Court activities and legal opinions; much information
> on other justices, including William O. Douglas, Hugo L. Black,
> Robert Jackson, Frank Murphy and Wiley Rutledge; notes on his

friend Louis D. Brandeis; an inside view of many legal and political matters, national and international affairs.

GAUSS, CHRISTIAN FREDERICK, 1878-1951   5422

THE PAPERS OF CHRISTIAN GAUSS. Edited by Katherine Jackson and Hiram Haydn. New York: Random House, 1957. 373 pp. Diary, pp. 45-127 passim.

Jun-Sep 1911. Princeton professor's walking tour through France, Switzerland and Italy with friend and colleague Percy Addison Chapman.

Aug-Sep 1914. A family sabbatical interrupted by World War I; harvesting hay in Switzerland in place of villagers called to the frontier; trip to Paris and description of chaos of war preparations.

1928. Sporadic entries covering his experiences as dean of Princeton; disciplinary matters; obvious concern for students' problems and well-being.

1941-1942 (with gaps). Effects of World War II on the university; the apparent suicide of a severely depressed student.

HALL, SHARLOT MABRIDTH, 1870-1943   5423

SHARLOT HALL ON THE ARIZONA STRIP. Edited by C. Gregory Crampton. Flagstaff, Ariz.: Northland Press, 1975. 97 pp. Diary, pp. 19-85.

Jul-Aug 1911. Woman's journey through northern Arizona as territorial historian in order to familiarize herself with all historic areas of the state; horseback travel and camping with guide Allen Doyle from Flagstaff to the Little Colorado, examining canyons explored by John Wesley Powell; a visit to the area where John Doyle Lee settled, planted fruit trees and operated a ferry and to sites of other early Mormon villages; across the Kaibab Plateau and into Zion Canyon, along the Virgin River and into mining districts of Cerbat Mountains; descriptions of animals, minerals and magnificent scenery of the rugged area; conversations with pioneers; notes on Paiute, Moqui and Navaho Indians; one of the earliest pictures of the area and its inhabitants, made by an adventurous woman, the first to hold public office in the state.

HOWARD, LAWRENCE C., b. 1894   5424

LOG OF THE EDWARD SEWALL. Salem? Conn.: 1958. 148 pp. passim.

Nov 1911-Mar 1912. Extracts from seventeen-year-old ordinary seaman's diary on the four-masted EDWARD SEWALL around the Horn from New York to San Francisco; daily routine of crew and officers, their relationships and grievances, demands on them during storms and accidents; good picture of Capt. Richard Quick, his command and foibles, his well-appointed quarters and books.

1912

ANON.   5425

In A DAY AT A TIME, edited by Margo Culley, pp. 204-207.

Sep 1912. Description of dreary and physically exhausting working conditions for women and children in a cannery; authenticity uncertain.

BENEDICT, RUTH FULTON, 1887-1948   5426

AN ANTHROPOLOGIST AT WORK: WRITINGS OF RUTH BENEDICT. By Margaret Mead. Boston: Houghton Mifflin, 1959. 583 pp. Diary pp. 56-79, 118-155.

Extracts in REVELATIONS: DIARIES OF WOMEN, compiled by Mary J. Moffat, pp. 148-162.

1912-1934 (with gaps). Anthropologist's infrequent but long introspective diary entries kept during two years' teaching before marriage; searching for meaning and happiness; reflections on the fate of being a woman; later, brief attempts to keep record of daily affairs and professional activity.

BRANHAM, L.B.   5427

Stauffer, Florence S., ed. "Branham's Diary." INDIANA HISTORY BULLETIN 50 (1973): 51-57.

1912-1931. Extracts from diary of a hotel keeper at Nappanee, proprietor of the Coppes Hotel; brief notes on people and events, especially related to local businesses, including his own.

BRYAN, MARY BAIRD, 1861-1930   5428

In THE MEMOIRS OF WILLIAM JENNINGS BRYAN, by William J. Bryan and Mary B. Bryan, pp. 320-326, 340-356, 415-449. Philadelphia and Chicago: John C. Winston, 1925. Reprint. New York: Haskell House, 1971. Port Washington, N.Y.: Kennikat Press, 1971.

1912-1920 (with gaps). Extracts dealing with public and personal life of her husband, William Jennings Bryan; harrowing rescue from PRINZ JOACHIM which went aground in the Bahamas, followed by Bryan's sponsoring legislation requiring round the clock radio service on ships; his campaigning for Woodrow Wilson in 1912, being appointed secretary of state, attending presidential inauguration and officially receiving the diplomatic corps with President and Mrs. Wilson at the White House; resignation over conflicting views on foreign policy relating to United States entry into World War I; campaign trips for women's suffrage and prohibition; attending Republican, Progressive and Democratic political conventions; a few notes on her own position as wife of secretary of state.

HOUSE, EDWARD MANDELL, 1858-1938   5429

THE INTIMATE PAPERS OF COLONEL HOUSE. Arranged as a narrative by Charles Seymour. Boston: Houghton Mifflin, 1926-1928. Reprint. St. Clair Shores, Michigan: Scholarly Press, 1976. 4 vols. passim.

1912-1919. Substantial diary extracts amid letters and other personal papers of Texas Democrat who became Woodrow Wilson's closest confidant and adviser; crucial involvement in formation of the cabinet, foreign relations of almost global scope, currency reform, freedom of the seas, the Pan-American Pact, the "Great Adventure" of United States emergence from isolationism and, above all, World War I, including prewar efforts, relations with allies, the Paris Peace Conference and the League of Nations; candid remarks on and dealings with Theodore Roosevelt, William Jennings Bryan, Franklin K. Lane, Walter H. Page, Robert Lansing, Albert S. Burleson, T.W. Gregory, James W. Gerard, generals Tasker H. Bliss and John J. Pershing and such foreign leaders as Count von Bernstorff, Sir Edward Grey, David Lloyd-George, Wilhelm II, Arthur J. Balfour, Lord Robert Cecil, Georges Clemenceau, Sir William Wiseman and others; various missions abroad for Wilson; an Atlantic crossing on the LUSITANIA shortly before its sinking; altogether, an important source on Wilson and the major figures and events of the period.

KAMBOURIS, HARALAMBOS K.   **5430**

Papanikolas, Helen, ed. and Vasilacopulos, C., trans. ''Oregon Experiences.'' OREGON HISTORICAL QUARTERLY 82 (1981):5-39.

1912-1915. Extracts from largely narrative diary of a Greek immigrant's experiences in Roseburg and elsewhere working in railroad yards, but also suffering long periods of unemployment; many references by name to fellow Greeks in the area; sending money home to his family; courtship by mail.

MOORE, ALICE   **5431**

Moore, Austin L., ed. ''The Last Eden: The Diary of Alice Moore at the XX Ranch.'' ANNALS OF WYOMING 41 (1969):63-81.

Jun-Aug 1912. Cheyenne girl's idyllic summer vacation camping with her family at the Williams Land and Livestock Company ranch in the Laramie Mountains; hospitality of the Williams family; enjoyment of walks, fishing, flowers, birds and animals; games and reading, including THE LAST DAYS OF POMPEII read aloud by her father, the Rev. Frank L. Moore; a good picture of happy family life.

MURPHY, ROBERT CUSHMAN, 1887-1973   **5432**

LOGBOOK FOR GRACE, WHALING BRIG DAISY. New York: Macmillan, 1947. 290 pp. Reprint. Time, 1965. 371 pp.

Jul 1912-May 1913. Whaling diary of an ornithologist who was to become a world authority on sea birds; notes kept aboard the DAISY, one of the last sail-powered whalers, mainly in Antarctic waters, of shipboard work and life; scientific observations on birds captured at sea and on land, particularly South Georgia Island; an entertaining and substantial diary.

MUSSER, ELISE FURER, 1877-1967   **5433**

Brooks, Juanita and Butler, Janet B., ed. ''Utah's Peace Advocate, The 'Mormona.' '' UTAH HISTORICAL QUARTERLY 46 (1978): 151-166. Diary, pp. 156-158.

1912-1914. Brief extracts from the diary of a Swiss immigrant who became a Mormon and intellectual and political leader in Utah; a trip to Washington, D.C., where she heard Helen Keller speak; in New York attending lectures at New York City College; references to her husband, Burton Musser.

Nov-Dec 1936. Extracts covering her experiences as the only woman delegate to the Buenos Aires Peace Conference; emphasis there on women's rights as well as peace, especially through the efforts of Doris Stevens; arrival of President Roosevelt at the conference.

PLUMMER, HENRY MERRIHEW, b. 1865   **5434**

THE BOY, ME AND THE CAT. Sharon, Mass.: Author, 1914. 103 pp. 2d ed. Rye, N.H.: Cyrus Chandler, 1961. 142 pp.

Oct 1912-Jun 1913. Diary of a cruise aboard the MASCOT, a thirty-year-old twenty-three foot Cape Cod catboat, undertaken by the diarist, his son and their cat; from New Bedford down the inland waterway to Miami and return; sailing details, food, hunting,

mishaps, sights and people along the way; an interesting adventure, colorfully recounted.

REYNOLDS, ALBERT, 1847-1913   **5435**

Buckholtz, C.W., ed. ''The Diary of Albert 'Death-on-the-Trail' Reynolds.'' MONTANA: THE MAGAZINE OF WESTERN HISTORY 35, no. 1 (1985):48-59.

Oct 1912-Feb 1913. Diary of the last few months in the life of a Glacier National Park forest ranger stationed on Lake McDonald; patrols throughout the area on foot, maintaining trails, enforcing park rules, making wildlife counts, guarding against poachers and herding starved deer to better forage; enduring cold, exhaustion and danger from grizzlies, etc.; suffering frozen feet which led to his death.

SMOOT, REED, 1862-1941   **5436**

Cardon, A.F. ''Senator Reed Smoot and the Mexican Revolutions.'' UTAH HISTORICAL QUARTERLY 31 (1963):151-163.

1912-1914. Extracts within article on Utah senator's assistance to Mormon colonists in Mexico during the revolt against Porfirio Diaz and unstable period following his overthrow; attempts in Washington, D.C., to arrange for arms shipments to colonists so they could defend themselves and to forestall United States intervention which might incite reprisals against American settlers.

1913

COPELAND, ESTELLA M.   **5437**

''Overland by Auto: Diary of a Family Tour from California to Indiana.'' INDIANA HISTORICAL SOCIETY PUBLICATIONS 26, no. 2 (1981):1-87.

May-Jul 1913. Diary kept by wife of Guy Copeland of a journey by car, partway in convoy with the William DeLameter family, from Watsonville, California, to their farm in Marion County, Indiana; route over roads ranging from adequate to barely passable and extremely dangerous; hotels and camping sights such as Roosevelt Dam; descriptions of Indians; added difficulty of caring for sick children.

DANIELS, JOSEPHUS, 1862-1948   **5438**

THE CABINET DIARIES OF JOSEPHUS DANIELS. Edited by E. David Cronon. Lincoln: University of Nebraska Press, 1963. 648 pp.

1913-1921. Diaries of secretary of the navy under Woodrow Wilson; almost encyclopedic coverage of national politics, foreign relations and defense policy of the period, including extensive material on World War I, the League of Nations and Council of National Defense; relations with Britain, France, Germany, Russia, etc; many references to his young assistant Franklin D. Roosevelt and to such other diverse figures as William Jennings Bryan, Newton D. Baker, William S. Benson, Bernard Baruch, Albert S. Burleson, Franklin K. Lane, Robert S. Lansing, William G. McAdoo, William S. Sims, etc., in addition to Wilson.

KOCH, HERBERT F.   **5439**

''The Flood of 1913.'' CINCINNATI HISTORICAL SOCIETY BULLETIN 25 (1967):136-149.

Mar 1913. Extracts describing University of Cincinnati student's participation in relief efforts at Hamilton, with long, vivid descriptions of destruction of property and loss of life; grim task of going from house to house recovering bodies.

SINTZENICH, ARTHUR H.C.   **5440**

Barnouw, Eric. "The Sintzenich Diaries." QUARTERLY JOURNAL OF THE LIBRARY OF CONGRESS 37 (1980):310-331 passim.

1913-? Article containing extracts from the voluminous diaries of an early motion picture cameraman, an English immigrant of German descent; many technical details of filming and references to actors and directors; long periods of unemployment and financial insecurity between films; in 1914, an African safari with Lady Grace Mackenzie for filming big game, an apparent romance, but her refusal later to pay his salary; pioneering in underwater cinematography for John Ernest Williamson; World War I service as a photographer and with the Signal Corps; subsequent work with D.W. Griffith, on whom his diaries provide considerable information; continued struggle to support his family between pictures.

STICKEL, FRED G., 1887-1969   **5441**

"Through the Morris Canal." NEW JERSEY HISTORY 89 (1971):93-114.

Jul 1913. Legislator's inspection tour by canal boat to help determine if the old canal should be abandoned in favor of increased railroad and highway development; comments on scenery, towns, factories, farms, roads, bridges and railways, as well as the condition of the canal and its water, locks and towpaths; a good picture of the end of the canal era.

1914

ALLEN, WILLIAM CHARLES, b. 1857   **5442**

A QUAKER DIARY IN THE ORIENT. San Jose, Calif.: Wright-Eley, 1915. 101 pp.

Sep 1914-Mar 1915. San Jose, California, Quaker's tour of the Orient on behalf of the International Peace Movement and as a missionary effort "on gospel lines according to the simple usage of conservative Friends"; travel with William B. Harvey to Japan, Korea, China and the Philippines, meeting with government officials in an effort to improve United States foreign relations, especially with Japan; preaching at schools and missions, visiting with missionaries of many denominations, with frequent references to Gilbert Bowles.

DELOACH, WILLIAM G., 1880-1967   **5443**

Neugebauer, Janet M. "The Diary of William G. DeLoach: A West Texas Farmer." WEST TEXAS HISTORICAL ASSOCIATION YEARBOOK 59 (1983):108-121.

1914-1964. Article containing extracts from the diaries of a Sudan, Texas, farmer, with brief periods in Oklahoma and Crosby County, Texas; a graphic depiction of the struggle of farming in the thirties, with dust bowl and the Depression forcing the loss of his

farm to "cold blooded land grafters"; sufficient recovery to buy another farm later; local incidents, recreations and social life.

FOYE, EVA N.   **5444**

"On Their Own in Yosemite." SIERRA 64, no. 3 (1979):18-26.

Jul-Aug 1914. A woman's diary of a camping and hiking trip with three friends; reactions of people at Miami Lodge that "we are very brave to start out without any men in the party"; campfires, the great outdoor cooking of Dr. Florence Sylvester, hot, tiring but satisfying hikes, scenery and wildlife; a good experience, with the diarist asking, "How will I ever be able to live under a roof again?"

FRASER, GEORGE C., 1872-1935   **5445**

Jett, Stephen C. "The Journal of George C. Fraser '93: Early Twentieth Century Travels in the South and Southwest." PRINCETON UNIVERSITY LIBRARY CHRONICLE 35 (1974):290-308.

1914-1922. Scant extracts within article describing extensive travel journals of a New York lawyer, a Princeton graduate with particular interest in geology, Indian life and photography.

GIBSON, HUGH, 1883-1954   **5446**

A JOURNAL FROM OUR LEGATION IN BELGIUM. Garden City, N.Y.: Doubleday, Page, 1917. 360 pp. passim.

A DIPLOMATIC DIARY. New York and London: Hodder and Stoughton, 1917. 296 pp. passim.

1914-1915. Narrative journal, with some dated entries, kept by secretary of the American legation in Brussels during German invasion and occupation of Belgium; a detailed picture of effects of war on civilians; relief efforts, particularly those of Herbert Hoover, chairman of the American Relief Committee; references to many diplomats, including United States ambassador Brand Whitlock, and complex international relations; a moving account of the last hours of Canadian nurse Edith Cavell before her execution by the Germans, despite Whitlock's efforts to secure a reprieve.

"A Journal from Our Legation in Belgium. "WORLD'S WORK 34 (1917):389-404, 541-552, 640-659; 35 (1917):70-79, 160-171.

Jul-Oct 1914. Extracts.

JAMES, WINIFRED LEWELLIN, 1876-1941   **5447**

A WOMAN IN THE WILDERNESS. New York: George H. Doran. London: Chapman and Hall, 1916. 291 pp.

1914-1915. Letter-diary of an Australian journalist living in Panama with her American businessman husband; trip in the first ship through the Panama Canal; Canal Zone social life, her attitudes toward black servants; views on women's suffrage; limited news of the war in Europe.

MORRISON, ANNA DALY, b. 1884   **5448**

DIARY. Boise, Idaho: Em-Kayan Press, 1951. 446 pp.

1914-1949. Revised diary of high-spirited, good humored woman who became wife of Harry Morrison, president of Morrison-Knudsen Company; courtship, marriage, working as secretary for the growing heavy construction business; accompanying her husband by buckboard and Model T Ford to construction sites, staying in all kinds of hot, dusty camps; amusing anecdotes of later travel by train, car and plane, meeting friends and business associates, shopping and sightseeing in major United States and foreign cities.

NIN, ANAÏS, 1903-1977   5449

The monumental life work, begun at age eleven, of a great diarist, a compulsive chronicler of her inner states as well as outward circumstances, whose diary became "my hashish, my opium pipe" as well as a means of capturing "the air of truth which cannot be imparted if it is not in the first casting"; a record of a life spent among writers, artists and musicians, chiefly in Paris and New York, with extended portraits of Antonin Artaud, Edmund Wilson, Truman Capote, Gore Vidal, Lawrence Durrell and, above all, Henry Miller; psychoanalysis with Rene Allendy and Otto Rank and work for a time with Rank as an analyist; reflections on beauty, friendship, love, artistic creation, dreams, fantasy and the predicaments and challenges of being human, female, a writer and especially the self-conscious builder of a life and persona that became Anaïs Nin.

LINOTTE: THE EARLY DIARY OF ANAÏS NIN. With a preface by Joaquin Nin-Culmell. New York: Harcourt Brace Jovanovich, 1978-1985. 4 vols.

1914-1931. Childhood and teenage diaries began when her beloved father, pianist Joaquin Nin, deserted the family; the move from Spain to New York, where the next lonely and formative years were spent; her "call" to become a writer, love of solitude and sense of her own differentness; early adult life in New York, Cuba and Paris; marriage to Hugo P. Guiler and beginnings of a literary career. Volume one translated from the French.

Extracts in SMALL VOICES, edited by Josef and Dorothy Berger, pp. 3-11.

Nov 1914-May 1915.

THE DIARY OF ANAIS NIN. Edited by Gunther Stuhlmann. New York: Swallow Press and Harcourt, Brace and World, 1966-1980. 7 vols.

1931-1974. The literary years in Paris and New York; later world travels as a celebrity.

Extracts in REVELATIONS: DIARIES OF WOMEN, compiled by Mary Moffatt, pp. 86-97.

Dec 1931. First meeting with and intensity of feeling for June Miller, wife of Henry Miller.

UNPUBLISHED SELECTIONS FROM THE DIARY. Athens, Ohio: D. Schneider Press, 1968. 43 pp.

1931-1934. Extracts on Henry Miller, Rene Allendy and others in Paris.

RHINE, LOUISA ELLA WECKESSER, 1891-1983   5450

SOMETHING HIDDEN: J.B. RHINE'S UNFINISHED QUEST. Jefferson, N.C.: McFarland, 1983. 287 pp. Diary, pp. 1-287 passim.

1914-1942 (with gaps.) Scattered diary extracts in a personal memoir of her evolving relationship with Joseph Banks Rhine, her marriage to him and their education together in botany at the University of Chicago; painfully moving through religious fundamentalism to careers devoted to teaching, counseling and psychical research at Duke University, the first institution to support a parapsychology laboratory; a few family notes.

SEEGER, ALAN, 1888-1916   5451

LETTERS AND DIARY OF ALAN SEEGER. New York: C. Scribner's Sons, 1917. 218 pp. Diary, pp. 1-165 passim.

Extracts in MEN WITHOUT MASKS, by Michael Rubin, pp. 54-63.

Oct 1914-Sep 1915. Service with French Foreign Legion as part of American Volunteer Corps; avid for action and somewhat romantic about war and the brotherhood of men fighting for a cause; great love for France, his adopted country.

STARLING, EDMUND WILLIAM, 1875-1944   5452

STARLING OF THE WHITE HOUSE: THE STORY OF THE MAN WHOSE SECRET SERVICE DETAIL GUARDED FIVE PRESIDENTS FROM WOODROW WILSON TO FRANKLIN D. ROOSEVELT. New York: Simon and Schuster, 1946. 334 pp.

1914-1941. Autobiography quoting extensively from diaries of man who was head of Secret Service through many administrations; United States entry into World War I; duties and reactions to work within the White House and on trips, outings, to church, plays and concerts with presidents; a raise in salary from $5.00 to $6.00 per day under Wilson; his discreet impressions of presidents and others in government; religious introspections of a devout Presbyterian.

WHITLOCK, BRAND, 1869-1934   5453

THE LETTERS AND JOURNAL OF BRAND WHITLOCK. Edited by Allan Nevins. New York and London: D. Appleton-Century, 1936. 2 vols. Journal, vol. 2.

1914-1921. World War I journal of minister and ambassador to Belgium; description of German invasion and occupation; endurance and heroism of the Belgian people; diarist's diplomatic work, relief efforts and social life; interactions with American and Belgian leaders, with extensive references to Woodrow Wilson, Herbert Hoover, King Albert of the Belgians and the Marquis de Villalobar; good descriptions of people, places and events; frank revelation of everyday life during war by a fine but reluctant diarist who complained of the "drudgery of the task, this diurnal recording of futile banalities that might better be forgotten."

WOOD, ERIC FISHER, 1889-1962   5454

THE NOTE-BOOK OF AN ATTACHE: SEVEN MONTHS IN THE WAR ZONE. New York: Century, 1915. 345 pp. passim.

Jul 1914-Jan 1915. Extracts from diaries and letters of an American architectural student in Paris at the outbreak of World War I, who became an attaché to Myron T. Herrick of the American embassy; four trips to the front observing French military operations at Marne, Aisne, Calais, Vitry-le-Francois, etc.; graphic and detailed descriptions, including his horrified reactions to seeing the dying, "frightful sights, and parts of them are often already mortified, as they lie in the straw, entirely occupied with breathing"; additional experiences and observations while bearing dispatches throughout Europe.

YOUNG, MARY SOPHIE, 1872-1919   5455

Tharp, B.C. and Kielman, Chester V., eds. "Mary S. Young's Journal of Botanical Exploration in Trans-Pecos Texas." SOUTHWESTERN HISTORICAL QUARTERLY 65 (1962):366-393, 512-538.

Aug-Sep 1914. Journal of one of several major field trips undertaken by University of Texas botany instructor, this time with student Carey Tharp; to west Texas by train, thence by carriage pulled by recalcitrant burros; good description of terrain, scenery, ranches and flora, as well as the logistics of camping, traveling and doing academic field work under difficult conditions; names of many ranch families in the area.

1915

ALLEN, JEROME L.   **5456**

"Leaves from a Greenland Diary." UNITED STATES NAVAL INSTITUTE PROCEEDINGS 68, no. 2 (1942):201-208.

May 1915. Extract praising tireless sled dogs who were the mainstay of a Navy commander's Greenland segment of the Crocker Land Arctic Expedition.

COOLIDGE, HELEN   **5457**

In A WAR DIARY IN PARIS, by John G. Coolidge, pp. 21-283 passim. Cambridge: Privately printed at the Riverside Press, 1931.

1915-1917. Diary entries interspersed with those of her husband, John Gardner Coolidge, special agent to the embassy in Paris; chiefly news of progress of the war, official and other social events; managing difficult living arrangements; attending Chamber of Deputies when Ribot announced America's declaration of war; charity work; trips to observe battlefront; a visit to Rome.

COOLIDGE, JOHN GARDNER, 1863-1936   **5458**

A WAR DIARY IN PARIS. Cambridge: Privately printed at the Riverside Press, 1931. 283 pp.

1915-1917. Diplomatic diary of special agent to the embassy in Paris at outbreak of World War I; chiefly war news and his work in charge of Ottoman interests until Turkey broke off relations; good report of ceremonies marking arrival of General Pershing in France; his personal opinions of American and other officials.

CUSHING, HARVEY WILLIAMS, 1869-1939   **5459**

FROM A SURGEON'S JOURNAL. Boston: Little, Brown, 1936. 534 pp.

"From a Surgeon's Journal." ATLANTIC MONTHLY 154 (1934):385-399, 590-601, 696-707; 155 (1934):102-116.

1915-1918. Harvard surgery professor's account of war service in France as part of the Harvard unit of American volunteer medical and ambulance personnel helping the French; notes on wounds and their treatment, especially head injuries; news from the front; efforts, which met with local resistance, to help the Red Cross establish an American base hospital on Boston Common; medical service at Dannes-Camiers with an American unit attached to the British Expeditionary Force, then with the American Expeditionary Force at Neufchateau; a long account, based on interviews, of a young officer's "psychneurosis in the line of duty."

DOYLE, LUKE CANTWELL   **5460**

In HISTORY OF THE AMERICAN FIELD SERVICE IN FRANCE, vol. 1, pp. 309-312.

Dec 1915. Account by Yale graduate from Worcester, Massachusetts, of difficult ambulance work in the Alsatian mountains at Mittlach.

FLORENCE, LELLA SECOR   **5461**

LELLA SECOR: A DIARY IN LETTERS. Edited by Barbara M. Florence. American Women's Diary Series, 1. New York: B. Franklin, 1978. 295 pp.

1915-1922. Daily events in the life of a World War I peace activist recorded in letters to her mother and sisters; writing and working for peace organizations, Henry Ford's Peace Ship, American Neutral Conference Committee, Emergency Peace Federation and suffrage movements; early years of marriage and the confining periods of caring for a young family with no help; moving to England, resuming her speaking and writing for Penal Reform League, British Labour party and birth control associations.

GALATTI, STEPHEN   **5462**

In HISTORY OF THE AMERICAN FIELD SERVICE IN FRANCE, vol. 1, pp. 312-313.

Dec 1915. Difficult winter ambulance service at Mittlach, Alsace, recorded by Harvard graduate from New York City.

GARRETT, GARET, d. 1954   **5463**

Cornuelle, R.C., ed. "Remembrance of the TIMES, from the Papers of Garet Garrett." AMERICAN SCHOLAR 36 (1967):429-445.

1915-1916. Extract of journalist's notes kept while he was editor of the editorial page of the NEW YORK TIMES; news of the sinking of the LUSITANIA and the ARMENIAN; the funeral of city editor Arthur Greaves; well-written and entertaining anecdotes revealing the characters of publisher Adolph S. Ochs and others at the TIMES.

GENET, EDMOND CHARLES CLINTON, 1896-1917   **5464**

AN AMERICAN FOR LAFAYETTE: THE DIARIES OF E.C.C. GENET, LAFAYETTE ESCADRILLE. Edited by Walt Brown. Charlottesville: University Press of Virginia, 1981. 224 pp.

1915-1917. Diaries of adventurous and patriotic young man from Ossining, New York, who deserted from the navy to see action in World War I and became the first American to die in combat after America formally entered the war; fighting with the French Foreign Legion in Champagne, transferring to Aviation Service, showing outstanding skill in training at Buc and Cazaux with good notes on various aircraft and aerial fighting; serving in Lafayette Escadrille, an all American squadron; frequent mention of aviators Edwin C. Parsons, James Rogers "Mac" McConnell and Raoul Lufbery; welcome diversion of leaves in Paris, often sharing his experiences with Capt. Frank Parker, military attache who was compiling information on air service; profound grief over McConnell's death and increasing despair over being jilted by girl friend at home.

"Leaves from a War Diary." NORTH AMERICAN REVIEW 224 (1927):270-285, 406-420.

1915-1917. Extracts.

GERARD, JAMES WATSON, 1867-1951   5465

FACE TO FACE WITH KAISERISM. New York: George H. Doran, 1918. 380 pp. Diary, pp. 55-128.

1915-1917. Diplomatic diary of ambassador to Germany, with entries illustrating events and attitudes in Germany leading to its resumption of unrestricted submarine warfare; many references to Wilson and his policies; war news from various fronts; meetings with high officials, including the Kaiser; attempts to relieve the condition of British prisoners; effects of war on German civilians; Germany's plan to attack the United States; early plots in Mexico, etc.; references to Col. Edward House; a picture of deteriorating United States-German relations prior to America's entry into the war.

GOLLINGS, ELLING WILLIAM, 1878-1932   5466

In BILL GOLLINGS: THE MAN AND HIS ART, by James T. Forrest, pp. 40-48 passim. Flagstaff, Ariz.: Northland Press, 1979.

1915-1931 (with gaps). Extracts of typical diary entries of cowboy and artist from Sheridan, Wyoming; daily activities on ranch and working with neighbors; notes on painting and selling his work.

NEWSOM, LYSIAS EVERETT, b. 1859   5467

DIARY OF A SOUTHERN TOUR IN MIDWINTER. Indianapolis: Printed by F.E. Brinkman, 1916. 12 pp.

Dec 1915-Jan 1916. Letter-diary of traveling agent for the Lackawanna Line, describing a train journey with his wife from Indianapolis to Key West; the sights of Chattanooga, Atlanta, St. Augustine, Daytona Beach, Palm Beach, Miami and the fledgling Miami Beach; boat trip to Cuba; from Tampa to Jacksonville via Florida's lake country; notes on climate, citrus groves, railways and Hoosiers settled in the Sunshine State; comments on lynching of blacks in Georgia.

PUTNAM, TRACY JACKSON   5468

In HISTORY OF THE AMERICAN FIELD SERVICE IN FRANCE, vol. 1, pp. 101-107, 291-302.

May-Dec 1915 (with gaps). Harvard graduate's experiences as a volunteer ambulance driver assisting French troops in Belgium and France; service in Alsace; the battle at Hartmannsweilerkopf.

SPEAKMAN, WILLIAM CYRUS, 1868-1930   5469

In MEMORIES, by Marie A.V. Speakman, 191 pp. passim. Wilmington, Del.: Greenwood Bookshop, 1937.

1915-1918. Occasional extracts from the diary of an American surgeon serving in France with the Wilmington Dental Ambulance; to France on the ROCHAMBEAU; treatment of French soldiers with severe facial and "dental" wounds; a meeting with Lucien Poincaré; some translations from diaries kept by his patients.

SPERANZA, GINO CHARLES, 1872-1927   5470

THE DIARY OF GINO SPERANZA, ITALY, 1915-1919. Edited by Florence C. Speranza. New York: Columbia University Press, 1941. Reprint. AMS Press, 1966. 2 vols.

1915-1919. Diary of an Italian-American intellectual, a lawyer turned writer, expert on Italian immigration and feature correspondent for the NEW YORK EVENING POST and the OUTLOOK;

a monumental account of his travels and observations in wartime Italy, with leisurely, sympathetic notes on virtually all aspects of Italian life, individuals and groups; his impressions of military, political and diplomatic situation and the effects of war on civilians; his work as a volunteer intelligence officer for the American Embassy.

1916

BARBER, WILLIAM MALTBY   5471

In HISTORY OF THE AMERICAN FIELD SERVICE IN FRANCE, vol. 1, pp. 324-334.

Jun 1916. Account kept by Oberlin College student from Toledo, Ohio, of his work as a volunteer ambulance driver transporting French wounded at Verdun; the shelling of his ambulance, severely wounding diarist and killing three of his already injured passengers.

BULLITT, ERNESTA DRINKER   5472

AN UNCENSORED DIARY FROM THE CENTRAL EMPIRES. Garden City, N.Y.: Doubleday, Page, 1917. 205 pp. London: S. Paul, 1918. 282 pp.

May-Sep 1916. Diary of residence and travel in Europe during World War I; frequent subjection to search of clothing and baggage; stay in Berlin, with observations on people and their attitudes; comparison of British and German newspaper reports of the war; social life and embassy activities; travels through Belgium, with notes on the effect of war and German occupation; experiences in Austria and Hungary, where she was again part of diplomatic social life through her husband, career diplomat William C. Bullitt.

"A Diary from Germany." WORLD'S WORK 33 (1916-1917):440-446.

May-Jul 1916. Extracts.

"Through Belgium and Austria." WORLD'S WORK 33 (1916-1917):553-560.

Jul-Sep 1916. Extracts.

KEOGH, GRENVILLE T.   5473

In HISTORY OF THE AMERICAN FIELD SERVICE IN FRANCE, vol. 1, pp. 457-467.

Jul-Sep 1916. Extracts from record of a volunteer ambulance driver from New Rochelle, New York; removing French wounded from the fighting at Cabaret to hospital at Dugny; constant danger from shelling and gas; terrible condition of the wounded.

LANSING, ROBERT, 1864-1928   5474

Grenville, J.A.S. "The United States Decision for War." RENAISSANCE AND MODERN STUDIES 4 (1960):59-81.

Dec 1916-Mar 1917. Article containing substantial extracts from the secret diaries of the secretary of state, kept during the period of American neutrality; a careful record of his attitudes and conversations, particularly involving his disagreements with President Wilson's League to Enforce Peace proposal; the crucial cabinet meetings leading up to severance of relations with Germany; Wilson's remarks and responses of cabinet members, including diarist's own speech in which he asserted that "we are at war now. Why not say so without faltering?"

LILLIE, WALTER HAMILTON   5475

In HISTORY OF THE AMERICAN FIELD SERVICE IN FRANCE, vol. 2, pp. 3-10.

Dec 1916-Jul 1917. Account by Harvard student from Boston of his volunteer ambulance service with French troops in Albania; difficulties of transporting wounded over muddy, shell-pocked mountain roads; good descriptions of a peasant wedding and funeral.

MARIS, CORA   5476

"Life at Pebble Quarry." NEVADA HISTORICAL SOCIETY QUARTERLY 25, no. 1 (1982):53-64.

1916-1919. Extracts from the diary of wife of Omer Maris recounting their experiences quarrying turquoise and copper ore in Ralston Valley; disappointment over lack of success and hardships of desert life.

MERIWETHER, LEE, b. 1862   5477

THE WAR DIARY OF A DIPLOMAT. New York: Dodd, Mead, 1919. 303 pp.

1916-1918. Journeys throughout France of special assistant to the American Ambassador responsible for inspecting prison camps to assure humane treatment of German and Austrian prisoners; minute picture of actual life in prison camps; military and civilian conditions in wartime France and his mounting sympathy for the plight of the French people; uncomfortable travel in unheated trains and worse accommodations.

OLDER, CORA MIRANDA BAGGERLY, 1873-1968   5478

DIARIES OF MRS. CORA BAGGERLY OLDER. Edited by Donna R. Harris. California History Center. Local History Studies, no. 7. Los Altos Hills? Calif.: Foothill Community College District, 1971. 32 pp.

1916-1923. Extracts from personal diary of wife of Fremont Older, editor of the SAN FRANCISCO BULLETIN; searching for California history, interviewing early settlers, including several survivors of the Donner party; the difficult time when her husband left the BULLETIN for the SAN FRANCISCO CALL; views on the draft, World War I, women's suffrage and prison reform; references to many notable Californians.

RAINSFORD, WALTER KERR   5479

"An American Ambulancier at Verdun." WORLD'S WORK 33 (1916-1917):183-194.

Jun 1916. Extracts of Harvard graduate's ambulance work in France; battles at Verdun and a graphic description of dangerous and exhausting rescue of wounded and ambulance driving.

SANGER, WILLIAM CAREY   5480

In HISTORY OF THE AMERICAN FIELD SERVICE IN FRANCE, vol. 1, pp. 496-504.

Dec 1916-Mar 1917. Diary extracts covering work of Harvard graduate from Sangerfield, New York, as a volunteer ambulance driver evacuating French wounded from the action near Verdun.

SEABROOK, WILLIAM BUEHLER   5481

In HISTORY OF THE AMERICAN FIELD SERVICE IN FRANCE, vol. 1, pp. 441-454.

May-Jul 1916. Extracts from account by Newberry College student from Atlanta of his work as an ambulance driver attached to French army at Verdun; admiration for French soldiers in the trenches.

STEVENSON, WILLIAM YORKE, b. 1878   5482

AT THE FRONT IN A FLIVVER. Boston and New York: Houghton Mifflin, 1917. 257 pp.

Extracts in HISTORY OF THE AMERICAN FIELD SERVICE IN FRANCE, vol. 1, pp. 168-187.

Mar-Nov 1916. Account of work as a volunteer ambulance driver kept by Philadelphia graduate of the University of Pennsylvania; the campaign in Somme, Verdun and Argonne areas; battle for Fleury; ghastly incidents of trench warfare and its casualties reported with occasional gallows humor; night-driving without lights and over shell-pocked and congested roads, transporting French wounded to field hospitals; great appreciation of the French for American volunteers.

1917

ANON.   5483

In THE 120TH FIELD ARTILLERY DIARY, edited by Carl Penner, pp. 1-536 passim. Milwaukee: Hammersmith-Kortmeyer, 1928.

1917-1919. Extracts from official regimental records and diaries of unidentified private soldiers of a largely Wisconsin unit during World War I; service in France under Col. Carl Penner; military operations in the Alsatian, Chateau-Thierry, Juvigny and Argonne theaters; a large and varied source on the experiences of officers and ordinary soldiers, with details from the homely to the heroic.

ANDREWS, AVERY DE LANO, 1864-1959   5484

MY FRIEND AND CLASSMATE JOHN J. PERSHING, WITH NOTES FROM MY WAR DIARY. Harrisburg, Pa.: Military Service, 1939. 291 pp. passim.

1917-1918. Extracts from diary of Pershing's assistant chief of staff at the headquarters of the American Expeditionary Force in France; administrative details, official functions, inspection travels and a surprising amount of social life; in addition to Pershing, references to many high officers, including Col. Theodore Roosevelt. Jr.

ASHE, ELIZABETH H., 1869-1954   5485

INTIMATE LETTERS FROM FRANCE, AND EXTRACTS FROM THE DIARY OF ELIZABETH ASHE. Rev. and enl. San Francisco: Bruce Brough Press, 1931. 224 pp. passim.

1917-1919. Diary of a nurse working for the Red Cross Children's Bureau in France; brief but highly evocative entries describing devastation of the countryside, birth of babies in bomb shelters, introduction of public health visiting concept, cooperation between French and American methods of medicine, exasperation with red tape and work with refugees and orphans; references to Dr. William Palmer Lucas.

Extract in A DAY AT A TIME, edited by Margo Culley, pp. 208-211.

Mar 1919. Relief work in Cambrai and Ypres.

BIDDLE, GEORGE, 1885-1973   5486

TAHITIAN JOURNAL. Minneapolis: University of Minnesota Press, 1968. 207 pp.

1917-1922. Brief selections from diary kept during World War I; two extended stays in Tahiti to concentrate on painting; island descriptions, people, customs, language, mythology and music; introspective observations on his emerging philosophy of art.

ARTIST AT WAR. New York: Viking Press, 1944. 241 pp.

Apr-Dec 1943. Diary kept as chairman of the War Department Art Advisory Committee to record scenes of World War II; going to Tunisia after selecting and dispatching artists to twelve fronts; sketching village life almost uninterrupted by war, returning refugees, convoys moving forward, medical corp trucks returning with wounded, Italian prisoners; to Sicily under contract with LIFE magazine after the art program was terminated by the War Department; entering Palermo with reconnaissance troops, seeing destruction and effects of war; as part of the Italian campaign of Fifth Army, having daily intimate contact with front line troops; in first car into Naples and with Second Battalion of the Fifteenth Regiment during most of their combat service in Italy; observations on soldiers, officers, generals Eisenhower, Mark Clark and Terry Allen, civlilians, and the many incongruities of war.

BIGELOW, DONALD FAIRCHILD   5487

In HISTORY OF THE AMERICAN FIELD SERVICE IN FRANCE, vol. 2, pp. 29-61.

Jun-Nov 1917. Extracts from letter-diaries of Princeton student from St. Paul, Minnesota; volunteer work as a transport driver hauling ammunition to the front, often in the dark, through deep mud and under shell fire; attack on Malmaison; a Fourth of July celebration; quotation from Alan Seeger's diary.

BOWERMAN, GUY EMERSON, 1896-1947   5488

THE COMPENSATIONS OF WAR. Edited by Mark C. Carnes. Austin: University of Texas, 1983. 178 pp.

1917-1918. Diary of Idaho man and Yale freshman in France and Belgium as member of American Ambulance Service; long, descriptive entries of the assignments of his section, number 585, moving from station to station, transporting wounded from field posts to hospitals, working under fire; an air battle with planes swooping only a few hundred feet overhead; thoughtful comments on war, fear and courage.

BRYAN, JULIEN HEQUEMBOURG   5489

In HISTORY OF THE AMERICAN FIELD SERVICE IN FRANCE, vol. 2, pp. 53-58.

Feb-Jul 1917. Extracts from record by Princeton student from Titusville, Pennsylvania, of his volunteer ambulance service in France; welcome news of United States declaration of war on Germany.

COLIE, FREDERIC RUNYON   5490

In HISTORY OF THE AMERICAN FIELD SERVICE IN FRANCE, vol. 2, 279-284.

Jun-Sep 1917. Extracts from the diary of Dartmouth student from East Orange, New Jersey; volunteer ambulance work in the Champagne region; death of Dartmouth friend Paul Gannett Osborn of wounds suffered in the shelling of his ambulance.

COOK, TRUMAN BLAIR   5491

"Merchant Marine, 1917-1918." OREGON HISTORICAL QUARTERLY 77 (1976):101-129.

Oct 1917-Aug 1918. Diary of an engineer on maiden voyage of the MADRUGADA, a sailing vessel equipped with engines; departure from Portland down coast to Arica, Chile, back to Callao, Peru, then north through Panama Canal; technical details of operating, maintaining and repairing troublesome engines on ship which "won't steam and won't sail"; stops at East Coast ports and, at Philadelphia, diarist's transfer to the S.I. ALLARD, a better ship.

COPELAND, PETER W.   5492

Grenier, Judson A. "A Minnesota Railroad Man in the Far East." MINNESOTA HISTORY 38 (1963):310-325.

1917-1918. Extracts, within article, from diaries and letters of a St. Paul member of the Russian Railway Service Corps sent to help reopen the Trans-Siberian Railway; extracts covering a long period in Japan en route to Vladivostok, with notes mainly on Japanese customs.

COWLEY, MALCOLM   5493

In HISTORY OF THE AMERICAN FIELD SERVICE IN FRANCE, vol. 3, pp. 91-99.

Jul 1917. Diary of Harvard student, later to be renowned author, of his experiences as a volunteer transport driver with the French troops; unloading of trucks under fire; a Fourth of July celebration.

CRAIG, HARMON BUSHNELL, d. 1917   5494

In HISTORY OF THE AMERICAN FIELD SERVICE IN FRANCE, vol. 1, pp. 259-271.

Jun-Jul 1917. Harvard student's work as a volunteer ambulance driver during action at Verdun; constant danger from shells and gas; unrelieved fatigue and ghastliness of transporting the dead and wounded.

CUNNINGHAM, ALFRED AUSTELL   5495

MARINE FLYER IN FRANCE. Edited by Graham A. Cosmas. Washington, D.C.: History and Museums Division, Headquarters, United States Marine Corps. For sale by the Supt. of Docs., United States Government Printing Office 1974. 43 pp.

Nov 1917-Jan 1918. Diary, kept by the first Marine Corps aviator, of a tour to observe Allied operations in France; Atlantic crossing on the ST. PAUL; wartime conditions in London and Paris; visits to and evaluations of French flying schools and air bases; encounter with American flyers of the Lafayette Escadrille; a combat mission with French pilots; visits to military sites in England; return home on the ST. LOUIS; interesting for personal views on people and conditions, as well as information on early military aviation.

DONALDSON, ROBERT ANDERS   5496

In HISTORY OF THE AMERICAN FIELD SERVICE IN FRANCE, vol. 2, pp. 412-422, 513-515.

Jul-Oct 1917. Extracts from articulate diary of Stanford student from Denver, recording his work as a volunteer ambulance driver; American Field Service training camp at May-en-Multien; action at Sermoise and attack on Malmaison; frantic work of removing French wounded from the front.

DUNN, HARRY LIPINCOTT   5497

In HISTORY OF THE AMERICAN FIELD SERVICE IN FRANCE, vol. 1, pp. 475-480.

May-Aug 1917. Brief diary of volunteer ambulance work in France, kept by University of California student from Santa Barbara.

ELY, DINSMORE, 1894-1918   5498

DINSMORE ELY; ONE WHO SERVED. Chicago: A.C. McClurg, 1919. 215 pp. Diary, pp. 1-38.

Jun-Jul 1917. Diary and letters of young American volunteer; amusements and submarine scares aboard ship crossing the Atlantic; arrival in France and sightseeing in Paris while awaiting admission to the Lafayette Escadrille; in training near Avord; reading, photography, the thrill of flying, a visit to Bourges and its cathedral of St. Etienne.

ESSIG, MAUDE FRANCES, 1884-1981   5499

Woolley, Alma S. "A Hoosier Nurse in France." INDIANA MAGAZINE OF HISTORY 82 (1986):37-68.

1917-1919. Article containing extracts from the diary of a Red Cross nurse from Elkhart assigned to Base Hospital Thirty-Two in France, nursing under conditions that occasionally reminded her of Florence Nightingale in the Crimea; the care of a variety of wounds and illnesses, with a detailed description of several treatments for victims of gas attack; working at least twelve-hour days, contending with frozen toilets, shortages of medicine and even beds, exhaustion and sickness among nurses, but a sense of pride and accomplishment in serving the wounded, who were "so patient and grateful for the little they receive."

FLOREZ, CARLOS DE   5500

"NO. 6": A FEW PAGES FROM THE DIARY OF AN AMBULANCE DRIVER. New York: E.P. Dutton, 1918. 150 pp.

Aug-Sep 1917. First impressions of an ambulance driver in France during World War I; daily routines, maintaining Fiat ambulances and carrying wounded and shell-shocked; describing the natural beauty of Lorraine region and rebuilding of Vitrimont; revealing

the mood and courageous spirit of the French in a gentle, literary style.

FRITZ, CHESTER, b. 1892   5501

CHINA JOURNEY: A DIARY OF SIX MONTHS IN WESTERN INLAND CHINA. Seattle: School of International Studies, University of Washington, 1981. 187 pp.

Vivian, James F., ed. "The Journal of Chester Fritz: Travels Through Western China in 1917." NORTH DAKOTA QUARTERLY 49, no. 2 (1981):9-120. Reprint. Grand Forks: University of North Dakota Press, 1981. 120 pp.

Feb-Jul 1917. Travel diary of a young North Dakota man, a recent graduate of University of Washington who initially went to China as a representative of the Fisher Flouring Mills of Seattle; an exotic journey mostly by sedan chair with pack horse caravans; through Yunnan Province, where he observed "the number of blind people, idiots, deformed people is appalling, while over half the people have goiter" and "filth and squalor everywhere"; lodging at village inns of dubious comfort and with missionaries or foreign officials, many of whom are named in the diary; through Kweichow, with notes on Miao aboriginal people as well as Chinese; in Szechwan Province, rich in natural resources; throughout his travels, descriptions of scenery, food, work, dwellings, clothing, markets, hospitality, condition of inns and roads, all manner of customs, discomforts and dangers, including bands of robbers; return to Shanghai by Yangtze riverboat with an escort of soldiers; notes on cities, towns and countryside along the river; a fascinating diary by an intrepid and observant young traveler who became a banker and millionaire gold and silver trader in the Orient.

GIBBS, GEORGE, 1861-1940   5502

Feist, Joe Michael, ed. "Railways and Politics: The Russian Diary of George Gibbs." WISCONSIN MAGAZINE OF HISTORY 62 (1979):179-199.

May-Oct 1917 (with gaps). Milwaukee railroad engineering expert's assignment as member of a commission to advise on restoration of the Trans-Siberian Railway, neglected because of World War I and Russia's internal upheavals; to Yokohama on the EMPRESS OF ASIA, thence to Vladivostok, their headquarters; notes on American and Russian military and railroad personnel; chaos of unmoved goods and cars; inspection tour the entire length of the railroad in a special car; dealings with Ambassador David R. Francis and the Railway Ministry; descriptions of Leningrad, then Petrograd, under wartime conditions; notes on the Root Commission activities of Alexander Kerensky, the Provisional Government, the July uprising, etc., with little apparent awareness of their significance.

GRIDER, JOHN MCGAVOCK, 1892-1918   5503

WAR BIRDS: DIARY OF AN UNKNOWN AVIATOR. New York: G.H. Doran, 1926. 277 pp. Garden City: Sun Dial Press, 1938. London: Temple, 1966. 166 pp.

1917-1918. World War I diary of sergeant and aviator; from Halifax to England on the CARMANIA with much merrymaking enroute; ground school at Oxford, which impressed him with its antiquity; machine gun and flying school; after-hours enjoyment of girls, pubs, castles, etc.; fond descriptions of various planes, including a Sopwith Pup, which he longed to fly; regular patrols in Viper Hispanos from base at Dunkirk; stunts and incidents involving a host of airmen named in the diary; details of air battles and an increasing number of deaths reported; the strain and tension of three or four flights a day showing in the entries just before he also became a casualty.

Springs, Elliott, "War Birds: Diary of an Unknown Aviator." AEROSPACE HISTORIAN 13 (1966):97-104; 14 (1967):37-41, 151-162, 219-225; 15 (1968):34-51.

1917-1918. Extracts.

Extracts in DIARY OF AMERICA, edited by Josef and Dorothy Berger, pp. 543-545.

Jun 1918. Description of air combat.

GRIERSON, JOHN MAXWELL   5504

In HISTORY OF THE AMERICAN FIELD SERVICE IN FRANCE, vol. 2, pp. 75-80.

Mar-Jul 1917. Account of his experiences in the Champagne offensive, by a volunteer ambulance driver from New York City.

HAMILTON, PERLEY RAYMOND, d. 1917   5505

In HISTORY OF THE AMERICAN FIELD SERVICE IN FRANCE, vol. 2, pp. 342-345.

Jul 1917. Extracts from the diary of a Clinton, Massachusetts, ambulance volunteer killed a few hours after the last entry; round-the-clock work under fire and on terrible roads during furious fighting at Glennes.

HARBORD, JAMES GUTHRIE, b. 1866   5506

LEAVES FROM A WAR DIARY. New York: Dodd, Mead, 1925. 407 pp.

1917-1918. A general's diary of service with the American Expeditionary Force as chief of Services of Supply; sailing to England on the luxurious BALTIC, on a zigzag course through the danger zone; a great welcome in France; much official business, luncheons, dinners, etc., with British and French officers; activities of Pershing; his functions at the general headquarters at Chaumont and action with the Marine Brigade at Verdun and Bellaue Wood; the Soissons offensive; notes on French families with whom he was billeted; a frank war diary in an informal, eloquent style.

HARLE, JAMES WYLY   5507

In HISTORY OF THE AMERICAN FIELD SERVICE IN FRANCE, vol. 2, pp. 16-26.

Jan-May 1917. Diary extracts of New York City ambulance volunteer's service with French troops on the Albanian front; terrible roads and fear of falling asleep at the wheel; death of section leader, Henry M. Suckley, of bombing wounds; interesting descriptions of Albanian peasants.

HOOD, REID, 1892-   5508

Chadbourn, Charles C., III. "The Diary and Letters of a North Louisiana Doughboy." NORTH LOUISIANA HISTORICAL ASSOCIATION JOURNAL 6 (1975):140-153.

1917-1919. Summary of diary with brief extracts covering his service with the Thirtieth Infantry, Third Division of the American Ex-

peditionary Force; fighting on the Hindenberg Line; occupation of Germany; rest and relaxation at Aix-les-Bains; journey home.

HURLBUT, JOHN BROWNING   5509

In HISTORY OF THE AMERICAN FIELD SERVICE IN FRANCE, vol. 2, pp. 285-289.

Jun-Oct 1917. Extracts from account of volunteer ambulance work by Dartmouth student from Hartford, Connecticut; action in the Champagne sector; the wounding and death of college friend Paul Gannett Osborn.

JATHO, CHARLES CONRAD   5510

In HISTORY OF THE AMERICAN FIELD SERVICE IN FRANCE, vol. 2, pp. 232-236.

Jun-Dec 1917. Notes by Albany, New York, student at Cambridge Episcopal Theological School serving as a volunteer ambulance driver in France; the devastation of Reims.

JOHNSON, HIRAM, 1866-1945   5511

THE DIARY LETTERS OF HIRAM JOHNSON. With an introduction by Robert E. Burke. New York: Garland, 1983. 7 vols.

1917-1945. Vast diaries of a long-time California Republican senator, formerly a leader in the Progressive party; notes on congresses and presidents from Wilson through Roosevelt and the events, issues and policies of their administrations, with his strong Progressive and isolationist predilections coloring many of his opinions; opposition to Wilson's signing of the declaration of war, reactions to World War I news and policy, concern over the Bolshevik takeover in Russia, opposition to the League of Nations; involvement with the opinions of Harding, Coolidge, Hoover and Roosevelt; intitial enthusiasm for the New Deal turning to disillusionment; misgivings about United States entry into World War II and, once in, a suspicion that American policy was being dictated by Churchill; postwar opposition to the United Nations; espousal of such causes as Boulder Dam and protective tariffs for California's specialty crops; active participation in Republican party affairs while continuing his interest in matters affecting his old Progressive colleagues Raymond Robins, Harold L. Ickes, Gifford Pinchot, etc.; several unsuccessful attempts to win Republican presidential nomination.

Levine, Lawrence W., ed. "The 'Diary' of Hiram Johnson." AMERICAN HERITAGE 20, no. 5 (1965):64-76.

1917-1944. Extracts selected particularly to show his reactions to a succession of presidents and Congresses and his isolationist and Progressive stance toward foreign policy.

Burke, Robert E. "Hiram Johnson's Impressions of William E. Borah." IDAHO YESTERDAYS 17, no. 1 (1973):2-11.

1917-1940. Article containing extracts relating to his long-time Republican colleague, Sen. William E. Borah of Idaho, and the politics of both.

JUDY, WILLIAM LEWIS, 1891-   5512

A SOLDIER'S DIARY: A DAY-TO-DAY RECORD IN THE WORLD WAR. Chicago: Judy, 1930. 216 pp.

1917-1919. War segment from a Chicago writer's lifelong diary; service under Gen. George Bell, for whom he worked as field clerk; basic training and monotonous camp life; on troop ship to

France, with account of action and army life there; references to many fellow officers and soldiers; reflections on courage and fear; notes on French civilians; a convincing picture of the horror and tedium of war and the endurance and resourcefulness of ordinary soldiers.

KIMMEL, MARTIN LUTHER, 1883-1971 5513

Brown, Moss K., ed. "To Be a Soldier." OREGON HISTORICAL QUARTERLY 75 (1974):241-269.

Sep-Dec 1917. Oregon enlisted man's diary kept during training at various camps, including Vancouver Barracks, Washington, Camp Green in Charlotte, North Carolina, Camp Mills, New York, and Camp Merritt, New Jersey; detailed descriptions of military training, duties and diversions and the conditions at each camp; opinions on his fellow soldiers and officers; philosophical reflections on war and patriotism and his own and others' reasons for enlisting.

LAHM, FRANK PURDY, 1877-1963 5514

THE WORLD WAR I DIARY OF COL. FRANK P. LAHM, AIR SERVICE. A.E.F. Edited by Albert F. Simpson. Maxwell AFB, Ala.: Historical Research Division, Aerospace Studies Institute, 1970. 271 pp.

1917-1919. Diary of officer sent to observe balloon schools and aerial operations in England and France and organize American balloon activities as chief of Air Service, Second Army, with headquarters at Toul; sailing on BALTIC to Liverpool; descriptions of training schools, bases and use of balloons by the British navy; on to France, observing balloon capabilities in third battle of Ypres; establishing balloon school at Cuperly; meeting many military men and Red Cross and YMCA civilians, such as President Wilson's daughter and war artist Georges Scott; entertaining Prince Albert, who was touring British front, at the aviation mess; going to Metz for triumphal entry of French troops; staying on in France after the war to act as host to riding teams from Allied nations who were participating in International Games for opening of Pershing Stadium; receiving Distinguished Service Medal from General Pershing; a great parade and review of all Allied troops on Bastille Day; return home on the LEVIATHAN.

LEACH, GEORGE E., b. 1876 5515

WAR DIARY. Minneapolis: Pioneer Printers, 1923. 205 pp.

1917-1919. Minnesota officer's World War I diary which he kept as a colonel of the 151st Field Artillery; action in France in the Baccarat and Marne areas and the defense of Châlon; gas attacks, trench warfare and casualties; diarist's admiration for the heroism of his men; frequent references to generals Charles McKinstry and Douglas MacArthur; brief period with the Army of Occupation on the Rhine, then home to Minnesota.

LEWIS, JAMES HENRY 5516

In HISTORY OF THE AMERICAN FIELD SERVICE IN FRANCE, vol. 2, pp. 149-150.

Sep 1917. Extracts from the diary of a Harvard student from Eastport, Maine; volunteer ambulance service at Verdun.

LILIENTHAL, DAVID ELI, 1899- 5517

THE JOURNALS OF DAVID E. LILIENTHAL. Introduction by Henry Steele Commager. New York: Harper & Row, 1964-1983. 7 vols.

1917-1981. Vast diaries of a veteran statesman and public servant; brief selections from 1917-1939, beginning when he was a student at DePauw University; thereafter, fairly complete entries on his activities, opinions and enormous and diverse accomplishments as director of the Tennessee Valley Authority, Atomic Energy Commission and the Development and Resources Corporation for technological development in the Third World: travels in numerous countries and a busy and lucrative period in the private sector; frank comments about Roosevelt, Truman, Kennedy, etc., and a host of other major figures in government, politics, foreign relations, domestic affairs, etc.; opinions about and involvement in critical issues and events over four decades, including an enduring concern about atomic energy and its environmental impact; family matters and restorative pastimes, such as gardening; considerable personal revelation; each volume in itself a compendium of the period covered and the entire journal, a textbook of public administration and an encyclopedia, from one highly involved perspective, of the raw materials of recent American history.

LOSH, WILLIAM JACKSON 5518

In HISTORY OF THE AMERICAN FIELD SERVICE IN FRANCE, vol. 2, pp. 90-93.

Mar-Jul 1917. Account of volunteer ambulance work by Stanford student from San Francisco; transporting French victims of a gas and liquid fire attack.

MACDOUGALL, ALBERT EDWARD 5519

In HISTORY OF THE AMERICAN FIELD SERVICE IN FRANCE, vol. 2, pp. 386-401.

Aug-Oct 1917. Substantial extracts from account by Harvard student from Flushing, New York, of his work as a volunteer ambulance driver attached to the French troops at Dugny; surgeons treating the wounded without anesthetic; German bombing of a hospital; visit to a French camp for German prisoners; his twenty-first birthday; great admiration for courage and fortitude of the French.

O'SHAUGHNESSY, EDITH LOUISE COUES 5520

MY LORRAINE JOURNAL. New York and London: Harper & Brothers, 1918. 195 pp.

Jun 1917-Jan 1918. Diary of woman in France as first American troops were arriving during World War I; effusive responses to the natural beauty of Lorraine—fields, parks, towns, churches, monuments—juxtaposed with the ruins of war; patriotic service in canteens in Bar-le-Duc and Chalons; notes on improvised hospitals, the desolate battlefield at Verdun, the aged and very young being cared for at Molitor; bits of sightseeing along the Marne, at Nancy, Vitrimont and Luneville; historical material, frequent quotes and conversations in French.

ALSACE IN RUST AND GOLD. New York and London: Harper & Brothers, 1920. 183 pp.

Oct.-Nov. 1918. Accompanying the French Military Commission from Paris to Alsace; more word pictures of scenes and villages, people, overheard conversations; daily life in Masevaux and near-by villages during last historic days of World War I which saw the final "re-Gallicizing of Alsace Lorraine."

PRESTON, JEROME   5521

In HISTORY OF THE AMERICAN FIELD SERVICE IN FRANCE, vol. 2, pp. 111-134.

Mar-Dec 1917.Extracts from the diary of a Harvard student from Lexington, Massachusetts; volunteer ambulance service at Verdun and Champagne; great admiration for courage of French infantrymen; moving descriptions and introspections; a diary showing considerable literary flair.

PUTNAM, ARTHUR JAMES   5522

In HISTORY OF THE AMERICAN FIELD SERVICE IN FRANCE, vol. 2, pp. 410-411.

Sep 1917. Account by Cornell student from Deposit, New York, of volunteer ambulance work with French troops at Sermoise.

RENDINELL, JOSEPH EDWARD, 1894-   5523

ONE MAN'S WAR: THE DIARY OF A LEATHERNECK. New York: J.H. Sears, 1928. 177 pp. passim.

1917-1918. Marine's diary and letters to his family; enlistment and leaving home for the first time; basic training at Parris Island, South Carolina; "crossing the pond"; action and inaction in France, "hauling manure for the frogs"; to the front, with trench warfare at Verdun and Belleau Wood, where the trench rats were "nice and fat from eating dead Germans and French"; notes on civilians including processions of refugees; dangerous scouting forays; the naive notes of an ordinary soldier enduring the dangers and discomforts of war.

ROGERS, HORATIO   5524

THE DIARY OF AN ARTILLERY SCOUT. North Andover, Mass.: Rogers, 1975. 268 pp.

WORLD WAR I THROUGH MY SIGHTS. San Rafael, Calif.: Presidio Press, 1976. 268 pp.

1917-1919. War diary of a Bostonian and Harvard student who was a corporal in Battery A, 101st Field Artillery, Twenty-sixth Division of the American Expeditionary Force; very brief notes of training camp, sailing on the ADRIATIC to France, further training in Brittany, then to the front; account of the Aisne-Marne offensive, St. Mihiel drive; a most welcome furlough and escapade after Armistice, knocking about towns and countryside; each entry elaborated in publication.

ROMEO, GIUSEPPE L., 1891-   5525

DIARY OF PVT. GIUSEPPE L. ROMEO. Tacoma, Wash.: Copeland and Son, Printers, 1919. 38 pp.

1917-1919. War diary of Italian immigrant; training at camps Lewis and Merritt; Atlantic crossing on the SCOTIAN to Scotland, train travel through England and by ship to Le Havre; further training in France, then to the front, with notes of action at Eclesfontain and Bar-le-Duc; illness and hospitalization; by train to Belgium and arrest for getting off without authorization; confinement to guardhouse, then court-martial and assignment to hard labor, en-

during poor food and ill treatment; return to his company, which was reviewed by General Pershing; a brief, unadorned account.

ROSS, GILBERT NELSON   5526

In HISTORY OF THE AMERICAN FIELD SERVICE IN FRANCE, vol. 2, p. 254.

Aug 1917. Note by Massachusetts Institute of Technology student from Brookline, Massachusetts, on German bombing of hospital at Vadelaincourt, where he was serving as a volunteer ambulance driver.

ROSS, KIRBY G.   5527

Povlovich, Charles A., ed. "Lest We Forget: World War I Diary of Kirby Ross." OREGON HISTORICAL QUARTERLY 84 (1983):5-28.

1917-1918 (with gaps). Portland man's diary of training and service with the Third Oregon, later 162nd United States Infantry; duties at Portland, Clackamas, etc.; from New York to France on the SUSQUEHANNA; at St. Nazaire, then to the front, with notes of trench warfare and casualties, including his friend Fred T. Merrill; Officers' Candidate School at Langres.

ROYCE, FRANK GRAY   5528

In HISTORY OF THE AMERICAN FIELD SERVICE IN FRANCE, vol. 2, pp. 237-242.

Jun-Sep 1917. Extracts from account by Cornell student from Fulton, New York, of his volunteer work as an ambulance driver transporting French wounded; his admiration for an elderly priest working as a stretcher bearer and for the spirit of the French troops.

SCHOEN, ERNEST RUDOLF   5529

In HISTORY OF THE AMERICAN FIELD SERVICE IN FRANCE, vol. 2, pp. 209-214.

May-Aug 1917. Diary of a Richmond, Virginia, ambulance volunteer and graduate of University of Virginia; action at Verdun; difficulty of getting ambulances to and from the trenches on roads choked with convoys; beauty of nature contrasted with scars of war; rather philosophical.

SHAW, ALPHEUS EDWARD   5530

In HISTORY OF THE AMERICAN FIELD SERVICE IN FRANCE, vol. 2, pp. 145-148.

Jun-Sep 1917. Account kept by Harvard student from Wilmington, Vermont, of volunteer ambulance work at Verdun.

SIRMON, W.A.   5531

THAT'S WAR: AN AUTHENTIC DIARY. Atlanta: Linmon, 1927. 277 pp.

1917-1918. Crichton, Alabama, officer's diary of monotonous days of training at Camp Gordon, Georgia, with 325th Infantry, Company E; aide-de camp to Gen. Marcus Cronin; stationed at Camp Upton, New York, with a few occasions for entertainments, dances and sightseeing in New York City; an incident of southern soldier's unwillingness to salute black officers; to England on the S.S. KARMALA; comments on poverty-stricken appearance of people in Liverpool and London; training for trench warfare in France and earning Distinguished Service Cross at front; hospitalization after exposure to mustard gas; rejoining his company at Argonne just before Armistice; a good view of daily life of a typical doughboy.

STRAUB, ELMER FRANK   **5532**

A SERGEANT'S DIARY IN THE WORLD WAR: THE DIARY OF AN ENLISTED MEMBER OF THE 150TH FIELD ARTILLERY (FORTY-SECOND (RAINBOW) DIVISION). Indiana Historical Collections, vol. 10. Indianapolis: Indiana Historical Commission, 1923. 356 pp.

1917-1919. Indiana University student's experiences, first in France attending to property and provisions for his division, then marching from camp to camp and to the Lorraine front; campaigns at Champagne and Meuse-Argonne; in Luxemburg at end of war, enjoying hot water and good food; whiling away time waiting to return home; accepting government offer to attend a European university and visiting Cologne, London and Liverpool while awaiting assignment, which was to University of Glasgow; living at Y.M.C.A. with much leisure, description of classes, sightseeing, shopping, theater and being entertained by tailor Murray Dewar at his home before returning to the United States on the MARTHA WASHINGTON.

STUHL, EDWARD, 1887-1984   **5533**

"From the Journals of Edward Stuhl." SISKIYOU PIONEER 5, no. 7 (1984):1-9.

1917-1961. Widely scattered extracts relating to Mount Shasta, Castle Crags and Castle Lake from journals of Hungarian-born naturalist and artist; natural history and scenery of the area; mountain climbing experiences.

SUTHERLAND, ROY   **5534**

In OUR SOLDIERS SPEAK, by William Matthews and Dixon Wecter, pp. 267-269, 291-295.

Apr 1917-Aug 1918. Extracts from Virginian's diary; last school days in Chattanooga, Tennessee; enlistment in Marine Corps and training at Parris Island, South Carolina, and Quantico, Virginia; off to France aboard the VON STEUBEN and collision with the AGAMEMNON; in the trenches in Verdun sector; wounding at Belleau Wood.

SWAN, WILLIAM DENNISON   **5535**

In HISTORY OF THE AMERICAN FIELD SERVICE IN FRANCE, vol. 2, pp. 11-15.

Jan-Mar 1917. Notes on volunteer ambulance service in Albania kept by Harvard student from Cambridge, Massachusetts; death of section leader Henry M. Suckley.

WALDNER, JAKOB, 1891-   **5536**

Schlabach, Theron, ed. "An Account by Jakob Waldner: Diary of a Conscientious Objector in World War I." MENNONITE QUARTERLY REVIEW 48 (1974):73-111.

1917-1918. A Hutterite's narrative and diary; from the Spring Creek Hutterite Community at Lewistown, Montana, to Camp Funston, Kansas, where he was held with a number of other Hutterites, Mennonites and other religious pacifists; physical and verbal harrassment, especially for refusal to work; an unsuccessful group effort at bribery for release; abhorence of camp violence,

including several murders, suicides and the hanging of three black soldiers accused of rape; religious reflections and references to many Hutterite pastors and fellow conscientious objectors. Translated from the German.

WEEKS, EDWARD AUGUSTUS   **5537**

In HISTORY OF THE AMERICAN FIELD SERVICE IN FRANCE, vol. 2, pp. 442-446.

Aug-Sep 1917. Brief notes of Cornell student from Elizabeth, New Jersey, serving as a volunteer ambulance driver at the St. Quentin front; descriptions of gassing victims.

WIGHTMAN, ORRIN SAGE, b. 1873   **5538**

THE DIARY OF AN AMERICAN PHYSICIAN IN THE RUSSIAN REVOLUTION. Brooklyn: Brooklyn Daily Eagle, 1928. 230 pp.

Jul-Oct 1917. Diary kept by a member of the American Red Cross mission to Russia, traveling throughout the country with photographer Harold Wyckoff and an interpreter; dated but rather narrative entries on the trip across Russia from Vladivostok on the Trans-Siberian Railway, with notes on people, customs and economic conditions; in Petrograd, where he reported demoralization, refusal to work and shortages of most necessities; comments on women soldiers and workers; impressions of Alexander Kerensky; a visit to the summer residence of the deposed czar; to Moscow and vicinity where he observed YMCA work; travel to Kiev and Odessa, with visits to hospitals; thence to the Rumanian front, with notes on condition of refugees and meetings with Rumanian generals.

1918

BAKER, HORACE LEONARD   **5539**

ARGONNE DAYS: EXPERIENCES OF A WORLD WAR PRIVATE ON THE MEUSE-ARGONNE FRONT. Aberdeen, Miss.: Printed by the Aberdeen Weekly, 1927. 122 pp.

Sep-Nov 1918. War diary of Monroe County, Mississippi, man serving in Company M, 128th Infantry, with entries beginning upon his arrival at Chatonrupt; exhausting marches "double-timing with full packs and stomachs not full," bombardments, shellings and gas attacks; going "over the top" in the Romagne offensive and subsequent action; religious reflections amidst the horrors of war.

BELLAMY, DAVID, 1888-1960   **5540**

"A Marine at the Front." AMERICAN HISTORY ILLUSTRATED 5, no. 10 (1971):30-42.

Jan-Nov 1918. Extracts from diary of American marine officer in France; the Toulon Sector, Verdun; battle of Belleau Wood; serving as adjutant and captain, Third Battalion, Sixth Marine Regiment, in the Aisne-Marne, or Soissons, offensive; Meuse-Argonne offensive; last days of war and celebration of the armistice; notes on destruction, morale, etc.

BONSAL, STEPHEN, 1865-1951   5541

UNFINISHED BUSINESS. New York: Doubleday, Doran, 1944. 313 pp. London: M. Joseph, 1944. 283 pp.

1918-1919. Diary of a foreign correspondent who became confidant and adviser to both President Wilson and Col. Edward M. House and was chosen to attend secret sessions of the Paris Peace Conference as Wilson's special interpreter of the unrecorded discussions; travels in Europe, with material on postwar conditions in Berlin, Vienna and other cities; extensive references to Léon Bourgeois, Georges Clemenceau and Jan Christian Smuts as well as Wilson and House; details of the Covenant of the League of Nations and Versailles Peace Treaty and concern for "unfinished business" that could lead to future problems in Europe; in Washington, D.C., for debate on ratification.

BOYLSTON, HELEN DORE   5542

"SISTER": THE WAR DIARY OF A NURSE. New York: I. Washburn, 1927. 202 pp.

1918-1920. Daily routines of a World War I nurse; long, fatiguing hours receiving wounded; relaxing with other nurses or enjoying a night out with a soldier; character sketches of nurses and patients; interesting comments on men's attitudes towards women; treating the whole event as an adventure and joining Red Cross to go to the Balkans after the war.

In TRAVELS WITH ZENOBIA, by Rose Wilder Lane and Helen Dore Boylston, edited by William Holtz, pp. 25-89. Columbia and London: University of Missouri Press, 1983.

Feb-Nov 1926 (with gaps). A letter-diary in which entries by her friend Rose Wilder Lane predominate; a funny and wildly adventurous journey from Paris to Albania in Zenobia, a maroon Model T Ford; travel conditions, people, inns and hotels; the heroic performance of Zenobia over bad roads and mountain terrain in France and Italy.

CAMPBELL, PEYTON RANDOLPH, 1894-1918   5543

THE DIARY-LETTERS OF SERGT. PEYTON RANDOLPH CAMPBELL. Buffalo, N.Y.: Pratt & Lambert, 1919. 142 pp.

Apr-Aug 1918. Diary of former advertising man for Pratt & Lambert now an enlisted man in World War I army; troopship life, machine gun, rifle and gas mask drills, steady move toward French front; locating little luxuries such as chocolate; life in the trenches; unaffected, cheerful conversational style.

CASEY, ROBERT JOSEPH, b. 1890   5544

THE CANNONEERS HAVE HAIRY EARS: A DIARY OF THE FRONT LINES. New York: J.H. Sears, 1927. 330 pp.

Aug-Nov 1918. Diary of commander of Battery A in the Third Illinois Field Artillery; action at Argonne, Romagne and Meuse; marches and trench warfare described in a rather jaunty manner, with the experience of wearing a gas mask resembling "a cold in the head, a dentist's chair in the days of the rubber dam, a gag, an inability to swallow, a nose filled with hot cinders, a hat four sizes too small," and the difficulty of getting horses to wear their gas masks.

GIMPEL, RENE, 1881-1945   5546

DIARY OF AN ART DEALER. Translated from the French by John Rosenberg. London: Hodder & Stoughton; New York: Farrar, Straus and Giroux, 1966. 465 pp.

1918-1939 (with gaps). Diary of a major French art dealer with an office in New York; particularly serving such American collectors as Joseph Widener, Henry C. Frick, the Rockefellers and the Carnegies; visiting galleries and other dealers, especially Roland Knoedler; a foreigner's view of a Fourth of July parade to bolster patriotic efforts for World War I; intimations of the coming of World War II; an appealing diary of a man who saw beauty, pathos and grotesqueness in both the paintings and people with whom he dealt.

GUTTERSEN, GRANVILLE, 1897-1918   5547

GRANVILLE: TALES AND TAIL SPINS FROM A FLYER'S DIARY. New York and Cincinnati: Abingdon, 1919. 176 pp.

Jan-Nov 1918. Diary of a young lieutenant impatient to get overseas with the Army Flying Corps; ground school at Austin, Texas; flying school at Ellington Field and San Leon Gunnery School at Houston; in New York awaiting orders to go to France when armistice was signed; recalled to Ellington Field where he died from complications of a cold; a breezy, bravado style.

HELM, EDITH BENHAM   5548

THE CAPTAINS AND THE KINGS. New York: Putnam, 1954. 307 pp. Diary, pp. 64-122.

Extracts in DIARY OF AMERICA, edited by Josef and Dorothy Berger, pp. 545-553.

Dec 1918-Jul 1919. Diary of Mrs. Woodrow Wilson's social secretary kept for James M. Helm, later her husband, while on two trips to France with President Wilson who was attending the Paris Peace Conference negotiations after World War I; behind the scenes views of persons, events, living arrangements and social functions; meeting many important figures including the kings and queens of England, Italy and Belgium; amusing incidents of a first time traveler among royalty; disappointment over missing, due to illness, the session of the Peace Conference at which League of Nations was adopted.

HOFFMAN, HARRY ADOLPH, 1898-1972   5549

Rosen, Benton H., ed. "The Diary of Harry A. Hoffman." RHODE ISLAND JEWISH HISTORICAL NOTES 6 (1973):327-359.

1918-1919. War diary of a Jewish soldier from Providence; basic training at Fort Wetherill made especially grueling by brutally cold weather; good description of routines of training; at the front in France during German counteroffensive of July 1918, with brief but graphic notes of marches and trench warfare; news of action in other regions; enjoyment of such rare and modest treats as baths and hot biscuits; news of armistice; "Slept last night, oh so beautifully. No shells to worry about, no guns to haunt my dreams"; references to various comrades; an unpretentious and moving diary.

IRVIN, FRANCIS L.   5550

In FRANCIS L. "SPIKE" IRVIN'S WAR DIARY AND THE HISTORY OF THE 148TH AERO SQUADRON AVIATION SECTION, by William

P. Taylor and F.L. Irvin, pp. 1-26. Manhattan, Kan.: Aerospace Historian, 1974.

> 1918-1919. Sergeant-major's account of his service with the 148th; foul accommodations on troop ship; in camp near Winchester, England, touring, socializing with locals and noting inadequate foodstuffs; in France under constant bombardment at Bruay where the squadron was assigned to No. 40 Squadron, R.A.F.; events, pilots' scores, casualties and leisure activities while stationed there and at other airfields near Dunkirk, Auxi-le-Chateau and Bapaume, etc.; visit to Paris; transfer to American front at Toul, attached to Second American Army; fraternizing with Germans at Metz after the surrender; at Colombey-les-Belles, working on squadron history; return home to Boston; brief but lively entries.

JONES, THEODORE K. 5551

Edwards, John Carver. "Sergeant Jones Goes to War." ARMY QUARTERLY AND DEFENSE JOURNAL 104, no. 1 (1973):61-71.

> Sep-Nov 1918. Extracts from the diary of a gunnery sergeant in the 320th Artillery, Eighty-Second Division, serving in France; the campaigns of St. Mihiel and the Argonne Forest.

KENNEY, GEORGE CHURCHILL 5552

"A Flier's Journal." AMERICAN HERITAGE 21, no. 1 (1969):46-57.

> 1918-1919. Extracts from journal of a flyer with the Army Signal Corps in France; high spirited and humorous; the hunting of a wild boar which turned out to be a peasant's pig; exciting accounts of photographic and combat missions, including crash landing when motor of his plane quit; recovery from wounds and return to flying.

KENT, ROCKWELL, 1882-1971 5553

WILDERNESS: A JOURNAL OF QUIET ADVENTURE IN ALASKA. New York: Putnam, 1920.

> Aug 1918-Mar 1919. Artist-adventurer's journal of life in a cabin on Fox Island with his nine-year-old son and an old prospector; daily exertions of survival, but a sense, too, of coziness and contentment; trips to Seward; notes on books, art, fatherhood, personal values.

GREENLAND JOURNAL. New York: I. Obolensky, 1962. 302 pp.

> 1931-1932. Adventures in Greenland of prolific author and artist; life, work, character of the people; moving vignettes of individuals, particularly of diarist's mistress; introspections and philosophical speculations.

LEE, BENJAMIN, 1894-1918 5554

BENJAMIN LEE, 2d: A RECORD GATHERED FROM LETTERS, NOTE-BOOKS, AND NARRATIVES OF HIS FRIENDS. By Mary Justice Chase. Boston: Cornhill, 1920. 333 pp. Diary, pp. 120-264.

> Jan-Sep 1918. Extracts from a navy aviator's diary; sailing to Liverpool on the NEW YORK; flying seaplanes for Naval Reserve Flying Corps; training and practice exercises; locating convoys; crash landing and being pulled from the sea near Plymouth; confiding to his diary details of illegal stunt flying.

MCELROY, JOHN LEE 5555

WAR DIARY OF JOHN LEE MCELROY. Camden, N.J.: Printed by Haddon Press, 1929. 50 pp.

> Sep 1918-Feb 1919. Diary of a first lieutenant in 315th Field Artillery, 155th Brigade; through Paris and Versailles to the front; the Metz offensive; incongruity of difficulty in getting food to the front but being sent champagne; clear details of positions; being in cold, drafty hospitals at Benoitevaux and Souilly for illness, not wounds; getting around France during crowded, postwar days; return to the United States on RIJNDAM and discharge at Camp Meade.

MAREK, GEORGE F. 5556

In OUR SOLDIERS SPEAK, by William Matthews and Dixon Wecter, pp. 271-275.

> Oct-Nov 1918. Diary of a seaman from Petersburg, Virginia, serving on the destroyer U.S.S. LUCE; convoy in the Atlantic; duties; sightseeing at Gibralter and Marseilles; submarine attacks and retaliation; sinking of H.M.S. BRITANNIA.

MEYER, ERNEST LOUIS, 1892-1953 5557

"HEY! YELLOWBACKS!" THE WAR DIARY OF A CONSCIENTIOUS OBJECTOR. New York: John Day, 1930. 209 pp. passim.

> Jul-Sep 1918. A few dated entries within the diaries and letters of a German-American political objector to military service in World War I; his expulsion from the University of Wisconsin and internment at camps Taylor and Sherman with Mennonites and other religious objectors; at Fort Leavenworth Penitentiary and in barracks confinement at Fort Riley; throughout, the suffering of abuse and torture and the deaths of some military prisoners.

MEYER, JACOB C. 5558

"Reflections of a Conscientious Objector in World War I." MENNONITE QUARTERLY REVIEW 41 (1967):79-96.

> Jul 1918-Jan 1919. Dated entries somewhat reconstructed from cryptic diaries and letters of a Wayne County, Ohio, Mennonite; interruption of Harvard graduate studies in history for internment at Camp Jackson, South Carolina; refusal to wear a uniform; pleading for the Amish to be exempt from shaving order; religious and scholarly reading; leading Bible study groups; references to Goshen College friends and events, fellow conscientious objectors and military personnel; a revealing diary of a future history professor at Goshen College and Western Reserve University.

PETERSON, IRA LEE, 1896- 5559

"Journal of a World War Veteran." WISCONSIN MAGAZINE OF HISTORY 8 (1924):199-220, 328-348.

> 1918-1919 (with gaps). Millard, Wisconsin, soldier's journal of service with the 128th Infantry in France; from New York on the COVINGTON; grueling marches, life in the trenches and offensives at Fismes and Verdun, with names of many casualties; his own wounds and treatment; Red Cross service prior to discharge.

PRATT, JOSEPH HYDE 5560

"Diary of Colonel Joseph Hyde Pratt, Commanding 105th Engineers, A.E.F." NORTH CAROLINA HISTORICAL REVIEW 1 (1924):35-70, 210-236, 344-380, 475-540; 2 (1925):117-144, 269-299.

May-Nov 1918. Letter-diary of an officer from Chapel Hill; by train for departure from Quebec on the transport TALTHYBIUS; fears of enemy submarine attack uppermost during Atlantic crossing; notes on England under wartime conditions; to France, with action in the Cassel area, thence to Ypres and the Poperinge Line; work on trenches, camps, gun emplacements, etc., and "laying the jumping off tape" before each battle, a dangerous procedure the diarist considered of dubious value; extensive travels in France, inspecting fortifications, with notes on devastation of various towns, especially Albert and St. Quentin; preparations for and charge through the Hindenburg Line and continuing action in the area.

ROBERTS, NORMAN   **5561**

In OUR SOLDIERS SPEAK, by William Matthews and Dixon Wecter, pp. 302-304.

Sep-Oct 1918. Extracts from diary of an Alexandria, Virginia, automobile mechanic, serving in the 168th Infantry, describing St. Mihiel offensive and a communion service in the Verdun woods.

RODERICK, MARY LOUISE ROCHESTER, 1889-1970   **5562**

A NIGHTINGALE IN THE TRENCHES. New York: Vantage Press, 1966. 289 pp.

1918-1920. Seattle, Washington, singer's volunteer tour of duty under YMCA National War Work Council, entertaining troops in France; singing in field hospitals and at the front lines; songs requested, including words to some popular army songs and poems; bombardments and other dangers; social life among French and American high command; marriage to Capt. David Morgan Roderick; a thoughtful and entertaining diary.

SERGEANT, ELIZABETH SHEPLEY, b. 1881   **5563**

SHADOW-SHAPES: THE JOURNAL OF A WOUNDED WOMAN. Boston and New York: Houghton Mifflin, 1920. 237 pp.

Oct 1918-May 1919. Account kept, probably for publication, by an American journalist who suffered compound fractures of both ankles on visit to battlefield of Mont-Bligny; emergency treatment at tent hospital, on train and at American Hospital of Paris at Neuilly; notes on numerous French and American visitors including Walter Lippmann; observations on doctors and nurses, the Red Cross, American soldiers and the hope they brought to France, the war and why it had to be; long analytical entries on the European situation, apprehension of postwar days, the arrival of President Wilson for the Paris Peace Conference and the ensuing dissension during negotiations.

SERONDE, JOSEPH   **5564**

"A Portuguese Cinema." ATLANTIC MONTHLY 125 (1920):676-687.

Nov 1918-Jan 1919. United States naval attache's account of diplomatic festivities in Lisbon celebrating the end of World War I, at first erroneously announced in the newspaper before the fact; the assassination of President Sidônio Paes and the brief revolution following, which attempted to restore former King Manuel to the throne; amusing but rather flippant and condescending.

SHERWOOD, ELMER W., 1897-   **5565**

In OUR SOLDIERS SPEAK, by William Matthews and Dixon Wecter, pp. 322-332.

In DIARY OF AMERICA, edited by Josef and Dorothy Berger, pp. 534-543.

Jul-Nov 1918. Extracts from Linton, Indiana, corporal's diary of campaign with the American Expeditionary Forces fighting with the Rainbow Division under Douglas MacArthur; battles at Chateau-Thierry, St. Mihiel and the Argonne; worry about his hospitalized horse; running across friends from his hometown; relishing the chance to clean up after days in the trenches; suffering when his comrades fell but carrying through with patriotic courage and flashes of humor.

SHOTWELL, JAMES THOMSON, 1874-1965   **5566**

AT THE PARIS PEACE CONFERENCE. New York: Macmillan, 1937. 344 pp. passim.

Dec 1918-Jul 1919. Diary of a Canadian-American historian and professor at Columbia describing his participation in the Paris Peace Conference; entries amid other material illustrative of the origins of economic and labor clauses of the peace treaties and providing a good picture of events, figures and debates of the Conference.

TAYLOR, LAURETTE, 1887-   **5567**

"THE GREATEST OF THESE---" New York: George H. Doran, 1918. 61 pp.

May-Jun 1918. Diary of an actress on tour to raise funds for the American Red Cross war effort; one night stands playing John Hartley Manners's OUT THERE in many major eastern and midwestern cities; uncomfortable train travel with little time between performances, humorous incidents, patriotism; raising over $600,000.

TUDURY, HENRY JETTON, 1885-1952   **5568**

Sullivan, Charles. "The Diary of Henry Jetton Tudury: Mississippi's Most Decorated Doughboy of World War I." JOURNAL OF MISSISSIPPI HISTORY 47 (1985):308-318.

1918-1919. Brief entries of Bay St. Louis war hero serving in France with the Fifty-ninth Infantry; action at the Marne, Verdun and Argonne Forest; exhausting marches; suffering a gas attack, which left him permanently impaired, at Chateau-Thierry; in Germany after the armistice; review of troops by General Pershing.

WHITE, VIOLA CHITTENDEN, 1890-1977   **5569**

PARTRIDGE IN A SWAMP: THE JOURNALS OF VIOLA C. WHITE. Edited by W. Storrs Lee. Taftsville, Vt.: Countryman Press, 1979. 255 pp.

1918-1941. Journals of a feminist poet, activist and literary scholar; homely daily events side by side with her thoughts on two world wars, reading, poetry and her own writing, political and economic issues, etc.; Peace party activities and opposition to United States entry into both wars; work on Socialist publications; experiences at McDowell Colony, Yaddo and Saratoga Springs; graduate work at Columbia University and doctorate at University of North Carolina; work as a librarian at Middlebury College; enjoyment of country walks and pageant of seasons in Vermont.

NOT FASTER THAN A WALK: A VERMONT NOTEBOOK. Middlebury: Middlebury College Press, 1939. 144 pp.

> 1930?-1931? Nature diary kept while she was a librarian at Middlebury; walks on the campus and surrounding countryside with sensitive notes on small details in the Thoreau manner; probably a condensation of several seasons.

WILSON, ELLIS E.   **5570**

"A Duffle Bag Diary of an American Red Cross Worker in France." ANNALS OF IOWA, 3d ser. 22 (1939-1941):64-76, 128-170, 201-247.

> Oct 1918-Jun 1919. Record kept by a Red Cross worker from Waterloo, Iowa; training and other preliminaries at Chicago, Sound Beach and Stamford, Connecticut, before departure for France on LA LORRAINE; work at St. Cyr and Paris, mainly supervising dispatching and maintenance of ambulances and other vehicles; visit of Woodrow Wilson to Paris; anecdotes about American soldiers, the French and Red Cross colleagues; bits of news about Peace Commission, Clemenceau, etc.; postwar sightseeing.

1919

ANON.   **5571**

THOSE WAR WOMEN. By one of them. New York: Coward-McCann, 1929. 283 pp.

> Feb-Aug 1919. Diary of an entertainer with the Women's Division of the American Expeditionary Forces in France just after World War I; chiefly a frivolous account of dining, dancing, outings and romances with officers.

ALLEN, HENRY TUREMAN, 1859-1930   **5572**

MY RHINELAND JOURNAL. Boston and New York: Houghton Mifflin, 1923. 591 pp.

> 1919-1923. Postwar journal of the commander of the American Army of Occupation in Germany; signing of Treaty of Versailles; celebrations in Paris and Brussels, thence to take up his post at Koblenz; mostly a record of complex diplomatic relations between the United States, Germany and France and their representatives, including French president Poincaré, Marshall Foch and American ambassadors Myron T. Herrick, Alanson B. Houghton and Hugh C. Wallace; diarist's concerns for the economic recovery of Europe; some social and family notes and such diversions as playing polo.

BANDHOLTZ, HARRY HILL, 1864-1925   **5573**

AN UNDIPLOMATIC DIARY, BY THE AMERICAN MEMBER OF THE INTER-ALLIED MILITARY MISSION TO HUNGARY. Edited by Fritz-Konrad Krüger. New York: Columbia University Press, 1933. 394 pp. Reprint. New York: AMS Press, 1966.

> Aug 1919-Feb 1920. Diary of an American general's participation in the mission to negotiate peace in Hungary and arrange for withdrawal of Rumanian troops; observations from a pro-Hungarian position; notes on proceedings and participation of British, French, Italian and other representatives, as well as United States colleagues Halsey E. Yates, Raymond Sheldon and James

T. Loree; social and cultural life in Budapest and enjoyment of opera, which he found in a surprisingly flourishing condition.

GOODHART, ARTHUR LEHMAN, 1891-   **5574**

POLAND AND THE MINORITY RACES. London: G. Allen & Unwin; New York: Brentano's, 1920. 194 pp.

> Jul-Sep 1919. Diary of Army captain appointed counsel to American Mission to Poland to investigate reported killing of Jews; long discourses on meetings with Jewish communities and Polish officials; impressive statesmanship of Ignace Paderewski; observing desperate economic conditions; hearing of persecutions and a variety of attitudes in individual cities; numerous national, religious and class conflicts of the Lithuanians, White Russians and Ruthenians with the new Polish state.

INMAN, ARTHUR CREW, 1895-1963   **5575**

THE INMAN DIARY: A PUBLIC AND PRIVATE CONFESSION. Edited by Daniel Aaron. Cambridge: Harvard University Press, 1985. 2 vols.

> 1919-1963. A diary of massive bulk, interest and importance kept by a wealthy and eccentric Boston invalid, a compulsive diarist who had "a curiosity about everything, perhaps an imagination," and hired informants to come and tell him about their lives, travels and events of the world outside his darkened cavern of an apartment, from which he emerged only for occasional chauffered forays in his 1919 open Cadillac; a private confession revealing his self-absorption, consuming desire to be famous, voyeuristic interest in the lives of others and some unattractive antipathies, including anti-Semitism; memories of his Atlanta childhood, references to his long-suffering wife, Evelyn Yates Inman, accounts of his dalliances with some of his women informants, and friendships, on his unusual terms, with a parade of interesting visitors and correspondents; a long-awaited publishing event providing a unique microcosm of much of American history, opinion and popular culture over four decades and a chronicle of a strange life which ended in suicide; a heroic editorial undertaking in which Inman's diaries had to be reduced to a fraction of the original without sacrificing their shape, diversity and unusual character.

MOFFAT, JAY PIERREPONT, 1896-1943   **5576**

THE MOFFAT PAPERS: SELECTIONS FROM THE DIPLOMATIC JOURNALS OF JAY PIERREPONT MOFFAT. Edited by Nancy Hooker. Cambridge, Mass.: Harvard University Press, 1956. 408 pp.

> 1919-1943. Extracts from journals of a diplomat whose career ranged from unsalaried apprentice secretary to full minister; detailed notes on his service in Poland, Japan, Switzerland, Turkey and Canada, with long periods in Washington, D.C.; analysis of the events and policies of two world wars and relations with a host of nations including Germany, Great Britain and France, as well as those in which he served; the League of Nations and various international meetings; extensive references to William C. Bullitt, Cordell Hull, Joseph Kennedy, Henry Stimson, Summer Welles and Franklin D. Roosevelt; marriage to Lilla Cabot Grew and a few pleasant notes on family life.

MORRIS, WALTER RIPTON, 1907-   **5577**

AMERICAN IN SEARCH OF A WAY. New York: Macmillan, 1942. 441 pp.

Extracts in SMALL VOICES, edited by Josef and Dorothy Berger, pp. 145-147.

1919-1942 (with gaps). Diaries kept from the age of twelve; brief childhood and adolescent notes, mainly of school problems, expanding into long introspective entries of youth and adulthood; romances, reading and intellectual aspirations; college and graduate school at University of Michigan, with considerable floundering in finding a focus for his interests and talents in music, writing and philosophy; feverish mental activity, as well as periods of depression "afraid to live and afraid to die" and "sick of my pale wanderings"; a seven year period in Gloversville, New York, while he tried to establish himself as a writer; political reflections, including a philosophical attraction to communism; reactions to war news; trips to New York City.

NOTEBOOK 2: BLACK RIVER. Englewood, N.J., 1949. 242 pp.

1942-1947. Writer's life, mainly at Englewood, New Jersey; endless introspections on life, art, literature, marriage and parenthood all mixed with the minutia of everyday existence; reactions to books read; trying to get his writing published.

THE JOURNAL OF A DISCARDED MAN. Englewood, N.J.: Knabe-North, 1965. 127 pp.

Dec. 1962-Jun 1963. Journal of graphic arts manager and writer experiencing unemployment caused by a company merger and frustrating months of discrimination because of his age in his search for a job; seeking advice and some comfort from fellow job seekers at the Forty Plus Club; filling the extra hours with errands and home chores; observations on the economic system and the value of work.

SHAW, LLEWELLYN DORRINGTON, 1904-1973   5578

Shaw, Alpha B., ed. "Dorry's Diary: Enderlin, North Dakota, in 1919." NORTH DAKOTA HISTORY 42, no. 3 (1975):19-25.

Apr-May 1919. Activities of a small town boy; hunting and trapping all manner of creatures, from frogs to muskrats; delivering newspapers, playing baseball, some school fights, a dance, class work and a Tarzan movie.

WILSON, EDMUND, 1895-1972   5579

THE TWENTIES: FROM NOTEBOOKS AND DIARIES OF THE PERIOD. Edited by Leon Edel. New York: Farrar, Straus, and Giroux, 1975. 557 pp.

1919-1929. Renowned author and critic's journals and working notebooks, interspersed with memoirs; an unsurpassed picture of the literary world of the twenties and life among the Greenwich Village literati, with extensive references to such friends as F. Scott Fitzgerald, John Peale Bishop, Edward E. Paramore, John Dos Passos, Elinor Wylie, etc.; an affair with Edna St. Vincent Millay and marriage to and divorce from Mary Blair; editorship of VANITY FAIR and NEW REPUBLIC; trips to Hollywood, Cape Cod, etc.; events of the day, including the Sacco and Vanzetti case; travel in Europe; intense creative effort and voracious reading mixed with bouts of depression and beginnings of a somewhat chaotic personal life.

THE THIRTIES: FROM NOTEBOOKS AND DIARIES OF THE PERIOD. Edited by Leon Edel. New York: Farrar, Straus, and Giroux, 1980. 753 pp.

1930-1940. Continued literary and personal pursuits of the increasingly acclaimed writer and critic; marriage to Margaret Can-

by, her death in an automobile accident, Wilson's "unsettled sexual life" and eventual marriage to Mary McCarthy; various literary activities, including work for the NEW REPUBLIC; travels throughout the United States observing effects of the Depression, especially among the locked-out coal miners in Pineville, Kentucky, whom he visited with Miner's Relief Committee; attendance at Roosevelt's inauguration; New Deal writings; exploration of communism, leading to visit to Russia on a Guggenheim Fellowship and publication of TO THE FINLAND STATION; interactions with Malcolm Cowley, E.E. Cummings, John Dos Passos, F. Scott Fitzgerald, Muriel Draper, Elizabeth Huling and others; life in New York City, Stamford, Connecticut, etc.

THE FORTIES: FROM NOTEBOOKS AND DIARIES OF THE PERIOD. Edited by Leon Edel. New York: Farrar, Straus and Giroux, 1983. 369 pp.

1940-1949. Continued reflections, notes for writing, literary friendships, etc., but few dated entries; divorce from Mary McCarthy and marriage to Elena Mumm Thornton; the deaths of F. Scott Fitzgerald and John Peale Bishop; a sad reunion with Edna St. Vincent Millay; extensive travels in Italy, where he met Santayana, Haiti and parts of America, including a visit among the Zuñi of New Mexico; war reporting for the NEW YORKER in England, Italy and Greece; life chiefly at Wellfleet, Cape Cod.

1920

BEST, MARY KINSLEY, b. 1885   5580

THE DIARY OF A PHYSICIAN'S WIFE. Rutherford, N.J.: Medical Economics, 1931. 1 vol., unpaged.

1920? Diary of the first year of medical practice, as seen by the doctor's rather doting wife; setting up an office and waiting room and hoping for patients, who trickled in rather slowly at first; house calls for a variety of ills and injuries; place of practice unspecified.

GUNNISON, ESTHER, 1893-1972   5581

Gunnerson, Dolores, ed. "Esther Gunnison: A Nebraskan at Oxford." NEBRASKA HISTORY 59 (1978):1-30 passim.

Nov 1920-Jul 1921. Extracts from diaries and letters of a young woman from Hamilton County who, upon graduation from Greeley State Teachers College, pursued her education at Oxford; to England on the LAPLAND; social life, courses and lectures at Oxford; tours of the colleges and throughout the area; trips to London for sightseeing, art, concerts, theater and literary sites, often with her former Greeley professor, Miss Frances Tobey; a delightful account of study and travel in England by an appreciative young American.

MARTIN, MARTHA, pseud.   5582

O RUGGED LAND OF GOLD. New York: Macmillan, 1953. 223 pp.

Extracts in REVELATIONS: DIARIES OF WOMEN, compiled by Mary J. Moffat, pp. 301-313.

1920? Undated diary kept during a winter alone in the wilderness of Alaska; being separated from her husband by a sudden storm; crawling back to her cabin after being injured in a landslide and tending her broken arm and leg; preparing to survive the severe winter weather; spending loving hours improvising a layette and giving birth to her baby alone; loneliness relieved by the joy of her baby daughter; her rescue by Indians arriving for their spring fish camp.

POWDERMAKER, HORTENSE   5583

In THE AMALGAMATED ILLUSTRATED ALMANAC, pp. 46-47. New York: Amalgamated Clothing Workers of America, 1924.

1920? Diary of two unspecified months recruiting women for Amalgamated Clothing Workers of America; joining social events to seek out leaders and gain their confidence.

ROBERTS, KENNETH LEWIS, 1885-1957   5584

I WANTED TO WRITE. New York: Doubleday, 1949. 471 pp.

1920? Autobiography containing many extracts from the diary of a journalist and writer of popular historical novels; his life as a young reporter in Boston and Europe and writing for military intelligence in Siberia; his decision to write fiction and account of the hard work, rewards and failures of a novelist's career; interesting research for his historical fiction which took him to Japan, Siberia, Italy, etc; social and intellectual life of Boston; relations with various publishers including George Horace Lorimer of the SATURDAY EVENING POST.

SHERIDAN, CLARE CONSUELA FREWEN, 1885-1970   5585

MAYFAIR TO MOSCOW. New York: Boni and Liveright, 1921. 239 pp.

RUSSIAN PORTRAITS. London: J. Cape, 1921. 239 pp.

Aug 1920-Jan 1921. Sculptor's diary of a trip from London to Moscow to execute portrait busts of Lenin, Trotsky and others at invitation of Lev Kamenev, Russian Communist leader, travel with Leonid Krassin, president of Soviet delegation to conclude trade treaty with England; political discussions during sittings, assessments of personalities, work and social life in Moscow; a unique view of Bolshevism.

MY AMERICAN DIARY. New York: Boni and Liveright, 1922. 359 pp.

Extracts in DIARY OF AMERICA, by Josef and Dorothy Berger. pp. 554-562.

Feb 1921-Jan 1922. In New York to complete publishing arrangements for MAYFAIR TO MOSCOW, lecturing on her Russian visit and experience, seeing artist's studios and society life; making primitive camping trip to Mexico with her six-year-old son, Dick; learning American filmmaking in Los Angeles as guest of Goldwyn studio; reunion with former Paris schoolmate who introduced her to Burlingame, California, and its superficial society; a vacation meeting with Charlie Chaplin.

1921

DUNBAR-NELSON, ALICE MOORE, 1875-1935   5586

GIVE US EACH DAY: THE DIARY OF ALICE DUNBAR-NELSON. Edited by Gloria T. Hull. New York: Norton, 1984. 480 pp.

1921-1931 (with gaps). Diary of black poet, clubwoman and political activist for black community; widow of poet Paul Dunbar and wife of Robert Nelson, struggling publisher of WILMINGTON ADVOCATE and later managing editor for WASHINGTON EAGLE; frequent notes on the financial plight of the former and of the column she wrote for the latter; activities in education, helping found the Industrial School For Colored Girls in Marshallton, Delaware, where she taught for a time and raising funds for Wilmington's Howar High School whose teachers were a large part of her social life; working for American Friends Inter-Racial Peace Committee and as a volunteer for several social service agencies; in demand as a speaker for women's clubs in the Washington, Baltimore and Philadelphia area; although constantly plagued by financial problems, the racism and sexism of the period, yet a part of a strong extended family and network of women friends who accomplished a great deal for the black community.

GOLDER, FRANK ALFRED, 1877-1929   5587

ON THE TRAIL OF THE RUSSIAN FAMINE. By Frank A. Golder and Lincoln Hutchinson. Stanford University, Calif.: Stanford University Press, 1927. 319 pp. Diary, pp. 27-126, 147-319.

1921-1923. Well-written impressions of member of American Relief Administration while traveling over much of Russia investigating best methods of relief from famine caused by drought; working against almost insurmountable obstacles, suspicious government, constant transportation delays, deceit and incompetence; traveling from Moscow headquarters to Riga, Samara, Astrakhan, the Ukraine, Petrograd, the Causcasus, South Russia and the Upper Volga.

HUTCHINSON, LINCOLN   5588

In ON THE TRAIL OF THE RUSSIAN FAMINE, by Frank A. Golder, pp. 127-146. Stanford University, Calif.: Stanford University Press, 1927.

Dec 1921-Jan 1922. With Frank Golder in the Ukraine as member of American Relief Administration supplying food for those suffering from famine in Russia; difficulties with the Ukrainian government which saw itself as an independent republic and not bound by Russian agreement for the A.R.A. to work in the whole country.

KOLB, ELLSWORTH L.   5589

Rusho, W.L., ed. "River Running 1921." UTAH HISTORICAL QUARTERLY 37 (1969):269-283.

Sep-Oct 1921. Diary of a boatman for United States Geological Survey mapping expedition through the dangerous Cataract Canyon of the Colorado; personnel, including Eugene Clyde LaRue, supplies and logistics of boating while surveying possible dam sites; notes and photographs of the area, which bisects the present Canyonlands National Park.

LONG, MARGARET, b. 1873   5590

THE SHADOW OF THE ARROW. Caldwell, Idaho: Caxton Printers, 1941. 310 pp. Rev. and enl. 1950. 354 pp.

Oct. 1921. A woman doctor's automobile trip through Death Valley with her friend Anne Martin, the first two women to venture into Death Valley alone: from Beatty, Nevada, and return through ghost town of Rhyolite, where they had some "ghostly experiences," to the Funeral Mountains, Furnace Creek, and across the Valley, camping en route; good descriptions of scenery and the moods of the desert.

MCGILL, VERNON   5591

DIARY OF A MOTOR JOURNEY FROM CHICAGO TO LOS ANGELES. Los Angeles: Grafton, 1922. 95 pp.

Oct 1921. Account of twenty-one day trip taken by diarist, his wife and daughter from Chicago to Los Angeles in a 1919 Wyllis Knight over Lincoln Highway and Santa Fe Trail; passing through Iowa, Nebraska, Kansas, Colorado, New Mexico and Arizona; daily entries covering scenery, towns, road quality, miles covered, car maintenance, sightseeing in Santa Fe and incidents along the way.

SLATE, EDITH ROHRBOUGH   5592

Slate, Edith Rohrbough and Howard, Geri Ellen, eds. "Our Automobile Trip to the West," OREGON HISTORICAL QUARTERLY 85 (1984):253-276.

May-Aug 1921. A woman's interesting diary of a move from Washington, D.C., to Alsea, Oregon, in a cozy and ingenious "house car" devised by her husband, Thomas Benton Slate; route, partly on Lincoln Highway; cooking, camping, care of children; problems with flat tires, unpaved and poorly marked roads; notes on scenery, towns and people en route, with diary ending in Nebraska when the vehicle overturned, damaged beyond repair, and the family was forced to continue by train.

WAYLAND, JOHN. W.   5593

"Marshall Foch Visits Richmond." VIRGINIA MAGAZINE OF HISTORY AND BIOGRAPHY 64 (1956):433-436.

Nov 1921. Extract covering visit of Marshall Ferdinand Foch to Richmond and the pageant staged in his honor; a parade of government dignitaries, brass bands, school cadets, Knights of Columbus, Red Cross nurses and "in due time and order were the Negro veterans."

1922

BEATON, CECIL WALTER HARDY, 1904-1980   5594

THE WANDERING YEARS; DIARIES: 1922-1939. London: Weidenfeld and Nicolson, 1961; Boston: Little, Brown, 1962. 387 pp.

THE YEARS BETWEEN; DIARIES: 1939-44. London: Weidenfeld and Nicolson, New York: Holt, Rinehart and Winston, 1965. 352 pp.

THE HAPPY YEARS; DIARIES: 1944-48. London: Weidenfeld and Nicolson, 1972. 248 pp.

THE STRENUOUS YEARS; DIARIES: 1948-55. London: Weidenfeld and Nicolson, 1973. 231 pp.

THE RESTLESS YEARS; DIARIES: 1955-63. London: Weidenfeld and Nicolson, 1976. 190 pp.

THE PARTING YEARS; DIARIES: 1963-74. London: Weidenfeld and Nicolson, 1978. 164 pp.

Abridgement. SELF PORTRAIT WITH FRIENDS: THE SELECTED DIARIES OF CECIL BEATON. Edited by Richard Buckle. New York: Times Books, 1979. 435 pp.

1922-1974. British photographer's witty and acerbic diaries; intimate portrayals of the glittering personalities of New York and Hollywood as subjects for his photography and as show business colleagues; costume design for MY FAIR LADY and GIGI; relationship with Greta Garbo; introspections of a man who was both public and private; extensive American content, as Beaton divided his productive years between the United States and Britain; an outstanding diary of a photographer, writer and theatrical designer.

CARROLL, GLADYS HASTY, 1904-   5595

TO REMEMBER FOREVER: THE JOURNAL OF A COLLEGE GIRL. Boston: Little, Brown, 1963. 306 pp. passim.

Aug 1922-Jun 1923. Bates College sophomore's journal written in long entries when she was at home during vacations to avoid anyone seeing it in her dormitory, interspersed with letters home, "to help me remember forever what went on and how I felt about it before my nineteenth birthday;" a combination of college life and friends, her aspirations to become a writer, a dramatic college closure and quarantine for scarlet fever; farm life in rural Maine with many warm descriptions and recollections of extended family members and events including the death and funeral of her grandfather.

ROMANOFF, ALEXIS LAWRENCE, 1892-1980   5596

DIARIES THROUGH WAR AND PEACE: ONE LIFE IN TWO WORLDS. Ithaca, N.Y.: Ithaca Heritage Books, 1977. 217 pp.

Feb-Mar 1922. Russian immigrant's brief impressions of America after arriving in New York from Shanghai.

Jul-Sep 1936. Embryologist's travel to international congresses in Germany, Denmark, Poland, and England giving papers on artificial incubation of birds' eggs; visiting universities, agricultural institutes and spending any leisure time in art museums.

Sep 1939-Apr 1940. A sabbatical from Cornell University to do research at Harvard; chiefly notes on libraries, laboratories, professors and research problems in biological sciences; news of the war; a professionally productive and satisfying period; brief notes while on leave at Yale; comparison of research methods and methods of teaching graduates at Harvard, Yale and Cornell.

Oct 1947-Jan 1948. Enjoying the resources of the Army Medical Library and the many art museums in Washington D.C., while on sabbatical.

WESTON, EDWARD, 1886-1958   5597

DAYBOOKS. Edited by Nancy Newhall. George Eastman House Monograph, no. 2. Rochester, N.Y.: George Eastman House, 1961-1966. 2 vols.

1922-1944 (with gaps). Photographer's private and personal journal, obviously an outlet for his emotions; his years in Mexico, with interest in the society and culture, particularly that of simple peasant people; references to Diego Rivera, Rafael Sala and other artists, to Senator Manuel Hernandez Galvan and to fellow-photographer Johan Hagemeyer; descriptions of bullfights, festivals, churches; return to California to life at Carmel and Point Lobos; personal and family affairs, great love for his sons, some references to women in his life; much on artistic and technical aspects of photography, attempts to explain his art and public reaction to it.

EDWARD WESTON; PHOTOGRAPHER: THE FLAME OF RECOGNITION. Edited by Nancy Newhall. New York: Grossman; Rochester, N.Y.: Aperture, 1965. 87 pp.

EDWARD WESTON: THE FLAME OF RECOGNITION. Edited by Nancy Newhall. New York: Aperture, 1971. 104 pp.

1922-1930. Extracts.

Extracts in MEN WITHOUT MASKS, by Michael Rubin, pp. 95-106.

1927-1944. Mainly a repetitious litany of love affairs past and present; occasional desire for permanence, but seeming inability to find it.

WIDTSOE, JOHN ANDREAS, b. 1872.   **5598**

Mortenson, A.R., ed. "A Journal of John A. Widtsoe." UTAH HISTORICAL QUARTERLY 23 (1955):195-231.

Sep 1922. Journal of an exploratory trip down the Colorado prior to and in connection with formation of the Colorado River Compact between states of the Colorado basin; travel with Utah State engineer R.E. Caldwell and others; a few notes on ranches and people en route; detailed descriptions of scenery, geology, camps, food and strategies of navigating the river; interesting as a document related to the history of water resource management, for its descriptions of many areas now submerged because of dams and for its comparison with John Wesley Powell's exploration.

1923

CROSBY, HARRY, 1898-1929   **5599**

SHADOWS OF THE SUN: THE DIARIES OF HARRY CROSBY. Edited by Edward B. Germain. Santa Barbara, Calif.: Black Sparrow Press, 1977. 304 pp.

1923-1929. Record of a suicidal poet's flirtation with death during expatriate life among Lost Generation writers in Paris and Spain; marriage, mistresses, use of opium, descriptions and introspections.

KENNEDY, ROSE FITZGERALD, 1890-   **5600**

TIMES TO REMEMBER. Garden City, N.Y.: Doubleday, 1974. 536 pp. passim.

1923-1970. Diary extracts within memoirs; her children's activities and antics; Boston politics and society; duties as wife of ambassador to England; involvement in election and presidency of her son John F. Kennedy; eightieth birthday celebration with Emperor Haile Selassie; her sustaining Catholic faith.

SMITH, BELLE HANNAH, 1882-1968   **5601**

Kuyper, Jerry, ed. "Belle's Diary," SOUTH DAKOTA REVIEW 16, no. 4 (1978-1979):79-88.

Apr-Jun 1923. Sanborn, Minnesota, farm wife's record of almost daily physical and verbal abuse by her husband, Jesse W. Howard, culminating in threats to kill her and himself; entries ending just before she left him and resumed her maiden name.

1924

FRASER, SALINE HARDEE   **5602**

Fraser, Marianne, ed. "One Long Day That Went on Forever." UTAH HISTORICAL QUARTERLY 48 (1980):379-389.

May 1924. A young girl's account, possibly reminiscence rather than diary, of an explosion at the Castle Gate Mine in Carbon County; the rescue operations and removal of bodies as she and other relatives of trapped miners waited through the day; casualties, including her father, Alma Nephi Hardee, and grandfather, Edward E. Jones.

HOWARD, ALICE STURTEVANT, b. 1878   **5603**

In THE YACHT "ALICE", by Henry Howard, pp. 111-189. Boston: Charles E. Lauriat, 1926.

Oct-Nov 1924. Diary kept by wife of Henry Howard and crew member of his yacht ALICE on maiden cruise from Staten Island, New York, to Miami, Florida, via inland waterways; negotiating locks and canals; seeking provisions and laundries in small villages along the way; enjoying the scenery and beautiful sunsets; taking care of business of American Merchant Marine Library Association.

MATTHIESSEN, FRANCIS OTTO, 1902-1950   **5604**

RAT AND THE DEVIL: JOURNAL LETTERS OF F.O. MATTHIESSEN AND RUSSELL CHENEY. Edited by Louis Hyde. Hamden, Conn.: Archon Books, 1978. 408 pp.

1924-1945. Unique journal in the form of letters between Harvard professor and literary critic Matthiessen and painter Cheney; homosexual love letters, as well as a record of enduring friendship and the creative processes of both; notes on friends, colleagues, places, teaching, writing and painting; Matthiessen's nervous breakdown and intimations of his eventual suicide.

MILLER, H. EARL, d. 1978   **5605**

"Edmonton Diary, 1924-1925." CONCORDIA HISTORICAL INSTITUTE QUARTERLY 54 (1981):74-81.

Oct 1924-Jul 1925. St. Louis Seminary student's experiences teaching at Concordia Junior College and preaching in local churches of the German Lutheran community at Edmonton, Alberta; by train from St. Louis and return, partly riding the rails; convention of the Christian and Missionary Alliance.

RICHARDS, EVA LOUISE ALVEY   **5606**

ARCTIC MOOD; A NARRATIVE OF ARCTIC ADVENTURES. Caldwell, Idaho: Caxton Printers, 1949. Journal, pp. 1-282 passim.

1924-1926. Journal extracts scattered throughout narrative of teacher's experiences at the Department of the Interior school in Wainwright, Alaska; teaching Eskimo children and serving as village midwife and nurse; descriptions of walrus and whale hunting; interesting vignettes of individual Eskimos and igloo life.

1925

BEEBE, CHARLES WILLIAM, 1877-1962   5607

THE ARCTURUS ADVENTURE: AN ACCOUNT OF THE NEW YORK ZOOLOGICAL SOCIETY'S FIRST OCEANOGRAPHIC EXPEDITION. New York and London: G.P. Putnam's Sons, 1926. 439 pp. Diary, pp. 384-425.

Feb-Jul 1925. Naturalist's record, augmented by entries of participant Ruth Rose, of a scientific voyage to the Galapagos Islands on the ARCTURUS; vivid descriptions of the plant, bird and animal wonders of the sea and various islands; an erupting volcano; investigation of the Sargasso Sea and Humboldt Current; notes on methods and equipment of oceanography; in port at St. George, Bermuda; a fine account notable for its literary style as well as scientific information.

FOSTER, LARIMORE, 1905-1925   5608

LARRY: THOUGHTS OF YOUTH. New York: Association Press, 1930; John Day, 1931. 152 pp. Diary, pp. 105-141.

Jun-Aug 1925. Diary kept by Ridgewood, New Jersey, youth, a promising student at Lafayette College, while on a ranch vacation in Arizona; working with families and cowboys on Flake and Turley ranches; camping, cow herding, breaking his own horse; a sense of initiation into manhood; admiration for his Mormon hosts and their religion; a celebration at Snowflake, Arizona; a reflective diary of a young man who was killed in a riding accident just before he was to return to college.

HEFFERNAN, LEO G., 1889-1956   5609

McMaster, R. K., ed. "Extracts from the Diary of Leo G. Heffernan: the Adventures of a Junior Military Aviator." AEROSPACE HISTORIAN 25, no. 2 (1978):91-102.

1925-1926 (with gaps). Extracts relating to military career from pioneer Army aviator's diary during schooling at Air Service Tactical School, Langley Field, Virginia, and Command and Staff School, Fort Leavenworth, Kansas; classes, marks, varied flying experiences including introduction to Martin Bomber and a balloon course; many classmates and officers mentioned; preceded by memoirs and concluding before completing school.

HOUGHTON, ADELAIDE LOUISE WELLINGTON,   5610
b. 1867

THE LONDON YEARS: THE DIARY OF ADELAIDE WELLINGTON HOUGHTON. New York: Privately printed at the Spiral Press, 1963. 274 pp.

1925-1929. Diary of wife of Alanson B. Houghton, ambassador to Britain; furnishing embassy and functioning as hostess for visits, teas, luncheons, parties, etc., frequently noting menus, stories told and gowns worn; decor of famous places; a vacation in Baden-Baden; return to New York, whereupon her husband lost a senatorial election; a pleasant diary in a polished, genteel style.

OLSEN, NILS ANDREAS, 1886-1940   5611

JOURNAL OF A TAMED BUREAUCRAT: NILS A. OLSEN AND THE BAE. Edited by Richard Lowitt. Ames: Iowa State University Press, 1980. 245 pp.

1925-1933. Journal of member and eventual chief of Bureau of Agricultural Economics; an inside picture of farm and economic policy formation during Coolidge, Hoover and early Roosevelt administrations; complex interactions with Henry C. Wallace, Henry A. Wallace, Arthur M. Hyde, Rexford G. Tugwell, Henry Morganthau, Jr., and others; activities of and Olsen's relations to the Federal Farm Board, Foreign Agricultural Service and Agricultural Adjustment Administration, in addition to his own bureau; a sense of frustration over confused and sometimes competing attempts of various agencies and bureaucrats to solve agricultural problems which began in the 1920's and worsened during the Depression; a useful economic and historical source.

SHERMAN, JANE, 1908-   5612

SOARING: THE DIARY AND LETTERS OF A DENISHAWN DANCER IN THE FAR EAST. Middletown, Conn.: Wesleyan University Press, 1976. 278 pp.

1925-1927. Exuberant and amusing diary, by the youngest member of the Denishawn Company, of a dance tour through the Orient; comments on Ruth St. Denis, Ted Shawn, and Doris Humphrey; theaters, hotels, sightseeing, performances and unfamiliar traveling conditions in Japan, China, India, Burma, Ceylon and Indonesia.

1926

BARTLETT, HARLEY HARRIS, 1886-1960   5613

THE HARLEY HARRIS BARTLETT DIARIES. Ann Arbor, Mich.: Privately published by K.L. Jones, 1975. 323 pp.

1926-1959. Diary of long-time professor of botany at the University of Michigan, director of the Botanical Gardens and collector of botanical specimens for the University Herbarium; academic life, faculty politics, including many references to President Alexander G. Ruthven and Ann Arbor social life; several botanical trips to the Philippines, with interesting notes on people and natural history, as well as to Haiti, Chile and Argentina; eclectic interests of a renaissance man who read widely and collected books, rarely missed a concert of the Detroit Symphony or a Michigan faculty recital and was an amateur musician; references to many of his graduate students, in whose academic and personal well-being he took a solicitous interest; World War II assignment directing an Army project in which servicemen conducted a Vegetational and Terrain Survey of Occupied Areas in the Pacific and Eastern Asia.

FUERTES, LOUIS AGASSIZ, 1874-1927   5614

ARTIST AND NATURALIST IN ETHIOPIA. By Louis A. Fuertes and Wilfred H. Osgood. Garden City, N.Y.: Doubleday, Doran, 1936. 249 pp.

Sep 1926-Apr 1927. Two views of a zoological expedition sponsored by Field Museum of Natural History and the CHICAGO DAILY NEWS, as depicted in diaries of expedition leaders, Fuertes, the artist and ornithologist, and Osgood, the mammologist; hiring and managing Ethiopian guides, with much bargaining over wages and wrangling between Christians and Moslems about division of tents and food; learning local lore and customs; meeting town and village leaders; in Addis Ababa for a reception by Prince Regent Ras Taffari, soon to become Haile Selassie; painting and collecting over four thousand specimens; notes on scenery, camps and wildlife of both northern and southern areas of a country not yet altered by European influences.

HRDLICKA, ALES, 1869-1943   **5615**

ALASKA DIARY. Lancaster, Pa.: Jacques Cattell Press, 1943. 414 pp.

1926-1931. Anthropologist's record of four Alaska expeditions sponsored by the Smithsonian Institution; notes on villages, physical types and measurements of Indians and Eskimos; customs, including much on burial; arts, archaeological sites, with excavation for skeletal remains in order to show how Asiatic man first came to western hemisphere; illnesses of Alaskan peoples; difficulties of travel, terrain and weather.

LANE, ROSE WILDER, 1886-1968   **5616**

TRAVELS WITH ZENOBIA. By Rose Wilder Lane and Helen Dore Boylston; edited by William Holtz. Columbia and London: University of Missouri Press, 1983. 117 pp. passim.

Feb-Nov 1926 (with gaps). Letter-diary kept by writer Rose Wilder Lane and her friend Helen Dore Boylston for Rose's mother, Laura Ingalls Wilder; an incredibly adventurous automobile journey from Paris to resettle in Albania; colorful, often humorous notes on people, inns and hotels, scenes, towns, etc.; the mechanics, literally and figuratively, of getting across France and Italy in Zenobia, their maroon Model T Ford; the amazing performance of the car over steep, potholed mountain roads in Italy and the sensations caused by Zenobia in villages where people had seldom seen cars; by boat across the Adriatic to Albania; ship to shore conveyance of Zenobia over narrow planks, with the grim Miss Boylston at the wheel and their French maid in hysterics on shore; setting up housekeeping in Albania in a venture which lasted less than two years; good descriptions of the country in a transition period, more military and controlled and less romantic than they recalled from an earlier trip.

LINDBERGH, ANNE MORROW, 1906-   **5617**

BRING ME A UNICORN. New York: Harcourt Brace Jovanovich, 1972. 259 pp. passim.

1926-1928. Young Englewood, New Jersey, woman's pleasant days, chiefly reading; sailing to Europe, with travels in France, Switzerland and England, sightseeing and shopping; student life at Smith College; aspirations to write; train travel to Mexico, where her father, Dwight Morrow, was ambassador; first meeting and plan to marry Charles A. Lindbergh; some personal, introspective outpourings to her diary.

HOUR OF GOLD, HOUR OF LEAD. New York: Harcourt Brace Jovanovich, 1973. 340 pp. passim.

1929-1932. The early years of her marriage and the difficulty of a shy woman adjusting to the publicity surrounding her famous aviator husband; learning to navigate, operate radio and take aerial photographs on survey flights while assisting to plan routes of Transcontinental Air Transport from New York to Los Angeles and Pan American Airways to Central and South America; tragic period of the kidnapping and murder of Charles, Jr., with the diary a means of releasing her grief.

LOCKED ROOMS AND OPEN DOORS. New York: Harcourt Brace Jovanovich, 1974. 352 pp. passim.

1933-1935. Readjustment after the kidnapping and murder of her first child, with trauma of testifying at the trial; search for privacy at the Morrow family estate in Englewood, New Jersey; birth of a second child; conflicting and painful emotions over own role and identity and the desire to do more than bask in her husband's fame; the rigors and even terrors of pioneer aviation, including transatlantic trip in a single engine seaplane mapping possible air routes; move to England; the cathartic importance of her diary.

THE FLOWER AND THE NETTLE. New York: Harcourt Brace Jovanovich, 1976. 605 pp. passim.

1936-1939. Her life in Europe, setting up homes in Kent, England, and on an island off the coast of Brittany; raising her children and accompanying Charles Lindbergh on official trips to Germany, Russia, India, etc.; a reflection of opinions current in embassies of Europe during prewar years; her own and her husband's reactions to Neville Chamberlain, Joseph Kennedy, George VI, etc., as well as Hitler and Göring; the difficulties of combining creative life as a writer with demands of marriage and child rearing, but determination to be unstinting with the needs of her family.

WAR WITHIN AND WITHOUT. New York: Harcourt Brace Jovanovich, 1980. 471 pp. passim.

1939-1944. Diaries covering the controversial period during which she and Charles Lindbergh lectured in support of an isolationist position toward United States involvement in World War II, with interesting glimpses of such like-minded leaders as John T. Flynn, Norman Thomas, Burton K. Wheeler and Joseph Kennedy; coping with the accusations of anti-Semitism and Nazi sympathies directed against her husband; family life with four children while living on Long Island, at Martha's Vineyard and Bloomfield Hills, Michigan; her growth as a woman and a writer.

MOTLEY, WILLARD, 1901-1965   **5618**

THE DIARIES OF WILLARD MOTLEY. Edited by Jerome Klinkowitz. Ames: Iowa State University Press, 1979. 196 pp.

1926-1943. Extracts from voluminous diaries of a black novelist, with entries beginning at age sixteen; life in a racially mixed Chicago neighborhood; school, sports, friendships, part-time work, literary club, etc.; youthful journeys to New York and Los Angeles, traveling mostly by bicycle, recording many experiences that influenced his stories and novels, including a jail stint in Cheyenne, Wyoming described at length; observations of Depression America and his own difficulties of survival on odd jobs while trying to write and sell his work; love problems and loneliness; reactions to books; personal opinions and philosophy.

1927

GOLDFELD, ABRAHAM   **5619**

THE DIARY OF A HOUSING MANAGER. Chicago: National Association of Housing Officials, 1938. 115 pp.

1927-1930. Diary of a young New York social worker in charge of managing Lavanburg Homes, a low income housing project on Manhattan's Lower East Side, financed by philanthropist Fred L. Lavanburg; management problems, maintenance of building, complaints of tenants, supervision of recreation and club activities of children and adults, referral of some needs to other social agencies; touching and personal, providing a microcosm of the sub-culture of Jewish immigrant poor, as well as urban social work.

HARRISON, JUANITA   **5620**

MY GREAT, WIDE, BEAUTIFUL WORLD. Arranged and prefaced by Mildred Morris. New York: Macmillan, 1936. 318 pp.

1927-1934. A black woman's leisurely travels around the world, often working her way as a maid; frank and colorful notes on London and Paris, most of the European countries, Turkey, India, China, Japan, etc.; traveling and staying in homes, small hotels or the YWCA; exuberant enjoyment of people, scenes, food, customs; appreciation of kindnesses shown her almost everywhere; adventures which no affluent tourist could ever buy described by a naive but natural writer; an outstanding travel diary, popular in its time.

"My Great, Wide, Beautiful World." ATLANTIC MONTHLY 156 (1935):434-443, 601-612.

1927-1935. Extracts.

In A DAY AT A TIME, edited by Margo Culley, pp. 223-225.

1935. Extract of discovering the excitement of Hawaii.

MEDRICK, GEORGE, 1893-   **5621**

Filippelli, Ronald L., ed. "Diary of a Strike: George Hedrick and the Coal Strike of 1927 in Western Pennsylvania." PENNSYLVANIA HISTORY 43 (1976):252-266.

Mar-Oct. 1927. Extracts from the diary of a Yugoslavian immigrant who became a coal miner and organizer for the United Mine Workers of America; travel throughout Allegheny, Fayette and Westmoreland counties to promote support for the strike, talking to striking miners and "scabs," meeting with Croatian and Serbian societies, etc.

1928

BARTHOLOMEW, ORLAND, 1899-1957   **5622**

In HIGH ODYSSEY, by Eugene A. Rose, pp. 153-154. Berkeley, Calif.: Howell-North Books, 1974.

Dec 1928-Apr 1929 (with gaps). Brief extracts of the first solo winter assault of Mount Whitney and the Muir Trail, an impressive feat of mountaineering skiing; notes on animal life, snow and weather conditions, temperatures.

BYRD, RICHARD EVELYN, 1888-1957   **5623**

LITTLE AMERICA, AERIAL EXPLORATION IN THE ANTARCTIC, THE FLIGHT TO THE SOUTH POLE. New York and London: G.P. Putnam's Sons, 1930. 422 pp. passim.

Sep 1928-Feb 1929. Establishment of the navy base at Little America, Antarctica; exploration involving ships, dog sleds and finally airplanes; geological work under Dr. Laurence M. Gould and weather observations; radio communication and the first flight over the South Pole; a good picture of the routine and discipline of Antarctic life, with strategies for surviving cold, pain and boredom; description of clothing, scientific equipment, food; personal glimpses of responsibilities and difficulties of leadership under harrowing conditions.

DISCOVERY: THE STORY OF THE SECOND BYRD ANTARCTIC EXPEDITION. New York: G.P. Putnam's sons, 1935. 395 pp. passim.

1932-1934. Extracts, within narrative, of Byrd's second expedition to the Antarctic; outfitting of ships BEAR OF OAKLAND and JACOB RUPPERT and voyage; journey by dog sled and tractor to Little America with explorations and scientific work from that base, including Byrd's winter alone at Advance Weather Base, closer to the South Pole; a few aerial operations.

ALONE. New York: G.P. Putnam's Sons, 1938. 296 pp. passim.

Mar-Aug 1933. Byrd's winter alone at Advance Weather Base between Little America and the South Pole; partly scientific, with much on Antarctic meteorology, and partly personal and philosophical; an important document of endurance and survival written up four years later, but containing large unaltered portions of the original diary.

DARBINIAN, REUBEN, 1883-1968   **5624**

Tashjian, James H., ed. "Two Newly-Discovered English Language Journals." ARMENIAN REVIEW 33 (1980):246-268; 34 (1981):147-173, 389-402.

1928-1932 (with gaps). Journals undertaken because "I have a very acute desire to speak and to write correct English" of an Armenian immigrant who was the longtime editor of the Armenian HAIRENIK DAILY of Boston; reactions to books, plays and politics, particularly the Hoover-Smith presidential campaign; Armenian news, people and causes; resignation from the HAIRENIK followed by unemployment and severe depression; suicide of his stepson, a promising pianist, and its disastrous effect on his depressive tendencies, marriage and social life; resumption of his post with the HAIRENIK; speaking engagements, with outlines and texts of speeches and editorials.

GREEN, JULIEN, 1900-   **5625**

DIARY, 1928-1957. Selected by Kurt Wolff. Translated by Anne Green. New York: Harcourt, Brace & World, 1964. 313 pp.

1928-1957. Extracts from the voluminous and introspective diaries of French novelist born in Paris of American parents; mostly his life and associations there, with references to André Gide, Gertrude Stein and others; remarks on books, music, art, the writer's task and, above all, his religious struggle, involving a return to Catholicism; trips to the United States with visits to New York, Washington, D.C., Baltimore, Savannah, etc., and to several universities where he lectured; important as a religious document and for the view it provides of Paris intellectual life over several decades.

LOW, ANN MARIE RIEBE, 1912-   **5626**

DUST BOWL DIARY. Lincoln: University of Nebraska Press, 1984. 188 pp.

1928-1937. Record of a young girl growing up in North Dakota during years of drought; love of horseback riding in open spaces on the farm; living in town with mother, sister and brother to go to school during winter months when roads were impassable; blistering hot summers, blizzards in winter; raising poultry to help earn college tuition; notes on professors, courses and her part-time library work at Jamestown College; continuing severe dust storms until there was no crop at all the year she graduated from college; teaching in small schools for meager salaries which she used for sister's and brother's education; increasing dismay at further damage to the beautiful countryside caused by army engineers for the Missouri Diversion Project, Biological Survey men and Civilian Conservation Corps, all at odds and proposing different solutions to the impossible plight of farmers; sensitivity to the particular ruggedness of her Stony Brook country and the people around her who loved it; a view at once of drought, the Depression, government programs and a young woman's maturing.

ROBERTS, DANIEL A., 1884-1974   5627

Roberts, Daniel J., ed. "A Chicago Political Diary." ILLINOIS STATE HISTORICAL SOCIETY JOURNAL 71 (1978):30-56.

> 1928-1929 (with gaps). Extracts from diary of an attorney for the West Chicago Park Commissioners, ward worker and friend of John Dill Robertson, Republican candidate for mayor of Chicago; complicated ward politics, machinations and rivalries; notes on Mayor William Hale Thompson, Thomas Curran, Fred Lundin and other Chicago political figures; meetings of the West Parks Board; many speaking engagements in connection with parks and city politics; various legal cases; awarding of contracts for extensive improvements to Humboldt Park, etc.

STANTON, MADELINE EARLE, 1898-1980   5628

Thomson, Elizabeth H., ed. "Madeline Earle Stanton, Disciple." JOURNAL OF THE HISTORY OF MEDICINE AND ALLIED SCIENCE 36 (1981):151-167.

> 1928-1933. Extracts from the diary of the longtime librarian at the Yale Medical Historical Library; entries made during her years as secretary to the pioneer neurosurgeon Harvey Cushing while at Harvard; scheduling patients, coordinating a large staff, managing his correspondence, helping with research and writing and putting up with his occasionally bad temper; reports on some of his surgical successes and failures; long, demanding workdays followed by care of her ill mother at home, with little time for social life; frequent money worries; moments of depression, leading to the anguished question: "Can anything be lonelier than the inarticulate woman?"; a keen interest in books and the beginnings of Dr. Cushing's medical history collection which became the basis of the Medical Historical Library; the record of a woman who had quietly become indispensible to a great man with little financial or personal reward.

1929

BLANTON, SMILEY, 1882-1966   5629

DIARY OF MY ANALYSIS WITH SIGMUND FREUD. New York: Hawthorn Books, 1971. 141 pp.

> Sep 1929-Jun 1930, 1935-1938 (with gaps). American psychiatrist's partial record of his initial analysis with Freud and further analysis and studies with him in Berchtesgaden and Vienna; an interesting revelation of Freud's methods during a period when he accepted as patients only those who planned to become analysts themselves; dreams and other content of the sessions; conversations indicative of friendship between the two; discussions of Jewish identity, etc.; awareness of the ominous increase of anti-Semitism in Germany and Austria.

JEFFERS, UNA CALL   5630

In TWO CONSOLATIONS, by Robinson Jeffers, pp. 1-2. San Mateo: Quercus Press, 1940.

> Oct 1929. Extract from journal of poet's wife describing Kelmscott, the home of William Morris.

McNEELY, SYLVIA, 1919-   5631

DIARY OF SYLVIA McNEELY. New York and Toronto: Longmans, Green, 1931. 121 pp.

Extracts in SMALL VOICES, by Josef and Dorothy Berger, pp. 112-117.

> 1929. Ten-year-old's frank and charming "diary" of daily life with her family; school, vacations, friends, enemies and "dum boys."

MARSHALL, ROBERT   5632

"Journal of Exploration of the North Fork of the Koyukuk by Al Retzlaf and Bob Marshall." FRONTIER: A MAGAZINE OF THE NORTH-WEST 11 (1931):163-175.

> Jul-Aug 1929. Exploration of the Koyukuk and Hammond river drainages and Brooks Range in northern Alaska; route terrain, especially difficult in swamps with pack horses; good descriptions of views from the Brooks Range; torment by mosquitoes and problems with bears, unfordable rivers and suddenly rising water; notes on geology and natural history of the area; an interesting and rugged adventure.

MEIGHEN, JOHN F.D., 1877-1957   5633

In BRING WARM CLOTHES: LETTERS AND PHOTOS FROM MINNESOTA'S PAST, collected by Peg Meier, pp. 288-298.

> 1929-1941. Extracts from Albert Lea, Minnesota, lawyer's diaries; family and business affairs showing little disruption during the Depression; travels to Europe and California; attendance at Democratic national conventions in 1932 and 1936; interest in radio, movies, national and world news.

OWEN, RUSSELL, 1889-1952   5634

SOUTH OF THE SUN. New York: John Day, 1934. 288 pp.

> 1929-1930. NEW YORK TIMES reporter's diary of the first Byrd South Pole Expedition; living and working in close quarters at Little America, with effects of long confinement and darkness of the Antarctic winter; boredom, pranks, quarrels, kindnesses and "interesting manifestations of character" among the international mixture of explorers, scientists, aviators, mechanics and dog drivers; informative notes on Antarctic aviation, especially the actual Polar flight, which diarist monitored from base camp by radio and transmitted to the TIMES; subsequent interviews with flyers; difficulties of finally getting off the ice barrier onto homebound ship.

1930

CHIDECKEL, MAURICE, b. 1876   5635

LEAVES FROM A DOCTOR'S DIARY. Nutley, N.J.: Hoffmann-La Roche and Roche-Organon, 1940. 99 pp.

1930? Baltimore physician's general practice experiences; entertaining descriptions of a wide range of patients; many humorous retorts from both the doctor and his patients.

DAVIS, LAVINIA RIKER, 1909-1961   5636

JOURNALS. New York: Privately printed, 1964. 168 pp.

1930-1951. Writer's journal; writing as a creative endeavor and ideas for books; family affairs and events; observations on people, ordinary and amusing incidents, overheard conversations, seasons, New York apartment living, Cape Cod summers and country living; uniqueness of reading aloud.

DEVOE, ALAN   5637

PHUDD HILL. New York: J. Messner, 1937. 153 pp. Journal, pp. 121-132.

Oct 1930? Extracts from nature writer's journal; mini-essays evoked by his daily walk in unidentified autumn woods.

KAHN, EDGAR A.   5638

JOURNAL OF A NEUROSURGEON. Springfield, Ill.: C. Thomas, 1972. 172 pp. Journal, pp. 37-60.

Feb-Dec 1930. Journal extracts of physician and professor at Michigan's University Hospital Neurosurgical Clinic; a picture of neurosurgery in its early days, the difficulties and limited results.

SETON, GRACE GALLATIN, 1872-1959   5639

LOG OF THE "LOOK-SEE": A HALF-YEAR IN THE WILDS OF MATTO GROSSO AND THE PARAGUAYAN FOREST, OVER THE ANDES TO PERU. London: Hurst & Blackett, 1932. 281 pp.

MAGIC WATERS: THROUGH THE WILDS OF MATTO GROSSO AND BEYOND, AUTOBIOGRAPHICAL LOG OF THE "LOOK-SEE." New York: E.P. Dutton, 1933. 281 pp.

Jun-Oct 1930? Diary of historian for a scientific expedition collecting specimens of insects, reptiles, birds and small animals; meeting and commenting on Brazilian women explorers; hazardous jungle camping and travel up Paraguay River through Mato Grosso; at conclusion of expedition continuing on alone over Andes, hunting with gun and camera, seeing Temple of the Sun in Bolivia and Lake Titicaca; attending First International Congress of Women in Chile; fascinating personal travel of an unescorted woman, with accounts of political, economic and business history.

1931

BARBOUR, MARY BIGELOW   5640

LEAVES FROM MY DIARY. Boston: Privately printed by Harvard University Press, 1932. 127 pp.

May-Jun 1931. Travel diary of a cruise through the Caribbean islands and through the Panama Canal to Acapulco and Baja California; meals, amenities, social life aboard ship and in port; some descriptions.

CARAWAY, HATTIE WYATT, 1878-1950   5641

SILENT HATTIE SPEAKS: THE PERSONAL JOURNAL OF SENATOR HATTIE CARAWAY. Edited by Diane D. Kincaid. Contributions in Women's Studies, no.9. Westport, Conn.: Greenwood Press, 1979. 151 pp.

Dec 1931-Jun 1932, Jan-Mar 1934. Journal of woman senator from Arkansas; initial impressions and work after assuming Senate seat upon the death of her husband and then becoming first woman to be elected to the Senate; comments, often uncomplimentary, on her colleagues' attire and long speeches; unexpected decision to run for re-election and the support of Huey Long; fascinating aspects of a curiously undistinguished Senate career.

MELVIN, LESLIE EDGAR   5642

Lee, Molly, ed. "I Beat the Arctic." ALASKA JOURNAL 13 (1983):3-64.

May 1931-Mar 1932. Diary of a young man's solo dogsled journey down the Arctic coast 1,500 miles, from Martin Point to Nome; on the HAZEL from Nome to Martin Point with August Masik and Harry Knudson; then the lonely, cold and difficult journey, sometimes losing his way, with "nothing but snow and mountains of ice in every direction", and often low on food and accepting timely help from hospitable Eskimos and far-flung settlers; arrival at Aarnout Castel's cabin on the brink of starvation; making igloos or sleeping on the ice; killing seals for himself and his dogs; at Barrow Point with his friend Oliver Morris, making a daring salvage expedition of the BAYCHINO; remainder of the journey to Nome, which included a mutiny by his hungry dogs.

POWERS, ELMER G., 1886-1942   5643

YEARS OF STRUGGLE: THE FARM DIARY OF ELMER G. POWERS. Coedited by H. Roger Grant and L. Edward Purcell. Ames: Iowa State University Press, 1976. 158 pp.

1931-1936. Substantial extracts from diary kept by Boone County, Iowa, farmer during disastrous years of drought and the Depression; regular farm work, low prices for crops and livestock, love of the soil and farm life; civic activities; foreclosures on farms; moods and reactions of diarist and his neighbors coping with tragedy; effects of New Deal legislation; an informative, articulate and touching record.

Grant, H. Roger and Purcell, L. Edward, eds. "A Year of Struggle." PALIMPSEST 57 (1976):14-28.

Jan-Sep 1936. Extracts illustrating multiple problems of 1936; the worst winter on record, followed by devastating drought; continued serious effects of the Depression.

1932

BOYD, JULIAN P.   5644

"The Southampton Meeting." NEW YORK STATE HISTORICAL ASSOCIATION PROCEEDINGS 31 (1933):5-12.

Oct-Nov 1932. Director's extracts from his diary of the annual meeting of the New York State Historical Association; a boat trip to Gardiners Island to see such historic sites as Conscience Point, where the first English settlers in New York landed, American Revolution and War of 1812 sites and an alleged spot where Captain Kidd buried a treasure; account of paper delivered and business transacted at the meeting.

CHEVALIER, STUART, 1879-1956   5645

A WINDOW ON BROADWAY: A JOURNAL OF OCCASIONAL NOTES ON THIS PRESENT SCENE AND WHAT MAY LIE BEYOND. Boston: Sherrill Press, 1936. 304 pp.

May-Oct 1932. A journal of one man's personal philosophy of living and dying; happiness in simplicity, human values, taking stock of ''the enduring satisfactions of life''; kept during period when he erroneously thought he had only a short time to live.

HATCH, OLIVIA PHELPS STOKES   5646

OLIVIA'S AFRICAN DIARY: CAPE TOWN TO CAIRO. Washington, D.C., 1980. 162 pp.

Jul-Dec 1932. Personal diary kept while on trip through Africa with her mother, her friend and photographer for the trip, Mary Marvin Breckinridge Patterson, and her father, Anson Phelps Stokes, who was visiting lecturer to the universities of the Union of South Africa and on tour of native schools and missions to study the general problem of race relations; congenial shipboard life on the WINCHESTER CASTLE to Cape Town; by automobile, train, riverboat and plane to universities, missions and sightseeing excursions in southern and eastern Africa; a good picture of British Africa in waning colonial period.

HURD, PETER, 1904-   5647

MY LAND IS THE SOUTHWEST: PETER HURD LETTERS AND JOURNALS. Edited by Robert Metzger. College Station: Texas A & M University Press, 1983. 408 pp. Diary pp. 85-108, 132-136, 261-334.

1932-1944 (with gaps). Scattered journal entries of artist and son-in-law of N.C. Wyeth, with some notes on Wyeth's influence on his early work and the social life at Chadds Ford, Pennsylvania; travel to Mexico to study Diego Rivera's procedures in fresco painting in anticipation of painting a mural for New Mexico Military Institute; service during World War II as artist-correspondent for LIFE magazine, first in England painting aircraft and airmen at their work; later authorized to travel anywhere the Air Transport Command could go; a few notes on Jamaica, Puerto Rico, South America, West Africa and Ascension Island.

LAMONT, CORLISS, 1902-   5648

RUSSIA DAY BY DAY: A TRAVEL DIARY. New York: Covici, Friede, 1933. 260 pp.

Jul-Sep 1932. Guided tour and diary of Russia by teacher and his wife, Margaret; sea travel aboard EUROPA and WELLAMO; by train and car through Leningrad, Moscow, Volga River and southern areas; visits to factories, collective farms and museums, with enthusiastic reports on Soviet policy and progress; frequent avowals of faith in the future of communism; dated entries, but a narrative, polemical style.

NOCK, ALBERT JAY, b. 1872?   5649

A JOURNAL OF THESE DAYS. New York: William Morrow, 1934. 309 pp.

1932-1933. Author's diary of impressions and observations on United States and European politics, government, political parties, economics, history, literature, music, nature, journalism, arts, travel to Europe and public figures.

JOURNAL OF FORGOTTEN DAYS. Hinsdale, Ill.: H. Regnery, 1948. 145 pp.

1934-1935. Continued commentary on American politics, education, religion, popular culture, journalism, books, and a changing society and traditions.

TIERNAN, LYNNE CARSON   5650

Glenn, Helen, ed. ''Journal of a Ranch Wife.'' FRONTIER AND MIDLAND 19 (1938-1939):258-276.

1932-1935 (with gaps). Diary of a young Montana ranch wife, begun on her wedding day, ''cowpuncher's wife, as was my mother before me''; some history of the ranch and area; humorous incidents and charming vignettes of family, ranch hands and neighbors; domestic and ranch work; the horrible summer of 1934 with its ''dust, wind, grasshoppers and starving, choking cattle''; a good picture of ranch life during the Depression.

1933

CLARK, EDITH K.O., 1881-1936   5651

''The Diary of Edith K.O. Clark.'' ANNALS OF WYOMING 39 (1967):217-244.

Extracts in A DAY AT A TIME, edited by Margo Culley, pp. 212-222.

Aug-Oct 1933, Jun-Sep 1934. Letter-diary of Buffalo, Wyoming, woman; building a summer log cabin on a homestead with the help of neighbors; horseback riding, hiking; enjoyment of both solitude and guests; good description of a harrowing forest fire; a breezy, colorful diary, giving an interesting picture of ranching and homesteading.

DODD, WILLIAM EDWARD, 1869-1940   5652

AMBASSADOR DODD'S DIARY. Edited by William E. Dodd, Jr. and Martha Dodd. New York: Harcourt, Brace, 1941. 464 pp. London: V. Gollancz, 1941. 452 pp.

1933-1938. Diplomatic and personal diary of University of Chicago historian and ambassador to Germany during the formative years of nazism; long, detailed entries indicating his concern about enthusiasm of many American visitors for what they regarded as progress under Hitler; evidence of increasing danger to Jews and the diarist's attempts to help Jewish intellectuals; conversations with or notes on such highly placed Nazis as Hitler, Goebbels, Göring and Von Neurath; references to Secretary of State Hull and other Americans; intimations of approaching war against incongruous backdrop of diplomatic social life, reading and intellectual interests; marvelous touches of observation and insight by a man who truly noticed things; an unselfserving, fascinating and significant diary.

FRANCIS, ROBERT, 1901-   5653

FROST: A TIME TO TALK. Amherst: University of Massachusetts, 1972. 100 pp.

1933-1935, 1950-1959. Poet's diary of his friendship and conversations with longtime mentor Robert Frost, mostly at Amherst; some biographical details, but mainly Frost's comments, both opinionated and wise, about poetry, people and the creative process; a delightful book in which the modest presence of the diarist is as interesting as his revelations of the great poet.

ICKES, HAROLD LE CLAIRE, 1874-1952   5654

THE SECRET DIARY OF HAROLD L. ICKES. New York: Simon and Schuster, 1953. 3 vols. Reprint. Da Capo Press, 1974.

1933-1941. An exhaustive record of public service as secretary of the interior and head of the Public Works Administration under Roosevelt; of special interest for Depression years, New Deal programs and early environmental and conservationist concerns, especially of Forest Service; clashes with business interests; prewar developments in Europe and Asia and early years of World War II; the Supreme Court; extensive notes on such influential Americans as Thomas G. Corcoran, James A. Farley, Felix Frankfurter, William Randolph Hearst, Harry L. Hopkins, Edward J. Kelly, Joseph P. Kennedy, Alfred M. Landon, Henry Morganthau, Jr., Gifford Pinchot, Franklin Delano Roosevelt, Henry A. Wallace, Benjamin V. Cohen, William O. Douglas, John Nance Garner, Cordell Hull, Fiorello H. La Guardia, John L. Lewis, Frank Murphy, Robert H. Jackson, Frank Knox, Ross T. McIntire, Frances Perkins, Henry L. Stimson, Wendell L. Wilkie and a host of other officials of all kinds; analysis, also, of activities of Hitler, Mussolini, Chamberlain, Churchill and other international figures; a major source for the Roosevelt years.

Extracts in DIARY OF AMERICA, edited by Josef and Dorothy Berger, pp. 585-593; TREASURY OF THE WORLD'S GREATEST DIARIES, edited by Philip Dunaway, pp. 394-401.

1933-1936.

KIRSTEIN, LINCOLN, 1907-   5655

FOR JOHN MARTIN: ENTRIES FROM AN EARLY DIARY. Dance Perspectives, 54. New York: Dance Perspectives Foundation, 1973. 55 pp.

Jun-Aug 1933. Extracts from diary of the founder of American Ballet, which later became the New York City Ballet; early experiences in Paris and London trying to paint and write; working with Romola Nijinsky on a biography of her husband, Waslaw; frequent association with and advice from composer Virgil Thomson; works of and gossip about prominent figures in the Paris dance, art, music and literary scene; ominous signs of Nazi oppression of artists in Germany; squabbles between Balanchine and Edward James over the ballet season at the Savoy in London and plans to bring Balanchine to America; a formative period for the American Ballet.

LANDRETH, EARL   5656

WASHINGTON DIARIES. New York: Vantage Press, 1964. 335 pp.

1933-1935. Personal diary of army major and secretary to the Puerto Rico Hurricane Relief Commission; lecturing at the War College, committee work assessing time required for war

readiness in case of emergency; reactions to news of international and domestic politics; regular notes on bills wending their way through Congress; the inauguration of Franklin D. Roosevelt; diarist's distrust of New Deal; everyday family activities and social life, children's interests, his wins and losses at bridge and the prices of stamps added to his collection.

MARTIN, ANNA   5657

AROUND AND ABOUT ALASKA. New York: Vantage, 1959. 94 pp. Diary pp. 15-23, 32-44.

Jul 1933. Missionary teacher's vacation boat trip around the Kenai Peninsula in Alaska; via Cook Inlet to Seldovia on a friend's small boat; continuing on the ALEUTIAN, a freighter taking salmon to Kodiak; observing the commercial fishing industry, scenery and visiting a Baptist mission on Woody Island.

1943-1944 (with gaps). Extracts of experiences while teaching at Savoonga, a village on St. Lawrence Island; Fourth of July and Christmas celebrations; notes on Eskimo villages, walrus hunting and the emergency delivery of medical supplies dropped by plane.

NICOLSON, Sir HAROLD GEORGE, 1886-1968   5658

DIARIES AND LETTERS. Edited by Nigel Nicolson. New York: Athenum; London: Collins, 1966-1968. 3 vols. American diary, vol. 1.

Extracts in DIARIES AND LETTERS, 1930-1964, edited and condensed by Stanley Olson, 436 pp. passim. New York: Atheneum, 1980.

Jan-Mar 1933. American portion of much longer diary of an English historian; lecture tour of the United States with his wife, novelist Vita Sackville-West; a hectic, but successful trip; observations on American scenery and manners, ravages of the Depression; meetings with such celebrities as the Lindberghs.

Sep-Nov 1934, Jun-Aug 1935. Visits to the United States to work on a biography of lawyer and diplomat Dwight Morrow, father of Anne Morrow Lindbergh; stays mainly at Englewood, New Jersey, and North Haven, Maine.

WORTHINGTON, MARJORIE MUIR, 1900-1976   5659

THE STRANGE WORLD OF WILLIE SEABROOK, New York: Harcourt, Brace & World, 1966. 249 pp. passim.

1933-1935. Extracts from writer's diary in biographical work on her husband, Willie Seabrook, during his years of suffering from alcoholism; visiting him at Bloomingdale Asylum for the Insane in White Plains, New York; moving to a farm in Rhinebeck, New York,following his recovery, where they both could write, enjoy the country and visit New York galleries and artistic and literary friends; diarist's retreat into writing when Willie returned to drinking heavily, was obsessed with the supernatural and withdrew to a private cabin for his bizarre, mysterious, possibly sadistic experiments with hired women.

1934

ANON.   5660

"Journal of a Relief Investigator." SOCIAL WORK TODAY 4, no. 2 (1936-1937):19-21; no. 3, 12-13; no. 4, 17-19; no. 5, 15-16; no. 6, 17-18; no. 7, 17-18; no. 9, 21-22.

Oct 1934-May 1935. Extracts from the diary of a Depression era social worker serving as an investigator in the New York City Emergency Relief Bureau; travels on foot delivering rent checks, clothing, blankets, food tickets, etc., and investigating eligibility among Jewish, Slavic, Italian, Irish and black tenement dwellers; descriptions of clients and their apartments and of colleagues, with characterization of social workers as "worn, careless, unimpressed with ourselves and our jobs, hopeless and disgusted"; impatience with social service red tape, city politics and the failings of capitalism.

SHIRER, WILLIAM LAWRENCE, 1904-   **5661**

BERLIN DIARY: THE JOURNAL OF A FOREIGN CORRESPONDENT. New York: Knopf, 1941. 605 pp.

1934-1941. Graphic daily record of Hitler's rise to power and the approach and beginnings of World War II; Hitler's speeches and charismatic effect on audiences; German land-grabs; Shirer's contacts with Goebbels, Göring, etc., as well as with ordinary Germans, diplomats, fellow journalists and American dignitaries; events in England, Austria, France, Czechoslovakia, Poland, etc.; a growing sense of disaster and evil.

END OF A BERLIN DIARY. New York: A.A. Knopf, 1947. 369 pp.

1944-1945. The liberation of Paris; death and funeral of Roosevelt; last days of the war in Europe, as reported in San Francisco; Truman's radio speech and conditions of surrender; diarist's trip to Berlin to observe postwar conditions and converse with German people; portions of secret German documents which shed light on Franco's relations with Hitler, the Munich appeasement, invasion of Norway, etc; account by aviator Hanna Reitsch, as written by an American interrogator, of Hitler's last days in hiding; extensive details on Nuremberg trials; early hopes for success of United Nations.

YURKA, BLANCHE, 1877-1974   **5662**

BOHEMIAN GIRL: BLANCHE YURKA'S THEATRICAL LIFE. Athens: Ohio University Press, 1970. 306 pp. Diary, pp. 188-201.

Aug-Sep 1934. Diary of a trip to Russia with New York Drama League aboard SOVTORGFLOT SIBIA in tourist third class cabin; good-natured description of ship travel and passengers, impressions of Leningrad and its citizens, Moscow and various theater productions seen there.

1935

CRILE, GRACE MCBRIDE   **5663**

SKYWAYS TO A JUNGLE LABORATORY: AN AFRICAN ADVENTURE. New York: W. W. Norton, 1936. 240 pp.

Nov 1935-Jan 1936. Woman's diary of accompanying her husband, George Crile, surgeon and research scientist, to East Africa; a view of early airplane travel from London to Paris, Alexandria, Khartoum, Nairobi and Maji Moto Camp, the jungle laboratory in the Great Rift Valley; details of camp layout and routine; protecting themselves from insects; collecting, dissecting and keeping records on many species of animals and birds; dress, coiffures and dancing of Masai and Mbulu people.

EISENHOWER, DWIGHT DAVID, 1890-1969   **5664**

THE EISENHOWER DIARIES. Edited by Robert H. Ferrell. New York: W. W. Norton, 1981. 445 pp.

1935-1967 (with gaps). Sporadically kept diaries and random notes of the general and president covering his military and political career with a fair degree of frankness; prewar years in the Philippines under Douglas MacArthur; assisting George C. Marshall in reorganizing the War Department; command of United States forces in Italy and North Africa and then of Allied forces in Europe, with considerable information on Normandy invasion, victory and demobilization during and after World War II; presidency of Columbia University; work with NATO; his decision to run for president and two terms in office; less than full information on many issues and personages of his administration, but some revelation of his personality and values; brief references to Thomas E. Dewey, John Foster Dulles, Harry Truman, etc.

HARRISON, FRANCIS BURTON, 1873-1957   **5665**

ORIGINS OF THE PHILIPPINE REPUBLIC. Tangier: Powderhouse Press, 1951. 521 pp. Edited by Michael P. Onorato. Data Paper - Southeast Asia Program, Cornell University, no. 95. Ithaca, N.Y.: Southeast Asia Program, Deptment of Asian Studies, Cornell University, 1974. 258 pp.

1935-1944 (with gaps). Private diary of former American governor general of the Philippines; cordial reception on return as advisor to President Manuel L. Quezon during first years of Philippine Commonwealth; the inauguration of Quezon; observations on political events, jockeying for positions of importance in government and business, transportation needs, economic conditions and self-sufficiency versus foreign commerce; acting as advisor again to Quezon and government in exile during war years; in Quebec for Eighth Conference of the Institute of Pacific Relations at Mont Tremblant, with sometimes amusing character sketches of delegates, frank opinion on meaning of the Atlantic Charter and the need for self-determination in Asia; a fine diary of politicians in action.

ROBINSON, DOROTHY ATKINSON, b. 1892   **5666**

DIARY OF A SUBURBAN HOUSEWIFE. By Dorothy Blake, pseud. New York: W. Morrow, 1936.

Extracts in DIARY OF AMERICA, edited by Josef and Dorothy Berger, pp. 593-596.

Jan-Nov 1935. Diary of housewife and long-time editor of WOMAN'S DAY; family life in Manhasset, Long Island; reflections on household tasks, children, her marriage; quiet satisfactions of a secure life.

IT'S ALL IN THE FAMILY. By Dorothy Blake, pseud. New York: W. Morrow, 1943. 279 pp.

1941-1942. The effect of the outbreak of World War II on her family; daughter rushing home from college to marry her naval officer sweetheart who was called to duty; son volunteering for Air Corps; maintaining a strong patriotic spirit in spite of shortages and rationing.

WALLACE, HENRY AGARD, 1888-1965   **5667**

Lowitt, Richard, ed. "Henry A. Wallace and the 1935 Purge in the Department of Agriculture." AGRICULTURAL HISTORY 53 (1979):607-621.

Jan-Feb 1935. Agriculture secretary's notes relating to controversy over contract with cotton farmers involving tenant policy and the balance of rights and powers between farmers and their sharecroppers; the eventual dismissal of Jerome Frank and other liberal lawyers by Chester Davis of the Agricultural Adjustment Administration; reaction to legal opinions of Frank and Alger Hiss; activities and views of Paul Appleby and Rexford Tugwell; a glimpse of complicated machinations at high levels of government.

THE PRICE OF VISION: THE DIARY OF HENRY A. WALLACE. Edited by John Morton Blum. Boston: Houghton Mifflin, 1973. 707 pp.

1942-1946. Candid, well-written diary of idealistic and sometimes controversial American leader, first as New Deal secretary of agriculture, then as vice president under Roosevelt and secretary of commerce; inside views on presidents Roosevelt and Truman and others at top levels of government; domestic and foreign policy matters, especially the conduct of World War II and beginnings of cold war; fascinating 1944 tour of Siberia and China.

WOODLEY, WINIFRED, pseud. 5668

TWO AND THREE MAKE ONE. New York: Crown, 1956. 167 pp.

1935-1955 (with gaps). Writer's diary of her work and life in a suburb of New York with a busy husband and three active children whose personalities emerge in the activities recorded; diarist's uneasiness over her roles as "the would-be intellectual and writer, and the outwardly conventional female" and feelings of failing to be the perfect mother.

1936

CILIBERTI, CHARLES, 1906- 5669

BACKSTAIRS MISSION IN MOSCOW. New York: Booktab Press, 1947. 127 pp.

1936-1938. Diary kept during three terms of service in Russia as chauffeur for Ambassador and Mrs. Joseph Davies; making friends with Russian employees at the embassy, learning to live under constant surveillance of secret police and grim, tense suspicion everywhere and establishing a strange relationship with Russian guards assigned to the ambassador; observations on Moscow and Leningrad; glimpses of life style of Russian officials when taking the Davies to Molotov's and Livitnov's country estates; trying to sound out common people's views on government and returning home with a strong appreciation for American freedom.

CUSTER, HOWARD N. 5670

Custer, Dale H. "A Document on the Second Johnstown Flood." PENNSYLVANIA HISTORY 30 (1963):347-354.

Mar 1936. Extracts within article describing a serious flood of the Conemaugh River at Johnstown, resulting in twenty-seven deaths and much property damage.

DAVIES, JOSEPH EDWARD, 1876-1958 5671

MISSION TO MOSCOW. New York: Simon and Schuster, 1941. 659 pp.

1936-1941. Confidential dispatches to the State Department, official and personal diary of American ambassador to Soviet Union; first impressions of Moscow, rundown churches and palaces housing workers and soldiers, introduction to the Kremlin and making official calls; judicial system and trials; visiting and reporting on industrial regions and farming; outrage over German propaganda and religious persecutions; concern over general war situation in Europe; unexpected and surprising conference with Stalin while making formal final call on President Kalinen; frequent interaction with Maxim Litvinov, Soviet ambassador to the United States; personal notes about social, cultural and sports events; collecting Russian paintings, icons and sacred relics which he eventually gave to the University of Wisconsin.

DUNHAM, KATHERINE, 1910- 5672

KATHERINE DUNHAM'S JOURNEY TO ACCOMPONG. New York: H. Holt, 1946. 162 pp.

1936. Diary kept by an anthropology student and dancer during one month on a Julius Rosenwald Travel Fellowship to the West Indies to study dance anthropology; experiences in village of Accompong in Jamaica, home of small group of Maroon people; learning native lore, adapting to and adopting native customs; field notes on agriculture, religion, government, music, dance and influence of western culture; her initiation into a cult.

HALSEY, MARGARET, 1910- 5673

WITH MALICE TOWARD SOME. New York: Simon and Schuster, 1938. 278 pp.

May 1936-Jan 1937. Woman's diary kept while she was traveling in Sweden, Norway and France with her husband, Henry Simon, and during a sabbatical in England; visiting typical tourist spots, finding a house in Yeobridge, close to Henry's work at University College Southwest in Exeter and learning the local customs of an English village; exaggeratedly clever style overrun with metaphor.

KELLER, HELEN ADAMS, 1880-1968 5674

HELEN KELLER'S JOURNAL. London: M. Joseph, 1938. 296 pp. Garden City, N.Y.: Doubleday, Doran, 1938. 313 pp.

Nov 1936-Apr 1937. Journal kept on ship and in England, Scotland and Paris soon after the death of her childhood teacher Anne Sullivan Macy; observations on and memories of many notable people; political affairs, particularly abdication of Edward VIII and the rise of nazism; keen response to nature and books; religious reflections.

ROBESON, ESLANDA GOODE, 1896-1965 5675

AFRICAN JOURNEY. New York: John Day, 1945. 154 pp. Reprint. Westport, Conn.: Greenwood Press, 1972.

Extracts in A DAY AT A TIME, edited by Margo Culley, pp. 226-247.

May-Aug 1936. Diary of Paul Robeson's wife, an anthropology student on a trip to Africa with their six-year-old son Pauli; from London to South Africa on the WINCHESTER CASTLE, with comments on patronizing treatment by passengers; in Africa, observations on colonialism, racism, working conditions in mining camps, living conditions in South African locations, cities, and villages; game reserves in south and east Africa; especial enjoyment of African women and grateful acceptance of their care during illness; meeting many people in her "old country" and challenging the idea that there is a "primitive mind" in Africans.

TILLICH, PAUL, 1886-1965   **5676**

MY TRAVEL DIARY: 1936; BETWEEN TWO WORLDS. Edited by Jerald C. Brauer. Translated by Maria Pelikan. New York: Harper & Row, 1970. 192 pp.

Apr-Sep 1936. Interesting record of German theologian's first return to Europe after his escape from Nazi Germany; Atlantic crossing, with good picture of passengers and ship social life; participation in ecumenical conferences at Oxford and Edinburgh; lecturing and enjoying social life in England, but worrying about British naivete concerning Nazi threat to Europe; through Holland, France, and Switzerland, where he lectured, met with intellectuals, renewed friendships with fellow German exiles and garnered reports of religious conditions in Germany; enjoying food, wine, conversation, art, nature, etc.; reflections on the intellectual, cultural, theological and political climate of Europe.

WEBER, JULIA, 1911-   **5677**

MY COUNTRY SCHOOL DIARY: AN ADVENTURE IN CREATIVE TEACHING. New York and London: Harper & Brothers, 1946. 270 pp. Reprint. New York: Dell, 1970.

1936-1940. Diary of a teacher at Stony Grove School, New Jersey, a one-room school with all grades and a variety of abilities; developing group and individual learning projects geared to each child's needs, using the environment and the community; managing the care of the school building and grounds; proudly watching increased self-esteem of students and the cooperation of appreciative parents.

WILLIAMS, W.S.   **5678**

Hofsommer, Donovan L., ed. "Steel Plows and Iron Men: The Illinois Central Railroad and Iowa's Winter of 1936." ANNALS OF IOWA, 3d ser. 43 (1976):292-298.

Jan-Feb 1936. Superintendent's record of struggle to keep Illinois Central open across Iowa during a winter of unrelenting blizzards and subzero temperatures; constant need for snow plow trains and men hired as shovelers; embargo against shipping perishable goods and livestock; rescue of passengers by bobsled.

1937

BERLE, ADOLF AUGUSTUS, 1895-1971   **5679**

NAVIGATING THE RAPIDS. Edited by Beatrice B. Berle and Travis B. Jacobs. New York: Harcourt Brace Jovanovich, 1973. 859 pp. passim.

1937-1971. Papers containing extracts from diaries recording a life of private law practice and public service as assistant secretary of state for Latin American affairs, ambassador to Brazil, a member of Roosevelt's "Brain Trust" for formulating New Deal policy, chairman of Kennedy's Task Force on Latin America, professor of law at Columbia, a founder of the Liberal party and chairman of the board of the Twentieth Century Fund; interactions with presidents from Roosevelt through Johnson and most of the in-

fluential figures of their administrations; considerable detail on developments preceding World War II and formation of United States policy before, during and after the war; emergence of the cold war and concerns with Asia and the Soviet Union; Latin American affairs and relations, particularly with Brazil and Cuba; extensive national and international travels and detailed references to Cordell Hull, Sumner Welles, Fiorello La Guardia and others.

HALE, BETTY MAY   **5680**

MY TRIP TO EUROPE. San Francisco: W. Kibbee & Son, 1938. 315 pp.

Mar-Aug 1937. Thirteen-year-old California girl's bubbly diary of a memorable trip to Europe; sailing on the CONTE DE SAVOIA and how she occupied her time; sights, shops, entertainment and food in major cities of Italy, France, England, Belgium, Switzerland, Germany, Denmark, Sweden, Norway and Scotland, a highlight being the procession after the coronation of George VI in London; diary ending with a newly awakened recognition of other countries in the world and a patriotic flourish in appreciation of America.

LINDBERGH, CHARLES AUGUSTUS, 1902-1974   **5681**

THE WARTIME JOURNALS OF CHARLES A. LINDBERGH. New York: Harcourt, Brace, Jovanovich, 1970. 1038 pp.

1937-1945. Famous aviator's journal, beginning with inspection tour of European air forces, convincing him of the superiority of German air power; activities and observations in London, Paris and Berlin, with access to political, military and diplomatic leaders; recommending an essentially isolationist position toward Nazi Germany and making antiwar speeches, which led to the erosion of his enormous popularity and his resignation from the Air Force Reserves and National Advisory Committee for Aeronautics; resuming Air Force service at the outset of World War II, flying many combat missions in the Pacific and working with Henry Ford on the construction of bombers; personal notes including social and family life in England, France and United States with many references to his wife, Anne Morrow Lindbergh, and sensitive support for her work as a writer.

"From THE WARTIME JOURNALS OF CHARLES A. LINDBERGH." AMERICAN SCHOLAR 39 (1970):577-613.

Sep-Oct 1938. Extracts covering attitudes and events in London, Paris and Berlin; meetings with Ambassador Kennedy to discuss the threat of war and the "military aviation situation in Europe"; comments on British fascist, Sir Oswald Mosley, Lord and Lady Astor, Lloyd George, Chamberlain and Churchill; Lindbergh's concerns about Britain's preparedness, especially in air power; meetings in Paris with Ambassador Bullitt and Jean Monnet; a trip to Berlin to confer with aviation experts and tour aircraft factories; a long conversation with Göring.

SANDERSON, EZRA DWIGHT, 1878-1944   **5682**

Crimmins, Terence R., ed. "The Sanderson Family and International Relations." STUDIES IN SOVIET THOUGHT 21, no. 1 (1980):31-38.

Aug 1937. Diary of Cornell University professor of rural sociology and head of rural research unit of the Federal Emergency Relief Administration; record of a conference in England entitled "Enlightenment on the Principles of Soviet Life and Society," which he attended at the behest of Harry Hopkins of the Federal

Writers Project; summaries of and his personal reactions to lectures, particularly those of Nickolai Natuschen whose "open admiration of Marx was somewhat disquieting", and to open discussion from the floor, some of which Natuschen silenced if in disagreement with his position; diarist's reluctance to share the prevailing optimism of many Western intellectuals for the likelihood that the Soviet system soon would overtake the West in "technological and intellectual superiority."

SCHNITZER, EWALD W., 1910-   **5683**

SELECTED ADVENTURES OF MY FIRST FIFTY YEARS. Idyllwild, Calif.: Strawberry Valley Press, 1974. 149 pp. Diary, pp. 29-39, 95-100.

Dec 1937-Jan 1938. Putney, Vermont, teacher's camping trip made with two colleagues; a cold first night at Gettysburg; contrasting luxurious estates of Virginia with poor plantations of Deep South and oil rich Texas; by Ford automobile on the Pan American Highway to Mexico City; enjoying hospitality and advice of language professor Mr. Dillon at University of Mexico, Rivera murals in Mexico City and Cuernavaca, as well as Palace of Cortez and beautiful gardens there; relaxing on beach at Acapulco, climbing Mount Popocatepetl; return trip of 1400 miles in thirty-two hours of continuous driving.

Aug 1959. Excursion through Greece with a travel group; notes on antiquities; sharing present experiences and memories of past ones with a new young friend.

SMEDLEY, AGNES, 1894-1950   **5684**

CHINA FIGHTS BACK, AN AMERICAN WOMAN WITH THE EIGHTH ROUTE ARMY. New York: Vanguard, 1938. 282 pp. passim.

Aug 1937-Jan 1938. Compilation of letters and diaries of a journalist traveling with Chinese communist troops during the Second Sino-Japanese War; incredible hardships, hunger, exhaustion; suffering of civilians and soldiers from disease and wounds; notes on peasant culture and condition; diarist's confidence in communism to alleviate China's misery; somewhat narrative style.

TISA, JOHN   **5685**

RECALLING THE GOOD FIGHT: AN AUTOBIOGRAPHY OF THE SPANISH CIVIL WAR. South Hadley, Mass.: Bergin & Garvey, 1985. 235 pp.

1937-1939. Autobiography containing substantial extracts from the diary of a young volunteer from Camden, New Jersey, who fought on the side of the Republic, serving as historian of the International Brigade; his minimal training followed by battle experiences at the Ebro Front and elsewhere; vivid descriptions of action, civilian conditions and the bombardments of Barcelona and Madrid; references to other Americans in the International and Abraham Lincoln brigades and to a brief meeting with Ernest Hemingway.

1938

DERLETH, AUGUST WILLIAM, 1909-   **5686**

VILLAGE YEAR: A SAC PRAIRIE JOURNAL. New York: Coward-McCann, 1941. 313 pp.

1938?-1940? Wisconsin author's journal of life in the town of Sac Prairie; snatches of conversation in the harness shop, drug store and on the street; vignettes of local people; nature observations; a pleasant picture of village and farm life.

VILLAGE DAYBOOK: A SAC PRAIRIE JOURNAL. Chicago: Pellegrini & Cudahy, 1947. 306 pp.

Jan-Dec 1946? Naturalist's continued observations of people and nature at Sac Prairie, Wisconsin, and surrounding countryside; a good picture of village and rural life.

KURTZ, WILBUR G., 1882-1967   **5687**

Harwell, Richard B., ed. "Technical Adviser: The Making of GONE WITH THE WIND." ATLANTA HISTORICAL BULLETIN 22, no. 2 (1978):6-131. Diary, pp. 27-129.

1938-1939 (with gaps). Letter-diary, written for family back in Atlanta, by artist and Atlanta/Civil War history buff who, on Margaret Mitchell's recommendation, was appointed technical adviser for the making of GONE WITH THE WIND: lengthy, detailed descriptions of his work; historical accuracy and inaccuracy in the film and reasons for each; props, costumes, sets, southern accents, red soil, etc.; designing Twelve Oaks and Tara and filming the burning of Atlanta; the casting of Scarlett O'Hara; meetings with David Selznick, William C. Mengies, Sidney Howard, James Wong Howe, George Cukor and other film notables; train trips across the country, with notes on accomodations and Southwest scenery; sightseeing in New York City and observing an anti-Semitic incident; notes on southern California and the Hollywood scene; a fascinating inside view of the creation of an epic.

WILSON, HUGH ROBERT, 1885-1946   **5688**

A CAREER DIPLOMAT, THE THIRD CHAPTER: THE THIRD REICH. Edited by Hugh R. Wilson, Jr. New York: Vantage Press, 1961. 112 pp. Reprint. Westport, Conn.: Greenwood Press, 1973. Diary, pp. 61-74, 94-100.

Feb-Nov 1938. Diary of ambassador to Germany during period of growing tensions leading to World War II; official activities which included meeting von Ribbentrop, Hitler, Göring and ambassadors from other countries; the surprise presentation to Charles Lindbergh of Service Cross of the Order of the German Eagle with Star.

Jan-May 1940. Extracts covering service on Advisory Committee on Problems of Foreign Affairs just before Pearl Harbor; notes on Lindbergh's speech on inter-American policy.

WOLFE, THOMAS, 1900-1938   **5689**

A WESTERN JOURNAL: A DAILY LOG OF THE GREAT PARKS TRIP. Pittsburgh: University of Pittsburgh Press, 1951. 72 pp.

"A Western Journey." VIRGINIA QUARTERLY REVIEW 15 (1939):335-357.

Jun-Jul 1938. Novelist's automobile tour through national parks of western United States; fragmentary but highly descriptive notes; some introspections.

Cracroft, Richard H.. "Through Utah and the Western Parks: Thomas Wolfe's Farewell to America." UTAH HISTORICAL QUARTERLY 37 (1969):291-306.

Jun-Jul 1938. Article containing extracts mainly of the Utah portion of his trip; Utah parks, Salt Lake City and unflattering views of Mormons and their culture.

1939

DEKOBRA, MAURICE, b. 1885   **5690**

SEVEN YEARS AMONG FREE MEN. Translated from the French by Warre B. Wells. London: T.W. Laurie, 1948. 280 pp.

1939-1946. Paris correspondent's "medley of impressions" during residence in America; contrasts, comparisons, praise and criticism; war, love, gangsters, radio talk shows, soap operas, literary life, Hollywood film stars, producers and stories; strikes during war, trade unions, newspaper columnists, Daughters of the American Revolution, Pearl Harbor, attitudes of Americans toward France; sobering comments on the entry of the nuclear age.

MERTON, THOMAS, 1915-1968   **5691**

SECULAR JOURNAL. New York: Farrar, Straus & Cudahy; Dell, 1959. 270 pp.

1939-1941. Reflections of the young Merton, then writer and teacher; his reading and writing, experiences with Catholic work in Harlem, a sojourn in Cuba, reactions to daily events of World War II; first inclinations toward becoming a Trappist monk; the chronicle of a journey toward religious vocation.

THE SIGN OF JONAS. New York: Harcourt, Brace, 1953. 362 pp.

Extracts in TREASURY OF THE WORLD'S GREAT DIARIES, edited by Philip Dunaway, pp. 209-217.

1946-1950. Diary conveying a sense of gaiety and freedom within the silent confines of the Trappist Monastery of Gethsemane, Kentucky.

THE ASIAN JOURNAL OF THOMAS MERTON. Edited by Naomi Burton, Patrick Hart & James Laughlin. New York: New Directions, 1973. 445 pp.

Oct-Dec 1968. Trappist monk's journal of a trip to India, Thailand, Tibet and Sri Lanka to implement monastic renewal throughout the world; kaleidoscope of impressions, observations, sights, conversations, poetry, quotations; meetings with Buddhist monastics, including the Dalai Lama in Tibet; concerns with Asian religions, wisdom and meditation.

NEWLIN, DIKA, 1923-   **5692**

SCHOENBERG REMEMBERED. New York: Pendragon, 1980. 369 pp.

1939-1941. Extracts from diary of precocious piano and composition student studying with Arnold Schoenberg at the University of California at Los Angeles at age sixteen; private lessons in composition as well as classes in composition, counterpoint and form and analysis with classroom incidents recorded in considerable detail; progressing to teaching assistant for Schoenberg; his teaching method and style, his moods, health, superstitions and humor, often at the expense of the students; his family and warm hospitality of his home; a good view of mentor and student and the beginning of a lasting relationship.

TURNBULL, AGNES SLIGH, 1888-1982   **5693**

DEAR ME, LEAVES FROM THE DIARY OF AGNES SLIGH TURNBULL. New York: Macmillan, 1941. 170 pp.

1939-1941. Family and personal life of author who confesses an attraction to "women's work"; introspections, miscellaneous reminiscences recalled by daily events; vignettes of people in her small town and its social life; affectionate anecdotes about her husband, daughter and the family dog.

VANDENBERG, ARTHUR HENDRICK, 1884-1951   **5694**

THE PRIVATE PAPERS OF SENATOR VANDENBERG. Edited by Arthur H. Vandenberg, Jr. Boston: Houghton Mifflin, 1952. 599 pp. passim.

1939-1949. Extracts from the diaries of Republican senator from Michigan; an illuminating document of the war and postwar years, revealing Vandenberg's political philosophy as it evolved from isolationism to bipartisan internationalism; reactions to major issues and events of the time, including the Dumbarton Oaks Conference; activities and opinions as chairman of the Senate Committee on Foreign Affairs and as delegate to the 1945 United Nations Conference at San Francisco and signer of the charter; work toward Marshall Plan and establishment of NATO; notes on presidents Roosevelt and Truman and the major figures of their administrations.

WARD, ORLANDO   **5695**

Gugeler, Russell A. "George Marshall and Orlando Ward." PARAMETERS: JOURNAL OF THE U.S. ARMY WAR COLLEGE 13 (1983):28-42.

1939-1941. Article containing extracts relating to General Marshall during part of his tenure as army chief of staff, as recorded by secretary of the general staff of the War Department; notes on military policy, needs and funding; criticism of Secretary of War Henry L. Stimson as "a doddering old man" and disapproval of some of Roosevelt's other appointees; relationship of the War Department with Congress.

WILDER, THORNTON, 1897-1975   **5696**

THE JOURNALS OF THORNTON WILDER. Edited by Donald Gallup. New Haven: Yale University Press, 1985. 354 pp.

1939-1961 (with gaps). Selections from journals kept "to discipline my thinking" and containing reflections on a vast array of literary, philosophical, psychological and ethical topics; travels, lectures, and work on SKIN OF OUR TEETH and THE ALCESTIAD at the MacDowell Colony, but, in general, very little about the events, scenes and people around him; mostly a revelation of the hard work and creative processes of an important writer.

Kramer, Hilton, ed. "From the Journals of Thornton Wilder." THE NEW CRITERION 4, no. 2 (1985):6-23.

1940-1954. Extracts relating to the difficulties of writing THE SKIN OF OUR TEETH; extended comments on works of Faulkner, Poe, Genet, Joyce, etc.; a birthday party for Robert Frost.

1940

BRINNIN, JOHN MALCOLM, 1916-   5697

SEXTET: T.S. ELIOT & TRUMAN CAPOTE & OTHERS. New York: Delacorte Press/Seymour Lawrence, 1981. 278 pp. passim.

> 1940-1953? Sketches distilled from a journal kept over many years; literary and personal anecdotes on Eliot, Capote, the Sitwells, Alice B. Toklas, etc.; travels in England and the United States, especially the Southwest.

BRUCKBERGER, RAYMOND LEOPOLD, b. 1907   5698

ONE SKY TO SHARE: THE FRENCH AND AMERICAN JOURNALS OF RAYMOND LEOPOLD BRUCKBERGER. Translated by Dorothy C. Howell. New York: P.J. Kenedy, 1952. 248 pp.

> 1940-1951. French Dominican's journals of his experiences in wartime France as a commando chaplain and later chaplain to the French Resistance; capture by the Gestapo and escape; Allied victory and postwar period; a sojourn in North Africa; voyage to America on the ILE DE FRANCE, thence to a monastery at Winona, Minnesota, and travels through the United States; reflections on religion, American civilization and mores, etc.

HEIDE, DIRK VAN DER, pseud.   5699

In SMALL VOICES, by Josef and Dorothy Berger, pp. 16-20.

> May-Sep 1940. Extracts from Dutch boy's diary of terrible first days of World War II in Rotterdam and being sent to America to stay with an aunt and uncle. Translated from the Dutch.

ISHERWOOD, CHRISTOPHER   5700

MY GURU AND HIS DISCIPLE. New York: Farrar, Straus, Giroux, 1980. 338 pp., passim.

> 1940-1976 (with gaps). English writer's diary mainly revealing his religious experiences under the guidance of Swami Prabhavananda in Los Angeles; initial meeting through fellow pacifist Gerald Heard; life at the Vedanta Center, teachings of the Swami and private meditation; departure from monastic life in order to pursue homosexual relationships and work as a film writer, but continued friendship with the Swami over many years, including a trip to India together; many references to his friend W.H. Auden and other literary people.

LAWRENCE, DAVID, 1888-1973   5701

DIARY OF A WASHINGTON CORRESPONDENT. New York: Kinsey, 1942. 356 pp.

> 1940-1942. Mainly a letter-diary of "impressions written to a relatively small group of persons" with some newspaper columns interspersed; such national matters as the Lend-Lease Bill, repeal of the Neutrality Law, congressional battles over the Selective Service Act; public reaction to mobilization for and events of World War II; diarist's observations on the New Deal and his strong support for Roosevelt's foreign policy and the League of Nations.

LEE, RAYMOND ELIOT, 1886-1958   5702

THE LONDON JOURNAL OF GENERAL RAYMOND E. LEE. Edited by James Leutze. Boston: Little Brown, 1971. 489 pp.

> 1940-1941. Diary of a United States military attache in London, providing a good picture of the British under war conditions, particularly Londoners living through the Blitz; extensive references to Churchill's policies, speeches and conversations and to such Americans as Harry Hopkins, William J. Donovan, ambassadors Joseph P. Kennedy and John Gilbert Winant and Gen. George C. Marshall; his reactions to American hesitation to enter the war and to the policies and leadership of Roosevelt; comments on United States relations with Russia, Germany and, of course, Great Britain.

LOOMIS, CHARLES P.   5703

"A Farmhand's Diary." MENNONITE QUARTERLY REVIEW 53 (1979):235-256.

> May 1940. Diary of a Bureau of Agricultural Economics researcher studying community stability and farming methods of Old Order Amish in Lancaster County, Pennsylvania; work as a farmhand for Moses Lapp and Christian King, who were involved in restoring unproductive farms previously owned by non-Amish; daily chores, family, social and religious life, health problems and attitudes, especially work ethic, of Amish.

1941

BERENSON, BERNARD, 1865-1959   5704

RUMOUR AND REFLECTION. London: Constable, 1952. 399 pp.

RUMOUR AND REFLECTION. New York: Simon and Schuster, 1952. 461 pp.

> 1941-1944. Diary of eminent Jewish art historian, author, collector and advisor to dealers and collectors; his expatriate life in Italy during World War II, often in hiding from Fascist-Nazi gangs, protected by a number of Italian hosts, at considerable risk to themselves; thoughts on art, books, history, civilization, war, Jews; reflections on people, places, old age; report of sadistic destruction of Florence and pillage where his personal art treasures were stored but miraculously spared.

ONE YEAR'S READING FOR FUN. New York: Knopf, 1960. 166 pp.

> Jan-Dec 1942. Record of books read while in seclusion as an alien in Italy during World War II; many hours reading privately or aloud with his wife Mary and secretary Nicky Mariano in his enormous private library; thoughts and perceptive comments chiefly on history, philosophy and literature.

SUNSET AND TWILIGHT. Edited by Nicky Mariano. New York: Harcourt, Brace & World, 1963; London: H. Hamilton, 1964. 547 pp.

> 1947-1958. Thoughts on living and historical persons in and out of his life; annoyance with the number of people who wanted to meet him and aware that he would resent not being "asked for an audience"; the need, even in his declining days, to fulfill himself with writing; a picture of an aged intellectual.

THE PASSIONATE SIGHTSEER. New York: Simon and Schuster; London: Thames, 1960. 200 pp.

> 1947-1956. Comments on particular works of art revisited in museums in Rome, Venice, Sicily, Tripoli, Calabria, Ravenna and Florence.

BOND, CHARLES R.   **5705**

A FLYING TIGER'S DIARY. By Charles R. Bond, Jr., and Terry Anderson. The Centennial Series of the Association of Former Students of Texas A&M University, no. 15. College Station: Texas A&M University Press, 1984. 248 pp.

1941-1942. Diary of a member of the famed Flying Tigers of the American Volunteer Group under Col. Claire L. Chennault initially assisting the Chinese war effort against Japan; full, rather narrative entries describing training at Toungoo, Burma, news of the bombing of Pearl Harbor and preparations for action; transfer to K'un-ming, China, for a cooperative United States, British and Chinese defense of the Burma Road; detailed description of aerial war against the Japanese; notes on squadron morale and discipline, ''bull sessions,'' etc.; many references to his and others' relations with Chennault and with flyers Robert Neale, Robert Little and George Burgard; considerable information on the P-40 fighter plane.

BRERETON, LEWIS HYDE, 1890-1967   **5706**

THE BRERETON DIARIES: THE WAR IN THE AIR IN THE PACIFIC, MIDDLE EAST AND EUROPE. New York: William Morrow, 1946. 450 pp.

1941-1945. General Brereton's record of aerial operations in Java, Australia, India, Egypt, North Africa, England and France, with much technical information on various bombers and fighter planes; notes on specific units, particularly the Ninth Air Force, and on generals Henry Arnold, Omar N. Bradley, Dwight D. Eisenhower, Douglas MacArthur, George C. Marshall and George S. Patton.

COULTER, NATALIE STARK, 1898-   **5707**

FORBIDDEN DIARY: A RECORD OF WARTIME INTERNMENT. Edited by Lynn A. Bloom. American Women's Diary Series, 2. New York: B. Franklin, 1979. 546 pp.

1941-1945. A diary begun at her home in Baguio, Philippines, as a series of letters to her mother, but continued as a hidden daily record during her family's years of imprisonment by the Japanese; fairly mild treatment at Camp Holmes, near Baguio, with greatest problem inadequate food, the basic Japanese army ration, which was of very poor quality; additional food provided by their Filipino servants, who still lived in their house, and eventually by commander Rokuro Tomibe, who arranged safe arrival of Red Cross food, clothing and medicine; services of Nellie McKim, a missionary's daughter, as camp interpreter and diplomat; notes on interpersonal relations of internees and interactions with the Japanese; organization of internees into Men's Committee and Women's Committee, with diarist rankled at women's political subordination; food, sanitation, school, medicine and living quarters, with men and women segregated, thus preventing family units living together until the last days of imprisonment; move to the old Spanish prison hospital at Manila and chaotic days of American liberation, including personal visit by General MacArthur; return to United States on the KLIPFON-TEIN; memorial service on ship for the death of Roosevelt; arrival in San Francisco and train trip to Boston, where she spent months in the Marine Hospital recovering from malnutrition and accompanying deficiencies.

''Forbidden Diary.'' AMERICAN HERITAGE 30, no. 3 (1979):78-95.

1941-1945. Extracts showing hunger, boredom, illness and her efforts to maintain the health and morale of her children; accounts of Japanese torture of male captives.

COWARD, NOEL, 1899-1973   **5708**

THE NOEL COWARD DIARIES. Edited by Graham Payn and Sheridan Morley. Boston: Little, Brown, 1982. 698 pp.

1941-1969. Diaries of versatile English playwright, also actor, composer and director; American content mainly involving work in New York and Las Vegas; fascinating personal and professional comments on such movie and stage stars as Gertrude Lawrence, Vivien Leigh, Lawrence Olivier, Marlene Dietrich and John Gielgud; discrete references to homosexuality; notes on many plays and films; an engaging and unpretentious diary providing an intimate picture of film and theater in England and America.

EHLERS, REGINALD GORDON MORRIS, 1886-   **5709**

DIARY OF THE SHIP'S SURGEON. Boston: Meador, 1944. 182 pp.

Aug-Nov 1941. Daily account kept aboard the TYLER, a passenger liner fitted out as a cargo boat; voyage from Wilmington to the Orient, with stops at Shanghai, Hong Kong, Manila, Singapore, Penang and Honolulu, returning to San Francisco; lengthy entries recording weather, events on ship and sightseeing in port; his opinions of Chinese, Japanese, unions, fellow officers and crew; news reports, especially concerning United States-Japanese tensions; notes on his work, reading, venereal disease and drunkenness among crew and dissension among the ship's personnel.

GEREN, PAUL FRANCIS, 1917-   **5710**

BURMA DIARY. New York and London: Harper & Brothers, 1943. 57 pp.

Dec 1941-Jul 1942. Compassionate, introspective, contemplative interpretation of the grueling journey from Rangoon, Burma to Assam, India, during Burma campaign of World War II; vain attempts to help sick and injured; discovering brotherhood of suffering.

KIKUCHI, CHARLES   **5711**

THE KIKUCHI DIARY: CHRONICLE FROM AN AMERICAN CONCENTRATION CAMP. Edited by John Modell. Urbana: University of Illinois Press, 1973. 258 pp.

Dec 1941-Sep 1942. Nisei graduate student's diary kept as part of the Japanese Evacuation and Relocation Study Project; a personal and graphic account of life at the Tanforan Assembly Center in California; effects of internment on Japanese culture and family life, education and careers; the diarist's articulate reflections about himself and his circumstances.

KOGAN, DAVID S., 1929-1951   **5712**

DIARY. Edited by Meyer Levin. New York: Beechhurst Press, 1955. 255 pp.

1941-1951. Diary of sensitive, intelligent boy growing up in a strong, closely knit Jewish family in Yonkers, New York; high school days followed by college at Cornell; finding both doubts and comfort in American Jewish way of life; candid thoughts on boy and girl friends, religions, literature, music, movies, art, politics and current events; great ideals and ambitions cut tragically short by death from lymphoma.

Extracts in DIARY OF AMERICA, edited by Josef and Dorothy Berger, pp. 609-617.

1943-1946. High school days, girls, family, pre-Rabbinical studies and occasional thoughts on World War II.

SMITH, CORNELIUS C.   5713

"...'A Hell of a Christmas.' " UNITED STATES NAVAL INSTITUTE PROCEEDINGS 94, no. 12 (1968):63-71.

Dec 1941. A Marine lieutenant's account of the bombing of Pearl Harbor; rescue of wounded and retrieval of bodies "out here, bobbing up and down like rubber dolls"; effects of the newly declared war on Hawaii civilians, including Japanese; memories of a happier Christmas the previous year.

STEIN, LEO, 1872-1947   5714

JOURNEY INTO THE SELF: BEING THE LETTERS, PAPERS & JOURNALS OF LEO STEIN. Edited by Edmund Fuller, New York: Crown Publishers, 1950. 331 pp. Journal, pp. 217-250.

1941-1944. Extracts from the largely psychological journals of Gertrude Stein's brother, a disappointed writer; thoughts on his crippling neurosis, psychoanalysis, old age, Christianity, the Bible, reading, writing and aesthetics; his life in Italy during the war, experiencing privations and danger; the battle of Florence; sketches of Italian villagers; anti-Semitism in Germany and Italy; a critical attitude toward the work of his sister.

STILWELL, JOSEPH WARREN, 1883-1946   5715

THE STILWELL PAPERS. Edited by Theodore H. White. New York: W. Sloane Associates, 1948. 357 pp. passim.

1941-1944. Extracts from the diaries and papers of the crusty hero of the Burma and China campaigns; hasty notes of action, decisions and opinions as commander of United States involvement in the Burma offensive, then when Burma fell to the Japanese, leader of a dangerous escape across the mountains to India; action as United States commander of Allied effort in southeast Asia under Mountbatten; commander of the Chinese army during recapture of northern Burma and frustration with his attempts to introduce reforms; considerable vituperation against Chiang Kaishek, T.V. Soong, Mountbatten and some of his American colleagues.

Extracts in DIARY OF AMERICA, edited by Josef and Dorothy Berger, pp. 598-602.

1942-1943. Chiefly his efforts to gain Chinese support in Burma.

SULZBERGER, CYRUS LEO, 1912-   5716

SEVEN CONTINENTS AND FORTY YEARS: A CONCENTRATION OF MEMORIES. New York: Quadrangle/The New York Times Book Company, 1977. 688 pp.

1941-1973. Abridged one volume edition of diaries.

A LONG ROW OF CANDLES: MEMOIRS AND DIARIES. 1934-1954. New York: Macmillan, 1969. 1061 pp.

1944-1954. Voluminous notes of journalist for NEW YORK TIMES, an observer of history on all continents; covering post World War

II problems and negotiations, NATO, civil war in Greece, founding of and decision on location of United Nations, Potsdam Conference, the birth of Israel, Republican and Democratic political conventions; on intimate terms with Roosevelt, Eisenhower, Harriman, Nixon, Truman, Charles E. Bohlen, Maurice Couve de Murvill, John Foster Dulles and Anthony Eden; official and personal reports on Marshall Tito, Haile Selassie, Josef Stalin, Maxim Litvinov and Russian-American relations.

THE LAST OF THE GIANTS. New York: Macmillan, 1970. 1063 pp.

1954-1963. His experiences and observations while writing foreign affairs column for NEW YORK TIMES; United States relations with France, Germany and China; great admiration for Churchill and De Gaulle; insights on world figures Georges Pompidou, Amory Houghton, John F. Kennedy, Nikita Khrushchev, Pandit Nehru, Konrad Adenauer and Dean Rusk; covering Geneva conference, 1955 and summit meeting of Big Four in Paris, 1960.

AN AGE OF MEDIOCRITY: MEMOIRS AND DIARIES, 1963-1972. New York: Macmillan, 1973. 828 pp.

1963-1971. Observations and interviews expanding to Third World and Communist figures and countries; Nicolae Ceausescu and Rumania, Fidel Castro and Cuba, Anwar Sadat and Egypt, King Hussein and Jordan, Salvador Allende and Chile; unsatisfactory interview with Yasir Arafat; policies on Vietnam; extensive secondhand information on Richard Nixon from Henry Kissinger.

POSTSCRIPT WITH A CHINESE ACCENT: MEMOIRS AND DIARIES. New York: Macmillan, 1974. 401 pp.

1972-1973. Ireland and its complicated political situation; Asian affairs culminating in a visit to China; the press, economic and agricultural conditions; being met and entertained by local revolutionary committees in Peking, Yenan, Sian, Shanghai and Hangchow; interview with Chou En-Lai; notes on Chinese relations with United States and Soviet Union.

VAUGHAN, ELIZABETH, 1905-1957   5717

THE ORDEAL OF ELIZABETH VAUGHAN: A WARTIME DIARY OF THE PHILIPPINES. Edited by Carol M. Petillo. Athens: University of Georgia Press, 1985. 312 pp.

1941-1945. Record kept by young mother forced into hiding in a hill camp with two small children after the invasion of the Philippines in World War II; located by the Japanese and interned first in a concentration camp in Bacolod, later moving on a crude oil ship to Santo Tomas concentration camp on the campus of the University of Manila; petty, humorous, incongruous events during years of stress, illness and progressively worse conditions until freed and returned to San Francisco; sensitive observations on confinement, deprivation and behavior by an observer trained as a sociologist.

1942

BIELIK, CASIMER   5718

In AMERICAN DIARIES OF WORLD WAR II, edited by Donald Vining, pp. 180-195.

1942-1944. Extracts of cryptic diary entries of a Wyandotte, Michigan, seaman, first class coxswain, later boatswain second class in Naval Armed Guard; duties, pranks, escapades while on leave; Old Neptune Day antics; chiefly in the Atlantic with a few notes while in the Mediterranean.

BIRNN, ROLAND R., d. 1942   5719

"A War Diary." AEROSPACE HISTORIAN 13 (1956):40-45, 98-103.

Feb-Jul 1942. Account by an Army Air Corps lieutenant of the stressful and frustrating period after the December 1941 Japanese attack on the Philippines; in Northern Territory, Australia, contending with heat, wretched food and insects without adequate planes and parts; at Daly Waters, "really a hole," where "General MacArthur came through the other day" bringing furniture and servants rather than pilots and mechanics; flying bombing raids and reconnaissance flights over New Guinea; casualties and low morale while stationed at Port Moresby; suffering "Dengue fever"; arrival of new planes, and diarist's death conducting final tests on his A-20.

BRUMMER, FRANCIS H.   5720

In AMERICAN DIARIES OF WORLD WAR II, edited by Donald Vining, pp. 133-143.

1942-1945. Extracts from diary of signalman third class on a number of ships; brief entries of dangerous action in the North Atlantic, once picking up survivors from the water near the North Pole.

BUNKER, PAUL   5721

In UNCOMMON VALOR, edited by James M. Merrill, pp. 369-371.

Jan-Mar 1942. Extracts from colonel's diary of the siege of Corregidor; notes on bombing raid and destruction; opinions on military operations, the British and Philippine independence.

BUTCHER, HARRY CECIL, 1901-   5722

MY THREE YEARS WITH EISENHOWER: THE PERSONAL DIARY OF CAPTAIN HARRY C. BUTCHER, USNR, NAVAL AIDE TO GENERAL EISENHOWER. New York: Simon and Schuster, 1946. 911 pp.

THREE YEARS WITH EISENHOWER: THE PERSONAL DIARY OF CAPTAIN HARRY C. BUTCHER, USNR, NAVAL AIDE TO GENERAL EISENHOWER. London: W. Heinemann, 1946. 748 pp.

1942-1945. Naval aide's massive and admiring account of Eisenhower during the European campaign; activities of and opinions about generals Marshall, Bradley, Clark, Smith and Patton, as well as Roosevelt, Churchill, Montgomery, De Gaulle, Hitler and a host of the key figures of the war in Europe; notes on various campaigns and movements; many social and anecdotal items.

DANIELS, JONATHAN, 1902-1981   5723

WHITE HOUSE WITNESS. Garden City, N.Y.: Doubleday, 1975. 299 pp. passim.

1942-1945. Occasional diary entries within narrative by Roosevelt's administrative assistant and later press secretary; an inside view of the people and politics of the time; war news, anecdotes and gossip.

FAHEY, JAMES J.   5724

PACIFIC WAR DIARY. Boston: Houghton Mifflin, 1963. 404 pp. Reprint. Westport, Conn.: Greenwood, 1974.

1942-1945. Diary of seaman first class from Waltham, Massachusetts; from Great Lakes Training Station in Chicago to assignment on MONTPELIER on which he served from first Allied offensive at Guadalcanal to last landing in Japan; drill with big guns en route to the South Pacific; descriptions of many battles and close calls in and around Solomon, Mariana and Philippine Islands, Borneo, China and Japan; names of many ships and where they saw action; hot days and sleepless nights; fear and tension of going into battle; admiration for comrades and officers; an emotional meeting with American, Australian, British and Dutch prisoners of war at Wakayama, bringing food, clothing and medicine.

Extracts in AMERICAN DIARIES OF WORLD WAR II, edited by Donald Vining, pp. 196-215.

Jan-Dec 1943. Battle at Tulagi; night attack on Shortland Islands; misery of hot battle stations on MONTPELIER; news of Japanese atrocities; welcome leave in Australia after a year on the ship; a visit by Eleanor Roosevelt and later by much admired Admiral Halsey.

HASSETT, WILLIAM D., b. 1880   5725

OFF THE RECORD WITH F.D.R. With an introduction by Jonathan Daniels. New Brunswick, N.J.: Rutgers University Press, 1958. 366 pp.

1942-1945. A White House staff member's inside journal of Roosevelt's life during the war years; a minute picture of what the president said and did, especially on secret trips away from the White House; revelations of his character, personality and interests; candid notes on many of the people surrounding him; war news; Roosevelt's failing health, death and funeral; a portrait of the president by an unabashedly partisan "Boswell."

HAYS, MARION PRATHER   5726

"From the Political Diary of an Unpolitical Person." ARKANSAS HISTORICAL QUARTERLY 36 (1977):158-191.

1942-1944. Diary of the wife of Brooks Hays, Democratic senator from Arkansas; a round of feting by "this dear city of Little Rock and all the lovely people who voted for us"; Washington social life, Baptist church activities, family events and war news; references to Sam Rorex, James William Fulbright and Hubert Humphrey; some of her husband's activities and views, especially the Hays-Fulbright bill and his opposition to the formation of the House Un-American Activities Committee.

LAIDLAW, LANSING STOUT, 1895-1966   5727

"Aleutian Experience of the MAD M." OREGON HISTORICAL QUARTERLY 80 (1979):31-49.

Dec 1942-May 1943. Letter-diary of Coast Guard coxswain from Portland; tour of duty on the ARTHUR MIDDLETON, transporting troops and supplies for the Aleutian campaign; Japanese bombing attacks while ship marooned on the rocks; aerial battles; frantic completion of airstrip for fighter planes; activities at Dutch Harbor; originally a long letter with dates added later by author.

MCCORMICK, VINCENT A.   5728

Hennesey, James. ''An American Jesuit in Wartime Rome.'' MID-AMERICA 56 (1974):32-55.

   1942-1945. Extracts, within article, from the diary of distinguished Jesuit living in Rome; his dealings with Americans Myron C. Taylor and Harold H. Tittman and other Allied diplomats; notes on the effects of bombing and wartime privations; reactions to activities and attitudes of the Pope and to Jesuit matters; the anguish of a loyal churchman disturbed by certain Vatican policies.

MCNAMARA, JOSEPH MICHAEL, 1911-   5729

In AMERICAN DIARIES OF WORLD WAR II, edited by Donald Vining, pp. 144-179.

   1942-1945. Extracts from diary of Danbury, Connecticut, naval machinist's mate second class, destroyer division; schooling in Boston where he took advantage of concerts and in Brooklyn with frequent trips to theaters in Manhattan; sea service on the ANTHONY in the Atlantic and Pacific where ship saw action in major sea battles at Efate, Bougainville, Guadalcanal, Saipan, Tinian, Guam, Eniwetok, Iwo Jima and Okinawa; vivid description of Japanese suicide planes, taking wounded from damaged ships and sea, ''a day of horror unbelievable''; low morale and growing nervousness after days of continuous battle; names and movements of many ships; much needed liberty enjoyed at Sydney; mention of engine problems caused by apparent sabotage during repair at Pearl Harbor; seeing devastation of Nagasaki before returning home on the CORBIESER.

MINOR, ANNE ROGERS, 1864-1947   5730

Gillikin, Jo. ''A Masterpiece in Modesty.'' CONNECTICUT HISTORICAL SOCIETY BULLETIN 49 (1984):73-81.

   1942-1946. Brief extracts from a diary kept in her last years of a somewhat overlooked Connecticut artist; almost daily references to painting, including subjects and media, as well as many other pursuits of an active, creative old age.

NATHAN, ROBERT, 1894-   5731

JOURNAL FOR JOSEPHINE. New York: A.A. Knopf, 1943. 142 pp.

   May-Sep 1942. Popular author's journal of a summer at Cape Cod; war news and his reactions and opinions interspersed with pleasant family life.

QUINN, MICHAEL A., 1895-   5732

LOVE LETTERS TO MIKE: FORTY MONTHS AS A JAPANESE PRISONER OF WAR. New York: Vantage Press, 1977. 331 pp.

   1942-1945. Diary kept in form of letters to his wife and family while prisoner of Japanese at O'Donnell and Tarlac in the Philippines, Karenko and Shirakawa on Taiwan, and Cheng Chia Tun and Mukden in Manchuria; treatment at each facility, transportation, daily routine, preoccupation with food, his own and companions' health, infrequency of reliable news, rumors; comfort in religious faith and maintaining Catholic services even in absence of a priest; long entries addressed to each child on his or her birthday, recalling memorable family events.

SCHLOSS, HARRY   5733

In AMERICAN DIARIES OF WORLD WAR II, edited by Donald Vining, pp. 269-285.

   1942-1945. Extracts from diary of a sergeant in Seventeenth Bomb Group, Thirty-fourth Bomb Squadron called Thunderbirds; gunnery school at Fort Myers; air mechanics training at Shepard Field; service in Africa and Sardinia flying sixty-two missions to Italy; rest camp at Capri; receiving Presidential Citation; names of many comrades.

SEAGRAVE, GORDON STIFLER, 1897-1966   5734

BURMA SURGEON. New York: W.W. Norton, 1943. 295 pp. passim. London: V. Gollancz, 1944. 159 pp. passim.

   Apr-May 1942. Diary extracts within memoir of a medical missionary to Burma who became army surgeon for Chinese troops under Gen. Joseph Stilwell; the battle of Burma and subsequent retreat to India covered in detail; heroism of Burmese nurses, Chinese soldiers and Quaker medics; a popular World War II classic.

SULLIVAN, JOSEPH P.   5735

''Diary Notes of an Army Quartermaster.'' QUARTERMASTER REVIEW 28, no. 1 (1948):38-40, 104-106.

   Dec 1942-Sep 1943. Quartermaster's observations in Algiers and Morocco.

TISDELLE, ACHILLE C.   5736

Morton, Louis, ed. ''Bataan Diary of Major Achille C. Tisdelle.'' MILITARY AFFAIRS 11 (1947):131-148.

   Feb-Apr 1942. A rare World War II diary kept for Maj. Gen. Edward P. King by an aide; entries covering the bombings of Corregidor, progress of operations on Bataan and surrender to the Japanese; laconic notes on American resistance while weakened by starvation and malaria; a detailed account of the surrender negotiations and interrogations; references to many officers and men, as well as Philippine allies; published entries ending at this point, although diary was continued, ingeniously concealed, through years in prison camps.

TOMITA, SAKU   5737

Cormack, Janet, ed.; Kodachi, Zuigaku and Heikkala, Jan, trans. ''Portland Assembly Center: Diary of Saku Tomita.'' OREGON HISTORICAL QUARTERLY 81 (1980):149-171.

   May-Jul 1942. Issei woman's account of two months in the Portland Assembly Center awaiting more permanent relocation; comfortable beds, but problems of boredom, scanty food, poor sanitation, crowding and sickness; diarist's enjoyment of seeing old friends and progress in her English classes; departures of people to various relocation camps.

TREGASKIS, RICHARD WILLIAM, 1916-   5738

GUADALCANAL DIARY. New York: Random House, 1943. 263 pp. Redhill, Surrey: Wells, Gardner, Darton, 1943. 191 pp.

   Jul-Sep 1942. International News Service war correspondent's diary describing the Marine invasion and worst days of jungle fighting on Guadalcanal during World War II; a vivid picture of the hardships and heroism of this kind of warfare.

INVASION DIARY. New York: Random House, 1944. 245 pp.

1943-1944. With the American troops during invasion of Sicily and Italy; daily events under fire as experienced by men at the front; suffering a head wound and reporting the shock of brain injury and the stages of recovery.

X-15 DIARY: THE STORY OF AMERICA'S FIRST SPACESHIP. New York: Dutton, 1961. 316 pp.

1959-1960. Tracing the development, first flights and accidents of the first vehicle designed to carry a person outside the earth's atmosphere and return; personal background information and the attending publicity of pilots Bob White, Scott Crossfield, Joe Walker and Charles Yeager.

VIETNAM DIARY. New York: Holt, Rinehart and Winston, 1963. 401 pp.

Oct 1962-Jan 1963. Journalist's coverage of the war in Vietnam; guerilla tactics contrasted with the war in Guadalcanal in 1942; special attention to the marines in action, with many names of soldiers included; little attention to the complicated controversy surrounding United States involvement in Vietnam.

WILKINSON, GERALD HUGH   **5739**

Thorne, Christopher. "MacArthur, Australia and the British, 1942-1943: The Secret Journal of MacArthur's British Liaison Officer." AUSTRALIAN OUTLOOK 29 (1975):53-67, 197-210.

1942-1943. Article containing generous extracts from the journal of an Englishman serving as liaison between MacArthur and various leading Australian and British officials during MacArthur's assistance in defense of Australia; reports of many conversations with him about people and plans; interesting view of his personality, character, strengths and defects; much on Australian campaign against the Japanese in New Guinea; MacArthur's reaction to war news from North Africa and Europe.

YOUNG, JAMES WEBB, 1886-   **5740**

THE DIARY OF AN AD MAN; 1943. Chicago: Advertising Publications, 1944. 256 pp.

1942-1943. Daily notes for a projected book on American business history from advertising point of views; continuing entries for a weekly column in ADVERTISING AGE; weekend notes mainly of seasonal events on diarist's farm; increasingly serious war news and home front shortages; written for an audience.

Extracts in DIARY OF AMERICA, edited by Josef and Dorothy Berger, pp. 596-597.

Jul-Oct 1942. Extracts regarding advertising, honesty and consumerism.

ZANUCK, DARRYL FRANCIS, 1902-1979   **5741**

TUNIS EXPEDITION. New York: Random House, 1943. 160 pp.

Nov-Dec 1942. Movie producer's account of his part in the North Africa campaign as a colonel with the Army Signal Corps and head of a unit assigned to film the action; at Gibralter, thence with Gen. Mark Clark to Algiers; description of the campaign across North Africa to the Tunisian front; the battle of Tebourba and action near Tunis.

1943

ANON.   **5742**

AND STILL WE CONQUER! THE DIARY OF A NAZI UNTEROFFIZIER. Edited by W. Stanley Hoole. University, Ala.: Confederate, 1968. 52 pp.

May-Dec 1943. German noncommissioned officer's diary of last days in North Africa, being captured at Protville and suffering miserable, overcrowded conditions, unbearable heat, blowing sand, insects and scant food until voyage on JOHN BROWN to Norfolk, Virginia, and Camp Shelby, Mississippi; by truck to farms in Alabama to harvest peanuts; monotony of camp life varied by birthday and anniversary celebrations; comments on abundant food, American "culture," propaganda, ignorance of world affairs and attitudes toward blacks; frequent assertions of German superiority; diary ending abruptly, probably confiscated. Translated from the German.

BOOKE, KENNETH E., 1918-1973   **5743**

In AMERICAN DIARIES OF WORLD WAR II, edited by Donald Vining, pp. 286-307.

1943-1944. Extract from diary of pilot of B-17 bomber serving with 407th Squadron, Ninety-second Bomb Group, Eighth Air Force; entries for each of thirty missions over Germany and France; good details of action, fears and losses, concluding "it was a damn rough racket and I'm glad it's over."

BROUGHER, WILLIAM EDWARD, 1889-1965   **5744**

SOUTH TO BATAAN, NORTH TO MUKDEN. Edited by D. Clayton James. Athens: University of Georgia Press, 1971. 207 pp.

1943-1945. Diary of a brigadier general who survived the Bataan Death March; command of the Eleventh Division on the central Luzon plain and at Bataan until its surrender; in prison camps at O'Donnell and Tarlac while still in the Philippines, then sent to prisons in Taiwan and at Mukden, Manchuria; although generally receiving better treatment because of rank, nevertheless suffering constant hunger and privations; the welcome arrival of Red Cross parcels after many delays; poems and notes on writing, reading, church services; maintaining hope with memories of family and friends and the solace of writing.

CHURCHILL, EDWARD DELOS, 1895-1973   **5745**

SURGEON TO SOLDIERS: DIARY AND RECORDS OF THE SURGICAL CONSULTANT, ALLIED FORCE HEADQUARTERS, WORLD WAR II. Philadelphia: Lippincott, 1972. 490 pp. passim.

1943. Diary extracts, scattered through medical record and memoir kept by distinguished surgeon who served in the North African-Mediterranean campaign; information ranging from high-level policy matters to such entries as, "Frosty and I ran both operating tables almost constantly, not finishing up until 4:00 a.m."; a conference in Tripoli with British doctors on the use of penicillin; admiring references to Kenneth and Frosty Lowry, with whom he treated Allied, German and civilian wounded in Algeria; descriptions of specific wounds, treatment and problems, with considerable controversy over treatment and medical policies, especially between the advocates of whole blood and plasma.

COZZENS, JAMES GOULD, 1903-1979   **5746**

A TIME OF WAR: AIR FORCE DIARIES AND PENTAGON MEMOS. Edited by Matthew J. Bruccoli. Columbia, S.C. & Bloomfield Hills, Mich.: Bruccoli Clark, 1984. 407 pp. passim.

1943-1945. Author's stateside experiences with the Air Force and Pentagon from which he drew some of the material for his Pulitzer Prize novel GUARD OF HONOR; work for the Office of Technical Information as a speech writer for Gen. Henry H. Arnold and others; responsibility for helping to shape official statements and press releases and prevent an occasionally garrulous officer from "shooting his face off" on sensitive issues; evident impatience with the complexities and absurdities of military organization.

DRURY, ALLEN, 1918-   **5747**

A SENATE JOURNAL. New York: McGraw-Hill, 1963.

1943-1945. Record kept by journalist and novelist during period when he was Senate reporter; notes on and analysis of domestic and foreign policy debates; his antipathy toward Roosevelt; sketches of many senators, including George Aiken, Alben Barkley, Walter George, James Murray, Claude Pepper, etc.; references to Truman; obviously, much material which provided background for his Senate novels.

ELLIS, LEWIS N.   **5748**

"Ploesti: A Pilot's Diary." AMERICAN HERITAGE 34, no. 6 (1983):77-83.

Jul-Sep 1943. Account of a massive low altitude bombing raid on Hitler's oil refineries at Ploesti, Rumania; a successful mission, but costly in men and planes.

FLOOD, MILFORD   **5749**

ARCTIC JOURNAL. Los Angeles: Wetzel, 1950. 459 pp.

Oct 1943-Jul 1944. Narrative journal of a crew member with Canadian Oil at Canol, Northwest Territories, on the Mackenzie River; digging holes for telephone poles and laying pipeline; camp life; problems with cold, monotonous diet, etc.; work details and much on the men and their interactions.

GUNTHER, JOHN, 1901-1970   **5750**

D DAY. New York: Harpers, 1943. 276 pp. passim.

Jul-Sep 1943. Journalist's narrative and diaries of action in the Mediterranean area during the invasion period, with entries covering his experiences at Algiers, Malta, Cairo, Istanbul, etc.; the Allied landing in Sicily; his close association with Eisenhower and impressions of Montgomery and others; the excitement and mechanics of being a war correspondent.

HARRIS, PAUL NELSON, 1914-   **5751**

BASE COMPANY 16. New York: Vantage Press, 1963. 201 pp.

1943-1945. World War II diary of a black navy man, beginning at the Naval Mine Depot, Yorktown, Virginia; thence to California where he was put in charge of a "colored" unit; difficulties when caught in the middle between white superiors and some of his black subordinates who refused to take orders from him and seemed bent on trouble; many references to the CALIFOR-

NIA, on which he had served earlier; a good picture of racial problems in the military and the apparent thwarting from above and below of the diarist's desire to do a good job.

JOSEPHS, RAY   **5752**

ARGENTINE DIARY: THE INSIDE STORY OF THE COMING OF FASCISM. New York: Random House, 1944. 358 pp. London: V. Gollancz, 1945. 342 pp.

1943-1944. Diary of American correspondent in Argentina for PM; daily events of the political scene, military dictatorship of Juan Perón, severing diplomatic ties with Axis countries, growing repression of Fascist style government through censorship of press, suppression of pro-democratic organizations and interference in universities.

LORD, CAROLINE M.   **5753**

DIARY OF A VILLAGE LIBRARY. Somersworth: New Hampshire, 1971. 269 pp.

1943-1960. Delightful diary of a librarian at Francestown, New Hampshire; brief, sometimes reflective notes on daily interactions with patrons of all ages and interests; good picture of New England village life and importance of the library.

LOVELL, FRANK   **5754**

In AMERICAN DIARIES OF WORLD WAR II, edited by Donald Vining, pp. 49-62.

Mar-May 1943. Extracts from diary of warrant officer attached to Ninth Infantry Division of Sixtieth First Army Battalion; Tunisia campaign in North Africa; in and out of foxholes during regular German raids; days of living on B and C rations; at the front of battle in Bizerte where he suffered a slight concussion.

MCCAUGHEY, ANNE, 1915-   **5755**

In AMERICAN DIARIES OF WORLD WAR II, edited by Donald Vining, pp. 82-106.

1943-1945. Extracts from diary of American Red Cross aide providing recreational and social service to patients at the Army's Fiftieth General Hospital, from Fort Carson, Colorado, to England, Scotland and France; notes on reactions to war, co-workers, bicycling in the country when off duty; observing racism and indicating a need to work on civil rights after the war.

MESECHER, THEARL, 1914-   **5756**

In AMERICAN DIARIES OF WORLD WAR II, edited by Donald Vining, pp. 343-373.

1943-1945. Extracts from prisoner of war diary of private first class from Iowa serving in Company I, 168th Infantry, Thirty-fourth Division and captured by Germans in Tunisia; long march to Tunis, by plane to Italy and by boxcar to Germany; in Stalag 7, moved to Stalag 5B at Friedrichshafen, doing hard construction work on one small meal each day; another move to Stalag 2B then to farms for harvesting; skimpy rations and clothing until Red Cross parcels began arriving; deteriorating morale as the months dragged on; wondering if he would become hardened by all the brutality he witnessed; "this lonely life is so terribly depressing."

ORIGO, IRIS, 1902-   5757

WAR IN VAL D'ORCIA. Introduction by Dennis Mack Smith. Boston: Godine, 1984. 239 pp.

1943-1944. Diary of an American-born woman married to an Italian and living on Tuscany farm during critical days of World War II; becoming almost completely self-sustaining, providing food and clothing for own family and community of farm laborers; sheltering children from the cities, Allied prisoners of war and partisans hiding in the woods; existing with little accurate news and many rumors as the German troops moved through Tuscany and the farm became front line for several days; forced to leave home with all the refugee children and return to destruction later; a shared misery recorded with small humorous and touching incidents.

PCTR, OTTO V., 1915-   5758

In AMERICAN DIARIES OF WORLD WAR II, edited by Donald Vining, pp. 75-81.

Mar-Apr 1943. Extracts from diary of private first class, Company I, 132nd Infantry, on Guadalcanal between engagements; Japanese air raid on Henderson Field.

STETTINIUS, EDWARD REILLY, 1900-1949   5759

THE DIARIES OF EDWARD R. STETTINIUS, JR. Edited by Thomas M. Campbell and George C. Herring. New York: New Viewpoints, 1975. 544 pp.

1943-1946. Diaries and calendar notes of industrialist-statesman, eventually secretary of state and representative to the United Nations; conversations with presidents Roosevelt and Truman; participation in Dumbarton Oaks, Yalta and San Francisco conferences; notes on Churchill, Stalin, Cordell Hull and James F. Byrnes; the Mexico City Conference of 1945; an important inside record of the making of United States foreign policy during and immediately after World War II, including the beginnings of the cold war.

STOVAL, ORAN C.   5760

Wagner, Robert L., ed. "The Odyssey of a Texas Citizen Soldier." SOUTHWESTERN HISTORICAL QUARTERLY 72 (1968):60-87.

1943-1944. Article containing extracts from the diary of a Bowie, Texas, engineer with the Thirty-sixth Division, Texas National Guard; action in Italy, southern France and Germany; the battle of Salerno and conditions in Italy; friction with rear echelon units, particularly the commander at Naples, Maj. General Arthur R. Wilson; Fifth Army's attempt to break German defenses at Cassino and ill-preparedness of Gen. Frank Otto Bowman; diarist's opinion that Gen. Mark W. Clark owed the success of the battle of Rome to Gen. Fred L. Walker but refused to give him credit.

1944

BAKER, RICHARD BROWN   5761

THE YEAR OF THE BUZZ BOMB: A JOURNAL OF LONDON, 1944. New York: Exposition Press, 1952. 118 pp.

May-Dec 1944. American civilian's record of life in London; his work in the French Duty Room of the Political Intelligence Department; fragments of war news, particularly bombing destruction of European cities, but mostly the effects of almost nightly bombing raids on London; trying to carry on work and social life amid constant fear and interruption; weekend walking tours in the country.

BEATTIE, EDWARD WILLIAM, 1909-   5762

DIARY OF A KRIEGIE. New York: Thomas Y. Crowell, 1946. 312 pp.

Sep 1944-May 1945 (with gaps). United Press correspondent's diary, kept with the thoroughness of a journalist while prisoner of Germans; capture in France, march to Strasbourg, by crowded train through Lahn Valley; imprisonment at Limburg under intolerable conditions, in Berlin at Stalag 3-D; after confiscation, resuming diary at Stalag 3-A at Luckenwalde with 17,000 prisoners of all nations; long descriptions of camp conditions, rampant rumors, bartering and everyone's preoccupation with food; character sketches of individuals; good observations on the views of each group of nationals on the war.

CHRISTENSEN, KEITH, 1921-   5763

In AMERICAN DIARIES OF WORLD WAR II, edited by Donald Vining, pp. 28-48.

Jun-Aug 1944. Extracts from Rapid City, South Dakota, soldier's diary in camp at Fort Carson, Colorado, with H Company of 201st Regiment; a sixty-day test of army rations under adverse mountain conditions; daily routines of marching, camping and medical tests; his situation described as "too hot, no privacy, too much cleaning and too much crap to take."

EDWARDS, RALPH G., 1920-   5764

In AMERICAN DIARIES OF WORLD WAR II, edited by Donald Vining, pp. 308-318.

Jan-May 1944. Extracts from diary of Ogdensburg, New York, sergeant with 717th Bomb Squadron, 449th Bomb Group, Army Air Corps; flying fifty missions from Grattaghi, Italy; record of each target, opposition encountered, success or failure and losses; admission of fear and gratitude each time the crew returned safely.

FORRESTAL, JAMES VINCENT, 1892-1949   5765

THE FORRESTAL DIARIES. Edited by Walter Millis. New York: Viking, 1951. 581 pp. London: Cassell, 1952. 542 pp.

1944-1949. Private diaries of secretary of navy and later defense; reports of cabinet and other meetings; opinions on and conversations with Roosevelt, Truman, Eisenhower, Averell Harriman, Robert A. Lovett, George C. Marshall and a host of other government and military figures; involvement in decision-making processes crucial to the final months of the war, the rebuilding of Europe and cold war relations with the Soviets; extensive material on the unification question, nuclear testing, the Berlin crisis, the Palestinian question and major aspects of war and peacetime defense policy; concerns about the increasing hold of communism on eastern Europe and China; travels in Europe; a valuable record of leaders, events and trends of the period; frustration and sense of failure which may have contributed to his suicide.

GILES, HENRY E.   **5766**

THE G.I. JOURNAL OF SERGEANT GILES. Edited by Janice H. Giles. Boston: Houghton Mifflin, 1965. 399 pp.

  1944-1945. Letter-journal of an Adair County, Kentucky, member of the 291st Engineer Combat Battalion, an enlisted man for whom an army uniform meant "not only that for the first time in my life I had clothes I wasn't ashamed of, but for the first time in my life I was somebody;" the strain of waiting in England for Normandy invasion, but a peaceful landing on Omaha Beach several weeks after D-Day; action and engineering work in France and Germany, with detailed account of the battle of the Bulge; serious morale problems because the chaotic "replacement depot system" caused long mail delays; many references to Robert C. Billington, David E. Pergrin and others.

GOLDMAN, PAUL   **5767**

In AMERICAN DIARIES OF WORLD WAR II, edited by Donald Vining, pp. 216-241.

  Mar-Jul 1944. Extracts from diary of Jewish pharmacist's mate first class from New York; from Boston to Plymouth, England; seeing evidence of bombing; moving between Dartmouth Harbor and France, delivering troops and picking up casualties; sightseeing in London while ship was being repaired.

GROH, GEORGE   **5768**

In DIARY OF AMERICA, edited by Josef and Dorothy Berger, pp. 602-605.

  Jun 1944. Extracts in military diary of intense fighting at Carenton, between Omaha and Utah beachheads.

GUNTHER, JOHN, 1929-1947   **5769**

In DEATH BE NOT PROUD: A MEMOIR, by John Gunther, pp. 229-249. New York: Modern Library, 1953.

  1944-1947 (with gaps). Scattered entries, within a book written by his famous journalist father, of the last years of young Gunther's life; medical treatment for malignant brain tumor; notes on school work, family and friends; an optimistic and courageous outlook.

HARKOVICH, MIKE, 1920-   **5770**

In AMERICAN DIARIES OF WORLD WAR II, edited by Donald Vining, pp. 381-415.

  Dec 1944-May 1945. Extracts from prisoner of war diary by Boise, Idaho, sergeant in Forty-fourth Bomb Group, Sixty-sixth Squadron, Eighth Air Force, shot down over Germany; seemingly endless, boring days in prison, playing cards, baseball and reading mysteries; preoccupation with food; thoughts of home and his wife; interest in latest song hits and musical group from the next compound; swapping rumors; noting psychological toll on some of his companions; wild celebration and days of confusion at liberation.

HASSLER, R. ALFRED   **5771**

DIARY OF A SELF-MADE CONVICT. Chicago: H. Regnery, 1954. 182 pp.

Extracts in MEN WITHOUT MASKS, by Michael Rubin, pp. 64-73.

  Jun 1944-Mar 1945. Prison diary of conscientious objector, literature secretary of Fellowship of Reconciliation and editor of FELLOWSHIP; an "unbelievably sterile routine" in Lewisburg, Pennsylvania, prison; reflections on prison life as "unrelenting tension and acute boredom" and on fellow prisoners; compassion for some who seem hopeless victims of circumstances and system.

LEWIS, CARROLL A.   **5772**

In AMERICAN DIARIES OF WORLD WAR II, edited by Donald Vining, pp. 319-328.

  Nov 1944-Jan 1945. Extracts from diary of Houston, Texas, first lieutenant with 379th Bomb Group based in England; details of eighteen missions, including a crash landing at an RAF base on Christmas eve followed by much partying the next day.

MAGINNIS, JOHN J.   **5773**

MILITARY GOVERNMENT JOURNAL: NORMANDY TO BERLIN. Edited by Robert A. Hart. Amherst: University of Massachusetts Press, 1971. 351 pp.

  1944-1946. Unusual account of American general's administration of civilian affairs in France, Belgium and Germany during final months of the war and after Nazi surrender; activities in Normandy, Ardennes, Hainaut and Berlin; dealings with local mayors and other officials to clean up towns, restore water and food supply and attend to health and sanitation problems; tense relations between Americans and Soviets during joint occupation of Berlin; historically important with much human interest.

MAZZA, MICHAEL   **5774**

In AMERICAN DIARIES OF WORLD WAR II, edited by Donald Vining, pp. 374-380.

  Aug 1944-Apr 1945. Extracts from prisoner of war diary of private from Haverhill, Massachusetts; after hospitalization in Hoenstein, Germany, being sent to Rowen to work on farms; on march for six weeks cut off from what little food supplies there were by Russians approaching from east and Americans from the west; welcome release by Americans; processed out at Camp Lucky Strike in France; return to a touching family reunion on Mother's Day.

RHINEHART, WALTER L., 1909-   **5775**

In AMERICAN DIARIES OF WORLD WAR II, edited by Donald Vining, pp. 244-250.

  1944-1945. Extracts from diary of naval officer from Washington, D.C., on destroyer in Pacific arena; routine duties; battle for Philippines, homesickness, eagerly waiting for mail and news of his young son.

SAIS, DESIDERIO J.   **5776**

In AMERICAN DIARIES OF WORLD WAR II, edited by Donald Vining, pp. 107-121.

  1944-1945. Extracts from Albuquerque, New Mexico, soldier's diary; in charge of trucks and amphibious vehicles, constantly moving from company to company in Anzio, Naples and Salerno; notes on local people; playing poker with his buddies; in France for Christmas mass at cathedral in Langres where it was so cold the altar boys wore gloves.

SAROYAN, WILLIAM, 1908-1981   **5777**

THE TWIN ADVENTURES. New York: Harcourt, Brace, 1950. 225, 285 pp. Diary, pp. 3-225.

Aug-Sep 1944. Author's diary which he kept while writing his novel, THE ADVENTURES OF WESLEY JACKSON, in London; experiences of living in wartime London; material on his work habits, reading, interests and diversions; some apparently psychosomatic problems during periods of high creativity.

SULLIVAN, WILLIAM J., 1917-   **5778**

In AMERICAN DIARIES OF WORLD WAR II, edited by Donald Vining, pp. 329-339.

Apr-Jun 1944. Extracts from diary of sergeant, 516th Squadron, 379th Bomb Group, Eighth Air Force; details of thirty missions to French and German targets, being hit on one, ditching in the water and being rescued in less than an hour.

1945

ASKIN, WILLIAM D., 1924-   **5779**

In AMERICAN DIARIES OF WORLD WAR II, edited by Donald Vining, pp. 251-265.

Jan-Mar 1945. Extracts from diary of yeoman second class on LST in Philippine engagement; trading with Filipinos who came alongside the ship in small boats; routine, boring office work on ship; many complaints about food, heat, crowding and bugs; enjoying a leave at Pearl Harbor, especially the "gorgeous" women at the canteen.

AYERS, EBEN A., d. 1977   **5780**

Farrar, Ronald. "Harry Truman and the Press: A View from the Inside." JOURNALISM HISTORY 8 (1981):56-62, 70.

1945-1953. Article containing extracts from diary kept by Truman's deputy press secretary; the president's opinions on the press, journalists and columnists, with Walter Lippmann receiving an extra share of colorful vituperation; accounts of press conferences; references to press secretary Charles G. Ross.

CAMPBELL, HELEN JONES   **5781**

DIARY OF A WILLIAMSBURG HOSTESS. New York: G.P. Putnam's Sons, 1946. 177 pp.

Jan-Nov 1945? Chatty diary, obviously written for publication, of the pleasures and problems of conducting tourists through buildings of restored Colonial Williamsburg; humorous incidents, effects on her family and black servants, who are depicted in stereotypical fashion.

ELLIS, EDWARD ROBB, 1911-   **5782**

In AMERICAN DIARIES OF WORLD WAR II, edited by Donald Vining, pp. 122-129.

Aug-Sep 1945. Extracts from diary of navy corpsman first class, serving in Okinawa, a former journalist; long, descriptive entries

of how things and people looked, what everyone did and the destruction of the cities.

EPSTEIN, BERNARD   **5783**

In AMERICAN DIARIES OF WORLD WAR II, edited by Donald Vining, pp. 416-423.

Jan-Apr 1945. Extracts from prisoner of war diary of Swampscott, Massachusetts, first lieutenant held at Oflag 79 in Brunswick, Germany; the liberation experience, finding hoarded food and remains of Red Cross parcels in Luftwaffe quarters though prisoners had suffered on scant rations; collecting souvenirs, flying out to Le Havre and Camp Lucky Strike, a tent city set up for processing liberated prisoners and returning them to the states.

GAYN, MARK J., 1909-   **5784**

JAPAN DIARY. New York: W. Sloan Associates, 1948. 517 pp.

1945-1948. Foreign correspondent's report of conditions and events in Japan during Allied occupation; press club and military headquarters in Tokyo; behind the scenes view of conflicts of the old feudal system and the attempt to introduce democracy; visits to villages; troubles and hopes of farmers; food shortages; war criminals and purges; intrigue and uncertainty in Korea; interviews with major and minor officials.

GEBHARD, ANNA LAURA MUNRO, 1914-   **5785**

RURAL PARISH! A YEAR FROM THE JOURNAL OF ANNA LAURA GEBHARD. New York: Abingdon-Cokesbury, 1947. 121 pp.

1945-1946? Diary, probably kept for publication, of a minister's wife in a rural Methodist parish serving three small churches; character sketches of people; difficulties and small successes; the flavor of small town life.

GILBERT, GUSTAV MARK, 1911-1977   **5786**

NUREMBERG DIARY. New York: Farrar, Straus, 1947. 471 pp.

Oct 1945-Jul 1946. Narrative diary of prison psychologist at the Nuremberg trial of Nazi war criminals; long interviews of and conversations with defendants in their cells and accounts of testimony during the trial; much on the attitudes and behavior of Hans Frank, Hermann Göring, Albert Speer and others; considerable information on their attitudes toward Hitler, the Nazi phenomenon, the war, concentration camps and the massacre of Jews; cross examination of witnesses; a fascinating and horrifying record.

JOHNSTON, RUSSELL R.   **5787**

POLAND 1945: A RED CROSS DIARY. Philadelphia: Dorrance, 1973. 171 pp.

May 1945-Apr 1946. Red Cross field director's diary kept while attached to postwar civilian relief in Warsaw and other Polish cities; travel to his assignment through Cairo, where he was on VE day; frustrating delays in Moscow with time to observe remnants of former grandeur and present destitution of citizens; the places, people, daily life, devastation and suffering during troubling days of Russian takeover in Poland; relief from loneliness and homesickness; fond memories of outings with his father, chiefly California hunting and fishing trips, with loving tributes to a "gentle, kindly man with a zest for living that kept him from growing old."

MELBY, JOHN FREMONT, 1913-   5788

THE MANDATE OF HEAVEN: RECORD OF A CIVIL WAR, CHINA 1945-49. Toronto: University of Toronto Press, 1968. 313 pp.

> 1945-1949. Extracts from diary of foreign service officer assigned to Chungking to "keep track of what the Russians were up to in China"; relations with numerous American, Chinese and Russian officials; travels to various Chinese cities; embassy social life and gossip; resignation of ambassador Patrick J. Hurley and appointment of George Marshall; much on Chou En-lai, Chiang Kai-shek, war and negotiations between Nationalists and Communists; serious effort to understand China and its problems, but with an urbane and slightly cynical humor.

SCHWARTZ, DORIS   5789

"My Three Months in Yokohama Harbor." YANKEE 45 (January 1981):83-87, 101-102.

> Sep-Nov 1945. Army nurse's life and work aboard hospital ship MARIGOLD at Yokohama just after Japanese surrender; physical and psychological condition of men recently released from prison camps; harrowing accounts of their experiences; their recovery from nutritional deficiencies and other illnesses.

TRUMAN, HARRY S., 1884-1972   5790

OFF THE RECORD: THE PRIVATE PAPERS OF HARRY S. TRUMAN. Edited by Robert H. Ferrell. New York: Harper & Row, 1980. 448 pp. passim.

> 1945-1962 (with gaps). A significant diary covering his presidency and retirement, entries beginning with the death and funeral of Roosevelt and the hectic days that followed; frank comments on domestic and foreign policy, national and world events, the cabinet and Congress; sometimes crusty opinions on people, including MacArthur and Eisenhower, as well as the "liars, trimmers and pussyfooters on both sides of the aisle in the Senate and the House"; political philosophy, personal values, religious views and pleasantly mundane family notes; mainly a revelation of Truman as a private man, humorous and unpretentious, not entirely at home with the grandeur and fuss of the White House; post-presidential years in Independence with travels to Europe, Hawaii, etc., but fewer diary entries.

MR. PRESIDENT: THE FIRST PUBLICATION FROM THE PERSONAL DIARIES, PRIVATE LETTERS, PAPERS, AND REVEALING INTERVIEWS OF HARRY S. TRUMAN. By William Hillman. New York: Farrar, Straus and Young, 1952. 253 pp. Diary, pp. 107-150.

> 1945-1949 (with gaps). Brief comments on affairs and persons of state.

Ferrell, Robert H., ed. "Truman at Potsdam." AMERICAN HERITAGE 31, no. 4 (1980):36-47.

> Jul-Aug 1945. Extracts covering the president's journey aboard the AUGUSTA; meeting with Churchill; horror of war-devastated Berlin; the historic meeting at Potsdam with detailed reactions to Stalin; ruminations on the Manhattan Project and intention to use atomic bomb against Japanese military targets only; thoughts on the "Polish Question," reparations and division of the spoils of war.

Mark, Eduard, ed. "'Today Has Been a Historical One': Harry S. Truman's Diary of the Potsdam Conference." DIPLOMATIC HISTORY 4 (1980):317-326.

> Jul 1945. Extract covering the conference and Truman's observations on Churchill and Stalin.

WORTIS, EMILY, 1938-   5791

In SMALL VOICES, by Josef and Dorothy Berger, pp. 27-29.

> Oct 1945-Jan 1946. Extracts from seven-year-old girl's first diary; brief entries about family and school.

1946

HORR, ALFRED REUEL, b. 1875   5792

THE LOG OF THE SCHOONER BOWDOIN. Cleveland: World, 1947. 140 pp.

> Jun-Jul 1946. Cleveland banker's adventures aboard the BOWDOIN as member of a volunteer crew composed of business and professional men, with Arctic explorer, Donald B. MacMillan, as captain; from Boothbay Harbor, Maine, up the coast of Labrador to edge of the Polar ice pack; navigating between icebergs; notes on Eskimos; an interesting picture of amateurs adjusting to seafaring life; dated but narrative entries.

MAUROIS, ANDRE, 1885-1967   5793

FROM MY JOURNAL. Translated from the French by Joan Charles. New York: Harper, 1948. 250 pp.

MY AMERICAN JOURNAL. London: Falcon Press, 1950. 250 pp.

> Jan-Dec 1946. French author's journal covering a teaching assignment in America and return to France; teaching of French and American literature at the University of Kansas City and Stephens College with interesting notes on his students, many of them returned veterans, and their attitudes, his courses and enjoyment of watching "some of these fine minds expanding"; references to many faculty, as well as literary and political contacts; reactions to American religious, social and racial attitudes and institutions; events of the time; return to Paris, with observations on postwar conditions and intellectual life in France and elsewhere in Europe; stories and aphorisms.

SYKORA, THOMAS ANDREW   5794

"A Seventeen Year Old Looks at the Lakes." INLAND SEAS 3 (1947):77-82, 180-184.

> Jun-Aug 1946? Lakewood, Ohio, boy's summer working on a Great Lakes bulk freighter; hard work of various kinds on board ship and unloading cargoes of coal and ore; a fierce storm; names of other freighters; some adventures in ports; an interesting diary of a well-spent summer.

1947

BEAUVOIR, SIMONE DE, 1908-1986   5795

AMERICA DAY BY DAY. Translated by Patrick Dudley. London: Gerald Duckworth, 1952. 295 pp. Reprint. New York: Grove, 1953.

Jan-May 1947. Journal of French intellectual's lecture and pleasure tour in America, somewhat reconstructed for publication; cities and scenes throughout the country, with special attention to New York, Washington,D.C., Chicago and Los Angeles; lecturing at universities; reflections on American mores and values and reactions to many people, identified only by initials.

Extracts in DIARY OF AMERICA, by Josef and Dorothy Berger, pp. 605-609.

Jan-Feb 1947. Manhattan seen through the eyes of a French visitor.

In PRAIRIE STATE, by Paul M. Angle, pp. 514-526. Chicago: University of Chicago Press, 1968.

May 1950. Extracts about Chicago as seen on walking tours with friends; luxury and squalor of various communities; ethnic populations, especially black.

DAY, DOROTHY, 1897-1980   **5796**

ON PILGRIMAGE. New York: Catholic Worker Books, 1948. 175 pp.

1947. Diary of founder of the Catholic Worker movement; daily pleasures on New York farm, the change of seasons, visits to daughters' homes in West Virginia and Pennsylvania; acceptance of no escape from ''woman's lot'' as homemaker; her philosophy of how to live and what to live by.

D'EÇA, FLORENCE L.   **5797**

THE DIARY OF A FOREIGN SERVICE WIFE. Taunton, Mass.: W.S. Sullwold, 1977. 333 pp.

1947-1958. Diary of a foreign service wife who accompanied her husband, Raul, a member of the International Information and Cultural Affairs Office, to Rio de Janeiro; assignment to Recife, finding and moving into a suitable house, struggling with Portugese language and communicating with servants; a recall to Rio for Quitandinha Conference just as life became somewhat settled; experiencing Carnival, Brazilian customs, diplomatic social life and entertaining American cultural ambassadors such as Aaron Copland, Blanche Thebom and the Minnesota Players; reassignment to Belo Horizonte to establish United States Information Service library, which suffered severe damage during anti-American protest; charity work for Baleia Hospital for tubercular children; high regard for the Seventh-day Adventist Clinic at Rio where she had emergency surgery.

DUSTOOR, PHIROZE EDULDJI, 1898-   **5798**

AMERICAN DAYS. With a foreword by Pearl Buck. Bombay: Orient Longmans, 1952. 325 pp.

1947-1948. Extracts, revised for publication, from diary of professor from University of Allahabad, India, on a tour of United States; shipboard contacts on voyage of MARINE ADDER to San Francisco; visiting and lecturing at universities, attending public and university lectures; cross-country train trip for Princeton's Bicentennial celebration; serving as a delegate to Fourteenth Conference of Rotary International; frank impressions of people, places, politics, customs and American institutions.

HOUSEHOLDER, VIC H.   **5799**

Ferrell, Robert H., ed. ''A Visitor to the White House.'' MISSOURI HISTORICAL REVIEW 78 (1984):311-336.

Feb 1947. Diary of an overnight stay at the White House of a war comrade and longtime friend of President Truman, there for the purpose of enlisting Truman's support for his company, American Rolling Mill Company, which was involved in labor disputes; detailed account of all facets of his visit and conversation; Truman's incredibly unguarded disclosure of intent to help influence the outcome of ARMCO litigation, his statement that Roosevelt had admitted severe illness in August of 1944 and his revealing of the number of atom bombs in the United States arsenal.

MALINA, JUDITH, 1926-   **5800**

THE DIARIES OF JUDITH MALINA. New York: Grove Press, 1984. 485 pp.

1947-1957. Diary of actress and founder, along with Julian Beck, of the Living Theatre during its stormy formative years; relationship with Beck and her parents; her mother's painful death from cancer; theaters and theater companies, chiefly in New York; thoughts on organizing pacifist-anarchist groups; arraigned with Dorothy Day and others for civil disobedience; a wide variety of artists, playwrights, poets, actors and musicians, with various interests in either the diarist or the idea of the juxtaposition of theater and politics; figures in her life including Paul Goodman, John Cage, Merce Cunningham, Alan and Serafina Hovhaness, Lester Schwartz, Philip Smith, Richard Stryker, Dylan Thomas, etc.

THE ENORMOUS DESPAIR. New York: Random House, 1972. 249 pp.

Aug 1968-Apr 1969. Experiences and impressions during the 1968-1969 American tour; her despair at the apparent failure of civil rights and peace movements; sketches of such friends as Allen Ginsberg, Salvador Dali and Serge Oblensky; observations on the American scene from a non-violent anarchist perspective.

O'BRIEN, MARGARET, 1937-   **5801**

In SMALL VOICES, edited by Josef and Dorothy Berger, pp. 74-79.

Jan-Mar 1947. Extracts from surprisingly normal childhood diary revealing more excitement about getting a radar signal ring with box tops than about being America's favorite child movie star.

1948

CRAFT, ROBERT, 1923-   **5802**

STRAVINSKY: THE CHRONICLE OF A FRIENDSHIP. New York: A.A. Knopf, 1972. 424 pp.

1948-1971. Selections from journal of Igor Stravinsky's companion and musical assistant; active schedule of recording sessions and concert tours with either Stravinsky or Craft conducting both in the United States and abroad; respites at Stravinsky's home in Hollywood and his candid remarks on many major artistic and political figures with whom he associated; details of an impressive recognition dinner, rare for an artist, given by President Kennedy; moving description of Stravinsky's funeral in Venice; a fascinating and revealing view of a musical career.

In DIALOGUES AND A DIARY, by Igor Stravinsky and Robert Craft, pp. 153-279. Garden City, New York: Doubleday, 1963. London: Faber, 1968.

1948-1962. Extracts.

In THEMES AND EPISODES, by Igor Stravinsky, pp. 159-352. New York: Knopf, 1966.

1949-1966. Extracts.

ELLIOT, JAMES, 1927-1956   **5803**

THE JOURNALS OF JIM ELLIOT. Edited by Elisabeth Elliot. Old Tappan, N.J.: Fleming H. Revell, 1978. 477 pp.

1948-1955. Diary of a missionary who was killed by the Auca Indians of Ecuador; Bible reading and meditations while a student at Wheaton College, Illinois; graduate work in linguistics; itinerant preaching for Plymouth Brethren; inner conflict over whether to combine marriage with dangerous and remote missionary work, then several years of marriage to Elisabeth Howard Elliot before his death.

LEWIS, ABIGAIL, pseud.   **5804**

AN INTERESTING CONDITION: THE DIARY OF A PREGNANT WOMAN. Garden City, N.Y.: Doubleday, 1950. 256 pp.

Extracts in A DAY AT A TIME, edited by Margo Culley, pp. 256-271.

Aug 1948-Jun 1949. Woman's diary of surprise at finding herself pregnant after being repeatedly told she could not bear children; changes in physical and emotional state, career and homemaking plans, husband and wife relationship; recounting the birth experience and discovering that delivery was not an end but the beginning of an exciting new experience.

MARSTON, OTIS   **5805**

"Running the Dolores River, 1948." COLORADO MAGAZINE 26 (1949):258-270.

May 1948. Adventures of two couples on a challenging river excursion by rowboat; much excitement navigating rapids; a few notes on scenery, camps, Indian caves, etc.

1949

BARTON, BETSY   **5806**

AS LOVE IS DEEP. New York: Duell, Sloan and Pearce, 1957. 144 pp.

1949-1955 (with gaps). Diary of a young woman confined to a wheelchair because of a crushed spine; coping with her handicap and then with her mother's illness and death from cancer; profound admiration for her mother's courage; her own isolation and bereavement, followed by the comfort of her family and growing acceptance of life and death.

BERNSTEIN, LEONARD, 1918-   **5807**

FINDINGS. New York: Simon and Schuster, 1982. 376 pp. Diary, pp. 144-147,

1949-1957 (with gaps). Very brief extracts on conception, realization and opening of WEST SIDE STORY; the challenge of treating a tragic story with the techniques of musical comedy.

COLE, MARGARET O'DONOVAN-ROSSA, 1887-   **5808**

GRANDMA TAKES A FREIGHTER: THE STORY OF AN ATLANTIC CROSSING. New York: Exposition Press, 1950. 104 pp.

Aug-Sep 1949. Account of a voyage to Germany and Belgium on the LENA LUCKENBACH as the only passenger and only woman aboard; learning ship jargon and enduring a few pranks from the crew, playing bridge, a fire drill; in ports of Bremerhaven, Hamburg, Antwerp, etc., watching unloading of cargo, sightseeing and exploring, often with the captain; noting the postwar devastation of Bremen.

GREEN, PARIS R.   **5809**

"Observations on a World Flight." ARKANSAS HISTORICAL QUARTERLY 8 (1949): 215-239.

Feb-Mar 1949. Travel diary of an airplane trip by Fayetteville man and his wife; stops in Hawaii, Tokyo, Shanghai, Hong Kong, Manila, Bangkok, Calcutta, Karachi, Cairo, Istanbul and Rome; some touristic notes but mainly textbook-type accounts of history and culture, plus his decidedly chauvinistic opinions on people and customs during a long, expensive trip which confirmed his satisfaction with being an American.

PEARSON, DREW, 1897-1969   **5810**

DIARIES. Edited by Tyler Abell. New York: Holt, Rinehart and Winston, 1974. 592 pp.

1949-1959. Journalist's diary containing material that could not be published in his regular columns, from Eisenhower's and Pershing's girl friends to Forrestal's madness; his own quarrel with Truman; references to presidents Johnson, Kennedy and Nixon, as well as senators Joseph R. McCarthy, Estes Kefauver, etc., and to Secretary of State John Foster Dulles.

PLATH, SYLVIA, 1932-1963   **5811**

In ARIADNE'S THREAD, edited by Lyn Lifshin, pp. 89-91.

Nov 1949. Diary extract on being seventeen; love and freedom, fear of getting older and having to make adult decisions.

THE JOURNALS OF SYLVIA PLATH. Edited by Ted Hughes and Frances McCullough. New York: Dial, 1982. 370 pp.

1950-1962. Selection from poet's journal selected to comprise about a third of the original; home life in Wellesley, Massachusetts, student days at Smith College and Cambridge University and teaching at Smith; her writing and publishing career; marriage to English poet Ted Hughes, fears of barrenness, but eventual births of children; life in England and Boston; reflections and musings about her aspirations, individual freedom and the special predicaments of women, the creative artist and the person blessed or cursed with sensitivity; depressions and dark moods described with increasing minuteness over the years; some painful thoughts about her mother and others formative to her life; therapy with Dr. Ruth Beuscher; reactions to the writing of others, particularly poets Adrienne Rich and Anne Sexton; entries ending several months before her death by suicide.

SALISBURY, HARRISON EVANS, 1908-   **5812**

MOSCOW JOURNAL: THE END OF STALIN. Chicago: University of Chicago Press, 1961. 449 pp.

1949-1953. Journal of a foreign correspondent for the NEW YORK TIMES admitted into Russia after a year and a half of no visas granted to American reporters; reporting what could be determined or surmised about the complex political situation during the height of the Stalin years and the cold war; relations with Yugoslavia and China; the death of Stalin and the changes that ensued; fluctuating importance of various figures in the government, such as Lavrenti Beriya, Molotov, Krushchev and Malenkov; personal notes on living conditions, cost and availability of consumer goods, theater, the Russian countryside and Easter; diary entries and dispatches to the TIMES with censors' cuts restored.

1950

GLUCKMAN, JANET   **5813**

In ARIADNE'S THREAD, edited by Lyn Lifshin, pp. 252-258.

1950? Jewish journalist's account of returning to Germany to visit her mother; observations on postwar conditions in East and West Berlin.

PARTON, MARGARET   **5814**

THE LEAF AND THE FLAME. New York: Knopf, 1959. 227 pp. London: Bodley Head, 1960.

1950?-1955? Private diary covering NEW YORK HERALD TRIBUNE journalist's five years in India; the mystery, beauty and staggering problems of that country; keen observations of scenes, situations and people, from Brahmans to untouchables, as well as Americans and British; such personal matters as the diarist's marriage, birth of a son and social life; analysis of Indian culture; sporadic dated entries, but no exact indication of years; a highly acclaimed book.

SMITH, CHARLES B.   **5815**

"Excerpts from a Test Pilot's Diary." UNITED STATES NAVAL INSTITUTE PROCEEDINGS 78, no. 2 (1952):131-135.

May 1950-Mar 1951. Navy pilot's account of experiences with the SF 12 K Project, with description of the plane and its performance under test conditions; conferences with the Kerry Aviation Corporation and navy engineers about modifications leading to certification of the "Monsoon" aircraft.

X, Doctor   **5816**

INTERN. New York: Harper & Row, 1965. 404 pp.

1950?-1951? Undesignated year in the life of an intern in what he calls Graystone Memorial Hospital; notes on other interns, doctors, nurses; his feelings about patients, himself, his work, frustrations, fatigue; a picture of the "dynamic process through which a doctor is made."

1951

CUCA, MARION, 1939-1953   **5817**

In SMALL VOICES, by Josef and Dorothy Berger, pp. 86-90.

1951-1952. Extracts from New York girl's diary of school, parties, organizing clubs and sleeping overnight with her girl friends; summer camp; boys; sensitivity toward the multi-ethnic neighborhood in which she lived.

KAHN, ARTHUR DAVID, 1920-   **5818**

SPEAK OUT! AMERICA WANTS PEACE. New York: Independence Publishers, 1951. 256 pp.

Mar-Oct 1951. Professor's speaking tour throughout the United States under auspices of the American Peace Crusade; meetings with Progressive party and labor groups; criticism of American rearmament, role in Korean War and cold war; reports of harassment by anti-Communists.

ROREM, NED, 1923-   **5819**

THE PARIS AND NEW YORK DIARIES OF NED ROREM. San Francisco: North Point Press, 1983. 399 pp.

1951-1961. Gifted composer's diary of years in France and North Africa; a self-portrait of an arrogant young man moving in the circles of the literary and artistic elite in Paris; comments on Georges Auric, Jean Cocteau, Virgil Thomson, Copland, Honegger, Bernstein, etc.; enjoying the patronage of Marie Laure Noailles; bits of gossip along with keen observations on the arts; pursuing his profession in New York but recording in his diaries chiefly his obsession with his personal importance, alcohol and homosexual lovers; ultimately a sad figure propounding questions that have elusive answers.

Extracts in MEN WITHOUT MASKS, by Michael Rubin, pp. 108-116.

1951-1961. Extracts painfully exploring feelings, including bereavement after being jilted by his homosexual lover.

THE PARIS DIARY. New York: Braziller, 1966. 240 pp.

1951-1955.

THE NEW YORK DIARY. New York: Braziller, 1967. 218 pp.

1955-1961.

THE FINAL DIARY. New York: Holt, Rinehart and Winston, 1974. 439 pp.

1961-1972. Commissions, composing, complaining; interaction with many musicians, especially singers performing his songs; profound grief over death of Viscomtesse de Noailles; frequent references to his own aging, what he had or had not accomplished; genuine love and appreciation for his family; pithy analysis of many musical works including his own; constant introspection; a glimpse into the mysteries of a creative mind.

SETTING THE TONE: ESSAYS AND A DIARY. New York: Coward-McCann, 1983. 383 pp. Diary pp. 60-85.

"Nantucket Diary." TRIQUARTERLY 40 (1977):184-207.

Jun-Sep 1974. Reflections on the deaths of Darius Milhaud, his neighbor Parker Tyler and others; his own aging; his Nantucket vacation "where the community is 101 percent heterosexual,

WASP, nonintellectual Republicans,'' none of whom, alas, had heard of Ned Rorem; interesting reactions to books and movies, art, the Quakerism in which he was raised; some bitter thoughts about the public reception of his music and published diaries.

ROUNDS, FRANK, 1915-   5820

A WINDOW ON RED SQUARE. Boston: Houghton Mifflin, 1953. 304 pp.

> 1951-1952. Journal of American Embassy attaché in Moscow; detailed and affectionate portrayal of many Russian people; attitudes, customs and situation under communism; notes on plays, ballets, concerts, libraries, museums, courts, etc.; travel mainly by train; a long analysis of a Shostakovich concert and predicament of Soviet artists; an interesting and illuminating journal.

STEINBECK, JOHN, 1902-1968   5821

JOURNAL OF A NOVEL. New York: Viking Press, 1969. 182 pp.

> 1951-1952. Letter-journal kept for his friend and Viking editor Pascal Covici, during the writing of EAST OF EDEN; of interest for what it reveals of Steinbeck's non-literary interests and pursuits, relations with those around him and his creative processes.

1952

ALBERTS, ROBERT C.   5822

THE SHAPING OF THE POINT: PITTSBURGH'S RENAISSANCE PARK. Pittsburgh: University of Pittsburgh Press, 1980. 247 pp. Diary, pp. 121-128.

> Jan-Sep 1952. Architect's office diary of time, place, and nature of his work on Point Park; details of a complex civic undertaking; ''converting imaginative drawings and proposals into blueprints on which contracts can be solicited and actual work performed.''

GINSBERG, ALLEN, 1926-   5823

JOURNALS: EARLY FIFTIES, EARLY SIXTIES. Edited by Gordon Ball. New York: Grove, 1977. 302 pp.

> 1952-1962. Extracts from poet's journal combining many dreams, musing, fantasies and experiences; a rather unsettled existence in New York and Berkeley and during travels to Mexico, France, Greece and Israel; much of interest on his friends William S. Burroughs, Jack Kerouac, Gregory Corso, Timothy Leary, etc., and conversations with Dylan Thomas and William Carlos Williams; homosexual attachments, the most enduring with Peter Orlovsky; various drug experiments, some related to his religious quest; drafts of poems and descriptions of scenes and people; an interesting journal, providing glimpses of one man's process of becoming a poet.

INDIAN JOURNALS. San Francisco: Dave Haselwood Books, 1970. 210 pp.

> 1962-1963. The poet's rambles through India with Peter Orlovsky; impressions of cities, villages, countryside, Hinduism, opium dens, tourist attractions and all manner of Indian people, from beggars to holy men; drug experiences and illnesses, including a revolting case of worms.

MITCHELL, CARLETON, 1910-   5824

PASSAGE EAST. New York: W.W. Norton, 1953. 248 pp.

> Jul 1952. Yachtsman's diary of the 1952 transatlantic race of the Royal Ocean Racing Club, in which his CARIBEE was the American entry; a colorful and detailed log and diary capturing the hard work, strain and exhilaration of sailing.

1953

HOPE, MARY   5825

TOWARDS EVENING. New York: Sheed and Ward, 1955. 178 pp.

> Jan-Dec 1953. Devout Catholic woman's religious reflections; frequent quotes or mention of reading classics of religious literature; thoughts on the aged in literature and art, especially saints; quiet acceptance of growing older, slowing down, facing loneliness and finding daily comfort in her devotions and prayers.

MERSON, MARTIN   5826

PRIVATE DIARY OF A PUBLIC SERVANT. New York: Macmillan, 1955. 171 pp.

> Feb-Jul 1953. Account of assistant to Robert L. Johnson, head of the International Information Administration during a tumultuous period; running head-on with Sen. Joseph McCarthy's efforts to control the State Department and to limit selection of American books supplied to libraries abroad to those reflecting his own ideology; Merson's and Johnson's often frustrated attempts to preserve a philosophy of intellectual and political freedom for American information services.

PRESCOTT, PETER S.   5827

A DARKENING GREEN: NOTES FROM THE SILENT GENERATION. New York: Coward, McCann, & Geoghegan, 1974. 222 pp.

> Jun 1953-May 1954. Extracts from an engaging diary of a Harvard freshman, later to be an editor of NEWSWEEK and literary critic, with narrative comment twenty years later; growing up, emotions of adolescence, anxiety about sex and the impact of his appearance on Radcliffe girls; notes on his instructors and hints of Harvard snobbery; a lack of political sophistication or involvement typical of his college generation.

SCHAFFER, DORI, 1938-1963   5828

DEAR DEEDEE: FROM THE DIARIES OF DORI SCHAFFER. Edited by Anne Schaffer. Secaucus, N.J.: Lyle Stuart, 1978. 222 pp.

> 1953-1963. Record of a brilliant girl's rapid and traumatic progression from adolescence to womanhood; college and graduate studies at Scripps, UCLA and Columbia often clouded by loneliness and her dissatisfaction with even the highest achievements; unsettling relationships, including a brief and devastating marriage to a homosexual and an exhilarating but ultimately disillusioning affair with a man twice her age; an abortion; high idealism leading to involvement in the civil rights movement and other causes; precocious reflections on books, ideas and values, particularly the predicament of the woman intellectual and her desire for her own identity as a scholar, yet longing

for a traditional Jewish marriage and family life; deaths of loved ones and other losses in rapid succession contributing to the final months of severe depression which preceded her suicide at age twenty-five.

1954

BELL, MARILYN, 1942- 5829

In SMALL VOICES, edited by Josef and Dorothy Berger, pp. 235-241.

1954-1955. Twelve-year-old's diary of school, skipping classes, playing in the band, playing basketball, mooning over movie idols, struggling with DAVID COPPERFIELD and introduction to Shakespeare in Crescent, Oklahoma, school; an ideal vacation in California.

CHILDS, MARQUIS WILLIAM, 1903- 5830

THE RAGGED EDGE: THE DIARY OF A CRISIS. Garden City, N.Y.: Doubleday, 1955. 251 pp.

Feb-Aug 1954. Journalist's account, "in diary form," of the last days of the Big Four foreign ministers' meeting in Berlin, the Geneva Conference and the breakdown of the European Defense Commununity Treaty; interviews with Jean Monnet, Konrad Adenauer and Paul Raynaud; notes and opinions on Claire Booth Luce, Mendés-France, John Foster Dulles, etc.; concern about the balance of power between democracy and communism; much on attitudes and activities of the American diplomatic community; stays in Berlin, Paris, Geneva, etc., and political developments in various European countries; a foreign relations document which reveals cold war tensions.

HAGERTY, JAMES CAMPBELL, 1909-1981 5831

THE DIARY OF JAMES C. HAGERTY: EISENHOWER IN MID-COURSE. Edited by Robert H. Ferrell. Bloomington: Indiana University Press, 1983. 269 pp.

1954-1955. Extracts from the diary of Eisenhower's press secretary; comments on activities and attitudes of the president and members of Congress and the cabinet; major and minor events, foreign relations and domestic issues of the period, with considerable material on the Quemoy-Matsu controversy, the Oppenheimer case, the downfall of Joseph McCarthy and developments in Vietman; extensive references to Richard Nixon, Sherman Adams, Herbert Brownell, William F. Knowland, Lewis L. Strauss, John Foster Dulles and others; a partial but useful picture of the period.

1955

GARDNER, DOROTHY WILLIAMS, 1904- 5832

FUN ON A FREIGHTER. New York: Vantage, 1957, 184 pp.

Jan-Apr 1955. Travel diary, edited for publication, of escapades of a middle-aged couple on a freighter trip with stops in Japan, Korea, Taiwan, Bangkok, Singapore and Hong Kong, recounted

in a breezy style; adventures in port; views of traveling companions and crew.

HARVEY, NIGEL 5833

AMID THE ALIEN CORN: AN INTREPID ENGLISHMAN IN THE HEART OF AMERICA. By Hugh Willoughby, pseud. Edited by Joseph L. Martin. Indianapolis: Bobbs-Merrill, 1958. 159 pp.

Extracts in TRAVEL ACCOUNTS OF INDIANA, compiled by Shirley McCord, pp. 281-286.

Sep 1955-Aug 1956. Engish agriculturalist's letter-diary describing his experience at Purdue University's graduate agricultural school; visits to farms; a cattle auction; interesting comparison with English agriculture, countryside and people; social life with farm families.

HESSE, EVA, 1936-1970 5834

Johnson, Ellen H. "Order and Chaos: From the Diaries of Eva Hesse." ART IN AMERICA 71, no. 6 (1983):110-118.

1955-1970 (with gaps). German immigrant's diary extracts relating to painting and its relation to her "goals, ambitions, satisfactions and frustrations"; frequent notes on what inspired her to work and the need for acceptance of her art.

MORROW, EVERETT FREDERIC, 1909- 5835

BLACK MAN IN THE WHITE HOUSE. New York: Coward-McCann, 1963. 308 pp.

1955-1960. Diary of President Eisenhower's administrative assistant for race and other special projects, the first black to hold an executive White House position; his speaking engagements, travels, daily activities, Washington social events, etc.; candid observations on colleagues Sherman Adams, Jim Hagerty, Gerry Morgan, etc., as well as on Eisenhower; his increasing discomfort with the administration's sluggish pace on civil rights.

STUART, JESSE, 1907- 5836

THE YEAR OF MY REBIRTH. New York: McGraw-Hill, 1956. 342 pp.

Jan-Dec 1955. Kentucky writer's journal kept during convalescence from a severe heart attack; resting at his farm home near Riverton, with time to reflect on life and death, religion, the love of family and friends and, above all, to enjoy nature; a pleasant, optimistic journal by a man who learned to treasure each day of life.

1956

CHARNLEY, JEAN 5837

AN AMERICAN SOCIAL WORKER IN ITALY. Minneapolis: University of Minnesota Press, 1961. 323 pp.

Feb-Jul 1956. Minneapolis social worker's diary kept when she was a consultant to Italian welfare agencies and schools of social work while on a Fulbright grant; genuine interest in the Italian people and concern for their social problems; the challenge of adapting her discipline to a different culture; humorous personal incidents with a new language, locating an apartment and getting around in Rome; written in a charming and lively style.

KIESLER, FREDERICK JOHN, 1896-1966   5838

INSIDE THE ENDLESS HOUSE: ART, PEOPLE AND ARCHITECTURE. New York: Simon and Schuster, 1966. 573 pp. passim.

1956-1964 (with gaps). Diary of an architect, sculptor and scenic designer; notes on art and artists, music and composers, concerts and operas; going to Israel to design shrine for Dead Sea Scrolls at University of Tel Aviv; traveling and speaking in Europe; seeing Brasilia in the construction stage; his art theories culminating in design for the ENDLESS HOUSE which is described in detail; ''all ends meet in 'Endless' as they meet in life.''

PEARSON, CAROL LYNN   5839

WILL I EVERY FORGET THIS DAY? Edited by Elouise M. Bell. Salt Lake City: Bookcraft, 1980. 130 pp.

1956-1965. Extracts from the personal diary of a young Mormon actress and playwright, with entries beginning during her senior year of high school; student life at Brigham Young University; studies, boyfriends, drama, writing and religious activities; introspections about womanhood, career, love; tour of Asia with her university drama group; teaching at Snow College and Brigham Young; travel in Europe, including the Soviet Union, and Africa; scriptwriting for Mormon Church films; fresh and interesting.

RODMAN, SELDEN, 1909-   5840

MEXICAN JOURNAL: THE CONQUERORS CONQUERED. New York: Devin-Adair, 1958. 298 pp.

Oct 1956-Apr 1957. Journal kept by poet and art critic of a six month sojourn in Mexico; notes on arts and artists, including José Clements Orozco, Diego Rivera, David-Alfaro Siqueiros and Rufino Tamayo; interest in history, politics and revolutions, with comments on such political figures as Lazaro Cardenas and Miguel Aleman; word pictures of the sights and sounds of Mexico.

1957

DONOVAN, JAMES BRITT, 1916-   5841

STRANGERS ON A BRIDGE: THE CASE OF COLONEL ABEL. New York: Atheneum, 1964. 482 pp.

1957-1962. Diary of court-appointed defense attorney for Rudolf I. Abel, accused of being a Soviet spy; development of the case, the trial and relationship of mutual respect that developed between lawyer and client; roles of Reino Haykanen, Abel's former assistant, and Judge Mortimer W. Byers; newspaper coverage of the entire episode; the exchange of prisoners on Glienecker Bridge in Berlin involving Abel, Francis Gary Powers and Frederick L. Pryor; an exciting diary which reads like a spy novel and provides information on United States-Soviet relations of the period.

ELIADE, MIRCEA, 1907-   5842

NO SOUVENIRS, JOURNAL, 1957-1969. Translated by Fred H. Johnson, Jr. New York: Harper and Row, 1977. 343 pp.

1957-1969. Extracts from journal of a Rumanian historian of religions, who took a post at the University of Chicago when his discipline was discontinued in Marxist universities; aspects of his American experiences; travels to the Orient, Europe and Mexico; interacting with contemporary figures such as Carl Jung, Nae Ionesco and Thomas Altizer; Paul Tillich's final lecture and death; notes on his classes, writing, speaking, ideas for future investigations, Christianity, myth and man; a glimpse into the range of interest and encounter of a great mind.

1958

CALISHER, HORTENSE, 1911-   5843

HERSELF. New York: Arbor House, 1972. 401 pp. Diary pp. 48-83; 129-232.

Sep 1958. Journal kept by author while lecturing on writing in universities in Japan, the Philippines and Thailand as International Educational Exchange Service professor; meeting officials, professors and students; visiting popular tourist spots and attending Japanese theater; comments on customs and American residents.

ERNST, MORRIS LEOPOLD, 1888-1976   5844

TOUCH WOOD, A YEAR'S DIARY. New York: Atheneum, 1960. 370 pp.

Aug 1958-Aug 1959. Extracts from diary kept in his seventieth year by a prominent lawyer and prolific author; a whirlwind of activities and impressions; public affairs and politics, world events, people, reading, reflection and writing; life in New York and Nantucket; journeys to Britain, France, Israel, Pakistan and Colombia; oblique references to the ''Galindez affair'' in the Dominican Republic and Ernst's involvement in its investigation; interest in causes of individual freedom and civil rights.

UNTITLED: THE DIARY OF MY 72ND YEAR. New York: Robert B. Luce, 1962. 272 pp.

Jan-Dec 1960. Continued diary of his busy life of public service and private law practice; wide reading, intellectual and cultural interests; personal and political philosophy; scenes and people around New York affectionately described; Maine and Nantucket sailing vacations; a pleasant diary of a man obviously enjoying his later years.

GALBRAITH, JOHN KENNETH, 1908-   5845

JOURNEY TO POLAND AND YUGOSLAVIA. Cambridge: Harvard University Press, 1958. 118 pp.

May 1958. Harvard economist's lecture tour under auspices of the University of Warsaw and the Polish Economic Society; visits to Warsaw, Lublin, Kraców and Belgrade; notes on economic conditions, agriculture, industry, academic institutions and people of all kinds; conversations with professors, students and officials; informal but substantive.

AMBASSADOR'S JOURNAL: A PERSONAL ACCOUNT OF THE KENNEDY YEARS. Boston: Houghton Mifflin, 1969. 656 pp.

1961-1963. Diplomatic and personal journal of period as Kennedy's ambassador to India; candid notes on Indian affairs and people; the border war with China and negotiations over Kashmir; dealings with Nehru; embassy social life; travels in India; concerns over developments in Vietnam and China; notes on Averell Harriman and Dean Rusk; news of Kennedy's assassination; an important diplomatic source and record of Kennedy administration.

A CHINESE PASSAGE. Boston: Houghton Mifflin, 1973. 143 pp. New York: New American Library, 1973. 127 pp.

Sep 1972. Account of campaigning for George McGovern in San Francisco and Hawaii, then traveling to China on a fact-finding tour with Wassily Leontief and James Tobin; descriptions, in a slightly wry style, of what he observed and whom he met; notes on economy and industrial output, the nature of work and decision-making, social organization, medical care, agriculture, etc.; visits to communes, described as clean, decent but grim, and to the University of Peking, where he lectured on economics; travel by train to Peking, Nanking, Canton, Shanghai, Hangchow and other cities, enjoying sightseeing, opera, acrobatic entertainments and other aspects of Chinese popular culture.

HARNWELL, GAYLORD PROBASCO, 1903-   **5846**

RUSSIAN DIARY. Philadelphia: University of Pennsylvania Press, 1960. 125 pp.

Jun-Jul 1958. Diary of physicist and president of the University of Pennsylvania, who with group of college and university presidents, visited universities, technical schools and medical institutes in Moscow, Leningrad, Tbilisi, Tashkent, etc.; technical and professional observations on higher education; interesting social encounters and the inevitable misunderstandings in traveling in a foreign country.

HOFFER, ERIC, 1902-   **5847**

WORKING AND THINKING ON THE WATERFRONT. New York: Harper & Row, 1969. 180 pp.

Jun 1958-May 1959. Journal of philosophical longshoreman and author; work on San Francisco Bay area docks; conversations and reading; ruminations of politics, human nature, American life, world affairs, literature, etc.; loneliness relieved by outing with his little godson Eric Osborne.

BEFORE THE SABBATH. New York: Harper & Row, 1979. 144 pp.

Nov 1974-Jun 1975. Widely varied thoughts recorded in diary form during his seventy-third year; attitudes on current events, American culture and pitfalls, national and international politics and history; reactions to a considerable range of books and articles; a few ruminations on old age.

HUGHS, JOSEPH HENRY, 1941-1963   **5848**

THE MAKING OF A COAST GUARD OFFICER: A COVENANT WITH HONOR. New York: Philosophical Library, 1966. 412 pp. passim.

1958-1963. Letters and diaries of a Catholic student at the Coast Guard Academy; friends, classes, tours of duty on various training ships; the rigors of naval training; descriptions of European ports; good picture of a young man's emerging values and maturity.

1959

BECK, FRANCES   **5849**

DIARY OF A WIDOW. Boston: Beacon Press, 1965. 142 pp.

1959-1962. Record of a young mother moving through shock, anger, frustration, and anguish after sudden death of her husband; courageously making a new life for herself and three young children; coping with the practical problems of moving, a new teaching job and children's illnesses; gradually coming to terms with the reality of death and finding love for another man.

KENDIG, DIANE   **5850**

In ARIADNE'S THREAD, edited by Lyn Lifshin, pp. 192-196.

1959-1978. Extracts from Cleveland, Ohio, woman's personal diary; childhood note on starting a diary; traumatic events such as an attempted rape; breakup with a boyfriend and serious burns from a gas oven explosion.

SHEPPE, WALTER   **5851**

In FIRST MAN WEST: ALEXANDER MACKENZIE'S JOURNAL OF HIS VOYAGE TO THE PACIFIC COAST OF CANADA IN 1793, by Alexander Mackenzie, pp. 319-336. Berkeley: University of California Press, 1962.

Jul 1959. Sheppe's record of his automobile journey along Mackenzie's route across Canada to the Pacific as preparation for his editing and annotating of Mackenzie's journal.

1960

BEVINGTON, HELEN SMITH, 1906-   **5852**

ALONG CAME THE WITCH: A JOURNAL IN THE 1960's. New York: Harcourt, Brace, Jovanovich, 1976. 223 pp.

1960-1969. Poet's impressions, noted monthly, of books and people; teaching at Duke; a sabbatical in Europe, with travel aboard the VULCANIA; reactions to events in the news; family matters; a number of poems scattered throughout.

THE JOURNEY IS EVERYTHING: A JOURNAL OF THE SEVENTIES. Durham, N.C.: Duke University Press, 1983. 208 pp.

1970-1979. Continued reflections of Duke University poet and teacher; mostly comments on people, books and travels, especially after her retirement in 1976; journeys to Russia, Italy, Yugoslavia, Greece, Australia, New Zealand, Hawaii, etc., with comments on the travels of others interwoven with her own; friendships, past and present, with many writers; a leisurely journey through the decade, full of memories, impressions and anecdotes.

GLASSER, HOWARD T.   **5853**

& ON FOR A TIME IN ULLAPOOL. Wakefield, R.I., 1960. 8 pp.

Aug 1960. Extract from diary of ballad collector kept during his search for ballads in Scotland; in Ullapool, a small village on Loch Broom, and vicinity; a delightful description of people and place.

PROUDFOOT, MERRILL   5854

DIARY OF A SIT-IN. Chapel Hill: University of North Carolina Press, 1962. 204 pp.

Jun-Jul 1960. Revealing diary of a white Presbyterian minister and college professor involved in marches, picketing and sit-ins to integrate lunch counters in Knoxville, Tennessee, stores; difficulties of applying nonviolent philosophy to inherently violence-prone situations; frank acknowledgement of tensions within the movement, as well as antagonisms from without, yet basically a cooperative and courageous effort of black and white, students, clergy and faculty.

1961

BERGER, JOSEF, 1903-   5855

POPPO. New York: Simon and Schuster, 1962. 192 pp. Diary, pp. 33-192.

Sep-Nov 1961. Writer's diary of extraordinary months of life with a nine-year-old Puerto Rican boy who had subtly captured his affection; the complications for him and his wife, Dottie, of being middle-aged parents; the love and affection on both sides; the agony and wishes of Poppo's mother Maria for his best interest; the ultimate victory of Poppo's love for Maria and the undertanding of the Bergers.

SEABORG, GLENN THEODORE, 1912-   5856

KENNEDY, KRUSHCHEV AND THE TEST BAN. By Glenn T. Seaborg with the assistance of Benjamin S. Loeb. Berkeley: University of California Press, 1981. 320 pp. passim.

1961-1963. Undated extracts within a book based on journals of the chairman of the Atomic Energy Commission under President Kennedy; an account of the negotiations which led to the Limited Test Ban Treaty; of interest not only for the test ban debate, but also for depiction of the relationship between Kennedy and Krushchev.

SOYER, RAPHAEL, 1899-   5857

DIARY OF AN ARTIST. Washington, D.C.: New Republic Books, 1977. 316 pp.

1961-1977. Artist's private diary and views on art and artists; influences, memories, the contemporary art scene and museums, especially the value of the Metropolitan Museum of Art; intimate interactions with peers, visiting major artists during a trip to Europe and Israel; great masterpieces seen through the words of a famous painter.

A PAINTER'S PILGRIMAGE. New York: Crown, 1962, 127 pp.

May-Sep 1961. Spontaneous journal entries of words and pictures kept while taking in the riches of European art museums; visits to modern studios and conversations with artists.

HOMAGE TO THOMAS EAKINS, ETC. Edited by Rebecca L. Soyer. South Brunswick, N.J.: T. Yoseloff, 1966. 183 pp.

1963-1965. Planning, problems and painting HOMAGE TO THOMAS EAKINS, a representational group portrait of American painters with Eakins' GROSS CLINIC in the background; comments on the artists and notes on conversations with Edward Hopper, Leonard Baskin, Lloyd Goodrich, Jack Levine, Moses Soyer, Edwin Dickinson and Reginald Marsh as they sat for studies for the painting.

SELF-REVEALMENT. New York: Random House, 1966. 116 pp. Maecenas, 1969.

1966-1967. Preparing for retrospective exhibition at Forum Gallery; sailing on OSLOFJORD to Scandinavian countries; interesting observations on passengers; revisiting museums in Europe; comments on writing involvement in the art world.

1962

ABRAMOWITZ, JACK, 1918-   5858

DIARY OF A SLOW LEARNER CLASS. Chicago: Follett, 1963. 48 pp.

Sep-Dec 1962. A history teacher's experience with slow learning high school students in an unspecified school; lessons, class discussion, problems and successes; many details of a variety of techniques for engaging students' attention, enhancing motivation and increasing learning of history and language skills.

BISSELL, HOWARD T., 1955-   5859

In SMALL VOICES, edited by Josef and Dorothy Berger, pp. 98-101.

Feb-Jul 1962. Extracts from diary of seven-year-old second grade boy; "probrums" at school and explanations of Mother's Day and Father's Day.

CLAPP, ARCHIE J.   5860

"Shu-Fly Diary." UNITED STATES NAVAL INSTITUTE PROCEEDINGS 89, no. 10 (1963): 42-53.

Apr-Aug 1962. Marine helicopter squadron commander's account of missions in support of Vietnamese troops in the Mekong Delta area; troop lifts to raid Vietcong strongholds; problem of "the VC mingling with the local population while they fired at us"; difficulties of jungle landings and of getting the diminutive Vietnamese men back up into the helicopters.

GIESE, VINCENT JOSEPH, 1923-   5861

JOURNAL OF A LATE VOCATION. Notre Dame, Ind.: Fides, 1966. 159 pp. Journal, pp. 36-69.

1962-1966. After service as lay worker in Chicago, deciding at age thirty-seven to study for Catholic priesthood at the Beda College, a seminary for belated vocations, in Rome; rigor of studies, special religious services, achievements of classmates, excitement and celebration of ordination; thoughts on the church and his calling.

GILROY, FRANK DANIEL, 1925-   5862

ABOUT THOSE ROSES. New York: Random House, 1955. 210 pp. Diary pp. 5-93.

1962-1964. Extracts from the diary of the playwright relating to his THE SUBJECT WAS ROSES; details of the drawn out negotiations to start production of the play, rehearsals with actors Jack Albertson, Irene Daily and Martin Sheen and director Ulu Grosbard right up to opening night at the Royale Theatre in New York; a view of artistic and financial uncertainties, the tension of last minute changes and both the involvement and detachment of the playwright.

GODWIN, GAIL, 1937-   5863

In ARIADNE'S THREAD, edited by Lyn Lifshin, pp. 75-85.

1962-1981 (with gaps). Extracts from author's journal; notes on working in London, writers and writing, editors, characters in novels; dreams; selling a book with observations on its progress and completion.

HORTON, DOUGLAS, 1891-1968   5864

VATICAN DIARY. Philadelphia: United Church Press, 1964-1966. 4 vols.

1962-1965. Daily notes by a Congregationalist who was an appreciative Protestant clergy observer at Vatican II; speeches, deliberations, arguments, moods ranging from inspiration to boredom, the emergence of leadership; a sense of the continuity and change, unity and diversity within the Roman Catholic Church.

1963

BROWN, ROBERT MCAFEE, 1920-   5865

OBSERVER IN ROME: A PROTESTANT REPORT ON THE VATICAN COUNCIL. New York: Doubleday, 1964. 271 pp.

Sep-Dec 1963. Diary of the debates, discussions and personalities of Vatican II as described by an official observer for the World Alliance of Reformed and Presbyterian churches; a pleasant, informative and sometimes humorous account by a sympathetic, though occasionally critical, observer.

JERSTAD, LUTE   5866

In EVEREST DIARY, by John Dennis McCallum, pp. 1-213 passim. Chicago: Follett, 1966. Reprint. Darby, Pa.: Scholars Reference Library, 1966.

Feb-Jun 1963. Personal diary of member of American Everest Expedition and one of first five Americans to conquer Everest; difficulties and exhilaration of mountain climbing.

JOHNSON, CLAUDIA ALTA TAYLOR, 1912-   5867

A WHITE HOUSE DIARY. New York: Holt, Rinehart and Winston, 1970. 806 pp.

1963-1969. Lady Bird Johnson's voluminous record of her years as first lady, beginning with the assassination of John F. Kennedy and ending with the inauguration of Richard Nixon; notes by a keen but gentle observer on luminaries of the Johnson administration, especially Hubert Humphrey, Robert McNamara and Dean Rusk; visits of heads of state, social and official occasions of all kinds; notes on major events, including the assassination of Sen. Robert Kennedy; her extensive travels and labors on

behalf of humanitarian and aesthetic causes; a good picture of marriage and family life under most unusual circumstances and of the character and personality of Lyndon Johnson.

L'HEUREUX, JOHN   5868

PICNIC IN BABYLON: A JESUIT PRIEST'S JOURNAL. New York and London: Macmillan, 1967. 301 pp.

Extracts in MEN WITHOUT MASKS, by Michael Rubin, pp. 83-92.

1963-1966. A former Jesuit's record of theology studies at Woodstock prior to ordination; satisfactions and pressures of his studies; loneliness and self-doubt giving way to an increasing sense of vocation; writing and publishing poetry; a touching, sometimes droll, and altogether charming journal.

ROBBEN, SUSAN, 1955-   5869

In SMALL VOICES, edited by Josef and Dorothy Berger, pp. 199-203.

1963-1964. Extracts from Levittown, New York, girl's diary; family, friends, school; a moppet's eye view of suburbia.

ROSSI, ALFRED   5870

MINNEAPOLIS REHEARSALS. Berkeley: University of California Press, 1970. 1 vol. (various pagings)

Mar-May 1963. Assistant director's log of daily rehearsals of HAMLET directed by Tyrone Guthrie for opening of the Tyrone Guthrie Theatre by the Minnesota Theatre Company; director's advice to actors, decisions on restaging, the notes after the rehearsals; a glimpse into the creative process and directing technique of an acknowledged master.

SMITH, ED   5871

WHERE TO, BLACK MAN? Chicago: Quadrangle Books, 1967. 221 pp.

1963?-1964? Diary of a black American serving with the Peace Corps in Ghana; high school teaching in several areas, as well as activities in Accra; interesting account of his varied experiences and impressions; observatins on race, tribalism, politics, the nonalignment question, social and cultural life, etc.; notes on his students and colleagues, both American and Ghanaian; reflections on himself and his identitiy as a black and an American; concerns for the future of Africa.

1964

COLEBROOK, JOAN   5872

INNOCENTS OF THE WEST: TRAVELS THROUGH THE SIXTIES. New York: Basic Books, 1979. 454 pp.

1964-1969. Australian journalist's ''observations, experiences, reading, conversations and interviews'' in a diary kept on extensive tour including New York, Boston and Berkeley, during fashionable dissent of the sixties; world political scene, radical movements, revolutionary currents, Communist power and subversion, all infused with the possibility or perhaps inevitability of an oppressive future.

DEMING, BARBARA, 1917-1984   5873

PRISON NOTES. New York: Grossman, 1966. 185 pp.

Extracts in A DAY AT A TIME, edited by Margo Culley, pp. 272-278.

Jan-Feb 1964. Diary of a woman jailed in Albany, Georgia, for participating in the "Quebec-Washington-Guantanamo Walk for Peace"; long narrative entries about companions imprisoned with her, other inmates, guards, fasting, recollections of other jail sentences; never giving up hope for success of nonviolent disobedience.

HARRIS, MARK, 1922-   5874

TWENTYONE TWICE: A JOURNAL. Boston: Little, Brown, 1966. 268 pp.

Nov 1964-Feb 1965. Narrative journal of a writer sent by the government as a special investigator for the Peace Corps in Africa; in Washington, D.C., for FBI clearance, with some comic opera elements there as well as during his African travels; a record which is more revealing of the diarist than of the Peace Corps.

MITCHELL, SUZANNE   5875

MY OWN WOMAN: THE DIARY OF AN ANALYSIS, by Suzanne Mitchell, pseud. New York: Horizon Press, 1973. 269 pp.

1964-1970. Personal diary of meetings with two therapists "in an effort to establish my own identity and to discover a more meaningful reason for being"; frustration, guilt, family and marital problems leading to divorce; returning to school, learning to face problems, to be alone yet not be lonely.

NAPEAR, PEGGY   5876

BRAIN CHILD: A MOTHER'S DIARY. New York: Harper & Row, 1974. 503 pp.

1964-1972. A mother's testament to success of controversial Doman-Delacato methods of the Institute for the Achievement of Human Potential in helping her brain damaged daughter to develop; the "patterning" of a child's brain by means of retracing normal steps of crawling and creeping, then years of sequential exercises assisted by parents and volunteers; wear and tear on family life; experiences with other parents of handicapped children, dealings and disillusionment with much of medical and educational establishment, delight in daughter's progress and frankness about discouragements.

SANTAMARIA, FRANCES KARLEN   5877

JOSHUA: FIRSTBORN. New York: Dial, 1970. 194 pp.

Mar 1964-Feb 1965. Young wife's personal journal of travel in Europe with her husband gathering material for articles and stories; extended stay in Athens preparing for birth of first child; humorous incidents of renting an apartment and shopping for a layette; frustrating experiences of being scorned by doctors for her questions about childbirth; settling on a natural childbirth clinic operated by Madame Kladaki; details of staff, service, patients and the birth experience; many romantic fantasies unveiled as she dealt with a foreign culture's life style, customs, society, attitude toward women and the care of infants; many notes on motherhood.

Extracts in REVELATIONS: DIARIES OF WOMEN, compiled by Mary J. Moffat, pp. 109-115.

Jan-Feb 1965. The special bond developing between mother and infant; the Jewish ceremony of circumcision.

1965

BLY, CAROL   5878

In ARIADNE'S THREAD, edited by Lyn Lifshin, pp. 261-268.

1965-1981. Extracts from journal of a writer and translator from Minneapolis; comments on society in small town rural America.

CHOUINARD, YVON   5879

In A TREASURY OF THE SIERRA NEVADA, edited by Robert L. Reid. pp. 300-307.

Jun 1965. Diary of first ascent of the Muir Wall on El Capitan in Sierra Nevada with companion T.M. Herbert; details of rock-climbing techniques; the exhilaration of becoming at home with the vertical environment despite physical and mental exhaustion from the climb and the cold, wet bivouacs.

HALL, PAMELA   5880

HEADS YOU LOSE. New York: Hawthorn Books, 1971. 148 pp. passim.

1965?-1968? Teenager's diary extracts of personal experiences with drugs; conflicts with her mother; the shock of being sent to a clinic in Spain, eventually recognizing the folly and danger of continued involvement with drug abuse; returning home and finding friends still caught in the drug scene by peer pressure, insecurity and boredom.

MCDANIEL, JUDITH   5881

In ARIADNE'S THREAD, edited by Lyn Lifshin, pp. 168-175.

1965-1975. Extracts from personal journal of feminist writer and critic on recognizing and accepting her lesbianism.

PARKS, DAVID, 1944-   5882

GI DIARY. New York: Harper & Row, 1968. 133 pp.

1965-1967. Diary of a black soldier in Vietnam with original entries amplified for publication; from the rigors and humiliations of boot camp, with notes on training and camp life, to Vietnam on a troop ship; relentless action and service as a radio operator; reflections on the war and wondering if he will ever get home; references to buddies killed or wounded, although names of people and units have been changed.

PILAT, OLIVER RAMSAY, 1903-   5883

LINDSAY'S CAMPAIGN: A BEHIND-THE-SCENES DIARY. Boston: Beacon Press, 1968. 348 pp.

May-Nov 1965. Diary of a NEW YORK POST reporter who volunteered to work for liberal Republican John Lindsay's campaign for mayor of New York; detailed notes on the issues, speeches and strategies; much on the personality, attitudes and values of the charismatic Lindsay, as well as on his opponents Abraham D. Beame and William F. Buckley; references to other political figures including Robert Kennedy, Jacob Javits, Robert Wagner, Lindsay's campaign manager Robert Price and others; the Lindsay family; newspaper coverage; interesting views of New York life and politics.

SULZBERGER, MARINA MAVROCORDATO, 1919-1976   5884

MARINA. Edited by C.L. Sulzberger. New York: Crown, 1978. 530 pp.

1965-1976 (with gaps.) Engaging personal diary, interspersed with letters, of charming Greek wife of Cyrus Sulzberger, foreign correspondent for the NEW YORK TIMES; vivid reports of travel in many countries of the world with her husband; colorful descriptions of her home and family in Spetsais, Greece; family life, chiefly in Paris, with the assorted joys and worries of raising two children;, seeing them through Harvard and Radcliffe during the Vietnam War period, including a visit to her son serving in Saigon and launching them into adult world; frequent entertaining and dining with major figures in world politics, including the John Kennedys, Charles Bohlen, Sargent Shriver and numerous other American and European dignitaries; a thoroughly delightful diary.

1966

BIHALY, ANDREW, 1934-1968   5885

THE JOURNAL OF ANDREW BIHALY. Edited by Anthony Tittle. New York: Crowell, 1973. 228 pp.

1966-1968. Introspective chronicle of loneliness and intense desire for love; attempts to ease problems with drugs; insights into life on lower east side of Manhattan in 1960's with references to horrors he experienced during World War II in a boys' school in Hungary.

DE MILLE, AGNES, 1905-   5886

RUSSIAN JOURNALS. Dance Perspectives, 44. New York: Dance Perspectives Foundation, 1970. 57 pp.

Jun-Jul 1966. Choreographer's experiences with American Ballet Theatre's tour in Russia with the expectation of introducing young Russian artists to developments in American dance; frustrations of all programming and printing decisions being made by the Russian government officials regardless of effect on artistic integrity; disastrous stage floor in second rate Moscow theater; inadequate rehearsal time with an orchestra unfamiliar with the music; cordial reception in Leningrad; difficulties with interpreters; descriptions of accommodations, service and visits to tourist spots.

FEINBERG, ABRAHAM L.   5887

RABBI FEINBERG'S HANOI DIARY. Don Mills, Ontario: Longmans, 1968. 258 pp.

Dec 1966-Jan 1967. Diary kept by rabbi on fact-finding mission of peace to Hanoi with Abraham John Muste, a retired Presbyterian minister, Martin Niemöller, a Lutheran pastor, and the Rt. Rev. Ambrose Reeves, assistant bishop of Chichester; brittle, biting comments on persons, the war, religion, the advisability of the mission; royal reception in Hanoi after muddled travel plans through Karachi and China; trying to separate propaganda from

truth; interview with Phan Van Dong and Ho Chi Minh who emphasized need for accepting four points of Geneva Agreement; interview with prisoners of war and great compassion for Vietnamese people.

GREENFELD, JOSH   5888

A CHILD CALLED NOAH. New York: Holt, Rinehart and Winston, 1972. Reprint: 1978. 191 pp.

1966-1971. A writer's moving account of the birth of his second son and the gradual realization that he is handicapped, with diagnoses ranging from retardation to autism; a round of treatment centers, hopes and disappointments; anger and crushing discouragement but refusal to despair; the effects of Noah and his severe problems on marriage and family life; an intimate and courageous diary.

A PLACE FOR NOAH. New York: Holt, Rinehart and Winston, 1978. 310 pp.

1971-1979. Continuing attempt to find adequate treatment and education for his mentally handicapped son and frustration with the medical and educational establishment; love and anger, exhausting efforts and small victories of daily family life; reflections on fatherhood, writing and being Jewish; eventually operating their own day care center for developmentally disabled children in Pacific Palisades, California.

HOAGLAND, EDWARD   5889

NOTES FROM THE CENTURY BEFORE: A JOURNAL FROM BRITISH COLUMBIA. New York: Random House, 1969. 273 pp.

Extracts in THE EDWARD HOAGLUND READER, edited by Geoffrey Wolff, pp. 49-75. New York: Random House, 1979; RIVER REFLECTIONS, edited by Verne Huser, pp. 90-92.

Jun-Aug 1966. New York writer's journal of a summer in Telegraph Creek, British Columbia, trying to reconstruct its history as a point on an abortive trans-world telegraph route; gold mining, telegraph and homesteading days; conversations with old timers about prospecting and trapping; notes on Indians past and present; marvelous character sketches of his hosts and guides; the difficulties of interviewing as a stutterer; a sensitive and refreshing book.

SALISBURY, CHARLOTTE Y.   5890

ASIAN DIARY. New York: Scribner, 1967. 158 pp.

May-Jul 1966. Asian impressions from a trip with her husband, Harrison Salisbury, associate editor of the NEW YORK TIMES; travel through Hong Kong, Cambodia, Thailand, Burma, India, Sikkim, Mongolia, Siberia and Japan, with descriptions of temples, food, entertainment, customs and clothes; her increasing distress over the Vietnam War.

CHINA DIARY. New York: Walker, 1973. 210 pp.

May-Jul 1972. Diary of travel in China with her journalist husband; details of hotels, food, entertainment, opera, travel conditions, farms, factories, schools and hospitals in the country and in major cities such as Peking, Xian, Yenan, Wuhan, Changsha and Shanghai.

CHINA DIARY: AFTER MAO. New York: Walker, 1979. 214 pp.

Aug-Sept 1977. Revisiting China and making comparison with previous trip; cultural climate following the overthrow of the Gang of Four; personal treatment in hotels; touring communes, schools and factories; soliciting opinions of Chinese people in Peking and cities in Mongolia.

TIBETAN DIARY. New York: Walker, 1981. 164 pp.

Jul-Aug 1980. Return to China; sightseeing and concluding complicated arrangements to travel in Tibet; when necessary provided with extra oxygen in the high altitude; evidence of poverty, Chinese propaganda and lack of understanding the people; visit to Johkang Temple, the seat of Tibetan Buddhism and the Potala, the extraordinarily rich palace of the Dalai Lama which had been damaged by Red Guards and was being laboriously restored; travel to Nepal and Katmandu over road built by Chinese.

TAYLOR, KATHRINE KRESSMANN   **5891**

DIARY OF FLORENCE IN FLOOD. New York: Simon and Schuster, 1967. 192 pp.

Nov 1966-Feb 1967. A moving and very personal chronicle of watching the rising Arno River flood the city of Florence followed by the tireless efforts of citizens and students to clean up and restore anything, especially art treasures, that could be salvaged.

1967

ELISOFON, ELIOT   **5892**

JAVA DIARY. New York: Macmillan, 1969. 298 pp.

Aug-Nov 1967. LIFE photographer's diary of assignment for photo-essay on wildlife, particularly an almost extinct one-horned rhinoceros, in the Indonesian nature reserve, Udjong Kulon; working through the bureaucratic hurdles to erect a game observation tower; trips into the jungle to photograph wildlife but never seeing the elusive rhino; fine descriptions of jungle camping, animals, birds, insects, coastal exploring, Indonesian life and food; interesting notes on camera equipment and photography.

GLUECK, NELSON, 1900-1971   **5893**

DATELINE: JERUSALEM. Cincinnati: Hebrew Union College Press, 1968. 134 pp.

Jun-Aug 1967. Diary of an archeologist, professor and president of Hebrew Union College; experiences in Israel, with notes on archeological excavations, as well as the effects of the 1967 Arab-Israel War on Jerusalem and Tel Aviv.

KRAMER, JERRY, 1936-   **5894**

INSTANT REPLAY: THE GREEN BAY DIARY. Edited by Dick Schaap. New York: World, 1968. 286 pp.

1967-1968. Daily actions and reactions of professional football player with the Green Bay Packers; one season, from training camp to Super Bowl.

MILTON, JOHN P.   **5895**

NAMELESS VALLEYS, SHINING MOUNTAINS; THE RECORD OF AN EXPEDITION INTO THE VANISHING WILDERNESS OF ALASKA'S BROOKS RANGE. New York: Walker; Toronto: Ryerson Press, 1969, 1970. 195 pp.

Jul-Aug 1967. Naturalist's Arctic expedition with companions Kenneth Brower and Steve Pearson to Brooks Range of Alaska; exploration of Sheenjek River region, Nameless Valley and National Arctic Wildlife Range; extensive notes on plants and animals, with great concern for potential environmental threat of oil development in wilderness areas; rigors of hiking and mountaineering in such inhospitable but magnificent terrain.

SWISHER, PETER NASH, 1944-   **5896**

A VIETNAM DIARY. Richmond: Hesperia Publication, 1975. 71 pp.

1967-1975 (with gaps). Officer's diary during Vietnam War; impressions and reflections on war, the cruelty of military men, helpless, hopeless Laotian villagers; a ten-day leave in Sydney, Australia; praise for conscientious officers, the real heroes who tried to maintain basic humanity while facing the reality of a senseless war.

TANNER, WILLIAM R.   **5897**

In YOU OWE YOURSELF A DRUNK: AN ETHNOGRAPHY OF UR-BAN NOMADS, by James P. Spradley, pp. 12-64. Boston: Little, Brown, 1970.

Aug 1967-Aug 1968. Sporadic but developed entries by an alcoholic in and out of jail "drunk tanks" and alcohol rehabilitation centers; considerable lore on how to survive in cities and on the road; wanderings throughout much of the United States; diary kept for anthropologist James P. Spradley as part of a study of Seattle, Washington, tramp subculture.

1968

ANELLO, BRUCE, 1947-1968   **5898**

In PEACE IS OUR PROFESSION, edited by Jan Barry, p. 26. Montclair, N.J.: East River Anthology, 1981.

Feb-Apr 1968. Brief extracts from diary of soldier in Vietnam on the hopelessness of a futile war.

BENNETT, JOAN FRANCES, 1949-   **5899**

In MEMBERS OF THE CLASS WILL KEEP DAILY JOURNALS: THE BARNARD COLLEGE JOURNALS OF TOBI GILLIAN SANDERS AND JOAN FRANCES BENNETT, by Tobi G. Sanders, pp. 93-153. New York: Winter House, 1970.

Extracts in A DAY AT A TIME, edited by Margo Culley, pp. 279-289.

Feb-Aug 1968. Diary kept as a class writing assignment by a black sophomore from South Carolina; thoughts on being a young woman and being black, memories of childhood, reactions to college life; highly introspective and sensitive.

BERRIGAN, DANIEL, 1921-   **5900**

NIGHT FLIGHT TO HANOI: WAR DIARY WITH 11 POEMS. New York: Macmillan, 1968. 139 pp. Diary, pp. 21-139.

Feb 1968. Diary of peace activist priest who traveled to Laos and North Vietnam with Howard Zinn to secure the release of three captured American fliers and to observe the effects of American involvement in Vietnam; delay in Vientiane with descriptions of life and encounters there; flight to Hanoi; notes on results of American bombings, interviews with American prisoners and with and with various North Vietnamese; much reflection revealing Berrigan's religious and moral convictions.

LIGHTS ON IN THE HOUSE OF THE DEAD: A PRISON DIARY. Garden City, N.Y.: Doubleday, 1974. 309 pp.

> 1970-1972. Imprisonment at Danbury, Connecticut, for destroying draft records during Vietnam War; rather than incidents, mostly reflections on religion, war and peace, American values, nonviolent resistance and its advocates, his reading and writing, etc.; notes on other prisoners in jail for various offenses and on the daily humiliation of prison life; admiration for his brother Philip and other peace activists.

BERRIGAN, PHILIP FRANCIS, 1923-   **5901**

PRISON JOURNALS OF A PRIEST REVOLUTIONARY. Edited by Vincent McGee. New York: Holt, Rinehart and Winston, 1970. 198 pp.

> May-Nov 1968. Introspections and observations of a Catholic priest and anti-Vietnam War activist while in prison at Baltimore, Maryland, and Lewisburg and Allenwood, Pennsylvania; trial and sentencing for burning of draft records.

WIDEN THE PRISON GATES: WRITING FROM JAILS. New York: Simon and Schuster, 1973. 261 pp.

> 1970-1972. Diary of imprisonment at Lewisburg Federal Penitentiary, Danbury Federal Correctional Institute and Dauphin County Jail for burning draft cards as protest of United States involvement in Vietnam; reflections on prison experiences, war and peace, nonviolent protest, American values, the church, etc.; references to his brother and fellow activist priest, Daniel Berrigan, Sr. Elizabeth McAlister, whom he later married, other members of the anitwar movement and various prisoners; trial for allegedly planning a kidnapping of Henry Kissinger.

FREEHAN, BILL, 1941-   **5902**

BEHIND THE MASK: AN INSIDE BASEBALL DIARY. Edited by Steve Gelman and Dick Schaap. New York: Maddick Manuscripts, distributed by World, 1970. 225 pp.

> Feb-Sep 1968. Catcher's diary of a baseball season with the Detroit Tigers, World Series champions; comments on teammates, emotions and exciting and disappointing moments of the game.

HASKINS, JAMES, 1941-   **5903**

DIARY OF A HARLEM SCHOOL TEACHER. New York: Grove Press, 1969. 149 pp.

> Sep 1968?-Jun 1969? Frank account of a young black teacher's discouraging year of teaching at Public School 92 in Harlem; extreme family, health and poverty problems of children; difficulties of teaching or learning amid classroom chaos and violence; incompetence and demoralization of some faculty and administrators; friction between black and white teachers; touching vignettes of individual children.

HUGHES, EILEEN LANOUETTE   **5904**

ON THE SET OF FELLINI SATYRICON: A BEHIND-THE-SCENES DIARY. New York: Morrow, 1971. 248 pp.

> Nov 1968-Jul 1969. LIFE correspondent's diary of observing Italian director Federico Fellini at work on his controversial version of Petronius' SATYRICON as it was filmed in Rome; much information on the personality, eccentricities and methods of Fellini, on the actors, colorful extras, sets, makeup, special effects, costumes, etc.

KEISTER, C.S.   **5905**

THE PRINCIPAL OF THE THING: A DIARY OF A HIGH SCHOOL PRINCIPAL. Philadelphia: Dorrance, 1970. 248 pp.

> Sep 1968-Jun 1969. Daily interactions with faculty, students parents; curriculum, student clubs, sports and social events at Hackettstown, New Jersey, High School; orderly, uninspired American secondary public education.

KIRKPATRICK, RALPH   **5906**

''From the Diary of a Spring Tour.'' PROSE 1, no. 1 (1970):93-110.

> May 1968. Harpsichordist's concert tour in East Germany, with interesting notes on performing and sightseeing in East Berlin, Dresden and points between; reactions to orchestras, concert halls and audiences; visits to bookshops and art museums; comments on people and their attitudes.

SANDERS, TOBI GILLIAN   **5907**

MEMBERS OF THE CLASS WILL KEEP DAILY JOURNALS: THE BARNARD COLLEGE JOURNALS OF TOBI GILLIAN SANDERS AND JOAN FRANCES BENNETT. New York: Winter House, 1970. 153 pp. Diary, pp. 1-92.

> Feb 1968. Diary kept as a class writing assignment; classes, conversations, impressions, introspections, affluent Jewish family life, a love affair and death of her boyfriend; a touching, sometimes sad diary, but with considerable humor.

SIEGEL, MARTIN   **5908**

AMEN: THE DIARY OF RABBI MARTIN SIEGEL. Edited by Mel Ziegler. New York: Maddick Manuscripts' distributed by World, 1971. 276 pp.

Extracts in MEN WITHOUT MASKS, by Michael Rubin, pp. 180-189.

> Dec 1968-Sep 1969. A Long Island rabbi's journal; struggle to find his own identitiy as a person and a rabbi; conflicts with his congregation especially over racial attitudes; his stand on the ''black anti-Semitism'' issue and support of black position in the New York City school conflict; his concern over suburban materialism of his community and congregation; routine duties, such as supervising the religious school, conducting services, bar mitzvahs, weddings, funerals, etc.; settling disputes; family problems including his wife's severe mental illness, requiring hospitalization, and his own soul searching as a result; loneliness, lack of friends, a sense of being an institution rather than a person.

YEZZO, DOMINICK   **5909**

A G.I.'S VIETNAM DIARY. New York: F. Watts, 1974. 92 pp.

> 1968-1969. Young soldier's tour of duty in Vietnam with First Air Cavalry Division; the sordid aspects of war; mixed emotions of fear, hate, excitement and love; combat, friendships, homesickness, sex, drugs and religion; a period of self-examination and maturing.

1969

BEARD, FRANK   **5910**

PRO: FRANK BEARD ON THE GOLF TOUR. Edited by Dick Schaap. New York: World, 1970. 323 pp.

Jan-Aug 1969. Professional golfer's account of such tournaments as the Masters, United States Open and Westchester Classic; vignettes of colleagues and competitors Arnold Palmer, Jack Nicklaus, Gary Player, etc.; ruminations on values and the effects of big money golf on personal and family life.

BRAUN, ERNEST   **5911**

In GRAND CANYON OF THE LIVING COLORADO, edited by Roderick Nash, pp. 65-75. San Francisco: Sierra Club; New York: Ballantine Books, 1970.

Sep 1969? Photographer's boat trip through the Grand Canyon; descriptive notes on scenery, vegetation and wildlife; adventures and mishaps navigating a succession of rapids; photographic challenges.

DEBUSSCHERE, DAVE, 1940-   **5912**

THE OPEN MAN: A CHAMPIONSHIP DIARY. Edited by Paul D. Zimmerman and Dick Schaap. New York: Random House 1970. 267 pp.

Aug 1969-May 1970. Diary, kept and edited for publication, of forward on New York Knickerbockers basketball team; training, games, plays, injuries; glory of being champions of National Basketball Association.

FERLAND, CAROL   **5913**

THE LONG JOURNEY HOME. New York: Knopf, 1980. 293 pp.

1969-1970. Extremely personal journal of thoughts the journalist could not speak, in addition to the record of her sessions during agonizing months of psychotherapy; interactions with staff and patients during hospitalization and at a mountain farm where she continued to see the doctor who finally led her to self-acceptance.

GRIFFIN, JOHN HOWARD, 1920-1980   **5914**

THE HERMITAGE JOURNALS. Kansas City: Andrews and McNeel, 1981. 231 pp.

1969-1972. A diary kept during stays at the Trappist Abbey of Our Lady of Gethsemane while working on a biography of Thomas Merton; living in Merton's modest hermitage and following his daily monastic routine, as well as immersing himself in his voluminous unpublished writings; reactions to the natural beauty of the place, the monks, the solitude and, above all, the life and significance of Merton; the diarist's own introspections and deepening Catholic faith; ill health which later forced him to give up the project.

JACKSON, THOMAS, 1942-   **5915**

GO BACK, YOU DIDN'T SAY "MAY I": THE DIARY OF A YOUNG PRIEST. New York: Seabury Press, 1974. 238 pp.

1969-1974 (with gaps). Episcopal priest's personal journal; work in Detroit ghetto and suburban New Jersey parish briefly recall-

ed; chiefly the events of his years at Athens as co-director with Tom Nicolls, of United Campus Ministry, University of Ohio; a taxing counseling load of student problems with marriage, pregnancy, sex and drugs compounded by serious and frustrating conflicts with local police and University president during student protests against the Vietnam War; closing of the University; the killings at Kent State; finding relief from the pressures with his wife and young family and a group of faithful friends; moving to California to develop a car wash business, which failed, intending to use the profits to establish a foundation to support social services; a sensitive and caring personality plagued with many doubts about the right direction for his life.

JAMES, NANCY ESTHER   **5916**

In ARIADNE'S THREAD, edited by Lyn Lifshin, pp. 222-227.

1969-1979. Extracts from journal of poet and teacher; death of her mother and reflections on mother-daughter relationships.

KIZER, CAROLYN   **5917**

"Pakistan Journal." HUDSON REVIEW 24 (1971):67-90.

Sep 1969. A poet's visit to Pakistan to address an international literary conference; papers by Northrup Frye and Ralph Russell; comments on Pakistani writers, politics, mores, sights and the logistics of getting about.

KUMIN, MAXINE   **5918**

In ARIADNE'S THREAD, edited by Lyn Lifshin, pp. 21-31.

1969-1970. Extracts from author's personal journal; notes on poems, stories or scenes she wants to write, other diarists and writers; family relationships.

LEVINE, STEPHEN   **5919**

PLANET STEWARD: JOURNAL OF A WILDLIFE SANCTUARY. Santa Cruz, Calif.: Unity Press, 227 pp.

1969-1970. A season as caretaker of Canelo Hills Cienega, Arizona, in area selected for wildlife sanctuary to be preserved in undisturbed state; poetic awareness of the land, observing the sensitivity of local people and insensitivity of thoughtless hunters and collectors; an impressive meeting with Joseph Wood Krutch.

SPIVACK, KATHLEEN   **5920**

In ARIADNE'S THREAD, edited by Lyn Lifshin, pp. 163-167.

1969-1979. Extracts from poet's personal journal; suffering over death of Robert Lowell; surviving a disintegrating marriage; comfort of supportive friends and her two small children.

1970

ANON.   **5921**

In FACE TO FACE TO FACE: AN EXPERIMENT IN INTIMACY, edited by Gordon Clanton and Chris Downing, 235 pp. passim. New York: E.P. Dutton, 1975.

Jul 1970-Mar 1971. Interspersed journals of three people, two women and a man, involved in a bisexual ménage á trois; mainly sexual experiences and attitudes, with a desire to be both "committed" and "experimental," including group sex and other "secondary" relationships; dated, but narrative entries of all three sounding curiously similar and abounding in the jargon of the period.

BAUER, HANNA — 5922

I CAME TO MY ISLAND. Seattle: B. Straub, 1973. 142 pp.

Jun-Jul 1970? Journal of woman teacher, psychologist and writer spending time alone on an unidentified island, probably in the San Juans, "getting in tune with herself"; speculations on how different cultures experience time and space; reactions to music; pressing through the first draft of a book on teachers and learning while enjoying the natural beauty around her.

COONS, WILLIAM R. — 5923

ATTICA DIARY. New York: Stein and Day, 1972. 238 pp.

1970-1971. Prison diary of English instructor at Skidmore and City University of New York in Attica Prison on an LSD charge; great rage not only against prison conditions, but American society and conventional values; lengthy introspections; notes on other prisoners, guards, etc.; ample indication of factors leading to the Attica Riot, which occurred just after diarist's release; monthy entries in narrative style.

CULBERTSON, MANIE — 5924

MAY I SPEAK? DIARY OF A CROSSOVER TEACHER. Edited by Sue Eakin. Gretna, La.: Pelican, 1972. 156 pp.

Jan-May 1970. White woman teacher's experiences during semester of teaching in all black Louisiana school after court-ordered integration; frustration, fear and prejudice followed by culture shock and surprise at poor facilities and lack of teaching materials; dedication to genuine educational achievement taking over as she discovers cooperative, willing students; ultimately a valuable, eye-opening encounter.

GOLDEN, JEFFREY, 1950- — 5925

WATERMELON SUMMER. Philadelphia: Lippincott, 1971. 152 pp.

Jun-Aug 1970, Apr 1971. Harvard student's diary of summer experiences as a volunteer worker at Featherfield Farm in Georgia, a New Communities Incorporated cooperative farm organized by black sharecroppers; culture shock, hot, exhausting days in the peanut and watermelon fields, a revealing view of racism and discrimination; in retrospect recognizing the experiment was neither a complete failure nor success but convinced of the value of cooperative institutions and discovering the summer had changed the direction of his life.

GREEN, KATE — 5926

In ARIADNE'S THREAD, edited by Lyn Lifshin, pp. 127-134.

Jun 1970. Extracts from author's private journal of the agonizing experience and subsequent emotions of having an abortion.

HAKE, LOIS M. — 5927

DIARY OF A BATTERED HOUSEWIFE. Independence, Ky.: Feminist Publications, 197-? 38 pp.

May-Sep 1970? Woman's diary of escape from marital violence; a history of growing awareness and the struggle to develop a positive self-image; a dated autobiographical narrative.

KIRK, JOHN T. — 5928

THE IMPECUNIOUS HOUSE RESTORER: PERSONAL VISION AND HISTORIC ACCURACY. New York: Knopf, 1984. 204 pp. Diary pp. 74-192 passim.

May-Sep 1970. Extracts from working journal of restorer of Daniel Bliss House, Rehoboth, Massachusetts, built around 1740; removing later additions, analyzing findings, using documents, paintings and oral history to discover and capture original plan and character of the house.

RANDALL, MARGARET RANDALL, 1936- — 5929

PART OF THE SOLUTION: PORTRAIT OF A REVOLUTIONARY. New York: New Directions, 1973. 192 pp. Diary, pp. 49-80.

1970-1972. A Socialist poet's experiences and approving observations in Cuba, noting its transition from "a society of consumers to a society of workers"; visits conducted by Communist party representatives to factories, schools, courtrooms, etc; reactions to Fidel Castro's speeches.

ROBERTSON, MARY ELSIE — 5930

In ARIADNE'S THREAD, edited by Lyn Lifshion, pp. 122-126.

1970? Extracts from journal of novelist and children's writer describing her experiences during psychoanalysis.

SCHUH, NITA — 5931

AFTER WINTER, SPRING: A CANDID GLIMPSE AT GRIEF AND HOPE. Plainfield, N.J.: Logos International, 1978. 85 pp.

1970? Selections from a woman's journal of working through grief during first year after death of her husband; automatically going through daily and seasonal activities; introspective searching; grasping any scant comfort and relying on her faith for a new hope.

STARKMAN, ELAINE — 5932

In ARIADNE'S THREAD, edited by Lyn Lifshin, pp. 228-233.

Apr-Jun 1970? Extracts from personal diary of a Jewish poet and college professor; notes on old age and having her mother-in-law move into her home.

WYSOCKI, SHARON — 5933

In ARIADNE'S THREAD, edited by Lyn Lifshin, pp. 43-51.

Jul-Oct 1970? Extracts from diary of a woman prison guard in a male correctional institution from first day on the job until resignation; reactions of prison staff and inmates as she acquired firsthand information on prison life with intent of becoming a prison counselor.

1971

LARREA, JEAN-JACQUES   5934

THE DIARY OF A PAPER BOY. New York: Putnam, 1972. 63 pp.

Nov 1971?-Feb 1972? A rather precocious ten-year-old's adventures delivering an unnamed New York newspaper; mainly problems with and revenges upon "stingy" customers; a few school matters.

LOOMIS, VIVIENNE, 1959-1973   5935

In VIVIENNE: THE LIFE AND SUICIDE OF AN ADOLESCENT GIRL, by John E. Mack and Holly Hickler, pp. 3-123 passim. Boston: Little, Brown, 1981. 237 pp.

1971-1973. A study containing diary extracts, letters and poems from the last two years in the life of a promising girl who committed suicide at age fourteen; family relationships with Unitarian minister father, artist mother and two older siblings in Melrose, Massachusetts; problems with self-esteem, friendships, an increasing sense of worthlessness; intense emotional attachments, especially to John May, a favorite teacher at Cambridge Friends School; journals and poems, discovered after her death, which reveal a level of reflection and writing far beyond her years.

MCLEOD, MERIKAY, 1946-   5936

BETRAYAL: THE SHATTERING SEX DISCRIMINATION CASE OF SILVER VS. PACIFIC PRESS PUBLISHING ASSOCIATION. Loma Linda, Calif.: Mars Hill, 1985. 356 pp.

1971-1975. Personal diary of editorial assistant at Pacific Press Publishing Association operated by Seventh-Day Adventists; from "being thrilled at the chance to edit books for God" through the grueling case of Silver vs. Pacific Press Publishing Association brought when she discovered gross inequity between men's and women's salaries in the company; winning the case but suffering disillusionment with church and press officials and the collapse of her marriage; inestimable support of her good friend and co-plaintiff, Lorna Tobler; letters, documents and editorial additions included.

RAINER, YVONNE   5937

WORK 1961-73. Halifax: Press of the Nova Scotia College of Art and Design; New York: New York University Press, 1974. 338 pp. Journal, pp. 173-188.

Jan-Feb 1971. Dancer's journal while in India on a fellowship from Experiments in Art and Technology; observations, reactions and feelings about dance, music, festivals, shrines, guides, teachers, cities and villages.

RUBIN, MICHAEL, 1835-   5938

IN THE MIDDLE OF THINGS: AN EXPERIENCE WITH PRIMAL THEORY. New York, Putnam, 1973. 255 pp.

1971? Record of three weeks of treatment as a resident patient at the Marin Center for Intensive Therapy after feeling that years of psychoanalysis had done little to relieve his bouts of depression, suicidal impulses and psychologically induced physical problems; the agony and release of "primal scream" sessions, but

periods of doubt about their lasting benefits; reflections on neurosis, childhood, his writing and teaching, his homosexuality, the nuclear family, various psychotherapies, etc.; an interesting and moving account of struggle to overcome some daunting emotional difficulties.

SARTON, MAY, 1912-   5939

JOURNAL OF A SOLITUDE. New York: W.W. Norton, 1973. 208 pp. Boston: G.K. Hall, 1979. 294 pp.

Sep 1971?-Sep 1972? A writer's solitary year at Nelson, New Hampshire; distress over recurrent depressions and rages and their damage to relationships; notes on other writers and on her own work, including its movement toward open portrayal of homosexuality; much reflection on the problems of the woman artist and on the difficulties and rewards of rural solitude; gardening as an "instrument of grace."

HOUSE BY THE SEA: A JOURNAL. New York: W.W. Norton, 1977. 287 pp. Boston: G.K. Hall, 1978. 389 pp.

Nov 1974-Aug 1975. Journal begun after her move from Nelson, New Hampshire, to York, Maine; growth in her appreciation of solitude, as well as friendship in person and through letters; the consolations of nature and gardening; the return of her creative powers after a hiatus of illness and depression.

RECOVERING: A JOURNAL. New York: W.W. Norton, 1980. 246 pp. Boston: G.K. Hall, 1981. 351 pp.

Dec 1978-Nov 1979. A record of recovery, both physical and spiritual, from a mastectomy, the bereavement of a failed relationship and disappointment over public misunderstanding of her work; a year of memories, particularly of her mother and others precious to her in the past; typically, a refreshing blend of such mundane matters as unanswered letters and maggots in the garbage pail with the poetic and philosophical aspects of her life.

AT SEVENTY: A JOURNAL. New York: W.W. Norton, 1984. 334 pp. South Yarmouth, Maine: J. Curley, 1984. 419 pp.

May 1982-May 1983. Journal begun on her seventieth birthday; a record of tasks, enjoyments and reflections; the demands of poetry readings, visitors, correspondence, domestic chores; balancing of needs for company and solitude, hard work and rest; enjoyment and stimulation of current friends and admirers and savored memories of past writers and mentors; the absolute requirement of beauty, found daily in her home, garden, ocean and woods; reflections on religion, on being seventy, a woman and a writer; a satisfying journal.

SMITH, FREDRICK W.   5940

JOURNAL OF A FAST. New York: Schocken Books, 1976. 216 pp.

Mar-Jun 1971. Journal of a fast undertaken as a means to spiritual growth and an aid to meditation; physical effects, metaphysical ruminations and a sense of identification with mystics and ascetics of the past.

STEINBERG, DAVID, 1942-   5941

FATHERJOURNAL. Albion, Calif.: Times Change Press, 1977. 90 pp.

Extracts in MEN WITHOUT MASKS, by Michael Rubin, pp. 138-148.

1971-1974. A young father's journal of child rearing experiences; his determination to be a nonstereotypical father and to share equally with his wife the work, joy and difficulties of caring for their baby son.

1972

AIKEN, GEORGE DAVID, 1892-　　　　　　　5942

AIKEN: SENATE DIARY. Brattleboro, Vt.: Stephen Green Press, 1976. 370 pp.

1972-1974. Views and values of the octogenarian Republican senator from Vermont; activities of the Foreign Relations Committee, with considerable comment on foreign policy issues and United States relations with various countries; his positions on agriculture, environmental issues, election practices, etc.; concerns about "so many imcompetent persons aspiring to high office," undue influence of American companies on politics and government of countries in which they operate, Vietnam War decisions, including renewed bombing of Hanoi; defense of Nixon and conviction that he should face impeachment rather than resign over the Watergate scandal; notes on early months of Ford's presidency; frequent references to senators Fulbright, Jackson, McGovern, Mansfield, Humphrey, and to Henry Kissinger; reactions to the deaths of Truman and Johnson; enjoyment of his home and garden at Putney, Vermont.

"The 'Down' Years 1972-74; a Senator's View." AMERICAN HERITAGE 27, no. 5 (1976): 26-31, 81-87.

1972-1974. Extracts relating to American corporations abroad, Vietnam, the questionable routes of many to political power, Watergate and Nixon's resignation, etc.

BRAUDY, SUSAN　　　　　　　　　　　　　　5943

BETWEEN MARRIAGE AND DIVORCE. New York: Morrow, 1975. 252 pp.

1972-1974. Journalist's diary of love affairs and a marriage breaking up; developing her career, free-lance work and a job with NEWSWEEK which ended by her being fired; making new networks of friends and beginning to feel a new confidence in managing her life alone.

"After the Marriage is Over." MS. 2, no. 10 (1974):48-51, 90-92.

1972-1973. Diary of a woman's adjustment to divorce; retrospective analysis of her marriage and possible reasons for its failure; her attitudes towards dating and casual sex, feminism and her career as a writer.

BREMER, ARTHUR H., 1950-　　　　　　　　5944

AN ASSASSIN'S DIARY. Introduction by Harding Lemay. New York: Harper's Magazine Press, 1972, 1973. 142 pp.

Extracts in MEN WITHOUT MASKS, by Michael Rubin, pp. 74-82.

Apr-May 1972. Diary kept by unemployed New York busboy who, two days after the last entry, shot and crippled Gov. George Wallace of Alabama; unsuccessful stalking of President Nixon; rambling, narcissistic introspections and sexual fantasies; a great sense of failure and a desire to be noticed, both for the assassination and for the diary, which he hoped would be "one of the most closely read pages since the scrolls in those caves."

CUOMO, MARIO MATTHEW, 1932-　　　　　5945

FOREST HILLS DIARY: THE CRISIS OF LOW-INCOME HOUSING. New York: Random House, 1974. 209 pp.

May-Oct 1972. Diary of Queens, New York, lawyer appointed by Mayor Lindsay as fact-finder and mediator in an incredibly complex and acrimonious community dispute over the city's decision to build low-income housing towers in Forest Hills, a middle-class Jewish community; a revealing and disturbing picture of governmental miscalculation, bureaucratic ineptitude, communication breakdown and racial and class conflict; Cuomo's conversations with residents of Forest Hills, leaders of the New York black community, city officials and academic outside observers; notes on somewhat farcical city hearings and on angry demonstrations; a sense of racial and class distrust exacerbated by poor planning and communication.

DIARIES OF MARIO M. CUOMO: THE CAMPAIGN FOR GOVERNOR. New York: Random House, 1984. 484 pp.

1980-1983. A highly personal and detailed record of his successful campaign for the governorship of New York; interesting, even suspenseful, account of the Democratic primary run against Edward I. Koch, mayor of New York, and the somewhat less exciting election campaign against Republican Louis E. Lehrman; the accumulated stress of fifteen-hour days; his refusal to compromise on his opposition to the death penalty; glimpses of rich ethnic diversity of New York City and varied populations of the state; considerable introspection revealing his political, social and moral values and personal doubts and struggles; the importance to him of family, Catholic faith and his Italian heritage.

KITMAN, SUSAN　　　　　　　　　　　　　　5946

"Diary of a Mad 12-Year-Old." MS. 1, no. 3 (1972):62-73, 123.

1972? Undated entries from a few weeks in the life of a precocious young feminist; school events, family and social interactions of a sexist nature and her reactions to them; her career and intellectual aspirations and views on future marriage and family life.

LYNCH, MARY ANN　　　　　　　　　　　　5947

In ARIADNE'S THREAD, edited by Lyn Lifshin, pp. 276-277.

Dec 1972. Extract from photographer's diary of incident in New York City Port Authority depot during holiday rush to escape the city, drunken man's attraction to her infant daughter.

MARIN, PETER　　　　　　　　　　　　　　5948

In MEN WITHOUT MASKS, by Michael Rubin, pp. 128-137.

Jul-Sep 1972. Diary extracts containing a man's rather minute examination of his marriage and his ambivalent feelings about it; a sense of the almost impossible burdens placed on modern marriage.

MINTY, JUDITH　　　　　　　　　　　　　　5949

In ARIADNE'S THREAD, edited by Lyn Lifshin, pp. 118-121, 215-217.

Sep 1972, 1977-1980. Extracts from journal of a Michigan writer and teacher's conversations with her thirteen-year-old son about his fear of death; a summer of serious accidents; introspections and tensions of being a teacher and giving poetry readings.

READ, JENNY, 1945-1976   **5950**

JENNY READ, IN PURSUIT OF ART AND LIFE. Edited by Kathleen Doyle. Burnsville, N.C.: Antioch University with Celo Press, 1982. 173 pp. passim.

> 1972-1976. Journal, interspersed with letters, of promising, young San Francisco sculptor; working in bookstore to support herself while developing her art; solid family support; introspective entries on life, death, art, dreams and images, personal relationships, religion; a significant journal of a young woman who was tragically murdered at the time her art was receiving recognition.

SEEGER, PETE   **5951**

"Song and Struggle: A Hanoi Diary." NEW WORLD REVIEW 40, no. 3 (1972):19-31.

> Mar 1972. Folk singer's impressions and experiences in Hanoi during a visit as guest of the Democratic Republic of Vietnam; notes on music and musicians, government officials and ordinary citizens; effects of the war; his admiration for the people, culture and political and economic system.

"Strummin' Banjo in North Vietnam." SATURDAY REVIEW 55, May 13, 1972, pp. 28-32.

> Mar 1972. Extracts covering his concerts and broadcasts, conversations with people, visits to schools, hospitals, villages, the Museum of War Crimes; observations of affection, cooperation and industriousness of the North Vietnamese.

VINING, ELIZABETH GRAY, 1902-   **5952**

BEING SEVENTY: THE MEASURE OF A YEAR. New York: Viking, 1978. 194 pp.

> 1972-1973. A novelist's diary begun on her seventieth birthday; her life in Kennett Square, Pennsylvania, and travels in Japan as a guest of the International Association of Playwrights, Editors, Essayists and Novelists; United States travels, lectures and literary conferences; reflections on both the problems and satisfactions of aging but the wish that she could "stop thinking about being old."

WHITEHURST, GEORGE WILLIAM, 1925-   **5953**

DIARY OF A CONGRESSMAN. Norfolk, Va.: Donning, 1983. 263 pp.

> 1972-1977. Virginia Republican congressman's diary; very detailed coverage of the period, with candid opinions on Richard Nixon, the Watergate affair, Spiro Agnew incident and Henry Kissinger, "the most articulate and intelligent man I have ever heard"; discussions of impeachment possibility and Nixon's resignation; meetings of the moderate Republican "Wednesday Group"; Armed Services Committee work; a visit to Mao's China, with extensive notes on travels and impressions; Gerald Ford's administration.

1973

AMATO, ANTONY, pseud.   **5954**

AFFAIR. By Antony Amato and Katherine Edwards, pseud., New York: G.P. Putnam's Sons, 1978. 188 pp.

1973-1975. Diaries kept and published pseudonymously by two lovers, a divorced man and a married woman, both professional writers attempting to collaborate on a novel; an account in explicit detail of an affair that lasted until they were caught by the woman's daughter, with unhappy results; contrived sounding.

COLEMAN, JOHN ROYSTON, 1921-   **5955**

BLUE-COLLAR JOURNAL: A COLLEGE PRESIDENT'S SABBATICAL. Philadelphia: J.B. Lippincott, 1974. 252 pp.

> Feb-Apr 1973. Haverford College president's two-month sabbatical odyssey as a blue-collar worker, first as ditch digger, finally as garbage collector; problems of finding jobs and lodging; reflections on work and education, personal and national values; conversations of coworkers.

COX, KATHLEEN   **5956**

" A Journal of the Unconscious." LAMP IN THE SPINE 9 (Spring/Fall, 1974): 58-77.

> Sep-Nov 1973. A woman's journal kept after hospitalization and various therapies had enabled her to become "stronger in myself"; emptying her mind and recording whatever images came into the "unconscious."

D'ARCY, PAULA, 1947-   **5957**

SONG FOR SARAH. Wheaton, Ill.: Harold Shaw, 1979. 124 pp.

> 1973-1979 (with gap). Young mother's excitement and joy of pregnancy, birth and first year of first child; suffering the reality of her husband's and daughter's death in a tragic automobile accident; struggling through sorrow to new understanding of faith and death.

DJERASSI, NORMA LUNDHOLM   **5958**

GLIMPSES OF CHINA FROM A GALLOPING HORSE. New York: Pergamon, 1974. 141 pp.

> May-Jun 1973. A visit to China with her husband, Carl Djerassi, who was lecturing at invitation of the Institute of Zoology; stays in Peking, Nanking, Wusih, Soochow, Shanghai, Hangchow and Canton; notes on historic places of interest, status and role of women, quality of food, clothing, etc.; a reception by Chou En-lai, during which he expounded on possibilities for United States-Chinese exchanges; visits to medical facilities, communes, schools, libraries, a tea plantation, etc.; diarist's admiration for cleanliness of cities and absence of crime, poverty and alcoholism, but concern about thought control and lack of individual expression.

DREW, ELIZABETH   **5959**

"A Watergate Diary." ATLANTIC MONTHLY 232, August, 1973, pp. 60-70.

> May 1973. A Washington correspondent's comments on and quotations from most of the principal figures of the Watergate affair, including President Nixon, during the period leading up to the Ervin hearings; a pastiche of news items and her analysis of them.

HALE, JOANNE   **5960**

"Shipyard Journal." LOG OF MYSTIC SEAPORT 25 (1973):52-58.

Jan-Feb 1973. Williams College student's account of working as a volunteer on the restoration of the L.A. DUNTON at Mystic, Connecticut, as part of the Williams "Man and the Sea" program.

HEMSCHEMEYER, JUDITH   **5961**

In ARIADNE'S THREAD, edited by Lyn Lifshin, pp. 218-219.

Jun 1973. Extract from journal kept by author and college professor on death of her mother.

MAGNUSON, JERMAINE   **5962**

CHINA DIARY: SENATOR AND MRS. MAGNUSON'S JOURNEY TO THE PEOPLE'S REPUBLIC OF CHINA. N.p.: Offset Printing, 1974? 44 pp.

Jun-Jul 1973. Brief description first of visit to Nixon home at San Clemente and of Mrs. Nixon as hostess, then of a trade tour of China as a spouse accompanying members of congressional trade delegation; hotels, meals, official banquets; visits to factories, agricultural communes, schools, Shanghai, Peking, the Great Wall, etc.

MURRAY, JUDITH MICHELE FREEDMAN, 1934-1974   **5963**

In ARIADNE'S THREAD, edited by Lyn Lifshin, pp. 97-105.

Sep 1973-Mar 1974. Extracts from author's diary; fears and pain during final illness of cancer.

RENNERT, MAGGIE   **5964**

SHELANU: AN ISRAEL JOURNAL. Englewood Cliffs, N.J.: Prentice Hall, 1979. 446 pp.

1973-1975. Journal of a self-described "gutsy grandmother" who emigrated to Israel; living first in a communal absorption center studying language and customs; moving into a private flat and learning to live with unaccustomed and annoying privations, at the same time developing an irrational love for the town of Beer-sheba; written in a jaunty style not without barbs at herself and the fledgling system.

WEBER, NANCY, 1942-   **5965**

THE LIFE SWAP. New York: Dial, 1974. 262 pp. passim.

1973? Diaries and letters of a New York journalist and "Micki," a Women's studies professor, who exchanged lives: homes, mates, lovers, friends, jobs, clothes, etc., for a month with predictably unsuccessful results.

1974

ARBLE, MEADE   **5966**

THE LONG TUNNEL: A COAL MINER'S JOURNAL. New York: Atheneum, 1976. 239 pp.

Sep 1974-Aug 1975. Diary of a year as a miner with the Nova Coal Company in Greenridge, Pennsylvania; difficulties of sup-

porting a young family after a carefree hippie life; views on miners and their families, social life and Catholic Church activities of a small mining town; diarist's complaints about the school system; a strike; sharing both the grueling daily work and desperate outlook for the future of coal miners.

CASSERLY, JOHN J., 1927-   **5967**

THE FORD WHITE HOUSE: THE DIARY OF A SPEECHWRITER. Boulder: Colorado Associated University Press, 1977. 374 pp.

1974-1976. Diary kept by a journalist who became a speech writer for President Ford; a quite intimate picture of an "unpretentious" president, his policies, strengths and weaknesses, the legacy of problems inherited from the Vietnam and Watergate eras; vignettes of many members of the White House staff, presidential advisers, the cabinet and other speech writers, with specific and frequent references to Milton Friedman, Alan Greenspan, Henry Kissinger, Ron Nessen, Robert T. Hartmann, Paul Theis, Donald Rumsfeld and others; notes on former president Nixon and future president Reagan; especially interesting for the hectic processes by which Ford speeches developed, the President's choices of writers and speeches for specific occasions and the fact of modern presidential rhetoric as a totally professional activity bearing little relation to the office or person.

DE VRIES, RACHEL   **5968**

In ARIADNE'S THREAD, edited by Lyn Lifshin, pp. 242-245.

Sep-Oct 1974. Extract from psychologist's journal of her experiences with women and children in Kenya while doing research on child development.

ELLIS, MARC H.   **5969**

A YEAR AT THE CATHOLIC WORKER. New York: Paulist Press, 1978. 140 pp.

Sep 1974-May 1975. Diary of a Jewish student whose concerns about poverty led him to spend the year after college at St. Joseph's Worker House in New York; routines, policies, dangers and shocks of a community devoted to clothing, feeding and sheltering the destitute of the Bowery area; interesting sketches of temporary and permanent residents, volunteer workers, staff and street people; conversations with the aged Dorothy Day and references to the CATHOLIC WORKER; the diarist's insights during a traumatic but valuable year.

NOUWEN, HENRI JOSEF MACHIEL, 1932-   **5970**

THE GENESEE DIARY: REPORT FROM A TRAPPIST MONASTERY. Garden City, N.Y.: Doubleday, 1976. 195 pp.

Jun-Dec 1974. Dutch-born priest's seven months, Pentecost through Advent, living in a Trappist monastery, Genesee, in upstate New York; a time to step back from teaching, writing, lecturing and claim solitude and a time to live the spiritual life under the expert tutelage of Abbot John Eudes; reflections on monastic life, inner freedom, obedience, submission; reading church fathers and contemporaries such as Thomas Merton.

¡GRACIAS! A LATIN AMERICAN JOURNAL. San Francisco: Harper and Row, 1983. 188 pp.

Oct 1980?-Mar 1981? Account of his efforts while in Bolivia and Peru to discover a possible missionary vocation in Latin America;

his life among the poor, sharing their condition and outlook; notes on churches, orphanages and prisons; reflections on the nature of the missionary task, morality, war, international politics, as well as his own spiritual quest; gratitude for the gifts gained through his Latin American pilgrimage.

POLIKOFF, JUDY   5971

EVERY LOVING GIFT: HOW A FAMILY'S COURAGE SAVED A SPECIAL CHILD. By Judy Polikoff as told to Michele Sherman. New York: G.P. Putnam's Sons, 1983. 271 pp. passim.

1974-1976. Diary within narrative kept by the mother of a brain-damaged boy; account of rehabilitation by a controversial method practiced at the Centre for Neurological Rehabilitation; the use of volunteers during every waking hour to "pattern" the child; difficulty of maintaining family life and relationships; ultimate vindication of the parents' determination to go to such lengths to help their son achieve a normal life.

THOMPSON, DANNY, 1947-   5972

E-6, THE DIARY OF A MAJOR LEAGUE SHORTSTOP. Minneapolis: Dillon Press, 1975. 248 pp.

Dec 1974-Sept 1975. The baseball season of a player in his third year of leukemia; relationships of players and managers, life in training camp and on the road with the Minnesota Twins.

TRUITT, ANNE, 1921-   5973

DAYBOOK: JOURNAL OF AN ARTIST. New York: Pantheon, 1982. 225 pp.

1974-1980. Sculptor's journal of unwinding after mounting two retrospective exhibits; working in the quiet and comfortable seclusion of artist's retreats at Yaddo and Ossabow Island; teaching, lecturing at various galleries and universities; life at her Washington, D.C., home with three almost grown children; autobiographical narratives side by side with record of her work in progress and the daily activity of keeping a busy household operating smoothly; insights of a mature artist, mother and woman.

UPTON, JOE, 1946-   5974

ALASKA BLUES: A FISHERMAN'S JOURNAL. Anchorage: Alaska Northwest Publishing, 236 pp.

Apr-Nov 1974? Journal of a fishing season in northwestern inland waterways from Seattle to the Lynn Canal in southeastern Alaska; descriptions and comments on the area fished, the boats, the catch or more often the lack of it, fishermen, scenery and his own cabin at Point Baker; observations on the declining fishing industry and some of the causes.

WEIDENFELD, SHEILA RABB   5975

FIRST LADY'S LADY: WITH THE FORDS AT THE WHITE HOUSE. New York: Putnam, 1979. 419 pp.

1974-1979. Serving as press secretary for Betty Ford with "unprecedented satisfactions, unbearable frustrations, and a first hand look at the world's most prestigious office building: The White House, Washington, D.C."; private life of the first family which was inevitably public, office politics, campaigning, vacationing at Vale; warm appreciation for Michael, Jack, Steve and

Susan; anxiety about Mrs. Ford's growing problem with medications; a revealing picture of a critical period for the nation, all in a popular, press release style.

1975

FLETCHER, DAVID JEFFREY   5976

MED SCHOOL MAYHEM. Chicago: F. Fergeson Productions, 1980. 345 pp.

1975-1977. Diary of an unusual medical student who achieved professional and public acclaim with his student research on "jogger's kidney"; completion of "pre-med" work at Knox College and medical training at Rush Medical College, Galesburg, Illinois; clinical experience as an army doctor in Hawaii; the publication of his research and resulting fame, complete with television interviews and talk shows; breezy notes on classes, tests, professors, fellow students, dramatic emergency room incidents, his love life, adventures on the talk show and television circuit; his admiration for the "practicing small town doctors" of Galesburg.

HERSEY, JEAN, 1902-   5977

A WIDOW'S PILGRIMAGE. New York: Continuum, 1979. 114 pp.

1975-1977. Writer and homemaker's diary from the initial sudden loss of her spouse of fifty years, through the grief, to a new independence in a different locale; accepting the sustaining love of family and friends; gaining comfort and strength in observing the renewing of life in her garden.

HORNER, JOYCE MARY, 1903-1980   5978

THAT TIME OF YEAR: A CHRONICLE OF LIFE IN A NURSING HOME. Amherst: University of Massachusetts Press, 1982. 207 pp.

Extracts in A DAY AT A TIME, edited by Margo Culley, pp. 292-304.

1975-1977 (with gaps). Sensitive descriptions and thoughts of a longtime English teacher at Mount Holyoke College, confined to a nursing home with severe arthritis and broken bones; accepting old age without fear, gaining inner strength from her interest in literature, music and politics, as well as vivid memories of summer vacations at Brighton, England, and on the Maine coast; continuing to write; notes on characteristics of other patients and on management of the nursing home.

LEE, LAUREL   5979

WALKING THROUGH THE FIRE! New York: Dutton, 1977. 113 pp.

Oct 1975-Jul 1976. Woman patient's experiences in the teaching hospital of University of Oregon Medical School, Portland, while battling Hodgkin's disease during her third pregnancy; moments of joy, sadness and humor in the encounters with doctors, nurses and other patients; birth of her daughter and conquering her illness only to be faced with divorce; strong Christian faith and triumphant spirit evident through poetic journal entries.

SIGNS OF SPRING. New York: Dutton, 1980. 118 pp.

1976-1978. With illness in remission, her new life as a single parent; amusing forays into the world of business when her first book was published, grateful for an income which allowed a home and car; devastating return of Hodgkin's disease, exhausting surgery and treatment, a suitor who ultimately could not handle both illness and children; comfort of her children and the triumph of another remission portrayed with wisdom and humor.

MOURNING INTO DANCING. New York: Dutton, 1984. 218 pp.

1980-1982. Supressing the ever present fear of return of Hodgkin's disease while busy with active, growing family; lecturing to women's groups; courtship and marriage which proved to be disastrous to everything but diarist's spirit, courage and faith.

PARKER, CAROL MONT   5980

"The Anatomy of a New York Debut Recital." PIANO QUARTERLY 24, no. 94 (1976):15-37.

ANATOMY OF A NEW YORK DEBUT RECITAL. Evanston, Ill.: Instrumentalist, 1981. 90 pp.

Extracts in ARIADNE'S THREAD, edited by Lyn Lifshin, pp. 32-36.

Aug 1975-Feb 1976. Pianist's thoughts and work at the piano in the months before debut at Carnegie Recital Hall; insights into music, teachers, especially Josef Fidelman, practicing, piano technique, memory; pre-concert tension and the exhilaration of seeing her name on the marquee.

ROSSER, PHYLLIS   5981

"Making Time: a Housewife's Log." MS. 4, no. 9 (1976):54-56, 87-88.

Aug 1975? An almost hourly diary of a suburban New Jersey housewife and free-lance writer; domestic chores and child care; a bit of reading when she had the chance; worry over sacrificing significant activities with her child for minutiae of domesticity.

WEINGARTEN, VIOLET   5982

INTIMATIONS OF MORTALITY. New York: Knopf, 1978. 242 pp.

1975-1976. Woman writer's personal journal of living with cancer, chemotherapy, fears, hopes; shielding her family from much of her anguish; finding release in writing.

1976

CAMPEN, RICHARD N.   5983

SANIBEL AND CAPTIVA, ENCHANTING ISLANDS. Chagrin Falls, Ohio: West Summit Press, 1977. 96 pp. Diary, pp. 13-15, 21-46.

Jan-Feb 1976, Jan 1977. Winter visitor's journal extracts, probably rewritten, accompanying photographs of two Florida gulf coast islands; description of long-time islander Clarence Rutland and his house; notes on residents, visitors, local history, beach strolls, arts and crafts, the Periwinkle Trailer Park, birding and shelling; a visit to Willis Combs, his arboretum and home; expeditions to the J.N. Darling Wildlife Preserve, Sanibel's wetlands preserve, the Bailey Tract and Captiva; confronting the problems of population growth.

COPPOLA, ELEANOR   5984

NOTES. New York: Simon and Schuster, 1979; Pocket Books, 1980. 288 pp.

1976-1978. Diary of wife of producer/director/writer, Francis Ford Coppola, during filming of APOCALYPSE NOW in the Philippines; making a documentary publicity film for United Artists while observing life on the set and behind the scenes, including actors Martin Sheen and Marlon Brando and cinematographer Vittorio Storaro; suffering both the professional and personal conflicts of an evolving and prolonged artistic production dealing with the senselessness of war in the context of a particular one, the Vietnam War, chronicling the events that ultimately changed the lives of those involved in the film; fine word pictures of scenery, everyday life in a jungle village, ritual ceremonies of Ifagaos, film personalities and the diarist's children.

In ARIADNE'S THREAD, edited by Lyn Lifshin, pp. 92-96.

1979-1981. Extracts on nature, children, women companions and work at her Napa Valley, California home.

HUNT, NAN   5985

In ARIADNE'S THREAD, edited by Lyn Lishin, pp. 142-148.

Oct 1976-Jan 1977. Extracts from poet's mid-life journal; analyzing a fellow poet's work; personal sense of loss on learning of Anaïs Nin's death.

LILLARD, PAULA POLK   5986

CHILDREN LEARNING: A TEACHER'S CLASSROOM DIARY. New York: Schocken Books, 1980. 262 pp.

1976?-1979? A kindergarten teacher's diary of experiences at Forest Lake Country Day School, using Montessori methods and materials in a highly challenging but relaxed classroom environment; interesting notes on individual children, their intellectual and social progress and ups and downs; many good days and a few bad ones for children and teacher.

MORAFF, BARBARA   5987

In ARIADNE'S THREAD, edited by Lyn Lifshin, pp. 52-54.

1976-1979. Extracts from potter's workbook; notes on glazes.

PENNINGTON, M. BASIL   5988

O HOLY MOUNTAIN! JOURNAL OF A RETREAT ON MOUNT ATHOS. Garden City, N.Y.: Doubleday, 1978. 291 pp.

May-Sep 1976. Journal of a Trappist monk from St. Joseph's Abbey, Spencer, Massachusetts, on an extended retreat at Mount Athos in Greece; the Orthodox monks' hospitality, daily regimen and work; the austere beauty of the holy mountain itself; interesting contrasts between Roman Catholic and Greek Orthodox monasticism and sprirituality; Father Pennington's own spiritual pilgrimage.

ROBSON, DEBORAH   5989

In ARIADNE'S THREAD, edited by Lyn Lifshin, pp. 316-319.

Apr-May 1976. Extracts from diary of a weaver and writer; notes on dyeing wool, weaving, constructing a dulcimer with makeshift tools; the beauty of spring weather in the Puget Sound region of Washington.

ROTH, GENEEN   5990

In ARIADNE'S THREAD, edited by Lyn Lifshin, pp. 182-187.

1976-1978. Extracts from the journal of a troubled young woman seeking understanding and self-acceptance in group psychotherapy at Esalen Institute and private therapy in California.

STINSON, ROBERT, 1941-   5991

THE LONG DYING OF BABY ANDREW. By Robert and Peggy Stinson. Boston: Little, Brown, 1983. 375 pp.

1976-1977. Parents' diary of their ordeal during the brief life or ''long dying'' of their premature baby; the state of neonatal intensive care, trauma for parents and family, suffering for the infant; questions on ethical aspects.

1977

ALCOSSER, SANDRA   5992

In ARIADNE'S THREAD, edited by Lyn Lifshin, 299-306.

Oct 1977-May 1978. Extracts from poet's journal of her travels in Montana giving poetry workshops supported by the National Endowment for the Arts; impressions of people and places.

ARVIO, SARAH, 1954-   5993

In ARIADNE'S THREAD, edited by Lyn Lifshin, pp. 246-251.

Sep 1977-Jan 1978. Extracts from woman's travel diary; impressions of Milan and Bari, Italy, Ivangrad, Yugoslavia, Paris and Hamburg.

CHESLER, PHYLLIS, 1940-   5994

WITH CHILD: A DIARY OF MOTHERHOOD. New York: T. Crowell, 1979. 288 pp.

1977-1979. Diary of Jewish, feminist, teacher and author; pregnancy with its attendant discomforts; uneasy interactions with her doctor and midwife; long hours of childbirth followed by fatigue and tensions of combining motherhood with her pre-child schedule of teaching, lecturing, writing and promoting her books; constant uncertainty of reliable child care and household help; puzzling over the altered relationships with husband, friends and feminist colleagues; continuing conflict with her own mother who wanted her to be a traditional stay-at-home housewife; her ''overwhelming and subtle loss in social status''; in spite of these realities, great joy in the love for baby Ariel.

COLAVIN-BRIDGES, FLORINDA   5995

In ARIADNE'S THREAD, edited by Lyn Lifshin, pp. 209-214.

1977-1979. Extracts from long reminiscent journal entries of conception of her daughter, separation from her husband and the lonely days of being a single parent.

DERRICOTTE, TOI   5996

In ARIADNE'S THREAD, edited by Lyn Lifshin, pp. 281-285.

Jul 1977-May 1978. Extracts from a black woman's diary of personal experiences living in an all-white neighborhood in Upper Montclair, New Jersey; racial discrimination in the Hartford Club.

DINE, CAROL   5997

In ARIADNE'S THREAD, edited by Lyn Lifshin, pp. 115-117, 177-181.

1977-1980. Extracts from personal journal of poet on lovers, her psychiatrist and radiation treatment for breast cancer.

EIDUS, JANICE   5998

In ARIADNE'S THREAD, edited by Lyn Lifshin, pp. 269-275.

Jun 1977-May 1978. Extract from journal of a Jewish writer and college professor from the Bronx; experiences while teaching in a midwest college; feelings of alienation and homesickness for New York.

HOGAN, LINDA   5999

In ARIADNE'S THREAD, edited by Lyn Lifshin, pp. 291-298.

1977-1978. Extracts from diary of Chickasaw woman and author; inner struggles with culture conflict.

KAHN, ELY JACQUES, 1916-   6000

ABOUT THE NEW YORKER AND ME: A SENTIMENTAL JOURNAL. New York: G.P. Putnam's Sons, 1979. 453 pp.

Jan-Dec 1977. Journal and memories of a prolific author, journalist and longtime staff writer for the NEW YORKER, with frequent references to editor William Shawn, Brendan Gill and scores of other literary folk; New York and Cape Cod social life; musings on politics, events and people; family matters; a leisurely journal full of anecdotes, gossip and opinion.

KNIGHT, ARTHUR WINFIELD   6001

''An Excerpt from the Diary of Arthur Winfield Knight.'' UNDER THE SIGN OF PISCES.'' 9, no. 2 (1979):15-17.

Jan 1977. Photographer's reflections on the death of Anaïs Nin and memories of three meetings with her; her efforts to conceal the effects of aging and to avoid photographs in later years.

LIFSHIN, LYN   6002

ARIADNE'S THREAD. New York: Harper and Row, 1982. 335 pp. Diary pp. 188-191, 329-333.

Apr 1977, 1978-1981. Extracts from journal of a poet and author; varied relationships with men; formulating the idea, planning, selecting and editing a book of diary extracts.

NORTON, EDWARD C.   6003

''Siege: A Striker's Diary.'' NIEMAN REPORTS 32 (1978):3-7.

Aug-Oct 1977. Record by NEW YORK DAILY NEWS reporter of strike against his paper and the NEW YORK TIMES; television news coverage; proliferation of ''strike papers''; legal predicament of Myron Farber; activities of newspaper tycoon Rupert Murdoch.

PASTAN, LINDA   6004

In ARIADNE'S THREAD, edited by Lyn Lifshin, pp. 312-315.

Sep 1977, Jun 1979. Extracts from poet's diary of plans to move to Nantucket followed by anxiety over perhaps locating the house too near the water.

PLAGENS, PETER, 1941-   6005

"Journal, Chicago Gig: The Artist Itinerant." ART IN AMERICA 66, no. 3 (1978):58-62, 137.

Apr 1977. Stint of an artist, teacher and critic as visiting artist at The Art Institute of Chicago; perceptions of undergraduate and graduate students and critiques of their work; personal ideas of teaching art and sharp criticism of current art education in colleges and universities.

SHANNON, ELIZABETH, 1937-   6006

UP IN THE PARK: THE DIARY OF THE WIFE OF THE AMERICAN AMBASSADOR TO IRELAND. New York: Atheneum, 1983. 358 pp.

1977-1981. Diary of a diplomat's wife which she kept while she and her husband, William Shannon, and their children were in Ireland; a lively account of social life, official functions, her involvement in the Irish women's movement, travels and enjoyment of the country and its people; the resourceful solving of problems and coping with unexpected, sometimes humorous situations; family matters, such as finding schools for her children, and their life in the ambassador's mansion in Phoenix Park, Dublin.

ZEIGER, LILA L.   6007

In ARIADNE'S THREAD, edited by Lyn Lifshin, pp. 197-206.

Jul-Aug 1977. Extracts from poet's diary kept while she was a resident fellow at the MacDowell Colony; notes on her work and interaction, or lack of it, with other colonists.

1978

ANON.   6008

"Diary of a Student Teacher." MUSIC EDUCATOR'S JOURNAL 65, no. 6 (1979):58-61.

Sep-Dec 1978? Meeting the teacher, principal and class; eagerness and frustrations, successes and failures of student teaching music in grades three through six.

ABBOTT, DOROTHY   6009

NOTHING'S CHANGED: DIARY OF A MASTECTOMY. New York: F. Fell, 1981. 214 pp. Diary, pp. 5-140.

1978-1980. A woman's record of her discovery of breast cancer, surgery and days of recovery; the trauma and fears; much needed support from husband and friends; honestly told, with many answers to the questions she asked of her doctors.

BANANA, ANNA   6010

ABOUT VILE. Vancouver, B.C.: Banana Productions, 1983. 106 pp. Diary, pp. 85-103.

Sep-Dec 1978. Diary of producer and director, along with Bill Gaglione, of Futurist Sound, a performance group, while on a European tour performing in galleries and spaces arranged by European friends through mail art network; notes on audiences in eastern and western Europe; interesting meetings and enter-

tainment by avant-garde artists, exchanging mail art, stamp art and viewing works in progress.

BLUM, ARLENE   6011

"Triumph and Tragedy on Annapurna." NATIONAL GEOGRAPHIC 155, no. 3. (1979):295-313.

Aug-Oct 1978. Extracts from mountain climbing diary kept by leader of the American Women's Himalayan Expedition, the first Americans to scale Annapurna I; success tragically marred by the deaths of two climbers from the second ascent team.

COHEN, WILLIAM S., 1940-   6012

ROLL CALL: ONE YEAR IN THE UNITED STATES SENATE. New York: Simon and Schuster, 1981. 344 pp.

1978-1979. Maine Republican's first year in the Senate; activities of Armed Services, Governmental Affairs and Indian Affairs committees; much on the Carter administration, including the Iran hostage crisis and SALT II deliberations; notes on Carter, Kissinger, Howard Baker, Robert Byrd, Gerald Ford, Gary Hart, Henry Jackson, Edward Kennedy, Edmund Muskie, John Stennis, John Tower and others; trips to China, Korea, Japan and Germany; efforts to maintain privacy and family life.

DI SPOLDO, NICK   6013

"Pages From a Prison Diary." CONFRONTATION 15 (1978):74-83.

May 1978? Extracts from the diary of an introspective prisoner; analysis of himself and prison life; reactions to books and reading; reasons for keeping a diary.

FISK, ERMA J.   6014

THE PEACOCKS OF BABQUIVARI. New York: Norton, 1983. 284 pp.

Dec 1978-May-1979. An amateur ornithologist's diary of documenting birds in Nature Conservancy property at head of Thomas Canyon, Pima County, Arizona; living in a deserted mountain ranch; problems with ranch cats, the resident peacocks and ground squirrels; isolated for a time by an unusual rain that flooded creek beds ordinarily used as roads into the canyon and closed major highways; learning to enjoy the quiet beauty ruled over by Baboquivari Peak, a mountain sacred to the Papago Indians.

HAMPL, PATRICIA   6015

In ARIADNE'S THREAD, edited by Lyn Lifshin, pp. 320-325.

1978-1980. Extracts from a Minnesota woman's diary; descriptions of the light on Lake Superior as it appears in summer months early in the morning, recorded regularly as a writer's exercise.

HERMAN, MICHELLE, 1955-   6016

In ARIADNE'S THREAD, edited by Lyn Lifshin, pp. 237-241.

Jul-Aug 1978. Extracts from author's diary while on vacation in Greenville, South Carolina, and the Blue Ridge Mountains; contrasts with New York City.

HOLDREN, SUSAN, 1959-1980   6017

In WHY GOD GAVE ME PAIN, by Shirley Holdren and Susan Holdren, pp. 22-104 passim. Chicago: Loyola University, 1984.

1978-1980. Young woman's brave battle with leukemia; continuing her studies at Ohio State University during periods of remission; faith, hope and courage which she shared with many patients during her hospital stays and which ultimately provided the strength for her family to cope with her death.

KINNICUTT, SUSAN   6018

In ARIADNE'S THREAD, edited by Lyn Lifshin, pp. 106-114.

Jan-Mar 1978. Extracts from author's journal relating clandestine meetings with a lover, her experience of anorexia nervosa and a friend's response to her novel.

LEE, ANDREA, 1953-   6019

RUSSIAN JOURNAL. New York: Random House, 1981. 239 pp. Vintage Books, 1984. 235 pp.

Aug 1978-May 1979, Sep 1980. Diary of a woman who accompanied her husband to Russia for his studies at Moscow State University; living and with Russian students in a dormitory, making friends; notes on the peasant market, steam baths, shortages of food and clothing, a wedding, Russian Easter service and the Soviet youth culture obsessed with jeans and rock music; clandestinely teaching English to emigrating Jews; later entry upon return to United States expressing her feeling of release from a subtle confinement yet missing life in the dormitory tower.

RUSS, MARTIN   6020

SHOWDOWN SEMESTER: ADVICE FROM A WRITING PROFESSOR. New York: Crown, 1980. 214 pp.

Sep-Dec 1978. Letter-Journal of a college professor at Carnegie Mellon University; advice to a new teacher on teaching writing; on relationship to students, to professional colleagues and to the administration laced with his battle for contract renewal which was refused because his consuming interest was teaching and writing rather than "initiating academic programs that can attract grants from outside the university (even when such programs aren't needed)."

RYAN, MARGARET   6021

In ARIADNE'S THREAD, edited by Lyn Lifshin, pp. 135-141.

Jul 1978-Jan 1979. Extracts from personal journal of poet, freelance writer and teacher of writing; thoughts, feelings, dreams and fears during first months of pregnancy.

SHEPHERD, LAURIE, 1950-   6022

A DREAMER'S LOG CABIN. New York: Dembner Books, 1981. 175 pp. Diary, pp. 21-131.

1978-1979. Young woman's diary of the hard work and sense of accomplishment in fullfilling her dream of building a log cabin in northern Minnesota; becoming part of a community of hardy people one of whom she joined in harvesting wild rice; coping with interminable rain and cold weather; experiencing the joy of moving into her cabin and living an uncomplicated life at her own pace.

ULLMAN, LESLIE   6023

In ARIADNE'S THREAD, edited by Lyn Lifshin, pp. 70-74.

Jun-Nov 1978. Extracts from poet's journal revealing emotions on winning Yale Younger Poets Award; agonies of a dissolving relationship with her lover.

WEIN, BIBI   6024

In ARIADNE'S THREAD, edited by Lyn Lifshin, pp. 62-69.

Mar-Apr 1978. Extracts from writer's journal during period of depression and struggle to resume writing.

1979

ARNOLD, ALAN, 1922-   6025

ONCE UPON A GALAXY. New York: Ballantine, 1980. 277 pp.

Mar-Nov 1979. Journal kept by publicist during filming THE EMPIRE STRIKES BACK, on sites in bitter cold Finse, Norway, and sets in Elstree, England and Marin County, California; notes on work and relationships of cast and large production staff; interviews with cast members Mark Hamill, Harrison Ford, Carrie Fisher, director Irvin Kershner, producer Gary Kurtz, story writer George Lucas, conceptual artist Ralph McQuarrie and others; observations on people as actors and characters; insights into the thought and artistry of twentieth-century space age special effects technology in moviemaking.

AUSTIN, NANCY   6026

"Diary of Three Mile Island Incident." SOCIAL EDUCATION 43 (1979):458-459.

Mar-Apr 1979. Camp Hill, Pennsylvania, woman's reactions to the Three Mile Island nuclear power accident; fears and uncertainties; the family's difficult decision to remain rather than to flee.

LEE, ROBERT   6027

CHINA JOURNAL: GLIMPSES OF A NATION IN TRANSITION. San Franciso: East/West, 1980. 115 pp.

Nov-Dec 1979. Sabbatical travels in China, with his family, of a Chinese-American professor at San Francisco Theological Seminary; by train, plane and bus to Peking, Nanking, Canton, Shanghai, etc., with an "Overseas Chinese" tour group; notes on cities, villages, communes, museums, schools and reopened churches, as well as effects of the Cultural Revolution; evidence of the emergence of a more open society; visit to the ancestral village and relatives of the diarist's wife.

LONGACRE, DORIS JANZEN   6028

LIVING MORE WITH LESS. Scottsdale, Pa.: Herald Press, 1980. 294 pp. Diary, pp. 9-11.

Jan-Nov 1979. Extracts from a Mennonite woman's diary showing her reactions to terminal cancer; religious reflections, concerns for her family and desire to stay well long enough to finish LIVING MORE WITH LESS, her second book.

MARSHALL, BOB   6029

DIARY OF A YANKEE-HATER. New York: F. Watts, 1981. 212 pp.

1979-1980. Baseball fan's observations on New York Yankees and their performance during one season; always rooting for the underdog and taking sly delight in their defeat by the Kansas City Royals at the end of the season; comments on controversial player Reggie Jackson and on various other sports in New York City.

SAGAN, MIRIAM, 1954-   **6030**

In ARIADNE'S THREAD, edited by Lyn Lifshin, pp. 286-288.

Oct 1979. Extract from a Boston woman's journal of her participation in demonstration at Seabrook nuclear power plant; clashes with the police and her reactions to the event.

SAURO, JOAN   **6031**

INNER MARATHON: THE DIARY OF A JOGGING NUN. New York: Paulist Press, 1982. 98 pp.

1979-1980. Roman Catholic nun's diary of everyday sights, sounds, sensations and spiritual observations seen and felt during her daily run; a mystical and mysterious view of life blending the commonplace and sublime.

SCHWARZ, VERA, 1947-   **6032**

LONG ROAD HOME: A CHINA JOURNAL. New Haven: Yale University Press, 1984. 284 pp.

1979-1980. Journal of a Stanford graduate student, well prepared by her extensive background in Chinese intellectual history, a member of the first group of Americans admitted to China under the United States-China cultural exchange agreement; a highly personal, evocative and even poetic presentation of her observations and experiences as she traveled through China; notes on people, scenes and institutions; the commune system and treatment of dissidents.

SMITH, BARBARA, 1946-   **6033**

In A DAY AT A TIME, edited by Margo Culley, pp. 305-309.

Feb-Jun 1979. Diary extracts revealing fears of a black, feminist, lesbian living in Boston during period when twelve black women were murdered; organizing women to exert pressure on law enforcement officers and educating women about self-defense; disgust with oppression and powerlessness, but finding moments of hope in a new kind of coalition of black and white, feminist and non-feminist, which she saw emerging over this issue.

SMITH, DWIGHT R.   **6034**

ABOVE TIMBERLINE: A WILDLIFE BIOLOGIST'S ROCKY MOUNTAIN JOURNAL. Edited by Alan Anderson, Jr. New York: Alfred A. Knopf, 1980. 246 pp.

Jun-Nov 1979? Journal of a professor of wildlife management and ecology at Colorado State University who spent summer and autumn in a log cabin above timberline in the Colorado Rockies; his observations of plants and animals and their adaptations to the harsh environment; his own adjustments to altitude, cold, wind and solitude; long hikes in the mountains; interesting observations on the natural and human history of the area, as well as religious and philosophical reflections; concerns about human impact on the fragile ecological system; a worthwhile human and scientific journal.

WALKER, THOMAS W.   **6035**

NICARAGUA IN REVOLUTION. New York: Praeger, 1982. Diary, pp. 81-91.

Jul 1979. Political scientist's account of five-day investigative sojourn in Nicaragua immediately following the fall of the Somoza government; from Los Manos on the Honduran border to Managua via Esteli; description of conditions, mood of people, actions of the Sandinistas; reports of former regiment's brutality.

1980

ANTIN, ELEANOR, 1935-   **6036**

BEING ANTINOVA. Los Angeles: Astro Artz, 1983. 87 pp.

Oct. 1980. Artist's diary of installation and performance at Ronald Feldman Gallery, New York City; self-obsession in attempt to portray an aging, black ballerina; an insight into performance art.

BROOKS, ANNE M., 1919-   **6037**

THE GRIEVING TIME: A MONTH BY MONTH ACCOUNT OF RECOVERY FROM LOSS. Wilmington, Del.: Delapeake, 1982. 40 pp.

THE GRIEVING TIME: A YEAR'S ACCOUNT OF RECOVERY FROM LOSS. Garden City, N.Y.: Dial, 1985. 40 pp.

1980? Painful month of a widow's stages of grief; her innermost feelings experienced when alone.

HENES, DONNA   **6038**

DRESSING OUR WOUNDS IN WARM CLOTHES: WARD'S ISLAND ENERGY TRANCE MISSION. Los Angeles: Astro Artz, 1982. 72 pp.

May-Jun 1980. Diary of author/artist's environmental art, entitled WARD'S ISLAND ENERGY TRANCE MISSION, at Manhattan Psychiatric Center; commentary on brutal style of works in sculpture garden; folkloric customs concerning universality of the magical connotations of knotting and healing; interactions with both patients and staff; long conversations with a doctor about sanity and insanity; an unconventional style artist's book.

ISAACS, HAROLD ROBERT, 1910-   **6039**

RE-ENCOUNTERS IN CHINA: NOTES OF A JOURNEY IN A TIME CAPSULE. Armonk, N.Y.: M.E. Sharpe, 1985. 192 pp.

Oct 1980. Journalist's diary of present-day China interspersed with reflections and memories of his experiences there in the thirties as editor of CHINA FORUM; revisiting at invitation of the Chinese Writers Association and meeting old friends who had suffered through the Cultural Revolution; notes on Peking Soong Ching-ling, Sun Yat-sen's widow and writers from his earlier experience.

LAPINSKI, SUSAN   **6040**

IN A FAMILY WAY. Boston: Little, Brown, 1982. 229 pp.

1980?-1982? A joint diary of an editor and her writer husband, Michael D. Hinds; decision to have a baby, pregnancy, childbirth and their daughter's first year; well-written, honest feelings of emotional changes, effect on their careers and respective work, new relationships with friends and family; learning to be parents, including several months of therapy for Michael who lacked a father as a role model.

MACIORA, JOSEPH C.V., 1959-   6041

AN ADVENTURE IN POLAND. New Britain, Conn.: Polish Genealogical Society of Connecticut, 1986. 53 pp.

Jul-Aug 1980. A young Polish-American's record of his tour of Poland by bus and train, visiting historic sites, churches, shrines, cathedrals, museums, etc.; the Auschwitz concentration camp; Warsaw, Krakow and other cities; visiting in homes of Polish people and making friends; attending lectures on the arts and culture; experiencing much that was of personal significance to him as a Pole and a Catholic, as well as of genealogical interest to his family.

MYERS, DARLENE   6042

In ARIADNE'S THREAD, edited by Lyn Lifshin, pp. 220-221.

May 1980. Extract from ballet dancer's diary on the death of her mother.

PICHASKE, DAVID   6043

THE JUBILEE DIARY. Peoria, Ill.: Ellis Press, 1982. 1 vol. unpaged.

1980-1981. Bradley College teacher and author's weekly retreats to Jubilee College State Park, Peoria, Illinois, original home of Jubilee College; thoughts on Philander Chase, first Episcopal bishop of Illinois and founder of Jubilee College, and his failed college; philosophical musings about seasonal changes of nature and their broader implications.

SICKMANN, ROCKY, 1957-   6044

IRANIAN HOSTAGE: A PERSONAL DIARY OF 444 DAYS IN CAPTIVITY. Topeka, Kan.: Crawford Press, 1982. 321 pp.

Feb 1980-Jan 1981. Marine sergeant's daily record of being held hostage by Tehran Polytechnic College students in Tehran, Iran; diary beginning on day ninety-two after blindfolds were removed and hands untied; boredom and monotony of days with nothing to do, homesickness, contradictory or false news from captors, lack of mail and uncertainty of release.

WALLACE, ISHMAEL   6045

In BETTER THAN SCHOOL: ONE FAMILY'S DECLARATION OF INDEPENDENCE, by Nancy Wallace, pp. 87-99. Burdett, N.Y.: Larson; New York: Distributed by Kampmann, 1983.

May 1980-Mar 1981. Extracts from a boy's diary of daily activities during second year of home schooling; writing plays and poems, extensive reading, piano lessons and great interest in music and composers; family fun and outdoor activities.

WALLACE, NANCY, 1950-   6046

BETTER THAN SCHOOL: ONE FAMILY'S DECLARATION OF INDEPENDENCE. Burdett, N.Y.: Larson; New York: Distributed by Kampmann, 1983. 256 pp. Journal, pp. 218-233.

1980? Extracts from journal of mother providing home schooling for son and daughter; a week at Suzuki Institute at the University of Maine with her son studying piano and her daughter studying violin; intense group and individual lessons; concerts; observing values and flaws of the Suzuki method.

Indexes

Name Index

*Numbers appearing in boldface type
indicate diarist entries*

A

Abbas II, Khedive of Egypt, 5331
Abbey, Charles Augustus, **3590**
Abbey, James, **3202**
Abbot, Charles Greeley, 5345
Abbot, Henry Larcom, **3548**
Abbott, Dorothy, **6009**
Abbott, Ethel B., **5133**
Abbott, Lemuel Abijah, **4542**
Abdul Aziz, Sultan of Turkey, 4988
Abel, Rudolf I., 5841
Aber, Martha Wilson McGregor, **5212**
Aberdeen and Temair, Ishbel Maria
    Marjoribanks Gordon, marchioness of,
    5312
Abert, James William, **2785**
Abramowitz, Jack, **5858**
Achenbach, Abbie Bright. See Bright,
    Abbie
Ackley, Richard Thomas, **3665**
Acton, John Emerich Edward Dalberg,
    3419
Adair, Cornelia Wadsworth Ritchie, **5023**
Adair, John, 5023
Adams, Ada. See Vogdes, Ada Adams
Adams, Annie. See Fields, Annie Adams
Adams, Cecelia Emily McMillen, **3336**
Adams, Charles Francis, 1807-1886,
    3651, 3763
Adams, Charles Francis, 1835-1915,
    3763, 5337
Adams, Edwin, 5040
Adams, George Russell, **4849**
Adams, Henry Brooks, 5415
Adams, J.J. **2826**
Adams, Jacob, **3821**
Adams, John Quincy, 2834
Adams, R.L., **4341**
Adams, Sherman, 5831, 5835
Adams, William, 3336
Addams, Jane, 5360
Adenauer, Konrad, 5716, 5830
Adler, George J., 3138
Affeld, Charles E., **4342**
Affeld, Frank Otto, 4342
Agapita, Don, 2878
Agassiz, Elizabeth Cabot Cary, **4749**
Agassiz, Ida. See Higginson, Ida Agassiz
Agassiz, Louis, 2927, 2985, 3586, 3612,

4749, 4786, 4871
Aggens, Steffen Heinrich, **4750**
Agnew, Samuel A., **4543**
Agnew, Spiro, 5953
Aiken, George David, 5747, **5942**
Aiken, William, 3652
Ainsworth, Charles G., 5342
Ake, Bill, 3982
Akin, James, **3337**
Albert I, King of the Belgians, 5453
Albert Frederick Arthur George, Prince.
    See George VI, King of Great Britain
Alberts, Robert C., **5822**
Albertson, Jack, 5862
Alcosser, Sandra, **5992**
Alcott, Amos Bronson, 3532, 4884
Alcott, Louisa May, 4261
Alden, Esther, pseud. See Allston,
    Elizabeth Waties and Pringle, Elizabeth
    Waties Allston
Aldrich, Lorenzo D., **3030**
Aldrich, Thomas Bailey, 3783
Alemán, Miguel, 5840
Alemany, José Sadoc, **3203**
Alexander, Edmund B., 3264
Alexander, Eveline Throop Martin, **4850**
Alexander, Sarah. See Lawton, Sarah
    Alexander
Alger, Russell Alexander, 5338
Alison, Joseph Dill, **3822**
Allen, Forest Rose. See Rose, Forest
Allen, Henry. See Allyn, Henry
Allen, Henry Tureman, **5572**
Allen, Jacob, 3284
Allen, James, 2783
Allen, Jerome L., **5456**
Allen, Lucy E., **4343**
Allen, Michael M., **3823**
Allen, Rufus, 3549
Allen, Terry, 5486
Allen, W.T., **3338**
Allen, William B., **3458**
Allen, William Charles, **5442**
Allende Gossens, Salvador, 5716
Allendy, Rene, 5449
Alley, Charles, **3824**
Allred, James, 3549
Allred, Reddick Newton, **2827**
Allston, Elizabeth Waties, **4344**. See also
    Pringle, Elizabeth Waties Allston
Allyn, Henry, **3420**

Alsip, Margaret Ann. See Frink, Margaret
    Ann Alsip
Alston, Lt. Col., **4345**
Altizer, Thomas, 5842
Alvord, Benjamin, 4602
Amato, Antony, pseud., **5954**
Amberley, John Russell, **4884**
Amberley, Katharine Louisa Stanley
    Russell, 4884
Ambler, James Markham, **5145**
Ambler, Lucy Johnston, **4033**, 4292
Ambler, Mary Cary. See Stribling, Mary
    Cary Ambler
Ames, Amos W., **4544**
Ames, Mary, **4751**
Ames, Michael, 4263
Ammen, Jacob, 3831
Amory, Charles Bean, **4752**
Anderson, Alexander Outlaw, 3180
Anderson, Andrew Jonathan, 4850
Anderson, Charles L., 3752
Anderson, George, 5379
Anderson, Isabel Perkins, 5232
Anderson, James M., 5351
Anderson, James W., **4545**
Anderson, John C., **4851**
Anderson, Larz, 5232
Anderson, Nicholas Longworth, **3500**
Anderson, Robert, 3761
Anderson, Samuel Thompson, **4346**
Anderson, William Wallace, **3591**
Andrews, Asa Walter, 5102
Andrews, Avery De Lano, **5484**
Andrews, Eliza Frances, **4546**
Andrews, Ellen Miriam Gibson, **5316**
Andrews, Ellie M. Butz, **4034**
Andrews, Emily Kemble Oliver Brown,
    5024
Andrews, Garnett, 4546
Andrews, George Lippitt, 5024
Andrews, Gilman A., **4347**
Andrews, Persis Sibley, **2786**
Andrews, W.H., **3825**
Andrews, William Albert, **5102**
Andrus, James, 4951
Anello, Bruce, **5898**
Angell, Truman O., **3339**
Angle, Helen M. Blondel, **5411**
Anna May. See May, Anna, pseud.
Anspach, John, 3286
Anthony, Susan Brownell, 2902, 3358,
    5142, 5307, 5312

Brooks, Anne M., **6037**
Brooks, Phillips, 2867
Broomall, Anna, 5294
Broshears, Catherine. See Maynard,
  Catherine Broshears
Bross, William, **5119**
Brother, Charles, **4564**
Brougher, William Edward, **5744**
Brouillet, John, 2915
Brower, Kenneth, 5895
Brown, Adam Mercer, **3209**
Brown, Alexander, **5080**
Brown, Alonzo, 4887
Brown, Andrew, 3357
Brown, Augustus Cleveland, **4565**
Brown, Benjamin, **3769**
Brown, David G., 3198
Brown, Dick, 3425, 3450
Brown, Emily Kemble Oliver. See
  Andrews, Emily Kemble Oliver Brown
Brown, Frank Mason, 5261, 5263
Brown, Henry Billings, **3551**
Brown, J. Robert, **3595**
Brown, Jabez, **4887**
Brown, James, 3404
Brown, James Berry, **3714**
Brown, James S., 3575
Brown, John, of Arkansas, **3596**
Brown, John, of California, **4065**
Brown, John, 1800-1859, 3379, 3621,
  3683, 3709, 3723
Brown, John Clifford, **5361**
Brown, John Evans, **3042**
Brown, John Henry, **3841**
Brown, John Lowery, **3210**
Brown, John Mason, **3842**
Brown, John W., **3348**
Brown, Joseph Emerson, 4438, 4546
Brown, Josephine Edith, **5293**
Brown, Leo G., **5271**
Brown, Nathan, **4066**
Brown, Orville Chester, 3552
Brown, Robert McAfee, **5865**
Brown, Spencer Kellogg, **3552**
Brown, Thomas Dunlop, **3432**
Brown, Warren, **3211**
Brown, William Carey, **5104**
Brown, William Harvey, **5214**
Brown, William Reynolds, **2788**
Browne, Charles Farrar. See Ward,
  Artemus
Browne, John Ross, **3634**
Browne, Thomas M., **4761**
Brownell, Herbert, Jr., 5831
Browning, Robert, 3569
Brownlow, Parson. See Brownlow,
  William Gannaway
Brownlow, William Gannaway, 3916, 4191
Brownson, Orestes, 3419
Bruce, Daniel E., **4067**
Bruce, Mazie, **5226**
Bruckberger, Raymond Leopold, **5698**
Bruff, Joseph Goldsborough, **3043**, 3046,

3133
Brummer, Francis H., **5720**
Brundage, Theodore, **5234**
Brundage, Victor D., 3522
Bryan, Francis T., **3044**
Bryan, Jerry, **5061**
Bryan, Julien Hequembourg, **5489**
Bryan, Mary Baird, **5428**
Bryan, William Jennings, 4329, 5298,
  5313, 5337, 5428, 5429, 5438
Bryant, Edwin, **2836**, 3054
Bryarly, Wakeman, **3090**
Bryce, James Bryce, **4956**
Buchanan. James, 2813, 3009, 3640,
  3735, 3755, 3761, 3815, 4441
Buchanan, Robert Christie, 3235
Buck, David, 4476
Buck, Eli, 4476
Buck, Lucy Rebecca, **3843**
Buck family, 3843
Bucke, Richard Maurice, 5249
Buckingham, Harriet Talcott, **3298**
Buckingham, Henry, 3298
Buckle, Charles M., **5202**
Buckley, James M., 3724
Buckley, Michael Bernard, **4957**
Buckley, William F., Jr., 5883
Buell, Don Carlos, 4207
Buell, George Pearson, 4695
Buffalo Bill. See Cody, William Frederick
Buhrer, George W., **4566**
Bulck, Luther E., **4762**
Bullard, Artemas, 2801
Bullard, William J., **4366**
Bullard, William S., 3490
Bullene, Thomas B., **5026**
Bullis, John Lapham, 5123
Bullitt, Ernesta Drinker, **5472**
Bullitt, William Christian, 5472, 5576,
  5681
Bullock, Stanley Henry, **5280**
Bunker, Henry C., 3115
Bunker, Paul, **5721**
Bunyard, Harriet, **4905**
Buoncoure, Levina. See Urbino, Levina
  Buoncuore
Burbank, Arthur R., **3045**
Burden, Florence Adele Sloane. See
  Sloane, Florence Adele
Burden, James Abercrombie, Jr., 5301
Burder, Thomas Henry Carr, 3347
Burdick, Cyrus, 3307
Burdick, John M., **4567**
Burgard, George, 5705
Burge, Dolly Sumner Lunt Lewis, **2917**,
  3844
Burge, Louisiana, **3844**
Burge, Thomas, 2917
Burger, Otis Kidwell. See Lewis, Abigail,
  pseud.
Burges, Samuel Edward, **3770**
Burgess, E.G., **4068**
Burgess, Hannah Rebecca Crowell, **3349**

Burgess, Perry A., **4852**
Burke, Curtis R., **4069**
Burke, Edmund, 5313
Burke, Richard Maurice, 3025
Burleson, Albert Sidney, 5337, 5429,
  5438
Burney, James, 3078
Burnham, Franklin J., **4568**
Burnham, Hiram, 4578
Burns, Amanda McDowell, **3845**
Burns, Anthony, 3487
Burnside, Ambrose Everett, 3016, 3869,
  3926, 3980, 4006, 4055, 4105, 4234,
  4263, 4296
Burr, Frederick H., **3324**
Burr, Nathan, 3087
Burrage, Henry S., **3846**
Burrell, Birney, **3433**
Burrell, Lyman, J., 3433
Burrough, John, 5249
Burroughs, John, 3504, 4900
Burroughs, William Seward, 5823
Burt, William A., 2953
Burtch, Mary Louisa. See Brewster, Mary
  Louisa Burtch
Burton, Anthony B., **4367**
Burton, Elijah P., **4569**
Burton, Richard Francis, **3771**
Burton, Robert Taylor, 3588, **4070**
Burwell, Colonel, 3426
Burwell family, 4063
Bush, A.L., 3055
Bushby, Arthur Thomas, **3670**
Buster, Samuel R., **4570**
Butcher, Harry Cecil, **5722**
Butcher, Thomas, **5318**
Butler, America Rollins, **3350**
Butler, Ashmun J., 3350
Butler, Benjamin Franklin, 3709, 3827,
  3869, 3894, 3901, 3911, 3917, 3985,
  4081, 4100, 4234, 4247, 4293, 4473,
  4542
Butler, Fanny. See Leigh, Frances Butler
Butler, Frances. See Leigh, Frances
  Butler
Butler, Frances Anne Kemble. See
  Kemble, Frances Anne
Butler, Julia. See Newberry, Julia Butler
Butler, Julia Colt, **5254**
Butler, Pierce, 3755, 4018
Butler, Pierce Mason, 2800
Butler, Sarah. See Wister, Sarah Butler
Butler, Sarah Davenport. See Davenport,
  Sarah
Butler, Sarah Elizabeth, **5105**
Butterfield, Daniel, 4006, 4234
Butterfield, Ira H., **3847**
Butz, Ellie M. See Andrews, Ellie M. Butz
Buzhardt, Beaufort Simpson, **3848**
Byers, Mortimer W., 5841
Byers, William N., **3351**
Bynum, G.W., **4368**
Byrd, Richard Evelyn, **5623**, 5634

Dale, Boone, 5379
Dale, Elizabeth. See Black, Elizabeth Dale
Dali, Salvador, 5800
Dallas, Francis Gregory, **3062**
Dallas, George Mifflin, 3651
Dally, Benjamin Hart, **5238**
Daly, Anna. See Morrison, Anna Daly
Daly, Augustin, 5127
Daly, Charles Patrick, 3869
Daly, Maria Lydig, **3869**
Damien, Father, 5217
Damien de Veuster, Joseph. See Damien, Father
Damon, Samuel Chenery, **3063**
Damon, Samuel M., 5135
Dana, Napoleon Jackson Tecumseh, 4205
Dana, Richard Henry, **5042**
Dandy, George Brown, 4508
Daniels, Arthur M., **4381**
Daniels, James, **4094**
Daniels, Johathan, **5723**
Daniels, Josephus, **5438**
Darbinian, Reuben, **5624**
Darcy, John Stevens, 3094
D'Arcy, Paula, **5957**
Darden, Annie B. Dillard, **3870**
Darragh, John, 4873
Dart, Lydia. See Moxley, Lydia Dart
Davenport, Jesse, 4531
Davenport, Sarah, **3064**
David, James C., **3363**
Davidson, Greenlee, **3508**
Davidson, James D., 3508
Davidson, John W., 3184
Davidson, Randall Thomas, Abp. of Canterbury, 5245
Davidson, W.J., **4095**
Davidson of Lambeth, Baron. See Davidson, Randall Thomas, Abp. of Canterbury
Davies, Joseph Edward, 5669, **5671**
Davies, Thomas Alfred, 4088
Davies, William Gilbert, **5170**
Davis, Alvah Isaiah, **3303**
Davis, Charles H., **4096**
Davis, Charles K., **5171**
Davis, Chester, 5667
Davis, Creed T., **4592**
Davis, George Thomas, 3869
Davis, Gilbert, 5151
Davis, Jefferson, 2888, 3621, 3688, 3794, 3837, 3848, 3858, 3928, 3929, 3944, 3967, 3985, 4007, 4077, 4132, 4317, 4351, 4395, 4404, 4560, 4737, 4769, 4829, 4832, 4839
Davis, Jefferson Columbus, 4415, 4695
Davis, John Shedden, **3364**
Davis, Josiah, 3221
Davis, Lavinia Riker, **5636**
Davis, Mark S., **4909**
Davis, Nicholas A., **3871**

Davis, Rebecca Whitby. See Ebey, Rebecca Whitby Davis
Davis, Sarah, **3220**
Davis, Stephen Chapin, **3221**
Davis, Sylvester, **3721**
Davis, Tamerlane, 3286
Davis, Varina Howell, 3794, 3858, 3944, 4314, 4546, 4769
Davis, Virginia. See Gray, Virginia Davis
Davis, William, **4593**
Davis, William P., **3872**
Dawes, Charles Gates, **5298**
Dawes, Henry Laurens, 2996
Dawes, Rufus Cutler, 5298
Dawes, Rusus R., **4097**
Dawson, George Mercer, **5012**
Dawson, Sarah Morgan, **4098**
Dawson, William Harrison, **4857**
Day, Agnes Lenora Gillespie. See Gillespie, Agnes Lenora
Day, David L., **3873**
Day, Dorothy, **5796**, 5800, 5969
Day, Gershom Bulkley, **3065**
Day, John, 3371
Deady, Matthew Paul, **4976**
Dearborn, Samuel Q., **4099**
De Bow, James Dunwoody Brownson, 3513, **4100**
Debusschere, Dave, **5912**
D'Eça, Florence L., **5797**
D'Eça, Raul, 5797
De Camp, Anna Maria. See Morris, Anna Maria De Camp
Decker, Harriet Page Wheeler. See Young, Harriet Page Wheeler Decker
Decker, Peter, **3066**
De Cotton, L., **5216**
Deery, Seraphine. See McGavock, Seraphine Deery
Deffeliz, Vicente, 3247
De Gaulle, Charles, 5716, 5722
De Jan, Winifred Lewellin James. See James, Winifred Lewellin
Dekobra, Maurice, **5690**
DeLameter, William, 5437
Delano, Alonzo, **3067**
Delany, John O'Fallon, **4101**
Delaware Dick. See Brown, Dick
DeLoach, Olivia Hill, **4594**
DeLoach, William G., **5443**
DeLoach family, 4774
De Long, Charles E., **3509**
De Long, George Washington, **5120**, 5145
De Massey, Ernest. See Massey, Ernest de e Mille, Agnes, **5886**
Deming, Barbara, **5873**
De Monteuil, Victor, 3926
Denig, Edwin T., 3553
Dennis, Ruth. See St. Denis, Ruth
Denny, John, 3313
Dent, Frederick T., 3047, 3095
Dent, Julia. See Grant, Julia Dent

Denver, James W., **3222**
Denzer, Valentine, **4595**
Derby, Emma C., **4888**
Derleth, August William, **5686**
Derricotte, Toi, **5996**
De Saussure family, 3913
Devereaux, Catherine Ann. See Edmondston, Catherine Ann Devereaux
Devereaux family, 3780
Devoe, Alan, **5637**
Devol, Bitha Marshall, 4889
Devol, William Dudley, **4889**
De Vries, Rachel, **5968**
Dewar, Murray, 5532
Dewey, Thomas Edmund, 5664
Dewolf, Charles Wesley, **4102**
Dewolf, David, **3068**
Dewolf, James M., **5067**
Díaz, Porfirio, 5337, 5436
Dibb, William Denton, **4103**
Dickens, Charles, 2927, 3783, 4473
Dickinson, Albert, **4382**
Dickinson, Arnell F., 3006, **3223**
Dickinson, Charlotte Humphrey, **3365**
Dickinson, Edwin, 5857
Dickinson, Emily, 2975, 3229, 3304, 3480, 5167
Dickinson, Henry Clay, **4596**
Dickinson, Lavinia Norcross, **3304**
Dickinson, Obed, 3365
Dickinson, Rudolphus S., 3224
Dickson, James, **4104**
Diebitsch, Josephine. See Peary, Josephine Diebitsch
Diederichs, Johannes F., **2920**
Dier, W. Arthur, **5013**
Dietrich, Marlene, 5708
Dietrich, Richard, 5100
Dill, Samuel Phillips, **4771**
Dillard, Annie B. See Darden, Annie B. Dillard
Dilts, Thomas Jefferson, 4652
Diman, Jeremiah Lewis, **3510**
Dimon, Theodore, **4105**
Dine, Carol, **5997**
Dinwiddie, David, **3439**
Dinwiddie, John, **3439**
Di Spoldo, Nick, **6013**
Dittes, Ben, 4525
Dix, Dorothea Lynde, 3859, 3934
Dix, John Adams, 3869
Dixon, Elizabeth. See Smith, Elizabeth Dixon
Djerassi, Carl, 5958
Djerassi, Norma Lundholm, **5958**
Doane, Gustavus Cheyney, **4960**, 4966
Doble, Abner, 3305
Doble, John, **3305**
Dodd, Ephraim Shelby, **4106**
Dodd, James McKee, **3874**
Dodd, William Edward, **5652**
Dodge, Henry Linn, 3170
Dodge, Mary. See Woodward, Mary Dodge

Garfield, Mollie. See Stanley-Brown, Mary Garfield
Garibaldi, Giuseppe, 3830
Garland, Hamlin, **5344**
Garner, John Nance, 5654
Garnett, James Mercer, **4618**
Garrard, Charles T., **3442**
Garrett, Garet, **5463**
Garrett, Henry A., **3887**
Garrett, Thomas Miles, **3089**
Garrison, Francis Jackson, **5182**
Garrison, William Lloyd, 3516
Garry, Spokan chief, 3324, 3511
Gary, Spokan chief. See Garry, Spokan chief
Gass, A.M., **3727**
Gatewood, Charles, 5223
Gatschell, Henry, 4995
Gault, William Perryander, **4129**
Gauss, Christian Frederick, **5422**
Gay, James Woods, **3309**
Gay, Martha. See Masterson, Martha Gay
Gay, Martin Baker, 3309
Gay, Mary Ann Harris, 4509
Gayle, Richard H., **4780**
Gaylord, Orange, **3234**
Gayn, Mark J., **5784**
Gebhard, Anna Laura Munro, **5785**
Gedney, John, **4130**
Geer, Allen Morgan, **3888**
Geer, Elizabeth Dixon Smith. See Smith, Elizabeth Dixon
Geiger, Vincent Eply, **3090**
Genet, Edmond Charles Clinton, **5464**
Genet, Jean, 5696
George VI, King of Great Britain, 5514, 5617, 5680
George, Thomas Bladen, **5386**
George, Walter Franklin, 5747
Gerard, James Watson, 5390, 5429, **5465**
Gerdemann, Hermann Philipp Wilhelem, **2851**
Geren, Paul Francis, **5710**
Gerity, Will S., **4962**
Gerolt, Friedrich von, Baron, 3869
Geronimo, Apache chief, 5135, 5223
Gerrish, Benjamin, **3728**
Gholson, Georgiana Freeman. See Walker, Georgiana Freeman Gholson
Gholson, Thomas Saunders, 4314
Gibbes family, 3913
Gibbon, John, 4756, 5058, 5062, 5068, 5077, 5084
Gibbon, Lardner, **3310**
Gibbs, Alfred, 4885
Gibbs, George, 1815-1873, **3091**
Gibbs, George, 1861-1940, **5502**
Gibson, Ellen Miriam. See Andrews, Ellen Miriam Gibson
Gibson, George Rutledge, **2852**, 4968
Gibson, Hugh, **5446**
Gibson, Walter Murray, **5217**

Gibson, William, 3291
Gibson, William J., **4619**
Gide, André, 5625
Gielgud, Sir Arthur John, 5708
Giese, Vincent Joseph, **5861**
Giesecke, Julius, **3889**
Gilbert, Alfred West, **3890**
Gilbert, Gustav Mark, **5786**
Gilboy, Bernard, **5173**
Gilchrist, Herbert, 5249
Gilchrist, Leonard Whiting, **4864**
Giles, Henry E., **5766**
Gill, Brendan, 6000
Gill, Harriet Tarleton, **3443**
Gillaspie, Ira Myron Bailey, **3891**
Gillespie, Agnes Lenora, **3371**
Gillespie, Anna Eliza Cook, **5363**
Gillespie, Emily Hawley, **3676**
Gillespie, Jacob, 3371
Gillespie, James, 3676
Gillespie, Josiah B., **5363**
Gillespie, Mary Ann., **5006**
Gillet, Orville, **4620**
Gillett, Edward B., 3487
Gillette, Warren C., **4963**
Gillmore, Quincy Adams, 4380
Gilman, Charles A., 5252
Gilman, Charlotte Perkins, 5164
Gilman, Daniel Coit, 3542
Gilman, James F., **5299**
Gilmer, Juliana Paisley, **2929**
Gilmer family, 4063
Gilpin, Mrs. John R., **5207**
Gilpin, William, 2844, 3835
Gilroy, Frank Daniel, **5862**
Giltner, Henry L., 3518
Gimpel, Rene, **5546**
Ginsberg, Allen, 5800, **5823**
Gist, States Rights, 4305
Gladden, Washington, 3831
Gladstone, William Ewart, 5042
Glasser, Howard T., **5853**
Glazier, Willard Worcester, **3892**
Glenn, R.G., 3247
Glisan, Rodney, **3235**
Glover, Amos, **3893**
Glover, Eli Sheldon, **5044**
Glover, Milton, 3300
Gluckman, Janet, **5813**
Glueck, Nelson, **5893**
Goddard, Robert Hutchings, **5345**
Godey, Laklin, 2803
Godfrey, Edward Settle, **5070**
Godwin, Gail, **5863**
Goebbels, Joseph Paul, 5652, 5661
Gold, William A., 3587
Golden, Jeffrey, **5925**
Golder, Frank Alfred, **5587**, 5588
Goldfield, Abraham, **5619**
Goldman, Paul, **5767**
Goldsborough, John Rodgers, **3444**
Gollings, Bill. See Gollings, Elling William
Gollings, Elling William, **5466**

Goodale, Ephrain, **5106**
Goodale, Fidelia Beach, 5106
Goodale, Greenleaf Austin, 5106
Goodale, I. Preston, **5346**
Goodell, William, 4066
Goodhart, Arthur Lehman, **5574**
Goodman, Paul, 5800
Goodman, Richard French, **3894**
Goodman, William Jefferies, **3605**
Goodnough, Ellen Saxton, **4865**
Goodnough, Ezra, **2796**
Goodnow, William E., 5035
Goodrich, Aaron, 3763
Goodrich, Lloyd, 5857
Goodridge, Sophia Lois, **3236**
Gordon, Andrew, **3092**
Gordon, Ellen. See Fletcher, Ellen Gordon
Gordon, Ishbel Maria Marjoribanks. See Aberdeen and Temair, Ishbel Maria Marjoribanks Gordon, marchioness of
Gordon, James A., 3741
Gordon, John B., 4546
Gordon, Julia Weber. See Weber, Julia
Gordon, Marquis Lafayette, **4131**
Gordon, Robert, **2930**
Gordon, Tommy. See Cardon, Thomas
Gorgas, Josiah, **4132**
Göring, Hermann, 5617, 5652, 5661, 5681, 5688, 5786
Gosse, Sir Edmund William, **5194**
Gottschalk, Louis Moreau, **3641**
Gould, Charles, **3093**
Gould, Jane Augusta Holbrook, **4133**
Gould, John Mead, **3895**
Gould, Laurence M., 5623
Gove, George S., **4134**
Gove, Jesse A., **3642**
Grabill, John H., **3896**
Gracie, Archibald, 3566
Grady, Henry Woodfin, 5248
Grady, Henry Woodfin Jr., 5248
Graham, Julia. See Ord, Julia Graham
Graham, Ziba B., **4398**
Granbury, Hiram Bronson, 4703
Grannis, John W., 4399
Grant, Frederick Dent, 4988
Grant, Julia Dent, 3869, 4503, 5026
Grant, Moses V., 2850
Grant, Ulysses Simpson, 2996, 3702, 3709, 3839, 3869, 3901, 3911, 4006, 4081, 4114, 4124, 4128, 4157, 4234, 4272, 4317, 4367, 4466, 4503, 4514, 4517, 4533, 4542, 4654, 4708, 4769, 4879, 4952, 5045, 5126, 5182, 5286
Graves, Ebenezer, **3445**
Gray, Charles Glass, **3094**
Gray, George, 5355
Gray, Henry, 3529
Gray, Kathie, **5071**
Gray, Richard L., **4135**
Gray, Samuel Howard, **4781**
Gray, Virginia Davis, **4400**

Hanna, Joseph A., 3373
Hanna, Marcus Alonzo, 5298
Hanna, Mark. See Hanna, Marcus Alonzo
Hanna, Oliver P., 5143
Hansbrough, P.M., 5263
Haraszthy, Agoston, **3906**
Harbord, James Guthrie, **5506**
Hard, Emma Catherine. See Taylor, Emma Catherine Hard
Hardee, Alma Nephi, 5602
Hardee, Saline. See Fraser, Saline Hardee
Hardee, William Joseph, 4091, 4255, 4275
Harder, Anna Frederike Luise. See Ogden, Anna Frederike Luise Harder
Hardesty, George Washington, **5107**
Hardie, Francis H., 5190
Hardin family, 3809
Harding, George Albert, **4144**
Harding, Warren Gamaliel, 5279, 5414, 5452, 5511
Hardy, Fanny Pearson. See Eckstorm, Fanny Pearson Hardy
Hargrave, Maria. See Shrode, Maria Hargrave
Harker, Mary Haines, **3448**
Harkness, James, **4145**
Harkovich, Mike, **5770**
Harlan, Aaron Word, **3238**
Harlan, Edward T., **4146**
Harlan, John Marshall, **5090**
Harlan, Wilson Barber, **4866**
Harland, W.D., **3907**
Harle, James Wyly, **5507**
Harmon, Appleton Milo, **2933**
Harmon, Ellen Gould. See White, Ellen Gould Harmon
Harned, Thomas Biggs, 5249
Harney, William Selby, 3583, 3584, 3642, 3665
Harnwell, Gaylord Probasco, **5846**
Harper, William Rainey, 5312
Harriman, Averell William, 5716, 5765, 5845
Harrington, Leonard Elsworth, **3908**
Harrington, Linus A., 3374
Harris, Benjamin R., **4624**
Harris, David, **4147**
Harris, Emily Jane Lyles, **4147**
Harris, Isaiah Morris, **3558**
Harris, James S., **3909**
Harris, Jeremiah Collins, **3314**
Harris, John H., **4148**
Harris, Lewis B., 3059
Harris, Mark, **5874**
Harris, Paul Nelson, **5751**
Harris, Thomas W., **3324**
Harris, Townsend, **3559**, 3561, 3869
Harrison, Benjamin, 5238
Harrison, Constance Cary, **4867**
Harrison, Francis Burton, **5665**
Harrison, Juanita, **5620**

Harrison, Mary Douglass Waring, **4409**
Harrison, Samuel Alexander, **3910**
Harrison, Thomas Skelton, **5331**
Harrison, William Gregory, **5138**
Harritt, Jesse, **2797**
Hart, Gary, 6012
Hart, H. Martyn, **5001**
Hart, Mary Samuella. See Curd, Mary Sam
Hart, William Jeremiah, **4979**
Harte, Bret, 3783
Hartman, George W., **2934**
Hartmann, J.A.H., **5195**
Hartmann, Robert Trowbridge, 5967
Hartsock, Andrew Jackson, **4149**
Hartsuff, George, 3546
Hartwood, William, 3690
Harvey, Charles, 3694
Harvey, Charles H., **3374**
Harvey, Charles Nigel. See Harvey, Nigel
Harvey, Clara Conger. See Conger, Clara
Harvey, Cordelia Adelaide Perrine, 4360
Harvey, James, 5097
Harvey, Mrs. Louis Powell. See Harvey Cordelia Adelaide Perrine
Harvey, Nigel, **5833**
Harvey, Susan Mitchell Hall. See Hall, Susan Mitchell
Harvey, William B., 5442
Harvey, Winfield Scott, **4911**
Harwood, Paul, 4874
Haskell, Leonidas, 3701
Haskell, Rachel Mitchell Clark, **4892**
Haskell, Thales Hastings, **3730**
Haskins, James, **5903**
Haskins, Nannie E., **4410**
Hassett, William D., **5725**
Hassler, R. Alfred, **5771**
Hasslock, Thekla Dombois, **2999**
Hastings, Lansford W., 2836, 2870
Hastings, Loren B., **2935**
Hasty, Gladys Winifred. See Carroll, Gladys Hasty
Hatch, Charles, 3750
Hatch, Olivia Phelps Stokes, **5646**
Hatch, Solomon, 3750
Hatfield, Robert Miller, **4625**
Haven, Alice Bradley, **2936**
Haven, Emily Bradley Neal. See Haven, Alice Bradley
Havens, Catherine Elizabeth, **3103**
Haviland, Thomas P., **4150**
Hawk, Ellen Maria Miller, **4411**
Hawkes, Edward, **5072**
Hawkes, George P., **4412**
Hawkins, Rush Christopher, 3926
Hawks, Esther, 3516, **4151**
Hawks, James D., **3104**
Hawks, John Milton, 3516, 4151
Hawkshurst, Robert, 3161
Hawley, Alpheus F., **4893**
Hawley, Emily. See Gillespie, Emily Hawley

Hawley, H.J., **3786**
Hawthorne, Nathaniel, 3347, 3783, 4514
Hay, John, 3799, **3911**
Hay family, 4774
Hayashi Noboru, Daigaku-No-Kami, **3519**
Hayden, Ferdinand Vandiveer, **3449**, 3584, 4868, 4999
Hayden, Jacob S., **3375**
Hayes, Benjamin Ignatius, **3105**, 3315
Hayes, Emily Martha Chauncey, **3315**
Hayes, Isaac Israel, 3002
Hayes, Lucy Ware Webb, 5142
Hayes, Rutherford Birchard, 2996, 3831, **5045**, 5046, 5090, 5142, 5365
Hayes, Webb C., **5365**
Haykanen, Reino, 5841
Haynes, Draughton Stith, **4152**
Haynes, James, 3189
Haynesworth, Malvina Arthur. See Arthur, Malvina
Hays, Brooks, 5726
Hays, Jack, 3076
Hays, John Coffee, 3078
Hays, Marion Prather, **5726**
Hazard, Lewis Ludlam, 4413
Hazard, Sarah Congdon. See Hazard, Sarah Congdon Hazard
Hazard, Sarah Congdon Hazard, **4413**
Hazen, William Babcock, 4582
Healy, Fred, **5183**
Healy, James Augustine, **3000**
Healy, M.A., 5283
Healey, Mary Jane Roach, **5183**
Healy, Michael A., 5183
Heap, Gwinn Harris, 3425, **3450**
Heard, Gerald, 5700
Hearst, William Randolph, 5654
Heartsill, William Williston, **3912**
Heath, Joseph Thomas, **2798**
Heffernan, Leo G., **5609**
Hegeman, George W., **4414**
Heide, Dirk van der, pseud., **5699**
Heinemann, F., **4626**
Heinrich, Charles, **3239**
Heintzelman, Samuel Peter, 3184, **3679**, 4293
Helm, Edith Benham, **5548**
Helm, James M., 5548
Helman, Howard, **4153**
Hembree, A.J., 3560, 3573
Hembree, Waman C., **3560**
Hemingway, Ernest, 5685
Hempstead, Junius Lackland, **4627**
Hemschemeyer, Judith, **5961**
Henchman, Augustus F., 3247
Hendryx, George W., 4476
Henes, Donna, **6038**
Henri, Robert, 5399
Henry, Patrick, 3725
Henry, William Seaton, **2799**
Henschen, August, 4990
Herbert, Hilary Abner, 4329
Herbert, T.M., 5879

Howard, Harlan Smith, **4420**
Howard, Henry, 5603
Howard, Jesse W., 5601
Howard, Lawrence C., **5424**
Howard, McHenry, **4421**
Howard, Oliver Otis, 3838, 4541, 4588,
 4631, 5089, 5104, 5117
Howard, Richard A., 3195
Howard, Sidney Coe, 5687
Howard, Waid, **4790**
Howard, William A., 3486
Howard, Winifred Mary De Lisle. See
 Howard of Glossop, Winifred Mary De
 Lisle Howard, Baroness
Howard of Glossop, Winifred Mary De
 Lisle Howard, Baroness, **5308**
Howe, Daniel Wait, **4422**
Howe, Henry, **4169**
Howe, Henry, 1811-1868, **4633**
Howe, Henry R., **5368**
Howe, Henry Warren, **3917**
Howe, James, **4423**
Howe, James Wong, 5687
Howe, William S.G., **3318**
Howell, Charles W., **4893**
Howell, John Ewing, **2802**
Howell, Rebecca Elizabeth. See Mace,
 Rebecca Elizabeth Howell
Howell, Saul Sylvester, **4913**
Howell, Varina. See Davis, Varina Howell
Howells, William Dean, **3378**, 3555, 5194,
 5218
Howison, Jane Briggs. See Beale, Jane
 Howison
Howland, William, 3304
Hoy, Philo Romayne, **3520**
Hoyt, Elinor Morton. See Wylie, Elinor
 Morton Hoyt
Hrdlička, Aleš, **5615**
Hubbard, Lucius M., 5419
Hubbell, Finley L., **4170**
Hubbert, Mike M., **3918**
Huddleston, David, **5002**
Hudgins, Mary T. Hunley. See Edwards,
 Mary T. Hunley Hudgins
Hudson, Henry James, **3644**
Hudson, John, **3246**
Hudspeth, James M., 2836
Huggins, Edward, **4964**
Hughes, Charles Evans, 5390
Hughes, Eileen Lanouette, **5904**
Hughes, Frank, **4171**
Hughes, John Taylor, **2858**
Hughes, Joseph Henry, **5848**
Hughes, Richard B., **5073**
Hughes, Ted, 5811
Huidekoper, Emma Cullum. See
 Cortazzo, Emma Cullum Huidekoper
Huish, Orson Pratt, **5348**
Hulbert, Eri Baker, **4791**
Hulin, Lester, **2940**
Huling, Elizabeth, 5579

Hull, Cordell, 5390, 5576, 5652, 5654,
 5679, 5759
Hull, Lewis Byram, **4634**
Hults, Ellsworth H., **4635**
Humphrey, Doris, 5612
Humphrey, Hubert Horatio, 5726, 5867,
 5942
Hundley, Daniel Robinson, **3919**
Hungerford, Benjamin Franklin, **4172**
Hunley, Mary T. See Edwards, Mary T.
 Hunley Hudgins
Hunnius, Carl Julius Adolph, **5074**
Hunt, Alexander Cameron, 3731
Hunt, E.N., 3997
Hunt, Ellen Elizabeth Kellogg, **3731**
Hunt, Emmett, **5139**
Hunt, Frances Caldern De La Barca,
 4792
Hunt, Henry Jackson, 4006
Hunt, Ida Frances. See Udall, Ida
 Frances Hunt
Hunt, Jefferson, 2869, 3145, 3156, 3162,
 3201
Hunt, Margaret. See McCormick,
 Margaret Hunt
Hunt, Nan, **5985**
Hunter, David, 4293
Hunter, Jesse D., 2832
Hunter, John C., 4263
Hunter, William W., **4173**
Huntington, William Henry, 4974
Hunton, John, **5014**
Hupp, Ormand, **3920**
Hurd, Peter, **5647**
Hurlbut, John Browning, **5509**
Hurlbut, Stephen Augustus, 4360
Hurley, Patrick Jay, 5788
Hurly, Kealing, **2941**
Huse, Charles Enoch, **3247**
Huse, Everett B., **4424**
Huson, Calvin, 3878
Hussein I, king of Jordan, 5716
Huston, Henry Clay, **3606**
Hutchings, James Mason, **3001**
Hutchins, Hapgood, 5382
Hutchinson, Lincoln, **5588**
Hutt, Charles Warren, **4636**
Hutt, Warren B., **4425**
Hutton, J.D., **3788**
Hutton, William Rich, **2942**
Hyatt, A.W., **4174**
Hyatt, Alpheus, **5151**
Hyde, Arthur M., 5611

I

Ibbetson, William H.H., **4175**
Ickes, Alonzo Ferdinand, **3921**
Ickes, Harold Le Claire, 5511, **5654**
Ide, Lucy A., **5108**
Imler, George R., **4637**

Ingalls, Eleazer Stillman, **3248**
Ingalls, William Bowers Bourn, **4793**
Ingersoll, E.J., **4426**
Ingersoll, Robert Green, 5359
Ingraham, Elizabeth Mary Meade, **4427**
Ingraham, James Edmundson, 5296
Inman, Arthur Crew, **5575**
Inman, Evelyn Yates, 5575
Inzer, John Washington, **4176**
Ionesco, Nae, 5842
Ireland, E.A., 5210
Irvin, Francis L., **5550**
Irving, Sir Henry, 5313
Irwin, Samuel S., **4428**
Isaacs, Harold Robert, **6039**
Isham, Giles S., **3114**
Ishatai, Comanche medicine man, 5051
Isherwood, Christopher, **5700**
Ismail I. See Ismail Pasha, Khedive of
 Egypt
Ismail Pasha, Khedive of Egypt, 4988
Ives, Joseph Christmas, 3492, **3645**
Ives, William, **2859**

J

Jackson, Claiborne F., 5174
Jackson, George Andrew, **3680**
Jackson, Henry Martin, 5942, 6012
Jackson, Henry R., 2899
Jackson, J. Thompson, 4178, **4429**
Jackson, Luther Washington, **4177**
Jackson, Mary Ellen. See Bailey, Mary
 Ellen Jackson
Jackson, Mitchell Young, **3379**
Jackson, Nannie Stillwell, **5274**
Jackson, Oscar Lawrence, **3681**
Jackson, Reggie, 6029
Jackson, Robert Houghwout, 5421, 5654
Jackson, Samuel McCartney, **4178**, 4429
Jackson, Sheldon, 5183, 5240, **5283**
Jackson, Stonewall. See Jackson,
 Thomas Jonathan
Jackson, Thomas, **5915**
Jackson, Thomas Jonathan, 3837, 3896,
 3912, 3928, 3929, 3944, 3997, 4062,
 4076, 4078, 4086, 4166, 4211, 4264,
 4285, 4361, 4395, 4769
Jackson, William Emsley, **5075**
Jackson, William Henry, **4868**, 4999
Jackson, William Hicks, 5312
Jacobs, Victoria, **3607**
Jacobs, William Plumer, **3682**
Jacobsen, James Robert, **5125**
Jaeger, Louis John Frederick, **3562**
James, Alice, 3783, 5109, **5259**
James, Charles Albert, **4981**
James, Edward, 5655
James, Frank Lowber, **5092**
James, Frederic Augustus, **4638**
James, Henry, 3783, **5109**, 5211, 5259

James, John, 3501
James, Nancy Esther, **5916**
James, Samuel, **3249**
James, Westwood Wallace, **3922**
James, William, 5109, 5259
James, Winifred Lewellin, **5447**
Jamieson, Milton, **2943**
Jamison, Matthew H., **4639**
Jamison, Samuel M., **3250**
Janzen, Doris. See Longacre, Doris
   Janzen
Jaques, John Wesley, **3923**
Jarvis, D.H., 5283
Jarvis, Francis Carr, 5349
Jarvis, Joseph Russell, **5349**
Jatho, Charles Conrad, **5510**
Javits, Jacob, 5883
Jay, Cornelia, **3924**
Jeffers, Robinson, 5630
Jeffers, Una Call, **5630**
Jefferson, Joseph, 3783
Jefferson, T.H., 2870
Jeffries, Lemuel, **3925**
Jemison, Robert Seaborn, **3521**
Jenkins, Foster Hooker, **3115**
Jenney, Walter Procter, 5048
Jernegan, Jared, 4914
Jernegan, Laura, **4914**
Jerstad, Lute, **5866**
Jervey, Susan Ravenel, **4794**
Jervey family, 4794, 4818
John, Enoch D., **4640**
Johns, Griffith, 3471
Johnson, Abby. See Woodman, Abby
   Johnson
Johnson, Andrew, 3694, 3709, 3794,
   3855, 3916, 3993, 4317, 4769, 4795,
   4871, 4912
Johnson, Andrew Jackson, **4430**
Johnson, Bushrod Rust, 4139
Johnson, Charles F., **3926**
Johnson, Charlotte Augusta Page, **3380**
Johnson, Claudia Alta Taylor, **5867**
Johnson, Edward, 4916
Johnson, Francis Marion, **4179**
Johnson, Hannibal Augustus, **4431**
Johnson, Hattie Carter, **4641**
Johnson, Henry H., **4432**
Johnson, Hiram, **5511**
Johnson, Jane, 3477
Johnson, John, **4642**
Johnson, John Lawrence, **3319**
Johnson, Jonathan Huntington, **4180**
Johnson, Lady Bird. See Johnson,
   Claudia Alta Taylor
Johnson, Lyndon Baines, 5810, 5826,
   5867, 5942
Johnson, Robert Livingston, 5826
Johnson, W.L., **4433**
Johnson, W.R., 3497
Johnson, Welcome A., **4434**
Johnson, William R., **5350**
Johnson, William S., **2944**

Johnston, Abraham Robinson, **2860**
Johnston, Adam S., **3927**
Johnston, Albert Sidney, 2945, 3507,
   3563, 3575, 3637, 3642, 3656, 3701,
   4769
Johnston, Eliza Griffin, **3563**
Johnston, James, 4894
Johnston, John Taylor, 3388, **4915**, 4974
Johnston, Joseph Eggleston, 3626, 3629,
   3646, 3866, 3929, 4072, 4077, 4125,
   4395, 4438, 4577, 4617, 4688, 4747,
   4819
Johnston, Mrs. Joseph E. See Johnston,
   Lydia McLane
Johnston, Lewis Saurin, **4435**
Johnston, Lucy. See Ambler, Lucy
   Johnston
Johnston, Lydia McLane, 3794
Johnston, Russell R., **5787**
Johnston, Thomas W., **4436**
Johnston, William Graham, **3116**
Johnston, William Preston, **2945**
Jolly, John, **3522**
Jones, Ada Millington. See Millington,
   Ada
Jones, Alfred Goldsborough, **3564**
Jones, Anna Wylly Habersham. See
   Habersham, Anna Wylly
Jones, Benjamin Franklin, **5046**
Jones, Burton Rensselaer, **5260**
Jones, Charles Colcock, 4643, 4671
Jones, Edward E., 5602
Jones, Grumble. See Jones, William
   Edmonson
Jones, Harriet, 3319
Jones, Jenkins Lloyd, **4181**
Jones, John Beauchamp, **3928**
Jones, Levi, 2829
Jones, Lucy, 2829
Jones, Mary. See Mallard, Mary Jones
Jones, Mary Sharpe. See Jones, Mary
   Sharpe Jones
Jones, Mary Sharpe Jones, **4643,** 4671
Jones, Nathaniel Vary, **2861**
Jones, Robert Elam, **4644**
Jones, Samuel Calvin, **4182**
Jones, Stephen Vandiver, **4982**
Jones, Theodore K., **5551**
Jones, Thomas Jefferson, **5152**
Jones, William Edmonson, 4329
Jonsson, Peter Johan, **4869**
Joplin, John, **2796**
Jordan, Stephen A., **4183**
Joseph, Nez Percé chief, 5303, 5079
Josephs, Ray, **5752**
Joslyn, Matilda. See Gage, Matilda Joslyn
Josselyn, Amos Platt, **3117**
Josselyn, Francis, **4184**
Joyce, Jacob O., 3468
Joyce, James, 5696
Juárez, Benito Pablo, 4981
Judah, Henry Moses, **2946**
Judd, A.N., **4645**

Judd, Charles H., 5153
Judd, Gerrit Parmele, 3118, 3446, 3555
Judge, William H., 5357
Judson, Harry Pratt, 5239
Judy, William Lewis, **5512**
Julian, George W., **4795**
Julian, John, 3360
Jumper, Captain, 4570
Jung, Carl, 5842
Junkin, Margaret. See Preston, Margaret
   Junkin

K

Kadashan, Tlingit chief, 5325
Kahn, Arthur David, **5818**
Kahn, Edgar A., **5638**
Kahn, Ely Jacques, **6000**
Kaji, Clara A. Whitney. See Whitney,
   Clara A.
Kalakaua, David, king of Hawaiian
   Islands, **5153**, 5217
Kalinen, Mikhail Ivanovich, 5671
Kambouris, Haralambos K., **5430**
Kamehameha III, king of the Hawaiian
   Islands, 3057
Kamehameha IV, king of the Hawaiian
   Islands, 3118, 3446, 3865, 4350
Kamehameha V, king of the Hawaiian
   Islands, 3118, 3555
Kamehameha, Lot. See Kamehameha V,
   king of the Hawaiian Islands
Kamenev, Lev Borisovich, 5585
Kamiakan, Yakima chief, 3511
Kamm, Charles, 3100
Kamm, Jacob, 3100
Kane, Elisha Kent, **3002**
Kane, Paul, **2862**
Kane, Thomas L., 3575
Kassler, George W., **4185**
Kautz, August Valentine, **3452**
Kean, Robert Garlick Hill, **3929**
Kearny, Philip, 4006
Kearny, Stephen Watts, 2785, 2791,
   2795, 2824, 2825, 2832, 2844, 2845,
   2852, 2853, 2860, 2861, 2900, 2905,
   3105
Keats, John, 5375
Keays, Elizabeth Parke, **4870**
Keays, Wilbur Parke, 4870
Keegan, Peter, **4186**
Keeler, Mary Ferguson, **5093**
Keeney, Jonathan, 3576
Keep, Oliver D., 4553
Kefauver, Carey Estes, See Kefauver,
   Estes Kefauver, Estes, 5810
Keiffer, Joseph Warren, 3831
Keiley, Anthony M., **4646**
Keister, C.S., **5905**
Keith, Blanche Yurka. See Yurka,
   Blanche

Laird, John Chamberlain, **3253**
Lamb, William, **4651**
Lamont, Corliss, **5648**
Lamont, Margaret, **5648**
Lamson, Joseph, **3383**
Lamson, Julina. See Smith, Julina Lambson
Landis, Charles Kline, 4331, **4916**
Landon, Alfred Mossman, 5654
Landreth, Earl, **5656**
Lane, David, **4191**
Lane, Emma Durant, **4965**
Lane, Franklin Knight, 5429, 5438
Lane, Harriet, 4441
Lane, Henry S., **2865**
Lane, Horace Greeley, **5322**
Lane, James H., 2997, 3619
Lane, James Henry, 3890, 3911
Lane, Larmon B., 4965
Lane, Rose Wilder, 5542, **5616**
Lane, William Carr, **3384**, 3412
Lang, Thomas Stackpole, 5161
Langford, Nathaniel Pitt, 4960, **4966**, 4999
Langhorne, Nancy Witcher. See Astor, Nancy Witcher Langhorne, Viscountess
Langsdale, George, 5313
Langworthy, Franklin, **3254**
Langworthy, Laura A. See Barnes, Laura A. Langworthy
Langworthy, Maria Welles. See Whitford, Maria Welles Langworthy
Lanier, Sidney, 3513, 4546
Lanman, Charles, **2866**
Lansing, Catherine Gansevoort. See Gansevoort, Catherine
Lansing, Robert, 5429, 5438, **5474**
Lanzit, Jacob Saul, **3684**
Lapham, Fannie Crosley, **5323**
Lapham, Nelson Turoe, 5323
Lapinski, Susan, **6040**
Lapp, Moses, 5703
Larcom, Lucy, **2867**
Large, Isaac Newton, 4939
Large, Samuel Pollock, **4939**
Larkin, Thomas, 2808
Larned, Charles H., 3486
Larned, William L., **4652**
Larrea, Jean-Jacques, **5934**
La Rue, Eugene Clyde, 5589
Lasselle, Stanislaus, **3124**
Lassen, Peter, 3043
Latham, Henry, **4871**
Latham, Henry C., **3935**
Latham, Milton Slocum, **3789**
Lathrop, David, **4192**
Lattie, Alexander, **2868**
Laub, George, **2805**
Lauman, Jacob Gartner, 4367
Laumiester, Francis, 3078
Lavanberg, Fred L., 5619
Law, J.G., **3936**
Lawrence, Abbott, 3329

Lawrence, Annie Bigelow. See Rotch, Mrs. Benjamin S.
Lawrence, David, **5701**
Lawrence, Gertrude, 5708
Lawrence, John, **4897**
Lawrence, Marian. See Peabody, Marian Lawrence
Lawrence, Mary Chipman, **3608**
Lawrence, Samuel, 3608
Lawrence, Sarah Tappan Doolittle. See Robinson, Sara Tappan Doolittle Lawrence
Lawrence, William, 5245
Lawrie, Arthur S., **3523**
Lawton, Alexander Robert, 4653
Lawton, Henry Ware, 5223
Lawton, Sarah Alexander, **4653**
Lawyer, Nez Percé chief, 3566
Lay, Henry C., **4654**
Layton, Christopher, 5193
Layton, Robert, 3033
Lazelle, Henry M., **3647**
Leach, George E., **5515**
Leaphart, C.W., **5394**
Leary, Timothy, 5823
Leasy, Henry, 3769
LeConte, Emma, **4655**
LeConte, Joseph, **4655**, **4656**
Lecouvreur, Frank, **3320**
Le Duc, William Gates, **4193**
Lee, Agnes, **3385**
Lee, Alice G. See Haven, Alice Bradley
Lee, Andrea, **6019**
Lee, Benjamin, **5554**
Lee, Charles, **4657**
Lee, Fitzhugh, 3962, 4111
Lee, Floride Clemson, **4441**
Lee, Francis Henry, **5110**
Lee, John Doyle, **2869**, 3432, 3701, 5423
Lee, Laurel, **5979**
Lee, Mary Ann Randolph Custis, 3944
Lee, Mary Charlton Greenhow, **4194**, 4468
Lee, Raymond Eliot, **5702**
Lee, Robert, **6027**
Lee, Robert Edward, 3385, 3524, **3609**, 3843, 3929, 3938, 3944, 3962, 3996, 4076, 4086, 4211, 4271, 4329, 4395, 4586, 4594, 4690, 4737, 4800
Lee, Mrs. Robert Edward. See Lee, Mary Ann Randolph Custis
Lee, Stephen Dill, 4338
Lee, William B., 3544
Lee, William Henry Fitzhugh, 3831
Lee, William Wallace, **4898**
Lee family, 3385, 4086
Leeder, Hepsey, 5132
Leeds, George, **3610**
Legrand, Julia Ellen. See Waitz, Julia Ellen Legrand
Lehrman, Louis E., 5945
Leigh, Coral E., 5241
Leigh, Frances Butler, 4018

Leigh, Vivien, 5708
Leighton, Caroline C., **4798**
Leighton, Rufus, 4798
Lenin, Nikolai, 5585
Lennon, Martin, **4442**
Lenoir, Walter N., 5275
Lenoir, Walter W., **3937**
Lenior family, 4782
Leon, Louis, **3938**
Leontief, Wassily, 5845
Leroux, Antoine, 3492
Leschi, Nisqually chief, 3452
Leslie, Frank, 3869
Leslie, Hyde, **5228**
Lester, Gurdon P., **4872**
Letteer, Alfred W., **4658**
Le Vert, Octavia Walton, **3457**
Levine, Jack, 5857
Levine, Stephen, **5919**
Levy, Eugene Henry, **4659**
Lewellin, Winifred. See James, Winifred Lewellin
Lewis, Abigail, pseud. **5804**
Lewis, Arthur, 5135
Lewis, Carroll A., Jr., **5772**
Lewis, Mrs. Charles C., 5277
Lewis, David G., 2950
Lewis, Dolly Sumner Lunt. See Burge, Dolly Sumner Lunt Lewis
Lewis, Edward J., **3790**
Lewis, Henry, **3007**
Lewis, James Henry, **5516**
Lewis, Jane Voorhees, **2950**
Lewis, John Llewellyn, 5654
Lewis, John Redman Coxe, **3458**
Lewis, Lawrence. See Lewis, John Redman Coxe
Lewis, Luna E. Warner. See Warner, Luna E.
Lewis, M.G., 2800
Lewis, Philip B., 3506
Lewis, Whitsel, **4660**
Lewisohn, Ludwig, 5382
L'Heureux, John, **5868**
Libbey, David Stone, **3386**
Lienhard, Heinrich, **2870**
Lies, Eugene, 3247
Lifshin, Lyn, **6002**
Lightner, Mary Elizabeth Rollins, **4443**
Liholiho, Prince Alexander. See Kamahameha IV, king of the Hawaiian Islands
Lilienthal, David Eli, **5517**
Liliuokalani, Lydia Kamekeha, Queen of the Hawaiian Islands, 5235
Lillard, Paula Polk, **5986**
Lillie, Walter Hamilton, **5475**
Lilly, Eli, 4071
Limeburner, Captain, 3295
Lincoln, Abraham, 2997, 3016, 3025, 3592, 3614, 3621, 3641, 3651, 3677, 3681, 3687, 3698, 3702, 3709, 3758, 3761, 3763, 3777, 3780, 3782, 3794,

McClernand, Edward John, **5077**
McClernand, John Alexander, 4367, 4523
McClintock, William A., **2875**
McClung, A.K., 2888
McClung, Zarah, **3391**
McClure, Andrew Samuel, **3463**
McClure, Elizabeth Ann Cooley, **2876**
McClure, James W., 2876
McClure, John, 2868
McClure, Thomas D., **3941**
McComas, Evans Smith, **4200**
McConnell, James Rogers, 5464
McConnell, Mac. See McConnell, James Rogers
McConnell, Robert, **5157**
McConnell, William, **3942**, 4817
McCook, Alexander McDowell, 3831
McCord, Henry J., **3130**
McCormick, Henry, **4802**
McCormick, Margaret Hunt, **4803**
McCormick, Richard Cunningham, 4803
McCormick, Robert, 3417
McCormick, Vincent A., **5728**
McCowen, Helen. See Carpenter, Helen McCowen
McCoy, Alexander, 3131
McCoy, James, 3381
McCoy, James, of New York, **4201**
McCoy, Samuel Finley, **3131**
McCreary, James Bennett, **4202**
McCulloch, Ben, 2952, 3841
McCulloch, Hugh, 4317
McCullough, Ben. See McCulloch, Ben
McDaniel, Judith, **5881**
McDiarmid, Joel Calvin, **4804**
MacDonald, Alexander Holmes, **3686**
McDonald, Andrew Young, **3943**
McDonald, Angus W., 4203
McDonald, Cornelia Peake, **4203**
MacDonald, David, **3687**
MacDonald, James, 3117
MacDonald, James Ramsay, 5298
McDougal, Charles, 3264
McDougal, Jane, **3132**
McDougal, John, 3078
MacDougall, Albert Edward, **5519**
McDougall, Jane. See McDougal, Jane
McDougall, Mrs. John. See McDougal, Jane
McDougall, Thomas, 5064
McDowell, Amanda. See Burns, Amanda McDowell
McDowell, Curtis, 3845
McDowell, Irvin, 3701, 3985, 4201
McDowell, Jackson, 3845
McDowell, Lafayette, 3845
McDowell, Mary, 3845
Mace, Rebecca Elizabeth Howell, **5314**
Mace, Russell Perry, **3793**
McElroy, John Lee, **5555**
McFadden, Thompson, **5032**
McGavock, Randal William, **3009**

McGavock, Seraphine Deery, 3009
McGavran, Mary Theodora, **5294**
McGehee, Valentine Merriwether, **4204**
McGill, Alexander T., 3392
McGill, George McCulloch, **3392**
McGill, Vernon, **5591**
McGillycuddy, Valentine T., **5078**
McGovern, George, 5845, 5942
McGregor, Martha Wilson. See Aber, Martha Wilson McGregor
McGrew, John S., 5135
McGuire, John P., 3944
McGuire, Judith White Brockenbrough, **3944**, 4228
McHenry, James, 3651
McIntire, Ross T., 5654
McIntyre, Benjamin Franklin, **4205**
Maciora, Joseph C.V., **6041**
McJury, John G., 5332
McKaig, Priscilla Ellen Beall, **3322**
McKaig, William Wallace, **3322**
McKay, David, 5249
McKay, William Cameron, **4873**
McKee, Rachel Jane Henry, 5088
M'Kee, Redick, 3091
McKeeby, Lemuel Clarke, **3258**
McKell, William James, **4667**
Mackenzie, Sir Alexander, 5851
Mackenzie, Grace, Lady, 5440
MacKenzie, Ranald S., 5051
Mackey, James F., **4668**
McKim, Nellie, 5707
McKim, Randolph Harrison, 4194, **4206**
McKinley, William, 3008, **3945**, 5218, 5298, 5313, 5337, 5355, 5370
McKinstry, Byron Nathan, **3259**
McKinstry, Charles Hedges, 5515
McKinstry, George, **2877**
Mackley, John, **3946**
McLane, Allen, 3046, **3133**
McLane, Lydia. See Johnston, Lydia McLane
MacLane, Mary, **5375**
McLean, Eugene, 3794
McLean, Margaret Sumner, **3794**
McLeod, Merikay, **5936**
McLoughlin, John, 2811
McMichael, James Robert, **4669**
MacMillan, Donald Baxter, 5792
McMillan, Esther Belle. See Hanna, Esther Belle McMillan
McMillen, Cecelia Emily. See Adams, Cecelia Emily McMillen
McMynn, Mrs. John Gibson, **4207**
McNair, Clement Vann, 3210
McNamara, Joseph Michael, **5729**
McNamara, Robert Strange, 5867
McNaught, John S., **5111**
McNear, James, 4547
McNeely, Sylvia, **5631**
McPherson, Aimee Semple, 5409
McPherson, James Birdseye, 4114, 4181, 4360, 4466

McQuarrie, Ralph, 6025
McQuig, John, **4940**
McVicar, Charles W., **4670**
McWilliams, William Joseph, **2951**
Macy, Anne Sullivan, 5674
Macy, William Madison, **4447**
Maddock, Sallie Hester. See Hester, Sallie
Maffitt, John Newland, **4208**
Maghee, Thomas G., **5016**
Maginnis, John J., **5773**
Magnuson, Jermaine, **5962**
Magnuson, Warren Grant, 5962
Magoffin, Samuel, 2878
Magoffin, Susan Shelby, **2878**
Magone, Joseph, 5117
Magoon, George D., **3393**
Magruder, John Bankhead, 3848, 4395, 4677
Maguire, Don, **5094**
Mahoney, Mary Manion, **5376**
Malenkov, Georgi, 5812
Malina, Judith, **5800**
Mallard, Mary Jones, 4643, **4671**
Mallory, Mary Alice Shutes, **4209**
Mallory, Samuel, **4672**
Mallory, Stephen Russell, 3866
Malone, Bartlett Yancey, **4210**
Mandelbaum, Asher, 4983
Mandelbaum, L., **4983**
Mandelbaum, Philip, 4983
Manigault, Louis, **3394**
Manion, Mary. See Mahoney, Mary Manion
Manly, Basil, **3688**
Manly, William L., 3145
Mann, Horace, 2902
Mann, Nehemiah Halleck, **4673**
Manners, John Hartley, 5567
Manning, John Laurence, 3858
Mansfield, Michael Joseph, 5942
Mansfield, Mike. See Mansfield, Michael Joseph
Mansfield, Richard, 5291
Mansur, W.H., **4674**
Manwaring, Joshua, **3734**
Marchand, John Bonnet, **3947**
Marchand, Josephine, 3388
Marcy, Henry Orlando, 4151, **4805**
Marcy, Randolph Barnes, 3047, **3134**, 3235, 3528, 3642
Marcy, William Learned, 2947, **3135**
Marek, George F., **5556**
Mariano, Nicky, 5704
Marin, Peter, **5948**
Maris, Cora, **5476**
Maris, Omer, 5476
Marjoribanks, Ishbel Maria. See Aberdeen and Temair, Ishbel Maria Marjoribanks Gordon, marchioness of
Markell, Catherine Susannah, **4211**
Markham, Stephen, 3485
Marks, Josephine Preston Peabody. See

Mitchell, Carleton, **5824**
Mitchell, Charles D., **4454**
Mitchell, Christine Funnemark. See Funnemark, Christine
Mitchell, David, 2886
Mitchell, Elisha, 3089
Mitchell, Margaret, 5687
Mitchell, Maria, **3467**, 4920
Mitchell, Rachel. See Haskell, Rachel Mitchell Clark
Mitchell, Robert Byington, 3831
Mitchell, Suzanne, **5875**
Mockett, Richard H., **4682**
Modh, Carl August, 3252
Modjeska, Helena, **5262**
Moerenhout, Jacob Antoine, **3010**
Moffat, Jay Pierrepont, **5576**
Moffat, Lilla Cabot Grew, 5576
Möllhausen, Heinrich Balduin, 3492, 3645
Molotov, Vyacheslav Mikhailovich, 5669, 5812
Moltke, Helmuth C.B. von, 4988
Monahan, Elmer Perry, **5403**
Monier, Henry D., **4220**
Monnet, Jean, 5681, 5830
Mont, Carol. See Parker, Carol Mont
Montgomery, Sir Bernard Law, 1st Viscount Montgomery of Alamein, 5722, 5750
Montgomery, John Berrien, 2791, **2808**
Moodie, Andrew, 3068
Moody, Dwight Lyman, 4715, 4978, 5060
Moore, Alice, **5431**
Moore, Charles B., **3468**
Moore, Coral E. Leigh. See Leigh, Carol E.
Moore, Ealy, **5295**
Moore, Edwin Marshall, 3141
Moore, Frank Lincoln, **5241**, 5431
Moore, James B., 5399
Moore, Jonathan L., **3571**
Moore, Josephus C., **3954**
Moore, Nancy E., **3955**
Moore, Nathaniel Fish, **2809**
Moore, Robert Augustus, **3956**
Moorehead, James W., **3957**
Moorman, Madison Berryman, **3263**
Moraff, Barbara, **5987**
Moran, Benjamin, **3651**
Moran, George Henry Roberts, **5112**
Moran, José Antonio, 4897
Mordecai, Emma, **4683**
Mordecai, William Y., **4313**
Morey, John, 3734
Morgan, Anna Belle, 4926
Morgan, Charlton H., 4408
Morgan, George P., **3958**, 3959
Morgan, Gerald Demuth, 5835
Morgan, Gerry. See Morgan, Gerald Demuth
Morgan, Henrietta Hunt, 4241
Morgan, James Dada, 4415
Morgan, James Morris, 4098

Morgan, John Hunt, 3518, 3589, 3892, 4091, 4202, 4241, 4255, 4345, 4444
Morgan, John Pierpont, 5279
Morgan, John S., **4455**
Morgan, Martha M., **3142**
Morgan, Martha Ready. See Ready, Martha
Morgan, Philip Hickey, 4098
Morgan, Sarah. See Dawson, Sarah Morgan
Morgan, Stephen A., 3958, **3959**
Morgan, Thomas, 4345
Morgan, William Ives, **3143**
Morgan family, 4241
Morganthau, Henry, Jr., 5611, 5654
Morison, Ellen Smith, 3144
Morison, James, **3144**
Morrell, Prudence, **2954**
Morrill, James, **4684**
Morris, Anna Maria De Camp, **3264**
Morris, Gouverneur, 3264
Morris, Oliver, 5642
Morris, Robert M., 3001
Morris, Walter Ripton, **5577**
Morris, William, 5630
Morrison, Anna. See Reed, Anna Morrison
Morrison, Anna Daly, **5448**
Morrison, Harry, 5448
Morrow, Dwight Whitney, 5298, 5617, 5658
Morrow, Everett Frederic, **5835**
Morrow, Henry Andrew, **4456**
Morrow, James, **3469**
Morse, Abner, **3572**
Morse, Bliss, **3689**
Morse, Edward Sylvester, **3612**
Morse, Elizabeth Wood. See Wood, Elizabeth
Morse, W.E.H., **3960**
Morton, Elias P., **4221**
Morton, Oliver Perry, 3882, 4589
Mosby, John Singleton, 3723, 3892, 4611
Moser, Henry, 4259
Moses, Sinkiuse-Columbia chief, 5117
Moses, Alice, 3940
Moses, Bernard, 5370
Moses, Eliza M., 3940
Moses, Wallace R., **5296**
Mosey, Albert Washington, **4222**
Mosier, Charles, **5332**
Mosley, Sir Oswald Ernald, 5681
Mosman, Chesley A., **4223**
Moss, A. Hugh, **4224**
Motley, Willard, **5618**
Mott, Lucretia, 3632, 5142
Mott, Richard, 3214
Mount, Mary Jane. See Tanner, Mary Jane Mount
Mountbatten, Louis Mountbatten, Earl, 5715
Mouton, Alfred, 4677
Moxley, Anson, 5096

Moxley, Lydia Dart, **5096**
Moyer, Lycurgus Rose, **4457**
Moyn, Clarissa, 4754
Mudd, Samuel, 4815
Mudge, Sarah W., **5113**
Muir, John, 3504, 4656, **4900**
Muir, Marjorie. See Worthington, Marjorie Muir
Mulford, Ami Frank, **5079**
Mullan, John, 3452, **3470**, 5044
Mulligan, James A., 3614
Mullins, John, **3797**
Mumford, William Taylor, **4458**
Munger, James F., **3265**
Munro, Anna Laura. See Gebhard, Anna Laura Munro
Munro, George C. **5285**
Munroe, Charles Kirk. See Munroe, Kirk
Munroe, Kirk, **5160**
Muragaki, Norimasa, **3735**
Murdoch, Rupert, 6003
Murphy, Frank, 5421, 5654
Murphy, Robert Cushman, **5432**
Murray, Charles E., 4144
Murray, James Edward, 5747
Murray, John, 2916
Murray, Judith Michele Freedman, **5963**
Muskie, Edmund Sixtus, 6012
Musser, Benjamin, **5377**
Musser, Burton, 5433
Musser, Elise Furer, **5433**
Mussolini, Benito, 5654
Muste, Abraham John, 5887
Mutsuhito, Emperor of Japan, 5153
Muzzall, Thomas Abram, **4874**
Myer, Nathaniel, **3471**
Myers, Darlene, **6042**
Myers, Jerome, 5399
Myers, John C., **4685**

N

Naglee, Henry Morris, 4214
Nah-co-mense, Cheyenne chief, 2785
Napear, Peggy, **5876**
Napoleon III, Emperor of the French, 3329, 4157, 4867
Napton, William Barclay, **5174**
Nash, William H., 4459
Nason, Elias, **3961**
Nathan, Robert, **5731**
Natuschen, Nickolai, 5682
Navajo, Havasupai chief, 5190
Neal, Emily Bradley. See Haven, Alice Bradley
Neal, Hannah, 3685
Neal, James, 3685
Neal, Samuel, 2842
Neale, Robert, 5705
Neese, George Michael, **3962**
Negley, James Scott, 3831
Nehru, Jawaharlal, 5716, 5845

Pierrepont, Edwards, 3869
Pierson, Marshall Samuel, **4697**
Pigman, Walter Griffith, **3270**
Pike, James Shepherd, **4473**
Pilat, Oliver Ramsay, **5883**
Pillow, Gideon Johnson, 2816, 2874, 3985, 4139
Pinchot, Gifford, 5511, 5654
Pinckney, William H.H., **4698**
Pineda, Manuel, 2932
Pitts, Florison, **4244**
Pitts, Joseph J., **4245**
Pius IX, pope, 4970, 4988
Pius XII, pope, 5728
Plagens, Peter, **6005**
Plath, Sylvia, **5811**
Platt, Jennie. See Barnitz, Jennie Platt
Player, Gary, 5910
Plumer, Samuel, 3257
Plummer, Henry, 4392, 4525
Plummer, Henry Merrihew, **5434**
Poché, Félix Pierre, **3529**
Poché, Sélima, 3529
Poe, Edgar Allan, 2922, 5696
Poe, James T., **4246**
Poincaré, Lucien, 5469, 5572
Point, Nicolas, **2960**
Polignac, Camille Armand Jules Marie, prince de, **4247**
Polikoff, Judy, **5971**
Polk, James Knox, **2813**, 2922, 2947, 3022
Polk, Mrs. James Knox. See Polk, Sarah Childress
Polk, Leonidas, 3109, 4072, 4125, 4395
Polk, Paula. See Lillard, Paula Polk
Polk, Sarah Childress, 4514, 4701
Pollard, Abigail. See Baldwin, Abigail Pollard
Pomeroy, Fernando E., **4248**
Pompidou, Georges, 5716
Poole, Charles A., **3972**
Poole, Fitch, Jr., **3153**
Poole, Theodore L., **4699**
Poor, John A., **2814**
Pope, John, 3505, 3852, 4097, 4293, 4317
Poppenheim, Mary Elinor Bouknight, **4813**
Porcher, Emma, **4814**
Porcher family, 4794
Porte, pseud. See Mathews, G.H.
Porte Crayon, pseud. See Strother, David Hunter
Porter, David Dixon, 4317
Porter, Fitz-John, 3661, 4149, 4293
Porter, George Loring, **4815**
Porter, Nimrod, **4700**
Porter, William Clendenin, **3973**
Posey, Alexander Lawrence, **5335**
Post, Charles A., **4474**
Post, Charles C., **3739**
Poston, Charles Debrille, **3271**, 3679,

3982
Potter, Edward Elmer, 4830
Potter, Helen Ward Brandreth. See Brandreth, Helen Ward
Potts, Benjamin F., 2996
Powdermaker, Hortense, **5583**
Powell, Frank, 3995
Powell, H.M.T., **3154**
Powell, John Wesley, 4933, **4944**, 4948, 4953, 4980, 4982, 4984, 4992, 4993, 5413, 5423, 5598
Powell, Lewis, 4824
Powell, Mildred Elizabeth, **4249**
Powell, Morris, 4984
Powell, Walter Clement, **4984**
Powell, William Henry, **3617**
Power, Ellen Louise, **4250**
Powers, Americus Windsor, 3618
Powers, Eliza Sears, 3746
Powers, Elmer G., **5643**
Powers, Elvira J., **4701**
Powers, Francis Gary, 5841
Powers, Mary Rockwood, **3618**
Pownall, Joseph, **3155**
Poyneer, George E., **5036**
Prabhavananda, Swami, 5700
Prather, Marion. See Hays, Marion Prather
Pratt, Addison, **3156**
Pratt, Joseph Hyde, **5560**
Pratt, Orson, 2885
Pratt, Orville C., **3015**
Pratt, Sarah, **3398**
Pratt, Teancum, **5175**
Preble, George Henry, **3476**
Prescott, Peter S., **5827**
Pressley, John G., **4251**
Preston, Caroline H., 2945
Preston, Jerome, **5521**
Preston, Margaret Junkin, **4252**
Preston, William E., **2961**, 3518, 4157
Preston family, 3858
Pretz, Alfred C., **3974**
Preus, Caroline Dorothea Margrethe Keyser, **2815**
Preus, Herman Amberg, 2815
Price, George Moses, **5176**
Price, John, 3683
Price, Lewis Richard, **3157**
Price, Morgan Philips, **4945**
Price, Robert, 5883
Price, Sterling, 2926, 3939, 4091, 4118
Price, William Edwin, 4945
Price, William Newton, **4702**
Prime family, 3924
Prince, Elizabeth Oakes. See Smith, Elizabeth Oakes
Prince, F.H., 5279
Pringle, Cyrus Guernsey, **4475**
Pringle, Elizabeth Waties Allston, **5389**. See also Allston, Elizabeth Waties
Pringle, Virgil Kellogg, **2882**
Pritchard, James Avery, **3158**

Proudfoot, Merrill, **5854**
Prouty, Anna S. See Wood, Anna S. Prouty
Prowse, William, 4547
Prude, Reuben H., **3693**
Pruyn, John van Schaick Lansing, **3694**
Pryor, Ann Whiting. See Fremont, Ann Whiting Pryor
Pryor, Frederick L., 5841
Pullman, George Mortimer, 5182
Pulsipher, John, **3575**
Pulszky, Ferencz, **3399**
Pumpelly, Raphael, 3982
Purdy, Frank, 5346
Putnam, Arthur James, **5522**
Putnam, George Palmer, **4946**
Putnam, Theodore L., **3740**
Putnam, Tracy Jackson, **5468**
Pyle, John S., 5294

Q

Quarles, William, 3578
Quezon y Molina, Manuel Luis, 5665
Quick, Richard, 5424
Quin, Ah, **5196**
Quincy, Josiah, 2834
Quincy, Samuel Miller, **4253**
Quinn, Michael A., **5732**
Quintard, Charles Todd, 4091, **4703**
Quitman, John Anthony, **2883**

R

Raasloff, Valdemar Rudolf, 3869
Rackleff, William Edward, **3159**
Rackleff, William R., 3159
Rae, George, **4816**
Raho, Blas, 3105
Rainer, Yvonne, **5937**
Rains, Sevier M., 5095
Rainsford, Walter Kerr, **5479**
Ralston, Elizabeth Fry. See Fry, Elizabeth
Ralston, William C., 3700
Ramsay, Alexander, **3160**
Ramsey, Alexander, 3323
Randall, Margaret Randall, **5929**
Randle, William G., **3400**
Randolph, George Wythe, 3929
Rank, Otto, 5449
Rankin, Alexander Taylor, **3741**
Rankin, Jeannette, 5337
Ranlett, Mrs. Charles E., **4704**
Ranous, Dora Knowlton Thompson, **5127**
Ransom, John L., **4476**
Ransom, Sophie. See Slack, Sophie Ransom
Rathbone, Thomas W., **4705**
Rathbun, Isaac R., **4254**

Sims, William Sowden, 5438
Sinclair, Harry Ford, 5279
Sinclair, John, **2894**
Singer, William, 2852
Sintzenich, Arthur H.C., **5440**
Siqueiros, David-Alfaro, 5840
Sirmon, W.A., **5531**
Sitgreaves, Lorenzo, **3279**
Sitting Bull, Hunkpapa Sioux chief, 4910
    5182
Sitwell family, 5697
Sjoborg, Sofia Charlotta, **4990**
Skaggs, Drennan C., 5335
Skelly, James, **2968**
Skousen, James M., 5193
Slack, Comfort I., **4499**
Slack, Sophie Ransom, 4499
Slate, Edith Rohrbough, **5592**
Slate, Thomas Benton, 5592
Slaughter, B.F., **4991**
Slaughter, G.W., 4930
Slaughter, Jack, 3448
Slaughter, Mary Haine Harker. See Har-
    ker, Mary Haines
Slaughter, Montgomery, 4263
Slaughter, William Alloway, 3486
Slayden, Ellen Maury, **5337**
Slayden, James Luther, 5337
Slemmons, John W., **5297**
Slettebo, Elizabeth Fedde. See Fedde,
    Elizabeth
Slidell, John, 3985, 3989
Slifer, Eli, **4274**
Sligh, Agnes. See Turnbull, Agnes Sligh
Sloan, Anna Marie Wall, 5399
Sloan, Dolly. See Sloan, Anna Marie Wall
Sloan, John, **5399**
Sloane, Florence Adele, **5301**
Sloat, John Drake, 2843
Slocum, Henry Warner, 4055
Small, Abner Ralph, **4722**
Smalls, Robert, 4304
Smedley, Agnes, **5684**
Smedley, Charles, **4500**
Smet, Pierre Jean de, 2821, 2960, 2995,
    3324, 4101, 4853, 4910
Smillie, James David, **4827**
Smith, Captain, 3084
Smith, Alden R., 5332
Smith, Alfred Emanuel, 5624
Smith, Andrew Jackson, 2869, 4523
Smith, Azariah, **2969**
Smith, Baldy, See Smith, William Farrar
Smith, Barbara, **6033**
Smith, Barbara Leigh. See Bodichon,
    Barbara Leigh Smith
Smith, Belle Hannah, **5601**
Smith, Benjamin Harrison, 3996
Smith, Benjamin T., **3995**
Smith, Charles B., **5815**
Smith, Charles W., **3280**
Smith, Cornelius, 2970
Smith, Cornelius C., **5713**

Smith, Dwight R., **6034**
Smith, E. Kirby. See Smith, Edmund
    Kirby
Smith, Ed, **5871**
Smith, Edmund Kirby, 3529, 4247, 4275,
    4395
Smith, Elias, **3747**
Smith, Eliza Marie Partridge. See Lyman,
    Eliza Marie Partridge Smith
Smith, Elizabeth Dixon, **2970**
Smith, Elizabeth Oakes, 3318
Smith, Ellen. See Morison, Ellen Smith
Smith, Ephraim Kirby, **2816**
Smith, Extra Billy. See Smith, William
Smith, Franklin Gillette, 4275
Smith, Frederick W., **5940**
Smith, George A., ship captain, 4947
Smith, George A., Utah settler, 2869
Smith, George Watson, **5116**
Smith, Gustavus W., 2874
Smith, Hannah, 3298
Smith, Harriet Amelia, **4501**
Smith, Harriet Newell Stevens, 4841
Smith, Hiram, 3298
Smith, Hyrum, 2805
Smith, Isaac Noyes, **3996**
Smith, Jacob, 4960
Smith, James West, **4502**
Smith, Jesse Nathaniel, **2895**
Smith, John, of California gold rush, 2832
Smith, John, English traveler, **5358**
Smith, John Henry, **4723**
Smith, Joseph, 2805, 2873
Smith, Joseph F., 5221
Smith, Julina Lambson, **5221**
Smith, Kirby. See Smith, Edmund Kirby
Smith, Levi Lathrop, **2971**
Smith, Lotan, 3582
Smith, Lucy P. Vincent, **4947**
Smith, Lucy Virginia. See French, Lucy
    Virginia Smith
Smith, Mary. See Berenson, Mary Smith
    Costelloe
Smith, Oliver, 2854
Smith, Orrin, 3253
Smith, Oscar B., **5081**
Smith, Philip, 5800
Smith, Robert Davis, **4275**, 4724
Smith, Sallie Diana, **4925**
Smith, Sarah Foote. See Foote, Sarah
Smith, Telamon Cruger Cuyler, **5248**
Smith, Thomas, 3059
Smith, Thomas Crutcher, **4276**
Smith, Uriah, 4841
Smith, Walter Bedell, 5722
Smith, William, 4330, 4833
Smith, William Austin, 4275, **4724**
Smith, William C.S., **3171**
Smith, William Farrar, 4234
Smith, William Wrenshall, **4503**
Smoot, Reed, **5436**
Smuts, Jan Christian, 5541
Snedaker, Morris Jackson, **3581**

Sneed, S.G., 5000
Snow, Erastus, **2972**, 3541
Snow, Francis Huntington, **5391**
Snow, J.E., **3802**
Snow, Taylor N., **3748**
Snowden, George Randolph, **4725**
Snowden, J. Hudson, **3803**
Snowden family, 4794, 4818
Snyder, Jacob R., **2817**
Snyder, John, 2880
Somerville, Mary Fairfax, 3467
Somoza Debayle, Anastasio, 6035
Soong, Ching-ling, 6039
Soong, T.V., 5715
Southwick, Thomas Paine, **4277**
Soyer, Moses, 5857
Soyer, Raphael, **5857**
Spain, David F., **3749**
Spalding, Henry Harmon, 2811, 2909
Spangler, Edward, 4815
Sparks, Jared, 2834
Spawr, Valentine, **4504**
Speakman, William Cyrus, **5469**
Spear, Laura Jernegan. See Jernegan,
    Laura
Spear, Virginia Belle Benton. See Benton,
    Virginia Belle ·
Spear, Willis, **5187**
Speed, James, 4317
Speer, Albert, 5786
Speer, William Henry Asbury, **4278**
Spencer, Cornelia Phillips, **4828**
Spencer, Lafayette, **3406**
Speranza, Gino Charles, **5470**
Sperry, Kate, **3997**
Sperry, William, 3491
Speyer, A., 2906
Spivack, Kathleen, **5920**
Spokan Garry. See Garry, Spokan chief
Spooner, John Pitcher, **3804**
Spotts, David L., **4926**
Spradley, James P., 5897
Sprague, Achsa W., **3172**
Sprague, William, 3846, 4879
Spreckels, Claus, 5217
Sprenger, George F., **4279**
Spring, Augusta Murray. See Knapp,
    Augusta Murray Spring
Springer, Austin D., **4280**
Sproston, John Glendy, **3535**
Sprunger, Caroline Tschantz, 5315
Sprunger, David, **5315**
Spurgeon, Charles Haddon, 4446, 4563,
    4888, 4946, 5278
Squire, Eugene Byrd, 5305
Squires, George Jackson, 5169
Stacey, Mary Banks, **5129**
Stacey, May Banks. See Stacey, Mary
    Banks
Stacey, May Humphreys, **3658**, 5129
Stager, Henry J., **4281**
Stalin, Joseph, 5671, 5716, 5759, 5790
Stamper, Issac J., **4282**

Walker, John G., 4394
Walker, Joseph Reddeford, 2803
Walker, Norman Stewart, 4314
Walker, Susan, **4315**
Walker, Thomas W., **6035**
Walker, William, 3308
Walker, William, **2819**
Walker, William Holmes, **3411**
Wall, Anna Marie. See Sloan, Anna Marie
  Wall
Wallace, Elizabeth McIntosh Curtis, **4520**
Wallace, George, 5944
Wallace, Henry Agard, 5611, 5654, **5667**
Wallace, Henry Cantwell, 5611
Wallace, Hugh Campbell, 5572
Wallace, Ishmael, **6045**
Wallace, Lewis, 5007
Wallace, Mary Austin; **4316**
Wallace, Nancy, **6046**
Wallace, Robert Bruce, 4316
Wallsh, Thomas F., **4521**
Walsh, John R., 5298
Walter, Mary Rowe. See Rowe, Mary
Walters, Archer, **3624**
Walters, Henry, 3388
Walters, William Thompson, 3388, 4974
Walton, Octavia. See Le Vert, Octavia
  Walton
Walton, Samuel, 3099
Ward, Mr., 4848
Ward, Artemus, 3651
Ward, Elisabeth Carolyn Vought, 3810
Ward, Harriet Sherrill, **3488**
Ward, Henry Dana, **2820**
Ward, John, **3412**
Ward, Joseph Richardson, **4522**
Ward, Lester Frank, **3810**
Ward, Orlando, **5695**
Ward, Sam. See Ward, Samuel
Ward, Samuel, **3761**
Ward, Smith G., 4397
Waring, Malvina Sarah Black, **4838**
Waring, Mary Douglass. See Harrison,
  Mary Douglass Waring
Warkentin, Bernard, 4998
Warmoth, Henry Clay, **4523**
Warner, Aaron, 2854
Warner, Agnes Stewart. See Stewart,
  Agnes
Warner, Horatio Gates, **3413**
Warner, J.J., 3105
Warner, Luna E., **4994**
Warner, William H., **2901**
Warre, Henry James, **2821**
Warren, Gouverneur Kemble, 3449, **3584**,
  4006, 4277, 4456
Warren, O.P., 3484
Wash, W.A., **4524**
Washburn, Henry Dana, 4960, 4966
Washington, Crawford, 3116
Washington, Ella More Bassett, **4743**
Washington, John Macrae, 3170
Washington, Lewis, 4743

Wassahu, Shoshoni chief. See Wassakee,
  Shoshoni chief
Wassakee, Shoshone chief, 3595
Waterman, Cameron D., 5292
Waterman, John O., 3100
Waterman, W.A., 3100
Watkins, Harry, **2822**
Watkins, Thomas C., **3907**
Watson, John, **5010**
Watson, Robert, **4008**
Watson, Walter A., **5250**
Watson, William J., **3183**, **3193**
Way, Phocion R., **3704**
Wayland, John W., **5593**
Wayland, Mrs. John Wesley, **4009**
Wayles, Martha. See Robertson, Martha
  Wayles
Wayman, John Hudson, **3414**
Weand, Henry K., **4839**
Webb, Beatrice Potter, **5360**
Webb, Creighton, 5301
Webb, Henry Livingston, 3033, 3034
Webb, Louis H., **4840**
Webb, Lucy Ware. See Hayes, Lucy
  Ware Webb
Webb, Sidney, 5360
Webber, Anna, **5168**
Webber, Emma, **4841**
Webber, Nathaniel, 3359, 3365
Webber, Thomas B., **4010**
Weber, Charles M., 2842
Weber, Julia, **5677**
Weber, Nancy, **5965**
Webster, Charles L., 3555
Webster, Daniel, 2854, 3016, 3228, 3341,
  3347
Webster, George B., **2998**
Webster, John Brown, **3705**
Webster, Kimball, **3194**
Webster, N.H., **4525**
Weckesser, Louisa Ella. See Rhine,
  Louisa Ella Weckesser
Weed, Stephen H., 3656
Weed, Thurlow, 3017, 3901, 4317
Weeks, Edward Augustus, **5537**
Weidenfeld, Sheila Rabb, **5975**
Weikert, Andrew J., **5100**
Weimer, John, **4744**
Wein, Bibi, **6024**
Weingarten, Violet, **5982**
Weinland, W.H., 5195
Weir, Robert, **3585**
Weitzel, Godfrey, 4482
Weld, Francis Minot, **3586**
Weld, Stephen Minot, **3661**
Welles, C.M., 3489
Welles, Gideon, 3894, 3993, **4317**
Welles, Sumner, 5576, 5679
Wellington, Adelaide Louise. See Hough-
  ton, Adelaide Louise Wellington
Wells, Daniel H., 5039
Wells, Edmond Hazard, **5338**
Wells, Emmeline B. Woodward, **5039**

Wells, Seth James, **4318**
Wendell, George Blunt, **3490**
Wendell, Mary Elizabeth Thompson.
  See Thompson, Mary Elizabeth
Wentworth, Hebron M., **4319**
Wentworth, John, 4605
Wescoat, Arthur Brailsford, **4526**
Wescoat, Jabez R., 4526
Wescoat, Joseph Julius, **4527**
Wesley, John, **3625**
West, Beckwith, **4320**
West, Calvin Brookings, **3491**
West, Duval, 5123
West, George Warren, 4142
West, John Camden, **4528**
West, Robert M., 4911
Westfall, Edward Dixon, **5222**
Westfall, J.D., 3912
Westinghouse, George, 5279
Weston, Daniel H., **4883**
Weston, Edward, **5597**
Wheaton, Charles Augustus, 2902
Wheaton, Ellen Douglas Birdseye, **2902**
Wheeler, Burton Kendall, 5617
Wheeler, George Montague, 5022
Wheeler, Joseph, 3892
Wheelock, Julia Susan. See Freeman,
  Julia Susan Wheelock
Whetten, Harriet Douglas, **4321**
Whipple, Alphonzo, **4322**
Whipple, Amiel Weeks, 2991, 3482, **3492**
Whipple, Charles W., **5266**
Whipple, Edwin P., 2927
Whistler, James Abbott McNeill, 3388,
  5354
Whitaker, Samuel T., 5393
White, Andrew Dickson, **3542**
White, Bob, 5738
White, Cornelius, 3085
White, Ellen Gould Harmon, 4841
White, George, 3470
White, Harriet Scovel, 4003
White, Henry, **4529**
White, Howard, 4943
White, J.M., 3037
White, James Springer, 4841
White, Katherine, **4323**
White, Lucy Hannah. See Flake, Lucy
  Hannah White
White, Sarah C., 4926
White, Thomas Benton, **4011**
White, Viola Chittenden, **5569**
White, William N., **2979**
White family, 4794, 4818
Whitefield, Edwin, **2903**
Whitehead, Lewis Young, **3493**
Whitehouse, Worthington, 5301
Whitehurst, George William. **5953**
Whiteley, Opal Stanley, **5400**
Whitford, Maria Welles Langworthy, **3662**
Whitford, Samuel, 3662
Whiting, Fred S., **4842**
Whiting, William Henry Chase, **3195**

C

military operations, Confederate, 4132, 4395
Alabama, 3244, 3897, 3977, 4072, 4077, 4125, 4176, 4183, 4235, 4275, 4438, 4590, 4609, 4674, 4724
Arkansas, 3529, 3885, 3903, 3904, 3912, 3965, 3973, 3992, 4002, 4113, 4118
Florida, 3822, 3825, 4527
Georgia, 3244, 3812, 3825, 3905, 4077, 4106, 4183, 4235, 4577, 4590, 4674, 4724, 4839
Indian Territory, 3903
Kentucky, 3244, 3589, 3872, 3874, 3904, 3922, 4002, 4021, 4106, 4116, 4127, 4202, 4282
Louisiana, 3529, 3903, 3912, 4174, 4235, 4463, 4498
Maryland, 4285
Mississippi, 3529, 3822, 3836, 3850, 3872, 3884, 3885, 3936, 3939, 3973, 4002, 4021, 4072, 4077, 4095, 4116, 4118, 4170, 4176, 4183, 4230, 4235, 4247, 4275, 4301, 4438, 4498, 4590
Missouri, 3885, 3939, 3973
North Carolina, 3244, 3586, 3825, 3866, 3905, 3909, 3938, 3993, 4008, 4069, 4076, 4125, 4183, 4251, 4272, 4356, 4453, 4506, 4527, 4724, 4819, 4840
Oklahoma, 3903
South Carolina, 3825, 3905, 4021, 4028, 4251, 4305, 4395, 4446, 4506, 4527, 4724
Tennessee, 3244, 3812, 3872, 3874, 3904, 3912, 3954, 4002, 4021, 4022, 4095, 4106, 4116, 4118, 4162, 4183, 4202, 4275, 4282, 4694, 4724
Texas, 3766, 3903, 3912, 3965, 3992, 4113, 4276
Virginia, 3825, 3866, 3871, 3874, 3902, 3938, 3953, 3958, 3959, 3993, 4008, 4021, 4022, 4035, 4042, 4069, 4076, 4125, 4148, 4159, 4210, 4217, 4251, 4272, 4356, 4361, 4368, 4401, 4421, 4453, 4464, 4492, 4519, 4527, 4528, 4629, 4670, 4686, 4694, 4763
Shenandoah Valley, 3854, 3896, 3902, 4022, 4313, 4329, 4330, 4377, 4468, 4592
West Virginia, 3851, 3996, 4016, 4159. See also Civil War, military operations, Confederate, Virginia
See also Civil War, campaigns and battles
Military operations, Union
Alabama, 3681, 3702, 3831, 3875, 3927, 3931, 3942, 3995, 4027, 4073, 4084, 4085, 4087, 4161, 4175, 4181, 4190, 4212, 4213, 4218, 4248, 4283, 4300, 4335, 4382, 4436, 4448, 4455, 4496, 4517, 4569, 4679, 4702, 4717, 4723, 4746
Arizona, 4143, 4298, 4389
Arkansas, 3832, 3900, 3933, 3981, 4031, 4102, 4115, 4167, 4189, 4205,

4218, 4223, 4237, 4244, 4289, 4324, 4400, 4418, 4447, 4455, 4536, 4620, 4647
California, 4298
Dakota Territory, 3857, 4014, 4236, 4381, 4385, 4390, 4397, 4405, 4471
Florida, 3108, 4079, 4151, 4221, 4226
Georgia, 3500, 3778, 3875, 3888, 3995, 4085, 4175, 4186, 4190, 4199, 4212, 4300, 4372, 4436, 4503, 4517, 4583, 4678, 4679, 4693, 4717, 4746
Indiana, 3702
Iowa, 4014
Kansas, 4189
Kentucky, 3500, 3689, 3702, 3809, 3831, 3832, 3879, 3891, 3893, 3907, 3927, 3931, 3942, 3946, 3977, 4011, 4013, 4027, 4052, 4059, 4060, 4067, 4071, 4082, 4083, 4084, 4085, 4087, 4122, 4169, 4175, 4186, 4190, 4191, 4212, 4213, 4222, 4248, 4283, 4286, 4300, 4328, 4349, 4504, 4554, 4580
Louisiana, 3830, 3839, 3875, 3917, 3964, 4112, 4165, 4182, 4205, 4218, 4225, 4227, 4232, 4239, 4244, 4262, 4270, 4283, 4293, 4303, 4310, 4418, 4447, 4459, 4482, 4494, 4554, 4761
Maryland, 3923, 4015, 4050, 4059, 4142, 4197, 4257, 4296, 4310, 4358, 4600
Minnesota, 4109, 4236
Mississippi, 3500, 3681, 3702, 3832, 3839, 3849, 3867, 3875, 3879, 3890, 3931, 3975, 3977, 3981, 4013, 4027, 4044, 4059, 4073, 4112, 4129, 4167, 4175, 4179, 4181, 4191, 4205, 4218, 4223, 4227, 4232, 4237, 4244, 4283, 4286, 4322, 4324, 4328, 4418, 4447, 4455, 4462, 4711
Missouri, 3599, 3701, 3818, 3832, 3849, 3875, 3890, 3900, 3907, 3933, 3941, 3943, 3946, 3977, 3981, 4031, 4068, 4115, 4167, 4182, 4189, 4205, 4218, 4223, 4289, 4447, 4647
New Mexico, 4185, 4298, 4389
North Carolina, 3826, 3873, 3926, 3934, 3990, 4026, 4081, 4084, 4085, 4131, 4168, 4300, 4333, 4430, 4484, 4505, 4555, 4651, 4657, 4668, 4702, 4721, 4839
Ohio, 4082
Oregon, 4047
Pennsylvania, 4130, 4149, 4257, 4274, 4310
South Carolina, 3879, 4032, 4079, 4081, 4085, 4131, 4214, 4221, 4226, 4380, 4508, 4522, 4830, 4839
Tennessee, 3500, 3681, 3689, 3702, 3778, 3809, 3824, 3831, 3839, 3849, 3867, 3875, 3879, 3888, 3890, 3891, 3893, 3927, 3931, 3942, 3946, 3975, 3977, 3986, 3995, 4027, 4044, 4052, 4059, 4067, 4071, 4073, 4082, 4083, 4085, 4087, 4122, 4129, 4161, 4175,

4179, 4181, 4186, 4190, 4192, 4195, 4199, 4212, 4213, 4222, 4223, 4227, 4244, 4248, 4283, 4286, 4300, 4322, 4328, 4335, 4364, 4366, 4372, 4379, 4391, 4402, 4415, 4422, 4426, 4430, 4448, 4451, 4454, 4496, 4516, 4517, 4569, 4580, 4589, 4598, 4678, 4702, 4711, 4717, 4721, 4745
Texas, 3942, 4182, 4205, 4218, 4244, 4335, 4447, 4455, 4761
Virginia, 3377, 3778, 3849, 3873, 3879, 3892, 3898, 3925, 3926, 3945, 3970, 3980, 3987, 4015, 4026, 4058, 4059, 4062, 4078, 4079, 4080, 4081, 4085, 4092, 4093, 4131, 4142, 4149, 4153, 4164, 4178, 4191, 4193, 4201, 4214, 4221, 4226, 4229, 4234, 4240, 4243, 4260, 4277, 4279, 4281, 4283, 4291, 4295, 4296, 4319, 4327, 4348, 4349, 4358, 4388, 4429, 4436, 4460, 4488, 4491, 4505, 4507, 4522, 4542, 4565, 4587, 4637, 4673, 4682, 4684, 4698, 4702, 4727, 4730, 4784, 4791, 4811, 4825, 4839
Shenandoah Valley, 3854, 3923, 3960, 4015, 4062, 4182, 4197, 4220, 4222, 4300, 4566, 4593, 4648, 4742
Washington, D.C., vicinity, 3899, 4005, 4142, 4164, 4191, 4327, 4565, 4696, 4702, 4707
West Virginia, 3817, 3831, 3883, 3960, 4011, 4197, 4222, 4705. See also Civil War, military operations, Union, Virginia
See also Civil War, campaigns and battles; Indian Wars of the West; Military operations in the West
Naval operations, Confederate, 4662
neutrality issues, 3993, 4126, 4208
by place
Atlantic, 3866, 3993, 4126, 4574
Caribbean, 3993, 4208
China Sea, 3993, 4126
Florida, 4053
Georgia, 4453
Gulf of Mexico, 3993, 4208
Indian Ocean, 3993, 4126
James River, 3866, 3993
Mississippi River, 4095
Mobile Bay, 4691
Red River, 4095
Savannah River, 4173
Trinity River, 4173
Virginia waters, 3950, 4217
Naval operations, Union, 4317
blockade, 4317, 4395
Atlantic, 3586, 3827, 3947, 3991, 4061, 4187, 4216, 4380, 4474, 4651
Gulf of Mexico, 4046, 4440, 4564, 4635
See also Civil War, blockade runners
neutrality issues, 3947, 4635
by place

Third, 4073, 4420
Sixth, 4181
Wisconsin infantry
  Fifth, 3852
  Sixth, 4097, 4406
  Tenth, 4207
  Eleventh, 3981
  Twelfth, 4679
  Thirteenth, 4198
  Fourteenth, 4286
  Twentieth, 4218
  Twenty-second, 4073, 4562
  Thirty-sixth, 4549
  Fortieth, 3986
  Forty-third, 4682
riots
  Boston, 4369
  New York City, 3805, 3869, 3925, 4039, 4395, 4493
  St. Louis, 3886
  Richmond, 4269
Sanitary Commission. See Civil War, United States Sanitary Commission
secessionists. See Secessionists
smuggling, 3529, 3681, 4608
soldiers, Confederate
  about, 3589, 3760, 3873, 3948, 3950, 4078, 4181, 4241, 4247, 4253, 4285, 4309, 4352, 4362, 4365, 4367, 4375, 4395, 4433, 4436, 4514, 4543, 4565, 4700
  books and reading, 3829, 3866, 3936, 4021, 4076, 4077, 4106, 4107, 4206, 4235, 4242, 4275, 4438, 4468, 4492, 4506, 4528, 4543, 4561, 4636, 4677, 4724
  drinking, 3905, 3956, 4008, 4021, 4095, 4235, 4271, 4308
  foreign-born, 3916, 4045, 4407
  gambling, 4271, 4276
  Jewish, 3938, 3940
  religious activities, 3896, 4072, 4076, 4091, 4110, 4116, 4210, 4251, 4464, 4468, 4519
  religious reflections, 3529, 3552, 3937, 4077, 4107, 4176, 4230, 4394, 4438, 4511, 4669
  sexual behavior, 3905, 4438
soldiers, Union
  about, 3503, 3724, 3950, 4278, 4309, 4343, 4364, 4391, 4400, 4409, 4438, 4502, 4517, 4543, 4546, 4582, 4588, 4707, 4734, 4833
  books and reading, 3500, 3809, 3830, 3888, 3917, 3926, 3934, 3953, 3984, 4178, 4181, 4244, 4296, 4324, 4342, 4364, 4379, 4418, 4422, 4433, 4504, 4543, 4554, 4619, 4639, 4647, 4690, 4722, 4741
  drinking, 3681, 3720, 3809, 3819, 3831, 3839, 3864, 3867, 3888, 3907, 3917, 3921, 3931, 3934, 3988, 4006, 4015, 4047, 4071, 4082, 4097, 4141, 4143, 4149, 4181, 4186, 4205, 4234, 4244,

4261, 4286, 4296, 4300, 4324, 4358, 4415, 4472, 4508, 4518, 4569, 4628, 4695, 4711, 4715, 4721, 4846
  foreign-born, 3701, 3824, 3849, 3926, 4073, 4186, 4298, 4342, 4383, 4474, 4566, 4587, 4600, 4649, 4714, 4741, 4783
  gambling, 3809, 3875, 3921, 4006
  Jewish, 3823
  religious activities, 3853, 3934, 3945, 3956, 3983, 4047, 4081, 4119, 4178, 4186, 4237, 4286, 4300, 4504, 4561, 4625, 4702, 4707
  religious reflections, 3702, 3824, 3934, 3945, 3984, 4081, 4119, 4177, 4505, 4657, 4668, 4678, 4702, 4722, 4741, 4772
  songs, 4200
  speculators, 3529, 3928, 4128, 4251, 4360
  spies
    Confederate, 3997, 4043, 4137, 4708
      execution of, 3980, 4106
    Union, 3552, 4311
      execution of, 4029
  sports, 3926, 4846
  suicides, 3923, 4081, 4141, 4174, 4216
  surrender at Appomattox, 3902, 4012, 4076, 4142, 4220, 4586, 4629, 4768, 4800
  surrender terms, 3681, 3882, 4234, 4142, 4317, 4688, 4746, 4769, 4807, 4819
  sutlers, 3907, 4069, 4088
  topography, 3816, 4293
  travel through the lines, 3950, 4231, 4271, 4481, 4654, 4734
  troop transport, Confederate, 3905, 3916, 3992, 4008, 4095, 4148, 4275
  troop transport, Union, 3839, 3875, 3881, 4013, 4031, 4081, 4142, 4181, 4283, 4303, 4335, 4430, 4678
    by ship, 3934, 3964, 4031, 4081, 4112, 4142, 4180, 4182, 4239, 4270, 4283, 4300, 4303, 4367, 4424, 4430, 4475, 4589, 4675, 4702
    Arago, 4310
    Creole, 4310
    Crescent, 4690
    Daniel Webster, 4254
    Expounder, 4032
    General Banks, 4205
    Georgia, 4032
    Hermon Livingston, 4738
    Illinois, 4165
    Jersey Blue, 4225
    McClellan, 4310
    Merrimack, 4262
    Milton, 4032
    Montebello, 4459
    New York, 3873
    Northerner, 4287, 4333
    R.R. Cuyler, 3864, 3881
    St. Mary's, 4165
    St. Patrick, 4199

    Saxon, 4121
    Superior, 4199
  uniforms, 3926, 4310, 4564
  United States Christian Commission, 3724, 4079, 4081, 4082, 4142, 4181, 4191, 4234, 4300, 4349, 4402, 4408, 4448, 4514, 4554, 4568, 4589, 4625, 4678, 4701, 4702, 4707, 4715, 4791, 4807
  United States Sanitary Commission, 3805, 3852, 3875, 3882, 3892, 3901, 4006, 4079, 4081, 4181, 4191, 4199, 4244, 4261, 4283, 4285, 4321, 4360, 4384, 4472, 4514, 4517, 4568, 4625, 4678, 4679, 4702, 4707, 4721
    fairs, 3782, 3869, 4006
  Weapons, 3681, 3838, 4367, 4380, 4428, 4447, 4740
Civil wars in
  China, 5788
  Greece, 5716
  Japan, 4061
Clergy, 2974, 2988, 3085, 3112, 3389, 3473, 3480, 3669, 4165, 4543, 4592, 4654, 4715, 4891, 4930
  Baptist, 3065, 3269, 3688, 4040, 4064, 4066, 4172, 4857
  Catholic. See Catholic priests, bishops, missionaries
  Church of God, 5409
  Congregational 2812, 2909, 3454, 5864
  Disciples of Christ, 4633
  Episcopal, 2820, 2839, 3610, 3884, 3944, 4206, 4375, 4703, 4907, 4976, 5001, 5243, 5245, 5915
  Free Methodist, 3654, 3978, 5260
  Friends, 5098
  Hutterite, 5021
  Indian, 3602, 3792
  itinerant, 2801, 2812, 2889, 2905, 3063, 3065, 3217, 3512, 3602, 3741, 3835, 4245, 4633, 5063, 5188, 5241, 5260, 5409
  Lutheran, 3080, 4037
  Mennonite, 4998, 5063
  Methodist, 2889, 2905, 3217, 3533, 3602, 3625, 3724, 3834, 3951, 4060, 4083, 4245, 4351, 4415, 4625, 4707, 4959, 5184
  Presbyterian, 2801, 3087, 3327, 3518, 3544, 3579, 3682, 3741, 3835, 3871, 4003, 4408, 4499, 4783, 4959, 5241, 5854, 5865
    Cumberland Presbyterian, 5378
  Unitarian, 5935
  United Brethren in Christ, 4149
  United Church of Christ. See Clergy, Congregational
  women, 3978
Clerks, 2928, 3668, 3720, 3810, 4262, 4372, 4848
Clipper ship travel, 3138, 3295, 3349, 3359, 3365, 3367, 3374, 3489, 3550, 3578, 3994

5576, 5652, 5665, 5671, 5679, 5688, 5788, 5820, 5845

about, 4988, 5232, 5367, 5370, 5446, 5454, 5502, 5564, 5610, 5669, 5671, 5728, 5797, 5830, 5884

Confederate States of America, 4024
English, 4956
French, 3010
Japanese, 3519, 3524, 3735, 3813, 3815
Russian, 5669

Discrimination. See Racial discrimination; Sexual discrimination

Disciples of Christ, 2996, 3299. See also Clergy, Disciples of Christ

Divorce, 3276, 3747, 4399, 5875, 5936, 5943, 5979

Dogsled travel, 3732, 4776, 5209, 5380, 5336, 5338, 5341, 5416, 5456, 5623, 5634, 5642

Draft. See Military service, Compulsory

Dreams, 2869, 3432, 3575, 3655, 3955, 4276, 4807, 5449, 5629, 5863, 5950

Drinking, 2991, 3089, 3226, 3374, 3465, 3489, 3562, 3572, 3647, 3777, 3985, 4885, 4907, 4931, 5709, 5947. See also Alcoholism; Drunkenness

Drinking in the army 2991, 3921, 4634, 4812, 4885, 4907. See also Civil War, soldiers, drinking

Droughts, 5311, 5587, 5626, 5643, 5650. See also Dust bowl

Drug use, 5823, 5880, 5885, 5975
hashish, 5136
LSD, 5923
opium, 4970, 5599, 5823

Duels, 3062, 3150, 3383, 3985
Broderick-Terry, 3497, 3685

Dumbarton Oaks Conference, 5694, 5759

Dust bowl, 5443, 5626. See also Droughts

Dutch in Iowa, 3113

Dutch in Michigan, 2978
See also Immigrants, Dutch

E

Earthquakes, 3257, 4624, 4700

Ecclesiastical trials, 3654

Eclipses, 3467, 3533, 4943

Ecologists, 6034

Economic conditions, 4871, 4945, 5360, 5577, 5611, 5649
Alaska, 3865
California, 5049
China, 5716, 5845
Illinois, 3758
Pennsylvania, 3810
Philippines, 5665
Poland, 5574, 5845
Russia, 5587
Texas, 3176
Washington, D.C., 3810
See also Confederate States of America,

economic conditions; Civil War, economic conditions

Economic policy, 5611

Economists, 5845. See also Women's diaries, economists

Ecumenical conferences, 5676

Editors, 5821, 5851, 5863, 6000. See also Newspaper and periodical editors; Women's diaries, editors

Education, 3322, 3347, 3419, 4871, 5649, 5955, 5649, 5955
by place
Africa, 5646
Alabama, 3759
Alaska, 5115, 5283
China, 5890
Delaware, 5586
Florida, 3513, 4151
Georgia, 3567, 3913
Hawaii, 2806, 2909
Indiana, 3778
Iowa, 3014, 4816
Montana, 4680
New Hampshire, 3627
New York City, 5903
Ohio, 3672, 3681, 3689, 4259
Oregon 3533
Pennsylvania, 3672, 3810, 4238
Russia, 5846
South Carolina, 3516, 4304, 4315, 4751
Tennessee, 3812, 4245, 4479,
Texas, 3176
Vermont, 3983
Virginia, 3314
Wisconsin, 3987, 4758
See also Colleges and universities; Schools; Teachers
exchange teachers, 5843
Montessori method, 5986
National Popular Education Board, 3014
Special, 5858. See also Schools for blind, deaf
Educators, 3949, 3951, 5283, 5484, 5950. See also Teachers; Women's diaries, educators

Electroplating, 3953

Emancipation. See Afro-Americans in the Civil War

Embryologists, 5596

Emigrant
accidents, 2907, 2940, 3207, 3251, 3391, 3420, 3441, 3474, 3593, 3752, 4133
guidebooks and advice, 2923, 3074, 3114, 3215, 3351, 3475, 4056

Emigrant journeys
Arizona from
Kansas, 5043
California, 2835, 2870, 2879, 2880, 2884, 2894, 3372, 3496
California from
Illinois, 3087, 3278, 3362, 3370, 3391, 3539
Indiana, 3107
Iowa, 3251, 3390, 3714, 4133, 4219

Kansas, 3636
Kentucky, 2836, 3403
Michigan, 3220, 3398
Missouri, 2817, 2837, 2877, 2898, 3105, 3106, 3443, 3595, 3649
Ohio, 3340, 3717
Texas, 4905, 4971
Wisconsin, 3418, 3488, 3618
Colorado from
Illinois, 3776, 4870, 4995
Missouri, 4107
Wisconsin, 4530
Kansas from
Massachusetts, 4994
Montana from
Illinois, 3366
Pennsylvania, 3366
Nevada from
Kentucky, 4537
Nebraska, 4355
Oregon, 2857, 2882, 3319, 3461, 3463, 3571
Oregon from
Illinois, 2935, 3023, 3234, 3303, 3313, 3331, 3333, 3334, 3336, 3352, 3360, 3420, 3474, 3495
Indiana, 2797, 2811, 2970, 3302, 3381, 3409, 3427, 3428, 3439, 3451
Iowa, 2940, 3337, 3351, 3406, 3455, 3471, 4200
Michigan, 3769
Minnesota, 4899
Missouri, 2802, 3193, 3309, 3350, 3389, 3404, 4931
New York, 3453, 3481
Ohio, 2893, 3261, 3298, 3301, 3327, 3361, 3402, 3460, 3491
Pennsylvania, 3483
Wisconsin, 3249
Texas from
Illinois, 4958
Tennessee, 3772
Utah, 2895, 2948, 3291, 3297, 3335, 3475, 3536, 4858
Utah from
Illinois, 2907, 2933
Iowa, 3624
Massachusetts, 3236
Minnesota, 4443
Nebraska, 2972
Washington from
Illinois, 4158
Michigan, 3342
Missouri, 3512, 5105
Ohio, 3261
Wisconsin, 5108
Wyoming from
Kansas, 3637, 5147
Montana, 5187
Nebraska, 5212
Emigrant parties
Belshaw, 3427
Birdsall, 3092
Bischoff, 5086

4812, 5105. See also Indian depredations; Whitman massacre
massacres of Indians by whites, 4392,
4716, 4797. See also Indian wars of the
West
medicine, 3432
missions, 2784, 2800, 2811, 2869, 2909,
2995, 3432, 3454, 3477, 3515, 3545,
3549, 3558, 3568, 3575, 3577, 3602,
3611, 3650, 3685, 3722, 3730, 3744,
3792, 4865, 4943, 4959
mounds, 5092
music and dance, 2821, 2985, 3305, 3323,
3566, 3801, 4809, 4927
oratory. See Indian councils and negotiations; Indian treaties
policy, 2819, 2996, 2997, 3134, 3188,
3293, 3384, 3412, 3420, 4903, 4935,
4952
population, 4952, 5290
pueblos. See Pueblos
religion, 3323, 3792. See also Indians,
Christian
removals
    Flathead, 2996
    Oneida, 4865
    Yakima, 5117
reservations, 2996, 3450, 3528, 3634,
3659, 3842, 4047, 4850, 4873, 4952,
5117
schools, 3792, 4123, 4943, 4959, 5074,
5318
scouts, 4809, 4873, 4942, 5058, 5062,
5064, 5068, 5077, 5089
slavery. See Slavery practiced by Indians; Slaves, Indian
superstitions, 2862, 2949, 4868
trails, 2953, 3392, 4531, 5044
treaties, 2897, 3323, 3634, 4294
    violations, 3634, 3743, 5027
    with
        Apache, 4797
        Arapaho, 4797
        Cheyenne, 4797
        Clear Lake, 3091
        Comanche, 2800, 3354, 4797
        Dakota, 3584, 3743, 5027
        Kiowa, 4797
        Liepan, 3354
        Navaho, 3170
    See also Indian councils and negotia-
    tions; Indian wars of the West, peace
    negotiations
Indian
    tribes
        Achowami, 3659
        Apache, 2845, 2860, 2991, 3037, 3078,
        3195, 3384, 3412, 3599, 3647, 3982,
        4143
        Arapaho, 4809, 4952, 5223, 4820, 4862
        Arikara, 2949, 3219, 3478
        Assiniboin, 2821, 2949, 2960, 3219
        Atsuqewi, 3659
        Bannock, 2821, 3057, 3611, 3650, 4932,
        5089, 5094, 5095, 5104, 5108, 5117

Blackfoot, 2949, 2960, 3219, 3366,
3478, 3498, 4056
Caw, 3450, 3577
Cayuse, 2915, 3566
Cherokee, 3134, 3210, 3279, 3528,
3568, 4123
Cheyenne, 3077, 3106, 3165, 3236,
3255, 3301, 3450, 3648, 4809, 4820,
4862, 4885, 4911, 4923, 4926, 4927,
4928, 4942, 5032, 5058, 5062, 5064,
5067, 5068, 5069, 5070, 5076, 5077,
5080
Chickasaw, 2800, 3671
Chinook, 2862
Chippewa, 3392
Choctaw, 3115, 3454, 3492, 3602, 3792,
3807
Coeur d'Alene, 3566
Comanche, 2785, 2800, 2906, 3096,
3134, 3279, 3354, 3492, 3528, 3626,
3671, 4926, 5004, 5032, 5051, 5097
Cowlitz, 2862
Cree, 2949
Creek, 2821, 3165, 3279, 5335
Crow, 2785, 2949, 3554, 3722, 3743,
4056, 4893, 4902, 5058, 5062, 5064,
5068, 5077, 5186
Dakota, 2783, 3795, 2836, 2882, 2949,
2972, 3077, 3083, 3125, 3173, 3178,
3207, 3236, 3280, 3301, 3313, 3362,
3375, 3403, 3478, 3553, 3583, 3584,
3668, 3722, 3743, 3857, 4014, 4236,
4381, 4385, 4390, 4397, 4405, 4471,
4547, 4603, 4645, 4652, 4809, 4820,
4862, 4885, 4910, 4927, 4991, 5027,
5031, 5058, 5061, 5062, 5064, 5067,
5068, 5069, 5070, 5077, 5080, 5082,
5084
Delaware, 2785, 3528
Deschutes, 3018
Digger, 2817, 2836, 3083, 3170, 3199,
3202, 3246, 3280, 3375, 3409, 3569
Five Civilized Tribes, 3897
Flathead, 2862, 2996, 3324
Fox, 2949, 3540
Goshante, 3801
Gros Ventre, 2949, 3219, 3478, 4056
Haida, 3512, 5213
Havasupai, 5190
Hopi, 3730, 5290
Iowa, 3540
Iroquois, 3732
Kickapoo, 3528, 3540
Kiowa, 2785, 3106, 3134, 3626, 3629,
3683, 4926, 5004, 5032
Klackamas, 2862
Kutenai, 3470
Kwakiutl, 5213
Makah, 4294
Mandan, 2949, 3478, 3668, 4645, 4853
Maricopa, 2860, 2991, 3030, 3054
Menominee, 3525
Modoc, 2659
Mohave, 3286, 3592

Mohegan, 5383
Moqui, 3432, 5423
Navaho, 2844, 2887, 3170, 3384, 3412,
3599, 4389, 4850, 4951, 5290, 5423
Nez Perce, 2811, 2862, 3298, 3439,
3478, 3566, 5079, 5089, 5094, 5095,
5100, 5303
Nisqually, 3634
Ojibwa, 3464
Omaha, 2949, 3255
Oneida, 4865
Osage, 3279, 4955
Paiute, 3450, 3545, 3708, 4307, 4980,
5095, 5104, 5117, 5423
Palouse, 3478, 3566
Pawnee, 2882, 2940, 2995, 3125, 3178,
3199, 3255, 3362, 3390, 3391, 3403,
3631, 4547, 4809, 4942
Pima, 2845, 2860, 2991, 3030, 3054,
4143
Potawatomi, 2836, 2949, 2995, 3163,
3178, 3194, 3375
Pueblo, 3384, 3412, 3492, 5134
Puyallup, 3634
Sac, 3540
Salish, 3478
Santee, 4014
Seminole, 2800, 3338, 3546, 5280
Shawnee, 2836, 3450, 3492, 3528, 3577,
3643, 3685
Shoshoni, 2836, 3170, 3291, 3409,
3575, 3595, 3611, 3650, 3708, 3801
Sioux. See Dakota
Snake, 3131, 3220, 3313, 3324, 3375,
3708, 4602, 4873
Spokan, 3470, 3478, 3566
Teton, 3219
Tlingit, 5325
Tsimshian, 5213
Ute, 2836, 2844, 3102, 3450, 3485, 4850,
4868, 4952
Wichita, 3134, 3528
Winnebago, 3253, 4943
Wyandot, 2819, 3131, 3163
Yakima, 3470, 3547, 3560, 3565, 3573,
3574, 5117
Yankton, 3219
Yellow Knife, 3732
Yukon, 3732
Yuma, 3645, 3184
Zuni, 2887, 3495, 5579
Indian wars, Seminole. See Seminole Wars
Indian wars of the West
    atrocities of both sides, 3037, 3565, 3573,
    3584, 4389, 4809, 4812, 4873, 5068,
    5069, 5117. See also Indian massacres
    campaigns and battles
        Arikaree. See Beecher Island
        Ash Hollow, 3583, 3584
        Bannock War, 5094, 5095, 5104, 5117,
        5108
        Beecher Island, 4923, 4928
        Birch Creek, 5117

M

Machinists, 3933, 4505

Magazines. See Newspapers and Periodicals

Mail routes and services, 2852, 2923, 3018, 3078, 3188, 3301, 3545, 3626, 3645, 4070, 4472, 4624, 4875, 5139, 5347
  Butterfield Overland Mail. See Overland Mail
  California Mail, 3549
  Eastern Mail, 3747
  Overland Mail, 3663, 3771
  Pony Express, 3656, 3747, 3771
  San Antonio-San Diego ("Jackass Mail"), 3704

Malnutrition, 5707, 5717

Manchurian crisis, 5298

Marines, 5495, 5523, 5534, 5540, 5713, 5738, 5860, 6044

Marital problems, 5875, 5920, 5943

Marital violence, 5601, 5927

Marriage
  attitude toward, 2982, 3128, 3672, 3676, 3720, 4411, 5142, 5948

Marshall Plan, 5694

Masons. See Freemasonry

Mayors, 3009, 3908

Mechanics, 3179, 3594

Medical
  interns, 5816
  schools
    Atlanta Medical College, 3951
    Eclectic Medical Institute, 3468
    Geneva University, New York, 2913
    Harvard, 3586
    Iowa Medical College, 4518
    Jefferson Medical College, 3518, 4113
    National Medical College, 4352
    New England Female Medical College, 4151
    Rush Medical College, 5976
    Women's Medical College of Philadelphia, 4989, 5294
  students, 2913, 3518, 5135. See also Women's diaries, medical students

Medicine, 2807, 2872, 3024, 3042, 3070, 3217, 3261, 3296, 3307, 3361, 3454, 3488, 3503, 3521, 3591, 3742, 3780, 3784, 3979, 4304, 4441, 4520, 4546, 4559, 4769, 5011, 5092, 5145, 5207, 5223, 5745, 5797
  air delivery, 5657
  amputations, 3591, 5016
  folk medicine, 2869, 4557, 4924, 5380
  hydropathic, 3672, 3720
  neonatal intensive care, 5991
  vaccination, 4917, 4943, 5135
  See also Illness; Medical aspects under individual wars; Spiritual healing

Meditation, 5691, 5700, 5940

Memorial Day, 3153, 3810, 4151

Ménage à trois, 5921

Mennonites, 4256, 4998, 5021, 5315, 5369, 5557, 5558, 6028. See also Hutterites

Mental hospitals
  Georgia, 3863
  Louisiana, 3529
  New York
    Bloomingdale Asylum for the Insane, 3214, 5659
    Manhattan Psychiatric Center, 6038
  Ohio
    Central Ohio Lunatic Asylum, 3378

Mental illness, 2930, 3080, 3214, 3257, 3361, 3378, 3421, 3618, 3676, 4919, 5382, 5604, 5944, 6038

Mercer Girls, 4854, 4878

Merchant Marine, 5491

Merchants, 3045, 3071, 3119, 3127, 3146, 3191, 3221, 3326, 3509, 3596, 3728, 3930, 3963, 4010, 4652, 4963, 4983, 5026, 5086, 5157, 5196. See also Businessmen; Gold rush, merchants and traders

Meteorites, 5321

Meteorology, 5623

Methodists, 2876, 2912, 2917, 2993, 3005, 3045, 3188, 3300, 3361, 3431, 3622, 3655, 3687, 3951, 4237, 4245, 5055, 5138, 5293, 5785
  about, 2918, 3399, 3400, 3558
  schism, 3654

Métis, 2783, 5012

Mexican War, 2883, 2911, 2941, 2947
  Alcalde of Monterey, California, 2790
  Bear Flag Revolt. See Bear Flag Revolt
  California Peace Commission, 2836
  campaigns and battles
    Bracito, 2886
    Buena Vista, 2799, 2888, 2892, 2952
    Cerro Gordo, 2840, 2849, 2874, 2899, 2951, 2961
    Chapultepec, 2840, 2937, 2951
    Churubusco, 2840, 2934, 2951
    Contreras, 2840, 2951
    Doniphan's expedition, 2858, 2886, 2887, 2906
    La Paz, 2932
    Matamoros, 2816
    Mexico City, 2934, 2944
    Molino del Rey, 2840, 2934
    Monterrey, Mexico, 2799, 2816, 2828, 2830, 2855, 2888
    Palo Alto, 2816
    Puebla, 2816, 2944
    Resaca de la Palma, 2799
    Sacramento, 2852, 2886
    Saltillo, 2816
    San Gabriel, 2845
    San Pasqual, 2845, 2856
    Santa Fe, 2844, 2887, 2926
    Vera Cruz, 2816, 2826, 2828, 2840, 2849, 2874, 2944, 2961
  chaplains, 2790
  civilians, 2829, 2878, 2888, 2906, 2922, 2929, 2932, 2944, 2949
  foreign participants, 2896, 2906

medical aspects, 2799, 2842, 2849, 2853, 2855, 2865, 2869, 2875, 2886, 2887, 2899, 2919, 2944, 2947, 2959, 2968

military operations
  Baja California, 2841, 2932
  California, 2790, 2791, 2808, 2832, 2833, 2841, 2842, 2843, 2845, 2853, 2856, 2858, 2860, 2861, 2900, 2906
  Mexico, 2799, 2808, 2816, 2826, 2828, 2840, 2852, 2858, 2865, 2874, 2875, 2878, 2881, 2886, 2888, 2892, 2897, 2906, 2918, 2919, 2934, 2937, 2943, 2944, 2946, 2951, 2952, 2961, 2984. See also Baja California
  New Mexico, 2824, 2825, 2844, 2845, 2852, 2853, 2858, 2860, 2869, 2886, 2887, 2900, 2926
  Texas, 2858, 2875

military units
  Army of the West, 2824, 2825, 2844, 2853, 2860, 2900
  Cambria Guards, 2968
  Eagle Artillery Company, 2863
  Fourth Artillery Regiment, 2918
  Georgia, 2899
  Illinois, 2826, 2899
  Indiana, 2865, 2892, 2910
  Kearny's Army of the West. See Army of the West
  Kentucky, 2850, 2875, 2919, 2961
  McCullough's Rangers, 2952
  Maryland, 2863, 2886
  Massachusetts, 2959, 3020
  Mississippi, 2888
  Missouri, 2887, 2906, 2926
  Mormon Battalion, 2827, 2832, 2833, 2861, 2869, 2896, 2904
  New Mexico, 2860
  New York, 2856
  North Carolina, 2929
  Ohio, 2943
  Palmetto Regiment, 2944
  Pennsylvania, 2840, 2864, 2881, 2934, 2951, 2968
  Seventeenth Rangers, 2855
  Shields' Brigade, 2826
  Spencer Greys, 2892
  Stevenson's Regiment, 2856
  Tennessee, 2849
  Texas, 2855
  Third Brigade, Second Division Volunteers, 2883
  Virginia, 2947
  Westmoreland County Guards, 2840, 2951

musicians, 2910

mutinies, 2856, 2899

naval operations, 2790, 2791, 2808, 2828, 2841, 2842, 2843, 2932

news, 2836, 2922

pillaging, 2850

political aspects, 2813, 2947

reconnaissance, 2845, 2932

N

NATO, 5664, 5694, 5716
National Geographic Society, 5283
National Guard
  Wisconsin, 5238
Natural disasters. See Droughts;
  Earthquakes; Floods; Volcanoes
Natural history, 3149, 3504
  Alaska, 3732, 4900, 5632
  Amazon Valley, 3310, 3316, 4749
  Antarctic, 5432
  Appalachian Mountains, 4997
  Argentina, 3691
  Arizona, 5423
  California, 2845, 2942, 3768, 3781, 4900,
    5533
  Canada, 3732
  Chile, 3691
  Colorado, 3727, 3737
  Florida, 4997, 5215, 5280, 5296, 5419
  Great Lakes, 2985
  Great Plains, 2785, 3420, 3629, 3653,
    3751, 5012
  Hawaii, 3364
  Idaho, 5403
  Indonesia, 5892
  Japan, 3397
  Kansas, 4994
  Maine, 5256
  Massachusetts, 4997
  Mexico, 2906, 4475
  Midway Islands, 5285
  Minnesota, 3007, 4457
  Mississippi Valley, 2949, 3594
  Missouri, 3520
  Missouri Valley, 2949
  Mongolia, 5289
  New Mexico, 2785
  New York, 2990
  Northwest, 3470
  Oklahoma, 3134, 5074
  Rocky Mountains, 3511, 6034
  South Dakota, 3219, 5031
  Southwest, 2981, 3033, 3384, 3425, 3653,
    3708, 4874, 4953, 4993
  Tennessee, 3396
  Texas, 3134, 5003
  Tibet, 5289
  Utah, 3173, 3246
  Vermont, 2957
  Western states, 3061, 3408, 3420, 3451,
    3479
  Wyoming, 5241
  Yellowstone, 4960, 4966, 5050
  Yosemite, 4900
  See also Expeditions, Botanical; Expedi-
    tions, Geological; Expeditions,
    Scientific
Naturalists, 2985, 3033, 3469, 3504, 3520,
  3622, 3732, 3751, 4749, 4900, 5151, 5285,
  5391, 5419, 5533, 5607, 5614, 5895, 6034.
  See also Women's diaries, naturalists

Nature diaries, 5569, 5637, 5686, 5740,
  5796, 5836, 6043
Nature reserves. See Wildlife conservation
Naval academies
  Confederate Naval Academy
    students, 4453, 4778
  United States Naval Academy, 3661,
    3873
    alumni, 3827
Naval Conference (1930). See London
  Naval Conference (1930)
Naval discipline, 3699
Naval Expedition to Paraguay. See Para-
  guay Expedition
Naval operations in the
  Arctic, 5120, 5456
  Atlantic
    Europe, 4890
    South America, 3699
  Pacific, 3062, 5282
    Asiatic Squadron, 5200
    China, 3617
    Japan. See Perry Expedition to Japan
    Puget Sound, 3062
    South Pacific Squadron, 3699
    See also individual wars
Navy Department, 4317
Navy personnel
  aides, 5722
  machinists, 5729
  seamen, 5718, 5724
  signalmen, 5720
Nazism, 5652, 5661, 5674, 5676, 5681, 5786
Neptune Day. See King Neptune's Day
Nervous breakdown. See Mentally ill
Neurosurgery, 5628, 5638
New Deal, 4945, 5414, 5511, 5579, 5643,
  5654, 5679, 5701
New Year's Day, 3516, 3852, 3862, 3935,
  4102, 4871
Newspaper
  correspondents. See Foreign correspon-
    dents
  publishers, 2790, 2852, 2926, 3841, 4200,
    4390, 4438, 5519
  reporters. See Journalists
Newspaper and periodical editors, 2922,
  2979, 3016, 3518, 3747, 3790, 3853, 3925,
  3928, 4066, 4998, 5063, 5210, 5355, 5579,
  5624
  about, 5248, 5287, 5478. See also Editors
Newspapers and periodicals, 3247, 3419,
  3555, 3901, 4379, 4466, 4551, 4631
  by name
    Advertising Age, 5740
    American Baptist and Freeman, 4066
    American Israelite, 5101
    Ashtabula Sentinel, 3378
    Atlanta Constitution, 5248
    Atlantic Monthly, 2587, 2927, 5211
    Barron's, 5279
    Bismarck Tribune, 5076
    Californian, 2790
    Catholic Worker, 5969

    Charleston Mercury, 3770
    Cheyenne Leader, 4754
    Chicago Daily News, 5614
    Chicago Tribune, 4360, 4906, 5119
    Como and Sentinel, 3070
    Concordia Empire, 5043
    Crescent, 3025
    Daily Citizen, 3760
    Daily Missouri Republican, 3106
    Deadwood Weekly Pioneer, 5073
    Deseret News, 3747, 5210
    Die Fackel, 2872
    Free Methodist, 5260
    Friends Intelligencer and Journal, 3477
    Gastonia Gazette, 5055
    Gold Hill Evening News, 3070
    Hairenik Daily, 5624
    Herald of Truth, 4998, 5063
    The Index, 4737
    Life, 5486, 5647, 5892, 5904
    Literary World, 2922
    London Times, 3985
    Monthly Friend, 3984
    New Orleans Daily Picayune, 3074
    New Republic, 5579
    New York Daily News, 6003
    New York Evening Post, 5470
    New York Herald Tribune, 5814
    New York Post, 5883
    New York Times, 3016, 4854, 5463,
      5634, 5716, 5812, 5884, 6003
    New York Tribune, 4473, 5281, 5355
    New Yorker, 5579, 6000
    Newsweek, 5943
    Ohio Spectator, 3737
    Ohio State Journal, 3378
    Outlook, 5470
    PM, 5752
    Philadelphia Press, 5399
    Plymouth Rock, 3070
    Raleigh Sentinel, 4828
    Reese River Reveille, 3070
    Review and Herald, 4841
    Rocky Mountain Advertiser, 4754
    Rocky Mountain Herald, 4754
    Rocky Mountain News, 4754
    Sacramento Union, 3555
    San Francisco Bulletin, 5478
    San Francisco Call, 5478
    Saturday Evening Post, 5584
    Sonoma County Independent, 4478
    Sonora Herald, 3051
    Soul Winner, 3518
    Southern Literary Gazette, 2979
    Vanity Fair, 5579
    Virginia City Daily Union, 3070
    Virginia City Territorial Enterprise,
      3070
    Virginia Daily Union, 3070
    Wall Street Journal, 5279
    The War Bulletin, 3841
    Washington Capital, 5281
    Washington Eagle, 5586
    Weston Journal, 2852

Pharmacists, 4962, 5767
Phi Beta Kappa, 3008
Philanthropists, 3396, 5110, 5222, 5244
Philippine Insurrection, 5350, 5370
  military units
    Engineer battalion, 5361
    22nd infantry, 5350
    31st volunteer infantry, 5365
  transport, 5365
Philosophers, 5330
Photographers, 3400, 3436, 4868, 4975,
  4980, 5263, 5342, 5348, 5393, 5413, 5594,
  5597, 5892, 5911, 6001
  See also War photographers; Women's
  diaries, photographers
Photography, 3942, 4181, 4984, 4999, 5219,
  5271, 5333, 5445, 5498, 5597, 5892
  of Indians, 4868, 4980, 4984
Phrenology, 2928, 3445, 3720
Physicians and surgeons, 3002, 3003, 3046,
  3096, 3101, 3106, 3133, 3144, 3146, 3148,
  3163, 3178, 3226, 3245, 3261, 3272, 3277,
  3307, 3342, 3384, 3414, 3466, 3518, 3736,
  3752, 3757, 3883, 3910, 4017, 4103, 4285,
  4755, 4790, 4873, 4898, 5011, 5092, 5218,
  5357, 5398, 5538, 5635, 5638
  about, 5392, 5628, 5816, 5976, 5994, 6038
  See also Women's diaries, physicians
  and surgeons
Physicians and surgeons, military, 3751,
  4876, 4917, 4991, 5016, 5051, 5067, 5112,
  5218, 5223, 5976
  Civil war
    Confederate, 3244, 3822, 3922, 3966,
     4113, 4492, 4590
    Union, 3585, 3838, 3852, 4073, 4105,
     4151, 4352, 4364, 4518, 4569, 4695,
     4708, 4805, 4815, 4822
  Mexican war, 2842, 2853, 2906
  World War I, 5459, 5469
  World War II, 5734, 5745
Physicians and surgeons, naval
  Civil war
    Confederate, 4662
    Union, 3586, 3991, 4061
Physicians and surgeons, ship, 2831, 2842,
  3182, 3469, 5145, 5200, 5385, 5709
Pianists, 3641. See also Women's diaries,
  pianists
Physicists, 5345, 5846
Pioneer graves, 3001, 3168, 3220, 3256,
  3268, 3272, 3283, 3301, 3336, 3362, 3370,
  3381, 3398, 3410, 3420, 3428, 3665, 4133,
  4483, 4537, 4603, 4847, 5075
Pioneers. See Emigrant journeys; Frontier
  and pioneer life; Gold rush; Overland
  journeys; Women's diaries, frontier and
  pioneer
Pirates, 3476, 3657, 5137
Plantation life, 2807, 3024, 3109, 3243, 3274,
  3503, 3623, 3638, 3698, 3784, 3858, 3915,
  3985, 4157, 5018
Plantation management, 2917, 2956, 2962,
  3024, 3306, 3394, 3499, 3621, 3633, 3677,

3688, 3698, 3705, 3742, 3780, 3784, 3915,
4111, 4268, 4309, 5191, 5389. See also
Farming
Plantation mistresses. See Women's
  diaries, plantation mistresses
Plantation overseers, 2956, 3306, 3394, 3499,
  3633
Plantations, 2917, 3632, 4061, 4250, 4342,
  4354, 4450, 4482, 4631, 4871, 4981
  cotton, 2962, 3109, 3633, 3915, 4786
  rice, 3394, 3677, 5389
  tobacco, 3499
  wheat, 3499
Plantations and estates
  The Apple Trees, 5408
  Arlington, 3385
  Ashtabula, 3503, 5191
  Ashwood, 4427
  Avenal, 4063
  Avon, 4404, 4622
  Beaulieu, 3905
  Beechwood, 3621
  Bel Air, 3843
  Belle Grove, 3723
  Belle Mead, 3499
  Belle Meade, 5312
  Belmont, 3623
  Belvoir, 2807
  Bremo Bluff, 2987
  Brokenburn, 3915
  California, 4526
  Castalia, 2807
  Castle Hill, 2807
  Cedar Grove, 4794
  Chatham, 4263
  Chemonie, 3306
  Cherry Grove, 4081
  Cismont, 2807
  Clifton, 4343
  Clover Lea, 4743
  Cloverfields, 2807
  Conneconara, 3780
  Cottonham, 4786
  Crescent Plantation, 4157
  El Destino, 2956
  East Hermitage, 3394
  Fair Lawn, 4136
  Fair Mont, 4479
  Forest Home, 4396
  Fort Hill, 4441
  Glen Welby, 4361
  Glencoe, 4520
  Gowrie, 3394
  Green Mount, 3784
  Grove Hill, 4063
  Hampton Hill, 3742
  Hascosea, 3780
  Haywood, 4546
  The Hermitage, 3995, 4198
  Inglewood, 3967
  Keswick, 2807
  Kinloch, 2807, 4309
  Linwood, 4098
  Looking Glass, 3780

  Malbourne, 3621
  Mexico, 4794
  Mi Casa, 4441
  Middleton Place, 4805
  Millward, 5018
  Montevideo, 4643, 4671
  Monticello, 3861, 4021
  Montpelier, 4138, 4468
  Morven, 4033, 4292
  Mount Hope, 4743
  Mount Vernon, 3244, 3347, 4108, 4124,
    4663, 4989
  Mulberry, 3858
  Music Hall, 2807
  Northampton, 4794
  Oakland, 4312
  Oakley, 4111
  Petite Anse, 3274
  Pine Bluff, 4546
  Pine Hill, 3513
  Pooshee, 3742, 4794, 4818
  Rivoli, 3503
  Rocky Hill, 4267
  Rokeby, 4268
  Rosewood, 4683
  Sandy Hill, 3858
  Society Hill, 3024
  Somerset, 4794
  Westover, 3698
  Woodboo, 2962
  Woodlawn, 4009
Planters, 2789, 2850, 2962, 2987, 3024,
  3394, 3621, 3638, 3666, 3677, 3688, 3698,
  3705, 3884, 4136, 4268, 4439, 4700, 4882.
  See also Women's diaries, planters
Playwrights, 5040, 5708, 5862. See also
  Women's diaries, playwrights
Plymouth Brethren, 5803
Poetry, 3780, 4690, 5992
Poets, 3025, 3569, 4136, 5194, 5335, 5451,
  5599, 5635, 5823, 5840, 5868. See also
  Women's diaries, poets
Polar ice pack, 5120, 5145, 5288, 5373, 5792
Police, 3206
Polish-Americans, 3901, 6041
Political campaigns, Presidential. See Presi-
  dential campaigns
Political conventions. See Political parties
Political parties, 5313
  American Party, 3596
  Copperheads, 3831, 4259, 4300, 4360,
    4362, 4715, 4723
  Democratic, 3614, 3728, 4329, 5414, 5429,
    5790, 5845, 5945
    national conventions, 3009, 3621, 5428,
     5633, 5716
  Free soil, 3012
  Liberal, 5679
  National Union Convention, 3016, 3709
  Peace Party, 4466
  Populist, 4329, 5224
  Progressive, 5428, 5511, 5818
  Republican, 3379, 3709, 3728, 3758, 4978,
    5045, 5184, 5218, 5238, 5298, 5307,

Q

Quakers. See Friends
Quemoy-Matsu controversy, 5831

R

Rabinnical studies, 5712
Rabbis, 5101, 5247, 5887, 5908
Race relations, 3118, 3516, 3913, 3993, 4151, 4237, 4617, 4685, 4769, 4882, 4912, 5337, 5793, 5835, 5871, 5903, 5908, 5925, 5945
  Africa, 5646
  military, 5531, 5751, 5755
  Poland, 5574
Racial discrimination, 5184, 5586, 5675, 5924, 5996, 6033
Racial integration, 5854. See also School integration
Railroad
  accidents, 3016, 3871, 3953, 4254, 5182
  contruction, 4908, 4937, 5196
  potential, 3086, 5119
  songs. See Songs, railroad
  surveys, 2897, 2981, 3003, 3004, 3086, 3246, 3422, 3426, 3436, 3447, 3450, 3478, 3479, 3492, 3505, 3527, 3548, 3743, 4359, 4885, 4986, 5261, 5263, 5271, 5296
  superintendents, 5678
  travel, 2801, 2807, 2809, 2872, 2883, 2895, 2954, 2958, 2996, 2999, 3029, 3093, 3148, 3157, 3174, 3194, 3214, 3244, 3269, 3276, 3299, 3307, 3317, 3325, 3328, 3332, 3347, 3351, 3384, 3393, 3396, 3407, 3419, 3442, 3466, 3467, 3481, 3487, 3508, 3530, 3531, 3556, 3572, 3601, 3625, 3631, 3638, 3641, 3652, 3656, 3658, 3660, 3685, 3687, 3701, 3708, 3735, 3755, 3767, 3773, 3815, 3842, 3956, 3971, 3985, 4057, 4076, 4100, 4121, 4135, 4331, 4448, 4537, 4701, 4856, 4859, 4886, 4887, 4904, 4916, 4931, 4935, 4945, 4955, 4956, 4959, 4968, 4972, 4975, 4994, 4998, 5001, 5009, 5021, 5023, 5025, 5034, 5044, 5047, 5050, 5093, 5099, 5112, 5118, 5119, 5133, 5135, 5140, 5157, 5158, 5165, 5170, 5178, 5185, 5186, 5188, 5202, 5210, 5211, 5225, 5230, 5251, 5281, 5300, 5305, 5319, 5362, 5364, 5379, 5394, 5405, 5410, 5448, 5467, 5567, 5798
  travel by
    Africa, 5646
    China, 5845
    England, 5386
    France, 5477
    Russia, 4988, 5538, 5820

  travel in
    private car, 5248, 5408, 5502
    "riding the rails", 5309, 5605
  workers, 5107, 5430, 5492, 5502
Railroads, 2979, 3502, 3537
  Atchison, Topeka and Sante Fe, 5107
  Atlantic and Great Western, 3651
  Atlantic and St. Lawrence, 2814
  Burlington and Missouri, 4937
  California Southern, 5196
  Cedar Rapids and Missouri, 4359
  Chicago, Burlington and Quincy, 5408
  Denver, Colorado Canyon and Pacific, 5261, 5263
  Galveston, Houston & San Antonio, 5123
  Illinois Central, 5678
  International & Great Northern, 5123
  Lackawanna Line, 5467
  Louisville and Nashville, 4071
  Northern Pacific, 2897, 4986, 4998, 5182, 5322
  Orange and Alexandria Railroad, 4076
  Pennsylvania, 5087, 5088
  Pennsylvania Canal and Portage, 3029
  St. Paul and Pacific, 4856, 4918
  South Florida Railroad Company, 5296
  Star Union National and Green Lines, 5238
  Texas & Pacific, 5123
  Trans-Siberian Railway, 5492, 5502, 5538. See also Russian Railway Service Corps
  Union Pacific, 4942
  Vineland, 4916
Ranch workers, 3070, 3374, 4904
Ranchers, 2842, 3430, 3514, 3537, 3615, 4307, 4374, 4672, 4897, 4931, 4954, 5009, 5017, 5107, 5187, 5197, 5211, 5227, 5257, 5272, 5273
Ranches and ranching, 4219, 4847, 5043, 5161
  Arizona, 4393, 5608
  California, 2806, 3171, 3247, 4954
  Colorado, 3718, 4897, 4904, 4987, 5319
  Mexico, 4981
  Montana, 3537, 5650
  New Mexico, 5009, 5017, 5034, 5107
  Nevada, 5410
  Oklahoma, 5074
  Oregon, 3309, 4931
  Texas, 3430, 3766, 4687, 5003, 5024, 5227, 5455
  Utah, 3575, 3611
  Wyoming, 5014, 5319, 5333, 5405, 5431, 5651
Range wars, 5009
Rape
  attempted, 5850
    See also Civil War, rape
Reading aloud, 5636, 5704
Reconstruction, 3394, 3709, 3742, 3810, 3830, 3901, 3911, 3929, 3993, 4157, 4317, 4320, 4473, 4769, 4777, 4819, 4871, 4884, 4912, 4950, 5045

  Alabama, 3688, 3866, 4091, 4846
  Florida, 3513
  Georgia, 2917, 3963, 4182, 4541, 4546, 4560, 4786, 4882
  Mississippi, 4846
  North Carolina, 3780, 4272
  South Carolina, 3503, 3677, 3895, 3913, 4751, 4821
  Virginia, 3720, 3723, 3800, 4004
    See also Carpetbaggers
Red Cross, 3343, 5542
  relief in Poland, 5787
  relief in Russia, 5538
  World War I, 4655, 5392, 5459, 5485, 5499, 5514, 5559, 5563, 5567, 5570
  World War II, 5707, 5744, 5755, 5756, 5783
Reindeer, 5183, 5283, 5329
Relief efforts, 3002, 5052, 5446, 5453, 5574, 5587, 5588. See also Red Cross
Religion, 3347, 3672, 3720, 3878, 3919, 5142, 5649, 5714, 5793, 5887, 5950
  Afro-American, 3108, 4003, 4081, 4151, 4181, 4237, 4315, 4546, 4701, 4751
  by place
    Alabama, 3688, 4000
    Arkansas, 5092
    California, 2790, 2806, 3063, 3065, 3066, 3070, 3179, 3200, 3203, 3330, 3579, 3685, 3686
    Chicago, 3614
    Colorado, 3741, 3835, 5241
    Europe, 4888, 5676
    Georgia, 2917, 2979, 3567, 3863, 3951, 4003, 4181, 4546, 4560, 4882
    Hawaii, 2806, 3127
    Indiana, 4807
    Iowa, 3685, 4237, 4913
    Kansas, 3685, 4245
    Kentucky, 3518
    Louisiana, 3529, 4114
    Maryland, 2872
    Massachusetts, 3229, 3480, 3586
    Minnesota, 3269, 3379
    Mississippi, 3785, 4114
    Missouri, 2801, 3779
    Montana, 4680
    Nevada, 3070
    New Hampshire, 3728
    New Jersey, 3005
    New York, 3001, 3358, 3542, 3805, 3869, 3924, 4066
    North Carolina, 3518, 4034, 4828
    Ohio, 2812, 2872, 2996, 3468, 3681, 4766
    Oklahoma, 3454, 3602, 3792
    Pennsylvania, 4037, 4149
    South Carolina, 3503, 3682, 3913, 4315
    South Dakota, 5158
    Tennessee, 3400, 3518
    Texas, 3176, 3766
    Utah. See Mormons
    Vermont, 2957, 3983

Religion, by place, continued

    Virginia 3314, 3518, 3723, 3784, 3837, 3944, 4025, 4063, 4074, 4269

    Washington, 3368, 3431

    Washington, D.C., 3859

    Wisconsin, 3572, 4633, 4679

    Wyoming, 4907, 5241

    See also Churches; Civil War, soldiers, religious activities; Clergy; individual denominations; Missions and missionaries; World's Evangelical Convention

    North Carolina, 3518, 4034, 4828

    Ohio, 2812, 2872, 2996, 3468, 3681, 4766

    Oklahoma, 3454, 3602, 3792

    Pennsylvania, 4037, 4149

    South Carolina, 3503, 3682, 3913, 4315

    South Dakota, 5158

    Tennessee, 3400, 3518

    Texas, 3176, 3766

    Utah, See Mormons

    Vermont, 2957, 3983

    Virginia, 3314, 3518, 3723, 3784, 3837, 3944, 4025, 4063, 4074, 4269

    Washington, D.C., 3859

    Washington, 3368, 3431

    Wisconsin, 3572, 4633, 4679

    Wyoming, 4907, 5241

    See also Churches; Civil War, soldiers, religious activities; Clergy; individual denominations; Missions and missionaries; World's Evangelical Convention

Religions, 5691, 5823, 5842

Religious

    conversions, 2975

    diaries, 2810, 2975, 3613

    reflections, 2867, 2871, 2876, 2888, 2917, 2919, 2920, 2928, 2936, 2955, 2974, 2992, 2993, 2996, 3005, 3012, 3031, 3078, 3112, 3120, 3123, 3128, 3140, 3149, 3152, 3165, 3186, 3205, 3230, 3239, 3299, 3333, 3336, 3346, 3385, 3424, 3435, 3460, 3495, 3503, 3504, 3516, 3544, 3567, 3572, 3580, 3585, 3608, 3621, 3627, 3672, 3677, 3682, 3686, 3711, 3720, 3742, 3746, 3756, 3779, 3782, 3799, 3800, 3811, 3831, 3835, 3845, 3863, 3882, 4007, 4063, 4090, 4231, 4292, 4404, 4475, 4517, 4520, 4560, 4611, 4643, 4666, 4721, 4807, 4829, 4841, 4869, 4913, 5035, 5056, 5149, 5164, 5334, 5388, 5536, 5539, 5625, 5674, 5803, 5825, 5836, 5900, 5901, 5914, 5939, 5979, 6028, 6031, 6034

    See also Civil War, soldiers, religious reflections

    revivals. See Revivals

    skepticism, 3421, 3477, 3555. See also Freethinkers

    visions, 2869

Relocation centers. See Japanese internment

Reporters. See Journalists

Rescue operations. See Emigrant relief

Resorts, 3698, 5242, 5281, 5300, 5362

Revivals, 3435, 3572, 3978, 5060, 5098, 5409. See also Camp meetings

Riots, 3468, 5046, 5087, 5088

River and lake boat accidents, 3011, 3614, 3685, 4383

River and lake boat captains, 2868, 3100, 3555

    Great Lakes captains, 5081, 5284

River and lake boat travel, 2792, 2793, 2801, 2804, 2807, 2809, 2812, 2859, 2876, 2883, 2904, 2910, 2919, 2939, 2951, 2954, 2958, 2968, 2978, 3001, 3011, 3032, 3038, 3042, 3045, 3081, 3093, 3095, 3107, 3113, 3117, 3148, 3158, 3168, 3174, 3194, 3197, 3213, 3219, 3227, 3234, 3235, 3237, 3244, 3253, 3257, 3263, 3269, 3271, 3280, 3284, 3287, 3291, 3294, 3299, 3302, 3311, 3315, 3317, 3323, 3332, 3347, 3348, 3357, 3370, 3375, 3392, 3393, 3407, 3419, 3428, 3442, 3452, 3460, 3461, 3466, 3467, 3468, 3481, 3496, 3509, 3521, 3523, 3536, 3537, 3556, 3558, 3566, 3579, 3581, 3603, 3605, 3631, 3632, 3644, 3681, 3685, 3691, 3692, 3704, 3708, 3712, 3715, 3739, 3763, 3767, 3773, 3796, 3802, 3842, 3956, 3985, 4101, 4121, 4135, 4144, 4145, 4158, 4198, 4265, 4409, 4443, 4528, 4537, 4547, 4672, 4680, 4701, 4779, 4789, 4816, 4837, 4852, 4853, 4856, 4859, 4864, 4872, 4883, 4886, 4893, 4925, 4998, 5023, 5029, 5031, 5044, 5117, 5119, 5190, 5261, 5263, 5280, 5336, 5362, 5419, 5501, 5646, 5794

    barge, 2960

    canoe. See canoe travel

    flatback, 2838, 2908, 4889

    mackinaw, 2985, 4851

    packet, 3658

River rafting, 5589, 5805, 5911

Road surveys and construction, 2795, 3044, 3077, 3170, 3173, 3195, 3422, 3425, 3470, 3511, 3630, 3658, 3673, 3743, 3752, 3788, 4531, 4535, 4801, 4820, 4849, 5319

Roads and trails

    Applegate's cutoff, 2857, 2882, 2940, 3023

    Bannock Mountain Road, 3173

    Barlow Road, 3351

    Beale's Road, 3286, 3425, 3658, 3673

    Bozeman Trail, 4713, 4852, 4855, 4862

    Bridger's Road, 3324

    California Trail. See Emigrant journeys, California; Gold rush, California; Overland journeys, California

    Carson Pass, 3259

    Cherokee Trail, 3757

    Chicago Turnpike, 2846

    Dalles and California Trail, 4531

    Egan Trail, 2923

    Gila Trail, 2991

    Hastings' Cutoff, 2836, 2870

    Hudspeth's Cutoff, 3045, 3185

    Humboldt River Road. See Gold rush, California

    Lander's Cutoff, 3714, 3847, 4603

    Lassen's Cutoff, 3043, 3046, 3094, 3117, 3129, 3133, 3160, 3194, 3233

    Lincoln Highway, 5591, 5592

    Meek Cutoff, 2797

    Mullan Road, 3452, 3470, 3842, 4056, 4101, 4103, 4145, 4265, 5044

    Old National Road, 3117

    Oregon Central Military Road, 4801

    Oregon Trail. See also Emigrant journeys; Gold rush, California; Overland journeys

    Pan American Highway, 5683

    Platte River Road. See Emigrant journeys; Gold rush, California; Overland journeys

    Republican River, 3077

    San Carlos, 3787

    Santa Fe-Gila River, 2853

    Sante Fe Trail, 2787, 2795, 2852, 2878, 2887, 3030, 3106, 3124, 3131, 3154, 3210, 3626, 3718, 3757, 5043, 5591. See also Emigrant journeys; Gold rush, California; Overland journeys

    Sibley's road, 4373

    Sidney-Deadwood Trail, 5125

    South Pass, 2795, 3039, 3057, 3067, 3094, 3116, 3117, 3129, 3161, 3164, 3185, 3282, 3283, 3289, 3717

    Southwestern Trail, 3078

    Spanish Trail, 3015, 3545

    Steam Wagon Road, 4868

    Sublette's Cutoff, 3233, 3255, 3272, 3275, 3313

    See also Military and government roads

Rockets, 5345

Romances, 3552, 3810, 3845, 4361, 5301, 5577, 5907. See also Courtship

Rotary International, 5798

Roundups

    cattle, 4307

    wild horses, 3430, 5124

Russian Railway Service Corps, 5492, 5502

Russian Revolution, 5538

Russians

    in Alaska, 3865, 4776, 5115, 5209, 5243

    See also Immigrants, Russian

S

SALT II. See Strategic Arms Limitation Talks II

Sabbaticals, Academic, 4350, 5422, 5596, 5673, 5852, 5955, 6027

Saddlers, 4022

Safaris, 5440

Utah Commission, 5210
Utah Expedition. See Utah War
Utah War, 3575, 3599, 3637, 3642, 3648,
3653, 3656, 3701
Utopian communities
Harmony Society, Indiana, 3207
"North American Phalanx," 3587
Reunion Colony, Texas, 3523, 3587

V

Vacations, 2809, 3464, 3698, 3802, 4962,
4965, 4987, 5029, 5038, 5281, 5292, 5300,
5362, 5388, 5411, 5431, 5657, 5731, 5829,
5844, 5983, 6016
Vatican II
Protestant observers, 5864, 5865
Vice Presidents, 5298, 5667
Vietnam War, 5716, 5738, 5884, 5890, 5896,
5898, 5900, 5942, 5951, 5984
aerial operations, 5860, 5909
aircraft. See Aircraft, Military
anti-war demonstrations, 5900, 5901,
5915, 5951
leaves, 5896
military operations, 5882, 5909
peace mission, 5887
Visions. See Religious visions
Vocation, 5861, 5868, 5915, 5970
Volcanoes, 5607
Mauna Loa, 2806
Mount St. Helens, 2821, 2862
Mount Wrangell, 5192
Volunteer work. See Charity work; Catholic
Worker Movement
Voyageurs, 2985, 3732

W

WPA. See Government bureaus and agencies, Work Projects Administration
Wagon travel, 2846, 2876, 2950, 3055, 3296,
3344, 3396, 3441, 3456, 3581, 3715, 3753,
3767, 4209, 4231, 4237, 4672, 4959, 4998,
5008, 5034, 5094, 5123, 5208, 5272, 5302,
5306, 5310, 5311, 5322, 5323, 5348, 5363,
5376, 5403. See also Emigrant journeys;
Gold rush; Freighting; Overland journeys; Wagons, wind-powered
Wagons
construction, 4082, 4256
wind-powered, 3739
Waitresses. See Women's diaries,
waitresses
Walking tours. See Foot travel; Hiking
War, 5486, 5488, 5512, 5513, 5563, 5704,
5896, 5984. See also names of individual
wars

War correspondents, 3985, 4360, 5076, 5579,
5738, 5750, 5762
War crimes, Civil War, 4844
trials, 3929
War crimes trials. See Nuremberg trials
War Department, 5695
War photographers, 5440
War with Mexico. See Mexican War
Washington's birthday, 3710, 3900, 3934,
4000
Water resources management, 5319, 5598.
See also Dams
Watergate affair, 5942, 5953, 5959
Weavers. See Women's diaries, weavers
Weddings, 3601, 3700, 3724, 3799, 4807,
5312, 5475, 6019. See also Shivaree;
Honeymoon
Welsh in
America, 4181
Nebraska, 3644
Whaling, 2796, 2982, 2983, 3048, 3139,
3151, 3265, 3356, 3585, 3608, 3697, 3706,
3804, 4880, 4914, 4919, 4947, 4985, 5114,
5137, 5385, 5432
Whaling ships
A. M. Simpson, 3697
A. R. Tucker, 4985
Addison, 3608
Ann Parry, 2796
Annie Bucknam, 3265
Arab, 2982
Benjamin Tucker, 3048
Clara Bell, 3585
Columbia, 3356
Daisy, 5432
Era, 5385
Florida, 3706
James R. Keller, 3804
Kate, 3697
Kathleen, 5137
Minnesota, 4919
Mount Welleston, 3804
Nautilus, 4947
Ocean Bird, 3697
Plough Boy, 3151
Rainbow, 3804
Roman, 4914
Tiger, 2983
Wanderer, 5114
Willis, 3139
White House, 3244, 3799, 4639
White House staff. See Presidential staff
Whitman massacre, 2905, 2909, 2915, 2964,
3018, 3470
Widowers, 5211, 5322
Widows. See Women's diaries, widows
Wife abuse. See Marital violence
Wilderness survival. See Survival, Wilder-
ness
Wildlife. See Natural history
Wildlife conservation, 5892, 5895, 5919,
5983, 6014
Wine cultivation, 3396, 3906

Women's associations, 3467, 3756, 5312,
5639, 6006
Women's diaries, 2786, 2847, 2878, 2885,
2902, 2929, 2950, 2954, 2975, 2983, 2986,
2999, 3060, 3132, 3140, 3190, 3205, 3304,
3312, 3315, 3322, 3328, 3329, 3346, 3358,
3381, 3387, 3396, 3448, 3457, 3464, 3477,
3513, 3524, 3550, 3577, 3632, 3664, 3700,
3723, 3726, 3729, 3760, 3773, 3777, 3779,
3782, 3794, 3799, 3800, 3808, 3840, 3843,
3854, 3858, 3862, 3863, 3869, 3870, 3876,
3877, 3915, 3924, 3944, 3950, 3955, 3968,
3997, 4007, 4009, 4018, 4019, 4030, 4033,
4041, 4063, 4074, 4075, 4089, 4090, 4098,
4137, 4147, 4154, 4155, 4156, 4157, 4194,
4198, 4203, 4207, 4211, 4228, 4231, 4241,
4249, 4250, 4255, 4259, 4264, 4292, 4311,
4314, 4316, 4338, 4339, 4343, 4376, 4400,
4404, 4409, 4440, 4441, 4445, 4450, 4461,
4481, 4485, 4517, 4541, 4546, 4581, 4582,
4585, 4588, 4594, 4608, 4611, 4641, 4653,
4655, 4661, 4666, 4671, 4683, 4704, 4706,
4734, 4743, 4753, 4767, 4774, 4786, 4794,
4798, 4803, 4807, 4813, 4814, 4818, 4821,
4823, 4824, 4826, 4828, 4835, 4841, 4877,
4878, 4881, 4888, 4920, 4921, 4968, 4987,
4990, 5008, 5023, 5030, 5035, 5038, 5054,
5056, 5059, 5083, 5093, 5113, 5118, 5128,
5133, 5142, 5156, 5167, 5169, 5177, 5181,
5208, 5226, 5230, 5240, 5245, 5251, 5256,
5259, 5265, 5267, 5277, 5281, 5288, 5300,
5301, 5312, 5314, 5316, 5359, 5362, 5371,
5376, 5383, 5395, 5396, 5402, 5411, 5412,
5428, 5433, 5437, 5444, 5447, 5448, 5476,
5478, 5520, 5582, 5592, 5603, 5616, 5630,
5639, 5640, 5646, 5663, 5673, 5737, 5757,
5781, 5804, 5808, 5825, 5828, 5832, 5850,
5873, 5875, 5876, 5877, 5884, 5890, 5891,
5913, 5927, 5956, 5957, 5958, 5964, 5971,
5990, 5993, 5995, 6009, 6022, 6026, 6030,
6046
actresses, 5127, 5262, 5567, 5571, 5662,
5800, 5839
about, 3777, 5313, 5904
Afro-American, 3516, 5586, 5620, 5675,
5996, 6033
anthropologists, 5426, 5672
art historians, 5057
artists, 5406, 5730, 5834, 6010, 6036,
6038
astronomers, 3467
authors, 2867, 2914, 2936, 3172, 3516,
4261, 4344, 4396, 4828, 4867, 5159,
5287, 5304, 5311, 5375, 5406, 5449,
5617, 5636, 5659, 5668, 5693, 5795,
5843, 5863, 5878, 5918, 5922, 5926,
5930, 5939, 5961, 5963, 5978, 5979,
5981, 5982, 5994, 5998, 6002, 6015,
6016, 6018, 6021, 6024, 6028. See also
Women's diaries, Novelists; Poets
blind, 5674
botanists, 5450, 5455
cannery workers, 4798, 5425
choreographers, 5886

Geographic Index

Geographic Index

Leavenworth, 2785, 2844, 2845, 2852, 2860, 2861, 2869, 2886, 2900, 2904, 2996, 3037, 3057, 3061, 3077, 3091, 3173, 3222, 3264, 3277, 3321, 3583, 3584, 3629, 3635, 3642, 3646, 3744, 4634, 4820, 4921, 5106, 5557, 5609
Lecompton, 3582
Lyon County, 4189
Manhattan, 3744, 5035
Mitchell County, 5168
Neosho River, 3597
Osage County, 3582
Osawatomie, 3552
Quindaro, 2997
St. Marys, 2995
Springhill, 4926
Topeka, 4921, 5165, 5281
Wabaunsee County, 3558
Wichita, 4926
Kansas River, 3003, 3004
Kentucky, 2850, 2875, 2919, 2954, 2961, 3214, 3244, 3353, 3500, 3689, 3702, 3809, 3831, 3872, 3874, 3879, 3891, 3893, 3907, 3922, 3927, 3931, 3936, 3942, 3977, 4002, 4011, 4013, 4021, 4027, 4052, 4057, 4059, 4060, 4067, 4069, 4071, 4082, 4083, 4084, 4085, 4087, 4106, 4116, 4122, 4127, 4161, 4175, 4186, 4190, 4191, 4199, 4209, 4212, 4213, 4222, 4233, 4247, 4275, 4283, 4286, 4297, 4300, 4328, 4345, 4349, 4436, 4547, 4554, 4580, 4675, 4701, 4857, 5090, 5836
Adair County, 4059, 5766
Albany, 4202
Augusta, 4744
Barbourville, 4275
Bardstown, 3529
Bloomfield, 4247
Bourbon County, 2875, 3442
Bowling Green, 4207
Clay City, 3518
Cloverport, 3403
Columbus, 3794, 3867, 3936, 4504
Covington, 4082, 4169
Danville, 3518
Fleming County, 2919
Fort Jefferson, 3946
Frankfort, 3581, 3842, 4297
Georgetown, 2945
Gethsemane, 5691, 5914
Glasgow, 3441
Hardin County, 3271
Harrison County, 4044
Hazel Green, 3518
Henderson, 4057
Hopkinsville, 4057
Lebanon, 4202, 4345
Lexington, 2836, 3442, 3518, 3809, 3936, 4069, 4241, 4247, 4248, 4275
Louisville, 3284, 3311, 3518, 3581, 3681, 3740, 3758, 3809, 3919, 3995, 4021, 4041, 4069, 4082, 4085, 4176, 4207, 4283, 4516, 4569, 4669, 4715,

4721, 4731, 4925, 5025, 5262, 5286
Mammoth Cave, 2958, 3467, 4925, 5185
Monticello, 3809
Munfordville, 3904, 4060, 4514
Newport, 3679
Nicholasville, 4082
Paducah, 4328
Paris, 4082
Perryville, 3500, 3689, 3831, 3832, 3904, 3927, 3931, 4021, 4023, 4052, 4116, 4213, 4275, 4297, 4300
Petersburg, 3158
Pineville, 5579
Pleasant Hill, 3589
Richmond, 3936, 4247, 4275
Riverton, 5836
Russellville, 5055
Sharpsburg, 3518
Shelby County, 3299, 4172
Shelbyville, 3284
South Union, 3955
Wayne Coutny, 3809
Kenya, 5968
Korea, 5200, 5442, 5784, 5832

L

Labrador, 5151, 5792
Lake Champlain, 3332, 5190
Lake Tahoe, 3729, 5118, 5135
Lake Titicaca, 5639
Lakes, Great. See Great Lakes
Laos, 5900
Liberia, 2938
Libya
  Tripoli, 5704, 5745
Louisiana, 3086, 3829, 3830, 3875, 3889, 3895, 3903, 3912, 3917, 3948, 3964, 4095, 4112, 4121, 4128, 4174, 4182, 4218, 4220, 4224, 4227, 4235, 4239, 4244, 4270, 4271, 4283, 4286, 4293, 4303, 4310, 4342, 4347, 4407, 4416, 4418, 4424, 4439, 4450, 4458, 4459, 4463, 4477, 4482, 4494, 4498, 4523, 4554, 4590, 4676, 4677, 4697, 4761, 4771, 4773, 4871, 5508, 5924
Alexandria, 3529, 4157, 4310, 4576
Ascension Parish, 3529
Atchafalaya Bay, 4038
Avery Island, 3274
Baton Rouge, 3917, 4046, 4098, 4165, 4225, 4258, 4303, 4310, 4418, 4744
Bayou Bouef, 4165
Bayou Lafourche, 4165
Bayou Teche, 3889, 4038, 4165, 4482
Brashear City. See Morgan City
Carrollton, 4180, 4205, 4303, 4447
Claiborne Parish, 4439
Clinton, 4098, 4235
De Soto Parish, 3155, 3693
Donaldsonville, 4258, 4310

Fort Burton, 4038
Fort Jackson, 4163, 4258
Fort St. Philip, 4163, 4258
Gilbert, 4898
Grand Coteau, 3529
Grand Encore, 4576
Homer, 3669
Jackson, 3529
Lafourche Parish, 3529
Lake Providence, 3839, 4227, 4360
Livingston Parish, 3529
Madison Parish, 3915
Mansfield, 3529, 3860, 3889, 3895, 3903, 4174, 4239, 4244, 4270, 4677, 4697
Monroe, 3529, 3875, 3915, 4312
Morgan City, 4310, 4482
Morganza, 3917, 4418
Natchitoches, 3529
New Orleans, 2793, 2823, 2840, 2904, 2934, 3001, 3018, 3033, 3074, 3076, 3096, 3114, 3148, 3242, 3271, 3284, 3315, 3348, 3467, 3475, 3550, 3616, 3632, 3674, 3760, 3762, 3773, 3777, 3880, 3889, 3904, 3985, 3993, 3917, 4007, 4024, 4046, 4057, 4098, 4100, 4128, 4157, 4165, 4232, 4237, 4244, 4258, 4262, 4271, 4293, 4310, 4467, 4659, 4691, 4846, 4871, 4965, 5025, 5040
Oak Ridge, 3915
Ouachita Parish, 4485
Pilottown, 4310
Plaquemine, 4418
Pleasant Hill, 3529, 3903, 4112, 4239, 4676, 4677
Pointe Coupee Parish, 3529
Port Hudson, 3850, 3917, 3973, 4072, 4095, 4114, 4128, 4163, 4165, 4180, 4225, 4232, 4235, 4258, 4262, 4303, 4310, 4416, 4423, 4424, 4432, 4437, 4447, 4482
Sabine Cross Roads. See Mansfield
St. Helena Parish, 3529
St. James Parish, 3529
St. Landry Parish, 4224
Ship Island, 3917
Shreveport, 4461, 4528
Trenton, 3915
Vermilion Bayou, 3529
Vidalia, 4114
Washington, 3529
West Baton Rouge Parish, 3829
West Feliciana, 4250

M

Mackenzie River, 5749
Madeira, 3462, 4120, 5229
Maine, 3895, 3960, 4142, 4184, 4214, 4319, 4400, 4431, 4575, 4578, 4722,

Geographic Index

4441, 4871, 4957, 4999, 5025, 5060, 5098, 5099, 5131, 5210, 5225, 5236

Nicaragua, 3032, 3152, 3305, 3393, 3413, 3417, 3434, 3555, 4755, 6035

Nile River, 3603, 4970

North Carolina, 3049, 3244, 3465, 3513, 3518, 3530, 3681, 3689, 3702, 3821, 3825, 3826, 3834, 3866, 3873, 3875, 3888, 3905, 3909, 3926, 3934, 3937, 3938, 3940, 3947, 3956, 3990, 3993, 3997, 4008, 4026, 4034, 4052, 4055, 4067, 4069, 4076, 4081, 4084, 4085, 4087, 4107, 4125, 4129, 4131, 4161, 4168, 4183, 4195, 4199, 4210, 4236, 4251, 4272, 4278, 4283, 4300, 4333, 4343, 4351, 4356, 4358, 4372, 4379, 4403, 4415, 4420, 4430, 4446, 4492, 4505, 4515, 4527, 4561, 4569, 4574, 4601, 4632, 4639, 4657, 4663, 4675, 4679, 4688, 4693, 4702, 4721, 4724, 4747, 4752, 4777, 4782, 4834, 4839, 4840, 4997, 5038, 5412

Albemarle Sound, 4061

Asheboro, 4034

Asheville, 3042, 3465, 4358, 4997, 5055, 5301

Averasboro, 4034, 4372

Bentonville, 3821, 4055, 4601, 4675, 4747

Bogue Island, 3909

Buckhorn, 3870

Cabarrus County, 3909

Cape Fear River, 4759

Carolina City, 3934, 4032, 4081

Chapel Hill, 3089, 3834, 3934, 4828, 5560, 5569

Charlotte, 3892, 3938, 4433, 4453, 4777

Confederate Point, See Federal Point

Davidson, 4034

Durham, 5450, 5852

Elizabeth City, 3926

Everettsville, 3862

Fayetteville, 4688

Federal Point, 4651

Fort Anderson, 4300

Fort Fisher, 4008, 4574, 4610, 4651, 4738

Gaston County, 4515

Gastonia, 5055

Goldsboro, 3586, 4148

Greensboro, 2929, 3993, 4690

Halifax County, 3780

Hamilton, 4333

Harnett County, 4034

Hatteras Inlet, 3827, 3862, 3917, 3926

Hertford County, 3828

Iredell County, 4034, 4076

Kinston, 4055, 4131, 4555

Lincolnton, 4834

Marion, 4272

Morehead City, 3934

Murfreesboro, 3828

New Bern, 3586, 3873, 3909, 3934,

4013, 4287, 4333

New Garden, 2988

Plymouth, 4333, 4484, 4561, 4657, 4668

Raleigh, 3780, 3956, 4055, 4272, 4283, 4430, 4433, 4724, 4819, 4828, 4950

Roanoke Island, 3873, 3926, 4013

Rockingham, 3243

Rocky Mount, 4138

Rutherfordton, 4272

Salem, 3515, 5038

Salisbury, 3868, 3880, 4300, 4358, 4559, 4606, 4623, 4638, 4722, 4770

Statesville, 4034

Tarboro, 4506

Union County, 4403

Washington, 3934, 4184, 4333

Wilmington, 3244, 3586, 3866, 4008, 4300, 4344, 4464, 4506, 4527, 4574, 4753

Wilson, 4506

Winton, 3926

Yadkin County, 4278

North Dakota, 3668, 3796, 4236, 4373, 4390, 4397, 4405, 4483, 4652, 4853, 4893, 4917, 4972, 4998, 5012, 5021, 5067, 5070, 5078, 5084, 5119, 5501

Bismarck, 5076, 5116, 5119, 5182

Devil's Lake, 2783, 4405

Enderlin, 5578

Fargo, 5182, 5201

Fort Abercrombie, 4056, 4236, 4390, 4866

Fort Abraham Lincoln, 5031, 5067, 5070

Fort Berthold, 3668, 5031

Fort Buford, 5031, 5037

Fort Pierre, 3219

Fort Rice, 4652, 4910, 4917, 4972, 4991, 5079

Fort Stevenson, 4903, 5031

Fort Union, 2949, 2960, 3037, 3219

Heart River, 4986

Jamestown, 5626

Kensal, 5626

Mapleton, 5201

Stony Brook, 5626

Whitestone Hill, 4471

Northwest Territories, 5416

Canol, 5749

Great Slave Lake, 5336

Mackenzie River, 3732

Norway, 5329, 5673, 6025

Nova Scotia, 3068, 4104, 4314

O

Ohio, 2872, 2903, 2943, 2954, 2996, 3031, 3146, 3214, 3327, 3340, 3500, 3508, 3681, 3689, 3817, 3821, 3831, 3883, 3890, 3893, 3925, 3931, 3945, 3967, 4011, 4013, 4027, 4069, 4082, 4092, 4108, 4129, 4161, 4199, 4202, 4212, 4213, 4222, 4266, 4300, 4332, 4335, 4345, 4349, 4362, 4364, 4367, 4379, 4402, 4417, 4433, 4454, 4466, 4469, 4477, 4516, 4530, 4598, 4634, 4647, 4650, 4663, 4667, 4685, 4693, 4705, 4729, 4742, 4817, 4975, 5071

Akron, 3487

Amelia, 4705

Ashland, 4011

Ashtabula, 3378

Ashtabula County, 3189

Athens, 5915,

Austinburg, 2992

Batavia, 2943

Belmont County, 4300

Berlin Heights, 4912

Butler County, 4259

Caldwell, 4786

Cambridge, 3260

Camp Chase, 3850, 3945, 4011, 4084, 4139, 4248, 4346, 4545

Canal Dover, 3642

Canton, 5294

Cardington, 3831

Chesterhill, 5334

Chillicothe, 3131

Cincinnati, 2792, 2812, 2851, 2872, 2893, 2958, 3283, 3288, 3311, 3323, 3357, 3401, 3466, 3468, 3558, 3658, 3681, 3704, 3712, 3890, 3931, 4021, 4041, 4169, 4514, 4745, 5025, 5101, 5171, 5247, 5408, 5439

Clarksville, 3558

Cleveland, 2872, 3689, 3745, 3817, 3892, 5792, 5850

Columbiana County, 4718, 5294

Columbus, 2918, 3066, 3266, 3378, 3831, 3945, 4082, 4202, 4364, 6017

Crawford County, 3942

Cumberland, 3083

Cuyahoga County, 3424

Dayton, 2812, 5262

Defiance, 3081, 3491

Delta, 3717

Elyria, 3424

Erie County, 3130

Felicity, 3270

Findlay, 3821

Gallipolis, 4685

Gibralter Island. See Great Lakes, Lake Erie, Gibralter Island

Greene County, 3374, 4693

Greenfield, 3288, 4634

Greentown, 4598

Guernsey County, 3460

Hamilton, 2812, 4259, 5439

Hocking County, 3681

Huron, 5081

Jefferson, 3378

Johnson's Island, 3850, 3919, 3967, 4107, 4135, 4139, 4176, 4246, 4278, 4306, 4346, 4416, 4441, 4513, 4524, 4685, 4773

5576, 5617, 5676. See also Alps
Berne, 5398
Geneva, 2974, 5716, 5830
Lausanne, 3924
Syria, 3138

T

Tahiti, 5486
Taiwan, 5732, 5744, 5832
Tennessee, 2999, 3049, 3178, 3244, 3500, 3513, 3518, 3681, 3689, 3702, 3724, 3778, 3787, 3809, 3812, 3821, 3824, 3829, 3831, 3839, 3849, 3850, 3867, 3872, 3874, 3875, 3879, 3890, 3891, 3893, 3897, 3904, 3912, 3916, 3927, 3936, 3942, 3946, 3954, 3956, 3975, 3977, 3986, 3992, 3995, 4002, 4021, 4022, 4023, 4027, 4044, 4052, 4057, 4059, 4067, 4071, 4073, 4082, 4083, 4084, 4085, 4087, 4091, 4095, 4106, 4116, 4118, 4122, 4125, 4129, 4161, 4162, 4175, 4179, 4181, 4183, 4186, 4190, 4192, 4195, 4198, 4199, 4212, 4213, 4222, 4223, 4227, 4236, 4245, 4247, 4275, 4282, 4283, 4286, 4300, 4301, 4322, 4328, 4335, 4362, 4364, 4366, 4372, 4379, 4395, 4402, 4415, 4422, 4426, 4430, 4436, 4438, 4448, 4451, 4454, 4479, 4496, 4498, 4503, 4511, 4513, 4516, 4517, 4519, 4555, 4569, 4572, 4573, 4580, 4589, 4590, 4598, 4609, 4675, 4678, 4689, 4694, 4701, 4702, 4703, 4711, 4717, 4721, 4724, 4740, 4747, 4752, 4819, 4950
Athens, 5055
Bedford County, 3954
Beersheba Springs, 4396
Bradley County, 3772, 4282
Camp Oakland, 2850
Chattanooga, 2986, 3809, 3821, 3831, 3931, 3933, 3942, 3992, 4055, 4084, 4091, 4176, 4181, 4212, 4266, 4351, 4364, 4415, 4438, 4448, 4514, 4516, 4530, 4715, 5467, 5534
Clarksville, 4057, 4410
Cleveland, 3920, 4364, 5409
Collierville, 4594
Columbia, 4275, 4703
Farmington, 4341
Fort Donelson, 3009, 3824, 3836, 3849, 3850, 3888, 3907, 3946, 3954, 3975, 4022, 4139, 4198
Fort Henry, 3009, 3824, 3850, 3888, 3907, 3975, 4198
Fort Pillow, 4096
Franklin, 3977, 4072, 4190, 4286, 4300, 4572, 4599, 4617, 4674, 4689
Hartsville, 4202
Henry County, 3400
The Hermitage, 3995, 4198

Jackson, 3888
Jasper, 5055
Johnsonville, 4702
Knoxville, 3180, 3879, 3916, 3990, 4055, 4159, 4161, 4191, 4202, 4282, 4362, 4412, 4415, 4464, 4529, 4555, 4702, 4721, 4950, 5854
Lookout Mountain, 3689, 3778, 3809, 3942, 3992, 3995, 4008, 4052, 4055, 4176, 4181, 4364, 4379, 4415, 4448, 4503
McMinnville, 4021, 4082
McNairy County, 4545
Maury County, 3795, 4183, 4624, 4700, 4703
Memphis, 2793, 2849, 2850, 3047, 3086, 3311, 3348, 3441, 3681, 3758, 3794, 3936, 3985, 4069, 4118, 4237, 4322, 4324, 4328, 4360, 4518, 4608, 5092, 5248
Missionary Ridge, 3689, 3702, 3778, 3977, 3992, 4008, 4052, 4161, 4176, 4190, 4199, 4283, 4364, 4379, 4415, 4448, 4503, 4577
Murfreesboro, 3500, 3821, 3831, 3867, 3891, 3931, 3942, 3977, 4021, 4027, 4069, 4084, 4106, 4162, 4190, 4202, 4204, 4212, 4213, 4255, 4275, 4422, 4495, 4517, 4715
Nashville, 2958, 3009, 3263, 3441, 3758, 3778, 3809, 3968, 3977, 3995, 4069, 4072, 4082, 4181, 4186, 4198, 4207, 4248, 4300, 4335, 4353, 4364, 4415, 4430, 4438, 4514, 4516, 4590, 4599, 4617, 4661, 4701, 4702, 4715, 4721, 4731, 4745, 5312
New Market, 3876, 4198
Old Fort, 3812
Paris, 3824
Pittsburgh Landing, 3500, 3822, 3829, 3836, 3839, 3849, 3875, 3888, 3890, 3893, 3907, 3931, 3936, 3942, 3946, 3975, 4023, 4177, 4179, 4230, 4275, 4301, 4322, 4328, 4332
Pulaski, 5055
Savannah, 3907
Sequatchie Valley, 4391
Shelby County, 4608
Shelbyville, 3227, 4071, 4395
Shiloh, See Pittsburgh Landing
Spring Hill, 3897, 4083
Stones River. See Murfreesboro
Strawberry Plains, 4358
Sumner County, 3468
Sylco Mountains, 3396
Thompson's Station. See Spring Hill
Tullahoma, 4379, 4745
Vineland, 3396
Warren County, 4021
Wartburg, 2986
Washington County, 3180
Watertown, 4696
White County, 3845
Tennessee River, 3946

Tennessee Valley, 5517
Terceira Island. See Azores
Texas, 2850, 2858, 2876, 2981, 3074, 3076, 3134, 3155, 3165, 3195, 3262, 3354, 3507, 3514, 3521, 3528, 3563, 3581, 3609, 3647, 3742, 3766, 3787, 3807, 3841, 3871, 3889, 3897, 3903, 3912, 3948, 3965, 3992, 4002, 4017, 4106, 4113, 4157, 4173, 4182, 4218, 4242, 4244, 4276, 4335, 4394, 4395, 4407, 4455, 4463, 4497, 4528, 4599, 4640, 4677, 4697, 4761, 4771, 4926, 4961, 4971, 5024, 5248, 5337, 5429, 5683, 5760
Amarillo, 5310
Austin, 3028, 3430, 3507, 3521, 5000, 5248, 5547
Beaumont, 4463
Ben Franklin, 5310
Bonham, 3727
Bosque County, 3766
Bowie, 5760
Brackettville, 4276
Brazos, 3096
Brazos River, 3528
Bremond, 4983
Brownsville, 3033, 3054, 4205, 4218, 4395, 4447
Cameron, 3441
Camp Ford, 3912, 4378, 4771
Camp Groce, 4378
Canton, 4677
Canyon, 5310
Channing, 5295
Chinati Mountains, 5123
Circleville, 3441
Clinton, 4276
Collin County, 4905
Corpus Christi, 5215
Crosby County, 5443
Dallas, 3441, 3523, 3587, 5248
Dockums, 5227
Eagle Pass, 3430
El Paso, 3044, 3078, 3195, 3501
El Paso del Norte, 2852, 2878, 3195
Ellis County, 3965
Elmendorf, 5222
Fort Belknap, 2899, 3134, 3528
Fort Bliss, 3647
Fort Clark, 5111, 5123
Fort Concho, 5097
Fort Davis, 3787, 5024
Fort Griffin, 4905
Fort Hudson, 3787
Fort McKavett, 3507
Fort San Saba, 4687
Fort Worth, 3408
Fredericksburg, 3195, 4276
Galveston, 2829, 3947, 4046, 4121, 4378, 4394, 4395, 4440, 4677
Grayson County, 3772
Green Lake, 3942, 4817
Harrisburg, 3059
Harrison County, 2855, 3705